MODERN AMERICAN LITERATURE

Volume I • A–G
Fifth Edition

St. James Press
AN IMPRINT OF GALE

DETROIT • LONDON

Joann Cerrito and Laurie DiMauro, *Editors*

Laura Standley Berger, Dave Collins, Nicolet V. Elert,
Miranda Ferrara, Kristin Hart, Margaret Mazurkiewicz, Michael J. Tyrkus
St. James Press Staff

Peter M. Gareffa, *Managing Editor, St. James Press*

Mary Beth Trimper, *Production Director*
Deborah Milliken, *Production Assistant*

Cynthia Baldwin, *Product Design Manager*
Eric Johnson, *Art Director*
Victoria B. Cariappa, *Research Manager*
Michele P. LaMeau, *Research Specialist*

Modern American Literature.—5th ed.
  p.   cm.
Includes bibliographical references and index.
Contents: v. 1. A-G — v. 2. H-O — v. 3. P-Z
ISBN 1-55862-379-5 (set). — ISBN 1-55862-380-9 (v. 1). —
ISBN 1-55862-381-7 (v. 2). — ISBN 1-55862-382-5 (v. 3).
  1. American literature—20th century—History and criticism.
PS221.M53   1998
810.9′005—dc21   98-38952
                                                  CIP

Printed in the United States of America

St. James Press is an imprint of Gale

10 9 8 7 6 5 4 3 2 1

FOREWORD TO THE FIFTH EDITION

This new edition of *Modern American Literature* represents a significant advancement in the series. These volumes collate all entries from the original three volumes of the fourth edition, published in 1960, with entries from the three supplements published in 1976, 1985, and 1997, so that all excerpts on a given author now appear in one place. Seventy new entries have been added, bringing the total number of authors discussed to 489, and bibliographies for all authors have been updated. In addition, the format has been simplified. Citations for journal articles now include the full source title, eliminating the need for the abbreviation key used in previous editions, and bibliographies now immediately follow author entries, rather than appearing in a separate section at the back of the book.

The compilers of this edition have built upon the notable efforts of previous editors, each of whom made significant contributions and additions. As in the past, entrants in the series, as well as the sources chosen for excerpting, have been carefully selected to provide broad and instructive overviews of the most significant authors of the modern period in American literature. New authors for this edition have been selected not only on the basis of their prominence but also on their presence in the contemporary curriculum. The richly diverse nature of American letters is reflected in the wide variety of genres represented, from the humorous contemporary tales of Andrei Codrescu to the contemplative nature essays of Annie Dillard to the literary and philosophical speculations of George Steiner. In addition, a concerted effort was made to broaden the cultural scope of the series by presenting discussion of the works of black, Hispanic, and Native American authors, including a number from earlier in this century whose works have until recently been undervalued or ignored, figures such as William Stanley Braithwaite, Paul Lawrence Dunbar, and Alain Locke. As in previous editions, every effort has been made to cull from brief reviews as well as lengthy critical evaluations, and from a wide variety of critical perspectives, showing wherever possible the evolution of an author's reputation and stature.

The function of this work continues to be the illumination of the works of American authors through the presentation of significant analyses. With its greater focus on multicultural authors and its streamlined format, this new edition will be even more useful to students and other researchers seeking critical perspectives on the most significant American writers of the twentieth century.

The editors would like to thank the many individuals and publishers who have generously granted permission to reprint their materials here.

ACKNOWLEDGMENTS

The editors wish to thank the copyright holders of the excerpted criticism included in this edition and the permissions managers of many book and magazine publishing companies for assisting us in securing reproduction rights. We are also grateful to the staffs of the Detroit Public Library, the Library of Congress, the University of Detroit Mercy Library, Wayne State University Purdy/Kresge Library Complex, and the University of Michigan Libraries for making their resources available to us. Following is a list of the copyright holders who have granted us permission to reproduce material in *Modern American Literature*. Every effort has been made to trace copyright, but if omissions have been made, please let us know.

A & W Publishers, Inc. From *The World of Raymond Chandler*, Miriam Gross, ed. Reprinted by permission of A & W Publishers, Inc. Copyright © 1977 by Weidenfeld and Nicholson. "The Illusion of the Real," copyright © 1971 by Jacques Barzun and Wendell Hertig Taylor.

Abyss Publications. From Hugh Fox, *Charles Bukowski: A Critical and Bibliographical Study*.

Hazard Adams. From article on Stafford in *Poetry*.

Phoebe Lou Adams. From article on Kinnell's *Black Light* in *The Atlantic Monthly*.

John W. Aldridge. From *After the Lost Generation*, published 1951 by McGraw-Hill Book Co. (Vidal). Used by permission of the author.

Charles Altieri. From article on F. O'Hara in *The Iowa Review*.

Amerasia Journal. Excerpt from "In the Shadows of a Diva: Committing Homosexuality in David Henry Hwang's M. Butterfly," by David L. Eng from *Amerasia Journal* 20:1, © 1994. Excerpt from "Approaches to Teaching Kingston's *The Woman Warrior*," by Hardy C. Wilcoxon from Amerasia Journal © 1994.

America. From article by Elizabeth M. Woods on Wilder. Copyright©1973 by America Press. Reprinted with permission of *America*. All rights reserved; James Finn Cotter on Shapiro. Reprinted by permission of America Press, Inc. © 1976. All rights reserved; James Finn Cotter on Merwin. Reprinted with permission of America Press, Inc. © 1983. All rights reserved; "William Kennedy" by James E. Rocks. Reprinted with permission of America Press, Inc., 106 West 56th Street, New York, NY 10019. © 1994. All Rights Reserved. "T. Coraghessan Boyle" by David Johnson. Reprinted with permission of America Press, Inc., 106 West 56th Street, New York, NY 10019. © 1994. All Rights Reserved. "Richard Bausch" by John Desmond. Reprinted with permission of America Press, Inc., 106 West 56th Street, New York, NY 10019. © 1994. All Rights Reserved. "Louise Erdrich" by John Desmond. Reprinted with permission of America Press, Inc., 106 West 56th Street, New York, NY 10019. © 1994. All Rights Reserved. "John Updike" by Lewis A. Turlish. Reprinted with permission of America Press, Inc., 106 West 56th Street, New York, NY 10019. © 1994. All Rights Reserved; v. 150, June 23-30, 1984. © 1984. All rights reserved. Reproduced with permission of America Press, Inc., 106 West 56th Street, New York, NY 10019.

The American Book Collector. From "The Search of an American Catholic Novel" by Bruce Cook, *American Libraries*, October 1973, page 549; copyrighted 1973 by the American Library Association. Reprinted by permission of the American Library Association (Sheed).

American Book Review. From article by Michael Benedikt on Ignatow; Candelaria, C. *J. S. Baca*. Illinois: American Book Review, 1990. Reprinted with permission. Weinreich, R. *William Burroughs*. Illinois: American Book Review, 1988. Reprinted with permission. White, Curtis. *Stephen Dixon*. Illinois: American Book Review, 1989. Reprinted with permission. Klinkowitz, J. *Stephen Dixon*. Illinois: American Book Review, 1989. Reprinted with permission. Spencer, Norman. *Henry Louis Gates*. Illinois: American Book Review, 1990. Reprinted with permission. Lenhart, Gary. *Alfred Chester*. Illinois: American Book Review, 1994. Reprinted with permission. Bingham, Sallie. *Alice Walker*. Illinois:

American Book Review, 1990. Reprinted with permission. Siegle, Robert. *Walter Abish*. Illinois: American Book Review, 1994. Reprinted with permission. Natt, Rochelle. *May Swenson*. Illinois: American Book Review, 1995. Reprinted with permission. V. 3, November-December, 1980; v. 14, December, 1992-January, 1993. © 1980, 1992-93 by The American Book Review. Both reproduced by permission.

American Examiner: A Forum of Ideas. From article by Bruce Curtis on Kopit.

American Humour. From article by T. Jeff Evans on De Vries.

American Library Association. From Richard K. Barksdale, *Langston Hughes: The Poet and His Critics*, reprinted by permission of the American Library Association, copyright © 1977 by the American Library Association.

American Literature. Alexander Marshall, ''William Faulkner: The Symbolist Connection.'' *American Literature*, 59:3 (October 1987), pp. 389–401. Copyright Duke University Press, 1987. Reprinted with permission. Jackson J. Benson, ''Ernest Hemingway: The Life as Fiction and the Fiction as Life,'' *American Literature*, 61:3 (October 1989), pp. 345–58. Copyright Duke University Press, 1989. Reprinted with permission. Mark Van Wienen, ''Taming the Socialist: Carl Sandburg's *Chicago Poems* and Its Critics,'' *American Literature*, 63:1 (March 1991), pp. 89–103. Copyright Duke University Press, 1991. Reprinted with permission. Catherine Rainwater, ''Reading Between Worlds: Narrativity in the Fiction of Louise Erdrich.'' *American Literature*, 62:3 (September 1990), pp. 405–22. Copyright Duke University Press, 1990. Reprinted with permission. Terri Witek, ''Robert Lowell's Tokens of the Self.'' *American Literature*, 63:4 (December 1991), pp. 712–28. Copyright Duke University Press, 1991. Reprinted with permission. Laura E. Tanner, ''Reading Rape: *Sanctuary and The Women of Brewster Place*.'' *American Literature*, 62:4 (December 1990), pp. 559–83. Copyright Duke University Press, 1990. Reprinted with permission. Forrest G. Robinson. ''A Combat with the Past: Robert Penn Warren on Race and Slavery,'' *American Literature*, 67:3 (September 1995), pp. 511–30. Copyright Duke University Press, 1995. Reprinted with permission. Barbara Foley, ''Jean Toomer's *Sparta*,'' *American Literature*, 67:4 (December 1995), pp. 747–76. Copyright Duke University Press, 1995. Reprinted with permission; v. 51, March, 1979. Copyright © 1979 Duke University Press, Durham, NC. Reproduced with permission.

American Notes and Queries. Excerpts from article on Robert Lowell by Jeffrey Meyers which appeared in *American Notes and Queries*. Copyright © 1990 by Erasmus Press.

The American Poetry Review. From articles by Robert Coles on Rukeyser, Frederick Garber on Stafford, Alicia Ostriker on Swenson, Alvin H. Rosenfeld on Ammons, Paul Zweig on Ignatow, Kevin Stein on James Wright, which appeared in *American Poetry Review*. Reprinted with permission of *The American Poetry Review* and the authors. From v. 5, May-June, 1976 for "Marvin Bell: Time's Determinant/Once, I Knew You" by Arthur Oberg; v. 8, November-December, 1979 for a review of "Ashes and 7 Years from Somewhere" by Dave Smith. Copyright © 1976, 1979 by World Poetry, Inc. Both reproduced by permission of the respective authors.

The American Scholar. From Shaun O'Connell, ''So It Goes'' Reprinted from *The American Scholar*, Volume 38, No. 4, Autumn, 1969. Copyright© 1969 by the United Chapters of Phi Beta Kappa (Vonnegut); Mark Schorer, ''Novels and Nothingness'' Reprinted from *The American Scholar*, Volume 40, No. 1, Winter, 1970–71. Copyright© 1971 by the United Chapters of Phi Beta Kappa (Didion); Susan J. Turner, ''The Anderson Papers.'' Reprinted from *The American Scholar*, Volume 39, No. 1, Winter 1969–70. Copyright © 1970 by the United Chapters of Phi Beta Kappa (Anderson); Philip Kopper, ''On the Campus.'' Reprinted from *The American Scholar*, 36, 4 (Autumn 1967). Copyright © 1967 by the United Chapters of Phi Beta Kappa. By permission of the publishers (Theroux); ''Modeling My Father,'' by Alexander Nemerov. Reprinted from The American Scholar, Volume 62, No. 4, Autumn 1993. Copyright © 1993 by the author.

American Studies. From article by David M. Fine on Cain. By permission of *American Studies* and the author.

American Theatre Association. From articles by Michael C. O'Neill on Kopit, Craig Werner on Rabe, from *Educational Theatre Journal and Theatre Journal*.

Américas. From Lee Holland, ''Homer and the Dragon.'' Reprinted from *Américas* monthly magazine published by the General Secretariat of the Organization of Americans States in English, Spanish, and Portuguese (Bukowski).

The Americas Review, v. XVI, Summer, 1988. Copyright © 1988 The Americas Review. Reproduced by permission of the publisher.

A. R. Ammons. From article on Strand in *Poetry*.

Anaya, Rudolfo A. From an introduction to *The Last of the Menu Girls*. By Denise Chavez. Arte Publico Press, 1986. Copyright © 1986 by Arte Publico Press. Reproduced by permission.

The Antioch Review. From article by David Bosworth on Vonnegut, Copyright © 1979 by The Antioch Review, Inc. First appeared in *The Antioch Review*, 37, 1 (Winter 1979). Reprinted by permission of the editors; for Saari, Jon. *William Styron*. Copyright © 1994 by the Antioch Review, Inc. First Appeared in the Antioch Review, Vol. 52, No. 1 (Winter 1994); v. XL, Spring, 1982. Copyright © 1982 by the Antioch Review Inc. Reproduced by permission of the Editors.

Archon Books. From G. H. Douglas, *H.L. Mencken: Critic of American Life*.

Ardis Publications. From W. W. Rowe, *Nabokov's Spectral Dimension*, © 1981 by Ardis Publications.

Arizona Quarterly. Selinger, Eric, ''John Ashbery.'' Winter 1991, p. 114. Reprinted with permission of Arizona Quarterly. Elliott, Emory, ''Robert Stone,'' Autumn 1987, p. 201. Reprinted with permission of Arizona Quarterly.

Edward Arnold Publishers, Ltd. From Brian Way, *F. Scott Fitzgerald and the Art of Social Fiction*, by permission of the publishers.

Art and Literature. From article by Bill Berkson on F. O'Hara

Arte Publico Press. From *Retrospace* by Juan Bruce-Novoa is reprinted with permission from the publisher (Houston: Arte Publico Press-University of Houston). 1990.

Art In America. From article by Morton Feldman on F. O'Hara.

Art News. From article by John Ashbery on F. O'Hara.

Robert Asahina. From article on Rabe in *Theatre*.

Associated Faculty Press, Inc. From Gary Q. Arpin, *The Poetry of John Berryman* (Kennikat Press, 1978, reprinted by permission of Associated Faculty Press, Inc.); article by Karen Sinclair in *Ursula K. Le Guin: Voyager to Inner Lands and to Outer Space*, Joe De Bolt, ed. (Kennikat Press. 1979, reprinted by permission of Associated Faculty Press, Inc.): Evelyn Gross Avery. *Rebels and Victims: The Fiction of Richard Wright and Bernard Malamud* (Kennikat Press. 1979, reprinted by permission of Associated Faculty Press, Inc. (Malamud).

Associated University Presses. From article by Willard Thorpe on Gordon in *Bucknell Review*; essay by Emily Mitchell Wallace in *William Carlos Williams*, Charles Angoff, ed., published by Fairleigh Dickinson University Press; from Carol Wershoven, *The Female Intruder in the Novels of Edith Wharton*, published by Fairleigh Dickinson University Press; Leonard Chabrowe, *Ritual and Pathos: The Theatre of O'Neill*, published by Bucknell University Press; Harry Williams, ''The Edge Is What I Have,'' *Theodore Roethke and After*, published by Bucknell University Press (Roethke); from Charles Altieri, *Enlarging the Temple: New Directions in American Poetry during the 1960s*, published by Bucknell University Press (Duncan).

The Atheneum Publishers, Inc. From *Alone with America: Essays on the Art of Poetry in the United States since 1950* by Richard Howard. Copyright © 1965, 1966, 1967, 1968, 1969 by Richard Howard (Ammons, Goodman, Meredith); from Margaret Brenman-Gibson, *Clifford Odets, American Playwright: The Years from 1906 to 1940.* Copyright © ©1981 by Margaret Brenman-Gibson. Reprinted with the permission of Atheneum Publishers.

The Atlantic Monthly. From Phoebe Adams, ''Portpourri.'' Copyright © 1966, by The Atlantic Monthly Company, Boston, Mass. (Kinnell); X.J. Kennedy, ''Translations from the American.'' Copyright © 1973, by The Atlantic Monthly Company, Boston, Mass. (Merrill); Melvin Maddocks, ''Paleface Takeover.'' Copyright © 1973, by The Atlantic Monthly Company, Boston, Mass, (Gardner); William Barrett, ''Reader's Choice, '' Copyright © 1962 by The Atlantic Monthly Company, Boston, Mass. (J. Williams); William Barrett, ''Reader's Choice,'' Copyright © 1962 by The Atlantic Monthly Company, Boston, Mass. (Price); Peter Davison, ''The New Poetry,'' Copyright © 1962 by The Atlantic Monthly Company, Boston, Mass. (Hollander); Peter Davison. ''New Poets,'' Copyright © 1963 by The Atlantic Monthly Company, Boston, Mass. (Swenson). Reprinted with permission.

James C. Austin. From ''Sinclair Lewis and Western Humor'' in *American Dreams, American Nightmares*, David Madden, ed.

George W. Bahlke. From *The Late Auden.*

Houston A. Baker, Jr. From article on Johnson in *The Virginia Quarterly Review.*

Howard Baker. From essay in *Sense and Sensibility in Twentieth-Century Writing*, Brom Weber, ed. (Porter); article on Gordon in *The Southern Review.*

Frank Baldanza. From article on Federic in *The Southern Review.*

Bantam Books, Inc. From Introduction by Richard Gilman to *Sam Shepard: Seven Plays.* Introduction copyright © 1981 by Bantam Books, Inc. By permission of Bantam Books, Inc. All rights reserved.

A. S. Barnes. From Bernard Sherman, *The Invention of the Jew*, published by Thomas Yoseloff (Fuchs).

Barnes & Noble. From Stephen D. Adams, *James Purdy.*

Rebecca Charmers Barton. From *Witnesses for Freedom* (Hurston).

Basic Books, Inc. From Introduction by Quentin Anderson et al., eds., to *Art, Politics, and Will: Essays in Honor of Lionel Trilling.* Copyright © 1977 by Basic Books, Inc. John Gardner, *On Moral Fiction.* Copyright © 1978 by Basic Books, Inc. (Updike).

Beacon Press. From *Stealing the Language* by Alicia Suskin Ostriker. Copyright © 1986 by Alicia Suskin Ostriker. Reprinted by permission of Beacon Press, Boston.

Calvin Bedient. From articles on West, on Oates in *Partisan Review.*

Belles Lettres: A Review of Books by Women, v. 10, Fall, 1994; v. 10, Spring, 1995. Both reproduced by permission.

Alfred Bendixen and Annette Zilversmit for Zilversmit on Wharton.

Bernard Bergonzi. From article on Warren in *The Southern Review.*

Best Sellers, v. 35, June, 1975. Copyright 1975, by the University of Scranton. Reproduced by permission.

Elizabeth Bishop. From essay in *Randall Jarrell 1914–1965*, Robert Lowell, Peter Taylor, Robert Penn Warren, eds.

Stephen A. Black, for the excerpt from his article on Thurber in *University Review*, Summer, 1966, which also appears in his book, *James Thurber, His Masquerades* (Mouton & Co.).

Black American Literature Forum. From articles by William H. Hansell on Hayden, Trudier Harris on Walker, Jack Hicks on Gaines; v. 24, Summer, 1990 for "W.E.B. Du Bois's Autobiography and the Politics of Literature" by William E. Cain. Reproduced by permission of the authors.

Black Sparrow Press. From Ekbert Faas, *Towards a New American Poetics: Essays and Interviews.* Copyright © 1978 by Ekbert Fass. By permission of Black Sparrow Press (Snyder). Excerpts from *Looking for Genet: Literary Essays and Reviews* by Alfred Chester. Copyright © 1992 by Herman Chester and reprinted with the permission of Black Sparrow Press.

Gus Blaisdell. From article on Connell in *New Mexico Quarterly.*

Robert Bly. From article on Ignatow in *The Sixties.*

The Bobbs-Merrill Company, Inc. From essays by Jacques Levy, by Michael Smith in *Five Plays* by Sam Shepard, Copyright © 1967 by Sam Shepard; essay by Elizabeth Hardwick in *La Turista* by Sam Shepard, Copyright © 1968 by Sam Shepard. Reprinted by permission of the publisher, the Bobbs-Merrill Company, Inc.

Boise State University. From Harry Russell Huebel, *Jack Kerouac*, Boise State University Western Writers Series. Bowling Green State University Popular Press. From Peter Wolfe, *Beams Falling: The Art of Dashiell Hammett*; article by Susan Wood on Le Guin in *Voices for the Future: Essays on Major Science Fiction Writers*, Vol. 2, Thomas D. Clareson, ed.

Bone, Robert. From Down Home: A History of Afro-American Short Fiction from Its Beginnings to the End of the Harlem Renaissance. Columbia University Press, 1988. Copyright © 1975 by Columbia University Press. Copyright © 1975 by Robert Bone. All rights reserved. Reproduced with permission of the publisher. From The Negro Novel in America. Revised edition. Yale University Press, 1965. Copyright © 1965 by Yale University. Copyright © renewed by Robert A. Bone in 1985. All rights reserved. Excerpted by permission of the author.

Book Week. For generous permission to reprint numerous excerpts from articles.

Book World-The Washington Post, August 11, 1974 by Doris Grumbach; August 5, 1984 for "Poets of Innocence and Experience" by Joel Conarroe. © 1974 Washington Post Book World Service/Washington Post Writers Group. Reproduced by permission of Russell & Volkeining, Inc. as agents for Doris Grumbach and by Joel Conarroe.

Georges Borchardt. Excerpts from *Automatic Vaudeville* by John Lahr. Copyright © 1984 and reprinted with the permission of Georges Borchardt, Inc.

Fred W. Bornhauser. From ''Poetry by the Poet,'' in *The Virgina Quarterly Review* (Kinnell, Meredith).

Boulevard. Excerpts from ''Autobiographies of the Present'' by Thomas Larson. Copyright © 1993 and reprinted with the permission of *Boulevard.*

Bowling Green State University Press. Excerpts from *Two Guns From Harlem* by Robert E. Skinner. Copyright © 1989 and reprinted with the permission of Bowling Green State University Press.

Bowling Green University Popular Press. From David H. Goldsmith, *Kurt Vonnegut.*

Robert Boyers. For article on Plath in *The Centennial Review.*

Brandt & Brandt Literary Agents, Inc.. From Gilbert A. Harrison, *The Enthusiast: A Life of Thornton Wilder*, copyright © 1983 by Gilbert A. Harrison. Reprinted by permission of Ticknor and Fields, a Hougton Mifflin company.

George Braziller, Inc. From *American Drama since 1918* by Joseph Wood Krutch; reprinted with the permission of the publisher. © 1939, 1957 by Joseph Wood Krutch; from *Character and Opinion in the United States* by George Santayana; reprinted with the permission of the publisher. Copyright © 1955 by

George Braziller, Inc.; from *R. Buckminster Fuller* by John McHale; reprinted with permission of the publisher. Copyright © 1962 by George Braziller, Inc.

Robert H. Brinkmeyer, Jr. From article on O'Connor in *The Southern Review*.

John Malcolm Brinnin. From article on Plath in *Partisan Review*.

John Brockman Associates. From Janice S. Robinson, H. D.: *The Life and Work of an American Poet*.

David Bromwitch. From article on Sexton in *Poetry*.

Cleanth Brooks. From article on Percy in *The Southern Review*.

Peter Brooks. From essay in *Romanticism: Vistas, Instances, Continuities*, David Thorburn and Geoffrey H. Hartman, eds., originally in *Paristan Review* (H. James).

Curtis Brown, Ltd. From foreword by Maxine Kumin to *The Complete Poems of Anne Sexton*.

Merle E. Brown. From *Wallace Stevens: The Poem as Act*.

Robert Brustein. From articles on Kopit, Guare, Mamet, L. Wilson in *The New Republic*.

Jerry H. Bryant. From articles on Gaines in *Iowa Review*, on Baldwin in *Phylon*.

Callaloo. From article by Todd Duncan on Gaines.

Cambridge University Press. From Jean Chothia, *Forging a Language: A Study of the Plays of Eugene O'Neill*; A. D. Moody, *Thomas Stearns Eliot, Poet*; article by A. Robert Lee on Himes in *Journal of American Studies*; article by John S. Whitley on Hammett from *Journal of American Studies*. Excerpts from *Hart Crane: The Context of "The Bridge"* by Paul Giles. Copyright © 1986 and reprinted with the permission of Cambridge University Press. Excerpts from *Modernism, Mass Culture and Professionalism* by Thomas Strychacz. Copyright © 1993 and reprinted with the permission of Cambridge University Press. Excerpts from *New Essays on the Sun Also Rises* by Linda Wagner-Martin (ed.). Copyright © 1987 and reprinted with the permission of Cambridge University Press. Excerpts from *The Cliffs of Solitude: A Reading of Robinson Jeffers* by Robert Zeller. Copyright © 1983 and reprinted with the permission of Cambridge University Press. Excerpts from *The Poetry of Marianne Moore* by Margaret Holley. Copyright © 1987 and reprinted with the permission of Cambridge University Press. Excerpts from *New Essays on "The Grapes of Wrath"* by David Wyatt (ed.). Copyright © 1990 and reprinted with the permission of Cambridge University Press. Excerpts from *The Long Poems of Wallace Stevens* by Rajeev S. Patke. Copyright © 1985 and reprinted with the permission of Cambridge University Press. Excerpts from *Modernist Quartet* by Frank Lentricchia. Copyright © 1994 and reprinted with the permission of Cambridge University Press. Excerpts from *Elizabeth Bishop's Poetics of Intimacy* by Victoria Harrison. Copyright © 1993 and reprinted with the permission of Cambridge University Press. Excerpts from *Elizabeth Bishop: The Biography of a Poet* by Lorrie Goldensohn. Copyright © 1992 by Cambridge University Press and reprinted with the permission of the author. Excerpts from *T. S. Eliot and Ideology* by Kenneth Asher, Copyright © 1995 and reprinted with the permission of Cambridge University Press. Excerpts from *Robert Lowell: Essays on the Poetry* by A. K. Weatherhead. Copyright © 1986 by Axelrod, Steven and Deese, Helen (eds.) and reprinted with the permission of Cambridge University Press. Excerpts from *New Essays on the Crying of Lot 49* by Bernard Duyfhuizen. Copyright © 1991 by Patrick O'Donnell (ed.) and reprinted with the permission of Cambridge University Press. Excerpts from *The Revolution in the Visual Arts and the Poetry of William Carlos Williams* by Peter Halter. Copyright © 1994. Reprinted with the permission of Cambridge University Press. Excerpts from *Elizabeth Bishop's Poetics of Intimacy* by Victoria Harrison. Copyright © 1993. Reprinted with the permission of Cambridge University Press.

Jonathan Cape Ltd. Tony Tanner, *City of Words* (Barth, Burroughs).

The Carleton Miscellany. From article by David Galler on Nemerov.

John R. Carpenter. From article on Snyder, Wakoski, in *Poetry*.

Paul Carroll. From *The Poem in Its Skin* (Ashbery, F. O'Hara).

Hayden Carruth. From articles on Berryman in *Nation*; on Bogan, on Merwin, on Schwartz, on Van Doren in *Poetry*.

Turner Cassity. From article on Howard in *Poetry*.

Catholic World. From article by Riley Hughes on Connell.

The Centennial Review. From article by Robert Boyers on Plath; Nicolaus Mills on Kesey; Cynthia Davis on Barth, Bernard Duffey on Sandburg.

Chicago Review. From "The Small, Sad World of James Purdy" by Paul Herr, published in *Chicago Review*, volume 14, Number 3, p. 19. Copyright © 1960 by *Chicago Review*; from articles by Bernard F. Rodgers, Jr., on Doctorow, H. C. Ricks on P. Bowles, Carl E. Rollyson, Jr., on Mailer, Linda Shell Bergmann on Reed, Richard Burgin on Singer, Robert von Hallberg on Snodgrass. Used by permission of the editors. For "Cynthia Ozick at the End of the Modern" by Andrew Lakritz. Copyright © 1994 Reprinted by permission of *Chicago Review*.

Chicago Tribune. For generous permission to reprint numerous excerpts from articles in *Book World, Chicago Sunday Tribune Book Review*; and September 13, 1987 for "Childhood Relived" by Catherine Petroski. © copyrighted 1987, Chicago Tribune Company. All rights reserved. Reproduced by permission of the author.

The Christian Century Foundation, for the excerpt from the review (of Thomas Merton's *Disputed Questions*) by C. Eugene Conover, copyright © 1961 Christian Century Foundation. Reprinted by permission from the January 18, 1961 issue of *The Christian Century*. For "Kesey and Vonnegut: Preachers of Redemption" by James Tunnell. Copyright © 1972 Christian Century Foundation. Reprinted by permission from the November 22, 1972 issue of *The Christian Century* (Kesey); for review of Henry Louis Gates's *Loose Canons: Notes on the Culture Wars* by John Ottenhoff. Copyright © 1994 Christian Century Foundation. Reprinted by permission from the January 19, 1994 issue of *The Christian Century*.

The Christian Science Monitor. From articles by Victor Howes on Fuller, on Gardner, on Howard, on Snyder, on Stafford. Copyright © 1968, 1970, 1971, 1972, 1974 The Christian Science Publishing Society; Robert Kiely on Sheed. Copyright © 1965 The Christian Science Publishing Society; Melvin Maddocks on Didion. Copyright © 1968 The Christian Science Publishing Society; Frederick Nordell on Bly. Copyright © 1963 The Christian Science Publishing Society. Excerpted by permission from *The Christian Science Monitor*; November 10, 1955. Copyright 1955, renewed 1983 by The Christian Science Publishing Society. All rights reserved. Reproduced by permission from The Christian Science Monitor./ September 4, 1992 for "As Others See The Vietnamese" by Kathleen Kilgore. © 1992 Kathleen Kilgore. All rights reserved. Reproduced by permission of the author.

CLA Journal. From articles by W. Edward Farrison on Hansberry, on Toomer; by Lance Jeffers on Bullins; v. XV, June, 1972; v. 16, September, 1972, copyright, 1972 by The College Language Association. Reproduced by permission of The College Language Association.

Leonard Clark. From article on Zukofsky in *Poetry Review*.

Gerald Clarke. From article on Vidal in *The Atlantic*.

John Clayton. From article on Brautigan in *New American Review*.

Samuel Coale. From article in *John Gardner: Critical Perspectives*, Robert A. Morace and Kathryn Van Spankeren, eds.

College and University Press. From Charles B. Harris, *Contemporary American Novelists of the Absurd* (Barth, Barthelme, Heller, Vonnegut).

Columbia University Forum, for the excerpt from Charles Alva Hoyt's article on Truman Capote, reprinted from *The Columbia University Forum*, Winter 1966, Vol. VIII, No. 1. Copyright © 1966 by

Columbia University in the City of New York. Columbia University Press. From Herbert Leibowitz, *Hart Crane*; George W. Nitchie, *Marianne Moore*; Onwuchekwa Jemis, *Langston Hughes: An Introduction to the Poetry*; June Schlueter, *Metafictional Characters in Modern Drama* (Albee); David Shapiro, *John Ashbery: An Introduction to the Poetry*; Susan B. Weston, *Wallace Stevens: An Introduction to the Poetry* © 1975, 1979, and 1977 by Columbia University Press. Reprinted by permission of the publisher.

Robert Combs. From *Vision of the Voyage: Hart Crane and the Psychology of Romanticism.*

Commentary. For excerpts from articles and reviews cited in the text, quoted from *Commentary*, by permission; Copyright © 1956, 1957, 1959, 1960, 1961, 1962, 1963, 1964, 1965, 1966, by the American Jewish Committee; from articles by Joseph Epstein on Dos Passos (January 1976), Pearl Bell on Piercy (July 1980), Ruth Wisse on Roth (September 1981). Reprinted from *Commentary*, by permission; all rights reserved. January, 1975 for "How Good is Alison Lurie?" by John W. Aldridge. Copyright © 1975 by the American Jewish Committee. All rights reserved. Reproduced by permission of the publisher and the author.

Commonweal. For generous permission to reprint numerous excerpts from articles, including articles by Michael True on Shapiro, George Hunt on Cheever, Robert Phillips on Howard, Richard M. Elman on Olsen, and Richard Kuczkowski on Sontag; v. CVI, October 12, 1979. Copyright © 1979 Commonweal Publishing Co., Inc. Reproduced by permission of Commonweal Foundation.

James M. Con. From article on Lardner in *The Virgina Quarterly Review.*

Concerning Poetry. From articles by Peter Cooley on J. Wright; Paul Cummins on Wilbur; Thomas Parkinson on Ginsberg; Richard K. Cross on Eberhart. Reprinted by permission of the editor; all rights reserved.

Confrontation. Excerpts from essay on Mary McCarthy by Martin Tucker which appeared in *Confrontation: A Literary Journal*, (Fall 1992), p. 360. Copyright © 1992 by Long Island University and reprinted with the permission of author. Excerpts from essay on Paul Bowles by Martin Tucker which appeared in *Confrontation: A Literary Journal*, (Fall 1991), pp. 337–38. Copyright © 1991 by Long Island University and reprinted with the permission of author. Excerpts from essay on Richard Ford by Martin Tucker which appeared in *Confrontation: A Literary Journal*, (Fall 1990), pp. 217–18. Copyright © 1990 by Long Island University and reprinted with the permission of author. Excerpts from essay on Alice Hoffman by Lee Mhatre which appeared in *Confrontation: A Literary Journal*, (Fall 1994), pp. 342–43. Copyright © 1994 by Long Island University and reprinted with the permission of author. Excerpts from essay on John Irving by Lee Mhatre which appeared in *Confrontation: A Literary Journal*, (Summer 1995), pp. 361–63. Copyright © 1995 by Long Island University and reprinted with the permission of author. Excerpts from essay on Lanford Wilson by Martin Tucker which appeared in *Confrontation: A Literary Journal*, (Spring 1992), pp. 246, 247, 255. Copyright © 1992 by Long Island University and reprinted with the permission of author. Excerpts from essay on Donald Barthelme by Martin Tucker which appeared in *Confrontation: A Literary Journal*, (Fall 1990), p. 216. Copyright © 1990 by Long Island University and reprinted with the permission of author.

Contemporary Poetry. From article by Claude J. Summers and Ted-Larry Pebworth on Howard. By permission of the editor.

Contemporary Review. From article by Rosalind Wade on Condon.

Cornell University Press, for the excerpt from *Jamesian Ambiguity and The Sacred Fount* by Jean Frantz Blackall, © 1965 by Cornell University. Used by permission of Cornell University; for the excerpt from *Hart Crane's Sanskrit Charge* by L. S. Dembo, © 1960 by Cornell University. Used by permission of Cornell University; for the excerpt from *The Theory of American Literature* by Howard Mumford Jones, © 1965 by Cornell University; for Austin Briggs, Jr., *The Novels of Harold Frederic*. Copyright © 1969 by Cornell University; for Charles Berger, "Vision in the Form of a Task: *The Double Dream of Spring*," in *Beyond Amazement: New Essays on John Ashbery*, David Lehman, ed., pp. 163–208. Copyright © 1980 by Cornell University. Used by Permission of the publisher, Cornell University Press.

John William Corrington. From Introduction to Charles Bukowski, *It Catches My Heart in Its Hands.*

Jonathan Cott. From essay on Purdy in *On Contemporary Literature*, Richard Kostelanetz, ed.

Malcolm Cowley. From article on cummings in *The Yale Review*.

The Crisis. From article by W.E.B. Du Bois on Toomer.

Critical Essays on Kurt Vonnegut. Excerpts from *Culture and Anarchy: Vonnegut's Later Career*, by D. Cowart. Reprinted with the permission of G. K. Hall & Co.

The Critical Quarterly. From articles by Damian Grant on Plath; Grevel Lindop on Simpson; D.P.M. Salter on Bellow; Tony Tanner on Vonnegut; Richard Bradbury on John Barth; Luke Spencer on John Berryman. Reprinted with the permission of *Critical Quarterly*.

Critique. For generous permission to reprint numerious excerpts from articles.

Crown Publishers, Inc. From *Rediscoveries*, edited with an introduction by David Madden. Copyright © 1971 by Crown Publishers, Inc. Used by permission of Crown Publishers, Inc. (Gaddis).

Cue. From article by Marilyn Stasio on Rabe.

The Dalhousie Review. From articles, by James Ballowe on Santayana: Alice Hamilton on McCullers.

Elizabeth Dalton. From article on Nobokov in *Partisan Review*.

Donald Davie. From essay on Olson in *The Survival of Poetry*. Martin Dodsworth, ed.

Arthur P. Davis. From From the Dark Tower: Afro-American Writers 1900-1960. Howard University Press, 1974. Copyright © 1974 by the College Language Association. Reproduced by permission of the publisher.

Cynthia Davis. From article on Barth in *Centennial Review*.

Delacorte Press. From essays by Joe David Bellamy, by John Somer, by Dan Wakefield in *The Vonnegut Statement*, Jerome Klinkowitz and John Somer, eds.

J. M. Dent & Sons Ltd. From Louis Sheaffer, *O'Neill: Son and Playwright*.

Denver Quarterly. From article by Joanne Greenberg on Kurt Vonnegut, Jr.'s *Mother Night*.

Andre Deutsch Ltd. From Roy Fuller, *Owls and Artificers* (Moore, Stevens); from John Updike, *Picked-Up Pieces* (Jong) and John Updike, *Hugging the Shore* (Bellow).

Diacritics. From article by Josephine Jacobsen on Ammons.

Roger Dickinson-Brown. From article on Momaday in *The Southern Review*.

Morris Dickstein. From article on Fuchs and Schwartz in *Partisan Review*.

Annie Dillard. From article on Connell in *Harper's*.

Millicent Dillon. From *A Little Original Sin: The Life and Works of Jane Bowles*.

Dissent. From articles by Ann Douglas on Farrell, Mark Caldwell on Susan Sontag. Reprinted with the permission of Dissent.

Melvin Dixon. From "Singing a Deep Song: Language as Evidence in the Novels of Gayl Jones" in Black Women Writers (1950-1980): A Critical Evaluation. Edited by Mari Evans. Anchor Press/Doubleday, 1984. Copyright © 1983 by Mari Evans. All rights reserved. Reproduced by permission of Doubleday, a division of Bantam Doubleday Dell Publishing Group, Inc.

Dodd, Mead & Company. From essay by Larry E. Thompson on Toomer in *The Harlem Renaissance Remembered*, Arna Bontemps, ed.

Doubleday & Company, Inc., from E. B. White's Introduction to *the lives and times of archy and mehitable* by Don Marquis. Introduction copyright 1950 by Doubleday & Company, Inc. Reprinted by permission of the publisher: excerpt from *O Rare Don Marquis* by Edward Anthony. Copyright© 1962 by Edward Anthony. Reprinted by permission of Doubleday & Company, Inc.: excerpts by Robert Gorham Davis, Alan R. Jones, and David L. Stevenson, from *The Creative Present*, edited by Nona Balakian and Charles Simmons. Copyright© 1963 by Nona Balakian and Charles Simmons. Reprinted by permission of Doubleday & Company, Inc.; excerpt from *The Theatre of the Absurd* by Martin Esslin. Copyright © 1961 by Martin Esslin. Reprinted by permission of Doubleday & Company, Inc.; excerpt from *Thomas Wolfe: A Biography* by Elizabeth Nowell. Copyright © 1960 by Doubleday & Company, Inc. Reprinted by permission of the publisher; for essay by Michael Benedikt on Drexler in *Theater Experiment*. Copyright © 1967 by Michael Benedikt; by William Van O'Connor on Gordon in *South*, Louis D. Rubin, Jr., and Robert D. Jacobs, eds. Copyright © 1961 by Doubleday & Company, Inc.; for William Barrett, *The Truants: Adventures Among the Intellectuals*. Copyright © 1982 by William Barrett. Reprinted by permission of Doubleday & Co. Inc. (Schwartz).

Ann Douglas. From article on Farrell in *Dissent*.

Dover Publications, Inc., for the excerpt from George Barkin's Preface to Ambrose Bierce: *Sardonic Humor of Ambrose Bierce*, Dover Publications, Inc., New York, 1963. Reprinted by permission of the publisher.

Robert Drake. From article on Price in *The Southern Review*.

Tom F. Driver, for the excerpt from his article on Edward Albee in *The Reporter* (Jan. 2, 1964), reprinted by permission of the author and his agent, James Brown Associates, Inc. Copyright © 1964 by The Reporter Magazine Company.

Martin Duberman. From articles on Bullins and Hansberry, on A. Miller in *Partisan Review*.

Bernard Duffey. From article on Sandburg in *Centennial Review*.

Duke University Press. From articles by Frank Baldanza on Purdy; L. S. Dembo on Zukofsky; Robert E. Fleming on Johnson; James W. Gargano on Wharton in *American Literature*; Louis Hasley on De Vries in *South Atlantic Quarterly*; Franklin Walker's essay on London in *Essays on American Literature in Honor of Jay Hubbell*, Clarence Gohdes, ed.; Frederick I. Carpenter on Jeffers; Dick Wagenaar on Lewis; Jane S. Bakerman on Morrison; Deborah G. Lambert on Cather in *American Literature*. copyright © 1977, 1978, 1981, and 1982; Frank Lentricchia, *Robert Frost: Modern Poetics and the Landscape of Self*, copyright © 1975: Mary Kathryn Grant. *The Tragic Vision of Joyce Carol Oates*, copyright © 1978, all of the above by Duke University Press, Durham. N. C. Patrick O'Donnell, ''The Thicket of Writing: On Stanley Elkin's Fiction,'' *Facing Texts: Encounters between Contemporary Writers and Critics*, ed. Heide Ziegler. Copyright 1988, Duke University Press, Durham, N.C. Reprinted with permission. Mimi Reisel Gladstein, ''Straining for Profundity: Steinbeck's *Burning Bright* and *Sweet Thursday*,'' *The Short Novels of John Steinbeck*, ed. Jackson J. Benson. Copyright 1990, Duke University Press, Durham, N.C. Reprinted with permission. Jerome Klinkowitz, *Donald Barthelme: An Exhibition*. Copyright 1991, Duke University Press, Durham, N.C. Reprinted with permission.

Jeffrey L. Duncan. From articles on West in *Iowa Review*.

Todd Duncan. From article on Gaines in *Callaloo*.

E. P. Dutton & Co., Inc., for excerpts from ''Lewis Mumford: American Prophet'' (*Harper's* June, 1952) by Van Wyck Brooks and Introduction to *The History of a Literary Radical and Other Papers* (by Randolph Bourne, published by Russell & Russell) by Van Wyck Brooks, permission is granted by E.P.Dutton & Co., Inc. on behalf of Mrs. Gladys Brooks; from *Fictions and Events* by Warner Berthoff; Copyright © 1971 by Warner Berthoff (Mailer, Nabokov). Excerpt on Mailer originally published in *New Literary History*; from Frank MacShane, *The Life of Raymond Chandler*, copyright© 1976 by Frank

MacShane; Townsend Ludington, *John Dos Passos: A Twentieth Century Odyssey*, copyright © 1980 by Townsend Ludington. Reprinted by permission of the publisher, E. P. Dutton, Inc.

Richard Eberhart. From article on Scott in *Poetry*.

Educational Theatre Journal. From article by Gil Lazier on Rabe.

Thomas R. Edwards. From article on Fiedler in *Partisan Review*.

Irvin Ehrenpreis. From "Ashbery and Justice" in *Poetries of America: Essays on the Relations of Character to Style*. Edited by Daniel Albright. The University Press of Virginia, 1989. Copyright © 1989 by the Rectors and Visitors of the University of Virginia Press. Reproduced by permission.

Encounter. From articles by Ronald Hayman on Bishop, on Olson, on Roethke, on Snyder; Theodore Weiss on W.C. Williams.

English. Excerpts from book review by Joan A. Burke of *Transformations* by Anne Sexton, in ''Transformations: Classics and Their Cousins.'' *English Journal*, March 1994. Copyright © 1994 by the National Council of Teachers of English. Reprinted with permission.

English Journal. From article by Janet R. Sutherland on Kesey; v. 61, December, 1972 for "Ray Bradbury and Fantasy" by Anita T. Sullivan. Copyright © 1972 by the National Council of Teachers of English. Reproduced by permission of the publisher and the respective authors.

English Language Notes. Excerpts from article on Nathanael West by Robert Wexelblatt, which appeared in *English Language Notes*. Copyright © 1988 and reprinted with the permission of *English Language Notes*.

English Literary History. Excerpts on Edith Wharton by Amy Kaplan. Copyright © Summer 1986, pp. 433–34, 453–54, by *English Literary History* and reprinted with the permission of the Johns Hopkins University Press.

English Studies. Excerpts from article on E. L. Doctorow by J. M. Bloom & F. R. Leavis which appeared in *English Studies*. Copyright © 1990 and reprinted with the permission of the Swets & Zeitlinger Publishers. Excerpts from article on Lanford Wilson by Logan Speirs which appeared in *English Studies*. Copyright © 1990 and reprinted with the permission of the Swets & Zeitlinger Publishers.

Epoch. From article by David Ray on Bly.

Esquire. From article by Malcolm Muggeridge on Brautigan. Reprinted by permission of *Esquire Magazine* © 1965 by Esquire, Inc.; from article by James Wolcott on Gardner. Reprinted with permission from *Esquire* (June 1982). Copyright © 1982 by Esquire Associates.

Essays in Literature. Excerpts from article on Mary Gordon by John M. Neary which appeared in *Essays in Literature*. Copyright © 1990 and reprinted with the permission of the publisher. Excerpts from article on Denise Levertov by Diane C. LeBlanc which appeared in *Essays in Literature*. Copyright © 1991 and reprinted with the permission of the publisher.

Sybill P. Estess. From article on Biship in *The Southern Review*.

Everett/Edwards, Inc., for excerpts from six essays in *Essays in Modern American Literature*, edited by Richard E. Langford, published by Stetson University Press in 1963; from essays by Dan Jaffee on Brooks; Jordan Y. Miller on Hansberry in *The Black American Writer*, C.W.E. Bigsby, ed.; Warren French on Purdy in *Essays in Modern American Literature*, Richard E. Langford, ed.; Warren French on Salinger and Donald Pease on Purdy in *The Fifties*, Warren French, ed.; Gerald Rabkin on Wilder in *The Forties*, Warren French, ed.; Michael J. Mendelsohn, *Clifford Odets: Humane Dramatist*. By permission of the publisher.

Extrapolation. Excerpts from *Isaac Asimov* by Clyde Wilcox. Copyright © 1990 by and reprinted with the permission of *Extrapolation*.

Eyre & Spottiswoode Ltd., for permission for the British Commonwealth for excerpts from *The Theatre of the Absurd* by Martin Esslin.

Faber and Faber, Ltd., for permission for world rights excluding the U.S.A. and Canada for excerpts from *The Dyer's Hand* by W. H. Auden; Saul Bellow's Foreword to *Recovery* by John Berryman; Denis Donoghue, *The Ordinary Universe* (Burke, Eliot, Fitzgerald, H. James, Jarrell, Moore, O'Neill, Pound, W.C. Williams); Hugh Kenner, *The Pound Era* (Pound); Julian Symons, *Bloody Murder* (Chandler, Hammett, Macdonald); Michael Alexander, *The Poetic Achievement of Ezra Pound*, by permission of the publishers.

Farrar, Straus & Giroux, Inc., for excerpts reprinted with the permission of Farrar, Straus & Giroux, as follows: from *Babel to Byzantium* by James Dickey. Copyright © 1956, 1957, 1958, 1959, 1960, 1961, 1962, 1963, 1964, 1965, 1966, 1967, 1968 by James Dickey; from *The King of the Cats* by F. W. Dupee; Copyright © 1963 by F.W. Dupee; from *The Collected Works of Jane Bowles*. Introduction copyright © 1966 by Truman Capote; from *A Reader's Guide to William Faulkner* by Edmond L. Volpe. Copyright © 1964 by Edmond L. Volpe; from *The Magic of Shirley Jackson*, edited by Stanley Edgar Hyman. Copyright © 1965, 1966 by Stanley Edgar Hyman; from *Doings and Undoings* by Norman Podhoretz. Copyright © 1958, 1964 by Norman Podhoretz; from *The Myth and the Powerhouse* by Philip Rahv. Copyright © 1949, 1950, 1951, 1952, 1953, 1954, 1955, 1956, 1957, 1958, 1960, 1963, 1964, 1965 by Philip Rahv; from the foreword by Saul Bellow from *Recovery* by John Berryman, Foreward copyright © 1973 by Saul Bellow; *Babel to Byzantium* by James Dickey. Copyright © 1956, 19578, 1958, 1959, 1960, 1961, 1962, 1963, 1964, 1965, 1966, 1967, 1968 by James Dickey (Ashbery, Kinnell, Meredith, Olson, Stafford); *Nathanael West: The Art of His Life* by Jay Martin. Copyright © 1970 by Jay Martin; *Doings and Undoings* by Norman Podhoretz. Copyright © 1953, 1954, 1955, 1956, 1957, 1958, 1959, 1962, 1963, 1964 by Norman Podhoretz (Goodman); Wilfrid Sheed's text and John Leonard's Foreword from *The Morning After* by Wilfred Sheed. Copyright © 1963, 1965, 19656, 1967, 1968, 1969, 1970, 1971 by Wilfrid Sheed and Foreword copyright © 1971 by Farrar, Straus and Giroux, Inc. (Coover); from Langston Hughes, *The Big Sea*, copyright 1940 by Langston Hughes, copyright renewed © 1968 by Arna Bontemps and George Houston Bass, reprinted by permission of Hill and Wang, a division of Farrar, Staraus & Giroux, Inc.; James Atlas, *Delmore Schwartz: The Life of an American Poet*, copyright © 1977 by Farrar, Straus & Giroux, Inc., reprinted by permission of Farrar, Straus & Giroux, Inc.

Feminist Studies. From article by Deborah Rosenfelt on Olsen, reprinted from *Feminist Studies*, 7, 3 (Fall 1981), by permission of the publisher, Feminist Studies, Inc., c/o Women's Studies Program, University of Maryland, College Park, MD 20742.

Suzanne C. Ferguson. From article on Barnes in *The Southern Review*.

Fontana Paperbacks. From Richard Poirer, *Mailer*.

Estate of Ford Madox Ford. From article on Gordon in *The Bookman*.

Gabrielle Foreman for her excerpt on Dove.

Fortress Press. From Wesley A. Kort, *Shriven Selves* (De Vries, Malamud, Styron, Updike).

Richard Foster. From essay on Fitzgerald in *Sense and Sensibility in Twentieth Century Writing*, Brom Weber, ed.

G. S. Fraser. From articles on Howard, on Zukofsky in *Partisan Review*.

Freedomways, v. 3, Summer, 1963; v. 20, 1980. Copyright © 1963, 1980 by Freedomways Associates, Inc. Both reproduced by permission.

Samuel French, Inc., for the excerpt from *New Theatres for Old* copyright, 1940, 1962, by Mordecai Gorelik, reprinted by special arrangement with Samuel French, Inc.; for the excerpt from the Introduction to *Peace on Earth*: copyright, 1933, by George Sklar and Albert Maltz, reprinted by special arrangement with Samuel French, Inc.

Jonathan Galassi. From article on Nemerov in *Poetry*.

Arthur Ganz. From article in *Tennessee Williams: A Collection of Critical Essays*. Stephen S. Stanton, ed.

Carol B. Gartner. From Rachel Carson. Frederick Ungar Publishing Co., 1983. Copyright © 1983 by Frederick Ungar Publishing Co., Inc. Reproduced by permission.

Addison Gayle, Jr. From essay on Faulkner, Styron in *Amistad 1*.

Genre. Excerpts from article on Truman Capote by Phyllis Frus McCord which appeared in GENRE. Copyright © 1986 and reprinted with the permission of the publisher. Excerpts from ''A Splintery Box: Race and Gender in the Sonnets of Gwendolyn Brooks'' by Stacy Carson Hubbard which appeared in GENRE. Copyright © 1992 and reprinted with the permission of the publisher.

Georgia Review. From articles by Daniel Hoffman on Sandburg, Benjamin Taylor on Sontag, reprinted with permission of the publisher; article on Saul Bellow by Greg Johnson which appeared in *The Georgia Review*. Copyright © 1991 by *The Georgia Review* and reprinted with the permission of the publisher. Excerpts from article on T. C. Boyle by Greg Johnson which appeared in *The Georgia Review*. Copyright © 1990 by *The Georgia Review* and reprinted with the permission of the publisher. Excerpts from article on Joyce Carol Oates by Sanford Pinsker which appeared in *The Georgia Review*. Copyright © 1991 by *The Georgia Review* and reprinted with the permission of the publisher. Vol. XLVII, Spring, 1993. Copyright, 1993, by the University of Georgia. Reproduced by permission.

Gettysburg Review. ''Robert Frost: The Symbols a Poem Makes,'' by D. Hoffman, first appeared in *The Gettysburg Review*, volume 7, number 1, and sections are here by the permission of the editors.

Henry Gifford. From essay in *Marianne Moore*, Charles Tomlinson, ed.

Richard Gilman. From Introduction to Rosalyn Drexler. *The Line of Least Resistance*.

Giovanni, Nikki. From "Afterword" in A Singer in the Dawn: Reinterpretations of Paul Laurence Dunbar. Edited by Jay Martin. Dodd, Mead & Company, 1975. Reproduced by permission of the author.

Hugh M. Gloster. From *Negro Voices in American Fiction*. University of North Carolina Press, 1948. Copyright 1948 by The University of North Carolina Press. Renewed 1975 by Hugh M. Gloster. Reproduced by permission of the publisher.

Going, William T. From *Essays on Alabama Literature*. The University of Alabama Press, 1975. Copyright © 1975 by The University of Alabama Press. All rights reserved. Reproduced by permission of the author.

Vivian Gornick. From article on Hellman in *Ms. Magazine*.

Kenneth Graham. From article on Berger in *The Listener*.

Graham House Review. Excerpts from article on Adrienne Rich by Terrence Des Pres which appeared in *Graham House Review*. Copyright © 1988 and reprinted with the permission of Graham House Review.

Granada Publishing Ltd. From C.W.E. Bigsby, *Confrontation and Commitment* (Hansberry).

Richard Gray. From *The Literature of Memory: Modern Writers of the American South* (McCullers, Styron).

Greenwood Press. From Margaret Perry, *A Bio-Bibliography of Countee P. Cullen*; from Barbara Christian, *Black Women Novelists*, reprinted by permission of the publishers (Morrison). *The Sleuth and the Scholar*, Rader and Zettler (ed.). Copyright © 1988 by Greenwood Press. Reproduced with permission of Greenwood Publishing Group, Inc., Westport, CT. *Silence and Narrative*, Janice L. Doane. Copyright © 1986 by Greenwood Press. Reproduced with permission of Greenwood Publishing Group, Inc., Westport, CT. *A Gertrude Stein Companion*, Bruce Kellner (ed.). Copyright © 1988 by Greenwood Press. Reproduced with permission of Greenwood Publishing Group, Inc., Westport, CT. *Political Mythology and Popular Fiction*, Yanarella and Sigelman. Copyright © 1988 by Greenwood Press. Reproduced with permission of Greenwood Publishing Group, Inc., Westport, CT. *Confronting Tennessee Williams' ''A*

Streetcar,'' Philip C. Kolin (ed.). Copyright © 1993 by Greenwood Press. Reproduced with permission of Greenwood Publishing Group, Inc., Westport, CT. *American Playwrights since 1945*, Scott T. Cummings/ Philip C. Kolin (ed.). Copyright © 1989 by Greenwood Press. Reproduced with permission of Greenwood Publishing Group. Inc., Westport, CT. *In the Mainstream*, Louis Harap. Copyright © 1987 by Greenwood Press. Reproduced with permission of Greenwood Publishing Group, Inc., Westport, CT. *A Search for a Post-Modern Theatre*, John L. DiGaetani. Copyright © 1991 by Greenwood Press. Reproduced with permission of Greenwood Publishing Group, Inc., Westport. CT. *With Ears Opening Like Morning Glories*, Carol Manning. Copyright © 1985 by Greenwood Press. Reproduced with permission of Greenwood Publishing Group, Inc., Westport, CT. *Literary Exile in the 20th Century*, Martin Tucker. Copyright © 1991 by Greenwood Press. Reproduced with permission of Greenwood Publishing Group, Inc., Westport, CT. *The Critical Responses to Dashiell Hammett*, Christopher Metress (ed.). Copyright © 1994 by Greenwood Press. Reproduced with permission of Greenwood Publishing Group, Inc., Westport, CT.

Bryan F. Griffin. From article on Irving in *The Atlantic*.

The Griffin, for the excerpt from ''Habit and Promise'' by R. P. Blackmur, p. 7 of *The Griffin*, March 1961, Volume 10, No. 3, The Readers' Subscription, Inc., Publishers, New York, 1961.

Grove Press, Inc. From Ruby Cohn, *New American Dramatists: 1960–1980)*; reprinted by permission of Grove Press, Inc. (Guare, L. Wilson).

Mel Gussow. From article on L. Wilson from *Horizon*.

Jay L. Halio. From articles on Hawkes, on Roth, on Taylor in *The Southern Review*.

G. K. Hall & Co. From Ray L. White, *Gore Vidal*, copyright © 1968; David Madden, *James M. Cain*, copyright © 1970; Edgar M. Branch, *James T. Farrell*, copyright © 1971; Martha Heasley Cox and Wayne Chatterton, *Nelson Algren*, copyright © 1975; Henry Chupack, *James Purdy*, copyright © 1975; James B. Scott, *Djuna Barnes*, copyright © 1976; Bob Steuding, *Gary Snyder*, copyright © 1976; Michael J. Hoffman, *Gertrude Stein*, copyright © 1976; Margaret B. McDowell, *Edith Wharton*, copyright © 1976; Charles D. Peavy, *Larry McMurtry*, copyright © 1977; Arthur Ford, *Robert Creeley*, copyright © 1978; Paul L. Gaston, *W. D. Snodgrass*, copyright © 1978; Robert Phillips, *William Goyen*, copyright © 1979; Alan Feldman, *Frank O'Hara*, copyright © 1979; Lillie P. Howard, *Zora Neale Hurston*, copyright © 1980; Ross Labrie, *Howard Nemerov*, copyright © 1980; Marie Henault, *Stanley Kunitz*, copyright © 1980; Robert Felgar, *Richard Wright*, copyright © 1980; Lois Gordon, *Donald Barthelme*, copyright © 1981; Gerald Pannick, *R. P. Blackmur*, copyright © 1981; Richard Anderson, *Robert Coover*, copyright © 1981; Bernetta Quinn, *Randall Jarrell*, copyright © 1981; Chari Davis, *W.S. Mervin*, copyright © 1981; Joseph Reino, *Karl Shapiro*, copyright © 1981; all of the above copyright by and reprinted with permission of Twayne Publishers, a division of G. K. Hall & Co.

From introduction by Stanley Trachtenberg in *Critical Essays on Saul Bellow*, Stanley Trachtenberg, ed., copyright © 1979; article by Daniel Walden in *Critical Essays on Arthur Miller*, James J. Martine, ed., copyright © 1979; article by G. F. Waller in *Critical Essays on Joyce Carol Oates*, Linda W. Wagner, ed., copyright © 1979; introduction by Scott MacDonald and article by Sylvia J. Cook in *Critical Essays on Erskine Caldwell*, Scott MacDonald, ed., copyright © 1981; article by Donald J. Greiner in *Critical Essays on Robert Frost*, Philip L. Gerber, ed., copyright © 1982; article by Howard Eiland in *Critical Essays on Philip Roth*, Sanford Pinsker, ed., copyright © 1982; article by John Gardner in *Critical Essays on William Styron*, Arthyr Casciato and James L.W. West III, eds., copyright © 1982; Article by Kathleen Verduin in *Critical Essays on John Updike*, William R. Macnaughton, ed., Copyright © 1982; article by Helen Hagenbüchle in *Critical Essays on Randall Jarrell*, Suzanne Ferguson, ed., copyright © 1983; all of the above copyright by and reprinted with permission of G. K. Hall & Co.

Barbara Hardy. From essay on Plath in *The Survival of Poetry*, Martin Dodsworth, ed.

Harper and Row, Publishers, Inc., for excerpts from *American Poetry Since 1945* by Stephen Stepanchev. Copyright © 1965, by Stephen Stepanchev. Reprinted by permission of Harper and Row, Publishers; Robert Lowell's Foreword to *Ariel* by Sylvia Plath. Copyright © 1966 by Ted Hughes; *Mortal Consequences* by Julian Symons. Copyright © 1972 by Julian Symons (Chandler, Hammett, Macdonald); *City of Words: American Fiction 1950–1970* by Tony Tanner. Copyright © 1971 by Tony Tanner (Barth, Burroughs); Rebecca Charmers Barton, *Witnesses for Freedom* (Hurston); Suzanne Juhasz, *Naked and*

Fiery Forms: Modern American Poetry by Women, a New Tradition, copyright © 1976 by Suzanne Juhasz, reprinted by permission of Harper & Row, Publishers, Inc. (Levertov, Plath, Sexton); introduction by Michel Fabre, *Richard Wright Reader*, Michel Fabre, ed.; Judith Kroll, *Chapters in a Mythology; The Poetry of Sylvia Plath*, copyright © 1976 by Judith Kroll, reprinted by permission of Harper & Row, Publishers, Inc.

HarperCollins. Excerpts from *Hemingway: A Biography* by Jeffrey Meyers. Copyright © 1985. Reprinted with the permission of HarperCollins. Excerpts from *The Dream at the End of the World* by Michelle Green. Copyright © 1993. Reprinted with the permission of HarperCollins.

Harper's Magazine, Inc., for the excerpt from ''The Riddle of John Dos Passos'' by Daniel Aaron, copyright © 1962 by Harper's Magazine, Inc. Reprinted from the March, 1962 issue of *Harper's Magazine* by permission of the author; for the excerpt from ''Lewis Mumford: American Prophet'' by Van Wyck Brooks, copyright © 1952 by Harper's Magazine, Inc. Reprinted from the June, 1952 issue of *Harper's Magazine* by permission of Mrs. Gladys Brooks; for the excerpt from the review of *Nova Express* (by William Burroughs) by Robert Hatch, copyright © 1964 by Harper's Magazine, Inc. Reprinted from the January, 1965 issue of *Harper's Magazine* by permission of the author; for the excerpt from the review of *The House of Five Talents* (by Louis Auchincloss) by Paul Pickerel, copyright © 1960 by Harper's Magazine, Inc. Reprinted from the October, 1960 issue of *Harper's Magazine* by permission of the author; for the excerpt from the review of *In Cold Blood* (by Truman Capote) by Rebecca West, copyright © 1966 by Harper's Magazine, Inc. Reprinted from the February, 1966 issue of *Harper's Magazine* by permission of the author; for the excerpt from the article by John W. Aldridge on Heller, copyright © 1979 by *Harper's Magazine*; all rights reserved; reprinted from the March 1979 issue by special permission; for the excerpt from the article by Paul Berman on Singer, copyright © 1978 by *Harper's Magazine*; all rights reserved; reprinted from the September 1978 issue by special permission; for the excerpt from the article by James Wolcott on Oates, copyright © 1982 by *Harper's Magazine*; all rights reserved; reprinted from the September 1982 issue by special permission.

Norman Harris. From article on Reed in *Obsidian*.

Rupert Hart-Davis Ltd., for permission for the British Commonwealth for the excerpt from *William James* by Gay Wilson Allen.

Harvard University. Department of English and American Literature and Language. From essays by Roger Rosenblatt on Hughes in *Veins of Humor*, Harry Levin, ed.; Gordon O. Taylor on Adams; Phillip M. Weinstein on H. James in *The Interpretation of Narrative*, Morton W. Bloomfield, ed.

Harvard University Press, reprinted by permission of the publishers as follows: from J. Hillis Miller, Jr., *Poets of Reality: Six Twentieth-Century Writers*, Cambridge, Mass.: The Belknap Press of Harvard University Press, Copyright © 1965, by the President and Fellows of Harvard College; from Walter Bates Rideout, *The Radical Novel in the United States, 1900–1954*, Cambridge, Mass.: Harvard University Press Copyright © 1956, by the President and Fellows of Harvard College; from Moses Rischin, *The Promised City: New York's Jews, 1870–1914*, Cambridge, Mass.: Harvard University Press, Copyright © 1962, by the President and Fellows of Harvard College; from Ernest Samuels, *Henry Adams: The Major Phase*, Cambridge, Mass.: The Belknap Press of Harvard University Press, Copyright © 1964, by the President and Fellows of Harvard College; from Theodora Ward, *The Capsule of the Mind: Chapters in the Life of Emily Dickinson*, Cambridge, Mass.: The Belknap Press of Harvard University Press, Copyright © 1961, by the President and Fellows of Harvard College; from Thomas H. Jackson, *The Early Poetry of Ezra Pound*; Helen Vendler, *On Extended Wings: Wallace Stevens' Longer Poems*; from Robert von Hallberg, *Charles Olson: The Scholar's Art*, reprinted by permission; Bonnie Costello, *Marianne Moore: Imaginary Possessions*, reprinted by permission; Robert G. O'Meally, *The Craft of Ralph Ellison*, copyright © 1980 by Harvard University Press, reprinted by permission; Ellen Fifer, *Nabokov and the Novel*, copyright © 1980 by Harvard University Press. Reprinted by permission.

Hawthorn Books, Inc. From essays by Robert Alter on Mailer; Donald B. Gibson on Baldwin, on Ellison; W. Gordon Milne on Dos Passos; Lewis A. Lawson on Faulkner in *The Politics of Twentieth-Century Novelists*, George A. Panichas, ed.

Alan Helms. From article on Ashbery in *Partisan Review*.

Calvin C. Hernton. From essay on Baldwin, L. Jones, Reed in *Amistad 1*.

David Higham Associates, Ltd. From article by Edith Sitwell on Purdy in *The New York Herald Tribune Book Section*.

William Heyen. From article on Levertov in *The Southern Review*.

Marianne Hirsch for her except on Morrison.

Baruch Hochman. From article on Singer in *Midstream*.

Daniel Hoffman. From article on Malcolm Cowley's *Bule Juniata in Poetry*, from article on Sandburg in *Georgia Review*.

Nancy Yanes Hoffman. From article on Sarton in *Southwest Review*.

The Hollins Critic. From articles by Eugene Chesnick on Percy; Peter Cooley on Plath; R. H. W. Dillard on Coover; Gale Flynn on Rich; Grace Farrell Lee on Singer; Judith Moffett on Merrill; Henry Taylor on Sarton; Gerald Weales on Kosinski; Robert Scholes on Hawkes; John Ditsky on Elkin; Miriam Fuchs on Barnes; Richard Kostelanetz on Stein; Henry Taylor on Meredith; Joel Connaroe on Berryman; and Daniel L. Zins on Doctorow; Michael Graves on James Wright; v. XIX, October, 1982; v. XXI, December, 1984. Copyright © 1982,1984 by Hollins College. Reproduced by permission of the publisher.

Holmes & Meier Publishers, Inc. From Patrick More, "Symbol, Mask and Meter in the Poetry of Louise Bogan," and Kathleen Woodward, "May Sarton and the Fictions of Old Age," in *Gender and Literary Voice,* Janet Todd. ed., by permission of Holmes & Meier Publishers, Inc., copyright © 1980 by Holmes & Meier Publishers, Inc., New York.

Holt, Rinehart and Winston. From Millicent Dillon, *A Little Original Sin: The Life and Works of Jane Bowles*, copyright © 1981 by Millicent Dillon; reprinted by permission of Holt, Rinehart and Winston, Publishers.

Horizon Magazine. From article by Mel Gussow on L. Wilson, reprinted from *Horizon Magazine*, Vol. 23, No. 5 (May 1980), copyright © 1980 by Horizon Publishers, Inc.

Horizon Press. Reprinted from *Standards: A Chronicle of Books for Our Time* by Stanley Edgar Hyman. Copyright © 1966, by permission of the publisher Horizon Press, New York (Purdy, Singer).

Houghton Mifflin Company. From Hyatt H. Waggoner, *American Poets from the Puritans to the Present* (Crane, Cummings, Frost, Roethke, Shapiro); foreword by Maxine Kumin to *The Complete Poems of Anne Sexton*, foreword copyright © 1981 by Maxine Kumin, reprinted by permission of Houghton Mifflin Company and Curtis Brown Ltd.; Janice S. Robinson, *H.D.: The Life and Work of an American Poet*, copyright © 1982 by Janice S. Robinson, reprinted by permission of Houghton Mifflin Company and John Brockman Associates; Gilbert A. Harrison, *The Enthusiast: A Life of Thornton Wilder*, copyright © 1983 by Gilbert A. Harrison, reprinted by permission of Ticknor & Fields, a Houghton Mifflin © company, and Brandt & Brandt Literary Agents, Inc.

Maureen Howard. From article on Bowles in *Partisan Review*.

Richard Howard. From articles on Auden in *Poetry*; on Rich in *Partisan Review*.

Howard University Press. From Authur P. Davis, *From the Dark Tower: AfroAmerican Writers 1900–1960* (Brooks, Johnson); from article by Darwin T. Turner in *James Baldwin: A Critical Evaluation*, Therman B. O'Daniel, Ed., © copyright 1977 by the College Language Association, with the permission of Howard University Press, Washington, D.C.

Irving Howe. From articles on Kosinski, on Plath in *Harper's*; essay on Singer in *On Contemporary Literature*.

The Hudson Review, for the quotations from *The Hudson Review*, which are copyrighted © 1957, 1958, 1959, 1960, 1961, 1962, 1963, 1964, 1965, 1966, 1967, 1968 by the Hudson Review, Inc.; from articles by Marius Bewley on Ammons in Vol. XXI No. 4 (Winter, 1968–69). Copyright © 1969 by the Hudson Review, Inc.; Hayden Carruth on *Trilogy* by H. D. (Doolittle) in Vol. XXVII No. 2 (Summer, 1974). Copyright © 1974 by The Hudson Review, Inc.; Hayden Carruth on Duncan, on Wakoski in Vol. XXI No. 2 (Summer, 1968). Copyright © 1968 by The Hudson Review, Inc.; Patrick Cruttwell on Winters in Vol. XXI No. 2 (Summer, 1968). Copyright © 1968 by The Hudson Review, Inc.; Ronald De Feo on *Gravity's Rainbow* by Pynchon in Vol. XXVI No. 4 (Winter, 1973–74). Copyright © 1974 by The Hudson Review, Inc.; William Dickey on Bogan, on Wilbur in Vol. XXII No. 2 (Summer, 1969). Copyright © 1969 by The Hudson Review, Inc.; Robert Garis on *Lost in the Funhouse* by Barth in Vol. XXII No. 1 (Spring, 1969). Copyright © 1969 by The Hudson Review, Inc.; Anthony Hecht on *Poems 3* by Dugan, on *The Blue Swallows* by Nemerov in Vol. XXI No. 1 (Spring, 1968). Copyright © 1968 by The Hudson Review, Inc.; Richmond Lattimore on *Adventure of the Letter 1* by Simpson in Vol. XXV No. 3 (Autumn, 1972). Copyright © 1972 by The Hudson Review, Inc.; Herbert Leibowitz on *New and Selected Poems* by Garrigue in Vol. XXI No. 3 (Autumn, 1968). Copyright © 1968 by The Hudson Review, Inc.; Herbert Leibowitz on *Planet News* by Ginsberg in Vol. XXII No. 3 (Autumn. 1969). Copyright © 1969 by The Hudson Review, Inc.; Herbert Leibowitz on *After Experience* by Snodgrass in Vol. XXI No. 3 (Autumn, 1968). Copyright © 1968 by The Hudson Review, Inc.; J. Mitchel Morse on Zukofsky in Vol. XXII No. 2 (Summer, 1969). Copyright © 1969 by The Hudson Review, Inc.; Neal J. Osborn, ''Toward the Quintessential Burke'' in Vol. XXI No. 2 (Summer, 1968). Copyright © 1968 by The Hudson Review, Inc.; William H. Pritchard on Jarrell, on *The Writing on the Wall* by Mary McCarthy in Vol. XXIII No. 2 (Summer, 1970). Copyright © 1970 by The Hudson Review, Inc.; William H. Pritchard on *The Fall of America* by Ginsberg in Vol. XXVI No. 3 (Autumn, 1973). Copyright © 1973 by The Hudson Review, Inc.; William H. Pritchard on Updike in Vol. XXI No. 2 (Summer, 1968). Copyright © 1968 by The Hudson Review, Inc.; Roger Sale on *The Collected Stories of Peter Taylor* in Vol. XXII No. 4 (Winter 1969–70). Copyright © 1970 by The Hudson Review, Inc.; John Simon on *A Moon for the Misbegotten* by O'Neill in Vol. XXVII No. 2 (Summer, 1974). Copyright © 1974 by The Hudson Review, Inc.; Louis Simpson on Stafford in Vol. XIV No. 3 (Autumn, 1961). Copyright © 1961 by The Hudson Review, Inc.; Patricia Meyer Spacks on Welty in Vol. XXV No. 3 (Autumn 1972). Copyright © 1972 by The Hudson Review, Inc.; Gerald Weales on *Fire Sermon* by Morris in Vol. XXIV No. 4 (Winter. 1971–72). Copyright © 1972 by The Hudson Review, Inc.; William H. Pritchard on Hollander, in Vol. XXVI. No.3 (Autumn 1973), copyright © 1973 by The Hudson Review, Inc.; Richard Pevear on Zukofsky in Vol.XXIX. No.2 (Summer 1976), copyright © 1976 by The Hudson Review, Inc.: Peter Glassman on Beattie, in Vol. XXX, No.4 (Autumn 1977), copyright © 1977 by The Hudson Review, Inc.: Maureen Howard on Morrison, in Vol. XXXI. No. 1 (Spring 1978), copyright © 1978 by the Hudson Review, Inc.: William H. Pritchard on Theroux, in Vol. XXXI. No. 3 (Autumn 1978), copyright © 1978 by The Hudson Review Inc., Richmond Lattimore on Hollander, In Vol. XXXII. No. 3 (Autumn 1979), copyright © 1979 by The Hudson Review, Inc.; ''An American Woman of Letters'' by Sonya Rudikoff in Vol. XLII, No. 1 (Spring 1989). Copyright © 1989 by The Hudson Review, Inc.; ''Why the Novel (Still) Matters'' by Alice Bloom in Vol. XLIII, No. 1 (Spring 1990). Copyright © 1990 by The Hudson Review. Inc. All selections reprinted by permission from *The Hudson Review*.

Humanist. Excerpts from article ''The Legacy of Isaac Asimov,'' by Pat Duffy Hutcheon, *The Humanist*, Mar./Apr. 1993. Copyright © 1993.

Indiana University Press. From essays by Anne Sexton, Ted Hughes in *The Art of Sylvia Plath*, Charles Newman, ed.; Ruby Cohn, *Dialogue in American Drama* (Albee, A. Miller, T. Williams); Rachel Blau DuPlessis in *Shakespeare's Sisters: Feminist Essays on Women Poets*, Sandra M. Gilbert and Susan Gubar, eds. (Rich); Richard Allen Blessing, *Theodore Roethke's Dynamic Vision*.

International Creative Mangement. From John Leonard's Foreword to Wilfrid Sheed, *The Morning After*, (Coover); articles by Earl Shorris on Algren, on Barthelme, on Gass in *Harper's Magazine*. Reprinted by permission of International Creative Management and Earl Shorris. First printed in *Harper's Magazine*. Copyright © 1972–73 by *Harper's Magazine*.

Iowa Review. From article by David Boxer and Cassandra Phillips on Carver.

Lee A. Jacobus. From eassy on L. Jones in *Modern Black Poets*, Donald B. Gibson, ed.

Fredric Jamison. From article on Chandler in *The Southern Review*.

Mrs. Randall Jarrell, for the excerpt from the review of *The Diamond Cutters* (by Adrienne Rich) by Randall Jarrell in *The Yale Review* (Autumn, 1956).

Johns Hopkins University Press, for excerpts from *ELH*, cited in the text; from article by Vivienne Koch on Gordon in *Southern Renascence*, Lewis D. Rubin, Jr., and Robert D. Jacobs, eds.; Mark Van Doren's Foreword to *The Selected Letters of Robinson Jeffers*, Ann N. Ridgeway, ed.; Calvin Bedient, Richard Allen Blessing in *Sylvia Plath: New Views on the Poetry*, Gary Lane, ed.; article by Hana Wirth-Nesher on Roth in *Prooftexts*. By permission of the publishers, Johns Hopkins University Press. Excerpts from article on D. Hwang by Linda Sarver which appeared in *Theatre Journal*. Copyright © 1995. Reprinted with the permission of the Johns Hopkins University Press.

James Weldon Johnson. From a preface to *The Book of American Negro Poetry*. Edited by James Weldon Johnson. Harcourt Brace Jovanovich, 1922. Copyright 1922, 1931 by Harcourt Brace Jovanovich, Inc.; renewed 1950 by Grace Johnson. Renewed 1950, 1959 by Mrs. Grace Nail Johnson. Reproduced by permission of the publisher.

D. A. N. Jones. From article on Bullins in *The Listener*.

Journal of American Studies. Excerpts from article on Susan Sontag by Liam Kennedy which appeared in *Journal of American Studies* (April 1990), Vol. 24. Copyright © 1990.

Journal of Modern Literature. From articles by A. Poulin, Jr., on Howard; Fred Moramarco on F. O'Hara, copyright © 1976 by Temple University; Rushworth Kidder on Cummings, copyright © 1979 by Temple University; Ann Edwards Boutelle on Hemingway, copyright © 1981 by Temple University; Stephen Jan Parker, ''Nabokov in the Margins: The Montreux Books.'' *JML*, volume 14, issue 1 (Summer 1987). Appears on pages 5–16. Permission is for page 5 only.

Journal of Narrative Technique. From article by Krystyna Prendowska on Kosinski, by permission; excerpts from essay by Elaine Orr. Copyright © Spring 1993 by and reprinted with the permission of The Journal of Narrative Technique.

David Kalstone. From article on Bishop in *Partisan Review*.

Kansas Quarterly. From article by George E. Kent on Angelou, Jonathan Holden on Chandler, by permission.

Frederick R. Karl. From essay in *The Achievement of Isaac Bashevis Singer*, Marcia Allentuck, ed.

Howard Kaye. From article on Winters in *The Southern Review*.

Alfred Kazin. From article on Oates in *Harper's*.

X. J. Kennedy. From article on Merrill in *The Atlantic Monthly*.

Hugh Kenner, for the excerpt from *The Invisible Poet: T.S. Eliot*.

Kent State University Press. From articles by Donald Palumbo on Burroughs, Dena C. Bain on Le Guin in *Extrapolation*. Copyright © 1979 and 1980 by Kent State University Press; reprinted by permission.

Kenyon Review. V. XI, Spring, 1989 for ''Ray-Rhymers, Shit-Burners, Transformation, and Grandpa Dave'' by Anthony Libby. Copyright 1989 by Kenyon College; reproduced by permission of the author. Excerpts from ''Portrait of a Lady: Isabella Gardner'' by Marian Janssen. First published in *The Kenyon Review*-New Series, Summer 1991. Excerpts from ''A World That Will Not Hold All The People: On Muriel Rukeyser'' by Suzanne Gadinier. First published in *The Kenyon Review*-New Series, Summer 1992. V. XIV, Winter, 1992 for ''Contemporary Poetics and History: Pinsky, Klepfisz, and Rothenberg'' by James McCorkle. Copyright 1992 by Kenyon College; reproduced by permission of the author. Excerpts from ''A Mysterious and Lavish Power'' by Sue Russell. First published in *The Kenyon Review*-New Series, Summer 1994. All rights reserved.

Baine Kerr. From article on Momaday in *Southwest Review*.

Edward Kessler. From *Image of Wallace Stevens.*

John O. Killens. From ''The Literary Genius of Alice Childress'' in *Black Women Writers (1950-1980): A Critical Evaluation.* Edited by Mari Evans. Anchor Press/Doubleday, 1984. Copyright © 1983 by Mari Evans. All rights reserved. Reproduced by permission of Doubleday, a division of Bantam Doubleday Dell Publishing Group, Inc.

Arthur F. Kinney. From essay on Faulkner in *The Southern Review.*

Kirk, Russell. From *Enemies of the Permanent Things: Observations of Abnormality in Literature and Politics.* Arlington House, 1969. Copyright © 1969 by Arlington House. Reproduced by permission of the Estate of Russell Kirk.

Kirkus Reviews, v. LII, July 1, 1984. Copyright © 1984 The Kirkus Service, Inc. All rights reserved. Reproduced by permission of the publisher.

William Kleb. From article on Shepard in *Theatre.*

Marcus Klein. From article on Gass in *The Reporter.*

Alfred A. Knopf, Inc. Excerpts from *James Baldwin* by David Leeming. Copyright © 1994 and reprinted with the permission of Alfred A. Knopf, Inc. Excerpts from *Metaphor and Memory* by Cynthia Ozick. Copyright © 1989 and reprinted with the permission of Alfred A. Knopf, Inc. Excerpts from *Louise Bogan: A Portrait* by Elizabeth Frank. Copyright © 1985 by Elizabeth Frank. Reprinted by permission of Alfred A. Knopf, Inc. Excerpts from *The Journals of John Cheever* by John Cheever. Copyright © 1990, 1991 by Mary Cheever, Susan Cheever, Benjamin Cheever, and Federico Cheever. Reprinted by permission of Alfred A. Knopf, Inc.

Kenneth Koch. From article on F. O'Hara in *Partisan Review.*

Michael Kreyling. From article on Price in *The Southern Review.*

Stanley Kunitz. From essay in *Randall Jarrell 1914–1965*, Robert Lowell, Peter Taylor, Robert Penn Warren, eds.

Thomas H. Landess. From *Larry McMurtry* (Steck-Vaughn, 1969).

Lewis Leary. From essay on Mark Twain in *Sense and Sensibility in Twentieth-Century Writing*, Brom Weber, ed.

Ruth Lechlitner. From article on Meredith in *Poetry.*

Thomas Le Clair. From article on Barth in *Texas Studies in Literature and Language.*

Richard Lehan. From article on Percy in *The Southern Review.*

George Lensing. From article on Lowell in *The Southern Review.*

John Leonard. From article on Yurick in *Life.*

Julius Lester. From Introduction to Lorraine Hansberry, *Les Blancs.*

J. C. Levenson. From article on Robinson in *The Virginia Quarterly Review.*

Philip Levine. From article on Merwin in *Poetry.*

Gloria Levitas. From article on Calisher in *The New York Herald Tribune Book Section.*

R. W. B. Lewis. From article on Purdy in *The New York Herald Tribune Book Section.*

Anthony Libby. From article on Bly in *The Iowa Review*.

Library Journal. From articles by john Alfred Avant on Oates; Robert S. Bravard on Reed; Richard M. Buck on Coover, on Horovitz; Bill Katz on Bukowski; Dorothy Nyren on Connell; Robert Regan on Wakoski; Jon M. Warner on Eastlake.

Laurence Lieberman. From articles on Dickey, on Duncan, on Garrigue, on Hughes, on Rexroth, on Rukeyser, on Shapiro, on Viereck, on J. Wright in *Poetry*. To be republished in *The Blind Dancers: Ten Years of American Poetry: 1965–75* by The University of Illinois Press.

Life Magazine, for the excerpt from ''A Cry of Loss: Dilemma Come Back'' by Tom Prideaux, *Life Magazine* © 1966 Time Inc.

Ruth Limmer. From article by Louise Bogan on Swenson, originally published in *The New Yorker* and republished in *A Poet's Alphabet* (McGraw-Hill, 1970), reprinted by permission of Ruth Limmer as Trustee of the Estate of Louise Bogan.

J. B. Lippincott Company. From *Native Sons* by Edward Margolies. Copyright © 1968 by Edward Margolies. Reprinted by permission of J.B. Lippincott Company (Baldwin, Cullen. Ellison, Himes, Hughes, R. Wright).

The Literary Review: An International Quarterly. From articles by Robert Miklitsch on Strand, reprinted from *The Literary Review*, Vol. 21, No. 3 (Spring 1978), pp. 357–59, published by Fairleigh Dickinson University; William F. Van Wert on Hawkes, reprinted from *The Literary Review*, Vol. 24, No. 1 (Fall 1980), pp. 37–39, published by Fairleigh Dickinson University; Marianne Boruch on A. Miller, reprinted from *The Literary Review*, Vol. 24, No. 4 (Summer 1981), pp. 548–49, 555, 560, published by Fairleigh Dickinson University; Paul R. Lilly, Jr., on Kosinski, reprinted from *The Literary Review*, Vol. 25, No. 3 (Spring 1982), pp. 390–91, published by Fairleigh Dickinson University.

Little, Brown and Co., for excerpts from books published by them, cited in text as Little; for the excerpt from *The Third Rose* by John Malcolm Brinnin, published by Atlantic-Little, Brown and Company; for the excerpt from *The Thought and Character of William James* by Ralph Barton Perry, published by Atlantic-Little, Brown and Company; for the excerpt from Alfred Kazin, *Contemporaries*. Copyright © 1958 by Alfred Kazin, by permission of Little, Brown and Co. in association with The Atlantic Monthly Press (Singer); Alfred Kazin, *The Bright Book of Life: American Novelists and Storytellers from Hemingway to Mailer*. Copyright © 1971, 1973 by Alfred Kazin, by permission of Little, Brown and Co. in association with The Atlantic Monthly Press (Burroughs, Capote, J. Jones, McCullers. Percy, Roth, Salinger, West); Louis Sheaffer, *O'Neill: Son and Playwright; Martin Gottfried, A Theatre Divided: The Postwar American Stage* (L. Wilson); Robert Coles, *Walker Percy: An American Search*, by permission of Little, Brown and Co. From *Look Homeward: A Life of Thomas Wolfe* by David Herbert Donald. Copyright © 1987 by Magnus, Ltd. By permission of Little, Brown & Company.

Liveright Publishing Corporation. From Waldo Frank's Foreword to Jean Toomer, *Cane*; Leon Katz's Introduction to Gertrude Stein, *Fernhurst, Q.E.D. and Other Early Writings*.

William Logan. From article on Hayden in *Poetry*, copyright © 1977 by William Logan, used by permission of the author. First published in *Poetry*.

Logbridge-Rhodes. From article by Dave Smith in *Homage to Robert Penn Warren*, Frank Graziano, ed.

London Magazine. From articles by Malcolm Bradbury on Purdy, Simon Raven on Selby, Alan Ross on Plath.

London Review of Books. Jeremy Harding's piece ''Junk Mail,'' first published in *London Review of Books*, volume 15, number 18, 23rd September 1996.

Los Angeles Times Book Review, February 5, 1989; March 29, 1992; April 12, 1992; April 17, 1994. Copyright, 1989, 1992, 1994, Los Angeles Times. All reproduced by permission.

Louisiana State University Press. From essays by Haskell Block on Stevens, on Tate; Leonard Casper on O'Connor; Olga W. Vickery on L. Jones in *The Shaken Realist*, Melvin J. Friedman and John B. Vickery, eds.; Herbert Schneidau, *Ezra Pound: The Image and the Real*; Lewis P. Simpson, *The Man of Letters in New England and the South* (Howells); Grosvenor Powell, *Language as Being in the Poetry of Yvor Winters*; James Justus, *The Achievement of Robert Penn Warren*; Robert S. Dupree, *Allen Tate and the Augustinian Imagination*; articles by Lewis P. Simpson on Faulkner, William Harmon on Ammons in *The American South: Portrait of a Culture*, Louis D. Rubin, Jr., ed.; Sherman Paul, *Repossessing and Renewing* (W. C. Williams); George S. Lensing and Ronald Moran, *Four Poets and the Emotive Imagination* (Bly, Stafford, J. Wright); Michael Kreyling, *Eudora Welty's Achievement of Order*; Louise Kertesz, *The Poetic Vision of Muriel Rukeyser*; Louis D. Rubin, Jr., *The Wary Fugitives: Four Poets and the South* (Ransom); Carol Shloss, *Flannery O'Connor's Dark Comedies: The Limits of Inference*; article by Ted R. Spivey in *The Art of Walker Percy: Stratagems for Being*, Panthea Reid Broughton, ed.; C. Hugh Holman, *The Loneliness at the Core: Studies in Thomas Wolfe*.

Jack Ludwig. From article on Singer in *Midstream*.

Thomas J. Lyon. From article on Snyder in *Kansas Quarterly*.

Macmillan Publishing Co., Inc. From Jerry H. Bryant, *The Open Decision* Copyright © 1970 by The Free Press, a Division of The Macmillan Company (Vonnegut); Denis Donoghue, *The Ordinary Universe*. Copyright © 1968 by Denis Donoghue (Burke, Eliot, Fitzgerald, H. James, Jarrell, Moore, O'Neill, Pound, W. C. Williams); Theodore L. Gross. *The Heroic Ideal in American Literature*. Copyright © 1971 by Theodore L. Gross (Ellison, Hemingway, Mailer, Salinger, R. Wright); John McCormick, *The Middle Distance*. Copyright © 1971 by The Free Press, a Division of The Macmillan Company (Anderson, Lewis); Gerald Weales, *The Jumping-Off Place*. Copyright © 1969 by Gerald Weales (Albee. L. Jones, Lowell, A. Miller, Shepard); Charles Doyle, *William Carlos Williams and the American Poem*.

Melvin Maddocks. From article on Gardner in *The Atlantic Monthly*.

Karl Malkoff. From article on Rexroth in *The Southern Review*.

Paul Mariani for his excerpt on Lowell.

The Markham Review. From article by Jean Frantz Blackall on Frederic; James Rambeau on Hurston.

The Massachusetts Review, for the quotations from *The Massachusetts Review*, which are copyrighted © 1965, 1966, by The Massachusetts Review, Inc.; for articles by Richard E. Baldwin on R. Wright. Copyright © 1973 by The Massachusetts Review, Inc.; E. M. Beekman on Chandler, on Hammett, on Himes. Copyright © 1973 by The Massachusetts Review, Inc.; William C. Fischer on L. Jones. Copyright © 1973 by The Massachusetts Review, Inc.; Josephine Jacobsen on Viereck. Copyright © 1968 by The Massachusetts Review, Inc.; Donald Junkins on Creeley. Copyright © 1968 by The Massachusetts Review, Inc.; Paul Mariani on W. C. Williams. Copyright © 1972 by The Massachusetts Review, Inc.; M. L. Rosenthal on Olson. Copyright © 1971 by The Massachusetts Review, Inc. All reprinted by permission from *The Massachusetts Review*; Wilburn Williams, Jr., on Hayden. Reprinted from *The Massachusetts Review*, © 1979 by The Massachusetts Review, Inc.

Harold Matson Company, Inc. From Steven Marcus's Introduction to *The Continental Op* (Hammett).

John R. May. From article on Chopin in *The Southern Review*.

Michael McClure. From essay in Sam Shepard, *Mad Dog Blues, and Other Plays*.

Jerome McGann. From article on Creeley in *Poetry*.

McIntosh and Otis, Inc., for permission for the British Commonwealth for the excerpt from *Ambrose Bierce* by Richard O'Connor, and for the excerpt from Jack London by Richard O'Connor.

David McKay Company. From essays by Robert Boyers on Jeffers; Jan B. Gordon on Frost; William Heyen on Snodgrass; John Logan on Cummings; H. R. Wolf on Robinson, in *Modern American Poetry*, Jerome Mazzaro, ed. Copyright © 1970 by the David McKay Company, Inc. Reprinted with permission of

Modern Language Association of America, for excerpts from the following articles, reprinted by permissions of the Modern Language Association: from Julia Cluck's "Elinor Wylie's Shelley Obsession," *PMLA*, LVI (Sept., 1941); from Stanley Greenfield's "The Unmistakable Stephen Crane," *PMLA*, LXXIII (December, 1958); from James G. Hepburn's "E. A. Robinson's System of Opposites," *PMLA*, LXXX (June, 1965); from Benjamin T. Spencer's "Pound: The American Strain," *PMLA*, LXXXI (December, 1966); from Frank Doggett, "The Transition from *Harmonium*: Factors in the Development of Steven's Later Poetry," *PMLA* 88. Copyright © 1973 by Modern Language Association of America; Philip L. Gerber, "The Financier Himself: Dreiser and C.T. Yerkes," *PMLA* 88. Copyright © 1973 by Modern Language Association of America; Paul N. Siegel, "The Conclusion of Richard Wright's *Native Son*," *PMLA* 89. Copyright © 1974 by Modern Language Association of America. Reprinted by permission.

Modern Language Quarterly. Kathleen Verduin. "Sex, Nature, and Dualism in *The Witches of Eastwick*," *Modern Language Quarterly*, 46:3 (September 1985), pp. 293–315. Copyright University of Washington, 1985. Reprinted with permission.

Modern Poetry Studies. From articles by Thomas A. Duddy on Zukofsky; Neil Schmitz on Reed; Ruth Quebe on Bishop; William Aiken on Ginsberg; Jean D. Rosenbaum on Piercy.

Ellen Moers, for the excerpt from her article on Theodore Dreiser in the *American Scholar* (Winter, 1963–64), to be published in her book, *Two Dreisers* (Viking).

Charles Molesworth. From article on Kinnell in *The Western Humanities Review*

John Rees Moore. From article on Warren in *The Southern Review*.

Edwin Morgan. From article on Thomas McGuane in *The Listener*.

William Morris Agency, Inc., for the excerpt from *Principles and Persuasions* by Anthony West, copyright © 1952 by Anthony West; for Robert Nemiroff's Foreword and James Baldwin's Preface in *To Be Young, Gifted and Black* by Lorraine Hansberry, adapted by Robert Nemiroff. Reprinted by permission of William Morris Agency. Inc. Copyright © 1969 by Robert Nemiroff and Robert Nemiroff as Executor of the Estate of Lorraine Hansberry and Copyright © 1969 by James Baldwin.

William Morrow & Company, Inc., for the excerpt from *Stephen Crane* by John Berryman, copyright © 1950 by William Sloane Associates, Inc.; for the excerpt from *Margaret Mitchell of Atlanta* by Finis Farr, copyright © 1965 by Finis Farr and Stephens Mitchell; Michel Fabre, *The Unfinished Quest of Richard Wright*. Copyright © 1973 by William Morrow and Company, Inc.; Hugh Kenner, *Bucky*. Copyright © 1973 by Hugh Kenner (Fuller); Alex de Jonge in *Vladimir Nabokov—A Tribute*, Peter Quennell, ed., published by William Morrow & Co., Inc., Publishers.

Mosaic. From article by Stanley Corngold on Kosinski in *Mosaic: A Journal of the Comparative Study of Literature and Ideas* published by the University of Manitoba Press, Volume VI, No. 4; article by Stephanie A. Demetrakopoulos on Nin in *Mosaic: A Journal for the Interdisciplinary Study of Literature*, 12, 2 (Winter 1978), 121–22; "Quantum Physics and the Ouija-Board: James Merrill's Holistic World View," by C.A. Buckley. This article originally appeared in *Mosaic: A Journal for the Interdisciplinary Study of Literature,* volume 26, number 2 (Spring 1993). "Between the wave and particle': Figuring Science in Howard Nemerov's Poems," by Miriam Marty Clark. This article originally appeared in *Mosaic: A Journal for the Interdisciplinary Study of Literature,* volume 24, number 4 (Fall 1990), published by the University of Manitoba, to whom acknowledgment is herewith made.

Mother Jones. From article by Katha Pollitt on Roth.

Ms. Magazine. From articles by Barbara Smith on Walker, *Ms. Magazine*, February 1974; Vivian Gornick on Hellman, *Ms. Magazine*, August 1976; Brigitte Weeks on Godwin, *Ms. Magazine*, January 1982; Gloria Steinem on Walker, *Ms. Magazine*, June 1982.

Lisel Mueller. From article on Snyder in *Poetry*.

Multicultural Review. Excerpts from the Joseph Milicia article on Kay Boyle which appeared in *Multicultural Review*, April 1992, p. 73. Copyright © 1992. Reprinted by permission of Greenwood Publishing Group, Inc., Westport, CT.

Philip Murray. From article on Wilbur in *poetry*.

The Nation. Excerpts from the Ray Gonzalez article on Rudolfo Anaya which appeared in *The Nation* magazine, July 18, 1994, pp. 98, 100. Reprinted with permission from *The Nation* magazine, © 1994 The Nation Company L.P. Excerpts from the Randall Kenan article on James Baldwin which appeared in *The Nation*, May 2, 1994, p. 596. Reprinted with permission from *The Nation* magazine, © 1994 The Nation Company L.P. Excerpts from the T. Solotaroff article on E.L. Doctorow which appeared in *The Nation*, June 6, 1994, p. 790. Reprinted with permission from *The Nation* magazine, © 1994 The Nation Company L.P. Excerpts from the Steven Moore article on W. Gaddis which appeared in *The Nation*, April 25, 1994. p. 505. Reprinted with permission from *The Nation* magazine.© 1994 The Nation Company L.P. Excerpts from the Jill Nelson article on H.L. Gates which appeared in *The Nation*, June 6, 1994. p. 795. Reprinted with permission from *The Nation* magazine, © 1994 The Nation Company L.P. Excerpts from the J. Montefiore article on Adrienne Rich which appeared in *The Nation*, Feb. 7, 1994, pp. 169–70. Reprinted with permission from *The Nation* magazine © 1994 The Nation Company L.P. Excerpts from the Barbara Kingsolver article on T.C. Boyle which appeared in *The Nation*, Sept. 25, 1955. pp. 326–27. Reprinted with permission from *The Nation* magazine, © 1955 The Nation Company L.P.

The Nation, New York, v. 208, February 24, 1969; February 2, 1970; v. 224, June 18, 1977; v. 225, September 17, 1977; v. 234, April 3, 1982; v. 235, November 27, 1982; v. 240, April 27, 1985; v. 243, November 1, 1986; v. 244, January 24, 1987; v. 244, May 16, 1987; v. 249, October 16, 1989; v. 250, January 1, 1990; v. 255, December 14, 1992; May 6, 1996. © 1969, 1970, 1977, 1982, 1985, 1986, 1987, 1989, 1990, 1992, 1996 The Nation magazine/ The Nation Company, Inc. All reproduced by permission.

The National Council of Teachers of English, for permission to use excerpts from articles in *College English*, cited in text; for permission to use excerpts from articles in *English Journal*, cited in text; for the excerpt from the article by Susan Friedman on Doolittle in *College English*.

National Poetry Foundation. From article by Carroll F. Terrell in *Louis Zukofsky: Man and Poet*, Carroll F. Terrell, ed.; articles by Mary Bryan, Gayle Gaskill in *May Sarton: Woman and Poet*, Constance Hunting, ed.

National Review, for excerpts from articles by John Dos Passos and Hugh Kenner, Guy Davenport on Didion, on Gardner, on Zukofsky: Theodore Sturgeon on Vonnegut: Geoffrey Wagner on Wilder, cited in text, permission granted by *National Review*, 150 East 35th Street, New York, N.Y. 10016.

Howard Nemerov. From *Reflexions on Poetry & Poetics* (Aiken, Burke).

Stella A. Nesanovich. From article on Tyler in *The Southern Review*.

The New Criterion. Excerpts from the James W. Tuttleton article on Edith Wharton which appeared in *The Nation*, March 1989, pp. 13–14. Reprinted with permission from *New Criterion* © 1989.

New Directions Publishing Corporation, for the excerpt from the Introduction by Leslie Fiedler to *The Lime Twig* by John Hawkes, copyright © 1949 by New Directions; for the excerpt from the Introduction by Albert Guerard to *The Cannibal* by John Hawkes, Copyright © 1961 by New Directions; for the excerpts from *Assays* by Kenneth Rexroth, copyright © 1961 by Kenneth Rexroth; and for the excerpt from the Introduction by Mark Van Doren to *Selected Poems* by Thomas Merton, copyright © 1959 by New Directions Publishing Corporation and Mark Van Doren; for Robert Creely's Introduction to *Charles Olson: Selected Writings* Copyright © 1966 by Charles Olson. Reprinted by permission of New Directions Publishing Corporation: *American Free Verse* by Walter Sutton. Copyright © 1973 by Walter Sutton. Reprinted by permission of New Directions Publishing Corporation (Snyder); for the excerpt from article by Mark Johnson and Robert DeMott in *Robert Duncan: Scales of the Marvelous*; Robert J. Berthoff and Ian W. Reid, eds., copyright © 1979 by New Directions Publishing Corporation, reprinted by permission of New Directions Publishing Corporation; article by Enid Veron in *A John Hawkes Symposium: Design and Debris*, Anthony C. Santore and Michael Pocalyko, eds., copyright © 1977 by New Directions Publishing Corporation, reprinted by permission of New Directions; excerpts from *Robert Creeley and the*

Genius of the American Common Place by Tom Clark. Copyright © 1993 by Tom Clark. Reprinted with the permission of New Directions Publishing Corp.

New England Review. From article by Ejner J. Jensen on Wilbur, *New England Review* 2, 4 (1980), 594–95; excerpts from the Allen Shepherd article on C. McCarthy which appeared in *New England Review*, Winter 1994, pp. 176–77, 178–79. Copyright © 1994.

New England Review and Bread Loaf Quarterly, v. 6, Winter, 1983 for "Marvin Bell: Essays, Interviews, Poems" by David Baker. Copyright © 1983 by Kenyon Hill Publications, Inc. Reproduced by permission of the author.

The New Leader, for the excerpts reprinted with permission from The New Leader of Feb. 15, 1965, April 16, 1962, April 30, 1962, Aug. 5, 1963, Feb. 15, 1965, Oct. 28, 1963, and April 11, 1966; from articles by Akbert Bermel on Bullins; Stephen Stepanchev on Wakoski; Shimon Wincelberg on Singer; Paula Meinetz Shapiro on Walker, Jan. 25. 1971, reprinted with permission from *The New Leader*; article by Pearl K. Bell on Irving, Nov. 25, 1974, reprinted with permission from *The New Leader*; article by Daphne Merkin on Updike, Dec. 4, 1978, reprinted with permission from *The New Leader*; G. Searles article on Ken Kesey which appeared in *The New Leader*, Jan. 14, 1991. pp. 20–21. Reprinted with permission of *The New Leader*, 1996. Copyright © the American Labor Conference on International Affairs, Inc. Excerpts from the John Simon article on Randall Jarrell which appeared in *The New Leader*, May 14–28, 1990. p. 13. Reprinted with permission of *The New Leader*, 1996. Copyright © the American Labor Conference on International Affairs, Inc. Excerpts from the Phoebe Pettingell article on Howard Nemerov which appeared in *The New Leader*, Dec. 30. 1994, pp. 27–28. Reprinted with permission of *The New Leader*, 1996. Copyright © the American Labor Conference on International Affairs, Inc. Excerpts from the George J. Searles article on John Updike which appeared in *The New Leader*, Oct. 1–15, 1990, p. 21. Reprinted with permission of *The New Leader*, 1996. Copyright © the American Labor Conference on International Affairs, Inc. Excerpts from the Stefan Kanfer article on August Wilson which appeared in *The New Leader*, May 4, 1992. p. 21. Reprinted with permission of *The New Leader*, 1996. Copyright © the American Labor Conference on International Affairs, Inc. Excerpts from the John Simon article on Mary McCarthy which appeared in *The New Leader*, June 1, 1992, pp. 23–4. Reprinted with permission of *The New Leader*, 1996. Copyright © the American Labor Conference on International Affairs, Inc. Vol. LV, October 16, 1972; v. LXXVI, April 5, 1993. © 1972, 1993 by The American Labor Conference on International Affairs, Inc. Reproduced by permission.

New Orleans Review. Excerpts from article on John Ashbery by Paul Munn which appeared in *New Orleans Review*, Copyright © 1992 and reprinted with the permission of *New Orleans Review*. Excerpts from article on Robert Bly by Jeffrey Alan Triggs which appeared in *New Orleans Review*. Copyright © 1992 and reprinted with the permission of *New Orleans Review*.

The New Republic. For articles by Calvin Bedient on Hawkes; Robert Brustein on Shepard; Lincoln Caplan on Buechner; William F. Clarie on Van Doren; Robert Coles on Salinger; Malcolm Cowley on Wilson; Louis Coxe on Garrigue; J. Michael Crichton on Vonnegut; James Finn on Kosinski; Lloyd Frankenberg on Goodman; Richard Gilman on Gass; Doris Grumbach on Sarton; Josephine Jacobsen on Levertov; Stanley Kauffmann on Doctorow, on J. O'Hara, on Rabe, on Saroyan; William Kennedy on Gardner; Hilton Kramer on Howard; W. T. Lhamon, Jr., on Pynchon; Robert Littel on Toomer; Townsend Ludington on Dos Passos; Irving Malin on Calisher; Saul Maloff on Algren, on Plath; Willie Morris on Capote; Herbert J. Muller on Mencken; Marjorie G. Perloff on Lowell; Jack Richardson on Kesey; Charles Thomas Samuels on Connell, on Vonnegut; Webster Schoot on Connell; John Seelye on Mailer; Charles Shapiro on Oates; Barbara Smith on Reed; John Wain on Cheever; James Walt on Hellman; Reed Whittemore on Auden, on Condon, on Cummings; Jonathan Yardley on Auchincloss, on Brautigan, on Faulkner, on London, on Sheed; anon on Malamud; Irving Howe on Olsen; Robert Brustein on Guare, Kopit, Mamet, L. Wilson; Richard Gilman on Malamud; Sontag; John Seelye on Piercy: Clancy Sigal on Elkin; Robert Scholes on Le Guin; Rosellen Brown on Ozick; Thomas LeClair on Gass; Josephine Hendin on Gardner; Joyce Carol Oates on Olsen; Nicholas Delbanco on Tyler; Noah Perrin on Cozzens; Daphne Merkin on J. Bowles; Edith Milton on Godwin; Harold Bloom on Hollander; Jack Beatty on Irving, Theroux; Bruce Allen on Morris; Ira Kapp on Berger; Ann Hulburt on Rossner; Leo Braudy on Sontag; Stefan Kanfer on Vidal; Helen Vendler on Sexton; Robert Alter on Malamud. Reprinted by permission of *The New Republic*, copyright © 1923, 1942, 1957, 1961, 1962, 1966, 1968, 1969, 1970, 1971, 1972, 1973, 1974, 1975, 1976, 1977, 1978, 1979, 1980, 1981, 1982, 1983 The New Republic, Inc. For v. 169, October 6, 1973; August 10 & 17, 1974; v. 178, February 11, 1978; v. 178, June 17, 1978; v. 191, October 8, 1984;

v. 198, May 16, 1988; v. 203, September 24, 1990; v. 203, December 31, 1990; v. 208, May 24, 1993. ©
1973, 1974, 1978, 1984, 1988, 1990, 1993 The New Republic, Inc. All reproduced by permission of The
New Republic.

New Statesman. From articles by Walter Allen on Sheed; A, Alvarez on Hansberry; Neal Ascherson on
Connel; Brigid Brophy on Calisher; Alan Brownjohn on Kinnell; Miles Burrows on Coover; Janice Elliott
on Zukofsky; Clive Jordan on Yurick; Susan Knight on Gardner; v. 74, October 20, 1967; v. 82, October
22, 1971; v. 96, December 1, 1978. © 1967, 1971, 1978 The Statesman & Nation Publishing Co. Ltd. All
reproduced by permission.

New Statesman & Society, v. 3, January 19, 1990; v. 6, December 3, 1993. © 1990, 1993 The Statesman
and Nation Publishing Co. Ltd. Both reproduced by permission of the publisher.

Newsweek, for excerpts from book reviews, copyright © Newsweek, Inc., Jan.-April, 1967; from articles
by Walter Clemons on Berger, on Lowell, on Pynchon; Arthur Cooper on Calisher; Rebert A. Gross on
Reed; Jack Kroll on Drexler, on Gass, on Rabe, on T. Williams; Peter S. Prescott on Auden, on Brautigan,
on Coover, on Doctorow, on Macdonald, on Ozick; Geoffery Wolff on Gass; Robert A. Gross on Angelou;
Jack Kroll on L. Wilson; Peter S. Prescott on Barth, Le Guin, Roth, and Walker; Raymond Sokolov on
Morrison. Copyright © 1968, 1969, 1970, 1971, 1972, 1973, 1974, 1975, 1976, 1977, 1978, 1980, 1981,
1982, 1983 by Newsweek, Inc. All rights reserved. Reprinted by permission. Vol. CIV, September 24,
1984. © 1984 Newsweek, Inc. All rights reserved. Reproduced by permission.

The New Yorker. From articles by Penelope Gilliatt on De Vries; Edith Oliver on Bullins, on Horovitz, on
Vonnegut, on Kopit, on Mamet; L. E. Sissman on McGuane, on Pynchon; Kenneth Tynan on Hansberry; v.
44, February 15, 1969 from "The First Hurrah" by Edith Oliver. © 1969 by The New Yorker Magazine,
Inc. Excerpted by permission.

New York Herald Tribune Weekly Book Review, July 10, 1960. Copyright © 1960 by The New York
Times Company. Reproduced by permission.

New York Magazine. From articles by John Simon, ''Rabe,'' copyright © 1973 by the NYM Corp, on
Kopit, L. Wilson, copyright © 1978, 1979 by News Group Publications, Inc. Excerpted with the
permission of New York Magazine.

The New York Review of Books, for excerpts from reviews dated 1964, 1965, 1966, 1967; from articles by
Robert M. Adams on Bathelme, on Fitzgerald; John Ashbery on Ammons; Eve Auchincloss on Calisher;
F.W. Bateson on Gardner; Joseph Brodsky on Kunitz; D. S. Carne-Ross on Gardner; Denis Donoghue on
Ashbbery, on Snodgrass, on Winters; Thomas R. Edwards on Baldwin, on Bukowski, on Mailer, on Reed;
Irvin Ehrenpreis on Wharton, on Updike; R. W. Flint on Kinnell; William Gass on Faulkner; Elizabeth
Hardwick on Plath, on Rahv; Geoffrey Hartman on Macarthy; V. S. Pritchett on Singer; Jack Richardson
on Kerouac, on Nabokov; Christopher Ricks on Coover, on Oates; Philip Roth on Malamud; Roger Sale on
Doctorow, on Elliott, on Fuller, on Mumford; Susan Sontag on Goodman; Stephen Spender on Ammons,
on Merrill, on Merwin; Jean Stafford on Chopin; Donald Sutherland on Stein; John Thompson on Heller;
Virgil Thomson on Bowles, on Stein; Rosemary Tonks on Garrigue; Gore Vidal on Auchincloss; John
Wain on Dahlberg; Michael Wood on Barth, on Connell, on Gass, on Drexler, on McGuane, on Mailer, on
Welty; for excerpts from essay on Sinclair Lewis by Gore Vidal which appeared in The New York Review
of Books, Oct. 8, 1992, pp. 14, 20. Excerpts from essay on Gore Vidal by Diane Johnson which appeared in
The New York Review of Books, Apr. 8, 1993, p. 25. Excerpts from essay on T. C. Boyle by Paul Auster
which appeared in The New York Review of Books, Jan. 17, 1991, p. 32. Excerpts from essay on Charles
Johnson by Gary Wills which appeared in The New York Review of Books, Jan. 17, 1991, p. 3. Excerpts
from essay on Robert Stone by Robert M. Adams which appeared in The New York Review of Books, Mar.
26, 1992, pp. 29–32. Excerpts from essay on Richard Ford by E. Hardwick which appeared in The New
York Review of Books, Aug. 10, 1995, pp. 11–14. Reprinted with permission from The New York Review of
Books. Copyright © Nyrev, Inc. 1963–1975; copyright © 1991–95 NYREV, Inc. Vol. IX, October 12,
1967; v. XXII, March 6, 1975; v. XXVI, April 19, 1979; v. XXXVI, February 16, 1989. Copyright © 1967,
1975, 1979, 1989 Nyrev, Inc. All reproduced with permission from The New York Review of Books.

The New York Times, for excerpts from reviews and articles in The New York Times Book Review,
Magazine, Arts & Leisure section, and daily New York Times cited in text, copyright © 1919, 1921, 1925,

The Ohio Review. From article by Richard Howard on Strand, originally published in *The Ohio Review*; excerpts on D. Levertov by Donald Revell. Copyright © Spring 1990. Reprinted with the permission of *The Ohio Review*.

Ohio State University Press. From Todd M. Lieber's *Endless Experiments: Essays on the Heroic Experience in American Romanticism* (Stevens. W.C. Williams); from Kathleen Woodward, *"At Last, The Real Distinguished Thing": The Late Poems of Eliot, Pound, Stevens, and Williams*, copyright © 1980 by the Ohio State University Press, all rights reserved; used by permission of the author and publisher (Eliot, Pound, Stevens, W. C. Williams).

Ohio University Press. From Max F. Schulz, *Black Humor Fiction of the Sixties* (Barth, Friedman, Pynchon); Sharon Spencer, *Collage of Dreams: The Writings of Anaïs Nin*; Benjamin Franklin V and Duane Schneider, *Anaïs Nin: An Introduction*; John O. Stark, *Pynchon's Fictions: Thomas Pynchon and the Literature of Information*; Laura Adams, *Existential Battles: The Growth of Norman Mailer*; Elizabeth Isaacs, *An Introduction to the Poetry of Yvor Winters*. Excerpts from *The Uncollected Edmund Wilson*, edited by Janet Groth and David Castronovo. Copyright © 1995. Reprinted with the permission of Ohio University Press.

The Open Court Publishing Company. From Roy Fuller. *Owls and Artificers* (Moore. Stevens).

Opportunity. From Article by Gorham B. Munsion on Toomer. Reprinted with Permission of the National Urban League.

Oregon State University. From article by Jackson J. Benson in *The Fiction of Bernard Malamud*, Jackson J. Benson, ed.

Alicia Ostriker. From article on Dugan in *Partisan Review*.

Peter Owen, Ltd., for permission for the British Commonwealth for excerpts from *The Landscape of Nightmare* by Jonathan Baumbach, *F. Scott Fitzgerald* by James E. Miller.

Oxford University Press (England), for the excerpt from *Image of the City and Other Essays* by Charles Williams; for permission for the British Commonwealth for the excerpt from *T.S. Eliot's Dramatic Theory and Practice* by C. H. Smith.

Oxford University Press, Inc., for excerpts, as follows: *The Colloquial Style in America* by Richard Bridgman. Copyright © 1966 by Richard Bridgman; from *The Poetry of Robert Frost* by Reuben Brower. Copyright © 1963 by Reuben A. Brower; from *Ezra Pound* by Donald Davie. Copyright © 1964 by Donald Davie; from *The Thought of Reinhold Niebuhr* by Gordon Harland. Copyright © 1960 by Oxford University Press, Inc.; from *Form and Fable in American Fiction* by Daniel G. Hoffman. Copyright © 1961 by Daniel G. Hoffman; from *The Partial Critics* by Lee T. Lemon. Copyright © 1965 by Lee T. Lemon; from *American Renaissance* by F. O. Mathiessen. Copyright © 1941 by Oxford University Press, Inc.; from *The Power Elite* by C. Wright Mills. Copyright © 1956 by Oxford University Press, Inc.; from *The New Poets* by M. L. Rosenthal. Copyright © 1967 by M. L. Rosenthal; from *The Modern Poets* by M. L. Rosenthal. Copyright © 1960 by M. L. Rosenthal; from *F. Scott Fitzgerald: The Last Laocoon* by Robert Sklar. Copyright © 1967 by Robert Sklar; from *The Poetry of W. H. Auden* by Monroe K. Speares, Copyright © 1963 by Monroe K. Spears; from *The American Historian* by Harvey Wish. Copyright © 1960 by Oxford University Press, Inc.; from *Harlem Renaissance* by Nathan Irvin Huggins. Copyright © 1971 by Oxford University Press. Inc. (Cullen, Hughes, O'Neill); *Richard Eberhart: The Progress of an American Poet* by Joel Roaches. Copyright © 1971 by Joel Roaches; *The Fabulators* by Robert Scholes. Copyright © 1967 by Robert Scholes (Vonnegut); *Dionysus and the City: Modernism in Twentieth-Century Poetry* by Monroe K. Spears. Copyright © 1970 by Monroe K. Spears (Berryman, Dickey, Ransom, Roethke, Tate); *Science and Sentiment in America: Philosophical Thought from Jonathan Edwards to John Dewey* by Morton White. Copyright © 1972 by Morton White (W. James, Santayana); David Kalstone, *Five Temperaments: Elizabeth Bishop, Robert Lowell, James Merrill, Adrienne Rich, John Ashbery*, copyright © 1977 by David Kalstone (Merrill, Rich); Richard Poirier, *Robert Frost: The Work of Knowing*, copyright © 1977 by Oxford University Press, Inc.; Cynthia Griffin Wolff, *A Feast of Words: The Triumph of Edith Wharton*, copyright © 1977 by Oxford University Press, Inc.; Richard H. King, *A Southern Renaissance: The Cultural Awakening of the American South, 1930–1955*, copyright © 1980 by Oxford University Press, Inc. (Wolfe). Excerpts from ''Whatever You Do Don't Go to the Joking,

Rhetoric and Homosexuality in the Orators,'' in *Auden Studies 2* by Richard Bozorth, ed. K. Bucknell and N. Jenkins. Copyright © 1994. All of the above reprinted by permission.

Cynthia Ozick. From an article on Calisher in *Midstream*.

Paideuma. From article by M. L. Rosenthal on Pound.

Pan American University. From article by James M. Haule in *James Dickey: Splintered Sunlight*, Patricia de la Fuente, ed.; article by Andrew Macdonald and Gina Macdonald in *Larry McMurtry: Unredeemed Dreams*, Dorey Schmidt, ed.

Papers on Language and Literature. Excerpts from the essay on William Styron by Daniel Ross which originally appeared in Papers on Language and Literature. Copyright © 1994.

Parnassus. From articles by Rosellen Brown on Sarton, Donald Davie on Lowell, R.W. Flint on Stickney, on Wheelwright, Diane Middlebrook on Ginsberg, Ralph J. Mills. Jr. on Eberhart, Levertov, and MacLeish; Eric Mottram on Levertov; M. L. Rosenthal on Creeley; Muriel Rukeyser on Sexton; Richard Saez on Merrill; Robert Stock on Nemerov; Helen Vendler on Rich; Larry Vonalt on Berryman; Robert Weisberg on Lattimore; Thomas R. Whitaker on Aiken; Bonnie Costello on Levertov; Margaret Atwood on Jong; Robert B. Shaw on Wilbur; Rosemary Johnson on Swenson; Guy Davenport on Olson; Alan Helms on Meredith; Paul Ramsey on Nemerov; excerpts from Evelyn Reilly's review on John Ashbery's *Flow Chart* which appeared in Volume 17, No. 2/Vol. 18, No. 1. Reprinted by permission of Parnassus.

Partisan Review, for excerpts from reviews and articles, cited in text, © 1941, 1947, 1951, 1959, 1961, 1962, 1964, 1965, 1966, 1967 by Partisan Review. Also from Calvin Bedient, ''Blind Mouths'' Copyright © 1972 by Partisan Review (Oates); Calvin Bedient, ''In Dreams Begin.'' Copyright © 1971 by Partisan Review (West); John Malcolm Brinnin, ''Plath, Jarrell, Kinnell, Smith.'' Copyright © 1967 by Partisan Review (Plath); Peter Brooks, ''The Melodramatic Imagination.'' Copyright © 1972 by Partisan Review (H. James); Elizabeth Dalton, ''Ada or Nana.'' Copyright ©1970 by Partisan Review (Nabokov); Martin Duberman, ''Theater 69.'' Copyright ©1969 by Partisan Review (Bullins, Hansberry); Thomas R. Edwards, ''The Indian Wants the Bronx.''Copyright © 1968 by Partisan Review (Fiedler): G. S. Fraser. ''The Magicians.'' Copyright © 1971 by Partisan Review (Howard): G. S. Fraser, ''A Pride of Poets.'' Copyright ©1968 by Partisan Review (Zukofsky); Alan Helms, ''Growing Up Together.'' Copyright © 1972 by Partisan Review (Ashbery); Maureen Howard, ''Other Voices.'' Copyright © 1968 by Partisan Review (Bowles); Richard Howard, ''Changes.'' Copyright © 1971 by Partisan Review (Rich); David Kalstone, ''All Eye.'' Copyright © 1970 by Partisan Review (Bishop); Kenneth Koch, ''Poetry Chronicles.'' Copyright © 1961 by Partisan Review (F. O'Hara): Norman Martien, ''I Hear America Singing.'' Copyright © 1971 by Partisan Review (Warren); Alicia Ostriker, ''Of Being Numerous.'' copyright © 1972 by Partisan Review (Dugan); Jane Richmond. ''To the End of the Night.'' Copyright © 1972 by Partisan Review (McGuane); Philip Stevick, ''Voice and Vision.'' Copyright © 1974 by Partisan Review, Inc, (Burroughs, Kosinski, Vonnegut); Tony Tanner, ''Bridsong.'' Copyright © 1972 by Partisan Review (Purdy); Alicia Ostriker, ''Shapes of Poetry.'' *Partisan Review*, 44, 4 (1977) (Hollander); Peter Brooks, ''Death of/as Metaphor,'' *Partisan Review*, 46, 3 (1979) (Sontag). Reprinted by permission of the authors and *Partisan Review*.

Passegiatta Press. See Three Continents.

Penguin. ''Gloria Naylor's Geography: Community, Class,'' by Barbara Christian, from *Reading Black, Reading Feminist* by Henry Louis Gates, Jr., Copyright © 1990 by Henry Louis Gates, Jr. Used by permission of Dutton Signet, a division of Penguin Books USA Inc. ''Cynthia Ozick'' by Tom Teicholz, from *Writers at Work, Eighth Series* by George Plimpton, editor, introduced by Joyce Carol Oates. Copyright © 1988 by The Paris Review, Inc. Used by permission of Viking Penguin Books USA Inc.

Pennsylvania State University Press. From James E. Miller. Jr., *T. S. Eliot's Personal Waste Land* (1977). By permission of The Pennsylvania State University Press, University Park, Pa.

Performing Arts Publications. From articles by Richard Coe, Michael X. Early, in *American Dreams: The Imagination of Sam Shepard*, Bonnie Marranca, ed.

David Perkins. From article on Auden in *The Southern Review*.

Marjorie Perloff. From Marjorie Perloff, *Frank O'Hara: Poet among Painters*, copyright © 1977 by Marjorie Perloff, copyright © 1979 by the University of Texas Press; originally published by George Braziller, used by permission of the author.

Phaidon Press, Ltd. From articles by Larzer Ziff and John Wain in *An Edmund Wilson Celebration*, John Wain, ed., published by Phaidon Press Ltd., Oxford, England, 1976. (American edition published by New York University Press and titled *Edmund Wilson: The Man and the Work.*)

Robert Phelps. From article on Goodman in *The New York Herald Tribune Book Section*.

Philosophy and Literature. For excerpts from article by Alan Collett on Truman Capote, © 10/89, pp. 289. Reprinted by permission of the Johns Hopkins University Press.

Phylon. From articles by Eugenia W. Collier on Johnson; Barbara Joye on Reed; S. P. Fullinwider on Toomer; and for v. XVIII, Second Quarter, 1957. Copyright, 1957, by Atlanta University. Reproduced by permission of PHYLON.

Robert Pinsky. From article on Strand in *Poetry*.

Playbill. Reprinted from *Playbill*, July 31, 1994. *Playbill* is a registered trademark of Playbill Incorporated, NYC. Used by permission.

Players Magazine (Editor Byron Schaffer, Jr.). From James R. Giles, ''Tenderness in Brutality: The Plays of Ed Bullins; James Hashim, ''Violence in the Drama of Tennessee Williams.''

PMLA, v. 105, January, 1990. Copyright 1990 by PMLA. Reproduced by permission of Modern Language Association of America.

Poetics Today. Wayne Pounds, ''The Postmodern Anus: Parody and Utopia in Two Recent Novels by William Burroughs,'' *Poetics Today*, 8:3–4 (1987), pp. 611–29. Copyright Porter Institute for Poetics & Semiotics, Tel Aviv University, 1987. Reprinted with permission.

Poet Lore. Excerpts from ''West of the Mississippi,'' by Edward Butscher which appeared in *Poet Lore*, Winter 1992.

Poetry. From Articles by Hazard Adams on Stafford; John R. Carpenter on Snyder, on Wakoski; Hayden Carruth on Bogan, on Merwin, on Schwartz, on Van Doren; Turner Cassity on Howard; Richard Eberhart on Scott; Daniel Hoffman on Cowley; Richard Howard on Auden; Ruth Lechlitner on Meredith; Philip Levine on Merwin; Laurence Lieberman on Dickey, on Duncan, on Garrigue, on Hughes, on Rexroth, on Rukeyser, on Shapiro, on Viereck, on J. Wright; Jerome McGann on Creeley; Lisel Mueller on Snyder; Phillp Murray on Wilbur; William Pritchard on Lowell; Ernest Sandeen on Blackmur; Robert B. Shaw on Meredith, on Tate; Barry Spacks on Dugan; Kathleen Spivack on Levertov; William Stafford on Brooks, on Olson; Dabney Stuart on Bukowski; Mona Van Duyn on Ashbery, on Rich, on Sexton; Alan Williamson on Lowell, on J. Wright. Copyright © 1944, 1962, 1963, 1964, 1966, 1967, 1968, 1969, 1970, 1971, 1972 by The Modern Poetry Association. Reprinted by permission of the editor of Poetry. Excerpts from the article on David Ignatow by David Wojahn first appeared in *Poetry*, copyright © 1995 by The Modern Poetry Association, and are reprinted by permission of the editor of *Poetry*. For v. CXXV, December, 1974 for ''The Big Machine'' by John R. Carpenter; v. CXLV, October, 1994 for a review of 'The Dead and the Living' by Linda Gregerson. © 1974, 1994 by the Modern Poetry Association. Both reproduced by permission of the Editor of Poetry and the respective authors.

Poetry Society of America Newsletter. Excerpts from article on Amy Clampitt by Jean Hanff Korelitz which appeared in *Poetry Society of America Newsletter*. Copyright © 1995. Excerpts from article on Amy Clampitt by Phoebe Pettingell which appeared in *Poetry Society of America Newsletter*. Copyright © 1995.

Laurence Pollinger, Ltd., for permission for the British Commonwealth for the excerpt from *The Third Rose* by John Malcolm Brinnin, published by George Weidenfeld & Nicholson, Ltd.

Cyrena N. Pondrom. From essay in *The Achievement of Isaac Bashevis Singer*, Marcia Allentuck, ed.

The Popular Press. *See* Bowling Green State University Popular Press.

Thomas E. Porter, S.J. From *Myth and Modern American Drama* (Albee).

Potpourri. Excerpts on William Stafford by Linda Rodriguez. Copyright © April 1993. Reprinted with the permission of Potpourri.

Prentice-Hall, Inc., for excerpts, as follows: from the Introduction to *O'Neill: A Collection of Critical Essays* by John Gassner, © 1964; from *Harvests of Change* by Jay Martin © 1967; from the Introduction to *Ezra Pound: A Collection of Critical Essays* by Walter Sutton © 1963; introduction by Stephen S. Stanton to *Tennessee Williams: A Collection of Critical Essays*, Stephen S. Stanton, ed., copyright © 1977; article by Arthur Ganz in *Tennessee Williams: A Collection of Critical Essays*, Stephen S. Stanton. ed., copyright © 1977; Introduction by Edward Mendelson to *Pynchon: A Collection of Critical Essays*, Edward Mendelson, ed., copyright © 1978; introduction by Robert Penn Warren in *Katherine Anne Porter: A Collection of Critical Essays*, Robert Penn Warren. ed., copyright © 1979; from essay by Donald E. Gibson on Hughes in *Modern Black Poets: A Collection of Critical Essays*, Donald E. Gibson, ed. Copyright © 1973 by Prentice-Hall, Inc.; Robert Nemiroff's Foreword in *To Be Young, Gifted, and Black: Lorraine Hansberry in Her Own Words*. Copyright © 1969 by Robert Nemiroff and Robert Nemiroff as Executor of the Estate of Lorraine Hansberry. Published by Prentice-Hall, Inc., Englewood Cliffs, New Jersey; essay by Charles Tomlinson in *Marianne Moore: A Collection of Critical Essays*, Charles Tomlinson, ed. Copyright © 1969 by Prentice-Hall, Inc., all of above by permission of Prentice-Hall, Inc., Englewood Cliffs. NJ07632.

Princeton University Library Chronicle. From article by Sherman Hawkins on Kinnell.

Princeton University Press. From Lillian Feder, *Ancient Myth in Modern Poetry*. Copyright © 1971 by Princeton University Press (Aiken, Eliot, Lowell, Merwin, Ransom); essays by Robert M. Adams, Michael Goldman, A. Walton Litz in *Eliot in His Time: Essays on the Occasion of the Fiftieth Anniversary of the Waste Land*, A. Walton Litz, ed. Copyright © 1973 by Princeton University Press; R. W. B. Lewis, *The Poetry of Hart Crane: A Critical Study*. Copyright © 1967 by Princeton University Press; Stuart Y. McDougal, *Ezra Pound and the Troubadour Tradition*. Copyright © 1972 by Princeton University Press; Jenijoy LaBelle, *The Echoing Wood of Theodore Roethke* (pp. 166–68), copyright © 1976 by Princeton University Press; Steven Gould Axelrod, *Robert Lowell: Life and Art* (pp. 11–12), copyright © 1978 by Princeton University Press; Lawrence Stapleton, *Marianne Moore: The Poet's Advance* (pp. 275–76), copyright © 1978 by Princeton University Press; John C. Kemp. *Robert Frost and New England: The Poet as Regionalist* (pp. 226–30, 235), copyright © 1979 by Princeton University Press; Michael André Bernstein, *The Tale of the Tribe: Ezra Pound and Modern Verse* (pp. 279–81), copyright © 1980 by Princeton University Press; Frank Doggett and Robert Buttel, eds. *Wallace Stevens: A Celebration* (pp. xi–xii, 275–76), copyright © 1980 by Princeton University Press. Reprinted by permission of Princeton University Press.

William H. Pritchard. From article on Lowell in *Poetry*.

Publishers Weekly. From the Jan. 18, 1985 issue of Publisher's Weekly, published by Cahners Publishing Company, a division of Reed Elsevier Inc. Copyright © 1985 by Reed Elsevier. From v. 237, November 2, 1990. Copyright 1990 by Reed Publishing USA. Reproduced from Publishers Weekly, published by the Bowker Magazine Group of Cahners Publishing Co., a division of Reed Publishing USA. From the Feb. 1, 1991 issue of Publisher's Weekly, published by Cahners Publishing Company, a division of Reed Elsevier Inc. Copyright © 1991 by Reed Elsevier. Reprinted from the June 22, 1995 issue of Publisher's Weekly, published by Cahners Publishing Company, a division of Reed Elsevier Inc. Copyright © 1995 by Reed Elsevier.

Purdue Research Foundation, for excerpts from *Modern Fiction Studies*, including Joyce Carol Oates on Updike, copyright © 1975; Keith Opdahl on Bellow, copyright © 1979; Hana Wirth-Nesher on Bellow, copyright © 1979; Bruce Michelson on Fitzgerald, copyright © 1981; Thomas LeClair on Gaddis, copyright © 1982, all by Purdue Research Foundation, West Lafayette, Indiana, U.S.A.

Raines & Raines. From James Dickey, *Babel to Byzantium*. Copyright © 1956, 1957, 1958, 1959, 1960, 1961, 1962, 1963, 1964, 1965, 1966, 1967, 1968 by James Dickey (Ashbery, Kinnell, Meredith, Olson, Stafford).

Random House, Inc., for the excerpt from *The Dyer's Hand* by W.H. Auden © Copyright 1962 by W.H. Auden. Reprinted by permission of Random House, Inc., for the excerpts from *A Piece of Lettuce* by George P. Elliott. Copyright © 1960 by George P. Elliott. Reprinted by permission of Random House, Inc.; for the excerpt from *Shadow and Act* by Ralph Ellison, Copyright © 1945 by Ralph Ellison. Reprinted by permission of Random House, Inc.; for excerpt from the Foreword by Clark Kinnaird to *A Treasury of Damon Runyon*. Copyright © 1958 by Random House, Inc. Reprinted by permission of Random House, Inc.; for excerpts from *Contemporary American Poetry* by Ralph J. Mills. © Copyright 1965 by Random House, Inc. Reprinted by permission; for excerpts from *Postscript to Yesterday* by Lloyd Morris. Copyright © 1947 by Lloyd Morris. Reprinted by permission of Random House, Inc.; for excerpt from *Father's Footsteps* by Damon Runyon, Jr. Copyright © 1953 by Curtis Publishing Co. Copyright © 1954 by Damon Runyon, Jr. Reprinted by permission of Random House, Inc.; for excerpt from the Introduction by Mark Schorer to *Selected Writings of Truman Capote*, © Copyright 1963 by Random House, Inc. Used by permission of Random House, Inc.; for excerpt from *The Autobiography by Alice B. Toklas* by Gertrude Stein. Copyright © 1933 and renewed 1961 by Alice B. Toklas. Reprinted by permission of Random House, Inc.; from A. Alvarez, ''Prologue: Sylvia Plath'' in *The Savage God: A Study in Suicide: The unwritten War* by Daniel Aaron. Copyright © 1973 by Daniel Aaron. Reprinted by permission of Alfred A. Knopf, Inc. (Bierce, Faulkner, Frederic, Howells, Twain); *The Confusion of Realms* by Richard Gilman. Copyright © 1963, 196, 1967, 1968, 1969 by Richard Gilman. Reprinted by permission of Random House, Inc; Steven Marcus's Introduction (Copyright © 1974 by Steven Marcus) to *The Continental Op* by Dashiell Hammett. By permission of Random House, Inc.; Carl Van Vechten's Introduction (Copyright © 1927 and renewed 1955 by Carl Van Vechen) to James Weldon Johnson, *The Autobiography of an Ex-Coloured Man*. Reprinted by permission of Alfred A. Knopf, Inc.; John A. Williams's essay on Himes in *Amistad 1*, John A. Williams and Charles F. Garris, eds.; Bernard Dick, *The Apostate Angel: A Critical Study of Gore Vidal*, copyright © 1974 by Random House, reprinted by permission of Random House, Inc.; John Updike, *Picked-Up Pieces*, copyright © 1975 by John Updike. Reprinted by permission of Alfred A. Knopf, Inc., originally published in *The New Yorker* (Jong); Charles A. Fecher, *Mencken: A Study of His Thought*, copyright © 1978 by Charles A. Fecher, reprinted by permission of Alfred A. Knopf, Inc.; article by Alistair Cooke in *On Mencken*, John Dorsey, ed., copyright © 1980 by Alfred A. Knopf, Inc., reprinted by permission of Alfred A. Knopf, Inc.; John Updike, *Hugging the Shore*, copyright © 1983 by John Updike, reprinted by permission of Alfred A. Knopf, Inc., originally published in *The New Yorker* (Bellow). Excerpts from *Henry Miller* by Leon Lewis. Copyright © 1986 by Schocken Books. Reprinted by permission of Schocken Books, published by Pantheon Books, a division of Random House, Inc. Excerpts from *The Devil at Large* by Erica Jong. Copyright © 1993 by Erica Jong. Reprinted by permission of Turtle Bay, a division of Random House.

Renascence. From article by Meta Lale and John Williams on Kosinski; from an essay on R. Wilbur by Gary Ciuba, © 1992/1993 by *Renascence*. Reprinted by permission of *Renascence*; from an essay on W. Percy by K. H. Westarp, © 1992 by *Renascence*. Reprinted by permission of *Renascence*.

Doug Rennie. Excerpts from article on Paul Auster by Doug Rennie which appeared in *Plant's Review of Books*. Copyright © 1994. Reprinted with the permission of Doug Rennie. Excerpts from article on John Cheever by Doug Rennie which appeared in *Plant's Review of Books*. Copyright © 1994. Reprinted with the permission of Doug Rennie.

The Review of Contemporary Fiction. Excerpts from article on Don DeLillo by Joseph Tabbi. Copyright © Fall 1991 and reprinted with the permission of the Review of Contemporary Fiction.

Kenneth Rexroth. From article on Goodman in *American Poetry Review*.

Paul R. Reynolds, Inc., for permission for the British Commonwealth for *O Rare Don Marquis* by Edward Anthony.

R. C. Reynolds. From article on McMurtry in *Southwest Review*.

Adrienne Rich. From article on Goodman in *American Poetry Review*; essay in *Randall Jarrell, 1914–1965*, Robert Lowell, Peter Taylor, and Robert Penn Warren, eds.

Jess Ritter. From essay on Heller in *Critical Essays on Catch-22*, James Nagel, ed.

Janice S. Robinson. From *H. D.: The Life and Work of an American Poet*.

James E. Rocks. From ''The Mind and Art of Caroline Gordon'' in *The Mississippi Quarterly*.

Deborah Rogers Ltd. From articles by Anthony Burgess on Calisher, on Eastlake in *The Listener*.

The Ronald Press Company, for the excerpt from *The Course of American Democratic Thought* by Ralph Henry Gabriel. Copyright © 1940, renewed 1968. The Ronald Press Company, New York.

Roger Rosenblatt. From essay on Hughes in *Veins of Humor*, Harry Levin, ed.

Mitchell D. Ross. From *The Literary Politicians* (Vidal).

Ross-Erickson, Inc., Publishers. From Paul Portugues. *The Visionary Poetics of Allen Ginsberg*.

Abraham Rothberg. From article on Snyder in *Southwest Review*.

Routledge & Kegan Paul, Ltd., for the excerpt from *Poetry and Belief in the Work of T.S. Eliot* by Kristian Smidt and for the excerpt from *T.S. Eliot and the Idea of Tradition* by Sean Lucy; for permission for the British Commonwealth for the excerpt from *Ezra Pound: Poet as Sculptor* by Donald Davie; for the excerpt from D. E. S. Maxwell, *Poets of the Thirities* (Auden). Excerpt from *Double Talk: The Erotics of Male Literary Collaboration*, by Wayne Koestenbaum (1989) (pp. 112–13 and 138–39).

Louis D. Rubin, Jr. From essays by James M. Cox on Twain, William Harmon on Pynchon, C. Hugh Holman on Lardner, Robert D. Jacobs on Faulker, Jay Martin on Bierce, Louis D. Rubin, Jr., on Mencken in *The Comic Imagination in American Literature*, Louis D. Rubin, Jr., ed.

Milton Rugoff. From article on Gaddis in *New York Herald Tribune Book Section*.

Jane Rule. From Lesbian Images. Doubleday, 1975. Copyright © 1975 by Jane Rule. Reproduced by permission of Georges Borchardt, Inc. on behalf of the author.

Rutgers University Press. From George W. Bahlke, *The Later Auden: From ''New Year Letter'' to ''About the House.''* Copyright © 1970 by Rutgers University press; Miller Williams, *The Poetry of John Crowe Ransom*. Copyright © 1972 by Miller Williams. Reprinted by permission of the author and Rutgers University Press. Karla F. C. Holloway, *Moorings and Metaphors*, copyright © 1992 by Karla F. C. Holloway. Reprinted by permission of Rutgers University Press. *The Playwright's Art*, Jackson R. Bryer, ed., copyright © 1995 by Rutgers, The State University. Reprinted by permission of Rutgers University Press.

Mariann B. Russell. From ''Evolution of Style in the Poetry of Melvin B. Tolson'' in *Black American Poets Between Worlds, 1940-1960*. Edited by R. Baxter Miller. University of Tennessee Press, 1986. Copyright © 1986 by The University of Tennessee Press. Reproduced by permission of The University of Tennessee Press.

St. Martin's Press, Incorporated. From George Garrett's essays on Connell, on Olson in *American Poetry*, John Russell Brown, Irvin Ehrenpreis, Bernard Harris, eds. By permission of St. Martin's Press, Inc. and Macmillan Co., Ltd; from Charles Doyle, *William Carlos Williams and the American Poem*; from Brian Way, *F. Scott Fitzgerald and the Art of Social Fiction*. Excerpts from *Saul Bellow: A Biography of the Imagination* by Ruth Miller. Copyright © 1991. Reprinted with the permission of St. Martin's Press, Inc. Excerpts from *The Fiction of Joseph Heller: Against the Grain* by David Seed. Copyright © 1989. Reprinted with the permission of St. Martin's Press, Inc. Excerpts from *The Postmodernist Allegories of Thomas Pynchon* by Deborah L. Modson. Copyright © 1991. Reprinted with the permission of St. Martin's Press, Inc. Excerpts from *Modern Novelists: John Updike* by Judie Newman. Copyright © 1988. Reprinted with the permission of St. Martin's Press, Inc. Excerpts from *Lillian Hellman: Her Legend and Her Legacy* by Carl E. Rollyson. Copyright © 1988. Reprinted with the permission of St. Martin's Press, Inc. Excerpts from *Radical Fictions and the Novels of Norman Mailer* by Nigel Leigh. Copyright © 1990. Reprinted with the permission of St. Martin's Press, Inc. Excerpts from *The American Novel* by A. Robert Lee (ed.). Copyright © 1989. Reprinted with the permission of St. Martin's Press, Inc. Excerpts from *Edith Wharton and the Art of Fiction* by Penelope Vita-Finzi. Copyright © 1990. Reprinted with the permission of St. Martin's Press, Inc. Excerpts from *Saul Bellow* by Peter Hyland. Copyright © 1993. Reprinted with the permission of St. Martin's Press, Inc. Excerpts from *Saul Bellow: A Biography of the Imagination* by

Ruth Miller. Copyright © 1991. Reprinted with the permission of St. Martin's Press, Inc. Excerpts from *David Mamet* by Dennis Carroll. Copyright © 1987. Reprinted with the permission of St. Martin's Press. Inc. Copyright © 1992 Ron Callan from *William Carlos Williams* by Ron Callan. Reprinted with permission of St. Martin's Press, Incorporated.

Salmagundi. From articles by Harold Bloom on Ashbery; Robert Boyers on Dugan; Henry Pachter on Goodman; Hyatt H. Waggoner on Ammons; Jerome Mazzaro on Ignatow; Richard Vine on Kunitz; excerpts from article on Robert Frost by Seamus Heaney. Copyright © Fall-Winter 1990–91 by *Salmagundi* and reprinted with the permission of the editors; excerpts from article on Stanley Kunitz by Terence Diggory. Copyright © Winter 1987 by *Salmagundi* and reprinted with the permission of the editors.

Ernest Sandeen. From article on Blackmur in *Poetry*.

San Francisco Review of Books. Excerpts from article on Terry McMillan by Myra Cole. Copyright © Fall 1992, pp. 20–21. Reprinted with the permission of *San Francisco Review of Books*. Excerpts from article on J. McInerney by S. Beacy. Copyright © Fall 1992, pp. 28–29, 30. Reprinted with the permission of *San Francisco Review of Books*. Excerpts from article on S. Shepard by E. Gillespie. Copyright © Fall 1993, pp. 12–14. Reprinted with the permission of *San Francisco Review of Books*. From v. VIII, Winter, 1983-84, "Good Luck in the New World" by Stephen Kessler. Reproduced by permission of the author.

Saturday Review. For generous permission to reprint mumerous excerpts from articles, copyright © 1948, 1959, 1961, 1963, 1964, 1966, 1968, 1969, 1972, 1976, 1977, 1979, 1980, 1981, 1982; also for v. 32, February 12, 1949; v. XLIII, July 23, 1960; v. 52, February 22, 1969. Copyright 1949, 1960, 1969 Saturday Review Magazine. © 1979, General Media Communications, Inc. Reproduced by permission of The Saturday Review.

Scarecrow Press, Inc. From Katherine Fishburn, *Richard Wright's Hero: The Faces of a Rebel-Victim*; Anne Z. Mickelson, *Reaching Out: Sensitivity and Order in Recent American Fiction by Women* (Godwin, Jong).

Richard Schechner. From article on Shepard in *Performance*.

Richard Schickel. From article on Doctorow in *Harper's Magzine*.

Duane Schneider. From article on Nin in *The Southern Review*.

Science Fiction Studies. From article by James W. Bittner on Le Guin; also from v. 15, March, 1988. Copyright © 1988 by SFS Publications. Reproduced by permission of the publisher.

Science Teacher. ''Isaac Asimov.'' *The Science Teacher*. Vol. 58, No. 2, pp. 71–73. Reprinted with permission from NSTA Publications, Jan. 1993, from *The Science Teacher*, National Science Teachers Association, 1840 Wilson Blvd., Arlington, VA 22201–3000.

Scott Meredith Literary Agency, Inc., for the excerpt from *Queen's Quorum* by Ellery Queen © 1951 by Little, Brown and Co. Reprinted by permission of the author and his agents, Scott Meredith Literary Agency, Inc., 580 Fifth Avenue, New York, New York 10036.

Charles Scribner's Sons. Reprinted by permission of Charles Scribner's Sons from *The Beat Generation* by Bruce Cook. Copyright © 1971 Bruce Cook (Brautigan, Kesey, Olson, Snyder).

The Seabury Press. From *With Eye and Ear* by Kenneth Rexroth. Copyright © by Herder and Herder, Inc. (Olson, Singer, Snyder); from *American Poetry in the Twentieth Century* by Kenneth Rexroth. Copyright © 1971 by Herder and Herder, Inc. (Ginsberg, Levertov, Moore, Wheelwright, W.C. Williams). Used by permission of the publisher, The Seabury Press, Inc.

Martin Secker & Warburg, Ltd., for permission for the British Commonwealth and Empire excluding Canada for the excerpts from *Shadow and Act* by Ralph Ellison, *Times Three* by Phyllis McGinley, *The Liberal Imagination* by Lionel Trilling, *Bright Book of Life* by Alfred Kazin (Burroughs, Capote, Jones,

McCullers, Percy, Roth, Salinger, West); *Contemporaries* by Alfred Kazin (Singer); *Nathanael West: The Art of His Life* by Jay Martin.

The Sewanee Review, for the excerpts from articles and reviews cited in text, copyright © 1950, 1951, 1953, 1955, 1957, 1958, 1959, 1960, 1961, 1962, 1963, 1964, 1965, 1966 by The University of the South; also for excerpts from articles by Dewey Ganzel on Hemingway; Caroline Gordon on O'Connor; F. H. Griffin Taylor on Lowell; William Hoffa on H. James; H. T. Kirby-Smith on Bishop; Thomas H. Landess on Meredith and Welty; Andrew Lytle on Gordon; Harry Morris on Bogan; Allen Tate on Ransom; Ruth M. Vande Kieft on O'Connor, copyright © 1949, 1968, 1969, 1970, 1971, 1972, 1973 by the University of the South; Lewis P. Simpson, "Malcolm Cowley and the American Writer," *Sewanee Review*, 84, 2 (Spring 1976), copyright © 1976 by the University of the South; Louis D. Rubin, Jr., "Not to Forget Carl Sandburg. . .," *Sewanee Review*, 85, 1 (Winter 1977), copyright © 1977 by the University of the South; Calvin Bedient, "Horace and Modernism," *Sewanee Review*, 85, 2 (Spring 1977), copyright © 1977 by the University of the South (Merwin); Denis Donoghue, "Trilling, Mind, and Society," *Sewanee Review*, 86, 2 (Spring 1978), copyright © 1978 by the University of the South; J.A. Bryant, Jr., "Allen Tate: The Man of Letters in the Modern World," *Sewanee Review*, 86, 2 (Spring 1978), copyright © 1978 by the University of the South; Tom Johnson, "Study Sense and Vital Humanism," *Sewanee Review*, 86,4 (Fall 1978), copyright ©1978 by the University of the South; (MacLeish); Louis D. Rubin, Jr., "Allen Tate 1899–1979," *Sewanee Review*, 87,2 (Spring 1979), copyright © 1979 by the University of the South; "Randall Jarrell and 'Poetry and the Age'" by Calvin Bedient. First published in the *Sewanee Review*, vol. 93, no. 1, Winter 1985. Copyright © 1985 by Calvin Bedient. Reprinted with the permission of the editor and the author.

Robert B. Shaw. From articles on Meredith, on Tate in *Poetry*.

Frank W. Shelton. From article on Gaines in *The Southern Review*.

Shenandoah. From articles by Lisel Mueller on Bly; M. L. Rosethal on Ammons; Herschel Gower on Taylor and Henry Sloss on Howard, both Copyright © 1977 by Washington and Lee University, reprinted from *Shenandoah: The Washington and Lee University Review*, with the permission of the editor.

Vernon Shetley. From article on Kinnell in *Poetry*.

Silver Burdett Press. For permission to reprint the excerpt by Nancy Shuker on Angelou.

Simon and Schuster, Inc., for the excerpts from *American Playwrights: 1918–1938* by Eleanor Flexner, copyright 1938, © 1966 by Eleanor Flexner; for the excerpt from *Mr. Clemens and Mark Twain* by Justin Kaplan, © 1966 by Justin Kaplan.

Lewis P. Simpson. From an article on Welty in *The Southern Review*.

Louis Simpson. From article on Snyder in *Harper's*.

Dave Smith. From article on Swenson in *Poetry*.

South Atlantic Review (formerly South Atlantic Bulletin). From article by Myra K. McMurry on Angelou in *South Atlantic Bulletin*.

South Carolina Review. From articles by Linda Wagner on Dickey and Levertov.

South Dakota Review. From articles by Charles A. Nicholas on Momaday; excerpts from the article on John Berryman by Jeffrey Alan Triggs. First published in the South Dakota Review, Summer 1988. Copyright © 1988 and reprinted by permission.

Southern Humanities Review. From articles by Ashley Brown on Gordon; James O. Hoge on Kesey; Alfred S. Reid on Shapiro; Max F. Schulz on Singer; James J. Thompson, Jr. on Caldwell; Frank W. Shelton, "Nathanael West and the Theater of the Absurd; A Comparative Study," *Southern Humanities Review*, 10, 3, (Summer 1976), 225, 231–34, copyright 1976 by Auburn University; Sidonie A. Smith, "The Song of a Caged Bird," *Southern Humanities Review*, 7, 4 (Fall 1973), 366-67, 374-75, copyright 1973 by Auburn University (Angelou); Robert Bly by Allen Hoey, copyright *Southern Humanities Review*

27, 2 (Spring 1993): 189–90. Also for v. XXV, Winter, 1991. Copyright 1991 by Auburn University. Reproduced by permission.

Southern Illinois University Press. From William J. Handy, *Modern Fiction* (Malamud); Leonard Lutwack, *Heroic Fiction: The Epic Tradition and American Novels of the Twentieth Century*. Copyright © 1971 by Southern Illinois University Press (Bellow, Hemingway); David Madden, *The Poetic Image in Six Genres*. Copyright © 1969 by Southern Illinois University Press (Oates, Shepard); Irving Howe, ''Daniel Fuchs' Williamsburg Trilogy; A Cigarette and a Window'' in *Proletarian Writers of the Thirties*, David Madden, ed. Copyright © 1968 Southern Illinois University Press; Matthew J. Bruccoli, ''Focus on *Appointment in Samarra*: The Importance of Knowing What You Are Talking About'' (F. O'Hara); Robert I. Edenbaum, ''The Poetics of the Private Eye: The Novels of Dashiell Hammett''; Herbert Ruhm, ''Raymond Chandler: From Bloomsbury to the Jungle—and Beyond,'' in *Tough Guy Writers of the Thirties*, David Madden, ed. Copyright © 1968 by Southern Illinois University Press; Gerald Weales, ''No Face and No Exit: The Fiction of James Purdy and J. P. Donleavy,'' in *Contemporary American Novelists*, Harry T. Moore, ed. Copyright © 1964 by Southern Illinois University Press; *The Confessional Poets* by Robert Phillips, Copyright © 1973 by Southern Illinois University Press (Plath); *In a Minor Chord* by Darwin T. Turner, Copyright © 1971 by Southern Illinois University Press (Cullen, Toomer); Darwin T. Turner, *Zora Neale Hurston: The Wandering Minstrel*; Introduction by Matthew J. Bruccoli to *Just Representations: A James Gould Cozzens Reader*, Matthew J. Bruccoli, ed. (published in conjunction with Harcourt Brace Jovanovich); article by John William Ward in *James Gould Cozzens; New Acquist of True Experience*), Matthew J. Bruccoli, ed.; David Cowart, *Thomas Pynchon: The Art of Allusion*; article by Samuel Coale in *John Gardner: Critical Perspectives*, Robert A. Morace and Kathryn Van Spankeren, eds. Reprinted by permission of Southern Illinois University Press.

Southern Literary Journal. Excerpts from article on Erskine Caldwell by Dan B. Miller. Copyright © Spring 1993 and reprinted with the permission of *Southern Literary Journal*. Excerpts from article on Z. N. Hurston by Janice Daniel. Copyright © Spring 1993 and reprinted with the permission of *Southern Literary Journal*. Excerpts from article on C. McCarthy by Andrew Bartlett. Copyright © Spring 1993 and reprinted with the permission of *Southern Literary Journal*. Excerpts from article on T. Wolfe by Ann Rowe. Copyright © Spring 1993 and reprinted with the permission of *Southern Literary Journal*.

Southern Quarterly. Excerpts from article on Cormac McCarthy by Alan Cheuse, ed. Arnold & Luce. Copyright © Summer 1992 by *The Southern Quarterly* and reprinted with the permission of the publisher, the University of Southern Mississippi. Excerpts from article on Cormac McCarthy by John Grammer, ed. Arnold & Luce. Copyright © Summer 1992 by *The Southern Quarterly* and reprinted with the permission of the publisher, The University of Southern Mississippi. Excerpts from article on Walker Percy by E. H. Oleksy. Copyright © Spring 1993 by *The Southern Quarterly* and reprinted with the permission of the publisher, The University of Southern Mississippi. Excerpts from article on Walker Percy by Gary M. Ciuba. Copyright © Spring 1994 by *The Southern Quarterly* and reprinted with the permission of the publisher, The University of Southern Mississippi. Excerpts from article on Reynolds Price by R. C. Fuller. Copyright © Winter 1994 by *The Southern Quarterly* and reprinted with the permission of the publisher, The University of Southern Mississippi. Excerpts from article on Anne Tyler by Barbara Harrell Carson. Copyright © Fall 1992 by *The Southern Quarterly* and reprinted with the permission of the publisher, The University of Southern Mississippi. Excerpts from article on Eudora Welty by Natalia Yakimenko. Copyright © Fall 1993 by *The Southern Quarterly* and reprinted with the permission of the publisher, The University of Southern Mississippi. Excerpts from article on Anne Tyler by Alice Hall Petry. Copyright © Fall 1992 by *The Southern Quarterly* and reprinted with the permission of the publisher, The University of Southern Mississippi.

The Southern Review. Excerpts from article on Tennessee Williams by W. Kenneth Holditch which first appeared in *The Southern Review*. Copyright © 1986. Excerpts from article on C. McCarthy by Terri Witek which first appeared in *The Southern Review*. Copyright © 1994. Excerpts from article on Reynolds Price by Ron Carlson which first appeared in *The Southern Review*. Copyright © 1994; v. 17, 1981 for ''Three Poets in Mid Career'' by Dana Gioia. Copyright, 1981, by the author. Reproduced by permission of the author.

Southwest Review. From articles by Gerald Burns on Snyder, on Wakoski; R. D. Reynolds on McMurtry; Abraham Rothberg on Snyder; Nancy Yanes Hoffman on Sarton; Baine Kerr on Momaday.

Barry Spacks. From article on Dugan's *Poems* in *Poetry*.

Patricia Meyer Spacks. From essay ''Free Women'' in *The Hudson Review* (Hellman).

The Spectator. From articles by Peter Ackroyd and McGuane; Alan Brien on Vonnegut; John Wain on Plath: Auberon Waugh on Brautigan, on Gardner; also v. 271, September 4, 1993. Copyright © 1993 by The Spectator. Reproduced by permission of The Spectator.

Spirit. From articles by Sally Andersen on Oates; Lynda B. Salamon on Plath.

Kathleen Spivack. From article on Levertov in *Poetry*.

The Springfield Union and Springfield Republican. From article by Richard McLaughlin on Purdy.

William Stafford. From articles on Brooks, Olson, and Swenson in *Poetry*.

Ann Stanford. From article on Swenson in *The Southern Review*.

Donald E. Stanford. From article on Porter in *The Southern Review*.

Stanford University Press. From William M. Chace, *Lionel Trilling: Criticism and Politics*.

Marilyn Stasio. From article on Rabe in *Cue*.

Steck-Vaughn Company. From Thomas H. Landess, *Larry McMurtry*.

Stein and Day. From Leslie A. Fiedler, *The Return of the Vanishing American*. Copyright © 1968 by Leslie Fiedler (Berger, Kesey); *The Collected Essays of Leslie Fiedler*. Copyright © 1971 by Leslie Fielder (Ginsberg, West). Reprinted by permission of Stein and Day Publishers.

George Steiner. From article on Plath in *The Reporter*.

Philip Stevick. From articles on Burroughs, on Kosinski, on Vonnegut in *Partisan Review*.

Dabney Stuart. From article on Bukowski in *Poetry*.

Studies in American Drama. Excerpts from article on Lanford Wilson by Gary Konas. Copyright © 1990 by *Studies in American Drama*. Reprinted with the permission of Ohio University Press.

Studies in American Fiction. Excerpts from article on Charles Johnson by Jonathan Little. Copyright © Autumn 1991 by *Studies in American Fiction* and Northeastern University and reprinted with permission. Excerpts from article on Toni Morrison by Elizabeth House. Copyright © Spring 1990 by *Studies in American Fiction* and Northeastern University and reprinted with permission. Excerpts from article on Joyce Carol Oates by Victor Strandberg. Copyright © Spring 1989 by *Studies in American Fiction* and Northeastern University and reprinted with permission. Excerpts from article on J. Cheever by M. D. Byrne. Copyright © Spring 1992 by *Studies in American Fiction* and Northeastern University and reprinted with permission. Excerpts from article on B. Malamud by V. Aarons. Copyright © Spring 1992 by *Studies in American Fiction* and Northeastern University and reprinted with permission.

Studies in American Humor. From Elaine Safer's ''The Allusive Mode, the Absurd and Black Humor in Bernard Malamud's *God's Grace*.'' *Studies in American Humor*, the annual journal of the American Humor Studies Association.

Studies in Black Literature. From article by Joan Bischoff on Morrison; Jeffrey Steinbrink on Ellison; Lloyd W. Brown on Hughes; also v. 6, Summer, 1975. Copyright 1975 by the editor. Reproduced by permission.

Studies in Short Fiction. For v. 23, Fall, 1986. Copyright 1986 by Newberry College. For Smith, Ernest J. ''John Berryman's Short Fiction: Elegy and Enlightenment.'' *Studies in Short Fiction* 30 (1993): 313–16. Copyright © 1993 by Newberry College. Reprinted by permission.

Studies in the Literary Imagination. From article by Pamela Shelden on H. James.

Studies in the Novel. From article by John M. Reilly on Toomer.

Walter Sutton. From eassy on Pound in *Sense and Sensibility*, Brom Weber, ed.

The Swallow Press, Inc., Chicago, Illinois, for the excerpts from *In Defense of Reason* by Yvor Winters and *The Last Analysis* by R. K. Meiners.

Swets and Zlitlinger. From article by G. A. M. Janssens on Bly in *English Studies*. See also *English Studies*.

Synergy. From article by Martha Bergmann on Bukowski.

Syracuse University Press. From Pamela White Hadas, *Marianne Moore: Poet of Affection*.

Tony Tanner. From article on Purdy in *Partisan Review*.

Taplinger Publishing Co., Inc. From articles by N. B. Hayles and by John P. Brennan and Michael C. Downs in *Ursula K. LeGuin*, Joseph D. Olander and Martin Harry Greenberg, eds.

Benjamin Taylor. From article on Sontag in *Georgia Review*.

Clyde R. Taylor. From essay on L. Jones in *Modern Black Poets*, Donald E. Gilbson, ed.

Gordon O. Taylor. From essay on Adams in *The Interpretation of Narrative*.

Walter Taylor. From article on Faulkner in *The Southern Review*.

Temple University Press. Excerpts from Terry Woods' *Lesbian and Gay Writing* edited by Mark Lilly. Copyright © 1990 by The Editorial Board Lumiere Press Ltd. Reprinted with the permission of Temple University Press.

Virginia R. Terris. From article on Rukeyser in *American Poetry Review*.

Texas A & M University. Excerpts from Katherine Anne Porter by Machann and Clark, eds. Copyright © 1990. Reprinted with the permission of Texas A & M University Press.

Thames and Hudson Ltd. From Richard Howard, *Alone with America* (Ammons, Goodman, Meredith); Ellen Moers, *The Two Dreisers*, for the excerpt from *Henry James—A Reader's Guide* by S. Gorley Putt.

Theater. From articles by Robert Asahina on Rabe, William Kleb on Shepard; Gordon Rogoff, ''Angels in America, Devils on Wings,'' *Theater* magazine, Vol. 24: 2, pp. 21, 24. Reprinted by permission of the publisher, Theater Magazine.

Three Continents. Excerpts from Valerie Harvey's ''Navajo Sandpainting'' in Ceremony, in *Critical Perspectives on Native American Fiction*, ed. Richard F. Fleck. Copyright © 1993. Reprinted with the permission of Three Continents Press (Passeggiata Press).

Tikkun. Excerpts from Jyl Lynn Felman's ''Lost Jewish Male Souls,'' May/June 1995. Excerpts from Robert Cohn's ''Mother Knew Best,'' July/Aug. 1994. Excerpts from James A. Miller's ''Letting It All Hang Out,'' Mar./Apr. 1995. Excerpts from Mark Schechner's ''Singer Ever After,'' Sept./Oct. 1994. Reprinted from TIKKUN MAGAZINE, A BI-MONTHLY JEWISH CRITIQUE OF POLITICS, CULTURE, AND SOCIETY. Subscriptions are $31.00 per year from TIKKUN, 251 West 100th Street, 5th floor, New York, NY 10025.

Time. From article by Robert Wernick on Gardner. Reprinted by permission from *Time*, The Weekly Newsmagazine. Copyright © 1970 Time, Inc.; for article by R. Z. Sheppard on Elkin. Reprinted by permission from *Time*. Copyright © 1971 Time, Inc.; R. Z. Sheppard on Auchincloss. Reprinted by permission from *Time*. Copyright © 1977 Time, Inc.; T. E. Kalem on T. Williams. Reprinted by permission from *Time*. Copy © 1983 Time, Inc.

Times Newspapers Limited. From anonymous articles on Berryman, on Bishop, on Buechner, on Creeley, on Frost, on Fuchs, on Merrill, on Mumford, on Nin, on Sandburg, on Saroyan, on Simpson, on Tate, on Wilbur; Caroline Blackwood on Heller; Russell Davies on Roth; Sylvia Millar on Caldwell; Robert Boyers on Gass, Malcolm Bradbury on J. O'Hara; Patricia Craig on Glasgow; George P. Elliott on Sontag; G. S. Fraser on Nemerov; Anthony Hecht on Wilbur; Eric Korn on De Vries; Zachary Leader on Taylor; Michael Mason on Burroughs; Helen McNeil on Olsen; Jay Parini on Eberhart and Rich; Louis Simpson on Dresier; Anne Stevenson on Piercy; Stuart Sutherland on De Vries; Julian Symons on Rexroth, reprinted from *The Times Literary Supplement* by permission.

Alan Trachtenberg. From article on Twain in *The Southern Review*; essay on H. Miller in *American Dreams, American Nightmares*, David Madden, ed.

Tulsa Studies in Women's Literature. Excerpts from Mary Titus's essay, "Murdering the Lesbian: Lillian Hellman's *The Children's Hour*," which appeared in *Tulsa Studies in Women's Literature*, Volume 10, Number 2 (Fall 1991). © 1991, The University of Tulsa. Reprinted by permission of the publisher.

Arlin Turner. From article on Twain in *The Southern Review*.

Twayne Publishers, Inc. From Morgan Gibson, *Kenneth Rexroth*, Thomas Gray, *Elinor Wylie*, Fred Moramarco, *Edward Dahlberg*, Vincent Quinn, *Hilda Doolittle (H.D.)*. Reprinted with the permission of Twayne Publishers, A Division of G.K. Hall & Co., Boston.

Twentieth Century Literature. From articles by Daniel J. Cahill on Kosinski; Francis Gillen on Barthelme; Richard Lehan on Fitzgerald; excerpts from Karen Jackson Ford's "Do Right to Write Right: Langston Hughes's Aesthetics of Simplicity." Copyright © 1992 and reprinted with the permission of *Twentieth Century Literature*. Excerpts from Kim McKay's "Double Discourse in John Irving's *The World According to Garp*." Copyright© 1992 and reprinted with the permission of *Twentieth Century Literature*. Excerpts from "Hearing Is Believing: Southern Racial Communities and Strategies of Story-Listing in Gloria Naylor and Lee Smith." by J. Donlon. Copyright© 1995 and reprinted with the permission of *Twentieth Century Literature*. Excerpts from the essay on Denise Levertov by Ronald R. Janssen. Copyright© Fall 1992 and reprinted with the permission of *Twentieth Century Literature*. Excerpts from the essay on Robert Lowell by Allan Johnston, Copyright© Spring 1990 and reprinted with the permission of *Twentieth Century Literature*. Excerpts from the essay on James Merrill by C. A. Buckley, Copyright© Winter 1992 and reprinted with the permission of *Twentieth Century Literature*. Excerpts from the essay on John Dos Passos by Joseph Fichtelberg. Copyright© Winter 1988 and reprinted with the permission of *Twentieth Century Literature*.

University of Alabama Press. From Richard Sugg, *Hart Crane's The Bridge*, published 1976 by the University of Alabama Press, copyright © 1976 by the University of Alabama Press.

University of California Press. From L. S. Dembo, *Conceptions of Reality in Modern American Poetry*. Copyright © 1966 by the Regents of the University of California (Olson); Frank Lentricchia, *The Gaiety of Language: An Essay on The Radical Poetics of W. B. Yeats and Wallace Stevens*. Copyright © 1968 by The Regents of the University of California (Stevens); Gerald Nelson, *Changes of Heart: A Study of the Poetry of W. H. Auden*. Copyright © 1969 by The Regents of the University of California; Hugh Kenner, *The Pound Era*. Copyright © 1971 by Hugh Kenner (Pound); Hugh Witemeyer, *The Poetry of Ezra Pound: Forms and Renewal, 1908–1920*. Copyright © 1969 by The Regents of the University of California; George T. Wright, *The Poet in the Poem: The Personae of Eliot, Yeats and Pound*. Copyright © 1960 by The Regents of the University of California (Eliot); Stephen Yense. *Circle to Circle: The Poetry of Robert Lowell*, copyright © 1975 by the University of California Press; Michael Alexander, *The Poetic Achievement of Ezra Pound*, copyright © 1979 by the University of California Press; Barry Ahearn, *Zukofsky's "A": An Introduction*, copyright © 1983 by the University of California Press. From *Safe at Last in the Middle Years: The Invention of the Midlife Progress Novel*, by Margaret Gullette, © 1988 by the Regents of the University of California Press. Reprinted by permission of the University of California Press. From *The Voice in the Margin: Native American Literature and the Canon*, by Arnold Krupat. © 1989 by the Regents of the University of California Press. Reprinted by permission of the University of California Press. From Charles Olson. *Selected Poems*, edited/translated by Robert Creeley, © 1993 by the Regents of the University of California Press, © 1987 Estate of Charles Olson and the University of Connecticut. Reprinted by permission of the University of California Press. From *The Voice in the*

Margin: Native American Literature and the Canon, by Arnold Krupat, © 1989 by the Regents of the University of California Press. Reprinted by permission of the University of California Press.

University of Central Arkansas Press. Excerpts on Lynette McGrath's ''Anne Sexton's Poetic Connections'' from Frances Bixler's *Original Essays on the Poetry of Anne Sexton*. Copyright © 1988 and reprinted with the permission of The University of Central Arkansas.

University of Chicago Press, for the excerpt reprinted from *American Judaism* by Nathan Glazer by permission of The University of Chicago Press, copyright © 1957 by the University of Chicago; for the excerpt by Malcolm Goldstein from *American Drama and Its Critics*, edited by Alan S. Downer, by permission of The University of Chicago Press, copyright © 1965 by the University of Chicago; for the excerpt from the Introduction by Josephine Herbst to *Gullible's Travels* by Ring Lardner by permission of The University of Chicago Press, Introduction copyright © 1965 by the University of Chicago; for the excerpt from Harold Bloom, *The Ringers in the Tower: Studies in Romantic Tradition*. Copyright © 1971 by Harold Bloom (Ammons); Chester E. Eisinger, *Fiction of the Forties*. Copyright © 1963 by Chester E. Eisinger (Gordon); Ruth R. Wisse, *The Schlemiel as Modern Hero*. Copyright © 1971 by The University of Chicago (Bellow, Friedman, Malamud, Roth); George Bornstein, *Transformations of Romanticism in Yeats, Eliot, and Stevens*, copyright © 1976 by the University of Chicago Press (Eliot, Stevens); Frank D. McConnell, *Four Postwar American Novelists*, copyright © 1977 by the University of Chicago Press (Barth, Pynchon); Mérie Borroff, *Language and the Poet: Verbal Artistry in Frost, Stevens, and Moore*, copyright © 1979 by the University of Chicago Press (Frost, Stevens); article by Elizabeth Fifer on Stein in *Signs*, Copyright © 1979 by the University of Chicago Press; from *Afro-American Literary Study in the 1990s* by Deborah E. McDowell. Copyright © 1980 by Deborah E. McDowell and reprinted with the permission of The University of Chicago Press. Excerpts from Blues, *Ideology and Afro-American Literature* by H. A. Baker, Jr. Copyright © 1984 by H. A. Baker, Jr. and reprinted with the permission of The University of Chicago Press. Excerpts from *Modernism and the Harlem Renaissance* by H. A. Baker, Jr. Copyright © 1987 by H. A. Baker, Jr. and reprinted with the permission of The University of Chicago Press.

University of Dallas. From Thomas H. Landess's Introduction to *The Short Fiction of Caroline Gordon*, Thomas H. Landess, ed.

University of Georgia Press. From essays by Charles T. Davis, William J. Free in *Edwin Arlington Robinson: Centenary Essays*, Ellsworth Barnard, ed.; William H. Note, *Rock and Hawk: Robinson Jeffers and the Romantic Agony*, copyright © 1978; Elizabeth Ammons, *Edith Wharton's Argument with America*, copyright © 1980; Ladell Payne, *Black Novelists and the Southern Literary Tradition*, copyright © 1981 (Ellison); article by Jane Flanders in *The Achievement of William Styron*, rev. ed., Robert K. Morris and Irving Malin, eds., copyright © 1981; Dick Davis, *Wisdom and Wilderness: The Achievement of Yvor Winters*, copyright © 1983, all the above by the University of Georgia Press, reprinted by permission of the University of Georgia Press. From *Toward Robert Frost: The Reader and the Poet* by Judith Oster, © 1992 by the University of Georgia Press. Reprinted by permission of the University of Georgia Press. From *Sacred Groves and Ravaged Gardens: The Fiction of Eudora Welty, Carson McCullers, and Flannery O'Connor* by Louise H. Westling, © 1985 by the University of Georgia Press. Reprinted by permission of the University of Georgia Press. From *Final Acts: The Creation of Three Late O'Neill Plays* by Judith E. Barlow, © 1985 by the University of Georgia Press. Reprinted by permission of the University of Georgia Press. From *The Inner Strength of Opposites: O'Neill's Novelistic Drama and the Melodramatic Imagination* by Kurt Eisen, © 1994 by the University of Georgia Press. Reprinted by permission of the University of Georgia Press. From *Randall Jarrell and the Lost World of Childhood*, by Richard Flynn, © 1990 by the University of Georgia Press. Reprinted by permission of the University of Georgia Press. From *Malcolm Cowley: The Formative Years* by Hans Bak, © 1993 by the University of Georgia Press. Reprinted by permission of the University of Georgia Press.

University of Illinois Press. From Sherman Paul, *Hart's Bridge* (Crane); John Vernon, *The Garden and the Map* (Barth, Burroughs, Pynchon, Roethke); Ruby Cohn in *Comic Relief: Humor in Contemporary American Literature*, Sarah Balacher Cohen, ed., copyright © 1978 (Albee, Shepard); James M. Mellard, *The Exploded Form: The Modernist Novel in America*, copyright © 1980 (Heller); Jerome Klinkowitz, *Literary Disruptions*, 2nd ed., copyright © 1980 (Kosinski); Thomas H. Schaub, *Pynchon the Voice of Ambiguity*, copyright © 1980; Introduction by Dave Smith to *The Pure Clear Word: Essays on the Poetry of James Wright*, Dave Smith, ed., copyright © 1982; article on Swenson by Dave Smith in his *Local Assays* (originally published in *Poetry*), copyright © 1985, all of the above by the Board of Trustees of the

University of Illinois; article by René Wellek on E. Wilson in *Comparative Literature Studies*. Excerpts from *Willa Cather and France* by Robert J. Nelson. Copyright © 1988. Reprinted with the permission of University of Illinois Press. Excerpts from *Splendid Failure* by Edward Brunner. Copyright © 1985. Reprinted with the permission of University of Illinois Press. Excerpts from *Reading Stanley Elkin* by Peter J. Bailey. Copyright © 1985. Reprinted with the permission of University of Illinois Press. Excerpts from *Marianne Moore: The Poetry of Engagement* by Grace Schulman. Copyright © 1986. Reprinted with the permission of University of Illinois Press. Excerpts from *Writing Pynchon* by Alec McHoul and David Wills. Copyright © 1990. Reprinted with the permission of University of Illinois Press. Excerpts from *Oedipus Anne: The Poetry of Anne Sexton* by D. H. George. Copyright © 1990. Reprinted with the permission of University of Illinois Press. Excerpts from *My Life as a Loaded Gun* by Paula Bennett. Copyright © 1990. Reprinted with the permission of University of Illinois Press. Excerpts from *Ride out the Wilderness* by Melvin Dixon. Copyright © 1987. Reprinted with the permission of University of Illinois Press.

University of Massachusetts Press. From Jay Parini. *Theodore Roethke: An American Romantic*, copyright © 1979 by the University of Massachusetts Press.

University of Miami Press. From Richard H. Rupp. *Celebration in Postwar American Fiction* (Agee, Baldwin, Cheever, Ellison, O'Connor, Salinger).

The University of Michigan Press, for the excerpt from *The Poetic Themes of Robert Lowell* by Jerome Mazzaro, copyright © 1965 by the University of Michigan; for the excerpt from *The Major Themes of Robert Frost* by Radcliffe Squires, copyright © 1963 by the University of Michigan; for the excerpt from *The Loyalties of Robinson Jeffers* by Radcliffe Squires, copyright © 1963 by the University of Michigan; for the excerpts from *The New England Conscience* by Austin Warren, copyright © 1966 by the University of Michigan.

University of Minnesota Press. From Gay Wilson Allen, *William James*. Copyright © 1970 the University of Minnesota; Louis Auchincloss, *Henry Adams*. Copyright © 1971 by the University of Minnesota; Warner Berthoff, *Edmund Wilson*. Copyright © 1968 by the University of Minnesota; Glauco Cambon, *Recent American Poetry* (Kinnell). Copyright © 1962 by the University of Minnesota: Merke E. Brown, *Kenneth Burke*. Copyright © 1969 by the University of Minnesota; Stanton Garner, *Harold Frederic*. Copyright © 1969 by the University of Minnesota; Lawrence Graver, *Carson McCullers*. Copyright © 1969 by the University of Minnesota; Leon Howard, *Wright Morris* Copyright © 1968 by the University of Minnesota; James Korges, *Erskine Caldwell*. Copyright © 1969 by the University of Minnesota; Erling Larsen, *James Agee*. Copyright © 1971 by the University of Minnesota; Frederick P. W. McDowell, *Caroline Gordon*. Copyright © 1966 by the University of Minnesota; Julian Moynahan, *Vladimir Nabokov*. Copyright © 1971 by the University of Minnesota; William J. Martz, *John Berryman*. Copyright © 1969 by the University of Minnesota; Jay Martin, *Robert Lowell*. Copyright © 1970 by the University of Minnesota; Earl Rovit, *Saul Bellow*. Copyright © 1967 by the University of Minnesota; Ben Siegel, *Isaac Bashevis Singer*. Copyright © 1969 by the University of Minnesota; Irvin Stock, *Mary McCarthy*. copyright © 1968; Irvin Stock, *Mary McCarthy*. Copyright © 1968 by the University of Minnesota; Charles Child Walcutt, *John O'Hara*. Copyright © 1969 by the University of Minnesota; Donald Pizer, *The Novels of Theodore Dreiser*. Warner Berthoff, *Hart Crane: A Re-Introduction* (University of Minnesota Press. 1989), pp. x–xi. Reprinted with the permission of The University of Minnesota Press. Nancy A. Walker. *A Very Serious Thing: Women's Humor and American Culture* (University of Minnesota Press, 1988), pp. 111–13. Reprinted with the permission of The University of Minnesota Press.

University of Missouri Press. From C. W. E. Bigsby, *Confrontation and Commitment* (Hansberry); Bettina Schwarzschild, *The Not-Right House: Essays on James Purdy*. By permission of the University of Missouri Press. Copyright © 1968 by Bettina Schwarzschild; Sanford Pinsker, *The Comedy That ''Hoits'': An Essay on the Fiction of Philip Roth*, Copyright © 1975; Stephen F. Milliken, *Chester Himes: A Critical Appraisal*, copyright © 1976; Robert Boyers, *Lionel Trilling: Negative Capability and the Wisdom of Avoidance*, copyright © 1977; Charles Molesworth, *The Fierce Embrace: A Study of Contemporary American Poetry*, copyright © 1979 (Ginsberg, Kinnell); Robert Boyers, *R. P. Blackmur; Poet-Critic*, copyright © 1980; Robert J. Begiebing, *Acts of Regeneration: Allegory and Archetype in the Works of Norman Mailer*, copyright © 1980; Mary Lynn Broe, *Protean Poetic: The Poetry of Sylvia Plath*, copyright © 1980; Neal Browers, *Theodore Roethke: The Journey from I to Otherwise*, copyright © 1982; David Packman, *Vladimir Nabokov: The Structure of Literary Desire*, copyright © 1982, all of the above by the Curators of the University of the Missouri, reprinted by permission of the University of Missouri Press.

The University of Nebraska Press. From D. J. Dooley, *The Art of Sinclair Lewis*. Copyright © 1967 by the University of Nebraska Press. Reprinted by permission of University of Nebraska Press; from articles by Robert Huff on Stafford; Debra Hulbert on Wakoski; Melvin Lyon on Dahlberg; Thomas Parkinson on Synder; Harold Witt on Aiken; Harriet Zinnes on Bly; anon. on Merwin in *Prairie Schooner*. Copyright © 1961, 1962, 1968, 1970, 1971, 1972, 1973 by University of Nebraska Press. Reprinted by permission from Prairie Schooner; from David Stouck, *Willa Cather's Imagination*, copyright © 1975; article by John W. Aldridge in *Conversations with Wright Morris: Critical Views and Responses*, Robert E. Knoll, ed., copyright © 1977; G. B. Crump. *The Novels of Wright Morris: A Critical Interpretation*, copyright © 1978; Robert C. Rosen, *John Dos Passos: Politics and the Writer*, copyright © 1981, all of the above by the University of Nebraska Press, reprinted, by permission of the University of Nebraska Press. Excerpts from a review on Don DeLillo by Lee Lemon from the Spring 1992 *Prairie Schooner*. Copyright © 1992 by the University of Nebraska Press and reprinted with the permission of University of Nebraska Press. Excerpts from *Hemingway's Quarrel with Androgyny* by Mark Spilka. Copyright © 1990. Reprinted with the permission of University of Nebraska Press. Excerpts from *Remember the Laughter: A Life of James Thurber* by Neil A. Grauer. Copyright © 1994. Reprinted with the permission of University of Nebraska Press.

University of Nevada Press. From *Many Californias: Literature from the Golden State*, edited by Gerald W. Haslam, copyright © 1991 by the University of Nevada Press. Reprinted with the permission of the University of Nevada Press.

University of New Mexico Press. From Cynthia D. Edelberg, *Robert Creeley's Poetry: A Critical Introduction*; Charles R. Larson, *American Indian Fiction* (Momaday).

University of North Carolina Press. From John M. Bradbury, *Renaissance in the South* (Gordon); Hugh M. Gloster, *Negro Voices in American Fiction* (Johnson); John Rosenblatt, *Sylvia Plath: The Poetry of Initiation*; Robert N. Wilson. *The Writer as Social Seer* (Baldwin, Hemingway, A. Miller); Forrest G. Read, *76: One Word and the Cantos of Ezra Pound*, copyright © 1981 by the University of North Carolina Press, used by permission of the publisher.

University of Oklahoma Press. From article by Howard Moss on Bishop in *World Literature Today*, 51, 1 (Winter 1977), copyright © 1977; Lothar Kahn on Singer in *World Literature Today*, 53, 2 (Spring 1979), copyright 1979, both reprinted with the permission of University of Oklahoma Press. Excerpts from *Other Destinies: Understanding the American Indian Novel* by Louis Owens. Copyright © 1992. Reprinted with the permission of University of Oklahoma Press. Excerpts from *N. Scott Momaday: The Cultural and Literary Background* by Matthias Schubnell. Copyright © 1985. Reprinted with the permission of University of Oklahoma Press. Excerpts from *Modernism, Medicine, and William Carlos Williams* by T. Hugh Crawford. Copyright © 1993. Reprinted with the permission of University of Oklahoma Press.

University of Pennsylvania Press. Excerpts from *John Barth and the Anxiety of Continuance* by Patricia Tobin. Copyright © 1992 and reprinted with the permission of University of Pennsylvania Press. Excerpts from *Mechanism and Mysticism* by Louis J. Zanine. Copyright © 1993 and reprinted with the permission of University of Pennsylvania Press. Excerpts from *Saul Bellow* by Ellen Pifer. Copyright © 1990 and reprinted with the permission of University of Pennsylvania Press. Excerpts from *Beyond the Red Notebook* by Dennis Barone. Copyright © 1995 and reprinted with the permission of University of Pennsylvania Press.

University of Pittsburgh Press. From *Mind of Winter: Wallace Stevens, Meditation, and Literature*, by William W. Bevis. © 1988 by University of Pittsburgh Press. Reprinted by permission of the University of Pittsburgh Press.

University of South Carolina Press. Excerpts from *Understanding Donald Barthelme* by Stanley Trachtenberg. Copyright © 1990. Reprinted with the permission of University of South Carolina Press. Excerpts from *Understanding Robert Bly* by William V. Davis. Copyright © 1988. Reprinted with the permission of University of South Carolina Press. Excerpts from *Understanding Randall Jarrell* by J. A. Bryant, Jr. Copyright © 1986. Reprinted with the permission of University of South Carolina Press. Excerpts from *Understanding William Kennedy* by J. K. Van Dover. Copyright © 1991. Reprinted with the permission of University of South Carolina Press. Excerpts from *Understanding Thomas Pynchon* by Robert D. Newman. Copyright © 1986. Reprinted with the permission of University of South Carolina Press. Excerpts from *Understanding Chicano Literature* by Carl R. Shirley and Paula Shirley. Copyright © 1988. Reprinted with the permission of University of South Carolina Press. Excerpts from *Understanding James Dickey* by Ronald Baugham. Copyright © 1985. Reprinted with the permission of University of South Carolina Press. Excerpts from ''*Alnilant*: James Dickey's Novel Explores Father and Son Relationships.'' in Ronald Buughman, ed., *The Voiced Connections* by William W. Starr. Copyright © 1989. Reprinted with the permission of University of South Carolina Press. Excerpts from *Understanding Contemporary American Drama* by William Herman. Copyright © 1987. Reprinted with the permission of University of South Carolina Press. Excerpts from *Understanding Kurt Vonnegut* by W. R. Allen. Copyright © 1990. Reprinted with the permission of University of South Carolina Press. Excerpts from *Understanding Gary Snyder* by Patrick D. Murphy. Copyright © 1992. Reprinted with the permission of University of South Carolina Press.

The University of Tennessee Press, for the excerpt from the article, ''Myth-making in America: 'The Great Stone Face' and *Raintree County*,'' by Boyd Litzinger in *Tennessee Studies In Literature*, Vol. VIII, edited by R. B. Davis and K. L. Knickerbocker, copyright © 1963 by the University of Tennessee Press. Excerpts from *Creating Faulkner's Reputation* by Lawrence H. Schwartz. Copyright © 1988 and reprinted with the permission of University of Tennessee Press. Excerpts from *Frost and the Book of Nature* by George F. Bagby. Copyright © 1993 and reprinted with the permission of University of Tennessee Press.

University of Texas Press. From article by Thomas Le Clair on Barth in *Texas Studies in Literature and Language*. copyright © 1973 by University of Texas Press; from Paul Christensen, *Charles Olson: Call Him Ishmael*. From *Faulkner's Marginal Couple: Invisible, Outlaw, and Unspeakable Communities* by John N. Duvall, Copyright © 1990. By permission of the University of Texas Press. From *Marianne Moore: Subversive Modernist* by Taffy Martin. Copyright © 1986. By permission of the University of Texas Press. From *Satire in Narrative: Petronius, Swift, Gibbon, Melville, and Pynchon* by Frank Palmeri, Copyright © 1990. By permission of the University of Texas Press. From *Grace Paley: Illuminating the Dark Lives* by Jacqueline Taylor. Copyright © 1990. By permission of the University of Texas Press. ''Humor, Subjectivity, Resistance: The Case of Laughter in *The Color Purple*'' by Carole Anne Taylor in *Texas Studies in Literature and Language*, vol 36:4, pp 462–63; by permission of the author and the University of Texas Press. ''Hysteron Proteron in *Gravity's Rainbow*'' by Steven Weisenburger in *Texas Studies in Literature and Language* vol 34:1; p 102; by permission of the author and the University of Texas Press. '''Mighty Strange Threads in Her Loom': Laughter and Subversive Heteroglossi in Zora Neale Hurston's *Moses, Man of the Mountain*'' by Christine Levecq in *Texas Studies in Literature and Language* vol 36:4: pp 438–40; by permission of the author and the University of Texas Press.

University of Toronto Press. From Balachandra Rajan, *The Overwhelming Question: A Study of the Poetry of T.S. Eliot*.

University of Washington Press. From A. Kingsley Weatherhead, *Edge of the Image*. Copyright © 1967 by the University of Washington Press (Olson); Rosemary Sullivan, *Theodore Roethke: The Garden Master*.

The University of Wisconsin Press. From Arthur B. Coffin, *Robinson Jeffers*; from articles of Bernard Benstock on Gaddis; John P. Farrell on Wilbur; Richard Lehan on Sheed in *Wisconsin Studies in Contemporary Literature*; by Alan J. Friedmand and Manfred Puetz on Pynchon; Blanche Gelfant on Kerouac, Robert von Hallberg on Olson; Howard M. Harper, Jr., on Kosinski; Norman Holland on Doolittle; Peter William Koenig on Gaddis; Samuel French Morse on Zukofsky, Marjorie G. Perloff on Kinnell, on O'Hara; Donald Sheehan on Howard in *Contemporary Literature*; *The Broken World of Tennessee Williams* by Esther M. Jackson; *Ellen Glasgow and the Ironic Art of Fiction* by Frederick P. W. McDowell, reprinted with permission of the copyright owners, the Regents of the University of Wisconsin; for the excerpts from articles in *Contemporary Literature* (formerly *Wisconsin Studies in Contemporary Literature*) cited in text, reprinted with permission of the copyright owners, the Regents of the University of Wisconsin and with permission of the University of Wisconsin Press; articles by Cynthia A. Davis on Morrison; Robert E. Fleming on J. Williams; Richard Jackson on Strand; Thomas Le Clair on Elkin and on Gardner in *Contemporary Literature*; article by Charles Russell on Burroughs in *Substance*. Copyright by the University of Wisconsin Press. Baker, Houston A., Jr. *Afro-American Poetics: Revisions of Harlem and the Black Aesthetic*. © 1988. (Madison: The University of Wisconsin Press.) Reprinted by permission of The University of Wisonsin Press. Wilson, Rob. *American Sublime: The Genealogy of a Poetic Genre*. © 1991. (Madison: The University of Wisconsin Press.) Reprinted by permission of The

1

copyright © 1975 by Donald Davie: Scott Donaldson. *By Force of Will: The Life and Art of Ernest Hemingway*, copyright © 1979 by Scott Donaldson.

The Village Voice. For generous permission to reprint from numerous articles from *The Village Voice* and *The Voice Literary Supplement*: Michael Feingold on Rabe; Jack Friedman on Bullins; John S. Friedman on Selby; Vivian Gornick on Didion; Julius Novick on Rabe, on Albee; Corinne Robbins on Horovitz; Michael Smith on Drexler; Gilbert Sorrentino on Zukofsky; Ross Wetzsteon on Mamet and Vonnegut; Michael Feingold on Guare; Terry Curtis Fox on Guare; Eliot Fremont-Smith on Irving and Roth; Eileen Blumenthal on Mamet; Michael Feingold on Mamet; Seymour Krim on Vonnegut; Vivian Gornick on Didion; Julius Novick on L. Wilson; Debra Rae Cohen on Purdy; Caryn James on Elkin: Khachig Tölölyan on Vonnegut; Laurie Stone on Rossner; Margo Jefferson on Ozick; Geoffrey Stokes on Theroux; Tom Carson on Algren. Reprinted with permission of the authors and *The Village Voice*, copyright © 1968, 1969; 1973, 1974, 1975, 1976, 1977, 1978, 1979, 1981, 1982, 1983 by The Village Voice, Inc.

Virago Press. Excerpts from *Willa Cather: A Life Saved Up* by Hermione Lee. Copyright © 1989 by and reprinted with the permission of Little Brown & Co. (UK).

The Virginia Quarterly Review. From articles by Houston A. Baker, Jr., on Johnson; Fred Bornhauser on Kinnell, on Meredith; James M. Cox on Lardner; J. C. Levenson on Robinson; anon. on Auchincloss, on Dickey, on McCarthy, on Taylor; Louis D. Rubin, Jr., on McCullers; Anne Hobson Freeman on Price, Jane Barnes Casey on Taylor.

Warwick Wadlington. From ''Pathos and Dreiser'' in *The Southern Review*.

Austin Warren. From article on Auden in *The Southern Review*.

Robert Penn Warren. From articles on Dreiser, on Ransom, on Twain in *The Southern Review*.

The Washington Post. For generous permission to excerpt numerous reviews and articles in *Book World*.

Robert Watson, for the excerpt from his review of James *Dickey's The Suspect in Poetry in Poetry*, Feb., 1966.

Donald Watt. From ''Burning Bright: 'Farenheit 451' as Symbolic Dystopia'' in *Ray Bradbury*. Edited by Martin Harry Greenberg and Joseph D. Olander. Taplinger Publishing Company, 1980. Copyright © 1980 by Joseph D. Olander and Martin Harry Greenberg. All rights reserved. Reproduced by permission of the author.

Wayne State University Press, for the excerpts reprinted from *Psychoanalysis and American Literary Criticism* by Louis Fraiberg by permission of the Wayne State University Press. Copyright © 1960 by the Wayne State University Press; for the excerpt from ''A Skeptical Music: Stevens and Santayana'' in *Criticism*, Vol. III, no. 3, Summer 1965 by David P. Young by permission of the Wayne State University Press; for the excerpt from Merle E. Brown, *Wallace Stevens: The Poem as Act*. Copyright © 1970 by Wayne State University Press. Thomas E. Porter, *Myth and Modern American Drama*. Copyright © 1969 by Wayne State University Press (Albee); J.S. Wolkenfeld, ''Isaac Bashevis Singer: The Faith of His Devils and Magicians,'' in *Criticism*. Copyright © 1963 by Wayne State University.

Gerald Weales. From articles on Vonnegut, on Horovitz in *The Reporter*.

Brom Weber, for the excerpt from *The Letters of Hart Crane, 1916–1932*, ed. Brom Weber, copyright © 1952 Brom Weber (University of California Press, 1965).

Brigitte Weeks. From article on Godwin in *Ms. Magazine*.

Weidenfeld and Nicolson. From A. Alvarez, *The Savage God* (Plath); Richard Gilman, *The Confusion of Realms* (Barthelme); Jacques Barzun in *The World of Raymond Chandler*, Miriam Gross, ed.

Philip M. Weinstein. From essay on H. James in *The Interpretation of Narrative*. Morton W. Bloomfield, ed.

Wesleyan University Press, for the excerpt from *The Plays of Thornton Wilder* by Donald Haberman, published by the Wesleyan University Press. Copyright © 1967 by Wesleyan University; for the excerpt from *H.L. Mencken: Literary Critic* by William H. Nolte, published by Wesleyan University Press. Copyright © 1964, 1966 by William H. Nolte; for the excerpt from essay by Ihab Hassan on Vonnegut in *Liberation*, Ihab Hassan, ed. Copyright © 1971 by Wesleyan University; Ruth Miller, *The Poetry of Emily Dickinson*. Copyright © 1968 by Ruth Miller Kriesberg.

Western American Literature. For articles by Jay Gurian on Berger; L. Edwin Folsom on Snyder; for v. XVI, February, 1982; v. 21, Winter, 1987; v. XXII, February, 1988; v. XXVIII, Summer, 1993. Copyright 1982, 1987, 1988, 1993 by the Western American Literature Association. Reproduced by permission. Excerpts of article on C. McCarthy by T. Pilkington which appeared in the *Western American Literature Journal*. Copyright © Winter 1993 and reprinted with the permission of publisher. Excerpts of article on T. McGuane by Nathaniel Lewis which appeared in the *Western American Literature Journal*. Copyright © November 1993 and reprinted with the permission of publisher. Excerpts of article on N. Scott Momaday by E. T. Smith which appeared in the *Western American Literature Journal*. Copyright © November 1993 and reprinted with the permission of publisher. Excerpts of article on Larry McMurtry by Ernestine P. Sewell which appeared in the *Western American Literature Journal*. Copyright © Winter 1993 and reprinted with the permission of publisher.

The Western Humanities Review. From ''The Rank Flavor of Bolld'' by Charles Molesworth (Kinnell).

Western Review. From article by Gerry Haslam on Eastlake.

Ross Wetzsteon. From ''The Genius of Sam Shepard'' in *New York Magazine*.

Whitson Publishing Co., Inc. From Henry C. Lacey, *To Raise, Destroy, and Create: The Poetry, Drama, and Fiction of Imamu Amiri Baraka (Le Roi Jones)*.

Mary Ellen Williams Walsh. From *A Vast Landscape: Time in the Novels of Thornton Wilder*.

Miller Williams. From *The Poetry of John Crowe Ransom*.

Alan Williamson. From articles on Lowell, on J. Wright in *Poetry*.

Brenda Wineapple. From article on Coover in *Iowa Review*.

Jack Wolkenfeld. From article on Singer in *Criticism*.

Women's Review of Books. Excerpts from the article on Audre Lorde by Barbara T. Christian first printed in *The Women's Review of Books*. Copyright © 1993 and reprinted with the permission of the author. Excerpts from article on Bobbie Ann Mason by Michele Clark which appeared in *Woman's Review of Books*. Copyright © March 1994 and reprinted with the permission of the author.

Women's Studies: An Interdisciplinary Journal. From article by Jaqueline Ridgeway on Bogan. Linda W. Wagner, ''Plath's *The Bell Jar* as Female *Bildungsroman*,'' *Women's Studies*, Vol. 12 (1986), pp. 55–68. Permission granted by The Gordon & Breach Publishing Group. Elizabeth Lennox Keyser. ''*A Bloodsmoor Romance*: Joyce Carol Oates' Little Women.'' *Women's Studies*, Vol. 14 (1988), pp. 211–23. Permission granted by The Gordon & Breach Publishing Group.

World Literature Today. Excerpts from article on John Berryman by Manly Johnson. Copyright © Summer 1990 by *World Literature Today* and reprinted with the permission of the Editor. Excerpts from article on Oscar Hijuelos by George R. McMurray. Copyright © Winter 1994 by *World Literature Today* and reprinted with the permission of the Editor. Excerpts from article on Charles Johnson by W. M. Hagen. Copyright © Spring 1991 by *World Literature Today* and reprinted with the permission of the Editor. Excerpts from article on Cynthia Ozick by Bernard F. Dick. Copyright © Spring 1990 by *World Literature Today* and reprinted with the permission of the Editor. For excerpts from v. 69, Spring, 1995. Copyright 1995 by the University of Oklahoma Press. Reproduced by permission.

The World Publishing Company, for the excerpt from *Carl Sanburg* by Harry Golden, reprinted by permission of The World Publishing Company, Copyright © 1961 by Harry Golden; for the excerpt from

F. Scott Fitzerald and His Contemporaries by William Goldhurst, reprinted by permission of the World Publishing Company Copyright © 1963 by William Goldhurst; for the excerpts from *After Alienation* by Marcus Klein, reprinted by permission of The World Publishing Company, Copyright © 1962, 1964, by The World Publishing Company.

Delbert E. Wylder. From article on Eastlake in *New Mexico Quarterly*.

Yale Review. From articles by Abraham Bezanker on Bellow; Marie Borroff on Meredith, on Merrill; Mary Ellmann on Ashbery; David J. Gordon on Gardner; Paul Edward Gray on Dickey; Laurence Lieberman on Howard, on Kinnell, on Kunitz, on Stafford; Louis L. Martz on Ammons, on Creeley, on Pound, on Wakoski, on Warren; Theodore Morrison on Frost; James W. Tuttleton on Wharton; Helen Vendler on Ammons, on Cummings; Robert C. Williams on Nabokov; James Wright on Meredith; Vincent Miller on Pound; Frank Kermode on Auden; Louis L. Martz on Hollander; Maureen Howard on Barthelme; David Thorburn on Beattie; John Hollander on Merrill. Copyright 1958, 1968, 1969, 1970, 1971, 1972, 1973 by Yale University. Reprinted by permission of *The Yale Review*, copyright by Yale University.

Yale University Press. From Robert A. Bone, *The Negro Novel in America* (Johnson, Toomer); John F. Lynen, *The Design of the Present* (Eliot); Raymond M. Olderman, *Beyond the Wasteland* (Kesey, Vonnegut); Robert A. Bone, *The Negro Novel in America* (Hurston); Kimberly W. Benston, *Baraka: The Renegade and the Mask*; Cleanth Brooks, *William Faulkner: Toward Yoknapatawpha and Beyond*, by permission of Yale University Press. Excerpts from Gilbert and Gubar, *No Man's Land* vol. 2. Copyright © 1989 and reprinted with the permission of Yale University Press.

Yale University, School of Drama. From Ren Frutkin, ''Sam Shepard; Paired Existence Meets the Monster,'' in *Yale Theatre*.

Mary Yost Associates, Inc. From Bruce Cook, *The Beat Generation* (Brautigan, Kesey, Olson, Snyder).

LIST OF ENTRANTS

Walter Abish
Kathy Acker
Henry Adams
Léonie Adams
James Agee
Conrad Aiken
Edward Albee
William Alfred
Nelson Algren
A.R. Ammons
Rudolfo Anaya
Maxwell Anderson
Robert Anderson
Sherwood Anderson
Maya Angelou
John Ashbery
Isaac Asimov
William Attaway
Louis Auchincloss
W.H. Auden
Paul Auster
George Axelrod

Irving Babbitt
Jimmy Santiago Baca
James Baldwin
Toni Cade Bambara
Russell Banks
Amiri Baraka
Djuna Barnes
Philip Barry
John Barth
Donald Barthelme
Richard Bausch
Charles Baxter
Ann Beattie
S. N. Behrman
David Belasco
Marvin Bell
Saul Bellow
Robert Benchley
Stephen Vincent Benét
Thomas Berger
John Berryman
Ambrose Bierce
Elizabeth Bishop
John Peale Bishop
R.P. Blackmur
Robert Bly
Maxwell Bodenheim
Louise Bogan
Arna Bontemps
Vance Bourjaily
Randolph Bourne
Jane Bowles

Paul Bowles
Kay Boyle
T. Coraghessan Boyle
Ray Bradbury
William Stanley Braithwaite
Richard Brautigan
Cleanth Brooks
Gwendolyn Brooks
Van Wyck Brooks
Rita Mae Brown
Sterling Allen Brown
Pearl Buck
Frederick Buechner
Charles Bukowski
Ed Bullins
Kenneth Burke
John Horne Burns
William Burroughs
Robert Olen Butler

James Branch Cabell
Abraham Cahan
James M. Cain
Erskine Caldwell
Hortense Calisher
Ethan Canin
Truman Capote
Rachel Carson
Raymond Carver
Willa Cather
Michael Chabon
Raymond Chandler
Denise Chavez
John Cheever
Charles W. Chesnutt
Alfred Chester
Alice Childress
Kate Chopin
John Ciardi
Sandra Cisneros
Amy Clampitt
Walter Van Tilburg Clark
Andrei Codrescu
Richard Condon
Evan S. Connell, Jr.
Marc Connelly
Pat Conroy
Robert Coover
Gregory Corso
Malcolm Cowley
James Gould Cozzens
Hart Crane
Stephen Crane
Robert Creeley

Countee Cullen
Edward Estlin Cummings

Edward Dahlberg
Samuel R. Delany
Don DeLillo
Floyd Dell
Bernard DeVoto
Peter De Vries
Pete Dexter
James Dickey
Joan Didion
Annie Dillard
Stephen Dixon
E. L. Doctorow
J.P. Donleavy
Hilda Doolittle
John Dos Passos
Rita Dove
Theodore Dreiser
Rosalyn Drexler
W.E.B. Du Bois
Alan Dugan
Paul Laurence Dunbar
Robert Duncan

William Eastlake
Richard Eberhart
Walter Edmonds
Lonne Elder
T.S. Eliot
Stanley Elkin
George P. Elliott
Ralph Ellison
Louise Erdrich
Martín Espada

James Thomas Farrell
Howard Fast
William Faulkner
Jessie Redmon Fauset
Kenneth Fearing
Edna Ferber
Lawrence Ferlinghetti
Leslie Fiedler
Harvey Fierstein
Dorothy Canfield Fisher
Vardis Fisher
Clyde Fitch
Dudley Fitts
F. Scott Fitzgerald
Robert Fitzgerald
John Gould Fletcher
Shelby Foote
Carolyn Forché

Richard Ford
María Irene Fornés
Wallace Fowlie
Waldo Frank
Harold Frederic
Bruce Jay Friedman
Robert Frost
Daniel Fuchs
Charles Fuller
R. Buckminster Fuller

William Gaddis
Ernest J. Gaines
Isabella Gardner
John Gardner
Hamlin Garland
Jean Garrigue
William H. Gass
Henry Louis Gates, Jr.
Jack Gelber
William Gibson
Allen Ginsberg
Nikki Giovanni
Ellen Glasgow
Louise Gluck
Gail Godwin
Herbert Gold
Paul Goodman
Caroline Gordon
Mary Gordon
William Goyen
Shirley Ann Grau
Paul Green
Horace Gregory
John Guare
A.B. Guthrie, Jr.

Marilyn Hacker
Donald Hall
Dashiell Hammett
Lorraine Hansberry
Robert Hass
John Hawkes
Robert Hayden
Alfred Hayes
Lafcadio Hearn
Joseph Heller
Lillian Hellman
Mark Helprin
Ernest Hemingway
O. Henry
John Hersey
Dubose Heyward
Oscar Hijuelos
Tony Hillerman
Chester Himes
Alice Hoffman
John Hollander
Israel Horovitz
Richard Howard

Sidney Howard
Irving Howe
William Dean Howells
Langston Hughes
Richard Hugo
Zora Neale Hurston
David Henry Hwang

David Ignatow
William Inge
John Irving

Shirley Jackson
Henry James
William James
Randall Jarrell
Robinson Jeffers
Sarah Orne Jewett
Charles Johnson
James Weldon Johnson
Gayl Jones
James Jones
Erica Jong
Donald Justice

MacKinlay Kantor
George Kelly
Adrienne Kennedy
William Kennedy
Jack Kerouac
Ken Kesey
Jamaica Kincaid
Sidney Kingsley
Maxine Hong Kingston
Galway Kinnell
Carolyn Kizer
Kenneth Koch
Arthur Kopit
Jerzy Kosinski
Alfred Kreymborg
Stanley Kunitz
Tony Kushner

Ring Lardner
Richmond Lattimore
John Howard Lawson
David Leavitt
Nelle Harper Lee
Ursula K. Le Guin
Denise Levertov
Meyer Levin
Philip Levine
Sinclair Lewis
Ludwig Lewisohn
Vachel Lindsay
Alain Locke
Ross Lockridge

Jack London
Audre Lorde
Amy Lowell
Robert Lowell
Alison Lurie

Dwight Macdonald
Ross Macdonald
Percy MacKaye
Archibald MacLeish
Haki R. Madhubuti
Norman Mailer
Clarence Major
Bernard Malamud
Albert Maltz
David Mamet
William March
Edwin Markham
John P. Marquand
Don Marquis
Paule Marshall
Bobbie Ann Mason
Edgar Lee Masters
F.O. Matthiessen
Peter Matthiessen
William Maxwell
Cormac McCarthy
Mary McCarthy
Carson McCullers
Phyllis McGinley
Thomas McGrath
Thomas McGuane
Jay McInerney
Claude McKay
Terry McMillan
Larry McMurtry
H.L. Mencken
William Meredith
James Merrill
Thomas Merton
W.S. Merwin
James Michener
Josephine Miles
Edna St. Vincent Millay
Arthur Miller
Henry Miller
Steven Millhauser
Ron Milner
Margaret Mitchell
N.Scott Momaday
William Vaughn Moody
Marianne Moore
Merrill Moore
Paul Elmer More
Christopher Morley
Wright Morris
Toni Morrison
Frederic Morton
Bharati Mukherjee
Lewis Mumford

Vladimir Nabokov
Ogden Nash
George Jean Nathan
Gloria Naylor
Howard Nemerov
Reinhold Niebuhr
Anais Nin
Marsha Norman
Frank Norris

Joyce Carol Oates
Tim O'Brien
Edwin O'Connor
Flannery O'Connor
Clifford Odets
Frank o'Hara
John O'Hara
Sharon Olds
Tillie Olsen
Charles Olson
Eugene O'Neill
Simon Ortiz
Cynthia Ozick

Grace Paley
Dorothy Parker
V.L. Parrington
Kenneth Patchen
Walker Percy
Marge Piercy
Robert Pinsky
Sylvia Plath
Katherine Anne Porter
Ezra Pound
J.F. Powers
Reynolds Price
E. Annie Proulx
James Purdy
Thomas Pynchon

David Rabe
Philip Rahv
Ayn Rand
John Crowe Ransom
Marjorie Kinnan Rawlings
David Ray
John Rechy
Ishmael Reed
John Reed
Kenneth Rexroth
Elmer Rice
Adrienne Rich
Conrad Richter
Elizabeth Madox Roberts
Kenneth Roberts
Edwin Arlington Robinson
Theodore Roethke

Ole Rölvaag
Judith Rossner
Henry Roth
Philip Roth
Constance Rourke
Muriel Rukeyser
Damon Runyon

J.D. Salinger
Sonia Sanchez
Carl Sandburg
George Santayana
William Saroyan
May Sarton
Murray Schisgal
Budd Schulberg
James Schuyler
Delmore Schwartz
Winfield Townley Scott
Hubert Selby
Anne Sexton
Ntozake Shange
Karl Shapiro
Irwin Shaw
Wilfrid Sheed
Sam Shepard
Robert Sherwood
Leslie Marmon Silko
Charles Simic
Neil Simon
Louis Simpson
Upton Sinclair
Isaac Bashevis Singer
Jane Smiley
W.D. Snodgrass
Gary Snyder
Susan Sontag
Gary Soto
Jean Stafford
William Stafford
Wilbur Daniel Steele
Lincoln Steffens
Wallace Stegner
Gertrude Stein
John Steinbeck
Wallace Stevens
Trumbull Stickney
Robert Stone
Mark Strand
William Styron
Harvey Swados
May Swenson

Amy Tan
Booth Tarkington
Allen Tate
Peter Taylor

Paul Theroux
Augustus Thomas
James Thurber
Melvin Tolson
Jean Toomer
Ridgely Torrence
Lionel Trilling
Mark Twain
Anne Tyler

John Updike

Mark Van Doren
John Van Druten
Mona Van Duyn
Thorstein Veblen
Gore Vidal
Peter Viereck
Kurt Vonnegut

Diane Wakoski
Alice Walker
Margaret Walker
Edward Lewis Wallant
Robert Penn Warren
Wendy Wasserstein
Eudora Welty
Glenway Wescott
Nathanael West
Edith Wharton
John Hall Wheelock
John Brooks Wheelwright
E.B. White
Reed Whittemore
John Edgar Wideman
Richard Wilbur
Thornton Wilder
C. K. Williams
John A. Williams
Tennessee Williams
William Carlos Williams
August Wilson
Edmund Wilson
Lanford Wilson
Yvor Winters
Thomas Wolfe
Herman Wouk
James Wright
Richard Wright
Elinor Wylie

Stark Young
Ray Young Bear
Sol Yurick

Louis Zukofsky

GENRE ABBREVIATIONS

Below are the abbreviations and terms used to indicate genres in author bibliographies. Bibliographies include all major works and collections, but are not intended to be exhaustive.

a	autobiography
	adaptation
anthol	anthology
art c	art criticism
b	biography
c	criticism
coll	collection
d	drama/play
e	essay
ed	editor, edition
h	history
	interview
j	journalism
juv	juvenile, children's literature
l	letters
	lecture(s)
m	memoir
misc	miscellany
n	novel, novella
nf	nonfiction
	opera libretto
p	poetry
	pamphlet
	photographs
pd	poetic drama, verse play
r	reminiscence
rd	radio drama
s	story, stories
scrp	screenplay
sk	sketches
t	travel writing
tr	translation
tv	television play, television drama

A

ABISH, Walter (1931–)

[Walter] Abish, born in Vienna, does not consider himself an exile writer since he left Austria when he was six years old. He received his first schooling in France and studied in private English schools in Shanghai, to which his Jewish family had fled with the fall of France. He became an American citizen in 1960.

Abish believes English is his native tongue since he has written only in English. His work, however, bears the mark of exilic experience both in its experimentation of authorial distancing from narrative material and in its subject content of isolated protagonists and weary world travelers. His best-known work, the novel *How German It Is* (1980), explores the anxiety of modern postwar Germany in its splintered geographic and spiritual states.

> Martin Tucker. *Literary Exile in the Twentieth Century* (Westport: Greenwood Press, 1991), pp. 47–48

For most of his career, Walter Abish has been one of those purposely irritating writers who welcome the label "experimental." His books declared, in everything from design to content, their expectation of a small, rigorously select audience. Rejecting the term "story" (which implies that most suspect of middlebrow elements, a plot), Abish instead called his shorter works "fictions." He favored arbitrary and noticeably literary devices, as in one of his early "novels," *Alphabetical Africa* (1974), which consists of fifty-one chapters titled from A to Z and back to A, each chapter relying heavily on words containing the designated letter. "X stands for experimental," one such chapter begins, "and for excretion, that is for plain shit on the trail." The critic is tempted to add: EXACTLY.

And then, in 1980, came a breakthrough, a sudden transformation. *How German It Is* was Abish's gesture in the direction of a wider readership. In contrast to the fragmented and alienated word clusters that he previously produced, it contained distinct characters, several plots, and a protagonist that you could practically identify with. Set in contemporary Germany, the novel reflected persuasively and intelligently on the postwar German mood of denial, with its superficial emphasis on material success and its underbelly of revolutionary politics. . . .

Now, thirteen years later, comes *Eclipse Fever*, another readable novel, if perhaps a less permanently valuable one. It marks Abish's belated departure from the avant-garde ghetto, his sudden eligibility for reviews in mainstream periodicals. It can also be read as a straightforward corporate-conspiracy thriller. To the readers of the highly convoluted *Alphabetical Africa*, this turn of events would have been inconceivable. It's as if James Joyce had followed up *Ulysses* not with *Finnegans Wake*, but with *The Ministry of Fear* and *Our Man in Havana*.

> Wendy Lesser. *New Republic.* June 21, 1993. p. 44

Abish is a moralist masquerading as a formalist. If *Eclipse Fever* lacks the bite of *How German It Is*, it is perhaps because the distant crimes of the Toltecs are less painful than our sharper memory of recent events in Germany, and our own lives are closer to German. And for all the elegance of the later novel, there is almost something faintly dated about the target of its satire. We are familiar with the premise of a predatory American culture victimizing other cultures and imposing our values but the suspicion seems inescapable that now the terms may be reversing; now it is Mexico with Chevrolet factories and a burgeoning GNP, and it is ourselves we see in Abish's Mexicans, depressed and eclipsed. Or perhaps this has been Abish's intention all along?

> Diane Johnson, *New York Review of Books.* September 23, 1993, pp. 39–40

Abish has been a most important voice to those who make new fiction, starring in ground-breaking treatments like those of Jerome Klinkowitz, lurking in the conversations of writers at lunch, cited or parodied (or both) frequently for the oulipolian experiment of *Alphabetical Africa*, for the postmodern subtleties of *In the Future Perfect*, and for "his avant-garde masterpiece" (as even the book jacket knows), *How German It Is*.

But who wrote *Eclipse Fever*? Blessed with Guggenheim and MacArthur foundation support, mightn't Abish have written just about *anything*? And perhaps he did. *EF* has everything going for it, including local color (Mexican), murder, an ingenue's journey into the world the rest of us know, literariness (the father writes, a Mexican critic awaits his visit, publishers and patrons and deals get prime space), glitter (the millionaire and his sex-starved wife), relevance (Mexican resentment at yankee domination, the trade in pre-Columbian artifacts, torture and corruption Out There). In fact, the book has all the elements you'd need for a Bestseller Construction Kit; it's a slick prospect for a film.

Maybe, finally, it is unreasonable to expect every novel a great writer gives us to be a breakthrough, for us, for him (or her, or them). *EF* is not an "F" because it's not as Abish as his most interesting (to me) work, nor is it an "A" because of its stylistic deftness and the wry shrewdness of its literary play; it is, like my alphabetical review, halfway "there," *EF* is also a course in best sellers that (should) ruin them for writers and readers. And, maybe, the lesson is that there aren't further surprises to be found in desublimating the conventions of culture and society—that we already know enough about them to change them, just not enough about ourselves to know why we don't. Alejandro ends the novel by entering the "sea of pale Spanish faces" with his own mestizo darkness itching him across (of course) his groin, the genesis of his "new" self a rash of social disease as he joins "his new family" rather than the mythic potency of the individual-as-phallus. "It must be nerves, he decided," overlooking like Francisco whatever is injurious to the function of the self, "and looked to the left and to the right to determine where he was to sit." *That* line is the future perfect of a thoroughly Abish ending.

> Robert Siegle. *American Book Review.* February–March, 1994, pp. 17, 27

Alien, uncanny, half-concealed: the art of Abish is ecliptic. (''I needed a society in which what I described wouldn't become self-evident,'' he writes in a yet unpublished interview. . .). Abish, I have said, defamiliarizes, de-creates, only to lure us into a space of lucid negativity. He does not offer us an exotic Mexico, that of D.H. Lawrence or Malcolm Lowry, say, nor a cathartic or redeeming landscape. He offers us an imaginary (that is, both essential and infinitely contestable) country. Thus, with Daedalian *hubris*, Abish permitted himself to visit Germany and Mexico only after he had written ''about'' them.

Ihab Hassan. *Southern Review*. Summer 1994, pp. 628–29

BIBLIOGRAPHY
Duel Site, 1970 (p); *Alphabetical Africa*, 1974 (n); *Minds Meet*, 1975 (s); *In the Future Perfect*, 1977 (s); *How German It Is*, 1980 (n); *Firsthand* [essay on artwork of wife, Cecile Abish], 1978; *99, The New Meaning*, 1990 (s, journal [with photos by C. Abish]); *Eclipse Fever*, 1993 (n)

ACKER, Kathy (1948–1997)

During the 1980s the younger readers and writers . . . and those others who had remained largely alienated from mainstream publishing were to be involved in considerable changes. The readers from the original baby-boom generation had by now become middle-aged and they remained largely responsible for supporting a plethora of small, independent publishing houses including the feminist, gay, and left-wing presses. The literary underground of experimentation and small presses had never quite gone away, even in Britain. (As Paul Valery had put it, ''Everything changes but the avant-garde''.) After William Burroughs, Kathy Acker was the only real inheritor of this bohemian tradition to cross over fully into the big-time publishing world. Acker, who lived for a long time in London, has commented on the lack of a literary ''underground'' in Britain: ''I came out of a poetry tradition—the Black Mountain poets, the Language Poets. No such traditions exist over here. The underground just isn't known here. I mean, a huge network that's been there for years and years . . . there's no such thing here.'' This is, of course, one of the reasons why English critics are so ill-equipped to deal with much of contemporary fiction, why English writing remains so mired in a parochial backwater. Acker suffered from a degree of misunderstanding from the British press that, she said, amounted to ''slander'' and that similarly stemmed from the lack of a strong British counterculture in writing. During the eighties the enormously diverse elements that comprised the American counterculture seemed to gather strength and show some indications of producing new writers. This American underground, which, as Acker points out, had never gone away over there, could be glimpsed by English readers in books and magazines like the Re/Search publications and Amok's Fourth Despatch catalogue. . . .

By the time the generation born in the postwar years grew up there were certainly immeasurably more opportunities for women to leave home and participate in experiments of every kind, artistic and sexual. In literature Patti Smith and Kathy Acker are obvious prototypes. . . . From the sixties onward. . . women's lives tended to go through a series of dizzyingly swift changes. Much art was of necessity preoccupied with the seismic changes wrought by feminism and it is only relatively recently that strong images of urban bohemian women—who cannot easily be dismissed as just ''feminists''—have started to emerge in fiction.

Elizabeth Young. In E. Young and Graham Caveney, eds. *Shopping for Space: Essays on America's Blank Generation Fiction* (New York: Grove Press–Serpent's Tail, 1992), pp. 6–7, 169–70

Acker's quest novels obsessively depict the search for individuality, for selfhood, in the context of the cultural construction of identity. For this search to proceed, Acker's protagonists must move beyond the border of culture to conceive of themselves as individuals, as other than complaint products of their culture. This quest, like the one Borges depicts, is unreasonable; it cannot be completed, for even in Acker's delirious narratives, it is impossible to step outside culture and thus to shed the culturally constructed self.

During a moment of revelation in the abortion scene that begins Acker's *Don Quixote*, the protagonist resolves to embark on such a quest for selfhood. Dressed in green paper and positioned on the operating table with knees raised as masked medical figures prepare to invade her body, she is struck with the sudden knowledge that her identity is not her own. This understanding moves her to adopt subversive strategies to disengage from the forces that have compelled her identity: ''When a doctor sticks a steel catheter into you while you're lying on your back and you do exactly what he and the nurses tell you to. . . you let go of your mind. . . .'' Once she can conceive of surrendering the constructed self, she can also formulate the quest to acquire her own ''name'': ''She needed a new life. She had to be named'' (9–10).

The quest for a new life and a name structures several of Acker's works. Yet unlike male quest novels, such as *The Magic Mountain* and *A Portrait of the Artist as a Young Man*, Acker's texts locate the means of acquisition outside culture, since they are unavailable in the context of patriarchy. To constitute the self differently, the quester must find an alternative site for such constitution. Acker moves her protagonists toward this site through the appropriation of male texts, a strategy she explains in the epigraph to part 2: ''Being born into and part of a male world, she had no speech of her own. All she could do was read male texts which weren't hers.'' The male texts represent the limits of language and culture within which the female quester attempts to acquire identify. Once inside the male text, the quester, by her very posture, subverts it: ''By repeating the past, I'm molding and transforming it.'' In the Borges story, replication is the issue. For Acker the appropriation of *Don Quixote* is a strategy of subversion. Her description of the textual appropriation used by Arabs applies to herself: ''They write by cutting chunks out of all-ready written texts and in other ways defacing traditions: changing important names into silly ones, making dirty jokes out of matters that should be of the utmost importance to us'' (39, 48, 25).

Acker's purpose in appropriating well-known texts is profoundly political. Through plagiarism, Acker proposes an alternative to the classical Marxist explanation of the sources of power. With Jean Baudrillard she believes that those who control the means of representation are more powerful than those who control the means of production. Plagiarism undermines the assumptions governing representation. . . . In plagiarizing, Acker does not deny the masterwork itself, but she does interrogate its sources in paternal authority and male desire. By placing the search for modes of representing female desire inside male texts, Acker and others clearly delineate the constraints under which this search proceeds. She also suggests that the alternative nature of, and location for, the missing contents in women's texts is in the not yet presented.

Ellen G. Friedman. "Where Are the Missing Contents? (Post) Modernism, Gender, and the Canon". *PMLA: Publications of the Modern Language Association of America.* March, 1993, pp. 243–44

BIBLIOGRAPHY
Ripoff Red, 1973 (p); *I Dreamt I Was a Nymphomaniac: Imagining,* 1974 (p); *The Childlike Life of the Black Tarantula: Some Lives of Murderesses,* 1975 (n); *The Persian Poems,* 1980 (p); *New York City in 1976,* 1981 (s); *Hello, I'm Erica Jong,* 1982 (n); *Great Expectations,* 1982 (n); *Implosion,* 1983 (p); *Portrait of an Eye,* 1983 (3 n: *The Childlike Life of the Black Tarantula; I Dreamt I Was a Nymphomaniac; The Adult Life of Toulouse Lautrec*); *Algeria: A Series of Invocations Because Nothing Else Works,* 1984 (p); *Blood and Guts in High School,* 1984 (n); *Don Quixote, Which Was a Dream,* 1986 (n); *Literal Madness,* 1988 (3 n: *Kathy Goes to Haiti,* 1978; *Pier Pasolini's My Death My Life* 1984; *Florida,* 1976); *Empire of the Senseless,* 1988 (n); *The Seven Cardinal Virtues,* 1990 (s); *In Memoriam to Identity,* 1990 (e); *Hannibal Lecter, My Father,* ed. S. Lotringer, 1991 (n); *My Mother: Demonology,* 1993 (n); *Pussy, King of the Pirates,* 1996 (n)

ADAMS, Henry (1838–1918)

The Education of Henry Adams, conceived as a study of the philosophy of history, turns out in fact to be an *apologia pro vita sua,* one of the most self-centered and self-revealing books in the language.

The revelation is not indeed of the direct sort that springs from frank and insouciant spontaneity. Since the revelation was not intended, the process is tortuous in the extreme. It is a revelation that comes by the way, made manifest in the effort to conceal it, overlaid by all sorts of cryptic sentences and self-deprecatory phrases, half hidden by the protective coloring taken on by a sensitive mind commonly employing paradox and delighting in perverse and teasing mystification. . . . The *Education* is in fact the record, tragic and pathetic underneath its genial irony, of the defeat of fine aspirations and laudable ambitions. It is the story of a life which the man himself, in his old age, looked back upon as a broken arch.

Carl Becker. *American Historical Review.* April, 1919. pp. 4245–6

In a manner he was a microcosm of American history, for what of history his family had not actually made, he had written or had

watched. America knew him not, but he had known America; and his autobiography stands in a class with that of Benjamin Franklin. He described it as "the education of Henry Adams," a process he seems to have abandoned in despair; but the reading of the book will give an American a European education, and a European an American one.

Shane Leslie. *Dublin Review.* June, 1919. p. 218

This gentleman from the House of Adams is preeminently a modern American scholar. He had a singular capacity for original research and polished presentation. He was both a student of history and a literary artist and in all his work he combined his abilities in the one with his powers in the other. To match his breadth and depth of knowledge he had a keen critical sense and a clear judicial mind. He had creative imagination, a sensitive appreciation of significant form, and a remarkable skill in removing the clutter of details and depicting essentials. He was a master of facts, pursuing his ideas with minute research and solid reasoning. He was a superb maker of phrases, but he sketched with accuracy and precision, coloring his narrative with his own personality and toning his portraits with insight and understanding.

Marian D. Irish. *American Scholar.* March, 1932. pp. 223–4

Henry Adams, very early, became too pessimistic and cynical to go on being a participant. He chose, instead, a place on the sidelines, and from there set about recording the minutes of all the unsavory transactions of America's public life. The picture of such proceedings which Adams drew, or at least suggested, in the *Education* is a final one. For not only were its revelations damning, but its sources were unimpeachable. It was the indictment of a supremely placed worldling who had listened at the most private keyholes, who had been told—or allowed to guess—the secrets of those who worked behind the scenes. Scarcely anyone else who did so little knew so much. Adams's indictment stands: the great documentary merit of the *Education* is its demonstration of what nineteenth-century America had become, and by what process, and on what terms.

Louis Kronenberger. *New Republic.* March 15, 1939. p. 156

Henry Adams recapitulated on American soil the romantic tradition of Europe. This tradition included aesthetic pessimism, in which framework he built up a personality-image which he came to enjoy artistically. The image was that of the failure, the heroic failure. He came to enjoy the spectacle doubly: on the stage as an actor, from the wings as an onlooker who revels in the gaping audiences. . . . Adams's failure was only a pen and paper failure. He wrote "a terribly ironic estimate of himself" because it pleased his artistic fancy to do so.

Max I. Baym. *American Scholar.* Winter, 1945. pp. 87–8

Pessimism was both a pose and a habit of mind with Henry Adams. Only fools and great statesmen were paid to be optimists. Furthermore, as Adams remarked, "no one can afford to pose as an optimist, short of an income of a hundred thousand a year.'' Adams had about twenty-five thousand and considered himself to be neither a great statesman nor a fool; thus, pessimism was for him the only dignified pose. And dignity was important, as well as required. However, something of his pessimism was genuine because his scientific and metaphysical speculations had convinced him that the cherished assumptions of his culture and tradition were totally wrong, and worse than useless; because by stubbornly defending the old notions of order, unity, the unique value of the individual, freedom of the will, one would only hasten the acceleration towards the inevitable catastrophe of all civilization.

> Gerrit H. Roelofs. *English Literary History*. Sept., 1950. p. 231

It is dangerously easy to overstress the near-tragic quality of the aging scholar, caught as never before in the impingement of beauty but knowing, too, the final ineffectuality of its comfort for one whose mind insisted on discovering monstrosity and chaos on every side. He still was one to relish good food and drink, to enjoy the company of handsome women and vigorous men and stimulate them by questions and banter. He was by no means the bitter, broken prophet that many critics, gullibly misreading his own account, have pronounced him to be. . . . One comprehends Adams most clearly as a man who to the last felt and not quite successfully defied the personal and universal disorder encroaching upon a sensitive dweller in the nineteenth and twentieth centuries. His dilemma was at once individual and typical.

> Robert A. Hume. *Runaway Star* (Cornell). 1951. pp. 35–6

He was very shy of self-revelation. Some of it came out, disguised, in the novels, biographies, and *History*. He could be more naked, for instance in *Esther* than in the first-person books, *Mont-St.-Michel* and *The Education*. *Democracy* is his political ordeal; *Esther*, his own, as well as his wife's religious plight. And where one might least expect to find it, in the heavily documented, nine-volume *History of the United States*, there are passages of lyrical intensity which tell us as much about the subjective Henry Adams as any of (his) letters.

> Elizabeth Stevenson. *The Nation*. Jan. 26, 1952. p. 87

Adams was not a likeable man; he was an important man. Like the intellectuals who would model themselves on his legend, he cultivated his snobbism too lovingly; he was something of what the Germans call *ein Besserwisser*; and his attitudes always seem a bit disassociated from his individual experience. In his own life he suffered the destructive split between literary and political vocations which has since become so prevalent. . . . But it was greatly to his credit that even as he submitted to this split, he did not approve of it; he knew that for the intellectual, health is possible only through a unity of the two parts, even if a unity in tension.

> Irving Howe. *New Republic*. Sept. 22, 1952. p. 26

The greatness of the mind of Adams himself is in the imaginative reach of the effort to solve the problem of the meaning, the use, or

the value of its own energy. The greatness is in the effort itself, in variety of response deliberately made to every possible level of experience. It is in the acceptance, with all piety, of ignorance as the humbled form of knowledge; in the pursuit of divers shapes of knowledge—the scientific, the religious, the political, the social and trivial—to the point where they add to ignorance, when the best response is silence itself. That is the greatness of Adams as a type of mind. As it is a condition of life to die, it is a condition of thought, in the end, to fail. Death is the expense of life and failure is the expense of greatness.

> R.P. Blackmur. *The Lion and the Honeycomb* (Harcourt). 1955. p. 95

Henry Adams had a rich and sensitive mind and was, behind his misanthropic exterior, a deeply humane individual. He had been formed rather rigidly in the heavy heritage of his Presidential ancestry and of New England dogma; and by the most subtle and delicate process he achieved, within his sensibility, a system of feathery balances, so that the discharge of his emotions might be propped by flying buttresses and filtered through his stained-glass windows. His mind was like the cathedrals he came to study; it was no accident that he turned to them.

> Leon Edel. *Saturday Review*. Dec. 10, 1955. p. 15

To agree that after his wife's death Adams devoted his talent to indicting the universe that had produced her and destroyed her is, of course, to over-simplify. Yet, once the *History* is finished, everything else of import seems to turn upon the theme of conflict between tranquillity and force. . . . This gifted man was in some sense the child of Byron and Voltaire. There was something in him elementary as well as ironical. A hostile critic might plausibly demonstrate that, because it was outrageous of the universe to deal with Mr. and Mrs. Henry Adams as the universe had done, the scholar would condemn the universe. The rebelliousness, the self-incrimination, the irony of the mature Byron are paralleled by Adams, the principal difference being that in the American these qualities were held in restraint as judgments, not hurled at the target as weapons.

> Howard Mumford Jones. *The Nation*. Dec. 24, 1955. pp. 558–9

Scenery, psychology, history, literature, poetry, art—all these are materials for the story he relates. But the controlling purpose of the narrative is to show, in its own form as in its subject, how vast a world can be found by the senses and how great a work the intellect may do when it serves the highest vision of the imagination and defies, knowingly, the terrors of fact which always beset that vision. Because the pilgrim-artist has discovered the realm of tragedy, the tourist-historian of *Mont-Saint-Michel and Chartres* works in a realm beyond that which can be marked out by any particular theory of history. The naïvete of the Romanesque, the refinement of the Transition, the scientific modernity of the Gothic all had their appeal to him because he saw them as phases of life which he had experienced in his role of human being as well as in his capacity as scholar. His aspiration expressed itself in the very shape of his composition, but the anguish of his doubt was also there, almost buried out of sight, in the continual presence of time that foreshadowed the end of love.

> J.C. Levenson. *The Mind and Art of Henry Adams* (Houghton). 1957. p. 288

Yet Adams's quest had led beyond the limits of either intellectual curiosity or the hope of fame (for he could satisfy neither) to bring him at last to that vantage point where the world of past and present took on that comprehensible form which gave him emotional and intellectual peace. If the journey from nineteenth-century Boston to twelfth-century Chartres had any meaning, it was expressed in the last subjective works, in the acceptance of the relativity of all historical interpretation, the tentativeness of all understanding. It was a conclusion, he must have known, no more valid than any other, a point of view for the time being useful and necessary. It made sense of what for Henry Adams was otherwise chaos. It explained, if it did not justify. One might wonder whether a study of history could ever do more than that.

> John C. Cairns. *South Atlantic Quarterly*. Spring, 1958. pp. 192–3

. . . he stands alone among all the thinkers of his generation, in having made a timely effort to understand the forces of science, technology, and politics that have brought us to the verge of a gigantic and irretrievable disaster. His eminence as a historian only emphasizes his loneliness as a social diagnostician. Adams' contemporaries, in the words of John Bigelow in 1899, regarded Adams as either "an inspired prophet or crazy," but they were no more disposed to heed his inspiration than to believe that his madness would, fifty years later, become the very criterion of sanity.

> Lewis Mumford. *The Virginia Quarterly Review*. Spring, 1962. p. 197

For [Adams], value or meaning is only conceivable as originating in final, impersonal ends. He cannot think of life as having meaning apart from a goal that is outside of and larger than the individual. This is the most fundamental and omnipresent manifestation of his Puritanism; it is a mental habit shaped by an obsessive need of his conscience to relate every event, every moral act, and every individual self to some ultimate and all-embracing unity. . . . [I]n reaching the end of his quest, he arrived at a colossal irony. For what Adams discovered was that life had no meaning; . . . Always pressing for certainty, for nothing less than an absolute certainty, he found it in universal death, an event no less meaningless than certain.

> George Hochfield. *Henry Adams: An Introduction and Interpretation* (Barnes and Noble). 1962. pp. 32, 139

Read as a novel of spiritual quest, an initiation romance of Adams's alter ego, the *Education* exhibits a structure of extraordinary complexity, moving simultaneously on many levels of meaning. The "Henry Adams" of the narrative is as protean as Whitman's "I" and contains its own multitudes. . . . The "air of reality" with which Adams invested the tragic hero of his autobiographical-philosophical romance is the product of a masterfully sustained illusion. Not that the author really undervalued his manikin; no theme is more often reiterated than that if he was wrong his fellows were even more mistaken. . . . Within his exacting inner world his pose of ignorance was no affectation, but in the world of his miserable fellow insects it was little more than the ironic condescension of the resolute schoolmaster setting traps for the complacent.

> Ernest Samuels. *Henry Adams: The Major Phase* (Harvard). 1964. pp. 353, 359

Only temperamentally and, in the narrow sense, biographically, did Adams seek out those avenues of silence where he could imagine the medieval world unified. But he knew more and better than this. He was not going to deny either the enthusiasm with which he and his friends had begun life in a "race for power" or the fact that they had miserably lost. . . . He knew he had had his historical neck broken. He grasped multiplicity not just as a term defining the inevitable movement of gold-bug capitalism to socialism and communism, not just as something scientists were beginning to define, not just as an antonym to twelfth century unity brought about by society's obedience to the laws of acceleration, not just as the chaos that would transform democracy into a form of totalitarianism, but as a master that simultaneously rendered impossible his personal scene of education and forced upon him definitions of education broader than himself or the teachings of his heritage. . . . The accelerated speed of forces has guaranteed that only ideas of education as subtle and flexible as Adams' can survive for as long as two generations; the problem now is not, as it once might have been, one of choosing the pot in which to be melted, but of learning how to swim in the big pot that is the only one large enough to contain all the forces at work.

> Roger Sale. *Hudson Review*. Autumn, 1965. pp. 430–2

I believe that Adams always misconceived his principal talent. He wanted the recognition of scientists for his theories in a field where he was not equipped to make any serious contribution. The picture of Adams, the descendant of presidents, a kind of early American "Everyman," a survival from the Civil War in the day of the automobile, traveling from one end of the globe to the other in quest of the absolute, pausing before Buddhas and dynamos, has so caught the imagination of the academic community that his biography, which he wrote as well as lived, has become, so to speak, one of his works, and his most fantastic speculations the subjects of serious theses. Yet to me his primary contributions to our literature were aesthetic. He is far closer to Whitman and Melville than to Bancroft or Prescott, and he is not at all close to Einstein.

> Louis Auchincloss. *Henry Adams* (Minnesota). 1971. p. 39

BIBLIOGRAPHY

(with Charles F. Adams) Chapters of Erie and Other Essays, 1871; *The Administration—A Radical Indictment!* 1872 (e); *Syllabus. History II, Political History of Europe from the Tenth to the Fifteenth Century*, 1874; (editor and contributor) *Essays in Anglo-Saxon Law*, 1876; *The Life of Albert Gallatin*, 1879 (b); *Democracy*, 1880 (n); *John Randolph*, 1882 (b); *Esther* [pseud. Frances

Snow Compton], 1884 (n); *History of the United States of America during the First Administration of Thomas Jefferson*, 1884; *History of the United States of America during the Second Administration of Thomas Jefferson*, 1885; *History of the United States of America during the First Administration of James Madison*, 1888; *History of the United States of America during the First Administration of Thomas Jefferson*, 1888 (first trade edition, corrected and revised); *History of the United States of America during the Second Administration of Thomas Jefferson*, 1890 (first trade edition, corrected and revised); *History of the United States of America during the First Administration of James Madison*, 1890 (corrected and revised); *History of the United States of America during the Second Administration of James Madison*, 1891; *Historical Essays*, 1891; *History of the United States of America*, 1891–92 (English edition); *Memoirs of Maran Taaroa Last Queen of Tahiti*, 1893; *Memoirs of Arü Taimai E Marama of Eimeo Terürere of Tooraai Terünui of Tahiti*, 1901 (by Tauraatua I Amo, Tahitian adoptive name of Henry Adams); *Mont-Saint-Michel and Chartres*, 1904 (h) (slightly revised, 1912); *The Education of Henry Adams*, 1907 (a) (slightly revised, 1918); *A Letter to American Teachers of History*, 1910 (e); *The Life of George Cabot Lodge*, 1911 (b); *The Degradation of the Democratic Dogma*, 1919 (e); *Letters to a Niece and Prayer to the Virgin of Chartres*, 1920; *A Cycle of Adams Letters, 1861–1865*, 1920; *Letters of Henry Adams, 1858–1891*, 1930; *Henry Adams and His Friends*, 1947 (letters); *Great Secession Winter of 1860–61, and Other Essays*, 1958; *A Henry Adams Reader*, 1960 (misc); *Documents Relating to New England Federalism*, 1969; *The Letters of Henry Adams*, 1982–88 (letters); *Sketches for the North American Review*, 1986 (e); *Supplement to the Letters of Henry Adams: Letters Omitted from the Harvard University Press Edition of the Letters of Henry Adams*, 1989 (letters); *The Correspondence of Henry James and Henry Adams*, 1992 (letters)

ADAMS, Léonie (1899–1988)

Hers is an accent which is as sensitive as it is strange, a register that seems to tremble with certain Elizabethan echoes but which vibrates with a lyric passion that proceeds from no other century but our own. Miss Adams is, as even the simplest of her poems reveals, a metaphysical poet; her most candidly declared descriptions blossom suddenly in an unearthly and intensified air. . . . One waits, with something greater than curiosity, for the successor to *Those Not Elect*. Meanwhile, it is almost enough to say that even where Miss Adams is least successful, she fails on a high plane and that, among the "emerging" lyricists none lead us to expect—and demand—more.

> Louis Untermeyer. *New Republic*. Nov. 25, 1925. p. 23

Leonie Adams takes us palpably into a world of her own. . . . All the poems in her book have the stillness, the faint lighting, the introspection and retrospection of an awakening at dawn when our labor is yet a dream and our dream has the burthen of labor. . . . But perhaps *High Falcon* is lacking in a quality that would fill up the measure of our admiration for a fine book of poetry. That quality is fulness. The moods that the poems come out of are real and

poignant, but again and again we wish they had been given a fuller body. Too often, the poet gives us the trees stripped bare. We want her sometimes to give us the tree with its leaves and fruits and a bird singing in the leaves. . . .

These poems do not clamorously tell us an emotional history; they are in undertones; they are for those who prefer cold airs and bare lands to noontide brilliancy and crowds and colors. They are not poems that can be taken in by a quick perusal; the reading of them must be accompanied by a certain meditation. They are poems of tragic life.

> Padraic Colum. *New Republic*. Dec. 18, 1929. p. 113

Those Not Elect, 1925, is an unusual first volume, though it owes a bit of its inspiration to classic metaphysicians. The Brooklyn mystic is a comparatively difficult poet by virtue of her devotion to the reflections of the mind over matter. Her exquisite psyche, aware of the inconsequence of man in eternity, ventures among problems abstruse to the average mind; but she molds her thought into concrete images. She rarely relaxes the high tension of her inquiry; there are no banal, and few colloquial lines along the way.

> Alfred Kreymborg. *Our Singing Strength* (Coward-McCann). 1929. p. 554

Her observations are on the whole free from remote astronomical and supernatural references, adhering instead to the city, the countryside of farms, the intimate landscape with many of its conventional properties retained, or of the pages of books. . . .

Natural sympathy has given Miss Adams' observations a rare opulence. She has explored the details of rural landscape and weather almost to the point of specialty. . . . The world is static, as the metaphysical observer requires it to be. In no poem may be found the impulsive capture of impression (together with the accompanying swell in phrase). . . . Miss Adams' virtue is of another order. She displays the persistent curiosity which pushes an analysis forward until it has achieved a perfect distillation of the essence of a perception. This is a clue to her spiritual bravery. It may be delayed by physical reticence, but it attains to freedom in the end.

> Morton Dauwen Zabel. *Poetry*. Feb., 1930. pp. 334–6

. . .certainly, Leonie Adams' re-creation of her world had a closer kinship to the revivals of a Gothic imagination in the poetry of the early and late nineteenth century than it had to metaphysical poetry. . . . The frequent use of the word "sweet," the "so sweet pain," and the adjective "cold," even the sound of her "airy shell" spoke of her mingled debt to and careful, attentive readings in the poetry of [Walter] de la Mare and Gerard Manley Hopkins.

> Horace Gregory and Marya Zaturenska. *A History of American Poetry* (Harcourt). 1946. pp. 297–8

Miss Adams's poetry is a difficult labor. Intensely compact, intensely intellectualized, and rigorously ascetic, it comes true, but it does not come easy. The matter, as she writes in "Sundown," is sanctified, "dipped in a gold stain." It seems doubtful that there can be a wide audience for Miss Adams's gold stain, but that there will always be a group of discerning and enthusiastic readers seems certain.

John Ciardi. *The Nation.* May 22, 1954. p. 445

The world of Leonie Adams is one of forms and pure relationships. Her gaze... is never intercepted by dreams, never blurred by mistiness. It is clairvoyant. She sees the formal rigor of all the things she looks at. And the emotion which these things generate, no matter how subtle or delicate it is, finds the exact word with which to express itself. Her poems... testify to a very real world of nature, and at the same time to a willful abstraction which isolates all the objects considered.... She is a watcher at the extreme edge of love and gentleness.... But she should be called the poet who has undertaken a metaphysical reintegration in a century when many poets, the surrealists especially, have been engaged in just the opposite process, that of disintegrating the cosmos.

Wallace Fowlie. *Commonweal.* Nov. 26, 1954. pp. 224–6

The present volume [*Poems: A Selection*] opens with 24 poems written since [1929], continues by reprinting nearly the whole of *High Falcon* (37 poems), and concludes by selecting 24 poems out of nearly 40 in her first volume, *Those Not Elect* (1925). The proportion is right: *High Falcon* shows her work consistently at its best, as in the famous "Country Summer"; though a few of her later poems, chiefly the shorter ones, display the same mysterious evocation of moods from piled-up images of green, sun, wind, and light.... Some of the longer pieces in the first section seem to suffer from incoherence and turgidity: they are too "poetic," too full of terms like "else-wending," "rime-bedabbled," "empery," "enduskings," and "ambient."

Louis Martz. *The Yale Review.* Winter, 1955. p. 305

BIBLIOGRAPHY
Those Not Elect, 1925 (p); *High Falcon and Other Poems*, 1929; *This Measure*, 1933 (p); (with others) *Lyrics of Francois Villon*, 1933 (tr); *Poems: A Selection*, 1954

AGEE, James (1909–1955)

Mr. Agee does a good deal to antagonize the reader. There are too many tongues, too many attitudes, too many awarenesses on the subjective side (perhaps defenses would be more precise); even the sincerity is too much, is too prostrate. And yet, visible through all this, are some unmistakable virtues: Mr. Agee, at times, writes brilliantly...; he is extraordinarily sensitive and aware and, above all, concerned with that deeper honesty that assembles before itself all those minute rationalizations and nuances of feeling that are always a kind of havoc inside ourselves.

Harvey Breit. *New Republic.* Sept. 15, 1941. p. 348

James Agee was born in the South and retains the pride and piety and love of language of the Southern writer.... Genius he surely

had; the trouble perhaps lay in his trying to read that genius into things not of his own making. In a vague way his instinct resembled that of Proust, whose genius was of a kind that could only portray genius, nothing but genius, whether in painters, duchesses, or elevator boys. Yet where Proust actually recreated his powers, Agee was content to delegate his.

F. W. Dupee. *The Nation.* April 28, 1951. p. 400

James Agee... was a writer who gave all of himself... to every medium that he worked in—poetry, fiction, reportage, criticism, movies, television. He was not only one of the most gifted writers in the United States, but such a natural as a writer that he found a creative opportunity in every place where drearier people pitied themselves for pot-boiling.... Agee was a writer who actually did better in popular and journalistic media—where certain objective technical requirements gave him a chance to create something out of his immense tenderness and his high sense of comedy than when he let himself go in purely speculative lyricism. He was a natural literary craftsman, not a literary intellectual, and it was only *avant-garde* associations that ever misled him. His most beautiful poems—like the title poem of his first book, *Permit Me Voyage*—are those which are most traditional in form.

Alfred Kazin. *New York Times Book Section.* Nov. 17, 1957. p. 5

Agee was a very gifted and versatile writer; his best-known work is *Let Us Now Praise Famous Men*, an account of sharecroppers in the depression, with photographs by Walker Evans. He wrote for motion pictures and was the finest critic of films this country has produced.... The most remarkable thing about Agee's new book—*A Death in the Family*—is that it is exactly the kind of novel that a great many people have tried to write and have not been able to bring off, at least not the way Agee does. The subject is extremely simple: a man dies. There is no plot or story, just an account of the reactions of his relatives and one friend. But the writing is brilliant, because it manages to be so sensitive to every nuance of emotion without ever going soft.

Paul Pickrel. *Harper's Magazine.* Dec., 1957. p. 88

The posthumously published *A Death in the Family* is Agee's final item of his career in letters, a novel on which he had been at work for eight years. It does not give him any new importance as an American writer, but it does bring to a delicate and satisfactory flowering his very great ability to create the qualities and nuances of private feeling.... There are moments of grief and loss in everyone's life which one cannot live with, but can only recover from. And they are, oddly, the moments when one recognizes one's feelings to have been most alive. The success of *A Death in the Family* is that it brings to the surface of the reader's consciousness these forgotten, rejected moments—his own tender, unusable anguish.

David L. Stevenson. *The Nation.* Dec. 14, 1957. pp. 460–1

The sternest criticism that can be made of these collected articles [*Agee on Film*] is that, from them, emerges not so much a critical intelligence or a Promethean appreciator of an art as a lovable and admirable man. Sometimes his lines soar; sometimes they merely gush. Sometimes his rhapsodic stabs penetrate to the heart; sometimes they flounder. He is given to meaningless distinctions. . . . But he had what is missing from most criticism today—of films and all arts: fierce intensity. The bitter image he leaves is not of a facile, corrosive cynic but of a blazing pessimist.

Stanley Kauffmann. *New Republic*. Dec. 1, 1958. p. 19

Throughout [*Agee on Film*], in which the best criticism by the late James Agee has been collected, there runs the assumption that the film is an art as well as a business—without, fortunately, any of the coterie cuteness about "art cinema". This assumption is apparent in the casual, unself-conscious way he uses the word "poem" to describe a film in which realism is lifted beyond itself into the aesthetic, in his use of other arts—music most often—in comparing effects, not means, and in his persistent discussion of superior films in terms of content *and* form, avoiding the ordinary preoccupation with content alone. . . . His descriptions of the photographic texture of films and his recognition of the ways the textures were used or misused are easily the most perceptive accounts of pure "seeing" that film criticism offers. . . . On the whole, *Agee on Film* is a long, literate, loving collection of one intelligent, sharp-eyed critic's very personal comments; it is also America's most important contribution to film criticism.

Gerald Weales. *The Reporter*. Dec. 25, 1958. pp. 38–9

[*A Death in the Family*] shows that Agee had the technical, intellectual, and moral equipment to do major writing. By "moral" which has a terribly old-fashioned ring, I mean that he believed in and—what is rarer—was interested in good and evil. Lots of writers are fascinated by evil and write copiously about it, but they are bored by virtue; this not only limits their scope but also prevents them from giving a satisfactory account of evil. In the novel, Jay Follett is a good husband and father, Mary is a good wife and mother, and their goodness is expressed in concrete actions. . . . The theme is the confrontation of love, that is carried to its highest possible reach, and death, as the negation of life and yet a necessary part of it. Only a major writer could rise to such a theme.

Dwight Macdonald. *Encounter*. Dec., 1962. p. 75

Agee in the rootlessness and disorder of Northern urban life sought always for order, definition, discipline, but he found there no firm tradition, no community of writers or intellectuals with whom he could ally himself. Though his career was lived during the Depression and World War II and the immediate postwar years, a time of strident political movements and intense ideological argument, he refused to assume an ideological "position". . . .

To all of his writing, whether journalism, movie scripts, or fiction, he brought the same sort of moral earnestness and what one critic has called "an almost religious sense of commitment to the truth". These qualities, it is clear enough, were stimulated and nurtured at that small church school in rural Tennessee and by the wise moral and spiritual guidance of a dedicated Episcopal priest, "my oldest and dearest friend," as Agee calls him in his letters. It is

the moral and religious aspect of the Southern story that forever haunted Agee, that he was forever telling, no matter what the subject.

Nash K. Burger. *South Atlantic Quarterly*. Winter, 1964. pp. 36–7

In the two novels [*A Morning Watch* and *A Death in the Family*] we see the essential quality of Agee's art. The novels are lyric—like the camera he understood so well, they focus on static scenes to portray universal reactions to human sorrow: guilt, courage, awakening, love. Such scenes work well. But the saddest thing about them, and about Agee's fiction in general, is his inability to believe in the present reality of his celebrations. They are of a certain time and place, protected, nurtured, and embalmed by memory. Agee's ideal world is a lost world, out of touch with present living. Even stylistically, none of Agee's abundant personal charm and vitality enters these books. In large measure, Agee's penchant for innocence is a death wish.

Richard H. Rupp. *Celebration in Postwar American Fiction* (Miami). 1970. p. 110

An intense desire to know himself marked Agee's work in the three great pieces of sustained prose that lie at the heart of his achievement. In *Let Us Now Praise Famous Men* Agee describes the process by which he came to a new and deep understanding of himself and his world. In *The Morning Watch* he looked back at himself as at the age of twelve he had come to an earlier appreciation of his own identity and importance. In *A Death in the Family* he looks even farther back and exposes the roots from which that twelve-year-old character had grown. And of the three works perhaps the frankest and most revealing is *A Death in the Family*. The young boy who is the central character in this novel is named Rufus, Agee's middle name which was the name he used almost exclusively in signing the letters to Father Flye.

Erling Larsen. *James Agee* (Minnesota). 1971. pp. 36–7

BIBLIOGRAPHY
Permit Me Voyage, 1934 (p); *Let Us Now Praise Famous Men*, 1941 (t); *The Morning Watch*, 1954 (n); *A Death in the Family*, 1957 (n); *Agee on Film*, Vol. One, 1958 (c); *Agee on Film*, Vol. Two, 1960 (c); *Letters of James Agee to Father Flye*, 1962, rev. ed. 1971; *The Collected Poems*, 1968; *The Collected Short Prose*, 1969; *The Last Letter of James Agee to Father Flye*, 1969; *Selected Journalism*, ed. Paul Ashdown, 1985; *Knoxville, Summer 1915*, 1986 (m); *Agee: Selected Literary Documents*, ed. Victor A. Kramer, 1996 (e)

AIKEN, Conrad (1889–1973)

He was master of a smooth limpid flow of verse narrative from the beginning. He did not have to learn and unlearn his technique. It was an authentic gift. Such a poet is rare enough even in England, still rarer in America. . . . Now it seems to me that, apart from his incontestable gifts as a prosodist and word-controller, Conrad Aiken's mind has up to the present worked on somewhat too narrow a basis. His poems, in short, are variations of but one idea—the idea of sexual disillusionment.

John Gould Fletcher. *Dial.* March 28, 1918. pp. 291–2

Apparently he believes in poetry as a craft, a sport, a profession—like boxing or magic—which must be thoroughly studied before it can be improved. He examines other poets accordingly, not to imitate them, but to learn their tricks. He never echoes. Sometimes he uses the devices of other poets as a vehicle for his own expression, but in any case he mingles them with devices of his own discovery so that he does not merely live in a tradition; he aids with his proper hands in building it.

Malcolm Cowley. *Dial.* Nov., 1922. p. 564

His has been a stubborn and, in many ways, heroic journey inward, following the Freudian stream. The political and social forces of our time have failed to touch him at his creative centers, though I do not doubt his intellectual awareness of them. What needs to be kept in mind is that the seemingly inexhaustible fertility of his imagination would seem to indicate that the course he has chosen may be, for him, the proper course. . . . His vision is of the shadows in the cave, and the cave itself impalpable as fog, of the swirling of phantoms, the dance of atoms, the blind gusts of desire. . . . What holds the dissolving cloudrack together is memory, the persistence of mind.

Stanley J. Kunitz. *Poetry.* May, 1937. pp. 103–4

Probably no poet has been more concerned with music than Conrad Aiken, or has used it more fruitfully. The interest is visible even in the titles of his poems, where we find nocturnes, tone-poems, variations, dissonants, and symphonies. . . . The formal arrangement of a good deal of his poetry is based on musical principles rather than on the more widely accepted poetic ones. His symbols are developed and combined in ways analogous to the composer's handling of themes. He has given us, here and there, enough information about the theoretical basis of his work to make it clear that the musical analogues are deliberately and skilfully cultivated. And, finally, this poetry based on music is alive with musical references which reinforce both the implications of its structure and a philosophy in which music is that epitome of the individual and the universe which it was to Schopenhauer.

Calvin S. Brown. *Music and Literature* (Georgia). 1948. p. 195

A story by Conrad Aiken is a horror wrapped in actuality, a fantasy all rooted and real, all rooted in a real detail. . . . Just as the structure of these stories characteristically develops in the effort of the material to assert a reality beyond or below its mundane shape, so their drama struggles to break over the edge of its own limitations. . . . We have, I think, no other body of contemporary fiction

like this—so centrally coherent, its very coherence derived from a contemplation of the intransigence of that incoherence that lies scattered on all sides of us, and above and below.

Mark Schorer. *New Republic.* March 31, 1952. pp. 19–20

As long ago as the First World War, Conrad Aiken was writing of the poet as being ''a curious blending of the psychoanalyst and patient.'' In novels, short stories, and a prolific poetry, all Aiken's work has exemplified the doctrine. He very early grafted upon traditional romanticism the golden bough of Freud. And somehow the undeviating process has made him one of the most distinguished unassessed writers of our era—perhaps the most distinguished.

Winfield Townley Scott. *Saturday Review.* Oct. 11, 1952. p. 26

Where other modern poets take the modern image of the cosmos as, at most, a point of departure, or a background irrelevant to human concerns and values, in Aiken's work it is always present as an inevitable awareness, as a kind of cold night which surrounds all things, like the sky itself. . . . But no matter how great the darkness, one cannot live by darkness. One must confront the darkness of existence—the silence of the stars, the depths of the atom, the gulf between each conscious being with all the attitudes which the imagination makes possible. This is the essential center of Aiken's poetry.

Delmore Schwartz. *New Republic.* Nov. 2, 1953. pp. 24–5

Aiken has sought his style in many directions, his experiments ranging from the diffuse allusiveness of Senlin to the archaic slam-bang theatrics of John Deth. Through every change, however, his devotion has been to the idea of the symphonic tone-poem, to a dissolving watery music, to a rain-swept and fog-abstracted landscape of the psyche. He has sought, in his own phrase, an ''absolute poetry.''

The weakness of that poetry seems to have centered from the beginning in its excess of melody and in the indefinitiveness of tone. . . . There is not much of the ''real world''—whatever that is—in Aiken, but certainly one is persuaded that he had found music for everything that dreams.

John Ciardi. *The Nation.* Nov. 14, 1953. p. 410

How does the bard sing? In the easiest external forms of any modern poet of stature. He sings by nature and training out of the general body of poetry in English. He writes from the cumulus of cliché in the language, always, for him, freshly felt, as if the existing language were the only reality outside himself there were. There is hardly ever in his work the stinging twist of new idiom, and the sometimes high polish of his phrasing comes only from the pressure and friction of his mind upon his metres. . . . Aiken depends on the force of his own mind and the force of metrical form to refresh his language. The cumulus upon which he really works is the cumulus of repetition, modulation by arrangement, pattern, and overtone. He writes as if the words were spoken to let the mind under the words sing. He writes as if it were the song of the mind that puts meaning in the words.

R.P. Blackmur. *Atlantic Monthly*. Dec., 1953. p. 82

He is in the tradition of Romantic poets from Shelley to Swinburne but with the manners and sensibility of one who knows London's twentieth-century Bloomsbury as well as Boston Common. If one thinks or speaks of such a thing as "poetic talent," there is more of that almost indefinable quality in a half dozen pages of Mr. Aiken's book (*Collected Poems*) than can be unearthed in whole volumes written by hundreds of his younger contemporaries. . . . As poet Mr. Aiken's gifts are rich and obvious, but the flaw among his gifts is not a superficial one. His deep lapses into flabby diction indicate that somewhere below the surface of his poems a flabby moral attitude exists.

Horace Gregory. *New York Times Book Section*. Dec. 20, 1953. p. 5

Whatever stature the work of Conrad Aiken may ultimately assume in the long run of criticism, we can affirm now, that he is one of the supreme technicians of modern English poetry. There are few writers, either in prose or in verse, who can challenge his mastery of language, who give us anything comparable to his assurance in controlling the most powerful and varied and nervous resources of expression. His writing has the inevitability of the highest art; it is, rhetorically, definitive.

Dudley Fitts. *New Republic*. Dec. 26, 1955. p. 19

Aiken is a kind of Midas: everything he touches turns to verse. Reading his poems is like listening to Delius—one is experiencing an unending undifferentiating wash of fairly beautiful sounds—or like watching a fairly boring, because almost entirely predictable kaleidoscope; a kaleidoscope all of whose transmutations are veiled, misty, watered-down. These are the metamorphoses of a world where everything *blurs* into everything else, where the easy, automatic, lyric, elegiac, nostalgic tone of the verse turns everything into itself, as the diffused. Salon photography of the first part of this century turned everything into Salon photographs.

Randall Jarrell. *The Yale Review*. Spring, 1956. pp. 479–80

. . . I want to show very briefly that . . . Aiken's fiction often issues from his own experience. I should first make it clear that Aiken drew details from his own life not as an easy way to fill in his narrative, but that he might relive (and so understand) the inner experience associated with those details. . . . Aiken would enrich not simply his awareness of himself, but also his ability to articulate that understanding with greater intensity. What experience he would use had, for the most part, been already stored up. He had now to explore and perfect by art what he would call in *Ushant* this "gold-mine of consciousness." He would make a myth out of himself. . . . Such novels as *Blue Voyage* and *Conversation*, and

stories like "The Last Visit" and "The Night Before Prohibition"—indeed nearly all of his fiction—explore the ego to reveal failures of honesty, kindness, and integrity.

Jay Martin. *Conrad Aiken: A Life of His Art* (Princeton). 1962. pp. 80–1, 86

Conrad Aiken has always had the nebulous quality of the admitted, congratulated poet who has never written Poems; that is, the poems do not *stick*, as poems; a general impression of excellence remains, of competence and skill. Lines come out and fix themselves, but can you fasten upon a poem of his, put it in your mind, and keep it there? It all flows away, beyond the margins; it ebbs, it is lost there. You look back again in the memory, and you have nothing left. . . .

There has always been about Aiken more of the literary figure, more of the distinguished man of letters of brilliant intellect, than of the poet. He is wordy and diffuse; the words and ideas spill on and on: . . . There is no drama, no story: the endless buzz, buzz, buzz of an Aiken poem. Yet suddenly we come up against the brilliance of an image so sharp, that we fall back breathless from contact with it; so fine, so enormous a mind, so dynamic and bitter an *intelligence*: . . .

Joseph Bennett. *Hudson Review*. Winter, 1963–4. p. 630

Blue Voyage seems to me the best of the novels, but that may be because I remember so well my first reading of it. At any rate it has considerable historical importance, for in it Aiken combined techniques that had been influenced by Joyce with insights that had been fostered by Freud. Countless novels have appeared in the past three decades that are indebted in one way or another to *Blue Voyage*. . . . The best parts of the novels are very much like the poems, but, as I have tried to point out, Aiken has many of the specific attributes of a writer of fiction—skill in dialogue, narrative force, a way of making his people recognizable even when they are mysterious. It is good to have his novels in print.

Granville Hicks. *Saturday Review*. Jan. 11, 1964. pp. 53–4

It is because Aiken has been so versatile and protean, has tried so many forms, and created so many verbal palaces, that he has lagged behind his sometimes less-endowed contemporaries. They were more single-minded. Aiken's houses are houses of words but also of cards, and somehow the internal monologues, in their endless clutter, do not give shape to people, only shadowy personages who talk too much. The conversations pyramid; they are often brilliant; but there are limitations even to good talk and Aiken errs by excess.

His novels therefore remain distinguished failures; they are object-lessons in the shortcomings of the internal monologue, and in the danger of using psychological theory to replace the lived experience—from which theory derives. Within the saturated literary qualities of Aiken's discipline there is the flaw of "everything"—there is the failure to capture the "epiphany" as Joyce did, or "the moment" as Virginia Woolf did.

Leon Edel. *New York Herald Tribune Book Section*. Jan. 19, 1964. p. 8

Not that he ever tried to kill his own active, generous and excitable conscience—who more scornful of the conscience-killers than he?—but rather that this thin mentalistic word "consciousness," for better or for worse, was to be his sign of everything generous, adventurous, dramatically, vigorously, and cleansingly outrageous. I think you must admit this to "get" Aiken, the man who successfully crossed the abyss between Santayana and Freud. . . . The younger novelists are catching up to Aiken and acting a lot more solemnly about it. Aiken is deeply, soul-stirringly *amusing*. . . . His "vaudeville of the psyche" enlists, in spurts and flashes, every kind of gusto that fiction has known.

R.W. Flint. *New York Review of Books*. Feb. 6, 1964. p. 13

The five novels that Conrad Aiken wrote between 1925 and 1940 were not much noticed at the time and one of them, [*A Heart for the Gods of Mexico*], was not even published in the United States, although in many respects it stands as his best. Now that they are available in one volume, we see not only that Aiken was one of the best American novelists of the period between the two World Wars, but that he still, a quarter of a century later, speaks to us with charm, vivacity and great acuity. . . . [The novels] have practically no plots, either in the conventional sense of a story or in the more highly developed sense of a structure of interacting moods, ideas and images. Nevertheless, they give the impression of being complete and integrated; the reader is never left with a feeling that the novels have failed to fulfill their inner necessity. . . . Aiken has confined himself to the simplest possible "verity": the conflict between the urgency and the obscenity of sex.

Hayden Carruth. *The Nation*. Feb. 17, 1964. pp. 171–2

A poet unconcerned with changing fashions, at the beginning playing vast iambic symphonies, and at the end, suites of lyrics, rarely varying the tone, [Aiken] isn't easy to take in a great dose like this one [*Collected Poems*]. . . . The mind sometimes wanders away, or it is mesmerized by the music, of star, water, leaf, web, tree, sleep, hill, needing more meat than beautiful sound or lovely repetition for its teeth to chew on.

He moves me most and keeps me riveted when he inserts characters in dramatic situations into his poems. . . . But sometimes the poetry is like a tone poem, or program music; we only get hints from the notes of what it is all about; themes recur, words and images do; but the composer himself has finished suffering elsewhere. The cry is evoked but we don't touch the man. This tendency to the abstract, when poetry was becoming more and more concrete and specific, put Aiken out of the running for popularity. He wrote for the ear (and many of these poems might benefit by reading aloud) when the eye had become the organ of the poem.

Harold Witt. *Prairie Schooner*. Fall, 1971. p. 267

It is in *Time in the Rock* that the concept of God as a projection of the many facets of the self is most fully developed. Here Aiken is even more explicit than in *Preludes for Memnon* in demanding that man give up what he regards as the delusions and false comforts of fantasy and live with a continual awareness of the beauty and power of the ephemeral in nature and man; he asks, moreover, that man recognize the symbolic nature of the "angels" and "churches" that have for so long served to distract him from the reality of chaos and death, and he demands a way of life that reflects man's consciousness of his own symbolic constructions. . . . Aiken expresses neither despair nor anger at this revelation of essential human narcissism; in fact, he seems to exult in his increasing awareness of the unconscious feelings expressed in traditional myths and to expose their nature and meaning with a kind of ruthless love for man, his "mad order," and the very symbols he uses to disguise its terrors. . . .

Recognizing that it is fundamentally man's "hunger" for security and grandeur that "shapes itself as gods and rainbows" (*Time in the Rock*, XVII), Aiken creates a new mythical concept: God is finally the symbolic expression of man's capacity for full consciousness of the anxieties, conflicts, and longings, the terror of his own limitations, and especially of death, which he has for so long repressed or acknowledged only in distorted and misleading forms; God is at the same time man's consciousness of all that he can achieve and enjoy in the face of the monstrous within himself and nature. The god in man functions in the poet when he employs the chaos of the unconscious mind as the material of creation, imposing order and beauty on its apparent formlessness.

Lillian Feder. *Ancient Myth in Modern Poetry* (Princeton). 1971. pp. 391–2

Ushant is the artistic reflexion of a life truly and fully and with difficulty lived, of a mind and conscience examined. Even its working out at 365 pages has a mythological appropriateness in this writer whose pious awareness of the cosmos is present even in domestic and daily doings; the Great Circle which he chose as the title of one of his novels being not only the path followed by Atlantic liners but also the circle of the year.

One more thing, a somewhat surprising result on reading *Ushant* again. For several days since, I've found that most any narrative I've picked up, by anyone at all, began to get itself woven into the fabric and symbolism of this one—an unexpected result of the echoing, musical method of composition, whereby Aiken may yet become the hidden author of a large part of our literature. All authors try to write the world, but only a very few succeed in teaching us how to read it.

Howard Nemerov. *Reflexions on Poetry & Poetics* (Rutgers). 1972. p. 96

As a prose poem—for in fact "essay" often *means* poem within this lightly encoded account of Aiken's life, just as "play" means novel and "novel" means this reflexive writing—*Ushant* joins the company of modernist works-in-progress, descendants of Wordsworth's *Prelude*, in which precariously narcissist voices move toward epic comprehensiveness as they try to name their own vocations. But unlike *The Cantos* or *Paterson*, *The Anathemata* or *The Maximus Poems*, this poem presents its "exfoliation" or "passacaglia" or "onomasticon" of metaphors through a lucid narrative and discursive style, focuses its evolutionary whirl in a long meditative moment (suspending more than five decades of a full life within a 365-page Joycean day of swirling shipboard introspection), and includes not only the matrix of experience from which it seems in the act of emerging but also its own critical explication. Rendering in public terms Aiken's private drama of "language extending consciousness and then consciousness extending language," *Ushant* aims to share in what D. [the protagonist] calls "the great becoming *fiat* in the poetic of the great poem of life." And surely no other modern American writing gives us with greater sympathy and wit the iridescent texture of that process. . . .

When Aiken allows cosmic rhyme to inform the particulars of his personal experience, the result is a serio-comic richness of tone, an intellectual complexity, and a vividness of detail that had never entered his verse.

Thomas R. Whitaker. *Parnassus*. Fall-Winter, 1972. pp. 60, 65

BIBLIOGRAPHY

Earth Triumphant and Other Tales in Verse, 1914; *The Jig of Forslin*, 1916 (p); *Turns and Monies and Other Tales in Verse*, 1916; *Nocturne of Remembered Spring*, 1917 (p); *The Charnel Rose, Senlin: A Biography, and Other Poems*, 1918; *Scepticisms*, 1919 (c); *The House of Dust*, 1920 (p); *Punch: The Immortal Liar*, 1921 (p); *Priapus and the Pool*, 1922 (p); *The Pilgrimage of Festus*, 1923 (p); *Priapus and the Pool and Other Poems*, 1925; *Senlin: A Biography*, 1925 (p); *Bring! Bring!* 1925 (s); *Blue Voyage*, 1927 (n); *Costumes by Eros*, 1928 (s); *Prelude*, 1929 (p); *Selected Poems*, 1929; *John Deth, A Metaphysical Legend, and Other Poems*, 1930; *Gehenna*, 1930 (e); *The Coming Forth by Day of Osiris Jones*, 1931 (p); *Preludes for Memnon*, 1931 (p); *And in the Hanging Gardens* . . . , 1933 (p); *Great Circle*, 1933 (n); *Landscape West of Eden*, 1934 (p); *Among the Lost People*, 1934 (s); *King Coffin*, 1935 (n); *Time in the Rock*, 1936 (p); *A Heart for the Gods of Mexico*, 1939 (n); *And in the Human Heart*, 1940 (p); *Conversation: or, Pilgrims' Progress*, 1940 (n); *Brownstone Eclogues*, 1942 (p); *The Soldier*, 1944 (p); *The Kid*, 1947 (p); *The Divine Pilgrim*, 1949 (p); *Skylight One*, 1950 (p); *Short Stories*, 1950; *Wake 11*, 1952 (p); *Ushant*, 1952 (a); *Collected Poems*, 1953; *A Letter from Li Po*, 1955 (p); *The Fluteplayer*, 1956 (p); *Mr. Arcularis*, 1957 (d); *A Reviewer's ABC*, 1958 (c) (published as *Collected Essays*, 1968); *Sheepfold Hill*, 1958 (p); *Collected Short Stories*, 1960; *Selected Poems*, 1961; *The Morning Song of Lord Zero: Poems Old and New*, 1963; *Collected Novels*, 1964; *A Seizure of Limericks*, 1964; *Cats and Bats and Things with Wings*, 1965 (p); *Collected Poems: 1916–1970*, 1970; *The Clerk's Journal*, 1971 [1911] (p); *Collected Criticism* (orig. *A Reviewer's ABC*), 1971; *Thee*, 1973 (p); *A Little Who's Zoo of Mild Animals*, 1977; *Selected Letters*, ed. Joseph Killorin, 1978; *Silent Snow, Secret Snow*, 1983 (s); *The Letters of Conrad Aiken and Malcolm Lowry, 1929–1954* , ed. Cynthia C. Sugars, 1992

ALBEE, Edward (1928–)

. . . Edward Albee . . . comes into the category of the Theatre of the Absurd precisely because his work attacks the very foundations of American optimism. . . . Albee has produced a play that clearly takes up the style and subject matter of the Theatre of the Absurd and translates it into a genuine American idiom. *The American Dream* . . . fairly and squarely attacks the ideals of progress,

optimism, and faith in the national mission, and pours scorn on the sentimental ideals of family life, togetherness, and physical fitness; the euphemistic language and unwillingness to face the ultimate facts of the human condition that in America, even more than in Europe, represents the essence of bourgeois assumptions and attitudes.

Martin Esslin. *The Theatre of the Absurd* (Doubleday Anchor). 1961. pp. 225-6

Strangely enough, though there is no question of his sincerity, it is Albee's skill which at this point most troubles me. It is as if his already practiced hand had learned too soon to make an artful package of venom. For the overriding passion of the play is venomous. There is no reason why anger should not be dramatized. I do not object to Albee's being "morbid," for as the conspicuously healthy William James once said, "morbid-mindedness ranges over a wider scale of experience than healthy-mindedness." What I do object to in his play is that its disease has become something of a brilliant formula, as slick and automatic as a happy entertainment for the trade. The right to pessimism has to be earned within the artistic terms one sets up; the pessimism and rage of *Who's Afraid of Virginia Woolf?* are immature. Immaturity coupled with a commanding deftness is dangerous. . . . Vividly as each personage is drawn, they all nevertheless remain flat—caricatures rather than people. Each stroke of dazzling color is super-imposed on another, but no further substance accumulates. We do not actually identify with anyone, except editorially. Even the non-naturalistic figures of Beckett's plays have more extension and therefore more stature and meaning. The characters in Albee's *The Zoo Story* and *Bessie Smith* are more particularized.

Harold Clurman. *The Nation*. Oct. 27, 1962. p. 274

Albee has a sense of character and drama that isn't ordinary. He can put two people on the stage and make them immediately lifelike: they respond to each other at once, which is exciting, especially since the response is usually revulsion. He handles demotic and clichéd speech in such a way that it seems fresh. He has a sense of humor which, though it is practically always exerted at the expense of his characters, can often make you laugh out loud. And best of all, he isn't afraid of corny theatricalism—in this of course he has the blessings and the precedent of contemporary French playwrights—and possesses an energy that never seems to flag.

Alfred Chester. *Commentary*. April, 1963. p. 297

As a maker of plots, Albee hardly exists. Both *The Zoo Story*, his first play performed in New York, and *Who's Afraid of Virginia Woolf?*, his most successful, are built upon an unbelievable situation—namely, that a sane, average-type person would be a passive spectator in the presence of behavior obviously headed toward destructive violence. . . . Whatever may be said against Albee . . . one must also say that his best is wholly theatrical. All his mistakes are theatrical mistakes. . . . I expect this instinct for the theatrical is what people really have in mind when they refer to Albee's talent. "Talent" is the wrong word, for the nature of a talent is to grow, and Albee shows no signs of that. He does show a theatrical instinct. . . . In his badly written plays he jabs away at life with blunt instruments. If his jabbing hit the mark, that would be another matter. But it doesn't, no more than does a child in the nursery when he tears up his toys. That is why Albee is the pet of the audience, this little man who looks as if he dreamed of evil but is actually mild as a dove and wants to be loved. In him America has found its very own playwright. He's a dream.

Tom F. Driver. *The Reporter.* Jan. 2, 1964. pp. 38-9

His first play, indeed, is not only within its limits a good and effective play; it is virtually an epitome, for good and for ill, of all his later original drama. . . . Since *The Zoo Story* does argue—not only through Jerry but through the action the play presents—that in mid-twentieth-century America the possibility of genuine intellectual understanding is lost beyond recall, consistency compels Albee to take great care that the events of his play be no more intellectually understandable to his audience than they are to Jerry and Peter; and I believe that his care has on the whole been rewarded; many of Albee's admirers have seemed to feel deeply for Jerry and Peter, but no one has claimed to know them. . . . Albee's comprehensive denial of intellect establishes a theatre incapable of resolution—a theatre suitable to fantasy, perhaps, but a theatre in which Albee's realism cannot help being inconclusive.

Melvin L. Plotinsky. *Drama Survey.* Winter, 1965. pp. 220-3

Probably the only way to save the play [*A Delicate Balance*] would be to dump all the harangues, and explanations, and most of the ideas, and to replace them with scenes. But scenes take longer to write. Those two people who are afraid of their own house are worth a play, and for the few minutes that they are treated comically (a la his own *American Dream*) Albee shows us what he might have done.

But he seems to have lost faith, or patience, in his own gift. Treated comically, these people are terrifying; treated seriously, they are nothing. Enough scraps and bits of bone can be found in the play to form the nucleus of a good surreal comedy: but they are kept rigidly apart by leadweights of preachment and unearned poetry.

Wilfred Sheed. *Commonweal.* Oct. 14, 1966. p. 56

Albee is progressing. *Who's Afraid of Virginia Woolf?* was about the emptiness that surrounds and threatens to swallow our relationships; *Tiny Alice* was about the void lurking behind our deepest beliefs; now, *A Delicate Balance* is about the nothingness, the bare nothingness of it all—it is a play about nothing. . . . What, one wonders, was the real motive behind *A Delicate Balance?* I, for one, still believe in Albee's perceptiveness and even in his talent (he did, after all, write *The Zoo Story* and *Virginia Woolf*); why would he hurtle into such utter pointlessness? It occurs to me that at least since *Virginia Woolf*, Albee's plays and adaptations have been viewed by many as dealing overtly or covertly with homosexual matters; Albee may have resolved here to write a play reeking with heterosexuality.

John Simon. *Hudson Review.* Winter, 1966–1967. pp. 627-9

This is probably going to be a difficult review to write and to read, so let me clear the decks with a deliberately unclear statement. Edward Albee's *Everything in the Garden . . .* is both extraordinarily flawed and extraordinarily engrossing. The latter remark the producers will doubtless quote, and the former will be remembered in my favor by at least my friends.

Mr. Albee is not merely our most hopeful playwright, our most promising playwright, our most interesting playwright—he is, quite simply, our best playwright. This is a position he won by virtue of *A Zoo Story* and *The Death of Bessie Smith*. Since then everything he has done has had to be regarded with seriousness and respect. . . .

Yet, in the final account this is a monstrously heavy handed account by Mr. Albee of a stealthily subtle play. If Mr. Albee wishes to sing us a song of social significance he should not choose such a shrill and hysterical falsetto.

Clive Barnes. *New York Times (daily).* Nov. 30, 1967. p. 60

Albee's version of *Everything in the Garden*, in short, is without interest, and I'm not concealing very well my reluctance to write about it. What continues to remain somewhat interesting, because unresolved, is the author's ambiguous relationship to his audience. As I have had occasion to remark somewhat too often, Albee's identity as a dramatist is highly uncertain. Lacking his own vision, he turns to adaptation; lacking his own voice, he borrows the voice of others. What has remained constant through his every change of style—through the progression of his influences from Genet to Strindberg to Pirandello to Williams to Ionesco to Eliot—is his peculiar love-hatred for those who attend his plays. Albee's desire to undermine the audience and be applauded for it is now leading him into the most extraordinary strategems and subterfuges, just as his desire to be simultaneously successful and significant has managed by now to freeze his artistic imagination. He has two choices, I think, if he is ever to create interesting work again: either to resolve this conflict, or to write about it. But both alternatives oblige him to become a great deal less masked, a great deal more daring, a great deal more open than he now chooses to be.

Robert Brustein. *New Republic.* Dec. 16, 1967. p. 27

In his one-act plays Albee often reaches into the vitals of American attitudes to strike at what he thinks sham and superficiality. In *The Zoo Story* he reveals the complacent businessman to be a vegetable incapable of experiencing any kind of real feeling; in *The American Dream* he presents our idealization of physical beauty and sexual power in all its vacuity. The validity of the satire in these plays rests on the exposure of the veneer that disguises fear, ruthlessness, savagery and self-interest without any attempt to solve the problems. There is always an implicit recognition of the depth of the problem. It cannot be solved by any quick panacea. . . . The conclusion of *Who's Afraid of Virginia Woolf?*, however, advocates a simple standard: no salvation from without, a reliance on "truth" and the resources of the personality. Though Albee sounds the "maybe" of caution with regard to the final situation of George and Martha, he also holds out a "romantic" hope that "it will be better." But the ironist of the first two-and-a-half acts has left his imprint on the play. There seems no reason why the old cycle of games should not begin again.

Thomas E. Porter. *Myth and Modern American Drama* (Wayne State). 1969. pp. 246-7

There are such strong surface dissimilarities among the Albee plays that it is easier and in some ways more rewarding to think of *The Zoo Story* in relation to Samuel Beckett and Harold Pinter and *A Delicate Balance* in terms of T.S. Eliot and Enid Bagnold than it is to compare the two plays, even though both start from the same dramatic situation: the invasion . . . of private territory. . . . Yet the comparison is obvious once it is made. Each new Albee play seems to be an experiment in form, in style (even if it is someone else's style), and yet there is unity in his work as a whole. . . .

Separateness is the operative word for Albee characters, for, even though his zoo provides suites for two people (*Who's Afraid of Virginia Woolf?*) or for more (*A Delicate Balance*), they are furnished with separate cages.

Gerald Weales. *The Jumping-Off Place* (Macmillan—N.Y.). 1969. pp. 28–30

Suspicion is born of Albee's very brilliance. His plays are too well crafted, his characters too modishly ambiguous, his dialogue too carefully cadenced. This is not to say that he writes perfect plays— whatever that may be—but his surface polish seems to deny subsurface search, much less risk. . . . Albee's plays are not devoid of suffering, and in any case one cannot measure the quality of a play by some putative pain of the playwright. Nevertheless, Albee's craftsmanship recalls the meditation of the disembodied voice of *Box*: "arts which have gone down to craft." And it is particularly ungrateful to turn his own finely modulated words against Albee. But just because his verbal craft *is* so fine, one longs for the clumsy upward groping toward art.

Ruby Cohn. *Dialogue in American Drama* (Indiana). 1971. pp. 168-9

All Over provides reason for being rather more sanguine about Albee's future than we have had the right to be for some years. His only two previous attempts at a fusion between his off-Broadway experimentalism and his Broadway naturalism were *Tiny Alice* and *A Delicate Balance*: the new play is a more honest piece of writing than the former and more original than the latter. He is still one of the most powerful influences in the American theatre, although he has not yet equalled the success of *Who's Afraid of Virginia Woolf?* and his three adaptations seriously damaged his reputation. The rival pulls of Beckett and Broadway have brought his talent dangerously near to disintegrating but there is still hope that it will recover.

Ronald Hayman. *Edward Albee* (Ungar). 1973. p. 138

Edward Albee's play *Seascape* . . . is fundamentally a play about life and resolution. It is that currently rare thing, a comedy rather than a farce, and it is a curiously compelling exploration into the basic tenets of life. It is asking in a light-hearted but heavy-minded fashion whether life is worth living. It decides that there is no alternative.

As Mr. Albee has matured as a playwright, his work has become leaner, sparer and simpler. He depends on strong theatrical strokes to attract the attention of the audience, but the tone of the writing is always thoughtful, even careful, even philosophic. . . . Mr. Albee is suggesting that one of the purposes of an individual human existence is quite simply evolution—that we all play a part in this oddly questionable historic process. So that the purpose of life is life itself—it is a self-fulfilling destiny. We have to come out of the water and get onto the beach, we have to live and we have to die, simply because life is about life.

Clive Barnes. *New York Times (daily)*. Jan. 27, 1975. p. 20

Unlike some other eminent playwrights, Mr. Albee has never been content merely to rework his old successes in new guises and present them as new plays. He has sometimes been accused of rewriting the old successes of others—*All Over*, for instance, sounded uncannily like a newly-unearthed late play by T.S. Eliot— but with *Seascape* he is certainly free of that accusation. The new play is short (less than two hours, with intermission), bizarre, and curious, and its strange premise is fraught with all sorts of implications and possibilities. But it seems unfinished, as if Albee had not quite known how to work out his intriguing premise.

Like *All Over*, his play, and *Box* and *Quotations from Chairman Mao Tse-tung*, the double bill before that, *Seascape* is very spare, very cerebral, very distanced, very uninvolved in the immediate intensities of experience. This is not necessarily a bad way to write plays, but none of these recent works of Mr. Albee have really been very satisfactory; perhaps he needs to get back into closer touch with himself.

Julius Novick. *The Village Voice*. Feb. 3, 1975. p. 84

Who's Afraid of Virginia Woolf?—song and play—conceals fear beneath a party surface. Far from a mere *dolce vita* of offensive couples, however, the drama of four characters terminates in an act of exorcism. Though Martha claims that George no longer knows the difference between truth and illusion, he finally kills their child of illusion in the last darkly comic scene of the play. When first heard, the Latin service for the dead sounds like camp parody, but it prepares for George's outrageous tale of the death telegram, corroborated by Honey. Unlike his namesake, Albee's George can tell a lie, but he implies that lies act in the service of truth. Possibly the dawn ending signals the birth of truth in marriage, and yet Martha's final words express fear rather than hope. Finally ambiguous, Albee's drama is comic not in its conclusion but in its verbal cruelties, lively colloquialisms, and such camp effects as Martha imitating Bette Davis, George imitating President Kennedy, a Latin burial service for an imaginary death, and a familiar tune with semi-nonsensical words—"who's afraid of Virginia Woolf?"

After *Virginia Woolf*, Albee's humor drains away. Like *Zoo Story*, *Tiny Alice* ends in death, but Julian, the would-be apostate, lacks the self-irony of Jerry, a prophet with a nickname. The opening scene seems to continue the three comic C's of *Virginia Woolf*—as Cardinal and Lawyer fence verbally; as they lapse into such slang as diddle, pig, loot; as they seem to play at law and church, rather than belonging to these professions. With the entrance of humorless Julian, however, comedy sputters into martyrdom (Albee apparently takes the martyrdom as seriously as does Julian, since he threatened to sue ACT for shrinking Julian's dying monologue). In *Virginia Woolf*, Martha says: "I have a fine sense of the ridiculous, but no sense of humor." Unfortunately, both senses have deserted Albee in his plays of the 1970's.

> Ruby Cohn. In *Comic Relief: Humor in Contemporary American Literature*, ed. Sarah Blacher Cohen (Univ. of Illinois Pr., 1978), pp. 284–85

Albee is far from affirming illusion as a way of life. The fact that there is a discernible—and recoverable—real self, when the layers of game play and fantasy are stripped from George and Martha, supports Albee's commitment to man's need to confront reality on its terms. Yet Albee does not without qualification decry the evils of illusion. Although ostensibly a realistic drama, *Who's Afraid of Virginia Woolf?* is supremely aware of itself as a play and manifests this awareness throughout. Where the illusion of George and Martha is dismissed as an unsatisfactory confrontation of reality, the illusion of their creator, Albee himself—i.e., the play—is upheld as a meaningful creation, for the play, unlike the escapist illusion of its central characters, leads toward truth rather than away from it.

That Albee is concerned not only with the relationship between reality and illusion with respect to patterns of life, but with the artistic process as well, is confirmed by an examination of the relationship between George and Martha on the one hand and Nick and Honey, their youthful guests, on the other, for this relationship is a microcosm of the relationship between play and audience and a statement of the positive function of art. . . .

Albee's metafictional characters, then, simultaneously deny the validity of illusion as a way of life and affirm the validity of illusion as art. Albee asks his audience to enter a world of illusion only as a means of discovery, because for Albee, the function of fiction, whether private or public, is to illuminate, not replace, reality.

> June Schlueter. *Metafictional Characters in Modern Drama* (Columbia Univ. Pr., 1979), pp. 83, 87

Despite the heaviness and seriousness of Albee's concern, it is the catholicity of his vision and technique that really distinguishes this play. Albee shows himself open and sensitive to all facets of the human condition: the serious, the funny, the physical, the metaphysical, the actual, and the illusionary. All of his devices deserve commendation: his wit; the purity of his style, so magnificent in its captivation and alteration of normal speech; and his lizard fantasy, through which he reveals the human reality. . . .

Seascape is not only a remarkable aesthetic achievement, but it is also a highly affirmative statement on the human condition. Albee, an American writer, seems to have employed the techniques of the European playwrights Pinter and Beckett, and transformed them so that he could make a highly personal statement, one almost

antithetical to their own. He seems to be saying that human life is worth living and that it is desirable to climb the evolutionary ladder in order to experience love, art, and the complexities of human interaction. It is desirable even if that means a certain loss of freedom, natural beauty, and the security possessed by the creatures of the sea. Albee has never made so affirmative a statement in his career; it is significant that *Seascape* should follow *All Over*, which dealt so heavily with death. With *Seascape*, Albee has, as if in a Lazarus-like rebirth of mind and spirit, magnificently affirmed life.

> Samuel J. Bernstein. *The Strands Entwined: A New Direction in American Drama* (Northeastern Univ. Pr., 1980), pp. 130, 134

The last great gift a parent gives to a child is his or her own death, and the energy underneath *Three Tall Women* is the exhilaration of a writer calling it quits with the past—specifically, the rueful standoff between Albee and his mother, the late Frances Cotter Albee, who adopted him only to kick him out of the family home, at eighteen, for his homosexual shenanigans and later to cut him out of her sizeable will. The play has earned Albee, who is sixty-six, his third (and most deserved) Pulitzer Prize, but the writer's real victory is a psychological one—honoring the ambiguity of "the long unpleasant life she led" while keeping her memory vividly alive. Far from being an act of revenge or special pleading, the play is a wary act of reconciliation, whose pathos and poetry are a testament to the bond, however attenuated, between child and parent. *Three Tall Women* bears witness to the son's sad wish to be loved, but with this liberating difference: the child is now finally in control of the parent's destiny, instead of the parent's being in control of the child's. . . .

In Act II, by an ingenious coup de théâtre, *Three Tall Women* expands from a parental cameo to a vista of decline. At curtain rise, A [one of three characters representing different ages of the mother figure] is still collapsed in bed but now has an oxygen mask over her face. B and C [the other two "stages" of the character] seem to have dressed up for their bedside vigil in period high fashion—B in pearls and an elegant gray frock with a full, pleated fifties skirt, and C in a layered ankle-length cream chiffon dress that evokes the twenties. Then, as B and C bicker about death, and the conversation drifts to the absence of a living will and why A didn't write one, A herself, in an elegant lavender dress, walks in from the wings. . . . The moment is electrifying. The body in the bed turns out to be a mannequin. In this theatrical filip, Albee goes from a familiar external reality to a bold interior one. B and C are now projects of A, who speaks rationally for the duration of the play, responding to different stages of her life. Albee's wonderful invention allows him both to incarnate A's narcissism and to lift the play from characterization to meditation. What we get is a kind of Cubist stage picture, where the characters are fragments of a single self. The device is at its most eloquent when the son appears, in preppy clothes and clasping freesias, to sit by his comatose mother in a dumb show of devotion.

> John Lahr. *New Yorker*. May 16, 1994, pp. 102, 103–4

One would think that 30 years of dismissive critical reviews and dwindling audiences might have been more than humbling enough for the one-time celebrated Bad Boy of Broadway. After all, Albee's not really had a solid commercial success since *Who's Afraid of Virginia Woolf?*, the marital slugfest which electrified audiences first on the Broadway stage in 1962 and later on the screen with Richard Burton and Elizabeth Taylor (who won the Best Actress Oscar for her role). And although this is Albee's third Pulitzer (the first, in 1967, was for *A Delicate Balance*, the second for 1975's *Seascape*), his distinctive voice has largely been absent from New York theater since 1983, after his play, *The Man Who Had Three Arms* failed on Broadway.

All that has swiftly changed for Albee through the unqualified success of *Three Tall Women*. . . .

While Albee is clearly pleased with the reception for *Three Tall Women*, he can't help but chide the idea that this somehow represents a comeback of sorts for him. After all, he's been writing plays all along, often directing productions of his own work at regional and university theaters and abroad. He's also been busy teaching young writers and supporting them and visual artists through his own private foundation based at his Montauk retreat. . . .

Albee says that he wrote the play over a four-month period in 1991, though it really took "55 years"—a reference to the long and tempestuous relationship which he had with his [foster] mother. . . .

Although Albee insists that he isn't the type of writer who usually draws on his own life for subject matter, he admitted that writing *Three Tall Women* was a form of exorcism for him. Speaking of his [foster] mother, he says, "She was destructive and contemptible, but there were reasons for her behavior, as there always are. Writing the play allowed me to understand her better, though I'm not sure I liked her any more or less than I already did.

"I just tried to get it all down," he adds. "It's the theme: What is worse than coming to the end of your life filled with regret? I was interested in the facts, man, just the facts: the good stuff, the bad, the misplaced pride. The facts carry implications with them."

Patrick Pacheco. *Playbill*. July 1994, pp. 33–34, 37

BIBLIOGRAPHY
The Zoo Story, 1958 (d); *The Death of Bessie Smith*, 1959 (d); *The Sandbox*, 1959 (d); *The American Dream*, 1960 (d); (with James Hinton, Jr.) *Bartleby*, 1961 (d); *Who's Afraid of Virginia Woolf?*, 1962 (d); *The Ballad of the Sad Cafe*, 1963 (d); *Tiny Alice*, 1964 (d); *Malcolm*, 1965 (d); *A Delicate Balance*, 1966 (d); *Everything in the Garden*, 1967 (d); *Box*, 1968 (d); *Quotations from Chairman Mao Tse-tung*, 1968 (d); *All Over*, 1971 (d); *Seascape*, 1975 (d); *Counting the Ways, and Listening*, 1977 (d); *The Lady from Dubuque*, 1980 (d); *Lolita*, 1981 (d); *The Man Who Had Three Arms*, 1983 (d); *Conversations*, 1988 (r, i.e., interviews); *Finding the Sun*, 1993 (d); *Selected Plays*, 1994; *Three Tall Women*, 1994 (d); *Fragments*, 1995 (d); *The Marriage Play*, 1995 (d)

ALFRED, William (1923–)

William Alfred's purpose in writing this verse play in four acts [*Agamemnon*] is not to make an adaptation of Aeschylus; he wishes to penetrate the myth itself, that "ambush of reality," that familiar place (he goes on to say in his preface) we might find in no matter how foreign a city. Thus he would work where Aeschylus worked, and where the imaginations of his "private" readers work, whether consciously or not; and he would make his play directly from—or in?—the life of that myth, and not from its literature. . . . What is sure is that he has done a fine play, with a few moments of really high distinction.

Henry Rago. *Commonweal*. Dec. 3, 1954. p. 259

The prime virtue of William Alfred's verse-drama, *Hogan's Goat*, is its absolute lack of shrewdness. It embodies none of the fashionable attitudes of the contemporary stage, whether commercial or avant-garde, and it is written with an ingratiating naïveté, as if the author had just emerged, play in hand, from a time capsule entered many decades before. . . . and while the blank verse is a little excessive in its use of simile, and a little unfamiliar in the mouths of Irish wardheelers, it is generally a serviceable dramatic instrument, especially as a source of invective.

For all its charm, however, the play is decidedly minor, mainly because it fails its own intentions. In the conflict between a young ambitious insurgent who wants to be mayor and the cynical, corrupt old incumbent who will use any device to keep his cherished office, Mr. Alfred has the opportunity to examine what has recently become an extremely important subject in America—the rise of Irish political power; but the author unfortunately gets sidetracked into writing pseudo-tragedy about his hubristic hero, concluding not with social-political insights but rather with a moral lesson about pride and selfishness. . . .

Robert Brustein. *New Republic*. Nov. 27, 1965. p. 46

To begin with, the . . . intention [of *Hogan's Goat*] is implied in such lines as "There are some things in life you can't take back"—the plot consequence of which is that not only the sinner but also the innocent are destroyed. Concomitant with this thought is the idea that in the quest for power lie the seeds of crime.

Further, the author wished to recreate the Irish Brooklyn of old with its mixture of religiosity, ignorance, provincial charm, fecklessness and brutality—the sweetly rancid festering of our ghettos in their growth and in their dissolution. Finally there is the purely literary striving . . . to envelop and elevate all this material through the use of modern verse forms, language which makes poetic patterns of the vernacular.

Harold Clurman. *The Nation*. Nov. 29, 1965. p. 427

I remember William Alfred reading, some dozen years ago in Harvard's Sanders Theatre, from his verse play, *Hogan's Goat*. I recall being impressed by his reading and unimpressed by his writing. The American Place Theatre has now given *Hogan's Goat* a compact and tidy production, but the play continues to be sprawling, sentimental melodrama decked out with verse that smacks of a Christopher Fry hopped up on Sean O'Casey. Oh, the heart is in the right place in this tale of an 1890 scandal that cost an eagerly aspiring immigrant-Irish publican the mayoralty of Brooklyn; and his passionate young spouse, her life. But plays do not live by heart and vaulting metaphors alone. . . . Nevertheless, this is not really an offensive play, merely a benighted one. It does, in any case, attempt to create plot and characters, and even if these Irish priests, politicos, ward-heelers, floozies, biddies, and bibbers have worn their garments of lovable local color hopelessly threadbare, and even if the romantic and political intrigues, clashes, and lightning revelations are smudged with the thumbprints of count-less popular dramatists, there is here an old-fashioned love of old-fashioned theatre for which one may heave a sympathetic sigh.

John Simon. *Hudson Review.* Spring, 1966. pp. 114–5

BIBLIOGRAPHY
Agamemnon, 1954 (pd); *Hogan's Goat*, 1965 (pd)

ALGREN, Nelson (1909–1981)

It is a novel about depressed people by a depressed man, and it is most convincing in its complete unity of action, mood, and form. . . . The whole narrative is pervaded by a feeling of loss rather than of bitterness or horror. And Algren's realism is so paced as to avoid the tedium of the naturalistic stereotype, of the literal copying of surfaces. He knows how to select, how to employ factual details without letting himself be swamped by them, and finally, how to put the slang his characters speak to creative uses so that it ceases to be an element of mere documentation and turns into an element of style.

Philip Rahv. *The Nation.* April 18, 1942. pp. 466-7

The scene in *Never Come Morning* that most people will remember is the rape of Bruno's girl in the cellar. . . . There are other scenes as brutal. . . . But the really good scenes are quieter; they are still lifes and genre pictures instead of being sensational films—the girls sitting around the juke box in Mama Topak's flat, the boys playing under the El, the look of Chicago streets in the rain, the tall corn growing between the slag heaps down by the river. It is this poetry of familiar things that is missing in the other Chicago novels and that shows the direction of Algren's talent. In spite of the violent story he tells—and tells convincingly—he is not by instinct a novelist. He is a poet of the Chicago slums, and he might well be Sandburg's successor.

Malcolm Cowley. *New Republic.* May 4, 1942. pp. 613-4

The point is that Algren's topical figures are failures even at vice. They are the underdogs of sin, the small souls of corruption, the fools of poverty, not of wealth and power. Even the murders they commit, out of blind rage or through sheer accident—or through another ironic twist of their impoverished destiny—are not impor-tant. . . . Thus Algren's work represents an extreme phase of the native American realism which opened in the 1900's. . . . And there are obvious limitations and aesthetic dangers in the social area and the kind of human material that Algren has made his own.

Maxwell Geismar. *English Journal.* March, 1953. pp. 124-5

A Walk on the Wild Side is in an American tradition of emotional giantism: its comedy is farce, its joys are orgies, the feats of its characters Bunyanesque, the sexuality is prodigious, their sorrow a wild keening almost too high for ordinary ears. Dove Linkhorn is pioneer stock gone bad, grown up and gone to seed, caught in a neon-lit jungle in a time of break-down. The picture of Dove burning out his dammed up, useless energies in a bonfire of lust and violence is one of the most extraordinary in contemporary fiction.

Milton Rugoff. *New York Herald Tribune Book Section.* May 20, 1956. p. 4

Algren's narrative . . . flickers to life only intermittently among the lay sermons and the miscellaneous information about jails and whorehouses. *A Walk on the Wild Side* is . . . documented, out of the same sense, I suppose, which compels popular magazine fiction, the notion that "truth" resides in avoiding inaccuracies; in knowing, for instance, exactly what equipment a New Orleans prostitute of the '30's would have had on her table. It is all part of the long retreat of the imagination before science, or our surrender to information.

Leslie A. Fiedler. *Partisan Review.* June, 1956. p. 361

The Man with the Golden Arm . . . seems to declare that admirable human qualities have little—or perhaps a negative bearing on social status and that the poetry of human relationships appears most richly where people are stripped down to the core of survival and have not strength or use for complicated emotions. Living on the barest edge of physical survival, his people simply have no use for vanity, sanctimoniousness, or prestige; being free and pure, their loves and affections are beautiful. . . . Society has become a jungle of viciousness and injustice beyond reclamation; only the waifs and strays merit attention because only they are capable of tender and beautiful feelings. One may be deeply moved by *The Man with the Golden Arm* but must, I believe, finally regard it as irresponsible and inaccurate—a sentimental contrivance that has little to do with reality but rather explores a cul-de-sac in the author's imagination.

Charles Child Walcutt. *American Literary Naturalism* (Minne-sota). 1956. pp. 298-9

The notion that prostitutes have hearts of gold is of course a literary cliché, and you will find it in much of the slumming fiction of the past, but nowhere in Algren's books is there any prostitute with a heart of gold. *Time*'s reviewer would find himself hard put to find a single line in *A Walk on the Wild Side*, or *Never Come Morning*, where prostitution is part of Algren's theme, that could be quoted or twisted to support the notion. Algren's prostitutes are people, good, bad, and indifferent, like any other women. If they perform a good deed or an unselfish act their motives are as mixed as those of any wife or sweetheart—or any businessman on the make for a buck. As for the bums, the charge of idleness is itself a cliché. It was always leveled against itinerant workers, "tramps," "hoboes," who followed the harvest or preferred pick-up jobs to punching a time-clock. For Dove Linkhorn in *Wild Side* it is work or starve from start to finish, and he is seldom idle. Far from being a bum in the *Time* reviewer's sense of the word (as distinguished from "people who work"), Dove is clearly intended to be a parody of the young man on the make for money and success. . . .

Lawrence Lipton. *Chicago Review*. Winter, 1957. pp. 6–7

Nelson Algren . . . has been fretfully silent, the fret manifested by occasional reviews, interviews, magazine pieces, comments, groans and gripes. A born writer, for one reason or another stalled in his vocation, may back and fill in this way. *Who Lost an American?* is the distillation of this fret, a collection of memories, notes, burlesques and prejudices in a book that is part fact, part fiction. . . .

The best thing in the book is Algren's personal rhythm—irreverent, funny, surreal, as if he has blended the lyricism of his early writing, "within a rain that light rains regret," with a tough meander and wail like that of funky jazz. Algren is a writer, the authentic poetic article; a fresh haircut strikes his eye as vividly as the murder of a Chicago poker player on a backstairs. It would be fine to discover him working once again on people whom he could feel in his blood and within an action that might carry his special melody.

Herbert Gold. *New York Times Book Section*. June 2, 1963. p. 23

There is something fundamentally dispiriting about *Who Lost an American?*, not because its inner feeling is irrelevant to life today—I do not believe it is—but because Algren, who is after all an accomplished writer, is so utterly helpless to turn this feeling into anything but a commonplace buffoonery. Caught between his own past, in which a deep identification with the social outcast and the working class was all but inseparable from his sense of literary vocation, and the present, in which money seems to brutalize equally those who have too much and those who have too little, Algren seems to have lost all sense of what useful literary tasks might remain open to him. His detestation of the prevailing moral atmosphere, not only of society at large but of the literary pretensions to which it has given rise, seems to have deprived him of his own seriousness as a writer.

Hilton Kramer. *The Reporter*. June 30, 1963. p. 47

No writer has been more relentlessly faithful to his scene and cast of characters than Nelson Algren. His scene is the "wild side," the "neon wilderness," the seamier sprawls of Chicago and its spiritual extensions across this broad land—America as Chicago. And his characters are the drifters and grifters, clowns and carnies, pimps and pushers, hustlers and hookers, gamblers and touts, junkies and lushes, marks and victims, conmen and shills, freaks and grotesques—the born losers who constitute a half-world, an anti-society to the society that never appears, not even as a sensed or felt presence, in Algren's work. Over the four decades of his life as a writer, scene and characters have never changed. Atmosphere, obsessions, talk, ways of putting in the time—all are fixed, held in suspension, dreamed and long after hazily recalled, caught not as they once were but as they are remembered, just as they are about to

dissolve and become ballads. The mythical time, whatever the calendar reads, is always the '30s, somewhere around the longest year of 1935.

Saul Maloff. *New Republic*. Jan. 19, 1974. p. 23

Nelson Algren hasn't written any novels for going on 20 years now—which is sad in a way. But it's not like he's been exactly idle in the years between: *The Last Carousel* is the third collection of short pieces he has published since his last novel. Unlike the other two (*Who Lost an American?* and *Notes from a Sea Diary*), this one contains a lot of short fiction. . . .

Algren's journalism is a little hard to tell from his fiction. They look a lot alike. Algren puts himself right in the middle of his non-fiction, too, sets scenes beautifully, and tells it all with dialogue and colorful details interwoven through the narrative. In other words, to give it a recently-stylish label, it's New Journalism—and Nelson Algren was writing it this way when Tom Wolfe was still at Yale working on his PhD in American Studies. This being the case and with journalism being exalted today in some quarters high above fiction as a mode of serious expression, I can't for the life of me figure out why he hasn't retained greater eminence.

Bruce Cook. *Commonweal*. Feb. 8, 1974. p. 469

The Man with the Golden Arm is an estimable novel which occupies an important position in Algren's development as a novelist. Though not so neatly constructed as *Never Come Morning*, it is more densely packed, more intense, and in some ways more mature. The humorous scenes lead straight to Algren's last major work, the uniquely comic *A Walk on the Wild Side*, which Algren and many of his critics consider to be his best novel. . . .

The Man with the Golden Arm is Algren's most comprehensive expression of his conviction that America's great middle class should be made to recognize the personal worth and dignity of the socially disinherited who do not live the spurious lives of the "business cats" and the country-club set, neither of whom has been willing to recognize "the world underneath." In writing such novels as *The Man with the Golden Arm*, Algren has blended Naturalistic Determinism "with a sympathy for his people that nevertheless cannot deter him from sending them to their miserable fates." In a style and language that are drawn directly from the world he depicts, he has "managed to impart a dignity to material which would be merely sordid in the hands of a lesser writer." He regularly insists that the "poetry" which characterizes his Realism is a natural poetry, one taken from the people themselves: "When I heard a convict who had just finished a stretch say, 'I made my time from bell to bell, now the rest of the way is by the stars,' if somebody was fusing poetry with realism it was the con, not me. My most successful poetry, the lines people threw back at me years after they were written, were lines I never wrote. They were lines I heard, and repeated, usually by someone who never read and couldn't write."

For this reason, despite the concreteness and authoritative detail of his prose, Algren is "more a singer than an explainer," one whose prose in *The Man with the Golden Arm* can become almost a "kind of incantation, like the chanting of ritual itself." In such a form, the curb and tenement and half-shadow world of Frankie and Sophie and Molly with its unforgettable smoke-colored rain, its musk-colored murmuring, and its calamitous light have brought the world underneath a bit closer to the middle-class American consciousness and conscience.

Martha Heasley Cox and Wayne Chatterton. *Nelson Algren* (Twayne, 1975), pp. 132–33

I have never quite met Nelson Algren—we talked on the phone once—but he has been a continuing influence in my life. He is the poet of the sad metropolis that underlies our North American cities; I was among those millions who caught an early chill there. Reading Algren didn't dispel the chill, but it did teach us to live with it and to look around us with deepened feelings and thoughts.

Algren's Chicago and the people who live in its shadows are still there. Algren is their tragic poet, enabling those who can read him to feel pain. And nearly everyone can read him. He writes with a master's clarity about the complex troubles of simple people, and not so simple people. Bruno Bicek and Frankie Machine and Steffi ''with the new city light on her old world face'' appear to be simple because Algren presents them with such understanding.

Algren came into the full use of his talent in the early years of the Second World War, which promised to open the way for a reassessment of our society. In full knowledge of the lower depths which had to be redeemed, Algren asserted the value of the people who lived in those depths. The intensity of his feeling, the accuracy of his thought, make me wonder if any other writer of our time has shown us more exactly the human basis of our democracy. Though Algren often defines his positive values by showing us what happens in their absence, his hell burns with passion for heaven.

Ross Macdonald. *New York Times Book Section*. Dec. 4, 1977, p. 62

A Depression-era naturalist who still pops up in surrealist anthologies, [Algren] never stopped believing that the human actions and emotions which make literature are inherently unclassifiable. He blew being a convincing muckraker by noticing that ''people without alternatives are forced to feel life all the way,'' which sounded better to him than what everybody else was doing; trading not feeling for not being forced. But then he botched being a good black humorist by missing the point that an awareness of the absurd is supposed to distance feelings and not heighten them. It's no accident that he was one of the few '30s writers to greet existentialism as reinforcement instead of deviation, and it's not surprising that he was drawn to the movement by liking the people first and their ideas later. . . . But throughout the '50s, whenever it dawned on critics that Algren didn't think of his characters as social ills to be cured, he was routinely attacked, by such people as Edmund Fuller, who also disliked *From Here to Eternity* because the hero was a ''slob.''

This bias must account for the comparative lack of reputation accorded *A Walk on the Wild Side*—which is Algren's best novel, an astonishing suspension of tragi-comedy within endlessly meshing webs of folklore, poetry, and dread. The closest analogy would be a blend of *Huckleberry Finn* with *The Threepenny Opera*, but that's

only an approximation; offhand, I can't think of any previous American book that's much like it, although dozens of writers, from Thomas Berger to Charles Bukowski, have been ransacking it for years. . . . *Wild Side* is a Depression novel in which the Depression isn't an economic situation or even a definable period, but a phantasmagoria that lifts the lid off the American character. Or, as Algren later put it, back then people couldn't *afford* inhibitions. . . .

But it's misleading to approach the book schematically. *A Walk on the Wild Side* confounds genres—its emotional effects are as various, caroming, and unmediated, as humanly scrambled, as emotion itself. And yet they're worked to such a dense, lucid level of magnification that they seem, at the same time, hallucinatory. The result is a slapstick disorientation that feels, against all reason, unquestionable. Stylistically, Wild Side is a kind of ultimate. Algren doesn't lend himself to being excerpted; his verbal devices, which conflate atmosphere, character, and meaning into one and the same thing, are seldom discrete. They're designed to stoke and build on themselves, and they reverberate through the whole length of the best *Neon Wilderness* stories, or, later, whole sections of *The Man with the Golden Arm*. In *Walk on the Wild Side*, Algren sustains the equivalent of a single jazz solo through an entire book. . . .

What makes Algren's work ambiguous, or disturbing, or simply puzzling to many people, I think, is that he doesn't feel any obligation to adopt a depersonalized solemnity toward his material. Yet his sardonicism, whimsicality, eccentric irony, and refractory high spirits never add up to displays of intellectual superiority. He's all there for his characters, opening himself and expressing the full range of his personality as a writer in order to be in touch with the full range of their lives as people. He asserts his own identity on their level, makes himself one of them by maintaining his individuality, which forces us to see them as individuals too, in a way that precludes simply having an intellectual attitude toward them: for Algren, do-gooding concern is as emotionally inadequate as disdain.

Tom Carson. *[The Village] Voice Literary Supplement*, Nov., 1983, pp. 16–17

In February [1980] he learned that he had been voted, however belatedly, into the American Academy and Institute of Arts and Letters, nominated by Donald Barthelme and seconded by Malcolm Cowley and Jacques Barzun. At first, when he told Canio [Pavone] about it, he seemed bitter about having been locked out for so long—should he even answer, could he hock the membership pin? Canio also remembered that Saul Bellow was mentioned, as if [Nelson] Algren believed that Bellow, who was rumored to have dismissed him as a tavern writer, had kept him out. But Pavone encouraged him to accept the nomination because he deserved it. In 1974, when he'd received the Award of Merit, he'd been cynical, but now Algren was happy, flattered, deeply satisfied. Heretofore he'd felt he was on some kind of American blacklist: his books sold abroad, and it was only in his own country that he was treated so badly. Suddenly he was being welcomed back into the literary world. It was *community* and being included that Algren craved, and that was what he found in Sag Harbor after all those lonely years in New Jersey and Chicago. . . .

More than a year after Algren's death, an American publisher for *The Devil's Stocking* had still not been found, and when Herbert

Mitgang mentioned this in *The New York Times Book Review*, Donald Fine renewed his offer to publish the last Nelson Algren novel, paying about half what he had originally offered. The novel appeared in 1983.

Algren's tombstone arrived with his name misspelled and had to be recut. And when the City of Chicago changed West Evergreen Street to West Algren Street, residents complained that the new address caused too much trouble. So the city changed it back again.

> Bettina Drew. *Nelson Algren: A Life on the Wild Side* (New York: G.P. Putnam's Sons, 1989), pp. 377, 380

Algren once was hailed as "the poet of the Chicago slums" and was considered by Ernest Hemingway to "rank among our best American novelists." An impressive collection of his Texas stories has just been published [*The Texas Stories of Nelson Algren*, ed. Bettina Drew]. . . . Influenced by a loving and cultivated sister, he formed an early interest in books, music, ballet, and the arts. In spite of his blue collar, uneducated background, Algren was determined to go to college. And so he did, graduating from the University of Illinois in 1931 with a degree in journalism. . . .

Making a decision to head south in search of work, Algren hitchhiked down to Texas, to New Orleans and back to Texas by box car. He took any available job: shilling for a crooked carnival, picking fruit, sorting peas and beans. This journey ended with a nightmare jail sentence for borrowing a typewriter from a deserted classroom. . . . Algren used many of his own experiences in writing these eleven powerful and tormented stories.

> Anne Geismar. *Anton Community Newspapers: Boulevard.* February 1996, p. 48

BIBLIOGRAPHY
Somebody in Boots, 1935 (n); *Never Come Morning*, 1942 (n); *The Neon Wilderness*, 1947 (s); *The Man with the Golden Arm*, 1949 (n); *Chicago: City on the Make*, 1951 (t) (new edition, 1968); *A Walk on the Wild Side*, 1956 (n); *Who Lost an American?* 1963 (t); *Conversations*, 1964; *Notes from a Sea Diary*, 1965 (m); *The Last Carousel*. 1973 (s); *The Devil's Stocking*, 1983 (n); *America Eats*, 1992 (cookery, Midwest); *Nonconformity*, 1994 (e); *The Texas Stories*, 1995 (s, e)

AMMONS, A.R. (1926–)

These poems [in *Expression of Sea Level*] take place on the frontier between what the poet knows and what he doesn't; perhaps that explains their peculiar life and sensitivity. They open to accommodate surprises and accidents. The poet's interest is extended generously toward what he didn't expect, and his poems move by their nature in that direction.

The poems are worked out, not by the application of set forms to their materials, but in an effort to achieve form—in accordance with a constant attentiveness to, a hope for, the possibility of form—the need of anything, once begun, to complete itself, meaningfully.

> Wendell Berry. *The Nation.* March 23, 1964. p. 304

Now, in the 1960s, poets are beginning to work towards an expansion of subject matter and a synthesis of style between the traditional forms and the open forms fostered by William Carlos Williams and others. The talented young poet A. R. Ammons . . . reveals some interesting aspects of that search. Ammons uses a variety of cadenced open forms to concentrate the kind of knowledge out of which he makes his images. He extends the subject of the poem by using a range of interesting facts, often scientific in character. At first some of his poems seem too prosaic, but reading them carefully one perceives that his facts build to a startling perception. . . . His rhythms do not sing; they separate and define. His tone is essentially philosophic, not dramatic, yet there is a distinctly individual quality to his diction.

> James Schevill. *Saturday Review.* July 4, 1964. pp. 30–1

The publication of A. R. Ammons' *Selected Poems* should bring him wider recognition than has come on the basis of his three previously published volumes. At forty-two Ammons is one of the most accomplished writers of his generation in America. His work, both in subject matter and execution, has certainty and assurance, and he possesses a creative intelligence perfectly aware of what it can do and what it ought not to try, and happily at ease within its recognized and accepted boundaries. Within those boundaries Ammons' poems speak with settled authority, and are not afraid of repeating themselves, which they often do with conviction and without monotony. In this respect he resembles Wallace Stevens a little, although in most other ways the minds of the two poets come through very differently. But as with Stevens, so with Ammons: when one begins to read him, the best way to understand one poem is to read a great many. This is usual with poets obsessed with one or two central themes in their work to which they return on every creative occasion. Once the clue to Ammons' master pattern is seized (and it is not at all difficult) his poems are unusually easy to read. Nevertheless, a reader wholly unacquainted with Ammons' poetry and coming across one or two of his poems for the first time—especially if they were from his earlier work—might understandably be a little puzzled.

> Marius Bewley. *Hudson Review.* Winter, 1968–9. p. 713

[Ammons] is decidedly his own man and possesses his own vision, his own accents, and even his own solicitude about the sheer sculptured *appearance* of each poem against its whitenesses and silences (once having examined a late and characteristic Ammons poem, you could never confuse his patterns with the patterns of anybody else). . . . Mr. Ammons just might be our finest contemporary "nature poet," always excepting the incomparable case of James Dickey. Sometimes he employs nature—landscapes and waterscapes, the being and grave motions of creatures—as a source for metaphors by which to trace out subtle generalizations about crucial human experiences, about the perplexities and mysteries of consciousness. On other occasions, he deliberately halts short after displaying for us—no negligible feat—the bright and resonant *thingness* of things. . . .

Mr. Ammons's best poetry will not heal us perfectly, of course. What could? Yet now and then it can return to us significant parts of our world and of ourselves, parts that we had always gazed at but had never before studied with loving closeness.

Robert Stilwell. *Michigan Quarterly Review*. Fall, 1969. p. 278

I am writing of Ammons as though he had rounded his first circle in the eye of his readers, and there is no other way to write about him, even if my essay actually introduces him to some of its readers. The fundamental postulates for reading Ammons have been set down well before me, by Richard Howard and Marius Bewley in particular, but every critic of a still emergent poet has his own obsessions to work through, and makes his own confession of the radiance. Ammons's poetry does for me what Stevens's did earlier, and the High Romantics before that: it helps me to live my life. If Ammons is, as I think, the central poet of my generation, because he alone has made a heterocosm, a second nature in his poetry, I deprecate no other poet by this naming. It is, surprisingly, a rich generation, with ten or a dozen poets who seem at least capable of making a major canon, granting fortune and persistence. Ammons, much more than the others, has made such a canon already. A solitary artist, nurtured by the strength available for him only in extreme isolation, carrying on the Emersonian tradition with a quietness directly contrary to nearly all its other current avatars, he has emerged in his most recent poems as an extraordinary master, comparable to the Stevens of *Ideas of Order* and *The Man with the Blue Guitar*. To track him persistently, from his origins in *Ommateum* through his maturing in *Corson's Inlet* and its companion volumes on to his new phase in *Uplands* and *Briefings* is to be found by not only a complete possibility of imaginative experience, but by a renewed sense of the whole line of Emerson, the vitalizing and much maligned tradition that has accounted for most that matters in American poetry. [1970]

Harold Bloom. *The Ringers in the Tower: Studies in Romantic Tradition* (Chicago). 1971. p. 261

Corson's Inlet ... opens with a poem that nicely illustrates the perfected diction Ammons has now achieved, a rhythmical certainty which does not depend on syllable-counting or even accentual measure, but on the speed and retard of words as they move together in the mind, on the shape of the stanzas as they follow the intention of the discourse, and on the *rests* which not so much imitate as create the soft action of speech itself. There is a formality in these gentle lines which is new to American poetry, as we say that there is a draughtsmanship in the "drip-drawings" of Pollack which is new to American painting: each must be approached with a modulated set of expectations if we are to realize what the poet, the painter is about. ... It is characteristic that so many of these poems ... take up their burden from the shore, the place where it is most clearly seen that "every living thing is in siege: the demand is life, to keep life." ... Ammons rehearses a marginal, a transitional experience, he is a littoralist of the imagination because the shore, the beach, or the coastal creek is not a *place* but an *event*, a transaction where land and water create and destroy each other, where life and death are exchanged, where shape and chaos are won or lost. It is here ... that Ammons finds his rhythms.

Richard Howard. *Alone with America* (Atheneum). 1971. pp. 11–4

The latest volume of A. R. Ammons, *Uplands*, is a better book than Stafford's [*Allegiances*], partly perhaps because it is slim. As usual, Ammons has treated himself with great critical rigor. These poems, like his earlier works, are primarily about the nature of human perception. Some readers might be tempted to say of him what is sometimes said of his mentor, Wallace Stevens, that his subject is poetry. This is true but only in the largest possible meaning of the word "poetry," for to both writers "poetry" is a way of describing the essence of human perception. In the poetry of Ammons one is constantly finding passages in which nature itself seems to be writing poems, that is, making creations that we see as having the kind of fluent form that Ammons seeks in poetry. ... Nature itself falls into forms as the rockslide reveals "streaks and scores of knowledge." Thus the rocks, the streams, the mountains, the pines, move through lines that only the human imagination can express. ... In its discipline and toughness of mind this volume would provide a good antidote for the loose and flimsy writing being done today by poets who feel that Whitman is now a license for any kind of verbal meandering.

Louis L. Martz. *The Yale Review*. Spring, 1971. pp. 413–4

At first sight A. R. Ammons seems a nature poet, and perhaps, with a difference, this is what he really is. He has the essential characteristic of the nature poet, which is to use observed pieces of nature as the reality of an organic order defending him against the reality of human disorder. ...

But, like Robert Frost, he is aware too of the evil within the natural order. ...

He passes the test of nature poets by doing very precise and beautiful things and by occasionally producing a line which has the effect of an explosion on the page. ... The new note in his observation is his sense of the impermanence of the permanent-seeming things. At their best, his poems give the feeling of the opaque being rayed through to make it transparent, the most solid being hollowed with tunnels through which winds blow, time undermining timelessness.

Stephen Spender. *New York Review of Books*. July 22, 1971. p. 4

Many of Ammons' poems are metaphysically framed sketches from nature. Some are realistic, some a kind of animated cubism, and some abstractly patterned. The "metaphysical" aspect is rather like that in Wallace Stevens: the same issue of reality and illusion. It almost seems obvious that Ammons' opening poem, "Snow Log," is a conscious allusion to Stevens' "The Snow Man," as a starting point from which *Uplands* goes on to explore possible directions of form and phrasing on a wider range than Stevens engaged himself with. Ammons does have certain advantages over Stevens: his knowledge of geological phenomena (an *experienced* knowledge) and his ability to use language informally and to create open rhythms. Everything he writes has the authority of his intelligence, of his humor, and of his plastic control of materials. What he lacks, as compared to Stevens, is a certain passionate confrontation of the implicit issues such as makes Stevens' music a richer, deeper force. There *is* a great deal of feeling in Ammons; but in the interest of ironic self-control he seems afraid of letting the feeling have its way, in the sense that Stevens lets his bitterness flood through "The Emperor of Ice-Cream." Stevens was certainly self-ironic, and hardly an emotional screamer, yet he *hated* the illusoriness of human ideals and understanding that the fact of death forced him to face. What Ammons presents is a certain delight or dismay at the imponderable, while at the same time he refuses to strike for effects of power we yearn for in a poet with such a mind and such an ear.

M.L. Rosenthal. *Shenandoah*. Fall, 1972. p. 88

In . . . extravagant and beautiful poems—verse essays really—Ammons maintains a virtuoso current of phrasing that embraces all types of vocabulary, all motions of thought, and leads us back now to Whitman and now to the accumulative (if hopefully cumulative) strain of Pound's *Cantos* or Williams's *Paterson*. Building on a non-narrative base, that is, on a will-to-words almost sexual in persistence, he changes all "flesh-body" to "wordbody" and dazzles us with what he calls "interpenetration"—a massively playful nature-thinking, a poetic incarnation of smallest as well as largest thoughts. . . .

No one in his generation has put "earth's materials" to better use, or done more to raise pastoral to the status of major art.

Geoffrey H. Hartman. *New York Times Book Section*. Nov. 19, 1972. pp. 39–40

Ammons' poetry is a poetry which is profoundly American, without being in any way limited by this characteristic. His use of language, his vocabulary and phrasing are utterly and flexibly American. The universal terms of science emerge accurately and naturally from the poems' roots.

The poetry can now be read in its bulk and ripeness. It is science-minded, passionately absorbed with the processes around the poet, the constant, complex, fascinating processes of water, wind, season and genus. But if Ammons' poetry is in the tradition of "nature poets," its essence is far different from the lyric, limpid joy of John Clare, or the *paysage moralisé* of Wordsworth, or the somber farmer-wisdom of Robert Frost, or the myth-ridden marvels of D.H. Lawrence's tortoises, serpents and gentians. Ammons sees the datum of nature as *evidence*; intricate, interlocking fragments of a whole which cannot be totally understood, but which draws him deeper and deeper into its identity. No poet now writing in English has so thoroughly created on the page the huge suggestion of the whole through its most minute components.

Josephine Jacobsen. *Diacritics*. Winter, 1973. p. 34

The fascination of [Ammons's] poetry is not the transcendental but his struggle with it, which tends to turn each poem into a battleground strewn with scattered testimony to the history of its making in the teeth of its creator's reluctance and distrust of "all this fiddle."

Reading the poems in sequence one soon absorbs the rhythm of making-unmaking, of speech facing up to the improbability of speech. . . . The movement is the same, from the visible if only half-real flotsam of daily living to the uncertainties beyond, but one

forgets this from one poem to the next; each is as different as a wave is from the one that follows and obliterates it. . . .

Much has been written about the relation of the so-called "New York School" of poets to the painting of men like Pollack, but in a curious way Ammons's poetry seems a much closer and more successful approximation of "Action Painting" or art as process. ("The problem is how to keep shape and flow.")

John Ashbery. *New York Review of Books*. Feb. 22, 1973. p. 4

What [Ammons] does is remarkable both in its sparseness and in its variety. One can't say "richness" because there is no sensual "give" in this poetry—but it does attempt an imitative re-creation, no less, of the whole variety of the natural world, if not, regrettably, of what Stevens calls its "affluence." But if, as Ammons seems to think, affluence is brought rather by the perceiving and receptive mind, as a quality, rather than inhering in nature itself (nature, who perceives herself singly, we may say, as an acorn here, a brook there, rather than corporately congratulating herself on all her brooks), then a poem attempting this ascetic unattributiveness must refrain from celebrating the multiplicity of the world in human terms. Why it should be so wrong to let in human gestalt-making is another question; Ammons permits himself entry when the poem is about himself, but he won't have any of those interfering adjectival subjectivities when he's occupied with morning-glories or caterpillars or redwoods. This discipline of perfect notation is almost monklike, and, monklike, it takes what comes each day as the day's revelation of, so to speak, the will of God.

Helen Vendler. *The Yale Review*. Spring, 1973. p. 420

Having sacrificed the dramatic, having dieted and professored his Romanticism, having drained off all but a wetting of the implicit, Ammons has left almost everything to his intelligence, the crispness of his language, the geniality of his tone, and the greatness of his subject, his *reasonable* approach to Romantic "spirituality." If the result is the "open" American counterpart of the closed Augustan verse essay—equally an *essay*—still in this reader's palm, at first weighing, it feels major. Though it has nothing of the feat about it it has scope, is original and blandly imposing. And to his linear discourse Ammons gives just enough "jangling dance" to shock "us to attend the moods of lips." Although almost nothing in the poem [*Sphere*] moves or ravishes, almost everything interests and holds—holds not least because it tests, and finds thin, the spiritual satisfactions available in being a conscious part of a universe afloat in nothingness. The talk is not desperate but, by and large, is just talk. The subject is not really in Ammons as the kind of happiness that threatens to swell into a yelp or surf onto silence. But Romanticism has always been in trouble; dissatisfaction is its nature; Ammons is doing what he can.

Calvin Bedient. *New York Times Book Section*. Dec. 22, 1974. pp. 2–3

To recognize . . . Ammons's affinities with Emerson, Dickinson, and Frost is not to reduce the pleasures of his poems but to heighten them. It is also to acknowledge that beyond these direct literary influences there are powerful currents of indirection that play perhaps a more major role still, sources of a more ancient and primal kind that inform the intellectual and emotional life of poetry at its deepest. . . .

For those who have a taste for this sort of thing—for poetry as an unravelling of meaning, a coming-apart or depletion of language—"Pray without Ceasing" may sustain interest, but more often than not the poem will have a hard time of it winning the fascination or affection of readers. At its core is a painful and bewildering renunciation of all significant sense—"it's/indifferent what I say"—the whole point being, one supposes, to reach bottom in order to know, and if possible still to praise, the ache of life in total descent. This plunge downward, into a "breakdown of pure forms," is announced in the poem's opening lines, which serve as a kind of program, or statement of intent, of what is to come:

done is to be undone: call me down from the high places

Yet after pondering the poems of this book [*Diversifications*]—and a very good book it nevertheless remains—it seems clear that "the high places" constitute Ammons's most proper place, that at his best he is a poet of the solitary and singular moment, that his truest translation of himself puts him, after all, on to the heights, at the farthest remove from the lowlands of communal grief.

Alvin Rosenfeld. *American Poetry Review.* July/Aug., 1976, pp. 40–41

Ammons impresses me as the best American poet now writing. He is the most versatile, his range is greatest, his excellence in the subsidiary arts included in poetry is the most distinguished, he is funny, and he has been wonderfully abundant. His published work now runs to almost a thousand pages, and he is nowhere near retirement. . . .

In his best poems, Ammons chips away at the oldest obstacle confronting American writers: the thing itself. Remotely in Eliot and Pound, indirectly in Stevens and Frost, and directly in William Carlos Williams, American-born writers have sought, sometimes with a desperation approaching hysteria, to escape the fictions of language and art so as to come as close as possible to the actual physical concrete things of the earth. . . . As purely as can be, Ammons belongs to the American tradition of using language and culture to reach ends that language and culture do not seem designed to reach. . . .

Ammons has emerged as the ideal heir to the strongest fortune of American poetry, and his work synthesizes the best experiments of all of his precursors, especially the ones who stayed at home—Whitman, Sandburg, Williams, Jeffers, Stevens, and Frost. With a southerner's innate skepticism and peculiarly efficient sense of irony, Ammons is at once the flattest of writers and the fanciest.

William Harmon. In *The American South: Portrait of a Culture*, ed. Louis D. Rubin, Jr. (Louisiana State Univ. Pr., 1980), pp. 342, 345

BIBLIOGRAPHY
Ommateum: with *Doxology*, 1955 (p); *Expression of Sea Level*, 1964 (p); *Tape for the Turn of the Year*, 1965 (p); *Corson's Inlet*, 1965 (p); *Northfield Poems*, 1966; *Selected Poems*, 1968; *Uplands*, 1970 (p); *Briefings*, 1971 (p); *Collected Poems: 1951–1971*, 1972; *Sphere: The Form of a Motion*, 1974 (p); *Diversifications*, 1975 (p); *The Snow Poems*, 1977; *Selected Poems, 1951–1977*, 1977, expanded edition, 1986; *Selected Longer Poems*, 1980; *A Coast of Trees*, 1981 (p); *Worldly Hopes*, 1982 (p); *Sumerian Vistas*, 1987 (p); *The Really Short Poems of A.R. Ammons*, 1990; *Garbage*, 1993 (p); *Rarities*, 1994 (p); *Stand-In*, 1994 (p); *The North Carolina Poems*, ed. Alex Albright, 1994; *Brink Road*, 1996 (p); *Set in Motion: Essays, Interviews, and Dialogues*, ed. Zofia Burr, 1996; *Glare*, 1997 (p)

ANAYA, Rudolfo (1937–)

In the novel [*Bless me, Ultima*], Antonio, symbolically both Christ and Odysseus, moves from the security and from the sweet-smelling warmth of his mother's bosom and kitchen out into life and experience. As he weighs his options—priesthood and the confinement represented by the farms of the Lunas', or the Marezes' freedom on the pagan seas of the llano—and as he grows from innocence to knowledge and experience, the *la llorona* motif figures both on a literal mythological level and as an integral part of Antonio's life.

As "literal" myth, *la llorona* is the wailing woman of the river. Hers is the "tormented cry of a lovely goddess" that fills the valley in one of Antonio's dreams. *La llorona* is "the old witch who cries along the river banks and seeks the blood of boys and men to drink." . . .

Antonio . . . elude[s] the death call of *la llorona*, and as he buries the owl, Ultima's spirit, he takes on the responsibility of the future in which he knows he must "buil[d] his own dream out of those things which were so much a part of [his] childhood" (p. 248). Antonio has avoided annihilation on the sheer cliffs of the Wandering Rocks—the fate of his brothers—and he has moved through the narrow strait and evaded the menace of Scylla and Charybdis as he comes to face the reality of his manhood.

Jane Rogers. "The Function of the La Llorona Motif in Anaya's *Bless Me, Ultima*." In Vernon E. Lattin, ed. *Contemporary Chicano Fiction* (Binghamton: Bilingual Pr., 1986), pp. 200, 205

[Rudolfo] Anaya, professor of English at the University of New Mexico, published in 1972 what may be the largest-selling Chicano novel to date. *Bless Me, Ultima* . . . is set in a small northeastern New Mexico town in the 1940s and is concerned with the maturation of a young boy, Antonio Marez, and his relationship with his spiritual guide, the Ultima of the title. She is a *curandera*, a wise woman, a dispenser of curing herbs and potions who also heals with spiritual advice and some "magic." She is present from the boy's earliest experiences of growing up—family conflict, school, religion, evil, and death. The novel is narrated in the first person by Antonio, but the perspective is from a later time, when the narrator is older and more experienced. It takes place in the span of one year, during which Antonio loses his faith in traditional religion but enters into a new, more profound spiritualism. . . .

There is much good in this novel: the beauty and magic of a wonderful New Mexico landscape, the legend of the Golden Carp (a god who becomes a fish in order to help his doomed people), and dream sequences as presentations of other dimensions of reality or as a means of foretelling the future. Anaya is adept at incorporating the rich folklore of his region, an element that is particularly important in the development of Chicano literature. . . .

Anaya's subsequent novels have not fared as well critically as his first, but this perhaps is because of the excellence of *Bless Me, Ultima*, and not so much because his other works are not sound. His second work, *Heart of Aztlan* (1976), is the story of Clemente and Adelita Chavez, who move to Albuquerque from the rural community of Guadalupe, a move they must make out of fiscal necessity. They settle in the downtown *barrio* of Barelas, where life is in stark contrast to their previous quiet and bountiful rural existence. . . .

With its grim portrayal of the disastrous results of rural Chicano migration to the big city, *Heart of Aztlan* is frequently classified as a work of social protest. The problem with the novel, according to many critics, is not so much a question of theme as one of craftsmanship.

Tortuga (Turtle, 1970) has fared better with the critics. The title refers to the protagonist, a sixteen-year-old paralyzed boy, so named because his body is encased in a hard, shell-like cast. The novel is a first-person narrative of his long recovery from a near-fatal accident. During the course of his hospital journey from illness to good health, Tortuga encounters many other crippled children, and an Ultima-like figure, Salomon, a mute who communicates with the boy through a telepathy process. . . . *Tortuga* is a novel rich with poetry, symbolism, dreams, and magical, mysterious characters.

> Carl R. Shirley and Paula W. Shirley. *Understanding Chicano Literature* (Columbia: Univ. of South Carolina Pr., 1988), pp. 104–7

After twenty-two years as the most important and influential Chicano novel ever written, although available only from a small press, Rudolfo Anaya's *Bless Me, Ultima* has been reprinted in hardcover and mass-market editions by Warner Books. A timeless work of youth and rites of passage, Tonatiuh-Quinto Sol's edition sold more than 300,000 copies in two decades of classroom use and word-of-mouth readership. Despite Anaya's impact as a storyteller and mentor for many Chicano writers and the fact that he is one of the best fiction writers in the United States, it has taken all this time for his work to reach a mass audience. Up to now, his books have appeared through small and university presses, which meant consistent publication but limited distribution. This was the norm for the majority of Chicano writers until recently. With the boom in Latino writers—I'm thinking of Cristina Garcia, Julia Alvarez, Dagoberto Gilb, and Denise Chavez, for example—will not have to ''pay dues'' for the length of time Anaya has. . . .

After all these years, *Bless Me, Ultima* endures because Anaya had the vision to see and capture the past, the present and the future of his people in one work of art. It is a difficult task to accomplish in fiction, yet Anaya did it with the same rare magnitude Gabriel Garcia Marquez effected in *One Hundred Years of Solitude*. *Bless Me, Ultima* is our Latin American classic because of its dual impact—it clearly defines Chicano culture as founded on family, tradition and the power of myth. Through Antonio and Ultima, we learn how to identify these values in the midst of the dark clouds of

change and maturity. *Bless Me, Ultima* also shows that, like Garcia Marquez, Anaya recognizes that the Latino world is fluid and mysterious and can only be recreated by playing with time and the unpredictable environment that surreal religious forces create in the lives of all, the young and the elderly, the isolated and the social, the powerful and the weak.

> Ray Gonzalez. *The Nation*. July 18, 1994, pp. 98, 100

BIBLIOGRAPHY
Bless Me, Ultima, 1972, rev. ed 1989, (n); *Heart of Aztlan*, 1976 (n); *Tortuga*, 1979 (n); *The Season of La Llorono*, 1979 (d); ed. (with Simon J. Ortiz) *A Ceremony of Brotherhood, 1680–1980*, 1981 (anthol of Mexican-American literature, c); *The Silence of the Llano*, 1982 (s); *The Legend of La Llorona*, 1984 (n); *The Adventures of Juan Chicaspatas*, 1985 (p); *A Chicano in China*, 1986 (a, t); *Who Killed Don José*, 1987 (d); *The Farolitos of Christmas*, 1987 (d); *Lord of the Dawn*, 1987 (n); *Flow of the River*, 1988 (e); *Albuquerque*, 1992 (n); *Man on Fire*, 1994 (e); *The Anaya Reader*, 1995 (misc); *Zia Summer*, 1995 (e); *Rio Grande Fall*, 1996 (n); *Jalamanta: A Message from the Desert*, 1996 (n); *Farolitos for Abuelo*, 1998 (juv); *Shaman Winter*, 1998 (n); *Conversations*, ed. Bruce Dick and Silvio Sirias, 1998 (i)

ANDERSON, Maxwell (1888–1959)

Mr. Anderson's uncommon virtues and regrettable shortcomings are once more visible (in *The Wingless Victory* and *High Tor*). Both contain much lovely song. Both . . . disclose a mind and a point of view infinitely superior to the playwrighting general. And the second combines with its other qualities a sound originality and a small measure of that precious after-image, a small measure of the day-after recollective warmth, which in its full is the stamp and mark of important drama. But both the superior second as well as the inferior first, lack the strong, taut, purple cords to tie up and bind closely into a whole their isolatedly commendable elements and their periodic stirring notes of dramatic music.

> George Jean Nathan. *Saturday Review*. Jan. 30, 1937. p. 19

Mr. Anderson, it seems to me, in his own plays has given the most striking confirmation of the obsolescence of verse technique. He is capable of writing well—in prose, and when he is close to real American speech. But in these recent plays he writes badly. I do not mean that he is technically incompetent; but he writes badly because English blank verse no longer has any relation whatsoever to the language or tempo of our lives, and because, as soon as he tries to use it, he has no resources but a flavorless imagery which was growing trite in our grandfathers' time.

> Edmund Wilson. *New Republic*. June 23, 1937. p. 194

Maxwell Anderson has been at his best, in recent years, when he was angry. But because his language lacks any basis for hope, for a constructive point of view towards what disgusts him, it must in the end turn back upon itself, and render him peevish and despairing.

Fine words and despair are not enough on which to nurture a dramatic talent; Anderson's latest plays show a marked decline. Yet his great gift is apparent whenever he permits himself to write immediately and simply about human beings.

> Eleanor Flexner. *American Playwrights* (Simon). 1938. pp. 128-9

In eleven plays "poetic" from beginning to end, Maxwell Anderson, America's chief verse writer for the theatre, has produced very little poetry.... Consciously or otherwise, Mr. Anderson seems more interested in arguing for his philosophy of life than in any particular happening, past or present. Each of the full-length plays turns upon a love story, essentially the same in all. A potentially perfect romance is frustrated by another need, political (the crown in *Elizabeth, Mary*, etc.), social (*Wingless Victory, Winterset*), or private (*High Tor, Key Largo*). While an assortment of contemporary topics are touched upon—the decay of aristocracy, race prejudice, class injustice, revolution, and absolution—the mechanism of the play is always the love affair, and the issue always a certain omnipresent danger of "dying within."

> Harold Rosenberg. *Poetry*. Jan. 1941. pp. 258–60

Maxwell Anderson's independence set him apart from his time. Not only as a literary craftsman—since he alone was writing poetic and romantic tragedies—but in other respects, he was an alien voice. In an age of increasing collectivism this voice could be heard praising individualism, independence, and the frontier spirit. In an age of increasing governmentalism he could still maintain that the best government was that which governed least. As the last champion of what almost amounts to a laissez-faire and rugged individualism, he is an isolated figure, almost an anachronism.

> Vincent Wall. *Sewanee Review*. July, 1941. p. 339

I am sure of this: the Anderson plays are declining in theatrical effectiveness but rising steadily in intellectual significance. If he is not an original thinker, Mr. Anderson has at least dug his teeth into a great subject; he has gradually moved beyond the crudely American conception of freedom as license to buy and sell anything at a profit to an Emersonian vision of the "infinitude of the private man." And always one feels—here is the peculiar appeal of the dramas—that he has achieved insight by staring hard at facts. Only Sean O'Casey among his contemporaries can hammer as much of the crude stuff of living into poetry for the stage.

> Edward Foster. *Sewanee Review*. Jan., 1942. p. 100

As Mr. Anderson's art matured . . . he evolved at the end of the first decade a working group of principles which were later stated as explicit theory.... This theory conceives of drama as having a high destiny, not only in its obligation to reflect a moral universe, but also in its function as inspirer of man's faith and as prophet of his future. The dramas Mr. Anderson wrote during his first decade did not fulfill these high purposes; nor did some of those he wrote during the second decade. But there are half a dozen plays from the later period which come close to his ideal and three or four which realize it fully; among the latter are *Mary of Scotland, Winterset,* and *Key Largo*.

> Allan H. Halline. *American Literature*. May, 1944. p. 81

Mr. Anderson really discovered himself, I think, in the historical plays. Here he developed his characteristic verse-form—a rather rough blank verse with a sort of tumbling, hurrying rhythm, like that of a tossing sea—a verse that can be used in colloquial realistic scenes, but that is capable of rising to high levels of imaginative beauty. Here also, through the study of historical figures and the attempt to recreate and interpret them, he gained a firmer grasp on character than he had shown in his earlier plays—a more penetrating insight, and greater skill in revealing character through speech. And here, too, I think he learned to simplify and clarify his story, just because the material with which he was dealing was so complex that severe simplification was necessary.

> Homer E. Woodbridge. *South Atlantic Quarterly*. Jan., 1945. p. 60

Many persons who do not count themselves among his most enthusiastic admirers would probably be willing to admit that he has succeeded more fully than any of our other dramatists in persuading a large popular audience to follow him gladly beyond the rather narrow circle of subjects, attitudes, and methods within which it has grown accustomed to remain confined.... Something of the same sort may be said of his verse which found ready comprehension in part because it did not, like so much modern poetry, require for its comprehension a familiarity with a modern tradition of which four-fifths of the theater-going public is completely ignorant. It has at least the primary virtue of dramatic verse inasmuch as it is easily speakable and easily understood when spoken.

> Joseph Wood Krutch. *American Drama since 1918* (Braziller). 1957. p. 305

BIBLIOGRAPHY

White Desert, 1923 (d); (with Laurence Stallings) *What Price Glory*, 1924 (d); *You Who Have Dreams*, 1925 (p); (with Laurence Stallings) *First Flight*, 1925 (d); *Outside Looking In*, 1925 (d); *The Buccaneer*, 1925 (d); *Three American Plays (What Price Glory, First Flight, The Buccaneer)*, 1926; *Sea-Wife*, 1926 (d); *Saturday's Children*, 1927 (d); (with Harold Hickerson) *Gods of the Lightning*, 1928 (d); *Gypsy*, 1929 (d); *Elizabeth the Queen*, 1930 (pd); *Night Over Taos*, 1932 (pd); *Both Your Houses*, 1933 (d); *Mary of Scotland*, 1933 (pd); *Valley Forge*, 1934 (pd); *Winterset*, 1935 (pd); *The Masque of Kings*, 1936 (pd); *The Wingless Victory*, 1936 (pd); *High Tor*, 1937 (pd); *The Star-Wagon*, 1937 (d); *The Feast of Ortolans*, 1938 (pd); *Knickerbocker Holiday*, 1938 (d, lyrics); *The Essence of Tragedy*, 1939 (e); *Key Largo*, 1939 (pd); *Eleven Verse Plays*, 1940; *Journey to Jerusalem*, 1940 (pd); *Candle in the Wind*, 1940 (d); *The Eve of St. Mark*, 1942 (d); *Storm Operation*, 1944 (d); *Truckline Cafe*, 1946 (d); *Joan of Lorraine*, 1947 (d) (also published as *Joan of Arc*, 1948); *Anne of the Thousand Days*, 1948 (pd); *Lost in the Stars*, 1950 (d, lyrics); *Barefoot in Athens*, 1951 (d); *The Bad Seed*, 1955 (d)

ANDERSON, Robert (1917–)

The main theme . . . [of *Tea and Sympathy*] is a defense of the special person in a society which tends to look askance at the "odd" individual, even the unpremeditated nonconformist. If the play has a message, it is to the effect that a boy like its protagonist may be more truly a man than those falsely rugged folk who oppress him.

The play also cautions us against prejudice, slander and false accusation—in a word, is a plea for tolerance. Naturally, we are all for it: every contribution in this direction is more than welcome. Yet in this regard I cannot help thinking that we have arrived today at a peculiar brand of tolerance. We tolerate the innocent! . . . Though now easily acceptable, a play like *Tea and Sympathy* is probably still regarded by many as adventurous and advanced, though it is actually primitive in its theme, characterization, and story development. It is, in fact, a very young play.

This is no adverse comment on it. It is the work of a young playwright, Robert Anderson, whose approach is honorably craftsmanlike and humane.

Harold Clurman. *The Nation*. Oct. 17, 1953. p. 318

Tea and Sympathy is a highly superior specimen of the theatre of "realist" escape. Superior in craftsmanship, superior in its isolation, combination, and manipulation of the relevant impulses and motifs. Its organization of the folklore of current fashion is so skillful, it brings us to the frontier where this sort of theatre ends. But not beyond it. So that one does not ask the questions one would ask of a wholly serious play. . . . Instead, one drinks the tea of sentiment and eats the opium of sympathy. . . . At every moment in the evening, one can say: this *has* to be a hit, or men are not feckless dreamers, the theatre is not a fantasy factory, and this is not the age of anxiety. . . . Anyway, it is a play for everyone in the family. The script is far better than most; folklore and daydream are not less interesting than drama. . . .

Eric Bentley. *New Republic*. Oct. 19, 1953. pp. 20–1

Among the season's most interesting offerings is Robert Anderson's *Tea and Sympathy*. Though Mr. Anderson (no relation of Maxwell Anderson) has had three plays produced, this study of a boy unjustly accused of homosexuality is his first hit. I can't pretend to believe completely in Mr. Anderson's play. I doubt if any boy of eighteen in these post-Kinsey days would reach his final year at boarding school without knowing the facts of life. I am confident that masters, worthy of being employed by such a school, would not accept the flimsy charge brought by a filthy-minded student or behave as these masters do after the charge is brought. And I am well aware that, if it were not a matter of saving a change of scenery, the final episode in all likelihood would not take place in the boy's dormitory room. I do know, however, that Mr. Anderson has a genuine flair for the theatre, that he can write fine individual scenes, and that he can hold an audience as I have seldom seen an audience held.

John Mason Brown. *Saturday Review*. Dec. 12, 1953. p. 45

Robert Anderson has not had a real success on Broadway since *Tea and Sympathy*. In *You Know I Can't Hear You When the Water's Running*, he deliberately set out to lower his insights and write something brightly commercial, something that people would like to see on Saturday nights. On their own terms—as lightweight sex plays—the four one-acts that comprise the package are successful at least half of the time.

Mel Gussow. *Newsweek*. March 27, 1967. p. 110

. . . Robert Anderson's *You Know I Can't Hear You When the Water's Running* begins with a very funny idea. . . . [O]ne is delightfully surprised to discover the sober author of *Tea and Sympathy* and a number of other anguished plays, has a flair for comedy.

However, the three playlets that follow are less pure comedy than the opening one. For while Anderson continues his comic invention, he permits it to become adulterated with his serious concern for problems of marital adjustment. . . . The playwright refuses to write a pure comic exercise and mixes in a certain naturalistic pathos.

It is probably inevitable that Mr. Anderson's work express his responsible recognition of the American scene. And if it strikes us as less entertaining than his free-swinging fun, it at least gives the evening character.

Henry Hewes. *Saturday Review*. April 1, 1967. p. 42

BIBLIOGRAPHY
Come Marching Home, 1945 (d); *Dark Horses*, 1951 (d); *The Eden Rose*, 1952 (d); *Love Revisited*, 1952 (d); *All Summer Long*, 1952 (d); *Tea and Sympathy*, 1953 (d); *Silent Night, Lonely Night*, 1959 (d); *The Days Between*, 1965 (d); *You Know I Can't Hear You When the Water's Running*, 1967 (d); *I Never Sang for My Father*, 1968 (d); *Solitaire. Double Solitaire*, 1972 (d); *After*, 1973 (d); *Getting Up and Going Home*, 1978 (d); *Theatre Talk: An Illustrated Dictionary of Theatre Terms and Definitions*, 1980 (ref); *The Last Act Is a Solo: A Play in One Act* , 1991

ANDERSON, Sherwood (1876–1941)

Winesburg, Ohio is a primer of the heart and mind, the emotions and the method of Sherwood Anderson. It is the most compact, the most unified, the most revealing of all his books. It is his most successful effort technically, for in it he has told the story of one community in terms of isolated short stories. . . . The author presents the impression that he is discovering for the first time the situations that he reveals to the reader, consequently he leads up to them as haltingly, as slowly as a child opening a door and entering an old, unused room. In the end the effect is cumulative and powerful.

Harry Hansen. *Midwest Portraits* (Harcourt). 1923. pp. 147–8

The thing which captures me and will not let me go is the profound sincerity, the note of serious, baffled, tragic questioning which I hear above its laughter and tears. It is, all through, an asking of the question which American literature has hardly as yet begun to ask. "What for?" ... It is that spirit of profound and unresisting questioning which has made Russian literature what it is, "Why? why? why?" echoes insistently through all their pages. . . . It echoes, too, in this book, like a great bell pealing its tremendous question to an unanswering sky, and awakening dangerously within one's self something that one has carefully laid to sleep—perhaps one's soul, who knows?

Floyd Dell. *Looking at Life* (Knopf). 1924. pp. 83–4

Winesburg, Ohio is a psychological document of the first importance; no matter that it is an incomplete picture of modern American life, it is an honest and penetrating one done with bold and simple strokes. These pictures represent the finest combination Anderson has yet achieved of imagination, intuition and observation welded into a dramatic unity by painstaking craftsmanship. They are one of the important products of the American literary renascence and have probably influenced writing in America more than any other book published within the last decade. They made and they sustain Anderson's reputation as an author worthy of comparison with the great short story writers.

Cleveland B. Chase. *Sherwood Anderson* (McBride). 1927. pp. 51–2

To the student of human nature under the conditions of provincial neo-Puritanism there must always belong a high interest to these documents with their toneless murmur as of one who has exhausted eloquence and passion and found them of no avail, with their tortured sense of life as a thing immitigably ugly and mean, with their delineation of dull misery so ground into the bone that it no longer knows itself for what it is. Nowhere in all these pages of Anderson will this student find a breath of freedom or of joy—never the record of an hour of either passion or serenity. Life is walled in; it is imprisoned from itself, from the sources without which it withers and dies. Who will knock down the walls? There is no one, least of all the author himself.

Ludwig Lewisohn. *Expression in America* (Harper). 1932. p. 484

(Hemingway and Gertrude Stein) disagreed about Sherwood Anderson. Gertrude Stein contended that Sherwood Anderson had a genius for using the sentence to convey a direct emotion, this was in the great American tradition, and that really except Sherwood there was no one in America who could write a clear and passionate sentence. Hemingway did not believe this, he did not like Sherwood's taste. Taste has nothing to do with sentences, contended Gertrude Stein.

Gertrude Stein. *The Autobiography of Alice B. Toklas* (Harcourt). 1933. p. 268

Anderson turned fiction into a substitute for poetry and religion, and never ceased to wonder at what he had wrought. He had more intensity than a revival meeting and more tenderness than God; he wept, he chanted, he loved indescribably. There was freedom in the air, and he would summon all Americans to share it; there was

confusion and mystery on the earth, and he would summon all Americans to wonder at it. He was clumsy and sentimental; he could even write at times as if he were finger-painting; but at the moment it seemed as if he had sounded the depths of common American experience as no one else could.

There was always an image in Anderson's books—an image of life as a house of doors, of human beings knocking at them and stealing through one door only to be stopped short before another as if in a dream. Life was a dream to him, and he and his characters seemed always to be walking along its corridors. Who owned the house of life? How did one escape after all? No one in his books ever knew, Anderson least of all. Yet slowly and fumblingly he tried to make others believe, as he thought he had learned for himself, that it was possible to escape if only one laughed at necessity.

Alfred Kazin. *On Native Grounds* (Reynal). 1942. pp. 210–1

Poor White belongs among the few books that have restored with memorable vitality the life of an era, its hopes and despairs, its conflicts between material prosperity and ethics, and its disillusionments, in a manner that stimulates the historical imagination. . . . No novel of the American small town in the Middle West evokes in the minds of its readers so much of the cultural heritage of its milieu as does *Poor White*; nor does Anderson in his later novels ever recapture the same richness of association, the ability to make memorable each scene in the transition from an agrarian way of living to a twentieth-century spectacle of industrial conflict with its outward display of physical comfort and wealth.

Horace Gregory. Introduction to *The Portable Sherwood Anderson* (Viking). 1949. pp. 16, 22

Read for moral explication as a guide to life, his work must seem unsatisfactory; it simply does not tell us enough. But there is another, more fruitful way of reading his work: as an expression of a sensitive witness to the national experience and as the achievement of a story teller who created a small body of fiction unique in American writing for the lyrical purity of its feeling. So regarded his best work becomes a durable part of the American literary structure. . . . While Steinbeck and Saroyan could enlarge on his occasional sentimentalism and Hemingway could tighten and rigidify his style, no American writer has yet been able to realize that strain of lyrical and nostalgic feeling which in Anderson's best work reminds one of another and greater poet of tenderness, Turgenev. At his best Anderson creates a world of authentic sentiment, and while part of the meaning of his career is that sentiment is not enough for a writer, the careers of those that follow him—those who swerve to Steinbeck's sentimentalism or Hemingway's toughness—illustrate how rare a genius sentiment still is in our literature.

Irving Howe. *Sherwood Anderson* (Sloane). 1951. pp. 249, 255

We must enter the realm of myth if we are to penetrate deeply into the form of *Winesburg*. . . . The myth of *Winesburg* concerns the legendary American small town, the town represented in the popular tradition as the lazy, gentle village of the Christian virtues. . . . The author's intention is to replace the myth of the small town Christian virtues with the myth of the "grotesques". It is important to remember that the "grotesques" are not merely small town characters. They are universal people, defeated by their false ideas and dreams. . . . The "grotesque" is neither misshapen nor abnormal. He is an unintegrated personality, cut off from society and adrift in his own mind.

> James Schevill. *Sherwood Anderson* (Denver). 1951. pp. 100–103

The exactitude of purity, or the purity of exactitude: whichever you like. He was a sentimentalist in his attitude toward people, and quite often incorrect about them. He believed in people, but it was as though only in theory. He expected the worst from them, even while each time he was prepared again to be disappointed or even hurt, as if it had never happened before, as though the only people he could really trust, let himself go with, were the ones of his own invention, the figments and symbols of his own fumbling dream. And he was sometimes a sentimentalist in his writing (so was Shakespeare sometimes) but he was never impure in it. He never scanted it, cheapened it, took the easy way; never failed to approach writing except with humility and an almost religious, almost abject faith and patience and willingness to surrender, relinquish himself to and into it. He hated glibness; if it were quick, he believed it was false too.

> William Faulkner. *Atlantic Monthly*. June, 1953. p. 28

Anderson's new approach to the Midwest drew its strength from humility and love. There was also the unabashed lyricism which, though it was to be transmuted in the later work by sympathy, here cut loose from the clogs of realistic convention. But particularly, the *[Mid-American] Chants* revealed a concentrated effort to make poetry out of Anderson's own language. This was simple and limited, frequently not sufficient to the demands he put upon it. In the *Chants*, for the first time, he came down upon his language, not to prune and order, but to let come from it whatever was, in nature, there. This was a part of his acceptance. He had felt in Gertrude Stein the achievement of poetry in the aggressively simple. And that, in a literary way, was where his own work must begin and end.

> Bernard Duffey. *The Chicago Renaissance in American Letters* (Michigan State). 1954. p. 205

What Anderson did for younger writers was to open vistas by finding new depths or breadths of feeling in everyday American life. Again with Whitman he might have boasted that he led each of them to a knoll, from which he pointed to "landscapes of continents, and a plain public road." He gave them each a moment of vision, and then the younger writer trudged off toward his separate destiny, often without looking back. Re-reading Anderson's work after many years, one is happy to find that its moments of vision are as fresh and moving as ever. They are what James Joyce called "epiphanies"; that is, they are moments at which a character, a landscape, or a personal relation stands forth in its essential nature or "whatness," with its past and future revealed as if by a flash of lightning. For Anderson each of the moments was a story in itself. The problem he almost never solved was how to link one moment

to another in a pattern of casuality, or how to indicate the passage of time.

> Malcolm Cowley. *New Republic*. Feb. 15, 1960. p. 16

If we approach the novel from the direction of George Willard, the young reporter presumably on the threshold of his career as a writer, instead of from that of the *subjects* of the sketches, *Winesburg* composes as a *Bildungsroman* of a rather familiar type the "portrait of the artist as a young man" in the period immediately preceding his final discovery of *métier*. In order to arrive at the rare excellence of *Winesburg*, we must first see that it is a book of this kind; and then we must go on to see in what ways it is not typical of the *genre*, for it is in the differences that Anderson's merits are revealed. An initial formulation of this difference would mainly call attention to Anderson's almost faultless holding of the balances between his two terms, artist and society, a delicacy that was perhaps made easier for him by the genuine uncertainty of his feelings. To put it bluntly, there are few works of modern fiction in which the artist's relations with ordinary men are seen with such a happy blend of acuity and charity, few works of any age in which the artist and ordinary men are seen so well *as fitting together* in a complementary union that permits us to make distinctions of relative value while at the same time retaining a universally diffused sense of equal dignity. We need look no further for the cause of the remarkable serenity of tone of *Winesburg*.

> Edwin Fussell. *Modern Fiction Studies*. Summer, 1960. pp. 108–9

Anderson's attitudes after 1912 remained basically unchanged. His heart lay in the rural simplicity of his youth, but it was the ideals rather than the facts, the feelings and the sentient newness of his Midwestern youth, that he wanted all his life to recapture. Armed with little more than a deep nostalgia for a way of life that could never be called back into being, he found in writing the sense of communion and sentient vitality he believed had been lost with the disappearance of the yeoman farmer and the tradesman. But his own regeneration could scarcely serve as a universal model; and, when he tried to prescribe sex and collectivism as workable popular alternatives to art, he invariably oversimplified both the nature and the problems of urban industrial society.

His thesis, to the end of his life, was that only a spiritual rebirth could save modern men from the machine; but he was never able to present his primitivistic modes of regeneration in convincing narrative terms. . . .

But Anderson's discouragingly long list of failures by no means diminishes the brilliance of his successes. If he failed as a sophisticated novelist, this failure was at least partly because he himself was not sophisticated, because he was a deeply involved purveyor of impressions and a man who suffered with his hurt and puzzled grotesques, and because he was not an intellectual or a detached observer and recorder of manners.

> Rex Burbank. *Sherwood Anderson* (Twayne). 1964. pp. 139, 141

As for the writing itself in *Sherwood Anderson's Memoirs*—I refer to the whole work, not just the somewhat difficult-to-identify new writing—there is much that is strong and free and good and that helps to extend one's view of Anderson's originality or to see better his relationship to some of his contemporaries (for example, William Carlos Williams and Dreiser) as well as to Whitman and Twain. There is added evidence here for the range of Anderson as a comic writer. His affinity with Twain in the "high and delicate art of how to tell a story" comes out more strongly when one can see in the narrative of the soldier boys in Cuba the same quiet, subversive humor of Twain's "The Private History of a Campaign that Failed"; and the new version of the story of Jacques Copeau's shirts touches the wild hilarity of Faulkner's humor. The narrative of Stella, the sister who took on the family after the mother's death, shows something in Anderson that has not, I think, been sufficiently remarked upon, an insight into human experience that goes far deeper than any cliché of buried lives.

Susan J. Turner. *American Scholar*. Winter, 1969–70. p. 158

Anderson's novelty lay in his appropriating to ordinary and sub-ordinary Americans a sensibility conventionally attributed to gorgeous young aesthetes or to Stephen Daedalus–like intellectuals. But the gestures of Anderson's passionate young woman stripping off her clothes and running out onto the street in the rain ("Adventure"), of his race track swipe who sees in the barroom mirror not his own face but a girl's, and of the same swipe becoming entangled in a horse's skeleton in the moonlight as he is pursued by Negroes intending rape ("The Man Who Became a Woman") are the gestures of Oscar Wilde, or more ludicrously, of Lautréamount rather than of Mark Twain. Anderson took from Twain a character and a tone. His boys and men are first Sherwood Anderson, and second Huck Finn. The tone, however, is violated by the persistent brooding, the search for the pastoral past, and the foggy, half-baked philosophizing that characterizes Anderson's indifferent average in fiction.

John McCormick. *The Middle Distance* (Free). 1971. pp. 22–3

BIBLIOGRAPHY
Windy McPherson's Son, 1916 (n); *Marching Men*, 1917 (n); *Mid-American Chants*, 1918 (p); *Winesburg, Ohio*, 1919 (s); *Poor White*, 1920 (n); *The Triumph of the Egg*, 1921 (s); *Many Marriages*, 1923 (n); *Horses and Men*, 1923 (s); *A Story Teller's Story*, 1924 (a); *Dark Laughter*, 1925 (n); *The Modern Writer*, 1925 (c); *Sherwood Anderson's Notebook*, 1926 (misc); *Tar, A Midwest Childhood*, 1926 (n); *A New Testament*, 1927 (p); *Hello Towns!* 1929 (e); *Nearer the Grass Roots*, 1929 (t); *The American County Fair*, 1930 (e); *Perhaps Women*, 1931 (e); *Beyond Desire*, 1932 (n); *Death in the Woods*, 1933 (s); *No Swank*, 1934 (e); *Puzzled America*, 1935 (e); *Kit Brandon*, 1936 (n); *Plays, Winesburg and Others*, 1937 (e); *Home Town*, 1940 (t); *Memoirs*, 1942; *The Sherwood Anderson Reader*, 1948; *The Portable Sherwood Anderson*, 1949, ed. Horace Gregory, 1972; *Letters of Sherwood Anderson*, 1953; *Return to Winesburg*, 1967 (misc, j); *Sherwood Anderson's Memoirs*, rev. ed., 1969; *The Buck Fever Papers*, ed. Welford Dunaway Taylor, 1971 (e); *Marching Men: A Critical Text*, ed. Ray Lewis White, 1972 (n); *Sherwood Anderson–Gertrude Stein*, 1973 (l, e); *Alice and The Lost Novel*, 1975 (n); *The "Writer's Book": A Critical Edition*, ed. Martha Mulroy Curry, 1975; *The Teller's Tales*, ed. Frank Gado, 1983 (s); *Selected Letters*, ed. Charles E. Modlin, 1984; *Letters to Bab: Sherwood Anderson to Marietta D. Finley, 1916–33*, ed. William A. Sutton, 1985; *The Sherwood Anderson Diaries, 1936-1941*, ed. Hilbert H. Campbell, 1987; *Sherwood Anderson: Early Writings*, ed. Ray Lewis White, 1989; *Sherwood Anderson's Love Letters to Eleanor Copenhaver Anderson*, ed. Charles E. Modlin, 1989; *Sherwood Anderson's Secret Love Letters: For Eleanor, A Letter a Day*, ed. Ray Lewis White, 1991; *Certain Things Last: The Selected Short Stories of Sherwood Anderson*, ed. Charles E. Modlin, 1992; *Winesburg, Ohio: Authoritative Text, Backgrounds and Contexts, Criticism*, ed. Charles E. Modlin and Ray Lewis White, 1996; *Southern Odyssey: Selected Writings by Sherwood Anderson*, ed. Welford Dunaway Taylor and Charles E. Modlin, 1997; *Sherwood Anderson's "Winesburg, Ohio": With Variant Readings and Annotations*, ed. Ray Lewis White, 1997; *The Egg and Other Stories*, ed. Charles E. Modlin, 1998

ANGELOU, Maya (1928–)

"What are you looking at me for? I didn't come to stay . . ." With these words—from a poem that she stumbled over during a church recital—Maya Angelou opens her autobiography [*I Know Why the Caged Bird Sings*] and conveys the diminished sense of herself that pervaded much of her childhood. The words were painfully appropriate. She and her brother were shuttled back and forth between their mother in the North and grandmother in the small town of Stamps, Ark. When she was 8, she was raped. She appeared in court, failed to tell the whole truth and, after her assailant was found dead, concluded that her words could kill. She retreated to silence. "Just my breath, carrying my words out, might poison people . . . I had to stop talking."

Yet, her few years of almost complete silence—she continued to speak to her brother Bailey—actually served her well; Miss Angelou—a former dancer, director and television scriptwriter who is now at work on her second novel—clearly heard, saw, smelled, tasted and seized hold of all the sounds and sights around her. Her autobiography regularly throws out rich, dazzling images which delight and surprise with their simplicity. . . .

But Miss Angelou's book is more than a tour de force of language or the story of childhood suffering: it quietly and gracefully portrays and pays tribute to the courage, dignity and endurance of the small, rural Southern black community in which she spent most of her early years in the 1930s.

Robert A. Gross. *Newsweek*. March 2, 1970, pp. 90, 90B

In [the] primal scene of childhood which opens Maya Angelou's *I Know Why the Caged Bird Sings*, the black girl child testifies to her imprisonment in her bodily prison. She is a black ugly reality, not a whitened dream. And the attendant self-consciousness and diminished self-image throb through her bodily prison until the bladder can do nothing but explode in a parody of release (freedom).

In good autobiography the opening, whether a statement of fact such as the circumstance of birth or ancestry or the recreation of a primal incident such as Maya Angelou's, defines the strategy of the narrative. The strategy itself is a function of the autobiographer's self-image at the moment of writing, for the nature of that self-image determines the nature of the pattern of self-actualization he discovers while attempting to shape his past experiences. Such a pattern must culminate in some sense of an ending, and it is this sense of an ending that informs certain earlier moments with significance and determines the choice of what experience he recreates, what he discards. In fact the earlier moments are fully understood only after that sense of an ending has imposed itself upon the material of the autobiographer's life. Ultimately, then, the opening moment assumes the end, the end the opening moment. Its centrality derives from its distillation of the environment of the self which generated the pattern of the writer's quest after self-actualization. . . . Her genius as a writer is her ability to recapture the texture of the way of life in the texture of its idioms, its idiosyncratic vocabulary and especially in its process of image-making. The imagery holds the reality, giving it immediacy. That she chooses to recreate the past in its own sounds suggests to the reader that she accepts the past and recognizes its beauty and its ugliness, its assets and its liabilities, its strength and its weakness. Here we witness a return to and final acceptance of the past in the return to and full acceptance of its language, the language a symbolic construct of a way of life. Ultimately Maya Angelou's style testifies to her reaffirmation of self-acceptance, the self-acceptance she achieves within the pattern of the autobiography.

Sidonie A. Smith. *Southern Humanities Review*. Fall, 1973, pp. 366–67, 375

I Know Why the Caged Bird Sings creates a unique place within black autobiographical tradition, not by being ''better'' than the formidable autobiographical landmarks described, but by its special stance toward the self, the community, and the universe, and by a form exploiting the full measure of imagination necessary to acknowledge both beauty and absurdity.

The emerging self, equipped with imagination, resourcefulness, and a sense of the tenuousness of childhood innocence, attempts to foster itself by crediting the adult world with its own estimate of its god-like status and managing retreats into the autonomy of the childhood world when conflicts develop. Given the black adult's necessity to compromise with prevailing institutions and to develop limited codes through which nobility, strength, and beauty can be registered, the areas where a child's requirements are absolute—love, security, and consistency—quickly reveal the protean character of adult support and a barely concealed, aggressive chaos. . . .

A good deal of the book's universality derives from black life's traditions seeming to mirror, with extraordinary intensity, the root uncertainty in the universe. The conflict with whites, of course, dramatizes uncertainty and absurdity with immediate headline graphicness. What intensifies the universalism still more is the conflict between the sensitive imagination and reality, and the imagination's ability sometimes to overcome. Maya and her brother have their reservoir of absurd miming and laughter, but sometimes the imagination is caught in pathos and chaos, although its values are frequently superior. . . .

The major function of the imagination, however, is to retain a vigorous dialectic between self and society, between the intransigent world and the aspiring self. Through the dialectic, the egos maintain themselves, even where tragic incident triumphs. In a sense, the triumph of circumstance for Maya becomes a temporary

halt in a process which is constantly renewed, a fact evident in the poetic language and in the mellowness of the book's confessional form. . . .

The uniqueness of *I Know Why* arises then from a full imaginative occupation of the rhythms flowing from the primal self in conflict with things as they are, but balanced by the knowledge that the self must find its own order and create its own coherence.

George E. Kent. *Kansas Quarterly*. Summer, 1975, pp. 75, 78

When Maya Angelou speaks of ''survival with style'' and attributes survival to the work of artists, she is talking about a function of art similar to that described by Ralph Ellison. . . .

Such an affirmation of life, a humanizing of reality, is Maya Angelou's answer to the question of how a Black girl can grow up in a repressive system without being maimed by it. Art protects the human values of compassion, love, and innocence, and makes the freedom for the self-realization necessary for real survival. Her answer, like Ellison's, skirts the reformer's question: is ''the cost of that style'' too high? In this sense she and Ellison are religious writers rather than social ones, for their ultimate concern is self-transcendence. It is unlikely that either would deny the practical value of the past twenty years' progress toward attainment of Negroes' full citizenship in America. But ultimately, as artists, their concern is with the humanity which must survive, and even assimilate into its own creative potential, such restrictions as these writers have encountered. For if this humanity cannot survive restriction, then it will itself become assimilated to the roles imposed upon it.

Myra K. McMurry. *South Atlantic Bulletin*. 41, 2, 1976, pp. 110–11

Maya Angelou . . . has achieved a kind of literary breakthrough which few writers of any time, place, or race achieve. Moreover, since writing *The Caged Bird Sings*, she has done so with stunning regularity, in *Gather Together in My Name*, in *Singin' and Swingin' and Gettin' Merry Like Christmas*. Now comes her uproarious, passionate, and beautifully written *The Heart of a Woman*, equal in every respect to *Gather Together in My Name* and only a shade off the perfection of her luminous first volume. As with any corpus of high creativity, exactly what makes Angelou's writing unique is more readily appreciated than analyzed and stated. It is, I think, a melding of unconcerned honesty, consummate craft, and perfect descriptive pitch, yielding a rare compound of great emotional force and authenticity, undiluted by polemic. . . .

Her ability to shatter the opaque prisms of race and class between reader and subject is her special gift.

David Levering Lewis. *Book World*. Oct. 4, 1981, p. 1

A journey that began in Stamps, Arkansas, has taken her to strange places in search of her self and a place that she can call home. It ends in Africa with the recognition that a person is not complete until she locates herself fully in her time (history) and her place (geography). The recognition of a self and the acceptance of one's place, no matter how grievous or repulsive its legacy, is the ultimate refuge of life—hence the celebration we encounter at the end of the text and the reason that God's children need traveling shoes. . . .

In 1970, when Angelou and Toni Morrison produced their first books, they were concerned with what it meant to be black and female in America. By 1986, they had enlarged their concerns to ask what it meant to be a black person in America, given the social, political, and economic constraints which mitigate against such development. Morrison's *Tar Baby* suggests that the black presence in America functions to prick America's unconscious (a 1981 "Benito Cereno" updated) and, like Maya Angelou, really begins to attack the ideological structures that keep these inhuman relations in place. The relationship that takes place between Jadine and son in the novel moves toward a recovery of the equilibrium between the Afro-American male and female that seem to be scuttled in most of the works of the 1970s and early 1980s.

There is a clarity, truth, and beauty that inform the autobiographical statement of Angelou and the particularity of her experiences that are collapsed back into the general experiences of her people. Her search for roots, her involvement with the politics of her people in the United States and Africa, give her work a depth that is absent in many other such works. For Angelou, as for Morrison, the pain and suffering of black women flow like tributaries into the rivers of their general pain, with the poignant demand that the black male be cognizant of their special pains. Theirs is a pain that possesses its own particularities.

Selwyn R. Cudjoe, "The Autobiographical Self Updated." In Henry Louis Gates, Jr., ed. *Reading Black, Reading Feminist* (New York: Meridian, 1990), pp. 301, 303–4

The promise of Africa, the part it plays in the construction of the Afro-American self, and the attempt to determine where the Afro-American belongs are the central concerns of *All God's Children*. To be sure, there is the recognition that "years of bondage, brutalities, the mixture of other bloods, customs and language had transformed us into an unrecognizable tribe" or that "an airline ticket to Africa would [not] erase the past and open wide the gates to a perfect future." Yet there is the major dilemma that many Afro-Americans faced in the 1960s: the recognition that they were cut off from the continuity of their past and hence were compelled to search for roots to supplement that loss. Angelou acknowledges her envy of those Africans who had remained on the continent and retained their culture intact. Even though they had been exploited by European colonialism they could still "reflect through their priests and chiefs on centuries of continuity." . . .

To the Afro-American, Africa remains a double-edged symbol, signifying the ancestral home and a sense of continuity, while America remains home, the site of a million humiliations. . . .

The five volumes of the autobiography offer numerous excellent examples of Angelou's skillful use of comic irony in describing her relationships with people. A sympathetic irony in dealing with other Blacks has characterized some of the most outstanding work in the Black American literary tradition from Douglass's *Narrative*, to Ralph Ellison's *Invisible Man* and the work of more recent Black writers like William Melvin Kelley, Ishmael Reed, Toni Cade Bambara, and Toni Morrison.

However, Angelou's effective use of self-parody is something new in Black autobiography and, thus, creates a unique place in Black autobiographical tradition. Through numerous excellent

examples of self-parody, in the first four volumes particularly, Angelou reveals her youthful silliness, her loneliness, her pretensions, her aspirations, and her instability. While most people encounter life, learn from experiences, and assume a more or less fixed set of postures toward reality, Angelou is unable to settle into security—not merely because life forces her to assume various roles, not merely because life whirls her along, but because, like the picaresque heroine, she is simply unable to keep to a set course. Angelou constantly lets go of the outer stability she sometimes finds because of the need for a vital tension between stability and instability. From the perspective of adulthood, she is able to parody this quality in her younger self for the purpose of analyzing that self. . . .

Yet nothing in Angelou's prose—not even the parody of self—is merely humorous for the sake of laughter. Behind the laughter is a vision of human weakness, an empathy for people's foibles and their efforts to retain some semblance of dignity in the midst of the ridiculous. One of the values of Angelou's autobiography is to be found in the fact that from *Caged Bird* to *Traveling Shoes*, through all of the experiences recreated and the observations recorded, the work remains both sensitive and poised, humorous and empathetic, realistic and unembittered.

Dolly A. McPherson. *Order Out of Chaos: The Autobiographical Works of Maya Angelou* (New York: Peter Lang, 1990), pp. 124–125

Perhaps it is fitting that we know so little about Maya's recent personal life. Certainly, after revealing, sometimes in painful detail, forty years of her life, she deserves some privacy. But more importantly, this lack of information makes us focus on her working life, on what she has accomplished as an artist—it is a breathtaking view of the talents of a creative and prodigious woman.

Maya's early lectures in the late 1960s and early 1970s were part of the black consciousness movement that was sweeping the nation. With the assassination of Martin Luther King, Jr., in 1968, blacks needed people who could speak about black cultural contributions to American society. Maya, along with many others, was able to translate black experience and reveal its richness. At the University of California at Los Angeles (UCLA), she articulated the blacks' contributions to American culture. . . .

These lectures, however, were not Maya's main endeavor. Play and screenwriting were taking up most of her creative energies. One of Maya's earliest and most successful writing projects was the screenplay *Georgia, Georgia* (1972). The story is about a black singer who tours Sweden and becomes fascinated by the white culture. Her companion, another black woman, angrily counters her friend's attraction to white society. Maya wrote the play as an attempt to portray black woman as they really are.

She has also spread her writing talents into television. In 1968, National Educational Television in San Francisco produced a ten-show series she wrote called *Black, Blues, Black*, which shows how African cultural traditions have influenced American life. Maya combined music, dance, drama, and narrative to show viewers how strongly African culture has permeated our daily lives.

Sister, Sister was a major television program Maya did for NBC in 1978. The two-hour program was a milestone for blacks in television because it was drama. There were comedy programs that featured blacks, but there was no serious drama at the time. . . .

With the success of *I Know Why the Caged Bird Sings*, Maya was able to begin publishing her poetry. Since 1971, she has published six volumes of her poems. Her latest book, *I Shall Not Be Moved*, was published in 1990. Many people feel that Maya's greatest strength as a writer lies in her prose, not her poetry. Her best poems use the speech patterns and rhythms of the black culture and contain the same energy and liveliness that her prose does. . . . Many critics feel that Maya's poetry can only be truly appreciated when it is read aloud by the poet herself. Her dramatic talents bring out the tension and sharp cadences in the poems, which the silent printed words cannot begin to convey.

Nancy Shuker. *Maya Angelou* (New York: Silver Burdett, 1990), pp. 108–10, 113–14

BIBLIOGRAPHY
I Know Why the Caged Bird Sings, 1970 (a); *Just Give Me a Cool Drink of Water 'Fore I Diiie*, 1971 (p); *Gather Together in My Name*, 1974 (a); *Oh Pray My Wings Are Gonna Fit Me Well*, 1975 (p); *Singin' and Swingin' and Gettin' Merry Like Christmas*, 1976 (a); *And Still I Rise*, 1978 (p); *Poems*, 1981; *The Heart of a Woman*, 1981 (a); *Shaker, Why Don't You Sing?*, 1983 (p); *All God's Children Need Traveling Shoes*, 1986 (p); *Poems: Maya Angelou*, 1986; *Now Sheba Sings the Song*, 1987 (p); *Conversations*, 1989 (r, i.e., interviews); *I Shall Not Be Moved*, 1990 (p); *On the Pulse of Morning*, 1993 (p); *Wouldn't Take Nothing for My Journey Now*, 1993 (p); *Complete Collected Poems*, 1994; *Phenomenal Woman*, 1994 (p); *My Painted House, My Friendly Chicken, and Me*, 1995 (juv); *Even the Stars Look Lonesome*, 1997 (e)

ASHBERY, John (1927–)

John Ashbery is one of the most original of contemporary poets. His four books of poems . . . are full of startling metaphors and fresh juxtapositions of words and perceptions. He keeps pushing the limits of language; he lives on the most thinly held, the most dangerous, frontiers. His impatience with the merely remembered phrase is evident in every line, though he occasionally uses a cliché to evoke a standard response which he then swamps with irony. He is not without antecedents and influences, however. He has gone to school to Wallace Stevens, from whom he gets both elegance and a furious concentration; to the French Surrealist poets, who have taught him to find fresh images in immersions in the subconscious; and to the "action" painters of the New York School of the 1950s, who have taught him to work with abandon at his canvas and to pray for happy accidents. But his voice is unmistakably his own; it is a voice that does not falter in a world of discontinuities.

Stephen Stepanchev. *American Poetry since 1945* (Harper), 1965. pp. 188–9

I assume that Mr. Ashbery's concern is to give the process of the mind as it moves through reflections, not merely the results of reflection. It is an extreme version of the common distinction between "a mind speaking" and "what is being said". But it is a

dangerous aesthetic, an inescapable temptation to bad work. When the dark is light enough, Mr. Ashbery writes with remarkable delicacy and ease, the meditation a lovely "wooing both ways" between landscape and mind. . . But the price is high, the subjective mode exorbitant.

Denis Donoghue. *New York Review of Books*. April 14, 1966. p. 19

John Ashbery is the Sphinx of the generation [of 1962]. Not only are all of his poems enigmas or simply impossible to understand but they appear to promise esoteric wisdom one finds nowhere else in American poetry. Fellow poets, critics and students admit to despair at ever discovering the key (if one exists) to the riddle of the poems in *The Tennis Court Oath* (1962) and *Rivers and Mountains* (1966). . . .

One quality most of Ashbery's poems share, on the other hand, is something like the peculiar excitement one feels when stepping with Alice behind the Looking Glass into a reality bizarre yet familiar in which the "marvelous" is as near as one's breakfast coffee cup or one's shoes being shined by an angel in the barbershop. In an Ashbery poem the marvelous is, in fact, the cup and the shoes—and the angel. His gift is to release everyday objects, experiences and fragments of dream or hallucination from stereotypes imposed on them by habit or preconception or belief: he presents the world as if seen for the first time. But the problem is: each poem is the first time in its own way unlike any past or future Ashbery poem. One way to read an Ashbery poem, it seems to me, might be to remember all one has felt or learned about poetry, including his poems—and then forget it and let the poem at hand do its own work.

Paul Carroll. *The Poem in Its Skin* (Follett). 1968. pp. 207–8

Like many folk tales, the idylls of Theocritus, the "Alice" books, *The Importance of Being Earnest*, the novels of Firbank and P. G. Wodehouse, *A Nest of Ninnies* is a pastoral; the world it depicts is an imaginary Garden of Eden, a place of innocence from which all serious needs and desires have been excluded.

It is possible, I think, that in our time pastoral is the genre best suited to pure fiction. . . .

A young novelist who is attracted by the pastoral should be warned, however, that it is extremely difficult to do well. I am not surprised to learn that, though *A Nest of Ninnies* is only 191 pages long, it took Messrs. Ashbery and Schuyler several years to write. Their patience and artistry has been well rewarded. I am convinced that their book is destined to become a minor classic.

W. H. Auden. *New York Times Book Section*. May 4, 1969. p. 20

Some Trees is made up of poems which display a great deal of irresponsible yet often engaging imagination. With one half of the mind feeling like a mystified but somehow willing accomplice, and the other half becoming more and more skeptical, one follows the bright, faddish jargon Ashbery talks with considerable obscure brightness, trying patiently, with some engagement, to decide which of several possible meanings each poem intends. The poems have over them a kind of idling arbitrariness, offering their elements as a profound conjunction of secrecies one can't quite define or evaluate. One doesn't feel, however, that Mr. Ashbery has been at great pains to fabricate these puzzles; on the contrary, this manner of writing seems perfectly natural to him, which must, I suppose, qualify him as an original of some sort. . . .

Though Mr. Ashbery enjoys a real facility with language, and is able to handle difficult forms, like the pantoum and the sestina, with remarkable ease, his poems amount to nothing more than rather cute and momentarily interesting games, like those of a gifted and very childish child who, during "creative play period," wrote a book of poems instead of making finger paintings. [1957]

James Dickey. *Babel to Byzantium* (Grosset). 1971. pp. 58–60

Ashbery's impressive talents, serving so brilliant and skeptical a mind, make for a difficult poetry; and it would be condescending to his accomplishment, as well as disingenuous, to ignore the difficulty. In his intense explorations into the fictions not only of an essential self but also of an essential art, Ashbery's discontinuous meditations often become intensely private, and at times inaccessible. As with earlier "visionary" poets like Blake and of course the later Stevens, with whom Ashbery is often linked and from whom he happily steals in a poem like "Chateau Hardware," it sometimes happens that the world of familiar objects and relations recedes. "You" designates a somewhat solipsistic "I," and everyone and everything else becomes a dimly-perceived "them" and "it." On these occasions, Ashbery's poetry runs the risk of vanishing into the imagined world of its own favorite dream, the risk of consulting only with its own motions, as its ideas and tones constantly dissolve into and out of one another like a beautiful drift of clouds. It's as if, sometimes, the poetry were so private and self-sufficient that it could dispense with the irksome necessity of an audience. . . .

It's exhilarating to watch Mr. Ashbery maintain his precarious balance on an "esthetic ideal" which seems to be raised higher with each new book. The latest, *Three Poems* (three extended meditations in prose), will excite aficionados of his work, but it probably won't, as an introduction, win him new converts.

Alan Helms. *Partisan Review*. Fall, 1972. pp. 624–5

Of the American poets now in mid-career, those born in the decade 1925–1935, John Ashbery and A. R. Ammons seem to me the strongest. . . . Ashbery goes back through Stevens to Whitman, even as Ammons is a more direct descendant of American Romanticism in its major formulation, which remains Emerson's. Otherwise, these two superb poets have nothing in common except their authentic difficulty. Ammons belongs to no school, while Ashbery can be regarded either as the best poet by far of the "New York School" or—as I would argue—so unique a figure that only confusion is engendered by associating him with Koch, O'Hara, Schuyler and their friends and disciples. . . .

The Coda of "The Recital" [in *Three Poems*] is a wholly personal apologia, with many Whitmanian and Stevensian echoes, some of them involuntary. . . . Against the enemy, who is an amalgam of time and selfishness, Ashbery struggles to get beyond his own solipsism, and the limits of his art. On the final page, an Emersonian-Stevensian image of saving transparence serves to

amalgamate the new changes Ashbery meets and welcomes. This transparence movingly is provided by a Whitmanian vision of an audience for Ashbery's art: "There were new people watching and waiting, conjugating in this way the distance and emptiness, transforming the scarcely noticeable bleakness into something both intimate and noble." So they have and will, judging by the response of my students and other friends, with whom I've discussed Ashbery's work. By more than 15 years of high vision and persistence he has clarified the initial prophecy of his work, until peering into it we can say: "We see us as we truly behave" and, as we can see, we can think: "These accents seem their own defense."

Harold Bloom. *Salmagundi*. Spring-Summer, 1973. pp. 103, 131

The first few books by John Ashbery contained a large proportion of a poetry of inconsequence. Borrowing freely from the traditions of French surrealism, and from his friends Frank O'Hara and Kenneth Koch, Ashbery tried out a fairly narrow range of voices and subjects. Subject matter, or rather the absence of it, helped form the core of his aesthetic, an aesthetic that refused to maintain a consistent attitude toward any fixed phenomena. The poems tumbled out of a whimsical, detached amusement that mixed with a quizzical melancholy. This aesthetic reached an extreme with *The Tennis Court Oath* (1962), a book in which no poem makes even the slightest attempt to marshal a rational context or an identifiable argument. Line follows line without the sheerest hint of order or apparent plan; this studied inconsequence delighted some readers at the time. But this is not a book to reread; seeing it outside the context of rebellion against the too-conscious aesthetic then fostered by academic poetry, it is difficult to understand why the book was published. . . . But reading the first four books together, one is struck by how precious are those poems that do make poetic sense, surrounded as they are by the incessant chatter of the poems of inconsequence. Slowly, however, it appears as if Ashbery was gaining confidence for his true project, and, as his work unfolds, an indulgent reader can see how it needed those aggressively banal "experiments" in nonsense to protect its frailty. Ashbery's later poetry often uses the traditions of prose discourse, but instead of a poetry of "statement" he has evolved a most tenuous, unassertive language. The first four books, one feels, would have turned out insufferably banal, or perhaps would have remained altogether unwritten, if Ashbery had faced his subject directly or made too various or rigorous demands on his limited language. . . .

What stands behind Ashbery's rather sudden succès d'estime is the triumph of a poetic mode. A mode demands less aesthetic energy than a truly individual style but usually offers more gratification than the average school or "movement." Ashbery's mode has what most modes have, a distinctive blend of sensibility, verbal texture, and thematic concerns. In each of these categories, or elements, a mode must not become too rigid; its sensibility cannot turn into a set of static attitudes, its verbal texture cannot be reducible to simple matters of vocabulary and verse forms, and its thematic concerns must allow for a range of subjects. Successful modes, then, thrive on their distinctiveness, their ability to be set off against a larger, more public set of expectations. But the moment this distinctiveness becomes too rigid, the mode slips into self-parody, consciously or unconsciously. Just when and how a mode calcifies (or what is less likely, fails to achieve a distinctive feel) is hard for literary historians to measure precisely, especially in contemporary literature.

Charles Molesworth. *The Fierce Embrace: A Study of Contemporary American Poetry* (Univ. of Missouri Pr., 1979), pp. 163, 181

Ashbery's best work, like the paintings of Jasper Johns, seems an intelligent if dark confrontation with the forces of the given. For Johns, the given may be an alphabet, target, flag, or map. For Ashbery, it is the world of degraded and charming cliché, doggerel, bad taste, Hollywood convention, newspaper prose, literary pietism, and metaphysical jargon. The central metaphysical-moral component in Ashbery's verse is its deadly withdrawal of the transcendental term and insistence on individual liberty. His image of the world does not lead to a hedonism pursued along the lines of an American pragmatic, though his ideas are as clear as a pragmatist's. . . . Ashbery's poetry, moreover, leads, as we have seen, through an excruciating evaluation of the possible consolations, cognitive and sensual, that are available. The poem is a difficulty, a resistance, and a critique. The final consolation for the poet may be, as with Stevens, the imagination. An imagination not of fragrance or of stippled sensibility nor of a late, bare, philosophical, and perhaps deluded penetration to *realia*, as in early and late Stevens. The imagination in Ashbery speaks of a constantly agitated *agon*. . . .

Man is locked in the unintelligible or barely intelligible labyrinth of language; one's art is forced to remain repetitive and solipsistic, and yet somehow adventurous. In discontinuous streams, in mistranslations, in suburban resentments and urban uncertainties, in action poetry, Ashbery leads ambiguity to the verge of nonsense and keeps it satisfactorily unredeemed.

David Shapiro. *John Ashbery: An Introduction to the Poetry* (Columbia Univ. Pr., 1979), pp. 12–13

No volume of Ashbery's is more crucially transitional than *The Double Dream of Spring* (1970). There are some poems in *Rivers and Mountains* (1966) that could have found a place in the later book: "These Lacustrine Cities" and "A Blessing in Disguise," to name two. But *The Double Dream of Spring* as a whole inaugurates a style, a mode of discourse—meditative, less harshly elliptical— that sets it off from the earlier volumes and creates a rhetoric for the subsequent poems to continue, but also to violate. (The poems of *Houseboat Days* [1977] seem to indicate an intention on Ashbery's part to complicate the style in the direction of a return to the elliptical mode.) More important, *The Double Dream of Spring* assumes a stance that Ashbery's later books have not repudiated— that of the poet of high imagination, the visionary. The stance is crossed with obliquity, no doubt: but its presence is undeniable and still astonishing to witness. We can say that in the densely charged lyrics of *The Double Dream*, and especially in its magnificent long poem "Fragment," Ashbery comes into his own and into his inheritance. . . .

Much of the difficulty readers have with Ashbery stems from problems in gauging his tone. The difficulty intensifies when it becomes a question of determining whether or not he is parodying a traditional literary *topos*. This way of posing the reader's alternatives sets up the question in a misleading way, although I think that

many readers do pose these terms in oppositional fashion. I think that seasoned readers of Ashbery learn not to demand of his poems that they move in a univocal direction: he can both parody and mean "seriously" at the same time, he both sees and revises simultaneously. At times he appears to war against the very idea of received tradition, even while acknowledging, by his refusal to give them up, that the old tropes embody a storehouse of poetic wisdom still alive for us today.

Charles Berger. In *Beyond Amazement: New Essays on John Ashbery*, ed. David Lehman (Cornell Univ. Pr., 1980), pp. 164–65

Ashbery delivers a universality attained primarily by chastening his English by placing it at one remove, trusting in its skeletal communicativeness. There is a kind of homeliness to the landscape of the poem, an assumption that elements of landscape are self-evident and self-evidently connected to the ways. . . "we live our lives" (a listing without further syntactical qualification suffices in both languages). Human history, despite our current urbanity, retains an anational quality: we recognize human archetypes and can concede to be part of the "we" that cannot help but read human import into landscape irrespective of the language used to represent it. Waves, wheat fields, forests, paths, stone towers, great urban centers are elemental icons in a sense, "things which translate without ambiguity," things whose aura of cultural particularity, if it exists at all, is a distant second to more important affinities across cultures and across languages.

Sara L. Lunquist. *Contemporary Literature*. Fall, 1991, pp. 410–11, 414

Flow Chart will rank as the culmination of Ashbery's obsession with the vital mechanics of literary tradition, the mysterious processes whereby poems and poets get saved, carried across time, repeated in different climates. He has always had explicit designs upon the canon, as Harold Bloom put it in his reading of "Wet Casements" and "Tapestry," an explicitness plaited in lines of the quirkiest subtlety. For many volumes now, Ashbery has displayed a startling copiousness in his ways of describing those transactions between past and future, between precursor and reader/poet, performed by any poet intent on "stellification." This last word comes at the end of "Syringa," an Orphic ode on the subject of the singer's own survival. Its unforgettable conclusion lays out the forces at work in what is weakly called "canonization," a process Ashbery sees as both monumental and haphazard, willed and fortuitous. The great originals must be repeated with a difference in order to last. . . .

Flow Chart is almost maniacally self-allusive, which may be its truest form of autobiography. And whether or not it images the end as a resolution, it is a hauntingly valedictory poem. Nor does Ashbery seem to regard the end open-endedly. The poem is studded with words such as judgment, verdict, account, reckoning, award, terms for the posthumous brokering of reputations that we might call literary survival—a stronger word than tradition. Ashbery seems to be following [Wallace] Stevens (hardly a surprise) by inventing figures to describe, and perhaps control, that invisible process.

Charles Berger. *Raritan*. Spring, 1992, pp. 130–31

In the case of Ashbery's haibuns, most American readers will recognize neither traditional or vestigial form. At a loss for clear antecedent, readers could accurately describe each of Ashbery's haibuns as a prose poem plus cryptic one-liners without end punctuation. They might guess that Ashbery is doing something with a form he adopted or adapted, and they would be correct. The haibun is a Japanese form mixing prose and haiku. The most famed practitioner of the form was Basho, whose *Narrow Road to the Deep North*, a travel diary in the form of haibun, is readily available in English. . . .

One effect of Ashbery's use of the haibun is potentially educative. As in certain allusions of Eliot or reworkings of non-Western traditions in Pound, we are invited to become better informed readers as we ponder the relations between a contemporary text and its possible antecedents.

Paul Munn. *New Orleans Review*. Spring, 1992, pp. 19, 21–22

At a time when all the big themes—the gods, the hero, the artist-hero, truth, the imagination, the past redeemed, the utopian dream—are definitely lowercase, it would seem to require a certain hubris to write a very long poem. Yet John Ashbery's new book-length poem, *Flow Chart*, fills its 216 pages unabashed. Innocent of themes and unencumbered by the mandates of coherence and unity, this poem can be accused, at most, of the quantitative hubris of a journal kept for decades. It is, in fact, characterized by a qualitative humility, if the Ashberyan refusal to "mean" can be described as such.

Perhaps, as suggested by its title, *Flow Chart* is less a long poem than a diagram or chart, a grid laid down over an endless flow of disrupted ruminations, literary fragments, pseudoconversations, pieces of argument, and other language objects, inviting us to look for patterns but not guaranteeing that there are any. This grid could have been laid down over any segment of the flow, since its boundaries and center are arbitrary. It marks out big squares of language only provisionally for the purposes of observation. . . .

It is, of course, this collagist's taste for discontinuity, exacerbated by the presence of false syntactical connectives, such as the "as" and "unless". . . that makes for the famous "difficulty" of Ashbery (about whose brilliance *and* sanity I have no doubts). And it is interesting how different it is to negotiate this difficulty in a very long poem than in the shorter ones. For while it might be possible to explicate the shorter poems in some conventional way if one were perversely impelled to do so, the reader of *Flow Chart* really has no choice but to give up the struggle for comprehension as we know it and let the flow of language take over. This induces a kind of reading more like drifting than swimming.

Such a shift in poetic initiative from "ideas" in the poet's mind to something generated by the very nature of "language" itself has been one goal of an avant-garde project for poetry traceable at least back to Mallarmé, carried forward by the Dadaists, and embraced today by the language poets as well as by French-influenced academic literary criticism. This shift is also implicit, if less radically demanded, in definitions of poetry that emphasize its density, compression, and thus "opaqueness," relative to the "transparency" of expository prose. In other words, expository prose disappears as you read it, whereas the material presence of

poetry and poetic prose cannot (or should not) be escaped. From this point of view, *Flow Chart* is exemplary. Scrupulously maintaining its hard, impenetrable surface of language, it provides few openings for a fall into mere comprehension.

Indeed, this extraordinary surface itself becomes the central experience of the poem. The discontinuities that loom so large in Ashbery's shorter poems, each asking for comprehension, each foiling comprehension in its unique way, in *Flow Chart* almost disappear, becoming only a small repeating pattern within a larger seamlessness.

Evelyn Reilly. *Parnassus*. vols. 17, no. 2; 18, no. 1, (1993), pp. 40, 43

Every age adores a few poets in whose work posterity maintains no interest. James Henry Leigh Hunt in his own time enjoyed much greater popularity (and better connections) than did Keats. Longfellow, Whittier, Holmes, and Lowell were much more popular than their almost exact contemporaries Whitman and Dickinson. Already the sun is setting on Sandburg, Cummings, MacLeish, and others of our century's passing fancies. Like sycophants who rise and fall with the political leaders they serve, such poets rise and fall with the Zeitgeist they feed. John Ashbery is such a poet, adored by the age because he says what it wants to hear, but destined for obscurity when the times change. His latest book, *And the Stars Were Shining*, shows why.

The first poem in the collection typifies the book as a whole. Its title, "Token Resistance," resembles many of the others in being formulaic and empty. Some are clichés ("The Favor of a Reply"), some the names of banal objects ("Gummed Reinforcements"), some imitations of famous title ("On First Listening to Schreker's *Der Schatzgraber*"), and some are common phrases ("Well, Yes, Actually"). Ironically it is the closest Ashbery comes in this book to a successful poem, because its long list of titles (each as silly as those used in the rest of the book) ends with an abrupt change of tone. The simple title, "The Father," opens the possibility of emotional or intellectual connections all the other titles, in the poem and in the book, avoid. Ashbery tries to make the title a distinctive element of his style (as it is in Wallace Stevens, for instance), but by falling into formulae he only makes it a *flaw* of his style. . . .

I do not mean to exaggerate the case. *And The Stars Were Shining* is not without its musical passages, its well-conceived images and turns of phrases. . . . Still, a best-case assessment of this book would make Ashbery a garrulous, minor Eliot who never found the Pound to prune his *Waste Land* or an affected Thomas Wolfe minus the Maxwell Perkins who could make his homeward-looking angel melt with truth. Ashbery has succumbed to the "creation without toil" that Yeats called "the chief temptation of the artist."

H.L. Hix. *New Letters*. Spring, 1994, pp. 6, 14

BIBLIOGRAPHY

Turandot, and Other Poems, 1953; *Some Trees*, 1956 (p); *The Poems*, 1960; *The Heroes*, 1960 (d); *The Compromise*, 1960 (d); *The Tennis Court Oath*, 1962 (p); *Rivers and Mountains*, 1966 (p);

(with James Schuyler) *A Nest of Ninnies*, 1969 (n); *Fragment*, 1969 (p); *The Double Dream of Spring*, 1970 (p); *Three Poems*, 1972; *Self-Portrait in a Convex Mirror*, 1975 (p); *Houseboat Days*, 1977 (p); *Three Plays*, 1978; *As We Know*, 1979 (p); *Shadow Train*, 1981 (p); *Apparitions*, 1981 (p); *Fairfield Porter*, 1982 (c); *A Wave*, 1984 (p); *Selected Poems*, 1985; *Red Grooms, a retrospective 1956–1984*, 1985 (catalogue); *Jane Freilicher: Paintings*, 1986 (e); *April Galleons*, 1987 (p); *Selected Poems*, expanded ed., 1987; *Reported Sightings: Art Chronicles 1957–1987*, 1989 (c); *Three Poems*, 1989; *Flow Chart*, 1991 (p); *Pierre Reverdy: Selected Poems*, 1991 (tr); *Raymond Roussel: Selections from Certain of His Books*, 1991 (tr); *Giorgio de Chirico: Hebdomeros and Other Writings*, 1992 (tr); *Hotel Lautreamont*, 1992 (p); et al., *Private Seven*, 1992 (anthol); *Ellsworth Kelly: Plant Drawings*, 1993 (c); *Three Books*, 1993 (p); *And the Stars Were Shining*, 1994 (p); *Pierre Martory: The Landscape Is Behind the Door*, 1994 (tr); *Can You Hear, Bird*, 1995 (p); *The Mooring of Starting Out: The First Five Books of Poetry*, 1997; *Wakefulness*, 1998 (p)

ASIMOV, Isaac (1920–1992)

Four changes in [Isaac] Asimov's future worlds have been traced to changes in the political and social culture. First, the growing awareness of diversity within worldwide communism and the decline of the cold war tensions produced a change in Asimov's vision of future galactic politics. . . . The later novels allowed for the possibility of detente.

Second, the increased politicization of the 1960s seems to have led to a greater emphasis on domestic politics . . . with greater detail.

Third, the counterculture cry for increased participatory democracy is echoed in a discussion of democratic political systems in the later books, replacing the corrupt empires and theocratic, plutocratic, and oligarchic governments of the early works. In addition to discussions of legislatures and elected executives, democracy: a vision of a universe in which all matter is intelligent and participates in decisions which affect its future.

Finally, the enormous changes in the role of women over the past thirty years are reflected in the greater role given to women in the later novels. Women in the early Asimov novels are principally daughters or wives of important actors; in the later novels they are central characters—and often are important political or scientific figures. In the early novels they are naive, frivolous, and often simpleminded, but in the later novels they are ambitious, intelligent, and strong. Indeed, the progressive liberation of Gladia in the later Robot novels seems to mirror the progress of feminist organizations in American politics.

Clyde Wilcox. *Extrapolation*. Spring, 1990. pp. 61–62

[*Asimov's Chronology of Science & Discovery*] In his inimitable style, in which authoritativeness is balanced by a light and humorous touch. Asimov gives the reader a vivid feel for history and demonstrates how science has shaped the world. His book brilliantly conveys the excitement of science and its importance through the years. The accelerating pace of scientific progress is reflected in the increasing number of entries provided for every year beginning with 1793. The book makes us realize how recent are many of the scientific and technological developments that seem to have always been with us.

George B. Kauffman. *Science Teacher*. February, 1991. p. 72

The underlying message in all of Asimov's writings is one of thoroughgoing humanism. . . . In his view, the universe can have meaning only insofar as its magnificent interconnections can be sensed, interpreted, and analyzed by human intelligence.

He confronted the issue of supernaturally based religious claims in his typically direct fashion, noting that no evidence has been uncovered by science that in any way points to divine guidance in the workings of the universe. Nor is there evidence of the existence of a soul or any other immaterial essence that sets humans apart from other animals and departs at death. While admitting that this does not amount to proof that such entities do not exist, he reminded us that the same applies to the case of Zeus, Marduk, Thoth, and a myriad other supernatural beings. . . .

Asimov sounded a stark warning concerning the need for a this-world focus. He argued that humanity can no longer afford to seek refuge in the false security of supernatural fantasy, for continued reliance on heavenly solutions could kill us all. Just as it is human beings alone who are destroying the world, he said, so it must be we alone who save it.

Pat Duffy Hutcheon. *Humanist*. March, 1993. pp. 4–5

BIBLIOGRAPHY
Select Bibliography The Foundation Trilogy, 1974 (3 n); *100 Great Fantasy Short Stories*, 1984 (s); *The Alternate Asimovs*, 1986 (n); *Prelude to Foundation*, 1988 (n); *The Asimov Chronicles: 50 Years of Isaac Asimov*, 1989 (s); *Asimov on Science: A 30-Year Retrospective*, 1989 (m); *The Asimov's Chronology of Science & Discovery*, 1989 (e, h); *The Tyrannosaurus Prescription & 100 Other Essays*, 1989 (e); *Nightfall*, 1990 (n); *The Complete Stories*, vol. 1, 1990; *Robot Visions*, 1990 (n); *Foundation and Empire*, 1991 (n); *Second Foundation*, 1991 (n); *Forward the Foundation*, 1993 (n); *Magic: The Final Fantasy Collection*, 1995 (s); *Gold: The Final Science Fiction Collection*, 1995 (s); *Yours, Isaac Asimov: A Lifetime of Letters*, ed. Stanley Asimov, 1995 (l)

ATTAWAY, William (1911–1986)

William Attaway's *Blood on the Forge* was reissued in 1969, the same year that saw the renascence of Jean Toomer's *Cane*, as well as the publication of several significant novels by contemporary Afro-American writers, such as Paule Marshall's *The Chosen Place, The Timeless People* and Ishmael Reed's *Yellow Back Radio Broke—Down*. Attaway's important but ignored book about the three Moss brothers, who leave the depleted farmland of Kentucky for the steel mills of Pennsylvania, poignantly but realistically tells the story of one facet of the Great Black Migration on during the first World War.

Blood on the Forge was originally published in 1941, only one year after *Native Son*, but Attaway does not deal with whiteness in character and symbol in the same terms that Richard Wright used. Attaway eschews the stereotypical; his white characters, with the exception of the sheriff and "Boss" Johnston, are essentially complex and well-rounded figures. Nor is whiteness his central symbol. The steel mill is. Big Mat, Melody and Chinatown are seduced North by the promise of jobs and decent wages, but are gradually beaten down and stripped of their manhood by the uncompromising and brutal, man-eating monster, the steel mill. Behind the faceless monster is the white power structure, manipulating the lives of white immigrants and black unskilled workers— who are shipped in by cattle car, a disgusting and dehumanizing experience—for the sake of feeding the mill and filling their coffers. The bosses are never seen; their power is felt mainly through their undertaking to set white worker against black, deputize strikebreakers and generally control through fear or famine.

Racism as an omnipotent factor does not exist in the lives of the three brothers after they leave Kentucky. At least for a time. They are accepted by the Slavs, the Irish and the Italians with whom they work in the mill; they drink, gamble and whore together. As a friend, old Zanski warns that they'll never be happy until they send for their families—a man needs children in his home and a wife to put up curtains—he admonishes. In a word, stability. But few black workers move out of the bunkhouse. Their separation from their past—rootedness in the soil, the folk, religion, family—is almost as complete as that of their ancestors who traveled to a new and ugly life in the dark bellies of slave ships instead of airless boxcars. When Mat does finally set up "housekeeping," it is with Anna, the Mexican prostitute, who wants an "Americano" because she is tired of "peons." (Anna suffers from the delusion that all "Americanos" are rich, regardless of color.) The three brothers are systematically unmanned by the dehumanizing process of forging steel. Chinatown is blinded in an accident which eats up the lives of fourteen men; Melody's hand is smashed so that he is no longer able to play his guitar; Big Mat is killed during the strike in which he has become an unwitting tool the bosses wield against the white workers. Earlier his skill and strength earned him the approbation of his fellow workers and the title "Black Irish"; later he comes to be "hated by his fellow workers. He was a threat over their heads. The women covered their faces at the sight of him, the men spat; the children threw rocks. Always within him was that instinctive knowledge that he was being turned to white men's uses. So always with him was a basic distrust of a white. But now he was a boss. He was the law. After all, what did right or wrong matter in the case? Those thrilling new words were too much to resist. He was a boss, a boss over whites."

There is very little about the unionizing process that the black workers, including the Moss brothers, understand or identify with. The backbreaking hazardous work in the mill has been a kind of salvation for them. Having sharecropped all of their lives, always on the verge of starvation, they are neither shocked nor dismayed by the twelve-hour day in the mill. At least they get paid. They have not begun to think about the possibility of better working conditions—an eight-hour day, better wages, unions—a fact that the Northern industrialists well knew and used to their advantage in controlling the "socialist" oriented, organizing aspirations of the

white immigrants: "Big Mat was not thinking about the labor trouble. Yet he knew he would not join the union. For a man who had so lately worked from dawn to dark in the fields twelve hours and the long shift were not killing. For a man who had known no personal liberties even the iron hand of the mills was an advancement."

One of the things that drives the Moss brothers North is the impossibility of paying of a $40 debt to Mr. Johnston, the landowner to whom they are perpetually in debt. Fear of the control the white boss has over their very ability to stay alive is a given with the black sharecropper. It inspires Mat's hate: "Deep inside him was the familiar hatred of the white boss." There are only a few stereotypical characters in *Blood on the Forge*. Mr. Johnston, the Kentucky landowner, is a classic bigot, indigenous to the South, but interestingly enough, he uses the black sharecroppers against the white just as the bosses in the northern mill use the black workers against the immigrants. Johnston explains to Mat why he doesn't have white sharecroppers work his land: "well, they's three reasons: niggers ain't bothered with the itch; they knows how to make it the best way they kin and they don't kick none." They don't "kick" because they have no recourse. If their anger gets out of control, the resultant violence always turns against them. When Mat explodes in anger and fury, killing the mule that killed their mother in the fields, he puts them all in Johnston's debt to the point of starvation. They don't run because they have no place to go, and Johnston thinks he can keep them from getting the "itch" by manipulation and innuendo, an "old Master" tactic, in the plantation tradition: "My ridin' boss tells me there some jacklegs around, lyin' to the niggers about how much work they is up North. Jest you remember how I treat you and don't be took in by no lies."

They don't get taken in by northern lies; they leave because they know southern truths. One of these truths is never to look at or touch a white woman. Melody knows that Mat has "more sense than to talk to a white lady"; Chinatown agrees: "It's dangerous. . . .' member young Charley from over in the next county got lynched jest cause he stumble into one in the broad daylight." Another of those old-fashioned southern truths is never strike a white man a semi-lethal blow. When the riding boss refuses to give Big Mat the mule Johnston has promised him ("If Mr. Johnston got good sense you won't never git another mule. . . . You'd be run off the land if I had my say. Killin' a animal worth forty dollars,' cause a nigger woman got dragged over the rocks—"), Mat in a blind rage strikes him down. Realizing that the man will live "to lead the lynch mob against him," Mat and his brothers reluctantly leave the land they have worked so lovingly yet for so little reward.

The white line drawn about their lives in the South is straight, clear, immovable. The Moss brothers are powerless to effect change, to shift that boundary in any direction, but they understand their role in the schema and derive some satisfaction from a sense of belonging to the land. Big Mat is a powerful man who seems to draw strength from the soil's blackness which is like his own. When he goes North he becomes unmoored, confused by the change in the pattern, but he adapts to the work better than his brothers, better even than the whites. What he doesn't understand is that hate can be generated to meet the needs of new situations. When the white workers become politicized enough to strike, more blacks are shipped in, in boxcars, and the brothers remember, identify with those men—"bewildered and afraid in the dark, coming from hate into a new kind of hate." Bo, the only black foreman, knows the pattern—they only send for black men when there's trouble.

Big Mat is a tragic figure, reminiscent of the one slave on every plantation who refused to be whipped by the soul driver, a man of tremendous physical power and courage who could never be submissive. As developed by the early black fictionists, he becomes the black hero or the "bad nigger," feared by everyone. Big Mat has some of these characteristics, but in *Blood on the Forge* he is also an Othello-like figure, proud, jealous, and formidable. And his blackness is played off against a white Iago, a sneaky little boss-sheriff who manipulates him by appealing to his new-found sense of manhood. "Deputize this man," the sheriff says, "assign him his hours. He won't need a club. Just give him a couple of boulders. He'll earn his four dollars Monday." Actually the bosses save the four dollars. Mat destroys and is destroyed, as so many are in the struggle for steel. Most of Attaway's characters—black, white, all shades of ethnic groupings—are handled well. Many have real nuances of complexity, including the two brothers, Chinatown and Melody, who are left derelict at the end; Anna, the grasping but pathetic Mexican girl; Zanski's granddaughter Rosie, a union sympathizer who turns prostitute for the scabs in order to support the starving strikers in her family; and Smothers, the black prophet of doom, who understands that all men will have to pay for ravaging the earth: *"It's a sin to melt up the ground*, is what steel say. *It's a sin.* Sicel bound to git everybody 'cause o' that sin. They say I crazy, but mills gone crazy 'cause men bringin' trainloads of ground in here and meltin' it up."

One of the tragic outcomes in the novel is the loss of continuity in the lives of the men who are almost human sacrifices to the industrial Moloch created by an unseen hand grasping for profits. And that hand is white. If we used to think that free enterprise meant freedom to exploit all the resources of our country—both human and natural—to destroy the land and leave it in waste, we have since been forced to change our minds. There is something very timely in Attaway's implicit warning, as Edward Margolies suggests in his introduction to the 1969 edition of *Blood on the Forge:* "Possibly he [Attaway] saw his worst fears realized in the rapid spread of industrial wastelands and the consequent plight of urban Negroes. From one point of view his feelings about the sanctity of nature now seem almost quaint in an age of cybernetics. Yet given what we are told is the dangerous pollution of our environment, who can tell but that Attaway may not have been right?"

What is most interesting about the "rediscovery" of such novels as *Blood on the Forge* is their contemporaneity. We have now, some twenty-eight years later, reached the point of no return in our violation of the environment and of each other. Yet we are as unseeing as Chinatown and the soldier at the end of the novel— "blind men facing one another, not knowing."

Phyllis R. Klotman. *CLA Journal*. June 1972, pp. 459–64

Undoubtedly, Mississippi's best known native-born black writer is Richard Wright. Wright's reputation, which has grown steadily since the publication of his *Native Son* in 1940, is justly deserved. Yet over the years, Wright's achievement has tended to overshadow and obscure the work of other Mississippi-born black writers. One of them whose work deserves to be better known is William Attaway. His *Blood on the Forge* (1941) is an excellent novel which stands up well when compared with any other fiction dealing with blacks written during the past three decades. . . .

Attaway's first novel, *Let Me Breathe Thunder*, appeared in 1939. It is the tough and tender story of two young box car wanderers and their love for a little Mexican waif. The major characters, Ed and Step, are rootless white men faced by [a] hard, precarious reality, yet still capable of dreaming and caring. They represent the large numbers of young people who drifted about America during the difficult depression years of the 1930's. They live from day to day, waiting for nothing in particular. Ed and Step are not professional hoboes given to pointing out the "romance of the road"; their single object is to stay alive and keep moving. They support themselves through brief stretches of farm work.

During a stop in New Mexico, Ed and Step meet an inarticulate Mexican boy named Hi-Boy. His wistful and trusting way soon breaks through their casual, seemingly tough veneer. Ed and Step appoint themselves the boy's guardian and take him on the road as they continue their roaming. Hi-Boy becomes an outlet for their affection and for the tenderness missing from their rootless lives. For Ed and Step, Hi-Boy's welfare comes to take precedence over all else. Quite naturally, when a Yakima Valley rancher wants to take Hi-Boy permanently into his family, Ed and Step are torn between their own need for the boy and their concern for his future.

Attaway's *Let Me Breathe Thunder* has some of the emotional force and equality of the relationship between George and Lennie in John Steinbeck's *Of Mice and Men* (1937). Less ably written, the book would be melodramatic and overly sentimental. But the characterizations are sure, the dialogue is crisp and natural, and careful attention is given to physical detail. All told, *Let Me Breathe Thunder* is a solid first novel and makes the point that a black writer can deal successfully with a work made up primarily of white characters.

Published in 1941, Attaway's second and best novel, *Blood on the Forge*, is set for the most part in an Allegheny Valley steel-mill community during World War One. During and for several months after the end of the war, a manpower shortage existed in the West Virginia and Pennsylvania steel industry. Attracted by wages of four dollars a day, many Southern farm blacks moved north to work in the mills. To these black tenant farmers living in a state of near peonage, the low wages of steel workers seemed like true riches. The prospect of enjoying greater social freedom provided an additional inducement for deserting the land.

This northward migration of blacks looking for a better life in the mill towns created problems for northern employers and labor leaders. At the time, unions were engaged in initial efforts to organize the steel industry on a closed shop basis. When strikes resulted, the employers relied increasingly on black strike breakers. The unions consequently watched the black influx with growing anxiety. Many white workers came to fear that they might be permanently displaced by blacks who were willing to accept lower wages and poorer working conditions.

Set against this background, *Blood on the Forge* is the story of three black brothers—Mat, Chinatown and Melody Moss—who abandon their worn-out tenant farm in Kentucky's red clay hills to work in an Allegheny Valley . The novel thus has a double theme: blacks coming with whites in an abnormal condition of the labor alike and men of the soil attempting to adjust to modern industrial life.

Mat, the eldest brother, at first appears to be making an adjustment to his new environment better than his brothers. Heretofore, he had stoically coped with life through his own understanding of the Bible. In the mill, his tremendous physical strength gains him a respect he had never gotten in the South. But Mat's new-found self-confidence proves to be an illusion. Discarding his Bible, be finds that his virility is not enough to sustain him. It counts for little with Anna, his Mexican mistress, who dreams of becoming the mistress of a wealthy mill owner. Playing on Mat's false sense of himself, the owners easily turn him against his fellow workers as they attempt to organize.

Chinatown, the hedonist, fares worse than Mat. Delighting in the sense, he spends his pay on corn whiskey, dice, and women. He is utterly dependent on his brothers. Of the three, he is hit the hardest physically by the harsh life of the mill worker. Eventually, he is left blind by an explosion in the mill.

The third brother, Melody, survives best. A musician in the South, he is still something of a poet after his move northward. But his new environment renders him impotent. His old songs don't seem to have any meaning any more; he is unable to play his guitar. Yet even though he appears at best indifferent to the manipulation of his fellow blacks by both the owners and white workers, he does manage to come through his Northern experience, unlike his two brothers, in one piece, physically and mentally.

Throughout the novel, Attaway reveals that the blacks' dream of greater social freedom in the mill towns is largely delusive. Many of their fellow white workers—especially the Slav and Irish immigrants—hate them and see them as a threat. When the union organizers appear, the employers easily manipulate the black workers into their camp. The blacks, being convinced that they are the lowest group in the racial pecking order, see their only chance of continuing on the job as bending to the desire of the owners.

Yet Attaway does not simply single out the blacks as the sole victim of the unjust conditions which he vividly portrays. He shows the European immigrants and native whites working under and being exploited by the same system of low pay, long hours, and unnecessary hazards to life and limb. He compassionately shows the blighted dream of the immigrants for a new life in America.

In *Blood on the Forge*, Attaway has mined a rich vein of human experience. His outlook is not very optimistic in this work, but he writes about his people knowingly and with warm appreciation. At once, his main characters are likable, humorous, bewildered, and stout-hearted. The dialogue sounds completely authentic.

Unfortunately, Attaway has published only the two novels considered above. The best of these, *Blood on the Forge*, has only recently begun to receive the critical recognition it merits. Edward Margolies has noted [in the introduction to the Collier Books' edition of *Blood on the Forge*] one of the reasons why Attaway's novel was largely ignored when it was first published: ''Appearing one year after Richard Wright's sensational *Native Son*, Attaway's book may have looked tame to an America preparing for another war and whose reading public had already found its Negro 'spokes-man' in the virile Wright.'' In any event, a careful reading of *Blood on the Forge* leads one to believe that, excepting Wright's *Native Son*, it is the strongest of black novels dealing with the plight of blacks and racial violence written during the inter-war period.

    L. Moody Simms. *Notes on Mississippi Writers*. Spring, 1975, pp. 13–18.

BIBLIOGRAPHY
Carnival, 1935 (d); *Let Me Breathe Thunder*, 1939 (n); *Blood on the Forge*, 1941 (n); *Hear America Singing*, 1967 (nf)

AUCHINCLOSS, Louis (1917–)

In this novel (*Sybil*), his first, Mr. Auchincloss shows many faults. His style is rather flat, and at times even clumsy; he has a sharp eye, but seldom describes what he observes with quite enough flair or wit. His heroine, furthermore, is a little too sensitive to ring true, a little too much the faithful recorder of her creator's feelings and ideas.

In spite of its limitations, however, *Sybil* is one of the most promising American novels in a long time. This is because Mr. Auchincloss succeeds in giving us vivid portraits of nearly every one of the people in his story. . . . Mr. Auchincloss shows them no mercy, spares them none of their faults, and yet manages to give a little twist of tenderness, an unexpectedly sympathetic turn, to each of them.

    James Yaffe. *The Yale Review*. Spring, 1952. p. vi

Apart from his knowledge of the law, Mr. Auchincloss probably knows more about traditional New York City society than any other good novelist now working. Furthermore, he seems to believe in the continuing importance of what is left of such society, and the values it attempts to preserve and hand down. It is precisely the background of such belief that makes his satirical jibes so entertaining, and makes the rather neat, foursquare world of his books so comfortable to read about. *The Great World and Timothy Colt* appeals in part, perhaps unintentionally, to the escapist impulse; but it also shows how traditional writing methods and social attitudes can throw a refreshing light on parts of the contemporary scene.

    John Brooks. *New York Times Book Section*. Oct. 21, 1956. p. 50

Louis Auchincloss . . . has a direct acquaintance with investment banking and . . . has made himself a skilful craftsman. In several novels and a couple of collections of short stories he has written authoritatively and persuasively about a small but important segment of American business. . . . Auchincloss is a deft prober, and he shows us how a sense of inadequacy and guilt can be created and how it can shape a life. To me the psychological problem to which he addresses himself in *Venus in Sparta* is less interesting than the ethical problem with which he was concerned in his preceding novel, *The Great World and Timothy Colt*. In its portrayal of a particular milieu, however, of a world in which there not only is money but has been money for several generations, the novel demonstrates that Auchincloss knows his stuff and knows how to use it to literary advantage.

    Granville Hicks. *Saturday Review*. Sept. 20, 1958. p. 18

It is obviously high time someone pointed out that he is one of our very best young novelists. This is far more than a matter of his knowledge of ''the highest stratum of American society'' or his alleged resemblance to Edith Wharton. It is true that Mr. Auchincloss knows a good deal about the successful and indifferent children of the earth . . . these people he represents with such complete and quiet understanding that it is easy to overlook their horror and their ultimate pathos.

What moves Mr. Auchincloss is the miracle of the developing heart flourishing incongruously in the great world. . . . Their honesty is his comedy.

Arthur Mizener. *New York Times Book Section.* Sept. 21, 1958. p. 4

Auchincloss has tried less for dramatic effect in this [*The House of Five Talents*] than in some of his books. His choice of an old lady as narrator is a happy one, because there is something old-fashioned in his writing, some sympathy with the past, that makes him more at ease in looking at the world through the eyes of an older character. Then too he is at his best not so much when he is trying for the big scenes as when his work is more essayistic—a brooding description of a family portrait by Sargent or the list of an old aunt's favorite topics of conversation. In some of his novels his presentation of characters is so much better than their actions that a reader who believes in them hardly believes in what they do, but in *The House of the Five Talents* they do not have to do very much.

Auchincloss has wit and intelligence and good taste, not necessary attributes of a novelist but nevertheless helpful. He is not overimpressed by the rich; I would guess that he knows people who have money and how they behave a good deal better than most writers who tackle the subject.

Paul Pickrel. *Harper's Magazine.* Oct., 1960. p. 102

It should be pointed out, I think, that when Louis Auchincloss calls attention to the novelist's duty to entertain he is not offering comfort to those who say, with their own little air of superiority, that they read to be amused but who really mean that they read to be put to sleep. Like the master himself [Henry James], Auchincloss asks these things of a good reader; a scrupulous attention to the page, a ready responsiveness to passion and to effects of power, an awareness of design, an appreciation of subtle wit, and, above all, a cooperative resourcefulness in using fiction to expand the panorama of society into one more stimulating than meets the sluggish eye. It is to this level of entertainment that he invites an audience and to it I hope that his witty and satisfying book [*Reflections of a Jacobite*] may guide many.

James Gray. *Saturday Review.* June 3, 1961. p. 38

As for *Portrait in Brownstone*, one may say that this is good standard Auchincloss. It moves in that well-heeled world of New York lawyers and financiers which is his particular hunting-ground—the world of Edith Wharton, I suppose, two or three generations later—and part of the satisfaction which it gives comes from the confidence it instils. This writer, you feel, really *knows* the people he writes about. Knows them, gets on well with them, but is quite independent enough to judge them: indeed, the picture he draws of intricate networks of selfishness and domination, deceptions and self-deceptions, is rather horrifying. It reminds me of early Galsworthy—not a comparison which will be taken nowadays as a compliment, but in fact Galsworthy before he went soggy, the Galsworthy of *The Man of Property* and *In Chancery*, was a much better novelist than his present obscurity would suggest.

Patrick Cruttwell. *Hudson Review.* Winter, 1962–63. p. 594

Though Auchincloss indicts fashionable society harshly (perhaps a bit too harshly), still his acid description of the social aquarium provides amusing as well as sober moments for the reader, for he, like so many novelists of manners, wields the weapon of satire most skillfully. Striking in an urbanely lethal way, he makes his "fish" wiggle before our eyes. . . . Fortunately, Auchincloss has the style—a fastidious and polished one—to complement his generally derisive attitude toward the aristocratic set. In the first place, his figures of speech, particularly the similes, possess sparkle and wit as well as appropriateness to the context. His description of the process of handling the closing papers—checks, bonds, mortgages, assignments, affidavits, guarantees, etc.—in a legal deal captures the ritualistic and elaborate nature of the performance by likening the shuffling of the papers across the long table to the "labored solemnity of a Japanese dance."

W. Gordon Milne. *University of Kansas City Review.* Spring, 1963. p. 183

Mr. Auchincloss always writes with urbanity. He knows the moods of New England and depicts them well; he knows the rivalries and pettiness of faculty life and the resentment and loneliness of boys who cannot be pushed. I think the older women in the book [*The Rector of Justin*], notably Mrs. Prescott, are more believable than the younger, such as Eliza Dean. But my deeper misgivings have to do with the form of the narration; the story begins in Brian's journal, then we have excerpts from a book by Horace Havistock, Dr. Prescott's oldest friend, who has come down to the school expressly to tell him that he must resign. Then we have a series of notes by David Griscam, followed by the memoir of Jules Griscam, his grandson and a black sheep of Justin. This shift from writer to writer is not contrived with enough individual divergence. I am not convinced that they would all take to paper this way; nor when they come to writing dialogue, that they would do it with the skill of an experienced novelist.

Edward Weeks. *Atlantic Monthly.* 1964. p. 133

Mr. Auchincloss loves novels, to read as well as to write. He becomes involved with plot, takes a personal interest in character, indulges a curiosity (and displays an expertise) about the subject of manners that place him in the company of such unabashedly Philistine critics (fellow novelists) as E. M. Forster and Mary McCarthy herself. His tone, even when critical, oscillates between the admiring and the deferential. . . . Mr. Auchincloss's slender study [*Pioneers and Caretakers*] opens up a more interesting question than that of the presumed limitations of women as writers of fiction: what have been their special gifts and strengths? What have women brought to fiction from their own unquestionably other, female experience, what have they done well that men have not? Mr. Auchincloss suggests—it is a very Victorian idea—that they have shown a persistent if not uncritical attachment to a regional homeland ennobled by childhood and ancestral associations. Against the dominant (in America) masculine fiction of rootlessness and rejection, he implies, women's fiction has provided a saving, a "more affirmative note" of conservatism.

Ellen Moers. *New York Times Book Section.* July 25, 1965. p. 1

The immediate setting of *The Embezzler* is as familiar as the story. It is Auchincloss' endlessly revisited Eastern urban, almost exclusively WASPish, upper-middle-class society, from about 1900 onward.... It is a world ... of well-conducted adulteries and a slow drying-up of moral resolve, a world that has its troubles and tremors, but is by no means on the brink of disaster—no apocalyptics here. It is solid, recognizable and something to be reckoned with, and has at least as valid a claim on our interest as the Brooklyn waterfront or a pad in California. If it is not deep enough to be explored in great depth, Auchincloss has been exploring it to the depth and width it possesses.... He does not dispute literary traditions; he revels in them, is nourished by them and seeks to perpetuate them. He has as fruitful a consciousness as Trollope about the particular tradition he is himself working in: the now darkening comedy of manners, with its established conventions and rhythms of action—and especially as practiced by a series of gifted Americans.

R.W.B. Lewis. *New York Herald Tribune Book Section.* Feb. 20, 1966. p.1

Yet American literature—as defined by the academic elite— seldom offers sympathetic reflections of home-grown aristocracies. The books of Henry James and Edith Wharton are prominent exceptions, though these writers spent most of their lives abroad. While the public enjoys upstairs-downstairs capers, most critics view money and manners as intellectually *déclassé*. Members of the top crust do not match the nation's heroic ideal: the rebellious romantic who spurns corrupting society to hunt his singular salvation in wild nature.

There are no such heroes in the fiction of Louis Auchincloss, and his romantics almost always pay for succumbing to egoism and stepping out of line. Auchincloss's novels and story collections (nearly one a year for 20 years) deal almost exclusively with New York City's white Anglo-Saxon Protestant haven of old name and old money, whose corridor of power runs from the brownstones and duplexes of the Upper East Side to the paneled offices of Wall Street. It is an influential, publicity-shy world where the rules of the game are hardened by tradition. The costs, and sometimes the rewards, of breaking these rules are the author's principal subject....

Auchincloss steers confidently through the world he knows so well. He telescopes time with delightfully gossipy character sketches and crisp vignettes. His prose is clear and judiciously cool, though his attempts to pump drama into drawing-room confrontations may lead to such awkwardness as ''But Ivy's words were still written like the smoke letters of an airplane announcing a public event across the pale sky of Clara's calm....''

Auchincloss's true dramatic moments are in exchanges of dialogue that he expertly stages to define his characters. It is this quality of closet theater that makes his work consistently entertaining—even when his sphere of wealth and privilege may seem hopelessly remote to most readers.

R. Z. Sheppard. *Time.* July 11, 1977, p. 76

Louis Auchincloss sees a lot. What he catches most suggestively, I think, are the dynamics of pride (and of vanity, arrogance, snobbishness and related failings). His work offers other pleasures, to be sure—a gallery of strikingly animated and intelligent women, a beautifully unaffected responsiveness to the claims of those who were here before us. (The portraits of the author's mother and father in *A Writer's Capital* are exceptionally loving.) And it's important not to give the impression, to readers who don't know his books, that some sort of moral hectoring or casuistry lies in wait for those who try them. In his novels Auchincloss usually offers a carefully constructed story, as well as much incidental observation, unsolemnly phrased, about social attitudes—for example, precisely how men of affairs look upon academics. This concern about entertaining is equally evident in his essays, which proceed not as sermons, but, frequently, as unpretentiously developed comparisons of one artist with another. I'm merely saying that, in my view, his writing is subtlest when it inquires into the moment-to-moment complications of self-regard—especially self-regard under pressure....

Gently he leads his readers toward comprehension of the nearly universal human helplessness before the passion that preoccupies him. With that comprehension come intuitions of the fundamental innocence of pride, even in lofty quarters. And the result is the banishment, unportentously managed, of the possibility—on this front at least—of moral condemnation or satiric putdown....

But literature also exists to help the powerless penetrate their own simplicity and corruption, to show forth the respects in which turbulence itself is another style of pride, and to alert people to the truth that any of us—the very rich not excluded—can be ruined by the temptation to be too hard on ourselves. Humorously, unobtrusively, the best of Louis Auchincloss's books nudge the reader toward such knowledge, which is why they will remain valuable.

Benjamin DeMott. *New York Times Book Section.* Sept. 23, 1979, pp. 7, 35

Watchfires works out its theme of liberation with such single-minded success that it carries Auchincloss out on the other side of what seems to have been a personal and artistic obsession that has consumed him ever since he started writing as a child.... Auchincloss writes about the rich the way Updike writes about the middle class, though without the stylistic flourishes. His own social and professional positions have given him an insight that makes his work unique in contemporary literature....

Watchfires ... is so strong, and in significant ways so different from his earlier work, that it is no longer possible to misperceive his achievement. *Watchfires* is warmer, more intense, more intimate than any book he has written previously. As a writer, Auchincloss seems newly open and vulnerable. Moreover, his characters all find some sort of liberation....

It is true that he is not a master stylist. He is capable of using a prefabricated phrase: describing someone who knows society ''like a book.'' And he can produce a rat's nest of a sentence: ''For if the old Puritanism of the Handys and Howlands had been diluted in her to the point of excluding the sin that existed only in the mind, or at least of ranking it as less culpable than its robuster brethren, the ancient sense of guilt had been replaced by an equally sharp horror of seeming ridiculous.'' But he is equally capable of a phrase that is both accurate and surprising....

The world Auchincloss writes about, the world of America's ruling class, is no smaller—and is, in fact, probably larger—than Faulkner's Yoknapatawpha County or Hardy's Wessex. And its influence is vast....

How good, finally, is *Watchfires*? How good is Auchincloss? Adding up his assets (complex characters; a persuasive, insider's vision of a rarefied but powerful world; an entertaining sense of narrative) and his debits (occasional stylistic infelicities) Auchincloss proves to be a sound, no-risk blue-chip, with reliable dividends.

David Black. *Saturday Review.* April, 1982, pp. 24, 28

[Louis] Auchincloss's great strength as a novelist is not invention. He does not create strange new worlds but remains, as Henry James once advised Edith Wharton to, "tethered in native pastures." He writes about the worlds he knows best. Though not all his characters are White Anglo-Saxon Protestants and not all his novels take place in New York City and environs, Auchincloss is usually concerned with upper-class characters or members of the bourgeoisie. As a reading of his autobiography *A Writer's Capital* will reveal, much of Auchincloss's fiction grows directly out of his own life and experiences. The autobiographical aspects of his work are often ignored; indeed, his career may be seen as a series of creative reinvestments of the capital of his early experiences. Despite the particular choices he has made, however, it is unfair to overemphasize the limitations of Auchincloss's world. Within an apparently small compass, there is great variety of character and situation. . . .

In addition to the large quality of his fiction—twenty novels and eight collections of stories—Auchincloss has also made significant contributions as a critic and popular historian. Perhaps his finest work of nonfiction is *A Writer's Capital,* a memoir of considerable charm and grace. As a practicing novelist, he writes authoritatively on James and Wharton. His knowledge of, and sympathy for, the tradition of the novel of manners, make his essays on O'Hara and Marquand, Proust, and Edith Wharton permanent contributions of scholarship. Yet, as his popular histories as well as most of his literary essays reveal, Auchincloss is essentially a generalist addressing a nonscholarly audience. At its best his criticism and historical writing introduces the average reader to the pleasures of the past while providing shrewd insights into characters and events. Auchincloss's achievements in nonfiction mark him as a true man of letters for our times.

Despite these achievements, Auchincloss will ultimately be judged by his fiction. Here the sheer body of his work is impressive, a sustained examination of which might be called the Auchincloss world: men in Wall Street law firms and investment houses, shy heroines and powerful matrons who must come to terms with the values of the tribe, insecure young men who must come to terms with familial expectations, and the terrors of success. Yet the quality of Auchincloss's individual novels and stories varies widely. His finest novels, however are all historical in some significant sense. . . . For Auchincloss's most acute commentaries on contemporary life, one must turn to his short stories. . . .

Throughout his work Auchincloss is also a moralist. . . . At points, too, especially in *The Rector of Justin* and the flawed but significant *I Come as a Thief,* his moral analysis includes religious themes.

Christopher C. Dahl. *Louis Auchincloss* (New York: Ungar Publishing, 1986), pp. 244–46

Few have more assiduously delineated the Eastern Seaboard aristocracy and business gentry than Louis Auchincloss, a lawyer-writer literally born on the inside track. In more than thirty volumes of fiction, he has cast an intimate, custodial eye over its caste habits

and turnings, occasionally, as in *The Rector of Justin,* producing a tale of considerable distinction. The latest novel [*Fellow Passengers*] continues the run. Dryishly ironic, Jamesian in allegiance if not flair, with touches of period Fitzgerald, it is craftsmanlike from start to finish.

Fellow Passengers weaves its ten "portraits" around the evolving life of Danny Ruggles, another scion of Old New York, another Auchincloss double—the lawyer who writes fiction. . . .

Auchincloss offers no Lambert Strether in Ruggles, no observing consciousness as interesting as the life under observation. But *Fellow Passengers* does duty enough, the nuance of American class behavior given by one who truly can be said to know.

Robert Lee. *The Listener.* Aug. 16, 1990, p. 33

BIBLIOGRAPHY
The Indifferent Children (pseud. Andrew Lee), 1947 (n); *The Injustice Collectors,* 1950 (s); *Sybil,* 1952 (n); *A Law for the Lion,* 1953 (n); *The Romantic Egoists,* 1954 (s); *The Great World and Timothy Colt,* 1956 (n); *Venus in Sparta,* 1958 (n); *Pursuit of the Prodigal,* 1959 (n); *The House of Five Talents,* 1960 (n); *Reflections of a Jacobite,* 1961 (c); *Portrait in Brownstone,* 1962 (n); *Powers of Attorney,* 1963 (s); *The Rector of Justin,* 1964 (n); *Pioneers and Caretakers,* 1965 (c); *The Embezzler,* 1966 (n); *Tales of Manhattan,* 1967 (s); *A World of Profit,* 1968 (n); *A Writer's Capital,* 1974; (m); *Reading Henry James,* 1975 (c); *The Winthrop Covenant,* 1976 (n); *The Dark Lady,* 1977 (n); *The Country Cousin,* 1978 (n); *Life, Law, and Letters,* 1979 (e); *Persons of Consequence; Queen Victoria and Her Circle,* 1979 (b); *The House of the Prophet,* 1980 (n); *The Cat and the King,* 1981 (juv); *Three "Perfect" Novels—and What They Have in Common,* 1981 (c); *Unseen Versailles,* 1981 (t); *Narcissa, and Other Fables,* 1982 (s); *Watchfires,* 1982 (n); *Exit Lady Masham,* 1983 (n); *The Book Class,* 1984 (n); *Honorable Men,* 1985 (n); *Diary of a Yuppie,* 1986 (n); *Skinny Island,* 1987 (s); *The Golden Calves,* 1988 (n); *The Vanderbilt Era,* 1989 (b); ed., *The Edith Wharton Reader,* 1989 (anthol); *Fellow Passengers: A Novel in Portraits,* 1989; *J.P. Morgan: The Financier as Collector,* 1990 (catalogue, great personal museum collections, b); *The Lady of Situations,* 1990 (n); *Love without Wings,* 1991 (b); *False Gods,* 1992 (fables); *Louis Auchincloss: Family Fortunes,* 1993 (n coll.); *Three Lives,* 1993 (n); *Collected Stories,* 1994; *The Style's the Man,* 1994 (c); *Tales of Yesteryear,* 1994 (n); *The Education of Oscar Fairfax,* 1995 (n); *The Man behind the Book,* 1996 (e, c); *"The Atonement" and Other Stories,* 1997

AUDEN, W.H. (1907–1973)

Mr. W. H. Auden is a courageous poet. He is trying to find some way of living and expressing himself that is not cluttered with stale conventions and that is at once intellectually valid and emotionally satisfying. In order to do so he is obliged to hack his way in zigzag fashion through a stifling jungle of outworn notions which obstruct progress. . . . The only difficulty in following him is that he seems to be perpetually mixing up two levels of experience, private and public. Publicly he tries to persuade us that the world is a farce, privately we feel that he regards it largely as a tragedy.

John Gould Fletcher. *Poetry*. May, 1933. pp. 110–1

Auden is a stylist of great resourcefulness. He has undoubtedly drawn heavily on the experimenters of the past decade, Eliot, Pound, Graves, and Riding in verse, and Joyce and Woolf (especially *The Waves*) in prose. But he is not an imitator, for very rarely has he failed to assimilate completely what the model had to give. He is not a writer of one style.

The lyrics written in short lines display an aptitude for economy of statement that is almost ultimate; he has sometimes paid for this by an insoluble crabbedness or a grammatical perversity in the unsuccessful pieces, but a few of this type are among his best poems. On the whole, he is most effective in the poems using a long line, poems where the difficulty his verse offers is more often legitimate, that is, derives from an actual subtlety of thought and effect rather than from a failure in technical mastery.

Robert Penn Warren. *Antioch Review*. May, 1934. p. 226

As a technical virtuoso, W. H. Auden has no equal in contemporary English or American poetry; and no equal in French, if we except Louis Aragon. There has been no one since Swinburne or Hugo who rhymed and chanted with the same workmanlike delight in his own skill. . . . He combines a maximum of virtuosity with . . . you could hardly say a maximum, but still a considerable density of meaning. . . . Whether you approach his work through his theology or his virtuosity, he is one of the most important living poets.

Malcolm Cowley. *Poetry*. Jan., 1945. pp. 202–9

In the poems written since Auden came to America the effects are clarified, the ambiguities have all but disappeared. The music hall improvisations which he favors—the purposeful blend of casual horror and baleful doggerel—sometimes make him seem the Freudian's Noel Coward; but the combination of acridity and banality is unsurpassably his own. No living poet has succeeded so notably in the fashioning of metropolitan eclogues. . . . The virtuoso has extended his range, and cleverness is no longer the dominant note. Versatile but no longer special, elaborate without being finicky. Auden has become not only the most eloquent and influential but the most impressive poet of his generation.

Louis Untermeyer. *Saturday Review*. Apr. 28, 1945. p. 10

The best poet of the Auden generation is Auden. His *Poems* (1930) reveal a new social consciousness in original rhymes, conversational or jazz techniques, and unlimited sensitivity. By these rhymes, and by suitable images of deserted factories, frontiers, invalid chairs, glaciers, and schoolboy games, Auden suggests the death of his class. Ideas for improvement, resembling those of D. H. Lawrence, stop short of Marx, who had little use for the individual change of heart that Auden prescribes.

William York Tindall. *Forces in Modern British Literature* (Knopf). 1947. pp. 56–7

We may sometimes feel that his view is distorted, that, for example, he thinks more are frustrated today than are in fact frustrated, or that he does not give sufficient weight, especially at present, to the surrounding evidence of human goodness as against the evidence of human sin. . . . Nevertheless, he is a significant figure, and in nothing more than in his sensitivity to the tensions of the age . . . Auden is at one of the frontiers of this anxiety-torn world; he is one of those who play out in themselves, with unusual and revealing clarity, struggles to which, whether we recognize it or not, we are all committed.

Richard Hoggart. *Auden* (Chatto and Windus). 1951. pp. 218–9

Auden's ideas have changed as strikingly as his way of life has remained the same. There is a dualistic idea running through all his work which encloses it like the sides of a box. This idea is Symptom and Cure. . . . The symptoms have to be diagnosed, brought into the open, made to weep and confess. . . . They may be related to the central need of love. . . . It is his conception of the Cure which has changed. At one time Love, in the sense of Freudian release from inhibition; at another time a vaguer and more exalted idea of loving; at still another the Social Revolution; and at yet a later stage, Christianity. Essentially the direction of Auden's poetry has been towards the defining of the concept of Love.

Stephen Spender. *Atlantic Monthly*. July, 1953. p. 75

Perhaps Auden has always made such impossibly exacting moral demands on himself and everybody else partly because it kept him from having to worry about more ordinary, moderate demands; perhaps he had preached so loudly, made such extraordinary sweeping gestures, in order to hide himself from himself in the commotion. But he seems, finally, to have got tired of the whole affair, to have become willing to look at himself *without doing anything about it*, not even shutting his eyes or turning his head away. In some of the best of his later poems he accepts himself for whatever he is, the world for whatever it is, with experienced calm; much in these poems is accurate just as observed, relevant, inescapable fact, not as the journalistic, local-color, in-the-know substitute that used to tempt Auden almost as it did Kipling. The poet is a man of the world, and his religion is of so high an order, his mortality so decidedly a meta-morality, that they are more a way of understanding everybody than of making specific demands on anybody.

Randall Jarrell. *The Yale Review*. Summer, 1955. p. 607

As our undoubted master of poetic resources, Auden has experimented with every device that would flat the poem into a true statement of the human position as he sees it. Meter, diction, imagery—every device of Auden's great skill (even his flippancy) is a speaking way of refusing to belie the truth with false compare. . . . In the native motion of his genius . . . Auden implicitly warns us away from the stereotyped affirmation of the good, the true, and the beautiful. He is not against the good, the true, and the beautiful, as some foolish critics have argued. Rather, he asks us to weigh these values in mortal fear of smudging them with prettiness, and with an instinctive recognition of the fact that, being human, our feelings are subtle, various, and often conflicting.

John Ciardi. *Saturday Review*. Feb. 18, 1956. p. 48

In a work of art, as in a man, we are best satisfied when we are confidently aware of a wholeness, or integrality, that underlies all the diverse and even conflicting elements. And we are most satisfied when there is a consistent thread running through the whole course of a man's life or the whole body of an artist's work.

In the case of Auden, it is our doubt on this point that makes us hesitant to class him with writers in whom we have this sense of wholeness or integrity. We do not take in his work the confident satisfaction that we do in the work of a Voltaire, a Swift, a Molière, a Wordsworth, a Keats, or a Browning. Or to take examples from the poets of our own time, we do not feel in his work the integrity that we feel in poets of lesser gifts—in Spender, or Marianne Moore, or in Robinson Jeffers; or in poets of comparable or greater gifts—Wallace Stevens, or Dylan Thomas, or Frost, or Eliot. Through a man's work we are reaching out to the man. And if it is true that the style is the man, we feel with these that we are making contact with at least as much of the man as shows in his work, and that we know sufficiently with whom we are dealing. With Auden we are not sure of this.

We know that he is a very gifted actor and mimic; and he has beguiled many an hour with his impersonations. But we cannot give ourselves up to him without certain reservations.

Joseph Warren Beach. *The Making of the Auden Canon* (Minnesota). 1957. p. 253

He can almost never do without this third element: the impersonal point of reference to which he directs the reader. It does not much matter whether this is society, literature, mythology or politics, or whether it is the subtle and elaborate game of serious light verse. Once he has an impersonal framework his real gifts come into action: his technical inventiveness, his striking but scrappy ideas, his great range of reading, his wit and, above all, his superb command of language.

These are rare gifts, stimulating and admirable. Yet somehow I can't, in the real sense, *agree* with Auden as I agree with Lawrence and Yeats. What he has positively to offer does not seem to matter much. I cannot, that is, get much from his work beyond the extraordinary ability and cleverness. He has caught one tone of his period, but it is a cocktail party tone, as though most of his work were written off the cuff for the amusement of his friends.

A. Alvarez. *Stewards of Excellence* (Scribner). 1958. pp. 104–5

It is remarkable that in *The Dyer's Hand* Auden is constantly able to do two things at once: to develop an argument about a literary subject which casts light on it and on literature in general, and simultaneously to develop a general moral or religious argument, with a particular relevance to the contemporary world. This is plainest in the section on Shakespeare, but I hope that my inadequate summary has indicated that it is characteristic of the whole book. In addition to their intrinsic interest and value, these larger themes and moral arguments supply the context within which

various of Auden's aphorisms and statements that have been puzzling or curious in some earlier form now are thoroughly intelligible. It becomes clear that he does not divorce poetry from truth and seriousness, as he has sometimes been accused of doing, and his emphasis on play, frivolity, the comic, and the fantastic takes on its full significance. The book offers a magnificent example of a mature and powerful intelligence, aware of its nature and limitations, casting fresh light upon individual works and writers, upon the perennial problems of criticism, and upon the nature of man. . . .

He is more like Dryden . . . than like most modern poets: he is a kind of maverick and extremely unofficial Anglo-American laureate, and, appropriately, writes much occasional verse. Like Dryden, he was much reproached for changes of faith and allegiance, and like him outmoded such reproaches by the tenacity and obvious sincerity of his convictions. Auden, too, has genuine modesty with regard to his own gifts, developing them with conscious craftsmanship but employing them prodigally and hence unevenly, so that high-minded critics accuse him of insufficient respect for his art.

Monroe K. Spears. *The Poetry of W. H. Auden: The Disenchanted Island* (Oxford). 1963. pp. 308, 337–8

Auden is pre-eminently the poet of civilization. He loves landscapes, to be sure, and confesses that his favorite is the rather austere landscape of the north of England, but over and over he has told us that the prime task of our time is to rebuild the *city*, to restore community, to help re-establish the just society. Even a cursory glance over his poetry confirms this view. Who else would have written on Voltaire, E.M. Forster, Matthew Arnold, Pascal, Montaigne, Henry James, Melville, and Sigmund Freud? On any one of them, yes, any poet might. But only a poet of civilization would write poems about them all. If one looks through the reviews and the criticism that he has published during the last thirty years, the case for calling Auden the poet of civilization becomes abundantly clear.

A great deal of this criticism is non-literary or only partially literary. Characteristically, it has to do with the problems of modern man seen in an economic or sociological or psychological context. Auden is everywhere interested in the relation of the individual to society, of the metaphysical assumptions implied by the various societies that have existed in history, and of the claims of history and of nature as they exert themselves upon the human being.

Cleanth Brooks. *Kenyon Review*. Winter, 1964. p. 173

He wants to try out what every poetic resource and every possible combination of poetic resources can mold out of the life of the present. As a deeply traditional poet, he can never be satisfied with a single style or a single kind of poem. Auden wants to compose every kind of poem, and he very nearly has. Even among the relatively few works this study has singled out for special consideration, his range of poetic strategy is imposing. A truer sense of his scope can be gained by reading seriatim through *The Collected Poetry*, limited though it is to works written by 1945. Auden's has been a sustained examination of our world through a complex series of prisms drawn from past poetries. As a result, not only can we now appreciate unsuspected beauties that he has drawn from familiar poetic elements, but we can measure our surroundings against a broader perspective that is as directly artistic as it is philosophic or religious. Auden has been the more effective for having long ago ceased to worry about stating profound or final truths in poetry. Instead he has concentrated on the ultimately more fruitful goal of perfecting each new amalgamation of poetic resources with experience.

John G. Blair. *The Poetic Art of W.H. Auden* (Princeton). 1965. pp. 186–7

I think I am the third poet the editor of this magazine has tried to get to review *The Dyer's Hand*, a major poet's assay of literary criticism, and it has taken me a year and a half to muster the bad judgment to try it. The gates of the book are defended by gargoyles of the superfluous critic. It is a work intended to reprove unnecessary criticism, and it does this both explicitly and by the performance of feats of insight and sensibility that I have come to feel (and the book has been around for almost three years now) are in fact *necessary* to modern thinking and feeling. . . . The last and highest opportunity a critic has to serve, Auden says, is to "Throw light upon the relation of art to life, to science, economics, ethics, religion, etc." The book does this, I feel, in the way only a complete and unique human personality can do.

William Meredith. *Poetry*. Nov., 1965. pp. 118, 120

The persona of [Auden's] early poems was an intense and interesting man. Central to his character was the need to know and, once he felt he had gained knowledge, the need to teach. The resultant effect of this "needing to" is a feeling of movement in the poems. We hear the voice of the persona admonishing us, as he moves from uncertainty to certainty and back to uncertainty, to look on ourselves and our world with hard, questioning eyes, accepting nothing as final, except death. . . .

If one were to give the above description of Auden's persona and verse to a prospective reader and then were to have him read the poems in *About the House* without telling him they were Auden's, his response would probably be, "What do these poems have to do with W. H. Auden?" The answer would be "Nothing," for although there are technical similarities between the work of the early Auden and that of the Auden of the sixties, the poems are written by what amounts to two different men and they show it; comparing them is like comparing the poems of Byron and Tennyson, or those of Pope and Blake.

The most important fact about the poetry of the "new" Auden, which one encounters for the first time in *Nones*, is the lack of tension between the poet and his experience. Both man and world simply are; no more, no less. The only problem, a nonmetaphysical one, is recognizing, accepting, and praising the existence of both.

Gerald Nelson. *Changes of Heart: A Study of the Poetry of W.H. Auden* (California). 1969. pp. 144–5

Auden's writing offers us a vision of the nature of personal being and becoming which is fully consistent with and an important contribution to an intellectual position underlying a significant body of twentieth-century literature. At the center of his thought and art in the later period is a vision of the nature of individual

action which is related to a dilemma central to the contemporary world, the fragmentation in belief of a whole civilization. If he is committed to one solution of that dilemma, it is not without an awareness of the difficulties and responsibilities of that commitment, nor is it without sympathy for those who do not wish to or cannot take upon themselves the problems of what Kierkegaard has called "the religious sphere." In man's weakness Auden sees his potentialities, and his art continues to be didactic in the best sense: it directed man toward knowledge of himself.

George W. Bahlke. *The Later Auden* (Rutgers). 1970. pp. 83–4

So many, so various, so handsome and so insinuating are the by-products of Auden's career among us that our indolence as well as our thirsty media risk persuading us that it is all one: one utterance altered, merely, according to the various circumstances of its occasion. This is not so. There is the poet Auden, who in this newest book [*City without Walls*] has added another dozen to the great poems in his canon, as well as a number of "pieces he has nothing against except their lack of importance"; and there is the witty, generous, rather bromidic public man we must not condescend to by allowing his good humor and his eccentricities . . . to obscure his greatness. Which is abundantly here and clear in this latest book so much under the sign of a consented-to mortality; from the title poem to the "Ode to Terminus," the book is concerned with boundaries, limitations, precarious identifications which make our life possible: that naming which was Adam's first task and Auden's to the last. Hence the famous and extraordinary vocabulary, and the wonderful meters, the alliterative spells and charms. . . .

Richard Howard. *Poetry*. Oct., 1971. p. 38

I think there is a sense in which Auden put himself on a shelf a good many years ago when his verse came reiteratively to proclaim man's incapacities, his inability to take charge, direct his fate; and indeed he has perhaps become our greatest poet of the shelf. But in the new volume [*Epistle to a Godson*] the shelf is even higher in the closet, and on it he sits meditating—with himself, or imaginatively with a few old friends. . . . His verse centers have usually been large and obvious like a statue in a park, with the poet's game one of sitting down in front of the statue and letting the sight of it develop in the mind a series of themes, projections, fancies. Thus it is a contemplative art, an art for a lonely and unbugged visionary on a park bench. Or shelf.

Reed Whittemore. *New Republic*. Sept. 23, 1972. p. 26

It is a common opinion among the English *literati* that Auden's later work is a collapse. I am so far from taking this view that I think an appreciation of Auden's later work is the only sure test for an appreciation of Auden, just as an appreciation of Yeats's earlier work is the only sure test for an appreciation of Yeats. You must know and admire the austerity which Auden achieved before you can take the full force of his early longing for that austerity—before you can measure the portent of his early brilliance. There is no question that the earlier work is more enjoyable. The question is about whether you think enjoyability was the full extent of his aim. . . . In his later work we see not so much the ebbing of desire as its transference to the created world, until plains and hills begin explaining the men who live on them. Auden's unrecriminating generosity toward a world which had served him ill was a moral triumph.

Clive James. *Commentary*. Dec., 1973. p. 58

His poetry alternated between socio-political and psychological modes of analysis, and he was likely to think that psychological ills are basic, political and social wrong derived from them. The process of diagnosis and healing, with which Auden was always so much concerned, had to start not with social institutions but with the human heart. Primarily he was a moralist, and the chief importance for him of psychological and sociological modes of thought was that they provided criteria of the good. . . .

Hawthorne has a story called "P's Correspondence" (*Mosses from an Old Manse*) in which an amiable madman gives an account of his meeting with the elderly Lord Byron. The letter is headed "London, February 29, 1845," and Byron, though fat and dull—a "mortal heap," in fact—is much improved morally. . . .

Byron, it emerges, is preparing a new collected edition, which is to be corrected, expurgated, and amended "in accordance with his present creed of taste, morals, politics and religion." None of the passages commended by the visitor would find a place in this new edition. P. concludes that Byron, having lost his passions, "no longer understands his own poetry.". . .

The application is plain enough, I believe; Auden came close to a point where he no longer understood his own poetry. I do not say that he exactly follows the pattern of development detected by Mr. P. in Byron and other writers; but something happened that made him close his mind, not to the earliest poetry so much as to that of the middle 'thirties. . . .

There is a genuine and sad perversity in this failure of Auden to understand himself. It is as if he came to find himself boring, or became unable to connect with himself, as in life he grew less and less able to connect with others. All those schemes and formulas he invented to systematize his views on everything from history to ethics—it was a habit early formed, as we see from some of the prose selections in this new book—served to fence him in, to prevent any real conversation with others, or with his former self. His earlier rhetoric failed later ethical tests, and in acquiring a poetic personality that could live with these faintly schoolboyish standards of truth-telling he lost all sense of the valuable strangeness of the personality it supplanted. . . .

And we old men who still think of the poems of the 'thirties as part of an almost incomparably good time for modern poetry— when you picked up the literary journals and read a late poem of Yeats, or *East Coker*, or a new Auden—are not going to sit idly by and allow it to be said that he was really in a bad patch of pretending, but eventually got it right; and that people will come to see that he did, abandoning their allegiance to the older texts and the banned poems. At least *The English Auden* will do nothing to strengthen that kind of propaganda.

Frank Kermode. *The Yale Review*. Summer, 1978, pp. 609, 612, 614

One cannot easily distinguish the poet from the poetry because Auden's life enters into his poetry and because the making of

poetry was at the center of that life. Furthermore, the plays, often in verse form and containing lyrics that have been separately published, are not detachable from any other part of the man's work. Finally, the prose criticism alternates with poetic passages, while its objects are, in large part, poetry and poetic theory. There are no watertight compartments in Auden's career; there is no way to isolate the forms and elements because he believed that intelligence and emotion, artfulness and honesty, game playing and moral clarity all had to be members of one community.

Among the last collections that he edited is the "commonplace book" entitled *A Certain World*. He said that it was the nearest thing to an autobiography that he would attempt. It amounts to excerpts, a sizable number of his favorite passages in both poetry and prose, all from other writers, but with some brief paragraphs he provided as introductions. This literary world is his own certain one, and the reader who wanders through it discovers not only a great deal about his critical taste but also how coherent this whole world is, even though it seems so various and comprehensive. The headings include Acronyms, Aging, Algebra, the Alps, Anesthesia, Brass Bands, Birds, Book Reviews, Calvin, Cats, Chiasmus, Choirboys, Christmas, Death, Dejection, Dogs, Dreams, Easter, Eating, Elegies, Eskimos, Forgiveness, God, Hands, Homer, Humility, Icebergs, Journalism, Kilns, Liturgy, Logic, Madness, Money, Numbers, Owls, Plants, Puns, the Renaissance, Roads, Saints, Spoonerisms, Tyranny, Voyages, and War. The last head of all is Writing. These are all matters of which Auden read with interest, and on which he could write. . . .

For all his recognizable idiosyncracy, Auden is an artist whose work is intended to be public, not romantically or cryptically personal; as Edward Mendelson has observed, he was determined to be a civic, not a vatic, poet. The integrity of his written work derives from its being at once the expression of a consistently recognizable mind but also its being devoted consistently to public purpose, seeking to cultivate the ordinary soil and in some small part, even, to redeem the time. Wisecracking, naughty, even self-indulgent at moments, he is, in the final analysis, a religious and moral artist.

Wendell Stacy Johnson. *W.H. Auden* (New York: Continuum, 1990), pp. 151–53

Auden called opera "the last refuge of the High style" among the arts that use words, the only one in which the grand manner had survived the ironic levelings of modernity. Unlike poetry, which always stops to reflect on the emotions that gave rise to it, the verse of an opera libretto, he said, gives immediate expression to willful feeling. For Auden, the unique combination of artifice and intensity in opera made it the ideal dramatic medium for both archetypal comedy and tragic myth. His libretti, most of them written in collaboration with Chester Kallman, present their mythical actions with a directness unlike anything in even his greatest poems. In their use of the simplest language of song to dramatize the most complex issues of history, psychology, and religion they surpass everything written for the musical theater in English and have few equals in the richer operatic traditions of Italian, German, and French.

Opera gave Auden the solution to a problem of dramatic poetry that he had been unable to solve in his early poetic plays, the problem of the proper voice for a poet who wants to write a public and heroic art as well as a private and intimate one. Poetry, he wrote in 1961, "cannot appear in public without becoming false to itself"; this was the conviction Auden had reached after his attempts to write public poetry in the 1930s. . . .

When Auden renounced as dishonest the grand style he had used in his public poems of the 1930s, he renounced only his use of that style in lyric and personal poetry, not the grand style itself. He still hoped to use it if he could find the proper vehicle. Around 1950 in "We, too, had known golden hours." the dedicatory poem to his book *Nones*, he wrote that "we" (the poem implicitly speaks for all who value the private realm) had known all the feelings that the grand style is best suited to express, "And would in the old grand manner / Have sung from a resonant heart." But the modern era had transformed the public realm from one of personal choice and action to one of mass necessity, where the grand manner now could do nothing more than endorse popular sentiment and political lies. The only authentic tones of voice that remained for poetry were private and quiet ones. . . .

The unstated answer, for Auden as poet, was in the grand style still possible in opera, and in libretti of the kind he had begun to write a few years before.

Edward Mendelson, ed. Introduction. In W.H. Auden and Chester Kallman. *Libretti, 1939–1973* (Princeton: Princeton Univ. Pr., 1993), pp. xi–xvii

This [Anthony Hecht. *The Hidden Law: The Poetry of W.H. Auden*] is almost the examination of Auden's poetry we've been waiting for. If that seems like damning with faint praise, it isn't. The deluge of books about Auden since his death has been strangely unsatisfying, as if the pleasure his work gives were felt by its exegetes as some sort of indulgence to be deplored. If one thinks sometimes of two Audens, the magician and the Censor, then the Censor seems to stand beside the desks of those who set out to criticize his work. The best books to date have been John Fuller's *Reader's Guide* and Justin Replogle's *Auden's Poetry*. Monroe K. Spears and Joseph Warren Beach have appeared as defending and prosecuting counsel, and Osborne's and Carpenter's biographies have both illuminated and darkened our view of his life. They should be read with more gossipy books to hand, especially Charles H. Miller's *Auden: An American Friendship* and Dorothy J. Farnon's *Auden in Love*, plus the tribute edited by Spender soon after Auden's death. I have hardly touched on the whole canon, much of it the grist of American academic mills. Edward Mendelson is our only safe guide through the chaos of Auden's texts, and as we make our way past the changes and suppressions, to say nothing of the poor proofreading and typesetting, we may feel like the theologians coping with early Church Fathers or musicologists deciding which score of Bruckner's is the urtext. Poor Bruckner was mutilated by others: Auden performed his own acts of butchery.

None of Auden's previous commentators except John Fuller and the early and hostile Francis Scarfe has been a professional poet. Anthony Hecht is not only that but also one of the finest creative artists in the second half of this century. He has no need to deck his commentary in those curatorial smartnesses which turns common sense on its head, or shroud it in the reductive jargons of theories. . . . He knows how odd Auden was in many ways but he knows something much more important—that Auden's poetic *oeuvre* is central to an understanding of twentieth century poetry, and that his unrepresentativeness as a man does not interfere with

his encyclopedic knowledge of human nature. As Hecht recognizes, Auden is wider in scope, more rounded in interest, more various in form than any of the rival figures writing in English in this century. . . . Auden alone mustered all the Muses' horses and roamed freely through our unpoetic century.

Peter Porter. *Poetry R.* Winter, 1993–94, p. 4

Auden's obsession with Eliot, like his obsession with Hardy, lasted about a year. During this period, he drew not only on Eliot, but also on the work of other modernists, such as Gertrude Stein, Virginia Woolf, Ezra Pound, and especially Edith Sitwell, whose influence on his work during 1926 is not easy to distinguish from that of Eliot. . . . Then in the late spring of 1927 he read, apparently at the suggestion of his friend Cecil Day-Lewis, some of the recent work of Yeats. He wrote to Isherwood that of the modern poets he was reading that summer term, "the later Yeats alone seems to me to be *at*." . . .

Auden passionately admired Yeats's mastery of language, but this mastery was married in his view to an eccentric vision. He felt profoundly ambivalent toward the vision which seemed to him far more subjective and esoteric than Wordsworth's. He was skeptical of its truth, but longed to share its power. Only after Yeats's death was Auden able to articulate this ambivalence. In "The Public v. the Late Mr. William Butler Yeats" (1939), he put Yeats on trial with the accusation: "In 1900 he believed in fairies; that was bad enough; but in 1930 we are confronted with the pitiful, the deplorable spectacle of a grown man occupied with the mumbo-jumbo of magic and the nonsense of India. . . . The plain fact remains that he made it the center of his work." Yet by offering in his essay the cases both for the prosecution and for the defense, Auden embodied his own equivocal attitude. In the end, the argument for the defense sets aside Yeats's beliefs on the ground that poets should not be judged for their ability to solve the problems of their generation, "for art is a product of history, not a cause." . . .

Auden's 1939 defense of Yeats underpins the all-important turn from political to private poet that he was then about to make in his own career. He was again using Yeats as a model, a poetical father of sorts; now it was by identifying Yeats's inadequacies, as he had once as a schoolboy identified Hardy's quite different inadequacies, that Auden at last prepared to set Yeats aside. . . .

Only a few days after his return from Yugoslavia in 1927, Auden wrote the now famous poem beginning "Who stands, the crux left of the watershed," in which Edward Mendelson has suggested he first discovered his own poetic voice. The journey abroad and the prolonged contact with his father triggered an important change in his writing; other, more important changes were to come after he left Oxford for good. . . . It was not until after Auden arrived in Berlin that he began steadily to produce mature, publishable work. Visiting home briefly in February 1929, he sent a copy of *Poems* [his first volume, 1928] to E.R. Dodds (he apparently gave copies to a number of friends at this time) with a letter saying that the second poem in the volume, the one beginning 'I choose this lean country,' is now completely rewritten as it is far too Yeatsian at present." He meant that he had already reworked it into a different poem beginning "From scars where kestrels hover." He had expunged the most obvious echoes of Yeats and added in his manuscript notebook "Berlin. Jan 1929" at the foot. He had also revised and redated several other contemporary pieces.

Fully aware that he had still been in the grip of his youthful obsession with Yeats when he composed "I choose this lean country," he was determined to progress toward something new. Alone in Berlin, cut off from family, friends, and familiar institutions, he had started to come to terms with the gift of his own weakness. The student began to transform himself into a master.

> Katherine Bucknell, ed. Introduction. *W.H. Auden: Juvenilia, Poems 1922–1928* (Princeton: Princeton Univ. Pr., 1994), pp. xlv–xlviii

Probably no work of Auden's has so consistently fascinated and troubled its readers as *The Orators*. For while it is easy to identify this book's major themes—social crisis and revolution, fascism, leadership, group movements—deciding what Auden is saying about such issues is another matter. Does he really mean it when he says, "All of the women and most of the men / shall work with their hands and not think again?" Or is he satirizing this Lawrentian ideal? Auden's comments about *The Orators* clarify little. In a 1932 letter he called it "a stage in my conversion to communism," but in 1966 he remarked: "My name on the title-page seems a pseudonym for someone else, someone talented but near the border of sanity, who might well, in a year or two, become a Nazi." Like another from the same essay, such comments are as coy as they are suggestive: "My guess today is that my unconscious motive in writing it was therapeutic, to exorcise certain tendencies in myself by allowing them to run riot in phantasy." Thus, the issue of the political valence of *The Orators*—which has been seen as fascist, antifascist, and simply confused—is also the issue of Auden's "seriousness." F.R. Leavis was responding to this quality of *The Orators* when he said that Auden "does not know just how serious he is."

In fact, these uncertainties—Auden's seriousness (or lack of it), his ambiguous politics, the question of the book's coherence—recall moments within *The Orators* itself. The anxiety about whether or not Auden is promoting fascism, for instance, recalls the Airman's concern over complicity with the enemy. Moreover, the weird messianic "He" of "The Initiates" has a "fondness for verbal puzzles," and the Airman of Book II fights the enemy with practical jokes. We might do well to hesitate before invoking criteria of aesthetic seriousness and ideological coherence in judging *The Orators*, because Auden is apparently flouting these readerly values. But if so, then what are the aesthetic and political rationales behind this book?

In this essay I shall argue that we can understand how and why *The Orators* troubles the standards by which it has been assessed only by exploring its treatment of homosexuality. Some studies of *The Orators* do refer to this subject—noting, for example, that the Airman is apparently homosexual—but same-sex desire has far more to do with why *The Orators* is a difficult, contradictory work than critics have realized. For the political implications of homosexuality in *The Orators* are themselves contradictory. Same-sex desire at once preserves the political order and makes the homosexual a criminal according to that order and this is the governing contradiction of Auden's "English Study."

> Richard Bozorth. "'Whatever You Do Don't Go to the Wood': Joking, Rhetoric, and Homosexuality in *The Orators*." In Katherine Bucknell and Nicholas Jenkins, eds. *Auden Studies* 2 (Oxford: Clarendon, 1994), pp. 113–14

BIBLIOGRAPHY

Poems, 1930 (revised 1932); *The Orators*, 1932 (e, p); *The Dance of Death*, 1933 (p); (with Christopher Isherwood) *The Dog Beneath the Skin*, 1935 (d); *Look Stranger!* 1936 (p); (with Louis MacNeice) *Letter from Iceland*, 1937 (p, e); *Spain*, 1937 (p); (with Christopher Isherwood) *On the Frontier*, 1938 (d); *Selected Poems*, 1938; *Ballad of Heroes* (words for Benjamin Britten's music), 1939; (with Christopher Isherwood) *Journey to a War*, 1939 (p, e); *Some Poems*, 1940; *Another Time*, 1940 (p); *New Year Letter*, 1941 (p) (American edition, *The Double Man*); *Hymn to St. Cecilia* (words for Benjamin Britten's music), 1942; *For the Time Being* (including *The Sea and the Mirror*), 1945 (p); *Collected Poems*, 1945; *The Dyer's Hand*, 1948 (e); *The Age of Anxiety*, 1948 (p); *Collected Shorter Poems, 1930–1944*, 1950; *The Enchafèd Flood*, 1951 (c); (with Chester Kallman) *The Rake's Progress*, 1951 (libretto); *Nones*, 1951 (p); *Delia*, 1953 (libretto); *Mountains*, 1954 (p); *The Shield of Achilles*, 1955 (p); *The Old Man's Road*, 1956 (p); *Making, Knowing and Judging*, 1956 (e); (with Chester Kallman) *The Magic Flute*, 1957 (libretto, tr); *Selected Poetry*, 1958; *Daniel* (verse narrative for the 13th century play), 1958; *W. H. Auden: A Selection by the Author*, 1958 (p); *Homage to Clio*, 1960 (p, c); *Five Poems for Music*, 1960; *Elegy for Young Lovers*, 1961 (libretto); *The Dyer's Hand*, revised edition, 1963 (e); *About the House*, 1965 (p); *Selected Shorter Poems, 1927–1957*, 1968; *Collected Longer Poems*, 1969; *Collected Shorter Poems*, 1969; *Secondary Worlds*, 1969 (e); *City without Walls*, 1970 (p); *A Certain World: A Commonplace Book*, 1970 (misc); (with Paul B. Taylor) *The Elder Edda*, 1970 (tr); *Academic Graffiti*, 1971 (p); *Epistle to a Godson*, 1972 (p); *Forewords & Afterwords*, 1973 (e); *Thank You, Fog: Last Poems*, 1974 (p); (with Leif Sjoberg) *Evening Land* (by Per Lagerkvist), 1975 (tr); *Collected Poems*, 1976; *The English Auden*, 1978 (p, e, d); *Selected Poems*, rev. ed., 1979; (with Paul B. Taylor) *Norse Poems*, 1981 (tr); *The Platonic Blow & My Epitaph*, 1985 (pamphlet); *Complete Works*, 8 vols., ed. Edward Mendelson, 1988–89, 1993; *Poems, 1927–1929: Facsimile of Original Notebooks*, 1989; *The Map of All My Youth*, 1990 (a); *Collected Poems*, ed. Edward Mendelson, 1991; *Juvenilia: Poems 1922–1928*, ed. Katherine Bucknell, 1994; *In Solitude, for Company: Auden after 1940, Unpublished Prose and Recent Criticism*, ed. Katherine Bucknell and Nicholas Jenkins, 1996 (misc)

AUSTER, Paul (1947–)

Paul Auster's *City of Glass*, one of the three remarkable novellas that make up his *New York Trilogy*, pushes the connotative significance of names in literary texts to an absurdist extreme. These three stories subject the clichés and stereotypes of the gumshoe detective story to a postmodernist skepticism about identity, causality, and meaning. Quinn himself [the protagonist] writes detective stories under the name of William Wilson, which happens to be the name of the eponymous hero of Poe's famous tale about a man in pursuit of his doppelgänger. Misidentified as "Paul Auster of the Auster Detective Agency," Quinn is seduced into acting the part, tailing a former professor called Stillman who has recently been released from prison and is feared by the client of Quinn, alias Wilson, alias Auster.... As if to demonstrate the point, Stillman deconstructs

Quinn's name, when they eventually meet, with a flow of whimsical free association. The connotations of Quinn stop nowhere, and therefore become useless to the reader as an interpretative key.

In the second story, "Ghosts," all the characters have the names of colors. . . . By this manifestly artificial naming system, Auster again affirms the arbitrariness of language, introducing it (arbitrariness) where it doesn't usually belong (fictional names). In the third story, "The Locked Room," the narrator confesses how he faked government censor returns, parodying the activity of a novelist. . . . In all three stories, the impossibility of pinning the signifier to the signified, of recovering that mythical, prelapsarian state of innocence in which a thing and its name were interchangeable, is replicated on the level of plot by the futility of the routines of detection. Each narrative ends with the death of despair of the detective-figure, faced with an insoluble mystery, lost in a labyrinth of names.

> David Lodge. *The Art of Fiction* (New York: Viking, 1992), pp. 38–39, 40

With thick, dark hair, smoky eyes, and brooding sensuality, forty-five-year-old New Yorker Paul Auster looks like a Tony Curtis upgrade. Since his dramatic 1982 memoir *The Invention of Solitude*, a reflection on the death of his joyless father ("a man without appetites . . . a tourist in his own life") that unintentionally exposed hidden horrors in his family's past, Auster has rapidly evolved from a shadowy experimental stylist into one of America's premier (but least known) living writers. He is, says *The New Republic*, "a man poised to write something momentous about our times."

His latest, *The Music of Chance* (1991), is vintage Auster—an eerie, captivating novel the plot of which turns on questions of identity and reality, often wandering haphazardly. On the surface, it reads like a potboiler, but hangs around in the mind like an unsettling dream you can't shake. . . .

Leaving his readers more questions than answers is an Auster trademark, one tattooed on his first universally praised work, *The New York Trilogy*, three novellas that form a brooding variation on the gumshoe genre. Each features detectives of sorts, a search of some kind, missing persons, and mistaken identities—but these are metaphysical whodunits where "What is real?" is as burning a question as "What's the scam?". . .

Because Auster's work is plutonium-dense with ambiguity, it will never float in the best-seller mainstream. But he's in good company.

> Doug Rennie. *Plant's Review of Books*. Winter, 1994, p. 15

Following his well-received *New York Trilogy*, Paul Auster broke free from the suffocating urban story with the help of that particularly demotic American genre, the road novel. In succeeding books, men drove out across the continent toward the newer version of the New World on the other coast. In *Mr. Vertigo*, he confines his characters to the spaces that lie in between. Despite determined efforts, they never make it either to New York or Los Angeles. Instead, they are caught in the ambiguities of small-town life in the Midwest.

Auster's New York City may have been claustrophobic, peopled by aspiring, doomed, and failed writers who spend more time at the window, watching and being watched, than they do before a sheet of paper, but he offers no contrasting rural idyll here. His is a profoundly agoraphobic Midwest—"A flatter, more desolate place you've never seen in your life.". . . This landscape provides the background to some curious travelers. In the 1920s of the novel. America is waiting to be shaped, though not, in all likelihood by "the Master," a Hungarian Jew living in Kansas, creating his own melting pot with stray characters found in circuses and won in poker games. The people are no less inscrutable than in Auster's New York. . . .

[His] theme, intriguing and at first well developed, is played out in a coda which brings the novel down to earth with [the protagonist] Walt. Grounded by puberty (only castration would allow him to fly on), Walt meets Dizzy Dean, a baseball hero of the 1930s who continued to play long after his skills had deserted him. The fictional Walt tries to preserve for posterity an unblemished career. This episode unfortunately helps draw attention to the difficulty Auster always has in getting out of stories. Several of his novels end, as this one does, with characters self-consciously writing the book which we are reading. These endings betray a curious uncertainty in writing which is otherwise so driven by confidence. Having put on a mesmerizing show, Auster hasn't quite learned Walt's routine, whereby you "bow—just once—and the curtain comes down."

> Peter Blake. *TLS: The Times Literary Supplement*. April 8, 1994, p. 20

Auster's postmodern self-fashioning odes do not end in aimless purposelessness or in a do-your-own-thing individualism. While he does not refuse to forsake the premodern notion of the individual so that a vestige of renaissance humanism can remain, he does examine in all of his fiction the consequences of actions taken in one's self-fashioning. Marco Stanley Fogg—MS—may be a life as work-in-progress, but his actions have impact on others, nonetheless. Auggie Wren instantaneously decided to be Ethel's grandson. "Don't ask me why I did it. I don't have any idea," he says. But once he takes an action, certain consequences follow. "Anything can happen": this phrase occurs in all of Auster's books and these books are examinations of struggles to find one's way, to make sense of this fact. This is why Auster is a major novelist: he has synthesized interrogations of postmodern subjectivities, explanations of moral causalities, and a sufficient realism.

> Dennis Barone. In *Beyond the Red Notebook* (Philadelphia: University of Pennsylvania Pr.) 1995, pp. 5–6

BIBLIOGRAPHY

Notebooks of Joseph Jourbert: A Selection, 1983 (tr); *Stéphane Mallarmé, A Tomb for Anatole*, 1985 (tr); *City of Glass*, 1985, *Ghosts*, 1986, *The Locked Room*, 1986; *The New York Trilogy*, 1990 (3 n); *In the Country of Lost Things*, 1987 (n); *The Invention of Solitude*, 1988 (n); *Disappearances*, 1988 (p); *Moon Palace*, 1989 (n); *The Music of Chance*, 1990 (n); *Ground Work: Selected Poems and Essays 1970–1979*, 1990; *The Art of Hunger: Essays, Prefaces, Interviews*, 1992 (e); *Leviathan*, 1992 (n); *Jacques Dupin: Selected Poems*, 1992 (tr); *Mr. Vertigo*, 1994 (n); "Smoke" and "Blue in the Face," 1995 (scrp); *Why Write?*, 1996; *Hand to Mouth: A Chronicle of Early Failure*, 1997 (m); *Lulu on the Bridge*, 1998 (scrp)

AXELROD, George (1922–)

The Seven Year Itch is funny, somewhat erotic, and in English. The sum of these virtues seems to be a smash hit, and a safe play to recommend to almost anyone who is looking for a pleasant evening's entertainment. What George Axelrod's romantic comedy amounts to is a series of *New Yorker* jokes attached to what (I am told) is a very true and rather ordinary situation—namely the light-hearted adultery of a happily married man while his wife and child are out of town for the summer. . . .

> Henry Hewes. *Saturday Review*. Oct. 13, 1952. p. 25

. . .*The Seven Year Itch* . . . is an ingenious, knowing, and very amusing sketch of a husband whose wife has gone to the country and has left him wide open to summer temptations in the city. The model upstairs comes down, the husband succumbs, and is thereupon beset by rosy daydreams in which the model throws herself at his feet, by counter nightmares in which his wife throws him out of the house, and by another set of fantasies in which his wife leaves him for another man who is paying her attentions in the country. It all ends happily as he rushes off for a connubial weekend. The piece is cleverly written. . . .

> Margaret Marshall. *The Nation*. Dec. 13, 1952. p. 563.

Will Success Spoil Rock Hunter? by George Axelrod . . . is a fantasy disguised as an ordinary farce. All farces are essentially fantastic, but in this case there is almost no pretense that the story is even fictitiously real: the central character is the Devil in the familiar form of a movie agent.

I believe I should have liked the play more if it had been presented as a fantasy—an entertainment which took even greater liberties with reality than farce permits. . . .

Some of the jokes are funny and there is . . . a bit of rancid ribaldry about many of them. I am a poor audience for these jokes because I consider most of the quips about Hollywood to be based on a lie. The joke about Hollywood's stupidity, madness, and immorality was effective as long as we believed that the people who made the joke had values which were not those of Hollywood—but this is no longer true. Motion pictures are a great industry at which many able people are hard at work, and the product of which most of us patronize. We now realize—if we never did before—that the majority of the people who scoff at Hollywood are extremely eager to become and remain part of its corruption, madness, etc.

> Harold Clurman. *The Nation*. Nov. 5, 1955. p. 405

BIBLIOGRAPHY
Beggar's Choice, 1947 (n) (published in 1951 as *Hobson's Choice*); (with others) *Small Wonder*, 1948 (sk); *Blackmailer*, 1952 (n); *The Seven Year Itch*, 1952 (d); *Will Success Spoil Rock Hunter?* 1955 (d); *Goodbye Charlie*, 1959 (d); *Where Am I Now—When I Need Me?*, 1971 (d)

B

BABBITT, Irving (1865–1933)

The distinction of Professor Irving Babbitt is that he endeavours to acquire the now unfashionable but not outworn Socratic virtues: he works for an attitude toward letters and the life of which letters are symptomatic that shall be comprehensive, cohesive and based upon perceptions of wholes.

This direction and this effort enables him to outrank almost all his colleagues in American literary criticism. . . . It is Professor Babbitt's Socratic merit that he has succeeded in charting the contemporary chaos and in construcing for himself a unifying attitude.

> Gorham B. Munson. *Criterion*. June, 1926. pp. 494–6

It is an unpleasant task to profess skepticism about the value of a group of writers who are aiming at the betterment of conduct. The philosophical difficulties that may inhere in Mr. Babbitt's particular defense of sane conduct, I do not feel myself competent to discuss. . . . The ethical code of the Humanists is probably sound enough, but, however sound these abstractions may be, they are of no use to the Humanists or to us so long as they retain the status of pure abstractions; the abstractions remain what Mr. Tate has called wisdom in a vacuum. The arbitrary and mechanical application of these principles to organic experience, whether the experience be literary or non-literary, does not constitute a discipline but rather a pedantic habit.

> Yvor Winters. *The Critique of Humanism*, edited by C. Hartley Grattan (Brewer). 1930. pp. 329–32

Professor Babbitt's doctrine is a compound of snobbery of the kind I find most irritating. Yet it has some elements in it of sense, even if these elements happen to be platitudes which my iceman, cigar dealer, grocer, butcher, bootlegger, garbage man and dentist already know; i.e., that it is best to keep temperate and thrifty, not to let your temper run away with you, not to make a nuisance of yourself, not to get up in the air over trifles, to see that your family gets properly fed and clothed, to pay your bills and not violate the laws. But what is new or Humanistic about that? Not a single person among my personal acquaintance has ever abandoned a child, although quite a few of them have read Rousseau.

> Burton Rascoe. *The Critique of Humanism*, edited by C. Hartley Grattan (Brewer). 1930. p. 123

There is no doubt that his aim is the same as that of Brunetière. He attacks the same multiform manifestations of naturalistic relativity. He agrees with him that "there is needed a principle of restraint in human nature (*un principe refrénant*)," that something must be opposed to "the mobility of our impressions, the unruliness of our individual sense, and the vagrancy of our thought." Brunetière, however, finally came to seek this principle of restraint in revealed religion. Babbitt does not deny that it may be found there, but the conversion of Brunetière, is for him an occasion for insisting that the immediate data of consciousness reveal such a principle of restraint at work within the individual, whether or not he believes in revealed religion. Thus Babbitt finds a way to ground his humanism purely on individualism.

> Louis J.A. Mercier. *The Challenge of Humanism* (Oxford). 1933. pp. 60–1

How perfectly he knew each of those great, queer but powerful beasts, the modernist ideas, how convincingly he set forth the origin, growth, and present shape of each. How admirably he described their skill in concealing themselves, or in appearing innocent while stalking their prey. And how he dissected them all, showing their powerful muscles, their great fangs, and their sacks of poison. . . . To hear him was to understand the modern world.

In his astonishing power of understanding and analysing his enemy, his skill in diagnosing the modernist disease, lies his unique importance.

> Hoffman Nickerson. *Criterion*. Jan., 1934. p. 194

The astonishing fact, as I look back over the years, is that he seems to have sprung up, like Minerva, fully grown and armed. No doubt he made vast additions to his knowledge and acquired by practice a deadly dexterity in wielding it, but there is something almost inhuman in the immobility of his central ideas. He has been criticized for this and ridiculed for harping everlastingly on the same thoughts, as if he lacked the faculty of assimilation and growth. On the contrary, I am inclined to believe that the weight of his influence can be attributed in large measure to just this tenacity of mind. In a world visibly shifting from opinion to opinion and, as it were, rocking on its foundation, here was one who never changed or faltered in his grasp of principles, whose latest words can be set beside his earliest with no apology for inconsistency, who could always be depended on.

> Paul Elmer More. *University of Toronto Quarterly*. Jan., 1934. pp. 132–3

His own manner of speech was of the substantial order, straight forward, unadorned, unimaged, owing its flashes of color either to quotations artfully interwoven or to the antics of a playful humor, which in lighter vein regaled itself by caricaturing and distorting any illogical statement or any lapse from good sense in one's hurried interjections. He had, in dialoguing, a mischievous fondness for playing out the game of argument to a finish and inflicting a sudden and disastrous checkmate on any unwary advances of his opponent—a process not always relished by those whose sense of humor was less active than his own.

> William F. Giese. *Antioch Review*. Nov., 1935. p. 78

Though Babbitt became identified in the public mind with one cause, that which bore the never fully elucidated name humanism, it was recognized in the academic world that he was also the proponent of a cause in one sense larger and more catholic—the cause of the humane study and teaching of literature. At Harvard he fought, in behalf of every American professor who believes that his function comprehends interpretation and criticism, against all who would restrict the academic office to fact-finding, fact-compilation, fact-reporting. Frequently viewed as a reactionary, he defended an academic freedom precious and perishable—the freedom to judge.

Austin Warren. *Commonweal*. June 26, 1936. p. 236

In exposing an idea he would often use a peculiar and significant gesture. His right hand, rising beside its shoulder with spread fingers and outward palm, would make short lateral pushes in the air. There was not the slightest volitant or undulatory motion of the arm—no concession to flying, no fluent gracefulness. Those shoves of the open hand into space—into the spaces of thought—were rigid and impersonal. They insisted that the principle on which he talked was patently universal, belonging to everyone and no one. As for wrong opposing notions, his fingers would sweep them down and away, one after another, while his tongue attacked them.

G.R. Elliott. *Antioch Review*. Nov., 1936. p. 41

His opinions were hard-set, his statements clean-cut and definitive. There was no budging him from his positions. This is what made him a precious friend for me, though I did not share in all his principles or judgments. He was the touchstone on which to assay your own thoughts, when you wanted the stimulus of contradiction—always based on deep reflection, fortified by vast learning, ordered by nimble didacticism. His militant spirit (equal to his athletic strength), and his dogmatic preemptoriness (marked on his deep-set features), displeased some. I felt always attracted to his decided personality. . . . The geniality of his smile and wink took away the sharp edge of his obstinacy.

C. Cestre. *Irving Babbitt*, edited by Frederick Manchester (Putnam). 1941. p. 55

The humanistic point of view is auxiliary to and dependent upon the religious point of view. For us, religion is Christianity; and Christianity implies, I think, the conception of the Church. It would be not only interesting but invaluable if Professor Babbitt, with his learning, his great ability, his influence, and his interest in the most important questions of the time, could reach this point. . . . Such a consummation is impossible. Professor Babbitt knows too much; and by that I do not mean erudition or information or scholarship. I mean that he knows too many religions and philosophies, has assimilated their spirit too thoroughly (there is probably no one in England or America who understands early Buddhism better than he) to be able to give himself to any.

T.S. Eliot. *Selected Essays* (Harcourt). 1950. pp. 427–8

BIBLIOGRAPHY
Literature and the American College, 1908 (e); *The New Laokoon*, 1910 (e); *The Masters of Modern French Criticism*, 1912 (e); *Rousseau and Romanticism*, 1919 (e); *Democracy and Leadership*, 1924 (e); *French Literature*, 1928 (e); *On Being Creative and Other Essays*, 1932; *The Dhammapada*, 1936 (tr); *Spanish Character and Other Essays*, 1940

BACA, Jimmy Santiago (1952–)

Martin & Meditations on the South Valley is . . . strikingly like other Chicano works in concept, theme, and motivation. Like them, it configures America in thoroughly Chicano/a (Latino/a) terms to reach, in this case, a poetic subjectivity that can only, ultimately, be private and self-revealing. In being so, however, it makes itself accessible to the reader outside. Just as we encounter, say, [Allen] Ginsberg or [Sylvia] Plath through the stark subjectivity of their words, so too do we apprehend [Jimmy Santiago] Baca through the directness of his persona, raw, inside his culture. . . .

Baca refus[es] to treat gender thoughtlessly as a category of received meanings and known terms. Intelligent in his approach, he understands gender as a condition that requires fresh contemplation and painstaking treatment if its rendering of men and women is to be as authentic and full as possible. He tries to comprehend the "misery" that made his parents abandon him, leaving him vulnerable as "field prey," and he succeeds in capturing the abject pathos of their self-destructions. In imagining experience from inside their skins and inside those of Caspar the Ghost, *la curandera Feliz*, Grandma Lucero, the *cholos* and *vatos locos* who are his peers, and all the other "real lives in the South Valley," Baca seeks a compelling honesty that means he cannot rely on conventional norms of sex and gender for his language and metaphor. He mostly succeeds, and often brilliantly. Where he doesn't, it is usually in a momentary lapse of diction, not at the profounder level of conceptualization. For example, the word *afterglow* is absolutely wrong to use in the description of a girl's sexual molestation, and in the crucial "Quarai" epiphany scene, it struck me as incomplete for Martin not to explicitly express his desire to love others, only his need to be loved, although his desire is implicit in the scene.

All in all, *Martin & Meditations on the South Valley* works superbly.

Cordelia Candelaria. *American Book Review*. January–February, 1990, pp. 15, 25

BACA: Yes. I'm currently finishing a novel and working on a book of poetry, but all of those things have been done on my terms, not out of pride or arrogance but mostly because I am so interested in the journey of self-discovery that I'm on. Despite the demands I encounter, I still find myself pretty much out here on this farm alone, and I can devise my own journeys, pick the tools I need, and go after things other people wouldn't go after. So I guess what I'm trying to say is that what has occurred over these past few years hasn't changed me much. What it's really reaffirmed is that the work I was doing before is the work I should be doing and I'm doing it now.

KEENE: So many people would love to be able to say what you are saying and mean it.

BACA: You know, it's a very hard way to go and it's not heroic in any sense of the word, but it is fulfilling. You do get up in the morning and feel a real power sense of the tree and the yard and the grass growing and the sun coming up, and you feel yourself very much a part of that whole, tenuous existence in the world, and it's not structured around a paycheck or insurance or tenure or grades or a new car. It's really sustained by a sense of appreciation for one's breathing and getting up and saying, "Hi, how are you?" and "Let's have a cup of coffee": the real small, simple pleasures in life.

KEENE: These small, simple pleasures run like motifs throughout all your poems, all your writings.

BACA: Yeah, the real, small pleasures in life. The idea of just seeing a man in prison who's condemned to die: I come out of the shower and it's nine o'clock and I see him napping and I look at his face, and there's a look on this man's face, on the face of a man who's going to die, that I think is more important for me than to go to work in a prison system and get brownie points. I would much rather go back to the cell and write about what I saw on the man's face. You know?

John Keene. Interview. In *Callaloo*. Winter, 1994, p. 49

One of the most talented voices in the contemporary scene of Chicano poetry, Jimmy Santiago Baca writes poetry that . . . offers a vision of Chicano identity that has a great deal to do with the terrible interplay between historical and contemporary political oppression. Baca brings to us images of violence and violation on a personal level. . . . While voicing an outrage characteristic of much Movimiento poetry, Baca's poetry moves beyond simply casting blame on "America" or "the system." The forms of oppression scrutinized by his poetry result from specific historical regimes in which indigenous values and peoples are erased through violence and malevolent neglect. Aztlan, within the logic of Baca's poetry, becomes a terrain inscribed by history, a terrain that marks but is also marked by the speaker and the subject of his poems. . . . In quick strokes, his poetry fills out the multiplicitous dramas, conflicts, and tensions evident in the lives of its subjects. The history that emerges is one in which the answers to cultural decimation do not descend from the heavens with the blast of trumpet. Salvation, where it exists, occurs on a personal level whereby individual rather than mass empowerment becomes the small response to the detribalization Baca's poetry addresses.

The collection *Black Mesa Poems* offers a series of poems written between 1986 and 1989 that reflect on the relations between humans, history, and land—the three concerns marking Aztlan in its various avatars. The poems construct a sense of history, not, as in [Rodolpho] Gonzales's poem [*I am Joaquin: an epic poem*], as an inertia-driven inevitability. History in Baca's poetry is dynamic and developing. It represents several currents within which Chicanos move and function. Rather than a singular trajectory leading directly from pre-Cortesian civilization through Mexican nationalism to contemporary struggle, history in *Black Mesa Poems* is a varied terrain marked by heterogeneity, a mosaic of violence and beauty that crystallizes in the land of the Black Mesa, a contemporary realm of Aztlan. . . .

Baca's poetry takes up and transforms a number of issues established by earlier poets of Aztlan: history, land, cultural reclamation, hope, advancement, the future. Renouncing apocalyptic or utopian visions of Aztlan, the land for Baca is the Black Mesa of New Mexico. It stands as a terrain that has been marked and crossed by the forces of history, by the players of that history, by the dreams and pains of those players. There is a great deal of interpenetration and fluidity in Baca's vision of history and its

relation to people and communities. History is constructed and reconstructed by humans through the poetry. In this imaginative reconstruction, the connection to the past and the claims to the present are reaffirmed. These claims are based less on the right of previous ownership and ancestry, though elements of this view are evident in Baca's poetry too. Rather, the claims rest on the simple fact that the land has marked and been marked by previous nomads and settlers. This interaction, played out through time and reconstructed through history, connects persons to place, present to past. Aztlan in Baca's poetry represents this rough terrain from which the past has been forged and into which, with resolve and with doubt, the Chicano is fated to proceed.

Rafael Perez-Torres. *Movements in Chicano Poetry: Against Myths, against Margins* (Cambridge: Cambridge Univ. Pr., 1995), pp. 77–78, 84

BIBLIOGRAPHY
Immigrants in Our Own Land, 1979 (p); *Martin & Meditations on the South Valley*, 1987 (p); *Black Mesa Poems*, 1989 (p); *Working in the Dark: Reflections of a Poet of the Barrio*, 1993 (a, e)

BALDWIN, James (1924–1987)

Go Tell It on the Mountain's beauty is the beauty of sincerity and of the courageous facing of hard, subjective truth. This is not to say that there is nothing derivative—of what first novel can this be said?—but James Baldwin's critical judgments are perspicacious and his esthetic instincts sound, and he has read Faulkner and Richard Wright and, very possibly, Dostoevski to advantage. A little of each is here—Faulkner in the style, Wright in the narrative, and the Russian in the theme. And yet style, story, and theme are Baldwin's own, made so by the operation of the strange chemistry of talent which no one fully understands.

J. Saunders Redding. *New York Herald Tribune Book Section*. May 17, 1953. p. 5

Few American writers handle words more effectively in the essay form than James Baldwin. To my way of thinking, he is much better at provoking thought in an essay than he is at arousing emotion in fiction. I much prefer *Notes of a Native Son* to his novel *Go Tell It on the Mountain*, where the surface excellence and poetry of his writing did not seem to me to suit the earthiness of his subject matter. In his essays, words and material suit each other. The thought becomes poetry, and the poetry illuminates the thought.

Langston Hughes. *New York Times Book Section*. Feb. 26, 1956. p. 26

His most conspicuous gift is his ability to find words that astonish the reader with their boldness even as they overwhelm him with their rightness.

The theme of *Giovanni's Room* is delicate enough to make strong demands on all of Mr. Baldwin's resourcefulness and subtlety. . . . Much of the novel is laid in scenes of squalor, with a background of characters as grotesque and repulsive as any that can be found in Proust's *Cities of the Plain*, but even as one is dismayed by Mr. Baldwin's materials, one rejoices in the skill with which he renders them. . . . Mr. Baldwin's subject (is) the rareness and difficulty of love, and, in his rather startling way, he does a great deal with it.

> Granville Hicks. *New York Times Book Section*. Oct. 14, 1956. p. 5

Giovanni's Room is the best American novel dealing with homosexuality I have read. . . . James Baldwin successfully avoids the cliché literary attitudes: over-emphasis on the grotesque and the use of homosexuality as a facile symbol for the estrangement which makes possible otherwise unavailable insights into the workings of ''normal'' society. . . . Baldwin insists on the painful, baffling complexity of things. . . . The complexities are of course most numerous in the treatment of the relationship between David and Giovanni. The void of mutual lovelessness . . . is the central pain of homosexual relationships.

> William Esty. *New Republic*. Dec. 17, 1956, p. 26

I'm sure that Baldwin doesn't like to hear his essays praised at the expense (seemingly) of his fiction. And I'm equally sure that if Baldwin were not so talented a novelist he would not be so remarkable an essayist. But the great thing about his essays is that the form allows him to work out from all the conflicts raging in *him*, so that finally the ''I,'' the ''James Baldwin'' who is so sassy and despairing and bright, manages, without losing his authority as the central speaker, to show us all the different people hidden in him, all the voices for whom the ''I'' alone can speak. . . . To be James Baldwin is to touch on so many hidden places in Europe, America, the Negro, the white man—to be forced to understand so much.

> Alfred Kazin. *Contemporaries* (Little). 1962. pp. 255–6

While any evaluation of Baldwin as writer must consider both his essays and his novels, it is, hopefully, for the latter that he will be remembered. Since the essays, for the most part, deal with contemporary problems, they will become historical; that is, again hopefully, they will cease to apply to current situations. Yet it is partly on the basis of the essays that one has faith in his value as a novelist, for some of the resources on which he must draw are revealed most sharply in the essays. What seems to be the case is that Baldwin has yet to find the artistic form that will reveal the mystery, that will uncover the truth he knows is there. If he does, if his intention and accomplishment become one, if his intellectual grasp is matched by his imaginative, he will be a writer whose measure it will be difficult to take.

> James Finn. *Commonweal*. Oct. 26, 1962. p. 116

James Baldwin has written, in *Another Country*, the big novel everyone has thought for years he had in him. It is a work of great integrity and great occasional power; but I am afraid I can do no more than the damned compact liberal majority has done, and pronounce it an impressive failure. Spiritually, it's a pure and noble novel; though it's largely populated by perverts, bums, queers, and

tramps, with only an occasional contemptible square interspersed, I wasn't much distressed by their comings, couplings, and goings. They are looking for love in some fairly unlikely ways and places, but the commodity is a rare one, and we can't afford to overlook possibilities. No, the book's faults are mainly technical. One of them has to do with the difficult question of dialect. Most of Mr. Baldwin's characters are of the hipster persuasion, or at least on the near fringe of hipsterism, and the patois he makes them talk has most of the faults of artifice and few of the merits of originality. In effect, their argot is dull and uninventive. We are supposed to feel about many of these characters that they're proud, sensitive, suffering souls; it is thoroughly depressing to find, when they open their lips flecked with anguish, that, man, they talk like trite. They're always mouthing about ''making it'' and if they could break the shackles of their degenerate dialect, it's indeed conceivable that they might make a phrase or an image or something.

> Robert M. Adams. *Partisan Review*. Spring, 1963. pp. 131–2

When Baldwin records, with finest notation, his exacerbated sense of what it is like to be a Negro; when he renders, with furious conviction, the indignities and humiliations which attend his every step, the stiffening and perpetual pressure which closes in upon a Negro simply because he is one; when he conveys his sense of the social climate by which the Negro comes despairingly to know, from earliest childhood, the atmosphere in which desperation is bred, that he is a pariah, a little more than animal, but less than human—then, I have no doubt, there can scarcely be a Negro who does not listen to him with full assent. But when we listen to any of Baldwin's voices—his passionately exhoratory warning or his pleading—it is not the voice, nor is it the tone of reason we are hearing, for Baldwin is not a ''reasonable'' man; it is a lamentation and a curse and a prayer.

> Saul Maloff. *The Nation*. March 2, 1963. p. 181

The largeness of purpose and gentleness of intention which Baldwin voices have brought a new climate, a new element, a new season, to our country in our time. That season, that climate, that element which are James Baldwin, they are now in the foreground of America's awareness. There is no way now that anyone can fail to recognize them, and to endure them, and to contend with them. They cannot be dismissed. It may even be that crops will have to be planted differently out of a consideration of this new season, or that quite new crops will have to be found which will flourish in the new climate, and that all the old fences and defences will be levelled by the fury of that new element. In his essays, his novels, his short stories, Baldwin has levelled the ground so that we may start anew.

> Kay Boyle in *Contemporary American Novelists*, ed. Harry T. Moore (Southern Illinois). 1964. p. 156

We should note that the title ''Another Country'' is lively with irony, for the novel presents a world as we know it but as it has not before been put in fiction to be seen, ''other'' by its ominous distance from what it ought to be and from real human needs, and then ''other'' as some private land where a handful of people have honored and renewed themselves. This tension epitomizes the book's role in Baldwin's vision. It does not cry out with the so bold and explicit warnings of "Letter from a Region in My Mind," but the prophet's tones there are really based in *Another Country*. An analogy is the way the self-reliance of "Civil Disobedience" is founded on the renewal and independence of vision Thoreau established at Walden. Baldwin had to discover his "distant land"—to use Thoreau's term—from which to see the essential unreality of New York. In this respect this third novel might be called the greatest of his liberal educations, just as it is the most informative for his audience. It is only from the distant land of *Another Country* that he can criticize the false land both toughly and compassionately, and the simultaneous violent content and delicate style in other work depends on this distance.

> Robert F. Sayre in *Contemporary American Novelists*, ed. Harry T. Moore (Southern Illinois). 1964 p. 167

To solve our national problem of racial tensions we must think clearly and plan soundly because we are in a delicate moment, when the anger of many Negroes is naked and the sorrows and guilts of whites more exposed. For Mr. Baldwin, regardless of *what* we say or try to do, Western civilization seems suspect and faltering. He allows the Negro scant susceptibility to the many problems which afflict whites—of identity, of religion, of survival, of intimacy and sexuality. The Negro is an outcast, plundered so long that his fate becomes an almost total historical judgment upon the white, Western world, a world which, according to Mr. Baldwin, knows very little about itself, because as he points out, it cannot understand the Negro. Yet, apparently the Negro can understand the white man, and can save him from his impending doom. The Negro, having given love to inadequate whites, is the crucial factor in finally enabling the white man to solve his problems of identity. There is a cynical medical and psychiatric core in me which must reject such an argument. The problems of "identity" and sexuality are simply too complicated for rhetoric of Baldwin's kind.

> Robert Coles. *Partisan Review*. Summer, 1964. p. 414

A "protest play," unfortunately, always has a hard time of it artistically, and even more so if, like Baldwin, the playwright doth protest too much. And not only too much but too much, too soon. Right at the outset [of *Blues for Mister Charlie*] we are clobbered with a tirade which is an inflammatory inventory of all the injustices toward the Negro, and, justified as these grievances are, they strike a false note: you do not paint a picture that is to be a work of art with air brush and poster paint—unless, that is, you are a pop artist—and Baldwin would shudder at the thought of having written a pop-art play. But that is what it is: agit-prop art.

Baldwin is undoubtedly one of our ablest essayists and literary journalists—terms I use with respect—but as a novelist he has always struck me as a failure, and a progressively worse one, at that. Somewhere hedged in by fact and opinion lies the domain of fiction, which is neither brute reality nor the spinning out of speculation, however profound or piercing. In fiction—and in drama, too—certain moods, experiences, states of being and insights achieve a solidity of texture through psychological exactness, tasteful selection of detail, architectural structuring, and (most important, though least definable) a poetic sensitivity to words. In these things, Baldwin is more or less deficient, and his assumption

of the mantle of embattled prophethood and the consequent thickening of his voice have made matters worse.

> John Simon. *Hudson Review*. Autumn. 1964. p. 421

Baldwin's writing, depending so much on the straightforward humane statement rather than on irony, wit, or the savage comic imagination of a Ralph Ellison, occasionally falls into platitude; but Baldwin is intuitive and courageous enough to know that this is where his chief strength lies—common experience uncommonly probed—so that while he occasionally expects the flat statement to do more literary work than it humanly can, I am still impressed by his maturity and understanding as a man. He knows life in a way that I can only call enlightened by Negro wisdom; it is the same older, deeper, seamier, finally larger grasp of suffering and reality that I have heard in the great Negro singers and have observed in certain subtly seasoned Negro acquaintances.

> Seymour Krim. *New York Herald Tribune Book Section*. Nov. 7, 1965. p. 5

The lives of the characters in these stories seem to possess an extra dimension of emptiness, because he sees them against the possibility of a very different kind of life: a life of ceremonies and mysteries touching the absolute. He is searching for another city and another country. Like the great moralizing novelists, he is a preacher; he writes to bear witness. It would be ridiculous, as well as rude, to tell him he should take another tack. My complaint is simply that the total hunger aching inside him has driven him on to invest certain aspects of secular life—notably sex—with a blasphemous grace, and, alas, the grace is artistically unconvincing. The beauty of the language in *Go Tell It on the Mountain* brought the hero's experience of salvation to life; and, faithful to the spirit of the blues, Baldwin left much of the book's anguish unresolved. But in recent works he has made larger and larger claims for his various instruments of salvation, while the instruments themselves have become less and less convincing. When, in *Another Country*, Baldwin gives us the word about the redeeming majesty of the orgasm—multiracial, heterosexual, or homosexual—you sense a lack of artistic control, to say nothing of a loss of common sense.

> Joseph Featherstone. *New Republic*. Nov. 27, 1965. pp. 34–5

When he is not playing the role of the militant Negro intellectual or proving his social relevance, and especially when he is not writing about the United States, James Baldwin is willing to recognize the importance of status and place and of a reasonable degree of hierarchy in an orderly and civilized society. He remarks approvingly that Europeans have lived with the idea of status for a long time. . . . But when he speaks of America, he insists that the past has no relevance, that the heritage of Western civilization is of questionable value, that what we have in this country must be unrelated to any past scheme of social order. . . . He is, as we might expect, suspicious or even resentful of Faulkner's identification with the place Mississippi—which makes it all the more interesting and ironic that Mr. Baldwin's own best work is the result of his marked (if unwilling) identification with Harlem.

> M.E. Bradford. *Georgia Review*. Winter, 1966. p. 439

In *Blues for Mr. Charlie*, Baldwin translates his apocalypse into concrete social terms. The race war is not yet quite upon us, but the play ends with preparation for a Negro protest march in a small Southern town in which its leader-minister keeps a gun in readiness concealed under his Bible. The alternatives are clear: love or violence, the Negro can wait no longer. Baldwin's theater resembles nothing so much—in form and fervor, at least—as the protest dramas of the radical left in the thirties. But the play is effective, for the emotions it arouses are specifically vindictive and personally embarrassing to his white audiences, which partly explains, no doubt, its failure on the Broadway stage. For Baldwin, the preacher, not only thunders at his audience's failure of social and human responsibility, but, far worse, he impugns their sexuality and depicts them as more terrified of the possibilities of life than the Negroes they persecute.

> Edward Margolies. *Native Sons* (Lippincott). 1968. p. 124

I do not take back what I said about Baldwin's having become a great writer—I've said it enough. But no matter how great he is, he does not seem to have anything new or different or progressive to say anymore. This could very well mean that, among other things, Baldwin has unwittingly or wittingly written himself into the very species personage that he has seemingly been trying to destroy, the species personage of The Father. Whether this is true or not, or whether it is true for a certain period, it is clear that he has necessitated if not nurtured into being a radically different set of black writers from himself and, alas, has been eclipsed by them.

Let me make one thing absolutely clear. These writers are not in competition with James Baldwin, nor are they in conflict with him. Nor can anyone take Baldwin's "place" as a writer, and certainly not as a black writer. Baldwin is an individual writer in his own right.

> Calvin C. Hernton in *Amistad I*, ed. John A. Williams and Charles F. Harris (Random). 1970. p. 213

Baldwin is saying in effect in this novel [*Another Country*] that we Americans have failed to live up to our professed moral commitments and that the innocence and puritanism of the country are largely at fault. This novel is like the essays insofar as Baldwin's stance is moral indignation. He is simply furious that America possesses the character it has. But what about more pertinent issues such as jobs, housing, health, education, etc.? What of the issues beyond the personal and the private? Baldwin is not so much concerned about these as about the moral issues. Hence his novel is about love, and only a moralist who does not grant the role of politics in determining the quality of life could believe that love is so central. . . . His most recent novel, *Tell Me How Long the Train's Been Gone*, reveals the same position. There Baldwin expresses sympathetic understanding of the political perspective, but clearly enough it is not his own.

> Donald B. Gibson in *The Politics of Twentieth-Century Novelists*, ed. George A. Panichas (Hawthorn). 1971. pp. 318–9

Baldwin certainly risked a great deal [in *If Beale Street Could Talk*] by putting his complex narrative, which involves a number of important characters, into the mouth of a young girl. Yet Tish's voice comes to seem absolutely natural and we learn to know her from the inside out. Even her flights of poetic fancy—involving rather subtle speculations upon the nature of male-female relationships, or black-white relationships, as well as her articulation of what it feels like to be pregnant—are convincing. Also convincing is Baldwin's insistence upon the primacy of emotions like love, hate, or terror: it is not sentimentality, but basic psychology, to acknowledge the fact that one person will die, and another survive simply because one has not the guarantee of a fundamental human bond, like love, while the other has. . . .

The novel progresses swiftly and suspensefully, but its dynamic movement is interior. Baldwin constantly understates the horror of his characters' situation in order to present them as human beings whom disaster has struck, rather than as blacks who have, typically, been victimized by whites and are therefore likely subjects for a novel.

> Joyce Carol Oates. *New York Times Book Section*. May 19, 1974. pp. 1–2

To read *If Beale Street Could Talk* as accurate social drama seems to me virtually impossible. I can't care as much as I want to about Fonny and Tish unless the system that victimizes them is described in a way that I can recognize. No one can doubt that terrible things are done to good and innocent black people. But Baldwin writes so flatly and schematically that he drives one to imagining ways in which his story might be more "believable.". . .

So one must try to read this novel allegorically, taking Tish and Fonny as Romeo and Juliet (as they're in fact teasingly called by some of their friends), cop-crossed lovers victimized by a repressive order whose exact workings don't really matter. They are credible and often affecting as lovers, but the fantasy on which Baldwin's allegory relies may disturb some of Baldwin's readers, particularly black ones: blackness in a white system becomes here a condition of helpless passivity, of getting screwed by the man; persecution and violation are emphasized so insistently and despairingly that enduring them becomes a kind of acceptance.

In fairness, I should say that Fonny is allowed to keep what manhood is possible for him by surviving confinement and escaping the homosexual rape he deeply fears that prison has in store for him. . . . But if Baldwin's political meanings carry an essentially sexual message, the frustrated rage in this novel needs a clearer relation to its inner subject. As it is, I unhappily suggest that an important and honorable writer has failed to make us believe in his vision of horrors that surely do exist, but outside his book.

> Thomas R. Edwards. *New York Review of Books*. June 13, 1974. p. 37

Without Wright's rage, or Ellison's intellectual distance, Baldwin is particularly exposed to hurt. He is tormented by the way he is treated, and he faces us with a chronicle of pain that is intensely personal. But his self-absorption, his intimate insights into his own anguish seem to be the sign of a final break-away from the old prison in which just such self-absorption was prohibited. In some ways, Baldwin's very personalism, with all its idiosyncrasies and neurotic ticks, comes closest of all to embodying the force that powers the liveliest thrusts in the Movement. For Baldwin is the first black writer to give real poetic depth to the polemics of black pride.

Sadly enough, his poetic powers have seemed to decline since his first novel, *Go Tell It on the Mountain*. But he gives us in that work an imaginative expression of the black struggle for self-awareness and the ascent toward self-affirmation that is both deeper and more explicit than that in either *Native Son or Invisible Man*. . . .

In the novels that he writes after *Go Tell It on the Mountain*—*Giovanni's Room* (1956), *Another Country* (1962), *Tell Me How Long the Train's Been Gone* (1968), and *If Beale Street Could Talk* (1974)—Baldwin seems to become more and more a spokesman for blackness and homosexuality. He moves toward the need for solutions, for a victory of darkness or light. He struggles increasingly against his early willingness to accept the mystery of his condition, and his fiction diminishes in quality accordingly. But no one can take from him his greatest achievement, the poetic interpretation of a new black consciousness and the expression of its complexities and paradoxes. Because it formulates so expressively the forces at work in the black culture during the early 1950s, because it engages social issues at a personal and emotional depth, *Go Tell It on the Mountain* will outlive most of Baldwin's essays, which have brought him, and quite justly, so much current attention.

> Jerry H. Bryant. *Phylon*. June, 1976, pp. 184, 186–87

In his dramas, James Baldwin has followed both paths of contemporary black playwrights—most consciously writing for white spectators when he seems to be denouncing them (*Blues for Mister Charlie*), most effectively creating for black audiences when he seems unaware of any audience (*The Amen Corner*). Yet the varying reactions to the two plays clearly illustrate the problem of the black playwright. Sensational, melodramatic, and written for whites, *Blues for Mister Charlie* provoked controversy that increased the attention accorded to it. The more thoughtful, more realistic, more credible *The Amen Corner* waited a decade for professional production, then appeared almost without comment. The question that arises is, Can a black be respected simultaneously as an artist and as a faithful portrayer of black life if his reputation depends upon an audience that neither knows nor cares about the world depicted by that black, but is concerned only with the effect of that world on the lives of white Americans?. . .

Baldwin's theme in *The Amen Corner* is not restricted to black people. The need for love and understanding is propounded as emphatically in *Another Country*, where Baldwin shows that white, middle-class people must learn to love each other. This theme, in fact, dominates Baldwin's work: human beings must learn to give themselves totally to other human beings if humankind is to survive. Nevertheless, he seems to develop this recurrent thesis more credibly within the traditionally religious context and church setting of *The Amen Corner* than in the topical, political situation of *Blues for Mister Charlie*.

In short, in *The Amen Corner* Baldwin achieved a success in theme and characterization surpassing his effort in *Blues for Mister Charlie*.

> Darwin T. Turner. In *James Baldwin: A Critical Evaluation*, ed. Thermon B. O'Daniel (Howard Univ. Pr., 1977), pp. 190, 193–94

James Baldwin has asked the most urgent and penetrating questions any modern novelist has asked about certain key patterns of human relationships. Deeply thinking and deeply feeling, he explores the possibilities of love, the inevitabilities of hate, and the bloody angles of race relations. And these fearsome interrogations are carried out in the harsh, tangible realities of urban America. Further, Baldwin treats all these confrontations as the substance of the artist's essential task—to dig into himself and into others for truths about the human condition and to report the truths accurately and unflinchingly. He has much to tell us about the social roles and the psychological and sexual identities of men and women; he reveals the meanings of blackness and whiteness, and of their commingling, in the United States. His mastery of style renders his many sad truths not palatable but palpable; we feel them on the nerve. It also colors his few joyous truths with a luminous intensity, with a thrilling energy of awareness. . . .

Baldwin's great merit, the artist's merit, as a chronicler of race relations in America is that he makes us see and feel the subjective realities of the national torment. Behind the tracts and statistics, the histories and sociologies and psychologies, there are breathing people; Baldwin takes us into their minds and hearts and forces upon us realizations that horrify and depress—but that may ultimately heal. Particularly in his two best novels, *Go Tell It on the Mountain* and *Another Country*, he examines the interior sense of race and class, driving home the implications of these blunt facts of existence. . . .

Baldwin makes vivid the consequences of racial subordination for individual behavior and for the contours of black personality. His art might be almost a dramatization of the analysis of black psychological functioning set forth by the psychiatrists Abram Kardiner and Lionel Ovesey in their provocative study *The Mark of Oppression*. They argue that the "mark" imposed by the long history of discrimination and enforced inequality contains the central elements of low self-esteem and aggression. Attempts to deal with these elements are a series of largely futile maneuvers, self-defeating in the main, as long as the social structure of injustice remains in place. Although the years since Kardiner and Ovesey's research and since the first publication of Baldwin's novels have been distinguished by some very important charges in educational and occupational opportunity and by the abolition of legal segregation, the damage and rage are still with us in significant quantities. Baldwin captures them as no other writer, black or white, has ever done.

> Robert N. Wilson. *The Writer as Social Seer* (Univ. of North Carolina Pr., 1979), pp. 89–91

What can one say after summarizing, sampling, analyzing and interpreting the work of James Baldwin and reactions to that work, except that here is a writer of exceptional range and power. What is sometimes lacking in aesthetic control over long art forms such as the novel is more than adequately made up for by concisely constructed scenes, descriptions, sentences. Some of Baldwin's habits are bound to be irritating to some readers—his use of profanity, his explicit and sentimental sex scenes, his castigation of white America, his seeming inability to rid himself of early religious training he finds bothersome but ingrained, his repetition of some ideas, phrases, scenes. But what emerges, nevertheless, from the whole of his work, is a kind of absolute conviction and passion and honesty that is nothing less than courageous.

When his work is joined with his life, the picture of courage grows. As we see Baldwin now victorious against the odds of poverty, race, stature, looks, homosexuality, publishing realities for black authors, it is needful to remind ourselves of the struggle that victory represents. We must remind ourselves because Baldwin has shared his struggle with his readers for a purpose—to demonstrate that our suffering is our bridge to one another. For an introduction to his life and work to do less than state that ultimate purpose behind everything Baldwin has written would be, I think, to do him a disservice.

Carolyn Wedin Sylvander. *James Baldwin* (Ungar, 1980), pp. 148–49

In truth, the way of life reconstructed in most of [James] Baldwin's novels is informed by a biblical imagination that is almost as bleak as that in *Native Son*. In *Go Tell It on the Mountain* (1953) the Grimes family has only a tenuous grip on reality due to the religiosity of the storefront Pentecostal church. In *Giovanni's Room* (1956) the subject of black culture is displaced by the moral and social problems of white homosexuals in Europe. In *Another Country* (1962) a tortuous series of racial and sexual encounters—white vs. black, homosexual vs. heterosexual, North vs. South, European vs. American—drives jazz musician Rufus Scott to suicide but becomes the rite of passage to self-understanding for his jazz-singing sister Ida and the social rebels of modern America who affirm bisexuality as the highest form of love. In *Tell Me How Long the Train's Been Gone* (1968) Leo Proudhammer contends with his private and public demons—heart condition, white mistress, black militant lover, racism, and the stultifying influence of his family—as he claws his way to salvation as a black actor. In *If Beale Street Could Talk* (1974) Tish and Fonny, the blues protagonists, are able to endure and transcend the agony of harassment in the ghetto and prison through love (personal and familial) and art (black music and sculpture). And in *Just above My Head*, Hall Montana, the first-person narrator-witness and older brother of the gospel-singing protagonist, testifies about the agonizing realities of human suffering and the ecstatic possibilities of love in the lives of those touched by his brother's journey on the gospel road.

As fascinating and ambitious as these novels are, only *Go Tell It on the Mountain, If Beale Street Could Talk*, and *Just above My Head* illuminate the matrix of shared experience of black Americans. But like [Richard] Wright, Baldwin focuses sharply on a single dimension of black culture. His emphasis, however, is not political but spiritual and sexual, not the terrifying possibilities of hatred, but the terrifying possibilities of love. In contrast to Wright's unrelenting narrative drive. Baldwin's short stories and novels are memorable for the soul-stirring eloquence and resonance of their pulpit oratory and black music as they plumb the depths of our suffering and the possibilities of our salvation. His use of the rhetoric, lore, and music of the black church show to their best advantage in his four collections of essays and in *Go Tell It on the Mountain*. But they are also organically significant in *If Beale Street Could Talk* and *Just above My Head*.

Bernard W. Bell. *The Afro-American Novel and Its Tradition* (Amherst: Univ. of Massachusetts Pr., 1987), p. 219

Far from being licentious and orgiastic—charges flung at him in the 1960s, especially after *Another Country*—Baldwin's sexual ethics are puritanical, in that he stresses the place of love and self-knowledge in every sexual event. . . .

Baldwin said many times, and repeated near the end of his life, that he was not "a believer." "If the concept of God has any validity or any use, it can only be to make us larger, freer, and more loving. If God cannot do this, then it is time we got rid of Him." These words were written in 1962, and his position had scarcely altered since.

But while he was not a believer in the sense of subscribing to a particular faith, or belonging to a specific church, his life was based on a faith that can only be called religious, just as his thought was infused with religious belief. His scripture was the old black gospel music.

James Campbell. *Talking at the Gates: A Life of James Baldwin* (New York: Viking, 1991), pp. 273, 281

Two of Baldwin's novels, *Another Country* and *Giovanni's Room*, deal centrally with gay relationships and issues of sexuality. The first-named of these is one of the great novels of our century. . . . The earlier work is interesting in its own right, but especially worth examining because it shows the author in the toils of certain prejudices from which, by the time of the later book, he had largely emancipated himself. Studying the two novels together is thus particularly interesting as it provides, among other things, a kind of chart of the author's intellectual, moral, and aesthetic development. . . .

Like Genet and [Tennessee] Williams, Baldwin always insists on love's fragility and transience. The novel's title has some relevance here, for "the room" in its cramped awkwardness is a symbol of the sexual panic and claustrophobia suffered by David. Its being far from the center, at [Place de] Nation [in Paris], signals what appears to David the peripheral experience of gay love. Giovanni has painted out the ground floor window and sits quite still next to it, in tension, when there are people to be heard on the other side of the window whom he cannot see—all of which is suggestive of gay closetry and secrecy. Giovanni's attempts literally to demolish part of the walls and build an alcove (that is, an extension) for books, is yet another (admittedly rather labored) symbol of the need to break out of the relationship.

The second aspect of *Giovanni's Room* which anticipates *Another Country* is the skillful presentation of character, in which the idea of people being fixed in any set of dispositions or traits is eschewed. . . .

This shifting of perspectives in relation to characters is mirrored by the nature of the episodes themselves. Rarely staying in the same emotional key, they move from gaiety to melancholy, from celebration to the funereal. . . .

Giovanni's Room is too embarrassed by the full implications of its subject matter. It enters bravely, but then shrinks away. It is, most significantly, informed by a collaborator's shame. But it is the beginning of the road which leads to one of the finest novels of our time.

Mark Lilly. *Gay Men's Literature in the Twentieth Century* (New York: New York Univ. Pr., 1993), pp. 144, 167

More than any other writer of his generation, white or black, gay or straight, man or woman, it would not be an exaggeration to say, James Baldwin exerted a moral hold on the American imagination nonpareil in the annals of this country's literature and its public debate for nearly four decades, a status clearly in league with that of Emerson and Thoreau and Douglass. (Though it must be noted that Baldwin never won any of the awards consonant with such distinction—the Pulitzer Prize, the National Book Award, the Nobel Prize.) Nonetheless, this author of six novels, several books of essays, three plays, and a number of short stories, this unusual looking, frail, high-strung, black, gay man did battle with the intractable American chimeras—racism, capitalism, brutality—with only a pen and a message, most simply, of love and redemption.

In one of his earliest published essays, "The Harlem Ghetto," he adjudges:

> In America, though, life seems to move faster than anywhere else on the globe and each generation is promised more than what it will get: which creates, in each generation, a furious, bewildered rage, the rage of people who cannot find solid ground beneath their feet.

That essay, written in 1948, has an uncanny relevance forty-six years later, especially in light of the Los Angeles riots of 1992, the rise of violent crime, the problems of the American penal system, escalating unemployment and the so-called Generation X and its dismal future prospects. From the beginning James Baldwin had a language and a style of delivery informed by his youthful training as a Pentecostal minister and by his intimate knowledge of the King James Bible and its voices in the wilderness of the Judeo-Christian tradition. In a great many ways he became an America Jeremiah warning us of impending doom, a Jonah in exile in the belly of France, a courageous Isaiah on the march in Selma, Alabama, a fiery Hosea on the television screen, from the radio, atop the speaker's platform. . . .

Clearly Baldwin's was a life and mind made for legend. And in our current age of MTV and personal computers and Scud missiles and virtual reality, it is difficult to remember exactly how much of a legend in his own time was the author of *The Fire Next Time*—that fiercely eloquent investigation into the Nation of Islam and exploration of religion and race and the American dilemma. Upon its publication in 1963, Baldwin was on the cover of *Time*, in *Life*, saturating the airwaves, a guest at the White House. Nor is it easy to comprehend the inexplicable daring and courage it took for a thirty-two-year-old black man to publish a novel about a love affair between two white men, *Giovanni's Room*, in 1956. America was about to lose her hateful illusion of innocence, and James Baldwin was undoubtedly one of her most passionate and looked-to Native Sons.

Randall Kenan. *The Nation.* May 2, 1994, p. 596

Baldwin was a writer who could combine the cadence of the King James Bible and Henry James in what he liked to call the "beat" of African-American culture. His audience was the whole "nation," and he incorporated the whole nation into his voice. His was the "voice in the wilderness" that preached the necessity of touching. In his personal life and his work, he took the side of those who were made into exiles and outcasts by barriers of race, sex, and class or who turned away from safety and chose the honorable path of tearing down such barriers. But he mourned for those who had created the barriers and had unwittingly allowed themselves to be destroyed by them.

David Leeming. *James Baldwin: A Biography* (New York: Knopf, 1994), p. xiii

BIBLIOGRAPHY
Go Tell It on the Mountain, 1953 (n); *Notes of a Native Son*, 1955 (e); *Giovanni's Room*, 1956 (n); *Nobody Knows My Name*, 1961 (e); *Another Country*, 1962 (n); *The Fire Next Time*, 1963 (e); *Blues for Mister Charlie*, 1964 (d); *Going to Meet the Man*, 1965 (s); *Tell Me How Long the Train's Been Gone*, 1968 (n); *The Amen Corner*, 1968 (d); (with Margaret Mead) *A Rap on Race*, 1971 (conversations); *No Name in the Street*, 1972 (e); (with Nikki Giovanni) *A Dialogue*, 1973 (conversations); *If Beale Street Could Talk*, 1974 (n); *The Devil Finds Work*, 1976 (e); *Little Man, Little Man: A Story of Childhood*, 1976 (juv); *Horse Fair*, 1976 (juv); *Just above My Head*, 1979 (n); *Evidence of Things Not Seen*, 1983 (j); *The Price of the Ticket: Collected Non-Fiction 1984–1985*, 1985 (misc); *Jimmy's Blues*, 1986 (p); et al., *Perspectives: Angles on African Art*, 1987 (interviews on African sculpture); *Conversations*, 1989 (r, i.e., interviews); *Early Novels and Stories*, 1998; *Collected Essays*, 1998

BAMBARA, Toni Cade (1939–1995)

A title with a religious allusion may seem inappropriate for an essay on the works of Toni Cade Bambara since religion, i.e., Christianity, as it is often depicted in the works of Black writers with their depictions of hair straightening, signifying in church, and preacher men—sometimes more physically passionate than spiritually—is conspicuously absent here. In fact, many of the usual concerns, about color and class, frequently found in the writings of other Black women prosaists, are absent. Bambara appears less concerned with mirroring the Black existence in America than in chronicling "the movement" intended to improve and change that existence. Like a griot, who preserves the history of his or her people by reciting it, Bambara perpetuates the struggle of her people by literally recording it in their own voices.

Her three major works of fiction, *Gorilla, My Love* (1972), *The Sea Birds Are Still Alive* (1977), and *The Salt Eaters* (1980), trace the civil rights movement in America from its inception, through its most powerful expression, to its loss of momentum. Each uses language to particularize and individualize the voices of the people wherever they are—on a New York City street, crossing the waters of the Pacific, amid the red salt clay of the Louisiana earth—and to celebrate their progress as they think, feel, and act in their struggle to be free.

But, paradoxically, while Bambara uses language to capture the speech patterns of the characters she idiomatically places in their time and space, Bambara eschews language, words, rhetoric, as the modus operandi for the people to attain their freedom. For Bambara, an innate spirituality, almost mystical in nature, must be endemic to the people if they are to have success. Her works juxtapose the inadequacy of language and the powers of the spirit, which needs no words to spread its light among the masses.

Ruth Elizabeth Burks. "From Baptism to Resurrection: Toni Cade Bambara and the Incongruity of Language." In Mari Evans, ed. *Black Women Writers* (Garden City, New York: Doubleday, 1984), pp. 48–49

Ultimately the genuinely modern writer "assumes a culture and supports the weight of a civilization." That assumption connects the present moment both to an immediate and to a remote past. From such a writer, we learn that whoever is able to live completely in the present, sustained by the lesson of the past, commands the future. The vitality of the jazz musician, by analogy, is precisely this ability to compose, in vigorous images of the most recent musical language, the contingencies of time in an examined present moment. The jam session, the ultimate formal expression of the jazz musician, is, on one hand, a presentation of all the various ways, past and present, that a tune may be heard; on the other, it is a revision of the past history of a tune, or of its presentation by other masters, ensuring what is lasting and valuable and useful in the tune's present moment and discarding what is not. Constructing rapid contrasts of curiously mingled disparities, the jam session is both a summing up and a part-by-part examination by various instruments of an integrity called melody. Now a melody is nothing more or less than the musical rendition of what a poet or a historian calls theme. And a theme is no other thing than a noticeable pattern occurring through time as time assumes its rhythmic cycle: past, present, and future. *The Salt Eaters* of Toni Cade Bambara is a modern myth of creation told in the jazz mode.

A narrative which opens with a direct question—"Are you, sure, sweetheart, that you want to be well?"—evokes from us an immediate response. In a time of ubiquitous pollution, unless we are head-buried geese, we answer: Yeah! By leave of our spontaneous response to an irresistible call (the mode of the jazz composer), we enter the improvising, stylizing, re-creative, fecund, and not-so-make-believe world of *The Salt Eaters*. That world, called Claybourne, Georgia, is in a state of definition and transition: "Claybourne hadn't settled on its identity yet. . . . Its history put it neither on this nor that side of the Mason Dixon. And its present seemed to be a cross between a little Atlanta, a big Mount Bayou and Trenton, New Jersey, in winter." But we enter Claybourne during its preparation for spring festival, and there we discover what resembles a splendid community marketplace: "Tables, tents, awnings, rides, fortunetellers, candy booths, gymnasts with mats, nets, trampolines, oil drums from the islands, congos from who knew where, flat trucks, platforms, pushcarts and stalls of leather crafts, carved cooking spoons, jewelry . . . flower carts, incense peddlers . . . kids racing by with streamers and balloons. . . Folks readying up for the festival" scheduled to begin when "Hoo Doo Man broke out of the projects with a horned helmet . . . and led the procession through the district to the Mother Earth floats by the old railroad yard." We discover that during festival, "People were supposed to write down all the things they wanted out of their lives—bad habits, bad debts, bad dreams—and throw them on the fire." Claybourne is in preparation for the rites of spring renewal. Yet in the midst of "the fugue-like interweaving of voices" resonant in the streets, we hear the voice of a street-corner preacher admonishing:

History is calling us to rule again and you lost dead souls are standing around doing the freakie dickie . . . never recognizing the teachers come among you to prepare you for the transformation, never recognizing the synthesizers come to forge the new alliances, or the guides who throw open the new footpaths, or the messengers come to end all excuses. Dreamer? The dream is real, my friends. The failure to make it work is the unreality.

The ominous cry of the street preacher, urging the community to recall its history, manifest its destiny, and heed its laws, intones the themes of its spring celebration: transformation, synthesis, and renewal.

As the community must engage its history in order to decipher the meaning of its own rituals—the rhythmic movement toward its destiny—so the individual self must engage its history in order to be well (whole); for if it does not, it hazards the loss of all that makes it whole. That loss is unaffordable and dread; it abates the power of regeneration.

The voice of the street preacher merges with the voice which has opened the narrative. That voice, its music "running its own course up under the words" is the Ebonic, mythopoeic voice of Minnie Ransom, "fabulous healer" of Claybourne, directly addressing Velma Henry, her patient, the celebrant, who enacts the meaning of the ritual that the entire community prepares to celebrate. It is through Velma's consciousness that we hear and observe everything that we know of Claybourne; it is Velma's personal transformation that we experience and that figures in the possibility of the community's renewal; it is through Velma's negation and acceptance of the actual and her pursuit of the possible that we learn the identity and enormous re-creative powers of those who have eaten salt together and who have learned to reconcile both the brine and the savor of life. . . .

Modernity, a jam session constructing rapid contrasts of curiously mingled disparities, is at once an extension of the past and a conduit of some future balancing of the best and worst of human possibilities. Thus, the child, also a passenger on the boat of refugees, snuggling close beside her mother as they grope their way topside to the deck searching a seat, is directed: "the passengers along the way grabbing the small hand and leading the child to the next hand outstretched." This child, like lil' Hazel and baby Jason and Raymond and Ollie and Manny and Patsy and Sylvia and Rae Anne and Horace and all the little girls becoming women and boys becoming men and the communities of the stories in *Gorilla, My Love* and *The Sea Birds Are Still Alive*, lives amid the scheme of oppositions played out in the great conjugation of past and present time mediating future possibilities.

It is this conjugation of time along with its referent—the salient features of a journey into experience conducted by a people who wrenched from a coherent past cast refugee upon a sea of circumstance confront incoherence and give it form—the Afro-American paradigm of creation—which *The Salt Eaters* evokes. Its cast of characters so far consummate the Bambara canon. Velma and Obie of the cast of *The Salt Eaters* are the energy of our possibilities while Campbell, Ruby, Jan, and company are the resources of our strength. Fred Holt, the bus driver of *The Salt Eaters*, is our worst choices able to be redeemed, while Dr. Meadows represents our ability to choose. The entire community of all of them is sufficient to defy the agents of destruction aligned around the malign power plant which seems to tower in their world. The valiant and gorgeous people of *The Salt Eaters* portray the strength of our past, available in the present, able to move our future.

As story, *The Salt Eaters* is less moving tale than brilliant total recall of tale. It is no blues narrative plucking the deep chords of the harp of our soul; no tale of anguish, struggle, lust, and love inspiring and conducting us toward mastery of the spirit and therefore mastery of the demon blues (and whites). It is not a declaration; rather it is an interrogation. It is not indicative in mood; rather it is subjunctive in mood. The novel, which is less novel than rite, begins with a question. It moves around a central word, *if*. *If* we wish to live, *if* we wish to be healthy, then we must *will* it so. *If* we *will* it so, then we must be willing to endure the act of transformation. *The Salt Eaters* is a rite of transformation quite like a jam session. The familiar tune is played, reviewed, and then restated in a new form.

In the tradition of fiction from which she works, Toni Cade Bambara's first novel faces fabulous first novels. Some among that rich opulence are William Wells Brown's *Clotel*, Du Bois's *Quest of the Silver Fleece*, James Weldon Johnson's *Autobiography of an Ex-Colored Man*, Jean Toomer's *Cane*, Langston Hughes' *Not without Laughter*, Zora Neale Hurston's *Jonah's Gourd Vine*, Richard Wright's *Native Son*, Ann Petry's *The Street*, James Baldwin's *Go Tell It on the Mountain*, Ralph Ellison's *Invisible Man*, Gwendolyn Brooks' *Maud Martha*, Paul Marshall's *Brown Girl, Brownstone*, Ishmael Reed's *The Free-Lance Pallbearers*, Toni Morrison's *The Bluest Eye*, and Charles S. Johnson's *Faith and the Good Thing*. All of these she knows and knows well. *The Salt Eaters* gestures to these and more. Many of these books belong to the company of the best ever written; all are global in their implications. More in the style of the zany brilliance of a Reed and the cultural ecology of a Johnson, *The Salt Eaters* does not pretend toward the simple splendor of the high elegant blues tradition. Though the work matches the encyclical inclusiveness of single works within that tradition, it dares a wrench. It subdues story, eschews fiction, not for fact but for act. It challenges us to renew and reform our sensibilities so that the high mode—the conquering healing power of main-line Afro-American fiction—can reemerge and become again our equipment for living—for life.

Eleanor W. Traylor. In Mari Evans, ed. *Black Women Writers* (Garden City, New York: Doubleday, 1984), pp. 58–60, 68–69

Although everyone knows instinctively that Toni Cade Bambara's first novel, *The Salt Eaters*, is a book that he or she must read, many people have difficulty with it. They get stuck on page ninety-seven or give up after muddling through the first sixty-five pages twice with little comprehension. Some cannot get past chapter one. Lost and bewildered, students decide that it is ''over their heads'' and wonder what made their teacher assign it in the first place.

There are compelling reasons for studying the novel. It is a daringly brilliant work that accomplishes even better for the 1980s what *Native Son* did for the 1940s, *Invisible Man* for the 1950s, or *Song of Solomon* for the 1970s: It fixes our present and challenges the way to the future. Reading it deeply should result in personal transformation; teaching it well can be a political act. However, Toni Cade Bambara has not made our job easy. *Salt* is long, intricately written, trickily structured, full of learning, heavy with wisdom—is, altogether, what critics mean by a ''large'' book.

At its literal-metaphoric center, Velma Henry and Minnie Ransom sit on round white stools in the middle of the Southwest Community Infirmary. ''The good woman Ransom,'' ''fabled healer of the district,'' is taxing her formidable powers with Velma, who has lost her balance and attempted suicide. The novel radiates outward in ever-widening circles—to the Master's Mind, the ring of twelve who hum and pray with Minnie; to the music room cluttered with staff, visitors, and assorted onlookers; to the city of Claybourne surrounding the Infirmary walls—a community which itself is composed of clusters (The Academy of the Seven Arts, the cafe with its two round tables of patrons, La Salle Street, the park); to the overarching sky above and the earth beneath steadily spinning on its axis. From the center, the threads web out, holding a place and weaving links between everything and everybody. At the same time, this center is a nexus which pulls the outside in—setting up the dialectic of connectedness which is both meaning and structure of the book.

Of the huge cast, certain characters stand out. There is M'Dear Sophie Heywood, Velma's godmother, who caught her at birth and has protected and praised her ever since. Now, she is so incensed with Velma's selfish nihilism that she has imposed silence upon herself and exited the circle/room, thinking back on her godchild as well as her deceased mate, Daddy Dolphy; on her son and Velma's almost-husband, Smitty, who was turned into an invalid by the police in a violent anti-war demonstration; and on her own bitter memories of being brutally beaten in jail by her neighbor, Portland Edgers, who had been forced to do so by guns and clubs. There is Fred Holt, the bus driver, ''brimming over with rage and pain and loss'' (and sour chili). Married as a youth to Wanda, who deserted him for the Nation of Islam, he now has a white wife Margie, who gives him nothing but her back. His misery is completed by the death of his best friend, Porter, a well-read conversationalist who was the only bright spot in Fred's days: Other important characters are Velma's husband Obie, whose ''image of himself [is] coming apart''; Dr. Meadows, a conscientious young M.D. who is pulling together his ''city'' versus ''country,'' his white westernized and ancient black selves; and a traveling troupe of Third World political performers called the Seven Sisters.

The rich cross section of variegated folks also includes less prominent characters such as Butch and Nadeen, two teenage parents-to-be; Jan and Ruby, activist women sharing a salad and organizing strategy; Donaldson, the inept FBI-CIA informant; and the list goes on. Some of these people appear onstage *in propria persona;* others are offstage fragments of memory. Some are quietly dead; others are roaming spirits. In many ways, these distinctions are false and immaterial, for everyone we meet takes up essential space, and there is no meaningful difference between their various states of corporeality/being/presence (a fact which confuses readers trying to keep the characters ''straight''). Old Wife, Minnie's ''Spirit Guide,'' is as ''real'' as Cora Rider grumbling in the music room. When Obie muses about his younger brother Roland, incarcerated in Rikers Island prison for raping a forty-six-year-old black woman, mother of four, Roland's voice and the woman's mopping up her own blood are as clear as Palma and Marcus hugging in the rain. And, like Velma, all of the major figures who need it undergo a healing change. . . .

Two versions of the future are given. One is an in-process sketch of a humanitarian society newly evolving from the death of ''the authoritarian age.'' The other is a nightmarish glimpse of ''everyone not white, male and of wealth'' fighting for burial grounds, of radioactively mutant kids roaming the stockaded streets killing ''for the prize of . . . gum boots, mask and bubble suit'' needed to breathe the contaminated air. Yes, there are "choices to be noted. Decisions to be made." This ultimatum is the burden of the question that Minnie repeatedly puts to Velma: "Are you sure, sweetheart, that you want to be well?"—for health entails taking responsibility for the self and the world we live in. Years after her healing, Velma "would laugh remembering she'd thought *that* was an ordeal. She didn't know the half of it. Of what awaited her in years to come."

Concern for a viable future explains the emphasis which Bambara places upon children, the succeeding generations. Unfortunately, they, too, are suffering from the vacuity of the age:

> there was no charge, no tension, no stuff in these young people's passage. They walked by you and there was no breeze of merit, no vibes. Open them up and you might find a skate key, or a peach pit, or a Mary Jane wrapper, or a slinky, but that would be about all.

They want a sweet, easy life, and they fight each other. Like their elders, they, too, have to be saved from and for themselves, for, as Old Wife declares, "The chirren are our glory."

As a self-described "Pan-Africanist-socialist-feminist," Bambara not only cares about children, but manifests a political consciousness which makes her a socially committed writer. It was quite some time, she says, before she "began to realize that this [writing] was a perfectly legitimate way to participate in struggle." Now she fulfills what Kalamu ya Salaam defines as the "responsibility of *revolutionary* Third World writers": "to cut through this [mass media] crap, to expose the cover-ups and ideological/material interests inherent in these presentations, and . . . to offer analysis, inspiration, information and ideas which . . . work in the best interest of Third World defense and development."

> Gloria T. Hull. In Marjorie Pryse and Hortense J. Spillers, eds. *Conjuring: Black Women, Fiction, and Literary Tradition* (Bloomington: Indiana University Press, 1985), pp. 216–19, 228–29

The question of identity—of personal definition within the context of community—emerges as a central motif for Toni Cade Bambara's writing. Her female characters become as strong as they do, not because of some inherent "eternal feminine" quality granted at conception, but rather because of the lessons women learn from communal interaction. Identity is achieved, not bestowed. Bambara's short stories focus on such learning. Very careful to present situations in a highly orchestrated manner, Bambara describes the difficulties that her characters must overcome.

Contemporary literature teems with male characters in coming-of-age stories or even female characters coming of age on male typewriters. Additional stories, sometimes written by black authors, indeed portray such concerns but narrowly defined within crushing contexts of city ghettos or rural poverty. Bambara's writing breaks such molds as she branches out, delineating various settings, various economic levels, various characters—both male and female.

Bambara's stories present a decided emphasis on the centrality of community. Many writers concentrate so specifically on character development or plot line that community seems merely a foil against which the characters react. For Bambara the community becomes essential as a locus for growth, not simply as a source of narrative tension. Thus, her characters and community do a circle dance around and within each other as learning and growth occur.

Bambara's women learn how to handle themselves within the divergent, often conflicting, strata that compose their communities. Such learning does not come easily, hard lessons result from hard knocks. Nevertheless, the women do not merely endure; they prevail, emerging from these situations more aware of their personal identities and of their potential for further self-actualization. More important, they guide others to achieve such awareness.

Bambara posits learning as purposeful, geared toward personal and societal change. Consequently, the identities into which her characters grow envision change as both necessary and possible, understanding that they themselves play a major part in bringing about that change. The ideal approximates the nature of learning described in Paulo Freire's *Pedagogy of the Oppressed*, in which he decries the "banking concept," wherein education becomes "an act of depositing, in which the students are the depositories and the teacher is the depositor." Oppressive situations define the learner as profoundly ignorant, not possessing valuable insights for communal sharing.

Although many of Bambara's stories converge on the school setting as the place of learning in formal patterns, she liberates such settings to admit and encourage community involvement and ownership. Learning then influences societal liberation and self-determination. These stories describe learning as the process of problem solving, which induces a deepening sense of self, Freire's "intentionality."

For Bambara the community benefits as both "teacher" and "student" confront the same problem—that of survival and prospering in hostile settings, without guaranteed outcomes. The commonality of problems, then, encourages a mutual sharing of wisdom and respect for individual difference that transcends age, all too uncommon in a more traditional education context. Bambara's characters encounter learning within situations similar to the older, tribal milieus. The stages of identity formation, vis-à-vis the knowledge base to be mastered, have five segments: (1) beginner, (2) apprentice, (3) journeyman, (4) artisan, and (5) expert.

Traditional societies employed these stages to pass on to their youth that information necessary to ensure the survival of the tribe, such as farming techniques, and that information needed to inculcate tribal mores, such as songs and stories. Because of Bambara's interest in cultural transmission of values, her characters experience these stages in their maturational quest. In her stories these levels do not correlate with age but rather connote degrees of experience in community. . . .

Toni Cade Bambara's stories do more than paint a picture of black life in contemporary black settings. Many writers have done that, more or less successfully. Her stories portray women who struggle with issues and learn from them. Sometimes the lessons taste bitter and the women must accumulate more experience in order to gain perspective. By centering community in her stories, Bambara displays both the supportive and the destructive aspects of communal interaction. Her stories do not describe a predictable, linear plot line; rather, the cyclic enfolding of characters and community produces the kind of tension missing in stories with a more episodic emphasis.

Her characters achieve a personal identity as a result of their participation in the human quest for knowledge, which brings power. Bambara's skill as a writer saves her characters from being stereotypic cutouts. Although her themes are universal, communities that Bambara describes rise above the generic. More fully delineated than her male characters, the women come across as specific people living in specific places. Bambara's best stories show her characters interacting within a political framework wherein the personal becomes political.

Martha M. Vertreace. In Mickey Pearlman, ed. *American Women Writing Fiction* (Lexington: University Press of Kentucky, 1989), pp. 155–57, 165–69

The nationalist-feminist ideology in *Seabirds* is not solely generated by depictions of characters. It is reinforced by narrative texture and form. As a body of race-and gender-specific narratives, these stories draw on various Afro-American cultural practices—the oral storytelling tradition, the use of folklore, and the reinscription of Afro-American music forms. The incorporation of these practices is evident in the narrative structure, point of view, and semiotic texture of the stories.

Bambara has spoken and written extensively on the influence of Afro-American music on her work. What is most striking about her appropriation of jazz in *Seabirds*, however, is its role in emphasizing and reinforcing the ideology of the text. Jazz performances generally begin with a statement of theme, are followed by improvisations or extreme variations, and conclude with reiteration and resolution. An analogous pattern structures each of the stories in this collection. In "The Apprentice," for example, the narrative begins with the narrator's anxiety about her mission, moves to an encounter between a young Black man and a white policeman, then moves to a senior citizen's complex, and finally to a Black restaurant. It then refocuses on the narrator's concerns and reveals her resolution to remain committed to political engagement. In "Witchbird," each fleeting reflection of Honey's extended blues solo constitutes a comment on some aspect of her life—her career, her past relationships with men, and her overall perception of herself. And in "Christmas Eve at Johnson's Drugs N Goods," Candy begins by reflecting on Christmas and a possible visit from her father, moves on to individual episodes largely focused on characterizations of the store's customers, and concludes with accepting Obatale's invitation to a Kwanza celebration.

This mode of narration serves a significant ideological function. In its highlighting and summarizing, as well as its glossing over certain episodes, the text produces its ideological content largely through clusters of events. Hence, in "Broken Field Running," the renaming process by which Black children discard their "slave names" and appropriate African names to define themselves with the context of Black culture, the police harassment symbolized by the police car cruising in the Black community, and the destructive effect of ghetto life depicted in the criminal activities of Black males form a montage, a cluster of images each one of which might be said to encode a particular aspect of ideology.

The narrative perspective, particularly as it reveals the narrator's relationship to the text's ideology, also contributes to the ideological construct. In *Seabirds*, as in *Gorilla*, the dominant narrative strategy is the apparently unmediated response of characters to the world around them. . . .

Gorilla and *Seabirds*, . . .while produced at historically different moments, are both structured by the desire to synthesize contending ideologies of Black cultural nationalism and feminism. With its submerged text, its positioning of girls and women as primary narrators, its eruption of women-defined issues and strategies of marginalizing Black males, *Gorilla* disrupts the apparent

unity of the world it seems to represent: an idyllic inner world of the Black community in which intraracial strife is minimal or nonexistent.

Seabirds identifies itself with the emergent feminist movement even in its dedication. The women in these stories possess a keen political awareness; the young girls have expanded their political consciousness; and Black male figures are even farther on the margins than they were in the earlier work. Tensions between nationalists and feminists are concretely presented in *Seabirds*, and the indeterminancy of the text is in the foreground.

The Salt Eaters, a work that bears all the traces of postmodern textual production, radically rewrites and displaces these earlier works. . . . [Its] central representations of madness and disillusionment, the increased antagonism between the sexes, and the triumph of an alternative culture displace the ambivalence of the earlier works and project a vision that is both dystopian and utopian.

Elliot Butler-Evans. *Race, Gender and Desire: Narrative Strategies in the Fiction of Toni Cade Bambara, Toni Morrison, and Alice Walker* (Philadelphia: Temple University Press, 1989), pp. 119–20, 122

BIBLIOGRAPHY
Gorilla, My Love, 1972 (s); *The Seabirds Are Still Alive: Collected Stories*, 1977 (s); *The Salt Eaters*, 1980 (n); *If Blessing Comes*; 1987 (n); *Deep Sightings and Rescue Missions: Fiction, Essays, and Conversations*, 1996 (misc)

BANKS, Russell (1940–)

In Russell Banks's previous novel *Continental Drift*, there occurred the summing-up sentence: "This is how a good man loses his goodness." The question as to how it happens is posed again in *Affliction*. Where *Continental Drift* framed the pressures on individuals and families in terms of the inexorable working out of the economic laws of supply and demand and accumulation, in the new novel the loss of goodness is placed in a longer perspective, one that begins to approach anthropology rather than history. . . .

Banks's statement about the cause of male inability to achieve a "decent," a "good" relationship to other people, and especially to women, is simplistic. Nevertheless, *Affliction* is a compelling depiction of a man unable to turn his best feelings and responses into words and behavior and who ends by repeating the violence done to himself as a child and adolescent. . . .

One cannot miss the note of mourning in *Affliction*. First of all, it's there for the wasted lives that make up history, but find no place in history. But in Banks's sympathy for his character there's also a sense of elegiac regret for the loss of the image, the model, of justness and strength portrayed, say, by John Wayne in *The Searchers*. Melancholy, but sufficient; able to live with his isolation as he returns to the desert; rejecting the settled life and ties of the homestead. The cinematic parallel to Wade Whitehouse [Banks's protagonist] would lie somewhere in the haunted amnesia of Harry Dean Stanton (coming out of the desert in *Paris, Texas*) and the confused, perverted honesty of Harvey Keitel in *Blue Collar*.

Martin Chalmers. *The Listener*. Sept. 13, 1990. p. 34

Rule of the Bone invites comparison not only with *Adventures of Huckleberry Finn* but also, somewhat unflatteringly, with *The Catcher in the Rye*. Bone is more generic and less funny than Holden Caulfield, and unlike Holden, he displays an odd immunity to pop culture. It's as if J. D. Salinger registered forty years in advance a commercialized teenage reality that Mr. Banks himself shies away from. Mr. Banks also falls short of Mr. Salinger's artistry in filtering acute psychological observation through vernacular distortion. But the comparison is not entirely fair. In his social and economic privilege, Holden Caulfield is so familiar to educated readers that Mr. Salinger can afford the luxury of subtlety. Bone, on the other hand, has had as little exposure to "sivilization" as Huck Finn did, and in order to rescue him from muteness Mr. Banks is compelled, a la Twain, to place him in fantastic situations. If the resulting story seems unrealistically bleak and its hero incompletely lovable—if you balk at the unrelenting depiction of white adults as selfish, cruel, and criminal—it's worth remembering that for kids like Bone the state of innocence to which Holden longs to return has never been an option: they would be happy to meet adults whose worst sin is phoniness. Intoxicating and unsparing, *Rule of the Bone* is a romance for a world fast running out of room for childhood.

> Jonathan Franzen. *New York Times Book Review*. May 7, 1995, p. 13

BIBLIOGRAPHY
Family Life, 1974 (n); *Hamilton Stark*, 1978 (n); *The New World*, 1978 (s); *The Book of Jamaica*, 1980 (s); *Trailerpark*, 1981 (s); *Continental Drift*, 1985 (n); *Success Stories*, 1986 (s); *Affliction*, 1989 (n); *The Sweet Hereafter*, 1991 (n); *Rule of the Bone*, 1995 (n); *The Relation of My Imprisonment: A Fiction*, 1996 (n); *Cloudsplitter*, 1998 (n)

BARAKA, Amiri (LeRoi Jones, 1934–)

LeRoi Jones's *Preface to a Twenty Volume Suicide Note* is close to the spirit of modern jazz. Like Allen Ginsberg, he improvises form and structure, but the principle is different. He tries something out, expands on it, repeats effects, drifts dreamily along wispy spirals of suggestion, grows tedious, pulls himself up short and does a beautiful solo for a minute or two. He has a natural gift for quick, vivid imagery and spontaneous humor, and his poems are filled with sardonic or sensuous or slangily knowledgeable passages set down on the run. If he can take his cleverness and facility in making momentarily vivacious effects a little in hand, he may acquire some of the character and incisiveness he now lacks. Meanwhile he represents an attractive current of youthful poetry that makes good use of the sparkling chatter and directness of his generation.

> M.L. Rosenthal. *The Reporter*. Jan. 3, 1963. p. 49

Blues People is a book of large ambitions. LeRoi Jones, poet, essayist, story writer and jazz critic, will not confine himself to the history of the development of the blues as music. He will not simply talk about blues people, how they felt in their double

exile—as Negroes and as artists—from a country they never left. He subtitles his book "Negro Music in White America" and from the first page we are informed of his larger sociological and anthropological interests and of his intention to show us the roots of blues in a people and their fate. . . . It is ironic that this gifted young poet, bent on fighting middle-class American culture in all its shabby superficiality, yields so willingly to that very culture's most vulgar jargon, its narrowest, pseudo-sociological mode of thinking. . . .

The book is most effective in its simple, direct information about blues music and its people, and its willingness to relate the suffering of generations of Negroes to the tenaciously redemptive power of their music. What was one kind of Hell, the author says, now turns into another as Negroes succumb to the blandishments of the white middle-class world. The blues and their successors in the several forms of jazz are thereby threatened. No less so, however, than the writer—living in that same world—who tries to do them justice.

> Robert Coles. *Partisan Review*. Winter, 1964. pp. 131–3

Read as a record of an earnest young man's attempt to come to grips with his predicament as Negro American during a most turbulent period of our history, *Blues People* may be worth the reader's time. Taken as a theory of American Negro culture, it can only contribute more confusion than clarity. For Jones has stumbled over that ironic obstacle which lies in the path of any who would fashion a theory of American Negro culture while ignoring the intricate network of connection which binds Negroes to the larger society. To do so is to attempt a delicate brain surgery with a switch-blade.

> Ralph Ellison. *Shadow and Act* (Random). 1964. p. 253. [*New York Review of Books*. Feb. 6, 1964]

His is a turbulent talent. While turbulence is not always a sign of power or of valuable meaning, I have a hunch that LeRoi Jones's fire will burn ever higher and clearer if our theatre can furnish an adequate vessel to harbor his flame. We need it.

He is very angry. Anger alone may merely make a loud noise, confuse, sputter and die. For anger to burn to useful effect, it must be guided by an idea. . . . With LeRoi Jones it is easy to say that the plight of the Negro ignited the initial rage—justification enough—and that the rage will not be appeased until there is no more black and white, no more color except as differences in hue and accent are part of the world's splendid spectacle. But there is more to his ferocity than a protest against the horrors of racism.

What we must not overlook [in *Dutchman*] is that, while this explosion of fury is its rhetorical and emotional climax, the crux of its significance resides in the depiction of the white girl whose relevance to the play's situation does not lie in her whiteness, but in her representative value as a token of our civilization. She is our neurosis. Not a neurosis in regard to the Negro, but the absolute neurosis of American society.

> Harold Clurman. *The Nation*. April 13, 1964. p. 383

That the play is preposterous on the literal level is obvious enough. Yet allegory or symbolism, to be effective, must first function properly on the literal level. But does *Dutchman* work even figuratively? Does the white society woo the Negro with a mixture of promises and rebuffs only to destroy him utterly when he shows his just resentment? Perhaps. But it looks to me as if resentment were finally beginning to pay off. Whites, moreover, have been treating Negroes with a simpler, though no less damnable, cruelty. They have been neither so Machiavellian, nor so psychotic, as *Dutchman* implies. Add to this Jones's often consciously arty language and the vacuity of his symbols: the girl plies her victims with apples, an assembly-line Eve; the title presumably refers to the Flying Dutchman, but whether this describes the girl, fatally traveling up and down the subway line, or the boy, needing to be redeemed by the true love of a white girl, is unclear and, in either case, unhelpful.

John Simon. *Hudson Review*. Autumn, 1964. p. 424

The revitalization of language is not simply a matter of *forcing* words to have meaning. How would we go about trying to resurrect lovely, individual, colossal? Not, surely, by involving them in compounds or extraordinary juxtapositions. But these forcing tactics are the ones Mr. Jones most easily employs; his effort is to wrench the word into a context where it must shudder, repent of its sins, and then take up wholesomely and whole-heartedly the New Life. The problem with such a technique is that it cannot be economical; so much of its effort must be spent on establishing the word in its new surroundings that there is little time left in which to use the word with skill, ease, and a belief in its rightness. It is like the renaming of the months in the French Revolution. The new names are naked and violent; they have no familiars, no body of accepted connotation which mediates between them and us. Because his poetry lacks such mediations, Mr. Jones must say things at length, must repeat them several times, in order that within the poem he can establish that familiarity which the previous convention could automatically depend upon.

William Dickey. *Hudson Review*. Winter, 1964–65. p. 592

. . .these two karate blows by LeRoi Jones display no talent at all—they are inspired primarily by race hatred. Larry Rivers' set for *The Toilet* consists of seven urinals; the scene is the boy's john of a predominantly Negro high school. There students congregate, during pauses in the educational process, to exchange insults and obscenities, and to gang up on unprotected students, usually "whiteys." The major victim of *The Toilet* is a Puerto Rican homosexual who, having sent a love letter to one of the Negroes, is brutally beaten, and then tossed, bleeding and unconscious, into one of the urinals. The Negro he loves—and who helped to mug him—returns surreptitiously at the end to cradle the victim's head in his lap and to sob over his prostrate form. This maudlin conclusion reveals a soft chink in the author's spikey armor, but still the play is not a drama but a psychodrama, designed for the acting out of sado-masochistic racial fantasies.

The Slave projects these fantasies into a Genet-like war between White and Black, which the Negroes are on the verge of winning.

Robert Brustein. *New Republic*. Jan. 23, 1965. pp. 32–3

LeRoi Jones is already familiar to New Yorkers as the author of some sensational little plays, and to readers of poetry as the author of some sensational little poems, and if his book on "Negro music

in white America" fails to be sensational, it is not because he has tried to keep it from being so, but because his accommodation of his subject has been couched—bedded down, in fact—in that language of all languages most refractory to sensationalism: the latest jargon of the social sciences. . . . Yet this fancy-talk of the social sciences is not used to describe or even to analyze, but to condemn and to despise. There are times when the belief in original virtue, a concept Mr. Jones has invented to oppose the original sin of being Black in White America, sounds either histrionic or professional, and in *Blues People*, for all its clever discussions of Armstrong and Beiderbecke, Bebop and Swing, Cecil Taylor and Ornette Coleman. . . , Mr. Jones does little more than attempt to create a system or dogma of evil and innocence by sheer classroom oratory.

Richard Howard. *Poetry*. March, 1965. pp. 403–4

Somewhere dimly beneath the surface [of *The System of Dante's Hell*], emerging it would seem only when Jones for whatever reason stops being arty and portentous, is a straightforward, rather moving description of what it meant for him to be Negro in his years of putting on flesh and ideas. . . . If these things derive from Ralph Ellison, they are not invalidated by that, and they have the virtue of being simply stated.

Richard Gilman. *New York Herald Tribune Book Section*. Dec. 26, 1965. p. 9

LeRoi Jones writes in the mood of the Prodigal Son who has returned at last to his blackness. He celebrates his homecoming in some 20 essays [*Home: Social Essays*], written between 1960 and 1965. . . . The early pieces, written between 1960 and 1963, are often arresting and sometimes persuasive. Thereafter Jones enters the fantasyland of black nationalism. . . .

About a third of the collection is devoted to literary subjects, and here Jones is distinctly at his best. . . . In his emphatic rejection of formal art, of tradition and of classical restraint, Jones betrays his affinity for that neo-Romantic permissiveness, that unbridled self-indulgence, which links him to the poets of the Beat generation.

We have finally to deal with five or six pieces which are not so much essays as fulminations. Ostensibly they announce the author's conversion to black nationalism; in reality they signal an esthetic breakdown, a fatal loss of artistic control. The prose disintegrates, the tone becomes hysterical, and all pretense of logical argument is abandoned. The style, shall we say, is severely disturbed.

Robert Bone. *New York Times Book Section*. May 8, 1966. p. 3

LeRoi Jones's *The System of Dante's Hell* (after two books of poems) is the traditional first-novel autobiography, but it plays with the form of fiction and the sentence structure of prose. The front of the book provides a kind of do-it-yourself structure for the whole novel, which we may impose, if we wish, on "chapters" of association-linked clauses and phrases. This outline is of the divisions and circles of Hell, and the novelist appears to be holding up against himself, like a costume, each type and sub-type of sin, seeing himself for a few pages as *that* sinner. . . . In its final pages the associational jumps narrow, the mind focuses on one action within one sequence of time, and a story appears like an island in the stream-of-consciousness. Powerful enough to reward any admirer of conventional fiction, it concerns a Negro soldier's attempt to sustain, for a little while, an illusion that society has opened at last to take him in, that he, the estranged, is wrapped in its warm cliches. . . .

What Mr. Jones, now that his plays have made him a public figure, is making here is a peace-offering to the hell of his own past and to the people who lived in it with him.

Mona Van Duyn. *Poetry*. Feb., 1967. pp. 338–9

Since all [Jones's] work is heavily autobiographical, his poetry and his fiction (particularly *The System of Dante's Hell*) show his attempt to escape the middle-class background which makes him feel like an oppressor of his own kind. It is in *Home*, however, that his journey can be seen most clearly. A collection of essays written at random over a five-year period, the book is given a shape of its own by the chronological arrangement of the pieces. They move from ''Cuba Libre'' (1960), in which he can still use the pronoun ''we'' meaning ''we Americans,'' to the essays of 1964 and 1965 where his identification is purely black and the prospect is destruction.

Gerald Weales. *The Jumping-Off Place* (Macmillan—N.Y.). 1969. p. 137

LeRoi Jones's *The System of Dante's Hell* . . . ostensibly consists of disconnected scenes and random thoughts or observations. Some early reviewers asserted that Jones used a pretentious title as an appeal to intellectuals. Yet, with meticulous precision, with broken but somehow poetic sentences, Jones does expose a Hell, a black ghetto thriving on incontinence, violence, and fraud, surrounded by ''white monsters'' who add to the torment of the Inferno and prevent escape. . . .

Yet in a very real sense Jones believes that he belongs in the Inferno which he himself has helped to build. He has witnessed and participated in the basest evil: ''heresy against one's own sources, running in terror from one's deepest responses and insights . . . the denial of feeling.''. . . In this urban Inferno the victims are not only tormented by their environment and their monsters but by each other, thereby removing the last trace of humanity. It is a city dominated by the Gorgon of Despair.

Olga W. Vickery in *The Shaken Realist*, ed. Melvin J. Friedman and John B. Vickery (Louisiana State). 1970. p. 157

In [Jones's] poetry, fiction, drama, criticism and scholarly works there is but one constant hammering—to be BLACK in America is to be REVOLUTIONARY. In *Dutchman*, *The Toilet*, and *The Slave*, three plays by LeRoi Jones, there is all the hatred, venom, brutality, profanity and downright insanity that whites have traditionally heaped upon the Negro; but now turned back upon whites. Whitman once said, ''A poet enlisted in a people's cause can make every word he writes draw blood.'' Jones, and those gathered about him, are not begging white society to love them. No. They are out to take their freedom and dignity as black men and to harass the white

world while, at the same time, inspiring the masses of big-city Negroes to the affirmation of their inherent beauty and worth, not as middle-class-oriented integrated Negroes, but as Black People.

Calvin C. Hernton in *Amistad I*, ed. John A. Williams and Charles F. Harris (Random). 1970. pp. 214–5

The prose tracts Jones has written in recent years, since the publication of *Black Magic Poetry*, have consistently urged a firm moral position for the black man, one which unites him with his Black brothers and one that turns its back on white corruption. The logic of this position was begun in the earliest poetry and developed through the struggles with [T.S.] Eliot's conception of God, and through the ultimate creation of an alternative to Eliot's moral view.

It may be said that one of Jones' solutions to the dilemma of what to do about Eliot's God, and what to do about the existential heroes of his comic book youth, is to supplant them both in his own person. . . . It may not be realistic to see Jones imagining himself as a kind of God, though he has seen black men as gods; but there is a curious passage near the end of *Black Magic Poetry* that suggests the temptation may be present. . . .

Perhaps it is merely a vatic pose Jones adopts in these poems, and he does not apotheosize himself at all. But there is a curiosity that lingers in the imagination regarding the name he has assumed since the publication of his poems, the Islamic name which appears in the ''Explanation'' to *Black Magic Poetry*. One wonders if God and the comic book heroes are dead forever, or if they have been absorbed into Jones' poetic unconscious wanting to poke out again. His name, Baraka, like Lorca's Duende, means many things. Its root is Hebrew: Brk, and it means a number of things: lightning, the blessed of God, virtue, inspiration, the muse.

Lee A. Jacobus in *Modern Black Poets*, ed. Donald B. Gibson (Prentice-Hall). 1973. pp. 125–6

There are enough brilliant poems of such variety in *Black Magic Poetry* and *In Our Terribleness* to establish the unique identity and claim for respect of several poets. But it is beside the point that Baraka is probably the finest poet, black or white, writing in this country these days. The question still has to be asked whether he has fulfilled the vocation set for him by his own moves and examples. He has called himself a ''seer'' (one familiar with evil is the way he defined it) and holy man, but hesitates to claim (while vying for it) the fateful name of prophet.

The prophet differs from the poet and other word-men in his role of awaking and sustaining among his people a vision of their destiny set beside the criteria of their deepest values in the most fundamental though significant language. A poet's obligation, by contrast, is to the integrity of his verbal rendering of his individual sensibility. The problem is whether Baraka's creative impulse, which is essentially underground, hip, urban, and avant-garde, can be made to speak for a nation of black people rather than for a set of black nationalists. Can he transcend the inclination to ad-lib on the changes of black consciousness . . . toward redefining that consciousness in the light of enduring values and in major works of sustained thought and imagination?

Clyde Taylor in *Modern Black Poets*, ed. Donald B. Gibson (Prentice-Hall). 1973. pp. 132–3

The Jones play [*A Recent Killing*] is uncouth in texture and performance, but it is nonetheless a play of considerable scope, power and, despite its harshness, sensibility. . . .

It seethes with passionate anger, with bursts of wild humor, with a consuming desire for expression. It explodes all over the place and, as usual with such hectic efforts, there is a quantity of debris— some of it ugly. But ugliness may also serve art's purposes: what is more important in this case is that the play teems with life. . . .

Most of the twenty-five scenes in this long play depict the world which creates the inevitability of its conclusion. Obviously cutting is required and loose ends should be tied up, and there are other things which may be argued against the play. Still, the faults are less significant than that the play is an American drama wrought from the bitter blood struggle of a man who can write, and writes not only about himself and his race but about the immediate environment in which we all dwell.

Harold Clurman. *The Nation*. Feb. 12, 1973. p. 218

A good many poets and critics don't like what's happened to the old LeRoi Jones, promising young Negro poet of *Preface to a Twenty Volume Suicide Note*. Baraka, obviously, is not interested in their opinions. Nevertheless, it is a mistake to dismiss him as an angry propagandist, as so many have done, because he appears to run against the literary grain. The old art of LeRoi Jones was written to be read. The new writing of Baraka is calculated to be heard—*how we sound*, he would say now—and his audience must have some sense of the Afro-American perspective from which his new writing issues. The black aesthetic which shapes his writing is neither lacking in artistic taste (strident, anti-poetic, uncontrolled, say the critics) nor in itself startlingly new. It only appears that way from a literary point of view, one that is in many respects incongruous to the cultural context upon which his stylistic rationale is based. What is remarkable, from a literary standpoint, is the range of innovation his political ideology and altered cultural consciousness have required of him as a writer. For Baraka, though, it is not remarkable at all, but only the result of an inevitable artistic transformation, the sure spelling out of his specific placement in the world as a black writer.

William C. Fischer. *Massachusetts Review*. Spring, 1973. p. 305

At the core of Baraka's art is the insistence upon the formlessness of life-giving energy and the energetic or fluid nature of all form. It is no wonder that events in his work are violent, his images often alarmingly brutal. The only fruition or finality honored is that of death, which produces a sudden enlargement of vision—the realization that personality, or the "deadweight" of any fixed idea or being, is inevitably annihilated by history's progress: "The only constant is change." . . .

Yet as the revelation and exorcism of self have given way to a communal orientation, Baraka has not abandoned his theatrical sensibility. On the contrary, he has sought an increasingly expansive theatre—the stage of world politics. His shifts—often perplexing and contradictory—leading from uncompromisingly separatist black nationalism to a more inclusive Pan-Africanism, and most recently to the embrace of international socialism, may be taken partly as an attempt to gain a broader world forum, and partly as

reflecting the need to fabricate new ideological roles for each change wrought by contemporary history.

Baraka has shown at every instant of his public career an intense commitment to those ideas and ideals he felt were integral to his motivating vision of life. Like James Brown, he has always been "an actor that is now." And it is by way of this ethos, with its equation of passion and significance, that Imamu Amiri Baraka creatively identifies himself with the evolving spirit of his people. . . .

Kimberly W. Benston. *Baraka: The Renegade and the Mask* (Yale Univ. Pr., 1976), pp. 261, 263

Perhaps more so than any other writer, Baraka captures the idiom and style of modern urban black life. The uniqueness and authenticity of his work is largely attributable to his thorough knowledge of the speech and music of urban blacks. In his best work, he exploits these two powerful and rich possessions of an otherwise weak and impoverished people. He shows, especially in his later works, an understanding of the full range of black speech patterns, an element which invigorates and renders dramatic even his short stories and poems. Baraka's flawless ear retained also the sounds of modern jazz, the most important artistic creation of black America. Along with the frequent evidence of the traditional jazz framework, we see also in the poems the following characteristics of modern jazz: spontaneity of line, moving by sheer suggestiveness of impetus; elliptical phrasing; polyrhythmic thrust. Although similar musical qualities have been attributed to the work of other modern American poets, the conscious and effective employment of these qualities cannot be questioned in Baraka's case, for his musical insights are not only integrated into the artistic methods of his plays, poems, and stories. They have been articulated in a number of perceptive essays, as well as the extremely important study *Blues People*. Throughout his literary career, Baraka has been concerned greatly with the sounds of black life. During the latter 1960's and early 1970's, this concern took on even more importance in his attempts to reach a largely non-reading audience. . . .

As we inspect the corpus of Baraka's writing, we are unavoidably aware of his faults—extreme privacy of reference, frequent experimental failure, and racist dogma, to name only a few. Nevertheless, we are also mindful of his merits—daring and frequently successful verbal approximations of jazz music, vibrant recreation of black speech, and a consummate portrayal of the black middle-class psyche. In spite of some obvious short-comings, Baraka, in the brief span of ten years, presented us with work of considerable promise. It is at least this writer's hope that the artist's increasingly myopic vision does not confirm the once-premature contention that "it is now necessary to inter him as a writer, young and kicking." However, at this point in his career, Baraka seems to be doing everything in his power to prove that grim prophecy sagacious.

Henry C. Lacey. *To Raise, Destroy, and Create: The Poetry, Drama, and Fiction of Imamu Amiri Baraka (LeRoi Jones)* (Whitston, 1981). pp. viii, 195–96

Since the early 1960s, the figure to be reckoned with in Black political life and art has been Amiri Baraka. Controversial, responsive to changing social ambience, he has articulated the riotous "language of the unheard" (to invoke Martin Luther King's definition) within a vernacular and a new idiom of radical solutions. A founder of the Black Arts Movement of the sixties, he propounded a view that was, as the late Larry Neal put it, "radically opposed to any concept of the artist that alienates him from his community.... The Black Arts Movement believes that your ethics and your aesthetics are one." Baraka's impact has been such that as early as 1973, Donald B. Gibson placed him among "major influences on Black poetry: (1) the Harlem Renaissance of the twenties; (2) the protest writing of the thirties as reflected in the work of Richard Wright; (3) the beat movement of the fifties; (4) the life and work of a single poet: Amiri Baraka.". . .

As an artist, Baraka wants "more than anything, to chart . . . change within myself." This constant mutability in the face of the changing world" (*Autobiography*, 18). And yet it is the reality of his changeless core that generates his vision. William J. Harris views him as a Manichaean and a vatic poet in the line of Whitman, Pound, [Kenneth] Patchen, and Ginsberg. In quest of philosophical truth, Baraka has turned to a variety of religious and political faiths. A serious artist, he has absorbed classical and modern literature, and contributes uniquely to art that is experimentally alive to its social and political content. He uses music and multimedia to further the accessibility and impact of his works, in order to convey to the people his messages of strength, resistance, and political instruction. Like a great dancer (or skater), he risks all with bold leaps and turns as evidenced by his plays *The Motion of History* and *Money: A Jazz Opera*, neither of which quite comes off theatrically, and *The Sidney Poet Heroical*, which does. His work has moved from concern with self and schools of white poetry to placement of that Black self in a national and world community, at the same time developing an experimental Black art rooted in traditions of language, music, and religious and secular rhetoric. . . .

Baraka's new book, *The Music*, clearly locates in its title his focus for present and future. It is Black music that has provided the lens, the cohesion, and the communication he has been pursuing as he "investigates the sun." This anthology of recent work, of [his wife] Amina's poetry and his own poetry, essays, and "antinuclear jazz musical," reveals a second and relatively new emphasis: Baraka as a poet/musician of praise—a lover of "The Music" (by which Black music is understood) and the family of Black musicians who create and interpret it, and a lover of his own family, itself consanguine within it.

D.H. Melhem. *Heroism in the New Black Poetry* (Lexington: Univ. Press of Kentucky, 1990), pp. 215, 217–18, 221

In the essay "Expressive Language," Baraka articulates the need for a new speech to undermine hierarchies of Western meaning; and he searches for this voice in African rhythms. Baraka feels that the twisting of meanings by dominant language forms has been a cause of great confusion and ignorance, both on the part of the dominated and the dominator, the latter having convinced himself that his distortions are justified and are, in effect, solid reasoning and no distortion at all. The Slave Trade was blessed by the religious and political leaders in Europe because, to them, the African was a heathen whose enslavement was therefore a natural punishment by God for his sinful nature. Projective verse as used by Baraka and other Third World writers attempts to tear down the hierarchical language structures which have consolidated that illusory view of Western superiority by overesteeming and inflating Western importance.

Like his Caribbean counterparts, Baraka also recognizes the need for creolization in poetic expression. He realizes that the black man is, after all, a product of mixed origins—African and European. Baraka notes, therefore, that socialization "which is rooted in culture depends for its impetus for the most part on the multiplicity of influences." This means that projective verse as a mode of articulating this ethnical reality is of paramount importance since, in order for a society and hence for a poem which mirrors that society to go in "many strange directions," the society or poem must contain a form of raison d'etre which harmonizes with the many-sidedness and which is creolized and open. Conventional, static forms are at best artificial for a people of plural background when they seek to reflect that plural world. Baraka realizes this when, in the essay "Hunting is not for Those Heads on the Wall," he points out that formal "artifacts made to cohere to preconceived forms are almost devoid of . . . verb value" (379).

Anthony Kellman. *Ariel*. April, 1990, pp. 55–56

BIBLIOGRAPHY
Preface to a Twenty Volume Suicide Note, 1961 (p); *Blues People*, 1963 (e); *Dutchman*, 1964 (d); *The Dead Lecturer*, 1964 (p); *The Slave*, 1965 (d); *The Toilet*, 1965 (d); *The System of Dante's Hell*, 1965 (n); *Home: Social Essays*, 1966; *Tales*, 1967 (n); *Four Black Revolutionary Plays*, 1969; *Black Magic Poetry*, 1969; *Slave Ship*, 1969 (d); (with Fundi [Billy Abernathy]) *In Our Terribleness: Some Elements and Meaning in Black Style*, 1970 (misc); *Jello*, 1970 (p); *Raise Race Rays Raze: Essays since 1965*, 1971; *Mad Heart and a Black Mass*, 1972 (d); *A Recent Killing*, 1973 (d); *Sidnee Poet Heroical*, 1975 (d); *Three Books*, 1975 (n, p, s); *The Creation of the New Ark*, 1975 (a); *Hard Facts*, 1978 (p); *The Motion of History, and Other Plays*, 1978; *What Was the Relationship of the Lone Ranger to the Means of Production?*, 1978 (d); *Selected Plays and Prose*, 1979 (d, e, s); *Selected Poetry*, 1979; *Reggae or Not!*, 1982 (p); *The Autobiography of LeRoi Jones*, 1984; *Daggers and Javelins: Essays 1974–1979*, 1984 (e); *The Music: Reflections on Jazz and Blues*, 1987 (e, m); *Visions of a Liberated Future: Black Arts Movement Writings*, 1989 (e); *The LeRoi Jones—Amiri Baraka Reader*, 1991 (misc); (with Thomas McEvilley) *Thornton Dial*, 1993 (e); *Heathens and Revolutionary Art*, 1994 (p, lecture); *Conversations*, 1994 (r, i.e., interviews); *Jesse Jackson and Black Peoplete Stories*, vol. 1, 1990; *Robot Visions*, 1990 (n); *Foundation and Empire*, 1991 (n); *Second Foundation*, 1991 (n); *Forward the Foundation*, 1993 (n); *Magic: The Final Fantasy Collection*, 1995 (s); *Eulogies*, 1996 (r); *Black Music*, 1998 (h, c)

BARNES, Djuna (1900–1982)

In the details of Djuna Barnes's stories there is a great deal of fine observation, clearly as well as beautifully phrased. It is the larger outlines of her stories that are obscure. This is perhaps because she sees in detail what the rest of us see, but feels about life as a whole differently from the rest of us. . . . The whole book (*A Book*), when one has ceased to ponder its unintelligibilities, leaves a sense of the writer's deep temperamental sympathy with the simple and mindless lives of the beasts: it is in dealing with their lives, and with the lives of men and women in moods which approach such simplicity and mindlessness, that she attains a momentary but genuine power.

Floyd Dell. *The Nation.* Jan. 2, 1924. pp. 14–15

If genius is perfection wrought out of anguish and pain and intellectual flagellation, then Djuna Barnes's novel *Nightwood* is a book of genius. In language, in philosophy, in the story it unfolds, she has woven a dark tapestry of spiritual and emotional disintegration whose threads never outrage each other in clashing disharmony. No gayety and no lights fall upon her pattern, which is not to say that her pages are devoid of laughter or humor. For humor she has in abundance but it runs deep in hidden places and the laughter it evokes is tragic. If she has been ruthless and cruel to herself in writing this book out of the rich essence of her knowledge and her thinking and her experience, she has the compensating reward of compelling the thoughtful reader into attention to what she has to say and her manner of saying it. Her prose is lyrical to a degree where it seems of another age and another world but at the same time it does not lose kinship with the earthiness of humans.

Rose C. Feld. *New York Herald Tribune Book Section.* March 7, 1937. p. 4

In her novel (*Nightwood*) poetry is the bloodstream of the universal organism, a poetry that derives its coherence from the meeting of kindred spirits. The "alien and external" are, more than ever, props; they form the hard rock on which Miss Barnes's metaphysically minded characters stand and let their words soar. The story of the novel is like the biological routine of the body; it is the pattern of life, something that cannot be avoided, but it has the function of a spring, and nothing more. It is in their release from mere sensation, or rather the expression of such an attempted release, that Miss Barnes's characters have their being.

Alfred Kazin. *New York Times Book Section.* March 7, 1937. p. 6

In *Nightwood*, as in the work of Braque and the later abstract painters, the naturalistic principle is totally abandoned: no attempt is made to convince us that the characters are actual flesh-and-blood human beings. We are asked only to accept their world as we accept an abstract painting. . . as an autonomous pattern giving us an individual vision of reality, rather than what we might consider its exact reflection. . . . The eight chapters of *Nightwood* are like searchlights, probing the darkness each from a different direction, yet ultimately focusing on and illuminating the same entanglement of the human spirit. . . . (*Nightwood*) combines the simple majesty of a medieval morality play with the verbal subtlety and refinement of a symbolist poem.

Joseph Frank, *Sewanee Review.* Summer, 1945. pp. 435, 438, 455–6

The Antiphon is unmistakably the work of a mind of distinction and stature. I was not so much moved as shaken by the spectres it raises. But is it, as a work of art, successful? Is it really comparable with Webster, or is the style a sham Jacobean, or a sham Eliot-Jacobean make. . . . The speeches of the characters are never, in the true

sense, dramatic, shaped by a living emotion. For all the sombre violence of imagery, they are aggregates of fancy, not imaginative expression proceeding from an inner unity of condition and thought.

Kathleen Raine. *New Statesman and Nation.* Feb. 8, 1958. p. 174

In *Nightwood*, published in 1936, Djuna Barnes gave us a novel of extraordinary and appalling force, a study of moral degeneration recited in a rhetoric so intensely wrought, so violent and so artificial, that it discouraged all but the hardiest readers and became a kind of symbol of sinister magnificence. *The Antiphon*, a verse play in three acts, repeats the oratorical modes of the novel, though with less obscurity and with some reduction of queerness. It is still difficult, perversely wayward; but it does make concessions to ordinary humanity, and there are in it moments of poetry and true excitement. It is scarcely a play: one cannot imagine it on any stage this side of Chaos and Old Night; but it is dramatic poetry of a curious and sometimes high order.

Dudley Fitts. *New York Times Book Section.* April 20, 1958. p. 22

In *Nightwood* the sentences are as heavy and intricate, as finely sewn as an old brocade, but their very grandeur serves only to muffle and disguise the human events they ostensibly depict. The whole tone and atmosphere of the novel are redolent of scandal, sin, and wayward confidence; everything about its language and setting promises extravagant revelations of the soul. Yet it remains curiously reticent and evasive, its characters fixed in a kind of verbal frieze. Reading it through again in this collection [*Selected Works*], I am reminded of how much more its author owes to Mr. Eliot than just a preface. The bogus aristocrats, the half-world of ambiguous sexuality, the self-conscious symbolism and mythic allusions as well as its fragmented shape, plainly remind us of the world of *The Waste Land*.

Hilton Kramer. *The Reporter.* July 5, 1962. p. 39

[Barnes's] world is a world of displaced persons—of an Armenian country boy on the lower east side of Manhattan, of Russian emigrés in Paris, Berlin, Spain, or New York, of Scandinavians or English in American farmland. They have abandoned national, racial, and ethical traditions; their human contacts are laceration. They lack even the integrity in isolation that comforts the characters of Hemingway or the early Faulkner, for they are estranged against themselves. Their aborted and ineffectual attempts to find meaning, order, or love are the subjects of the stories. Technique, as well as subject, marks the stories as extraordinary.

Readers who find the verbal pyrotechnics of *Nightwood*, or of the 1927 novel, *Ryder*, or of *The Antiphon* too often merely talky and falsely rhetorical will discover in most of the stories a fusing of experience and idea. Economy is especially characteristic of the revised versions collected in the *Selected Works*, where verbal fat has been pared away, and objects, persons, and actions flash out with chilling precision. This is not to say, of course, that the stories are easy to read; on the contrary, like those of Katherine Mansfield and Katherine Anne Porter—which technically many of them resemble—they retain their meaning in a very dense texture, where each detail is significant and essential to the whole. And in spite of *Nightwood*'s relatively wide circulation they are generally unknown today.

Suzanne C. Ferguson. *Southern Review*. Winter, 1969. p. 27

Miss Barnes's themes have consistently taken the modern world to task, but her techniques reflect her careful study of the past. She has been influenced in diction and vocabulary by the Bible, Chaucer, Shakespeare, Donne, Milton, Fielding; by the literature of Manners, Sterne, and Joyce. With some justice, we may state that she has also admired these writers and their works for structural reasons. From the start of her longer work, she became an experimenter with fictional forms which tend to fragment, superimpose, juxtapose, or intertwine her thematic and plot lines. The episodic character of both her early and later models appears in the "spatial" quality or unorthodox arrangement of her material into forms which resist the linear-as-chronological schema typical of fictional narratives. . . .

I am not entirely persuaded as to the novelty of her structure. The picaresque novel, a very old form, is both episodic and susceptible to rearrangements of time; and certain chapters recount events occurring during the same time as other events described in previous chapters. A clearer sense of Barnes's purpose is obtained by considering time thematically rather than structurally. As interested in time rearrangements as she may be, Miss Barnes is much more interested in time as it relates to the degenerating patterns of Western society. She does not write, at the expense of theme, for the sake of creating poetic language; for both theme and style are important for her creation of her desired effect.

In turn, later writers, particularly those noted less for their popularity than for their craftsmanship, appear to have been influenced in varying degrees by Barnes's writings. For example, Faulkner showed evidence that we have indicated of having been influenced by Barnes as he sought to achieve the ideal of feminine beauty in his later novels, such as *The Hamlet*, *The Town* and *The Mansion*. Barnes is cited in the introduction to John Hawkes' novel *The Cannibal* as having influenced that writer stylistically, and Anais Nin's novels have been said to reflect such an influence.

As such conventions of the nineteenth century novel as its linear plot and its "realistic" characters are increasingly displaced by the challenges of our frighteningly changing times and people, we can anticipate that discerning readers as well as writers hopeful of improving their craftsmanship will turn in growing numbers to Miss Barnes's works for instruction.

James B. Scott. *Djuna Barnes* (Twayne, 1976), pp. 141–42

Djuna Barnes's middle vision comes to its fullest expression in *Nightwood*; that . . . immaculate novel is indeed a masterpiece. To let it stand alone as representative of a full career, however, is to deprive the novel of a good share of its merit. *Spillway* and *The Antiphon*, rather than being blind thrusts in new directions, follow from *Nightwood* in a precise and logical way. It may even be argued that *The Antiphon* is a work of comparable value insofar as it gives final shape to Miss Barnes's central themes. Certainly both companion volumes to *Nightwood* in *The Selected Works* greatly amplify the themes and stylistic attainments of their predecessor. Likewise, the uneven and sometimes flawed work before *Nightwood*,

if seen with attention to the emergence of qualities that finally cohere in the novel, may reveal merits that have been overlooked. Even the early popular journalism, seeming hardly to bear upon a cryptic and subjective novel of 1936, may suggest something of what was to follow. . . .

In all, *Nightwood* is Djuna Barnes's central work, if not her only achievement of distinction. The book's trans-generic mode enables Miss Barnes to focus the themes and stylistic techniques that had been forming for years into a cohesive whole. It is completely consistent with the earlier work in form and themes, only more concentrated and intricately worked within its selective range. It brings the aims of the novel perhaps as close as possible to those of poetry, particularly with respect to the poetic image. It remains to be seen whether or not *The Antiphon*, a similar attempt in the genre of verse drama, is as successful. But *Nightwood* is a masterful work architecturally and linguistically, comparable to the works of Joyce and Eliot among the moderns, and to those earlier writers quoted or echoed in the novel itself. Like Malcolm Lowry's *Under the Volcano* and William Gaddis's *The Recognitions*, equally neglected works of similar merit, nearly every phrase in it is distinctive and functional, essential to the whole.

Louis F. Kannenstine. *The Art of Djuna Barnes: Duality and Damnation* (New York Univ. Pr., 1977), pp. xviii, 126

Barnes's reputation rests essentially on *Nightwood* (1936). A powerful novel of marriage, adultery, and betrayal, it should not be mistaken for a domestic narrative in the Updike manner, where failures can be comprehended and new beginnings achieved. Focusing on bogus aristocrats and American expatriates in Europe during the 1920s and 1930s, this is a nightmarish world, off kilter and surreal. Its inhabitants lose the object of their love, Robin Vote, and are unable to find an outlet or spillway for their anguish. Almost like puppets, they are set into frenetic motion and new behavioral patterns by forces from within their unconscious. These include sudden transvestism and bisexuality, metamorphoses of personality, and schizophrenia, all placed against juxtaposed times and swift changes in setting. Complex techniques such as these, along with eccentric characters, have led critics to associate Barnes with experimental forms and especially with anti-realism. But she is not a one-book author, and therefore she should be examined in the larger context of other important works. Though more traditional, they still reveal characters and conflicts that are the foundation of *Nightwood*, as well as her dexterity in using vastly differing styles. *A Book* (1923) and *A Night among the Horses* (1928) consist of short stories, poems, and one-act plays that, unlike *Nightwood*, are concise and even traditionally narrated. But it is here that themes such as the severed self and the atomized self are introduced. . . .

Whatever the techniques—traditional or experimental—Barnes's work is concerned with ways of being reconciled to life's random misfortunes. In the stories of *Spillway* there is often an emotional "spillway" that rechannelizes feelings of helplessness and isolation. Its specific form may not be pleasurable, yet still it exists as an alternative to the completely isolated personality. For some characters who are whirled about by stimuli they never quite understand, the spillway is passivity or acquiescence, while for others it is a private fantasy, endless travel, or psychological regression. Whatever the case, the suffering begins with detachment from origins.

Miriam Fuchs. *Hollins Critic*. June, 1981, pp. 2–3

BIBLIOGRAPHY
A Book, 1924 (misc); *Ryder*, 1928 (n); *Nightwood*, 1936 (n); *The Antiphon*, 1958 (pd); *Selected Works*, 1962; *Ladies Almanack*, [1928] 1972 (n); *Vagaries Malicieux*, 1974 (e); *Greenwich Village as It Is*, 1978 (t); *Smoke, and Other Early Stories*, 1982; *Creatures in an Alphabet*, 1982 (p); *Interviews*, 1985; *Atlantic Monthly the Roots of the Stars: The Short Plays*, 1995; *Nightwood: The Original Version and Related Drafts*, 1995 (n); *Poe's Mother: Selected Drawings of Djuna Barnes*, 1995; *Short Stories: Selections*, 1996

BARRY, Philip (1896–1949)

Mr. Barry has had the best preparation that America can give. He has been educated by our professors and theorists and has built upon the foundation thus attained with experience in the hard school of Broadway. If he allows nothing to turn him aside from it, he may yet write a great play. . . . His knowledge of the technique, his ability to write sincere and moving dialogue, his poetic sensitivity, the acting quality of his work, his varied experience, all forecast an achievement of which America may be proud.

> Carl Carmer. *Theatre Arts*. Nov., 1929. p. 826

The characteristic cleverness and brightness of Philip Barry's dialogue have tended to obscure the similarity of pattern of his plays. He deals for the most part with the individual's revolt against conventional pressure for social conformity and attempts to force him into a pattern of behavior to which he is inimical. Most frequently his antagonist is "business" and everything it stands for: its goal, way of life, its hostility to originality and individuality. To Barry "big business" represents everything he abhors in modern life.

> Eleanor Flexner. *American Playwrights* (Simon). 1938. p. 249

Before the emergence of S.N. Behrman, Mr. Barry was our best writer of polite comedy. The true gift was his, but he valued it so little that he was said to have only contempt for *Paris Bound*, one of the earliest as well as one of the best of his pieces, and he gradually sacrificed success to two tendencies incompatible not only with the spirit of comedy but also, it would seem, with each other. Increasingly Mr. Barry became a snob and a mystic. His later plays were full of yearning elegants who seemed equally concerned with the meaning of the universe and with what the well-dressed man will wear—in his head as well as on it.

> Joseph Wood Krutch. *The Nation*. Dec. 24, 1938. p. 700

I carefully reread what Mr. John Anderson, Mr. John Mason Brown, and Mr. Brooks Atkinson had in their various columns seen fit to record (about *Here Come the Clowns*). . . . I was compelled to admire the diffused and sociable precision with which they expressed their respect for the playwright's intentions, past achievements, forward-looking subject matter and approach, and the equally exact conveyance of the tedium they felt at his present effort. Each of these reviews of theirs conveyed also the sense we get of fine intervals as such, of genuine and thrilling inventions now and then. . . . That the critics wished the author well was clear, and wished his play well, and clearly too they could not find their way in it. Which . . . is pretty much the way I feel about it.

> Stark Young. *New Republic*. Dec. 28, 1938. p. 230

On the whole Mr. Barry has written an interesting play (*The Philadelphia Story*), with shrewd touches of character, and much humour. Moreover, Mr. Barry's heart and brain are both on the side of the angels, which is something in this day of inverted values in the theatre. . . . Also Mr. Barry can write admirable dialogue, though at times his tendency to preciosity is evident. In fact this latter tendency is his greatest artistic sin. But despite this fault Mr. Barry has written his best comedy since *Holiday*, though not his finest play—that is *Here Come the Clowns*.

> Grenville Vernon. *Commonweal*. April 14, 1939. p. 692

Phil was as serious at heart as he was gay on the surface. He was at once a conformist and a non-conformist, a sophisticate and a romantic. He was a good American from Rochester who never ceased to be Irish. The accent of his spirit, regardless of the accent of his speech, remained Gaelic. The fey quality was there, the ability to see the moon at midday. He had the Irish gift for both anger and sweetness, and the Irish ferment in his soul. He was a Catholic whose thinking was unorthodox and restless. Even in his comedies, when apparently he was being audacious, he employed the means of Congreve to preach sermons against divorce which would have won a Cardinal's approval.

> John Mason Brown. *Saturday Review*. Dec. 24, 1949. p. 26

Barry was essentially a writer of comedy, and repartee was his stock in trade. He did however aspire to a greater seriousness, and there are passages in *Hotel Universe* and *Here Come the Clowns* which indicate ability in that direction. The difficulty, whenever he attempted heavier fare, was that he seemed to walk on tiptoe, perhaps in fear that he would be laughed at, and his work always seems to be trying to anticipate that possibility by getting in the first laugh. It moves gingerly among the more disturbing moral problems, darting and feinting, always ready to withdraw into the security of a smart remark, as though to indicate that the author has not lost his sense of humor or got himself out of his depth.

> Walter Kerr. *Commonweal*. Jan. 26, 1951. p. 398

Barry's was a healing art at a time when dramatic art was mostly dissonance. Perhaps Barry felt the need for healing too greatly himself to add to the dissonance and to widen the rifts in the topography of the modern, specifically contemporary American, scene. Whatever the reason, and regardless of the risk of indecisiveness, Barry sought balm in Gilead, found it somehow, and dispensed it liberally—and with gentlemanly tact. . . . It was not the least of Barry's merits, a mark of both his breeding and manliness, that his manner was generally bright and brisk and that the hand he stretched out to others, as if to himself, was as firm as it was open.

John Gassner. *Theatre Arts*. Dec., 1951. p. 89

Certainly it falls far short to dismiss Barry as a witty writer of high comedy of manners, bantering, facile, and superficial. He was that and more. Beneath his flippancy and "chit-chat" was a sensitive and deeply spiritual writer coming to grips with the psychology of his times and expressing a yearning for maturity and emotional wholeness. No other American playwright was able to transmute the raw elements of unconscious life into a work of art so delicate, so subtly ingratiating, and so fresh in form, as did Philip Barry. If these are the criteria of greatness, *Hotel Universe* belongs among the great plays.

W. David Sievers. *Freud on Broadway* (Heritage). 1955. p. 211

BIBLIOGRAPHY
A Punch for Judy, 1921 (d); *You and I*, 1923 (d); *The Youngest*, 1924 (d); *In a Garden*, 1925 (d); *White Wings*, 1926 (d); *John*, 1927 (d); *Paris Bound*, 1927 (d); (with Elmer Rice) *Cock Robin*, 1928 (d); *Holiday*, 1928 (d); *Hotel Universe*, 1930 (d); *Tomorrow and Tomorrow*, 1931 (d); *The Animal Kingdom*, 1932 (d); *The Joyous Season*, 1934 (d); *Bright Star*, 1935 (d); *Spring Dance*, 1936 (d); *War In Heaven*, 1938 (n); *The Philadelphia Story*, 1939 (d); *Liberty Jones*, 1940 (d); *Without Love*, 1942 (d); *Foolish Notion*, 1944 (d); *Second Threshold*, 1951 (d)

BARTH, John (1930–1990)

The recent monstrous novel of John Barth, . . . *The Sot-Weed Factor*, could scarcely have been written by a European, because it involves a *new* concept rather than a variation on an existing one. . . . It presents itself as a "historical novel," or again, as a "joke on historical novels," and each guise is strong enough that the work may be, and is, read as either. It is also, like *Finnegans Wake*, a proof of what cannot be done, or else the reason for no longer doing it; theoretically at least, the existence of *The Sot-Weed Factor* precludes any further possibility for the "historical novel." This does not mean that the book is one to be especially recommended; readers familiar with the extraordinary art of Mr. Barth's earlier novel, *The End of the Road*, will probably find *The Sot-Weed Factor* prolix and overwhelmingly tedious. This is, of course, an integral part of the book's destructive function. . . ; Mr. Barth's sense of humor, in short, is an extremely advanced one.

Terry Southern. *The Nation*. Nov. 19, 1960. p. 381

The mark of style in [*The Sot-Weed Factor*] is untiring exuberance, limitless fertility of imagination (fancy, if you prefer), a breathless pace of narrative that never lets the reader rest or want to rest. Superficially one might say that our author "imitates" seventeenth century style, but he doesn't really; he only makes us think he does. He thereby avoids the stiffness of pedantry and at the same time

gets a flavor of the antique. The aim . . . is burlesque—even the apparently inordinate size of the book is a joke. It was a dangerous joke, but he gets away with it. He burlesques the aged conventions of fiction—mistaken identity, "the search for a father," true love, and all the rest—with merciless ingenuity. No moral purpose is discoverable, no arcane "significance," simply fun.

Denham Sutcliffe. *Kenyon Review*. Winter, 1961. p. 184

Primarily, John Barth is a novelist of ideas. The situations in his comic works are always directed toward establishing his twin themes of the individual's quests for value and identity in a world of gratuitous events. Clearly aligned with existentialist conceptions, Barth, nevertheless, denies a formal knowledge of philosophy and prefers to describe himself as "reinventing" ideas to cope with his view of the modern world. . . .

The Sot-Weed Factor is Barth's most complete and satisfactory treatment of his themes of value and identity. Here his approach is primarily a negative one. Through the destruction of a false ideal of innocence, Barth establishes his picture of man as a complex, emotional and sexual being and stresses the value of sympathetic ties between men.

Part of Barth's success in *The Sot-Weed Factor* comes from the book's form. As opposed to his first two novels which are realistic treatments of bizarre situations, the third novel is purposely artificial.

John C. Stubbs. *Critique*. Winter, 1965–66. pp. 101, 108

If we can measure literary achievement at all, we can measure the value of a novel by the extent to which it succeeds in the impossible task of getting the sloppy richness of life into the satisfying neatness of artistic shape.

By any such standard, *Giles Goat-Boy* is a great novel. Its greatness is most readily apparent in its striking originality of structure and language, an originality that depends upon a superb command of literary and linguistic tradition rather than an eccentric manipulation of the "modern." . . .Barth employs the traditional patterns of myth, epic and romance to generate a narrative of extraordinary vigor and drive. At the same time, he freights this narrative with ideas and attitudes in combinations so varied and striking that the reader is torn between stopping to explore the book's philosophical riches and abandoning himself to the pleasure of immersion in a story. . . .

Robert Scholes. *New York Times Book Section*. Aug. 7, 1966. pp. 1, 22

I got into a kind of rage of disappointment when the genius who wrote *The End of the Road* took up the fad for self-imprisonment in funny language. *The Sot-Weed Factor* and *Giles Goat-Boy* are unreadable, and I can swear to this because I read them through. So when John Barth's new collection of short pieces, *Lost in the Funhouse*, arrived my heart sank, and I left it on the shelf for a long time. . . . And now I've read *Lost in the Funhouse* with great pleasure and hardly know where to look. Because of my needless fears, I haven't given the book the attention it deserves, so I can only hazard first impressions. There may be a more significant relation than I have grasped between the folksy short stories about boyhood on the Eastern Shore and the deliberately bizarre excursions into the style of Borges, Beckett, Kafka and mock-epic, but I have a hunch that the structural pretensions are pure put-on. In any case, most of Barth's language has come back to genuine, and very funny, life. The spoofs of "fiction about fiction about fiction" manage, in a way I couldn't have predicted from the laborious imitations of the two previous novels, to be funny on this familiar subject and seriously interesting too, and both in new ways.

Robert Garis. *Hudson Review.* Spring, 1969. pp. 163–4

Since neither *Giles Goat-Boy* nor *The Sot-Weed Factor* is a "proper" novel but "imitations-of-novels," they do not offer representations of reality at all but representations of representations of reality, removing them at least twice from the world of "objective reality" and further emphasizing their artificiality in the process. Thus Barth uses artificiality to expose artificiality. By presenting a farcical and exaggerated version of the world, not as the world is, but as it is erroneously conceived to be, Barth mocks the false conception and suggests cosmic absurdity by inversion.

Charles B. Harris. *Contemporary American Novelists of the Absurd* (College and University). 1971. p. 116

Barth's early narrators demonstrate an independence of mind from the omnipotence of environment which in one sense is a state much to be desired. On the other hand they are presented as suffering from a nihilism which excludes them from confident participation in life, and which is to be seen as a curse or a blight. At the same time that equivocal mental and verbal freedom which they "enjoy," and which allows them to be completely arbitrary in the patterns they choose, is the freedom increasingly exercised by Barth himself. His tendency to sport on lexical playfields increases in his following books. In these "floating operas" signs tend to become more important than their referents, and the impresario of fictions, John Barth, plays with them in such a way that any established notions of the relationship between word and world are lost or called in doubt. Barth is indeed one of the great sportsmen of contemporary fiction.

Tony Tanner. *City of Words* (Harper and Row). 1971. p. 240

In his last three works of fiction, Barth systematically debunks the idea of progress by showing that life is existentially absurd, by showing that the individual, society, and cosmos are all inherently chaotic. He then demonstrates the foolishness of acting on notions about transcendental correspondence, for such idealism will quickly destroy both man and his society. As an alternate to such notions of idealism and progress, Barth stresses the actuality of cyclical correspondence. According to the cyclical pattern, man and his society must pass from innocent notions about the goodness of life and about the individual's role as a saviour-hero to a more mature, tempered, and somewhat cynical view necessary in order to formulate an appropriate way to create meaning for the individual and harmony for a society. Finally, however, Barth does not demonstrate any permanence or absolute merit in such maturity, for senility, death, and decay are the ultimate rewards for the individual and his civilization. Even so, life will probably continue in

correspondingly similar cycles for generations, centuries, millenniums, and substantially longer periods of time.

Gordon E. Slethaug. *Critique.* 13, 3, 1972. pp. 27–8

I had always thought that Barth's mind was more interesting than any of his books so far—it was perceived, through the books, of course, but it could be perceived as being let down. *Chimera* makes me think that this is precisely the impression the books have all set out to create. The texts suggest an author who, for all his narrative meddling and jugglery, is aloof from them, better than they are, and the clumsy gags and the frequent silliness only confirm this feeling. All intentional, an aristocracy of bad taste, a disdain for the world's terms. . . .

Barth is not obscure or difficult, and he can be very funny . . . and the moral dimensions by no means disappear in the trickiness. He is suggesting in *Chimera*, for example, that love is a terrible risk, an almost certain loss, given our own and others' experience in the matter, but that the risk can be redeemed by the quality of spirit with which it is taken. . . .

But Barth won't take this kind of risk with his writing: won't free it and master it, won't let it loose from the safe zones of pastiche. It is as if he would rather not know where the limits of his talent lie, were happier with the thought of being a brilliant man repeatedly betrayed by his books.

Michael Wood. *New York Review of Books.* Oct. 19, 1972. pp. 34–5

In *Lost in the Funhouse* [Barth] transcends the agonizing efforts at self-definition of Ebenezer, Burlingame, and George Goat-Boy, and the equally traumatic biographies of the Maryland tales, and comes to rest in the serene Borgian acceptance of an identity that has no confirmatory existence apart from its fictional entity. Indeed, the mark of Borges's "The Immortal" is everywhere impressed in Barth's paradigmatic renderings of the myths of Narcissus, Menelaus, and the archetypal poet anonymous. His skeptical acceptance of the permanence of multiplicity, of even the possibility that one's self is but the dream of another insubstantial being, becomes the only viable strategy for confronting the Great Labyrinth, both human and cosmic. In parody alone may the artist hope to find a successive form that dissemblingly confirms continuation in time. To retell the old myths, to come paradigmatically ever closer to a great contemporary like Borges (as these stories so patently do), and to lampoon the anti-Gutenberg cries of McLuhan and company (as these stories also do) is to maintain the fiction of continuity and the reality of person in the limited persistence of the word, is finally, if nothing else, to give aesthetic validity to life.

Max F. Schulz. *Black Humor Fiction of the Sixties* (Ohio Univ. Pr.). 1973. p. 40

The irony of the novel [*The Sot-Weed Factor*] consists in the fact that it is based on the model of *Tom Jones*, and on all the assumptions the world of *Tom Jones* makes, but that its hero, Ebenezer Cooke, achieves disillusionment, not identity, at the end. The very concept of "identity" is called into question by the novel. No one in the novel is what he appears to be; Bertrand, Ebenezer's valet, poses as Ebenezer aboard ship; Burlingame poses as Lord Baltimore, Colonel Peter Sayer, Timothy Mitchell, and Nicholas Lowe. The overwhelming complexity and richness of the novel derive partly from this substitution of illusion for identity. All of the complicated, shifting interconnections of the plot and the political intrigues it involves are brought a step beyond *Tom Jones*: the threads of the plot never are tied up neatly in *The Sot-Weed Factor*, and facts never do dovetail. The maze of the plot, from the overview of the reader, verges on the condition of a labyrinth, the condition in which the consistent identity of the world exists in a shattered state. The space of *The Sot-Weed Factor* is apparently the same kind of map space as in *Tom Jones*, but cracks in this space are always opening up, and they open into voids.

> John Vernon. *The Garden and the Map* (Illinois). 1973.
> pp. 63–4

Barth's solution to his distaste for necessity is to create imaginative alternatives to reality—*The Sot-Weed Factor, Giles Goat-Boy*—with characters whose fictionalizing approach to life he shares. With their own arbitrariness and finality, these alternatives dramatize the irresponsibility of fiction to any man's factual and reasonable truth. They and their heroes, who make their lives into fanciful floating operas, are amoral. The only limiting provision of this value—the fictionalization of experience—is that it work: psychologically to protect, aesthetically to interest. The floating-opera man does not want to give himself away but does want to interest others. For Barth's characters it is a way of living in the world while retreating from it. For Barth as a novelist it is a way of writing a book without the curse of sincerity, a way of having protean secrets protected by protean disguises.

Barth's parody of aesthetic form is one of these disguises. What seems to be an attack on fiction itself is actually a critique of the solidification or rationalization of the aesthetic process into an abstract construct. The aesthetic or fictionalizing process is fluid and willful; it breaks up or ignores traditional values and conventions, which may seem to have a rational basis, to control one's experience.

> Thomas Le Clair. *Texas Studies in Literature and Language*.
> Winter, 1973. p. 722

The typical Barth character . . . embarks upon a voyage of thought and passion whose goal is to discover the "real" self, the "real" experience, underlying the fictions in which he is imprisoned. For Barth, the novel begins when a character becomes conscious of himself as an actor, puppet, and perhaps inventor of his own life-drama. Therefore, the plot of Barth's novels is largely the plot of discovering the underlying myths, the archfictions which will allow us to live with the smaller, less satisfying fictions of everyday life and still to believe in ourselves as conscious, creative agents. . . .

Barth's career, indeed, is a progression toward precisely such a mythic vision of the inauthentic condition of modern man: an evolution of style, theme, and subject which ends—for the present—in a severe, allegorical approach that describes the modern dilemma of writer and reader most efficiently by a retelling and inversion of the most ancient and "irrelevant" of legends. There is a surprising corollary to this evolution—as Barth's fictions become more and more obsessively "mythic," they also become lighter,

more truly comic, more open to the possibilities of life and to the chances of escaping the infinite vortices of self-consciousness.

> Frank D. McConnell. *Four Postwar American Novelists*
> (Univ. of Chicago Pr., 1977), pp. 115–16

Make no mistake: [*Letters*] is a daunting book. Amid the fabulist fictions which have, in the past twenty years, sprouted at every hand, it rises like a monument—a monument being, of course, a construction that demands attention but is not itself alive. Patience, Shakespeare tells us, sat on a monument, and that is one of the things the reader can do with *Letters*, but whatever he does with it, he had better bring Patience along for company. Again, make no mistake: this longest and most complex of John Barth's novels is really an awesome performance. Like Nabokov's *Ada*, Pynchon's *Gravity's Rainbow* and Gaddis's *J.R.*—the only contemporary novels other than Barth's own to which it may be fairly compared—*Letters* is brilliant, witty, at times erudite, and damn near unreadable as well. The reader's jaw drops in amazement, then remains locked in the yawn position. . . .

Put briefly, Barth's intention here is to write a novel which will serve as a sequel to all five of the books he had written prior to embarking on this one, and to do so in the form of an epistolary novel, a genre he well knows was exhausted nearly two centuries ago but which he will revivify by means of all manner of alphabetical, anagrammatical and numerological games. . . .

Barth cannot write a dull page and there is much here that is delightful, but by writing a great many very similar pages, and drawing so heavily on material he has exhausted before, he becomes very quickly dull. . . .

And yet: it is impossible to dislike the book. Perhaps, given the perspective a reviewer can never immediately enjoy, I'll look upon it with more affection. Barth is as inventive and as muscular a writer as we have just now. Faint-headed readers may not finish *Letters*, but no one who cares for fiction can ignore it altogether.

> Peter S. Prescott. *Newsweek*. Oct. 1, 1979, pp. 74, 76

John Barth's fictions have always used male-female relationships to explore questions of identity. Barth's characterizations have escaped criticism, however, because his fictions have gradually abandoned the pretense of realism, in favor of parodic and self-conscious techniques. The "self-reflexive" approach allows Barth to explore the deeply traditional structures—the myths—that he finds at the heart of fiction, of experience, and of perception. This pursuit of fundamental form has led him to a mythic definition of male and female identities, one that underlies all the work but becomes most explicit in *Chimera*. The notions of gender identity revealed in Barth's work are important first because they *are* traditional; they reflect the assumptions inherent in a male-centered mythology. But Barth extends the myth, employing it as metaphor for the condition of the artist/perceiver. That "new" myth contains more than the dangers of the old male-female dichotomy; it is a fascinating example of the ways that contemporary subjective relativism can support a myth even more deadening to women. Thus Barth's ideas of gender identity are important not only in illuminating his own fictional views, but also in tracing the emergence of old sex roles in new disguises. . . .

Barth wants to show the paradoxical nature of life, but keeps coming down on one side of the paradox, unable to resolve the polar tensions without surrender of one pole. A perspective so heavily weighted in favor of the ''masculine,'' conceptual, creative pole can hardly celebrate ''feminine'' principles, particularly when the narrative itself displays the triumph of idea over fact, scheme over ambiguous life. Barth's preference for the ''male'' side eliminates even the power suggested by the mythic dichotomy, reducing the potent innerness of the Earth Mother to the ''vacuum'' of the not-self, and reducing the energy of the Muse to the mimicry of the mirror-self. The result is female characters who are always seen from outside, who are reduced to symbols, symbols moreover of the non-human aspects of life, and who are denied power even in that area by narrative insistence on the creative male perceiver.

Cynthia Davis. *Centennial Review*. Summer, 1980, pp. 309, 321

There is so much that is appealing, even wise, in *Sabbatical*, that if I finally found it irritatingly cute, I hope the shortcoming is mine, not the author's. John Barth certainly has the right stuff. He can, as Saul Bellow once prescribed, put a spin on words, but it seems to me that in *Sabbatical* he has not so much hammered out a novel as proffered a long and convoluted academic write. Seductive here, touching there, but ultimately confusing. Unsatisfying. Undone, perhaps, by its own cleverness, a highly refined propensity for literary games and riddles. . . .

For all its self-consciousness, plentiful footnotes pedantic or ponderous, and showy literary references, *Sabbatical* has been built on a frame of very stale convention. Which is to say, at the novel's end—well, no, it doesn't end, it stops—the author and his black-eyed Susan are (wait for it) about to sit down and write the novel we have just read with, as the blurb writer coyly puts it (wink, wink), a little help from the author.

Mordecai Richler. *Saturday Review*. June, 1982, p. 67

Letters, with its central image and metaphor of the Tower of Truth rising over a university campus but inexorably sinking into the marshland even as it was built, was an extended and general discussion of the state and status of American culture and literature which, of necessity, concluded inconclusively. Even its one (apparently) definite death, that of Todd Andrews as he stood atop the tower at the moment of its explosive destruction, has been withdrawn and he is to be found sailing through the pages of *The Tidewater Tales*.

Sabbatical, taking its start from the final page of *Letters*, is a study of a retired CIA operative writing his memoirs as a revenge on the Company's more heinous deeds. Along the way, the Vietnam War, abortion, the role of US secret service in South America, the pollution of the James River, the state of contemporary fiction and criticism are all discussed within the frame of a preambulatory narrative. All these discussions contribute obliquely to the central question of the book: whether, in the face of the present direction the world is taking, the two central characters of the novel should reproduce themselves biologically as well as literally.

The Tidewater Tales replays and reworks that ground situation, . . . and pays homage to the fictional character whom Barth sees as

the goddess of the art of narrative by introducing her into the text as a player in the game.

Richard Bradbury. *Critical Quarterly*. Spring, 1990, pp. 66–67

At the probable risk of some arbitrariness, one can distinguish four major functions of myth in *Chimera*. The first may be labeled the demystification of myth as spiritual, cultural, or historical heritage. Next, and contradictory so far as reader expectancy is concerned, is the defamiliarization of myth as received tale. The third function is what might be called the radicalization of myth as self-parody. This activity is not only characteristically Barthian but also involves a doubling of paradigms or schemas and a perceived referentiality to either or both of the first two functions. The final function— although, as we shall see, there is also a function of the functions— is the restoration of myth as unbounded narrativity. This activity bears closely on the nature of Barth's work since *Chimera*, most notably *Letters* and *The Tidewater Tales* with their virtually inexhaustible inventiveness compounded with replication.

John Vickery. *Modern Fiction Studies*. Summer, 1992, p. 429

The conceit of John Barth's new novel [*Once upon a Time: A Floating Opera*] (if novel it is; it's as much a memoir) concerns a fountain pen. ''Nothing fancy about it,'' Barth says. ''It's a no-nonsense, British-made Parker, burgundy plastic barrel, brushed steel cap with arrow-shaped clip and some sort of polished gray stone let into the top, point neatly cowled by the lower barrel in a clean modernist style, nib alloyed of platinum and iridium for hardness and corrosion resistance. But I was impressed by the manufacturer's recommendation that the pen be used exclusively by its owner, since over time the rub shapes itself to its user's penmanship and thus writes evermore smoothly.''

This precise description of a *modernist* pen occurs, within a longer passage in which Barth describes in loving detail his working methods—how he must write in an old binder he bought in his undergraduate days, how he must place plugs in his ears to shut out all sound, etc. Throughout, Barth comments on his novels, their sources, their critical reception. But what little story he offers concerns his pen, his mourning over its loss, and its eventual replacement—all tricked out in ''arias,'' ''acts,'' ''duets,'' and the like, although any resemblances to an opera are purely mechanical.

Somewhere near page 100, Barth and his wife begin their voyage. It's much the same voyage undertaken in *Sabbatical* (1982) and *The Tidewater Tales* (1987), twin books telling the same story from different premises, but, in any case, featuring a voyage around Chesapeake Bay by a man and woman. There's more trouble with the plot than usual in *Once upon a Time*, however. . . .

Perhaps Barth is pretending; with his immense talents, he could write a great story if he chose. He'd rather speculate on what sort of story he'd have if he had one. . . .

Once upon a Time is the most postmodern of all of Barth's novels. No character with an interesting or sympathetic internal life is presented; Barth seems incapable of such a creation. No major theme is undertaken—not even, with any thoroughness, Barth's own aging. There is nothing here, in the end, but writing.

John Mort. *New L.* Spring, 1994, p. 6, 7

BIBLIOGRAPHY

The Floating Opera, 1956, rev. ed. 1967 (n); *The End of the Road*, 1958 (n); *The Sot-Weed Factor*, 1960, rev. ed. 1967 (n); *Giles Goat-Boy*, 1966 (n); *Lost in the Funhouse*, 1968 (s); *Chimera*, 1972 (n); *Letters*, 1979 (n); *Sabbatical: A Romance*, 1982 (n); *The Literature of Exhaustion*, 1982 (c); *The Friday Book; or, Book-Titles Should Be Straightforward and Subtitles Avoided: Essays and Other Nonfiction*, 1984; *Roadside America*, 1986 (t); *The Tidewater Tales*, 1987 (n); *The Last Voyage of Somebody the Sailor*, 1991 (n); *Once upon a Time: A Floating Opera*, 1994 (autobiographical n); *Further Fridays: Essays, Lectures, and Other Non-Fiction, 1984–1994*, 1995 (misc); *Death in the Funhouse*, 1995 (n); *On with the Story*, 1996 (s)

BARTHELME, Donald (1931–1989)

Come Back, Dr. Caligari by Donald Barthelme is a hard wild controlled collection of poker-faced perversities, working a kind of drollery which automatically precludes the intimate effects but pinwheels and sky-rockets spectacularly across its own landscape. Occasionally Mr. Barthelme falls into a mode which can best be described as that of a pop artist in prose; these stories are studded with solemn absurdities from ads, comic-books, mail-order catalogs, record-blurbs, and instruction-leaflets. . . .

The characters rise like automata to their formal speeches and jerky actions, then subside; it makes not only for the cruel funny, but, oddly, for a desolate landscape littered with pathetic fragments of useless speech-patterns. It is a book written as if with verbal components from a used-car graveyard; its most striking effects come from disparity, inconsequence, and incongruity.

> Robert M. Adams. *New York Review of Books*. April 30, 1964. p. 10

On its most available level *Snow White* is a parodic contemporary retelling of the fairy tale. More accurately, the tale is here refracted through the prism of a contemporary sensibility so that it emerges broken up into fragments, shards of its original identity, of its historical career in our consciousness *Disney's cartoon film is almost as much in evidence as the Grimm story* and of its recorded or potential uses for sociology and psychology—all the Freudian undertones and implications, for example. Placed like widely separated tesserae in an abstract mosaic construction, the fragments serve to give a skeletal unity to the mostly verbal events that surround them, as well as a locus for the book's main imaginative thrust.

The only thing resembling a narrative is that the book does move on to fulfill in its own very special way the basic situation of the fairy tale. But Barthelme continually breaks up the progression of events, switching horses in midstream, turning lyricism abruptly into parody, exposition into incantation, inserting pure irrelevancies, pure indigestible fragments like bits of stucco on a smooth wall, allowing nothing to *follow* or link up in any kind of logical development. . . .

Fiction, Barthelme is saying, has lost its power to transform and convince and substitute, just as reality has lost, perhaps only

temporarily (but that is not the concern of the imagination), its need and capacity to sustain fictions of this kind. [1967]

> Richard Gilman. *The Confusion of Realms* (Random). 1969. pp. 45, 47

Barthelme's stories are . . . unnatural acts. They are attempts—mocking attempts—at narrative in a time that is shapeless and that affords no principle of selection. Like William Burroughs, Barthelme creates a new kind of fiction by frustrating, spoofing, or aggressively ignoring the expectations—of situation, development, denouement—raised by the old. He is light-minded with a vengeance; or, if light-mindedness is indeed an illness, militant mockery is its slightly feverish principle. Hence these stories [*Unspeakable Practices, Unnatural Acts*], though so much like play, are not quite free. They mock contemporary life, they mock the art of fiction itself, not in simple exuberance, and certainly not in full comic gaiety but in a somewhat painful merriment and with ever so slightly a feeling of having to vomit.

> Calvin Bedient. *The Nation*. May 27, 1968. p. 703

Barthelme's only novel to date, *Snow White*, is an extended parody, an ingenious "put-on" that is perhaps the purest example of Camp yet published. Barthelme, however, does not emphasize artifice at the expense of meaning, as Sontag's definition of Camp would lead one to expect. On the contrary, *Snow White* demonstrates as few novels can the indissolubility of form and content in the novel. To be sure, the form of Barthelme's Camp masterpiece—the ways he manages and arranges character and incident and the use he makes of language—does obscure all coherent meaning or "content" in the novel, but this is precisely Barthelme's point. In writing a novel devoid of "meaning" in the traditional sense of that term, Barthelme denies the possibility of meaning in an absurd world. The form of his novel thus becomes an analogue to the absurd human condition.

> Charles B. Harris. *Contemporary American Novelists of the Absurd* (College and University). 1971. pp. 124–5

Barthelme's importance as a writer lies not only in the exciting, experimental form, but in the exploration of the full impact of mass media pop culture on the consciousness of the individual who is so bombarded by canned happenings, sensations, reactions, and general noise that he can no longer distinguish the self from the surroundings. Barthelme's metropolis is rapidly reaching the state where the media are the man. As refuge the individual finds only unquestioning acceptance of contradictory states on the one hand, or specialized and meaningless abstractions on the other. Though wisdom and insight may exist here, the mass media have reduced everything to the same level of slightly shrill importance, and thus, paradoxically, to the same level of trivia. In the constant barrage of equally accentuated "nownesses," the individual loses all sense of priorities, and thus, caught between undifferentiated fact and equally meaningless abstractions, his world is that horror envisioned by one of E. M. Forster's characters in *A Passage to India* where every thing exists and nothing has value.

As a writer, Barthelme also asks about the arts in such a city and finds the artist too is trapped. Striving to achieve aesthetic distance, to get above the level of mere phenomenon, the artist finds that his works aren't accepted by a world bent on "fact" or that his efforts at perspective have produced only the borrowed, traditional or trivial and are thus unrelated to the world they should represent.

> Francis Gillen. *Twentieth Century Literature*. Jan., 1972. pp. 37–8

Barthelme's stories are normally made up of fragments seemingly associated at random; the closer they come to narrative development, character portrayal or any other conventional purpose, the more overtly they signal their fragmentation. Barthelme may separate the parts of a story with numbers or blank space, or interpose graphic divisions. Earlier writers have drawn similar attention to the formal arbitrariness of fiction—one thinks of Sterne, who also favored graphic intrusions and blank space, or Thackeray, who said in *Vanity Fair* that his characters were puppets—but not even contemporary meta-fictionists like Borges go so far in insisting that the reader take the story as a made object, not a window on life.

Although Barthelme's strategies vary in significance from story to story, they all spring from a common impulse. He is very conscious that formulas achieve familiarity and that familiarity breeds inattention. Though he wishes that literature could still provide insight and inspiration as it did in the great, mercifully unselfconscious days of a writer like Tolstoy . . . he is also aware that modern readers have experienced too much literature to respond freely to the old modes, so he free associates to "make it new." While less theoretical contemporaries resort to marginal subject matter, idiosyncratic viewpoints or shocking language, Barthelme uses formal dislocation to achieve this goal.

> Charles Thomas Samuels. *New York Times Book Section*. Nov. 5, 1972. p. 27

Donald Barthelme either takes pills, does dope, drinks an awful lot, or has one of the unique literary imaginations of the present age. I think it's the latter. . . .

Calling Donald Barthelme's work fiction doesn't do the job. They're writings . . . in search of their own definition, fiction essays on themes that are secret or haven't been announced. They usually have no plots, no characters we can identify from life, no formal beginnings or endings. They're all event, condition, attitude expressed from the viewpoint of a bright and detached stone-head. Some sentences run on for 200 words in quest of a subject. Like poems, his tales seem to plead for reading aloud. They're for feeling and effect, not narration. . . .

While other writers struggle with identity problems and questions or reality, Barthelme has found the magic. Reality doesn't exist. Identity is a costume. . . . His fairy tales . . . should be viewed as you would modern painting. Enjoy the color. Feast on the textures, shapes, patterns. Muse over the combinations.

Yet like contemporary art and music, Barthelme's writing rides on the back of its social source. The pointless talk and intense self-consciousness of his characters, the barbaric juxtapositions of the sacred and the profane, the expensive junk, laminated vocabularies and suspended judgments of his tales—all point to a cultural cellar

in which Barthelme sits thinking. So much so a Skinnerian psychologist could make a case for Barthelme as delivery boy for the dreams of the body neurotic of the U.S.A.

> Webster Schott. *Book World*. Nov. 5, 1972. p. 3

Sadness is a collection of Barthelme's recent stories, his dreams, his toys. Perhaps because he has illustrated one of them with literal montage, it is the art of collage that Barthelme's technique evokes for me—the scissoring and pasting of borrowed images, bringing them into new contexts and thus forming a new reality, but a reality taking half its meaning from the old contexts. Barthelme cites Leninist-Marxist thought knowledgeably, and what we are talking about (not necessarily as a consequence) is a dialectical art, which is to say a revolutionary art. Which is not to say a political art, one that services a revolution, but an art that stages its own strictly apolitical upheaval.

Barthelme is no political man. Mementos abound of Borges and Beckett, who belong also to the grand toymaker tradition of Klee and Calder. The world inhabited by these men is the echo chamber, the hall of mirrors, the palace of art, the House of Usher. Theirs is a closet, a palace revolution. Theirs is a highly objective, even cerebral world, yet these artists make themselves felt nonetheless. We are aware of Barthelme's presence in these stories, whether as an unhappy husband, a man on an operating table, or a mysterious, modern incarnation of St. Anthony. The landscape is bleak, evoking the unpleasant, flat horizons of surrealistic paintings; yet we also detect the familiar features of Barthelme's native East Texas.

> John Seelye. *Saturday Review*. Dec., 1972. p. 66

In the past few years, half masquerading as Thurber's ghost, Donald Barthelme has slipped into the preconscious of contemporary fiction through the pages of *The New Yorker*. Both Thurber and Barthelme draw on a self-indulgent yet acidly ironic fantasy life in which they triumph over their enemies and find innocent pleasures they prefer to call guilty. . . .

In five collections of stories and one novel, he has established not so much a milieu of places and characters, nor a recognizable style, as an elusive tone. . . . For several years now Barthelme has been sprinkling his texts with modishly doctored engravings and old prints that reinforce his mood [between the fantastic and the comic]. Even without them his most characteristic passages recall Max Ernst's pre-surrealist collages, and also the stunning slow-motion farce-epics of the Bread and Puppet Theater. . . .

For those who prefer to use the handrail of plot when they step off onto the dark stairs of fiction, *The Dead Father* offers more to hold onto than Barthelme's earlier fiction. Even so, he snatches away our security after only a few steps.

> Roger Shattuck. *New York Times Book Section*. Nov. 9, 1975. pp. 1–2

To turn . . . to Donald Barthelme's *The Dead Father* may induce culture shock. This cold short narrative is written at an extreme distance from life, out of literary models and the author's idea of a defunct avant-garde. *The Dead Father* is God, we are told at one point, but the tyrannic authority of the past will do. It seems clear only that Barthelme finds clarity simplistic and is enchanted with the attenuated jokes of modernity. Here may be found his Lucky speech, his *Watt* palaver, his Joycean flourishes, his Kafkaesque dream, etc. It's all very cynical and chic, like Woody Allen's posture of the twirp taking on the big guys once again. Here the novel itself is a *shtick*. Barthelme is adroit and must know the dangers he runs in his use of the literary forebears he fears and admires. The awe is still in him and he cannot bring himself to real parody. The book is boring and difficult to no purpose. The little snigger we get from recognizing the Beckett line is like that Model T in *Ragtime*. Real freedom, if that is what Barthelme is seeking in laying the image of the father to rest, will come in a release of his comic talent from the merely fashionable. He is ingenious in dealing with the madness of sophisticated urban life but he is not yet angry enough to dig out from under the clods of pastiche that muffle his own voice.

Maureen Howard. *The Yale Review*. Spring, 1976, pp. 408–9

As though to offer an alternative to our immersion in fixed roles and clichés, and our inevitable imprisonment in the fixed structures of language, he subjects the written and spoken forms of language to endless experimentation and parody. Most typically, he literalizes metaphor, which shocks the reader into an awareness of both his own uncreative use of language and its rich possibilities. Barthelme evokes through his verbal arrangements, in fact, a universe—unborn until then, untapped in his reader's consciousness. He creates, especially up through *The Dead Father*, a unique form of comedy, with language as its subject, the emblem of man's relationship to other men and to the universe. It is a comedy, moreover, that is wildly funny, as it is liberating and educative. In some of his more recent work—with either its literalizations of metaphysical issues (which create a unique form of fable) or with its new dialogue forms—he creates an even more poetic and diffuse style. One may associate the brilliant verbal collage with the earlier and main body of his writing, and the more ineffable, infinitely suggestive and polyphonic techniques of poetry and musical composition with some of the more recent material. . . .

Barthelme is wonderfully interesting and funny: more important, he is remarkably liberating. Our pleasure comes not in figuring out how his people use words, or the sources of his parody, but rather we revel in his dazzling and endlessly provocative verbal textures. He may be aware that language constricts and that the mind tends to operate in structures, but he is unique in creating for us through his wonderful elegance the great and abundant world. He demands a sophisticated reader, for the better read and more sensitive to language and style one is, the more fun he will have, since Barthelme seems to have read everything. Unlike Eliot, however, whose literariness was didactic and in many ways, an end in itself—because it pointed back to a time of former value— Barthelme's vast information is but his means of stimulating us to a recognition of the limitations as well as the meanings of past formulations. Ultimately, Barthelme wishes us to break free and take pleasure in the world his thick textures evoke.

Lois Gordon. *Donald Barthelme* (Twayne, 1981), pp. xi–xii, 33

Barthelme can probably write any way he wants to. He has chosen to remain a comic writer whose subject matter is disorder. (This

phrase will fit Voltaire, Twain, and Beckett.) He has given no hint of a predilected order, and I can't think of one that wouldn't depress him. He accepts the absurdity of everything with the clarity of a saint or the absoluteness of a nihilist. He does not bereave us of our intelligence, our wit, our material comforts. He lets us keep every advantage we have against an absurd and futile existence, and proceeds to show us the absurdity and futility of our best and brightest, especially these.

His method is simplicity itself. There are no more contexts. Every attempt at ceremony parodies itself. Barthelme relocates our world back in Eden, apple in hand, wiseacre snake hissing psychiatry, advertising, marketing, personality tips, economics, weight watching, art appreciation, group therapy, our lovely brassy swinging culture from Philosophy 700 (Kierkegaard to Sartre) to bongo drums in the subway. But we feel suddenly naked, embarrassed, and unwelcome in the garden. Barthelme doesn't know why we feel this way either, but he can focus our feeling into a bright point that can raise a blister.

Guy Davenport. *Book World*. Oct. 25, 1981, p. 5

In a tale like "The Educational Experience" [Donald] Barthelme enlarges the perspective of his art. This story becomes nothing less than a work of conceptual art, a three-dimensional art event depicting the origins of the disillusionment and sense of failure that the personal acknowledges in "See the Moon." As in stories like "Me and Miss Mandible," "The Sergeant," and "The School," the tale blames its narrator's educational experience for misleading and brutalizing him. It transforms a four-year college curriculum into an intellectual gymnasium in which students exercise to quotations from history and literature and hurdle over new discoveries in solid-state physics like athletes in a track event. This education rewards speed and efficiency in its students but totally fails to suggest the ways human knowledge might develop their imaginations. Consequently, the students are processed from this assembly line with great cynicism about learning, thinking, and feeling. "The Educational Experience" functions as a story about the dubious process of contemporary education and the confusions it causes in those who manage to survive it. Moving from descriptions of the strenuous obstacles these students encounter to the trivial fragments of information they are made to assimilate, the tale emerges as both a piece of conceptual art and an action painting that uses words from strikingly different vocabularies to instruct, admonish, and direct its students into regimented lives.

Wayne B. Stengel. *The Shape of Art in the Short Stories of Donald Barthelme* (Baton Rouge: Louisiana State Univ. Pr., 1985), p. 204

In *The Dead Father*, the rejection of the past comes about through a journey no one is anxious to make and which will leave matters in much the same condition as when they began. Barthelme thus reduces the conflict from one of heroic enactment to that of repetitive statement, allowing neither, as in comedy, the triumphant celebration of youth over age nor, as in tragedy, the transcendence of necessity through understanding. Nurturing and destructive, omnipotent and ineffectual, tyrannical as well as bewildered, vulnerable no less than vindictive, the Dead Father is a figure of undiminished sexual appetites and vague unfulfilled longings, whose farcical attempt to perpetuate his own myth invites an ambivalent response. Almost from the start, it undercuts its own resonance by substituting for the ritual gesture or expression an uncertain questioning about how effectual such gestures or expressions have been. . . .

The discontinuity of the elements suggests that the narrative principle is more onomastic, or naming, than visual. Neither the objects named nor the relationships between them are arranged in any necessary order by combining the parts to afford some perspective or by widening the view of landscape. Nor is order determined by the evolving character of one or another of the actors as a consequence of what happens to them. They are, rather, allowed simply to remain side by side. In Barthelme's fiction, then, juxtaposition proves to be regressive rather than developmental. The Dead Father's acquiescence in his burial punctuates the loss of the symbols of his authority; it is not caused by that loss or even illuminated by it.

Stanley Trachtenberg. *Understanding Donald Barthelme* (Columbia: Univ. of South Carolina Pr., 1990), pp. 188–89, 199–200

Barthelme's new novel, *The King*, finished three months before his death last year, is an Arthurian fable of human poses and pretensions. Set in a land and time in which Arthur, Guinevere, knights, tournaments, jesters, and tents mingle with Franklin and Eleanor Roosevelt, Winston Churchill, Lord HeeHaw, submarines, bombs, and ubiquitous radio waves, the fabulistic stream of Barthelme consciousness wanders into plots of ripe fruits of satire. Barthelme's barbs and witty touches of parallelism in all ages of human history abound in this short fiction: what he is after is a knowing of human foibles, a compassionate forgiveness of them, and ultimately the unknowing of human contradiction by acceptance of its nature. All remains the same at the end of Barthelme's fiction: Arthur and Guinevere in separate tents of activity, the knights on various legs of journeys round the table of discontents, the world during its Second Great War in a cataclysm that already has passed a first phase. Yet just as much as the remains are the beginnings that Barthelme's fiction poses: awareness of human need to move forward into constructs of understanding without forgoing old clubs of association.

Martin Tucker. *Confrontation*. Fall, 1990–Winter, 1991, p. 216

In Barthelme . . . postmodern must also mean post-Freudian; identifiable "thought structures," "phantasies," "wish-creations," and typical patterns, as they are isolated and defined in the classical psychoanalytic literature, guide Barthelme to the kind of personal and intertextual material with which he works, influence his modes of wit and humor, and frame the narrative problems that generate that remarkable variety of experimental solutions to which the critics have rightly pointed. Appreciating Barthelme's revisionary project opens the way to seeing his fragmentary discourse as less a refraction of postmodern disarray than as an effect of a more or less disguised and intensely polemical dialogue with modernism's

foremost "cartographers of the mind" and theorists of the father-son relation—fathers and sons are Barthelme's flood subject, after all.

Michael Zeitlin. *Contemporary Lterature*. Summer, 1993, pp. 185–86

BIBLIOGRAPHY
Come Back, Dr. Caligari, 1964 (s); *Snow White*, 1967 (n); *Unspeakable Practices, Unnatural Acts*, 1968 (s); *City Life*, 1970 (s); *The Slightly Irregular Fire Engine*, 1971 (juv); *Sadness*, 1972 (s); *Guilty Pleasures*, 1974 (s); *The Dead Father*, 1975 (n); *Amateurs*, 1976 (s); *Great Days*, 1979 (s); *Sixty Stories*, 1981; *Overnight to Many Distant Cities*, 1983 (s); *Paradise*, 1986 (n); *Forty Stories*, 1987; *The King*, 1990 (n); *The Teachings of Don B.*, ed. Kim Herzinger, 1992 (coll); *Not-Knowing: The Essays and Interviews of Donald Barthelme*, ed. Kim Herzinger, 1997 (coll)

BAUSCH, Richard (1940–)

In Bausch's latest novel, *Violence* (1992), the ghost of his abusive father is awakened in Charles Connally when he narrowly escapes death in a convenience-store holdup. The discovery of his own capacity for violence, and his cowardice, unhinges Connally so that he *almost* follows his father's path of violence. But some mysterious exorcising spirit, centered in his ability to forgive his mother for her past failings and in the love of his pregnant wife Carol, saves him. Baush counterbalances the paralyzing dark forces with small, inexplicable gestures of healing that enable his characters to carry on.

Bausch's fictional subject is the American middle class, with its complicated relationships between young couples, parents and children, and relatives. These relationships are continually tested to the breaking point. . . . Bausch deftly shows the quirky, mysterious eruptions of grace that testify to the resilience of the human spirit.

John F. Desmond. *America*. May 14, 1994, p. 11

For the most part, the United States, as depicted by Richard Bausch in *Aren't You Happy for Me?* remains a civilian society. Its problems are personal and familial. Racial and religious conflict, and the ownership of the nation, tend not to arise. If some of Bausch's characters are touched by the economy in the form of unemployment, and thus are aware of class, they are inclined to interpret this in terms of personal realities. Politics, in the longest piece, "Spirits," is what a lecherous drunken professor at a small private college used to be involved in and famous for, back in the Kennedy era.

Richard Ford's introduction to this first British collection aligns Bausch's work with a tradition of realism reaching back to "that old Midwesterner, Chekhov," and it is true that Bausch's direction of the reader's interest is so discreetly persuasive that it takes a while for the stories' real peculiarity to emerge—namely the combination of highly articulate characters and their characteristic lack of curiosity about anything beyond their immediate orbit. . . .

The weariness and frequently inexplicable sense of loss which unify the population of *Aren't You Happy for Me?* have lessons to offer, one of them being not to expect to derive much happiness from the growth of understanding. Yet the effect is far from wearisome. The unfussy polish and economy of Bausch's stories could seem like mere accomplishment of a not unfamiliar sort, but phrases and scenes resurface in the mind, demanding that the whole collection be reread, its lines of kinship seen afresh. Bausch's novels should now be made available in Britain, too.

Sean O'Brien. *TLS: The Times Literary Supplement*. July 21, 1995, p. 21

BIBLIOGRAPHY

Real Presence, 1980 (n); *Take Me Back*, 1981 (n); *The Last Good Times*, 1984 (n); *Aren't You Happy for Me?*, 1985 (s); *Spirits and Other Stories*, 1987 (s); *Mr. Field's Daughter*, 1989 (n); *The Fireman's Wife and Other Stories*, 1990; *Violence*, 1992 (n); *Rebel Powers*, 1993 (n); *Rare & Endangered Species*, 1994 (s); *Selected Stories*, 1996; *Good Evening, Mr. and Mrs. America, and All the Ships at Sea*, 1996 (n); *In the Night Season*, 1998 (n)

BAXTER, Charles (1947–)

Although *Through the Safety Net* is only his second collection of stories and he has yet to publish in the large circulation "name" magazines, Charles Baxter must be counted among one of our best short fiction writers. The author of these eleven stories is a mature, accomplished writer, as evident in "Winter Journey" and "Surprised by Joy." The suggestive title of the collection unites the stories and has many referents, including the title story and the Reaganomic notion that beneath society stretches a safety net, really. The most telling referent, however, appears in "A Late Sunday Afternoon at the Huron." . . .

Baxter's characters, though falling through a spiritual abyss, have known a mild happiness. As they fall, they can still remember a happiness, or at least they can conjure one. Some even land safely.

Baxter celebrates in his falling characters that ability to acknowledge the life in those who still balance upon the tightrope. In "The Eleventh Floor," an alcoholic commercial writer, Mr. Bradbury, is shrouded in a cynical indifference to the world, and not until Mr. Bradbury recognizes the deep, sexual love between his son and his son's lover does life affect him. . . .

Having spent the latter part of his life in an alcoholic blur, blindly falling, Mr. Bradbury may not be redeemed by his understanding, for he has merely drawn open his own frailty. Yet for someone who is falling, parting the curtains to see the world is a worthy act. Baxter does not gratuitously play with his subjects. Rather, he proffers the hope and possibility that another net will gather beneath the falling, provided that those who fall are humane enough to recognize their own vulnerability.

Through the Safety Net is not a collection of Carverean stories of good, inarticulate people living bad lives; neither do these stories wallow in modern malaise; neither are they simple regional tales. Baxter's Michigan is inhabited by cars, half-employed workers, burned-out graduate students, half-sane school teachers, would-be painters, dogs, young boys, and angels—a Michigan meriting

forgiveness and blessing. Life is affirmed, even when living is grievous or bitter. In a time in which many short stories are written either as thinly veiled autobiography or as *l'art pour l'art* exercises, these stories are profound in how Baxter brings back authority to the teller of the tale. In short, he has something to say *for* us, and he takes on that moral responsibility with humor, wisdom, and compassion.

James Brock. *Studies in Short Fiction*. Fall, 1986, pp. 459–60.

"Life can only be understood backwards," Kierkegaard once observed, "but it must be lived forwards." Backward into memory and childhood—that is the direction taken by Charles Baxter's highly accomplished first novel [*First Light*]. Like the Broadway shows *Merrily We Roll Along* and *Betrayal*, *First Light* consists of a series of episodes that recede further and further into the past, and with each backward step, the reader is granted further insight into the characters' lives. The process is not unlike the one used by psychiatrists: as ancient family history is sifted, clues are yielded that shed new light on the present. In one's beginnings are found seeds of what is yet to come.

As he has already demonstrated in two impressive collections of short stories, *Harmony of the World* and *Through the Safety Net*, Mr. Baxter possesses an intuitive understanding of the hazards and rewards of domestic life—especially as practiced by survivors of the 60's. In *First Light*, he trains his gifts of sympathy and observation on a single family, the Welches of Five Oaks, Mich. More specifically, his focus is on Hugh Welch, a Buick salesman, and his brilliant sister, Dorsey, who left home to become a famous astrophysicist.

When we first meet Dorsey, she's just returned for a Fourth of July visit to her hometown, with her new husband and her deaf son, Noah, in tow. Hugh, it seems, has been dreading the visit for days: though he's spent his life "watching over" his kid sister, he's recently begun to doubt that she needs his help at all. To make matters worse, he's already taken a decided dislike to her husband, Simon, a glib, self-conscious actor who seems to be constantly putting him down. Indeed, the initial impressions that Simon and Dorsey make on the reader is less than positive: Dorsey comes across as a snobbish academic who patronizes her working-class brother, and Simon strikes us as a self-absorbed fool, a small-town cad who not only cheats on Dorsey all the time but also likes to boast about it.

"All I ever wanted," Hugh tells Dorsey, "was to make sure . . . that you were all right. You know: safe."

"That's sweet," she replies, echoing a sentiment expressed by many of the characters in *Through the Safety Net*. "But it won't ever work. Not for me. It hasn't ever worked. Besides, there's no safety in safety. So I might as well live with Simon. You and I, Hugh—we've been divorced, haven't we? Can brothers and sisters get divorces from each other? I think they can, and I think we got one."

From this nervous, nearly adversarial exchange, Mr. Baxter slowly draws us into Dorsey's and Hugh's past; we begin to understand just how this "divorce" has occurred. Over the years, after all, Dorsey and Hugh have drifted into different worlds. As their paths have diverged, their memories of each other have become uncomfortable reminders of what they once were—and might have been.

Having elected to stay in Five Oaks and marry a girl he dated in school, Hugh now leads a simple, tactile life: though his marriage has devolved into a passionless routine, punctuated with occasional motel room liaisons, he still derives a blunt, unaccommodated pleasure from selling Buicks, and he enjoys renovating the house he inherited from his parents. "To record the passage of time through his life," writes Mr. Baxter, "Hugh alters his house room by room. He surrounds himself with the work of his hands."

Dorsey, in contrast, has gone on to study the cold, starry skies. She has made a life for herself in the cerebral spheres of academia, fulfilling all the brave, high expectations of her parents and teachers. She has worked for her doctorate, had a disturbing affair with her mentor, a brooding physicist named Carlo Pavorese, and borne his child, Noah. In the wake of those events, she has abruptly married Simon, a willful, self-absorbed man, in whose adolescent pranks she delights.

The men in Dorsey's life are drawn, by Mr. Baxter, in uncharacteristically broad strokes; they tend to feel more like generic types than individuals. Carlo is a caricature of the mad genius—tormented, brilliant and domineering—while Simon seems like a shallow alter ego of Hugh. Where Hugh is adept with his hands, Simon is inept; where Hugh is earnest and sincere, Simon is posturing and phony, etc.

Happily enough, the two-dimensionality of these fellows doesn't really bother us, so wrapped up are we in the story of Dorsey and Hugh. As the novel progresses, the retreat into their past accelerates; we see their youth and childhoods revealed, like rapidly turned pages in a snapshot album. Dorsey's appeal to Hugh for help, as she lies alone in a hospital room with her newborn baby; Dorsey's delivery of the valedictory speech at the Five Oaks high school; Hugh's growing reputation as a ladies' man in Five Oaks; Dorsey's difficulty finding a date for the school dance, her sense of being a social outcast; Hugh's dazzling performance as a hockey player, in front of his adoring sister's eyes; Dorsey's fascination, as a child, with the stars and planets of the nighttime sky.

In reading of these events, we see why Dorsey and Hugh each made the choices that they did, how their childhood dreams were translated into adult decisions. We see how Hugh looked for Dorsey in his wife, Laurie; how Dorsey's hero worship of her brother led her to pick men so different in temperament and talents. In fact, by orchestrating tiny details of observation and larger emotional patterns, Mr. Baxter makes us understand both the shifting balance of power that has occurred between Dorsey and Hugh over the years, and the bonds of affection and shared experience that unite them. The result is a remarkably supple novel that gleams with the smoky chiaroscuro of familial love recalled through time.

Michiko Kakutani. *New York Times*. August 24, 1987, p. C13.

The 13 stories in *A Relative Stranger*, all quietly accomplished, suggest a mysterious yet fundamental marriage of despair and joy. Though in one way or another each story ends in disillusionment, the road that leads us to that dismal state is so richly peopled, so finely drawn, that the effect is oddly reassuring.

The much-praised author, Charles Baxter, has published a novel, *First Light*, as well as two previous collections of stories *Harmony of the World* and *Through the Safety Net*.

Many of the male protagonists in this new collection are confused and timid souls in search of something to believe in; they are all intelligent and sensitive, yet somehow unexceptional. By contrast, the women around them tend to be strong and colorful people who accept life easily—and whose impatience with the men is manifest.

In "Prowlers," Pastor Robinson manages to tolerate a visit by his wife Angie's lover, an abrasive person named Benjamin; when the visit is over, Angie muses to her husband that she and Benjamin know all each other's secrets. Robinson gently protests: "You know my secrets." Angie: "Sweetheart, you don't have any secrets. You've never wanted a single bad thing in your life."

Characters like Robinson have the fatal transparency of goodness, a passive blamelessness that may in itself be a tragic flaw. This hapless virtue has a parallel in Cooper, the hero of a story called "Shelter." Cooper is a generous soul who becomes so involved with the homeless—entirely out of brotherly love, a quality he refuses to recognize in himself—that he puts the autonomy of his own family in danger.

Anders, a Swedish businessman in "The Disappeared," finds his childish expectations of America are crippled by his relationship with a stranger in Detroit. Fenstad is a teacher whose pallid devotion to logic is no match for his mother's irrational vitalities (significantly, the story's title is not "Fenstad" but "Fenstad's Mother"). Warren, in "Westland," is hanging around the zoo one day when he meets a teen-age girl who announces that she wants to shoot a lion. She doesn't do it, but in a bizarre echo of the girl's words, Warren later fires shots at the local nuclear reactor to protest the fouling of the environment. It's another portrait of impulsive, undirected goodness, and again its medium is a heartbreaking ineffectuality.

One story that stands out from all the others, in both style and theme, is "The Old Fascist in Retirement," an elegant fictional imagination of Ezra Pound's latter days in Italy. The bitterness of the title contrasts with the rather sympathetic portrait the story contains; the underlying message (so familiar) may be that Pound was not really evil, only deeply confused. If so, then the old poet begins to look like a version—augmented, to be sure, by his peculiar genius—of Fenstad or Cooper or Robinson: a good, articulate man who tragically failed to understand something fundamental about the social contract.

In the powerful title story, "A Relative Stranger," a man discovers late in life that he has a brother. Both men, as infants, were given up for adoption. It appears that two lost souls are headed for a joyful reunion. Yet fraternity turns out to be a burden, another of nature's unpardonable hoaxes; the two brothers are wholly incompatible. One of the brothers says: "I was always homesick for the rest of the world. My brother does not understand that. He thinks home is where he is now."

Few of the protagonists in this collection would make the brother's mistake (if it is one). They are the temperamentally homeless, the ones who look off in amazement as other people accept the conditions of the everyday world without even the murmur of an existential question. If these stories have a common theme, it may be this abiding failure, in leading characters, to imagine what is most real. By contrast, Charles Baxter's chronicling of such human debilities represents a continuing triumph of the imaginative will.

William Ferguson. *New York Times Book Review*, October 21, 1990, p. 18.

[You'd] hurt nothing at all by introducing yourself to Charles Baxter's *A Relative Stranger*. Straight out, let's announce this reviewer is a fan, and in these pages reviewed an earlier work, *Harmony of the World*. Baxter just gets better. Where Rick Hillis dazzles the eye and Daniel Stern makes mind play, Charles Baxter writes straight for the heart. His style is unassuming. Metaphors are rare. There are no pyrotechnical displays of language. All proceeds via understatement, a style that leaves unadorned sadness and passion in stark relief against the page. This prose is glass.

In "Westland," in circumstances that have nothing to do with his job, when a social worker becomes involved with a dysfunctional family he gains possession of a small pistol. He fires it four times at the blank wall of a nuclear reactor. Driving home he finds himself behind a car with a green bumpersticker that reads: "CAUTION: THIS VEHICLE EXPLODES UPON IMPACT!" and the social worker thinks, "That's me. . . . I am that vehicle." Many lesser writers, having achieved such a moment, would have quit, but Baxter always works his material completely, squeezing every final nuance from his characters and plot. . . .

"The Disappeared" is the story of a Swedish engineer, Anders, summoned to Detroit by General Motors to discuss his work in metal alloys. He is fascinated by America, "especially its colorful disorderliness." His ambition is "to sleep with an American woman in an American bed," and once his business is completed, he has three days in "a wide-open American city, not quite in the wild West, but close enough to suit him." Now, most American readers will know that Anders would have been safer in Wichita, Dodge City, or even Tombstone in 1880 than on the streets of contemporary Detroit. Doormen and cab drivers give him warning, but Ander's ignorance makes him fearless. He meets a woman, of course, and being unsure of racial identifications he is mystified by what race she may be. She is one of the Last Ones, a member of the Church of the Millenium, "where they preach the Gospel of Last Things."

Detroit eventually turns on him, of course. Anders comes to feel "that he must get home to Sweden quickly, before he becomes a very different person, unrecognizable even to himself," and he steps out of a building into air "which smelled as it always had, of powerful combustible materials and their traces, fire and ash." A very American landscape.

As an author, Charles Baxter is a rare representative of an endangered species—the American writer obsessed with defining the American character. That's a theme that to many seems so presumptuous, so vast and overdone, that they have retreated to neo-regionalism, taking refuge from the Whitmanesque impulses that have shaped so much of our literature, hiding in the more manageable landscape of a specific time and place. But Charles Baxter returns to the bigger theme again and again, and thank goodness. As we change, we need new voices that will redefine us anew.

In other stories, Baxter exquisitely explores relationships between two people, relationships that are always uneven.

In the title story, a man who was an adopted child meets another man who informs him they are brothers. "Fenstad's Mother" describes an elderly woman who is, because of her humanistic Old Left Politics, more dynamic, more at ease, more compassionate, and more alive than her son, a teacher, can ever hope to be. And each of "Three Parabolic Tales" explores how men and women need and abuse each other. The first story is about a young couple,

the second about middle age, the third about an older man and wife. The stories make a lovely trio.

A Relative Stranger is a rich display of Charles Baxter's talents. The intelligence behind the prose is so quiet and so muted, that the reader is never aware of the contrivance of Art. The stories just seem to *be*, sprung fully grown and fully armored, just as they are, and imagining alternatives—that they might have once been something else that the writer judged, revised and refinished—seems impossible.

Introduce yourself to Charles Baxter if you don't already know him. You can never tell what might come of it. Give yourself a reward.

Perry Glasser. *North American Review*. December, 1990, pp. 60–4.

Often when short-story writers go to write novels they get jaunty. They take deep breaths and become brazen—the way shy people do on wine. Donald Barthelme becomes mythic and parodic, Alice Munro boldly seamsterly (stitching novels from stories). Andre Dubus asks us to reconsider the novella (as an equivalent form). Perhaps Grace Paley has shown the greatest bravado of all in simply not bothering.

Charles Baxter, whose three brilliant collections of short stories (*Harmony of the World, Through the Safety Net* and *A Relative Stranger*) may place him in the same rank as the above writers, constructed his first novel in reverse chronology. *First Light* (1987), the hauntingly detailed story of a brother and sister from Five Oaks, Mich., is an intricate unknotting, a narrative progression backward in time toward the moment when the boy, Hugh, first touches his infant sister's hand. It is a strategy intended, no doubt, to make the form Mr. Baxter's own, as well as to show the inextricability of sibling ties. Now, in his second novel, *Shadow Play* the novel is no longer a form to be seized and remade, but a capacious place in which to move around. Mr. Baxter is looser, less strict. The narrative has not been trained; Mr. Baxter indulges it, affectionately musses its hair, lets it go where it may. The result is, paradoxically, both a more conventionally constructed novel and a more surprising and suspenseful book.

Shadow Play is primarily the story of Wyatt Palmer, a fiercely bright and artistic boy who grows up to find himself stuck in the most pedestrian of existences, by day a bored government bureaucrat, by night a tired-husband, father and homeowner. When a chemical company called WaldChem sets itself up in town and pressures the city management (for the sake of the local economy, of course) to look the other way as health regulations are violated, Wyatt is suddenly and precariously placed at the center of a drama involving ethical behavior in "postethical" times.

In a contracting economy, too many citizens of Five Oaks appear willing to make a devil's pact: health for cash; lives for jobs. As assistant city manager, Wyatt would like to "notify the state that the on-site waste management guidelines and regulations and licensing restrictions are being violated."

But the head of WaldChem is a high school buddy; Wyatt plays golf with him; he has given Wyatt's wayward foster brother, Cyril, a job in the plant. And, as the city manager tells Wyatt, "the times are against you." By remaining quiet and polite and helpful to those around him, Wyatt strikes a most unholy bargain—with himself as well as with the world. He is no longer his troubled brother's troubled keeper; he is a member of the audience. As Mr.

Baxter wrote in *First Light*, "No one knows how to do that in this country, how to be a brother."

Not unlike Shirley Jackson's story "The Lottery," Mr. Baxter's *Shadow Play* takes large themes of good and evil and primitive deal making, and situates them in municipal terms and local ritual. He is interested in those shadowy corners of civilization in which barbarity manages to nestle and thrive. The America of this book has become a kind of hell. "The houses gave off a dingy little light, the light of I'm-not-sorry-for-anything, the light of Listen-to-me. . . . That way you didn't even need eternal fire."

Shadow Play is also an examination of how the Midwestern values of niceness, passivity, helpfulness and just-going-along can contribute to the rot and demise of a community. When Wyatt's foster brother develops lung cancer while holding down his custodial job at the plant, Wyatt is impassive. "They didn't have to make WaldChem so dangerous, those bastards," rages the dying Cyril. "They could have made it safer."

"You smoked, Cyril," Wyatt replies quietly. "You smoked cigarettes all your life." It is a response so wicked in its neutrality that later "he stood in his own living room, repressing the impulse to scream." "The verdict on him, he now knew, was that he was obliging and careless, an accessory." When Wyatt agrees to help Cyril commit suicide (one is reminded here of a fellow Michigander, Dr. Jack Kevorkian) he has not only enacted the central metaphor of the book but effectively set himself up for a nervous breakdown, one replete with tattoo, adultery, arson and a move to Brooklyn!

This last is no amusing little fillip; in the geographical paradigm of Mr. Baxter's book, New York City is Eden as anti-Eden. Here the fruit of the tree of knowledge is not rotting in anyone's driveway. There are no driveways; the trees were cut down years ago. The good fight has long since been waged and lost, and here one can live in something akin to aftermath if not to peace. As a boy Wyatt had memorized a map of the New York subway system, and as a young man he lived there as an artist, a painter of shadow portraits; now, in New York with his family, he can resume where he left off before the heart and hinterland so rudely interrupted him. He can attempt something *un*-Midwestern, something unthwarted, adventurous, something like a coda, a twilight sequel; in unecological times, an ecology of hope and loss.

One of Mr. Baxter's great strengths as a writer has always been his ability to capture the stranded inner lives of the Middle West's repressed eccentrics. And here, in his second novel, he is a full throttle. The character of Wyatt's mother is a figure of alleged madness, but (whether it speaks to Mr. Baxter's talent or should because for this reader's concern) the passages that give voice to her insanity are lucid, lovely, sympathetic: "She knew that birds sometimes agreed or disagreed with their names but she kept that information to herself." "Angels," she thinks, "were so vain, so pretty. They wore coral earrings and distressfully unassembled hats." When Wyatt brings his mother to New York, and, she finds the life of a bag lady a congenial one, Mr. Baxter treats this with a certain heartening dignity rather than a forlorn condescension.

He also gives much of the book over to the voice and point of view of Wyatt's bright, quirky Aunt Ellen, who functions as a sapient observer of the world of the novel. She believes not in a benevolent God but in a God of pure curiosity; moreover, she believes she is writing the Bible of that God. "There is absolutely no love coming to us from that realm," she says of the more traditional deity. "None at all. You might as well pray to a telephone pole."

Aunt Ellen, even more than Wyatt, is the moral center of the book—hers is the most trenchant of the solitudes fashioned and recorded here. That Mr. Baxter can traverse gender and offer such a deep and authentic rendition of a woman's voice and thoughts should not in itself be remarkable in contemporary fiction, yet still it is.

Because his work doesn't offer itself up in gaudy ways for popular consumption or intellectual play (theorists and critics have failed to descend en masse with their scissors and forks), Mr. Baxter has acquired the reputation of being that rare and pleasurable thing: a writer's writer. He has steadily taken beautiful and precise language and gone into the ordinary and secret places of people—their moral and emotional quandaries, their typically American circumstances, their burning intelligence, their negotiations with what is trapped, stunted, violent, sustaining, decent or miraculous in their lives. In writing about ordinary people he derives narrative authority from having imagined farther and more profoundly than we have, making his literary presence a necessary and important one, and making *Shadow Play* a novel that is big, moving, rich with life and story—something so much more than a writer's anxious vacation from shorter forms.

Lorrie Moore *New York Times Book Review*. February 14, 1993, pp. 7–8.

BIBLIOGRAPHY
Chameleon, 1970 (p); *The South Dakota Guidebook*, 1974 (p); *Harmony of the World*, 1984 (s); *Through the Safety Net*, 1985 (s); *First Light*, 1987 (n); *A Relative Stranger*, 1990 (s); *Imaginary Paintings and Other Poems*, 1990 (p); *Shadow Play*, 1993 (n); *Believers*, 1997 (s); *Burning Down the House*, 1997 (e)

BEATTIE, Ann (1947–)

Something of Updike's attentiveness to ordinary human encounters distinguishes Ann Beattie's *Chilly Scenes of Winter*, a fine first novel which records the reluctant passage into adulthood of a twenty-seven-year-old survivor of the Woodstock generation. The novel incorporates characters and situations Beattie had treated earlier in her *New Yorker* stories, nineteen of which have been gathered under the title *Distortions* and released as a companion to the novel. But the novel is a more interesting and significant performance, richer in psychological nuance and in documentary power. Though there are many isolated passages in *Distortions* that exhibit Beattie's descriptive care and her talent for truthful dialogue, only one of the stories, "Snake's Shoes," has the sustained authority of the novel. One reason for the novel's superiority is that it is less tendentious than the stories, less confined by neo-absurdist attitudes toward contemporary experience. The novel is thus less somber than the stories and registers on every page a lively, generous alertness to the antic or comic in human relations. The characters in *Chilly Scenes* are respected more consistently than their counterparts in the stories, and although their vivid idiosyncrasies are always comically before us, what is odd or distinctive in their behavior belongs to their personalities, is rooted in Beattie's powers of observation and dramatic representation. Too often in the stories, in contrast, one feels the pressure of a surrealist program, the influence of Barthelme and Pynchon, behind the author's choice of details or in the often schematic resolution of her plots.

Chilly Scenes is written in the present tense and relies heavily on dialogue and on a purified declarative prose not unlike good Hemingway, but much funnier. This disciplined young novelist takes care to differentiate even her minor characters, and one of her most memorable cameo players declares herself only as a voice through the telephone—a nervous, guilty mother trying to trace her wayfaring daughter in two brief conversations that momentarily distract the protagonist during this final winter of his prolonged adolescence. The hero himself is wonderfully alive: a gentle bewildered man, extravagantly loyal to old friends and to the songs of the 'sixties, drifting through a final nostalgia for the mythologies of adversary selfhood he absorbed in college and toward an embarrassed recognition of his hunger for such ordinary adventures as marriage and fatherhood. The unillusioned tenderness that informs Beattie's portrait of her central character is a rare act of intelligence and mimetic art.

David Thorburn. *The Yale Review.* Summer, 1977, pp. 585–86

I can think of no other American writer save Thomas Pynchon who has found so wide and respectful an audience so early in her career. No one who has a serious interest in contemporary fiction can fail to be aware of Beattie's abrupt and alarming stories. Their publication in book form [*Distortions*] marks, I believe, a genuine event in the national life.

I suppose that one first feels struck by Beattie's consummate technical virtuosity. Her frigid prose, the shocking inexorableness of her humor and narrative designs, the macabre and spare efficiency of her thought, conspire to project her tales as actual—if rather awful—occurrences of modernist existence. I have called Beattie's prose cold: but one must read this most wicked and witty writer very closely indeed. It is true that she assembles as subjects a grotesque community of dwarfs, fats, gargoyles, and sluts, a bizarre collection of the lonely, the disoriented, and the dispossessed. Never, though, does she permit her figures to seem merely apathetic or aimlessly malcontent. Nor does she ever dismiss them as freaks. Beattie constructs her stories from within a soft and subtle sensibility of sympathy, participation, and hopefulness. She understands that, however capricious or queer, her characters' pains have their origin less in the morasses of individual neurosis than in the insipidity of the culture at large, the withering vapidity of the historical processes which envelop one and with which one must manage to coexist in some sort of emotional relation. It is the sign of her extraordinary intelligence and gentleness that Beattie considers her fictionalized people to be as human as their author; that she regards her own suffering as conterminous with that of her roughly satirized characters.

Beattie comprehends, this is to say, that we are driven into our misery and peculiarity because, appropriately, we cannot accommodate the abstraction and absurdity which surround us. Her characters fervently want to feel; especially they long to love. But the rapidity and monstrousness of contemporary history, the dearth of external supports for even the minimal impulses of human life, seem to the stories' people to invalidate the very possibility of achieving affective experience.

Peter Glassman. *Hudson Review.* Autumn, 1977. p. 447

The characters who populate [*Secrets and Surprises*] came of age during the 1960's. They are, on the whole, a nice-looking bunch of people who have never suffered from any of the basic wants. Most of them, for reasons often unexplained, share a mistrust of passion and conversation. . . . They exist mainly in a stateless realm of indecision and—all too often—rather smug despair. . . .

Frequently, in these stories, things are substitutes for the chancier commitment to people; things people buy or live with or give one another are asked to bear the responsibility of objective correlatives, but too often they become a mere catalogue of trends. The reader is left holding an armful of objects and wondering what emotional responses they were meant to connect him with.

Perhaps the best level on which to enjoy these stories is as a narrative form of social history. Miss Beattie has a coolly accurate eye for the *moeurs* of her generation. . . . But a sharp eye for *moeurs* doesn't add up to a full fiction any more than the attitude of irony can be said to represent a full human response.

Gail Godwin. *New York Times Book Section.* Jan. 14, 1979. p. 14

In the six years since her work first began to appear in *The New Yorker*, Ann Beattie has become for many readers the representative young American novelist and short-story writer. Her two collections of stories—*Distortions* (1976) and *Secrets and Surprises* (1979)—and her novel *Chilly Scenes of Winter* (1976) won the praise of critics and reviewers and of older and established writers as diverse as John Updike and Mary Lee Settle. But her cultural significance lies as much, if not more, in the devotion and self-recognition she inspires among younger readers: people in their twenties and early thirties who graduated from college as the Sturm und Drang of the 60's faded into the anxious laid-back narcissism of the late 70's.

Her new novel at once confirms her status and marks a considerable advance on her previous work: *Falling in Place* is stronger, more accomplished, larger in every way than anything she's done, and its publication is a fitting occasion for a look at both her work and her curious celebrity.

Her fiction has none of the usual gimmicks and attractions that create a cult: it's not conspicuously witty or bizarre or sexy or politically defiant or eventful; in fact, it offers so colorless and cool a surface, so quiet a voice, that it's sometimes hard to imagine readers staying with it. Her subject matter, too, is deliberately banal: she chronicles the random comings and goings of disaffected young people who work in dull jobs or drop out, and spend a lot of time doing and feeling practically nothing except that low-grade depression Christopher Lasch has called the characteristic malaise of our time. This tepid nihilism or defeated shopping-mall consumerism is depicted in a deadpan, superrealistic style: I am not a camera but a videotape machine.

Of course, banality has many literary uses. But Ann Beattie's gray subaqueous world has none of the existential terror of Samuel Beckett's seemingly banal subject matter, or the hidden menace of Harold Pinter's social banality; there's none of the esthetic delight and wit of Donald Barthelme's intentionally banal, pop-art verbal collages, or of the apocalyptic and fully orchestrated angst, the doomed banality of Joan Didion's novels and essays. Ann Beattie's sad, bleak books are a far cry from the zany, black-humored flights of such earlier cult writers as Kurt Vonnegut or Richard Brautigan. The characters who populate the works of such recent "younger" novelists as Robert Stone, John Irving, Mary Gordon or Leslie Epstein seem in comparison as brightly colored and energetic as the characters in a Verdi opera. . . .

Inevitably these studies in domestic sorrow recall the stories of J.D. Salinger or John Cheever or John Updike: Ann Beattie's world, like theirs, is a miserable suburban purgatory inhabited by grieving wraiths. But the extraordinary literary color, shape and motion that animate the work of those older New Yorker writers are qualities Ann Beattie turns away from. Her stories are defiantly underplayed and random, trailing off into inconsequentiality, ending with a whimper or, at best, an embarrassed grin. And unlike her predecessors, she has no grand conservative vision buried deep in the background of her books. . . .

Her books exhibit a kind of Quaalude schizzy artistry; they're held together by an angry adolescent's sharp-eyed, deadpan delivery—less is more, right?—by an irony so uniformly spread around the imagined world that nearly all color and feeling are leached away, an irony that becomes a kind of self-defensive verbal tic, an irony without reference to any higher, deeper, unironically embraced standards, not even esthetic standards. . . .

Yet nothing Ann Beattie has written could quite prepare us for her new novel, *Falling in Place*. It's like going from gray television to full-color movies. Not that her themes or settings have changed that much, but there's a new urgency to the characters' feelings and a much greater range and number of characters and points of view. . . .

> Richard Locke. *New York Times Book Section*. May 11, 1980. pp. 1, 38

Compared to the earlier stories, these [in *The Burning House*] are less grotesque, more narrowly and intensely focused, more accomplished; they are also less outrageous and less outraged and more sympathetic to their characters. The mood is not bloody-minded; rather it is sorrowful. Most of the stories are about the process of separating, but there are no causes proposed, only effects, and thus no one is seen as responsible for the pain. The result is a certain moral attenuation. This is not hell but limbo, which some writers have located on the moon: That's where the space cadets end up.

No one is better at the plangent detail, at evoking the floating, unreal ambiance of grief. I would say Ann Beattie is at her best here, except that I think she can do even better. One admires, while becoming nonetheless slightly impatient at the sheer passivity of these remarkably sensitive instruments. When that formidable technique is used on a subject large enough for it, the results will be extraordinary indeed. Still, that's like caviling because Wayne Gretsky misses one shot. If Miss Beattie were a ballerina you could sell tickets to the warm-ups.

> Margaret Atwood. *New York Times Book Section*. Sept. 26, 1982, p. 34

Although her celebrated short stories depend on the conventions of episode and implication, Ann Beattie's novelistic imagination sends its spirals out from carefully elaborated structural premises. In her last novel, *Picturing Will*, she studied the dynamics of family life by using a five-year-old boy as a reference point and occasional focus for what were, finally, less chapters than adjacent panels, each rendered with a somewhat different scale, perspective, and point of view.

Her new novel, *Another You*, has a more ambitious blueprint. We could simplify it by imagining a narrowing cone laid on its side, with another widening cone superimposed on it. The first represents the dominant narrative, which tracks the fraying relationship of Marshall and Sonja Lockard, a childless couple living in a small New England college town. The other is the epistolary unfolding of a tale from the past. . . .

Another You is a novel of the present that is somehow written out of the sensibility of the 1970s, the decade so deftly portrayed in Ms. Beattie's earlier work. Marshall in particular comes across as locked in period amber. . . .

But there is a larger problem. While Ms. Beattie's structural conception is enticing enough to ponder, the narrative feels skewed. The basic plot of Marshall and Sonja's story is, finally, not very interesting; its characters and events smack too much of the myriad campus adultery novels of an earlier time. Meanwhile, the other material, the tale slowly divulged by the letters, has far greater potential. *Another You* has its moments, since Ms. Beattie is ever vigilant about the feints and ruses by which we live. But here she has not done full justice to her premise of causes and their late-blooming effects.

> Sven Birkerts. *New York Times Book Review*. Sept. 24, 1995, p. 12

BIBLIOGRAPHY
Chilly Scenes of Winter, 1976 (n); *Distortions*, 1976 (s); *Secrets and Surprises*, 1978 (s); *Falling in Place*, 1980 (n); *The Burning House*, 1982 (s); *Where You'll Find Me*, 1986 (s); *Picturing Will*, 1989 (n); *What Was Mine*, 1991 (s); *Another You*, 1995 (n); *My Life, Starring Dara Falcon*, 1997 (n); *Park City*, 1998 (s)

BEHRMAN, S. N. (1893–1973)

In this American play (*The Second Man*) the talk is fresh, the epigrams are not machine made but seem spontaneous and in keeping with the character, and there is a merry note of satirical burlesque in the melodramatic episodes introduced into the story. . . . This play may owe much to *The Importance of Being Earnest* (as it owes something, also, to *Man and Superman*), but it is no mere rehash of ancient styles. It is much more ironic Yankee burlesque-comedy of Hoyt and Cohan touched with literary distinction and a hint—just a pleasant hint—of thoughtfulness.

> Walter Prichard Eaton. *New York Herald Tribune Book Section*. June 26, 1927. p. 12

Mr. Behrman . . . remains one of the few playwrights that we have ever had in America who does not cause embarrassment to dramatist, actors, and audience, when he indulges in brains or sophisticated statement. . . . He is one of those rare authors in the theatre who do not mistrust civilized society and do not think that Times Square must understand or no tickets will be sold. He has sensed the fact that in our theatre there is a genuine opening for such dramatists as might leave the mass of theatre-goers confounded or displeased; for him the French proverb, "Pour les sots acteurs Dieu créa les sots spectateurs,'' extends to audiences and plays, and he has taken the bold risk of failing in his own way instead of failing in somebody else's.

Stark Young. *New Republic*. Dec. 28, 1932. p. 188

The remarkable thing about Mr. Behrman is. . . the clarity with which he realizes that we must ultimately make our choice between judging men by their heroism or judging them by their intelligence, and the unfailing articulateness with which he defends his determination to choose the second alternative. . . . Mr. Behrman's plays are obviously ''artificial''—both in the sense that they deal with an artificial and privileged section of society and in the sense that the characters themselves are less real persons than idealized embodiments of intelligence and wit. . . . No drawing room ever existed in which people talked so well or acted so sensibly at last, but this idealization is the final business of comedy.

Joseph Wood Krutch. *The Nation*. July 19, 1933. pp. 74–6

You must grant S.N. Behrman the privilege of writing plays on his own terms, if you want to enjoy them in the theatre. His dramas have little plot and less action. People come and go as often as they do in other men's plays; they meet and part and meet again, but they do so because the conversation—which is the alpha and omega of Behrman's playwriting—needs a shift in emphasis or in attack, rather than because of any change in the aspect of the situation. You cannot fairly say that his plays are ''not about anything,'' for they fairly bristle with the contemporary, social, economic, controversial things they are about. But his drama is in his talk, and it would be well for people who think they do not like ''talky'' plays to consider carefully what Behrman can do with talk, before they decide too definitely that many words never made a play.

Edith J.R. Isaacs. *Theatre Arts*. April, 1936. p. 258

Behrman is a man of rather emotional, almost lyrical and, if you will, sentimental nature, embarrassed by a sense that this nature is not quite smart enough for the society in which he finds himself and in which he would like to occupy a favored place. Thinking of himself—and he is preoccupied with the subject—he is ready to weep, but society, he believes, would consider such behavior unseemly. Looking at the world, he is almost ready to cry out or at least to heave so profound a sigh that the sound might be construed as a protest, so he suppresses his impulse and flicks our consciousness with a soft with that contains as much self-depreciation as mockery. He tries to chide his world with a voice that might be thought to belong to someone else—a person far more brittle, debonair, urbane than he knows himself to be.

Harold Clurman. *New Republic*. Feb. 18, 1952. pp. 22–3

Something deeper than style alone distinguishes him from our many purveyors of light entertainment, including those who have at one time or another made a specialty of skepticism and debunking. That something is his habit of balancing the score. It makes him not merely a judicious but an acute playwright rather than a

merely congenial one. He always remains *two* men; one man makes the positive observations, the second proposes the negative ones. . . . Berhman's art of comedy, including his so-called comic detachment, consists of an ambivalence of attitudes that has its sources in the simultaneous possession of a nimble mind and a mellow temperament.

John Gassner. *Theatre Arts*. May, 1952. pp. 96–7

Providence Street, the background for most of (*The Worcester Account*), is the scene of Mr. Behrman's early life. . . To one who comes, as I do, from a similar place, the half-ghetto of the American city, these people are immediately familiar. I recognize them in Mr. Behrman's skillful reproduction and wonder why they often appear shortened, flattened, and lacking in vigor and primitive idiosyncrasy. They have been written of with charm and in the process have emerged somewhat tamed and weakened. Somehow the charm does not seem to belong to them; it is not their native charm but one which the author has lent them, returning to them after long separation. The air of nostalgia which pervades the book is often appealing but many times emphasizes the quaintness of Providence Street rather than its difficulty and poverty.

Saul Bellow. *Saturday Review*. Nov. 20, 1954. p. 41

. . .Behrman has never been seriously considered as a comedian of ideas. One reason may be that he sets his plays in drawing rooms. His drama moves in that international half-world in which art and intellect meet money, in which celebrity, notoriety, or wealth is a necessary entree. Invariably, the dramatic situation against which the conflict of ideas is played is one that involves the discovery or dissolution of love, and there is always a central female character, who could be and often was played by Ina Claire. When an elegantly dressed play, with articulate and often amusing lines, is centered on a character who is played by an extremely sophisticated actress, it is not surprising that substance is ignored for surface.

There is another, and probably more important, reason why the ideas in Behrman's plays have been passed over. The bulk of his plays were written in the 30's and his objectivity, if taken seriously, would have been completely unacceptable in that decade. Basically conservative, Behrman stood on middle ground, trying to hold on to the area, once staked out by humanists, in which tolerance of ideas and of human weakness could flourish. His plays show a fascination and a distaste for the man who becomes completely absorbed in himself or his beliefs—the complete egoist or the convinced idealist.

Gerald Weales. *Commentary*. March, 1959. p. 256

Here, then, is Mr. Behrman, during the last three years of Max's life, assiduously visiting Rapallo, armed with what I take to have been an invisible notebook. He has constructed his portrait [of Max Beerbohm] round these visits, and with the cleverness of a superlative photographer he has timed his shots so that he can, at will, step into the picture himself. The final chapter is headed ''The Last Civilized Voice.'' But Max's voice was not the last. Mr. Behrman has a voice of his own, and its pitch is exactly right for the matter in hand. He catches Max's inflexions to the life, and he adds his own very personal wit. Nothing in the world is harder than to be both amusing and affectionate throughout 300 pages; but that is precisely what Mr. Behrman has accomplished.

Alan Pryce-Jones. *New York Herald Tribune Book Section.* Oct. 2, 1960, p. 1

S.N. Behrman's *Lord Pengo*, based loosely on Mr. Behrman's study of Duveen, is based equally loosely on the requirements of the stage. . . .

The true picaresque hero is a psychologist as well as a rascal: Lazarillo de Tormes, as a mere child, realizes that "there are many people in the world who run away from other folks only because they don't know themselves." It is on similar psychological perceptions that Pengo operates, but the trouble is that suave, persistent, slow-working wiles are not the stuff dramas are made on. Epics and novels, yes; but not plays, which need conflict. So Mr. Behrman drags it in the shape of a rebellious son complete with appropriate platitudes ("I don't seem to get a chance to talk to you, Father!"). Out of love for Pengo, Mr. Behrman, moreover, neglects the other characters, and clients, in any case, are not ideal dramatic fare. Devoted but tough female secretaries, for that matter, have long since had their day.

Despite urbane dialogue and some bubbles of iridescent fun, *Lord Pengo* is weighed down with *longueurs* and fillers and a general feeling of fatigue.

John Simon. *Hudson Review.* Spring, 1963. pp. 83–4

Already famed as a dramatist and author of the highly successful *Portrait of Max*, Mr. Behrman here [*The Suspended Drawing Room*] brings together a collection of short pieces originally done for the *New Yorker*. Included are two essay-impressions of London during, and just following, the last war. The remainder of the volume is devoted to seven character sketches. . . . Mr. Behrman, through deft skills, removes the reader from shackling reality and introduces him to other times and unforgettable characters. . . . The really satisfying feature is the clever selection of the perfect detail. Finding London during the war too large a vista for his small canvas, he chooses to describe only the bomb shelters and in doing so, he captures the horror and senselessness of the bombings, while also clearly revealing the indomitable spirit of the English.

Richard K. Burns. *Library Journal.* Aug., 1965. p. 3290

BIBLIOGRAPHY
(with Kenyon Nicholson) *Bedside Manners*, 1924 (d); (with Kenyon Nicholson) *A Night's Work*, 1926 (d); *The Second Man*, 1927 (d); *Meteor*, 1930 (d); *Brief Moment*, 1931 (d); *Biography*, 1933 (d); *Three Plays* (*Serena Blandish, Meteor, The Second Man*), 1934; *Rain from Heaven*, 1935 (d); *End of Summer*, 1936 (d); *Wine of Choice*, 1938 (d); *Amphitryon 38*, 1938 (d, tr); *No Time for Comedy*, 1939 (d); *The Talley Method*, 1941 (d); *The Mechanical Heart*, 1941 (d); *The Pirate*, 1943 (d); *Jacobowsky and the Colonel*, 1944 (d, tr); *Dunnigan's Daughter*, 1946 (d); *I Know My Love*, 1952 (d, tr); *Jane*, 1952 (d); *Duveen*, 1952 (b); *The Worcester Account*, 1954 (a); *Fanny*, 1955 (d, tr); *The Cold Wind and the Warm*, 1959 (d); *Portrait of Max*, 1960 (b); *Lord Pengo*, 1963 (d); *But for Whom Charlie*, 1964 (d); *The Suspended Drawing Room*, 1965 (t); *The Burning Glass*, 1968 (n); *People in a Diary*, 1972 (m); *Tribulations and Laughter*, 1972 (m)

BELASCO, David (1859–1931)

Belasco's contribution to the American drama is that of a producer and stage director rather than that of an author. His plays—mostly melodramas—have little permanent value, but as a creator of stage-effects, in elaboration of detail, in arrangement of action and stage pictures, he is recognized to be without a master in the modern theatre.

Arthur Hornblow. *A History of the Theatre in America* (Lippincott). 1919. p. 340

David Belasco, with his passion for thoroughness, was particularly instrumental in giving a certain substantial illusion to the box-set interior, and eliminating the most grossly artificial features from exteriors. But this revolt was solely in the direction of naturalism. It did not start with the desire to bring the setting into closer harmony with the spirit of the play, but only with the object of making the scene more natural. It removed the worst absurdities of Nineteenth Century staging; but in its later elaboration it provided distractions quite as foreign to the substance of the drama. In the pursuit of the natural, Belasco and others began to build scenes so finely imitative, so true to the surface appearances of life, that the audience often forgot the play in wonder at the photographic perfection of the setting.

Sheldon Cheney. *The Art Theatre* (Knopf). 1925. pp. 189–90

Beginning in 1893 with his first great success, *The Girl I Left Behind Me* (by Belasco and Franklin Fyles), he won a national reputation for colorful plays produced with meticulous Naturalism. . . . It is impossible not to see in Belasco the return of that cycle which would bring back Naturalism to the bathos of Romanticism from which it had once emerged. . . . Belasco's melodramas had an admixture of sweetness and light in a blend to which, it is likely, he had a unique claim. If any social criticism remained, it was reduced to a whisper. . . .

Belasco used an idiom newer than that of his Romantic predecessors. The acting was believable in comparison with nature; the settings were infinitely more lifelike than in the past. But underneath both the Romantic stereotype was there for any alert observer to see. By the time Naturalism received its American expression at the hands of Belasco, it was no longer a life-storming technique.

Mordecai Gorelik. *New Theatres for Old* (Samuel French). 1941. pp. 160–3

The [Henry C.] De Mille-Belasco collaborations were playwrought before they were playwritten. Except for experimental snatches, dialogue was held in abeyance until character had been conceived and developed and situations devised and arranged in elaborate detail. Most of the actual writing was done by De Mille, most of the planning and dramatic construction by Belasco. The preliminary discussions over and the development of the action clear in their minds, the two men repaired to the theater and staged the play. De Mille sat at a table in the front row of the orchestra; Belasco on the stage impersonated all the characters in the situations which had been plotted. Such dialogue as had been written down was primarily a point of departure, a means by which the situations were set in motion. The dialogue which emerged in final form sprang less from the preliminary speeches than from the situations in action; the determining factor was stage effectiveness. De Mille would read a few lines; Belasco would set them in motion, suggest alterations, omissions, and enlargements to fit stage business.

> Robert H. Ball. Introduction to *America's Lost Plays*, vol. 17 (Princeton). 1941. p. xii

As a playwright Belasco had his training in a rough-and-ready school, where action and strong, simple motives were dominant. Although in the course of his life he passed through many phases, and although he adapted himself somewhat to changing styles and points of view, he never relinquished his fundamental belief in simplicity of motive and strength of situation as the basic factors in drama. A direct approach to the human heart was his chosen path, and from that path he never strayed. Many of his plays disclosed a love of the morbid, but his morbidity was natural, not decadent. Even his sensuousness escaped the charge of perversion.

Realistic effect was his forte. Knowing that, he could indulge his fancy, for to a showman like Belasco the theater is primarily a place where the implausible is made plausible. In print many of his plays seem today too implausible, but plausibility in the theater is a variable thing, and in their day, presented by the hand of the master, they were plausible. History is consistent on that point.

> Glenn Hughes and George Savage. Introduction to *America's Lost Plays*, vol. 18 (Princeton). 1941. pp. x–xi

A consideration of the plays written, rewritten, adapted, arranged and produced by David Belasco . . . might lead one to believe that the work of this extraordinary man was more closely related to the development of modern American drama than it actually was, but it is impossible to determine the precise extent of his cooperation with other writers in all the plays to which his name is attached, either as sole author or collaborator; and even where his share as playwright is relatively clear, what he added as director and stage manager rather obscures his role as writer. . . . Even such picturesque and more or less "original" plays as *The Girl of the Golden West* . . . and *The Return of Peter Grimm*. . . , are little more than local-color pastiches written largely to exhibit his own virtuosity as director and the special talents of his actors.

> Barrett H. Clark. *A History of Modern Drama* (Appleton-Century). 1947. p. 652

Working with highly theatrical, sentimental plays (mostly of his own authorship), he directed and set them with consummate "naturalism." He exactly reproduced a Child's restaurant down to a cook flapping pancakes in the window; he cluttered the setting of *The Return of Peter Grimm* with hundreds of theatrically extraneous properties "because that was the way the room would be". . . he erected complete rooms beyond the entrances of a setting in

order to help the actors acquire a strong sense of illusion as they traversed these extra rooms on their way to the stage; he expected actors to "engross themselves in their parts"; and he kept his electricians busy developing lighting equipment that would more nearly reproduce natural light.

Like the painted actuality of Romanticism, this extreme Naturalism defeated its purpose because it drew attention to the setting instead of providing an environment that strengthened the believability of the dramatic action.

> H.D. Albright, William P. Halstead, Lee Mitchell. *Principles of Theatre Art* (Houghton). 1955. p. 162

For this Belasco was a clever man—the cleverest, and by all odds, in the native theatre—and, doubtless chuckling up his sleeve, for it is impossible to imagine him deceived by his own tin-pantaloonery, he witnessed the canonization of his simple humbug and through that simple humbug the canonization of himself by the absorbent rhapsodists. But this was yesterday. . . . Mr. Belasco has contributed one—only one—thing for judicious praise to the American theatre. He has brought to that theatre a standard of tidiness in production and maturation of manuscript, a standard that has discouraged to no little extent that theatre's erstwhile not uncommon frowsy hustle and slipshod manner of presentation.

> George Jean Nathan. *The Magic Mirror* (Knopf). 1960. pp. 59, 62

In the days of Belasco realism, every effort was made to produce the effect of reality on the stage. For this the late David Belasco should be praised rather than condemned, for he came into the theatre as an innovator at the turn of this century, and at a time when lighting and scenery were in the age of innocence. However, he ultimately made realism an end in itself, which defeated his original purpose.

> Lawrence Langner. *The Play's the Thing* (Putnam). 1960. p. 160

BIBLIOGRAPHY

The Creole, 1876 (d); *Olivia*, 1878 (d); (with James A. Herne) *Within an Inch of His Life*, 1879 (d); *Drink*, 1879 (d); (with James A. Herne) *Hearts of Oak*, 1879 (d); *Paul Arniff, or, The Love of a Serf*, 1880 (d); *The Eviction*, 1881 (d); *La Belle Russe*, 1881 (d); *The Stranglers of Paris*, 1881 (d); *The Lone Pine*, 1881? (d); (with Peter Robinson) *The Curse of Cain*, 1882 (d); *American Born*, 1882 (d); *May Blossom*, 1882 (d); *Valerie*, 1886 (d); *The Highest Bidder*, 1887 (d); (with Clay M. Greene) *Pawn Ticket No. 210*, 1887 (d); (with Henry C. DeMille) *The Wife*, 1887 (d); (with Henry C. DeMille) *Lord Chumley*, 1888 (d); (with Henry C. DeMille) *The Charity Ball*, 1889 (d); (with Henry C. DeMille) *Men and Women*, 1890 (d); *Miss Helyett*, 1891 (d); (with Franklyn Fyles) *The Girl I Left Behind Me*, 1893 (d); *The Younger Son*, 1893 (d); *The Heart of Maryland*, 1895 (d); (with Clay M. Greene) *Under the Polar Star*, 1896 (d); *Zaza*, 1898 (d, tr); *Naughty Anthony*, 1899 (d); (with John Luther Long) *Madame Butterfly*, 1900 (d); *DuBarry*, 1901 (d); (with John Luther Long) *The Darling of the Gods*, 1902 (d); *Sweet Kitty Bellairs*, 1903 (d); (with John Luther Long) *Adrea*, 1904 (d);

The Girl of the Golden West, 1905 (d); (with Richard Walton Tully) *The Rose of the Rancho*, 1906 (d); (with Pauline Phelps and Marion Short) *A Grand Army Man*, 1907 (d); *The Lily*, 1909 (d, tr); *The Return of Peter Grimm*, 1911 (d); (with Alice Brady) *The Governor's Lady*, 1911 (d); *The Secret*, 1913 (d, tr); *My Life Story*, 1914 (a); (with George Scarborough) *The Son Daughter*, 1919 (d); *The Theatre Through the Stage Door*, 1919 (r); *Kiki*, 1921 (d, tr); *A Souvenir of Shakespeare's The Merchant of Venice*, as presented by David Belasco, at the Lyceum Theatre, Dec. 21, 1922, 1923; *The Comedian*, 1923 (d, tr); *Laugh, Clown, Laugh*, 1923 (d, tr); *Plays Produced under the Stage Direction of David Belasco*, 1925 (c); (with Willard Mack) *Fanny*, 1926 (d, tr); *Mimi*, 1928 (d); *Six Plays (Madame Butterfly, DuBarry, The Darling of the Gods, The Girl of the Golden West, The Return of Peter Grimm)*, 1928; *The Heart of Maryland, and Other Plays*, 1941

BELL, Marvin (1937–)

[Bell] often deploys barrages of surrealistic humor, somewhat in the manner of Mark Strand or James Tate. . . .

[Any] use of humor in an essentially serious poem requires a kind of intelligence which is rare among poets, though poets often praise it: . . . Bell not only [sees himself and his] surroundings clearly but [renders] them without overinflation. [He has] the ability to make sense, rather than gratuitous use, of more or less subjective imagery. . . .

Bell's range—the variety of themes, tones and line lengths which he has mastered—is quite wide. The inclusion of the sixteen earlier poems [in *A Probable Volume of Dreams*] shows how far Bell has extended his range since they first appeared. His voice is sometimes evasive, often idiosyncratic, so that the reader is simultaneously engaged and kept, for a time, at a distance. This effect is sometimes achieved by means of a device which Strand and Tate also use; I mean the use of an addressed "you" who is more like a translated "I". The style of those poems is lean, with short lines and sentences which carry an economy of emotion which would constrict if it were not for Bell's control over the placement of ironies. . . . The conscientious wit which keeps the earlier poems from going flat has also directed the development of Bell's style toward the more discursive poems which are collected for the first time in this book. The economy remains, but the range of emotion and the depth of exploration are increased; the resulting poems are characterized by longer lines and a more inclusive vision. Even the surrealistic humor has been extended to include such verbal exuberance as [a poem] . . . spoken by a poet who is "locked in / the English Department". . . .

Bell's poems move out from a great variety of departure points; in this limited space, I cannot give a fair indication of his versatility. He is concerned with war, love and the kinds of mental life in which a poet and teacher is caught up. He approaches these subjects as a man remembering, thinking and believing. If his music is low key, it is almost always appropriate to his themes.

"Toward Certain Divorce," which is among the best poems in the volume, is a narrative meditation spoken by a visitor in the home of a man and a woman who are planning to separate. The last few lines are typical of the later, more discursive style; they show that a poet, if he is strong enough, can handle the problem of

sentimentality, not by avoiding it but by facing it squarely and earning his use of it.

> Henry Taylor. *The Nation*. February 2, 1970.

[From *A Probable Volume of Dreams* through *The Escape into You* and *Residue of Song*]—the three most important books of Marvin Bell which have been published so far—we discover the poet crafting his poems in structures which keep reminding us just how much artifice is involved, and how much wit is needed to keep the poem afloat and the reader at once near and at bay. What proves telling is seeing which poems from Bell's limited edition of *Things We Dreamt We Died For* . . . get left out of *A Probable Volume of Dreams*: the poems tend not merely to be the weaker ones, but the less distanced ones in which there is insufficient strategy to manage where the poet-father must walk, "foot by foot," both on earth and in heaven.

If the most recent poems of Bell, those still uncollected in book form, have begun to indicate changes in both the life and the art, there are lines of continuity as well as lines of departure. Some of Bell's preferences are ingrained and resonant enough for his best poems, whatever the vintage, for us to know that if they shout back and forth at one another there will be response and commerce. . . .

Stanza by stanza, sequence by sequence, and book by book, Bell reminds us that he is intent on exploring the relationships among love, art, and some public, moral realm which demands faces and postures of another kind. . . .

The latest work of Bell shows a predilection, still, for using a poetry of wit in order to address concerns of morality and aesthetics. But what is changed is Bell's ability to join that kind of poem to a poem that is more lyrical, sometimes more lyrically elegiac than he had wished or managed to be before. . . .

The poetic strategies are still elaborate, even when the poet seems to walk most lightly or softly. But "license" now seems in the service of greater good: the "exclusive calculations," "sensational airwaves" and "interchangeable frequencies" of some of the past work have settled into Bell's celebration of the fact that the self has held together, that the wife and sons have not been lost in order to allow the poet to satisfy some false, wilful Romanticism in his own time.

Nor is sadness, or Bell's corner on sadness, gone. But he has begun to see sadness more in terms of joy. If happiness is an unfashionable contemporary American poetics, Bell is unafraid to start writing a new lyric which tells us we had better ascertain "who is doing the crying," and just how happy we are.

> Arthur Oberg. *American Poetry Review*. May-June, 1976, pp. 4–8.

Marvin Bell does love poetry. He loves the very idea of it. And in *Old Snow Just Melting*, his new collection of essays and interviews, he loves writing and talking about poetry and does so with a joy and an obvious commitment that are contagious. . . .

Old Snow Just Melting . . . brings together twenty-one essays with such titles as "I Was a Boston (Marathon) Bandit (On Assignment)" and "Learning from Translations" and four interviews including "The University Is Something Else You Do" and "Self Is a Very Iffy Word for Me." All were, he points out, done on assignment, including eleven essays written from 1974 to 1978 for

The American Poetry Review, published here under the title "*Homage to the Runner.*" Even the titles indicate the range of subjects in these pieces, from teaching to Hugo to pain, and the range of attitudes, playfulness-going-to-seriousness (as he might say). . . .

I do think you will be disappointed if you expect, in *Old Snow Just Melting,* a book of criticism. And you will be disappointed if you expect a fully drawn, straightforward statement of poetics; this is more a poetics-in-the-making. If you can give Bell a little room, though, as you do that old friend who takes so long to tell a "simple" story, the one who winds around and forgets and gestures wildly and maybe even invents a little, you will be doubly rewarded. After all, when your friend finally finishes his story, haven't you learned more than the story itself? Haven't you learned something about your friend?

Now a couple of years old, *These Green-Going-to-Yellow* is to my mind one of Marvin Bell's best books of poetry. . . . In a day of hermit-poets, watered-down confessional poets, self-absorbed poets, diary-poets and poets-of-the-private-language, Bell's richly populated poems are a welcome return back to the world of people. By my count, in fact, all but two of the thirty-one poems in *These Green-Going-to-Yellow* include characters other than the speaker. . . .

What the people in Bell's poems have to contend with is indicated in the title. *These Green-Going-to-Yellow* identifies the natural and inevitable decay of the world: trees die here, and birds, and pigs; the seasons change; people pass away and are missed; wars claim lives faster than ever. Maybe it is only a coincidence, but many of Bell's best poems here are those in which the speaker both admits to loss (or meanness or decay) and then tries to give back something to fill the void. In the beautiful "The Hedgeapple," the speaker and his friends have nearly taken a hedgeapple from a woman's tree. . . . The poem ends in a gesture of unabashed guilt-going-to-generosity, since he cannot bear to have almost stolen "someone else's treasure.". . .

Bell's form is relaxed, even rambling at times. His voice is casual, but is capable of the beauty that clear language can bring. Only infrequently in these poems do I sense Bell allowing his form too much leisure or his voice too much ease. ["To an Adolescent Weeping Willow"], though, typifies such temptation. . . . The poem ends with the speaker's realization of the fallacy of his own metaphor—that the easy-moving tree and his hard-working father aren't alike. But Bell's language is a touch too easy too. I think Bell is less effective . . . when he depends too much on the momentum and character (even charm) of his style to make up for looseness. In fact, hasn't this been identified as a problem of many poets from the generation just prior to Bell's: that, having struggled to develop recognizable and convincing styles, they sometimes seem satisfied, simply and almost always ineffectively, to imitate themselves? I certainly don't think it's a problem for Bell generally. But I don't want it to become one either. He has come far already, and his poems, at their best, are among our current best.

David Baker, *New England Review and Bread Loaf Quarterly,* Winter, 1983, pp. 332–36.

BIBLIOGRAPHY
Two Poems, 1965 (p); *Things We Dreamt We Died For,* 1966 (p); *Poems for Nathan and Saul,* 1966 (p); *A Probable Volume of Dreams,* 1969 (p); *The Escape into You: A Sequence,* 1971 (p); *Woo Havoc,* 1971 (p); *Residue of Song,* 1974 (p); *Stars Which See,* 1977 (p); *These Green-Going-to-Yellow,* 1981 (p); *Old Snow Just Melting: Essays and Interviews,* 1983 (misc); *Segues: A Correspondence in Poetry,* with William Stafford, 1983 (p); *Drawn by Stones, by Earth, by Things That Have Been in the Fire,* 1984 (p); *New and Selected Poems,* 1987 (p); *Annie-Over,* with William Stafford, 1988 (p); *Iris of Creation,* 1990 (p); *The Book of the Dead Man,* 1994 (p)

BELLOW, Saul (1915–)

The Victim. . . is hard to match in recent fiction, for brilliance, skill, and originality. . . . *The Victim* is solidly built of fine, important ideas; it also generates fine and important, if uncomfortable, emotions.

Diana Trilling. *The Nation.* Jan. 3, 1948. pp. 24–5

Reading *The Adventures of Augie March* in 1953 must be a good deal like reading *Ulysses* in 1920. . . . Tentatively: Saul Bellow is perhaps a great novelist, *The Adventures of Augie March* perhaps a great novel. If *The Adventures of Augie March* is great, it is great because of its comprehensive, non-naturalistic survey of the modern world, its wisely inconclusive presentation of its problems; because its author dares to let go (as so many very good and very neat modern writers do not); because the style of its telling makes the sequence of events seem real even when one knows they couldn't be; because the novel is intelligently and ambitiously conceived as a whole that esthetically comprehends its parts; because it is an achievement in and a promise of the development of a novelist who deserves comparison only with the best, even at this early stage of his development.

Harvey Curtis Webster. *Saturday Review.* Sept. 19, 1953. pp. 13–4

If such a novel is to be fully effective the sense of dramatic improvisation must be a dramatic illusion, the last sophistication of the writer, and . . . the improvisation is really a pseudo-improvisation, and . . . the random scene or casual character that imitates the accidental quality of life must really have a relevance, and . . . the discovery, usually belated, of this relevance, is the characteristic excitement of the genre. That is, in this genre the relevance is deeper and more obscure and there is, in the finest examples of the genre, a greater tension between the random life force of the materials and the shaping intuition of the writer.

It is the final distinction, I think, of *The Adventures of Augie March* that we do feel this tension, and that it is a meaningful fact.

Robert Penn Warren. *New Republic.* Nov. 2, 1953. p. 22

Saul Bellow's new novel is a new kind of book. The only other American novels to which it can be compared with any profit are *Huckleberry Finn* and *U.S.A.,* and it is superior to the first by virtue of the complexity of its subject matter and to the second by virtue of a realized unity of composition. In all three books, the real theme is

America, a fact which is not as clear in this new book as it is in its predecessors, perhaps because of its very newness. . . . *The Adventures of Augie March* is a new kind of book first of all because Augie March possesses a new attitude toward experience in America: instead of the blindness of affirmation and the poverty of rejection, Augie March rises from the streets of the modern city to encounter the reality of experience with an attitude of satirical acceptance, ironic affirmation, and comic transcendence of affirmation and rejection.

Delmore Schwartz. *Partisan Review*. Jan., 1954. pp. 112–3

Henderson the Rain King differs from *Augie March* in many interesting ways. In the earlier novel Bellow uses a loose structure to illustrate, through a long series of essentially realistic episodes, the vast possibilities of contemporary life. Beginning in poverty and illegitimacy, Augie ranges far, horizontally and vertically, to end in uncertainty. Henderson, on the other hand, born to every advantage, has lived fifty-one years of unquiet desperation. Of Augie's kind of patient pilgrimage he has never been capable. He is driven by the voice that cries, "I want, I want," and the story of his search is both romantic and dramatic. I cannot say that *Henderson the Rain King* is a better book than *Augie March* the denseness of the experience in the earlier novel is something almost unparalleled in contemporary literature. But it is a wonderful book for Bellow to have written after writing *Augie March*. It is a book that should be read again and again, and each reading, I believe, will yield further evidence of Bellow's wisdom and power.

Granville Hicks. *Saturday Review*. Feb. 21, 1959. p. 20

Anyone unfamiliar with Mr. Bellow's earlier work would, I think, immediately recognize from a reading of *Henderson* why so many of our best critics consider him the most important American novelist of the postwar period. For one thing, it contains a wealth of comic passages that bear comparison with the wild, grotesque humor we find in some of Faulkner's stories, and for another it is endlessly fertile in invention and idea. Beyond that, however, this is by all odds the most brilliantly written novel to have come along in years. Mr. Bellow has finally been able to discipline the virtuosity that ran away with *Augie March*, and the result is a prose charged with all the vigor and vitality of colloquial speech and yet capable of the range, precision, and delicacy of a heightened, formal rhetoric.

Norman Podhoretz. *New York Herald Tribune Book Section*. Feb. 22, 1959. p. 3

Seize the Day is Bellow's one exercise in pure naturalism. He takes a character ill-equipped for life, whose mistakes become more and more unredeemable as he grows older, and lets him sink under their weight. But is this really the end for Tommy? . . . Is the consummation referred to in the last sentence some kind of new beginning spiritually? What is the "heart's ultimate need" referred to so cryptically?

Robert Gorham Davis in *The Creative Process*, ed. Nona Balakian and Charles Simmons (Doubleday). 1963. pp. 126–7

For some time now the critical consensus has been, expressed not so much formally in writing as in the talk of literary circles, that *Seize the Day*, published some eight years ago, was his best single performance. *Herzog* is superior to it, I think, even if not so tightly organized and in fact a bit loose on the structural side. For one thing, it is a much longer and fuller narrative than *Seize the Day*, which is hardly more than a novella. For another, it is richer in content, in the effective disposition of tone and language, as well as in intellectual resonance and insight of a high order into the make-up of modern life—insight into what is really new and perhaps all too hazardous about it in its strange, almost inconceivable, mixture of greater freedom and maddening constriction.

Above all, this novel positively radiates intelligence—not mere brightness or shrewdness or that kind of sensitiveness which sometimes passes for mind among us. It is a coherent, securely founded intelligence—a real endowment—of genuine intellectual quality which, marvelously escaping the perils of abstraction, is neither recondite nor esoteric. It is directed towards imaginative ends by a true and sharp sense of the pain that rends the human world of its ills, both curable and incurable, and equally by a bracing, unfailing sense of irony and humor serving to counteract such chronic vulnerabilities of intelligence as over-solemnity of mind on the one hand and perversity of sensibility on the other.

Philip Rahv. *New York Herald Tribune Book Section*. Sept. 20, 1964. p. 1

Willy nilly, then, all these later heroes of Bellow are gluttons for suffering—for what suffers is still alive and still has the possibility of renewal. They are all also trying to reach the deeper sources of grief and impulse, to reconstitute the past in order to shed it, to clear away the cultural conditioning that has deflected them from a simple understanding of their desires. Herzog's case, however, is a much more complicated one. He has so many roles and images and is so divided among them that simplicity is impossible. A child of the immigrant ghetto, to which his heart is still tied, he has written his first and only book on *Romanticism and Christianity*. A bookish, urban type, he has tried to turn himself into a New England country squire. A scholar, a foot-loose intellectual, a lover of fancy women, he is also a dutiful man around the house and a patient caretaker of his wife's neurosis. No wonder he has problems of identity. He is a Romantic who sets great store by "the heart"—a term that is constantly on his mind—but he is also a Rationalist who has more principles of ethics than Spinoza.

Theodore Solotaroff. *Commentary*. Dec., 1964. p. 63

In both *Augie March* and *Henderson* Bellow has run down well before the end: Augie, after the trip to Mexico, only sits around and has others tell him who Augie March is; Henderson, save for the great scene with the frogs, barely survives the trip to Africa. Technically Bellow has solved this problem by cheating, for in *Herzog* he does not really begin his story until half way through. Herzog's life is slowly gathered, then he has it snapped in a terrifying courtroom scene, and this propels him from New York to Chicago and enables Bellow to march home to a stunning triumph in the last third of the book. But this solution is not just a technical one and is not really cheating at all. For Augie and Henderson the only way to see right side up is via primitivism, and Bellow seems to have realized or discovered that primitivism was for him more theoretically than actually valid. The answer in *Herzog* is quite different: a novel of ideas and a hero who feels his having come to the end of the line so well that the touters of the Void can be sneered at if only because they cannot reckon with Herzog's narcissism and buoyancy.

The result is the first or at least the largest step taken beyond Lawrence and the romanticism that is bought at the terrifying expense of fear and loathing of human kind. Dignity must go and without any accompanying comic reassurance—Herzog must scurry like a rat from his will and need to be kept in shelter, and he must end in silence. But the gains are great: a repeated and convincing insistence that the equation of reality with evil is sentimental and a demonstration that existentialism is only the most recent attempt of the romantic to be respectable and aristocratic.

Roger Sale. *Hudson Review*. Winter, 1964–65. pp. 617–18

If there is one thing the American theatre cannot afford to throw away, it is a play. And yet after twenty-eight painfully eked-out performances, Saul Bellow's *The Last Analysis* had to close, as though it were another confection, another soufflé that did not quite rise to the occasion. The truth is that the production was frightful, but no amount of superimposed opacity could obscure the underlying translucence and purity; what was here being rejected was rarer than a pearl in an oyster; a play in a Broadway playhouse.

I am not saying that Bellow's farcical fantasy about a once hugely successful comedian restaging his life as a closed-circuit TV show for an audience of psychiatrists at the Waldorf-Astoria, in order to shed light on the terrible disease Success, is a flawless dramatic creation. But there are things in it that we must hold dear. There is, first of all, the intense rhetoric that makes the word become flesh before our very ears and eyes: such throbbing flesh that it scarcely matters if the personages uttering it are somewhat less than people. Nor does it matter all that much (though it does matter) that this galaxy of galvanic words does not compose itself into a well-shaped entity; this, at least, is a case where the sum of the parts is greater than most other wholes.

John Simon. *Hudson Review*. Winter, 1964–65. p. 556

To a considerable degree the novel [*Herzog*] does work as a rather conventional drama of alienation, though this is precisely what Bellow doesn't want it to be. It is about the failure of all available terms for interpretation and summary, about the intellectual junk heap of language by which Herzog-Bellow propose dignities to the hero's life and then as quickly watch these proposals dissolve into cliché. A similar process goes on in *Augie*, against the competition of an anxious and often phony exuberance, and it was there that Bellow began to fashion a comic prose which could bear the simultaneous weight of cultural, historical, mythological evocations and also sustain the exposure of their irrelevance. His comedy always has in it the penultimate question before the final one, faced in *Seize the Day*, of life or death—the question of what can be taken seriously and how seriously it can possibly be taken. The result, however, is a kind of stalemate achieved simply by not looking beyond the play of humor into its constituents, at the person from whom it issues, at the psychological implications both of anyone's asking such questions and of the *way* in which he asks them. It

seems to me that Bellow cannot break the stalemate with alienation implicit in his comedy without surrendering to the Waste Land outlook and foregoing the mostly unconvincing rhetoric which he offers as an alternative. That is why his comic style in *Herzog*, even more than in *Henderson* or *Augie*, is less like Nathanael West's than like that of West's brother-in-law, S.J. Perelman.

Richard Poirier. *Partisan Review*. Spring, 1965. pp. 270–1

Let me, then, put down what I will not discuss: a few rejected theses which may find themselves the center of despair in an otherwise capable Master's Essay. Let me reject: (a) that Bellow probes the meaningful questions of our times; (b) that his Jewishness is crucial to his success as a writer; (c) that his heroes help us see ourselves as we really are; (d) that his imagination and inventiveness give pleasure by themselves; and (e) that he is to be identified closely with his own heroes. Any of these propositions is capable of being maintained; any is perhaps true. The only difficulty is that they are irrelevant to discussing Bellow *as a novelist*. They can change our feeling or commitment to the novels, but they cannot change our judgment of the novels. *Herzog* is not a vehicle for philosophical speculations nor an embodiment of the mores of particular subcultures nor an attempt toward mass therapy in the guise of education nor an object of entertainment and titillation nor a wheelbarrow for the burden of autobiography. Or, of course, it may be all these things; but what makes *Herzog* a novel is, simply, that its form gives it a unique significance.

James Dean Young. *Critique*. Spring-Summer, 1965. p. 8

If [the Bellow hero] is a victimized figure, he is a victim of his own moral sense of right and wrong—his own accepted obligation to evaluate himself by standards that will inevitably find him lacking . . . Bellow's heroes suffer intensely and rehearse their agonies at operatic volume for all to hear. "I am to suffering what Gary is to smoke," says Henderson. "One of the world's biggest operations." But it would be a serious mistake to confuse this characteristic reaction of the Bellow hero with one of passive lamentation or self-pitying surrender. Even in his partly sincere and partly mock self-revilings, he is determined to believe that "human" means "accountable in spite of many weaknesses—at the last moment, tough enough to hold." And in final effect, none of Bellow's heroes actually resigns himself to his suffering. Painfully they climb again and again out of "the craters of the spirit," ridiculing their defeats with a merciless irony, resolved to be prepared with a stronger defense against the next assault that is sure to come.

Perhaps this aspect of Bellow's work has been the least appreciated by contemporary critics. Some have interpreted his thematic preoccupation with the sufferer as a device of compromise, a "making do," or accommodation—an argument which implies that Bellow is gratuitously surrendering the heroic ideal of a fully instinctual life to the expediency of flabby survival within the status quo. But this, it seems to me, is precisely to miss the moral point and to misread Bellow's deliberate irony. Trained in anthropology, Bellow is quite willing to regard the species *man* as merely one of the evolutionary products of nature and natural processes. But Bellow is determined to insist on the qualitative difference between *man* and the other sentient species that nature has produced.

Earl Rovit. *Saul Bellow* (Minnesota). 1967. pp. 12–3

The last four novels of Saul Bellow are devoted to a single theme: the effort of a perplexed man to discover enough of himself and reality to continue living in a time of personal and public crisis. Introspection, or the nervous exercise of a contemporary consciousness, is the means of discovery for the disturbed hero and forms the substance of the novels. To supply a narrative ground for the intellectualization and verbalization of his introverted characters, Bellow uses the metaphor of the journey of the man of many troubles, Odysseus. Each of his heroes finds himself alienated from father, wife, and children and undertakes a journey of return in the course of which he experiences death and learns important philosophical lessons. . . . It is the development of different kinds of introspection and the astonishing variety of the journey devised for each new wanderer that is the measure of Bellow's genius and the constant delight of his readers.

> Leonard Lutwack. *Heroic Fiction* (Southern Illinois). 1971. pp. 88–9

It is difficult to imagine where Bellow will go from here. The development that is clearly recognizable throughout his work concerns not only language and characterization but also the approach to the form of the novel. As the characters grow older, more mature, and more ''human''—a term that means to Bellow an increasing awareness and appreciation of the qualities that enable the individual as well as mankind to ''survive''—the language becomes more controlled, more concise, more elegant, with greater emphasis being placed on the subliminal emotional content of each single word. As is natural in this context, the joyfulness and exuberance, the undauntable love of life that characterized *The Adventures of Augie March* and *Henderson the Rain King*, gradually diminish.

This is also the result of the growing importance of ideas in Bellow's later work. Remembering, evaluating, imagining, and reinterpreting become the protagonists' main ''business'' in life, a development that clearly indicates Bellow's changing attitude toward the novel. Artistic self-expression has become of secondary importance compared to the unending stream-of-thought processes contained in *Herzog* and *Mr. Sammler's Planet*. These novels are not only the comprehensive records that ''compulsive witnesses'' of their own lives have taken down, they also represent Bellow's effort to turn the novel into a medium of inquiry.

> Brigitte Scheer-Schäzler, *Saul Bellow* (Ungar). 1972. p. 127

In a lecture given in London in 1971 Richard Poirier attacked Saul Bellow for being ''unmodified by reality and unable to admit radical alienation.'' It is perhaps possible to see something of this rejection of reality in those sections on sex and youth from *Mr. Sammler's Planet*. In the novel not one young person has anything really lasting or positive to offer; they are all flawed for Mr. Sammler by their dirt, their smell, or their slogans. It is at least partly true that in his admiration for the old liberal Bloomsbury values (not so far, perhaps, from some radical ideals) personified in Artur Sammler ''the old fashioned, sitting sage'' Bellow is unconsciously withdrawing to a safer, more civilized and more reassuring age. There is no doubt that many young Americans do identify Bellow with a Jewish intellectual élite which is just as dedicated to sustaining social inequalities as, say, General Motors. The radical

view—implied by Poirier—says that intellectuals like Bellow are cut off from what is going on around them with the consequence that their writing is more or less irrelevant. They are exercising in a void.

The danger in this extreme view of the writer's purpose—the kind of view that Sartre has come to hold—is that the novel must be a social tract keeping up with events of the times and not imaginatively leaping ahead. This can be just as stultifying as leaving important things out. And to ask the novelist to include everything radical groups regard as ''significant'' would be absurd. Even so, it does seem odd that in a novel that so carefully sets out to describe recent events Bellow makes no mention of the Vietnam War, something which has, by any standard, made an enormous difference to the way Americans feel about themselves.

> D.P.M. Salter. *The Critical Quarterly*. Spring, 1972. p. 64

It may be because Bellow cannot bring into single dramatic focus his optimism about man and his pessimism about the conditions of life that his characters so often seem schizophrenic and the endings of his novels disappointingly equivocal. His protagonists are men of goodwill and high hopes who make their way through a hellish wasteland in which they are forced to suffer every imaginable kind of humiliation and injustice. Yet at the end, in spite of everything, they are still seekers and believers. . . .

In *Humboldt's Gift* Bellow has still not found a way of successfully reconciling these contradictory attitudes and the two kinds of material in which they are expressed. But he does manage to cope with them more effectively than he has been able to do in any of his previous novels. The protagonist, Charles Citrine, confirms one's impression that Bellow's views of the nature of human existence are becoming increasingly mystical and may eventually find a formally religious framework. Citrine is a student of anthroposophy, a doctrine which maintains that through self-discipline cognitional experience of the spiritual world can be achieved, and his meditations on such a possibility become a significant yet unobtrusive leitmotiv of the world. But the critical point is that Bellow treats them throughout as meditations only. They are not required to bear a major thematic weight as are the speculative materials in the earlier novels. Therefore, Bellow's inability to reconcile them with his secular materials does not become problematical, since Citrine merely retreats from time to time into his meditations and at best only holds out hope that they may eventually lead him to a perception of spiritual truth.

> John W. Aldridge. *Saturday Review*. Sept. 6, 1975. p. 24

Most critics, I think, would agree that Saul Bellow's greatest difficulty lies in his plots. He rewrote *Herzog* thirteen times, he tells us, turning it like ''a prayer wheel''; and in *Mr. Sammler's Planet* and *Humboldt's Gift*, he seems to have thrown up his hands: contrivance and improbability in these novels will do. Why? Why does the man who so brilliantly crafted *Seize the Day* now accept something rough, unsymmetrical, and even corny?

One answer is obvious: Bellow has always flirted with the loose or episodic. *The Adventures of Augie March* was a smash hit, and *Humboldt* is in many ways a return to the earlier ''fantasy holiday,'' as Bellow called it in the 1950s. Bellow has two modes: intense, closely textured, moral; and light, energetic, open. *The*

Victim, *Seize the Day*, and, yes, *Herzog* represent the former while *Augie March*, *Sammler*, and *Humboldt* represents the latter. Bellow clearly finds great pain in his plots and is tempted for good or ill to cut loose, to stop worrying about his novel's shape. Fiction should be *interesting*, he believes, and even fun, like the old Chicago cornball humor he loved in Vaudeville and gave a try at in his play *The Last Analysis*. Simply put, Bellow fears the dangers of constriction, of polishing the life out of a work. . . .

Bellow's most obvious obstacle to plot lies in the fact that he is a realist—perhaps the reason that he wants a plot in the first place. A novel such as *Herzog* reflects Bellow's need for distance from his material, which is usually autobiographical, we're told, and embodies Bellow's struggle to control what amounts to a superabundance of material, a realistic world so weighty with detail that it's most oppressive. Plot in Bellow's work is hard won, wrested from a confusing density and multiplicity of people, ideas, events, and sensation. It's so hard won that we might well claim that the struggle *is* the plot, as all the protagonists seek to move from the overwhelming richness of experience to some kind of peace and clarity.

Here Bellow's very strength creates the obstacle, for no one catches the specifics of face and light and city as well as he. His texture is so intense, so vivid, that he must be tempted continually to write for the page. At the same time, such intensity must threaten to overthrow his plot—surely he struggles to control it. And much the same might be said of his characters. . . .

So Bellow loves energetic, driven characters who have a size and vitality that make them hard to control—so hard to control that the protagonist finds himself bullied by them, shoved about, as each tries to pull him *his* way.

And then the characters are inseparable from their ideas, which also fill Bellow's pages with a confusing abundance. Bellow often has sought a plot that would contain a number of ideologies and has imagined a quest that is mental, as he seeks to dramatize nothing less than the act of thinking. And yet there are too many thoughts finally for the plot line to be easy, since it is an *idea* after all which provides the shape of a novel. . . . In a way, Bellow is a victim not only of our present distrust of any plot, but of our incredibly high demands for the ones we do accept. The New Critics have taught us to demand that a conclusion end a novel in a memorable way, summarizing all that went before and illuminating it, crystallizing the whole book in a single glowing image or scene. Never mind that such a scene near the end of a long traditional novel might well break the tone. We're perfectionists when we talk about structure and accept only an inspired unity. It's fitting, in view of such conflicts and inconsistencies, that Bellow forge his successful plots from the very obstacles that have plagued him.

> Keith Opdahl. *Modern Fiction Studies*. Spring, 1979. pp. 15, 17, 28

In his exploration of stereotypes in *Mr. Sammler's Planet*, Bellow turned away from the Jewish milieu that dominated his earlier fiction and American Jewish writing generally—Jewish immigrant life in the ghettos of America's large cities or the second and third generation move to the suburbs and assimilation. Instead, he chose a painful "other" for the Americanized Jewish community—the life of a survivor of Nazi atrocity, a man returned from the dead and the madness of the Holocaust and deposited in the insane landscape of urban America in the '60s. If the flight to the suburbs is in part a

flight away from the visibility of human failure and suffering in cities, then a novel about a survivor of genocide living on the deteriorating upper West Side of New York City is bound to be disturbing to many Jewish readers, seeking more obvious images from their own lives. But more importantly, a novel about several Jewish survivors of Nazi persecution that does not present suffering as ennobling, but rather as crippling, undercuts any sentimental myths about hard won moral lessons or the spiritual rewards of tragedy. Instead, Bellow does present a vision of human community and moral accountability, but *despite* suffering, not because of it.

Mr. Sammler's Planet is Bellow's most Jewish novel because it deals directly with the most important events of Jewish history in this century—the Holocaust, the state of Israel, and American Jewry's relation to both. Moreover, the major values embodied in the novel are basic tenets of Jewish life, although they are not exclusively Jewish: a reverence for life and an unwavering belief in human survival under any circumstances; an emphasis on reason and human intellect, part of a long tradition of interpretation and commentary on scripture; a preference for good deed and actions over contemplation, the concept of *mitzvoth*. These values—which constitute a rejection of despair, irrationalism, or madness as illuminating and consciousness for its own sake—are the components of Saul Bellow's humanistic vision of the world and run counter to what he has defined as literary modernism.

> Hana Wirth-Nesher and Andrea Cohen Malamut. *Modern Fiction Studies*. Spring, 1979, p. 61

Bellow's resistance to alienation has for the most part taken the form of an individual's struggle to define those qualities which identify him as human, qualities which, for Bellow, emerge sometimes in opposition to, sometimes as a function of, the belief that goodness can be achieved only in the company of other men. In exploring these alternatives, Bellow has demonstrated an overriding concern for the ordinary circumstances of daily reality. "While our need for meanings is certainly great," he has written, "our need for concreteness, for particulars, is even greater." In approaching the reality of individuals who actually live and actually die, however, Bellow has evidenced a good deal of anxiety about a facticity that smothers the imagination. "The facts begin to crowd me," Henderson complains, "and soon I get a pressure in the chest." Bellow has responded to the same pressure. American fiction, he complained not long after the publication of *Henderson* [*the Rain King*], had become characterized by a concern for documentation animated neither by the theoretical structure that informed Zola's naturalism nor the feeling or the view of fate that described Dreiser's social novels. More recently, he has objected to the accountability to fact which the society holds the demands of the artist no less than of the scientist or the technical expert in any field. Writing of the difficulty of the artist in a modern, technological society, Bellow has remarked that "the artist has less power to resist the facts than other men. He is obliged to note the particulars. One may even say that he is condemned to see them." In this shift from the artist's need to the social demand for fact as a compelling principle of composition, Bellow anticipated a tendency which, as Pearl K. Bell has recently noted, has come to extend even to the popular novel—Bell cites as representative examples Arthur Hailey's *Wheels*, James Michener's *Centennial*, James Clavell's *Shogun*, and prominently, Herman Wouk's *War and Remembrance*—which formerly defined itself by a concern for narrative movement.

Though Bellow continues to insist on the importance of giving weight to the particular, such weight, he argues, need not be in quantifiable terms any more than art should fulfill a compensatory function in restoring the alienated modern individual to psychic health. Rather, factual authority proceeds from an imaginative faculty that, with Henry James, Bellow insists must maintain its regard for the story as story and must express man's "intuition that his own existence is peculiarly significant.". . .

Accordingly, despite his concern for social conditions, Bellow has shown little interest in specific social movements or political issues. Environment has functioned less as an influence on events and characters than as a projection of their inner conflict, a symbol as well as an agent of inhuman darkness. Bellow's protagonists are thus placed in a social environment but oppressed by personal and natural forces that obscure the resulting tensions by developing them in oblique relation to their framing situations. . . .

There is, then, in Bellow's fiction a fundamental division between a moral concern for the way things look and feel and an insistence on a more meaningful ideality, antecedent to such everyday striving and projected by characters indistinguishable from the authorial voice, whose narrow consciousness of a world displaces its portrayal through an independent perspective.

Stanley Trachtenberg. In *Critical Essays on Saul Bellow*, ed. Stanley Trachtenberg (G.K. Hall, 1979), pp. xiii–xiv

The good thing about *The Dean's December* . . . is that it is by Saul Bellow, and therefore possesses wit, vividness, tenderness, brave thought, earthy mysticism, and a most generous, searching, humorous humanity; the bad thing about it, or at least not so good, is that it also is *about* Saul Bellow, in an uncomfortable, indirect, but unignorable way. . . .

Bellow believes in the soul; this is one of his links with the ancients, with the great books. At the same time, like those great books, he feels and conveys the authentic heaviness in which our spirits are entangled; he has displayed for thirty years an unsurpassedly active and pungent awareness of the corporeal, of the mortal, of human creatureliness in all its sexual and assertive variety. He is not just a very good writer, he is one of the rare writers who when we read them feel to be taking mimesis a layer or two deeper than it has gone before. His lavish, rippling notations of persons, furniture, habiliments, and vistas awaken us to what is truly there. Such a gift for the actual is not unnaturally bound in with a yen toward the theoretical; for how do we see but by setting ourselves to see? From *Augie March* on, a sense of intellectual quest moves Bellow's heroes and is expected to move his readers. The quest in *The Dean's December* is narrow enough to meet concentrated resistance. . . .

Bellow has it in him, great poet and fearless mental venturer that he is, to write one of those unclassifiable American masterpieces like ''Walden.'' But such a book must ramify from a firm, simple center, and this *The Dean's December* does not possess.

John Updike. *New Yorker*. Feb. 22, 1982, pp. 120, 127–28

By general critical agreement, Saul Bellow is the strongest American novelist of his generation, presumably with Norman Mailer as his nearest rival. What makes this canonical judgment a touch problematic is that the indisputable achievement does not appear to reside in any single book. Bellow's principal works are: *The Adventures of Augie March*, *Herzog*, *Humboldt's Gift*, and in a briefer compass, *Seize the Day*. The earlier novels, *Dangling Man* and *The Victim*, seem now to be period pieces, while *Henderson the Rain King* and *Mr. Sammler's Planet* share the curious quality of not being quite worthy of two figures so memorable as Henderson and Mr. Sammler. *The Dean's December* is a drab book, its dreariness unredeemed by Bellow's nearly absent comic genius.

Herzog, still possessing the exuberance of *Augie March*, while anticipating the tragicomic sophistication of *Humboldt's Gift*, as of now seems to be Bellow's best and most representative novel. And yet its central figure remains a wavering representation, compared to some of the subsidiary male characters, and its women seem the wish-fulfillments, negative as well as positive, of Herzog and his creator. This seems true of almost all of Bellow's fiction: A Dickensian gusto animates a fabulous array of secondary and minor personalities, while at the center a colorful but shadowy consciousness is hedged in by women who do not persuade us, though evidently once they persuaded him.

In some sense, the canonical status of Bellow is already assured, even if the indubitable book is still to come. Bellow's strengths may not have come together to form a masterwork, but he is hardly the first novelist of real eminence whose books may be weaker as aggregates than in their component parts or aspects. His stylistic achievement is beyond dispute, as are his humor, his narrative inventiveness, and his astonishing inner ear, whether for monologue or dialogue. Perhaps his greatest gift is for creating subsidiary and minor characters of grotesque splendor, sublime in their vivacity, intensity, and capacity to surprise. They may be caricatures, yet their vitality seems permanent. . . . This helps compound the aesthetic mystery of Bellow's achievement. His heroes are superb observers, worthy of their Whitmanian heritage. What they lack is Whitman's Real Me or Me Myself, or else they are blocked from expressing it.

Harold Bloom. Introduction in Harold Bloom, ed. *Saul Bellow* (New York: Chelsea House, 1986). pp. 1–2

Bellow is in some ways the least fashionable of contemporary novelists. While modern and postmodern writers have been shaping the novel into something enclosed, labyrinthine, and narcissistic, he has adhered generally to the more open stylistics of nineteenth-century realism. While Jewish novelists have been chronicling their American experience and becoming a group presence in the bookstalls, he has rejected the label of Jewish writer and insisted upon the label *American*. While masters of the novel have been plumbing the minds of the insane, the disaffected, and the neurotic, he has given us thoughtful fictions about the urban intellectual. Thought itself is really both the subject and the strategy of Bellow's fiction. . . .

This commitment to thought establishes Bellow as America's most obviously intellectual novelist. No writer now living has explored with greater subtlety and intensity than he the terrain where overburdened consciousness, intellectual fervidness, and moral anxiety come together. No writer has caught more tellingly the intellectual temper of the age—its sense of material disorder, its shrinking from mental excess, its fear of final reckonings. Yet Bellow's novels are not in any sense philosophical disquisitions tricked out in story form. The life of the mind moves dramatically toward catharsis rather than toward some ultimate QED in his novels, his focus always the lived through experience of ideas. Nor is Bellow insensitive to the shadows that hang over commitment to thought in our culture. His most cerebral characters suffer from intellectual shell shock, and so great is their suffering that Bellow might almost be thought to warn us off the territory. . . .

More than any living American writer, Bellow commands our respect for his stubborn attempt to reconcile the human mind with a nature that ill accommodates it and an experience that surfeits it. We are richer that he engages us in the endeavor.

> Robert F. Kiernan. *Saul Bellow* (New York: Continuum, 1989), pp. 233, 235

In consequence of which, one is obliged to put a riddle: if you found this book of stories (*Him with His Foot in His Mouth*) at the foot of your bed one morning, with the title page torn way and the author's name concealed, would you know it, after all, to be Bellow?. . . Omitting, then, extraterritorial interests not subject to the tractable laws of fiction . . . would you recognize Bellow's muscle, his swift and glorious eye?

Yes, absolutely; a thousand times yes. It is Bellow's Chicago, Bellow's portraiture—these faces, these heads!—above all, Bellow's motor. . . .

To this thickness of community and these passions of mind Bellow has added a distinctive ingredient, not new on any landscape, but shamelessly daring just now in American imaginative prose. Let the narrator of ''Cousins'' reveal it: ''We enter the world without prior notice, we are manifested before we can be aware of manifestation. An original self exists, or, if you prefer, an original soul.'' Bellow, it seems, has risked mentioning . . . the Eye of God. . . .

This metaphysical radar (suspiciously akin to the Eye of God) ''decodes'' Saul Bellow, and these five ravishing stories honor and augment his genius.

> Cynthia Ozick. *Metaphor and Memory* (New York: Alfred A. Knopf, 1989), pp. 50–57

The first female to serve as the protagonist of a Bellow novel, Clara [in *A Theft*] has endured the marital disappointments and failures that befall most of her male predecessors; she is however, neither bitter nor scornful of the possibilities for love. As restless and troubled (she has twice attempted suicide) as any of Bellow's heroes, she has this singular advantage. Like Henderson's wife Lily, Clara regards love as the fundamental fact of being. . . .

As the central figure and intelligence in *A Theft* Clara Velde radiates energy and warmth. . . . Further contributing to the sanguine atmosphere of Bellow's latest work are the passages of high-spirited comedy, and sexual parody, that recall his earlier fiction. Once more, the absurdities of twentieth-century life prove laughable as well as grotesque. . . .

As the creator of all these seekers after ''real being,'' Bellow still honors the novel's incapacity to deliver ''absolutes.'' Affirmation of soul's ''natural knowledge'' is always dramatic and personal, the protagonist (and his author) making no claims for ''objective truth.'' In the earlier novels, especially, Bellow's protagonists

scarcely understand their struggle for awareness. And in the later novels—whether the protagonist begins his search, like Sammler, in a state of intense inner conflict, or, like Corde, already has an inkling of his tie to creation—the internal harmony he achieves is always precarious, besieged unrelentingly by the chaotic forces of twentieth-century life. As acutely aware as a Corde, a Herzog, or a Sammler of the sheer mass of ''objective'' evidence bearing down, with crushing force, on the fragile ''internal facts'' of human attachment, Saul Bellow continues, nonetheless, to articulate the ''shamelessly daring'' language of connection. In each successive novel, and with increasing boldness from *Mr. Sammler's Planet* on, he has pitted the art of his fiction against the grain of contemporary ''head culture''—defying the leaden authority of its reigning idols.

> Ellen Pifer. *Saul Bellow: Against the Grain.* (Philadelphia: Univ. of Pennsylvania Pr., 1990), pp. 179–80, 184–85

Saul Bellow presents this collection of occasional works of nonfiction [*It All Adds Up: From the Dim Past to the Uncertain Future*] modestly—he calls it ''not a reliquary but a gathering of some of the more readable essays''—but most readers are likely to receive it otherwise. Though it is for his fiction that we most honor Bellow, the voice in which he speaks is always distinctively his own no matter what the genre that he chooses to use. A new book by Bellow is always to be valued, even if it is not a novel and not, technically, ''new'': thus it is with *It All Adds Up*, the only nonfiction collection he has published in a career that now embraces a half-century.

Few readers need to be told that Bellow is a person of pronounced and prickly views. In the decades since *Herzog* made its rather startling appearance, he has not been reluctant to use his fiction to cast a gloomy light upon the modern world. In a few instances this has produced novels more notable for their crankiness than for their art, perhaps most self-evidently *The Dean's December*, but it also has charged them with a fierce and insistent energy. Reading them, one is much aware of the author's powerful, commanding presence, a presence entirely unlike any other in contemporary American literature.

Certainly it pervades the two and half dozen pieces herein collected. To call them essays is a bit of a stretch since they include several lectures and a couple of transcribed interviews, but they are indisputably Bellow. They are the work of a man who says, ''I come of a generation, now largely vanished, that was passionate about literature,'' and who has spent much of his adult life trying to figure out ''the place of poets and novelists'' in ''American society as it is now and the mixture of mind and crudity it offers.'' That, in one form or another, is the question he explores in the meatiest of these pieces. . . .

On no subject does Bellow write more passionately than this. Clearly he has been sustained by his conviction that there is something more to American life than what we see and that it is the responsibility of the artist to search for it. Knowing that, we can understand all the more clearly the . . . fierce energy and insistent energy of his fiction; it derives from his determination, no less strong in his eighth decade than it was in his third, to track down that elusive but ever alluring truth.

All of which serves as a useful reminder of the implacable seriousness that is at the heart of Bellow's artistry, but it should not distract us from the great humor that reverberates throughout his work.

> Jonathan Yardley. *San Francisco Examiner*. March 30, 1994, p. C–5

BIBLIOGRAPHY
Dangling Man, 1944 (n); *The Victim*, 1947 (n); *The Adventures of Augie March*, 1953 (n); *Seize the Day*, 1956 (n, s, d); *Henderson the Rain King*, 1959 (n); *Herzog*, 1964 (n); *The Last Analysis*, 1964 (d); *Mosby's Memoirs*, 1968 (s); *Mr. Sammler's Planet*, 1970 (n); *Humboldt's Gift*, 1975 (n); *To Jerusalem and Back*, 1976 (t); *The Portable Saul Bellow*, 1977 (s, n); *The Dean's December*, 1982 (n); *Him with His Foot in His Mouth, and Other Stories*, 1984; *More Die of Heartbreak*, 1987 (n); *Summations*, 1987 (address at Bennington College); *The Bellarosa Connection*, 1989 (n); *A Theft*, 1989 (n); *Something to Remember Me By*, 1991 [two novellas and a story: *The Bellarosa Connection, A Theft*]; *It All Adds Up: From the Dim Past to the Uncertain Future*, 1994 (e); *The Actual*, 1997 (n)

BENCHLEY, Robert (1889–1945)

Mr. Benchley has a genuine sense of the ridiculous; he passes through the semi-intelligent world of the business office, the city room, the theatre, with an amused appreciation of its vanities; he takes an absurd pleasure in his grimaces and horseplay not so much because they make others laugh but because they are required of him by the pompous stupidities of civilized existence. Unhappily he has had to fill two hundred and fifty pages with this sort of thing. In half that number he could have published all of his parodies, including the "Christmas Afternoon," which is very good, "From Nine to Five," "Football," a few of his little farces, and all of the pages between the flyleaf and the contents page. He would have succeeded in omitting all of the distressing bits quoted by his friends as the best things in the book.

> Gilbert Seldes. *Dial*. Jan., 1922. p. 95

Here . . . is Robert C. Benchley, perhaps the most finished master of the technique of literary fun in America. Benchley's work is pure humor, one might almost say sheer nonsense. There is no moral teaching, no reflection of life, no tears. What Benchley pursues is the higher art of nonsense and he has shown in it a quite exceptional power for tricks of word and phrase.

> Stephen Leacock. *The Greatest Pages of American Humor* (Doubleday). 1936. p. 233

Along comes Robert Benchley like those hardy perennials, [P.G.] Wodehouse and [E. Phillips] Oppenheim. When I was still in college in 1921 . . . I read *Of All Things*, which I still consider his best and freshest book. . . . He is popular now, and I believe that he syndicates his articles. At any rate, they are seriously the work of the serious humorist; still funny, but too much of the same thing to make one laugh anew. Yet those who do not know Mr. Benchley

and his illuminator, Mr. Gluyas Williams (never better than in this role), have missed something unduplicated in American humor. He can write on anything, and does. Falling flat, Mr. Benchley is sharper than all his imitators. . . . He is a rare and natural wit who . . . writes too much and too often.

> David McCord. *The Yale Review*. Autumn, 1936. p. 81

The man seems to be a humorist, and yet the Pagliacci undertones are seldom absent. . . . Generalizations about Benchley are dangerous. . . . But surely spontaneity is the key to his particular form of mental disorder. The man is spontaneously cuckoo. . . . Still, he says some pretty acute things. . . . I have said that Benchley seems to be a humorist, and right now, in order to give Bob a break, I want to retract that "seems." Maybe "humorist" isn't the right word either. All I know is, he makes you laugh.

> William Rose Benét. *Saturday Review*. Jan. 8, 1938. p. 7

"Is Robert Benchley a solar myth?" That is the question little knots of curious people, as well as curious knots of little people, have been asking ever since Mr. Benchley traded in his quill for an Actor's Equity card and abandoned the craft of writing. It has often been said—and it is being said again right at this minute—that the Ice Age of American humor began the moment he stopped practicing letters. For the sad fact is that when Benchley went out of business he forgot to appoint a successor. He just locked up the store and threw away the key. . . .

In this, his latest garland [*Benchley Beside Himself*], Mr. Benchley proves again what needs no confirmation, that for sheer guile and sprightliness he leaves his competitors, imitators and apostles tied to a tree. Whether you begin with "Polyp With a Past," or the masterly inquiry into Negro folksong . . . or any one of twenty others, it is a dead cert you will wind up clawing at your collar and emitting a series of strangled little yelps.

> S.J. Perelman. *New York Times Book Section*. June 13, 1943. p. 2

. . .in past years I was probably afraid to read him for fear of finding out how many of my own humorous bits had already been written by the Master. I think that most humorists today must humbly admit to the same indebtedness.

Benchley *was* humor. His writings were only one of the outward and visible evidences of the inner grace, the divine essence. . . . Benchley *did* give out a radiant glow; his friends and his millions of readers *did* warm themselves and feel better because of his presence. But he was not one to be operated by a switch; he was a flame, capable of leaping out of the fireplace and bitterly searching the hypocrite, the pretentious, the inhuman.

> Donald Ogden Stewart. *The Nation*. Oct. 16, 1954. p. 343

To read *The Benchley Roundup* . . . is to reread some of the most laughable prose of the past thirty years and to be reminded of how much we still miss Bob Benchley. He had the most ingenious way of submitting himself to exasperation. The causes of his annoyance he would describe with wonderful accuracy, and with a slow burn. . . . [But] the worm always turns, in a Benchley essay; the moment comes when the gentle sufferer can stand no more, and this is the fun of the thing—to see him rise in his wrath and impale the nuisance with the deftest of phrases.

>   Edward Weeks. *Atlantic Monthly*. Nov., 1954. p. 88

Benchley was a highly subjective writer, and most of what he wrote was conditioned by his feelings about himself. Among his gifts was the ability to set these feelings down neatly and precisely. . . . He was willing, even eager, to make fun of himself, provided he was reasonably sure that others would know what he was talking about, but he was reluctant to do anything that appeared to be straining to make the point.

>   Nathaniel Benchley. *Robert Benchley* (McGrawHill). 1955. p.2

It's pretty hard to find anything dated in his gallery of cheerful incompetents failing calamitously to adapt themselves to modern man's living habits, and his genial, bumbling authorities lecturing on how to figure income-taxes, raise babies, sub-let apartments, control crime, take vacations, vote, train dogs, and other subjects susceptible to hilarious exploitation. . . . Very properly "kindliness" has been used more than any other word to describe the basic quality of Benchley fun-making. . . . He could also express a cold, virtuous anger in his writing. A lot of unscrupulous reporters and editors felt the bite of Robert Benchley's contempt in the acid comments on current journalism which *The New Yorker* frequently published above the sobriquet of Guy Fawkes.

>   Marc Connelly. *New York Herald Tribune Book Section*.
>   Nov. 13, 1955. pp. 1, 13

Benchley's Little Man has an integrity that can be strained but never quite broken; it gleams sullenly through his foggiest notions. In *The Neurotic Personality of Our Time*, Karen Horney says that one refuge of the intellectual sort of neurotic is a detachment in which he refuses to take anything seriously, including himself. The self-mockery of Benchley's fictive double is never carried to the point where he loses his wholesome awareness that man's environment was made for man, not he for it, and if things don't seem that way (here the reformer speaks)—well, things had better be changed. Miss Horney also states that the neurotic feels a compulsion to be liked. Benchley's double is less concerned with being liked than with preserving his integrity and his ethical vision.

>   Norris W. Yates. *The American Humorist* (Iowa State).
>   1964. p. 246

BIBLIOGRAPHY
Of All Things, 1921 (e); *Love Conquers All*, 1922 (e); *Pluck and Luck*, 1925 (e); *The Early Worm*, 1927 (e); *20,000 Leagues Under the Sea, or, David Copperfield*, 1928 (e); *The Treasurer's Report and Other Aspects of Community Singing*, 1930 (e); *No Poems, or, Around the World Backwards and Sideways*, 1932 (e); *From Bed to Worse, or Comforting Thoughts about the Bison*, 1934 (e); *Why Does Nobody Collect Me?* 1935 (e); *My Ten Years in a Quandary and How They Grew*, 1936 (e); *After 1903—What?* 1938 (e); *Inside Benchley*, 1942 (e); *Benchley Beside Himself*, 1943 (e); *Benchley—Or Else!* 1947 (e); *Chips Off the Old Benchley*, 1949 (e); *The Benchley Roundup*, 1954 (e)

BENÉT, Stephen Vincent (1898–1943)

John Brown's Body . . . is as good as knowledge, sincere personal feeling, and Mr. Benét's particular literary expertness, could make it. To argue that it is more than this, would be quite specially unjust. It is a popular patriotic epic of essentially the same order as Noyes's Elizabethan Odyssey; regarded as a grand historical poem like *The Dynasts*, it would be a heavy disappointment. All the virtues of readability, romantic charm, reminiscent pathos, it has in abundance; the higher virtues that one might expect of such a performance, it very definitely lacks. It lacks these partly because it is not organized and controlled, as such a poem would be, by a clear and sweeping philosophic vision; partly because it is not directed for all its competence, by a rigorous and corrective artistic purpose.

>   Newton Arvin. *New York Herald Tribune Book Section*.
>   Aug. 12, 1928. p. 2

John Brown's Body has been called among other things an epic and it has been compared, not unfavorably, to the *Iliad*. Mr. Benét himself has no such pretensions. . . . The poem is not in any sense an epic; neither is it a philosophical vision of the Civil War; it is a loose episodic narrative which unfolds a number of unrelated themes in motion picture flashes. In spite of some literary incompetence in the author and the lack of a controlling imagination, the story gathers suspense as it goes and often attains to power.

>   Allen Tate. *The Nation*. Sept. 19, 1928. p. 274

Epic is too heroic a word, no doubt, to stand alone as descriptive of this poem (*John Brown's Body*); a word associated too loftily with Homer and Virgil, with Dante and Milton; suggestive of masterpieces of the past, whose royal rhythms carry mythical gods and heroes through magical exploits. Mr. Benét's poem is a kind of cinema epic, brilliantly flashing a hundred different aspects of American character and history on the silver screen of an unobstrusively fluent and responsive style.

>   Harriet Monroe. *Poetry*. Nov., 1928. p. 91

Stephen Benét has the true gift of poetry, and he has a scope and energy of ambition that is rare among poets in this practical age. . . . Even where Benét's poetry is not so fine, it is sustained by a fine sincerity—by the poet's own heart honestly feeling all that is felt—and it is adorned with interruptions of excellent lyrical song. All these virtues compel one to judge *John Brown's Body* by the standards of great art. And as a great work of art, I think the book fails. . . . It is a sophisticated book, an intellectual book, full of complicated, diverse and extremely up-to-date ideas. Only as a whole it lacks idea. It lacks attitude. It lacks the unity that is imparted by an intention.

>   Max Eastman. *Bookman*. Nov., 1928. p. 362

Mr. Benét keeps to the middle of the road in his verse as in his thinking. Neither an innovator nor an imitator, he is an able craftsman who draws upon sources both old and recent. With some lapses his poetry is interesting, perceptive, and in good taste. . . . He is the critical historian who shrinks from the half-truths and savageries of prophecy and partisanship; lacking the evidence for a final judgement, he is content to chronicle. As such he has his place and a not undistinguished one; for an honest chronicler who is also a skilful poet is better than a score of false prophets without art.

Philip Blair Rice. *The Nation.* July 18, 1936. pp. 81–2

His verse is a survival of an abundant native line; it has become a virtual guide-book of native myth and folklore, their place-names, heroes, humours, and reverences. . . . Mr. Benét derived, through Lindsay, from the bardic romantics who held sway in American poetry for over a century. . . .In America this tradition, in its homeliest form, was the living authority of text-books and family anthologies all the way from Neihardt, Riley, and Markham, back through Hay, Harte, and Miller, to the bearded dynasties of Longfellow and Bryant—a succession hostile to eccentric talent or refined taste, scornful of modernity or exotic influence, once the pride of the burgeoning Republic, and now chiefly a source of cheerful embarrassment to teachers and blushing incredulity to their students. Mr. Benét has aspired from his school-days to a place in this old American line.

Morton Dauwen Zabel. *Poetry.* Aug., 1936. pp. 276

Mr. Benét, when not writing hundreds of pages of flat free verse, can be a poet, and can tell a first-rate story when not wrestling with attitudes towards history. I think posterity will treat him much like Stevenson. Some will ignore him; the young will treasure his adventure tales, especially *Spanish Bayonet*; and most people will like his ballads, love poems, and prose fantasies. At his unpretentious best he is a writer of sure skill and simple charm. But his efforts as interpreter of the American scene and the world crisis will be tactfully forgotten. No matter how fertile their imagination, little of worth results when writers who do not feel *prophetically* the power of ideas attempt to express social and historical truths.

Frank Jones. *The Nation.* Sept. 12, 1942. p. 218

He was in sheer fact the poet so urgently called for by our last national poet, the first to chant songs for and of all America, Walt Whitman. And unlike Walt Whitman, whose prophetic symbolism could be read by the people only in single poems and passages, he broke through the ivory wall and was read (as Whitman prophesied some American would be) by the population at large. It seems probable that no writer of poetry in English has ever been read by so many in his lifetime—not even Longfellow—as was Stephen Benét. And while he was popular, he never wrote down to his public. He gave them his best, and it was good.

Henry Seidel Canby. *Saturday Review.* March 27, 1943. p. 14

His life was a model, I think, of what a poet's life should be—a model upon which young men of later generations might well form

themselves. He was altogether without envy or vanity. He never considered appearance, or tried to present himself as anything but what he was, or paid the least attention to the prevalent notions of what a poet ought to be. Also, and more important, he was truly generous. . . .Moreover, his generosity was not a moral quality alone. It was an intellectual quality as well. . . . It was this warm and human concern with things seen, things felt beyond himself, which gave him his quality as a poet.

Archibald MacLeish. *Saturday Review.* March 27, 1943. p. 7

Stephen Vincent Benét's death was a particular loss because he added to the variety of American poetry. His contribution of the historical narrative was unique, since few practiced it and no other approached his success. It is important to define his effort. He was not interested in mouthing the word "America." . . . Benét's deep regard for the United States of America was based not on a feeling of blood and earth, but on an honest belief in this country as remarkably permitting human freedom. He knew the misery and corruption, and you'll find them in his books. But, stronger than any other motive, you will find Benét's fascination with the effort of these states to be a place where that reckless and distorted word "liberty" actually means individual right and intellectual exemption.

Paul Engle. *Poetry.* Dec., 1943. p. 160

Whatever may be the eventual position of Benét's work in the ranks of American letters, one suspects that it will persist, in a quiet way, pretty far forward, despite the cyclical clamor as advance guards change. . . . Stephen Vincent Benét had a faith and a delight in people and a belief that they could come to good ends. And it is precisely this faith and delight and belief that distinguish his work from that of most of his noisier contemporaries, that make his storied people stand out. . . . Benét's people exist in an older context . . . a context of accomplishment; of reaffirmation of the ancient and necessary faith that man not only can defeat his devils but can act with decency toward his fellows.

Robeson Bailey. *Saturday Review.* Jan. 4, 1947. p. 16

BIBLIOGRAPHY
Five Men and Pompey, 1915 (p); *The Drug Shop*, 1917 (p); *Young Adventure*, 1918 (p); *Heavens and Earth*, 1920 (p); *The Beginning of Wisdom*, 1921 (n); *Young People's Pride*, 1922 (n); *The Ballad of William Sycamore*, 1923 (p); *King David*, 1923 (p); *Jean Huguenot*, 1923 (n); *Tiger Joy*, 1925 (p); *Spanish Bayonet*, 1926 (n); *John Brown's Body*, 1928 (p); *The Barefoot Saint*, 1929 (s); *Ballads and Poems, 1915–1930*, 1931; (with Rosemary Benét) *A Book of Americans*, 1933 (p); *The Story of the United Press*, 1933 (j); *James Shore's Daughter*, 1934 (n); *Burning City*, 1936 (p); *The Magic of Poetry and the Poet's Art*, 1936 (e); *The Devil and Daniel Webster*, 1937 (s); *Thirteen O'Clock*, 1937 (s); *Johnny Pye and the Fool-Killer*, 1938 (s); *The Ballad of the Duke's Mercy*, 1939 (p); *Tales Before Midnight*, 1939 (s); *The Devil and Daniel Webster*, 1939 (d); *The Devil and Daniel Webster*, 1939 (libretto); *Nightmare at Noon*, 1940 (p); *Dear Adolf*, 1942 (sk); *A Child Is Born*, 1942 (d); *Selected Works*, 1942; *Selected Poetry and Prose*, 1942; *Twenty-five Short Stories*, 1943; *Western Star*, 1943 (p); *America*,

1944 (h); *We Stand United and Other Radio Scripts*, 1945; *The Last Circle*, 1946 (s, p); *Selected Letters*, 1960

BERGER, Thomas (1924–)

[*Crazy in Berlin* is] a first novel of exceptional merit. . . . Indeed, I know of no book by an American that searches more earnestly the meaning of the Nazi convulsion and its aftermath in order to discover their wider applications. . . . Mr. Berger gives us a wealth of characterization, but more of the basis of character read deeply and truly. . . . Behind this work, there is a fine intelligence; this is a book written from the vantage of maturity. The quality of the writing itself is varied. Mr. Berger has a sure sense of the ludicrous; seriousness lights up with mockery; ideas can take the shape of sensual images. Berlin itself, its cellars, streets, and ruins stand before us. If the movement of the book is slow, that, too, may become part of our pleasure in it. But sometimes the writing is unclear or, to put it more accurately, is congested with meaning. Nor has Mr. Berger always organized his materials to best effect; we are threatened with a surfeit of valuable matter. Still, this book is in most ways a solid achievement, an original novel of unquestionable power.

Gene Baro. *New York Herald Tribune Book Section*. Oct. 26, 1958. p. 12

Two novels [*Crazy in Berlin* and *Reinhart in Love*] hardly provide an adequate basis for judgment on an author like Thomas Berger. Criticism must make allowances for its own errors just as it must allow for the unexpected turns in a writer's craft. But two novels also amount to a kind of self-declaration. The declaration, I think, is of a double import: it reveals something about Berger's singular talent, and it illuminates a new trend of American fiction.

Berger's primary concern is the individual in a world of cunning appearances and uncertified realities. Power and Fraud rule that world, distorting appearances and realities, pressing man to the limits of his sanity, and pressing on him the guilt-ridden role of victim or aggressor. But threats also contain their own answer, and shields may be fashioned of weapons. Man's response, therefore, is to adopt a stance of knowing craziness, resilient simplicity, or defensive defenselessness. These are the qualities Reinhart possesses. Nor is it an accident that his patron's day, so Berger says, is April First, Fool's Day.

Ihab Hassan. *Critique*. 5, 2, 1962. pp. 14–5

However late or early in the day it may be for the Western novel, Thomas Berger has just written a really noble one [*Little Big Man*], something really new. . . . In about the same way that Faulkner delivers the old South to the ken of a jaded but renewable imagination, Berger delivers the West. He took on an apparently impossible task and made the dead bones live, not by stringing them together and jerking the strings to make them dance, but by showing how we dream "anonymously and communally" as Mann once put it, finding, by a prophetic leap, the common ingredients our regressive dream of the West shared with the

dreams of those vanished Indians and a boy kidnapped from a wagon train. And oh, that Wild West dream is funny, magically and marvelously funny as Berger recreates it, like an embarrassment and a rapture we never knew quite how to confess.

R.V. Cassill. *Book Week*. Oct. 25, 1964. p. 2

Sometimes . . . the new Western anti-heroes shrink in size until they move through the vastness of the West more like the dwarfed Julius Rodman of Edgar Allan Poe than any movie version of the Cowboy Hero. . . . Thomas Berger's Little Big Man is precisely what his name declares: a shrimp with sharp wits and an enormous spirit—though in a showdown he prefers to depend more on those wits than that spirit, as, for instance, in encounters with the sort of large, icy killer he knows he cannot outdraw. . . . Indeed, all of the "historical" characters in *Little Big Man* are undercut and debunked by a kind of merciless geniality that is likely to mislead the unwary reader about the real nature of the novel.

One reviewer, for example, quite inappropriately described *Little Big Man*, just after it appeared, as "exciting, violent, and ribald . . . ranks with *The Big Sky* and *The Oxbow Incident*." But it has neither the moral earnestness of the latter nor the easy realism of the former, only a desire to demonstrate how, for all its pathos and danger, the West was and remains essentially *funny*. . . . Berger is not so brutal and extreme in this regard, so totally nihilistic as David Markson, or even John Barth: but he, too, cannot resist drawing almost anything he happens to know into the circle of his ridicule.

Leslie A. Fiedler. *The Return of the Vanishing American* (Stein and Day). 1968. pp. 160–1

Berger's *Killing Time* is (need I say it?) a picaresque, bleakly comic account of the world's malevolent absurdity, with a Holy Fool at the centre, much bizarre violence and sex, philosophic dialogues, and a style that is mannered and glittering. . . .

The effects Mr. Berger achieves are lurid, yet economical and intelligent. His situations are presented in a bright, harsh light, with a related blackness that you can feel. His tone is sardonic and reflective, aloof, yet without any of the onanistic snickerings of a James Purdy. His characters are all too subtly, even elaborately analysed to be simple grotesques. And yet the effect of the whole book is of a distant and somewhat cerebral brilliance. Our interest is in texture and the to-and-fro of argument rather than in a felt predicament. Even the violence and the misery are appreciated almost as exciting colours, not as human experiences. And the persons and events are so extreme, so spasmodic, that we cease to take even the ideas—the Quest for Being—very seriously. So much novelty and so much inconclusive cleverness defeat their purpose of making us question our lives, and come close to providing a very superior kind of science fiction.

Kenneth Graham. *The Listener*. May 16, 1968. pp. 639–40

Little Big Man is a great novel because it portrays western "society" in the nineteenth century as it really was—violent, yes, but also absurd, melodramatic, incongruous. Its author never sacrifices his imagination to realism. At the same time it is scrupulously accurate as to places, dates and events, the results of the ''60 or 70 accounts of Western reality'' which Berger says he read ''to reinforce my feeling for the myth.'' It is also ''the Western to end all Westerns'' which Berger intended it to be, because it splendorizes the West with love and imagination. Far from discarding any of the choice western properties, Berger has turned them inside out, revealing one by one the possibilities of a western literary art.

Jay Gurian. *Western American Literature*. Winter, 1969. p. 296

Vital Parts confirms Berger's rank as a major American novelist, one whose stylistic fecundity, psychological insight, and social knowledge are seemingly inexhaustible. Reinhart continues to move, clownlike, through his familiar world of ''asymmetrical impulses, like a laughter hopelessly mad, hopelessly free,'' large in physique, generosity, honesty, gullibility, optimism, and capacity for enduring psychosocial wounds. . . .

A comic allegorist of the worthwhile Middle American, skillfully wielding a colloquial diction and rhythm of extraordinary expressiveness, Thomas Berger is one of the most successful satiric observers of the ebb and flow of American life after World War II. His prolificacy promises a continued development of the tragicomic mode of vision, something American literature badly needs to compensate for the over-extended silence of such formerly active writers as Ralph Ellison, Joseph Heller, and Thomas Pynchon.

Brom Weber. *Saturday Review*. March 21, 1970. p. 42

In the shifting landscape of Thomas Berger, man is constant, that is to say, hopelessly the prisoner of himself and his pathetically limited vision. All ideology, all hope of genuine change is false since, alas, ''The 'public' is a collection of individuals though politicians pretend otherwise.'' That is the heart of his irony, and that is why his comedy is too bitter for general popularity, though not, in my opinion, too bitter to be called great (despite occasional lapses into archness, occasional strain in the purely slapstick passages). Under the cold, correct surface of his prose—which, employed to render absurdity, creates the fundamental tension of his work—lies one of the most genuinely radical sensibilities now writing novels in this country. Next to the devastation he wreaks in his quiet way, a public anarchist like Reinhart's fellow Cincinnatian, Jerry Rubin, seems pip-squeak indeed. *He* thinks there is hope; Carlo Reinhart and Thomas Berger know there is only the possibility of replacing present delusions with new ones.

Richard Schickel. *Commentary*. July, 1970. p. 80

Berger's settings and characters in all his novels are plausible rather than apocalyptic. His satire refuses to make an alliance between reader and author against an oppressive, ugly ''them.'' Paul Krassner once wrote that ''the ultimate object of satire is its own audience,'' and Berger's integrity arranges that no reader— male chauvinist, militant feminist or in between—can emerge from *Regiment of Women* unscathed. All of Berger's main characters— Georgie Cornell here, Jack Crabb in *Little Big Man*, Carlo Reinhart in *Crazy in Berlin, Reinhart in Love* and *Vital Parts*—are moved more by circumstances than by some passionate belief or lack of

belief. Berger's clearest outrage is reserved for anyone who presumes to sit in moral judgment on another, and his central characters are all slammed about by beings more certain than they about the location of truth. . . .

Berger's own style, with its tendency to absorb the speech rhythms of his characters and its unwillingness to stand apart from them, is especially suited for such themes. Since *Little Big Man*, especially, he has concentrated on exploring the possibilities and revealing the secrets of everyday language with a deep wit and feeling that transforms our awareness of the language we really use much more than does the flamboyance of a writer bent on asserting his personal style. *Killing Time* may be Berger's most brilliant effort to engage in this truly poetic task of renovating the language we speak. But *Regiment of Women* is a brilliant flame from the same sources of energy.

Leo Braudy. *New York Times Book Section*. May 13, 1973. pp. 6–7

Thomas Berger understands one of the cardinal principles of silent-film comedy, the excruciating approach to an anticipated collision averted by a hair-breadth swerve at the last moment into a fresh kettle of fish. His timing and control are impeccable.

Sneaky People is a book full of secrets and surprises. . . . Each melodramatic twist is short-circuited by an unlooked-for response. . . . Over all this shines the sun of a dusty Midwestern city at the end of the Depression: daily life is lovingly remembered and recreated in exact detail. On a first reading, *Sneaky People* is exhilaratingly bawdy and tricky. A second reading arouses a different feeling: this is Thomas Berger's tenderest, most touching work.

Walter Clemons. *Newsweek*. April 28, 1975. p. 79

Thomas Berger's fifth novel [*Who Is Teddy Villanova?*] is mainly a parody of detective thrillers; his well-known *Little Big Man* was a parody of Westerns. According to the jacket copy, in *Who Is Teddy Villanova?* we will recognize the familiar ''seedy office,'' ''down-at-the-heels shamus,'' ''procession of sinister, chicane, or merely brutal men and scheming, vicious, but lovely women'' and a ''sequence of savage beatings.'' All this is true. The novel contains much that is conventional in detective thrillers. Still, one needn't know the books of Dashiell Hammett or Raymond Chandler in order to appreciate Berger's witty burlesque of their characters and situations.

Berger's style, which is one of the great pleasures of the book, is something like S.J. Perelman's—educated, complicated, graceful, silly, destructive in spirit, and brilliant—and it is also something like Mad Comics—densely, sensuously detailed, unpredictable, packed with gags. Beyond all this, it makes an impression of scholarship—that is, Berger seems really to know what he jokes about. This includes not only Hammett and Chandler, but also Racine, Goethe, Ruskin, Elias Canetti, New York and the way its residents behave. Essentially, then, Berger's style is like itself insofar as it is like other styles. And his whole novel—in its wide ranging reference to cultural forms both high and pop—is like a huge verbal mirror. Its reflections are similar to what we see in much contemporary literature—hilarious and serious at once.

Leonard Michaels. *New York Times Book Section*. March 20, 1977, p. 1

Thomas Berger belongs, with Mark Twain and Mencken and Philip Roth, among our first-rate literary wiseguys. Savvy and skeptical, equipped with a natural eloquence and a knack for parody, he has been expertly flinging mud at the more solemn and self-important national myths for 20 years. In *Little Big Man*, the best-known of his books—for, alas, the usual reason—he brilliantly savaged the legendary American West. *Who Is Teddy Villanova?*, perhaps the funniest 300 pages of 1977, took on the world of the tough-guy detective novel. For all its clowning, it performed a serious service in deflating the bloody and rather vainglorious cult of Bogart-out-of-Philip Marlowe. Mr. Berger's method, with these and the other mythical landscapes he has explored in his nine novels, is to set them down in his droll, relentlessly straight-faced prose, so as to empty them of romance, and let the brutal/crummy facts stare out. His pages swarm with bawdy puns and slapstick and bookish in-jokes; but even at his most absurd, his intrinsic tone is that of a hard-nosed realist who won't let the myths distort his essentially grouchy idea of the way things really are.

Grouchy, emphatically, is the word. In a review of Mr. Berger's Reinhart books—*Crazy in Berlin*, *Reinhart in Love*, and *Vital Parts*—Richard Schickel pointed out what is distinctive about Mr. Berger as a satirist. It is that he is more piqued by Good than by Bad. Doing good in a world that is mostly bad can have bizarre or disastrous consequences. This wry paradox is at the heart of Mr. Berger's interest in Good King Arthur and his Knights of the Round Table, and in their incorrigibly noble chivalric code. *Arthur Rex*, Mr. Berger's newest novel, is his splendid, satiric retelling of the legend of Camelot. . . .

Mr. Berger's revisions are most authentic, most profound, when the admixture of parody is strongest. At those times—a good three-fourths of the book—he is never merely a parodist after all, but also a compelling yarn-spinner in his own right; a Tolkien for the worldly indeed, stripped of their 19th-century sentiment by the author's deeply anti-Romantic ways, the stories have a leaner, more strident look than they have had in a long time. Not T.H. White's *The Once and Future King*, nor John Steinbeck's mostly antiquarian version, but Thomas Berger's *Arthur Rex* is the Arthur book for our time.

> John Romano. *New York Times Book Section*. Nov. 12, 1978, pp. 3, 62

It is a mystery of literary criticism that Thomas Berger, one of the most ambitious, versatile, and entertaining of contemporary novelists, is hardly ever mentioned in the company of America's major writers. He is a wit, a fine caricaturist, and his prose crackles with Rabelaisian vitality. His phenomenal ear for oddnesses of speech appropriates as readily the grey malapropisms of the silent majority in *Reinhart in Love* . . . as the winning tall-tale garrulousness of *Little Big Man*, a savory reminiscence of the Cheyenne Indians in frontier days. . . .

Moreover, it cannot be said that he ever writes from a universal, or even an ordinary eye-level perspective. He is a magic realist; . . . Berger's focus, his grasp of detail, is sharper and smaller than life. He will allow something infinitesimal to catch his eye and brood upon it, even as he overlooks a larger emotion or design. In the past the disturbing effect of this was somewhat offset by the sheer cascade into his bulky novels of tangy physical images, raunchy episodes, and eccentric wayside characters with an extravagant gift of gab. In his new book, *Neighbors*, there are no such fringe benefits. This strange exasperating little story has been pared down to the taunting colloquy among four characters on a dead-end street in an unnamed suburb. We see them through a pane that is blindingly clear and yet so distorting as to make them seem demented. . . .

He is in fact terrifyingly methodical and consciously satanic in this psychological chiller whose hero is victimized mainly by his own weakness and ambivalence. The plot dramatizes a conviction Berger has held for a long time. In the fictional foreword to *Little Big Man*, the narrator observes: "Each of us, no matter how humble, from day to day finds himself in situations in which he has the choice of acting either heroically or craven." Is Berger telling us in *Neighbors* that cravenness, uncertainty about our own feelings, breeds aggression in others? That obsequiousness is really distrust, and once suspected will be returned in kind? *Neighbors* is a cool study in taking advantage, a chess game in which each move is followed inexorably by the countermove the player leaves himself open for. The victim is at the mercy of some force not larger than himself as happens in Kafka's *The Trial* but, far more grueling, exactly equal to himself. That is to say, everyone gets his just psychological deserts.

> Isa Kapp. *New Republic*. April 26, 1980, pp. 34–35

BIBLIOGRAPHY

Crazy in Berlin, 1958 (n); *Reinhart in Love*, 1962 (n); *Little Big Man*, 1964 (n); *Killing Time*, 1967 (n); *Vital Parts*, 1970 (n); *Regiment of Women*, 1973 (n); *Sneaky People*, 1975 (n); *Who Is Teddy Villanova?*, 1977 (n); *Arthur Rex*, 1978 (n); *Neighbors*, 1980 (n); *Reinhart's Women*, 1981 (n); *The Feud*, 1983 (n); *Nowhere*, 1985 (n); *Being Invisible*, 1987 (n); *The Houseguest*, 1988 (n); *Changing the Past*, 1989 (n); *Orrie's Story*, 1990 (n); *Meeting Evil*, 1992 (n); *Robert Crews*, 1994 (n); *Suspects*, 1996 (n); *The Return of Little Big Man*, 1999 (n)

BERRYMAN, John (1914–1972)

In terms of what he is doing he has considerably more control than [Randall] Jarrell, but it is possible that the control is premature. For example, too many of his poems go off into the fixed direction of the meditative convention of Yeats: at his comparatively early age he seems to have got set in the tone of pronouncement and prophecy, with the result that his powers of observation are used chiefly for incidental shock. Yet his line has more firmness and structure than Jarrell's, and there is a sense in which he is more mature: he is not afraid to commit himself to systematic and even solemn elaborations of metaphor.

> Allen Tate. *Partisan Review*. May–June, 1941. p. 243

John Berryman . . . is a complicated, nervous, and intelligent writer whose poetry has steadily improved. At first he was possessed by a slavishly Yeatsish grandiloquence which at its best resulted in a sort of posed, planetary melodrama, and which at its worst resulted in monumental bathos. . . . [His] latest poetry, in spite of its occasional echoes, is as determinedly individual as one could wish. Doing things in a style all its own sometimes seems the primary object of the poem, and its subject gets a rather spasmodic and fragmentary treatment. The style—conscious, dissonant, darting; allusive, always over-or under-satisfying the expectations which it is intelligently exploiting—seems to fit Mr. Berryman's knowledge and sensibility surprisingly well, and ought in the end to produce poetry better than the best of the poems he has so far written in it, which have raw or overdone lines side by side with imaginative and satisfying ones.

Randall Jarrell. *The Nation*. July 17, 1948. pp. 80–1

John Berryman has at least in a limited degree the gift for language . . . , but it is frustrated by his inability to define his theme and his disinclination to understand and discipline his emotions. Most of his poems appear to deal with a single all-inclusive topic: the desperate chaos, social, religious, philosophical, and psychological, of modern life, and the corresponding chaos and desperation of John Berryman. No matter what the ostensible subject, this is commonly what emerges, and most of the poems are merely random assortments of half-realized images illustrating this theme.

Yvor Winters. *Hudson Review*. Autumn, 1948. p. 404

Homage to Mistress Bradstreet is a long poem written in fifty-seven stanzas—except for two they are of eight lines each—on the subject of Anne Bradstreet, 1612–1672, wife to Simon Bradstreet (colonial governor of Massachusetts after her death), and perhaps America's—almost surely Massachusetts'—first poet. . . . Its triumph, what makes it so very interesting, is the curious diction employed, a truly personal speech which without seeming archaic neither seems quite contemporary: it is a strange, and touching, going-out from oneself, a feeling-back into our common past. The tensions of the present poem exist in the unfolding of a double mystery: that of life and death, of the past and present. . . . The poem is somewhat uneven. But at its best the mystery is embodied in lines that (if one might presume a little) ought to have pleased George Herbert.

Ambrose Gordon, Jr. *The Yale Review*. Winter, 1957. pp. 299–300

The poems [in *77 Dream Songs*] that strike me as being best . . . I read as marvelous play by a passionate, despairing, cracked, erudite, utterly poetic genius. Moreover, though they are called dream songs, and though they are apparently supposed to be the dreams of a character ''Henry'' (who, in 17 of the poems, is joined by ''Mr. Bones''), I do not read the poems as songs, nor can I read many of them as dreams; and I read Henry and Mr. Bones as being no more than playful half-masks for John Berryman, Halloween masks covering only the eyes and part of the cheeks. In a strange way, the poems do not mean anything much; that is, their value comes not from any ideas or emotions or experiences or things they refer to and derive from; it comes from the virtuosity of the poet. They are pure poets' poems: even one with few devices and disguises is still so contrived (in the best sense) that the anguish

which the poem may be about affects the reader less than the poet's artifice.

George P. Elliott. *Hudson Review*. Autumn, 1964. p. 458

Basically both *Mistress Bradstreet* and *Dream Songs* are memory pieces, historical complements. In the first Berryman simultaneously affirms and denies the faith of our fathers; in the second he stumbles about the shards. *Mistress Bradstreet* is the old America, the puritan symmetry, ritual, and worldly disgust, reset with the Songs of Solomon. *Dream Songs* is where we are now: a finky sophistication, unexpiated guilt, those collision-course thrills the American dream assumes. The dream itself is a tyrannical cliché, a vaudeville for Fort Knox. Again and again, interpreting the American scene, past or present, Berryman, even with all his highly individualized tics, takes on its contrary pulls, its mocking lawlessness and hidebound creeds. There is throughout all of Berryman a double movement, a wrenched, wistful backing away and sticking close: Berryman, the artful dodger, in love with the enemy, the pop world's loony pursuits; and Berryman, the shut-in scholar, accumulating the saving remnants. . . .

Robert Mazzocco. *New York Review of Books*. June 29, 1967. p. 14

A case could be made, I think, for the thesis that sexual curiosity and the writer's need to find a self outside his own skin are the driving force behind this poem [*Homage to Mistress Bradstreet*]. It rises to its highest points when his imagination is entirely released toward the satisfaction of his curiosity—that is, when he not only envisions Anne's physical experience but identifies with it and, as it were, finds her language for her. The passionate climax at the center of the poem, in which the two poets are imagined in a transport of discovery of each other, through speech and through love, creates Anne as in a frenzy of desire and guilt. The naive fantasy in which the poem begins has now become a vision of the torment of religious conscience in conflict with sexual need. . . . The physical ardor and stormy melancholy of Anne, and her death-horror that makes itself felt more and more forcibly, are a means for Berryman to objectify his feelings more simply than he does through the several voices of the *Dream Songs*—which are, after all, only private voices despite his attempt to keep them distinct.

M.L. Rosenthal. *The New Poets: American and British Poetry since World War II* (Oxford). 1967. pp. 129–30

Despite career-long unevenness in the quality of his work, John Berryman has become a major American poet, has achieved a permanency that places him in a group with Theodore Roethke and Randall Jarrell. Berryman, it seems to me, has taken on the whole modern world and has come to poetic terms with it. At the same time he has taken on himself, and has come to poetic terms with that too. He has seen the wreck of the modern world (or, better, the modern world insofar as it is a wreck) and the wreck of his personal self in that world. He is not a pessimist but has, rather, what we would have to call a tragic view of human life—with good reason for holding it. Yet, not surprisingly, the tragic view finds its complement in a comic view, his wild and so often devastatingly effective sense of humor. He is preeminently a poet of suffering and laughter.

William J. Martz. *John Berryman* (Minnesota). 1969. p. 5

The minstrel show was both a genuine kind of folk art and popular entertainment in nineteenth-century America, and a crowning symbol of the oppression of the Negro because it reduced him to the role of comic sycophant. Berryman's use of it is effective because it brings up automatically both the American past and contemporary issues of race, civil rights, and the like; perhaps more important, it also represents the poet as exploited entertainer (though with multiple ironies, romantic and other), making jokes out of his gruesome and harrowing experiences.

The *Dream Songs* are very varied and attractive, often dramatic, with much humor and a vivid awareness of the surfaces (as well as the depths) of contemporary life. There is a ''Lay of Ike'' and a ''Strut for Roethke'' and other satiric and nostalgic ones; and there are confessional poems about breakdowns, fears of nuclear war, and the like. . . . But, as the title confesses, there is no unifying structure. In most of them, the method is essentially the same as that of *Homage to Mistress Bradstreet*, a double point of view in which the poet is partially identified with the dramatic character in the past but also retains his focus on the present. But while with *Homage to Mistress Bradstreet* there was the external narrative of Anne Bradstreet's life to serve as framework, with built-in aesthetic and larger relevances in the facts of her being the first American poet and a Puritan, there are no such points of reference in *The Dream Songs*.

Monroe K. Spears. *Dionysus and the City* (Oxford—N.Y.). 1970. pp. 248–9

I always thought his earlier poems, with their surface jumpiness, had no metric at all, or scarcely any; they move, not with the basic, consistent cadence of essential poetry but only with their own meretricious push and thrust of hyperbolic and unexpected phrasing. They move, stiltlike, on Berryman's peculiar rhetoric. Now in the new poems [*Love & Fame*], where the language is simpler, I see my feeling confirmed, for with a modified rhetoric the lack of meter is more than ever obvious. . . .

As for diction, we have on the one hand Berryman's well-known colloquial cuteness . . . and on the other his deliberate archaisms, inversions, the use of fusty words like ''moot'' and ''plaint.'' Archness, what we used to call the sophomoric: in parts of *The Dream Songs* he almost brought it to a pitch intense enough to make an honest effect. . . . Yet must ''fresh idiom'' mean ''twisted and posed''? And does language ever add to ''available reality''? We know the danger of that old fatuity; and doubly dangerous it was for Berryman, I think, because it led him, in its arrogance and his own, to infer, by transversion or contraction or mere muleheadedness, that *poetry* as well as verse might be manufactured if only one could invent a fresh idiom in language twisted and posed. This is an oversimplification, more would need to be said in any comprehensive discussion of Berryman's work, but it is still very close to the heart of the matter; and the proof, I believe, lies on every page of his books.

The time has come, surely, to say that Berryman's poetry is usually interesting and sometimes witty but almost never moving,

and that in spite of its scope and magnitude it lacks the importance that has been ascribed to it in recent years by many critics, editors and readers.

Hayden Carruth. *The Nation*. Nov. 2, 1970. pp. 437–8

Delusions, Etc. was already in proof when John Berryman jumped off a bridge in Minneapolis onto the frozen Mississippi last January. So there is no question of its being a ragbag of uncollected work hastily gathered up as a memorial. The book is as he wanted it, the order of its poems and the emotional emphasis all his. Which seems to point to the fact that, up to the end, he was fighting against the way of dying he finally chose. For the emphasis is on the faith he had regained after 43 years away from the Roman Catholic Church. So *Delusions, Etc.* begins and ends on a religious note, as though to defend himself against his own depression.

In all truth, it is not the religious note of a genuinely religious man. Berryman's poems to God are his least convincing performances: nervous, insubstantial, mannered to a degree and intensely argumentative. It is as though he had continually to reassure himself of his belief, or to reassure the Deity if He happened to be listening. There is, of course, a distinguished tradition for this kind of verse: John Donne and Hopkins, Berryman's great hero, were continually arguing with God in the tone of voice of men who knew that there was a lot to be said on both sides. But Berryman had a quirkier sensibility, less rigorous and logical than associative, diffuse, at times a bit scatterbrained. . . .

As the middle sections of *Delusions, Etc.* show, his real gift was different, less armored, less comforting and emerging only slowly in his maturity. Essentially, it was a gift for grief. He had always been a poet of profound unease, touchy and irritable, as if his nerve ends were too close to the surface.

A. Alvarez. *New York Times Book Section*. June 25, 1972. p. 1

No other poem in the twentieth century possesses the scope, the complexity, the grief and joy of life, in quite the marvelous and meaningful way that Berryman's *Dream Songs* does.

For all its wonder, *The Dream* Songs took its toll on Berryman. Not only was the composition of it long and painful, but also its completion signaled for him, I think, the end of his most ambitious poetic work. There was no way at fifty-four that he would ever write another long poem, and despite the fact that he published two collections of poems after *The Dream Songs—Love & Fame* (1970) and the recent, posthumous *Delusions, Etc.*—he was, at his death in January 1972, engaged in writing a novel, collecting a group of his literary essays for publication, and preparing to launch into his long-in-progress critical biography of Shakespeare—all worthy literary endeavors yet none requiring the talents of the poet.

If *Love & Fame* and *Delusions, Etc.* do not add significantly to Berryman's stature as a poet, they do provide some excellent individual lyrics and, more importantly, further perspectives on the themes Berryman developed in his major works.

Larry Vonalt. *Parnassus*. Fall–Winter, 1972. p. 182

[Berryman] was a full professor now, and a celebrity. *Life* interviewed him. The *Life* photographer took 10,000 shots of him in

Dublin. But John's human setting was oddly thin. He had, instead of a society, the ruined drunken poet's God to whom he prayed over his shoulder. Out of affection and goodwill he made gestures of normalcy. He was a husband, a citizen, father, a householder, he went on the wagon, he fell off, he joined A.A. He knocked himself out to be like everybody else—he liked, he loved, he cared, but he was aware that there was something peculiarly comical in all this. And at last it must have seemed that he had used up all his resources. Faith against despair, love versus nihilism had been the themes of his struggles and his poems. What he needed for his art had been supplied by his own person, by his mind, his wit. He drew it out of his vital organs, out of his very skin. At last there was no more. Reinforcements failed to arrive. Forces were not joined. The cycle of resolution, reform and relapse had become a bad joke which could not continue.

Saul Bellow, Foreword to *Recovery* by John Berryman (Farrar). 1973. p. xiv

There was nothing to keep Berryman from going on with *The Dream Songs*. Two appeared in his posthumous volume; and a thousand more might have come out in his lifetime. Henry might have grown into a public figure like Mr. Dooley, airing his moods and opinions from day to day before an audience that had learnt what to expect. In the way of general ideas and moral insights Berryman has little that is fresh to offer. Neither is he a phrase-maker, nor a magician with words. It is emblematic that a child-hood disease should have weakened his hearing, because his ear for rhythm is undistinguished. For all his talent and learning. Berryman could not come near the intellectual style of Auden or the middle-aged Lowell. Once he had circulated the most sensational facts of his private life, his richest treasure was the ironic drama of Henry's diary.

So it strikes one as a hero's mistake that Berryman should have turned his back on this invention and chosen a simpler exploitation of auto-analysis for his last two books. . . .

The coherence of the last books cannot replace the pleasures of *The Dream Songs*: their deliberate humour and indirection; view-points that never stand still; a tone that hops from aspiration to bathos. In the last poems, the strongest humour seems unintention-al; it would be cruel to deal seriously with their serious argument; their inarticulateness is painfully artless. Having discovered that his sensibility could bewitch us, Berryman made the error of growing solemn about it; and the reader's attention must move back from the poet's attitude to his mind.

It is somehow fitting that his final book should find its noblest moments in a tribute to Beethoven since Berryman took seriously the idea of "the mysterious late excellence which is the crown/of our trials & our last bride" (*Dream Song*), an excellence that he admired in Yeats, Williams, and Goya, as well as in Beethoven. That his own last books are not among his most impressive is, of course, distressing, and we are left with the inevitable speculations about where his art would have taken him had he chosen to live—he was, after all, only fifty-seven when he died. Whether he would have gained "the crown of our trials" is impossible to say, though *Delusions, Etc.*, which seems to be the product of a mind at the end of its tether, suggests that this is unlikely. The only thing we can be certain of, however, is that he would have surprised us with an altogether unexpected mode—he never repeated himself, each of his books being as different from the one that precedes it as that

book, in turn, is from its immediate predecessor. Who would have predicted that *Delusions, Etc.*, would follow *Love & Fame*, that *Love & Fame* would emerge from the *Songs*, that the songs themselves would be the next step after *Mistress Bradstreet*? Anyone willing to speculate on the sort of work Berryman might have written in his sixties (or seventies!) is either clairvoyant or reckless.

What we do know, of course, is that his final books, whatever their virtues (and these, particularly in the case of *Love & Fame*, are considerable), represent a falling off from his strongest work. We should not regret their existence, however, disappointed as we may be that they are not more consistently fine. Nor should we, in our haste to evaluate Berryman's overall achievement, attach undue importance to these rather desperate works. To do so would be to lose sight of the fact that this man, whatever his personal and aesthetic crises, gave us the *Sonnets* and *Homage to Mistress Bradstreet*.

Joel Connaroe. *Hollins Critic*. Oct., 1976, pp. 11–12

The "typical" Berryman poem presents a character radically at odds with his environment who, through a process of suffering and self-examination, comes to a realization of the importance of either love or work or both. In both cases it is the character's responsibili-ty to the culture which is rescued from the threats of irresponsibility (on the personal level, usually sex, drink, aggression or the desire for death; on the cultural level, aggression in any number of forms). Stated in other terms, Berryman's characters go through a process of rebellion and submission, finding, however, in that submission a means of triumph. The world doesn't change (or changes in only relatively minor ways), but the character finds a satisfactory means of adapting to it. Mistress Bradstreet, Henry, and the Berryman of the late poems submit to the needs (and joys) of the family and the will of God.

This is grossly oversimplified, of course, and stated so simply leaves out much of what makes Berryman's poetry valuable. For such simple solutions are not and cannot be arrived at simply, and it is the presentation of the enormous and complex difficulties, caused by both internal and external factors, that distinguishes Berryman's work. . . .

Gary Q. Arpin. *The Poetry of John Berryman* (Kennikat, 1978), pp. 10–11

Almost from the beginning of his work on *The Dream Songs*, Berryman felt urged to confer a structure upon the poem. He succeeded best in commending certain models to the interest of its unfolding. Provoked by what he took to be the conventional exigencies of the long poem, he tried to inject a plot into material which had little intrinsic narrative direction apart from that of the natural order of events. . . . He wanted to submit the Songs (the sections of the poem) to the discipline of sequence and succession. He felt it important for them to imply a story. Continuity alone, whether of form and style, or of the creative life which the Songs composed, was just not enough. His aim was to impose an absolute form on a poem constituted by multiple occasions. . . .

He could not help looking ahead, however, trying to anticipate the nature of the work. He needed to control the direction of its progress (which was a type of wanting to control his own life), not to surrender it; to project its plot (and then to enforce it), rather than to allow it self-definition. The effort to chart the poem to a determinative point was in most respects a losing one, for its true character was that of chance, of segmented insights, and of occasional lucubrations. While working on his second volume of Dream Songs in 1966, Berryman told Jonathan Sisson that *His Toy, His Dream, His Rest* "has to be composed out of whatever I save." The statement may be seen as tantamount to an admission that his structural principle was one of elimination, of chance and discovery. During the following year he gave all his time to writing more and more Songs, with the result that Book VII came to be seriously (and perhaps pointlessly) distended with sections ordered and written more on the principle of a diary. Because of that difference of approach, the work as a whole is unbalanced and desultory in structure.

John Haffenden. *John Berryman: A Critical Commentary* (New York Univ. Pr., 1980), pp. 6–7

The central experience of *77 Dream Songs* is certainly that of loss. Berryman himself, looking back from the perspective of the later dream songs of *His Toy, His Dream, His Rest*, described Henry as "a white American in early middle age sometimes in blackface, who has suffered an irreversible loss" (Prefatory Note). Just what the "loss" is, however, is not a simple question. Like Hamlet's notoriously mysterious motivation, for which there is no clear "objective correlative," the loss that motivates Henry's *Weltschmerz* is never definitely located, though there are a number of possibilities hinted at in different "series" of poems: the loss of sex or love, the loss of religion, the loss of friends and fellow poets. . . .

This despair, which is not motiveless but certainly in search of adequate motivation, is the real mystery of Berryman's later work, and it consumes the literate pose of his persona. Somewhat paradoxically, our best insights into its cause come not in the fully realized poems about Henry, but those poems where Berryman drops the mask and speaks of what is transparently his own grief. The death wishes and suicidal hints come into focus when Berryman forces himself to consider the event in his life no pose could ironize or mitigate, the suicide of his father. Significantly, the penultimate poems . . . deal with his father's death and Berryman's inability to come to terms with it.

Jeffrey Alan Triggs. *South Dakota Review*. Summer, 1988, pp. 61, 67

Berryman's poetry, as he says of T.S. Eliot's, is "grievous and profound beyond a single poet's." As for readers, they "will have to follow, wherever, wherever." Berryman's making, unmaking and remaking of sound, sense, and self, his ferocity and tenderness; his songs, satires, petitions, lamentations, and blues require adept readers. His world is Cervantine, Shakespearean, and Joycean. Like Walt Whitman, the American poet he most resembles, Berryman delights equally in tragedy and comedy. He is proud and humble, learned and primitive, nervy and nervous, fantastic and realistic. His characters are victims and masters, self-pitying and brave, lecherous and loving, responsible and irresponsible, alienated and connected. He takes quite literally Coleridge's definition of the "secondary Imagination" that "dissolves, diffuses, dissipates, in order to re-create." He is a poet of Keatsian "Negative Capability" in which the poet, as Keats says, "is capable of being in uncertainties, mysteries, doubts, without any irritable reaching after fact and reason." He believes that intensity, in Keats's words, is "capable of making all disagreeables evaporate."

Charles Thornbury. *John Berryman: Collected Poems 1937–1971* (New York: Farrar, Straus & Giroux, 1989), pp. xviii–ix

Consider what Berryman did with language "twisted and posed." He provides some leads to sources, such as blackface dialogue, the torturous verbal knots and density of Hopkins's terrible sonnets, jazz and the blues, Shakespeare (especially *King Lear* and *The Tempest*), languages he received already twisted, needing to be twisted again and "posed"—that is, given a context and set off. These hints about what went into his linguistic recipe are interesting enough, but more so is what he does not mention, sources such as Krazy Kat, archie and mehitabel, the Katzenjammer Kids, and Pogo, all richly endowing the daily scene of his times with comedy and satire. They contribute a zaniness of language, comic rebelliousness, freshness, and color to Berryman's poetic medium. Whether they make some contribution to the stock of "available reality," however, depends in part on how one perceives the grounding of these popular works in fantasy, escape, and the absurd—all to be expected in works of popular culture. Tristan Corbiere, an influence Berryman enthusiastically acknowledged, belongs perhaps to this group.

In the list of motives for writing poetry referred to above Berryman insists that poetry takes place "out near the end of things," where life and language (whatever) can be made or remade—that is, transformed, *changed*.

Manly Johnson. *World Literature Today*. Summer, 1990, p. 424

The same qualities that made Berryman a brilliant teacher—attention to detail, an authoritative voice, the willingness to do his homework—also made him an outstanding literary critic, as can be seen in the posthumously published collection *The Freedom of the Poet* (1976), which gathers essays, lectures, reviews, and even short stories originally written over a thirty-year period. The earliest piece, on Yeats's plays, first appeared in the *Columbia Review* in 1936, when Berryman was still an undergraduate. . . .

That Berryman was deeply serious about literature is proven on every page of this book. He has as much contempt for nonserious writing, for "the popular boys," as he has admiration for the real thing—and the real thing is, by its nature, intellectual. . . .

Clearly Berryman himself was an intellectual; one of the most impressive characteristics of his critical writing is how well and how completely he did his homework. In areas that I am able to judge, the record is striking. . . .

The problem of the artist's relationship to his audience is, for Berryman, an especially tricky one in America. It may well be that serious art is an elite, rather than a popular, preoccupation—elite in the sense that one must have both intelligence and education to understand and appreciate serious works of art. Berryman makes it very clear that this is his perspective in his essay on Ring Lardner. . . . As Berryman says, "It is a disconcerting feature of much American literary art that either it's so closely bound up with the world of popular entertainment that the boundaries are not easy to fix, or else. . . it has no relation to the world at all.''. . .

It may well be that John Berryman himself succumbed to some of these dangers late in his own career. He loved to be treated as a celebrity, gave indiscreet interviews to large-circulation magazines, and even wrote a series of poems (in *Love & Fame*) that seem more nearly addressed to a popular than a serious audience.

> Peter Stitt. In Richard J. Kelly and Alan K. Lathrop, eds. *Recovering Berryman: Essays on a Poet* (Ann Arbor: Univ. of Michigan Pr., 1993), pp. 45–46, 55

Berryman's major achievement in short fiction is ''Wash Far Away,'' drafted in the 1950s but discovered and published only after his death. The title is from Milton's ''Lycidas,'' a text that figures prominently in the story. Along with *Recovery*, ''Wash Far Away'' is Berryman's most extensive prose treatment of the theme of loss and regeneration, and whereas the novel treats of experience late in its author's life, the partially autobiographical story draws to an event that took place early in his career as a writer and teacher. In 1939 Berryman met and summered with Bhain Campbell, a fellow aspiring poet, and the two men taught and roomed together, along with Campbell's wife, during the 1939–40 academic year at Wayne University (later Wayne State) in Detroit. But by late 1940 Campbell was dead from cancer. The loss was a major one, and the character of Hugh in the story is largely modeled on Campbell. This biographical parallel adds a third layer to the text, a story of a man dealing with loss while attempting to teach one of the great poems of loss. . . .

Awareness of a dead self and the desire for reinvigoration matters, for ultimately the teacher's challenge is not so much to conquer loss as it is to find self-significance. . . . In the process of coping with loss, a rebirth of self has begun. Berryman repeatedly alludes in his unpublished papers to what he saw as a clear connection between loss and freedom, death, and rebirth.

> Ernest J. Smith. *Studies in Short Fiction.* Summer, 1993, pp. 313–16

BIBLIOGRAPHY
Poems, 1942; *The Dispossessed*, 1948 (p); *Stephen Crane*, 1950 (b); *Homage to Mistress Bradstreet*, 1956 (p); *77 Dream Songs*, 1964 (p); *Berryman's Sonnets*, 1967 (p); *Short Poems*, 1967; *His Toy, His Dream, His Rest*, 1968 (p); *Homage to Mistress Bradstreet, and Other Poems*, 1968; *The Dream Songs*, 1969 (p); *Love & Fame*, 1970 (p); *Delusions, Etc.*, 1972 (p); *Recovery*, 1973 (n); *The Freedom of the Poet*, 1976 (s, e); *Henry's Fate, and Other Poems*, 1977; *We Dream of Honour*, 1988 [letters to his mother]; *Collected Poems 1937–1971*, 1989

BIERCE, Ambrose (1842–1914?)

His stories are their own justification. We may not agree with the method that he has chosen to use, but we cannot escape the strange, haunting power of them, the grim, boding sense of their having happened—even the most weird, most supernatural, most grotesquely impossible of them—in precisely the way that he has told them. . . . Mr. Ambrose Bierce as a story teller can never achieve a wide popularity, at least among the Anglo-Saxon race. His writings have too much the flavour of the hospital and the morgue. There is a stale odour of mouldy cerements about them. But to the connoisseur of what is rare, unique, and very perfect in any branch of fiction he must appeal strongly as one entitled to hearty recognition as an enduring figure in American letters.

> Frederic Taber Cooper. *Bookman.* July, 1911. pp. 478–80

There was nothing of the milk of human kindness in old Ambrose; he did not get the nickname of Bitter Bierce for nothing. What delighted him most in life was the spectacle of human cowardice and folly. He put man, intellectually, somewhere between the sheep and the horned cattle, and as a hero somewhere below the rats. His war stories, even when they deal with the heroic, do not depict soldiers as heroes; they depict them as bewildered fools, doing things without sense, submitting to torture and outrage without resistance, dying at last like hogs in Chicago, the former literary capital of the United States. So far in this life, indeed, I have encountered no more thorough-going cynic than Bierce was.

> H.L. Mencken. *Prejudices: Sixth Series* (Knopf). 1927. p. 261

With his air of a somewhat dandified Strindberg he combined what might be described as a temperament of the eighteenth century. It was natural to him to write in the manner of Pope: lucidity, precision, ''correctness'' were the qualities he adored. He was full of the pride of individuality; and the same man who spent so much of his energy ''exploring the ways of hate'' was, in his personal life, the serenest of stoics. The son of an Ohio farmer, he had no formal education. How did he acquire such firmness and clarity of mind? He was a natural aristocrat and he developed a rudimentary philosophy of aristocracy which, under happier circumstances, might have made him a great figure in the world of American thought. But the America of his day was too chaotic.

> Van Wyck Brooks. *Emerson and Others* (Dutton). 1927. p. 152

In his stories . . . the events are narrated with restraint, the descriptions have no excessive details, for the various details are ''constituents'' of the atmosphere and nearly every word is necessary for the realization of the detail. As a rule, Bierce aims to obtain the total and enduring effect by means of atmosphere, and in many stories it would be unsafe to say that the narrative has greater importance than the impression or the conviction that he wishes to ''flow'' from the stories; in some instances, he allows us to view an action from several points of vantage. He has a delicate sense of the shades of meaning and of strength in words; therefore, he puts the right word in the right place. The style, in brief, is excellent.

> Eric Partridge. *London Mercury*. Oct., 1927, p. 637

If his name lives, it is within the range of probabilities that it will be as a tradition of wit, courage and decency. Whatever judgement may be passed on his work, it does not affect the important fact that Bierce was one of the most provocative figures of his generation. One cannot reflect on the facts of his life without coming to entertain an admiration for his splendid courage and indomitable spirit. To those of us in the West who have watched the fate of his reputation with a peculiar and personal interest, it has always been a source of satisfaction to realize that dead, absent or unknown, he has survived his critics and that he has even bettered his enemies who pursued him into Mexico, ''to feast on his bones.''

Carey McWilliams. *Ambrose Bierce* (Boni). 1929. p. 335

The fame of Ambrose Bierce ultimately will rest upon his literary work as a whole. That his distinction as an author is not confined to his short-stories alone is apparent, for his fame as a writer was firmly established before any of them were written; they but extended his renown. To be sure, I hold these stories to be the greatest ever published in any language. . . . But Bierce was a great artist in all that he wrote; he was no better in one branch of literature than he was in another, poetry excepted—and his verse that was not poetry was yet the best of verse. So numerous were his literary activities, embracing so many classifications of literature—more classifications well done than any other author in all time achieved— that I find it impossible to isolate any one classification and say that his fame will endure mainly because of his contributions to that particular field.

Walter Neale. *Life of Ambrose Bierce* (Neale). 1929. pp. 453–4

Rejecting violently the novel, realism, dialect, and all use of slang, humorous or otherwise, Bierce stood firmly for the short story, romance, and pure English produced through intense, self-conscious discipline. Bierce was first and foremost a disciplinarian. He placed great emphasis on the technique of fiction and verse. He was constantly eager to be correct, and to see that others were correct even in the details of punctuation. . . . He sought, like Poe, to make a single vivid impression upon the reader. To that end he eliminated all extraneous references. Furthermore, each story is a complete world in itself, controlled by the writer's logic, not by the illogicality of life. Since Bierce saw no point in reproducing the flat tones of ordinary life, he found an interesting topic only in the impingement of the extraordinary or the unreal on the normal course of events.

C. Hartley Grattan. *Bitter Bierce* (Doubleday). 1929. pp. 118, 121–2

If it be objected that Poe's characters seldom seem lifelike, what must be our objection to Bierce? They have absolutely no relevant characteristics that strike us as human, save their outward description; it is never for the character's sake but always for the plot's sake that a Bierce story exists. Bierce was interested, even more than Brown, Poe, or Melville, in the *idea* of the story—seldom in the human significance of it. In fact some of the stories exist essentially for the whiplash ending, which in Bierce's handling antedated O. Henry. But the Bierce story can be reread with some profit for there is real evidence of a technician's hand.

George Snell. *AQ*. Summer, 1945. p. 51

It is fitting that someone should be born and live and die dedicated to the expression of bitterness. For bitterness is a mood that comes to all intelligent men, though, as they are intelligent, only intermittently. It is proper that there be at least one man able to give penetrating expression to that mood. Bierce is such a man— limited, wrong-headed, unbalanced, but in his own constricted way, an artist. He will remain one of the most interesting and eccentric figures in our literature, one of our great wits, one of our most uncompromising satirists, the perfecter of two or three new, if minor genres: a writer one cannot casually pass by.

Clifton Fadiman. *Saturday Review*. Oct. 12, 1946. p. 62

Along with Poe, Bierce was one of those rare birds in American literature—a Dandy in Baudelaire's sense of the term. The Dandy opposes to society, and to the human world generally, not some principles but himself, his temperament, his dreamed-of depths, his talent for shocking, hoaxing, and dizzying his readers. An aesthetic Enemy of the People, Bierce exploited whatever was most questionable in his personality, dramatizing his sense of guilt and perdition in theatrical horrors and a costume of malice. . . . Out there in his West Coast newspaper office Bierce was somehow seized by the hypnosis of evil and defiance that has inspired so much of modern literature from symbolism to Dada and Surrealism.

Harold Rosenberg. *The Nation*. March 15, 1947. p. 312

Like Swift he was driven by a passion for clarity; he simply could not write a muddy sentence. Like Swift, too, he was obsessed by a fierce determination to be precise and was, so to speak, a lexicographer by instinct. Not only does the *Dictionary* contain the best of Bierce's satire but it also reveals some of his underlying preoccupations.

Most readers of *The Devil's Dictionary* are so entertained by Bierce's wit that they fail to notice the recurrent themes. Politics, for example, was high on the list of subjects that most frequently engaged his attention. Bierce lived and wrote in a period when American politics were turgid, fatuous, and corrupt—the period from ''the bloody shirt'' through ''rum, romanism and rebellion'' to ''Remember the Maine!'' An idealist by temperament, he had recoiled violently from the bombast and corruption of the post-Civil-War decades. He liked to convey the impression that he regarded practical politics with complete disdain. But almost single-handedly he defeated the attempt of the Southern Pacific Railroad to make a final raid on the federal treasury—in the fight over the so-called Funding Bill in 1896—and in doing so had a strong case made for the public ownership of railroads.

Carey McWilliams. Introduction to *The Devil's Dictionary* by Ambrose Bierce (Hill and Wang). 1957. p.vii. [1952]

While Bierce was read and admired by many another writer, it is difficult to see his work as a direct influence on the journalistic style of later practitioners, few of whom possessed his skill. The same factors which formed his techniques—the cynicism which allowed him to live with conditions he felt himself powerless to affect; his fascination with words and their syntactic combinations as opposed to straight reporting styles—could have led others to imitate him unconsciously. But the imitations, conscious or unconscious, lacked Bierce's distinguishing mark, the tone of arrow-like contempt, because they were assumed as an artificial way of dismissing the troubles of the world. Bierce's tone was a natural outgrowth of a personality so shocked by war that it held itself together only by the compulsive demonstration that meaningless slaughter contained all the meaning there was.

Larzer Ziff. *The American 1890s* (Viking). 1966. p. 170

It was his precise recollection of atmosphere, the limpid clarity of his description of physical setting that gave his Civil War stories such a startling air of realism. Mencken considered him the "first writer of fiction ever to treat war realistically." Certainly he was the first to show that heroism had no place in the scientific slaughter which war had become even in his time. Both in his short stories and in his nonfictional sketches he conveyed the reality of Shiloh, Stones River, Chickamauga, Kenesaw Mountain and Franklin as no other writer has. . . .

If he is rediscovered in the near future, it will likely be as the first notable exponent of black humor in America. Prudish as he was in anything written for publication, he would be offended at inclusion in such raffish company. Anything bordering on the pornographic evoked an outcry for rigid censorship and harsh penalties from Bierce. Today's black humorists could, however, meet him with profit. He is their natural father.

Richard O'Connor. *Ambrose Bierce* (Little). 1967. pp. 5, 7

Bierce's tales of war are not in the least realistic; they are, as he doubtless intended them to be, incredible events occurring in credible surroundings. Triggered like traps, they abound in coincidences and are as contemptuous of the "probable" as any of Poe's most bizarre experiments. Bierce's soldiers move in a trance through a prefigured universe. Father and son, brother and brother, husband and wife, collide in accidental encounters. The playthings of some Power, they follow a course "decreed from the beginning of time." Ill-matched against the outside forces assailing them, they are also victimized by atavistic ones. Bierce's uncomplicated men-at-arms, suddenly commandeered by compulsive fear or wounded by shame, destroy themselves.

Yet each of Bierce's preposterous tales is framed in fact and touched with what Poe called the "potent magic of verisimilitude." Transitions from reality to surreality seem believable not only because the War was filled with romance and implausible episodes but also because of the writer's intense scrutiny of war itself. The issues of the War no longer concerned him by the time he came to write his soldier stories. They had practically disappeared in the wake of history. But the physical and psychological consequences of constant exposure to suffering and death, the way men behaved in the stress of battle—these matters powerfully worked his imagination, for the War was only meaningful to Bierce as a personal experience. If war in general became his parable of pitifully accoutered man attacked by heavily armored natural forces, the Civil War dramatized his private obsessions.

Daniel Aaron. *The Unwritten War* (Knopf). 1973. p. 184

It was not simply that [Bierce] had learned to despise social ideals of any sort, and to have "a conscience uncorrupted by religion, a judgment undimmed by politics and patriotism, a heart untainted

by friendships and sentiments unsoured by animosities." More than this, the world, as he perceived it, took on a threatening aspect; like the musket ball, it attacked his head, his reason. The terrain of reality which he plotted—he was a topographic officer—he saw filled with traps. Where others saw a handsome prospect, he saw danger lurking and always assumed that beneath pleasing appearances was a threatening reality. He was convinced, in short, that reality was delusory. By emphasizing mind he attempted to preserve mind, always threatened by physical obliteration or mental deception; he defended the mind, and in doing so, took as his major theme the *growth of reflection*, the compulsion to scrutinize and observe.

This might have been a tragic theme, for reflection leads to a deeper and deeper penetration of delusion and at last to the conviction that all is delusion—that, ultimately, as Bierce said in a late letter, "nothing matters." Reality, Bierce did conclude in *The Devil's Dictionary*, was "the dream of a mad philosopher," the logical product of irrational minds, and therefore absurd—"the nucleus of a vacuum." But he treated this conviction comically, and employed humor to expose the absurdities of his deluded contemporaries and the institutions delusions created and perpetuated. In short, he preserved his own mind by ridiculing the crazed world that questioned his sense and sensibility.

Jay Martin in *The Comic Imagination in American Literature*, ed. Louis D. Rubin, Jr. (Rutgers). 1973. p. 196

BIBLIOGRAPHY
The Fiend's Delight, 1872 (fables and aphorisms); *Nuggets and Dust*, 1872 (fables and aphorisms); *Cobwebs from an Empty Skull*, 1874 (fables) (printed in 1893 as *Cobwebs*); *The Dance of Death*, 1877 (e); *Tales of Soldiers and Civilians*, 1891 (s); *The Monk and the Hangman's Daughter*, 1892 (n); *Black Beetles in Amber*, 1892 (p); *In the Midst of Life*, 1892 (n); *Can Such Things Be?* 1893 (s); *Fantastic Fables*, 1899; *Shapes of Clay*, 1903 (p); *The Cynic's Word Book*, 1906 (printed in 1909 as *The Devil's Dictionary*); *A Son of the Gods*, 1907 (s); *The Shadow on the Dial*, 1909 (e); *Write It Right*, 1909 (c); *Collected Works*, 1909: I *Ashes of the Beacon— The Land Beyond the Blow—For the Ahkoond—John Smith, Liberator, Bits of Autobiography*; II *In the Midst of Life*; III *Can Such Things Be?*; IV *Shapes of Clay*; V *Black Beetles in Amber*; VI *The Monk and the Hangman's Daughter—Fantastic Fables*; VII *The Devil's Dictionary*; VIII *Negligible Tales—On With the Dance— Epigrams*; IX *Tangential Views* (e); X *The Opinionator* (c); XI *Antepenultimata* (e); XII *In Motley—King of Beasts—Two Administrations—Miscellaneous*; *My Favorite Murder*, 1916 (s); *A Horseman in the Sky*, 1920 (s); *The Letters of Ambrose Bierce*, 1922; *Ten Tales*, 1925 (s); *Collected Writings*, 1946; *The Enlarged Devil's Dictionary*, 1967; *The Ambrose Bierce Satanic Reader*, 1968 (j); *Complete Short Stories*, 1970; *Selected Works*, 1973; *Twenty–One Letters of Ambrose Bierce*, 1973; *Skepticism and Dissent: Selected Journalism from 1898–1901*, 1980; *A Vision of Doom: Poems*, 1980; *The Civil War Short Stories of Ambrose Bierce*, 1988; *One of the Missing: Tales of the War between the States*, 1991; *The Moonlit Road, and Other Ghost and Horror Stories*, 1998; *A Sole Survivor: Bits of Autobiography*, 1998

BISHOP, Elizabeth (1911–1979)

Elizabeth Bishop is spectacular in being unspectacular. Why has no one ever thought of this, one asks oneself; why not be accurate and modest? Miss Bishop's mechanics of presentation with its underlying knowledge, moreover, reduce critical cold blood to cautious self-inquiry. . . . With poetry as with homiletics tentativeness can be more positive than positiveness; and in *North and South* a much instructed persuasiveness is emphasized by uninsistence. . . . At last we have someone who knows, who is not didactic.

> Marianne Moore. *The Nation.* Sept. 28, 1946. p. 354

The augury of Miss Bishop's early poems has been fulfilled in a small body of work which is personal, possessed of wit and sensibility, technically expert and often moving.

The distinction of the poetry. . . has been most often its insistence on the opacity and impenetrable presence of the object, whose surfaces will yield, to a pure attention, not sermons, but details. . . . The happiest consequence of this kind of work will be the refreshment it affords the language (which becomes impoverished by the moralizing of descriptive words) and the sense it gives of immense possibility opening; as if from playing checkers we now come to chess, we delightedly may foresee combinations endlessly intricate, and the happier for going beyond the range of conscious intention a good deal of the time. But there are consequences less cheerful as well: one of them is triviality, or you may call it the want of action, where the poem never becomes so much as the sum of its details and so, in two senses, fails to move; another closely related, is the inspired tendency to believe all things possible to a clever precision and a dry tone.

> Howard Nemerov. *Poetry.* Dec., 1955. pp. 181–2

Miss Bishop's world is opulent, but in the most unexpected and most humble ways. As a poet, she gives order to this opulence. She enumerates it. She stabilizes the shudder, the nerve, the reflection, the pleasure and the irradiation. . . . In this poetic world there is nothing merely invented. There is no fantasy and no delirium. There are embellishments, in the best tradition, but what is embellished is always true. What is sanctioned is what has been found to be authentic. . . . Elizabeth Bishop is a partisan in the world.

> Wallace Fowlie. *Commonweal.* Feb. 15, 1957. p. 514

She never moralizes. She is not interested in the abstract truth at the end of the road, but in the concrete truths that lie along the way—the shape of a tree, the look of gently broken water in the morning sunlight, or the appearance of an old fish half-in half-out the boat. Her truths are the truths of a bowl of peaches by Cézanne, a wheat field by Van Gogh, a lady playing the lute by Ter Borch. The reader must therefore be interested in the manner in which she selects or "filters" her subject, in the tonality she achieves, in her massing of the details into significant form. Her best poems do reveal moments of vision, but she inserts them so unpretentiously amid carefully and skillfully selected objective details that a careless reader easily misses them. Her vocabulary, too, is so utterly free from pomposity that its accuracy and suitability to the occasion is not at first

apparent. Only rarely is she obscure, but on these rare occasions it is an obscurity arising from reticence rather than from a desire to mystify or to conceal lack of thought. She never forces a poem beyond its limits, nor herself to assume a pose that is unnatural. In this lies her strength, a strength with limitations.

> James G. Southworth. *College English.* Feb., 1959. p. 214

Elizabeth Bishop is modest, and she is dignified. Because she is modest, she has not presumed to assign to her artistic sensibilities an importance incommensurate with their value. Hers may be a minor voice among the poets of history, but it is scarcely ever a false one. We listen to it as one might listen to a friend whose exceptional wisdom and honesty we gratefully revere.

Because Elizabeth Bishop is dignified she has been reluctant to fling her troubles at the world; she prefers always to see herself with a certain wry detachment. As a result, her poems are occasionally artificial; there is sometimes a coy archness which undermines the strength of her deeper perceptions. On the other hand, her tone savors more good manners than of mannerism. She would not insult us as she tells us the often unflattering truth. . . .

Elizabeth Bishop is a realist, but she sees miracles all the time. In her poems it is as if she were turning again and again to say to us: "If man, who cannot live by bread alone, is spiritually to survive in the future, he must be made to see that the stuff of bread is also the stuff of the infinite." The crumb which becomes a mansion in "A Miracle for Breakfast" is more than a clever poetical conceit. It is a symbol of hope in a world which can be bearable—for some mysterious reason—in spite of its evils.

> Anne Stevenson. *Elizabeth Bishop* (Twayne). 1966. pp. 126–7

Already, when her first book, *North and South*, was published in 1946, she was the tourist, the curious, sympathetic and delighted observer of place and custom, animal, and person, and the interaction between them which gave them identity and character. Now, twenty years later, she still has the eye for detail, the capacity for detachment, the sense for the right word and the uncanny image, and the mental habit that imposes order, balance, and clarity on everything she sees. But this third book [*Questions of Travel*] holds more yet: a greater richness of language, a grasp of proportion and progression that makes every poem appear flawless, and an increased involvement between the "I" of the traveler and the "it" and "thou" of landscape and stranger. As the sense of place becomes ever more insistent, the questions of travel are asked more openly and urgently, including the final, inevitable one: where is home? Miss Bishop does not provide answers. Her eagerness to discover, examine, and celebrate "the sun the other way around" exists for its own sake: her answers are the poems themselves.

> Lisel Mueller. *Poetry.* Aug., 1966. p. 336

Questions of Travel is her first collection since 1955, and it shows her at the full maturity of her powers. There are 19 poems, many of them first-rate—it's not a term that comes easily—and there is a long prose story of childhood, "In the Village," whose wide-eyed lucidity charges details with emotions and meanings.

Miss Bishop's method astonishes with its flexibility; within plain wrappers, it registers an extraordinary range of experience. It can deal with Trollope's journal, or the life of the slums of Rio; it can face death in Nova Scotia, control the rainy season in a metaphor, take a close look at virtually anything, and tell the fantastic story of the Amazonian villager who decides to become a witch. The method—since it is a vision—suits itself to a variety of forms, to the ballad or the sestina, to the quatrain and to the stanza built of rhythms that refine and elaborate those of casual speech. In short, Miss Bishop can entertain artificialities without losing her directness; her genius is for seeing clearly. This book is a formidable achievement.

Gene Baro. *New York Times Book Section*. March 26, 1967. p. 5

[Bishop's] poems often resemble short stories both in the way that she weds action to visual detail, and in the way she makes characters emerge clearly from very few details. She creates people out of scraps of their conversation, pointing it affectionately and ironically with her rhythms . . .

These forty-four poems [*Selected Poems*] show how much she has developed in the twenty-five years they cover. The lines tend to get shorter as she becomes more economical with her adjectives and in "At the Fishhouses" she starts moving out from the immediate experience—an encounter with an old fisherman—to more general questions. . . .

In the later poems, her canvases get bigger and the interrelationships between characters and their physical environments subtler. In the Mexican poems, the sound is no more resonant than before, but the meaning is. Her analyses go deeper and she comes more to evaluate experiences at the moment of describing them, sometimes, as in "Questions of Travel" by the simple expedient of asking what she'd have missed if she hadn't had them.

Ronald Hayman. *Encounter*. July, 1968. p. 71

The poems in *Questions of Travel*, and some of the new poems first printed in *The Complete Poems* are so clear they seem spoken by someone fresh from dreams, just awake. Many of them describe a country where the truth is almost as strange as dreams and to which the forms of legend and ballad ("The Riverman"; "The Burglar of Babylon") seem entirely appropriate. Humble figures are described in an understated, humorous fashion, and yet take on a mythical air, like the tenant Manuelzinho or the seamstress who grows to be like one of the Fates, Cloth nourished in their midst. But nothing is overdone or beyond the daily exercise of composing oneself. Here, I think, is the point at which Miss Bishop's poems are most provocative. Finally their technique is the opposite of the poetic journal, Lowell's latest urgent attempts at registering character in verse. Registering, transmitting, is the *Notebook*'s strongest effect, these poems which end in blazing nightmares, clear vision frayed by underground warnings. Miss Bishop's instinct—from which so much of the modern poetic interest in character derives—is something else: without ever abandoning the feelings of the moment, continually aware, constantly using verse to master the flood of the particular, she writes poetry to compose rather than expose the self. Doing that, her *Complete Poems* makes us alive again to what poetic *composition* is—both something private and something shared.

David Kalstone. *Partisan Review*. Nov. 2, 1970. p. 315

Elizabeth Bishop is constantly brought back to the particularities of earth: thus she is "contemplative." Yet her poems also demonstrate a search for understanding, for transcendence, for epiphany. She is a meditative poet. "Sandpiper," then, is strangely different from Blake's poem to which it alludes. For Bishop is more likely to find in grains of sand simply the marvel of various color (as the sandpiper does at the end of her poem) than she is "the world" as does Blake. Such "worlds" as those of color and infinite variety which the sandpiper sees in the sand do become for him transcendent "minute and vast and clear." Even with her apparent search for "vision," however, Bishop is much more likely to see the properties in a wild flower in some new way which provides self-understanding than she is to see them as "heaven," as does Blake—who is certainly the more visionary of the two poets. . . .

What characterizes Elizabeth Bishop's sensibility is a coalescence of realistic description and personal imagination. Her poetry results from a careful process of "looking." Such seeing is reflected in her accurate images. Experienced as maps to her own experiences, however, Bishop's poems emerge as a record of her own manner of seeing things as they are and more often than not of the carefully evolved epiphanic insights into their particular meaning for her.

Sybil P. Estess. *Southern Review*. Autumn, 1977, pp. 721, 726

Admiring action, there may be behind Bishop's poems a fear of passivity in itself: the reduction of the status of the observer to that of the excluded. If one were to try to station the writer behind a movie camera in these poems, it would be hard to say from just what angle the movie was being shot. The object is everything, the viewer and the viewer's position—except by inference—the merest assumption. Yet how remarkably consistent that lens is, how particularly keen the eye behind it! There is a great deal to be said for scope, but more to be said, I think, for the absolutely achieved. These poems strike me as ageless; there are no false starts, no fake endings. None of the provincial statements of youth, none of the enticements of facility are allowed to enter. Starting with "The Map," we are in the hands of an artist so secure in the knowledge of what makes and doesn't make a poem that a whole generation of poets—and remarkably different ones—has learned to know what a poem is through her practice. She has taught us without a shred of pedagogy to be wary of the hustling of the emotions, of the false allurements of the grand. Rereading these poems, how utterly absent the specious is! There is no need to revise them for future editions, the way Auden revised and Marianne Moore revised and Robert Lowell revised. Nothing need be added, nothing taken away. They constitute a body of work in which the innovative and the traditional are bound into a single way of looking. From a poet's point of view, these poems are the ones of all her contemporaries that seem to me most to reward rereading.

Howard Moss. *World Literature Today*. Winter, 1977, p. 33

The dignity and precision of Elizabeth Bishop's poetic delivery rely largely upon her imagery of detachment, an imagery that takes interior dilemmas and expresses them in terms of the exterior world of nature. In *Questions of Travel* such imagery draws the individual poems into a recognizable unity not only by physical recurrence, but also, more importantly, by complementing and interweaving the major themes. These themes (or, alternately, the dilemmas or questions of the title) include the permanent realm of the potential in human life, the puzzles of epistemology, and the temporary resolutions of the imagination. Corresponding to these themes, the categories of imagery are, respectively, images of transformation, of frames, and of suspension. Despite my abstract nomenclature, the imagery, by which I mean the entire physical world presented in the poem and not just its figurative language, consists of quite concrete, often ordinary objects. For instance, the imagery of transformation revolves mainly around water; of frames, around colors; and of suspension, around birds. Very rarely do the birds, colors, or water grow into deliberate symbols; instead, they serve more humbly as indicators of the interdependence of theme and imagery.

Ruth Quebe. *Modern Poetry Studies*. 10, 1, 1980, p. 68

In the last years of her life, Elizabeth Bishop wrote poems that reflected a new belief in naturalistic narrative, stories that weave together dream states and old conversations, and a return to the ancient riddles of identity and human isolation. Published three years before her death in 1979, *Geography III* sounds something of a valedictory note, and yet it rehearses a familiar theme with renewed vigor: the tonic value of dreams. Practicing a secular form of rememberment and salvage, the poet initially looks backward to a child's first unsettling awareness of her body and then forward through evocations of lost love, to rueful intimations of mortality. Midway in this lyrical journey, Bishop stops to remember the way grandparents "talked/in the old featherbed" about "deaths and sicknesses," about friends who "died in child-birth" or "took to drink" or lost their sons "when the schooner foundered." The voices that first found their way into her dreams now find a place in her art, and they go on and on, "talking in Eternity" ("The Moose," *Collected Poems*, 171–72).

The foundered schooner, the shipwrecked life, or troubled mind is the burden, the ever-present bass line that runs through the poet's compositions. Against this central theme, Bishop introduces the sound of quiet affirmation and endurance. Muted, it can be heard in every crafted line, in each preserved detail from the past, but it comes through clearly, unmistakably, in "The Moose," a poem twenty years in the making.

Marilyn May Lombardi. *The Body and the Song: Elizabeth Bishop's Poetry* (Carbondale: Southern Illinois Univ. Pr., 1991), p. 218

To the figure of the moralist lurking in her mind and work, Bishop also added the figure of the scientist, and did this quite naturally and with fairly little fuss. In Bishop's love of patient description we have a persuasive example of a Wordsworthian wise passivity, of a Keatsian negative capability; in her fidelity to the ideal of the scholar-dreamer-artist content to bring to bear all of one's human resources of eye, hand, and mind to the chosen task, she resembles the best of her predecessors, her aesthetic generously syncretic. Like the sun that shines in her "Large Bad Picture," no matter what the worked intention of the artist may turn out to be, Bishop's governing principle of light is "comprehensive and consoling."

Her fondness for Darwin's minute attentions testify to the enlarging effect of the dedicated mind. In Bishop's preoccupation

with small, successive acts, we seem to be given a license to join a series of words like *small, understated, determined, modest*, and so on: the words weave a moral figure that goes on the one hand, back to the religious energies of the wealth of the harvest that springs from the mustard seed, and on the other back to Blake's romanticism. She may have mocked Blake with her scatterbrained sandpiper, and feared the disintegrative forces that a myopic obsession with the grains or atoms of life can summon. Yet this fear seems countered by the awesome release of powers that Blake describes in his "Auguries of Innocence" as "a World in a Grain of sand [. . .] Infinity in the palm of your hand / and Eternity in an hour." Bishop's cool pragmatism, skeptical self-possession, and determined secularism, however, prevent any lifting abstractions from drift or dilution. Yet it is finally a transfigurative energy that Bishop recognizes. In her crucial description of that slide into the unknown, that "self-forgetful, perfectly useless concentration" that is, after all, the moment of epiphany, it seems important to recognize the large and generous view of human effort that her words, all of her words, imply.

Lorrie Goldensohn. *Elizabeth Bishop: The Biography of a Poetry* (New York: Columbia Univ. Pr., 1992), p. 286

Why object relations? It has been my contention that this revisionary psychoanalytic model offers a particularly advantageous method for reading poetry. Specifically, I argue that reading Bishop through object-relations theory yields a number of insights; foremost among them, an understanding of the psychodynamics of literary influence relations as they work themselves out between Bishop and her most formidable predecessor, Marianne Moore. In addition to the individual insights provided through such an approach, one can discern a larger, revisionist conceptualization of poetic influence through the lens of object relations. Particularly, one can understand the workings of influence not in the agonistic mode of Freudian theory but through the dynamics of gift exchange, the feelings of envy and gratitude that emerge from the originary primal scene, and the infant's nursing at her mother's breast. The conflictual responses that result from this experience— fear that the mother may prove insufficient, pleasure when a reciprocal balance of supply and demand has been reached, anxiety that the breast may be robbed of sufficient resources, bemusement at the site of the feeding and the rejecting breast—all can be transposed to the modulations of literary creativity and the interrelationship between the poet and her literary predecessor. . . .

Consequently, my foregoing discussion of Bishop's "Efforts of Affection" investigates the forces of envy and gratitude that operate in the daughter-poet's psyche as it traces the rhetorical strategies Bishop evokes to negotiate her way between the potentially destructive power of envy and the rehabilitative force of gratitude. The bemusement Bishop experiences when she meditates on Moore is itself useful, Klein would argue, for it allows Bishop the space afforded by *misrecognition*, thus enabling Bishop to survive the ambiguous double binds of a mother who simultaneously gives and withholds.

If envy and gratitude are the primary, polar emotions that dominate the originary site of poetic influence, then related feelings of loss, mourning, and reparation govern literary productivity itself. At the heart of Bishop's work lies a desire to make restitution, to find a compensatory gift that will make up to the wounded, abandoning mother all that her daughter has paradoxically lost. The desire to make reparations stems from the interior need to replenish the self, to find a way to survive the first and most crucial loss, that of the mother. Any writer's work may thus be read as the product of the desire to make reparation. Interestingly, Bishop makes this search for reparation itself the *theme* of much of her strongest work as she delineates the longing that finds it origins in her sense of loss. . . .

Object relations, however, offers us more. By investigating the interpsychic processes that govern a writer and her precursor, we can begin to decipher patterns that illuminate our own experience as readers. For all of us, as readers, are affected by the formative process of life at the mother's breast. The individuating psychodynamics of one reader-writer's (in this case, Bishop's) relation to her parent and her parental texts affords us access to the processes that inform reading relationships more generally. If we understand reading as a process of reparation, a revisionist procedure of re-making what we read, then analysis of that process of revision enables us more accurately to assess the distinctive psychic life of any individual reader. Reading Bishop reading Moore, therefore, enables us to pinpoint more precisely than heretofore not simply Moore's and Bishop's mutual poetic origins, but the specific turns that differentiate Bishop from Moore, thereby shedding light on the distinctive workings of Bishop's *intrapsychic* life.

Finally, reading Bishop through Moore enables us to trace an alternative paradigm to male, modernist tradition, a paradigm based upon a female-centered model for literary influence that traces the processes of influence relations in terms of the pre-Oedipal stage, thereby acknowledging the primary importance of the mother and hence the literary foremother.

> Joanne Feit Diehl. *Elizabeth Bishop and Marianne Moore: The Psychodynamics of Creativity* (Princeton: Princeton Univ. Pr., 1993), pp. 106, 108–10

The world of the adult, even more than that of the child, is beguiling but unsettlingly diverse. Though most comfortable generating poetry from domestic images of her childhood, Bishop, like other perceptive people, was drawn to subjects, images of people and landscapes, language, and themes best defined by their otherness. How she explores this material, and the problem of why her poetry about African-American and Brazilian folk life compares poorly to her portraits of North American ancestral provincials are the issues of this chapter. From the perspective of her mastery of the conventions of English-language poetry, Bishop re-invents herself in an alien context. Working from romantic-modern traditions and expectations established by Wordsworth, Emerson, Hopkins, [W. C.] Williams, and Frost, including the reinvigoration of the pastoral mode, she attempts to advance her grasp of dailiness to illustrate, if not penetrate, aspects of culture from which she remains emotionally estranged. She juxtaposes familiar cultural images and constructs with those of the exotic cultures of Key West and Brazil, and, in the process, generates tropes of self-realization in which she herself becomes "more truly and more strange." She becomes an "experience-distant" field-worker attempting to illuminate what Clifford Geertz has called "concepts that, for another people, are experience-near."

Bishop eventually reverses interior and anterior stances and learns to see herself as an alien (as the section titles of *Questions of*

Travel suggest), a perpetual guest. The self-realization, however, earned in the struggle with an unmoored childhood and migratory adulthood furthers that quest for the fully grasped moment, which would be accomplished only in "Crusoe in England." The challenge of these poems of provincial relocation, as with much of her work, is to transcend romantic conventions of the picturesque and the sublime and exact a language adequate to reconstitute, in a deconstructive landscape, a viable self-realization. Yet like Adrienne Rich's attempt to identify herself with an American slave (see "From an Old House in America"), Bishop's gestures would often be troubled by what Aldon Nielsen in *Reading Race* has labeled "presumptive identification[s]" with the "racial other."

> C.K. Doreski. *Elizabeth Bishop: The Restraints of Language* (New York: Oxford Univ. Pr., 1993), pp. 102–3

Within the dialogue of her translations Bishop discovers intimate guides to Brazil. Likewise, her own writing about Brazil, where cultural and political differences meet, asserts in its tones, structures, and thematic insights that representation is in part a collaborative effort. Her relationships extrinsic to the writing, with a Brazilian poet, friend, or guide, make vitally complex her enactment of subject-subject relationships within the piece. Just as Ruy led Bishop repeatedly to revise her impressions during their trip to Vigia, and the community watch for the burglar on the loose as well as her research on the socioeconomics of Rio framed her ballad, so her outsider's distance from the voices along the Rio São Francisco or in the Brazilian mines colored her representations of these experiences. Within the ballad, then, Bishop's double point of view allows her to set the observing burglar beside the observing rich, for a moment erasing the difference that seems so inevitably to divide them. Within the story, Bishop-as-tourist converses with Ruy-as-guide, each investing the desires and interpretations of the other with the shades of his and her difference. Alert to the situatedness of speakers and subjects throughout her writing on Brazil, Bishop may not hear the words being called by the "maddening little women" or the squatter's children at play, but her poems inevitably concern themselves with the dynamics that bind and distance her speakers and her subjects in relationships of power, possession, and love.

> Victoria Harrison. *Elizabeth Bishop's Poetics of Intimacy* (New York: Cambridge Univ. Pr., 1993), p. 182

The publication of Elizabeth Bishop's *Selected Letters* [in England, *One Art*, ed. Robert Giroux] is a historic event, a bit like discovering a new planet or watching a bustling continent emerge, glossy and triumphant, from the blank ocean. Here is an immense cultural treasure being suddenly unveiled—and this hefty selection is only the beginning. Before the millennium is out, Bishop will be seen as one of this century's epistolary geniuses, like that modernist Victorian Gerard Manley Hopkins, whom she lovingly admired and learnt from. . . .

The long, competitive love which existed between Bishop and Lowell, the parabola of her relationship with Marianne Moore, are the best examples in *One Art* of this dynamic textuality. Very many letters derive their fascination from this type of dialogic energy—a momentary, sometimes momentous communicativeness that stretches them like soap bubbles sent up into the sunlight of unrepeatable relationships where each letter occurs as a historic moment whose taut nowness can be immensely exciting.

Tom Paulin. *TLS: The Times Literary Supplement.* April 29, 1994, p. 3

For most of her writing life, Elizabeth Bishop was known for not wishing to be known. Where other poets muscled their careers to centerstage, she hovered in the wings. Where others importuned their audience with news of their private sorrows, she remained impressively tight-lipped. A near-contemporary of the so-called confessional poets, poets such as Robert Lowell and John Berryman, she once said of them: "You just wish they'd keep some of these things to themselves."

"Closets, closets and more closets" was Bishop's response to the gay liberation movement. Her friends knew that she was lesbian, and also that she was alcoholic, but she herself liked to believe that each of these dispositions was a secret. Certainly her poems gave no clues. And since Bishop spent most of her career outside the United States, mostly in Brazil, and took little part in homeground literary politics, there was not much word of mouth to go on. Her geographical self-exile seemed perfectly in tune with her habits.

Ian Hamilton. *New Republic.* Aug. 8, 1994, pp. 29, 34

BIBLIOGRAPHY
North and South, 1946 (p); *Poems: North and South & A Cold Spring*, 1955; (with the editors of *Life*) *Brazil*, 1962 (t); *Questions of Travel*, 1966 (p); *The Ballad of the Burglar of Babylon*, 1968 (juv); *The Complete Poems*, 1969; *Geography III*, 1976 (p); *The Diary of "Helena Morely,"* 1977 (tr); *The Complete Poems, 1927–1979*, 1982; *The Collected Prose*, 1984 (m, s); *One Art: Letters*, 1994; *Conversations*, ed. George Monteiro, 1996 (interviews); *Exchanging Hats*, ed. William Benton, 1996 (paintings)

BISHOP, John Peale (1892–1944)

His tradition is quite evidently aristocratic. He prefers the fine, the delicate, the rare in character or in performance. Several of the poems have to do with the aristocracy of the South. I do not think, however, that one can accuse Mr. Bishop of snobbery. Through the poems runs the realization that, regardless of preference, the time has come when the fine flower of aristocracy is decadent, that terrible though this process may be, aristocracy must now be reinvigorated by contact with more primitive and ignorant class-es. . . . He shrinks a little from the common herd, but he does not entirely deny them.

Eda Lou Walton. *The Nation.* Feb. 7, 1934. pp. 162–3

There is, then, the contemporary preoccupation with styles (not simply style), with metrical forms, and with the structure of the line. But Bishop, of all the modern poets who take this approach,

feels the least uneasiness about a proper subject matter. There is no one subject, no one scene, nor a single kind of imagery coming from a single subject or scene: every poem, as I say, is a new problem. And Bishop feels no inhibition in the presence of any kind of material.

Allen Tate. *New Republic.* Feb. 21, 1934. p. 52

One would surmise, even without the specific information, that his acquaintance with French poetry of the later nineteenth century is immediate, and not second-hand through Eliot and Pound. But it seems that Eliot, Pound, and Yeats have done something to define the precise use Bishop has made of these and other models. And it is not that Bishop has merely re-adapted current techniques; it is that he has written with the same attitudes from which those techniques were developed. The principle of unification to be detected in the attitudes behind the present poems is not so much the unification of a single personality or a philosophy or a fundamental theme, as it is the unification that a period affords its various fashions.

Robert Penn Warren. *Poetry.* March, 1934. p. 345

Mr. Bishop is one of the school of Eliot and Pound; he has the sense of an individual poem as being something as separately well made as a vase or a candlestick, a sense hardly to be found in Jeffers or Sandburg. . . . The range of Mr. Bishop's achievement is not great: a few detached observations sensitively recorded over a number of years; but he understands the meaning of craftsmanship. He knows that for words to take on the illusion of life there must be the precarious marriage between content and form.

F. O. Matthiessen. *The Yale Review.* Spring, 1934. p. 613

I believe that John Peale Bishop has written one of the few memorable novels of this decade (*Act of Darkness*). . . . Mr. Bishop has chosen his material with the same care that he devotes to the writing of a poem; and since he is a poet of unusual sensibility, one finds in his prose an admirable restraint in the use of the so-called "poetic" image and vocabulary. There is fine economy of words in his paragraphs; and by effective inversion of adjectives his prose cadence is of highly individual (but not spectacular) quality. I believe these matters were of concern to Mr. Bishop in the writing of his novel—and not whatever social implications it may contain. He had, however, something to say which was a record of experience, and the fact that he has said it well produced a narrative of continuously exciting revelation.

Horace Gregory. *New York Herald Tribune Book Section.* March 10, 1935. p. 7

This sensitive re-creation of adolescence (*Act of Darkness*), poetic, obviously autobiographical, Proustian in conception although not in style, introduces a new Southern novelist. . . . If I have read the novel aright, it is this: That body and spirit are not one but two that move along parallel lines, supplementing each other to form a track. . . . *Act of Darkness* must by all means be set down as a superior book. There is power behind its sensitivity. And in its best passages this first novel achieves distinction.

Fred T. Marsh. *New York Times Book Section.* March 17, 1935. p. 6

Mr. Bishop is one of the few men now writing in America or elsewhere who recognize the privileges, tests, and ordeals of the aesthetic discipline. . . .The unity in (his) poems derives from his effort to return, after widely eclectic experiences in art and the sophistication of New York and Paris, to his native roots and loyalties, his moral plight as an individual, and to the recovery of his local habitation and a name. . . . Mr. Bishop still respects the impersonal discipline and objective moral sense of his symbolist teachers. His work asks to be considered as poetry before it makes its appeal as a private history or an American document. . . . His work has everything that taste, finish, and conscience can give it.

Morton Dauwen Zabel. *The Nation.* April 12, 1941. pp. 447–8

It is difficult enough to describe Mr. Bishop's essential talent. It is a rather unusual combination of the scholar and the sensualist. The intellectual today likes his learning and the lyricist, of course, loves his love poems. There is a bad separation. Mr. Bishop thinks what he feels, he experiences actually what ideally he knows as a scholar, he can be at the same time serenely intellectual and terribly sensual. . . . He combines one's feeling with one's thinking.

Peter Monro Jack. *New York Times Book Section.* Jan. 4, 1942. p. 5

Bishop's basic theme is the loss of form, the loss of myth, the loss of a pattern. . . . It is true that Bishop's poetry is often poetry about poetry, but then Bishop's conception of poetry is more profound than the man-in-the-street's essentially "literary" conception. The problems of writing poetry and the problems of a formless and chaotic age become at many points identical. . . . Certainly none of Mr. Bishop's problems would be solved by his abandoning his theme. . . . Or by giving up a concern for "form." Indeed, the most successful of Bishop's poems are precisely those which exploit his theme most thoroughly and which are most precisely "formal."

Cleanth Brooks. *Kenyon Review.* Spring, 1942. pp. 244–5

One of Bishop's great merits was to have realized his limitations and, unlike so many other American writers, to have preferred perfect minor achievement to over-ambitious failure. In this way he turned a defect of destiny into an aesthetic virtue. He was that rare thing in American literature, a true type of the second-order writer who, though incapable of supreme creative achievement, keeps alive a sense for the highest values. It is this type of writer whom the French delight to honor, recognizing their importance for the continuance of a vital cultural tradition; and this is perhaps one reason why Bishop felt so powerful an attraction for French culture.

Joseph Frank. *Sewanee Review.* Winter, 1947. pp. 106–7

We have been used to hearing this West Virginian dismissed as *too* typical, i.e., too derivative on the one hand, too immersed in class consciousness (upper level) on the other; yet his essays and poems in their progress . . . amply display an original mind and reveal the generous, passionate, humane personality finally emerging from beneath the successive masks of the "provincial," the dandy, the snob, the ironist. . . . Toward the end, the romantic exile came home to his own idiom, and achieved in his poetry a density of meaning projected with classic purity of tone.

Gerard Previn Meyer. *Saturday Review.* Oct. 2, 1948. p. 24

As a poet he is, perhaps, not obscure; his life was outwardly serene but it conceals a sensibility that was courageously tortured; conditions that look identical seem simultaneously to have hamstrung his talents and set him free. He is infinitely discussable, for he raises (how forcibly I was not aware) the crucial problems of writing now, in America, as well as the adequacy of available solutions. He is more pertinent, both in achievement and mechanism, than, say, Kafka. The achievement matters but the torture is instructive, for it is the torture of the creative will, persistently willing to will, but the will being again and again dissipated, and reviving, being frittered or smashed, but always returning.

William Arrowsmith. *Hudson Review.* Spring, 1949. p. 118

BIBLIOGRAPHY
Green Fruit, 1917 (p); (with Edmund Wilson) *The Undertaker's Garland*, 1922 (s, p); *Many Thousands Gone*, 1931 (s); *Now With His Love*, 1933 (p); *Act of Darkness*, 1935 (n); *Minute Particulars*, 1935 (p); *Selected Poems*, 1941; *Collected Poems*, 1948; *Collected Essays*, 1948; *Selected Poems*, 1960

BLACKMUR, R.P. (1904–1965)

Blackmur is preoccupied with pure poetry. . . . His metrics have the individuality of the classic composers of chamber music. . . . The joints of his moods with everyday are thin at times, and one must be alert with utter inner poise to hear or to heed him. A whole page of print, which yesterday opened vistas, today will seem blank until tomorrow it opens wider. Always the subject matter . . . illustrates human subterfuge from oblivion and ruse against the unavoidable futility of existence. . . . Even as he finds home Way Down East and in the Hub where landscape and men exhausted smile and move and speak with grace unknown to their past times of strength, so does he universally at once express and comment upon a cultural decadence.

John Brooks Wheelwright. *New Republic.* July 21, 1937. p. 316

Specifically and primarily, the method can be described as that of taking hold of the words of the poem and asking two very important questions: (1) Do these words represent a genuine fact, condition, or feeling? (2) Does the combining of these words result in "an access of knowledge"? Knowledge in the full sense, one must add, for something must be made known "publicly," "objectively," in terms which any intelligent reader, with the proper effort, can grasp; as distinct from terms and language used "privately," "personally," "subjectively." Now of the two questions, it is the first that Blackmur emphasizes and the second which he often neglects. The discrete parts—sentences, phrases, single words (which are sometimes counted)—are the main object of his attention. The way in which they combine is sometimes an afterthought (though this is less so in the more recent essays).

Delmore Schwartz. *Poetry.* Oct., 1938. p. 30

With a critic like Richard P. Blackmur, who tends to use on each work the special technique it seems to call for, and who at one time or another has used almost every type of criticism, the difficulty of placing any single way of operating as his "method" is obvious. What he has is not so much a unique method as a unique habit of mind, a capacity for painstaking investigation which is essential for contemporary criticism, and which might properly be isolated as his major contribution to the brew. . . . Blackmur is almost unique in his assumption that no demand for knowledge the poet makes on the serious reader (that is, the critic) is unreasonable, and that if he doesn't have the information he had better go and get it.

Stanley Edgar Hyman. *Poetry.* Feb., 1948. pp. 259, 262

The writing . . . is nervous, extraordinarily complex in texture, and urgent with a kind of religious New England cantankerousness that one has scarcely heard in contemporary verse since the too early death of John Wheelwright—not that I mean to imply that Mr. Blackmur derives from Wheelwright (the debt, if it exists, must surely be reckoned the other way around), but that the vibrant originality of the one stirs memories of the other, *discordes concordantes.* . . . I am saying, in short, that Mr. Blackmur, extraordinarily difficult though he can be, is a poet *sui generis*; and the *genus* is rare and important.

Dudley Fitts. *Saturday Review.* March 20, 1948. p. 28

These are poems of the most extreme situations possible, of a constricted, turned-in-upon-itself, contorted, almost tetanic agony: the poet not only works against the grain of things, but the grain is all knots. . . . Sometimes the pain is too pure to be art at all, and one is watching the nightmare of a man sitting in the midst of his own entrails, knitting them all night into the tapestry which he unknits all day. But there is in the poems, none of that horrible relishing complacency with which so many existential thinkers insist upon the worst; the poems try desperately for any way out, either for the Comforter—*some* sort of comforter—or else for that coldest comfort, understanding.

Randall Jarrell. *The Nation.* Apr. 24, 1948. p. 447

Again and again, until it touches a note of hysteria and one wonders at such insistence, Mr. Blackmur speaks out against his anathema—expressive language. He makes constantly an appeal to reason, which in poetry is objective form. . . . The fact is, Mr. Blackmur has been attempting as difficult a critical job as was ever conceived. . . . Perhaps Mr. Blackmur's fearful note is near to the

cry of those who push analysis to the limit of reason. And perhaps, as I think, he has been pushed himself into statements that exceed his purpose, as when he says, for instance, that poetry is "language so twisted and posed in a form that it not only expresses the matter in hand but adds to the stock of reality.". . . Mr. Blackmur arrives, by way of the back stairs, at a sort of higher romanticism, where we children of his prior, or downstairs enlightenment are likely to feel timid or ill at ease.

Hayden Carruth. *The Nation.* Jan. 10, 1953. p. 35

In recent years as a Professor of English at Princeton he has become the fountainhead of a distinctly personal and highly original school of criticism. His standards are high, his language fluent, though sparse, and on occasion recondite, and he pays extraordinary attention to minute detail; his work represents a constant searching of the mind for the highest amount of intellectual pressure and insight it will yield.

During these years Mr. Blackmur has, in reality, gone to the school of his own bold intelligence and allowed himself that free and full "response to experience" he deems to be the first duty of a critic.

Leon Edel. *New York Times Book Section.* April 17, 1955. p. 4

The alienated artist is . . . ordinarily forced into one of two possible roles: that of the lonely prisoner in a personal "ivory tower," or that of a prophet without honor, a rather owlish Cassandra.

To some extent, perhaps, R. P. Blackmur fills both these roles. . . . While he has not abandoned the technique of "criticism of criticism" which is often regarded as a kind of hallmark of modern ivory-towerism, he is essentially engaged in a work of public persuasion, evangelical, almost apocalyptic. . . . Criticism should turn, Mr. Blackmur, believes, from poetry, which, as poetry, seems to him to have declined in value for us, to the novel, which he regards as the most significant literary form now and in the future. The ideal which he sets before the critic is thus a synthesis of Coleridge and Aristotle.

John F. Sullivan. *Commonweal.* May 13, 1955. p. 159

Mr. Blackmur is all these things: poet, rhetorician, evangelist, university teacher, a lover of words, master of a weighted vocabulary. It is surely the poet in him and equally the rhetorician which makes one, reading this book, hate the things Mr. Blackmur hates: formula, methodology, pre-judgement, slogan. And love the things he loves; the acts behind such words as imaginative, plastic, symbolic, responsive, actual, form. It is also the poet in Mr. Blackmur which makes him use, quite freely and without quotation marks, phrases which he has remembered from such writers as Henry James, Melville, Thomas Mann, Ransom, and Santayana: sacred rage; compositional centre; operative consciousness; the sense of life; the shock of recognition; the outsider; a poet nearly anonymous; a philosopher almost a poet. There are other phrases, including 'disconsolate chimera', which appear to be quotations from Mr. Blackmur himself.

Denis Donoghue. *Twentieth Century.* June, 1957. pp. 540–1

In criticizing poetry, his concern is not with pattern but with language. He knows what words or groups of words affect him, and he wants to know why they affect him. He is aesthetic about words and carries them back into the poet's mind and forth into his own with a relished complexity that is as obscure and seemingly chaotic as anything in modern poetry.

Basically Blackmur is an impressionistic critic rapturizing over words and images. However, his raptures do cling to a theory that is worked out precisely as his impressions develop into speculations (which they often do). It is quite possible, to be sure, that the complicated verbiage of his essays fools one into suspecting more precision than is actually present, and sometimes one is startled by a dangerous overemphasis or even a contradiction, but the theory is there and can be described.

Maurice Kramer. *College English*. May, 1961. p. 553

Blackmur has tried to recreate in his own way Arnold's vision of the "future of poetry," first by encouraging against the current of modern pragmatization and secularization a passion and a reverence for sensed mysteries; and second by discovering works of literature, whether for audience or artist, as experiences which put that passion and reverence into formal relation with the sense of the mysteries, with this discovered relation perhaps finally to be considered a kind of "knowledge." It was something as ambitious and esoteric as this that Blackmur had in mind when in "The Lion and the Honeycomb" he wrote, with a rather irrelevant metaphoric humility for one who is nothing if not virtuoso, that the critic as "go-between" ought to disappear "when the couple are gotten together."

Blackmur's first task, to cultivate the mysteries, is very materially aided by his style. Rhythmic incantation, allegorical indirection, the mystical rhetoric of pun and paradox—these are the sorts of techniques creating in his criticism its distinctive aura of priestly and prophetic power.

Richard Foster. *The New Romantics* (Indiana). 1962. p. 98

Beside him, [Allen] Tate and [John Crowe] Ransom are boring indeed, and their styles, compared to his, are never capable of the resonance and suggestiveness that finally is essential to the literary essayist who is only incidentally a critic. From the early pieces on modern poets and the magnificent omnibus reviews now in *The Expense of Greatness* to the Byzantine labyrinths of the later essays on James and Eliot, Blackmur has shown that he can elevate the characteristic gestures of the New Criticism to a self-sustaining art. There is, furthermore, a wit in him which is quite uncharacteristic of the others.

Roger Sale. *Hudson Review*. Autumn, 1962. pp. 478, 480

To identify the tradition that links Blackmur with [Henry] James and [Henry] Adams one could do worse than adopt the term Blackmur himself uses when discussing the 1920s—"bourgeois humanism." This may suggest the New Humanists but Blackmur's struggle with modern literature was not merely polemical like theirs which left them free to dismiss or condemn it. Rather, since he had himself suffered the cultural crises that produced it, he understood how the "malicious knowledges" of the time, notably psychology and anthropology, had undermined man's faith in his rationality, had delivered him over to the "great grasp of unreason," and had set him to inventing the "techniques of trouble." Yet he believed that the great modern writers (particularly Joyce, Eliot, Mann, Yeats, and Gide) managed to create out of the remnants of the humanist tradition an "irregular metaphysics" which secured a measure of control over the irrational forces which had been unleashed.

One of the two major centers of formative power in Blackmur's thinking about America was, then, the literature of the twenties. This book [*A Primer of Ignorance*] shows that the other was his encounter with foreign, mainly European, culture concretized through his sojourns abroad in the 1950s. These provided the finishing touch to his already wide self-education, not changing his fundamental bourgeois humanism, but only "improving" it. What he found when he began to contemplate America in the presence of European culture can be exemplified in the comparison he draws in "The Swan in Zurich" between the New York City Ballet and the Ballet of Sadler's Wells and other European companies: the American troupe's "excessive commitment to mere technique" in contrast to the technical imperfections but greater human warmth of the European performances. This discovery of American devotion to pragmatic abstractions at the cost of the more personalized values and greater cultural density of Europe strikingly corroborates the earlier testimonials of Hawthorne, James, and Adams.

Ernest Sandeen. *Poetry*. Aug., 1968. pp. 357–8

Blackmur was a poet. He published in his lifetime three volumes of verse and hoped that some of his work at least would stand. At present he has almost no readers. At a time when so little poetry is read, it is not surprising that a small voice like Blackmur's should not be heard. Some critics, like Denis Donoghue, in an introduction to a recent collected edition of the poems, regret that we have forgotten Blackmur and urge us to discover the poetry for ourselves. But Donoghue is a fine critic, and even he cannot persuade us that there is much in Blackmur to compel sustained attention. "Sometimes the knowledge in Blackmur's poems is not his own but what he recalls of Hopkins' knowledge," he concedes. Or one hears the music of Eliot, or Pound, or Yeats: "But mostly the knowledge is his own." Perhaps. But then, the issue is not whether Blackmur occasionally broke free of his models and wrote in a voice that sounded more like his own than theirs. The fact is that, even in his best poems, Blackmur sounds more like a man who wants to write poetry than like a true poet. . . .

For Blackmur, ideas could be as interesting as they were for another sort of critic entirely. And he showed, in his later work especially, that politics and cultural institutions could be quite as absorbing to the literary mind as poems or stories. We go on with the question of content here because it is so central to our concern with poetical thinking. The content Blackmur could not honor was a content that was nothing but a sentiment, an attitude or an idea. He was ready to accept that certain ideas were more attractive than others, or that a particular attitude would readily serve the gifts of a particular poet. But in themselves these ideas or attitudes were not the facts that could inspire a final sympathy or allegiance. Eliot's mind was a fact in the more final sense, his better poems an enactment of his sensibility that would stand, permanently, as an emblem of a certain kind of possibility realized. Call it the possibility of a mind divided against itself but working strenuously all the same at a wholeness it associated with utter singleness of purpose.

> Robert Boyers. *R. P. Blackmur: Poet-Critic* (Univ. of Missouri Pr., 1980), pp. 8–9, 64–65

Blackmur's contribution to literature may be found in the form of the critical essays he wrote during the later phases of his career. The Library of Congress essays, in particular, represent the form of the critical essay that marks his unique contribution. These essays were his attempt to raise criticism to a new plane of discourse.

Briefly put, Blackmur attempted to incorporate into these essays an expression of his aesthetic experience of literature and of culture. Thus, in effect, he tried to ''open'' the form of the critical essay by giving equal emphasis to the nonrational expression of his own experience. Prior to Blackmur's practice, critical essayists had always tried to be, with more or less success, proponents of rational thinking. Blackmur, however, made the irrational, the emotional, part of the critical essay. . . .

Blackmur did not mean to discount the rational understanding of his essays. Rather, he sought what he thought should be a *total* experience that included the irrational with the rational. In this desire he was seeking for the art of criticism what modern artists had sought for painting, poetry, the novel, and music. Blackmur did not want his criticism to point to an experience but to *be* an experience. In this way he extended the scope and the form of literary criticism.

In addition to raising criticism to the level of a legitimate art form, Blackmur also contributed a whole body of work that will have permanent value as long as there is a Western culture. Throughout his work Blackmur questioned the lack of standards to judge not only art but life, liberty, and the pursuit of happiness. He was against the democratic inclusiveness of the spirit that meant whatever is done must perforce be ''creative.'' At the same time he agonized over the question of creativity and its manifestations in a democratic, romantic age. In his own work he applied the scrupulosity he admired so much in Henry Adams; that is, he took pains to give his essays a ''form'' as well as a content. Put another way, Blackmur thought he could control unbridled romantic effusions of spirit by insisting upon a rigorous attention to form.

All of his work has a certain tension that derives from this conflict between form and content, reason and imagination. Blackmur fought the same battle that every twentieth-century artist has fought and must fight. His particular art form was criticism, but it could have been poetry or the novel. In the last analysis, his work must be seen as his unique attempt to create order and meaning out of the undifferentiated chaos of the spirit. So Blackmur becomes one with the many who have built their own edifices of meaning through art.

> Gerald J. Pannick. *Richard Palmer Blackmur* (Twayne, 1981), pp. 155–57

BIBLIOGRAPHY

The Double Agent, 1935 (e); *From Jordan's Delight*, 1937 (p); *The Expense of Greatness*, 1940 (c); *The Second World*, 1942 (p); *The Good European, and Other Poems*, 1947; (with others) *Lectures in Criticism*, 1949; *Language as Gesture*, 1952 (c); *The Lion and the Honeycomb*, 1955 (e); *Anni Mirabiles, 1921–25*, 1956 (e); *Form and Value in Modern Poetry*, 1957 (c); *New Criticism in the United States*, 1959 (e); *Eleven Essays in the European Novel*, 1964; *A Primer of Ignorance* 1966 (e); *Poems*, 1977; *Dirty Hands; or, The True-Born Censor*, 1977; *The Revival*, 1979; *Henry Adams*, 1980 (c); *Studies in Henry James*, ed. Veronica A. Makowsky, 1983 (c); *Selected Essays*, ed. Denis Donoghue, 1986; *Outsider at the Heart of Things*, ed. James T. Jones, 1989 (e)

BLY, Robert (1926–)

Robert Bly is one of the leading figures today in a revolt against rhetoric—a rebellion that is a taking up of the Imagist revolution betrayed, a reassertion of much of the good sense Pound brought to poetry—but also a movement which has in it much that is perfectly new. The new is found in a pure form in the work of Robert Bly and of his friend James Wright; it is not an easy aesthetic to describe; it can be found only in a response to their poems. . . .

[Bly's] is a poetry, I decided at last, that returns the reader to its subjects, a poetry of excitement primarily about a certain kind of life and vision to which the poem directs attention rather than stealing attention from that experience. Hence, this work is profoundly dependent upon the nature of reality—it reflects a choice of subjects and a judgment on them as experiences. Although all poets take into themselves parts of the exterior world and put them back in what is, to say the least, a rearrangement, Bly is committed more totally than most poets to their subjects for two reasons. The choice of his images, the excitements, the celebrant realities, is a mannered or narrowed one; and the intensity of that choice is such that it is opinionated—it expresses a judgment about what life and poetry should be. If, then, the poet should be one who rejoices at solitude, nature, the sullen beauty of the provinces and of our history, then as advocate of that vision he is not and cannot be the poet who celebrates sickness, glamorizes Miltown, smog and hypochondria. For Bly—and in this respect he is a visionary—the words of poems are real—they *are* expressways or ditches, cornrows or streetlamps, bathtubs or mailboxes; a poem is a chosen world.

> David Ray. *Epoch*. Winter, 1963. p. 186

Robert Bly's first collection, *Silence in the Snowy Fields*, impresses because of its purity of tone and precision of diction. It is not until we begin to feel that Mr. Bly could do more, when the monotonous simplicity of many of the poems starts to pall and takes on a programmatic character (after all he edits a polemical magazine, *The Sixties*, that we become dissatisfied. This artful diction is heavily indebted to early Stevens . . . but we miss the cunning backdrop that the simpler poems of *Harmonium* surely have. . . . Bly's characteristic development is to begin a poem with a simple narrative or descriptive *donnée* and then proceed through modulations more or less subtle, to an overwhelmed, even apocalyptic end.

> D. J. Hughes. *The Nation*. Jan. 5, 1963. p. 17

[Bly] is a poet of Western space, solitude, and silence. He writes poems about driving a car through Ohio, hunting pheasants, watering a horse, getting up early in the morning, and watching

Minnesota cornfields, lakes, and woods under the siege of rain, snow, and sun. His distinction in treating these subjects lies in the freshness of his "deep images," which invest the scene he describes with an intense subjectivity and a feeling of the irremediable loneliness of man, who can never make contact with the things of the world. . . .

It is evident that Robert Bly's theory and practice cohere. His poetic voice is clear, quiet, and appealing, and it has the resonance that only powerful pressures at great depths can provide.

> Stephen Stepanchev. *American Poetry since 1945* (Harper). 1965. pp. 185–7

Mr. Bly's poems . . . divide into poems of the inner and the outer. He does not deal with the relationship of one to the other, or not very often; usually, he writes of each separately and in opposite tones. His poems about present-day America, especially its political life, tend to be harsh and dissonant, and their sadness has a bitterly sharp edge, except for those dealing directly with the inhumanity of the Vietnam war, which are informed by deep compassion. The poems about the inner world, on the other hand, are slow-moving and quietly, intently joyful; they do not wish to come to grips with experience, but rather to let it flow by, to see it without forcing it. Mr. Bly is trying to free his diction of all rhetorical trappings, whether they be of the long-established or the current orthodoxies, in order to write simply, to render "the light around the body," the *feeling* of the experiences unencumbered by any literal setting. The approach is essentially mystical.

> Lisel Mueller. *Shenandoah*. Spring, 1968. p. 70

The Light around the Body is one of the most significant American volumes to be published in years. Maybe literary America is waking up. Maybe it has learned that "inwardness" is not necessarily looking at one's navel, listening to "the way they ring the bells in Bedlam" à la Sexton or tortuously describing the abnormalities of one's aunt or father. The seemingly uncontrollable malignant forces around us do indeed lead us to look inward, but it is at the least sentimental and at the most destructive of the creative self to allow that inward eye complete authority. . . .

There are many poems in the book with obvious and open political content. Such poems as "Those Being Eaten by America" . . . "Smothered by the World," or such poems with specific references to recent and dubious episodes in American history as "Sleet Storm on the Merritt Parkway," "The Great Society," and the whole third section of the book with its poems on the Vietnam war—such poems are not mere propaganda poems, poems like those written freely in the 30's. They are not merely doctrinal. Although they are social protest poetry, they are not simplistic and doctrinaire. They are deeply poetic. They fulfill the needs of art, not those of politics. These poems, it must be remembered, are being written after the symbolists, the post-symbolists, written at a time in all the arts when the chief subject matter is art itself. The aesthetic emphasis is apparent here too, but it is an emphasis not on a sterile impersonality; not on a narrow formalism, or a fetishist autonomy of the work of art; not on disengagement, but on a reality stemming from a concerned, emotional self, inward and released,

and from an outward self, yearning for a "glimpse of what we cannot see,/Our enemies, the soldiers and the poor."

> Harriet Zinnes. *Prairie Schooner*. Summer, 1968. pp. 176, 178

Bly . . . has been in the forefront of the politicalization of contemporary American poetry, and his objectives and his zeal may well have our full sympathy. On the other hand, the apolitical tradition of American poetry since the 1930's has proved very hard to break through. Political ideology and political action have shown a habit of losing the excitement of political oratory in the tight, economic medium of poetry; the effect is often one of simple-mindedness. . . .

Considering the odds Bly is facing, his performance is admirable. . . .

The Light around the Body marks an advance over *Silence in the Snowy Fields*. The advance is perhaps most economically described as a success of subject-matter. There is an attractive and contagious commitment about these poems which occasionally gives rise to a grim, grotesque humor which was absent from the earlier poems. . . .

The best of Bly's poems . . . achieve an original expression of his personal gloom and his sorrow for a world which "will soon break up into small colonies of the saved."

> G.A.M. Janssens. *English Studies*. April, 1970. pp. 128–31

For those who recognize that it is nations and not individuals that make war, Robert Bly's new book may be the best examination of our motives during the debacle in Vietnam. *Sleepers Joining Hands* looks at the dominion of chaos and death over recent American life and tries to discern its whole meaning, as if at last we have got far enough into it or beyond it to understand what happened, and as if we will not be devastated again by any more surprises. . . .

He can speak quietly of terrible things in a way that produces genuine chills. . . .

The spectacle of power is beautiful, and Bly can illustrate by the ominous unleashing of it that man's frail moral nature is inadequate for the enormous consequences of his acts. Bly can show, calmly, literally, how we writhe to defend our minds against this tragic knowledge, rationalizing, denying and generalizing our sins until viciousness appears demanded of us and we drive ourselves toward insanity.

> David Cavitch. *New York Times Book Section*. Feb. 18, 1973. pp. 2–3

Bly is . . . the mystic of evolution, the poet of "the other world" always contained in present reality but now about to burst forth in a period of destruction and transformation. Bly's poetry of the transformation of man follows logically from his early poetry of individual and private transcendence. Repeatedly, *Silence in the Snowy Fields* announces an "awakening" that comes paradoxically in sleep, in darkness, in death, an awakening depicted in surrealist images as compelling as they are mysterious, evasive. Bly's sense of mystical transformation is not really completely articulated until, primarily in the 1967 collection, *The Light around the Body*, it achieves an apocalyptic dimension, the awakening no longer individual or private, but part of the spiritual evolution of the race.

This general awakening, like the analogous experience of the isolated mystic, comes in the long dark night of a dying civilization. The poems of ecstatic prophecy in *The Light around the Body* achieve much of their force by juxtaposition with the poems of political despair which dominate the collection. Constantly and convincingly Bly suggests that the psychological impact of Vietnam on America is as destructive as the physical presence of America in Vietnam. . . .

But the confluence of physical and psychological or spiritual in Bly is most striking when he depicts the paradoxically evolutionary aspects of apocalypse, apocalypse now considered not as end but as process.

Anthony Libby. *Iowa Review.* Spring, 1973. pp. 112–3

The late 20th century converges on Robert Bly from every side. In *Sleepers Joining Hands*, there is a seething cauldron of ecological devastation, genocide in Vietnam, Consciousness III, the long shadow of the Indian wars, the changing roles of the sexes. He is peculiarly the seer both of the present moment and the possible future.

In a few lines he can catch the essence of vast migrations and enormities. . . .

Alive and terrifying as this poetic vision is, in some ways it is surpassed by the long prose section which adduces vast amounts of anthropological evidence to prove that all societies were originally matriarchal, and that the Great Mother (including the castrating type, the Teeth Mother) is reemerging into the consciousness of Western man after being suppressed for millennia.

Chad Walsh. *Book World.* April 1, 1973. p. 13

The stimulus injected by Robert Bly into the poets of the Emotive Imagination has not been solely as translator, editor, and theoretician. *Silence in the Snowy Fields*, a 1962 collection of poems which had appeared earlier over a period of almost ten years in the magazines, was the first volume demonstrating extensively the realized potentialities of the Emotive Imagination. Bly's second volume, *The Light around the Body*, demonstrated his expanding interest in political poetry. The 1973 volumes *Jumping Out of Bed* and *Sleepers Joining Hands* disclose his enduring predilection for the Emotive Imagination, even as the political poems have diminished as a result of America's disengagement in Vietnam.

Bly's success as a poet depends of course on the quality of the individual poems, but . . . his own work has been indisputably shaped by his long interest in and translation of poets like [Pablo] Neruda and [Georg] Trakl. Moreover, his poetry also inevitably becomes a kind of illustration of his own poetics, outlined, as we have also seen, in scores of essays and reviews. When Bly says, for example, that a poem is "something that penetrates for an instant into the unconscious," one expects his own verse to show how that is so. . . .

In the past quarter-century of Bly's publication of poetry, he appears to have found reinforcements of and elaborations upon a fundamental method which sprang up almost at once in his work and which was clearly worked out by the time of his first volume in 1962, *Silence in the Snowy Fields*. He has not departed radically from the use of the Emotive Imagination as we have defined it, and his work, perhaps more than the other poets treated here, represents a continuing and long-range experimentation with its resources.

Most of Bly's poems are whimsical and minor; they have no pretensions of being anything else. Frequently his political verse manages to go little beyond bald propaganda. His poetry finally belongs in the same context as his translations, as well as his criticism and editing. As an indefatigable man-of-letters, in the best sense of the term, Robert Bly has been a vital phenomenon in American poetry since mid-century.

George S. Lensing and Ronald Moran. *Four Poets and the Emotive Imagination* (Louisiana State Univ. Pr., 1976), pp. 71, 85

My sense of Bly's poetry is that it exhibits the skill it does because of its author's high seriousness, but such a sense can only be averred, not demonstrated. However, we can register the characteristic energy of Bly's lyrics by exploring them as resolutions (not solutions, in the sense of problems disposed of, but resolutions, in the sense of a consciousness articulated) through which two apparently opposing compulsions redefine one another. One of these compulsions is most visible as theme, the other as style. Thematically, the concerns of meditative poetry, namely the structures of consciousness and the relation of fact and value, outline the range and subject of these poems. Poetry for Bly offers a criticism of life, but a criticism available only through discipline, by a rectification of thought and feeling. Bly's antiwar poetry doesn't settle for expressing humanistic values; rather, he alleges that the grossest forms of false consciousness are necessary for such inhumanity as a war to occur and that only through a fundamental relearning of the world can it be prevented. This accounts for Bly's aggressive, sometimes intemperate modernism: he sees the poet simultaneously as a solitary craftsman and as a moral scourge. . . .

What I think Bly's poetry enacts, especially in the strengths and weaknesses of *Camphor*, is the persistent desire of American poets simultaneously to celebrate the body and to incorporate the universal energies, thus making them available to all. How to domesticate the sublime? Bly's answer seems to be to deify the *truly* immediate, that is, the data of consciousness understood not as thought, but as bodily sensation. Bodily presence and process—the purview of natural history, with its emphasis on seeing, on turning the given into a specimen by an act of loving attentiveness to detail and change—thus become equated with bodily ecstasy—the evidence of religion, with its proffered hope that the bodies of men and women can become one body, which will manifest, in a Blakean way, the transforming and divine energies of the universe.

Charles Molesworth. *The Fierce Embrace: A Study of Contemporary American Poetry* (Univ. of Missouri Pr., 1979). pp. 116, 138

The theme of the father-son relationship. . . . [Robert] Bly has discussed in depth what might be seen as the background to the poems in *Black Cat* on several occasions. Here is a summary of his views: "Historically, the male has changed considerably in the past thirty years." The 1950s male "was vulnerable to collective opinion" and "lacked feminine space . . . lacked compassion, in a way that led directly to the unbalanced pursuit of the Vietnam War. . . . Then, during the '60s, another sort of male appeared."

The war "made men question what an adult male really is. And the women's movement encouraged men" until "some men began to see their own feminine side and pay attention to it." Still, the "grief and anguish in the younger males was astounding" and "part of the grief was remoteness from their fathers." Now, "it's possible that men are once more approaching [the] deep male" in the psyche, "the *deep* masculine".... "A few years ago I began to feel diminished by my lack of embodiment of the fruitful male, or the 'moist male'.... The absorption with the mother may last ten, fifteen, twenty years, and then rather naturally, a man turns toward his father."

This focus on the father as the first "transformer" of his son's energies is, ideally, followed by exposure to a "wise old man," who "assumes the role of a shaman" and teaches the boy "artistic curiosity and intellectual discipline values of spirit and soul, the beginnings of a rich inner life." This stage should be followed by an "intensive study of mythology."

> William V. Davis. *Understanding Robert Bly* (Columbia: Univ. of South Carolina Pr., 1988), pp. 137–38

Bly himself is aware of the problem of isolation in such personal poetry, and admits as much in a comment on the *Snowy Fields* poems: "I don't feel much human relationship in these poems, and the hundred thousand objects of twentieth-century life are absent also" (*Selected Poems* 27). He claims that his purpose was "to gain a resonance among the sounds," as well as "between the soul and a loved countryside." This vein being worked, his solution was to follow Neruda toward the "impure" poetry of politics. The Vietnam War, of course, provided his occasion.... In an essay on political poetry, Bly speaks of the need of a poet, once he has fully grasped his own concerns, to leap up to the "psyche" of the nation: "the life of the nation can be imagined ... as a psyche larger than the psyche of anyone living, a larger sphere, floating above everyone. In order for the poet to write a true political poem, he has to be able to have such a grasp of his own concerns that he can leave them for a while, and then leap up into this other psyche." This statement acts both as an apology for the poems of *Snowy Fields* and as a program for the poems of *The Light Around the Body* (1967) and *The Teeth Mother Naked at Last* (1970).

> Jeffrey Alan Triggs. *New Orleans Review.* Fall-Winter, 1992, p. 164

Iron John, then, grows not only out of Bly's experience during the past decade in the men's movement but out of the central meanings of his life.... His devotion to asserting and cultivating the primalness and primacy of the imagination in a highly domesticated and institutionalized literary culture has led him to view the condition of men in similar terms and to apply the learning he has acquired in the archeology and anthropology of the imagination to remedy it. This authority is finally what makes *Iron John* a serious, ground breaking book....

Also, *Iron John* has a lot of specific insight and lore to teach men and employs a very effective method. It takes an old story and gives it a new spin, thereby enlisting the child in us who is still most open to learning and the adult who is keen to escape from his own banality. Along with combining therapy for men, or at the very least clarity, with a course in the world mythology and ethnography

of male initiation, *Iron John* is also a spiritual poetry reading in which the words of Blake and Kabir, Rumi and Yeats and many others join Bly's own poems as a kind of accompaniment to the text.

> Ted Solotaroff. "Captain Bly". In William V. Davis, ed. *Critical Essays on Robert Bly* (Boston: G.K. Hall, 1992), pp. 262–63

Perhaps no one has excited greater single-handed influence on the course of mainstream American poetry since the early sixties than Robert Bly. The rise of creative writing programs coincided with Bly's energetic and broadcast polemicizing on behalf of a vision of a poetry revolutionized, internationalized, and politicized. The simultaneous escalation of the war in Vietnam gave Bly even wider exposure and influence. His essays spoke to a generation impatient with the status quo, irritated at the slowness of change, and enraged at the obduracy of an obsolete establishment. How easy it was to spill politics into poetry; the injustice of the war, of a national posture revealed in the Civil Rights movement, made Bly's message all the more urgent. And it didn't hurt that the ideas he advocated for poetry were easily applied in poetry workshops: focus on the image, on its psychological and political resonance, with little attention to the forms of verse, other than discarding the traditional (what worse condemnation?) trappings of rhyme and meter. Even the models he proposed were tailored to the political climate; Central Americans, Spanish surrealists, wild-eyed and free-spirited political activists or at least licensed outsiders.

Bly's essays are best read in light of this historic context. To this end, the essays bear the date of their initial publication. The essays from the first of the book's three divisions, "Looking for Dragon Smoke," represent his thinking from the sixties through the early seventies, "sum[ming]up," as Bly writes, "the platform of viewpoint of my magazine, *The Fifties, The Sixties,* and *The Seventies*." The second section consists of essays on twelve of Bly's contemporaries, culled from reviews and, in some instances, combining shorter reviews of a poet across a span of many years. Finally, "Educating the Rider and the Horse" concentrates on the evolving shape of American poetry over the past thirty or so years. Most interesting here are the essays, composed in the eighties, wherein Bly levels a critical eye at the workshop mentality's effect on American poetry.

> Allen Hoey. *Southern Humanities Review.* Spring, 1993, pp. 189–90

BIBLIOGRAPHY

Silence in the Snowy Fields, 1962 (p); *The Sea and the Honeycomb*, 1966 (p); *The Light around the Body*, 1967 (p); *The Teeth-Mother Naked at Last*, 1970 (p); *Sleepers Joining Hands*, 1972 (p); *Jumping Out of Bed*, 1973 (p); *Friends, You Drank Some Darkness*, 1975 (tr); *Old Man Rubbing His Eyes*, 1975 (p); *Leaping Poetry*, 1975 (c); *The Morning Glory*, 1975 (p); *This Body Is Made of Camphor and Gopherwood*, 1977 (p); *This Tree Will Be Here for a Thousand Years*, 1979 (p); *Talking All Morning*, 1980 (e); *Truth Barriers, by Tomas Tranströmer*, 1980 (tr); *Selected Poems of Rainer Maria Rilke*, 1981 (tr); *The Man in the Black Coat Turns*,

1981 (p); *The Eight Stages of Translation*, 1982 (c); *A Voyage to the Well*, 1984 (fairy tales, d); *Loving a Woman in Two Worlds*, 1985 (p); *Selected Poems*, 1986; *Waking from Newton's Sleep*, 1986 (e); *Juan Ramón Jiménez: Lights and Shadows*, 1987 (tr); *Tomas Transformer: Selected Poems 1954–1986*, 1987 (tr); *Of Solitude and Silence: Point Reyes Poems*, 1989; *Iron John: A Book about Men*, 1990 (m, e); *American Poetry; Wilderness and Domesticity*, 1990 (c); *Angels of Pompeii*, 1992 (p); *What Have I Ever Lost by Dying?: Collected Prose Poems*, 1992; *Meditations on the Insatiable Soul*, 1994 (p); *The Soul Is Here for Its Own Joy*, 1995 (e); *Hammering Iron*, 1995 (e); *The Sibling Society*, 1996 (e); *Morning Poems*, 1997 (p); *Holes the Crickets Have Eaten in Blankets*, 1997 (p); *The Maiden King: The Triumph of the Feminine*, 1998 (e); *Hunger, by Knut Hamsun*, 1998 (tr)

BODENHEIM, Maxwell (1893–1954)

His verse is Chinese. It does not resemble Chinese poetry; it is not a direct and unfigured commentary on nature; quite the contrary. It is Chinese in etiquette rather, being stilted, conventional to its own conventions, and formally bandaged in red tape. It is a social gathering of words; they have ancestries and are over-bred; they know the precepts of the Law and take delight in breaking them. Meeting together they bow too deeply, make stiff patterns on paper or silk, relate their adventures in twisted metaphor and under an alias, sometimes jest pompously behind a fan. They discovered irony late in life.

Bodenheim is a master of their ceremony and arranges it with an agile fantasy which takes the place of imagination.

Malcolm Cowley. *Dial*. Oct., 1922. p. 446

He has humiliated nouns and adjectives, stripped them of their old despotisms and loyalties, and of the importance which ages of power as vehicles of broad emotions had given them over the minds of poets and men. He has given them the roles of impersonal figures tracing his mathematics of the soul. His words are sharp, neatly strung, with tapping consonants and brief unemotional vowels, like the chip of a fatal chisel. . . . Metaphysics is a man's choice of his own *mise en scene*—in Bodenheim's poems it is an arctic light in which his brilliant images accept their own insignificance as finalities, yet are animated by the macabre elation which has thrown them into relief.

Louis Grudin. *Poetry*. Nov., 1922. pp. 102–4

Here is a ferocious anti-sentimentalist. I am not sure how much of a poet Mr. Bodenheim is. What I am sure of is that his work is honest—honest to the point of mocking at its own honesty—and that it never mistakes a state of sentiment for one of intense feeling. . . . Mr. Bodenheim is, as the stinging acidity of his style betrays, less concerned anyway with feeling than with thought. Life is to him a boundless paradox, an irony of defeat, a bitter act of treachery. Alike in his method of writing, his attitude to society at

large, and his defiant individualism, he reveals the poet preoccupied with moral, rather than aesthetic values.

John Gould Fletcher. *Freeman*. Jan. 30, 1924. p. 502

One has a picture of Bodenheim as ring master, cracking his savage whip over the heads of cowering adjectives and recalcitrant nouns, compelling them to leap in grotesque and unwilling pairs over the fantastically piled barriers of his imagination. It is a good show—particularly for those who have not seen it too often. . . . He is still—if I may take my metaphor out of the circus—the sardonic euphuist; his irony leaps, with fascinating transilience, from one image to another. . . . But, for all his intellectual alertness, the total effect is an acrobatic monotony: what started as a manner is degenerating into a mannerism.

Louis Untermeyer. *Bookman*. April, 1924. pp. 220–1

Though his sensitive feeling for words betrays him sometimes into preciosity, mostly he makes it serve his purpose. For his is an art of veiled and egoistic emotions, in which the immediate subject, be it a lady or a buttercup or the rear porch of an apartment building reflects, like an actor's practice-mirror, the poet's swiftly changing expressions and attitudes. . . . With Mr. Bodenheim it is the one all-engrossing phenomenon of the universe. Standing before the mirror, he is kindled to frozen fires of passion over the ever-changing aspects of his thought in its mortal sheath; he is intrigued—nay, moved to the white heat of ice by the subtle workings of his mind, trailing off from the central unreal reality there visible out to nebulous remote circumferences of an ego-starred philosophy.

Harriet Monroe. *Poetry*. March, 1925. pp. 322–3

His poems frequently testify to the fact that he has had, and that he is capable of emotion; but they are almost never a direct expression of emotions. Rather, they are an analytic recollection of such states of mind; and the effect, in the hands of the curious word-lover that Mr. Bodenheim is, is odd and individual and not infrequently pleasing. In his simpler and less pretentious things, when he merely indulges his fancy, as in ''Chinese Gifts,'' he can be charming. Here the verbalist and the cerebralist momentarily surrender, the colder processes are in abeyance, and the result is a poetry slight but fragrant. But for the rest, one finds Mr. Bodenheim a little bit wordy and prosy. One feels that he works too hard and plays too little; or that when he plays, he plays too solemnly and heavily.

Conrad Aiken. *New Republic*. June 1, 1927. p. 53

To consider Mr. Bodenheim at all is very much like considering a prickly pear; one never knows when he is going to get a thorn run through his finger. Still, like the prickly pear, once the combative surface is pierced an edible and tasty (albeit faintly acidulous) fruit is to be discovered. In other words, Mr. Bodenheim has his values, his poetical accomplishments (of no mean order, either), his impalpable connotations, and his savage satirical zest that is quite often salty enough to delight the victim. Together with his value he has drawbacks. Now these drawbacks are mainly on the surface, as the thorns of the prickly pear are. They are evidenced mainly in an undue suspiciousness of the world at large, in an instinctive gesture of defense that reveals itself in a consistent offensive, in an emphatic disgust for the commonplaces and courtesies of polite living and in a passion for cerebralism that sometimes goes to such lengths as to defeat its objective.

Herbert Gorman. *Saturday Review*. June 18, 1927. p. 912

Maxwell Bodenheim's book of poems (*Bringing Jazz*) might well be used as a starting point for a definition of jazz esthetics. First of all, it provides a particular kind of superlative entertainment that depends almost entirely upon the titillations of jazz rhythm and the impact of a brilliant, quickly assimilated image. . . . Next we see that Bodenheim's specific brand of irony which he has employed throughout his work, including the discovery of the American underworld in his novels, is converted into a jazz medium. . . . In spite of the many attempts to capture jazz rhythm with all its essentials intact and at the same time to create actual poetry, we have but two successful examples of this style, both significant because they display a like precision in technique: T.S. Eliot's ''Fragments of an Agon: Wanna Go Home, Baby?'' and a selection of three or four poems from *Bringing Jazz*.

Horace Gregory. *New Republic*. March 12, 1930. p. 107

Mr. Bodenheim is all personality. He has become a legendary figure of Bohemianism, a vague mixture of Greenwich Village orgies and soapbox oratory. Of course he is neither one nor the other. He is a poet entirely writing about himself and when he seems to be writing about the injustice of the world and the wretched social system of the world he is still writing about himself, as one might almost say, a willing and masochistic victim. He takes upon himself the whole burden of the worker's complaint against the capitalist's way of making his life. . . . His poems are largely a set of grievances, and they have their value. . . . Their value, in so far as it is a value, is in personality, not at all in communism or in religion but in one's self. . . . It is the quick, involved and rude life that Mr. Bodenheim writes of, his own life, not necessarily correlated with the life of our time.

Peter Monro Jack. *New York Times Book Section*. March 29, 1942. p. 4

BIBLIOGRAPHY
Minna and Myself, 1918 (p); *Advice*, 1920 (p); *Introducing Irony*, 1922 (p); *Blackguard*, 1923 (n); *The Sardonic Arm*, 1923 (p); *Crazy Man*, 1924 (n); *The King of Spain*, 1924 (p); *Replenishing Jessica*, 1925 (n); *Against This Age*, 1925 (p); *Ninth Avenue*, 1926 (n); *Returning to Emotion*, 1926 (p); *Georgie May*, 1927 (n); *Sixty Seconds*, 1929 (n); *Bringing Jazz*, 1930 (p); *A Virtuous Girl*, 1930 (n); *Naked on Roller Skates*, 1931 (n); *Duke Herring*, 1931 (n); *Run, Sheep, Run*, 1932 (n); *Six A.M.*, 1932 (n); *New York Madness*, 1933 (n); *Slow Vision*, 1934 (n); *Lights in the Valley*, 1942 (n); *Selected Poems*, 1946; *My Life and Loves in Greenwich Village*, 1954 (a)

BOGAN, Louise (1897–1970)

Under a diversity of forms Miss Bogan has expressed herself with an almost awful singleness. . . . One can be certain that experience of some ultimate sort is behind this writing, that something has been gone through with entirely and intensely, leaving the desolation of a field swept once for all by fire. But the desolation is not vacancy or lassitude. The charred grass is brilliantly black, and the scarred ground is fascinating in its deformity. There still is life, hidden and bitterly urgent.

Mark Van Doren. *The Nation*. Oct. 31, 1923. p. 494

Miss Bogan's themes are the reasons of the heart that reason does not know, the eternal strangeness of time in its period and its passage, the curious power of art. Her mood is oftenest a sombre one, relieved not by gaiety but by a sardonic wit. She is primarily a lyricist. . . . It is the spirit's song that Louise Bogan sings, even when her subject is the body. The texture of her verse is strong and fine, her images, though few, are fit, her cadences well-managed. . . . Implicit in her work is the opposition between a savage chaos and the world that the ordering imagination, whether directed by the intellect or the heart, controls.

Babette Deutsch. *Poetry in Our Time* (Holt). 1932. pp. 238–9

There are bitter words. But they are not harassingly bitter. . . . There are paralleled series of antithetical thoughts, but the antithesis is never exaggerated. . . . There are passages that are just beautiful words rendering objects of beauty. . . . And there are passages of thought as static and as tranquil as a solitary candle-shaped flame of the black yew tree that you see against Italian skies. . . . There is, in fact, everything that goes to the making of one of those more pensive seventeenth century, usually ecclesiastical English poets who are the real glory of our two-fold lyre. Miss Bogan may—and probably will—stand somewhere in a quiet landscape that contains George Herbert, and Donne and Vaughan, and why not even Herrick?

Ford Madox Ford. *Poetry*. June, 1937. pp. 160–1

I hope she now decides to make some change in her theory and practice of the poet's art. Together they have been confining her to a somewhat narrow range of expression. Her new poems—meditative, witty, and sometimes really wise—suggest that she has more to say than can be crowded into any group of lyrics, and that perhaps she should give herself more space and less time. Most American poets write too much and too easily; Miss Bogan ought to write more, and more quickly, and even more carelessly. There are poems, sometimes very good ones, that have to be jotted down quickly or lost forever.

Malcolm Cowley. *New Republic*. Nov. 10, 1941. p. 625

Miss (Leonie) Adams and Miss Bogan were surely sisters in the same aesthetic current; and while I must confess that I have often wondered why that sisterhood insisted on wearing its chastity belt on the outside, poetry nevertheless remains wherever the spirit finds it.

But—speaking as one reader—if I admire objectively the poems of the first three (the earlier) sections of Miss Bogan's collection, with the poems of section four, I find myself forgetting the thee and me of it. . . . Miss Bogan began in beauty, but she has aged to magnificence, and I find myself thinking that the patina outshines the gold stain. . . . Miss Bogan sees into herself in the late poems—and not only into herself, but deeply enough into herself to find within her that jungle—call it the Jungian unconscious if you must—that everyone has in himself.

John Ciardi. *The Nation*. May 22, 1954. pp. 445–6

The virtues of her writing which have been most often spoken of are, I should suppose, firmness of outline, prosodic accomplishment, chiefly in traditional metrics, purity of diction and tone, concision of phrase, and, what results in craft from all these, and at bottom from a way of seizing experience, concentrated singleness of effect. . . . A large part of their moral force derives from the refusal to be deluded or to be overborne. The learning of the unwanted lesson, the admission of the hard fact, a kind of exhilaration of rejection, whether of the scorned or the merely implausible, the theme appears in the earliest work. . . . It is an art of limits, the limit of the inner occasion and of the recognized mode.

Leonie Adams. *Poetry*. Dec., 1954. pp. 166–9

Women are not noted for terseness, but Louise Bogan's art is compactness compacted. Emotion with her, as she has said of certain fiction, is "itself form, the kernel which builds outward from inward intensity." She uses a kind of forged rhetoric that nevertheless seems inevitable. . . . One is struck by her restraint—an unusual courtesy in this day of bombast.

Marianne Moore. *Predilections* (Viking). 1955. p. 130

Miss Bogan's volume. . . is not the volume of a poet for whom verse is merely a pastime, a diversion; the care with which the details have been selected and ordered. . . is the care of devotion. . . . All this is fine and dandy, and it may properly lead—as it has led—to observations about the importance of cultivating a poetry of care in a careless world. . . .(Yet) some of the critics . . . have noted a coldness here, an overscrupulousness there, and a general absence of the warm rhetoric of persuasion in poems so strenuously dedicated to the "verbal discipline."

Reed Whittemore. *Sewanee Review*. Winter, 1955. p. 163

Miss Bogan is one of our finest poets. She has written twenty or twenty-five poems that are unforgettable; they may be the best of their kind in American literature. And what we get from them, I think, aside from our delight, is the recognition of her basic poetic wisdom. She has not resisted her temptations, for she has seen that resistance can produce only poems which are crafty and correct but rarely interesting. Instead she has yielded; she has taken her temptations as they came, and has outsmarted them. Let the poem be conventional, public, and occasional, since that is the mask one must wear—so she might have spoken—but let each poem reveal

just enough of a private inner violence to make the surface move without breaking. A passionate austerity, a subtle balance; and only perfect poetic attention, far beyond technique, could attain it.

Hayden Carruth. *Poetry*. Aug., 1969. p. 330

To write as a woman of things that concern woman would have meant to me [as a young writer] soft prose, fine writing and poetical musings by three-named lady writers. I intended to avoid all of it. But Louise Bogan suggested something deeper: a lack of options as part of the condition of being a woman, a narrow life chosen by women because they were unwilling, if not unable, to take risk. And yet wasn't there something of a risk in the act of being the person who wrote the poem?. . .

For these are the cries of a woman—cries against the turning of luck or of bad timing, and they speak of the ability to face the mirror or the bottle, of the courage to go to the "mad-house" (as she called it in a letter to Theodore Roethke) when life went down on her and she could not pull herself up alone any more. There is a loss implied in these poems for all women who are alone and aging; that final loss when there is no one to turn to again at night in bed under the covers, when there is no one to hold you against the dark.

Nancy Milford. *New York Times Book Section*. Dec. 16, 1973. p. 1

It is [a] constant conflict between will and authority that shapes Bogan's poems. Because she herself unconsciously represented some of the strictures her spirit rebelled against, only form and symbol can express the tight, concentrated emotion of the unconscious struggling with the conscious. Although she strove always to make her poetry something beyond the narrowly personal and to cast out "small emotions with which poetry should not, and cannot deal," to be objective (a note on the worksheet indicating the poems to be published in the volume *The Sleeping Fury* says ". . . they must be as objective as possible"), it is often the personal emotion of the poet that informs the poem and gives authenticity to it. The emotion which is distanced by formal structures, sometimes distanced to the point of a "mask," a male persona, operates to illustrate the inherent conflict that the poem is really about. . . .

Her use of lyrical stanzas with second and fourth lines of rhyme or slant rhyme link the intellectual content of the poem with the subjective response to rhythm and sound. The appeal is to both the conscious and unconscious, and the imagery is of both: the images of the conscious of the first two stanzas and the images of the unconscious in the last two ("whispers in the glassy corridor" is especially wonderful in combining sound, imagery, and meaning). The tone is one of unhappy questioning rather than of being "contented with a thought/Through an idle fancy wrought." Her poem wonders about the human state that, by implication, is ruled by the same "forms and appetites" as the rest of nature, but aspires to more and therefore suffers. . . .

Louise Bogan once made the comment that highly formal poetry has always been obscure because the universe is difficult. Her own formal poetry is an acknowledgment of that difficulty, that obscurity, and of the complexity of modern truth.

Jacqueline Ridgeway. *Women's Studies*. 5, 2, 1977, pp. 141, 147–48

Louise Bogan was a poet who matured during the first half of this century and who embraced traditional forms, masks, and mythologies. Compared to contemporary women poets, she is neither direct, personal, or particular. Yet buried under the metrical decorum, the masks, the symbols, and the reticence of her poetry is a person who is painfully aware of her situation as a woman, and who tries to escape it. . . .

The strongest desire in Bogan's poetry has Emersonian overtones: she wants to recover a sense of wholeness in the face of the human passion for destructive analysis. Bogan dislikes anything that the human mind superimposes on the world because human interpretations or analyses are distortions of the unity of nature and experience. Her clearest expression of this dislike is in "Baroque Comment.". . .

"Masked Woman's Song" is extremely oblique and can only be understood by sifting it through the motifs in her other poems. . . . In Bogan's poetry men are always threatening or betraying. They try to pin women to words in "The Romantic," try to trap women in those forms "Coincident with the lie, anger, lust, oppression and death in many forms" in "Baroque Comment," and try to reduce women to heartless, emotionless servants who "return, return,/To meet forever Jim home on the 5:35," in "Evening in the Sanitarium.". . .

In ["Masked Woman's Song"] . . . Bogan writes that men have overthrown the constructive values of life, like freedom and love, and have forced women to live, out of fear, at a distance, masked from the varieties of experience and the wellsprings of life. But such an interpretation must be made between the lines: Bogan's attitude toward men, as ever, is obscured by her restrained and elliptical style. Her true feelings are blurred by symbol, distanced by masks, muted by form.

Today, needless to say, such a style is rare, if not impossible, in a feminist poet. Where free verse is the exception in Bogan's poetry, something like a sigh of relief in a wasteland of anxiety and repression, most contemporary women poets use free forms as a matter of course, for their spontaneity, directness, and freedom from objectification and unwanted literary associations. But contemporary women poets have much less to fear than Bogan did; feminism is more secure now and support groups abound. Yet Louise Bogan was one of the earlier women poets who pointed to a way out of the strangling forms and mentalities of traditional verse. If for no other reason than that, her life and her poetry deserve our interest and attention.

Patrick Moore. In *Gender and Literary Voice*, ed. Janet Todd (Holmes and Meier, 1980), pp. 67–69, 78–79

When Farrar, Straus & Giroux . . . published a new collected edition in 1968, *The Blue Estuaries: Poems 1923–1968*, Louise Bogan's life as a poet came to an end.

Bogan had dedicated *Selected Criticism: Poetry and Prose* "To Maidie Alexander, daughter, and friend," and she now dedicated what she knew to be her final book of poems "To the memory of my father, mother, and brother." Her depression had been at least in part an attempt to connect with them, and this dedication acknowledged the bridge between her life's work and her love for her family. The poems in the sixth and last section of the book were Bogan's final fruits, and of two kinds, primarily. There were

occasional poems, like those in the final section of *Poems and New Poems*, and simple, severe lyrics. Some were old poems, written or put down as first drafts as long ago as 1940; others had been written after 1948, about the time, that is, that Bogan had stopped thinking of herself as a *practicing* poet. Poems had come thereafter one at a time, for the most part, with long intervals in between.

Many of these later poems are in free verse, and in them Bogan arrives at a middle ground between formal rigor and the looser, more open feeling May Sarton had encouraged her to strive for. In "The Dragonfly," for instance, written sometime in the fall of 1961, she worked with short free-verse lines in a delicate line of Thoreauvian naturalism. Its inspiration was a picture postcard of a dragonfly Ruth Limmer had sent her from Detroit, but she wrote the poem on commission for the Corning Glass Company—wrote it to order, that is!—and a piece of Steuben Glass was carved to illustrate it. She was fond of the poem, which, she informed Miss Limmer, was completely "based on FACT."

Her formal poems were correspondingly natural in diction.

Elizabeth Frank. *Louise Bogan* (New York: Alfred A. Knopf, 1985), pp. 400–401

A profound change in Louise Bogan's relationship to all poets came with her appointment as a poetry critic of *The New Yorker* in 1931. Bogan complained a great deal about the job: It interfered with her creative life; it reminded her that she was primarily self-taught, not as well-educated, in the formal sense, as most of the people with whom she associated; most important, . . . she was determined to be "honest" as she saw and put "standards" above friendship. . . . In 1931 then she was forced to take a public stand on poetry; this necessarily included an assessment of women poets. The task no doubt helped her to formulate in a coherent and sustained way her ideas about the special province of women of letters. Her reviews are invaluable to us as a record of one distinguished woman poet's response to American poetry from the twenties through the sixties.

Her strong public stance had a particularly marked effect on her relationships with women. For example, Bogan's reviews of Edna St. Vincent Millay's poems in the late thirties put an end to their friendship. . . . To understand the complexity of friendships and rivalries between "exceptional" white women in New York City in the twenties and the thirties, we need to be acutely aware of historical moment and context. This was the post-Suffrage era, the age, in sophisticated circles, of the "free woman." Feminist analyses of the lives of American women in the late twenties and thirties are only now beginning to emerge, but it is surely too simple to say that feminism died utterly after the color, the class, the economic situation, and the location of the women involved. In New York, the white, middle-class, upwardly mobile woman saw it was in her interests to identify publicly more with men than with women. . . .

This, then, was the complex setting for Louise Bogan's poetry: a modernist milieu that had no great expectations for the work of women; subtle relationships among women poets, sometimes rivalrous, sometimes supportive; a powerful post as a critic, which led Bogan to think and write about the relationship of poetry by women to past and present traditions; her own experience of poetry and life, coupled with a shift in poetic taste in the forties, which in turn prompted a passionate defense of the gift of women's "heart" to poetry.

Gloria Bowles. *Louise Bogan's Aesthetic of Limitation* (Bloomington: Indiana Univ. Pr., 1987), pp. 38–39, 64

BIBLIOGRAPHY
Body of This Death, 1923 (p); *Dark Summer*, 1929 (p); *The Sleeping Fury*, 1937 (p); *Poems and New Poems*, 1941; *Achievement in American Poetry, 1900–1950*, 1951 (c); *Collected Poems*, 1954; *Selected Criticism*, 1955; (with Elizabeth Roget) *The Journal of Jules Renard*, 1964 (tr); *The Blue Estuaries*, 1968 (p); *A Poet's Alphabet*, 1970 (c); *What the Woman Lived*, 1973 (l); *Journey around My Room: The Autobiography of Louise Bogan*, ed. Ruth Limmer, 1980

BONTEMPS, Arna (1902–1973)

Arna Bontemps' first venture in fiction [*God Sends Sunday*] is to me a profound disappointment. It is of the school of "Nigger Heaven" and "Home to Harlem." There is a certain pathetic touch to the painting of his poor little jockey hero, but nearly all else is sordid crime, drinking, gambling, whore-mongering, and murder. There is not a decent intelligent woman; not a single man with the slightest ambition or real education, scarcely more than one human child in the whole book. Even the horses are drab. In the "Blues" alone Bontemps sees beauty. But in brown skins, frizzled hair and full contoured faces, there are to him nothing but ugly, tawdry, hateful things, which he describes with evident caricature.

One reads hurriedly on, waiting for a gleam of light, waiting for the Sunday that some poor ugly black God may send; but somehow it never comes; and if God appears at all it is in the form of a little drunken murderer riding South to Tia Juana on his back.

W.E.B. Du Bois, *The Crisis*. September, 1931, p. 304.

In that limited and almost barren field known as the negro novel, Arna Bontemps's *Black Thunder* fills a yawning gap and fills it competently. Covering all those skimpy reaches of Negro letters I know, this is the only novel dealing forthrightly with the historical and revolutionary traditions of the Negro people.

Black Thunder is the true story of a slave insurrection that failed. But in his telling of the story of that failure Bontemps manages to reveal and dramatize through the character of his protagonist, Gabriel, a quality of folk courage unparalleled in the proletarian literature of this country. . . .

Black Thunder is mainly the story of Gabriel, who believes in the eventual triumph of his destiny in spite of all the forces which conspire against it. He is convinced that God and the universe are on his side. He believes he must and will lead the Negro people to freedom. He seems to have no personal fear and no personal courage. He thinks, dreams, and feels wholly in terms of Negro liberation. . . . When considering Gabriel solely as an isolated individual, he seems sustained by an extremely foolish belief in himself; but when one remembers his slave state, when one realizes

the extent to which he has made the wrongs of his people his wrongs, and the degree in which he has submerged his hopes in their hopes—when one remembers this, he appears logically and gloriously invincible. . . .

Gabriel believes [in the uprising], he believes even when he is caught; even when the black cowl is capped about his head, even when the ax swings, he believes. Why? For me the cardinal value of Bontemps's book, besides the fact that it is a thumping story well told, lies in the answer to that question. Perhaps I am straying further afield than the author did in search for an answer. If I do, it is because I believe we have in *Black Thunder* a revelation of the very origin and source of folk values in literature.

Even though Gabriel's character is revealed in terms of personal action and dialogue, I feel there is in him much more than mere personal dignity and personal courage. There is in his attitude something which transcends the limits of immediate consciousness. He is buoyed in his hope and courage by an optimism which takes no account of the appalling difficulties confronting him. He hopes when there are no objective reasons or grounds for hope; he fights when his fellow-slaves scamper for their lives. In doing so, he takes his place in that gallery of fictitious characters who exist on the plane of the ridiculous and the sublime. Bontemps endows Gabriel with a myth-like and deathless quality. And it is in this sense, I believe, that *Black Thunder* sounds a new note in Negro fiction, thereby definitely extending the boundaries and ideology of the Negro novel.

Richard Wright. *Partisan-Review and Anvil*. February, 1936, p. 31.

God Sends Sunday follows *Nigger Heaven* in its emphasis upon sex and fast living, but differs in its introduction of a main character who is a celebrated jockey and a prodigal libertine in the racing centers of the Mississippi Valley. . . .

In its abandonment of the Harlem background, *God Sends Sunday* exemplifies a new trend in fiction showing the influence of *Nigger Heaven*. Besides, more than any other novel in the Van Vechten tradition, it avoids race consciousness.

[Another novel by Bontemps, *Black Thunder*,] treats the abortive slave insurrection under Gabriel Prosser in Virginia in 1800. . . .

The underlying thesis of *Black Thunder* . . . is that Negro slaves, with the exception of a small number bound in mind as well as in body, had an obsessive love of freedom. . . .

Black Thunder is written with restraint and detachment. Bontemps portrays slaves, freedmen, planters, and French radicals with impartiality, showing no disposition to glorify pro-Negro nor to traduce anti-Negro characters in the book. Miscegenation on the Southern scene is not blinked. Furthermore, Bontemps succeeds in weaving Gabriel's uprising into the web of state and national life. . . . Although *Black Thunder* is not without blemish, A. B. Spingarn is quite correct in his observation that the book is "the best historical novel written by an American Negro."

Also a record of the Negro's quest for freedom is Bontemps' second historical novel, *Drums at Dusk*, an account of the black insurrection which resulted in the independence of Haiti and the emergence of Toussaint L'Ouverture.

Bontemps paints a vivid picture of social upheaval and class prejudice in tropical San Domingo. Struggling for control are the wealthy elite, the low-class whites, and the free mulattoes. The aristocrats, dominating slaves who outnumber all other inhabitants by nearly ten to one, keep their positions secure by intimidating the blacks and playing them against the mulattoes. . . . Miscegenation is rampant, as lecherous aristocrats frequently manifest a preference for ''chocolate'' and openly flaunt their yellow mistresses. . . . In brief, *Drums at Dusk*, a worthy successor to *Black Thunder*, is another vivid illustration of the richness of the Negro's past as a source for historical fiction.

> Hugh M. Gloster. In *Negro Voices in American Fiction* (University of North Carolina Press, 1948).

Arna Bontemps is a transitional figure whose novels bear the mark both of the Negro Renaissance and of the depression years which follow. . . . A minor poet during the 1920s, Bontemps turned later to fiction, history, and books for children. He has written three novels, of which the first *God Sends Sunday* (1931), is an unadulterated product of the Negro Renaissance. The setting of the novel is the sporting world of racetrack men and gamblers, of jazz and the shimmy, of fights and razor carvings. His historical novels, however, which deal with slavery times, reflect the mood of the Depression era. By choosing slave insurrections as a basis for his plots, Bontemps stresses an aspect of slavery which was emotionally appealing to the rebellious thirties. . . .

The narrative technique [of *Black Thunder* (1936)], which conveys the action by a progressive treatment of the participants, is reminiscent of the novels of Dos Passos. The plot is developed in fragments, through short chapters which open with the name of the character under consideration. From this constant shift in point of view, the reader must piece together the full panorama. It is a technique especially suited to the presentation of complex historical events, and Bontemps employs it skillfully. At its best, this technique requires deft characterization, since the action of the novel is constantly refracted through a new consciousness, which the reader must understand in its own right. . . .

Arna Bontemps' second historical novel, *Drums at Dusk* (1939), is in every respect a retreat from the standards of *Black Thunder*. Deriving its plot from the Haitian slave rebellion which brought Toussaint l'Ouverture to power, the novel is unworthy of its subject. In writing of a successful rebellion, Bontemps is deprived of the dramatic power of tragedy, and he discovers no appropriate attitude to take its place. Upon a highly romantic plot he grafts a class analysis of society which is post-Marxian and flagrantly unhistorical. Frequently lapsing into crude melodrama, he embroiders his narrative with all of the sword-play, sex, and sadism of a Hollywood extravaganza.

> Robert Bone. In *The Negro Novel in America*, revised edition, Yale University Press, 1965, pp. 120–52.

Bontemps' poems [collected in *Personals*] make use of several recurring themes: the alien-and-exile allusions so often found in New Negro poetry; strong racial suggestiveness and applications; religious themes and imagery subtly used; and the theme of return to a former time, a former love, or a remembered place. On occasion he combines in a way common to lyrical writing the personal with the racial or the general. Many of these poems are protest poems; but the protest is oblique and suggestive rather than frontal. Over all of Bontemps' poetry there is a sad, brooding

quality, a sombre ''Il Penseroso'' meditative cast. In *Personals* there are no obviously joyous or humorous pieces.

The poems of Arna Bontemps lack the clear, unambiguous statement of those of his contemporaries: McKay, Cullen, Hughes. There is modern obscurity in these verses, and the so-called meaning often eludes the reader. Their craftsmanship, however, is impressive. The reader somehow feels a certain rightness in Bontemps' lines, that what he has said could not be expressed otherwise. There is a quiet authority in these poems.

> Arthur P. Davis. *From the Dark Tower: Afro-American Writers 1900–1960*. Howard University Press, 1974. pp. 83–9.

Arna Bontemps was a prolific, versatile writer whose books were trailblazers for the award-winning works of many of today's black writers—among them Virginia Hamilton, Ashley Bryan, Rosa Guy, Leo and Diane Dillon, and Gwendolyn Brooks. Bontemps's lasting legacy is his writing for children at a time when there were few books written by blacks for black children. His first was *Popo and Fifina,* written with Langston Hughes whom he met during the Harlem Renaissance in the 1920s. Popo and Fifina, ages eight and ten, are appealing, resourceful children of a Haitian family in a seacoast town. Their father is a fisherman who still finds time to make a red kite, their mother trains them in daily chores, their uncle introduces them to the art of wood designing. The setting is lush and tropical, sunny with mangoes and parrots, vibrant with sudden storms and the midnight music of drums in the forest.

Bontemps turned to Alabama for his next two stories. *You Can't Pet a Possum* is about eight-year-old Shine Boy and his pup Butch who get into trouble but are saved by Aunt Cindy, who finally agrees to let Butch join the family as long as he doesn't act as though he owned the house. ''Do, I'm gonna take a stick and run him raggedy,'' threatens Aunt Cindy in the local vernacular. (Although he used it occasionally in his writing, Bontemps found the Negro dialect mostly offensive and demeaning.) The second story, *Sad-Faced Boy,* is about Slumber and his two brothers who hitchhike to Harlem to visit their uncle. The boys with harmonica, guitar, and drum form a successful band, and have adventures in the library and the subway, but come cold weather, thoughts of cotton and ripe persimmons soon send them back to their cabin in Alabama. *Sad-Faced Boy* was the first children's book in which Bontemps touched on the ''lonesome boy'' theme. He admitted that it was partly autobiographical in origin; as a boy he had looked in vain for lonesome boy stories.

Years later Bontemps explored this theme more fully in the haunting lyrical story *Lonesome Boy*. Bubber is so passionately devoted to his silver trumpet that he blows it loud, fast, and high everywhere he goes. His Grandpa warns him, ''It ain't good to go traipsing around with a horn in your hand. You might get into devilment.'' Bubber grows up still playing his trumpet, all the way down to New Orleans where he plays to his heart's content until the eerie night he learns the meaning of his Grandpa's warning. The mystifying, opaque ending makes the story memorable and tantalizing.

The Fast Sooner Hound, co-written with Jack Conroy, is a lively humorous picture story about a long-legged, lop-eared hound who would ''sooner run then eat.'' He wins a bet for his master by outrunning the Cannon Ball, the fastest train on wheels.

Bontemps's finest achievement is *Story of the Negro,* a book he wished he had had when he was in high school. It is a comprehensive, powerfully written history of the causes and consequences of slavery from the earliest times. The cruelty, suffering, and humiliations are heartbreaking; the struggles, survivals, and triumphs are extraordinary. The book demonstrates that from Aesop to Martin Luther King Jr., slaves and blacks have sought to arouse the conscience of the nation and the world.

> Mary Silva Cosgrave. In *Twentieth-Century Children's Writers*, ed. Laura Standley Berger (St. James Press, 1995).

BIBLIOGRAPHY

God Sends Sunday, 1931 (n); (with Langston Hughes) *Popo and Fifina, Children of Haiti*, 1932 (juv); *You Can't Pet a Possum*, 1934 (juv); *Black Thunder*, 1936 (n); *Sad-Faced Boy*, 1937 (juv); *Drums at Dusk*, 1939 (n); (with Jack Conroy) *The Fast Sooner Hound*, 1942 (juv); (with Jack Conroy) *They Seek A City*, 1945 (s), also published as *Any Place but Here*, revised edition, 1966; *We Have Tomorrow*, 1945 (juv); *Two Harlems*, 1945 (e); *Slappy Hooper, the Wonderful Sign Painter*, 1946 (juv); *Story of the Negro*, 1948 (juv); *Free and Easy*, 1949 (d); *Buried Treasures of Negro Art*, 1950 (e); *George Washington Carver*, 1950 (juv); *Chariot in the Sky: A Story of the Jubilee Singers*, 1951 (juv); *How I Told My Child About Race*, 1951 (e); (with Jack Conroy) *Sam Patch, the High, Wide, & Handsome Jumper*, 1951 (juv); *The Story of George Washington Carver*, 1954 (b); *Lonesome Boy*, 1955 (juv); *Frederick Douglass: Slave, Fighter, Freeman*, 1959 (juv); *Personals*, 1963 (p); *Famous Negro Athletes*, 1964 (juv); *Mr. Kelso's Lion*, 1970 (juv); *Free Atlantic Monthly Last: The Life of Frederick Douglass*, 1971 (juv); *Young Booker: The Story of Booker T. Washington's Early Days*, 1972 (juv); *The Old South: "A Summer Tragedy" and Other Stories of the Thirties*, 1973 (s)

BOURJAILY, Vance (1922–)

There are tenderness and violence in Mr. Bourjaily's story, the genuine, not the movie-advertisement kind, and there is much more than that. There is a lot about a generation that is without much hope, that has never known stability, that found, even in [World War II], not much to inspire a thinking man. I hope a lot of people will read *The End of My Life*; I'm sure almost everybody will enjoy it, despite its faults, which are numerous and obvious, and I'm equally certain that Bourjaily is going to write other and better novels. He has done an almost first-rate job with this one.

> Merle Miller. *Saturday Review*. Aug. 30, 1947. pp. 17–8

In literary terms, *The End of My Life* stands as a transitional novel squarely between the two generations. Its early lyricism that is so much in the spirit of the old war writing gives way to the dead futility at its end that anticipates the spirit of the new war writing. The development of Skinner through the novel, from the confident cynicism of his prewar attitude to the self-destructive horror induced in him by the reality of war, sets the pattern of the new writing as surely as if he had written it himself. It shows how the discovery of war's truth carried this generation beyond the narrow but highly effective literary frame of simple disillusion and left

them with an acute but essentially inexpressible awareness of the complex ills of their time.

> John W. Aldridge. *After the Lost Generation* (McGraw). 1951. pp. 131–2

Vance Bourjaily's first novel, *The End of My Life*, had a slightly anachronistic flavor. It told of a second world war that was something of a lark, with ironic sad young men going to Africa to make funny conversation and die. With its extreme youthfulness it constituted a poignant memorial to the wide-eyed college intellectual of the last days of the New Deal.

The Hound of Earth reveals a writer purified of most of the postures of extreme youth. The mocking bright-boy melancholy . . . has been succeeded by a frighteningly immediate, perversely humorous perspective upon contemporary American problems of conscience. . . .

This novel is sometimes arch, as in the romance of its moral suicide; it is frankly sentimental at times and then abandons itself to whimsey. . . . But for the most part it holds in balance its humor and its pathos—this tension is the special note of Bourjaily's style— and endures past a first reading as an effective drama about how difficult it is to be both responsible and an individual in contemporary America.

> Herbert Gold. *The Nation*. July 23, 1955. p. 79

All the characters in Vance Bourjaily's novel *The Violated* . . . pursue contemptible ideals insofar as they pursue anything other than love affairs. This enormously long, soggily earnest book is the more exasperating because it contains enough brilliant flashes to keep the reader hoping for better things.

According to Mr. Bourjaily, his novel is about a group of people who are "violated . . . by their inability to communicate, to love, to comprehend, to create—violated by neurotic commitments to preposterous goals or, more tragically, to no goals at all." This is a perfectly accurate description of the three men whose dreary careers are followed over some thirty years, and also of everyone connected with them, and this is the book's weakness. . . . The nervous, inquisitive rootlessness of late adolescence is well conveyed, but the disabilities that prevent these characters from attaching themselves to the world as they grow older are nebulous. . . . They seem to be people congenitally incapable of coming to grips with anything. . . .

While it is possible to admire the skill with which Mr. Bourjaily writes, and respect his concern for the unhappy people he writes about, it is difficult to share his assumption that the plight of these unaccountable cripples is worth 599 pages.

> Phoebe Adams. *Atlantic Monthly*. Oct., 1958. pp. 90–1

The Violated seems to me a failure, but an interesting one, if only because of the way in which Mr. Bourjaily's courage and ambition lead him to repeated troubles. He has chosen to write one of those full-scale, lavishly detailed narratives composed of parallel and intersecting levels. Such a technique, borrowed from the social novel of the early years of the century, assumes that society is distinctly, even rigidly stratified; that its component classes are intrinsically interesting and worth observing; that a novelist can arrange a conflict between members of these classes which will be dramatic in its own right and representative of larger issues; and that thereby the narrative can finally be brought to a coherent climax.

But for the material Mr. Bourjaily has chosen—the lives of pitiful and bewildered drifters during the past two decades—these assumptions do not operate with sufficient force. His central characters are not distinctive enough, either in social or personal qualities, to warrant separate strands of narrative. As they collapse into each other's lives, the successes of one indistinguishable from the failures of the other, they create a smudge of sadness at the very point where the novel demands tension and clarity. Like the postwar society they reflect, these characters are too much of a sameness, so that one wearies of their presence almost as quickly as one credits their reality.

Irving Howe. *New Republic*. Nov. 10, 1958. p. 17

Bourjaily's first two novels were . . . "symbolic." The main character in *The End of My Life* . . . is made to stand for an entire generation. As he gradually comes to lose all his feeling for other people, and thus all his desire for life, he represents in extreme . . . the effects of the war. . . . But Bourjaily's last two books have made every attempt to eschew these metaphorical devices, and for this reason they stand apart from most American fiction. . . . The characters, events, and ideas in *Confessions of a Spent Youth* are held together by a tone of detached yet committed inquiry and by a conversational style that moves easily from quiet humor to unobtrusive lyricism.

Harris Dienstfrey. *Commentary*. April, 1961. pp. 360–2

Vance Bourjaily in *The Man Who Knew Kennedy* . . . is examining the meaning of the event [the assassination of Kennedy] for the generation to which Kennedy belonged, and his novel is the story of a part of that generation. . . . In an earlier novel, *The Hound of Earth*, one I have always liked, Bourjaily also made a historic event his center—the explosion of the atom bomb over Hiroshima. . . . Bourjaily's most recent novel, on the other hand, *Confessions of a Spent Life*, seems to grow almost entirely and directly out of his own experience. His strength, whether his approach to a novel is subjective or objective, is his familiarity with American manners in the postwar world. It is really, of course, only a small segment of American experience that he presents in *The Man Who Knew Kennedy*; but such as it is, he gives it life.

The book is extremely readable, and in part, despite its solemn theme, it is charming. . . . What mildly bothers me about the book is that parts of it seem to me a little slick in a way that Bourjaily's earlier novels haven't been.

Granville Hicks. *Saturday Review*. Feb. 4, 1967. pp. 35–6

BIBLIOGRAPHY
The End of My Life, 1947 (n); *The Hound of Earth*, 1955 (n); *The Violated*, 1958 (n); *Confessions of a Spent Youth*, 1960 (n); *The Unnatural Enemy*, 1963 (e); *The Man Who Knew Kennedy*, 1967 (n); *Brill among the Ruins*, 1970 (n); *Country Matters: Collected Reports from the Fields and Streams of Iowa and Other Places*, 1973 (e); *Now Playing at Canterbury*, 1976 (n); *A Game Men Play*, 1980 (n); *The Great Fake Book*, 1986 (n); *Old Soldier*, 1990 (n); (with Philip Bourjaily) *Fishing by Mail: The Outdoor Life of a Father and Son*, 1993 (l)

BOURNE, Randolph (1886–1918)

Here was no anonymous reviewer, no mere brilliant satellite of the radical movement losing himself in his immediate reactions: one finds everywhere, interwoven in the fabric of his work, the silver thread of a personal philosophy, the singing line of an intense and beautiful desire.

What was that desire? It was for a new fellowship in the youth of America as the principle of a great and revolutionary departure in our life, a league of youth, one might call it, consciously framed with the purpose of creating, out of the blind chaos of American society, a fine, free, articulate cultural order. That, as it seems to me, was the dominant theme of all his effort, the positive theme to which he always returned from his thrilling forays into the fields of education and politics, philosophy and sociology. . . . Here was Emerson's "American scholar" at last, but radiating an infinitely warmer, profaner, more companionable influence than Emerson had ever dreamed of, an influence that savored rather of Whitman and William James. He was the new America incarnate, with that stamp of a sort of permanent youthfulness on his queer, twisted, appealing face.

Van Wyck Brooks. Introduction to *The History of a Literary Radical and Other Papers* by Randolph Bourne (S.A. Russell). 1956. [1919]. pp. 3–4

He discovered new educational experiments; new pathfindings in philosophy and literature; new flights in politics and musical art. To the problems of each field he seemed to bring the whole sum of his former experience, his deep intuition and sure sense of fact, sharp comprehension, quick imaginativeness, and pleasure in the sensuous. And through this liberal delivery, the reports of his discoveries, whether they assumed the shape of a description of the schools in Gary or of a review of a novel, of a whimsical account of friends, children, teachers, or a serious discussion of the future of American culture, became, almost always, experiments in themselves, new theories of facts, new keen images of reality. Bourne could speak with equal sureness, humanity, lightness on a dozen different topics; and his talk itself, like his book-reviewing, was a sort of adventure.

Paul Rosenfeld. *Dial*. Dec., 1923. p. 552

Already he is more or less a legend to many persons who have not even opened his books and do not know that they contain all the germs of the new spirit. But even a casual examination will prove that those germs are there. Touchingly prophetic, Bourne felt the coming struggle before it had become evident to less subtle observers. During his brief, vivid life he managed to utter some significant reflection upon almost every topic which vitally concerns the age. He wrote of religion, the state, property, the arts, education.

> Carl and Mark Van Doren. *American and British Literature Since 1890* (Century). 1925. p. 123

All of this work [of Bourne] represented the very first quality in the journalism of ideas, but for the most part, it was still journalism. His view of life was maturing, deepening, not yet ready for rounded expression, it was still a promise.... Randolph Bourne was precious to us because of what he was, rather than because of what he had actually written.... He will never occupy the place of a great teacher, but one feels that potentially he had exactly that office, and that in ten years, in twenty years, he would have distilled out of such pain and frustration as only a crippled man can know, a new image of beauty and perfection.

> Lewis Mumford. *New Republic.* Sept. 24, 1930. pp. 151–2

He was very deformed. Not alone was he dwarfed and hunchbacked: his face was twisted, he had a tortured ear, his color was sallow and his breathing was audible and hard. He walked in a cape that hid him. He took a chair for the first time in your presence, let fall the black shroud about him, and revealed a form so mangled that you despaired ever to find sufficient ease for the sort of conversation his immediately brilliant mind demanded.

But the magic of Randolph Bourne was not separate from his poor body, and at once you knew this. This is why, in writing of this splendid spirit, it is meet to dwell upon his misery. Within half an hour, your discomfort was gone—so miraculously gone that your mind was prone to look about for it. But whenever, in the future, awareness did return of the grotesque shape in which this spirit was imprisoned and was doomed to walk, it was intellectual altogether: the mind needed to stir the senses with the thought of it, while the senses moved in full ease within his presence.

> Waldo Frank. *In the American Jungle* (Farrar and Rinehart). 1937. pp. 59–60

His book-reviews tended always to be critical essays on the social roots of a man's thinking. They were radical in the sense that they were unsparing in the application of the critical canons they chose. Not that Bourne lacked a breadth of sympathy: his essay on Cardinal Newman had in it generosity and enjoyment. But the main direction of his mind was more exacting.... His attacks on the Philistines among novelists and critics . . . had a joyful abandon. He was, in a sense, an American Matthew Arnold, with a touch of Nietzsche's "gay science," who had studied Veblen and delighted in him. His writing, like Veblen's, was ironic: and I am using the term here in Bourne's sense of irony—as flowing from a democracy of the literary realm in which no idea can plead privilege or immunity from a drastic deflation.... His attack on the liberal intellectuals of his day and on their role in bringing America into the war was one of the most scathing in American political literature. Bourne was pacifist in his deepest convictions; he was

also a democrat in the truest cultural sense. The war crossed his grain on both counts.

> Max Lerner. *Twice A Year.* 1940–1941. pp. 65, 68

Above all Bourne was the perfect child of the prewar Enlightenment; when its light went out in 1918, he died with it. Afterward his story seemed so much the martyrology of his generation that the writer was lost in the victim. Yet even when one goes back to Bourne's books—not merely his bitter and posthumously published collections of essays, but his early studies of contemporary youth, education, and politics—it is not hard to see why Bourne must always seem less a writer than the incarnation of his time. For from his first book, *Youth and Life*, to the *Impressions of Europe* which he wrote on a fellowship abroad and his books on education and the Gary schools, Bourne proved himself so inexpressibly confident of a future established on the evangelicisms of his period, so radiant in his championship of pragmatism, art, reason, European social democracy, and the experimental school, that he now seems a seismograph on which were recorded the greatest hopes and fiercest despairs of his time.

> Alfred Kazin. *On Native Grounds* (Reynal). 1942. pp. 183–4

The key to the bewildering variety of essays and book-reviews which Bourne poured out in the short space of his career lay in their literary quality. He drew strength from the forces which were rapidly transforming the country; he was eager to assist that transformation. But his articles dealing with city and town planning, feminism, Americanization, and college reform—though keen and even startling, although based on solid studies in education, sociology, and political science—were essentially fragments. They served to show the impact of new social developments on a sensitive mind. Bourne's literary essays, on the other hand, were not only thought through, but made up a collection of work which could bear examination years later.

> Louis Filler. *Randolph Bourne* (American Council on Public Affairs). 1943. p. 79

From a pragmatic standpoint Randolph Bourne was a tragic failure. In possession of all the intellectual qualifications for leadership, well on his way towards a position of power and influence, he deliberately rejected the world at a time of crisis and assumed the role of an outcast crying in the wilderness. With the Kaiser's military might let loose over Europe, with democratic society in grave danger, he quixotically expounded a pacifistic anarchism. It might even be argued that the poison of perversity had early entered his spirit and embittered his entire life's experience. From his first passionate attacks on the folkways and activities of the older generation he proceeded in a contrary direction which logically ended in his uncompromising opposition to a war which the best minds accepted as the lesser of the dire alternatives confronting the country. For all his native gifts, he was only a negative and fanatical eccentric.

History, however, will deal more fairly with him. For he belongs not with the politicians but with the prophets. What matters in his case was not his reaction to daily events nor his judgment of temporal affairs but his energetic stimulation of minds and his vision of the good life. Few Americans possessed his enthusiasm for the deepending and enrichment of our indigenous culture. He early sought to remove the layer of rust and rot which crusted the minds of many Americans.

> Charles Madison. *Critics and Crusaders* (Holt). 1947. pp. 440–1

Like Socrates he was a creative critic who placed his faith in the education of youth, education built around a fresh, intense, and on-going examination of society. Bourne's life was all of a piece. Consistency was its badge. One can refer, as we shall see, to any part of his career without worry of finding contradictions in thought or method. He called continually for social progress through social enrichment.

Contrary to the misreading of critics, the core of Bourne's philosophy was neither the relation between political power and cultural creation nor a naive faith in a revolutionary mass move-ment of youth against the older generation. The root of Bourne's thinking was the conviction that modern times need a modern religion, a reestablishment of values and methods.

> A.F. Beringause. *Journal of the History of Ideas*. Oct., 1957. p. 598

The only public issues that engaged Bourne's imagination for very long were questions, not of politics, but of culture: education, feminism, the rebellion of youth. . . . [A]ll his works came back in one way or another to the fact which from childhood had burned itself into Bourne's consciousness, the gap between the genera-tions. . . . Bourne thought he was repudiating politics, and he attacked other progressives as having subordinated everything else to political concerns; and yet his own conception of politics as a ''means to life'' represented an extension of the political into the most intimate areas of existence. To say that politics was of no use unless it could improve the very tone and quality of people's private lives was to argue in effect that every aspect of existence was ultimately a question for political decision.

> Christopher Lasch. *The New Radicalism in America* (Knopf). 1965. pp. 83, 90

Bourne had also begun to make literary experiments. Half a dozen of his ''portraits,'' some satiric, some almost poetic, were pub-lished in *The New Republic*. Like Henry Adams, he was captivated by the feminine mystique, and felt keenly the energy and the vitality and the attraction of women. He wrote of the suffragettes with a tartness. . . . But he wrote also of their longings and of their loneliness. He wrote of young men who played the violin, who spent long hours reading in the cavernous halls of the Forty-second Street Library. His portraits were not ''grotesques,'' as Sherwood Anderson would call his sketches of *Winesburg, Ohio*; they were wistful and lonely. Bourne's people were not yet adrift in Dos Passos' pulsating world; they were not yet ''lost'' in Paris cafes. They were at once gay and sad. Bourne was a poet of solitaries, of

the ironic, idealistic young people who had not yet had the war cross their lives.

> Lillian Schlissel. Introduction to *The World of Randolph Bourne* (Dutton). 1965. pp. xxviii–xxix

BIBLIOGRAPHY
Arbitration and International Politics, 1913 (e); *Youth and Life*, 1913 (e); *The Tradition of War*, 1914 (e); *The Gary Schools*, 1916 (j); (with others) *Towards an Enduring Peace*, 1916 (e); *Education and Living*, 1917 (e); *Untimely Papers*, 1919 (e); *The History of a Literary Radical and Other Papers*, 1920 (e); *War and the Intellec-tuals*, 1964 (e); *The World of Randolph Bourne*, 1965

BOWLES, Jane (1917–1973)

There is nothing propagandistic or topical in Jane Bowles's *In the Summer House*, . . . which is not the only reason I prefer it to most of the plays I have seen this season. Its author has an original writing talent and a not at all stock sensibility. It may even be deemed a paradox that I like the earlier or wackier part of the play better than the last part, in which the characters are resolved with the aid of a little off-the-cuff psychoanalysis. . . . The aimless dialogue, the sadly abstract atmosphere of the first part of *In the Summer House*, is lovely, colorful and strangely evocative: it spins a melody of the trivial and ''pointless'' which emanates from the semiconsciousness of rather ordinary folk with a primitive direct-ness that is essentially poetic.

> Harold Clurman. *The Nation*. Jan. 16, 1954. p. 58

Surrounding Mrs. Bowles's art is an effluvium of chic despair which will alienate many readers. On the other hand, her work can easily be overvalued since it combines proud idiosyncrasy with a rather startling prescience (her novel, *Two Serious Ladies*, . . . forecast the current vogue of comic gothicism). When that book first appeared here, reviewers could damn it with a clear con-science: modernism had not yet become an obligatory mass fash-ion. . . . Today in the United States, where the cultivated reader feels duty-bound to be affronted, Mrs. Bowles's controlled derision is likely to seem the definitive force of civilized disgust.

Surely her indictments have an easy inclusiveness. Like her husband Paul, Mrs. Bowles writes tight little anecdotes about the pull of bestiality, an unexpected form of self-fulfillment. Like her husband's stories, hers pit the weak against the strong, the right-eous against the sensual, only to record a general rout. Though her tales lack his intellectual clarity, they have greater charm.

> Charles Thomas Samuels. *New York Review of Books*. Dec. 15, 1966. p. 38

. . . I saw *In the Summer House* three times . . . because it had a thorny wit, the flavor of a newly tasted, refreshingly bitter bever-age—the same qualities that had initially attracted me to Mrs. Bowles's novel, *Two Serious Ladies*. . . . And yet, though the tragic

view is central to her vision, Jane Bowles is a very funny writer, a
humorist of sorts—but *not*, by the way, of the Black School. Black
Comedy, as its perpetrators label it, is, when successful, all lovely
artifice and lacking any hint of compassion. Her subtle comprehension of eccentricity and human apartness as revealed in her work
require us to accord Jane Bowles high esteem as an artist.

Truman Capote. Introduction to *The Collected Works of
Jane Bowles* (Farrar). 1966. pp. viii–ix

It is to be hoped that she will now be recognized for what she is: one
of the finest modern writers of fiction, in any language. . . . Mrs.
Bowles's seemingly casual, colloquial prose is a constant miracle;
every line rings as true as a line of poetry, though there is certainly
nothing ''poetic'' about it, except insofar as the awkwardness of
our everyday attempts at communication is poetic. This awkwardness can rise to comic heights, and in doing so evoke visions of a
nutty America that we have to recognize as ours. . . .

In her later stories Mrs. Bowles has played down the picaresque
local color she used to such effect in the novel. . . . As in all her
work, it is impossible to deduce the end of a sentence from its
beginning, or a paragraph from the one that preceded it, or how one
of the characters will reply to another. And yet the whole flows
marvelously and inexorably to its cruel, lucid end; it becomes itself
as we watch it. No other contemporary writer can consistently
produce surprise of this quality, the surprise that is the one essential
ingredient of great art. Jane Bowles deals almost exclusively in this
rare commodity.

John Ashbery. *New York Times Book Section*. Jan. 29, 1967.
pp. 5, 30

It is difficult to imagine—especially in these days of celebrity-
authors—a writer who would actually *prefer* a limited readership,
but then Jane Bowles is not like other writers. She is original to the
point of being unnerving, and it seems entirely possible that she
wrote as much with the intention to exclude as to include. She is
fated to remain a specialized taste because hers goes beyond a mere
idiosyncrasy of style, an identifiable semantic tic like Donald
Barthelme's or William Gass's. One is tempted to make comparisons—to Ivy Compton-Burnett for the entrenched habit of irony, to
Carson McCullers for the use of the grotesque—but they don't
really hold up: she is both more human than the former and less
sentimental than the latter. Bowles's voice is an uncompromisingly
independent one and it bespeaks a vision of life so unflinching as to
challenge most of our assumptions.

To read *My Sister's Hand in Mine* is to submit to a demanding
presence. Jane Bowles is one of those writers who can truly be said
to inhabit a country of her own making. Although the specific
geographical location might change, the emotional terrain is characteristically depleted, and one comes away with an unsettling
image of projected solitude. . . .

Jane Bowles is a capricious weaver of spells; her stories often
end as though they were about to begin again somewhere else—
now you see the magic, now you don't. Perhaps that is because her
fiction is conceived at such a rarified altitude; her characters are
living in domesticated penal colonies. . . .

There is a persistent mystery at the heart of Jane Bowles's
fiction. What is amazing, finally, is that fiction so intentionally

whimsical, even perverse, should reverberate the way Bowles's
does, igniting sparks of recognition on every page.

Daphne Merkin. *New Republic*. Feb. 11, 1978, pp. 30–31

If there is one common denominator in Mrs. Bowles's work, it is
women's relentless search for autonomy and self-knowledge, for
release from all conventional structures. And a demonic, frenzied
search it becomes in Mrs. Bowles's hands. . . .

Of the 20th-century novelists who have written most poignantly
about modern women's independence from men—Colette, Lessing,
Kate Chopin, Jean Rhys, Jane Bowles come immediately to
mind—the last three are consummate artists who have each spent
several decades buried in oblivion. . . . As for Jane Bowles, whose
oeuvre also concerns a redefinition of female freedom, a considerable silence has attended her work since the production of her play
In the Summer House 25 years ago, not-withstanding the critical
acclaim she has received. . . .

The theme of women's independence, and its frequent coeffi-
cients of solitude and potential destruction, have more often than
not been limned with Lessingesque earnestness in a socio-realistic
setting. So Mrs. Bowles's oeuvre is all the more unique because of
its Grand Guignol hilarity, its constant surprises, and a blend of
realism and grotesqueness that occasionally recalls Ronald Firbank.
There is extraordinary tension between the sturdy, supernormal
physical world she describes and the gloriously unpredictable,
fantastic movements of the eccentric personages who inhabit it. . . .

Mrs. Bowles's acerbic genius for the *outré* does not leave it any
grounds for comparison with Radclyffe Hall's sentimental tale
[*The Well of Loneliness*]. Neither are her heroines' precipitous
declines caused by any preference for lesbianism, for they seem as
asexual as they are independent and nomadic, turning to the flesh as
a symbol of independence without appearing to enjoy one moment
of it. Their gloriously uninhibited carousing, their voluptuous
liberation from all male discipline . . . has much more to do with a
return to the permissive sexual androgyny of juvenile bonding than
with any sexual preference. It is this very childlike playfulness that
gives Mrs. Bowles's work its fey power and its luminous originality, and that may disconcert readers fond of predictably ''female,''
''mature'' heroines. . . .

In Mrs. Bowles's work, the traditional novelistic struggle
between weak and strong characters ends inevitably in a draw. The
rigorous pursuit of autonomy, and a rueful acceptance of its often
tragic consequences, is the only heroic goal. For even the strongest
are unmade by their failure to take into account ''the terrible
strength of the weak,'' and follow an equally drunken downward
path to wisdom. There is a severe avoidance of all moralizing. It is
left to the individual reader to determine whether Mrs. Bowles's
heroines were better off in the shelter of their repressive marriages
and inhibited spinsterhoods than in the anarchy of their libertinage.

Francine du Plessix Gray. *New York Times Book Section*.
Feb. 19, 1978, pp. 3, 28

From the time she was a child Jane had had the sense of sin—a sin
that she could never define except to say that it was hers and
original, that which separated her from others. Her life had been
spent in the doubleness of the knowledge of that sin and the evasion
of the knowledge. She had been obsessed by Elsie Dinsmore and

yet had mocked Elsie's obedience to her father and her even greater obedience to Jesus. She had read Simone Weil's work over and over, feeling an identity with her, but then she had laughed and said, "But I have a sensual side too." For years she had spoken about sin and salvation—no one understood it. Most people thought it was Jane being funny, as when she'd said, "Most of all I want to be a religious leader," and then laughed and said, "But of course I'm not."

That sin which she took to be her destiny was inseparable from her imagination. Her writing became both the evidence of the sin and also—by some turn within her—the religious sacrifice that was its expiation. In her work, from the beginning, the themes of sin and salvation were unrelenting: in the words of Miss Goering as a child, baptizing Mary, "Dear God . . . make this girl Mary pure as Jesus Your Son"; in the words of Miss Goering at the end of her journey, ". . . is it possible that a part of me hidden from my sight is piling sin upon sin as fast as Mrs. Copper-field?"; in the words that tell of Sadie's life, "She conceived of her life as separate from herself; the road was laid out always a little ahead of her by sacred hands. . . ."

If in the earliest works there was a double edge—the sense of belief and the other side of belief, both present and united by her wiles—as the years went on, as her work became only unfinished work, the voices of sin and salvation became more urgent. "My life is *not* my own," Bozoe Flanner screams at Janet Murphy. "Have you missed the whole point of my life?" And of a woman in an unfinished play, Jane wrote: "She believes that she has a second heart and because she believes this she can accept a lie and protect it—Her wild clinging to this false trust is a result of her not wishing to discover that she has only one heart after all. . . . She guards her false trust in order not to fall into her single heart—The single heart is herself—it is suffering—it is God—it is nothing. . . ."

> Millicent Dillon. *A Little Original Sin: The Life and Works of Jane Bowles* (Holt, Rinehart and Winston, 1981), pp. 414–15

BIBLIOGRAPHY
Two Serious Ladies 1943 (n); *In the Summer House*, 1954 (d); *Collected Works*, 1966 (n, d, s); *Feminine Wiles*, 1976 (s, d, letters); *My Sister's Hand in Mine* [expanded edition of *Collected Works*], 1978 (n, d, s); *Out in the World: Selected Letters of Jane Bowles, 1935–1970*, 1985

BOWLES, Paul (1910–1986)

There is a curiously double level to this novel. The surface is enthralling as narrative. It is impressive as writing. . . .In its interior aspect, *The Sheltering Sky* is an allegory of the spiritual adventure of the fully conscious person into modern experience. . . .Actually this superior motive does not intrude in explicit form upon the story, certainly not in any form that will need to distract you from the great pleasure of being told a first-rate story of adventure by a really first-rate writer.

> Tennessee Williams *New York Times Book Section*. Dec. 4, 1949. pp. 7, 38

Once again, Mr. Bowles has written a frightening book. Only now there is an important difference. The *shock* is present, but is no longer a device. It is a conclusion justified by the hashish delirium that is the one possible resolution of Dyar's existentialist pilgrimage into the unknown interior of himself. If Mr. Bowles takes the chance of losing the *voyeurs* in his audience by this new discipline, he asks of others that he be judged more specifically on his merits.

These merits are considerable, but of a technical and exterior sort. Mr. Bowles, who is an accomplished composer, presents his characters contrapuntally. What each is doing at a particular moment is artfully disclosed. The theme of one is offered first and then followed by his antiphonal response to another whose theme has already been given. But only sensibility joins them, and a terrible rootlessness.

> Leonard Amster. *Saturday Review*. March 15, 1952. p. 21

Mr. Bowles's stories and novels are the work of an exposed nerve. The pain is felt before the experience. There is a perennial dryness and irony in American literature of which Bowles is the latest and most sophisticated exponent; it has the air of premature cynicism, prolongs the moment when civilisation itself becomes entirely anxiety and disgust. . . .Bowles has been properly compared with D. H. Lawrence, for he has a marvelous eye for the foreign scene as it comes to the eye of the rich, rootless wanderer. He is also a brilliant collector of items of human isolation in its varying degrees of madness, and he is intellectually disapproving of both the isolated man and the man who has merely the apparent solidarity and gregariousness of the urban creature. . . .Where Bowles fails is that in reducing the Lawrence situations. . .to a kind of existentialist dimension, he has made them merely *chic*. The moral passion has vanished; even passion has gone.

> V.S. Pritchett. *New Statesman and Nation*. July 12, 1952. p. 44

Bowles is an obsessionist, and his obsession may be simply stated: that psychological well-being is in inverse ratio to what is commonly known as progress, and that a highly evolved culture enjoys less peace of mind than one which is less highly evolved. . . .It is no accident that the three novels and that fifteen of the seventeen stories in *The Delicate Prey* have a foreign setting. Nor is it true, as has sometimes been charged, that Bowles is merely indulging in a pointless exoticism, for not only are the settings foreign, they are usually primitive as well. For this reason he chooses such remote locales as a small town in the Sahara, a Colombian jungle, a river boat winding painfully through the interior of an unidentified Latin-American country. And in nearly all of his work the tension arises from a contrast between alien cultures: in a typical Bowles story, a civilized individual comes in contact with an alien environment and is defeated by it.

> Oliver Evans. *Critique*. Spring-Fall, 1959. p. 44

The abysses and furies of the human psyche; the fragile, provisional nature of the civilized instincts; the lure of the primitive and the inhuman; the sadness of deracinated people; the underground warfare of marriage and friendship; the lonely divisions between desire and behavior, between having and holding, between one hand and the other hand; the modern world's contagions of angst, dread, deadness: all these strains of the existentialist vision are dramatically presented in Bowles' earlier work and come to a classic statement in his novel, *The Sheltering Sky*, one of the most beautifully written novels of the past twenty years and one of the most shattering. . . .

. . .*The Time of Friendship* brings together his first collection of stories in more than twenty years. Most of them are effective, several are memorable, but only one seems to me to break fresh ground. This is the long title story in which Bowles abandons his rather static view of primitivism, and moves beyond his somewhat fatigued fascination with its timeless mysteries and perversities, to write about post-colonial Algeria. . . .

The story is as complex in the telling as any Bowles has written; what is so strange and moving is its benignity. What it portends for his future work, I don't profess to know. But it's good to find him writing a tender story and one which strengthens his grip on contemporary experience. Perhaps the world is moving too fast for even his nihilism to have the last work. It's nice to think so.

Theodore Solotaroff. *New Republic*. Sept. 2, 1967. pp. 29–31

Reading *The Time of Friendship*, Paul Bowles's new collection of stories, I was aware of a career honest in its aims but only occasionally swinging free of a steady performance. Unlike Tennessee Williams' attempts at unmanageable forms, Bowles sticks with what he can do. Here are the gothic tales with their meaningless violence and seedy Arab settings which repeat the formula established in *The Delicate Prey* seventeen years ago. Here are the macabre Saki endings and the landscapes beautifully tuned to an indefinable melancholy. The stories are always carefully written but, for the most part, they are too self-contained and seldom have anything to match the atmosphere of frenzied desolation that drives through *The Sheltering Sky* to make it Bowles's masterpiece. He is still involved with his ideas of twenty years ago but he has lost his passion for them. The existential experience of *The Sheltering Sky* can never seem dated, but many of the empty exotic scenes in *The Time of Friendship* depend upon a bleak modernity which has worn thin even for Bowles.

Maureen Howard. *Partisan Review*. Winter, 1968. p. 149

Paul Bowles has produced a large body of work, only a fraction of which is represented in the *Collected Stories*. He has published poetry, four novels, an autobiography and two travel essays. He has taped and translated an impressive number of oral stories in Moghrebi, a North African dialect. These translations are an achievement in themselves and also play a central part in the development of his short fiction. Bowles is moreover a composer of some standing, and has recorded a large collection of North African music. Nevertheless, fiction is the central pillar of his work, and his autobiography, poetry and journalism are only interesting galleries attached to the central structure, ornamental perhaps, but hardly essential. His novels have excellent qualities but only his first, *The Sheltering Sky*, deserves to be classed with the short fiction. . . .

The majority of the stories published in Bowles's first collection, *The Delicate Prey*, already exhibit a mature sense of subject

and of technique. "A Distant Episode" is one of the best of these stories. The title reminds the reader that the events described are far removed from the west. It is an initiation story (Bowles has written a number of these), a meeting between the rule-bound west, represented by "the Professor," and the violence of North Africa. The Professor is a professor of linguistics; preoccupied by the structure of Language, he is incapable of communication. . . .

Like the Professor in "A Distant Episode," Bowles may seem to have returned to his starting point, surrealistic description having been replaced by kif dreams and automatic writing by oral texts. But to see his career as static or circular is a mistake. The early surrealism was an act of violence towards language, a literal dismembering. The stories collected here redirect this violence, allowing dismemberment an uneasy coherence. The seventeen-year-old could only appropriate a style; the intervening years have created a master capable of appropriating a culture.

H. C. Ricks. *Chicago Review*. Spring, 1980. pp. 83, 85, 88

[William Carlos] Williams' characteristically trenchant observation of one of Bowles' techniques is one that holds true for all the novels and short stories that Bowles has published since *The Sheltering Sky*: he is an author who works to avoid cliché by confronting his materials, not by sidling past them with the help of the codified tics and patterns of "fine writing." His work is unsettling, but rarely because of the raw materials, the content, of his stories. Rather, it is the acutely conscious attempt to deal with these materials honestly that enables him to transcend the content that, in other hands, might be the stuff of sensation or didacticism.

The language of Bowles' fiction is reticent and formal, but often brutal in its flat candor. No wonder Williams admired him. Over his work there lies a barely visible "haze" of anxiety or terror. His characters, once embarked upon the adventures that he invents for them, carry them through to the end; there is no point in a Bowles story at which one can say, with any certainty, *there* is where the story takes its turn. His stories do not take "turns," but follow strait and undeviating paths, the beginnings of which are anterior to their first words. We "come in" on them, as it were.

It is as if Bowles has made a compact with his readers, one that assumes that he and they know that people are weak, vacillating, self-serving, envious, and often base, as well as being, more often than not, irrational because of fixed and unexamined beliefs in country, class, religion, culture, and so on. Granting the existence of this compact, the stories may be seen as inevitable, their characters not so much caught in a web of problems as playing out, so to speak, their hands. In a curious way, the stories may be seen as modern variations on the Jonsonian use of medieval "humours." . . .

[He] is most at home in his work in a North African setting, usually Moroccan, and . . . most of his stories have to do with Arabs or with Arabs and their dealings with Americans or Europeans. I would say that much of Bowles' power and clarity, his freshness and eschewal of the banal has come about because he uses this material without resorting to condescension, awed delight, or sociological analysis: the specific world of Morocco is *there*.

Nowhere in Bowles do we find any hint of the exotic. His Arabs don't think of themselves as such, but as people who live the lives that have been given them. The brilliance of Bowles' work is rooted in the fact that his prose takes his non-western world for granted, and this matter-of-fact attitude is tacitly held in subtle opposition to what might be called the reader's expectations. We bring our great bag of *idées fixes* to Bowles' Morocco, and he calmly proceeds to empty it in front of us. Furthermore, Bowles' western characters are often seen to be carrying that same bag in the stories in which they appear: their reward for this cultural error is usually disaster. . . . He does what the good artist everywhere does: solves the problems he has created for himself with the same tools used to create the problems. He is responsible to his work and not to the dim flickerings of "taste." These are distinguished stories indeed.

Gilbert Sorrentino. *Book World*. Aug. 2, 1981, pp. 3, 6

With his wife, Jane Bowles, he became a legendary example of the gilded expatriate—a sojourner who seemed to fit into the most exotic places; meet the most fascinating people; and go on to tell of his experiences in a manner cool and haunting. The manner cloaked the unpleasant, particularly the rigors of travel in primitive places and the emotional conflicts of the main parties in Bowles's adventures. At the same time the manner made possible the exhibition of the magnificent unconventional beauties available to the nomadic life Bowles had led. What emerges from his autobiography, *Without Stopping*, and his journal, *Days: Tangier Journal 1987–1989*, is the portrait of a man who cannot feel at home unless he has recourse to solitude, and for whom solitude must mean periodic journeying into unknown territories. In an earlier century Bowles might be called a romantic and compared to Byron or Sir Richard Burton. Today, he may be characterized as an example of the homeless virus that afflicts the gifted and sends them into exiles of the spirit, those who seek in their chosen rootlessness an insight into their condition and an acceptance of it.

Bowles, if judged by his autobiography, is a kindly man, much more so than he is in *Days; Tangier Journal 1987–1989*, which is a piquant, witty, and sometimes acerbic account of daily jousting with an increasingly larger public. Bowles is also a man who has tried to do his best by meeting responsibilities to his parents, wife, friends, employers, and public, and yet at the same time he has consistently tried to escape from the net of personal and professional demands. His way is a subtle and magnificent coil of escape; few are capable of practicing it well, for the process is monastic in its dues; its rewards, while inwardly palpable, are not outwardly evident.

Without Stopping then tells the story of a man who has determined his life's mission as seeing as much of the world as he can feel, and to utilize that rich experience in his music and writing. He tells, for example, the anecdote of an artist who put a collection of work under his pillow before he went to sleep in order to absorb it when he could no longer concentrate on it in a waking state. This anecdote and other revelations Bowles puts forth are fascinating precisely because he is low-keyed in his narration: much is clearly being withheld while much is subtly rendered in a sheltering style.

There is also plenty of gossip in his work: Bowles is aware of his need to sell to a public, but the real value of his autobiographical and travel writings are to be found elsewhere.

Martin Tucker. *Confrontation*. Fall, 1991, pp. 337–38

To the expatriates who landed there after World War II, the International Zone of Tangier was an enigmatic, exotic, and deliciously depraved version of Eden. A sun-bleached, sybaritic outpost set against the verdant hills of North Africa, it offered a free

money market, and a moral climate in which only murder and rape were forbidden. Fleeing an angst-ridden Western culture, European emigrés found a haven where homosexuality was accepted, drugs were readily available, and eccentricity was a social asset.

But the decadence of the infidels who drifted to Tangier was offset by a singular thread in the city's complex fabric—the mysticism of its native Muslims. Paul Bowles, the most prominent of the literary exiles who settled in Tangier, was acutely aware of its spiritual undercurrent. "I relish the idea that in the night, all around me in my sleep, sorcery is burrowing its invisible tunnels in every direction, from thousands of senders to thousands of unsuspecting recipients," he wrote. . . .

Taken with the promise of worldly pleasures in an occult setting, a flock of other Western intellectuals assembled in Tangier after Bowles embarked on his self-imposed exile in 1947. Along with Jane Bowles, the idiosyncratic writer whom he married in 1938, Paul became a magnetic force in a scene enlivened, at various junctures, by Truman Capote, Tennessee Williams, William Burroughs, Brion Gysin, Allen Ginsberg, and Jack Kerouac. Over a period of two decades, they saw—and wrote about—the city from a remarkable range of perspectives: For twelve months of his four-year sojourn, the gaunt Burroughs, languished in a male brothel, where he "had not taken a bath . . . nor changed my clothes or removed them except to stick a needle every hour in the fibrous gray wooden flesh of terminal addiction.". . .

Few modern settings have offered such an alchemical blend of primitivism and sophistication, and few have spawned so many provocative tales. And while the spirited, raffish port has long since deteriorated into a desultory tourist town, Europeans who find themselves there still sit for long hours in its cacophonous cafes, talking of Paul and Jane and the tawdry glory that was Tangier. Most of the visitors never knew the Bowleses, but that hardly seems to matter; we have all become fellow travelers in a world ruled by entropy, and it was Paul who mapped the course. . . .

Paul Bowles never stopped complaining about his adopted home. At the end of 1990, he was lamenting the fact that the Villa Nouvelle had been marred by construction projects that would never be finished, and that the price of cookies at the Fez Market jumped from one week to the next. He talked about the absurdities of Moroccan bureaucracy, and he shuddered over the gloomy weather. But if some failed to see how Tangier had held him for so long, Bowles knew why he had stayed on after Jane had died: "Tangier," he said, "is like a gong that rang [forty] years ago. I still hear the resonance."

Michelle Green. *The Dream at the End of the World* (New York: HarperPerennial, 1993 [1992]), pp. xi–xii, xiv, xvi, 344

BIBLIOGRAPHY
The Sheltering Sky, 1949 (n); *The Delicate Prey*, 1950 (s); *Let It Come Down*, 1952 (n); *The Spider's House*, 1955 (n); *Yallah*, 1958 (t); *The Hours after Noon*, 1959 (s); *Their Heads Are Green and Their Hands Are Blue*, 1963 (t); *Up above the World*, 1966 (n); *The Time of Friendship*, 1967 (s); *Love with a Few Hairs, by Mohammed Mrabet*, 1968 (tr); *Scenes*, 1968 (p); *The Thicket of Spring*, 1971 (p); *Without Stopping*, 1972 (a); *Three Tales*, 1975 (s); *Things Gone & Things Still Here*, 1977 (s); *Collected Stories, 1939–1976*, 1979; *Next to Nothing: Collected Poems, 1926–1977*, 1981; *Points in Time*, 1982 (s); *Mohammed Mrabet: Marriage with Papers*,

1986 (tr); *A Distant Episode: Selected Stories*, 1988; *Unwelcome*, 1988 (s); *Days: Tangier Journal 1987–1989*, 1991 (m); *Too Far from Home*, ed. Daniel Halpern, 1993 (a, misc); *In Touch*, 1994 (l); *The Portable Paul and Jane Bowles*, ed. Millicent Dillon, 1994 (misc)

BOYLE, Kay (1903–1992)

Anyone . . . whose standards of the short story are not the standards of the correspondence school will appreciate that the work of Miss Boyle, for simple craftsmanship, is superior to most of that which is crowned annually by our anthologies. Anyone with an ear for new verbal harmonies will appreciate that Miss Boyle is a stylist of unusual taste and sensibility. It is time, therefore, to cease to regard her as a mere lower case révoltée and to begin to accept her for what she is: more enterprising, more scrupulous, potentially more valuable than nine-tenths of our best-known authors.

Gerald Sykes. *The Nation*. Dec. 24, 1930. p. 711

Gertrude Stein and James Joyce were and are the glories of their time and some very portentous talents have emerged from their shadows. Miss Boyle, one of the newest, I believe to be among the strongest. . . . She sums up the salient qualities of that movement: a fighting spirit, freshness of feeling, curiosity, the courage of her own attitude and idiom, a violently dedicated search for the meanings and methods of art. . . . There are further positive virtues of the individual temperament: health of mind, wit and the sense of glory.

Katherine Anne Porter. *New Republic*. April 22, 1931. p. 279

She is one of the most eloquent and one of the most prolific writers among the expatriates; her work is always finished in the sense that her phrases are nicely cadenced and her imagery often striking and apt; her characters are almost always highly sensitized individuals who are marooned or in flight in some foreign country, banded together in small groups in which the antagonisms often seem intense beyond their recognizable causes. . . . It is noteworthy how much Kay Boyle gets out of the casual coming together of her people, what untold dangers and mysterious excitement she finds in their first impressions of each other—out of the tormented relationships and the eventual flight.

Robert Cantwell. *New Republic*. Dec. 13, 1933. p. 136

Kay Boyle is Hemingway's successor, though she has not that piercing if patternless emotion which is what we remember of Hemingway at his best. It is significant that both writers received their literary training in Paris, as did Henry James, that they are familiar with deracinates and those casual sojourners in Paris whose search is for the exciting and the momentary. Each has the observational facility of the newspaperman, with the poet's power

of meditating on life; their work stands out from any other type of fiction written in any other country, in both content and technique.

Mary M. Colum. *Forum*. Oct. 1938. p. 166

To my mind, the chief defect in Miss Boyle's equipment as an artist is to be traced to her lack of a subject which is organically her own; and by an organic subject I mean something more tangible than a fixed interest in certain abstract patterns of emotion and behavior. Being in possession of an elaborate technique and having developed disciplined habits of observation, Miss Boyle seems to be able to turn her hand to almost anything. As a result one feels all too often that she is not really involved with her themes, that she has not conceived but merely used them.

Philip Rahv. *The Nation*. March 23, 1940. p. 396

In her best work, it seems to me, her style is never noticeably brilliant; it is always subdued, always subservient to the creation of scenes and characters. One seldom feels, either, that Miss Boyle's stories or novels have been carpentered to fit a carefully worked out thesis. The best of her fiction is convincing and lifelike; the "meaning," seldom forced or imposed, rises—or seems to rise—naturally out of characters and actions, as though the author had actually observed the people and events just as she writes about them. . . . [S]he appears to be deeply committed to some ideal of social equality, personal freedom, universal tenderness or love—it is difficult to label what is usually subtle and complex—and she sees in the world about her the brutal violation of those who embody these ideals. Again and again in her fiction we are shown sensitive individuals, who respond to life feelingly rather than conventionally, attacked and defeated by tough, well-insulated barbarians flying the banners of custom and tradition.

William Stuckey, *Minnesota Review*. Fall, 1960. p. 118

Kay Boyle has added eighteen poems from the last ten years to her earlier work in verse that culminated in the long 1944 poem *American Citizen*; these *Collected Poems* are elusive but—as always in the poetry of a writer whose characteristic achievement is in prose—they offer a reliable thematic index to Miss Boyle's preoccupations over the years: she aspires to be, doubtless is, a good European, the kind of person who knows the right café to sit in front of, the interesting wine to order, a hard ski slope to descend, an easy man to love. Her landscapes, both American and European, are made into emblems of the wild heart, the behavior of her animals likened to the actions of men. It is not entirely fair, by the way, to refer to her "earlier work in verse," since so many of these difficult pieces are experiments in mixing verse with extended prose passages; indeed, however obscure it may be, such prose is always firmer and, if not more deeply felt, then more dramatically honed than the verse, which in even the very latest poems is without much spine or spring, though Miss Boyle has spirit and to spare.

Richard Howard. *Poetry*. July, 1963. pp. 253–4

Put simply, Kay Boyle's theme is nearly always the perennial human need for love; her design is woven from the many forms the frustration and misdirection of love may take. Her style and the care with which she limns a setting are, as they inevitably must be with a creative artist, but vehicle and adjunct for her central meaning. Although on occasion she may have forgotten the artistic obligation in exchange for sheer virtuosity (always a danger for the virtuoso), using her style to bedazzle rather than to aid vision, or letting exotic setting obscure the human situation with which she is dealing, in her better fiction, style, setting, and theme for a seamless web in which all the threads are held under a precise tension.

Richard C. Carpenter. *Critique*. Winter, 1964–65. p. 65

She is the author of 13 novels, some of them very good, but she is not quite a major novelist. Her major medium has always been the short story and the novelette. (And it is typical of this aristocrat, whose earlier work lay in the tradition of Edith Wharton and Henry James, not to use the fashionable word, novella.) But even here, she was in the early thirties, a writer of superior sensibility—or so I thought—using a foreign scene more successfully than her native one, and belonging, in essence, both to the expatriate line of James and Wharton and to that later "lost generation" of the 1920's.

What this new collection of Miss Boyle's short stories and novelettes does prove is that while all of the speculation above is somewhat true, none of it is really true, or profoundly true. She has all these elements in this new collection of her mature work. But, as in the case of every first-rank writer, she rises above the disparate elements in her work or in her temperament, to become something else. What *Nothing Ever Breaks Except the Heart* proves, in short, is that Kay Boyle has at last become a major short-story writer, or a major writer in contemporary American fiction, after three decades of elusiveness, sometimes of anonymity, almost of literary "classlessness," while she has pursued and has finally discovered her true metier. . . . To her earlier vision of sensibility, she has added what every first-rate writer must have, a standard of human morality—and the fact that human morality is usually, if not always, related to a specific social or historical context.

It is this familiar concept, missing in so much current and "new" American fiction, that is embodied in the magnificent stories of her maturity.

Maxwell Geismar. *New York Times Book Section*. July 10, 1966. pp. 4, 16

Kay Boyle's contemporaries in the twenties and thirties assumed she would be one of the literary stars of her generation. In a review in *The The Nation*, Gerald Sykes said of her in 1930, "It is time . . . to cease to regard her as a mere lower case revoltee and to begin to accept her for what she is: more enterprising, more scrupulous, potentially more valuable than nine-tenths of our best-known authors.". . .

But acclaim for Kay Boyle's work nearly always has been contained within small circles. Her only popular success was *Avalanche*—the book that, on literary grounds, probably least deserved it and which earned her the damaging ridicule of that influential critic, Edmund Wilson. Despite her distinguished and prolific career, her work is not widely known today, and only a handful of her books remain in print. . . .

Her reputation has also suffered at the hands of critics who repeatedly devalued her work on the basis of its subject matter. It appears as though her subject matter—often the trials of a woman

alone groping for an identity and a context in which to live—simply did not interest critics concerned with more "substantial" issues. . . .

As a young avant-garde expatriate, she wrote, "I have no religion, except that of poetry, and in Poe, Whitman, and William Carlos Williams I recognize the apostles of America." She always has had much in common with the nineteenth-century American romantics, perhaps more than she has recognized. This romantic perspective is another constant that binds together the works of diverse material and style that make up her canon. From the beginning of her career to the present day, she has insisted upon experiencing life firsthand, ignoring any "middlemen" of letters, religion, or philosophy. She has believed in overstepping the confines of institutions and traditions and in spurning the dictates of convention and "common sense." She has placed her faith in the intuition and the imagination and believed that no time has ever been more significant than the present instant.

Sandra Whipple Spannier. *Kay Boyle: Artist and Activist* (Carbondale: Southern Illinois Univ. Pr., 1986), pp. 214, 220, 221

"Primarily a poet" according to her own assessment, Kay Boyle has, nonetheless, been praised mostly as a writer of short stories, novels, and memoirs—when indeed this remarkable American artist has been acknowledged at all by the literary establishment. Her career has had a rather astonishing span: She was a member of the *transition* group in the Paris of the 1920s and a friend to many of the famed of those days; sojourner in various parts of Europe before and after World War II; opponent of McCarthyism back in the U.S.; a heroic inspiration to her students at San Francisco State during the most turbulent days of the Vietnam era. The diverse spirits of all these times—except perhaps the 1950s—flash forth memorably in the free verse of her new collection of poems dated variously between 1916 and November 1990. Boyle strongly favors the form of the address or verse letter: These poems are directly "to" or at least "for" a quite varied group of persons. . . . M.L. Rosenthal pronounced the poems of Boyle's 1970 volume to be "museums of select political, moral, and social attitudes," but the best of these later poems seem not dated at all in their fierce expressions of an aging woman against injustice. . . . In "A Poem for Vida Hadjebi Tabrizi," for example, Boyle, reading a poem of Babette Deutsch, feels a spiritual contact with her friend across a continent, but feels even more the spirit of another woman conjured up, an Iranian political prisoner. Some of the *communiqué* poems of the 1920s and 1930s are more cryptic/private in their intent (or we are farther from their politics), but they often contain striking images that may owe more to her "idol" Rimbaud than to her friend and avowed influence, [W.C.] Williams. Especially noteworthy are several experiments mixing prose poetry with free verse.

Joseph Milicia. *Multicultural Review*. April, 1992, p. 73

BIBLIOGRAPHY

Wedding Day, 1929 (s); *Plagued by the Nightingale*, 1931 (n); *Devil in the Flesh*, 1932 (tr); *Year Before Last*, 1932 (n); *Gentlemen, I Address You Privately*, 1933 (n); *The First Lover*, 1933 (s); *My Next Bride*, 1934 (n); *Death of a Man*, 1936 (n); *The White Horses of Vienna*, 1936 (s); *Monday Night*, 1938 (n); *A Glad Day*, 1938 (p); *The Youngest Camel*, 1939, rev. 1959 (juv); *The Crazy*

Hunter, 1940 (s); *Primer for Combat*, 1942 (n); *American Citizen*, 1944 (p); *Avalanche*, 1944 (n); *A Frenchman Must Die*, 1946 (n); *Thirty Stories*, 1946; *1939*, 1948 (n); *His Human Majesty*, 1949 (n); *The Smoking Mountain*, 1951 (s); *The Seagull on the Step*, 1955 (n); *Three Short Novels*, 1958; *Generation without Farewell*, 1960 (n); *Nothing Ever Breaks Except the Heart*, 1966 (s); ed. and tr., *The Autobiography of Emanuel Carnevali*, 1968; *Being Geniuses Together, 1920–1930*, 1968 (rev. ed. of Robert McAlmon memoir [1938]); *Testament for My Students*, 1970 (p); *The Long Walk at San Francisco State*, 1972 (e); *The Underground Woman*, 1975 (n); *Fifty Stories*, 1980; *This Is Not a Letter*, 1985 (p); *Words That Must Somehow Be Said*, 1985 (e); *Life Being the Best*, 1988 (s); *Collected Poems*, 1991

BOYLE, T. Coraghessan (1939–)

T. Coraghessan Boyle is perhaps . . . most resourceful in making use of . . . comic forms, and [he is] temperamentally aligned with [Philip] Roth and other "wild" humorists (Woody Allen also comes to mind in his view of contemporary America). In [*The River Is Whiskey*], Boyle's third collection, the comedy derives from bizarre situations and characters, but above all from the author's corrosive wit and inventive use of language, virtues which are notable throughout these zany, energetic stories. What if a man in pursuit of fame were to transform himself into a human fly? What if a young woman were to follow the concept of "safe sex" to a grotesque extreme? What if a public relations man were assigned to improve the "image" of the Ayatollah Khomeini? Boyle pursues such questions with near-manic intensity even as he exerts careful control over his narrative structures, many of which are reminiscent of Twain in their combination of boisterous humor and a piercing commentary on their contemporary experience.

Boyle combines a wealth of detail about 1980s America with a keen awareness of literary tradition: his stories are furnished with compact discs, cellular phones, home security systems, and specific details about our food and drink, clothing, and entertainment; yet they also allude to fairy tales and the Faust legend, to Hemingway and Joyce and Kafka. Like many of the so-called minimalist writers, he has a fondness (at times excessive) for mentioning brand names, but his obsessive documentation of contemporary reality does establish a connection—as most minimalists either fail or refuse to do—between that reality and the spectrum of Western literary tradition, as if to place contemporary America within the ongoing progression of human folly.

Greg Johnson. *Georgia Review*. Winter, 1990, p. 714

The strength of *East Is East* lies in the story of Hiro, where Boyle's previously demonstrated talent for comic-grotesque invention comes into play. One of the funniest episodes occurs when a rich, garrulous, Japanophile old woman, Ambly Wooster, takes Hiro into her beach house under the impression that he is Seiji Ozawa. The cultural confusions multiply, as do the vigorously narrated mishaps that befall Hiro in his desperate attempts to leave the island and reach the City of Brotherly Love. While there is a considerable degree of Waugh-like cruelty in the fate Boyle metes out to his antihero, who follows the example of Mishima to its bloody

conclusion, Hiro himself is engaging enough to provide a pathos at the end that in no way clashes with the comedy that precedes it. This is an exuberant reworking of the innocents abroad theme that goes back at least as far as Voltaire's *L'Ingenu*.

Paul Auster. *New York Review of Books*. January 17, 1991, p. 32

That a writer such as Boyle, invariably fascinated by quirky human behavior, chose John Henry Kellog for his focal historical character in the novel [*The Road to Wellville*] is no surprise. But curiously, though his title is taken from one of C.W. Post's most famous slogans, only John Henry Kellog appears as a character in *The Road to Wellville*. Post and W.K. Kellog are simply mental irritations to the hyperactive doctor [protagonist], enemies to be dealt with, vanquished, outlived.

In place of Post and W.K. Kellog, Boyle offers several wholly fictional characters, rather ordinary ones even for historical fiction and certainly for Boyle, who has earned a reputation for creating more entertaining and plausible representations of humanity than these turn out to be. . . .

One measure of historical fiction is a novel's success in keeping readers from slipping outside the plot to dwell on the historical plausibility of the events portrayed. With a Hawthorne or Faulkner, it simply doesn't occur to one to ask, "Is this true—could this really happen?" Readers do not pause to ask such questions of *World's End*, Boyle's 1987 novel that quite deservedly won the PEN/Faulkner award. But in *The Road to Wellville*, Boyle deliberately goads just these questions from readers. The regimen is too preposterous, the daily menu too ludicrous to have ever been taken seriously—even by such creatures as inhabit Boyle's fictive world. Even in a satire.

David R. Johnson. *America*. April 23, 1994, pp. 20–21

T.C. Boyle has proved himself time and again a canny storyteller at home with the offbeat and borderline grotesque; he applies his same sly skills here to characters heavily soiled with the grit of real life. The novel [*The Tortilla Curtain*] gamely addresses what has probably always been the great American political dilemma: In a country that proudly defines itself as a nation of immigrants, who gets to slam the door on whom? Boyle cuts to the heart of this question by describing two different nations, rich and poor, which occupy the same space but are often invisible to each other. Delaney's wife, Kyra, a powerhouse realtor, presides over a world of empty, immaculate mansions waiting to be sold. She clicks on high heels through these great halls admiring the space, without thinking once of homelessness. Kyra has a bleeding heart all right—it really gets her dander up to see a poor overheated pet locked in a car. But with a wave of her hand she scatters the labor exchange that is Cándido's lifeline, because the sight of those people hanging around is bound to affect property values. Meanwhile, Cándido crouches on the other side of the class wall, seeming to accept the excesses of *gabacho* wealth as an outlandish inevitability as he tries not to starve. In one of the book's many moments of fierce black comedy, he ponders the ethics of stealing food and crockery from a dog. . . .

What Boyle does, and does well, is lay on the line our national cult of hypocrisy. Comically and painfully he details the smug wastefulness of the haves and the vile misery of the have-nots. It doesn't seem to dawn on anyone in this novel that opulence next to starvation is brutally immoral, but the reader can hardly escape that conclusion. Red-blooded Americans of every stripe all find themselves rooting for Cándido and América, right up to the rip-roaring deus ex machina ending that screams out that we are all in this together.

Barbara Kingsolver. *The Nation.* Sept. 25, 1995, pp. 326–27

BIBLIOGRAPHY

Descent of Man, 1979 (s); *Water Music*, 1981 (n); *Budding Prospects: A Pastoral*, 1984 (n); *Greasy Lake*, 1985 (s); *World's End*, 1987 (n); *If the River Was Whiskey*, 1989 (s); *East Is East*, 1990 (n); *The Road to Wellville*, 1992 (n); *Collected Stories*, 1993; *Without a Hero*, 1994 (s); *The Tortilla Curtain*, 1995 (n)

BRADBURY, Ray (1920–)

Ray Bradbury has drawn the sword against the dreary and corrupting materialism of this century; against society as producer-and-consumer equation, against the hideousness in modern life, against mindless power, against sexual obsession, against sham intellectuality, against the perversion of right reason into the mentality of the television-viewer. His Martians, spectres, and witches are not diverting entertainment only: they become, in their eerie manner, the defenders of truth and beauty. . . .

[Bradbury] thinks it . . . probable that man may spoil everything, in this planet and in others, by the misapplication of science to avaricious ends—the Baconian and Hobbesian employment of science as power. And Bradbury's interior world is fertile, illuminated by love for the permanent things, warm with generous impulse. . . .

Bradbury knows of modern technology, in the phrase of Henry Adams, that we are "monkeys monkeying with a loaded shell." He is interested not in the precise mechanism of rockets, but in the mentality and the morals of fallible human beings who make and use rockets. He is a man of fable and parable. . . .

Bradbury is not writing about the gadgets of conquest; his real concerns are the soul and the moral imagination. When the boy-hero of *Dandelion Wine*, in an abrupt mystical experience, is seized almost bodily by the glowing consciousness that he is really alive, we glimpse that mystery the soul. When, in *Something Wicked This Way Comes*, the lightning-rod salesman is reduced magically to an idiot dwarf because all his life he had fled from perilous responsibility, we know the moral imagination.

"Soul," a word much out of fashion nowadays, signifies a man's animating entity. That flaming spark the soul is the real space-traveller of Bradbury's stories. "I'm alive!"—that exclamation is heard from Waukegan to Mars and beyond, in Bradbury's fables. Life is its own end—if one has a soul to tell him so. . . .

[The] moral imagination, which shows us what we ought to be, primarily is what distinguishes Bradbury's tales from the futurism of Wells' fancy. For Bradbury, the meaning of life is here and now, in our every action; we live amidst immortality; it is here, not in some future domination like that of Wells' *The Sleeper Awakens*, that we must find our happiness. . . .

What gives [*The Martian Chronicles*] their cunning is their realism set in the fantastic: that is, their portrayal of human nature, in all its baseness and all its promise, against an exquisite stage-set. We are shown normality, the permanent things in human nature, by the light of another world; and what we forget about ourselves in the ordinariness of our routine of existence suddenly bursts upon us as fresh revelation. . . .

In Bradbury's fables of Mars and of the carnival [in *Something Wicked This Way Comes*], fantasy has become what it was in the beginning: the enlightening moral imagination, transcending simple rationality. . . .

The trappings of science-fiction may have attracted young people to Bradbury, but he has led them on to something much older and better: mythopoeic literature, normative truth acquired through wonder. Bradbury's stories are not an escape from reality; they are windows looking upon enduring reality. . . .

Russell Kirk. *Enemies of the Permanent Things: Observations of Abnormality in Literature and Politics.* Arlington House, 1969. pp. 116–20, 120–24.

Elements of what may be called "fantasy" were present in Ray Bradbury's works from the beginning of his writing career. His own recent remark distinguishing science fiction from fantasy in literature is that "science fiction could happen." This implies, of course, that fantasy could not happen. But in today's world, where change occurs at such rapid rate, nobody would venture to state dogmatically that any idea is incapable of realization. Therefore, whether or not a work of literature is fantasy becomes more a matter of the author's intention rather than a matter measurable by objective criteria. This is especially true of an author such as Bradbury, who by his own admission writes both science fiction and fantasy.

Bradbury's own brand of fantasy apparently came to birth in the world of the carnival. His imagination was nurtured with carnival imagery. . . . Whenever a travelling circus or carnival came through Waukegan in the 1920s and early 1930s, Bradbury and his younger brother were always present. . . .

[The] carnival became for him a sort of subconscious touchstone for a whole system of moods and images which emerged later in his writings. As a result, the carnival world can be thought of as a clearinghouse for Bradbury's imagination—the place where he goes for his symbols when he is writing a tale of horror, nostalgia, fantasy, or some combination of the three. . . .

But of Bradbury's tales [during the 1940s] more were horror than fantasy. Perhaps he would regard an attempt to distinguish between horror and fantasy in his works as mere semantic quibbling. The difference, it seems to me, can almost be described as a matter of levity. In the horror tales, he was completely serious and trying his best to achieve a shock effect upon his readers. In the best of these, he probably succeeded because he also achieved, in the writing process, a shock effect upon himself. He was trying to exorcise something in himself as he wrote. Thus his horror tales were not written to enable his readers to escape, but rather to cause them to suffer so that they might be cleansed. . . . The fantasy stories, on the other hand, allow the readers' spirits to expand rather than to contract, as is the effect in the horror tales. The thrust of his effort seems to lie in the creation of a mood, and, lost in this mood, the readers can escape to a Secondary World. . . .

The theme running through [*Something Wicked This Way Comes*] is that Evil is a shadow: Good is a reality. Evil cannot exist except in the vacuum left when people let their Good become not an active form, not a pumping in their veins, but just a memory, an intention. As Bradbury has indicated in other stories and articles, he feels that the potential for evil exists like cancer germs, dormant in all of us, and unless we keep our Good in fit condition by actively using it, it will lose its power to fight off the poisons in our system. . . .

Love is the best humanizing force man possesses, Bradbury seems to be saying. . . .

The idea of the healing powers of love is perhaps most beautifully expressed in the story "A Medicine for Melancholy" (1959). The story is almost a parable. A young girl in eighteenth-century London is slowly fading away before the eyes of her concerned parents. No doctor is able to diagnose her illness, and finally in desperation they take her, bed and all, and put her outside the front door so that the passersby can try their hand at identifying what is wrong with her. A young Dustman looks into her eyes and knows what is wrong—she needs love. He suggests that she be left out all night beneath the moon, and during the night he visits her and effects a cure. In the morning the roses have returned to her cheeks and she and her family dance in celebration. . . .

[This] idea, or moral, if that is a better word, . . . seems to be at least implicit in the majority of Bradbury's stories from the late 1950s until the present. He did not cease to be a teacher when he stopped writing science fiction, but he did place a moratorium upon the more evangelistic kind of moralizing which he was practicing in the late 1940s and early 1950s. Now, at last, his own sense of values seems to have become completely at one with his art. . . .

Anita T. Sullivan. *English Journal*. December, 1972, pp. 1309–14.

If Bradbury's ladders lead to Mars, whose chronicler he has become, or to the apocalyptic future of *Fahrenheit 451*, the change is simply one of direction, not of intensity. He is a visionary who writes not of the impediments of science, but of its effects upon man. *Fahrenheit 451*, after all, is not a novel about the technology of the future, and is only secondarily concerned with censorship or book-burning. In actuality it is the story of Bradbury, disguised as Montag, and his lifelong love affair with books. . . .

"Metaphor" is an important word to Bradbury. He uses it generically to describe a method of comprehending one reality and then expressing that same reality so that the reader will see it with the intensity of the writer. His use of the term, in fact, strongly resembles T. S. Eliot's view of the objective correlative. Bradbury's metaphor in *Fahrenheit 451* is the burning of books; in "*The Illustrated Man*", a moving tattoo; and pervading all of his work, the metaphor becomes a generalized nostalgia that can best be described as a nostalgia for the future.

Essentially a romantic, Bradbury belongs to the great frontier tradition. He is an exemplar of the Turner thesis, and the blunt opposition between a tradition-bound Eastern establishment and Western vitality finds itself mirrored in his writing. The metaphors may change, but the conflict in Bradbury is ultimately between human vitality and the machine, between the expanding individual and the confining group, between the capacity for wonder and the stultification of conformity. These tensions are a continual source for him, whether the collection is named *The Golden Apples of the*

Sun, *Dandelion Wine*, or *The Martian Chronicles*, Thus, to use his own terminology, nostalgia for either the past or future is a basic metaphor utilized to express these tensions. Science fiction is the vehicle.

Ironic detachment combined with emotional involvement—these are the recurring tones in Bradbury's work, and they find their expression in the metaphor of "wilderness". To Bradbury, America is a wilderness country and hers a wilderness people. . . .

For Bradbury the final, inexhaustible wilderness is the wilderness of space. In that wilderness, man will find himself, renew himself. There, in space, as atoms of God, mankind will live forever. Ultimately, then, the conquest of space becomes a religious quest. The religious theme in his writing is sounded directly only on occasion, in such stories as "The Fire Balloons", where two priests try to decide if some blue fire-balls on Mars have souls, or "The Man", where Christ leaves a far planet the day before an Earth rocket lands. Ultimately the religious theme is the end product of Bradbury's vision of man; the theme is implicit in man's nature.

Willis E. McNelly. In *Voices for the Future: Essays on Major Science Fiction Writers, Vol. 1*, ed. Thomas D. Clareson. Bowling Green University Popular Press, 1976, pp. 167–75.

"It was a pleasure to burn," begins Bradbury's *Fahrenheit 451*. "It was a special pleasure to see things eaten, to see things blackened and *changed*." In the decade following Nagasaki and Hiroshima, Bradbury's eye-catching opening for his dystopian novel assumes particular significance. America's nuclear climax to World War II signalled the start of a new age in which the awesome powers of technology, with its alarming dangers, would provoke fresh inquiries into the dimensions of man's potentiality and the scope of his brutality. . . . The opening paragraph of Bradbury's novel immediately evokes the consequences of unharnessed technology and contemporary man's contented refusal to acknowledge these consequences.

In short, *Fahrenheit 451* (1953) raises the question posed by a number of contemporary anti-utopian novels. In one way or another, Huxley's *Ape and Essence* (1948), Orwell's *Nineteen Eighty-Four* (1948), Vonnegut's *Player Piano* (1952), Miller's *A Canticle for Leibowitz* (1959), Hartley's *Facial Justice* (1960), and Burgess's *A Clockwork Orange* (1962) all address themselves to the issue of technology's impact on the destiny of man. In this sense, Mark R. Hillegas is right in labeling *Fahrenheit 451* "almost the archetypal anti-utopia of the new era in which we live." Whether, what, and how to burn in Bradbury's book are the issues—as implicit to a grasp of our age as electricity—which occupy the center of the contemporary mind.

What is distinctive about *Fahrenheit 451* as a work of literature, then, is not what Bradbury says but how he says it. With Arthur C. Clarke, Bradbury is among the most poetic of science fiction writers. Bradbury's evocative, lyrical style charges *Fahrenheit 451* with a sense of mystery and connotative depth that go beyond the normal boundaries of dystopian fiction. Less charming, perhaps, than *The Martian Chronicles*, *Fahrenheit 451* is also less brittle. More to the point, in *Fahrenheit 451* Bradbury has created a pattern of symbols that richly convey the intricacy of his central theme. Involved in Bradbury's burning is the over-whelming problem of modern science: as man's shining inventive intellect sheds more and more light on the truths of the universe, the increased knowledge he thereby acquires, if abused, can ever more easily fry his planet to a cinder. Burning as constructive energy, and burning as apocalyptic catastrophe, are the symbolic poles of Bradbury's novel. Ultimately, the book probes in symbolic terms the puzzling, divisive nature of man as a creative/destructive creature. *Fahrenheit 451* thus becomes a book which injects originality into a literary subgenre that can grow worn and hackneyed. It is the only major symbolic dystopia of our time.

> Donald Watt. In *Ray Bradbury*, Martin Harry Greenberg and Joseph D. Olander, eds. (Taplinger Publishing Company, 1980), pp. 195–213.

Ray Douglas Bradbury is probably the first American writer of science fiction to become widely known outside the field. Although his reputation rests in considerable part on two early novels, *The Martian Chronicles* (1950) and *Fahrenheit 451* (1953), many of his short stories are perennial anthology favorites. His fiction is noted for its poetic and lyrical qualities, but he has also written a number of dramatic works.

Bradbury was born in Waukegan, Illinois, in 1920; after some nomadic years his family settled in Los Angeles in 1934 and Bradbury has lived there ever since. His long residence on the West Coast notwithstanding, the Midwest of his boyhood is a persistent image in his work: a small-town American utopia of the past with green lawns, shady streets, and friendly neighbors. The image pervades his quasi-autobiographical novel *Dandelion Wine* (1957), and in *The Martian Chronicles* the Martians cruelly use it to enchant and destroy spacemen from Earth.

In the 1940s Bradbury made his way into large circulation magazines like *Collier's* and the *Saturday Evening Post*. The poetic quality of his work seemed to burst the confines of the genre, which made purists uncomfortable. Bradbury was in fact one of the few science fiction writers of note then who was neither a disciple of John W. Campbell, Jr., the innovative editor of *Astounding Science Fiction*, nor possessed of a technical or scientific education. His prize-winning short stories of the late 1940s led to his first novel, *The Martian Chronicles*, in 1950.

In form *The Martian Chronicles* is more a sequence of episodes (some had been previously published) than a novel. They stretch from 1999 to 2026, as the native Martians are destroyed by an Earth-borne plague (chicken pox), and Earth itself is made uninhabitable by nuclear holocaust. A few survivors flee to Mars: in the last chapter a man promises to show his children the true Martians and points to their own reflections in a pool of water.

Free water on Mars suggests that Bradbury's red planet is a poetic image, not a scientific fact. Strict definers of science fiction have had difficulty with Bradbury's inattention to scientific probability, and with attitudes in his fiction which seem downright antiscientific. Yet Bradbury's concern is not with science in the abstract but with the human use or abuse of it. Science and technology, as represented in his fiction, are often the occasion for displays of human pride and folly, which is only to say that much of Bradbury's work is satire, a posture characteristic of science fiction. One of Bradbury's best-known short stories, "The Veldt," illustrates the point: the Hadleys have put a technologically advanced playroom in place of their own care for their children. Their

indifference finally kills them as the simulated African landscape becomes all too real.

That was futuristic enough for 1950, but generally the face of Bradbury's fiction is turned firmly toward the past, as in the idyllic portrayals of mid-America in perhaps the 1920s. In another noted short story, "The Sound of Thunder," a time traveler is actually shot for altering the past, so precious it seems. In one sense, his fiction warns us about what we can lose.

The future world of *Fahrenheit 451*, for example, is one in which firemen set fires; they burn books. In the totalitarian regime postulated, effective thought control means destroying the heritage of the past, the knowledge that can make human beings wise and free. But this picture of a repressive dystopia ends with praise for the irrepressible human spirit: some people refuse to abandon their past. They memorize great literary and philosophical works; they carry within themselves and in a way become Swift or Thoreau or Thomas Love Peacock.

Since the 1960s Bradbury has turned from science fiction and fantasy to poetry (his *Collected Poems* appeared in 1982), drama, including productions of his own plays, and mystery fiction: his *Death is a Lonely Business* came out in 1986. Clearly Bradbury is a versatile writer, but the science fiction which established his name remains a poetic blend of the pastoral and the scientific, of the nostalgic and the satiric.

> Michael N. Stanton. In *Reference Guide to American Literature, 3rd editon*,, ed. Jim Kamp (St. James Press, 1994).

When asked how he would like to be remembered by future generations, Ray Bradbury once replied "as a magician of ideas and words." Indeed, Bradbury is such a magician, and he is one of the twentieth century's most important storytellers and allegorists. An author who writes from personal experience and cultural inheritance, who relies on the history of ideas and free word association, and who threw his first million words away, Bradbury has proven himself a warlock of words and a teller of universal tales that incorporate myths, beliefs, themes, rituals, and character types that define both American and world cultures.

Bradbury's short stories, novels, stage plays, screen plays, poems, and radio plays appeal to all ages, and his dexterity with issues of youth and age, and coming-of-age, make his writing significant and meaningful to a wide-ranging public. He has always drawn heavily from his personal experience, making autobiography the largest overriding thematic element of his work. Bradbury is a visionary who is sensitive to the emotions and idiosyncrasies and wonders that comprise the human experience. If at times the logic of his stories is suspect, his ability to solve the human equation makes these logistic errors insignificant.

> Garyn G. Roberts. In *Twentieth-Century Young Adult Writers, 1st edition,* ed. Laura Standley Berger (St. James Press, 1994).

BIBLIOGRAPHY
Dark Carnival, 1947 (s); *The Meadow*, 1947 (d); *The Martian Chronicles*, 1950 (s); *The Illustrated Man*, 1951 (s); *Fahrenheit 451*, 1953 (n); *The Golden Apples of the Sun*, 1953 (s); *The October Country*, 1955 (s); *Dandelion Wine*, 1957 (n); *The Day It Rained Forever*, 1959 (s); *A Medicine for Melancholy*, 1959 (s); *Something*

Wicked This Way Comes, 1962 (n); *The Anthem Sprinters and Other Antics*, 1963 (d); *The Machineries of Joy*, 1964 (s); *The World of Ray Bradbury*, 1964 (d); *The Autumn People*, 1965 (s); *The Wonderful Ice-Cream Suit*, 1965 (d); *The Pedestrian*, 1966 (d); *Tomorrow Midnight*, 1966 (s); *Christus Apollo*, 1969 (d); *I Sing the Body Electric!*, 1969 (s); *Old Ahab's Friend, and Friend to Noah, Speaks His Piece: A Celebration*, 1971 (p); *Leviathan 99*, 1972 (d); *When Elephants Last in the Dooryard Bloomed: Celebrations for Almost Any Day in the Year*, 1973 (p); *Long after Midnight*, 1976 (s); *The Bike Repairman*, 1978 (p); *The Foghorn*, 1977 (d); *Where Robot Mice and Robot Men Run round in Robot Towns*, 1977 (p); *Twin Hieroglyphs That Swim the River Dust*, 1978 (p); *The Author Considers His Resources*, 1979 (p); *The Aqueduct*, 1979 (p); *The Attic Where the Meadow Greens*, 1980 (p); *The Veldt*, 1980 (d); *The Haunted Computer and the Android Pope*, 1981 (p); *Imagine*, 1981 (p); *The Love Affair*, 1983 (p); *A Memory of Murder*, 1984 (s); *Death Is a Lonely Business*, 1985 (n); *The Toynbee Convector*, 1988 (s); *A Graveyard for Lunatics: Another Tale of Two Cities*, 1990 (n); *Zen in the Art of Writing*, 1990 (e); *Yestermorrow: Obvious Answers to Impossible Futures*, 1991 (e); *The Smile*, 1991 (n); *Green Shadows, White Whale*, 1992 (n)

BRAITHWAITE, William Stanley (1878–1962)

William Stanley Braithwaite is the Negro poet who unquestionably stands next to Dunbar. Dunbar found entrance into Stedman's American anthology; Braithwaite, who came upon the stage a little too late for this, is represented in Jesse B. Rittenhouse's *Little Book of Modern Verse*. Braithwaite is even better known for his critical work than for his poetry. In addition to editing anthologies of Elizabethan verse, Georgian verse, and Restoration verse, he has, since 1913, collected and edited yearly anthologies of magazine verse that have been of great service to all people interested in contemporary poetry. These books, together with his yearly reviews of contemporary poetry, have undoubtedly helped create a larger and more appreciative audience for contemporary American poets. His own poems have appeared in a number of the best magazines and have been collected in two volumes, *Lyrics of Love and Life* (1904), and *The House of Falling Leaves* (1908). A highly sensitive estheticism is the keynote of his poetry. In this sense, as well as in lyric ability, he suggests Sidney Lanier. In finish and grace his poems are superior to those of Dunbar; they are superior also in another and less important respect—literary allusiveness. Braithwaite has a superior savoir faire in handling literary background that is probably due to his longer and more intimate associations with books and writers. His poems have grace, but he is too idealistic for humor. He has a sense of human fate and the seriousness of life, but he falls far short of the knowledge of life and the sympathetic interest in human types that Dunbar possessed. Like Shelley (his principal master, along with Keats), he is idealistic to a fault. His poetry is too much "out of time and out of space"—there is too much seclusion from the problems and men of his own day. His genuine and obvious refinement affords a pleasant contrast to much that is crude and raw in the more controversial writers but does not fully compensate for a deficiency in definite,

tangible substance. His poems, some of which have been set to music, have a fine lyric quality, and the idealism of such poems as "Nympholepsy," "A Song of Living," and "The Eternal Self" is both sincere and inspiring. The poems, especially in the first volume, are often slight, and of no particular individual weight or ethical value, but his second volume shows a considerably greater depth of feeling and widening of interest. "In a Grave Yard," "A Little Song," "By an Inland Lake," and "It's a Long Way" are lyrics from the first volume that would be no discredit to the best contemporary poets. Among the best poems in the second volume are "From the Crowd," which describes a poignant lyric impression, "A Song of Living" and "The Eternal Self." His later poems show a still higher technical finish and a mystical tendency that sometimes oversteps the bounds of rational comprehension.

Whether Mr. Braithwaite derives this tendency from his reading of Blake or from certain obscure strains in recent British and American poetry, it is one of the factors that sharply differentiates him from most of the other poets represented in this book. He himself objects, justly, to having his poems classed indiscriminately as "Negro" poetry. Just as the Caucasian really predominates in the poet's racial inheritance, so the non-racial is the striking characteristic of his verse. His poems have no more of the Negro race in them than the poems of Longfellow or Bryant; in fact, paradoxically, they have less, by reason of their remoter connection with the substantial realities of ordinary life. There is very little real passion in Braithwaite's poetry; on the contrary there is an exquisite restraint which seems rather to avoid vigorous emotional expression and prefers instead a fine lyric suggestiveness.

Newman Ivey White. In *An Anthology of Verse By American Negroes*, ed. Newman Ivey White and Walter Clinton Jackson, 1924. Reprint by The Folcroft Press, Inc., 1969 pp. 1–26.

An older generation remembers the large annual anthologies of poetry collected by William Stanley Braithwaite of Boston. A veritable sleuth of rhyme, he read every publication large or small, near or remote in which a poem was published. He loved poetry and his attitude toward the new writer was generous and encouraging. Happy was the young poet to learn that he had won the approving eye of Braithwaite. It is fitting that Braithwaite should be given his just rewards as a poet as well as for his labors as a servant of the muse. His anthology selections are too inclusive to win lasting approval but they are a valuable reference. He is a more discerning taskmaster of his own poems than he was of the work of the poets he gathered in the highways and byways.

Braithwaite is a versatile craftsman, who can open his tool box and fashion a good sonnet, quatrain, or couplet with an admirable deftness. His talent as story-teller is shown in "Fugue in Gardenia," and the philosophic ballad "Sandy Star." One of his most effective poems is the psalm "Off the New England Coast" an eloquent prayer which concludes with the affirmative plea—

Not an inch of thy Beauty to perish,
not an ounce
thy Might to be lost.

Mr. Braithwaite's scope as a poet is limited, and his rhetoric shows no electric images, nor dramatic power. His gift is as quiet and consistent as the pleasure it evokes. To Braithwaite, noble servant of the muse and occasional rider of Pegasus, all lovers of poetry should give thanks.

The Saturday Review of Literature. February 12, 1949, p. 31.

[William Stanley Braithwaite] attained prominence as critic and anthologist. His leading reviews for the *Boston Transcript,* his anthologies of magazine verse, published yearly from 1913 to 1928, and a collection of Elizabethan verse mark him as a critic of great sensibility. Braithwaite's poetry, however, is of greater pertinence to this study. He is the most outstanding example of perverted energy that the period from 1903 to 1917 produced.

Various explanations have been given for the oddity which a study of certain Negro poets like Braithwaite presents, but not one takes into account the pressure of the age. It is not considered that the expression of certain thoughts, feelings, and ideas was denied if they wished the hearing of an important audience. No one of the explanations mentions that all but one of these poets wrote better verse on material that in the very nature of things was (rather than is) Negro material. Braithwaite is the exception. On this general head, Countee Cullen has something to say in the preface to *Caroling Dusk:* "Since theirs [Negro writers] is also the heritage of the English language, their work will not present any serious aberration from the poetic tendencies of their time . . . for the double obligation of being both Negro and American is not so unified as we are often led to believe." Also, and apparently by way of explanation, Braithwaite's autobiographical sketch has this to say: "I inherited the incentives and ideals of the intellect from an ancestry of British gentlemen." Further, it might be pointed out that he was born in Boston and has lived most of his life in Massachusetts. These remarks are definitely offered in the nature of excuses for divergence from the racial norm of creative ends.

Most of the Negro poets who from nearly the beginning of the century to the middle years of the World War turned their talents toward traditional poetic material—love, birth, death, beauty, grief, gladness—without any thought of their racial background developed a sort of dilettantism, a kind of love of display of poetic skill, and experience, and knowledge. In this their verse is comparable to the tricky poetics of the Cavaliers. It is bright and light, but without substance—Chinese fireworks.

> Lolotte, who attires my hair,
> Lost her lover. Lolotte weeps;
> Trails her hand before her eyes;
> Hangs her head and mopes and sighs,
> Mutters of the pangs of hell.
> Fills the circumambient air
> With her plaints and her despair.
> Looks at me:
> "May you never know, Mam'selle,
> Love's harsh cruelty."

Now this is pretty and skillful poetry, but it is not poetry afire with the compelling necessity for expression. No passion (even slightly remembered in tranquillity) of pain or joy, no spring of pure personal knowledge or conviction justifies it. It is just "lines expressing something or other."

Mr. Braithwaite set the pace for this particular school. It is not enough, however, to say that he seems to be merely a dilettante. He is both much more and much less than that—but it is not quite clear what or how much. In the *Poetic Year* for 1916, he wrote: "All this life that we live, this experience that we have of the world, are but footnotes to reality. . . . Ever since the beginning man has tried to translate the language of the spirit—the invisible, immaterial character of another existence that is as real as our own." Despite his brave, plain words, his translation of the language of the spirit leaves much to be desired in the way of clarity, and he seems never to have understood the "footnotes to reality." His poems mark the path of his steady progress into the rare atmosphere of the spiritual world. . . .

J. Saunders Redding. *To Make a Poet Black*, 1939. Reprinted by Cornell University Press, 1988, pp. 49–92.

BIBLIOGRAPHY
Lyrics of Life and Love, 1904 (p); *The House of Falling Leaves with Other Poems*, 1908 (p); *The Story of the Great War*, 1919 (e); *Selected Poems*, 1948 (p); *The Bewitched Parsonage: The Story of The Brontes*, 1950 (b); *The William Stanley Braithwaite Reader*, 1972 (misc)

BRAUTIGAN, Richard (1935–1984)

The best thing about Richard Brautigan's first published novel [*A Confederate General from Big Sur*] is the language, which is consistently more inventive and delicate than you might expect from one of the so-called "beats.". . . His metaphors alone make Brautigan's novel worth reading. . . . Brautigan's characters aren't violent, like Kerouac's. They are selfish, irresponsible, but they harm no one and do not obviously "rebel." . . . The writer is as freely experimental as his characters. He gives us a choice of several written endings, and he dots the narrative with italicized flashbacks to the Civil War, which was "the last good time this country ever had." It all makes for good whimsical reading. Perhaps, however, *A Confederate General from Big Sur* might have been more than merely whimsical if there had been more tension between the imagined society and the one we all live in, or between the writer's fancy and his reason.

Arthur Gold. *Book Week.* Feb. 14, 1965. p. 18

Mr. (if I may be so bold and square as to accord him the prefix) Richard Brautigan, in his novel *A Confederate General from Big Sur*, provides as good an account as has come my way of Beat life and humor; though the latter, I have to admit, won from me no more than the kind of wintry smile I habitually wore during the five sad years that I was editor of *Punch*.

Big Sur is, of course, hallowed ground to admirers of Henry Miller's writings, a Beat shrine, if ever there was one. A glimpse is caught in *A Confederate General from Big Sur* of Mr. Miller collecting his mail, and provides the only point in the narrative when the giggling stops and a respectful silence momentarily descends. Otherwise the novel consists of a series of bizarre (perhaps it would be politer to say picaresque) adventures, sometimes salacious, sometimes narcotic, and sometimes pettifoggingly criminal.

Beats, according to Mr. Brautigan's account, are heathen, parasitic, dirty and idle. They are the devil's anchorites, covered with the lice of unrighteousness, and eating the bitter bread of boredom and vacuity. Only an occasional bout of fornication relieves the tedium of their days, and even that is precluded when they are too high to perform. As a protest against the American way of life, theirs would seem to lack point. They are but a waste product of what they affect to despise; refusing to participate in the feast of affluence, they grovel and crawl under the table and about the guests' legs in search of crumbs, cigarette butts and voyeur ecstasies. Poor Beats! Mr. Brautigan has convinced me that we are better without them.

Malcolm Muggeridge. *Esquire.* April, 1965. p. 60

Brautigan . . . is funny, but seldom satiric, sometimes bored but hardly ever angry, frequently happier than you but never holier than thou. . . . Alas for the hazards of being reviewed: Brautigan at secondhand is all too likely to sound merely whimsical and cute. He is not; what underlies these games is a modern fatalism, not maudlin fatheadedness. . . . [In *In Watermelon Sugar*] the spun-sugar simplifications of organized happiness and the naïve placidity of the narrator are repeatedly darkened by our perception of real misery, jealousy, frustration and unrequited love. It is more complicated technically and more disturbing emotionally than the earlier works, and it suggests that you should, while reading all the Brautigan now available, look forward to the Brautigan yet to come.

J.D. O'Hara. *Book World.* Jan. 11, 1970. p. 3

I'll call [Brautigan] a novelist because it is for his novels, *A Confederate General from Big Sur* and *Trout Fishing in America*, that he is best known. There are no books quite like them and no writer around quite like him—no contemporary, at any rate. The one who is closest is Mark Twain. The two have in common an approach to humor that is founded on the old frontier tradition of the tall story. In Brautigan's work, however, events are given an extra twist so that they come out in respectable literary shape, looking like surrealism. *A Confederate General from Big Sur* is a kind of Huck Finn–Tom Sawyer adventure played out in those beautiful boondocks of coastal California where Jack Kerouac flipped out in the summer of 1960. But it is with *Trout Fishing in America* that Brautigan manages to remind us of Mark Twain and at the same time seem most himself. As you may have heard, this one is not really about fishing, but it is really about America. In the book—call it a novel if you will—whopper is piled on dream vision with such relentless repetition that the ultimate effect is a little like science fiction.

Bruce Cook. *The Beat Generation* (Scribner). 1971. p. 206

The cover of *Trout Fishing in America* is important. It shows a young couple in front of the statue of Benjamin Franklin in San Francisco's Washington Square. The girl is dressed in a long skirt, high boots, wire-rimmed glasses, and a lace hair band; the man is wearing a nineteenth-century hat, a vest and black coat over his

paisley shirt and beads. He too has wire-rimmed glasses. With his vest and glasses, with her boots and lace, they look like something out of an earlier America. They reflect the nostalgia which permeates this book: for a simpler, more human, pre-industrial America. Brautigan knows it's gone. But some of the values in this book are derived from this kind of nostalgia. Brautigan has created a pastoral locked in the past, a pastoral which cannot be a viable social future.

I want to live in the liberated mental space that Brautigan creates. I am aware, however, of the institutions that make it difficult for me to live there and that make it impossible for most people in the world. Brautigan's value is in giving us a pastoral vision which can water our spirits as we struggle—the happy knowledge that there is another place to breathe in; his danger, and the danger of the style of youth culture generally, is that we will forget the struggle.

John Clayton. *New American Review.* No. 11, 1971. pp. 67–8

Trout Fishing in America is a solid achievement in structure, significance, and narrative technique. For all its surface peculiarity, moreover, the book is centrally located within a major tradition of the American novel—the romance—and is conditioned by Brautigan's concern with the bankrupt ideals of the American past. Its seemingly loose and episodic narrative, its penchant for the marvelous and the unusual, its pastoral nostalgia—all of these things give it that sense of "disconnected and uncontrolled experience" which Richard Chase finds essential to the romance-novel. Brautigan's offhand manner and sense of comic disproportion give to the narrative an extravagance and implausibility more suited to the fishing yarn and tall-tale than to realistic fiction. Lying just below the comic exuberance of the book, furthermore, is the myth of the American Adam, the ideal of the New World Eden that haunts American fiction from Cooper to the present. The narrator of *Trout Fishing in America* is Leatherstocking perishing on the virgin land that once offered unbounded possibility, modern man longing for the restoration of the agrarian simplicity of pioneer America. That a life of frontier innocence is no longer possible adds to the desperate tone and comic absurdity of the narrator's frustrated excursions into the American wilderness.

Kenneth Seib. *Critique.* 13, 2, 1971. p. 71

[*A Confederate General from Big Sur* is] much better than *Trout Fishing in America*, which is the only other [Brautigan book] I have read. Its narrative may be pointless, but at least events follow one another in chronological sequence. Some hippies and their girls and a rich madman settle in a cabin in Big Sur and that's about it. They frighten away the frogs with alligators and have quite a nice time. The dialogue is relaxed, with occasional zany excursions into the pot vocabulary, which I like. Sometimes, even, it is enlivened by the sour wit one finds in Virginia Woolf's saner moments: "I've heard that the Digger Indians down there didn't wear any clothes. They didn't have any fire or shelter or culture. They didn't grow anything. They didn't hunt and they didn't fish. They didn't bury their dead or give birth to their children. They lived on roots and limpets and sat pleasantly out in the rain."

Does this not remind one of Woolf's description of the Great Frost? Whether it does or not, Mr. Brautigan writes five thousand times better than Kerouac ever did, and could easily produce some modern equivalent of W. H. Davies's *Autobiography of a Super-Tramp* with a little more effort, a little more discipline and a little less of the semiarticulate exhibitionism which is what people apparently mean nowadays when they talk of "creative" writing.

Auberon Waugh. *Spectator.* Feb. 27, 1971. p. 287

Right now Brautigan is riding high. He is the Love Generation's answer to Charlie Schulz. Happiness is a warm hippie. . . .

That the young should have taken so passionately to Brautigan is not surprising. He is the literary embodiment of Woodstock, his little novels and poems being right in the let's-get-back-to-nature-and-get-it-all-together groove. His exceedingly causal, off-hand style is wholly vogue, and I readily concede that there is a certain charm about it and him. . . .

[*The Abortion*] is diverting, and Brautiganites will find in it their usual joys. The lovable Brautigan himself is on hand as always, his own hero, talking about love and peace and the beauties of nature. The book is modestly funny, can be read in a matter of an hour or so, and will not hurt a soul.

Jonathan Yardley. *New Republic.* March 20, 1971. p. 24

The stories [in *Revenge of the Lawn*], many of them only a paragraph or two long, are characterized by that Brautigan blend of simplicity, humor, surrealism, nostalgia, and bittersweetness that endeared Saroyan to an earlier generation of Americans. The simplicity is sometimes cloying and the nostalgia sometimes veers into the sentimental, but these are small faults if you enjoy Brautigan, as I do, enormously; if you don't, they'll madden you and make him seem dead-pan precocious and wildly self-indulgent. If you're a woman, you will also be maddened by the exaggerated Beat Generation attitudes toward women that linger here.

Sara Blackburn. *Book World.* Nov. 28, 1971. p. 2

Revenge of the Lawn is really one vision of people who have drowned their feelings and live underwater lives. For Brautigan's fishermen do not want to catch trout so much as they want to be like them. . . . Going underwater, underground, inside, Brautigan people live with no passionate attachment to anyone or any place and never permit themselves to feel a thing. But in Brautigan's scheme withdrawal can be a strategic maneuver. . . . Brautigan makes cutting out your heart the only way to endure, the most beautiful way to protest the fact that life can be an endless down. *Revenge of the Lawn* is not Brautigan's best book. But it has the Brautigan magic—the verbal wildness, the emptiness, the passive force of people who have gone beyond winning or losing to an absolute poetry of survival.

Josephine Hendin. *New York Times Book Section.* Jan. 16, 1972. p. 7

The most laconic of these new writers, Richard Brautigan is perhaps best known for *A Confederate General from Big Sur, Trout Fishing in America,* and *In Watermelon Sugar,* as well as for his poetry. Lucid, precise, whimsical, idyllic, Brautigan develops a unique fragmentary style: his "chapters" are sometimes no longer than his chapter headings. Yet beneath the surface of happy love

and naïve humor, the reader feels the lurking presence of loss, madness, death, feels some great blankness enfolding the rivers and wrecking yards of Brautigan's America. Mocking the conventions of fiction, Brautigan engages both silence and speech in his rigorous art, spare as a haiku. A Californian, he has some affinities with the Zen sweetness of Snyder and Kerouac; but his knowledge of the dark also recalls Hemingway.

Ihab Hassan. *Contemporary American Literature* (Ungar). 1973. p. 171

On first reading Richard Brautigan's *In Watermelon Sugar,* one senses that something extraordinary has happened to the form of the novel, to the intellectual and aesthetic conventions to which we have become accustomed. Brautigan's work is jigsaw puzzle art that demands more than close reading; it demands an active participation by the reader, a reconstruction of a vision that has been fragmented but warmed by a private poetic sensibility. Three avenues of accessibility, the novel as a utopian instrument, the analogues to the Garden of Eden, and natural determinism converge and create a frame for Brautigan's novel.

Brautigan has created the utopian dream for the post-industrial age of affluence, beyond IBM, and finally beyond curiosity. His longings, unlike other utopian ideals, have no claim on progress, no uplifting of the material condition of man, no holy wars to redistribute the physical wealth, no new metaphors for survival based on the securing of human necessities, and no emotional nirvanas. Other utopian dreamers have responded directly to the events of their age, but Brautigan is responding to the cumulative ages of man, and no response can be significant for him that does not place the entire past on the junk heap (the forgotten works). Nothing will do but a fresh start, with a fresh set of assumptions; *In Watermelon Sugar* takes us back to the beginning, for this is Eden, with its syllabic and accented soul mate iDEATH, reconstructed.

Harvey Leavitt. *Critique.* 16, 1, 1974. p. 18

Like Kurt Vonnegut, Richard Brautigan is beloved by college kids. Each is admired for his tenderness toward human vulnerability, for his pose of the faux naif, for his air of sweet inexpressible sadness. The difference between them is that Brautigan is a singularly careful writer. . . . [He] is a miniaturist who broods about death, who builds his novels from small self-contained blocks. He cannot entirely avoid coyness or dead-end digressions. Yet he conveys a sense of spare economy, of humorous or graceful lines eased in almost imperceptibly. . . . *The Hawkline Monster* is rather more of a pastiche, more of a parody than any of Brautigan's other fictions. It lacks the complexity, the more evanescent refractions of his best book, *Trout Fishing in America.*

Peter S. Prescott. *Newsweek.* Sept. 9, 1974. p. 82

BIBLIOGRAPHY

A Confederate General from Big Sur, 1964 (n); *The Pill versus the Springhill Mine Disaster,* 1969 (p); *In Watermelon Sugar,* 1969 (n); *Trout Fishing in America,* 1970 (n); *Rommel Drives on Deep into Egypt,* 1970 (p); *The Abortion,* 1971 (n); *Revenge of the Lawn,* 1971 (s); *The Hawkline Monster,* 1974 (n); *Willard and His Bowling Trophies,* 1975 (n); *Willard and His Bowling Trophies,*

1975 (n); *Loading Mercury with a Pitchfork*, 1976 (p); *Sombrero Fallout: A Japanese Novel*, 1976; *Dreaming of Babylon: A Private Eye Novel, 1942*, 1977; *June 30th, June 30th*, 1978; *The Tokyo-Montana Express*, 1980; *So the Wind Won't Blow It All Away*, 1982 (n)

BROOKS, Cleanth (1906–1994)

Modern Poetry and the Tradition is sound without being sententious; it is suggestive yet precise; it avoids the temptation of sensationalism and the opposite extreme of stodginess. Mr. Brooks writes lucidly rather than brilliantly about the reach of the image . . . and goes to some length to explain the "difficulty" of modern poetry and the reader's resistance to it. . . . All in all, this is the work of a scholar who is sensitive to every nuance of feeling and every change of pitch, Mr. Brooks is a probing analyst, but he is not a pedant. His work, reflecting his subject, is allusive rather than simple and straightforward, complex but clear.

> Louis Untermeyer. *Saturday Review*. Jan. 13, 1940. p. 17

One test of a critical theory is its range of enlightenment. Mr. Brooks is illuminating about Eliot and Yeats, but neglects certain poets altogether—D. H. Lawrence, for example, who is certainly witty, or Laura Riding who is certainly intellectual. He may say that they are not good poets—though I should disagree with him—but it is up to him to show why, and their omission makes me doubt if his theory is equipped with the necessary critical tools. . . . Admirable as far as it goes, his criticism of the propagandist view of art fails to account for its success not only among hack critics but quite good artists. In my opinion the social-significance heresy is a distortion of a true perception, namely, that the *Weltanschauung* of a poet is of importance in assessing his work, and that there is, after all, a relation, however obscure and misunderstood, between art and goodness.

> W.H. Auden. *New Republic*. Feb. 5, 1940. p. 187

Poetry is assumed to rest within a sacred circle, from which historical and psychological considerations on the critic's part are exorcised as profane. To this illiberal outlook Brooks gives the name "humanism." A core of vigorous understanding is thus surrounded with inhibitions by no means always free from intellectual morbidity. Order becomes for Brooks almost an obsession. . . . Brooks is imprisoned in a cage. He suffers from the familiar limitations of narrow and dogmatic doctrines; yet within these limits he frequently writes with admirable discernment.

> Henry W. Wells. *Saturday Review*. April 12, 1947. p. 50

Mr. Brooks suggests that poetry is great in proportion to its power to contain and reconcile whole systems of conflicting values. Truth in poetry is dramatic, determined by a right relation to its context. By studying the interior structure of poems it should be possible for criticism to discriminate the greatest poems from the less great and so to prepare the way for a new history of poetry based not on

extraneous considerations but on solid observations of poems as poems.

Mr. Brooks's studies in the structure of poetry are masterly exercises in the kind of close critical explication that enriches our appreciation of the poems examined and confers a new dignity on the work of the poet.

> George F. Whicher. *New York Herald Tribune Book Section*. Apr. 20, 1947. p. 2

There was developed in the quarter-century between the wars both a system of criticism and a sensibility of poetry, the one fitting and predicting the other, which when they wanted a sanction invoked Donne and when they wanted a justification exhibited Eliot or Yeats. It is not surprising, therefore, that this criticism and this sensibility should bend backwards and try a testing hand on all the poetry that lay between Donne and Eliot. This is what Mr. Brooks tries for. . . . He reads the poems as if their problems were the same as those found in a new quartet by Eliot or a late poem of Yeats; and for his readings he uses the weapons of paradox, irony, ambiguity, attitude, tone, and belief.

> R.P. Blackmur. *New York Times Book Section*. June 8, 1947. p. 6

Either I imperfectly understand Mr. Brooks's theory of poetry . . . or there is nothing very new about it. A poem, I take it, cannot contain one thing only: out of several things it makes its single effect. Some of these, we learn, are *different* from others. In the laboring of this, "paradox" behaves like an acrobat. I share Mr. Brooks's interest in the history of English poetry and his resistance to the critical relativists, but to pinch the diversity of observable phenomena into a single set of terms or insist on anything resembling a unanimity of style seems to me to be indiscreet, or worse. Worse, because it will blind you.

> John Berryman. *The Nation*. June 28, 1947. p. 776

If there is one formulation which seems to him more suitable than others, for it recurs oftenest, it is that which asserts that the unity of poetic language has the form and status of a verbal paradox. He has always liked to stand and marvel at paradox—"with its twin concomitants of irony and wonder"—while I think it is the sense of the sober community that paradox is less valid rather than more valid than another figure of speech, and that its status in logical discourse is that of a provisional way of speaking, therefore precarious. We do not rest in a paradox; we resolve it. . . . As a literary critic he has a hollow scorn for the procedures of logic, which he generally refers to as the procedures of "science"; and he advises the scientists in effect that they cannot understand poetry and had better leave it alone. But this is to underestimate the force of logic in our time and, for that matter, the great weight of the rational idea in western civilization.

> John Crowe Ransom. *Kenyon Review*. Summer, 1947. pp. 437–8

I do not question . . . that "irony," in Brooks's sense of the term, is a constant trait of all good poets, and I should have no quarrel with him had he been content to say so and to offer his analyses of texts as illustrations of one point, among others, in poetic theory. What troubles me is that, for Brooks, there are no other points. Irony, or paradox, is poetry, *tout simplement* its form no less than its matter; or rather, in the critical system which he has constructed, there is no principle save that denoted by the words "irony" or "paradox" from which significant propositions concerning poems can be derived. It is the One in which the Many in his theory—and there are but few of these—are included as parts, the single source of all his predicates, the unique cause from which he generates all effect.

R.S. Crane. *Modern Philology*. May, 1948. pp. 226–7

It may be making virtues of natural limitations, but Brooks's style seems a deliberately plain, steady, utilitarian style. The critical commentary does not emulate but only serves the poem, assists it in the performance of its "miracle of communication," like the disciples distributing the bread and fish.... If one can avoid thinking of a critical essay as properly either a contest or an amorous exercise between the author and the reader, Brooks is perhaps simply trying very earnestly to be precise about what he is saying, and again, not saying. Further, he makes no pretensions. One perfectly good reason for putting it plainly might be that he thinks it is a plain thing he has to say.

John Edward Hardy. *Hopkins Review*. Spring, 1953. pp. 160–1

There have even been objections from within the ranks to intrusions of "personality" into the critical labor. Cleanth Brooks, a New Critic whose style has always been efficient and spare, and who—aside from a catch-word or two—has contributed nothing to the poetry of New Criticism, once defended to Alfred Kazin the supposed "impersonality" of the New Critic (a supposition not easily supported outside Brooks' own work) and indicated his opposition to criticism that attempts "rivalry with the work of art."

Richard Foster. *The New Romantics* (Indiana). 1962. pp. 186–7

For whom, then, has Mr. Brooks caused his book The Hidden God *to be published in hardback?*

For a hypothetical "Christian looking at modern literature," who, he says, ought to find in that literature "a great deal that is heartening and helpful."...

Is it Mr. Brooks' assumption, then, that his Christian reader has special difficulties with such a writer as Yeats?

It is: and with most other great modern writers; for many who are aware that a great modern literature exists "continue to dismiss it as merely sensational, violent, meaningless, or nihilistic." It is his hope that he can induce such readers to approach and perhaps digest this literature....

Is Mr. Brooks' effort then wasted?

No effort of so skilful a propagandist for literacy is ever wholly wasted. Ultimately those who must read will read, and will find out what they must read; and if Mr. Brooks can do no more with a segment of the rest, he will at least inhibit their too ready prattle about what they have not read or read imperfectly, and hence reduce their power to drive dedicated readers into rebellion against

what is represented to them as Christianity. So at least one may pray.

Hugh Kenner. *National Review*. Aug. 13, 1963. pp. 109–10

... in *The Hidden God* Mr. Brooks, who is one of modern criticism's most distinguished practitioners of exacting verbal analysis, has chosen the broad view, and he offers us a series of essays on five major twentieth-century writers. These pieces, enclosed between an introductory and a concluding chapter, make up a little book that forsakes stringent inspection of the single text for a general reassessment of what is centrally definitive in the work of Hemingway, Faulkner, Yeats, Eliot, and Robert Penn Warren.... Mr. Brooks wants most cautiously to forego any claim that we are confronted with some sort of crypto-Christianity in the fiction of Hemingway and Faulkner or in the poetry of Yeats and Warren. He claims only that many of the great writers of our time are engaged by the essential problems of Christianity, that their work can be significantly illumined by reference to Christian premises—and this is brilliantly demonstrated by a sensitive marshaling of a solid body of evidence.

Nathan A. Scott. *Saturday Review*. Sept. 28, 1963. p. 60

... Mr. Brooks's study [*William Faulkner*] gives the impression of striving to do nothing less than to set the entire world of Faulkner scholarship, criticism, and appreciation in order. Since I have nothing like the space necessary to discuss his thesis in detail, suffice it to say that he is arguing principally that Faulkner is a writer whose Southern quality has been ignored to the detriment of accurate critical understanding. More specifically, Mr. Brooks places the community at the center of both Faulkner's life and work where it provides simultaneously a moral impetus and touchstone. In working out his thesis Mr. Brooks uses a multifaceted method. Thus, he attacks technical questions in a scholarly manner, as when he works out the time sequence of *Sanctuary*. He also devotes considerable space to correcting earlier critics guilty of either factual or interpretative errors. And, finally, he employs both the impressionistic and what might loosely be called the history of ideas approaches.... [T]hough he has many astute things to say— he is particularly rewarding on *The Unvanquished*—the general impression is one of a very uneven critical performance, one whose dominant trait seems to be that of extreme nervousness. It is this that seems to be back of the testy and selective treatment of critics, the hesitant and yet insistent reference to authors and concepts only tenuously related to Faulkner, and the largely unnecessary (in a scholarly work) stress on the immediacy of Faulkner's power as a writer. From all of this, one is led to conclude that Mr. Brooks has no real critical rationale for the study of fiction, or at least none of the order of coherence he has so ably demonstrated in the past with regard to poetry.

Olga W. Vickery. *American Literature*. Nov., 1964. pp. 380–1

Cleanth Brooks's work is significant not only because it is extremely influential, but also because it has, until recently, persistently advanced a single, coherent theory despite the author's awareness of its limitations. Much literary criticism since the 1920's has been theoretically irresponsible; it has tossed out theories and terminologies, then immediately denied or ignored them. Brooks's work, on the other hand, illustrates the virtues and vices of theoretical consistency. Most of his criticism develops from three sets of terms: irony (and its near equivalents, paradox and wit), drama, and metaphor (or one of its variants). Irony creates unity in variety and helps to establish aesthetic distance; drama achieves both variety and distance; metaphor fuses meanings and removes the object from reality. Brooks has, then, two criteria for aesthetic value—structure (the combination of unity and complexity) and aesthetic distance. His varied but related critical machines are built to show that if a poem has a certain kind of complex structure and achieves a certain distance, it is a good poem.

Lee T. Lemon. *The Partial Critics* (Oxford). 1965. p. 139

BIBLIOGRAPHY

(with Robert Penn Warren) *Understanding Poetry*, 1938 (c); *Modern Poetry and the Tradition*, 1939 (c); *The Well-Wrought Urn*, 1947 (c); (with Robert Penn Warren) *Modern Rhetoric*, 1950 (c); (with W. K. Wimsatt) *Literary Criticism: A Short History*, 1957 (c); *The Hidden God*, 1963 (c); *William Faulkner: The Yoknapatawpha Country*, 1963 (c); (with John Thibaut Purser and Robert Penn Warren) *An Approach to Literature*, 1964 (c); *A Shaping Joy: Studies in the Writer's Craft*, 1971 (c); *The Poetry of Tension*, 1971 (c); ed. (with R. W. B. Lewis and Robert Penn Warren) *American Literature: The Makers and the Making*, 1973 (c); *William Faulkner: Toward Yoknapatawpha and Beyond*, 1978 (c); (with Robert Penn Warren) *Understanding Fiction*, 1979 (c); *William Faulkner, First Encounters*, 1983 (c); *The Language of the American South*, 1985 (c); *On the Prejudices, Predilections, and Firm Beliefs of William Faulkner*, 1987 (e); *Historical Evidence and the Reading of Seventeenth-Century Poetry*, 1991 (c); *Community, Religion, and Literature*, 1995 (e); *Cleanth Brooks and Robert Penn Warren: A Literary Correspondence*, ed. James A. Grimshaw, Jr., 1998 (l); *Cleanth Brooks and Allen Tate: Collected Letters, 1933–1976*, ed. Alphonse Vinh, 1998 (l)

BROOKS, Gwendolyn (1917–)

All in all, despite the fact that this first book [*A Street in Bronzeville*] has its share of unexciting verse, there are considerable resources evidenced for future work. Miss Brooks, to use one of her own phrases, "scrapes life with a fine-tooth comb." And she shows a capacity to marry the special quality of her racial experience with the best attainment of our contemporary poetry tradition. Such compounding of resources out of varied stocks and traditions is the great hope of American art as it is of American life generally.

Amos N. Wilder. *Poetry*. Dec., 1945. p. 166

This little book of poems [*A Street in Bronzeville*] is both a work of art and a poignant social document. It is doubly effective on both scores because it seems such delightfully artless art and (in spite of its razor edges) so innocent of deliberation in its social comment. Simply out of curiosity, let us say, the reader begins a stroll down that unnamed Street. Almost immediately, and with no coercion on

the part of the author, we abandon our present identity and become one of the denizens of Bronzeville. . . . Oddly enough, we never feel sorry for these neighbors as we move among them. We know them instead. What we feel is not pity but sympathy—an extension of our capacity for aliveness and awareness of being.

Starr Nelson. *Saturday Review*. Jan. 19, 1946. p. 15

The work of this young Chicago poet never fails to be warmly and generously human. In a surly and distempered age one is genuinely grateful to Miss Brooks for the lively and attractive spirit that sallies forth from her poems. In contrast to most of her contemporaries, she is neither ridden by anxiety nor self-consumed with guilt. There is in her work a becoming modesty. Though the materials of her art are largely derived from the conditions of life in a Negro urban milieu, she uses these incendiary materials naturally, for their intrinsic value, without straining for shock or for depth, without pretending to speak for a people. In reading this second volume [*Annie Allen*] by the author of *A Street in Bronzeville* I have been impressed by how little of the energy that should go into the building of the work has been diverted to the defence of the life.

Stanley Kunitz. *Poetry*. April, 1950. p. 52

With a few exceptions when straightforward narrative takes over, [*Maud Martha*] is presented in flashes, almost gasps, of sensitive lightness—distillations of the significance of each incident—and reminds of Imagist poems or clusters of ideograms from which one recreates connected experience. Miss Brooks' prose style here embodies the finer qualities of insight and rhythm that were notable in her two earlier books of poetry (her *Annie Allen* received the Pulitzer Prize), and gives a freshness, a warm cheerfulness as well as a depth of implication to her first novel. In technique and impression it stands virtually alone of its kind.

Hubert Creekmore. *New York Times Book Section*. Oct. 4, 1953. p. 4

Nothing vague here [in *The Bean Eaters*], nothing European, nothing mystical. These poems, generous and full of humanity, rattle with verbs and jangle with action. Their images are everyday; their subjects are poor people (often Negroes), the dreams of the downtrodden, the frustrations of the meek.

Yet, for all the worthiness of their themes and their aims, you will probably find them incomplete as poems. Miss Brooks appears more concerned to condemn social injustice and to draw sympathetic character portraits than to write poems that echo on every level, and as a result she repeats the same kind of statement too often for poetic truth.

Peter Davison. *Atlantic Monthly*. Sept., 1960. p. 93

She has a warm heart, a cool head and practices the art of poetry with professional naturalness. Her ability to distinguish between what is sad and what is silly is unfailing, and she deals with race, love, war and other matters with uncommon common sense and a mellow humor that is as much a rarity as it is a relief. Sometimes she is overly sentimental or gets too involved with furniture and ephemera, but on the whole this selected volume [*Selected Poems*]. . . is a pleasure to read.

Carl Morse. *New York Times Book Section.* Oct. 6, 1963. p. 28

Gwendolyn Brooks does the thing that so few poets anywhere can do, and that is to take a really spoken language and make it work for her. Most everyone writes a ''writing'' language, but in her work, there are all the familiar cadences and sounds of speech, right down to the bone-hard rhetoric of the 1960s. . . . I say that her technique is really useful to her because in addition there is visible a whole person behind her poems, and you always feel that she ''writes committed.'' She is one of the very best poets.

Bruce Cutler. *Poetry.* March, 1964. pp. 388–9

Coming to Gwendolyn Brooks, we find a writer avowedly a spokesman, and in this sense a writer who ''looks in'' to a group. . . . Indulging a fancy to make a point, one could say that Gwendolyn Brooks writes in the confidence and momentum of a tradition that *intends to be* established. Put it this way: there is a language that goes with current city events, or there are languages that attempt to hold that existence in human perspective that is local, indigenous. In Gwendolyn Brooks's writings there is this determination to see what is, not to opt for any falsity, and not to abandon the risk of individual judgment either. The result is a special kind of complexity. Sometimes the poems are confusingly local in reference; they shimmer with strong feelings that surface abruptly. But throughout there is implied a steady view, an insight.

William Stafford. *Poetry.* March, 1969. p. 424

It's too soon to say anything definitive about the work of Gwendolyn Brooks. Perhaps she hasn't yet written the poems that will stand out a hundred years from now as her major ones. But she has already written some that will undoubtedly be read so long as man cares about language and his fellows.

There have been no drastic changes in the tactics and subjects she has dealt with over the years. It's doubtful if future critics will talk about the early and the late Brooks, not unless she strikes out into much different territory after 1969. What one observes is a steady development of themes and types.

Her poetry is marked by a number of central concerns: black experience; the nature of greatness; the way in which man expresses his needs, makes do, or lashes out. Ordinarily the view is one of delicate balance, that of a passionate observer. The poems strike one as distinctly those of a woman but always muscled and precise, written from the pelvis rather than the biceps. [1969]

Dan Jaffe in *The Black American Writer,* vol. 2, ed. C.W.E. Bigsby (Penguin). 1971. p. 93

In recent years . . . Gwendolyn Brooks has abandoned her former integrationist position and moved steadily towards a black nationalist posture. With this ideological change, there has come a parallel shift in verse techniques. Influenced by the young black revolutionary writers of the 1960's, Miss Brooks has given up, not

all, but many of the conventional forms used in her early publications. For one thing, like other modern poets, she employs rhyme very sparingly. Perhaps her most popular form now is the kind of flexible, unrhymed verse paragraph found in the volume *In the Mecca.* . . . Perhaps the most effective element in her poetic technique is word-choice. With strong, suggestive, often-times unusual words—words that startle the reader—Gwendolyn Brooks weaves a brilliant poetic tapestry. Never sentimental, never a mouther of clichés, she brings to any subject the freshness and excitement which characterize good poetry—and good poets.

Arthur P. Davis. *From the Dark Tower: Afro-American Writers 1900 to 1960* (Howard). 1974. pp. 192–3

[Gwendolyn] Brooks's religious faith is ambivalent regarding the supernatural. Yet it is deeply humanistic. Her apocalyptic imagery has a counterpart of stability, but its force is dynamic; its permanence, change. ''Divorce''—from nature, as decried by [W. C.] Williams and followers like Charles Olson: from God, as mourned in Eliot; from Stevens—is transformed by Brooks into a concern with divorce from human dignity. Her work cries out against the subjugation of blacks, which may have inflicted more physical than spiritual damage, while it has hurt whites spiritually. Brooks embodies caritas, expressed in the poetic voice as it articulates a racial and communal system. Hers is a unified sensibility, pragmatic and idealistic, shaped, in part, by the needs which it ventures to meet. This kind of artistic courage, risking ''the highest falls,'' is shown by a poet of the first rank, a major poet.

Brooks meets the criteria for major status on all four levels: craft and technique; scope or breadth; influence of the work in style, content, or productivity, upon others; and influence of the poet upon others. . . . She has extended language itself, as Whitman did, by imaginative compounding, word-coinage, and the use of black English vernacular. She belongs to that select category [Ezra] Pound called ''the inventors,'' the highest classification of poets who create and expand formal limits and, thereby, taste itself.

D.H. Melhem. *Gwendolyn Brooks: Poetry and the Heroic Voice* (Lexington: Univ. Pr. of Kentucky, 1987), p. 237

Brooks joined Hughes not only in turning to the black urban folk for subject matter, but in their similar roles as observer-participants. As Hughes indicated, although he had early written lyrics about ''love, roses and moonlight, sunsets and snow,'' he felt that such ''lyric poetry'' contradicted much of his and his people's everyday experience. In his ''social'' as opposed to ''lyric'' poems, he found that ''sometimes, certain aspects of my personal problems happened to be also common to many other people. And certainly, racially speaking, my own problems of adjustment to American life were the same as those of millions of other segregated Negroes'' (''Adventures'' 205). Hughes thus combined individual and public perspectives to become participant-observer. When Brooks uses the figure ''pen'' for Hughes she is applauding the writer soaked in the life of his people who grasps and records that life in all its multi-faceted complexity: the poet keeps the folk's dream alive.

Brooks too saw in her work a preponderance of a different kind of lyric—one with social implications. ''I believe I have written more 'Kitchenette building' type poems than I have written about birds singing and feeling sorry for a girl who's temporarily overwhelmed by grief'' (*Report from Part One*, 158). Brooks also minimizes the interiority of her poetry when she describes herself as a ''Watchful Eye, a tuned Ear, a Super-reporter'' (*Mecca* jacket). These metaphors reveal the poet's desire to hone her skills so as to shape artistic equivalencies of the urban folk. As she says, ''the city is the place to observe man *en masse* and in his infinite.''

> Mariann Russell. *Langston Hughes Review*. Spring, 1988, pp. 31, 32–33

Maud Martha, Gwendolyn Brooks's only novel, appeared in 1953, the same year that *Go Tell It on the Mountain*, James Baldwin's first novel, was published. By that time, Brooks had already published two books of poetry, *A Street in Bronzeville* (1945) and *Annie Allen* (1949), for which she won the Pulitzer Prize. But although she was an established poet, Brooks's novel quietly went out of print while Baldwin's first publication was to become known as a major Afro-American novel. Brooks's novel, like Baldwin's presents the development of a young urban black into an adult, although Brooks's major character is female and Baldwin's is male. Brooks's understated rendition of a black American girl's development into womanhood did not arouse in the reading public the intense reaction that Baldwin's dramatic portrayal of the black male did. Yet Paule Marshall (whose 1959 novel, *Brown Girl, Brownstones*, is considered by many critics to be the forerunner of the Afro-American woman's literary explosion of the 1970s), would in 1968 point to *Maud Martha* as the finest portrayal of an Afro-American woman in the novel to date, and as a decided influence on her work. To Marshall, Brooks's contribution was a turning point in Afro-American fiction, for it presented for the first time a black woman not as a mammy, wench, mulatto, or downtrodden heroine, but as an ordinary human being in all the wonder of her complexity.

Why is it that *Maud Martha* never received some portion of the exposure that Baldwin's novel did, or why is it still, to this date, out of print, virtually unknown except to writers like Marshall and a small but growing number of black literary critics? Even within the context of black studies or women's studies, Brooks's novel is unknown or dismissed as ''exquisite,'' but somehow not particularly worthy of comment. One could say, of course, that *Maud Martha* was not significant enough to receive such attention. However, comments such as Marshall's tend to nullify that argument. Or one could say that Brooks's accomplishment as a poet overshadowed, perhaps eclipsed, her only novel, although the novel shares so many of her poetic characteristics that one would think that it would attract a similar audience. I am inclined to believe that, ironically, the fate of the novel has precisely to do with its poetic qualities, with the compressed ritualized style that is its hallmark, and as importantly, with the period when it was published.

> Barbara Christian. ''Nuance and the Novella.'' In Maria K. Mootry and Gary Smith, eds. *A Life Distilled: Gwendolyn Brooks, Her Poetry and Fiction* (Urbana: Univ. of Illinois Pr., 1989), pp. 239–40

[Her mother] Keziah was to say of Gwendolyn's poems: ''The poetry she wrote during her early teens was the type that appealed to all rhyme-lovers, but it was not the kind the critics select when

awarding prizes.'' Looking back herself, Gwendolyn affirmed this judgment. In *Negro Story*, she stated that she had known nothing of the ''technical possibilities [of poetry] until she was 24.'' That would have been in 1941, when she was participating in the writing workshops of Inez Stark Boulton—an experience that contributed much to her writing progress. But when her comments about lack of technical knowledge before the 1940s is quoted to her today, she is puzzled, pointing out that she had read the *Winged Horse* anthology by 1932 and had by then begun to understand certain technical points from reading critics such as Louis Untermeyer. She had in 1933 written to James Weldon Johnson, the famous black writer of the Harlem Renaissance, and sent him some of her poems. In one of his two letters of response, he told her that she had talent but needed to read modern poetry. She had by then read Langston Hughes and Countee Cullen and other black writers in Cullen's anthology, *Caroling Dusk*, and in Robert Kerlin's *Negro Poets and Their Poems*. . . .

Not until the late 1930s did Gwendolyn make systematic and concentrated raid upon the storehouse of modern poetic techniques. And the raids were to increase under the influence of the Boulton workshop in 1941 and 1942 because it supplied what she had not had before: a systematic exposure of her faults and a coherent point of view regarding the assets of the modern poetry movement.

A reader who wanders into the juvenilia and the apprentice work by chance is likely to be startled. By 1931 there is a precocious body of work that predicts the early rise of a brilliant poet. The poet as delighted rhymester exists up to the latter part of 1935, during which period some development can be ascertained. The 1937–38 period shows a greater freedom of language, which the poet needed to get solidly into her own feelings. The progress became rapid in the 1940s.

> George E. Kent. *A Life of Gwendolyn Brooks* (Lexington: Univ. Pr. of Kentucky, 1990), pp. 22–23

Gwendolyn Brooks's use of the sonnet form in her poetry of the 1940s and 50s signals her status as inheritor and critic of two Renaissance traditions, one originating in Europe during the fourteenth century and the other in Harlem around 1912. According to Henry Louis Gates, Jr., the texts of every Afro-American writer ''occupy spaces in at least two traditions: a European or American literary tradition, and one of the several related but distinct black traditions. The 'heritage' of each black text written in a Western language is . . . a double heritage'' (4). For Brooks, this doubleness in the text doubles yet again over the question of gender; the feminine voice in Brooks's poems, as in the lyric generally, is necessarily dislocated, occupying uneasy ground between the Western tradition's figurations of poetic authority and its representations of silent women. Brooks's ambivalent relation to literary tradition is dramatized in her revision of a single form from two separate traditions, one white, one black, and both predominantly male. . . .

In her revision of English Renaissance conventions, Brooks succeeds in making of the sonnet a vehicle for her own form of complaint, a poetry of power trespassing on the restricted ground of the traditionally male, and white, sonnet. In her extension of the Harlem Renaissance's political concerns to include the construction of gender and the politics of form, she insists on the ideological nature of both the subject and its language. While petitioning for power in the world, Brooks acts out this appropriation at the level of the poem. By forcing the sonnet's shackled and corseted form to embody questions of race and gender, she forces us to recognize the ideological power of form itself, as well as the subversions which that same power makes possible.

> Stacy Carson Hubbard. "'A Splintery Box': Race and Gender in the Sonnets of Gwendolyn Brooks." *Genre.* Spring, 1992, pp. 47, 63

BIBLIOGRAPHY

A Street in Bronzeville, 1945 (p); *Annie Allen*, 1949 (p); *Maud Martha*, 1953 (n); *Bronzeville Boys and Girls*, 1956 (p); *The Bean Eaters*, 1960 (p); *Selected Poems*, 1963; *Selected Poems: In the Time of Detachment, in the Time of Cold* [Civil War Centennial Commission of Illinois], 1965 (p); *In the Mecca*, 1968 (p); *For Illinois 1968: A Sesquicentennial Poem*, 1968; *Riot*, 1969 (p); *Family Pictures*, 1970 (p); *Aloneness*, 1971 (p); *Jump Bad*, 1971 (p); *The World of Gwendolyn Brooks*, 1971 (collected works); *Aurora*, 1972 (p); *Report from Part One: An Autobiography*, 1972; (with Keorapetse Kgositsile, Haki R. Madhubiti, and Dudley Randall, *A Capsule Course in Black Poetry Writing*, 1975 (e); *Beckonings*, 1975 (p); *Primer for Blacks*, 1980 (p); *To Disembark*, 1981 (p); *Young Poet's Primer*, 1981 (e, c); *Black Love*, 1982 (p); *Very Young Poets* [writing manual], 1983 (e); *Mayor Harold Washington [and] Chicago, The I Will City*, 1983 (p); *The Near-Johannesburg Boy*, 1986 (p); *A Life Distilled*, 1987 (e); *Blacks*, 1987 (coll); *Gottschalk and the Grande Tarantelle*, 1988 (p); *Winnie*, 1988 (p); *Children Coming Home*, 1991 (p); *Report from Part Two*, 1996 (a)

BROOKS, Van Wyck (1886–1963)

He seems to wake up every morning and regard America, and everybody who ever wrote in America, or who signified anything in American life, with fresh, eager, and ever-interested eyes. His mind perpetually revolves around the idea of a national culture in America, and he pursues all sides of the subject with such a vividness of interest and vividness of language, that when you have read three or four of his books, you begin to believe that the creation of such a culture is one of the few causes left worthy of the devotion and self-sacrifice of men.

> Mary M. Colum. *Dial.* Jan., 1924. p. 33

He, more than any one else, more even than Mr. H. L. Mencken, has created a certain prevalent taste in letters, a certain way of thinking about literature.

This eminence, though I feel it has been won through default, has been graced by estimable qualities of Mr. Brooks. He has scholarship which becomes imposing when applied to the waste land of American letters. . . . Happily, Mr. Brooks has a style at the service of his erudition and historical consciousness. . . . What is wrong with Mr. Brooks and what is wrong with nine-tenths of American critical writing is no less than a deficiency in the sense of

proportion. . . . It lacks a standpoint which is high enough for the vision of contributory elements melting into a major and vital organism.

> Gorham B. Munson. *Dial.* Jan., 1925. pp. 28–9, 42

He has been the most influential critic of the past twenty years. His early work was the principal factor in the erection of the lofty cultural standards that have encouraged the rise of a mature, serious, philosophical criticism. The effect of his later work was not so praiseworthy, for it led to the embittered subjectivity of Lewis Mumford's *Melville* and Matthew Josephson's *Portrait of the Artist as American.* . . . In any event, for good or bad, something of Brooks has seeped into almost every American critic under fifty (including even the Marxist, Granville Hicks). There is no better testimony to his fine mind, his exquisite taste, his integrity and unselfishness.

> Bernard Smith. *New Republic.* Aug. 26, 1936. p. 72

When all is said and done, Mr. Brooks's achievement remains a prodigious one, conceived with audacity and carried out with extraordinary skill. In reading his literary history, one has a sense that Mr. Brooks has repeopled the American continent. On his benign Judgment Day, the dead arise from their graves, throw off their shrouds and become flesh and blood again, ready to take their place in eternity. The writer who in his youth called for a usable American past has, in the full tide of maturity, created that past for us; and has shown us that it was far richer, far sweeter, far more significant than we could, in our rebellious, dissident, adolescent days have dreamed of. To the writer who has accomplished this great feat, we owe unending admiration and gratitude.

> Lewis Mumford. *Saturday Review.* Nov. 8, 1947. p. 13

Brooks has made so many switches in his forty years of writing and his nineteen books that it is difficult to perceive any consistent pattern. He has been an aesthete, a socialist, a Freudian, a manifesto-writer, a Jungian, a Tolstoyan book-burner, and finally a compiler of literary pastiche and travelogue for the Book-of-the-Month Club. He has moved from total arty rejection of America and its culture to total uncritical acceptance. He has occupied almost every political and philosophic position of our time, and called them all "socialism." Nevertheless, there is a consistent pattern to his work, from his first book to his last, but it is a method rather than a viewpoint, the method of biographical criticism.

> Stanley Edgar Hyman. *The Armed Vision* (Knopf). 1948. pp. 106–7

It is always said that Mr. Brooks is "readable." This means that his style is pleasant and his anecdotes are delightful. Now Mr. Brooks's prose does have very agreeable manners, it has the air of well-tempered conversation. And his little stories are often charming. . . . We could wish for so civilized a "desire to please" in the writers of the humorless, perspiring little essays in some of American literary journals. But the chit-chat is too often without edge, where edge is needed: good form does not demand such a sacrifice. And the anecdotes come too close to being the whole of the book; so much so that for me they cease to be "readable," they are too dense on the page, they are so many acres of underbrush.

Henry Rago. *Commonweal*. March 28, 1952. p. 619

It is a complex personality, that of a cosmopolitan bent at all costs on being a glorious provincial. We can discuss all the high qualities, those that make him our genuine "man of letters"—in the old-fashioned sense of the term—since the death of Howells. He has a style and manner, a sense of picturesque, a feeling for the anecdote as a work of art. He has a genuine relish for the idiosyncrasies and the *bizarréries* of literary bohemia and a tendency to suffuse with a pastel optimism even the dark moments in the lives of our great writers.

Leon Edel. *New Republic*. March 22, 1954. p. 20

By his own account of childhood and youth Brooks is the heir of culture and breeding; in this sense he is perhaps the last great disciple of the genteel tradition in our letters. But what is heroic and admirable in all this is the rejection of his own tradition in favor of the new forces which have appeared in our society since the 1850's. And his affirmation of our central "Western" line of progressive or radical thought extends even to his praise of the "vulgarian immigrant" Dreiser. We know this vein of American thought is at present in eclipse, with both our literary critics and our politicians. When—or perhaps, in more desperate moments, *if*—our mood changes, Brooks will be seen as a major spokesman for our literature who is indifferent to leadership but who has never relinquished his "position." How could he? It is inside himself.

Maxwell Geismar. *The Nation*. Apr. 3, 1954, p. 283

After *The Ordeal of Mark Twain*—and after "America's Coming-of-Age" and "Letters and Leadership," essays that Brooks wrote in the same period—there was a second renaissance, not so rich as the first in great personalities, perhaps not so rich in great works, but still vastly productive; it was a period when American writers once again were able to survive and flourish in their own country. The *Ordeal* and the essays had helped to make it possible. How much they had helped it would be hard to decide; one would have to know all the apprentice writers of the time who read them, and what the writers told their friends, and how the *Ordeal* in particular affected their ideals of the literary vocation. I can testify from experience, however, that the climate of literature seemed different after Brooks had spoken. He had given courage to at least a few writers, and courage is hardly less contagious than fear.

Malcolm Cowley. *New Republic*. June 20, 1955. p. 18

As anyone would expect who has read Van Wyck Brooks's definitive volumes about the writer in America from 1800 to 1915 or his *John Sloan*—or, for that matter, any of his books—the chief trouble with *The Dream of Arcadia* is the embarrassment of riches it contains. Like all of his books, his account of American writers and artists in Italy from 1760 to 1915 is packed with detail, full of quotable quotations, wealthy in insights dropped casually even in footnotes. Before one begins to read, he wonders whether the subject is enough for a full-length book; before he finishes he

realizes that here compressed is material for several volumes—the history of what Italy has meant to the American artist and, through him, to American culture as a whole.

Harvey Curtis Webster. *Saturday Review*. Sept. 27, 1958. p. 19

The Ordeal of Mark Twain is one of the earliest books in which a prominent American critic makes use of psychoanalytic ideas, although they furnish him neither the central theme of the book nor its chief method. . . .

The foundation of the book, however, does not seem to me to be wholly psychological, since it gives at least as much stress to social factors in the America of the Gilded Age and to Mark Twain's relationships with friends and business associates as it does to the primary bases of these in the family constellation. The book, consequently, may be characterized as a combination of criticism and biography using a method which is a combination of sociology and psychology. Its intention is to show the stultifying effect of psychic trauma, maladjustment, and frustration induced by adverse social conditions upon Mark Twain's latent artistic ability. This it does by tracing the ineffectual struggle which he waged against their combined power.

Louis Fraiberg. *Psychoanalysis and American Literary Criticism* (Wayne State). 1960. pp. 120–1

Even though Brooks did not know [William Dean] Howells as Howells knew Clemens, he has imparted to this volume something of the tone that Howells imparted to *My Mark Twain*. In its special fashion, Brooks's *Howells* is a masterpiece by one who has actually experienced a part of Howell's world and has vicariously lived in all of it as an indefatigable reader and writer.

But with a reminiscence done by a friend and contemporary we only ask on the factual level whether the author has remembered right or not. With the quasi-reminiscence that Brooks has done we are entitled to know something of his sources. Of these he tells us only a little in his prefatory note, asking readers to trust him rather than oblige him to fill another volume with "the usual scholarly apparatus."

George Arms. *American Literature*. Jan., 1961. pp. 478–9

As a biographer, Van Wyck Brooks believes that there is a fundamental relationship between the lives men lead and the things they do. He is primarily a chronicler and an *evoker*; he likes an atmosphere and a background. And he works, as biographers must, in mosaic, putting together bits and pieces of information as best he can to demonstrate human accomplishment. To be sure, we are sometimes too aware of the separate pieces; and sometimes a piece is fitted the wrong way, or is out of place. But Brooks' studies, compared with our giant biographies, exemplify the art of concision.

The shortcomings of Van Wyck Brooks' portraits stem from his reluctance to probe into the why and how of human endeavor. This seems to reflect his eternal optimism and faith in man's will to struggle and to succeed—and a particular faith in America's "coming of age."

Leon Edel. *New Republic*. Sept. 17, 1962. p. 14

As a critic, a single dissenting voice, he realized that he couldn't do much "to change the whole texture of life at home." He might, however, do something to change our conception of the writer in America, and the writer's conception of his own task, always with the aim of encouraging himself and others to do better work, the best that was in them. To this aim he devoted himself with admirable consistency and—let it be recorded—with an amazing degree of success.

There is one field in which the success can be measured. When we think of the contempt for American authors, mixed with ignorance about them, that prevailed in universities during the reign of Barrett Wendell; when we contrast it with the reverence for many of the same authors that is now being proclaimed in hundreds of scholarly monographs each year, as well as being revealed statistically by the multiplication of courses in American literature—while living writers share in the glory reflected from the past by being invited to the campus as novelists or poets in residence—we might also remember that Brooks had more to do with creating the new attitude than anyone else in the country.

Malcolm Cowley. *Saturday Review*. May 25, 1963. p. 18

Brooks was not the critical Pollyanna that those New Critics who have read little by him maintain. Nobody in all our critical writings so far has been so perceptive about the faults of our writings and, indeed, of our whole literary tradition. Read *The Wine of the Puritans* (1908) and read *America's Coming-of-Age* (1915), and see what intelligent, well-informed, well-mannered criticism of our literary products can be. Brooks loved, but he also knew. Brooks searched for things to praise, but he was not blind to things not worthy of praise. Sometimes, indeed, he was so disappointed in many of the things he found that he overstated his disappointment—to take it back years later in his massive and magnificent five volumes about the *Makers and Finders* of our literary culture.

Charles Angoff. *Literary Review*. Autumn, 1963. p. 31

It has become the fashion today to regard the earlier work of Van Wyck Brooks as his main achievement. It is as the author of *America's Coming of Age, Letters and Leadership*, and the studies of Mark Twain, Henry James and Emerson, books of protest and of criticism, that he makes his chief appeal to the younger generation. And it is true that these are the books that cleared the air for a more wholesome creative life in America and tilled the ground in which many vigorous talents were able to take root. In his emphasis on our native note, as opposed to the then prevalent literary provincialism, his courageous holding up of the mirror to our spiritual life, his insistence upon the cultural communion out of which great literature arises, and his early discernment of the deep cleft, in the American soul, between idea and practice, Van Wyck Brooks was a forerunner, a voice crying in the wilderness. But this was only one part of his achievement. He had been a pioneer. Now he saw his vision coming true, and turned to the other and essential task that lay ahead: to bring to life for us our entire literary heritage, to exhibit the pageant of genius in our country, and give us, in his own phrase, "a usable past.". . . This was the second and greater part of the achievement of Van Wyck Brooks, a man in quest of the truth; truly, a man driven by the furies.

John Hall Wheelock. *Library Chronicle*. Winter, 1965. p. 4

The clue to Brooks' way of thinking may be found in his remark that "Allston liked to contemplate extremes and try to fill, imaginatively, the space between." So, for example, he gives us "highbrow" and "lowbrow," and the mediating term, "middlebrow." More often, however, there is no mediation but only opposition, as in the "creative life" *vs.* the "acquisitive life." Here, Brooks, a master polemicist, has followed his own advice to critics to find the deep, irreconcilable "opposed catchwords"; and in what follows we realize that his melodramatic way of seeing is supported by an equally melodramatic way of feeling.

Sherman Paul. *New Leader*. Feb. 15, 1965. p. 20

It may be said that after *America's Coming-of-Age, Letters and Leadership* (1918), and *The Literary Life in America* (1927), his three deservedly famous manifestoes, he never wrote a whole book in his own person, but always masked himself in the identities of those about whom he wrote, or invented an alter ego, as in *Oliver Allston* (1941). This is also true of *An Autobiography* which in part reads like left-over notes from his literary chronicle. Yet he is capable for short stretches of an ordered amplitude and downrightness which puts us to shame.

Quentin Anderson. *New Republic*. April 17, 1965. p. 15

BIBLIOGRAPHY
(with John Hall Wheelock) *Verses by Two Undergraduates*, 1905; *The Wine of the Puritans*, 1908 (e); *The Malady of the Ideal: Obermann, Maurice de Guérin and Amiel*, 1913 (e); *John Addington Symonds*, 1914 (b); *America's Coming-of-Age*, 1915 (e); *The World of H.G. Wells*, 1915 (b); *Letters and Leadership*, 1918 (e); *The Ordeal of Mark Twain*, 1920 (b); *Paul Gauguin's Intimate Journals*, 1921 (tr); *Jean Jacques Rousseau* (by Henri-Frederic Amiel) 1922 (tr); (with Eleanor Stimson Brooks) *Some Aspects of the Life of Jesus from the Psychological and Psycho-analytic Point of View* (by Georges Bergner), 1923 (tr); *Henry Thoreau, Bachelor of Nature* (by Léon Bazalgette), 1924 (tr); (with Eleanor Stimson Brooks) *Summer* (vol. II of *The Soul Enchanted*, by Romain Rolland) 1925 (tr); *The Pilgrimage of Henry James*, 1925 (b); *Emerson and Others*, 1927 (e); *Mother and Son* (by Romain Rolland) 1927 (tr); *The Road* (by André Chamson), 1929 (tr); *Roux the Bandit* (by André Chamson) 1929 (tr); *The Crime of the Just* (by André Chamson) 1930 (tr); *Sketches in Criticism*, 1932 (c); *The Life of Emerson*, 1932 (b); *Three Essays on America* (*America's Coming-of-Age, Letters and Leadership, The Literary Life in America*, 1934 (e); *The Flowering of New England, 1815–1865*, 1936 (h) (revised edition, 1946); *New England Indian Summer, 1865–1915*, 1940 (h); *Our Literature Today*, 1941 (c); *The Opinions of Oliver Allston*, 1941 (n); *The World of Washington Irving*, 1944 (h); *The Times of Melville and Whitman*, 1947 (h) (second edition, 1953); *A Chilmark Miscellany* 1948; *The Confident Years, 1885–1915*, 1952 (h); *The Writer in America*, 1953 (c); *Scenes and Portraits*, 1954 (r); *From a Writer's Notebook*, 1955 (e); *Makers and Finders (The Flowering of New England, New England Indian Summer, The World of Washington Irving, The Times of Melville and Whitman, The Confident Years)*, 1955 (h); *John Sloan: A Painter's Life*, 1955 (b); *Helen Keller*, 1956 (b); *Days of the Phoenix*, 1957 (r); *The Dream of Arcadia*, 1958 (h); *Howells: His Life and World*, 1959 (b); *From the Shadow of the Mountain*, 1961

(r); *Fenellosa and His Circle*, 1962 (b); *An Autobiography (Scenes and Portraits, Days of the Phoenix, From the Shadow of the Mountain)*, 1965

BROWN, Rita Mae (1944–)

For those who think fiction is not the place to sermonize, *Rubyfruit Jungle* is often too blatantly preachy. Molly, the main character, has been a radical lesbian from birth, refusing all the conventional limitations of being a girl. In play she says, ''I got to be the doctor because I'm the smart one and being a girl don't matter.'' Faced with the requirement to please others, she counters with, ''I care if I like me, that's what I really care about.'' These assertions are the sort also to be found in the new, right-minded literature for children being published by feminist presses. There is nothing wrong with them. Nor is there anything wrong with Molly's sermonizing to a friend who feels limited by her background in what she can do with her life. . . . But the earnestness would weigh heavily if the book were not lifted by arrogant humor, never-mind-the-consequences fury, and transcending tenderness. . . . The film Molly makes of her adopted mother as a thesis for her degree is the device by which Molly transcends the bitterness she might otherwise have fixed on, for the film is the real portrait of a woman who did what she could in a narrow, prejudice-ridden world from which she had no way of escape. At the same time, it underlines the remarkable gifts of defiance and intelligence which have marked Molly for freedom. *Rubyfruit Jungle* is a far shout from the maimed religious and psychological apology of *The Well of Loneliness* and, as propaganda, healthier, for protest is a more accurate weapon against bigotry than special pleading. Rita Mae Brown is ready to play without a handicap. . . .

Jane Rule. *Lesbian Images*. Doubleday, 1975, pp. 183–96.

Ever since *Rubyfruit Jungle*, her tough-talking, tenderhearted story of a girl who loves girls, Rita Mae Brown's subject has been the misfit between human passions and societal conventions. Imagine a Rubens nude trying to squeeze into a size 6 corset, and you've got the comic futility and wasteful pain that Miss Brown sees in the effort to confine desire within one standard form: respectable heterosexual marriage. In her view, sexuality is a first cousin of imagination, involving an irrepressible urge to honor and rival the crazy abundance of life.

Unexamined heterosexuality, in *Rubyfruit Jungle*, is a pressure cooker of far-out fantasies. The most dogged champion of decency in the small town of her boisterous novel *Six of One* is discovered, at age 80, to keep pornography under his mattress. And in Miss Brown's latest novel, *Southern Discomfort*, nearly all the good husbands of 1918 Montgomery, Ala.—including the judge and the chief of police—relieve the pressures of propriety chez Banana Mae Parker and Blue Rhonda Latrec, prostitutes of Water Street.

For Miss Brown, such duplicity is the stuff of human comedy. But her last two novels boasted women characters who dared to tell the naked truth and to love whom they pleased. . . . There is no such character in *Southern Discomfort*—no embodiment of passion triumphant, of fearless love and guiltless pleasure—and the novel is stronger for it.

Rita Mae Brown still believes in the fundamental innocence of passion, but for the first time she gives the old adversaries—rules, roles, prohibitions, limitations—a grudging respect, a kind of equal time. . . .

It's rare to say that a book would be better if it were longer but I suspect that in a less impatient era *Southern Discomfort* would have been a 700-page epic that slowly revealed the roots of character and the intertangling of disparate lives. As it is, the book often seems abrupt and arbitrary, jump-cut as if it were a two-hour movie. Lacking space to let us discover her major characters at their living, Miss Brown flatly tells us who they are: ''Hortensia wanted control over everybody and everything.'' It's a while before these authorial puppets come to life. Meanwhile, minor characters, like Hercules's boxing manager, Sneaky Pie, are so vivid that they cry out for more space. The plot moves in fits and starts. A fistfight between mother and son is perfectly rendered, but a later, even more crucial scene of violence is rushed and anticlimactic. The reader is left feeling charmed, moved—and a little bit cheated.

Annie Gottlieb, *New York Times Book Review*. March 21, 1982, pp. 10, 29.

In Rita Mae Brown's *Rest In Pieces*, every house, barn, shop, rectory and civic building in the tiny Virginia hamlet of Crozet seems to have a resident cat. One sees in such details the fine paw of Sneaky Pie Brown, Ms. Brown's cat., who gets co-author credit for this cozy tale and who bears ''an uncanny resemblance'' to one of its heroines, the ''wonderfully intelligent'' Mrs. Murphy, a tiger cat who resides with the town postmistress, Mary Minor (Harry) Haristeen.

When she isn't lording it over the other animals on Harry's farm, Mrs. Murphy trains her formidable intellect on the appalling case of a corpse (''No fingerprints. No clothes. . . . No head'') that turns up in bits and pieces all over town, just as a handsome stranger with a dark secret comes to Crozet and takes a friendly interest in Harry. The suspense isn't exactly killing, but it gets us jumpy enough to look over our shoulders in church.

Ms. Brown's earthy prose breathes warmth into wintry Crozet and pinches color into the cheeks of its nosy, garrulous residents. ''How close it made everyone feel,'' Harry muses on their funny nicknames, ''these little monikers, these tokens of intimacy.'' It is the shattering of this intimacy by acts of violence that Ms. Brown examines so thoughtfully, creating such an enchanting world of Crozet that we shudder to see any more of its citizens in their graves. Or caught with red hands.

Marilyn Stasio. *New York Times Book Review*. September 6, 1992, p. 17.

BIBLIOGRAPHY

The Hand That Cradles the Rock, 1971 (p); *Rubyfruit Jungle*, 1973 (n); *Songs to a Handsome Woman*, 1973 (p); *In Her Day*, 1976 (n); *A Plain Brown Rapper*, 1976 (e); *Six of One*, 1978 (n); *Southern Discomfort*, 1982 (n); *Sudden Death*, 1983 (n); *High Hearts*, 1986 (n); *Poems*, 1987 (p); *Bingo*, 1988 (n); *Starting from Scratch: A Different Kind of Writer's Manual*, 1988 (e); *Wish You Were Here*, 1990 (n); *Rest in Pieces*, 1992 (n); *Venus Envy*, 1993 (n); *Dolley: A Novel of Dolley Madison in Love and War*, 1994 (n); *Murder at Monticello; or, Old Sins*, 1994 (n); *Pay Dirt*, 1995 (n); *Riding*

Shotgun, 1996 (n); *Murder, She Meowed*, 1996 (n); *Rita Will*, 1997 (m); *Murder on the Prowl*, 1998 (n); *Cat on the Scent*, 1998 (n)

BROWN, Sterling Allen (1901–1989)

[As a college teacher, Sterling Brown] recalls that he learned as much about language from his students as they learned from him. He was fascinated by the talk and the songs of his students and their parents; they were intrigued by this lanky, athletic professor who took seriously the local lore. The students brought to class local champion singers and talkers. . . . Another brought Brown the first blues records he had ever heard.

Thus Brown began his collection of black folk songs and sayings. He realized that worksongs, ballads, blues, and spirituals were, at their best, poetical expressions of Afro-American life. And he became increasingly aware of black language as often ironic, understated and double-edged. Obviously, more than pathos and humor was expressed in the stinging couplet from the spirituals: "I don't know what my mother wants to stay here fuh, / This ole worl' ain't been no friend to huh." Where in American writing about Afro-American life was this compressed, direct eloquence being equalled? And no one seemed to be writing about the man who might sing these blues lines: "I hear my woman calling some other man's name, / I know she don't want me, but I answers jus' de same." Early on, Brown knew that he would try to render black experience as he knew it, using the speech of the people. He would not, because of white stereotyping, avoid phonetical spellings (although as the years passed, these "dialect" spellings seemed less and less necessary). His goal was not to run from the stereotype, but to celebrate the human complexity behind the now grinning, now teary-eyed mask.

Brown's poetry comprises a portrait gallery of Afro-Americans. The few whites who appear are seen in relation to their darker brethren. For the blacks there are certain joys and satisfactions. There is laughter—not just the grim "laughing to keep from crying"—but belly laughter which may have nothing to do with social ills and frustrations. But in Brown's poetry the scene from which comedy or tragedy must be squeezed is an absurd and gloomy one. . . .

Perhaps Brown's greatest strength lies not in his grim surveying of the American scene, but in his portraits of the people who persevere in spite of everything. . . .

For Brown, folklore serves the function classically attributed to literature; it is functional, instructive, saving. . . . Blacks survived slavery, segregation, and prejudice by clinging to the hopeful, rugged values expressed in the songs of their fathers. . . .

Brown's poetic vision is riotously funny, hopeful, meditative—and ultimately dubious, tragical. . . .

Robert G. O'Meally. *The New Republic*. February 11, 1978, pp. 33–6.

[Most of the poems in Sterling Brown's *The Collected Poems of Sterling A. Brown* were composed in dialect and] had as their subjects distinctively black archetypal mythic characters as well as the black common man whose roots were rural and Southern. Mr.

Brown called his poems "portraitures," close and vivid studies of a carefully delineated subject that suggested a strong sense of place.

These portraitures the poet renders in a style that emerged from several forms of folk discourse, a black vernacular that includes the blues and ballads, spirituals and worksongs. Indeed, Mr. Brown's ultimate referents are black music and mythology. His language, densely symbolic, ironical and naturally indirect, draws upon the idioms, figures and tones of both the sacred and the profane vernacular traditions, mediating between these in a manner unmatched before or since.

But it is not merely the translation of the vernacular that makes his work so major, informed by these forms though his best work is; it is rather the deft manner in which he created his own poetic diction by fusing several black traditions with various models provided by Anglo-American poets to form a unified and complex structure of feeling, a sort of song of a racial self. Above all else, Mr. Brown is a regionalist whose poems embody William Carlos Williams's notion that the classic is the local, fully realized. . . . Mr. Brown boldly merged the Afro-American vernacular tradition of dialect and myth with the Anglo-American poetic tradition and . . . introduced the Afro-American modernist lyrical mode into black literature. . . .

Reading this comprehensive edition, I was struck by how consistently [Mr. Brown] shapes the tone of his poems by the meticulous selection of the right word to suggest succinctly complex images and feelings "stripped to form," in Frost's phrase. Unlike so many of his contemporaries, Mr. Brown never lapses into bathos or sentimentality. His characters confront catastrophe with all of the irony and stoicism of the blues and of black folklore. What's more, he is able to realize such splendid results in a variety of forms, including the classic and standard blues, the ballad, the sonnet and free verse. For the first time, we can appreciate Mr. Brown's full range, his mastery of so many traditions.

Henry Louis Gates, Jr. *New York Times Book Review*. January 11, 1981, pp. 11, 16.

[Brown's] poetry was collected in anthologies as early as James Weldon Johnson's *The Book of American Negro Poetry* (1922), and, like Johnson himself and Langston Hughes, he set about disrupting the patently false and banal image of the docile American Negro with his charming *patois*, artificially stylized and mimicked by the whites in the minstrel shows still popular in the 1920s and 1930s. Johnson says in his preface on Hughes and Brown that they "*do* use a dialect, but it is not the dialect of the comic minstrel tradition or the sentimental plantation tradition; it is the common, racy, living, authentic speech of the Negro in certain phases of real life."

Brown uses original Afro-American ballads such as "Casey Jones," "John Henry," and "Staggolee" as counterpoint for his modern ones, but the portent of his ironic wit should not be underestimated, for it is actually a tool to shape an ironic, infernal vision of American life as Hades: "The Place was Dixie I took for Hell," says Slim in "Slim in Hell." The American Negro is heralded not as Black Orpheus but as modern tragic hero Mose, a leader of *all* people while futilely attempting to save his own: "A soft song, filled with a misery/Older than Mose will be." In "Sharecropper" he is broken as Christ was broken; his landlord "shot him in the side" to put him out of his misery; he is lost and wild as Odysseus in "Odyssey of a Big Boy"; and found again:

Man wanta live
Man want find himself
Man gotta learn
How to go it alone.

Though small in quantity, Brown's poetry is epic in conception; his ballad, blues, and jazz forms are the vehicles for creative insight into themes of American life.

> Carol Lee Saffioti and Dayana Stetco. In *Reference Guide to American Literature, 3rd edition*, ed. Jim Kamp (St. James Press, 1994).

BIBLIOGRAPHY
Outline for the Study of the Poetry of American Negroes, 1931 (c); *Southern Road*, 1932 (p); *The Negro in American Fiction*, 1938 (c); *Negro Poetry and Drama*, 1938 (c); *The Last Ride of Wild Bill and Eleven Narrative Poems*, 1975 (p); *The Collected Poems of Sterling A. Brown*, edited by Michael S. Harper, 1980 (p)

BUCK, Pearl (1892–1973)

She is entitled to be counted as a first-rate novelist, without qualification for the exotic and unique material in which she works. . . . This is the elemental struggle of men with the soil.

The design is filled out with richness of detail and lyric beauty. If now and then there is a straining for effects of biblical poetry, more often there is poignancy in the simple narrative of simple, rude events. . . . Most of all there is verity.

> Nathaniel Peffer. *New York Herald Tribune Book Section*. March 1, 1931. p. 1

Such a novel as *The Good Earth* calls at once for comparison with other novels of the same general design—novels of the soil on the one hand and novels concerning Oriental life on the other. Any such comparison brings out the fact that despite Mrs. Buck's very good narrative style, despite her familiarity with her material, her work has a certain flatness of emotional tone. . . . Mrs. Buck is undoubtedly one of the best Occidental writers to treat of Chinese life, but *The Good Earth* lacks the imaginative intensity, the lyrical quality, which someone who had actually farmed Chinese soil might have been able to give it.

> Eda Lou Walton. *The Nation*. May 13, 1931. p. 534

It ought to be very moving to a Western reader. There is only one difficulty. Romantic love is a fake center of psychology to ascribe to the typical Oriental man or woman, reared in the traditional bondage to quite different ideals. Although romantic love is second nature to the Western woman, trained to it by the traditions of a thousand years, it would not even be understood by an old-fashioned Chinese wife. By placing the emphasis on romantic love,

all Confucian society is reduced to a laughable pandemonium. . . . *The Good Earth*, though it has no humor or profound lyric passion, shows good technique and much artistic sincerity. Thus, it is discouraging to find that the novel works toward confusion, not clarification. . . . Mrs. Buck, the daughter of a missionary, refuses from the start of her book to admit that there is such a culture as Confucianism.

> Younghill Kang. *New Republic*. July 1, 1931. p. 185

There is a firm unity in her work which makes its component parts not easily distinguishable, . . . an identification with one's characters so complete and so well sustained is rare in fiction. . . . The language in which Mrs. Buck presents this material . . . is English—very plain, clear English; yet it gives the impression that one is reading the language native to the characters. . . . Mrs. Buck never, I think, uses a word for which a literal translation into Chinese could not be found. . . . Whether any novelist can be in the very first flight who depicts a civilization other than his own, I do not know. . . . But we may say at least that for the interest of her chosen material, the sustained high level of her technical skill and the frequent universality of her conceptions, Mrs. Buck is entitled to take rank as a considerable artist.

> Phyllis Bentley. *English Journal*. Dec., 1935. pp. 791–800

Mrs. Buck is clearly not the destined subject of a chapter in literary history, and would be the last to say so herself. . . . [But] *The Good Earth*, the first volume bearing that name, not the trilogy, is a unique book, and in all probability belongs among the permanent contributions to world literature of our times. . . . It is a document in human nature, in which questions of style—so long as the style was adequate, and of depth—so long as the surfaces were true and significant—were not important. It did not have to be as well written as it was, in order to be distinguished. . . . We do not wish to be unjust to Mrs. Buck. Her total achievement is remarkable even though it contains only one masterpiece.

> Henry Seidel Canby. *Saturday Review*. Nov. 19, 1938. p. 8

Although *The Good Earth* was among the most popular books of the 1930's—ranking just after *Gone with the Wind* and *Anthony Adverse*—and although it has received more prizes and official honors than any other novel in our history, there are still literary circles in which it continues to be jeered at or neglected. . . . It is the story of Wang Lu, a poor farmer who becomes a wealthy landlord, but it is also a parable of the life of man, in his relation to the soil that sustains him. The plot, deliberately commonplace, is given a sort of legendary weight and dignity by being placed in an unfamiliar setting. The biblical style is appropriate to the subject and the characters.

> Malcolm Cowley. *New Republic*. May 10, 1939. p. 24

It is a quarter of a century since Pearl Buck wrote a novel which, perhaps more than all earlier books combined, made the outside world Chinaconscious. In *The Good Earth* millions of Westerners first met the Chinese people as they really feel and think and behave. . . . Before 1930 many Americans pictured the Chinese as queer laundrymen, or clever merchants like Fu Manchu, or heathens sitting in outer darkness; few believed they could greatly influence our own fate. Since then historical events have taught us otherwise—and among those ''events'' Pearl Buck's book might well be included. Her more than two dozen novels, translations, and nonfiction books interpreting traditional and revolutionary Asia have fully justified the early award to her of the Nobel prize in literature.

> Edgar Snow. *The Nation.* Nov. 13, 1954. p. 426

Throughout her writing life, Pearl Buck has been building bridges of understanding between an old and a new civilization, between one generation and another, between differing attitudes toward God and nationality and parenthood and love. Not all Miss Buck's bridges have withstood the weight of problems they were designed to bear. But *The Good Earth* will surely continue to span the abyss that divides East from West, so long as there are people to read it.

> Virgilia Peterson. *New York Times Book Section.* July 7, 1957. p. 4

Mrs. Pearl Buck has been enveloped in a kind of critical and popular literary personality which has very little to do with what she actually writes. To the professional critic, she is suspiciously prolific and some what single-minded. To the political extremists, she is subversive just because she has been so prescient on Asian affairs. Her sense of Asian politics and society results in such accurate predictions that it is, by the logic of the extremist, a clear-cut evidence of her advocacy of what has happened.

The Living Reed will confirm both the critic and the extremist in their views. To a wide public, it will be the most powerful and informative book Mrs. Buck has written in some years. *The Living Reed* retains Mrs. Buck's sense of tradition, her deep commitment to the family scanned over several generations as a microcosm of larger social configurations, and her almost visceral feel for how the civil Leviathan can crush the bones of mere mortals.

> Eugene Burdick. *New York Herald Tribune Book Section.* Sept. 15, 1963. p. 5

The reason Miss Buck has refused to keep pace with modern techniques is not far to seek. She is following the old-fashioned Chinese story practice of emphasizing event and characterization. And yet there is a dichotomy even here. In the 1930's her best fiction was objective, and the didactic element was usually muted or subordinated. When written in this vein, her work takes on force and meaning. After 1939, however, she breaks away from objectivity; didacticism becomes a dominant feature, and the quality of her work declines. If she had followed the same form of imitation of the Chinese novel type in her post-Nobel Prize writing, her work after 1939 might have reached the significance of her earlier productions. Increasing humanitarian interests brought a lack of *vraisemblance* and demonstrated the inadvisability of distorting what Thomas Hardy calls ''natural truth'' for the purpose of stressing didactic points. A growing sentimentalism also makes

itself felt more and more in her later writing, and this attitude is detrimental to the highest artistry.

> Paul A. Doyle. *Pearl S. Buck* (Twayne). 1965. p. 151

Written about a quarter century ago, around the time when Pearl Buck's *The Good Earth* was winning a Pulitzer, and, with her other work, a Nobel award, this novel [*The Time Is Noon*] was once set in type, only to have publication canceled with her approval—because, supposedly, it was ''too personal.''. . .

The parts that ordinary novelists do well stump this author, unfortunately; the parts that stump the others she handles wonderfully. Her villains are completely unbelievable—as if, in fact, she never really knew one. The minister father who steals the money hoarded by his wife, the farmer-husband and his doltish family, the scoundrel of a church organist are right out of dime novels. But her good people, customarily skimped or short-changed in fiction, often come touchingly, dramatically alive. . . .

> W.G. Rogers. *New York Times Book Section.* Feb. 19, 1967. p. 44

BIBLIOGRAPHY

East Wind: West Wind, 1930 (n); *The Good Earth*, 1931 (n); *Sons*, 1932 (n); *The Young Revolutionist*, 1932 (n); *The First Wife and Other Stories*, 1933 (s); *All Men Are Brothers*, 1933 (tr); *The Mother*, 1934 (n); *A House Divided*, 1935 (n); *House of Earth* (*The Good Earth, Sons, A House Divided*), 1935 (n); *The Exile*, 1936 (b); *Fighting Angel*, 1936 (b); *This Proud Heart*, 1938 (n); *The Chinese Novel*, 1939 (c); *The Patriot*, 1939 (n); *Other Gods*, 1940 (n); *Today and Forever*, 1941 (s); *China Sky*, 1941 (n); *Dragon Seed*, 1942 (n); *The Promise*, 1943 (n); *Twenty-Seven Stories*, 1943 (s); *The Exile, Fighting Angel*, 1944 (b); *Portrait of a Marriage*, 1945 (n); *Pavilion of Women*, 1946 (n); *Far and Near: Stories of Japan, China and America*, 1947 (s); *Peony*, 1948 (n); (with Eslanda Goode Robeson) *American Argument*, 1949 (conversations); *Kinfolk*, 1949 (n); *The Child Who Never Grew*, 1950 (e); *God's Men*, 1951 (n); *The Hidden Flower*, 1952 (n); *Come, My Beloved*, 1953 (n); *My Several Worlds*, 1954 (a); *Imperial Woman*, 1956 (n); *Letter from Peking*, 1957 (n); *Long Love*, 1959 (n); *Command the Morning*, 1959 (n); *Fourteen Stories*, 1961 (s); *Hearts Come Home*, 1962 (s); *A Bridge for Passing*, 1962 (m); *Satan Never Sleeps*, 1962 (n); *The Living Reed*, 1963 (n); *Stories of China*, 1964; *Death in the Castle*, 1965 (n); *Children for Adoption*, 1965 (e); *People of Japan*, 1966 (t); *The Time Is Noon*, 1967 (n); *To My Daughters With Love*, 1967 (e); *The New Year*, 1968 (n)

BUECHNER, Frederick (1926–)

There is a quality of civilized perception [in *A Long Day's Dying*], a sensitive and plastic handling of English prose and an ability to penetrate to the evanescent core of a human situation, all proclaiming major talent. . . .

The author's main objective seems to be to explore the implications of sensibilities which operate without a clearly perceived moral base. This is, of course, one of the central themes of modern fiction: it is, in a sense, the sole theme of such a novelist as Virginia Woolf. But Mr. Buechner goes at it in his own way, probing into each incident until he has presented it in all its delicate significance, using background and setting to develop a tone in the light of which action and even dialogue take on new and richer meanings.

Yet this is not a fussy or a pretentious novel. The line of action moves clearly and steadily ahead, and modulations of the emotional pattern are achieved deftly and without any discursive speculation or brooding prose.

> David Daiches. *New York Times Book Section.* Jan. 8, 1950. p. 4

It is truly as if Buechner had written [*A Long Day's Dying*] to fulfill an assignment in a Creative Writing course. Not only does he seem to have memorized a list of the exact ingredients that must go into a "significant" modern novel, but he seems to have gone to the library and set out consciously to collect them. He appears, furthermore, to have been exceedingly careful to choose only those which are in particularly special favor at the moment and of which his instructor would be absolutely certain to approve.

> John W. Aldridge. *After the Lost Generation* (McGraw). 1951. p. 222

There is a deceptive air of ease about [*The Return of Ansel Gibbs*]. There are pages of witty and urbane conversation which are a pleasure to read, but every passage serves to advance the plot, to develop characters that live and feel and interact. Mr. Buechner is an abundant writer: epigrams, aphorisms, skilful and original imagery enliven his prose.

There is a quality of distinction about Frederick Buechner's writing which might best be compared to the gleam of hand-polished old silver—as opposed to the chromium gloss of much of the "sophisticated" writing being done today.

> A.C. Spectorsky. *Saturday Review.* Feb. 15, 1958. p. 21

. . . Buechner's very interesting, perhaps over-subtle attempt is evidently to show how the springs of Gibbs' decisions flow and function, how underneath the perplexing movements of the mind of a "rational man" the deep currents of emotion and intuition may carry him to his real destiny. . . . Buechner's style, as others have remarked of his earlier books, is often noticeably "Jamesian." Sometimes it echoes James's arch manipulations of phrases and attitudes, sometimes his comma-laden, packed attempts at precision. Occasionally it is overwrought. . . . In this novel there is less of the seemingly deliberate attempt to create bizarre situations than in *A Long Day's Dying* . . . or *The Season's Difference*. . . . Despite faults in both conception and execution, the maturity of tone and the skill with which it is constructed make *The Return of Ansel Gibbs* the firmest and clearest of his works.

> Edwin Kennebeck. *Commonweal.* April 11, 1958. pp. 53–6

[*The Return of Ansel Gibbs*] is a dialectical novel of ideas. . . a readable, upstanding and ambitious member of the school. Mr.

Buechner gained a somewhat unfair reputation for "Jamesian" preciosity in 1950 with *A Long Day's Dying* which he is now, and successfully on the whole, trying to shake off. As a job of intellectual and emotional plotting, in which events are arranged to force the characters to reveal themselves as candidly and concisely as they know how, it is very well done.

Mr. Buechner once again locates us in the mainstream between Wall Street and the East sixties, with climatic side trips to Washington, Harlem and big-time TV. But the real axis of the novel is that which ran, and may still run, between Stevensonian liberalism and a tragic (or "pessimistic") view of life derived from, or resembling, [Reinhold Niebuhr's] analysis of history and morals. . . . We are still in the familiar Buechner atmosphere of rather chic good living, good eating and genteelly tough-minded conversation. . . . But a novel of ideas as well-conceived can survive such things.

> R. W. Flint. *New Republic.* June 23, 1958. p. 29

. . . the tone of *The Final Beast* . . . is religious and moral throughout—so much so at times that he seems almost to be moralizing. Yet it is a fine and moving novel, deeply and quietly felt, even though Mr. Buechner has unnecessarily complicated an essentially simple story. . . . The ironic moralities here are patent: the gossips of a New England town have been more destructive than the German concentration camps that the old woman had been able to survive; and the destroying instrument is a child who thought he was befriending the man of God.

> William Barrett. *Atlantic Monthly.* Feb., 1965. pp. 140–1

He is like Salinger and Updike: all three are deft, charming and sensitive writers, but they all tend to suppose that those virtues automatically confer value on the people and situations they are writing about. Since that is not necessarily so, their work often turns into a merely narcissistic display of deftness, charm and sensitivity. They are all good at depicting wayward and vulnerable characters, but since they are all tempted to suppose that waywardness and vulnerability are in themselves manifestations of moral sanctity, we are constantly being called on to admire their characters, no matter how seedy they may otherwise be and no matter how much harm they do to themselves or to others.

> Howard Green. *Hudson Review.* Summer, 1965. pp. 285–6

For a clergyman to become a novelist is one thing, but for a presumably decadent novelist to become a clergyman (and a Presbyterian at that) is less easy to encompass. Still, it is a fact of life like martyrdom and malnutrition, and if we are to read Buechner's novels with the respect they deserve, we have to accept that there is a very definite connection between his two vocations. . . . His references are often literary or mythic, although he began in the second novel to make remarkable use of ordinary events infused with new meaning, as in the fine scene in *The Season's Difference* in which the dotty old clergyman, playing Statues with the children, re-enacts the Fall. In *A Long Day's Dying*, the symbols are either literary or bizarre, and they are usually overexplained. The style, once considered a virtue of the book, seems now one of its weaknesses. The novel is still absorbing in its own right, but in retrospect it is primarily interesting as a starting point for Buechner's later work. If the end of the book is a little ambiguous, if the birds that abound are symbols of grace as well as of sex, it may be pointing beyond life as a long day's dying. In general, however, it is a picture of the world after the Fall.

In all three of the later novels, Buechner is concerned with the possibility of being born again. . . . The inspiriting power in *The Season's Difference* and *Ansel Gibbs* becomes explicitly Pentecostal in *The Final Beast*.

Gerald Weales. *The Reporter*. Sept. 9, 1965. p. 46

Black comedy and benign intentions do not very often mix well in a novel. Frederick Buechner's success in delivering to us the bizarre and the seamy details of the American backlands, with a weird, curiously absorbing, humour, is plain in almost everything he writes; yet the talent is shared by a host of American novelists of his generation and younger, is emulated in scores of zany *pièces noires* about the Great American Nightmare. Where Mr. Buechner differs is in his anxiety to reconcile, in as subtle and unobvious a way as possible, these horrors with a plausible affirmative view. He is a Christian novelist, taking pains to weave into the sick, alarming, ludicrous fabric of his plots some strand of allegory which will, if one listens with care, make the wretchedness bearable.

In his last novel, *The Entrance to Porlock*, the ghastliness somewhat outweighed the hope. It may be his real gain in technical assurance, in his control of an elegant deadpan style, in sheer entertainment value, which makes *Lion Country* so much more satisfying: a strange, serene balancing act which blends successfully at last the satirical talent and the moral purpose.

TLS: The Times Literary Supplement. Jan. 10, 1971. p. 1165

Open Heart is an ingenious and glorious metaphor of Christian messianism. But it is both more and less than this: a novel; and its ways are the ways of the novel. . . . Bebb is no theorem or metaphysics. Bebb lives—whether the world is felt to be hallowed or not—with an antic and radiant insatiability; he reminds one a little of Thomas Mann's Joseph. And Buechner is, by his own lights and in some of the most masterly comic prose being written in America, sanctifying the profane. Fraud is only a seeming; suffering and frailty are the means of our purification, and death is not death but eternal life. For me (for whom the Messiah has not yet come), these are illusions, and therefore how hard being a Christian seems!

Cynthia Ozick. *New York Times Book Section*. June 11, 1972. p. 36

Love Feast, the third volume of a trilogy, completes a process of self-recognition and revelation for Buechner. Its relationship to the earlier books, *Lion Country* and *Open Heart*, is paradoxical, for in those books the precision of language, the strength, inventiveness and whimsy of character, and the story itself promised a resolution Buechner doesn't manage gracefully in *Love Feast*. But it is still a novel of contemporary wit and elegance, full of small truths and unexpected mysteries. As Yeats said, out of our quarrels with ourselves comes poetry. . . .

Buechner's faith seems as stark and mysteriously natural as the desert. No dogma confines his writing, no credo fixes his characters for judgment. He claims to be a part-time Christian, yet to him the messages of Christ show themselves often, even in peculiar, mundane circumstances. In fact Buechner's sense of God and Christian teachings has a vigorous and fanciful quality, born of the Testaments and a conviction that "the language of God is metaphor" and that religion must be learned through story.

It is not surprising, then, that *Love Feast* closes artificially, when we no longer expect resolution to a tale we should have known all along would lead to new chapters and defy conventional ending.

Lincoln Caplan. *New Republic*. Jan. 25, 1975. pp. 27–8

BIBLIOGRAPHY
A Long Day's Dying, 1950 (n); *The Season's Difference*, 1952 (n); *The Return of Ansel Gibbs*, 1958 (n); *The Final Beast*, 1965 (n); *The Magnificent Defeat*, 1966 (e); *The Hungering Dark*, 1969 (e); *The Entrance to Porlock*, 1970 (n); *The Alphabet of Grace*, 1970 (e); *Lion Country*, 1971 (n); *Open Heart*, 1972 (n); *Love Feast*, 1974 (n); *The Faces of Jesus*, 1974 (e); *Treasure Hunt*, 1977 (n); *Telling the Truth: The Gospel as Tragedy, Comedy, and Fairy Tale*, 1977 (c); *Peculiar Treasures: A Biblical Who's Who*, 1979 (b); *The Book of Bebb*, 1980 (n); *The Sacred Journey*, 1982 (a); *Now and Then*, 1983 (a); *A Room Called Remember: Uncollected Pieces*, 1984 (sermons); *Brendan*, 1987 (n); *Godric*, 1987 (n); *Whistling in the Dark: An ABC Theologized*, 1988 (meditations); *The Wizard's Tide*, 1990 (juv); *Telling Secrets*, 1991 (a); *The Clown in the Belfry: Writings on Faith and Fiction*, 1992 (misc); *The Son of Laughter*, 1993 (n); *Wishful Thinking: A Seeker's ABC*, 1993 (meditations); *The Longing for Home: Recollections and Reflections*, 1996; *On the Road with the Archangel*, 1997 (n); *The Storm*, 1998 (n)

BUKOWSKI, Charles (1920–1994)

It is not, after all, Bukowski's subjects or his imagery, it is not his point of view or his neostoic attitudes that make his poetry remarkable and almost without parallel in our time—it is his voice, the rhythms and the characteristics of his own idiom that distinguish him from his contemporaries. He has replaced the formal, frequently stilted diction of the Pound-Eliot-Auden days with a language devoid of the affectations, devices and mannerisms that have taken over academic verse and packed the university and commercial quarterlies with imitations of imitations of Pound and the others. Without theorizing, without plans or schools or manifestos, Bukowski has begun the long awaited return to a poetic language free of literary pretense and supple enough to adapt itself to whatever matter he chooses to handle. What Wordsworth claimed to have in mind, what William Carlos Williams claimed to have done, what Rimbaud actually did in French, Bukowski has accomplished for the American language. . . .

There are no sweet endings in Bukowski's world. Because, unlike the Brothers Grimm and their contemporary followers, Bukowski recalls that no one lives happily ever after: there are cancers and bullets; there are psychotic nightmares and tabloids full of excellent suicide motives. There is a world of chrome and neon, concrete and steel in which human beings are trapped like flies, like ants, like dissenters in the collapsing rooms of the Inquisition: sooner or later the question is asked, the answer given—and, the answer always being wrong in the end, the sentence carried out.

John William Corrington. Foreword to *It Catches My Heart in Its Hands* by Charles Bukowski (Loujon). 1963. pp. 5, 9

No Establishment is likely ever to recruit Bukowski. He belongs in the small company of poets of real, not literary alienation, that includes Herman Spector, Kenneth Fearing, Kenneth Patchen and a large number of Bohemian fugitives unknown to fame. His special virtue is that he is so much less sentimental than most of his colleagues.

Yet there is nothing outrageous about his poetry. It is simple, casual, honest, uncooked. . . .

Bukowski is what he is, and he is not likely to be found applying for a job with the picture magazines as an Image of Revolt. Unlike the Beats, he will never become an allowed clown; he is too old now, and too wise, and too quiet. More power to him.

Kenneth Rexroth. *New York Times Book Section.* July 5, 1964. p. 5

Some have likened the muscular music of Charles Bukowski to that of the early Sandburg, but the skidrow—mission stiff—greasy spoon—rented room bard is the only one of his kind. He cannot be classified or yoked with any other poet, living or dead.

And poet he is. One who can make words dance and roar like an earthquake or whisper softly like a Spring breeze freshening the fetid air of the streets where men past caring sleep fitfully in flophouse cubicles. In *Cold Dogs in the Courtyard* the death of a cockroach, "blind yet begotten with life, a dedicated wraith of pus and antennae," inspires an eloquent commentary on the human condition. Again, in *Crucifix in a Death-Hand*, Bukowski has "something for the touts, the nuns, the grocery clerks, and you. . . ."

Jack Conroy. *ABC.* Feb., 1966. p. 5

In Bukowski's world there is little wonder, and beauty has its foundations deeply sunk into ugliness. He took LSD once and was impressed—but not all that much. He drinks a lot but never glows rosily, instead his vision is getting greyer and greyer as he moves further and further into the completely rationalistic view of the mechanics-dominated world that rusts, wheezes and threatens at any moment to completely collapse.

He provides a necessary counterbalance to the hippy lotus-eater worldview of love, long hair and Ultimate Love. He works in the Post Office eight hours a night, he hasn't lost track of the work-a-day (or night) America which is the only reality for too many Americans. At the same time he has avoided that ivy-covered outlook of the college-town-based Platonic poets who read the daily newspapers through the double-layered glass walls of their air conditioned literary museum. He's an authentic, the real-thing,

because he talks from the vantage point of the pavement, the dog biscuit factory, the whore house, the park bench, the run-down room with the shabby shade and worn-out rug stretched feebly across the sagging floor. He represents a kind of stepped-up reality in relation to the beats because he never tried to make the running-down American world sing or shout or chant—and they did. He just makes it talk. And if you listen to what it's saying it pays off. You don't go through the looking glass (for a change) but sweat it out in the real world on this side.

Hugh Fox. *Charles Bukowski: A Critical and Bibliographical Study* (Abyss). 1969. pp. 94–5

Buk, as he is known to "little mag" readers, is by now an American legend. Even those who merely hover near the underground press know of him as a unique blend of Whitman, Miller, and Dylan Thomas. With two years of college and countless drunks behind him, he now approaches his 50th year as a clerk in a Los Angeles post office—much to the dismay of the postal inspectors. Since he began chopping out poetry at age 35, he has appeared in every important "little" from one coast to the other; the bibliographies read like an ongoing history of the little magazine. Two major books have been published by Jon and Louise Webb of the Loujon press, but he's yet to find a large, established publisher. Thus the work of one of America's most original, hard-hitting, and imaginative poets probably is available in only a few libraries.

The Days Run Away Like Wild Horses over the Hills . . . should now bring Bukowski the attention he deserves. His language is sensitive, harsh, yet always accessible to the most turned-off layman. Even the failures are a hell of a lot better than the works of many modern, better-known poets published today.

Bill Katz. *Library Journal.* May 15, 1970. p. 1848

Charles Bukowski never did escape from California. Certainly he is quite unimaginable anywhere else, and he is still out there on the West Coast, writing poems and stories about his five decades of drinking, screwing, horse-playing, and drifting around, proving defiantly that even at the edge of the abyss language persists. "A legend in his own time," the cover of his new collection of stories [*Erections, Ejaculations, Exhibitions and General Tales of Ordinary Madness*] calls him, and that seems fair. . . .

He writes as an unregenerate lowbrow contemptuous of our claims to superior being. Politics is bullshit, since work is as brutalizing and unrewarding in a liberal order as in any totalitarian one; artists and intellectuals are mostly fakes, smugly enjoying the blessings of the society they carp at; the radical young are spiritless asses, insulated by drugs and their own endless cant from any authentic experience of mind or body; most women are whores, though *honest* whores are good and desirable; no life finally works, but the best one possible involves plenty of six packs, enough money to go to the track, and a willing woman of any age and shape in a good old-fashioned garter belt and high heels.

He makes literature out of the unfashionable and unideological tastes and biases of an average Wallace voter. And that sense of life is worth hearing about when it takes the form not of socko sex-and-*schmertz* but of blunt, unembarrassed explanation of how it feels to be Bukowski, mad but only north-north-west, among pretentious and lifeless claims to originality and fervor.

Thomas R. Edwards. *New York Review of Books*. Oct. 5, 1972. pp. 21–3

The loose forms and cool, anarchic voice favored by so many of the Beats were not confined to them. Charles Bukowski, for instance, a writer associated with the urban sprawl of Los Angeles, uses a cryptic, free-floating line and an off-hand, casual idiom to describe the other America: life among the underclass, the bums, dropouts, and dispossessed who cast a cold eye on the national dream of success. "I am not aiming high," Bukowski admits in one of his poems, "/I am only trying to keep myself alive / just a little longer." This is true enough, in a sense. There are no large gestures in his work: he simply tries to record things as they pass in a downbeat, laconic, or even sardonic, way. However, this commitment to the notion of the writer as recording instrument does not inhibit judgment. Bukowski is a frustrated moralist, slyly reminding us of what Rexroth has called "the unfulfilled promises of 'Song of Myself' and *Huckleberry Finn*." Nor does it limit the range of his voice. His poems are sometimes documentaries, alive with grubby detail ("Men's Crapper"), and at others strange and bizarre to the point of surrealism ("The Catch"). This reflects a common impulse among contemporary writers: the sense that the extraordinary landscapes of postwar America can only be accommodated by a vision ready to use both fact and fantasy—the eye of the camera, with its disposition for empirical detail, and the inner eye of the fabulist, alert to nightmares and magic. "Our history has moved on two rivers." the novelist Norman Mailer has observed. . . .

How can American writers now navigate these two rivers? Mailer asks. How can they invent a language adequate to a reality that incorporates Harlem and Hollywood, the Vietnam War and MTV, Richard Nixon, Charles Manson, and Colonel Oliver North? The answer, suggested by a writer like Bukowski, is a mixture of naturalism and surrealism: demonstrating a willingness to write the facts down and to attend to the "ecstasy and violence" that generated those facts, to gravitate between outer space and inner, documentary and dream.

Richard Gray. *American Poetry of the Twentieth Century* (Essex: Longman, 1990), pp. 306–7

Charles Bukowski was in essence a writer with one character and one story. His familiar protagonist, Henry Chinaski, was a hard-drinking, unsuccessful writer, living in Los Angeles, who liked women for their old-fashioned attributes, and whose main cerebral activity, when not writing unsellable work, was studying the racing form. Bukowski is usually compared to Hemingway and Henry Miller, but Chinaski takes his place in a line of American fiction heroes, from Huckleberry Finn to Sergeant Bilko, whose message is their mischief.

Bukowski died in March this year, aged seventy-three. He had published his first short fiction in 1944, in the respected *Story* magazine, but it was not until three decades later, when Black Sparrow Press began publishing his work, that he gained a cult following, which turned into unexpected commercial success. While this was a welcome turn of events for Bukowski, it was bad news for Chinaski. For the two were essentially one, and it was a

paradox of Bukowski's appeal that his success, from a reader's point of view, depended on failure. *Pulp*, which is published posthumously, is probably the worst thing he ever wrote. It's a Chandler spoof (itself a tired genre), with a touch of the supernatural, and some waves in the direction of literary heroes (a predictably sexy female hires Chinaski to track down Celine, last spotted in a Hollywood bookshop). Plotting was not within Bukowski's technical range—his picaresque novels are frankly episodic—and while *Pulp* gestures pitifully in that direction, the signals soon become unreadable, and the book descends into nonsense. A better idea of Bukowski's strength can be gained from *Run with the Hunted: A Charles Bukowski Reader*, edited by John Martin, an anthology of material taken from novels, stories, and poems published over the past twenty-five years.

James Campbell. *TLS: The Times Literary Supplement*. August 19, 1994, p. 21

BIBLIOGRAPHY

Flower, Fist and Bestial Wail, 1961 (p); *Longshot Pomes for Broke Players*, 1962 (p); *Run with the Hunted*, 1962 (p); *It Catches My Heart in Its Hands*, 1963 (p); *Cold Dogs in the Courtyard*, 1965 (p); *Crucifix in a Death-Hand*, 1965 (p); *Confessions of a Man Insane Enough to Live with Beasts*, 1965 (misc); *All the Assholes in the World and Mine*, 1966 (m); *Poems Written before Jumping Out of an 8 Story Window*, 1968 (p); *At Terror Street and Agony Way*, 1968 (p); *Notes of a Dirty Old Man*, 1969 (misc); *The Days Run Away Like Wild Horses over the Hills*, 1970 (p); *Erections, Ejaculations, Exhibitions and General Tales of Ordinary Madness*, 1972 (s); *Mockingbird Wish Me Luck*, 1972 (p); *Fire Station*, 1973 (p); *South of No North*, 1973 (p); *Burning in Water, Drowning in Flame*, 1974 (p); *Post Office*, 1974 (p); *Life and Death in the Charity Ward*, 1974 (p); *Factotum*, 1975 (n); *Love Is a Dog from Hell: Poems 1974–1977*, 1977; *Women*, 1978 (n); *Play the Piano Drunk Like a Percussion Instrument until the Fingers Begin to Bleed a Bit*, 1979 (p); *Shakespeare Never Did This*, 1979 (t); *Dangling in the Tournefortia*, 1981 (p); *Ham on Rye*, 1982 (n); *Hot Water Music*, 1983 (p); *Bring Me Your Love*, 1983 (p); *Going Modern*, 1983 (p); *Talking to the Mailbox*, 1984 (p); *War All the Time: Poems 1981–1984*, 1984; *There's No Business*, 1984 (s); *Barfly: The Continuing Saga of Henry Chinaski*, 1984 (n); *You Get So Alone at Times That It Just Makes Sense*, 1986 (p); *The Movie "Barfly"*, 1987 (scrp); *The Roominghouse Madrigals*, 1988 (p); *Hollywood*, 1989 (n); *Septuagenarian Stew*, 1990 (s, p); *The Last Night of the Earth Poems*, 1992; *Run with the Hunted*, 1993 (misc); *Screams from the Balcony: Selected Letters, 1960–1970*, 1993; *Pulp*, 1994 (n); (with Ken Price) *Heat Wave*, 1995 (p); *Living on Luck: Selected Letters 1960s–70s*, ed. Seamus Cooney, 1995; *Confession of a Coward*, 1995 (m); *Betting on the Muse*, 1996 (p, s); *Bone Palace Ballet*, 1997 (p); *The Captain Is Out to Lunch and the Sailors Have Taken over the Ship*, 1998 (m)

BULLINS, Ed (1936–)

The American Place Theater has made another important find, Ed Bullins, author of three one acts, *The Electronic Nigger, and*

Others. . . . Unlike the general run of young playwrights, Bullins does not spend most of his time showing what a whiz he is at creating monologists who gab endlessly in back rooms about their cranky existences. He gives his attention to the impact of one character on another, the blood of drama, not its gristle.

The least formally structured of his plays, *A Son, Come Home,* happens to be the least effective. . . .

He comes into his own with the title play. *The Electronic Nigger* presents a young Negro novelist, Jones, conducting his first evening class in what prospectuses describe as Creative Writing I. Jones proudly tells his mixed garland of middle-aged and youthful students, "You won't be graded on how well you write, but on how you grow in this class." Unluckily for him, one student turns out to be a verbose know-it-all who disrupts the lesson and steals the allegiance of the other students. . . .

Clara's Old Man, which winds up the trio, is one of the best short American plays I have come across: realistic in manner yet throbbing with weirdness and driven by bursts of extravagant invention that make a definition by genre seem impertinent.

Albert Bermel. *New Leader.* April 22, 1968. p. 28

The white problem in America is at the core of all Bullins's work. He denies being a working-class playwright: he is from the criminal class. All the other men in his family have been in prison. He is the only one who went to high school, who went to college; but he claims that working people in Harlem like his surrealist, intellectual plays.

The Electronic Nigger is not straight propaganda. An evening class in literary expression is being gently conducted by Mr. Jones, a novelist: the session is interrupted by a penologist, Mr. Carpentier, who spouts large generalisations in technical language—not unlike Marshall McLuhan's—and takes over the class, until Jones's head is full of noise and Carpentier is leading pupils in a mechanical goose-step, bawling abstract inanities. (All this is well staged, in-the-round, with life-like acting shifting slowly to an expressionist style, with a climax of disciplined noise and nightmare.) Neither Jones nor Carpentier is white. During the clash, Jones at one point appeals to Carpentier as his "black brother," but the latter denies being black. A white pupil calls him "Uncle Tom" and a black pupil says: "No. It's for me to say that."

D.A.N. Jones. *The Listener.* Aug. 22, 1968. p. 253

It fascinated me that *In the Wine Time,* produced by an organization consciously devoted to Black Power [the New Lafayette Theater], was the only "black" play I saw this season not obsessed by Whitey. There were, to be sure, occasional references, but the central purpose of the play was "to celebrate the Black experience" *for fellow blacks.* This is no more nor less than the New Lafayette's official credo promised, but it is always a surprise when rhetoric and practice coincide.

Clarity and fidelity of purpose, however, have never yet guaranteed artistic success. *In the Wine Time* does not reverse my opinion of last season (based on an evening of Bullins' short plays done at the American Place) that his reputation has outpaced his performance. On the one hand, *In the Wine Time* is attenuated—a one-acter

stretched into three—yet, on the other, its melodramatic ending is insufficiently prepared for, and is even at odds with the desultory humor and fitful tensions that precede it.

Martin Duberman. *Partisan Review.* No. 3, 1969. pp. 489–90

Ed Bullins, out of Genet via LeRoi Jones, writes like a man trying to dislodge a big white monkey from his back. His obsession is the corruption of black integrity by white values. His plays are composed like effigies, specially designed to torture his enemies, and based on the magical assumption that if one destroys the symbol often enough, the reality will also get impaired. Like the vendettas of LeRoi Jones, they belong less to the convention of art than they do to the world of black magic. Which is precisely why they are so fascinating in the theater.

Charles Marowitz. *New York Times Theater Section.* April 13, 1969. p. 3

Ed Bullins' *In New England Winter* . . . is compounded of sudden spurts of anger, violence, and passion, and spurts, just as sudden, of wit and humor, tenderness, and, finally, mystery. Like Mr. Bullins' *The Pig Pen* . . . the play opens up, to a certain extent, once it is over—when we realize, for example, that what seemed to be a prologue is actually an epilogue, and that everything that follows leads up to it. . . .

The plot is the least of it. Mr. Bullins' details of character and speech and behavior make up a whole style of living, especially when they are specific and precise. They are so strong that we take everything else on trust, and his language often makes poetry out of the casually obscene vernacular of his actors. The people and their feelings about one another are what give the play its depth.

Edith Oliver. *New Yorker.* Feb. 6, 1971. p. 72

Crazy dark laughter envelops all the proceedings [in *The Duplex*], but the meaning is frightful. It is not simply a matter of revealing the horrid messiness typical of most ghettos, whatever the color of their inhabitants; there is something more damaging beyond the specifics of promiscuous fornication, smoking of pot, gambling, drunkenness, outbursts of physical brutality, irresponsibility and wrecked lives. What is really being exposed is our civilization.

Bullins flatters no one and directly accuses no one. He offers hardly any preachment or "propaganda." His method is largely realistic. . . .

What makes *The Duplex* so telling is that, apart from their native humanity, all of its characters are fundamentally abandoned people. What ails them is not due solely to white indifference, incomprehension or hostility but to a deprivation in the soil of sound values, which are not supplied by America because it has not for a long time actually possessed them.

Harold Clurman. *The Nation.* March 27, 1972. p. 412

In the best of Bullins' work, he is creating a tradition for black drama to follow, helping to create a fearlessness, a self-acceptance.

There is no sensational spooning up of filth nor is there sentimentality; instead there is the searing eye of unsentimental analysis. And subtlety, so that when one reads *Clara's Old Man*, one is reminded of the principle that in the presence of artistic greatness, the surface of a play does not necessarily reveal its depths; the depths are suggested rather than stated. And there is implicit direction; though Bullins' working class in his best work does not have conscious direction, one senses a kind of godly principle, a kind of holiness and enormous energy and power, and one perceives that all that is needed is a harnessing force, a wise and compelling leadership, and sweeping changes will be made. There is another artistic principle: that a great work of art must suggest the awesome potentialities of man for growth: this principle too is a spine of Bullins' best work.

There is thus great strength and great confusion in Bullins' working class, of whom one could say: in great chaos, great strength; in great lostness, the potentiality of decisive direction; in compulsive suicide, powerful life.

Lance Jeffers. *CLA Journal*. Sept., 1972. p. 34

Beyond the political activism and the racial consciousness of his plays (which are, of course, what Bullins most values in them), there is another side. *In the Wine Time, In New England Winter, Goin' a Buffalo*, and other Bullins plays create a mood of lost innocence, purity, and beauty that is universally meaningful. In fact, the dramatist creates in most of his work a counter-mood to that which dominates the actual dialogue—there is a sense of once-glimpsed loyalty, sensitivity, and romance which the ghetto reality of the setting makes impossible to attain. This obbligato of tenderness is so overpowered by the brutality of the ghetto that it exists in the plays as something once envisioned, but almost forgotten, by one or two main characters. The theme of a brutal reality destroying human dreams of tenderness and romance is, of course, a common one in twentieth century literature—black and white—and requires no specifically Black consciousness to respond to it. The three Bullins plays are, however, striking illustrations of this theme.

James R. Giles. *Players*. Oct.–Nov., 1972. p. 32

The Reluctant Rapist is Theatre of Cruelty on every level. And this is especially so when considering the book as a literary object. The writing is *bad*. Not bad-ass. Just bad. It reads like an appointment book (I went here, ate this, fucked that) rather than a work of fiction. It makes no attempts to penetrate to its characters' motivational cores. The prose itself creates no illusions. Neither does it reveal any. Politically, psychologically, linguistically, *The Reluctant Rapist* barely exists.

But at the level of etiology this novel does manage to exert a morbid fascination. The book's cantus firmus—entwined with Stevie Benson's near constant erection—is that not only is it right to humiliate women, but that no matter what they say they actually enjoy it! The idea seems to be that much like a sassy child will love a good whuppin' now and then, so will women love an occasional good raping. Especially the white ones—who have been unfairly denied their full share of degradation by an unenlightened society.

Jack Friedman. *The Village Voice*. Oct. 25, 1973. p. 35

The Reluctant Rapist is a handbook to the plays. As a playwright, Bullins rips, tears, rapes; he blows apart black life. As a novelist, he explains what the ripping, tearing, and raping are all about. They are the acts of a lover in deep need of blasting away the conventional faiths and beliefs to expose the truthful, irreducible center so that he and his beloved may at last be free. Steve Benson the rapist is a metaphor of Ed Bullins the playwright. And Steve's story is a reassembling of the bits from the exploded bombs and tearing beak. . . . The conventional order of events is one of those beliefs that has to be destroyed. And Bullins is successful in destroying it, in fusing the past with the present, in giving us the feeling of living the past again from the standpoint of the present and seeing the future infuse the past.

Jerry H. Bryant. *The Nation*. Nov. 12, 1973. p. 504

BIBLIOGRAPHY
Goin a Buffalo, 1968 (d); *A Son, Come Home*, 1968 (d); *The Electronic Nigger*, 1968 (d); *Clara's Old Man*, 1968 (d); *In the Wine Time*, 1968 (d); *Five Plays*, 1968; *The Duplex*, 1970 (d); *The Pig Pen*, 1970 (d); *The Hungered One*, 1971 (s); *In New England Winter*, 1971 (d); *The Fabulous Miss Marie*, 1971 (d); *Four Dynamite Plays*, 1972; *The Theme Is Blackness*, 1972 (d); *The Reluctant Rapist*, 1973 (n); *House Party*, 1973 (d); *New/Lost Plays*, 1993 (anthol)

BURKE, Kenneth (1897–1993)

Kenneth Burke is one of the few Americans who know what a success of good writing means—and some of the difficulties in the way of its achievement. . . . *The White Oxen* is a varied study, as any book where writing is the matter, must be. American beginnings—in the sense of the work of Gertrude Stein, difficult to understand, as against, say, the continuities of a De Maupassant. It is a group of short accounts, stories, more or less. They vary from true short stories to the ridiculousness of all short stories dissected out in readable pieces: writing gets the best of him, in the best of the book: "The Death of Tragedy" and "My Dear Mrs. Wurtlebach."

William Carlos Williams. *Dial*. Jan., 1929. pp. 6–7

Burke's approach to symbolism is not susceptible of verification, and depends for its convincing force on his ability to make the reader perceive immediately the author's intuitions. This is to say that the method is essentially a-scientific if not unscientific. A generation of readers brought up on the facile technique of popularized psychoanalysis will no doubt find this method acceptable. But even those who look with suspicion on the explosions of an imagination uncontrolled by a scientific governor must frequently adjudge Burke's intuitions to be happy hits indeed, often throwing a burst of light on the dark pockets of our social scene.

Eliseo Vivas. *The Nation*. Dec. 25, 1937. p. 723

If he suffers from a restraint, I should think it a constitutional distaste against regarding poetic problems as philosophic ones. I suppose his feeling would be that poetry is something bright and dangerous, and philosophy is something laborious and arid, and you cannot talk about the one in terms of the other without a disproportion and breach of taste. . . . He has a whole arsenal of strategies, like the German general staff, who are said to have whistling bombs if they like, and whose campaigns rest upon a highly technical and sustained opportunism. . . . He is perspicuous and brilliantly original, and I would venture to quarrel with no positive finding that he makes, but only with his proportions, or his perspective.

John Crowe Ransom. *Kenyon Review*. Spring, 1942. pp. 219, 237

Mr. Burke's distinction as a critic is twofold. First, he is a man of amazing learning, who knows how to use his learning unpedantically and, if necessary, with a dose of irony. Second, he is that very rare thing among critics: a man who examines creative manifestations without *parti pris*, who does not put his own intention before the intention of the poet but carefully scrutinizes the mind of the agent as embodied in the act. His erudition aids him in treating literature universally, i.e. each particular literary instance is brought into relation with the whole body of *Weltliteratur*; while his patient ingenuity manages to disengage the hidden cross-references and ambiguities of each work.

Francis C. Golffing. *Poetry*. March, 1946. p. 339

Mr. Burke's courage is not purely of the theoretical kind. He dares to translate his doctrines into very definite instances, although his purpose is not indoctrination. He is fighting for free thought and free speech at a time when these are denounced as un-American activities. . . . It is a great comfort to find one who, ignoring the stampede, dares to say: "So help me God, I cannot otherwise." There are enough clear-sighted and vigorous pronouncements in this book (*A Rhetoric of Motives*) to insure the wrath of Senator McCarthy; if the Senator could understand them.

Albert Guerard. *New York Herald Tribune Book Section*. July 23, 1950. p. 8

He started from literary criticism (after writing two books of fiction); he has provided us with many brilliant examples of the critic's art; and yet the most brilliant of all the examples is possibly his essay on *Mein Kampf*, in which he explains Hitler's strategies of persuasion. In other words the quality of his intention does not depend on the literary greatness of his subject; and when his literary subject happens to be a great one, as in another brilliant essay, on *Venus and Adonis*, he may not even discuss the qualities that make it a masterpiece. He is more interested in mechanisms of appeal, as in the Hitler essay, and in the disguises of social attitudes, as in the *Venus and Adonis*. We could, however, go further and say that his real subject is man as a symbol-using animal.

Malcolm Cowley. *New Republic*. Sept. 14, 1953. p. 17

Burke's gift as a poet is. . . real. His word play is true mortal-fun, and his ear for a rhythm is rich and right. He does especially well in

ending a poem on a kind of dissolving rhythm. Not with a bang but a whimper, perhaps, but the whimper sings. Above all, the poems, when put together, generate the sense of a real person—learned, bourbony, getting on to mortality as a bit of a hard case but still, and always, sweet on life. I like both the cantankerousness and the sweetness; one flavors the other. No one should have trouble believing that Kenneth Burke's despairs are humanly real.

John Ciardi. *The Nation*. Oct. 8, 1955. pp. 307–8

Throughout his writings Burke seems to have effected a neat "conversion downwards" of phenomena into terms. His system is, it seems to me, essentially a verbal one which treats words at what is often a great distance from the reality of things and people. It would be interesting. . . to study Burke semantically and to examine, among other things, the fluctuations in verbal level which he employs. His theory of poetic performance leads through the ascending order: poetry, act, motive, power, reality. This scale might well be applied to his critical system. Were this to be done, I have the impression that we would find it to be as much a poetic as a critical performance.

Louis Fraiberg. *Psychoanalysis and American Literary Criticism* (Wayne State). 1960. p. 200

Kenneth Burke . . . combines the methods of Marxism, psychoanalysis, and anthropology with semantics in order to devise a system of human behavior and motivation which uses literature only as a document or illustration. The early Burke was a good literary critic, but his work in recent decades must rather be described as aiming at a philosophy of meaning, human behavior, and action whose center is not in literature at all. All distinctions between life and literature, language and action disappear in Burke's theory. He seems to have lost all sense of evidence in his recent analyses of poetic texts. Thus he interprets Coleridge's "Ancient Mariner" as "ritual for the redemption of his drug," and Keats's "Ode on a Grecian Urn" he reads in terms of the identity of love and death, of capitalist individualism and Keats's tubercular fever, in almost complete disregard of the text. A system which plans to embrace all life ends as a baffling phantasmagoria of bloodless categories, "strategies," "charts," and "situations."

Rene Wellek. *The Yale Review*. Autumn, 1961. p. 109

It would be a mistake not to see Burke's work in its historical context, not to realize that all of his books are verbal acts upon a historical scene, and that the dramatistic system as a whole is a humanist's counter-statement offered to the public at large as a reaffirmation of *human* purpose and as a means of "purifying war" (man's greatest rational lunacy) so that each person, in his own way, may *peacefully* and intelligently pursue the better life.

Since 1945, Burke has worked with missionary zeal to spread the good word (dramatism) that came to him upon completing the work started in the 1930's when he first began his study of communication and dedicated himself to the attainment of peace through knowledge. . . . As a theory of language, dramatism attempts to isolate and study the essence of language and, by systematically examining the uses to which man puts it, to isolate and study the essence of man and the drama of human relations. One of the main conclusions reached is that man's views of himself, other men, nature, society, and God are language-ridden—that man necessarily views everything through a "fog of symbols."

W. H. Rueckert. *Kenneth Burke and the Drama of Human Relations* (Minnesota). 1963. p. 161

. . .because Miss [Marianne] Moore was a person with roots in the American resurgence, in those lyric years when poets sought to revive and rephrase Whitman's messianic spirit, during her turn as editor [of *The Dial*] she achieved one splendid feat. She recognized Kenneth Burke as the critic who might well map a path along a middle road to the heavenly kingdom. Deciding that *The Dial*'s Award should go to Burke, she did not celebrate Burke's arrival there. Rather she hoped to dramatize the ways in which Burke exercised the highest care and accuracy and diligence. . . . in pursuit of the life of letters. In her view, he was the one American critic who possessed technique and sensibility enough to reconcile letters and culture, science and imagination in a single theory of literary value which is simultaneously a theory of human virtue in a comprehensive but probably not final sense of that bloody word.

William Wasserstrom. *The Western Humanities Review.* Summer, 1963. p. 262

Kenneth Burke's *The Rhetoric of Religion*, like everything else that Mr. Burke has written, is highly original, brilliantly stimulating, infinitely suggestive, and ultimately baffling. Mr. Burke is so thoroughly *sui generis* that it is difficult to fit him into any contemporary philosophical pigeon-hole; but if he belongs anywhere, it is certainly with those who have restored the symbolic imagination to a central place in modern thought. Mr. Burke's attention has always centered on the emotive, psychic, and ethical-moral needs of the human spirit, and on the "symbolic actions" by which these needs are expressed. Much of the paradoxical originality of his thinking comes from applying concepts taken from the study of magic or religion and employing them to characterize completely secular historical and cultural phenomena. If a good deal of modern thought has been engaged in debunking, or, to be more formal, in "demythification"—that is, the interpretation of one or another "sacred" ideology in terms of "profane" categories—then Kenneth Burke might be said to have adopted the opposite tack of "remythification."

Joseph Frank. *Sewanee Review.* Summer, 1964. p. 484

Like Freud, Burke looks forward to a modification in our experience of guilt. Unlike Freud, however, he does not trace the origins of suppressed guilt-feelings to events in prehistory, recapitulated during the first few years of life; nor does he look upon religion precisely as a mass-neurosis, no better at promoting an ideal inner strength than the individual neuroses of secular men. For Burke, on the contrary, guilt is endemic to *any* human condition: it is virtually identical with the unacknowledged self-hatred that must accompany man's conflict with himself, nature, his fellowmen. . . .Man's

life comprises not only physical motion but also symbolical action; one can quarrel with one's father or, like Hume, write a book denying the real, substantial power of antecedent causes. Burke doesn't mean to challenge the autonomy of philosophic effort by such interpretations; he means rather to argue the presence of poetic motives in metaphysical thought—means, that is, to underwrite poetry as the archetype of symbolic action generally, because it offers not only symbolical experiences but also appropriate symbolical expiations.

Alvin C. Kibel. *American Scholar.* Spring, 1965. pp. 304–5

A book [*Towards a Better Life*] so absorbed with style and stylization had better be well-written. Mr. Burke's prose, which has been known to develop opacities, displays here a translucent elegance and humor, but the novel isn't just fine writing. It is, in addition, beautifully expressive writing, with a vein of mockery at work under the formal turns of phrase. . . . *Towards a Better Life* is likely to count more, in future histories of American literature, than any given dozen of its soggier contemporaries.

A word here, in celebration of Mr. Kenneth Burke. He has been among us so long in so many capacities, and to such pervasive effect, that it is easy to lose track of how much the literary temper of our time owes to him. In whatever genre, his work has always carried the strong stamp of his individuality; he has never dissolved it into pap for the multitude or codified it into tablets for quick absorption by graduate students. He has never made it with a book club; he has never seemed ashamed of being learned. The subtlety of his critical work has challenged, its perversity has provoked, its original insights have opened up immense corridors of thought.

Robert M. Adams. *New York Review of Books.* Oct. 20, 1966. p. 33

We ask a prosaic question: what kind of book [*Towards a Better Life*] are we reading? It is certainly not a novel, nor was it meant to be. In ascriptions of this kind we are well advised to consult Northrop Frye's account of the several forms of prose fiction. Then it appears that Burke's book is not a freak, a sport of Nature, but an example of a distinguished tradition, the anatomy. . . . The masterpieces of the genre include *A Tale of a Tub, Candide*, the *Anatomy of Melancholy, Headlong Hall*, and *Brave New World*. . . .

It is not enough to say that *Towards a Better Life* is beautifully "written," if by this praise we mean to consign the book to an anthology of Prose Style. However peculiar its origin, it is in fact one of the most moving books in modern literature, as well as one of the purest anatomies.

Denis Donoghue. *The Ordinary Universe* (Macmillan—N.Y.). 1968. pp. 214–5

If speculative in life, language, or literature, then you can hardly miss with *Language as Symbolic Action*, a rich and culminative work. Burke is still coming on with further developments, in this book and for future ones, but is meanwhile expressing his most important positions, it seems to me, more thoroughly and unmistakably than ever before, with the illustrations and exemplifications sufficient in length and detail, brilliant in quality. Although *Towards a Better Life* has more than enough appeal as art, it will inevitably be of added interest because of its network of relationships to a major career in criticism—one that except for recent memory of KB's pious plumbings around the word itself might have been labelled (rather than libelled) ''solid gold.'' But golden or not, encomiums are not easy to avoid as an unusually productive and unusually successful life's work refines to quintessence, the artificer in fine fettle for completing the contract.

Neal J. Osborn. *Hudson Review*. Summer, 1968. p. 321

If there is a title peculiarly fitting to Burke in all his work, it is one dear to Burke himself, the title of rhetorician. Burke is a rhetorician in a double sense: whatever he considers, he considers it rhetorically as an instance of rhetoric. Rhetoric, as I am thinking of it, is the use of words to evoke a specific emotion or state of mind. Whatever Burke studies, this is what he finds it to be, whether it is open propaganda, the Constitution of the United States, psychoanalysis, philosophy, or even pure poetry. Dialectics itself he defines as a kind of rhetoric; it is ''all enterprises that cure us by means of words.'' Pure poetry differs from other forms of rhetoric only in the sense that the state of mind it evokes is an end in itself, whereas ordinary rhetoric evokes a state of mind which is to lead to practical consequences.

The objective of Burke's own rhetoric is a consistent one: to evoke a state of oneness among men. If he can convince us that we are all rhetoricians, that we are all using words combatively for our own purposes, he will have purified our warlike natures by evoking in us a feeling of our final oneness.

Merle E. Brown. *Kenneth Burke* (Minnesota). 1969. p. 7

Most simply put, [Burke] can get more thoughts out of a book than anyone else can, evoking in his reader time after time a mixed attitude of surprise, gratitude, and chagrin—''yes, of course, why couldn't I have seen it for myself?''—while at the same time, in the same gestures, often in the very same sentences, he is developing a method and a terminology which the reader, if he will, can master for application elsewhere. . . .

There is an enthusiasm in all this that sometimes comes near enough to madness: criticism as rhapsody, or *furor poeticus*. Nor do I mean that in disparagement, though aware that some writers would; for among the most appealing things about Burke, to my mind, is the sense he has, the sense I get from reading him, that thought, if it is to matter at all, must be both obsessive and obsessively thorough, that thinking, if it is to salvage anything worth having from chaos, must adventure into the midst of madness and build its city there.

Howard Nemerov. *Reflexions on Poetry & Poetics* (Rutgers). 1972. p. 84

BIBLIOGRAPHY
The White Oxen and Other Stories, 1924; *Death in Venice*, 1925 (tr); *Genius and Character* (by Emil Ludwig), 1927 (tr); *Saint Paul* (by Emile Baumann), 1929 (tr); *Counterstatement*, 1931, 2nd ed. 1968 (c); *Towards a Better Life*, 1932, 2nd ed. 1968 (n); *Permanence and Change*, 1935 (e); *Attitudes towards History*, 1937, rev. ed. 1959, 3rd ed. 1984 (e); *The Philosophy of Literary Form*, 1941 (c); *A Grammar of Motives*, 1945 (e); *A Rhetoric of Motives*, 1950 (e); *Book of Moments*, 1955 (p); *Poems 1915–1954*, 1955; *The Rhetoric of Religion*, 1961 (e); *Perspectives by Incongruity*, 1963 (e); *Collected Poems, 1915–1967*, 1967; *Language as Symbolic Action*, 1967 (c); *The Complete White Oxen*, 1968 (s); *Dramatism and Development*, 1972 (ph); *The Philosophy of Literary Form: Studies in Symbolic Action*, 1974 (c); *The Selected Correspondence of Kenneth Burke and Malcolm Cowley, 1915–1981*, ed. Paul Jay, 1988; *On Symbols and Society*, ed. Joseph R. Gusfield, 1989 (c)

BURNS, John Horne (1916–1953)

Mr. Burns writes unevenly, perhaps deliberately so, sometimes using the shock technique of photographic realism, sometimes employing a kind of stylized symbology, but always with telling effect. In [*The Gallery*], his first novel, Mr. Burns shows a brilliant understanding of people, a compassion for their frailities and an urge to discover what inner strength or weaknesses may lie beneath the surface.

J. D. Ross. *New York Herald Tribune Book Section*. June 8, 1947. p. 5

The appreciation of the Italian people grows occasionally into something like a sentimental idolatry. The bitterness against American crudity comes close in places to a youthful intolerance. And the steady stress upon sex . . . grows into what looks like an inadvertent concentration upon one aspect of human experience as if it were the sole aspect. The genuine love and understanding which marks much of [*The Gallery*] are, indeed, in a real way, vitiated by what appears a far too simple, far too easy falling back upon both sexual activity and a kind of vague, wistful brotherliness.

Richard Sullivan. *New York Times Book Section*. June 8, 1947. p. 25

In *The Gallery* John Horne Burns absorbs the soldier's idiom into a spacious narrative prose that modifies but does not dominate the language. It is an appropriate device, as the matter of the book is the mental confusion and emotional disruption of our American soldiers abroad. . . . On the one hand (Burns) is uneasy and guilty about the smug, provincial, materialist life in America, and shocked by the conduct of many American soldiers. . . . On the other hand, his sympathy with the Neapolitans is generous and ingratiating, and his affection for them is too specific and imaginative to be merely sentimental. . . . One regrets that he didn't employ his human insight and talent for social analysis to go beyond a just indignation and consider whether even American boorishness and immaturity couldn't be the reverse of certain substantial national virtues.

John Farrelly. *New Republic*. July 7, 1947. p. 28

[*The Gallery*] is not a book for little boys in any school, but for adults who recognize the truth and know good writing when they see it, and who do not object to blatant four-letter words. The author's place in American war fiction seems certain. Compared with *The Gallery* . . . *Three Soldiers*, the novel that started off the realistic fiction of the First World War, was a fragrant and tender lily.

Harrison Smith. *Saturday Review*. Feb. 14, 1948. p. 7

The central love affair of the novel, through which Guy Hudson finally realized the difference between sex and love, is not altogether convincing. What is apparent, however, just as in the English sophisticates, is the dominant sexuality of the novel, and a sexuality that finds expression in harsh and even violent terms. There is an inverted Puritanism in Mr. Burn's work, and a remarkably sophisticated sense of evil and malice.

Maxwell Geismar. *Saturday Review*. Apr. 2, 1949. p. 16.

Mr. Burns was not far enough removed from his experiences to be capable of relating them without an excess acidity. Consequently his attack is not pointed as directly as it might have been. His book is too long, and a few of his most acute and penetrating observations are obscured by paragraphs of unleashed fury which become rather tedious.

Virginia Vaughn. *Commonweal*. Apr. 29, 1949. p. 76

John Horne Burns is one of those American writers who believe in shock treatment. To judge by *Lucifer with a Book* he is a satirical moralist rather than a novelist. He has much of Henry Miller's rich comic gift, a fluency which amounts at times to lallomania, a passion for scatological images and a strong tendency to preach. It is not always easy to discover, in this whirlwind of words, just what Mr. Burns is preaching about, but one thing seems to emerge clearly; nothing is so dangerous and destructive as virginity of mind and body and, until this impediment has been removed, preferably by rape, no one can begin to live.

Antonia White. *New Statesman and Nation*. Nov. 5, 1949. p. 520

The Gallery is a hybrid book, made up of two kinds of material set in two different literary devices that are never fused. The affirmation of values in the "Promenades" is consistently thwarted by the negation of values in the "Portraits"; and the non-dramatic treatment of the one is in the end completely overcome by the tensely dramatic treatment of the other. There is one step that Burns might have taken to ensure his point. He might have disregarded altogether the innate potentialities of the material he put into the "Portraits" and twisted the action in such a way that the book would have been forced to end on an affirmative note . . . but it would have meant a deliberate falsification of the truth as he saw it, and Burns was too scrupulous an artist for that.

John W. Aldridge. *After the Lost Generation* (McGraw). 1951. pp. 145–6

Each of (his) three books owes its degree of power to the author's ability to write exquisitely observed *mot*-filled prose which lends a stylish quality to every incident, even ones which might better have been omitted for reasons of taste. And common weaknesses stem mostly from the fact that Mr. Burns, the angry moralist, appears to be in conflict with Mr. Burns, the detached artist.

James Kelly. *New York Times Book Section*. Sept. 7, 1952. p. 4

BIBLIOGRAPHY
The Gallery, 1947 (n); *Lucifer with a Book*, 1949 (n); *A Cry of Children*, 1952 (n)

BURROUGHS, William (1914–1997)

The ten episodes from William S. Burroughs' *Naked Lunch* [which had appeared in *Big Table*, a magazine]. . . is writing of an order that may be clearly defended not only as a masterpiece of its own genre, but as a monumentally moral descent into the hell of narcotic addiction. . . . [The] writing does, to be sure, contain a number of four-letter words, but the simple fact is that such obscenities—if obscenities they are—are inseparable from the total fabric and effect of the moral message. . . .

What Burroughs has written is a many-leveled vision of horror. . . . And only after the first shock does one realize that what Burroughs is writing about is not only the destruction of depraved men by their drug lust, but the destruction of all men by their consuming addictions, whether the addiction be drugs or over-righteous propriety. . . . Burroughs is not only serious in his intent, but he is a writer of great power and artistic integrity engaged in a profoundly meaningful search for true values.

John Ciardi. *Saturday Review*. June 27, 1959. p. 30

Naked Lunch belongs to that very large category of books . . . whose interest lies not in their own qualities, but in the reception given to them in their own time. In itself, *Naked Lunch* is of very small significance. . . . From the literary point of view, it is the merest trash, not worth a second glance. What is worth a glance, however, is the respectful attitude that some well-known writers and critics have shown towards it. . . .

The only writer of any talent of whom Burroughs occasionally manages to remind one is the Marquis de Sade; but if one turns to the pages of Sade after *Naked Lunch* the resemblance soon fades, since Sade, however degenerate he can be at times, has always some saving wit and irony. Burroughs takes himself with a complete, owlish seriousness; indeed, in his opening section he seems, as far as one can make out through the peasoup fog of his prose, to be offering the book as some kind of tract against drug addiction. . . . Altogether, *Naked Lunch* offers a very interesting field for speculation, both pathological and sociological. No lover of medical textbooks on deformity should miss it.

John Wain. *New Republic*. Dec. 1, 1962. pp. 21–3

In its theme and techniques, the novel is open to misunderstanding by the highbrow Philistine (an animal possessed of a highbrow sophistication and a lowbrow taste). It is finally concerned with the extremes of horror in human life; and, therefore, it takes its place in that literary tradition preoccupied with the possibilities of emotional experience. . . . The effect of the book is Kafkaesque—a simultaneous sense of stark terror and reeling comedy. . . . In short, *Naked Lunch* is one of the more truly original and exciting pieces of prose to emerge from the fifties. It is precisely these elements that [John] Wain, in his youthful senility, is incapable of seeing.

Richard C. Kostelanetz. *New Republic*. Dec. 15, 1962. p. 30

According to literary legend, Allen Ginsberg, while visiting Burroughs in his Paris apartment sometime during the 1950s, found the floors littered with hundreds of sheets of paper that Burroughs had scrawled on while high on heroin. Ginsberg, it is said, gathered the papers together, read them with reverence, and put them into the form, or rather sequence, they now have. He needn't have bothered to sort them, since the book would have almost the same effect if he had shuffled the manuscript like a deck of cards. . . . It is all somehow a work of spite, a work of revenge—revenge against beer bottles and God, against matchsticks and love, against war and peace and Tolstoy and fingertips and sealing wax. Some of it is funny and some of it marvelously dirty, but it just goes on and on; it begins to sound like the whine of a girl who's been stood up. It begins to sound like a tantrum.

Alfred Chester. *Commentary*. Jan., 1963. pp. 90–1

The best comparison for the book, with its aerial sex acts performed on a high trapeze, its con men and barkers, its arena-like form, is in fact to a circus. A circus travels but it is always the same, and this is Burroughs' sardonic image of modern life. The Barnum of the show is the mass-manipulator, who appears in a series of disguises. *Control*, as Burroughs says, underlining it, *can never be a means to anything but more control—like drugs*, and the vicious circle of addiction is re-enacted, worldwide, with sideshows in the political and "social" sphere—the "social" here has vanished, except in quotation marks, like the historical, for everything has become automatized. . . .

The phenomenon of repetition, of course, gives rise to boredom; many readers complain that they cannot get through *The Naked Lunch* and/or that they find it disgusting. It *is* disgusting and sometimes tiresome, often in the same places. . . . Yet what saves *The Naked Lunch* is not a literary ancestor but humour. Burroughs' humour is peculiarly American, at once broad and sly.

Mary McCarthy. *Encounter*. April, 1963. pp. 94–6

It is easy enough to treat such a book [*The Ticket that Exploded*] as pathology, or to take the fact that Burroughs exists and is widely read and part of a literary movement as warning that some sort of counter-action is necessary. But this is not a literary judgment, and may be, as Sartre argued in the case of Jean Genet's early work, an inhumane one. We cannot know what the vision means unless we experience it totally, giving ourselves up to it as we do to other works of art, with suspension of disbelief and—in this instance—of

distaste. We must confront Burroughs as a free being who in some sense chose to have his kind of life and write his kind of book. Our solemn, almost religious duty is to reach the bottom of his experience, take on the burden of it, see ourselves in it, temporarily *be* Burroughs. There may even be hypocrisy in pretending it is a burden. Some of the violence and filth is an expression of Swiftian disgust at the way things are. But obviously, as was true of Swift, the author delights in such imaginings. If we read the book properly we can feel the pleasure also—or learn to.

Robert Gorham Davis. *Hudson Review*. Summer, 1963. p. 281

The element of humor in *Nova Express*, as in *Naked Lunch* and his two other novels, has moral strength of historic proportions, whereby the existentialist sense of the *absurd* is taken to an informal conclusion. It is an absolutely devastating ridicule of all that is false, primitive, and vicious in current American life: the abuses of power, hero worship, aimless violence, materialistic obsession, intolerance, and every form of hypocrisy. . . .

His attunement to contemporary language is probably unequalled in American writing. Anyone with a feeling for English phrase at its most balanced, concise, and arresting cannot fail to see this excellence. . . . Compared to Burroughs' grasp of modern idiom in almost every form of English . . . the similar efforts of Ring Lardner and of Hemingway must be seen as amateurish and groping.

Terry Southern. *New York Herald Tribune Book Section*. Nov. 8, 1964. p. 5

Naked Lunch records private strategies of culture in the electric age. *Nova Express* indicates some of the "corporate" responses and adventures of the Subliminal Kid who is living in a universe which seems to be someone else's insides. Both books are a kind of engineer's report of the terrain hazards and mandatory processes which exist in the new electric environment.

Burroughs uses what he calls "Brion Gysin's cut-up method which I call the fold-in method." To read the daily newspaper in its entirety is to encounter the method in all its purity. Similarly, an evening watching television programs is an experience in a corporate form—an endless succession of impressions and snatches of narrative. Burroughs is unique only in that he is attempting to reproduce in prose what we accommodate every day as a commonplace aspect of life in the electric age. If the corporate life is to be rendered on paper, the method of discontinuous nonstory must be employed.

Marshall McLuhan. *The Nation*. Dec. 28, 1964. p. 517

William Burroughs' popular reputation dates back only about two years. At that time Mary McCarthy and Norman Mailer proclaimed his talent in a moment of intemperate enthusiasm and Burroughs' most famous book, *Naked Lunch*, was subsequently published in this country in the general lapse of censorship restrictions. Burroughs' first book had appeared some ten years earlier under the pseudonym William Lee. This was entitled *Junk* and is now available in a paperback edition called *Junkie* under Burroughs' own name.

Junk is a more or less journalistic account of the experiences of a drug addict. It rises, however, considerably above the general literary level of sensational *exposé*. It is an authentically macabre vision of Hell and the flat literalism of the writing makes it more appalling in some ways than Burroughs' later accounts of the same material. . . .

Naked Lunch is the *Revelation* of an irreligious world. Its apocalyptic vision is more than the raving of a mind distraught by drugs. It is a terrible book in the true sense of the word. Even its humor and its pornography are streaked with blood and terror. . . . But it is not possible to dismiss it as mere pathology. It is a "serious" book for all its surface wise-cracking and toughness; it is serious in that it is a total vision of man in the universe, an existentialist attempt to extract meaning from total horror. . . . Unfortunately, the independent talent which expressed itself so powerfully in *Naked Lunch* has become, in *Nova Express*, the silliness of extreme hipsterism.

William James Smith. *Commonweal*. Jan. 8, 1965. pp. 491–2

The "color" [in *Nova Express*] changes from time to time as Burroughs feeds into his verbal kaleidoscope the major forms of science fiction: space mercenaries, time distortion, exotic symbiosis, galactic catastrophe, supergadgetry, and lost worlds. For all I know, he may have used existing texts; certainly he cribs (quite honestly, it should be said) from Kafka, T. S. Eliot and others, mixing their phrases into the plastic phantasmagoria. The effect after a time is pleasantly hypnotic. . . . At intervals, timed to check complete blackout, sense pops out of the amalgam; sometimes it is funny, more typically it is outrageous along the lines of Burroughs's well-established scatology. . . .

I'll accept his premise that we're being flummoxed out of our honest animal senses by high powered manipulators, and I think he is right to be sore about it. The trouble is that in his zeal to conjure with words he has produced what looks more like an abstract decoration than a terrible warning.

Robert Hatch. *Harper's Magazine*. Jan., 1965. p. 91

Burroughs is clearly writing, as does any novelist, his spiritual autobiography. Some novelists tell it through controlled fantasy, using the objective resources of action and invented character. Others disguise their own lives and write romanticized autobiographies, punishing their enemies and rewarding their friends (or sometimes the reverse). And a few, like Kafka and Burroughs, use neither plot nor personal career to carry the essential burden, but fly into fantasy, nightmare, persuaded dream. In *The Soft Machine* it is as if Burroughs does not trust the power of his nightmares. He jiggles and toys with them; he repeats naggingly; he eliminates the degree of sanity which makes the irony cut.

Herbert Gold. *New York Times Book Section*. March 20, 1966. p. 4

Burroughs's ideas are serious and interesting, and on the basis of the long interview in *Paris Review* (Fall 1965) one can see that he is one of the most intelligent and articulate writers in America today. And his experiments do produce some distinctive effects. Many passages in his books can catch something of the atmosphere of dreams in which vivid fragments of hallucinatory vividness rise and fade in utter silence, leaving one with the curiously abstract experience of witnessing concretions which do not impinge. Echoes, portents, disturbing details, flicker out at us, not as parts of legible propositions but as parts of a drifting turbulence with intensities and intermittences beyond the grasp of syntax. . . .

To escape from words into silence and from mud and metal into space is Burroughs's version of a well-established American dream of freedom from conditioning forces. It would perhaps be obtuse to ask what mode of life would be adopted in silent space. We are being given the morphology of an emotion as much as a literal prescription, when Burroughs exhorts us to shed all verbalizations and leave the body behind.

Tony Tanner. *City of Words* (Harper). 1971. pp. 130, 134

Burroughs is the great autoeroticist of contemporary fiction, the man who writes to stock up his private time machine. The "absurdity," the world-craziness which he claims to reproduce in its comic disorganization, consists in dislodging all the contents of his mind in a spirit of raw kaleidoscopic self-intoxication. These rapid shifts and indiscriminate couplings of scenes take place in Burroughs's books as if they were violently oscillating and exploding in the telescopic eyepiece of an astronomer who just happens to be gloriously soused.

Alfred Kazin. *Bright Book of Life* (Little). 1973. p. 263

Burroughs' novels . . . become diabolical maps, maps whose surfaces have been so intersected with conflicting directions, so cut up, that they are unreadable; they are maps of hell. Even the "conflicting directions," the sense of surrealistic contradiction in Burroughs, are finally neutralized by a cut-up world, a world existing in pieces that can't relate to each other enough to contradict. This is more true of the two later novels, *Nova Express* and *The Ticket That Exploded*, than it is of *Naked Lunch* and *The Soft Machine*. In *The Soft Machine* Burroughs makes his best use of cut-ups by establishing with them a dynamic rhythm of cohesion and fragmentation that becomes the experience of the novel. In the later novels, however, cut-ups come to seize their own space, to have less to do with other sections of the novels, except as waste bins to catch those sections when they drop. They become stagnant pools of amputated language and space through which the reader has to wade.

The amputation of language and space becomes also, at its extreme, an amputation of the body. Although the body in Burroughs is reified into two principles, an organic and a mechanical one, the mechanical is the final condition of the body, since even purely organic life, the body as blob, eventually swallows itself and falls into mineral existence, into death. Thus the objectification of the body in realism becomes in Burroughs a total dismemberment of the body, an explosion of it into separate existence, into pieces whose parts are all equal to each other and equal to any other object in the vicinity. This is the final condition of realism: schizophrenic atomism, living in pieces, in a world of pieces.

John Vernon. *The Garden and the Map* (Illinois). 1973. pp. 108–9

It is an extremely demanding way to write a book, to begin to do something different every five pages or so, and to bring it off requires not only skill but virtuosity of a very high order. The greatest likelihood is that the book will seem frightfully uneven, demonstrating that its author does some things better than others, which seems to me very much the case with *Exterminator!*. Another likelihood is that a book so discontinuous will seem, at its end, not to have been structured but only to have grown by accretion, like a scrapbook, and this too seems to me the case with *Exterminator!*. For all of its brutality, there is so much comic-strip stylization to its whores, pimps, junkies, presidential advisers, and scientologists, that the brutality never seems quite persuasive. The most chilling aspect of the book, in fact, seems to me the dust jacket photograph of Burroughs himself, gaunt, riven, Lazarus returned from the dead. Nothing in the art of *Exterminator!*, despite moments of great verve and inventiveness, seems to me commensurate with the implicit vision behind those hollow eyes.

Philip Stevick. *Partisan Review*. No. 2, 1974. p. 306

In *Naked Lunch* and its three less well-known sequels, *The Soft Machine*, *Nova Express*, and *The Ticket That Exploded*, William Burroughs weaves an intricate and horrible allegory of human greed, corruption, and debasement. Like Orwell's *1984* and Huxley's *Brave New World*, Burroughs' four works, taken collectively, seize on the evils or tendencies toward a certain type of evil that the author sees as being particularly malignant in his contemporary world and project them into a dystopian future, where, magnified, they have grown monstrous and taken on an exaggerated and fantastic shape. And like these classics of dystopian fiction, Burroughs' works are more novels of ideas that cleverly utilize the trappings of science fiction than they are what most people would consider ''pure and simple'' science fiction.

Even to the sophisticated reader they are troublesome puzzles; they are clearly more impenetrable than most popular literature. . . .

Significantly, this is not to say that they are without meaning or story, or that they are not imitations of life. But these elements are both realized differently here than they are in more conventional fiction. Although they share the same themes, metaphorical images, characters, and stylistic approach, this quartet—Burroughs' most serious novels—becomes more bizarre and takes on more of the appearance of science fiction as the novels progressively clarify and develop the author's thought. Each volume contributes to a single plot—or rather combines with the others to suggest the elements of what little plot there is. Thus, they may each be considered sections of one large work that encompasses them all.

Burroughs experiments with a style that has its closest analog in the cinematic technique of montage, although that technique is here most radically employed. He juxtaposes one scene with another without regard to plot, character, or, in the short view, theme to promote an association of the reader's negative emotional reaction to the superficial content (sexual perversion, drug abuse, senseless violence) of certain scenes with the implied narrative content (examples of ''addictions'': to drugs, money, sex, power, i.e., the allegory) of others. One clear instance of this technique is Burroughs' treatment of homosexuality, a practice that, while it is repeatedly equated with excrement and death (and is likely to have a negative connotation in the minds of most readers), is also endlessly juxtaposed to various addictions, particularly heroin addiction. The theory is that if such juxtapositions recur often enough, the feeling

of revulsion strategically created by the first set of images will form the reader's attitude toward the second set of examples.

Donald Palumbo. *Extrapolation*. Winter, 1979, pp. 321–22

William Burroughs' novels provide the most graphic and extreme expression of anarchic idealism and rage in contemporary literature. His characters are incessantly beset by forces of exploitation which push them into lives of addiction, self-destruction and progressive dehumanization. Rarely do they perceive either what is happening to them or their own participation in their degradation. Most accept uncritically the propaganda broadcast by the media, the institutions of social control, the ''Time, Life, Fortune Monopoly,'' the ''reality studios,'' or the political groups of *Naked Lunch*—the Liquifactionists, Divisionists and Senders, all of whom are intent on replicating themselves through their victims or dominating people's thoughts by instilling a single pattern of cognition and expression in society.

But Burroughs also suggests that to struggle against social control means to battle against one's prior identification with it—and, even more distressing, that to actively oppose the enemy insures that one remains defined by them: for as long as one is obsessed with fighting the opposition, one is not free of it. In Burroughs' novels, the greatest danger is thus to allow oneself to become rigidly defined by something external to oneself, for then one's identity is restricted and vulnerable. Consequently, the individual must not only disrupt the reality studios, but continuously disorient himself and his language to prevent his life from being controlled by anything except immediate, personal will. Against the institutions of control, Burroughs sends his anarchists, terrorists and the ''Nova Police'' who expose what is taken for reality for the grotesque horror it is. Against the three political parties of *Naked Lunch*, he pits a fourth, the Factualists, whose job it is to reveal in the most brutal—and often pornographic—terms the truth of our normal lives. The Factualists, however, cannot substitute an alternative vision, for Burroughs trusts no codified message or program, which might then be co-opted or become an authoritarian voice in others' lives. All the Factualists can do is disrupt and expose reality to force people to recognize themselves for what they are both before and after they accept a version of the ''reality film''—''dying animals on a doomed planet.'' Paradoxically then, precisely what sends people into addiction—their fear of chaos and pain, their sense of personal fragmentation and insignificance—becomes the means and the basis of their cure. Disruption, chaos, violence and exposure are what one must learn to live in. Only those strong enough to exist without external support, without a rigid identity, will survive.

Charles Russell. *Sub-stance*. No. 27, 1980, p. 321

The truth is that the attempt to rescue Burroughs for literary respectability by representing him as a satirist is hard to carry through convincingly.

It entails an insistence that the erotic and violent materials in the novels, and perhaps also the drugs, are generally there to instil disgust (a word Burroughs uses and invites the use of) and fear. But when these motifs are so widely distributed in the book, with such invariant wording, it is hard to feel that a strong local meaning attaches to them. . . .

As Burroughs implies, disgust is irrelevant to the sexual effect of a motif. An erotic context will subdue a disgust that might otherwise have arisen. Erotic imagery is a poor weapon for the satirist, for its tendency is not to sharpen our aversion to, but to reconcile us with, what is morally or physically repugnant. In fact all three of the kinds of material in Burroughs which excite desire and subdue disgust—sex, physical violence, and drugs—are at various points in the novels used affirmatively.

Cities of the Red Night perhaps carries Burroughs's utopianism further than do any of its predecessors. A change in history is fantasized whereby "pirate communes" (of a kind pioneered in reality by Captain Mission in the early eighteenth century) successfully establish themselves in Central America, and with their fraternal, egalitarian doctrines dislodge the Spanish, and are posed for a global expansion. The commune leaders are vigorously active homosexuals; their military successes are due to an early invention of the cartridge and the explosive shell (suddenly envisaged by one of the characters at the climax of an act of buggery), and citizens are kept loyal and resilient through an efficient distribution of opium (so much for the execrated "junk pyramid" of *Naked Lunch*).

The utopian narrative cannot sustain itself, and is shown to collapse back into something more macabre, disorderly, and recognizably Burroughs. What follows is perhaps more "satirical," but the juxtaposition with the earlier chapters, and the characteristic libration between horror and relish, produce the true Burroughs manifold of feeling: that ambivalence of the libertarian versus the eccentric and misanthropic. . . .

It is part of the abrupt and disconcerting sense of design which can crop up in a Burroughs novel that the final journey through the cities follows a progression which is announced many pages, and many hallucinatory episodes, earlier. Similarly, the quite orthodox first chapter of the book, which seems to have been lost sight of, is all at once referred to ten pages from the end. In *Naked Lunch* Burroughs undoubtedly developed a remarkable technique (whether by recording his dreams, using cut-up methods, or however) for getting on paper a very special kind of connected but free fantasy. It is essentially the repetition of that technique which *Cities of the Red Night* and the other novels have to offer. Burroughs's books, for all their afflatus, have a way of making the reader sit back and ponder, quite coldly: "How was that done?" The technique is not that new, either. It has very little to do with Jonathan Swift, but much to do with another Irishman. The present-tense, pantomimic rendering of the gruesome fantasy exemplified in the hanging sequences—and indeed their content—was first explored (and in this instance set in a thoroughly designed context) by Joyce in the "Circe" episode of *Ulysses*.

Michael Mason. *TLS: The Times Literary Supplement*. March 27, 1981, p. 333

William Burroughs today lives in Lawrence, Kansas, caring lovingly for his cats. If the image of him rocking and reflecting scratchy-voiced on his porch in the final moments of the documentary *Burroughs* is an accurate portrayal, he's come a long way from his period of addiction, when he was known as "El Hombre Invisible," through his years as granddaddy of the Beat Generation and social philosopher cum superstar. Hardly that tired image of the old druggy who gets off on hung boys, he's . . . well, a respectable elder gentleman—with just a few strange (and possibly dangerous) habits like shooting target practice into plywood, for

example. But shootist is only one of the many personae of the kaleidoscopic Burroughs mythology. Another is "the old writer," afflicted with writer's block and living in a boxcar on an abandoned dump: William S. Hall, the central intelligence of the recently published *The Western Lands*—the last book in the trilogy that began with *Cities of the Red Night* (1981) and *The Place of Dead Roads* (1984).

An ingenious adventure involving the usual sex, drugs, and violence, *The Western Lands* is the most playful and self-consciously literary of Burroughs's late works. William S. Hall wants to "write his way out of death" by dreaming up words that are not his own. Mired in the junk heap of his own cliches, he wishes to transcend them, and in so doing transcend the deadening imagery of our civilization. A typical Burroughs surrogate who believes that no one owns words, Hall appropriates lines from Shakespeare and pulp fiction alike. And Burroughs frames the whole in the oldest, best-established literary motifs, grail legends, pilgrimages in the manner of Chaucer's *Canterbury Tales*, and poetic sequences like T.S. Eliot's *The Waste Land*. . . .

Many ask, why does anyone—especially a woman—want to read this: I say, it's the most stimulating, exciting writing around. Burroughs once again proves himself to be a master storyteller who has found a way to wed his fragmentary stylistics to a unified and highly structured narrative. Even as far back as the recently published *Queer* (1985), written in 1951, he was beginning to invent the story within the story, the routines that would become high satire in *Naked Lunch* (1959). With this aesthetic strategy Burroughs hopes to find the way out of time that propels a good deal of his work. . . . In his fiction, Burroughs has worked out his theories, taking the narrative out of time and into space.

Regina Weinreich. *American Book Review*. November–December, 1988, p. 1

Burroughs's attitude toward language and the practice of the writer betrays the view that literary invention is authorized by a plenitude existing fundamentally outside language. . . . Burroughs often treats the practice of writing oneself out of Western civilization as a preparatory act for a genuine transfiguration of culture and society, and to this extent he might be seen as maintaining—despite his sympathy for polytheism—the Christian doctrine of life on this earth as a preparation for the life to come. Burroughs, one senses, would really *like* to be out in space, mutating, and he resorts to writing as the only available *supplement* for this accomplishment. More fundamentally, Burroughs's antipathy to time—to the culture of the One God, the God who has all the time in the world and before whom, therefore, everything ultimately must perish through having been already anticipated—entails a disdain toward writing itself as an irreducibly temporal medium. Leaving time entails leaving the word; but Burroughs can only articulate the need to stop articulating. Hence the air of bad conscience about Burroughs's books: writing is still something that happens in lieu of action. This double bind is symbolized by Burroughs's obsessive use of ellipses, which represent not simple pauses but active attempts to stop speech so as to point to something beyond it—namely space. . . .

Burroughs's critique of metaphysics contains metaphysical motifs and gives expression to metaphysical desires. His critique of the either-or proposition rests upon the claim that it conceals a more fundamental order—the liberating truths of space and eternity as opposed to the oppressive lies of time and causality. Space, the absence of the constraints imposed by time and causality, is the realm where everything is possible and hence permitted. But Burroughs cannot think the leap from the time of language to that of space except in forms that indict themselves as temporalized narratives. He therefore resorts to nostalgia—for the truly marginalized outlaws, for pre-modern civilization, and even for the future. Yet the nostalgic yearning to escape time is as Heidegger teaches, the most metaphysical desire there is. And to avoid coming to terms with the limits of postmodern subversion, as practiced by contemporary literary theory, Burroughs must finally resort to fantasies of enemies, monsters, and other power addicts who serve as focuses of evil and whose ritual elimination might enable a new becoming to take place. In this sense, Burroughs continues the obsession with isolating and purging "responsibility for evil" that William E. Connolly has identified as a central trope of Western moralists and their critics; and he offers an ironical reversal of the "political demonology"—the creation of monsters who threaten our freedom—that Michael Rogin has located at the center of American political culture. In his conviction that the political is entirely absorbed by the undoing of authority and that, once all public power has been thoroughly delegitimated, life, in its "pregnant" synchronicity, will take care of itself, Burroughs, and the practices of postmodern subversion he masterfully exemplifies, remains decisively within the tradition.

Frederick M. Dolan. *CL. 32*, no. 4, Winter, 1991, pp. 548–50

The monstrous and unreadable nature of much of [Burroughs's] fiction, the careful management of the revolt and the rationed nightmare of exile have returned him, with profit, to the great plains of American orthodoxy: home at last with honors to a nation of yawning Penelopes. He is nowadays mostly approved of and even the dismissals are a kind of homage. Pottering around his white woodframe house in Kansas and dressing, according to his biographer Barry Miles, from the L.L. Bean catalogue, Burroughs is nowadays a sedate American figure: an oddball reactionary, a gun handler, a bit of an anti-Semite, a sentimentalist—he says of his cats that "they just opened up a whole area of compassion in me"—and, crucially, an American male who dispatched the American woman at a stroke.

As far as mind and metabolism go, Burroughs is the party who stuck his head under the wheels of a freight train or got flushed out of a jumbo jet toilet and lived, in a manner of speaking, to tell the tale. His endurance can be seen as superhuman or animal, but scarcely human. What general object it served, beyond Being Bill Burroughs, is not clear. In the last letter of the volume, making yet another of his points, he seems to hazard a one-line teleology: "In this game the point is to lose what you have, and not wind up with someone else's rusty load of continuity." That, like many of the things he says, is good and memorable, yet one remains in doubt whether he ever really understood the purpose of ghastly stamina—which puts him squarely in the animal camp, if not with the circus act. As for his fellow creatures, they are to be found not in the entomologist's nightmare, as David Cronenberg would have it, but in the homestead paradigm of the old American TV series. Burroughs belongs, along with Lassie and Champion the Wonder Horse, in a dignified menagerie of beasts who have performed incredible feats with only an inkling of what they were about.

He has something of their loyalty as well. On the whole, he has stood morosely by his own shortcomings, while snapping bravely at the heels of those who deride his books. Rich or not so rich, he has kept a keenly aristocratic distaste for materialism and a contempt for corporate America. His mortuary humor has remained intact. (Paranoia, he said when he was living behind a series of locked doors on the Bowery ten years ago, is "having all the facts.") He has been prepared occasionally, on issues like El Salvador, to speak up for the dispossessed—although what upset him most in the TV news clips was the pitiful state of the FMLN's small arms.

The rest is largely a case of standing things on their heads. Burroughs has played the shaman to more than one tribe and managed, in the role of healer, to help a few of them on the road to ruin. Most readers of *Naked Lunch* would probably agree that they got ill while he got better—which is one way to interpret Dr. Benway's magnificent remark in the early part of the novel: "Want to cure anybody of anything, find out who doesn't have it." Over the years, Burroughs has also done away with some rather helpful distinctions between craving and satisfaction, boredom and terror, pleasure and aversion. It has always been hard to tell whether he is the survivor standing on his own grave, or the dead man under his shoes.

Jeremy Harding. "Junk Mail." *London Review of Books*. Sept. 23, 1993, pp. 18–19

BIBLIOGRAPHY
Junky (pseud. William Lee), 1953 (n); *The Naked Lunch*, 1959 (n) (American edition, *Naked Lunch*, 1962); *The Exterminator*, 1960 (n); *Minutes to Go*, 1960 (n); *The Soft Machine*, 1961 (n); *The Ticket That Exploded*, 1962 (n); *Dead Fingers Talk*, 1963 (n); *The Yage Letters* (to Allen Ginsberg), 1963; *Nova Express*, 1964 (n); *The Job*, 1970 (interviews, with Daniel Odier); *The Wild Boys: A Book of the Dead*, 1971 (n); *Exterminator!*, 1973 (misc); *The Last Words of Dutch Schultz*, 1975 (n); *Mayfair Academy Series More or Less*, 1973 (s); *Book of Breeething*, 1975 (e); *Cobble Stone Gardens*, 1976 (p); (with Brion Gysin) *The Third Mind*, 1978 (c); *Blade Runner: A Movie*, 1979 (screenplay); *Ah Pook Is Here*, 1979 (n, e); *Roosevelt after Inauguration*, 1979 (e); *Port of Saints*, 1980 (n); *Cities of the Red Night*, 1981 (n); *The Place of Dead Roads*, 1984 (n); *The Burroughs File*, 1984 (misc); *Mind Wars*, 1985 (n); *Queer*, 1985 (n); *The Adding Machine*, 1985 (e); *The Western Lands*, 1987 (n); *Tornado Alley*, 1988 (n); *Interzone*, 1989 (n); *The Cat Inside*, 1992 (b); *The Letters of William S. Burroughs, 1945–1959*, 1993; *My Education: A Book of Dreams*, 1995 (a); *With William S. Burroughs: A Report from the Bunker*, 1996; *Word Virus: The William S. Burroughs Reader*, 1998

BUTLER, Robert Olen (1945–)

For the Vietnamese immigrants in Robert Olen Butler's stories, distance is sentient. It buzzes inside them like a crossed telephone line, a haunting syncopation under the forthright American rhythms they are trying to learn.

Butler's Vietnamese live, for the most part, in waterside communities in Louisiana: Lake Charles, Gretna, Versailles. The author himself lives and teaches in Lake Charles. Ever since he went to Saigon in 1971 as an Army linguist, he found his personal and literary vocation—unlike other writers there—less in exploring what it felt like to be an American in Vietnam than in what it felt like to Vietnam to have Americans there.

It is the Vietnamese voice that he seeks and that, in these stories, he has so remarkably and movingly found. What it means for these expatriates to come to a new country and function in it is more the setting than the theme. Butler writes essentially, and in a bewitching translation of voice and sympathy, what it means to lose a country, to remember it, and to have the memory begin to grow old. He writes as if it were his loss, too.

The 15 stories in *A Good Scent from a Strange Mountain* differ considerably in weight and complexity. One or two are brief lyrics. In "Mid-Autumn," a mother speaks to her unborn baby about a village boy she passionately loved and who was killed; and of the calmer love she feels for her husband, an American soldier who brought her to the United States. She tells a fairy tale about a prince who came down from the moon, who longs to get back and cannot, but who finds the Earth good in its own way.

There is the romance of a New Orleans bar girl and an American who fell in love with Vietnam during the war. His passion for her memories allows her to become a contented American housewife. Another romance takes place between a waitress and an older man, a Polish Jew who becomes her mentor in overcoming the strangeness of America.

These stories are graceful but a little too easy in their emotional movements and their lessons. Others are harsher and more effective. In "Open Arms," the Vietnamese narrator recalls serving as translator in an American-Canadian program to turn captured Viet Cong into informants. One day, they bring in Thap. He is a man of tragedy; his wife and children were killed in a Viet Cong raid on a village. His burning devastation contrasts with the sleek South Vietnamese major who takes part in his interrogation.

"If I was the major," the narrator recalls, "I'd feel very nervous because the man beside him had the mountain shadow and the steady look of the ghost of somebody his grandfather had cheated or cuckolded or murdered 50 years ago and he was back to take him." Thap's tragedy is too big; his first allegiance had betrayed him. Now his new allegiance betrays him in a different way, a casual, pragmatic American way.

The sense of loss among the expatriates is played out in different fashions. In one story, the narrator has become a successful businessman, and put aside his memories of Vietnam to concentrate on his American future. The price he pays is emotional blankness. He dearly loves his wife, who lives closer to her memories, but when he embraces her, she is no more real to him than the itch in his ankle or his agenda for the next day.

The wife's grandfather arrives for a visit. She remembers how he used to carry her on his back; he represents all the tradition she left behind. Her excitement is dashed when he fails to remember her or to take any interest in anything except their new car. Her desolation spurs the husband to a redeeming leap of imagination; he hoists her up on his back and gallops around their garden.

There is poignancy in many of the stories, but, except perhaps in one or two, Butler avoids sentimentality. A principal reason for this, and one of his main strengths, is his ability to speak in his characters' voices—an almost perfect English but with odd strains and inflections—and to discover what they discover without foreknowledge or patronage.

One story is pure comedy. The narrator is a solemnly insignificant man with a beautiful and restless wife. In Vietnam, he ran a network of informants for the Americans. He used his position to warn off potential rivals; if they paid no attention, the Americans would receive a report of Viet Cong activity just where the rival worked or walked. An aerial attack would follow.

In America, of course, the narrator has no such power. So when a Vietnamese rival begins paying court to the wife, the reprisal has to be different. It is hilariously elaborate and utterly effective.

In a collection so delicate and so strong, the title story stands out as close to magical. It is narrated by Dao, an expatriate who is nearly 100 and lives with his daughter. His thoughts wander between past and present; he will die any day.

"Ho Chi Minh came to me again last night, his hands covered with confectioners' sugar," the story begins. Dao, so near death and with an unquiet memory of the past, receives visits from the ghost of Vietnam's founding leader. They had been roommates in Paris during World War I. Both had worked in the kitchen of the great chief Escoffier, Ho Chi Minh as an apprentice pastry cook. Ho's passion was his country's liberation; Dao remembers him putting on an ugly and ill-fitting bowler hat—and furious at having to do it—to go out to Versailles where the Peace Conference was taking place, and try to get the ear of Woodrow Wilson.

The two men went their different ways. The narrator became a Hoa Hao Buddhist, a sect of austere unworldliness. Its meditations take shape around the phrase: "A Good Scent From a Strange Mountain." Ho, of course, chose revolution.

Ghost and dying man are now together, each with his own sense of incompletion. The narrator has lived spiritually apart from his country's tragedy. And Ho? He was never able to make a successful pastry glaze. Thinking of politics, he failed to listen properly to Escoffier. He used confectioners' instead of granulated sugar.

Through the words of Dao, Butler holds the two failures in equilibrium. To neglect a revolution and to neglect a glaze are two aspects of human limits. "I was only a washer of dishes but I did listen carefully when Monsieur Escoffier spoke," Dao says. "I wanted to understand everything. His kitchen was full of such smells that you knew you had to understand everything or you would be incomplete forever."

Richard Eder. *Los Angeles Times Book Review*. March 29, 1992, pp. 3, 7.

For three decades Vietnamese have played the foils in an American psychodrama. We venture, we kill, we dream, we regret, we make peace; they smile their innocent or sinister smiles. One of the Vietnamese characters in Robert Olen Butler's first collection of short fiction gives a bitter self-portrait through distorting American eyes: "We were fascinating and long-suffering and unreal or we were sly and dangerous and unreal."

A Good Scent From a Strange Mountain goes a long way toward making the Vietnamese real, and its method is bold: each of the 15 stories is told in the first person from the viewpoint of a Vietnamese transplanted from the Mekong Delta to the Louisiana bayou. The Americans have become foils; it's the Vietnamese who are now at the center, haunted by the past, ambivalent about their hosts, suffering sexual torments, seeking a truce in their various wars.

This reversal makes for a less hyperbolic kind of story than most American fiction and film about the war in Vietnam and its aftermath. In their new home on the Gulf Coast these Vietnamese are often visited by old ghosts and legends, but the war itself is on the periphery, a given. Unlike Americans, they don't pick at the horrors they've survived and there's hardly a word of politics. Their memories are dominated instead by bittersweet sense experience: in "Preparation" a woman readying her friend's corpse for burial combs and envies the beautiful hair she combed and envied when they were girls in Saigon.

Vietnam, where Mr. Butler served as an Army linguist fluent in the language, is the setting for two of his six novels— *The Alleys of Eden* and *On Distant Ground,* which share common characters. They are the work of a writer who is intoxicated by Vietnam and the Vietnamese, who loves what has alienated so many other Americans, including novelists: the strange lingual tones, the ambiguity of relations in an ancient and complex society, the teeming nighttime streets of Saigon. The heroes of both novels withdraw from the war—one as a deserter, the other as a traitor of sorts—in favor of personal ties, to a South Vietnamese woman and a Vietcong prisoner. Vietnam is where these Americans become more compassionate, not more cruel, and the memory of Vietnam keeps them in the grip of a powerful nostalgic longing for the smell of market food, the flesh of a lover or the face of a lost child.

In his stories Mr. Butler confers this longing on his Vietnamese characters. And in doing so he manages to make them completely original, with quirky interests and odd obsessions, as distinct from one another as from the Americans they brush against.

In "Fairy Tale" a bar girl, remembering what a delicacy apples were in Saigon, thinks how, like apples in America, sex has become too abundant for her to savor it: "You take a bite now and you can make yourself remember that apples are sweet, but it is like the apple in your mouth is not even there. You eat too many apples and all you can do is remember them." In "Snow," a spinster with little hope of ever marrying expresses a different shade of melancholy: "There are other Vietnamese here in Lake Charles, Louisiana, but we are not a community. We are all too sad, perhaps, or too tired. But maybe not. Maybe that's just me saying that. Maybe the others are real Americans already."

Probably not. These Vietnamese—even the businessman in "Relic" who swears that "America is the land of opportunity"—seem to live their real lives in the past and the supernatural. In the title story, an old man preparing for death is visited by the ghost of Ho Chi Minh in search of memories. Ho's hands are covered in the sugar he baked with when the two men worked at a [Paris] hotel in 1917. In spite of the Communist victory, Ho's ghost confesses: "I am not at peace."

The dying man, whose relatives have brought Vietnamese political murder to New Orleans, asks Ho, "Are there politics where you are now, my friend?" The implicit answer is that there are only memories, that it's the burden of the dead to recover them all, that sugar is as important as war. The dying man finally understands Ho's restlessness. . . .

To become complete, these dislocated men and women return in memory and imagination to Vietnam, where folk tales narrated within the stories often illuminate their present condition. An expectant mother who lost her first lover in Vietnam tells her unborn American child a fairy tale: an emperor went to the moon and found happiness there, but after returning to earth he could never go back; he could only remember. A South Vietnamese soldier is saved from Vietcong ambush by a beautiful woman's ghost; later, when he finds the ghost to thank her; she devours him; and the man telling the story on a Greyhound bus feels devoured, too, in his uneasy American exile.

The intricacy of these stories, and of most of the collection, lies in their motifs, not in psychological insight. Mr. Butler uses the narrative surprises and symbolic imagery of folklore, and as in folklore his meanings can be both simple and opaque. The longest and most ambitious of the stories, "The American Couple," comes much closer to the familiar terrain of contemporary fiction. But to do so it has to give its Vietnamese woman narrator an essentially American consciousness. In the shifting tensions of two couples spending a day together at a Mexican resort—one Vietnamese, one American, of whom the husband is an obsessive Vietnam vet—Mr. Butler loses in focus and compression what he gains in complexity. Nothing in "The American Couple" is quite as vivid as the sugar on Ho Chi Minh's ghostly hands.

But there are risks in the simpler tales. They sometimes tend toward melodrama: large, obvious emotions are generated by manipulations of plot. And Mr. Butler can't always resist sentimental endings. Since these weaknesses also show up in his two war novels, they're more than just functions of taking on so many convincingly Vietnamese points of view. But in the absence of sophisticated, familiar, telling ironies, and within the limits of what even this most sensitive American writer *can* know about his Vietnamese characters, he's often left with crude resolutions. At least three stories end happily ever after in at long last love.

One of the strongest stories, "The Trip Back," shows Mr. Butler's art at its most moving and problematic. A businessman drives to the Houston airport to pick up his wife's grandfather, just emigrated from Vietnam. On the way home, the old man expresses interest in little other than the businessman's car, which has induced a memory of driving from Saigon to Hanoi years before. "This man beside me was rushing along the South China Sea," the businessman thinks. "Right now. He had felt something so strong that he could summon it up and place himself within it and the moment would not fade." The grandfather has returned so vividly to the deep past that he has no memory of the granddaughter he's about to be reunited with. And the businessman begins to dread that when his own time comes he won't "die well," that his own life will be reduced to "the faint buzz of the alarm clock beside my bed," that "I may be prepared to betray all that I think I love the most." He's afraid that he'll end up remembering even less than the grandfather—without his homeland, without his wife.

In the end, he overcomes his wife's grief at being forgotten with a simple gesture, meant to be poignant, that seems inadequate to the profundity of his crisis. It takes a little away from an almost perfect story. But *A Good Scent from a Strange Mountain* is remarkable not for its flaws, but for how beautifully it achieves its daring project of making the Vietnamese real.

George Packer. *The New York Times Book Review.* June 7, 1992, p. 24.

Robert Olen Butler's *A Good Scent From a Strange Mountain* makes deeper and truer sense of the bittersweet life of exiled Vietnamese. He concentrates on Westernized families who escaped in 1975. The only American fiction writer who has delved deeply into the lives and psyches of these new Americans, Butler is fluent in Vietnamese, and it shows. It's refreshing to see this ancient and subtle language used with respect instead of GI pidgin.

Each of Butler's stories forms a poignant monologue. The Vietnamese characters take center stage and speak as if justifying their existence. Sometimes this didacticism is intrusive, but it may be unavoidable; the world view of the characters differs so greatly from that of the audience. Butler's characters appear to have adapted well to American life, but they nonetheless bear an overwhelming sense of loss.

In their nostalgia, guilt, and pain, they are no different from Westerners who have experienced wrenching traumas. But Vietnamese traumas find their outlet in a spirit world—a mental universe of unseen, powerful forces. This alternative reality occasionally intrudes at moments of stress and dislocation: A translator in the war wonders if a turncoat Viet Cong is really a demon; a lonely housewife discovers that her grandfather's soul has transmigrated into a parrot; an elderly, dying man converses nightly with the ghost of his old comrade Ho Chi Minh.

Though Butler's book excels in presenting Vietnamese life, he is an outsider. It's too soon for the Vietnamese themselves to tell their stories. Like all immigrants, the first generation is preoccupied with survival. The next generation of Vietnamese-Americans will produce anthropologists, sociologists, and journalists with a foot in both cultures.

Kathleen Kilgore, *The Christian Science Monitor*. September 4, 1992, p. 12.

BIBLIOGRAPHY

The Alleys of Eden, 1981 (n); *Sun Dogs*, 1982 (n); *Countrymen of Bones*, 1983 (n); *On Distant Ground*, 1985 (n); *Wabash*, 1987 (n); *The Deuce*, 1989 (n); *A Good Scent from a Strange Mountain*, 1992 (s); *They Whisper*, 1995 (n); *Tabloid Dreams*, 1996 (s); *The Deep Green Sea*, 1997 (n)

C

CABELL, James Branch (1879–1958)

That he says impeccably his say is indisputable; that he says it for only a few is undebatable. . . . He is . . . enjoyed only by those who possess a certain scholarship plus a but slightly secondary interest in fiction plus a mental kinship that recognizes the aptness of his means.

> Blanche Williams. *Our Short Story Writers* (Moffat). 1920. p. 23

Mr. Cabell, by questioning the reality of reality, has been naturalized in the world of dreams till he moves about there without the scruples lasting over from another allegiance. Thus the beauty of his Poictesme is double-distilled. Those lovers of beauty who must now and then come down to earth for renewal will occasionally gasp in Poictesme, wishing the atmosphere would thicken and brilliant colors change. But always Poictesme hangs above the mortal clouds, suspended from the eternal sky, in the region where wit and beauty are joined in an everlasting kiss.

> Carl Van Doren. *James Branch Cabell* (McBridge). 1925. p. 83

Here at last is an American novelist with a culture and style of his own, a conscious artist and a man of letters. . . . Cabell . . . is an adept at artistic writing, the only prose writer in American fiction who cultivates style for its own sake. . . . He likes to call himself a classic, classic in style, though romantic in inspiration. . . . Cabell's ideal is harmony, clearness and grace. He moves within fiction as if it were a natural element and not as in a quarry where he is painfully hewing out stones.

> Régis Michaud. *The American Novel Today* (Little). 1928. pp. 202–3

The high repute of the works of Mr. Cabell has not been attacked by critics, partly out of a faint snobbishness; partly for the amusing reason that those who were fit to criticize him found him almost impossible to read, and lastly because scholarship and love of good prose seemed too rare in America to be discredited on other grounds without a pang. His prose is, indeed, not only correct but constantly graceful in diction and liquid in rhythm. The trouble is that there is nothing in all these romances for the mind to grasp; one fumbles in a sunny mist; one hopes from page to page to come upon something either sharp or solid; that hope is soon abandoned and next it becomes clear that even the grace of this style is often falsely arch and knowing or effeminate and teasing. The style, in brief, is married to the matter and both are *articles de luxe*, like gorgeously enameled cigarette étuis diamond and ruby-studded, or riding crops with jeweled handles.

> Ludwig Lewisohn. *Expression in America* (Harper). 1932. p. 531

This Virginian gentleman and genealogist could hardly be expected either to approve of life in the United States or to feel that he was under any obligation to improve it. Instead he has converted his petulant disgust into a melodramatic pessimism. . . . The artist has a function in this mad world, Mr. Cabell argues; it is to create beautiful illusions, which alone make life endurable. But, far from occupying himself with the dissemination of dynamic lies, Mr. Cabell has devoted all his talents to attacking man's illusions. He is, then, a fraud, for neither his romanticism nor his pessimism is genuine. He is a sleek, smug egoist, whose desire to be a gentleman of the old school breeds dissatisfaction with the existing order, but who has not enough imaginative vigor to create a robust world in which deeds of chivalry and gallantry are performed. Instead he has written mild little fantasies, carefully baited with delicate obscenities.

> Granville Hicks. *The Great Tradition* (Macmillan). 1933. p. 221

His own style is indubitably established, consciously dependent on archaism, but dependent for relief on marked and homely modernisms. On the whole it is attractive, and sometimes it is charming. But it is pedantic in phrasing and in dispensable detail. Knowing that fancy is more important than fact in the tales, the reader is annoyed and distracted by circumstantial matters of chronology and genealogy that delay action and throw no light on motivation.

The notable fact about Cabell in the modern pageant has been his persistence in playing his own role until through ability and cooperation of the censors he achieved a wide hearing. He ought to be taken as seriously as he takes himself, which is not very seriously, for his tongue as a rule is ostentatiously in his cheek.

> Percy H. Boynton. *Literature and American Life* (Ginn). 1936. pp. 799–800

Critics have persisted in putting Cabell into the wrong category. They have repeatedly called him a romanticist, bent upon escape. They refuse to see that his extravanganzas of Poictesme are all allegories. He is as close to the modern pulse as the most intense realist, and as alarmed over it. He is a humorist, a wit, a satirist, an intellectual, a classicist. And he is a characteristic twentieth-century pessimist. He is right in the thick of life, and he is so disgusted with it that he can see nothing sensible to do except laugh. If he is a romanticist bent upon escape, then so were Aristophanes, Rabelais, Ben Jonson, Congreve, Voltaire, Mark Twain, and Anatole France.

> Vernon Loggins. *I Hear America* (Crowell). 1937. p. 287

Unlike that other artificer of the medieval. Thomas Chatterton, Cabell never persuaded himself; and he had no need to persuade his readers. They wanted just what he gave them: the touch of life bereft of life's prosaic sordidness; an easy road to wisdom; a masquerade of the soul in which, by mocking the daydreams of the great herd, one could liberate and enjoy one's own. Cabell did not pretend to be an ''escapist'' he was a realist whose cynical appreciation of reality encouraged him to make it ridiculous. By dismissing the superficial world of the present, he illuminated its pathos lightly and fleetingly. . . . The critical Babbitts might think Cabell a satanic figure, but he was not even attempting to *épater le bourgeois*; he sought only to amuse him. Reading his books, good middle-class fathers and citizens, like good middle-class undergraduates, enjoyed the luxury of a depravity that was as synthetic as breakfast cereal, and as harmless.

Alfred Kazin. *On Native Grounds* (Reynal). 1942. pp. 233–4

BIBLIOGRAPHY

The Eagle's Shadow, 1904 (revised edition, 1923); *The Line of Love*, 1905 (s) (revised edition, 1921); *Gallantry*, 1907 (s) (revised edition, 1922); *Branchiana*, 1907 (h); *The Cords of Vanity*, 1909 (n) (revised edition, 1920); *Chivalry*, 1909 (s) (revised edition, 1921); *Branch of Abingdon*, 1911 (h); *The Soul of Melicent*, 1913 (n) (revised edition, titled *Domnei*, 1920); *The Rivet in Grandfather's Neck*, 1915 (n); *The Majors and Their Marriages*, 1915 (h); *The Certain Hour*, 1916 (s); *From the Hidden Way*, 1916 (p) (revised edition, 1924); *The Cream of the Jest*, 1917 (n) (revised edition, 1922); *Jurgen*, 1919 (n); *Beyond Life*, 1919 (e); *The Judging of Jurgen*, 1920 (c); *Joseph Hergesheimer*, 1921 (c); *Figures of Earth*, 1921 (n); *The Jewel Merchants*, 1921 (d); *Taboo*, 1921 (sk); *The Lineage of Lichfield*, 1922 (c); *The High Place*, 1923 (n); *Straws and Prayer-Books*, 1924 (e); *The Silver Stallion*, 1926 (n); *The Music from Behind the Moon*, 1926 (s); *Something About Eve*, 1927 (n); *Works*, 1927–1930; *The White Robe*, 1928 (s); *Ballades from the Hidden Way*, 1928 (p); *The Way of Ecben*, 1929 (n); *Sonnets from Antan*, 1929 (p); *Some of Us*, 1930 (e); *Townsend of Lichfield*, 1930 (c); *Between Dawn and Sunrise* (selections), 1930; *These Restless Heads*, 1932 (e); *Special Delivery*, 1933 (e); *Smirt*, 1934 (n); *Ladies and Gentlemen*, 1934 (e); *Smith*, 1935 (n); *Preface to the Past*, 1936 (c); *Smire*, 1937 (n); *The King Was in His Counting House*, 1938 (n); *Of Ellen Glasgow*, 1938 (e); *Hamlet Had an Uncle*, 1940 (n); *The First Gentleman of Virginia*, 1942 (n); (with A. J. Hanna) *The St. Johns*, 1943 (h); *There Were Two Pirates*, 1947 (n); *Let Me Lie*, 1947 (e); *The Devil's Own Dear Son*, 1949 (n); *The Witch Woman*, (*The Music from Behind the Moon, The Way of Ecben, The White Robe*), 1949 (n); *Quiet, Please*, 1952 (e); *As I Remember It*, 1955 (r); *Between Friends*, 1962 (letters)

CAHAN, Abraham (1860–1951)

As Mr. Cahan is a Russian, and as romanticism is not considered literature in Russia, his story [*Yekl*] is, of course, intensely realistic. It could not be more so indeed than Mr. [Stephen] Crane's stories, and it is neither more nor less faithful than these. The artistic principle which moves both writers is the same; but the picturesque, outlandish material with which Mr. Cahan deals makes a stronger appeal to the reader's fancy. He has more humor than the American, too, whose spare laughter is apt to be grim, while the Russian cannot hide his relish of the comic incidents of his story. It is mainly not at all comic, however, but tragical as the divorce of the poor little Russian wife can make it, though the reader is promptly consoled by her marriage with a man worthier of her than Jake the Yankee. He goes away and weds the Americanized

"Polish snope" whom he had flirted with before his wife came out to him. . . .

I had almost forgotten to speak of his English. In its simplicity and its purity, as the English of a man born to write Russian, it is simply marvelous.

> William Dean Howells. *New York World*, July 26, 1896, in Clara M. and Rudolf Kirk. *American Jewish Historical Quarterly*. Sept., 1962. p. 52

He is a humorist, and his humor does not spare the sordid and uncouth aspects of the character whose pathos he so tenderly reveals. Poor, workworn, ambitious, blundering, grotesque lives they mostly are which he deals with, but they have often a noble aspiration, to which he does justice with no straining or vaunting. The rich Jew going home to his village in Poland to get a husband for his Americanized daughter, whose ideal is to marry an "uptown feller," and bringing back a dreamy young Talmudist, who turns agnostic on his hands; the prosperous pedlar who sends to his native place, where he has been the byword and laughing-stock, and demands the daughter of the wealthy distiller in marriage; the young Russian wife, whose heart goes from her work-dulled husband to the student they have taken for a lodger to eke out their pitiful fortunes; the Yiddish bride who imagines spending all her savings on a wedding supper in the vain hope that the guests will bring gifts enough to set her up in housekeeping—such are the materials which the author handles so skillfully that he holds the reader between a laugh and a heartache, and fashions into figures so lifelike that you would expect to meet them in any stroll through Hester-street. It will be interesting to see whether Mr. Cahan will pass beyond his present environment out into the larger American world, or will master our life as he has mastered our language. But of a Jew, who is also a Russian, what artistic triumph may not we expect?

> William Dean Howells. *Literature*. Dec. 31, 1898, in Clara M. and Rudolf Kirk. *American Jewish Historical Quarterly*. Sept., 1962. p. 41

And for a background that immense Russia, a country which has produced the greatest novelists and is the most illiterate of Europe, a nation of nations whose history is stained with the blood of conquered races and massacred sects. It is from this rich mine that Mr. Cahan has selected with an artist's care his material. But in *The White Terror and the Red* we have something far more interesting than a narrative of sensational episodes, or a gallery of interesting types, more valuable than a vivid picture of melodramatic history in the making. We have a work of art of the highest class.

It was reserved for a Russian realist to do full justice to the subject, and Mr. Cahan is a Russian and a realist. He is concerned with life. His literary god is the truth as he sees it, and because he is an artist and his theme throbs with passionate human interest, he has succeeded in writing a novel which bears out the bright promise of his earlier work.

> Edwin Lefevre. *Bookman*. April, 1905. p. 187

The White Terror and the Red is, as far as I know, the first important novel which has applied the general spirit of Russian fiction to the literal facts of the revolution [of 1879–81]. Mr. Cahan has been enabled to do this by virtue of an exceptional position. He is a Russian, living in America, and writing in English. He is, therefore, not limited by the despotism of the Russian government, as the Russian writers are. He is one of the very few men not now in Russia who combine with genuine literary ability an inside knowledge of the facts leading to the assassination of the Czar. In his book the Russian realistic method and the Russian idealistic spirit have for the first time been applied to the direct and literal facts of the revolution.

This directness of approach Mr. Cahan has had. *The White Terror and the Red*, is, therefore, at once a genuine historical novel, dealing with the events which resulted in the assassination of the Czar, and a genuine realistic novel, a rare combination.

Hutchins Hapgood. *Critic*. June, 1905. p. 561

The portrait of David Levinsky is a portrait of society, not simply of the Jewish section of it, or of New York, but of American business. And business is business whether done by Jew or Gentile. If Levinsky is a triumphant failure, he is so because American business, which shaped him to its ends, is, viewed from any decent regard for humanity, a miserable monster of success. Not that Levinsky is an abstraction, or that the novelist is forcing a thesis. Far from it. . . . Mr. Cahan is an artist; he knows how to think through his characters, by letting them do the thinking, as if it were their affair and not his.

John Macy. *Dial*. Nov. 22, 1917. p. 522

Of this East Side world, with its thick vitality, and push against the city, Mr. Cahan has drawn a picture of incomparable vigor, richly documented, admirably proportioned. This, you say, is the very life which corresponds to what the outsider can only see in street and shop and through his imagination. You are immersed in the life of the family, the synagogue, the sweatshop, the cafe, the theatre, the socialists and intellectuals. And you witness it through the eyes of a man of vigor and intelligence, David Levinsky, who is engaged in mastering, appropriating, nourishing his senses and ambitions by means of that life. Consider Mr. Cahan's art in the light of his opportunity for propaganda. For he makes his hero not a socialist but an exploiter who has no sympathy with the helpless workers from whom he has come, who fights the unions, is afraid of socialism, and remains unregenerate to the last, justifying his "individualism" by the Darwin and Spencer he had read during the intellectual ferment of the sweatshop. . . . Mr. Cahan makes him tell the story in rich human detail, as an understandable human being. You are no more appalled at David's tyrannies and greeds than David is himself. Yet in David's unperceptive reactions to the women he desires, in his annoyance at the radicals and "intellectuals," Mr. Cahan makes a subtle back-fire of criticism more deadly than the most melodramatic socialist fiction.

R.B. *New Republic*. Feb. 2, 1918. pp. 31–2

There is no question whatever that the work of Abraham Cahan, Yiddish scholar, journalist, novelist, belongs to the American nation. As far back as the year in which Stephen Crane stirred many

sensibilities with his *Maggie*, the story of an Irish slum in Manhattan, Mr. Cahan produced in *Yekl* a book similar and practically equal merit concerning a Jewish slum in the same borough. But it and his later books *The Imported Bridegroom and Other Stories* and *The White Terror and the Red* have been overwhelmed by novels by more familiar men dealing with more familiar communities. The same has been true even of his masterpiece, the most important of all immigrant novels, *The Rise of David Levinsky*. It, too, records the making of an American, originally a reader of Talmud in a Russian village and eventually the principal figure in the cloak and suit trade in America. But it does more than trace the career of Levinsky through his personal adventures: it traces the evolution of a great industry and represents the transplanted Russian Jews with affectionate exactness in all their modes of work and play and love—another conquest of a larger Canaan. Here are fused American hope and Russian honesty. At the end David, with all his New World wealth, lacks the peace he might have had but for his sacrifice of Old World integrity and faith. And yet the novel is very quiet in its polemic. Its hero has gained in power; he is no dummy to hand maxims on. Moving through a varied scene, gradually shedding the outward qualities of his race, he remains always an individual, gnawed at by love in the midst of his ambitions, subject to frailties which test his strength.

The fact that Mr. Cahan wrote *David Levinsky* not in his mother-tongue but in the language of his adopted country may be taken as a sign that American literature no less than the American population is being enlarged by the influx of fresh materials and methods.

Carl Van Doren. *Contemporary American Novelists, 1900–1920* (Macmillan). 1922. pp. 144–5

Cahan's absorbing interest in literature has been one of the reasons that the standard of literary criticism as well as the quality of fiction printed in the *Forward* has always been high. . . . Cahan has mellowed somewhat with the years, but in the old days he was considered a bit of a tyrant in the office. Writers often had what they considered their best copy mercilessly derided as "fancy," and were told that the editor didn't want "any Carusoes in the office." Reporters who lapsed into polysyllables or put style ahead of content had to stand by helplessly while Cahan called upon the elevator man, or some other representative of the paper's readers to judge the disputed passage. If the man was unable to understand the copy it was thrown away or rewritten.

J.C. Rich. *American Mercury*. Aug., 1947. pp. 175–6

I have purposely refrained from treating David Levinsky as a fictional character and have spoken of the novel as though it were the actual memoir of an American Jew, in tribute to Cahan's power of characterization. Such immediacy of revelation is the novel's strongest quality, and Levinsky is made to talk about himself not only with an authentic accent, but with a motive in disclosure verging on something sly—precisely as such a man would talk. This well known and widely respected businessman tells the truth about himself, his love affairs, his efforts to outsmart the unions, the way other men tell lies—to see if he can get away with it! But as fiction, Cahan's writing lacks continuity: his transitions from subject to subject tend to be abrupt, with a perseveration in the linking of sex and economics. . . . Often the trains of thought collide within the single paragraph, business plowing into everything else. True, Levinsky's mind would work this way, and the habit would also serve him the purpose of saying, "I may not be doing so well with the girls—but think of the money I'm making." (Though business is meaningless to Levinsky, one of the most touching insights of the novel is provided by Cahan's showing how he succumbs to a businessman's vulgarity of tone and manner, and berates himself for the weakness.)

Isaac Rosenfeld. *Commentary*. Aug., 1952. p. 135

And if one had to select a single person to stand for East European Jews in America, it would be Abraham Cahan, the editor of the *Jewish Daily Forward*. . . . In one of his novels, the best yet written about American Jewish life, we are given a vivid and convincing picture of the helplessness and irrelevance of East European Judaism in the America of the early years of the mass immigration. We read in *The Rise of David Levinsky* of how a young Russian Jewish yeshiva student, learned and pious, emigrates to this country. On the boat he eats no forbidden food and prays daily. In America he seeks out and finds solace in the synagogue established by the people from his home town. But he also moves inevitably from one transgression to the next. First his earlocks are cut off, then he shaves, soon he abandons the synagogue in favor of night school and English studies. And soon nothing is left—and with practically no soul-searching.

Nathan Glazer. *American Judaism* (Chicago). 1957. pp. 68–9

This perceptive Russian intellectual shared in all the experiences of his fellow immigrants: he was factory hand, lecturer, teacher of English, labor organizer, law student, and socialist preacher. But from the outset he cultivated literary ambitions. In his first year Cahan mailed an article describing the coronation of Tsar Alexander III to the *New York World* and it was promptly published. By the mid-1880's Cahan's journalistic career encompassed the Russian, Yiddish, and English fields. . . . In 1896 his first novel, *Yekl, A Tale of the Ghetto*, was published by Appleton's. . . . His novel, despite the high praise of William Dean Howells, brought him no royalties. Women, who constituted the major market for novels, devoured knightly romances but had no interest in immigrant stories; furthermore, an unmoral love story that alluded to sex was taboo.

Moses Rischin. *The Promised City: New York's Jews, 1870–1914* (Harvard). 1962. p. 124

BIBLIOGRAPHY
Yekl: A Tale of the New York Ghetto, 1896 (n); *The Imported Bridegroom and Other Stories of the New York Ghetto*, 1898 (s); *The White Terror and the Red*, 1905 (n); *Raphael Naarizoch*, 1907 (n) (in Yiddish); *The Rise of David Levinsky*, 1917 (n); *Bletter von Mein Leben*, 1926–31 (a) (5 volumes, in Yiddish); (with others) *Socialism, Fascism, Communism*, 1934 (e); *Scholum Asch's Neier Veg*, 1941 (c) (in Yiddish)

CAIN, James M. (1892–1977)

Every so often a writer turns up who forces us to revalue our notions of the realistic manner, for, no less than reality itself, it is relative and inconstant, depending on the period, the fashion, the point of view. There is the feeling of realism, of intense realism, in James M. Cain's work, and yet he cannot be compared to such diverse types of realists as Zola, Ibsen, Sandburg, Dreiser, or Hemingway. It is the hard-boiled manner that has been heralded for some time, and is now upon us. . . . Cain can get down to the primary impulses of greed and sex in fewer words than any writer we know of. He has exorcised all the inhibitions; there is a minimum of reason, of complexity, of what we commonly call civilization, between an impulse and its gratification. In the broadest sense he is no asset as yet to American literature, for he adds nothing in breadth, but only in intensity, to our consciousness of life.

Harold Strauss. *New York Times Book Section*. Feb. 18, 1934. p. 8

The Postman Always Rings Twice . . . is a brutal story of adultery and murder whose appropriate setting is a wayside filling-station in California. Up to a certain point it rings horribly true: the bungled attempt at murder, the unsuccessful crime, the maggots of mutual suspicion that begin to prey on the guilty partners. But then Mr. Cain begins to make things up. He has almost succeeded in showing two triumphantly evil people—the reader is uncomfortable but can't let the story drop—When his intention falters: he converts his two villains into another Paolo and Francesca and rings down the curtain on a Hollywood-tragic ending. *The Postman Always Rings Twice* is a short, meretricious but exciting book; it does not pretend to tell the whole story, but it does pretend to tell nothing but the truth.

T.S. Matthews. *New Republic*. Feb. 28, 1934. p. 80

In the theatre they call it "pace." Mr. Cain had phenomenal pace in his story *The Postman Always Rings Twice*, and he demonstrates this gift again in *Serenade*. And another thing. There is no use being too nice about the fact that what gives Mr. Cain's novels their intensely readable quality is their deliberate and even brutal sexual honesty. . . . Mr. Cain is a real writer who can construct and tell an exciting story with dazzling swiftness—one of our hard-boiled novelists whose work has a fast rhythm that is art.

William Rose Benet. *Saturday Review*. Dec. 4, 1937. p. 5

Cain deals with ciphers, picturesque cardboard characters whom he cuts into attractive designs. He has certain specific knowledges that he draws on in all his novels: the workings of the law, the inside of the restaurant business and the world of music. . . . He has a few favorite themes: fate, the relationship of art and sex, and particularly the relationship of sex and violence. All his books give the sense of having been pieced together skillfully out of these shiny bits of glass, having no organic existence or internal necessity.

Stanley Edgar Hyman. *New Republic*. Oct. 6, 1941. p. 442

... in his work there is clearly a difference between sensationalism for its own sake and the effects sought by a writer obviously concerned with style and technique, even when the basic premise is violence. And it is truly an astonishing style, rippling and easy in a nervous sort of way, the people talking as such people would talk, the writing vivid and direct. . . . For when Mr. Cain's faults have all been pointed out—and the principal one is that character doesn't matter much in his writing—the pertinent fact remains: when he is at the top of his form it is all but impossible to put down the story he is telling.

> John K. Hutchens. *New York Times Book Section.* April 18, 1943. p.7

The elements of a Cain novel add up to a kind of bogus tragedy, in which ill luck takes the place of fate. Perhaps here is one reason why the illusion of life is so strong in *The Postman.* Luck has no place in tragedy, but it has ample scope in our daily lives. At any rate, the illusion of life is there, so strong that we accept any number of details which, in another book, would thoroughly spoil the reader's pleasure. . . . What we have in *The Postman* is a dose of unattenuated violence, describable in the jargon appropriate to the dignity of the book as possessing "terrific punch." If the book were one of greater dignity and higher seriousness, we would stop talking of punch and begin to discuss "impact" or "concentration of effect." Such suddenly delivered impact is commonly recognized as one of the essentials of tragedy. Cain's books do not strike a tragic note, however, because the violence in them is not endowed with any sort of moral significance. We are aware of his violence not as something which we must accept because it is a part of Man's Fate, but as something for a clever writer to play tricks with.

> W.M. Frohock. *The Novel of Violence in America* (Southern Methodist). 1950. pp. 97–9

Bemused by violence, Americans like to feel out, Cain says, all the nuances of the cliché "There but for the grace of God go I." To involve the reader more intimately in the social communion with violence, ritualized by mass media reportage, Cain deals with characters just removed from the gangster and private eye milieu. . . . Cain admires the clear, hard, cold mind, and thrusts his characters into actions in which their daring and know-how enable them to meet any challenge. His typical hero is an "educated roughneck": a meat packing executive, an insurance agent, a bank executive, an engineer. But even his boxers, farmers, and mechanics prove adroit. These men crave praise and are sometimes immobilized, momentarily, by condemnation. . . .

Tough optimism is clearly expressed in all of Cain's writing. At times he is cynical and satirical, but the American brand of masculine romanticism is also active, and occasionally even sentimentality intrudes. In Cain's world, chance, luck, coincidence, gamble and counter-gamble, risk, audacity, and the ability to improvise upon the given serve his characters, but usually end in defeating them. While he is capable of creating finely drawn moral dilemmas, as in *Mignon*, he is primarily interested in the *action* produced by them and their impact on character rather than in elaborating upon facets of the abstract issues.

> David Madden in *The Thirties*, edited by Warren French (Everett Edwards). 1967. pp. 68–9

Though Cain writes out of the social and literary milieu that produced the deliberate attacks of the proletarian novelists, Cain never deals directly, as we have noted, with society's ills. While in several novels the relevance of Cain's characters to a larger social context is fairly intimate, his most effective social criticism emerges from his treatment of another interest—character portrayal, handled statically in the essays; dramatically, in the dialogues; narratively, in the novels. But, in all three genres, it is the dramatic thrust of characters in action that intrigues him; and they add up to an impressive gallery of American public types. . . .

While there seems to be no serious intention nor artistic conception at the heart of any of his sixteen novels, [Cain] does exhibit in his work a strange mingling of serious and of popular elements which he has made his own; and he has always, in his own way, been serious about craft. A writer of unfortunate faults, he is an interesting example of the author who often lets his journalistic temperament blur his creative field of vision. But, if his vision of life never becomes sharply focused, controlled, or conceptualized, it is obviously heightened and exaggerated to create effects that are often poetically compressed. While Cain seldom rises above certain commercial elements and never seems quite to step over the threshold into novelistic art, as it is normally conceived, his novels are valuable illustrations of the concept of the "pure" novel.

Certainly Cain's art, more than anything else, moves even the serious reader to almost complete emotional commitment to the traumatic experiences Cain renders; and this artistic control convinces me that without his finest novels—*The Postman* [*Always Rings Twice*], *Serenade*, *Mildred Pierce*, and *The Butterfly*—the cream of our twentieth-century fiction would be thinner. Straddling realism and expressionism, he often gives us a vivid account of life on the American scene as he has observed and experienced it; and, in his best moments, he provides the finer vibrations afforded by the esthetic experience. Cain the entertainer may fail to say anything truly important about life, but he takes us through experiences whose special quality is found in no other writer's work.

> David Madden. *James M. Cain* (Twayne, 1970), pp. 164, 175–76

In the Twain-Crane-Dreiser-Hemingway tradition, Cain successfully made the leap from journalism to fiction although he never abandoned magazine writing. Journalism not only provided him with some knowledge of a number of career fields but, more significantly for his craft, helped him achieve the compression, tautness and detached objectivity which, coupled with his sensational and brutal subject matter, characterize his writing and link him with other "tough guy" writers of the period. . . .

Cain's L.A. novels, drawing on this tradition, express the collective and destructive fantasies of the depression decade and turn these fantasies into nightmares. All of his heroes and heroines are self-destructively driven by sexual passion, a too-consuming love or an overpowering desire for material possessions. Such hunger is always the force driving them to desperate acts. Cain's pattern is to give his protagonists the temporary illusion of victory and then to take everything away from them. . . .

What defeats Cain's heroes . . . is not what defeats Fitzgerald's: the truth that the dream, once realized, can neither be preserved nor recaptured. For Cain the characters are defeated because their dreams are in direct conflict with those of others. Each character is yoked to, and set against, another—Frank and Cora, Mildred and Veda, Walter and Phyllis—and destroyed because the other is more ruthless, more clever or simply more determined. The pairs are suicidally tied to each other by passion, greed and jealousy. . . . There is never a chance they will get away with anything. . . .

For Cain, who arrived in Los Angeles soon after the Crash and remained through the Depression, the city came to represent the betrayed dreams of the whole nation. In the boom years hundreds of thousands had come seeking their fresh starts and new beginnings—a detached house, open space, mobility, good climate, renewed health and a piece of the wealth. The dream seemed within grasp. Fortunes, real and rumored, were being made in real estate, restaurants, oil and movies. Where the dream was most fervently believed and seemed closest to fulfillment, the collapse was more painful. Cain gave us a sense of what it was like to live, work and dream in Los Angeles in the thirties. His restless, driven and self-destructive heroes and heroines remind us of the hunger and the desperation that were a part of that not-so-distant past.

> David M. Fine. *American Studies*. Spring, 1979, pp. 27–29, 33–34

BIBLIOGRAPHY
Our Government, 1930 (sk); *The Postman Always Rings Twice*, 1934 (n); *Serenade*, 1937 (n); *Mildred Pierce*, 1941 (n); *Love's Lovely Counterfeit*, 1942 (n); *Three of a Kind (Career in C Major, The Embezzler, Double Indemnity)*, 1943 (n); *Past All Dishonor*, 1946 (n); *Butterfly*, 1947 (n); *The Moth*, 1948 (n); *Galatea*, 1953 (n); *Mignon*, 1962 (n); *The Magician's Wife*, 1965 (n); *Money and the Woman: The Embezzler*, 1968 (n); *The Institute*, 1976 (n); *Hard Cain*, 1980 (s); *The Baby in the Icebox*, 1981 (s); *Cloud Nine*, 1984 (n); *The Enchanted Isle*, 1985 (n); *60 Years of Journalism*, 1985 (j); *Sinful Woman*, 1988 (n); *Jealous Woman*, 1988 (n); *The Root of His Evil*, 1988 (n)

CALDWELL, Erskine (1903–1987)

It is as difficult for an outsider as it is for Mr. Caldwell to find in his work any systematic, even any conscious doctrine. He has not shaped himself by reasoning and he does not make up stories to prove abstract points. . . . (His stories) somehow sound as if they had been invented a long time ago and cherished in the popular memory, waiting for the hand of art if it should chance upon them. Mr. Caldwell, handling these matters, partly goes back to a manner at least a hundred years old. Again and again he brings to mind the native humorists before Mark Twain, when American humor had not yet been sweetened but was still dry, blunt, and broad. . . . It is in Mr. Caldwell's choice of heroes and in the boldness with which he speaks of their love and religion that he goes beyond any of the older humorists.

> Carl Van Doren. *The Nation*. Oct. 18, 1933. p. 444

I have denied that Caldwell is a realist. In his tomfoolery he comes closer to the Dadaists; when his grotesqueness is serious, he is a

Super-realist. We might compromise by calling him over all a Symbolist (if by Symbolist we mean a writer whose plots are more intelligible when interpreted as dreams). . . . I am not by any means satisfied by the psychoanalytic readings of such processes to date, though I do believe that in moralistic fantasies of the Caldwell type, where the dull characters become so strangely inspired at crucial moments, we are present at a poetic law court where judgements are passed upon kinds of transgression inaccessible to jurists, with such odd penalties as no *Code Napoléon* could ever schematize.

> Kenneth Burke. *New Republic*. April 10, 1935. p. 234

Mr. Caldwell is said to think of himself as a realist with a sociological message to deliver. If that message exists I fail to find it very clearly expressed in the present play (*Journeyman*). . . . But there is no point discussing what a work of art means or whether or not it is "true to life" unless one is convinced that the work "exists"—that it has the power to attract and hold attention, to create either that belief or that suspension of disbelief without which its "message" cannot be heard and without which its factual truth is of no importance. And to me the incontrovertible fact is that both Mr. Caldwell's novels and the plays made from them do in this sense "exist" with an uncommon solidarity, that his race of curiously depraved and curiously juicy human grotesques are alive in his plays whether or not they, or things like them, were ever alive anywhere else.

> Joseph Wood Krutch. *The Nation*. Feb. 12, 1938. p. 190

His intention . . . seems to be that of arousing sympathy for Southern tenant farmers, black and white. I believe this intention is good and that nothing effective will be done to correct the bad conditions now prevailing throughout the South until the sympathy of the nation is aroused. At the same time, I am convinced that sympathy is not enough. There must be some real understanding, and the ideas in people's minds must have some correspondence with actual conditions as they exist. If the picture of tenant farmers and of poor people in the South generally, as rendered in *God's Little Acre* and *Tobacco Road* are authentic, then there is little which can be done by landlord or tenant, by government or God, unless, of course, Mr. Caldwell's writings should so arouse the interest of the Deity that he would then proceed to make tenant, landlord, and land over again.

> W.T. Couch. *The Virginia Quarterly Review*. Spring, 1938. p. 309

The chief theme of Caldwell's writing is the agony of the impoverished land, which has now so nearly reached a state of complete exhaustion in large sections of the old South that it is only a matter of time (he thinks) when the dust storms will cross the Mississippi and extend the desert to the east. This is the material basis for the social conditions which he sets forth in his stories. But, of course, it is the people who interest him as a student of human nature; and with the people, it is not so much their material sufferings as the moral degradation which follows steadily on the decline of their material well-being. It is the illiteracy passed on from generation to generation of those who cannot find time to go to school or have not clothes to wear to school. . . . It is the shiftlessness and irresponsibility wrought by habitual want of hope.

Joseph Warren Beach. *American Fiction 1920–1940* (Macmillan). 1941. p. 223

Erskine Caldwell is two writers, both good of their kind, and one a sort of genius in his own narrow field. They collaborate on most of his books, but with conflicting aims; and the result is that reading some of his novels . . . is like a week-end visit to a bickering household. ''I am a social novelist,'' says the first Caldwell. . . . The second Caldwell does not talk about his aims, and in fact he isn't completely conscious of them; but sometimes, pushing his twin brother away from the typewriter, he begins pounding out impossible fancies and wild humor.

Malcolm Cowley. *New Republic*. Nov. 6, 1944. p. 599

Where Faulkner's supreme dimension is time, Caldwell's is space, and the whole quality of their art lies distinguished in these separate dimensions. Plot, being essentially a matter of space, becomes of necessity Caldwell's sphere of operations, and though his characters are seldom nuanced and the range of his emotions remains pretty narrow, he handles incident and action and spatial movement with a skill that holds the reader to attention. . . .

Yet the exigencies and narrowness of space landlock Caldwell's writing, and make it, despite its clearer and firmer outlines, more limited and less important than Faulkner's. It demonstrates that a mastery of plot linked to a cargo of social significance is not enough to establish a great reputation. Though Caldwell impresses his readers, he does not haunt them in the sense of lingering in their imaginations or compelling them to read him a second time.

Leo Gurko. *The Angry Decade* (Dodd). 1947. pp. 138–9

It's a shame that Erskine Caldwell in his new novel, *Claudelle Inglish* . . . is still imitating Caldwell in this, his thirty-eighth book. Since *Tobacco Road* (1932) he has written a series of vivid if uneven accounts of life and lust in the backwoods South. The South has not liked its picture as taken by the Georgia-born novelist.

But neither the South nor Mr. Caldwell can maintain the same indignation in the same form for twenty-seven years. As long ago as 1940 Clifton Fadiman suggested Caldwell was ''beginning to repeat himself,'' and the quality of repetition has ranged from pretty good to pretty bad. Lately it has been pretty bad. . . .

It is said Caldwell was bitter when Broadway received *Tobacco Road* as comedy, yet humor has always seasoned the raw taste of his plots and social commentary in an up-again, down-again career. Both are tried in the same way in *Claudelle Inglish* but the lesson is no longer about the South or a bad economic system. It is about the dullness of the same joke and the same cry of protest too often repeated in the same tone.

Doris Betts. *Saturday Review*. May 2, 1959. p. 25

Like most best selling authors, Erskine Caldwell tends to be patronized or ignored by academic critics and serious readers.

Many know of *Tobacco Road* and *God's Little Acre*, but tend to dismiss them as merely popular or salacious novels. Few seem to know the full range of the man's work: his text-picture documentaries, such as the remarkable *North of the Danube*; his charming books for children; his neglected *Georgia Boy*, a book that stands with Faulkner's last work as one of the finest novels of boyhood in American literature; and his short stories, some of which rank with the best of our time. A brief study cannot fully redress the indiscriminate neglect of readers and critics (nobody will argue that all Caldwell's works are valuable, or that all need to be considered at length); but I will indicate briefly the achievement of Erskine Caldwell, in an attempt not only to do justice to the writer, but to prevent if possible another disgrace in American letters: the sort of disgrace we visited on Melville, forgotten for years; the sort of disgrace we seem to be visiting on Phelps Putnam, Delmore Schwartz, and other good poets now almost entirely out of print, as well as on Glenway Wescott (who remembers that first novel, so highly praised by Ford Madox Ford?).

James Korges. *Erskine Caldwell* (Minnesota). 1969. p. 5

Caldwell's portrayal of Southern religion can be summed up . . . in the three themes of fatalism, poverty of ethic, and sexuality, but does Caldwell's account coincide with historical reality? In most of his work Caldwell can plead poetic license, but in *Deep South* he sheds the cloak of the novelist and becomes a combination of reporter, historian, and autobiographer. With surprising consistency, both in *Deep South* and in the fictional works, Caldwell captures the essence of Southern revivalistic religion. The latent sexuality which he brings to the surface has certainly been a feature of the Southern religious scene, especially of the more fervent brands of fundamentalism. Caldwell's emphasis on the ethical barrenness of Southern religion penetrates to the very heart of the South's religious difficulties. Finally, Caldwell ferrets out the curious Southern blend of John Wesley and John Calvin, of evangelicalism tinged with fatalism.

Caldwell's picture is, of course, partial. Southern life and Southern religion are far more complex than they appear in Caldwell's pages. But Caldwell makes no claim to the completeness of the historian. Rather, he fictionalizes important features of the Southern religious scene, and in so doing creates a fictional religious world which, in its approximation to reality, furnishes an invaluable aid to the historian of the South. . . .

James J. Thompson, Jr. *Southern Humanities Review*. Winter, 1971. p. 43

When all is said and done, how significant a writer is Caldwell? The critical consensus, as of 1979, was that he is an interesting, but unquestionably minor figure, whose work never fulfilled his early promise. And yet, as we have seen, this consensus is largely a result of a consistent failure on the part of Caldwell commentators to deal with Caldwell on his own terms. Of course, even the most careful attention to the ways in which Caldwell's aesthetic functions in his work does not negate the fact that this work has limitations, some of which are a direct result of the aesthetic itself. For one thing, there are certain kinds of reading pleasure Caldwell does not provide, even at his best. The enjoyment of re-reading a story or novel, carefully exploring its subtleties until its full implications are apparent—an enjoyment Faulkner, Hemingway, Bellow, and so many of the most respected contemporary writers give us again and again—is almost entirely absent from the experience of reading Caldwell. By and large, rereading a Caldwell story or novel not only fails to uncover subtleties missed the first time through, it eliminates the suspense originally generated by our curiosity about what the characters might do next. To put it another way, once we've finished a Caldwell story, it ceases to be "fiction"—at least according to Caldwell's definition—and becomes memory. Secondly, since Caldwell's fiction is centered entirely on his characters' statements and actions, we do not experience the exploration of fictional forms which makes Stein or Faulkner enjoyable volume after volume. Third, no matter how many of Caldwell's books we read, we do not grow aware—as we do, say, in Eliot or Hardy or Steinbeck—of a World View, a model against which we can measure our interpretations of our own experience. . . .

In the final analysis, Caldwell has as much to offer us—despite his perfectly obvious "limitations"—as any other first-rate modern writer. Working within an unusual but cogent definition of fiction, he has created dozens of interesting stories characterized by a courageous willingness to be honest about the mysterious complexities of human lives and by a determination to communicate the fruits of his intensive observation in a form which is clear enough, direct enough, and powerful enough to be read, understood and vividly remembered for years by both trained literary critics and lay readers . . . I believe [Caldwell] . . . is a great writer, and he may be the most refreshingly unpretentious great writer we've ever had.

Scott MacDonald. In *Critical Essays on Erskine Caldwell*, ed. Scott MacDonald (G.K. Hall, 1981), pp. xxix, xxxi–xxxii

Any final assessment of Caldwell's contribution to the documentary genre in America must rest on the work he did in the 1930s, when he developed the techniques that have served him throughout his literary career. He recognized from the outset that documentary truth has more kinship with the authenticity of fiction than with scientific poll-taking and therefore never assumed a factitious air of disinterestedness about the material he recorded. Documentary and nonfiction writing has always been for Caldwell partisan, personal and highly selective; his imagination has played as vital a part in it as his conscience and observation. Yet there are clear stylistic and ideological distinctions between Caldwell's fiction and nonfiction. Despite the obvious inventive quality of much of his reporting which has led several of his critics to label it fiction, Caldwell maintains a separate persona, vocabulary, technique and even point of view in his nonfiction. While the fiction is almost consistently notable for the author's disengaged stance from the "antics and motivations" of the characters, the nonfiction permits an intrusive author, calling attention to his presence, his awkwardness, his anger and his sympathy. The more sophisticated vocabulary of the nonfiction reveals to what extent the ingenuous style of the fiction is a consciously contrived technique, while the tendency to separate comedy from degradation in the nonfiction suggests a different ideological purpose—reform rather than despair for the victims of economic and racial exploitation. While the underlying vision of human nature and society, especially as symbolically manifested in the South, is consistent in all his work, it is in the nonfiction that the intensity of Caldwell's moral purpose is most evident; by developing a carefully wrought, inventive literary method for his documentary reporting, he has succeeded in his best works, in negating the conventional distinction between effective propaganda and genuine aesthetic merit.

Sylvia Jenkins Cook. In *Critical Essays on Erskine Caldwell*, ed. Scott MacDonald (G.K. Hall, 1981), pp. 390–91

Unsustained by the adrenaline of his early public sensation, the literary vitality of Erskine Caldwell now depends on just two works, *Tobacco Road* (1932) and *God's Little Acre* (1933), the only major titles among his almost sixty books available in the paperback format necessary for classroom study and the limited immortality that it confers. To that short list I would add, at a minimum, the story cycle *Georgia Boy* (1943), currently out of print. The case for this recommendation may be expressed syllogistically. First, in order best to judge a writer's achievement, we must include a judgment of his work at its finest. Second, both Caldwell and a quorum of commentators have cited his stories as his best work and the *Georgia Boy* collection as the apex of his achievement in the form. Therefore, for our own enrichment and in fairness to Caldwell, we need to resurrect *Georgia Boy* for the extended reconsideration it deserves.

Although some critics have dismissed *Georgia Boy* as flawed and trivial, the book's structural integrity and the thematic depth should rank it with another major American story cycle, Sherwood Anderson's *Winesburg, Ohio*. Far from being a loosely articulated constellation of simple stories, *Georgia Boy* is unified by contrapuntal characterization and a related animal motif, by dialogue refrains, by a complexly comic tone calling for varied reader responses, and by the twofold theme of coming of age in the South and the South's coming of age—a theme developed through a deceptively naive narrative perspective that requires our careful examination of the title itself. . . .

When Erskine Caldwell told an interviewer in 1986 that the stories here are "not in any way autobiographical," he almost certainly meant only that the specific incidents are fabrications and that his own stable parents had not stood as models for the elder Stroups. In 1983, however, Caldwell left no doubt that his personal experience of boyhood had been the inspiration for this book. After citing *Georgia Boy* as a favorite work, he described it as follows: "This was a whole series of short stories I wrote as the result of looking back at my early life and a playmate who happened to be a black boy. . . . That was a sort of landmark [for me] as far as writing was concerned, because I wrote it purely for the fact that I wanted to go back and think about my early life." Thus, even if *Georgia Boy* is not personal history, it is a kind of spiritual autobiography—the more significant of the two because that is the material of mythology, which we value above the historical record.

Not since before the revival of academic interest in Erskine Caldwell's writings over the last decade has *Georgia Boy* been available in a paperback edition. For classroom study, the book, in effect, does not exist. . . . Certainly, there are other works by Caldwell that deserve to be brought back. The novels *Journeyman* (1935), *Trouble in July* (1940), and *Tragic Ground* (1944) all have champions; and many voices have praised his early stories. The combinative advantages of the story-cycle form, however, set *Georgia Boy* apart from, and arguably above, these other works. It is distinguished, moreover, by a complex structural and stylistic weave and by the many variations on its major theme played by an instrumental narrator whose personal simplicity is the book's greatest sophistication. For these reasons and others, if I had to

choose just a single Caldwell work for regeneration, I would
unhesitatingly select the too-long neglected *Georgia Boy*.

Ronald Wesley Hoag. In Edwin T. Arnold, ed. *Erskine
Caldwell Reconsidered* (Jackson: Univ. Pr. of Mississippi,
1990), pp. 73, 83– 84

[T]o write Caldwell off as a second-rate pornographer, a facile
humorist, or an outdated proletarian is to make a judgment on a
body of work whose most essential quality is its defiance of any
such conventional terms of assessment—of literary categories,
schools of thought, and ethical and aesthetic labels. When French
critics asserted that ''no one is more American than Erskine
Caldwell,'' they referred not merely to the hard-boiled style and
brutal pessimism associated with American naturalists, but to
Caldwell's affinity for the macabre, the irrational, and the subversive that undermined all certainty about the nature of his fiction,
tingeing tragedy with farce and comedy with horror. His work thus
resists coherent schemes of interpretation, a situation that Caldwell
appeared to exacerbate by his continual mocking disparagement of
the pursuit of criticism and by his efforts throughout his life to
present a simplified and contradictory public image of himself, in
interviews and autobiographies, that effectively kept the riddle of
his literary world intact. . . .

By the end of Caldwell's long life, in 1987, he had passed
through notoriety, fame, neglect, and even, eventually, a certain
amount of honorific ceremony. From Poland he received the Order
of Cultural Merit; France made him Commander of the Order of
Arts and Letters. In Japan, he was honored at a banquet given by the
Erskine Caldwell Literary Society; and at home, finally, he was
made a member of the American Academy of Arts and Letters.
There was also a modest revival of scholarly and critical interest in
Caldwell's work, although it still remains largely omitted from the
classroom anthologies that mark successful admission into the
great tradition of American literature, despite his remarkable skill
in producing dozens of short stories that seem eminently suitable
for such selection. By being ''particularly American,'' Caldwell
had proved perhaps too crafty and recalcitrant to be satisfactorily
assimilated and classified.

This exclusion of Caldwell means, however, the loss of a unique
and audacious voice that explored aspects of life hitherto rarely
approached in American literature. He exposed the depravity of
poor people's lives with the venom of a naturalist and then held
them up to moral irony and incongruous humor. He noted laconi-
cally the search for spiritual transcendence in his fellow mortals
and the frenzied sexual channels into which it was so often
diverted. He observed the powerful instinct of human sexuality and
saw how readily it might be bartered or exploited for money,
transformed into obsessions, or confused into foolish whims. He
portrayed individuals as variously irrational, foolish, and vicious,
but he attacked fiercely a social system that exposed them to
hunger, disease, and persecution. He envisioned an absurd world,
but always insisted that not all of its cruel manifestations were
beyond cure. He did this in a style that seemed so simple as
continually to risk banality, for only in such a context could his
startling dissonances and incongruous juxtapositions have their full
impact. He was a powerful imagist and a wildly inventive creator of
character and incident. If the greatest successes of his career in
short stories, novels, and nonfiction were concentrated largely in
the twelve years between the publication of *American Earth* in

1931 and *Georgia Boy* in 1943, his earlier preparation for them was
enlightening; and his later work, especially in the 1960s, was often
intriguing. Many of these later novels about women and blacks
were written well in advance of, and often well beyond the realm
of, the verities of current feminist and civil rights thinking; but
verities and certainties were never Caldwell's mode, even in his
most dedicated proletarian period, unless mixed with more disconcerting and oblique attitudes. . . .

Though in his later work Caldwell lost the stimulus of the
intellectual context of the Great Depression and tried rather unsuccessfully to broaden his fictional realm, in his major work of the
1930s and 1940s he created a dissonant and defiant literary vision
of poverty and social powerlessness. He simultaneously invoked
naturalistic theories and undermined them; he was disconcertingly
simple in his narration yet complex in his meaning; he relished
vulgarity and reviled the circumstances it was forced to dwell in;
and his fiction finally refused, much like the poor themselves, to
accommodate itself to any comfortable category, either aesthetic
or political.

Sylvia Jenkins Cook. *Erskine Caldwell and the Fiction of
Poverty* (Baton Rouge: Louisiana State Univ. Pr., 1991),
pp. 2, 4–5, 284

In 1946, William Faulkner named Erskine Caldwell as one of
America's five greatest novelists. This was not considered an
unusual comment. With the publication of *Tobacco Road* in 1932
and *God's Little Acre* in 1933, Caldwell attracted a following of
distinguished literary critics. Malcolm Cowley was only one of
many who ranked him alongside F. Scott Fitzgerald, Faulkner, and
Thomas Wolfe. Cowley later wrote that Caldwell ''had a greater
natural talent for telling stories than anyone else in his generation.''
. . . Many critics shared the opinion of the *Baltimore Sun* reviewer
who felt that Caldwell had surpassed both Faulkner and Wolfe in
his depictions of Southern life. Across America, universities offered seminars on his fiction, and eager doctoral candidates analyzed every aspect of his thought. As late as 1960, Caldwell was
under serious consideration for the Nobel Prize in literature. . . .

Caldwell's writing would always draw the loudest cry from
those who found his work obscene or pornographic. Outraged
citizens picketed theaters that dared show his plays, and high-
minded city councilmen found political capital in banning his
books. Boston's ''Committee for Decency'' targeted Erskine Caldwell as America's ''chief purveyor of filth.'' When *God's Little
Acre* was seized from bookstore shelves in New York and declared
''obscene'' by the New York Society for the Suppression of Vice,
Caldwell took his complaint to the state Supreme Court. With the
help of testimony from such literary lions as H. L. Mencken and
Sherwood Anderson, he was acquitted, and his case became a
landmark on First Amendment litigation. . . .

Today, Erskine Caldwell is virtually forgotten by scholars and
popular readers alike, and he surely represents one of the greatest
disappearing acts in our literary history. To date, there is no full-
scale biography of Caldwell in print, and until now, no fiction that
so impressed the literary scholars of his day. Sylvia Cook's *Erskine
Caldwell and the Fiction of Poverty* represents not only a renewal
of interest in this all but disregarded artist but, happily, a sophisticated and intelligent starting point for meaningful, contemporary
debate on his work.

Part of Caldwell's critical decline resulted from the sheer volume of poor writing he did, both before and after his valuable contributions of the 1930s and early 1940s. Reading this immense body of work—over one hundred short stories, thirty novels, and twelve books of nonfiction—is a massive undertaking, and to Cook's great credit, she has mined from this enormous corpus valuable insights into Caldwell's creative vocabulary.

Dan B. Miller. *Southern Literary Journal*. Spring, 1993, pp. 112–14

BIBLIOGRAPHY
The Bastard, 1930 (n); *Poor Fool*, 1930 (n); *In Defense of Myself*, 1930 (e); *American Earth*, 1931 (s); *Tobacco Road*, 1932 (n); *Mama's Little Girl*, 1932 (s); *God's Little Acre*, 1933 (n); *We Are the Living*, 1933 (s); *A Message for Genevieve*, 1933 (s); *Journeyman*, 1935 (n); *Kneel to the Rising Sun*, 1935 (s); *Some American People*, 1935 (e); *Tenant Farmer*, 1935 (e); *The Sacrilege of Alan Kent*, 1936 (s); (with Margaret Bourke-White) *You Have Seen Their Faces*, 1937 (e); *Southways*, 1938 (s); (with Margaret Bourke-White) *North of the Danube*, 1939 (t); *Trouble in July*, 1940 (n); *Jackpot*, 1940 (s); *Say! Is This the U.S.A.?* 1941 (t); *All-Out on the Road to Smolensk*, 1942 (j); *All Night Long*, 1942 (n); *Georgia Boy*, 1943 (n); *Tragic Ground*, 1944 (n); *Stories*, 1944; *A House in the Uplands*, 1946 (n); *The Sure Hand of God*, 1947 (n); *This Very Earth*, 1948 (n); *Place Called Estherville*, 1949 (n); *Episode in Palmetto*, 1950 (n); *Call It Experience*, 1951 (a); *The Humorous Side of Erskine Caldwell*, (selections), 1951; *The Courting of Susie Brown*, 1952 (s); *A Lamp for Nightfall*, 1952 (n); *Complete Stories*, 1953; *Love and Money*, 1954 (n); *Claudelle*, 1955 (n) (American edition, *Claudelle Inglish*, 1957); *Gretta*, 1956 (n); *Gulf Coast Stories*, 1956 (s); *Certain Women*, 1957 (n); *When You Think of Me*, 1959 (s); *Jenny by Nature*, 1961 (n); *Men and Women* (selected stories), 1961; *Close to Home*, 1962 (n); *The Last Night of Summer*, 1963 (n); *Around about America*, 1964 (t); *In Search of Bisco*, 1965 (e); *The Deer at Our House*, 1966; *In the Shadow of the Steeple*, 1967 (n); *Miss Mamma Aimee*, 1967 (n); *Summertime Island*, 1968 (n); *Deep South*, 1968 (m); *The Weather Shelter*, 1969 (n); *The Earnshaw Neighborhood*, 1971 (n); *Annette*, 1973 (n); *Afternoons in Mid-America*, 1976 (e, t); *The Black & White Stories of Erskine Caldwell*, 1984; *With All My Might: An Autobiography*, 1987; *Conversations*, 1988 (r, i.e., interviews); *Midsummer Passion & Other Tales of Maine Cussedness*, 1990 (s); *Call It Experience: The Years of Learning How to Write*, 1996 (r); *The Stories of Erskine Caldwell*, 1996; *Men and Women*, 1998 (n)

CALISHER, Hortense (1911–)

[*False Entry* is] the work of a writer who knows what she wants to do and how she wants to do it. The style, at least at first, seems rather mannered, and indeed it is involved and allusive, but the further one goes, the more one recognizes how beautifully it suits her purpose. . . .

Identity is not given us; it is something that we either do or do not achieve. That Miss Calisher can take this familiar truth and

make of it something fresh and exciting is proof of her deep insight and her mastery of a most difficult method. Despite her unconventional method of telling her story, Miss Calisher knows how to make use of the traditional arts of the novelist. . . . If her aim is to explore deeply the mysteries of a particular person, she is able to bring minor characters on the stage in such a way that we can see them clearly. The novel rewards the closest possible reading, but it can give a more casual kind of pleasure, too.

Granville Hicks. *Saturday Review*. Oct. 28, 1961. p. 17

Hortense Calisher's second novel [*Textures of Life*] attempts, and pretty well pulls off, something of a *Golden Bowl*. This one could not be symbolised by the extravagant *objet d'art*, with its bizarre flaw, conceived by James. Miss Calisher's material is the American bourgeoisie at home, and the textures of the lives she interweaves are homely. Here is a Golden Bowl in, so to speak, basketwork. But the working is Jamesian indeed in firmness of structure and subtlety of superstructure. Sometimes she uses the master's very idiom—not in pastiche but as legitimately and creatively as Tiepolo used Veronese's. . . .

In James's nexus the Prince is admittedly not up to the other three. Yet it is not simply as a weak character that he lets the dance down. Weak characters can be boldly portrayed; but James is too relenting towards the Prince to make him a Vronsky or a George Osborne; the weakness lies not only in the Prince but in James—where it is perhaps a weakness for Italian young men, or just for princes. Miss Calisher's construction has a comparable flaw, and again in the younger generation. *Jeune premier* parts are always the hardest to do. Her David may not properly exist—there is little to him but a trick of letting his glasses slide down his nose—but he is waved into being by adroit sleight of hand. It is Elizabeth, reacting against her mother's "taste," bohemianly disregarding material objects except such as she herself, as a sculptor, makes, in whom one suspects a lightweightness of character and a college-girl pretentiousness of intellect—which the author seems not to realise. With the older couple Miss Calisher can do no wrong. The vivid, invalid's life of David's father, the vaguer but penetrating vision of Elizabeth's mother—she splendidly creates both and superbly counter-poises them. Miss Calisher is not only that rarity, a talented novelist, but that double-blossomed rarity, a talented novelist who is serious about art.

Brigid Brophy. *New Statesman*. Sept. 13, 1963. p. 326

Hortense Calisher's *Extreme Magic*, a novella and a number of short stories, is a collection remarkable for uneven achievement. The sensibility is extremely feminine—in the faintly pejorative sense—and the talent diaphanous. . . . The writing is sometimes skillfully evocative, the nuances suggestive, the imagery just; but then there are ornaments (many of them) as trashy as "the river gave a little shantung wrinkle." . . . But there are two stories, "The Rabbi's Daughter" and "The Gulf Between," that are harmoniously true and moving—even substantial—because they rise from authentic experience: in this case cultivated, haute-bourgeois, upper-West-Side Jewish life, a little down on its uppers. Miss Calisher has a real sense of a past . . . she can show where things come from; what people really are; how they feel; how they affect one another; why what happens happens.

Eve Auchincloss. *New York Review of Books*. June 25, 1964. p. 17

[In *Journal from Ellipsia*] Hortense Calisher expends a great many words on a sophisticated science-fiction theme, and these words are not cleanly bolted into clear but complex structures so much as—as though they were all made of some colloidal substance— allowed to stick into great lumps, like long-forgotten sweets shaken out of a paper bag. Admittedly her literary problem is the representation of communion between two worlds—one here, one *out there*—and the effect of cotton wool coming out of, or being stuffed into, desperately communicating mouths may be regarded, by some readers, as appropriate. But the book, besides being very long, is very hard to read, and one wonders whether it was all worth it. What happens in *Journal from Ellipsia* is this: an androgynous creature from beyond tries to break through into this world; it contacts Janice, a beautiful anthropologist, who now wants to break out of this world into the one beyond. Her story is told, as it were, posthumously—the unearthly talking machine, the top arguing scientists, the throwing of the ball of narration to different players (including the one from out there). There are British characters, and they tend to speak in what I call the toodle-pip idiom, an American invention. This, in a book about intergalactic communication, makes everything said seem more implausible than it ought to.

Anthony Burgess. *The Listener*. April 21, 1966. p. 589

The New Yorkers is a miraculous novel in that it is exactly equal to its ambition. For the first fifty or even hundred pages its ambition is hidden or apparently denied. You think you are reading a futility— another perhaps wise but old-style novel "rich in texture," "closely worked," patient beyond easy disclosure, afflicted with the paradox of a choking capaciousness. Then begins the extraordinary glimmer of Design, and very rapidly there is evidence of something new—newly against the grain of expectation.

The miracle is not in the language, which, though controlled and self-aware, is occasionally formally florid, like porcelain. Sentence by sentence it does not always distinguish itself. Yet the method of its obliqueness. its internal allusions, echoes, and murmurings, all this is uncommonly cunning and thick with the ingenuities of discovery. The miracle is nevertheless not in the language but in the incredible spite—everything is spited, from literary fashion straight up to the existentially perceived cosmos. If the anti-novel can be defined in part as spiting expectations, then Calisher's concept of it belongs with Nabokov's. Like other "New" novels. *The New Yorkers* is also about itself—which is to say it aspires to fool, to lead, to play tricks with its own substance. But unlike others, especially unlike the most intelligent—for what is more intelligent than a novel by, say, Susan Sontag?—Calisher's novel is *about* intelligence. Or, better yet, Intelligence.

Cynthia Ozick. *Midstream*. Nov., 1969. p. 77

Hortense Calisher . . . is one of our most substantial yet elusive writers. By any narrow or literal definition, she is becoming less

and less a strictly narrative artist. Her characters are boundless states of mind. Nor does she structure books conventionally: *Queenie* doesn't move; it spins, pausing for scenes, pausing for ideas. Mrs. Calisher appears also to borrow imaginatively from the other arts, giving the reader the feel of the dance, of the mobile, of sculpture. In *Queenie*, probably the most light-hearted of her novels, she has made a tripping entry into the mind of a present-day young girl, and has with wit and spirit fashioned a kind of ballet around the story of Queenie's coming of sexual and intellectual age.

The story unwinds in the form of tapes addressed to various "interlocutors," including the admissions dean of "Hencoop College" in New York. God, a Hencoop professor in whom for a time Queenie reposes some faith, and finally the President of the United States. . . .

The book overflows with ideas, couched in sparkling aphorisms. Touching on the generation gap, the sexual gap, the abysmal political gap, the communication gap. As the device of the tapes suggests, the story is, among other things, about someone who wants to have a good talk with *Someone*.

Lucy Rosenthal. *Saturday Review*. April 3, 1971. p. 34

Like any good writer, Hortense Calisher keeps a reader on the move. She has a "style," though it worries her when people say that, because for some it implies surface, a glib veneer with nothing beneath it. But she needn't worry. Her intelligence shows without aid of italics and block capitals. To be "carried away" is not in her case to be swept off into rhetorical clouds of Chestertonian pomp, but to be led on by the imagination into fresh perception, awe and an occasional all-out celebration. . . .

Hortense Calisher is a creator of voices, moods, states of mind, but not of worlds. Her fiction, like her autobiography [*Herself*], sends us back into the world we know; it may refresh and enhance it, but it does not, even for a moment, obliterate or remake it. This is not to say that she is, in some old-fashioned sense, a realist. On the contrary, rather than fabricating reasonable facsimiles of "things as they are," she takes certain "scenes" for granted and lets her quick wit and marvelous imagination play over them. If we know a bit about the scenes she selects, we're likely to find her works beautifully agile and astute. If not, she is not about to hammer the parts together for us.

Robert Kiely. *New York Times Book Section*. Oct. 1, 1972. pp. 3, 20

Calisher is a shrewd observer of our social ills—displacements of youth, futilities of the rich—but she is more than a naturalist noting easy details, cataloging crimes or sins. She is a maker of fictions; she insists on private consciousness—even when this consciousness is extreme, obsessive, and "poetic". [*Eagle Eye*] is a powerful indictment of social wrongs by an odd hero who may see less (or more) than he believes. . . . Calisher stuns us with the "magic forbidden leaps" of her imagination. She forces us to enter—and withdraw from—her narrator's mind; she offers few clues to his ultimate condition. But by testing us with her sharp vision she emerges here as a true creator—an eagle of fiction-makers.

Irving Malin. *New Republic*. Nov. 3, 1973. p. 26

In this novella [*The Man Who Spat Silver*], we are dealing with a private event. The probing of this woman's inner space is achieved with intelligence and original imagery. It is a story that will have appeal to intellectual puzzle solvers. At times the writer's penchant for playing with words and form become self-conscious. The split personality, the bizarre dreams, the hallucinatory details of the mythical figure are the stuff of literary techniques used widely today, and [Hortense] Calisher is following in the footsteps of her personal and her generation's manners and fondness for peculiar techniques. In her novella some of the techniques begrudge the revelation of their mysteries as well as clarify the issues. The reader must work hard to carve a path through the mysteries. The rewards of the effort are what may be called illuminated mystery.

Lee Mhatre. *Confrontation*. Fall, 1989, p. 86

Hortense Calisher, known primarily as a "writer's writer," has been turning out works of serious fiction for over forty years. Her eleven novels, six collections of short stories and novellas, and two autobiographical works have been consistently, sometimes lengthily, reviewed. . . . But despite her reputation as a significant voice in American fiction she has received neither popular acclaim nor, excepting two doctoral dissertations, in-depth critical analyses. The absence of the first is understandable enough: Calisher's dense and quirky fictions are not the stuff of which bestsellers are made. Reasons for the critical silence are less easy to come by. One possibility lies in the resistance of her works to easy categorization: she is not, in any narrow sense, a woman's writer, a Jewish writer, or a New York writer. She is, however, a writer known for her distinctive, even idiosyncratic, style. Especially when surveying Calisher's career, reviewers single out her style—usually summed as "convoluted," "elliptical," or "Jamesian"—as the one constant. They rarely situate a new novel within Calisher's canon, let alone the context of contemporary fiction. As a result, each new work seems, notwithstanding its stylistic signature, sui generis.

It is certainly true, as a number of her reviewers have remarked, that Calisher's subject matter covers a vast range of territory. Yet however varied the novels' imaginative worlds, a thematic continuity exists that, for too long, has gone unnoticed. It was not until a 1987 *Paris Review* interview that Calisher, recalling the unique physical sensation of her childhood's trolley rides, referred to that theme's presence in her fiction. . . .

For the next forty years Calisher has spun out variations on that theme: her protagonists may yearn for if not the true place then at least a firmly manageable one in which to stay put, but by novel's end or novella's end, they come out into a world that promises not a safe place, but an open-ended journey. That reviewers have failed to grasp that theme's all-pervasiveness—the thematic centrality of, simultaneously, rites of passage and of extradition—only underscores her achievement. That they have failed to see that style is not something imposed on subject matter, but, rather, the perfect vehicle for and embodiment of her life's theme, has resulted in an unfortunate stereotyping of Calisher the consummate stylist.

Calisher's impressive range, the variousness of story, character, and structure, have vitalized a theme which, by nature of its very universality, could easily have conjured up cliché upon cliché. . . .

Calisher has always savored contradictions and dualities. Hester Elkin of the autobiographical stories is the first of many protagonists to experience the necessarily painful pull between mutually

exclusive ways of being in the world. . . . To be in-between is to be in motion and, thus, fully alive, capable of changes in direction.

On one level, Calisher's own sense of in-betweenness is reflected in her character's names. . . .

On the one hand, Calisher seems bent on explaining and encompassing the self and the world in elegantly attenuated sentences reminiscent of James, Hugo, the Bible. On the other hand, equally representative sentence fragments bespeak a resolutely modern consciousness that is always (literally, it would seem) brought up short by the impossibility of ever really articulating and communicating experience. . . .

The "outdoors-indoors blend" that Calisher has known and savored since childhood, from an early awareness of her household's encompassing eras and temperaments, may, in part, explain why it is so difficult to securely "place" her in a literary context. Her subjects—but not her themes—reflect the times she lives in. Her style may straddle eras and genres, yet her voice is distinctly her own.

Kathleen Snodgrass. *The Fiction of Hortense Calisher* (Newark: Univ. of Delaware Pr., 1993), pp. 11–12, 116–17

What does the novelist of manners do in a world without privacy, without secrets, in which it seems that anything can be said anywhere? What happens to a writer with a mastery of nuance, a fine attentiveness to the things not said, to her characters' unvoiced knowledge of one another's knowledge? For it's a mastery that seems to have no place in our age of televised confessionals.

Nevertheless it's appropriate to the landscape of Hortense Calisher's twenty-first book and nineteenth volume of fiction. The movie king of her title [*In the Palace of the Movie King*] is Paul Gonchev, born in Vladivostok, reared in Kyoto, who has chosen, however improbably, to base his career in Albania. Gonchev makes exquisite pseudodocumentaries about great cities for a country that has shut the door on the outside world. . . .

The best parts of *In the Palace of the Movie King* show how a psychology born of a leisured world in which private life seemed all can be used to register a society in which it seems to count for nothing. Or rather one where the very power of the state gives privacy a value it may no longer have for us. . . .

There are some fine scenes throughout: the opening, the Albanian chapters, and late in the novel an extraordinary account of a California earthquake. Yet too often the details she picks to document America's national mood just don't fit. . . .

In the Palace of the Movie King is a kind of love song to an ever-changing America, where to be an exile, both free of and weighted down by one's past, is the national fate. One wants to like Ms. Calisher's latest novel, but its very contemporaneity makes it seem quite oddly out of touch.

Michael Gorra. *New York Times Book Review*. February 20, 1994, p. 12

BIBLIOGRAPHY
In the Absence of Angels, 1951 (s); *False Entry*, 1961 (n); *Tale for the Mirror*, 1962 (s); *Textures of Life*, 1963 (n); *Extreme Magic*, 1964 (s); *Journal from Ellipsia*, 1965 (n); *The Railroad Police, and The Last Trolley Ride*, 1966 (s); *The New Yorkers*, 1969 (n); *Queenie*, 1971 (n); *Herself*, 1972 (a); *Standard Dreaming*, 1972

(n); *Eagle Eye*, 1973 (n); *The Collected Stories*, 1975; *On Keeping Women*, 1977 (n); *Mysteries of Motion*, 1983 (n); *Saratoga, Hot*, 1985 (n); *The Bobby Soxer*, 1986 (n); *Age*, 1987 (n); *Kissing Cousins*, 1988 (a); *The Man Who Spat Silver*, 1989 (novella); *In the Palace of the Movie King*, 1993 (n); *In the Slammer with Carol Smith*, 1997 (n); *The Novellas of Hortense Calisher*, 1997 (coll)

ETHAN CANIN (1960–)

It is far harder to compress plot, character, and atmosphere into a compact order than to sprawl over a novel's length. That is the rare talent of a good short story writer. It is all the more remarkable that Ethan Canin has managed to write four short stories [in *The Palace Thief*] that are a pleasure to read the first time around and in two instances are worthy of anthologizing so that they can be reread for years to come.

The narrators in [two of the stories] "The Accountant" and "The Palace Thief" are riveting in their quiet ways because they have the fascination of dormant volcanos that erupt without warning and then return to their quiescent state. The transcending value of these two stories is not the unexpected revolt by these characters against their lifelong passivity but their reaction to and rumination on their distinct moment of rebellion. Above all, it is the characters' own surprise and the subsequent struggle to reconcile their lives, their values, and their concept of themselves with their singular eruption out of the pattern of conformity and restraint. As they subside again into passivity, their inability to comprehend what led them to act and their complementary inability to understand what they know with certainty, that they will never rebel again, binds the reader to them. It is the nearly universal human ability to glimpse but never fully to command one's destiny. As the accountant reflects, "I suppose I was wondering, although it is strange for me to admit it, why, of all the lives that might have been mine, I have led the one I just described."

Of all the lives that Ethan Canin may lead, let us hope he chooses to lead the life of a writer.

Barbara Milbauer. *Confrontation*. Fall, 1994–Winter, 1995, pp. 341–42

BIBLIOGRAPHY
Emperor of the Air, 1988 (s); *Blue River*, 1991 (n); *The Palace Thief*, 1994 (s)

CAPOTE, Truman (1924–1984)

Other Voices, Other Rooms abundantly justifies the critics and readers who first hailed Capote as a writer of exceptional gifts. . . . Capote's sensibility is as notable as his insight, and its range is impressive, for it enables him to describe elements of physical environment that would be scarcely perceptible to most of us; yet these elements, however unnoticed, are recognized by the reader as authentic, and indisputably present. But although his descriptive writing is masterly, it is his ability to create and interpret character—to increase both the scope and depth of our understanding of ourselves and others—that yields the major excellences of *Other Voices, Other Rooms*. . . . It is not only a work of unusual beauty, but a work of unusual intelligence. In it, readers will establish contact with one of the most accomplished American novelists to make his debut in many a season.

Lloyd Morris. *New York Herald Tribune Book Section*. Jan. 16, 1948. p. 2

Even if Mr. Capote were ten or twenty years older than he is, his ability to bend language to his poetic moods, his ear for dialect and for the varied rhythms of speech would be remarkable. In one so young this much writing skill represents a kind of genius. On the other hand, I find myself deeply antipathetic to the whole artistic-moral purpose of Mr. Capote's novel. . . . For it seems to me to create a world of passive acceptance in which we are rendered incapable of thinking anybody responsible for his behavior in any department.

Diana Trilling. *The Nation*. Jan. 31, 1948. pp. 133–4

Other Voices, Other Rooms is easily the most exciting novel to come from America this year. Though one of its chief characters is what is customarily referred to by reviewers as "decadent," both he and the rest of the characters in this emotional story of the South make the average character in contemporary American fiction seem perverted by comparison. For the only moral standard that literature knows is the truth, and it is truthful intensity of Mr. Capote's book that makes it so remarkable. . . . He has dared to write of life in all its complex splendor and to tell of the human heart, and yet he has triumphed without sinking into romanticism or departing from any of the desired standards of taste and maturity. . . . But what ensures its success is the quality of Mr. Capote's writing, which is very high indeed, and original without being exhibitionist or obscure.

Robert Kee. *Spectator*. Nov. 19, 1948. pp. 674–6

If the Mad Hatter and the Ugly Duchess had had a child, and the child had almost grown up, these are almost the kind of short stories he could be expected to write. . . . Who wants, really, to crawl back into the twilit cave and roll the papier-mâché stone over the doorway? Who would want to let Alice's wonderland serve as the myth around which he organized his adult life? . . . With these reservations, however, one must fairly assert for these stories a kind of triple power: a mind at times disciplined toward poetry, with a special skill at naming; a pleasant and only slightly grotesque humor, and an ability to suggest, as in the novel, the outlines of haunted personalities.

Carlos Baker. *New York Times Book Section*. Feb. 27, 1949. p. 7

As a teller of tales he has a peculiar and remarkable talent. . . . In his hands the fairy tale and ghost story manage to assimilate the attitudes of twentieth-century psychology without losing their integrity, without demanding to be accepted as mere fantasy or explained as mere symbol. . . . In Capote's stories the fairy world, more serious than business or love, is forever closing in upon the skeptical secure world of grown-ups.

> Leslie A. Fiedler. *The Nation*. April 2, 1949. pp. 395–6

Mr. Capote's second novel, *The Grass Harp*, remains within the extreme limits of what we call Gothic, but it is a sunlit Gothic, an aberrant form with a personality, an agreeable personality, entirely its own. . . . Mr. Capote keeps his story beautifully under control. His story has elements of allegory, it expounds a rather simple, basic statement concerning the nature of love. . . . In the beginning of the novel one does catch whiffs of the well-known Southern decay, but the book is not concerned with morbidity. It is a light, skilful, delightful story.

> Oliver La Farge. *Saturday Review*. Oct. 20, 1951. pp. 19–20

One thing about Truman Capote . . . that one notices right off is that he looks a little like a toy. That's what some people *say*, anyway. If he is a toy, he nevertheless has a mind that would turn those big thinking cybernetic machines green with envy. As a matter of fact, his mind has enough good steel in it to turn too many human beings the same violent color—and it has, no doubt about it. Mr. Capote's appearance is lamblike but all intellectual bullies are warned not to be deceived.

> Harvey Breit. *New York Times Book Section*. Feb. 24, 1952. p. 29

The dichotomy of good and evil exists in each Capote character just as the dichotomy of daylight and nighttime exists in the aggregate of his stories. We might almost say that Capote's stories inhabit two worlds—that of the realistic, colloquial, often humorous daytime and that of the dreamlike, detached, and inverted nocturnal world. This double identity must be viewed with a double vision because Capote's stories can be interpreted either psychologically or as an expression of a spiritual or moral problem. In either case, whether the story be realistic or fantastic, the central focus is on the moment of initiation and the central character is either adolescent or innocent.

> Paul Levine. *The Virginia Quarterly Review*. Autumn, 1958. p. 602

The form of *Breakfast at Tiffany's* approaches perfection. It has pace, narrative excitement, a firm and subtle hold on the sequence of events from the first backward glance to the final salutation. A novelette in scope, it still manages to treat a subject usually accorded the fuller scope of the picaresque novel with marvelous selectivity. The point of view, the tone, the style herald no technical discoveries in the field of fiction: they simply blend to make the subject spring to life.

> Ihab Hassan. *Radical Innocence* (Princeton). 1961. p. 254

Among the surprising qualities of Truman Capote's mercurial talent and a quality that is made very plain by such a selection from the entire body of his work as this [*Selected Writings*] is its range, the variety of its development over the nearly twenty years in which the author has been publishing. A prose of many moods, it is equally at ease in situations of black nightmarish horror and of high, often hilarious comedy, and perhaps its single constant quality is the unerring sense of style. By style one means, when speaking of Capote's work, not only the right words in the right places, but the body of detail precisely and freshly observed and the varieties of the speaking human voice accurately heard and quintessentially reported.

> Mark Schorer. Introduction to *Selected Writings of Truman Capote* (Random). 1963. p. vii

This [*Breakfast at Tiffany's*] novella's similarities to Isherwood's Sally Bowles have often been noted. The difference is more revealing. Isherwood's story is quintessential social-political history. This is quite beyond Capote who, for all the war-time detail, delivers finally a relatively isolated portrait of a romantic figure in quest of the perennial romantic grail, utter happiness. . . .

. . .His concluding essay [in *Selected Writings*] on Brooklyn Heights—written for *Holiday* in a manner quite different from his own pointillist travel pieces—proves yet once more that he is a literary actor, good only when he gets the right part. Capote's writing depends on which magazine commissions him or which author he is imitating. There is no clear personal imprint. The only generalization possible is that, so far, he is at his best with humorous observation. . . . His fiction is strongest, most vital, when it resembles his best non-fiction. It is noteworthy that he is now at work on a long examination of a Kansas murder case. . . . Almost half of this collection is non-fiction; the book on which he has been engaged for some years is non-fiction. Perhaps he has recognized that his forte is in using his artistic abilities on factual material, and in that self-recognition may be the pleasant end of a search. For this collection is the record of a man trying out many voices in many rooms.

> Stanley Kauffmann. *New Republic*. Feb. 23, 1963. pp. 22, 24

It is to Mr. Capote's disadvantage that every book he writes turns into what our great grandmothers used to call "a pretty book." He knows that ours is a bloodstained planet but he knows also that it turns on its axis and moves round the sun with a dancer's grace, and his style defines the dancer as ballet-trained. For this reason Mr. Capote is often not taken as seriously as he should be, and it is possible that his new book, *In Cold Blood*, may be regarded simply as a literary *tour de force* instead of the formidable statement about reality which it is. . . . That Mr. Capote has invented nothing and recorded with a true ear and utter honesty is proved by the conversations in the book. The inhabitants of Holcomb, Kansas, do not on any page engage in the subtle and economical dialogue Mr. Capote ascribes to the characters in his novels. They speak the words which reporters hear when they interview the participants in prodigious events, and listen to with embarrassed ears. The stuff is corny, yet not just corny. The corn is celestial. Even the cleverest writer who tries to invent it achieves an obvious fakery, which is quite absent from this book.

> Rebecca West. *Harper's Magazine*. Feb., 1966. p. 108

The author [of *In Cold Blood*] is .., deeply concerned with his people and the six lives that were lost. To this he adds an acute and sympathetic interpretation of their behavior. Indeed, one feels throughout the book that he is in the company of a highly perceptive, very civilized man who wants to understand but has no desire to instruct, judge, or condemn. The literary form may not be new, but, it must be conceded, this self-restraint assuredly is.

But the special brilliance of the achievement lies in the writing. This serves flawlessly and effortlessly the purposes of the narrative. . . . But the author's resources go far beyond narrative. The main actors are visible in all dimensions and precisely as they must be seen for the purposes of the history.

> John Kenneth Galbraith. *The Reporter*. March 10, 1966. p. 58

Much has been made, in the unprecedented hullabaloo that surrounded the publication of *In Cold Blood*, of that book's inaugurating a "new literary genre." . . .

What Mr. Capote thinks he has discovered is already known to the world by a different name: history. History is the art of telling the truth, selectively (so that the reader may not strangle on vast accumulations of data) and gracefully (so that the reader will want to read in the first place). That is what Mr. Capote has done. If it is objected that history is usually concerned with larger issues, reflect what the similar ordeal of a 15th century family might be worth today to the historian, if he were lucky enough to find it written in such careful and well-authenticated detail. . . .

What Mr. Capote wants to do for his history, I take it, is what the novel can do for its subject matter: present it so compellingly that it escapes its relatively narrow base into universal significance. That is a commendable ambition in the historian, who is far more than the novelist committed to specifics. It is in terms of this problem that I apprehend Aristotle's dictum that poetry is truer than history. Even so, the best historians have always been able to present their facts so creatively and suggestively as to make small incidents serve great generalizations.

> Charles Alva Hoyt. *Columbia University Forum*. Winter, 1966. p. 53

Why . . . did Capote honor himself by calling [*In Cold Blood*] in any sense a "novel"? Why bring up the word at all? Because Capote depended on the record, was proud of his prodigious research, but was not content to make a work of record. After all, most readers of *In Cold Blood* know nothing about the case except what Capote tells us. Capote wanted his "truthful account" to become "a work of art," and he knew he could accomplish this, quite apart from the literary expertness behind the book, through a certain intimacy between himself and "his" characters. Capote wanted, ultimately, to turn the perpetually defeated, negative Eros that is behind *Other Voices, Other Rooms* into an emblematic situation for our time.

> Alfred Kazin. *Bright Book of Life* (Little). 1973. pp. 210–1

It is [Capote's] attention to style, to the extraordinary pull of places, to all the fleeting wisps of the past that give [*The Dogs Bark*] a durability far beyond the perfunctory compendia of pieces with which publishers stay in the graces of their good writers when those writers are between big books. . . . This is less a guidebook for the millions of aspiring journalists and city-room entrepreneurs in the land who wish to break the shackles, than a self-charting of a courageous literary life, a life of stamina, and despite the misleading public appurtenances, of course, of considerable solitude. If the "new journalism," which moves from one symposium to the next, has in fact become something more than we had bargained for (some of its exponents now belittling the act of fiction and poetry as irrelevant, obliterating in one fairly broad sweep some of the deepest impulses of the human blood), then *The Dogs Bark* is an effective answer, for while much of it does indeed stand on "reporting," it is at the core a great deal more ambitious: it is the written geography of an imaginative artist.

> Willie Morris. *New Republic*. Nov. 3, 1973. p. 22

Readers who accept the idea that Capote's early writing should be categorized as romance can then dismiss irrelevant issues. They are the people who find Capote's second book remarkable in its voyage into the human psyche via the route of the romance. *A Tree of Night and Other Stories* is like a heavily woven tapestry of different depths that draws one from layer to layer. The collection contains stories in both a light and dark mode. Although Capote was never again to publish stories of the latter kind, some of the characteristics appear in other works, and some of the characters surface under other names in the fiction of the past decade.

Capote has spoken of his work as belonging to cycles in his development as a writer. He labels *Other Voices, Other Rooms* at the end of the first cycle, and he places *A Tree of Night and Other Stories* in the second. During the ten-year period of his second cycle, his most varied and prolific, he wrote the autobiographical story, "A Christmas Memory"; *The Grass Harp*, a novel which he also turned into a play; "House of Flowers," a short story which later became a musical comedy; essays and portraits, *Local Color* and *Observations*; film scripts for *Beat the Devil* and *The Innocents*; a nonfiction, comic, book-length travel report, *The Muses Are Heard*; and finally, the very popular novel, *Breakfast at Tiffany's*.

Capote's third cycle, corresponding to the decade of the sixties, was devoted primarily to the preparation and writing of *In Cold Blood*, although during that time he also published two of his well-known pieces, "A Thanksgiving Visitor," which is a spin-off from "A Christmas Memory," and "Among the Paths to Eden," one of his best short stories, and one which led some critics to predict, incorrectly, that this was the direction his future fiction was to follow.

Much has been written about *In Cold Blood*, its genre, its style, its narrator. Every conceivable type of study of the book has been undertaken. In interviews Capote continues to explain the genesis of the book and his interest in developing a new art form. During the time that he was writing articles on a regular basis for *The New Yorker*, particularly those that became *The Muses Are Heard*, he developed a strong interest in narrative journalism. He decided he wanted to expand reporting into something more meaningful, to create a work which combined journalism and fiction. When his attention was piqued by a news story of the murder of a Kansas family, he felt that he had found the subject matter to experiment with a different type of novel. The result was Capote's most noted book and greatest literary achievement, to which he gave the designation, the "nonfiction novel." Other writers, American and European, have been using similar techniques since Capote introduced them; yet, he is bitter about the failure of some critics to acknowledge his contribution in devising a new theory of writing. One of those he singles out is Norman Mailer, who, Capote says, was disparaging of the form, yet quickly saw the value of it for his own work and wrote a number of nonfiction novels. Whether or not sufficient credit is given to Capote for his innovativeness, nobody can question the impact the book has had.

Helen S. Garson. *Truman Capote* (Ungar, 1980), pp. 7–9

Music for Chameleons consists of a brief autobiographical introduction, then six short stories followed by a novella; and it ends with seven "Conversational Portraits."... Despite [Capote's] claims, the technique is (mercifully) innovatory only in one or two superficial and formal ways; in many more important ones it is a brave step back to older literary virtues. He now writes fiction increasingly near fact, and *vice versa*. In practice this means that he is very skillfully blending the received techniques of several kinds of writing....

If all one required of a writer was high stylishness, a marvelous eye and ear, a far from contemptible degree of self-honesty, and a piquant readability in all he attempts, then one cannot fault Mr. Capote. He is as good as sheer literary intelligence can make a writer. What he seems to me to lack (and what raised his French models above being *only* great stylists) is a literary heart, which requires not only magnanimity but a patience with ordinariness, the gray muddle of average existence.

He speaks in his foreword of wanting to assimilate into his new style of writing all he has learned from "film scripts, plays, reportage, poetry, the short story, novellas, the novel." The odd man out here, the awkward fit, is surely that last thing. It is the very length and diffuseness of the novel that allows the growth of deeper feelings in both writer and reader; and creating such feelings in the short story is the most difficult Indian ropetrick in fiction. Yet all the truly great masters (most famously James Joyce in *The Dead*) have accomplished it, and as I read these glittering and always entertaining stories I found myself wondering why Mr. Capote came close at times, but never quite made it.... Of one thing I am certain: Contemporary literature would be much, much duller and poorer without him.

John Fowles. *Saturday Review*. July, 1980, pp. 52–53

In his later nonfiction Capote continues to assume an objective point of view, only this time eschewing omniscience entirely and acknowledging the perceiving "I," In "Hello Stranger" (*Music for Chameleons*), he presents without commentary a conversation with a friend who confesses a strange sexual indiscretion. The sketch is constructed around the interview form itself—"TC's" question followed by "George's" answer—with a minimum of connecting description. The surface of the story and of the man who tells it are presented, without explicit interpretation, for us to judge.... Acknowledging the "I" in its act of observation calls our attention to the opaqueness of surfaces we must interpret for ourselves.

Chris Anderson. *Midwest Quarterly*. Spring, 1987, pp. 348–49

BIBLIOGRAPHY
Other Voices, Other Rooms, 1948 (n); *A Tree of Night*, 1949 (s); *Local Color*, 1950 (t); *The Grass Harp*, 1951 (n); *The Grass Harp*, 1952 (d); *House of Flowers*, 1954 (d); *The Muses Are Heard*, 1957 (t); *Breakfast at Tiffany's*, 1958 (n); *Observations*, 1959 (commentary on photographs by Richard Avedon); *Selected Writings*, 1963; *A Christmas Memory*, 1966 (m); *In Cold Blood*, 1966 (j); *The Thanksgiving Visitor*, 1968 (m); *The Dogs Bark*, 1973 (j); *Music for Chameleons*, 1980 (s, e, a); *One Christmas*, 1983 (s); *Children on Their Birthdays*, 1985 (juv); *Answered Prayers: The Unfinished Novel*, 1986 (n); *A Capote Reader*, 1987 (misc); *Conversations*, 1987 (r, i.e., interviews); *I Remember Grandpa: A Story by Truman Capote*, 1987

CARSON, Rachel (1907–1964)

When poets write about the sea their errors annoy scientists. When scientists write about the sea their bleak and technical jargon paralyzes poets. Yet neither scientists nor poets should object to *The Sea around Us*. It is written with precision more than sufficient for its purpose, and its style and imagination make it a joy to read....

[Miss Carson] must have read many bristling books about tides and ocean currents and felt the thrill and mystery that lie deeply buried in them. She must have learned how to talk with oceanographers, those salty and crusty scientists who go down to the sea in ships to probe the sea's insides. While doing all this she must have read a fine variety of literature, for her chapters are headed by unusually apt quotations from authors as diverse as Homer, Matthew Arnold and The Venerable Bede.

The product of Miss Carson's learning is a book packed with information expressed in charming language. She tells how old the sea is and how all life came from it. The land in those old years was as bleak as the mountains of the moon, but the sea was as full of churning life as it is today. Then, little by little, plants learned to live on land. Animals followed to eat them. At last land animals developed that could sail on the sea in ships and measure the flowing tides and drop ingenious instruments into the deep ocean basins. Those prying animals are the oceanographers, Miss Carson's friends.

Miss Carson has other friends, and she obviously loves them all. She tells with a gardener's tenderness of the "blooming" of the northern seas, a magic moment in spring when the winter-chilled surface water sinks into the depths. Bottom water rises, bringing to the surface the salts that are needed by all living things. Then microscopic plants (diatoms) sprout by billions and trillions. Slightly larger animals multiply to devour them. Shrimps, squids, fish and whales struggle for the living broth and add their young to enrich it. Everybody eats everybody, and Miss Carson enjoys and describes it all....

Miss Carson loves mysteries too, and the sea has plenty of them. She tells of the black depths where no ray of light ever penetrates. All sorts of strange things live there, she says. Besides the giant squid that are hunted by sperm whales, the deeps are swarming with mysterious creatures that have, so far, evaded man's efforts to capture them. They are known only by clues picked up by the most modern instruments. What are these deep-living phantoms? How big are they? How shaped? Miss Carson seems glad that she does not know, and her reader is glad too.

The sea is alive with rhythm and cycles, some of them centuries long. This branch of science is formidable, but Miss Carson explains it in language that is soft and disarming. . . .

Each of Miss Carson's chapters is worth sampling and savoring, and her book adds up to enjoyment that should not be passed by. Every person who reads it will look on the sea with new pleasure. He will know that it is full of lights and sounds and movements, of sunken lands and mountains, of the debris of meteors, of plains strewn with ancient sharks' teeth and the ear-bones of whales.

Jonathan Norton Leonard, *New York Times Book Review*. July 1, 1951, p. 1.

The Edge of the Sea lacks the organ tones of Miss Carson's *The Sea around Us*. It deals not with the sea as a majestic whole but with the narrow strip of part-time sea bottom that rings the land between high and low tide marks. No habitat on earth is more fiercely contended; none supports more teeming and more varied life. The tidal strip has, also, a philosophical importance. It was the cruel training ground where sea creatures learned to live on the hostile land. Miss Carson points out forms that are making that great transition today and also a few that are returning from the dry land to the sea.

The Atlantic Coast of the United States, the author explains happily, has almost every kind of shore, from the hard rocks of Maine, pounded by icy surf, to the coral reefs and mangrove swamps of the tropical Florida keys. She seems to love the Maine coast best, and she takes her readers there when the tide is high and the waves are tossing spray among the shoreside junipers. No sea creatures are in sight except the waiting gulls. "But the gulls," says Miss Carson, "know what is there."

When the ebb begins (Miss Carson can *hear* the tide turn) she and the gulls follow the water line down the dripping rocks. The gulls are looking for clams and crabs big enough to be edible. There is nothing too small for Miss Carson to note and make interesting. She points out a dark line high on the rocks. It was drawn by blue-green algae, perhaps the oldest plants on earth, and it is likely that the rocky shores of one billion years ago had that same dark line.

Little by little the sea retreats, followed by Miss Carson. She pays loving respects to each species as it emerges: the crowding barnacles, the rock weeds, the mussels, starfish, snails and crabs. Each has a fascinating history and each its own way of life. Most of the animals are carnivorous, eating each other and smaller things with untiring gusto. This slaughter is not horrifying. Clams do not cry for mercy when fierce whelks bore holes in their shells. Even when there is visible struggle Miss Carson takes it philosophically. It is part of the feeding cycle, the steady mainspring of life. . . .

On Carolina beaches and limey Florida reefs Miss Carson shows her readers the beauty and oddness of the living things peculiar to those places: eyeless worms that prowl through the mud glowing with phosphorescence, bright colored clams that dance in the surf, sea urchins that point their venomous spines toward an approaching shadow. Each form is stranger than the last; there is no end of strangeness.

Miss Carson's book is beautifully written and technically correct. People who get bored by too much lolling on beaches should read it as a guide book. All around them, even beneath them,

are fascinating worlds. A little wading, searching and poking will open their doors.

Jonathan N. Leonard. *The New York Times Book Review*. October 30, 1955, p. 5.

The enduring quality of the sea is a central theme of Miss Carson's writing; the sea which almost, but not quite, subjugates and dominates the land; the vast and unplumbed sea from which life as naturalists see it sprang; the sea, pressing always against the land, lapping higher, until, in some shadowy future, more and more land crumbles away again into the sea, and material life marches once more into the watery depths from which it came.

In *The Edge of the Sea*, Miss Carson's latest book, the enduring quality of the sea again is a theme, though in a different way. In this book Miss Carson has left the deep sea world, in which the sperm whale and giant squid, titans of the deep, battle in a midnight abyss, and has turned toward the shore, to that intertidal world which belongs at high tide to the sea and at low tide to the land. . . .

Though the author preserves in this book the essential mystery of the sea, *The Edge of the Sea* portrays a world more nearly understandable to the average reader than is the deep water world of *The Sea around Us*. The intertidal world has been glimpsed by every reader who has walked along a beach or sea coast. If that beach has been a sandy one in the temperate zones, the reader will remember strings of kelp and other weeds along the high tide line, will have marveled at the structure of minute shells, will have watched the primordial horseshoe crab tracing its way across the sands, will have seen a dozen forms strange and new to him. . . .

The Edge of the Sea is pitched, perhaps, in a lesser key than was *The Sea around Us*, if only because of the intertidal world is a more limited subject than was the whole sea itself. In her new book, however, Miss Carson's peri is as poetic as ever, and the knowledge she imparts is profound. *The Edge of the Sea* finds a worthy place beside Miss Carson's masterpiece of 1951.

Harry B. Ellis. *The Christian Science Monitor*. November 10, 1955, p. B8.

It is characteristic of the imbalance in Carson's reputation that although many have praised her as a scientist who wrote like a poet, she is not recognized as a significant literary figure, much less given her place in the pantheon of American writers with Henry David Thoreau.

From her earliest occasional writing, through the four major books, to her latest speeches, Carson's work is of a piece in substance, artistry, and underlying philosophy. But even beyond this, her life and work together formed an artistic whole. Preparation, dedication, and her sense of vocation as an artist interlocked with her sense of mission as a moral and social person. . . .

As naturalist and writer, she is a literary descendant of Thoreau. In personal terms, although they shared a certain reclusiveness, her life seems the opposite of his. Thoreau claimed to have lived the life he "might have writ," even though he did commit many careful words to paper. Carson's life was in her work, except for the part she devoted to her family. . . .

Carson's major books form changing patterns of pairs. The first, *Under the Sea-Wind*, and the second, *The Sea around Us*, focus on the oceans, while the third, *The Edge of the Sea*, and the fourth, *Silent Spring*, concentrate on the land. . . .

In poetic effect, *Under the Sea-Wind* is the highest point on the incline, with the next two books sacrificing some loveliness to the cause of instruction, although the balance remains tilted to the artistic. With its concentration of unpleasant facts, *Silent Spring* is at the lowest point of Carson's poetic writing, yet is still a book of spare beauty with passage of lyrical brilliance. . . .

Silent Spring began as an exposé of the dangers of pesticides but came close to becoming the major ecological work Carson had wanted to write. As in all her work, style and structure relate organically to the particular subject, but *Silent Spring* is nonetheless an extension of the motifs and themes of earlier books. When Douglas Costle, as Administrator of the United States Environmental Protection Agency, declared that Rachel Carson "sounded the alarm about environmental dangers," he credited not *Silent Spring* alone, but "her unique, empathetic presentation of the workings of nature in *Under the Sea-Wind, The Sea around Us, The Edge of the Sea*, and finally *Silent Spring*". . . .

[Carson's] claim to a place in literature as well as history rests on all her books, each an individually realized achievement representing a different kind of writing, all testifying that she possessed what William Beebe considered the "*ideal* equipment for a naturalist writer of literary natural history.". . .

> Carol B. Gartner. *Rachel Carson*. Frederick Ungar Publishing Co. 1983.

BIBLIOGRAPHY
Under the Sea-Wind: A Naturalist's Picture of Ocean Life, 1941, revised 1952 (nf); *The Sea around Us*, 1951, revised 1966 (nf); *The Edge of the Sea*, 1955 (nf); *Silent Spring*, 1962 (nf); *The Sense of Wonder*, 1965 (nf); *The Rocky Coast*, 1971 (nf); *Silent Spring Revisited*, 1987 (nf)

CARVER, Raymond (1938–1988)

In most of these 22 short fictions [*Will You Please Be Quiet, Please*] the objects of Raymond Carver's close attention are men and women out of work or between jobs, at loose ends, confused and often terrified. If they are kids, they play hooky. Husbands and wives lie beside each other in bed, touch cautiously, retreat, feign sleep, lie, each bewildered by what has just happened and by what might happen next. The stories themselves are not at all confused; they have been carefully shaped, shorn of ornamentation and directed away from anything that might mislead. They are brief stories but by no means stark: they imply complexities of action and motive and they are especially artful in their suggestion of repressed violence.

No human blood is shed in any of these stories, yet almost all of them hold a promise of mayhem, of some final, awful breaking out from confines, and breaking through to liberty. . . .

In his choice of plots and materials Mr. Carver is in the modernist train of Kafka. Odd and threatening messages come as though by magic through the mails or by telephone. Strangers invade one another's lives and offer preposterous challenges to one another. In the customary literary execution of such procedures,

identities shift, characters are misled into taking enemies as friends, conspiracies develop or are, at the least, apprehended. Mr. Carver, by contrast, anchors his men and women, his children, even his dogs and cats, in stable identities. With a speed common to all his stories he fixes the special tic or manner he wishes to develop: "I was out of work," says the narrator of "Collectors" in the story's first sentence. "But any day I expected to hear from up north. I lay on the sofa and listened to the rain. Now and then I'd lift up and look through the curtain for the mailman."

> Geoffrey Wolff. *New York Times Book Section*. March 7, 1976, pp. 4–5

Compared to the more "mannered" writers of the sixties and seventies—Barth, Pynchon, Barthelme, for example—Carver's style seems ingenuously simple, almost photo-realistic. Even the prose of Grace Paley and Leonard Michaels, both considered exemplars of lean, taut language, seems positively lush, almost Baroque in resonances and allusiveness, when held up to that of Carver. The temptation is to classify Carver as a throwback to an earlier era, say, of Anderson, Lardner and Hemingway. Although he derives from and to some extent reminds us of these earlier writers, there's a crucial difference. The sensibility here is clearly postmodern: beyond the flat quality of the Hemingway hero struggling to preserve an identity in the dreary vastness of the wasteland, beyond the psychological frameworks of Anderson's stories, beyond the comic satire of Lardner. Carver's simple language is a disguise, as is Harold Pinter's, for the emotional violence lurking beneath neutral surfaces. . . .

Like most of us, his characters aren't heroes. They don't teach us how to behave nobly or honorably or even intelligently in moments of crisis. Like the voyeurs they are or resemble, Carver's characters shy away from dramatic confrontation, they avoid existential tests of character. These people are completely removed from Mailer's or Hemingway's preoccupation with masculine assertion. Although there are showdowns in these stories, no one really wants them to occur. Betraying wives are threatened with bodily harm, but rarely do their husbands actually make good on their threats. . . .

Nothing happens because in the main Carver's dissociated characters prefer it that way. Living in a world of unarticulated longing, a world verging on silence, they may even, like the couples in "Neighbors" and "Will You Please Be Quiet, Please?," consider themselves "happy." But such happiness is fragile, Carver tells us. Something or someone always happens along to disturb the uneasy equilibrium, forcing a sudden confrontation with a hidden or suppressed part of the self. The disturbance itself acts as a trigger to larger revelations of self-alienation.

> David Boxer and Cassandra Phillips. *Iowa Review*. Summer, 1979, pp. 81, 83–84

Raymond Carver's America is helpless, clouded by pain and the loss of dreams, but it is not as fragile as it looks. It is a place of survivors and a place of stories. People live to tell their tales and the tales of others. "Things are better now," they say. "I am sitting over coffee and cigarettes at my friend Rita's and I am telling her about it." "That was in Crescent City, up near the Oregon border. I left soon after."

Mr. Carver is the author of two volumes of short fiction and two books of poetry, as well as other works in limited editions. His writing is full of edges and silences, haunted by things not said, not even to be guessed at. He has done what many of the most gifted writers fail to do: He has invented a country of his own, like no other except the very world, as Wordsworth said, which is the world of all of us. It is an American world, of course, littered with place names, credit, convertibles, Stanley Products, sunburst clocks, shopping centers, Jell-O, motels, Almond Roca, baseball caps, trips to Reno, Elks, Indian reservations, beckoning spaces of Western country and children with names like Rae and Melody. But there are simple, central solitudes and bewilderments here too: local enough, but not the property of any one nation. ''I could hear my heart beating. I could hear everyone's heart. I could hear the human noise we sat there making...'' ...

Mr. Carver's first book of stories [*Will You Please Be Quiet, Please?*] explored a common plight rather than a common subject. His characters were lost or diminished in their own different ways. The 17 stories in *What We Talk about When We Talk about Love* make up a more concentrated volume, less a collection than a set of variations on the themes of marriage, infidelity and the disquieting tricks of human affection. . . .

''Things change,'' a character says in [one] story, and this is the dominant note in the book. People lose track of who they were and what they wanted, mislay their lives and are startled by their memories. . . .

In other stories it is the failure of speech, rather than its absence, that does the talking: ''He wanted to say something else. But there was no saying what it should be.'' ''There were things he wanted to say, grieving things, consoling things, things like that.'' In the last story in the book a husband leaving home insists that he wants to ''say one more thing. . . But then he could not think what it could possibly be.''

The point is not that words are inadequate, or that actions speak louder. It is that the desire to talk can be perceived as a need, and that need has its fluency, makes use of any language that comes to hand. This is a troublesome fact for a writer, but Mr. Carver does not dodge it. ''She seemed anxious, or maybe that's too strong a word.'' Only a very delicate stylist would worry about the strength of ''anxious'' and the milder, perhaps unnamable quality of feeling that hides behind this attempt at description. In Mr. Carver's silences, a good deal of the unsayable gets said.

Michael Wood. *New York Times Book Section*. April 26, 1981, pp. 1, 34

Mr. Carver has been mostly a writer of strong but limited effects—the sort of writer who shapes and twists his material to a high point of stylization. In his newest collection of stories, *Cathedral*, there are a few that suggest he is moving toward a greater ease of manner and generosity of feeling; but in most of his work it's his own presence, the hard grip of his will, that is the strongest force. It's not that he imposes moral or political judgments; in that respect, he's quite self-effacing. It's that his abrupt rhythms and compressions come to be utterly decisive. . . .

Cathedral contains a number of similar stories, very skillful within their narrow limits, written with a dry intensity, and moving, at their climaxes, from the commonplace to the unnerving. . . .

These stories yield neither the familiar recognitions of realistic narrative nor the ambiguous motifs of symbolic fiction. They cast us adrift, into a void on the far side of the ordinary. Ordinary life is threatening; ordinary life is the enemy of ordinary people.

Behind Mr. Carver's stories there are strong American literary traditions. Formally, they summon remembrances of Hemingway and perhaps Stephen Crane, masters of tightly packed fiction. In subject matter they draw upon the American voice of loneliness and stoicism, the native soul locked in this continent's space. Mr. Carver's characters, like those of many earlier American writers, lack a vocabulary that can release their feelings, so they must express themselves mainly through obscure gesture and berserk display.

It's a meager life that Mr. Carver portrays, without religion or politics or culture, without the shelter of class or ethnicity, without the support of strong folkways or conscious rebellion. It's the life of people who cluster in the folds of our society. They are not bad or stupid; they merely lack the capacity to understand the nature of their deprivation—the one thing, as it happens, that might ease or redeem it. When they get the breaks, they can manage; but once there's a sign of trouble, they turn out to be terribly brittle. Lacking an imagination for strangeness, they succumb to the strangeness of their trouble.

A few of Mr. Carver's stories—''They're Not Your Husband,'' ''Where I'm Calling From'' and ''A Serious Talk''—can already be counted among the masterpieces of American fiction; a number of others are very strong. But something of the emotional meagerness that he portrays seeps into the narrative. His art is an art of exclusion—many of life's shadings and surprises, pleasures and possibilities, are cut away by the stringency of his form. . . .

I think Mr. Carver is showing us at least part of the truth about a segment of American experience few of our writers trouble to notice. Neoconservative critics, intent upon pasting a smile onto the country's face, may charge him with programmatic gloom and other heresies, but at his best he is probing, as many American writers have done before, the waste and destructiveness that prevail beneath the affluence of American life. . . .

Cathedral shows a gifted writer struggling for a larger scope of reference, a finer touch of nuance. What he has already done makes one eager to read his future work.

Irving Howe. *New York Times Book Section*. Sept. 11, 1983, pp. 1, 42–43

INTERVIEWER: *Ray's [Raymond Carver] last story, ''Errand''—I thought I could always recognize a Ray Carver story.*

RICHARD FORD: You can't though—by which I don't mean that you can't sometimes recognize a story of his by its ''style.'' But you couldn't *always* do it. He could surprise you. His work—his style—changed. That's an unfortunate thing about the terms *Carver Country* or *Carveresque* as a putative literary description. Most of the sightings that people took on Ray's style—by which I mean, particularly, the length and cadence of his sentences, the length of his stories—those sightings mostly are from *Will You [Please] Be Quiet, Please?*—his first book.

Do you believe they are overlooking his later work?

FORD: Well, *What We Talk about When We Talk about Love*, his next book, contained stories of longer duration, sentences of less clipped cadences. Some stories in that book were edited and revised so that they *seemed* superficially more like earlier stories. But I'd already seen them in manuscript, and I knew them in the original. . . . By the time Ray's third book of stories (*Cathedral*) had been published . . . the kind of normal changes that go on in any writer's style as one gets older and learns more and uses things up, and as the demands on one's sentences become different and perhaps greater—these changes were evident. The style and cadence of Ray's sentences had changed. He could still write *short* stories, but he could do more, too—and would've done a great deal more.

People who love Ray's stories sometimes remember them as seeming more alike than they really are; as in all things, love often prospers through the agency of a kind of restrictiveness. But Ray was a more various writer than many of his fans give him credit for. His sympathies enlarged. As he became, in his life, more comfortable and had a more ample life, his stories became more ample.

> Richard Ford. In Sam Halpert, ed. *When We Talk about Raymond Carver*, (Layton, Utah: Peregrine Smith Books, 1991), pp. 146–47

INTERVIEWER: *You've said that you have high regard for his stories. But beyond that, what do you see in his work?*

JAY MCINERNEY: One of the things that hasn't been mentioned enough is that each of his major collections represented a different stage in his development. That was not frequently noticed. People kept discovering him, as if he'd just been born. That is to say, even the *New York Times* review of his second book, *What We Talk about When We Talk about Love*, was actually a review of his first book. And so we were disappointed that the reviewer treated it all as one lump.

This collection—What We Talk about When We Talk about Love—*wasn't this the one where the stories seem pared down to a bare minimum?*

MCINERNEY: Yes, this was the collection that fixed a stereotyped image of minimalism to his work. The collection went very far in exploring how much can be left out in a story—the old Hemingway notion. In fact, so much was left out that Ray subsequently published these stories in their original, and to me, more satisfying longer versions.

Do you find his earlier work preferable to his later?

MCINERNEY: I wouldn't pick one period over another. To me, it's remarkable to see the continuity *and* the development. That is to say, by the time Ray published his first book, he knew what he was doing. I suppose nothing could have the impact on me that ''Will You Please Be Quiet, Please?'' did, because it was like a bolt out of the blue. For some of us it must have been like picking up *In Our Time* for the first time—suddenly this very new language, this wonderful new idiom. It's the world as you always suspected, but you never realized it was, until you read the book. It had an incredible impact, and I suppose I'll always love that book, especially as it hit me so hard.

> Jay McInerney. In Sam Halpert, ed. *When We Talk about Raymond Carver*, (Layton, Utah: Peregrine Smith Books, 1991), p. 47

To be inside a Raymond Carver story is a bit like standing in a model kitchen at Sears—you experience a weird feeling of disjuncture that comes from being in a place where things *appear* to be real and familiar, but where a closer look shows that the turkey is papier-mâché, the broccoli is rubber, and the frilly curtains cover a blank wall. In Carver's fiction things are simply not as they appear.

Or, rather, things are *more* than they appear to be, for often commonplace objects—a broken refrigerator, a car, a cigarette, a bottle of beer or whiskey—become transformed in Carver's hands, from realistic props in realistic stories to powerful, emotionally charged signifiers in and of themselves. Language itself undergoes a similar transformation. Since there is little authorial presence and since Carver's characters are often inarticulate and bewildered about the turns their lives have taken, their seemingly banal conversations are typically endowed with unspoken intensity and meaning. Watching Carver's characters interact, then, is rather like spending an evening with two close friends who you know have had a big fight just before you arrived: even the most ordinary gestures and exchanges have transformed meanings, hidden tensions, emotional depths.

> Ewing Campbell. *Raymond Carver: A Study of the Short Fiction* (Boston: Twayne, 1992), p. 98

BIBLIOGRAPHY
Winter Insomnia, 1970 (p); *Put Yourself in My Shoes*, 1974 (p); *At Night the Salmon Move*, 1976 (p); *Will You Please Be Quiet, Please?*, 1976 (s); *Furious Seasons*, 1977 (s); *What We Talk about When We Talk about Love*, 1981 (s); *Cathedral*, 1983 (s); *Fires: Essays, Poems, Stories*, 1983; *Dostoevsky*, 1985 (scrp); *Where Water Comes Together with Other Water*, 1985 (p); *Ultramarine*, 1986 (p); *Bill Burke Portraits*, 1987 (e, accompanying photo album); *In a Marine Light*, 1987 (p); *Where I'm Calling From*, 1988 (s); *Elephant*, 1988 (s); *A New Path to the Waterfall*, 1989 (p); *Conversations*, 1990 (r, i.e., interviews); *No Heroics, Please*, 1992 (misc); *All of Us*, 1996 (p)

CATHER, Willa (1873–1947)

Miss Cather's mind is basically static and retrospective, rich in images of fixed contours. . . . The characteristic quality of her mind . . . is not its puritanism or its idealism, but something deeper in which these are rooted. She is preeminently an artist dominated by her sense of the past, seeking constantly, through widely differing symbolisms, to recapture her childhood and youth. A sort of reverence for her own early years goes, hand in hand, with her Vergilian ancestor-worship; and out of this has flowered her finest work.

> Clifton Fadiman. *The Nation*. Dec. 7, 1932. pp. 564–5

In *My Ántonia*, Ántonia Shimerda . . . became the symbol of emotional fulfillment in motherhood on a Western farm. The thesis was arresting, appearing as it did in 1918 at the very moment when farm and village life were coming under the critical eyes of the novelists intent upon exposing its pollution. Without satire or bitterness and with only a little sentimentalism, Willa Cather pictured a strong character developing under severe difficulties which would crush a less heroic soul, surviving the most primitive hardships in a sod hut, toiling like an ox in the field with the men, enduring want, cut off from ordinary pleasures, withstanding betrayal and the cheap life as a hired girl in a village, and emerging at last after such desperate conditions to a triumphant serenity as mother to a healthy group of shy, awkward but happy and laughing boys who are content with their life on the farm.

Harlan Hatcher. *Creating the Modern American Novel* (Farrar and Rinehart). 1935. p. 66

A Lost Lady, Miss Cather's most explicit treatment of the passing of the old order, is the central work of her career. Far from being the delicate minor book it is so often called, it is probably her most muscular story, for it derives its power from the grandeur of its theme. Miss Cather shares the American belief in the tonic moral quality of the pioneer's life; with the passing of the frontier she conceives that a great source of fortitude has been lost.

Lionel Trilling in *After the Genteel Tradition*, ed. Malcolm Cowley (Norton). 1937. p. 55

Miss Cather's style, grave, flexible, a little austere, wonderfully transparent, everywhere economical, is wonderfully apt for her purposes. There are certain things, to be sure, it cannot do. It cannot register wit or amusement or even humor, save rarely; it never rises to passionate indignation; it lacks earthiness, despite Miss Cather's profound belief in a normal relation with the earth. Dialogue, as she reports it, is seldom more than adequate. But within its boundaries it is beautiful writing, liquid to the ear, lucent to the eye. . . . There are few to whom the adjective "classic" can be more truly applied, for beneath the quick sympathy there is a Roman gravity, a sense of the dignity of life which contemporary fiction . . . has mainly lost.

Howard Mumford Jones. *Saturday Review*. Aug. 6, 1938. p. 16

Willa Cather's traditionalism was . . . anything but the arbitrary or patronizing opposition to contemporary ways which Irving Babbitt personified. It was a candid and philosophical nostalgia, a conviction and a standard possible only to a writer whose remembrance of the world of her childhood and the people in it was so overwhelming that everything after it seemed drab and more than a little cheap. Her distinction was not merely one of cultivation and sensibility; it was a kind of spiritual clarity possible only to those who suffer their loneliness as an act of the imagination and the will. . . . Later, as it seemed, she became merely sentimental, and her direct criticism of contemporary types and manners was often petulant and intolerant. But the very intensity of her nostalgia had from the first led her beyond nostalgia; it had given her the conviction that the values of the world she had lost were the primary values, and everything else merely their degradation.

Alfred Kazin. *On Native Grounds* (Reynal). 1942. pp. 250–1

From beginning to end, the Cather novels are not stories of plot, but chronicles, given a depth and significance lacking in the merely historical chronicle by that "sympathy" which leads to a perfect interplay of environment and character.

Her art was essentially a representation of this reaction between the soul of man and its environment. That is why the best of her stories are told against the land. . . . Her own absorption in her people and her land creates the suspense that she herself has

felt. . . . She is preservative, almost antiquarian, content with much space in little room—feminine in this, and in her passionate revelation of the values which conserve the life of the emotions.

Henry Seidel Canby. *Saturday Review*. May 10, 1947. pp. 23–4

From the whole range of Cather's values, standards, tastes, and prejudices, her tone is that of an inherent aristocrat in an equalitarian order, of an agrarian writer in an industrial order, of a defender of the spiritual graces in the midst of an increasingly materialistic culture. . . . Selecting and enhancing the most subtle effects of wealth, she has, rather like Sam Dodsworth's wife, either looked down upon or ignored the whole process of creating wealth. Writing so discreetly about the age when business was a personal adventure, she has neglected to mention the most typical forms of the adventure.

Maxwell Geismar. *The Last of the Provincials* (Houghton). 1947. pp. 217–8

Death Comes for the Archbishop is a historical novel; it is also a regional novel and a deliberately picturesque novel, with natural description helping to set the emotional tone. . . . The ritual and beliefs of the Catholic Church, the heroic activity of missionary priests, and the vivid colors of the southwestern landscape combine to produce a new kind of warmth and vitality in her art. . . . Yet one wonders whether this lively creation of a golden world in which all ideals are realized is not fundamentally a "softer" piece of writing. . . . There is, it is true, a splendid sympathy in the treatment of the characters and a most genuine feeling for the period and natural setting in which the action is laid. But there is no indication here of an artist wrestling successfully with intractable material. The material is all too tractable, and the success, though it is real, seems too easy.

David Daiches. *Willa Cather* (Cornell). 1951. p. 105

Mr. Maxwell Geismar wrote a book about her and some others called *The Last of the Provincials*. Not having read it I do not know his argument; but he has a case: she is a provincial; and I hope not the last. She was a good artist, and all true art is provincial in the most realistic sense: of the very time and place of its making, out of human beings who are so particularly limited by their situation, whose faces and names are real and whose lives begin each one at an individual unique center. Indeed, Willa Cather was a provincial as Hawthorne or Flaubert or Turgenev, as little concerned with aesthetics and as much with morals as Tolstoy, as obstinately reserved as Melville. In fact she always reminds me of very good literary company. . . . She is a curiously immovable shape, monumental, virtue itself in her work and a symbol of virtue—like certain churches, in fact, or exemplary women, revered and neglected.

Katherine Anne Porter. *The Days Before* (Harcourt). 1952. pp. 72–3

Miss Cather's central theme is that of people who pull themselves up by their bootstraps. . . . The inner voice of the early novels of Willa Cather suggests this fascination with, and need to describe, various forms of success—but also certain forms of failure. The drive to power in these books is overriding, with the result that the novels contain no complicated plots, no complexity of human relationships, no love affairs that we can take seriously. Her heroines, those women with feminized masculine names, Alexandra, Ántonia—and the name Alexandra itself reminds us of one of history's greatest conquerors—have tenacious wills and an extraordinary capacity for struggle.

> Leon Edel. *Willa Cather: The Paradox of Success* (Library of Congress). 1960. p. 8

What she did not want to admit was that the heroic ideal is impossible in the age of the machine; this was the real source of her animus against science, technology, and the industrial revolution. . . . Willa Cather was unwilling to give up her belief in hero worship; when she saw it failing in the modern world, rather than adopt some other view she made a villain of life. . . . Because of Willa Cather's aversion to conflict and because the whole impulse of her being tended toward the expression of a single unified emotion or mood, I have regarded her novels as being not novels at all in the conventional sense but extended lyrics in prose.

> John H. Randall. *The Landscape and the Looking Glass* (Houghton). 1960. p. 372

The country has shrunk, and our sense of the weight and relevance of Willa Cather's observation of Nebraska has shrunk with it. Nebraska is no doubt still there, but as a distinct imaginative possibility it has for the moment simply disappeared. As in so many other cases we are left confronting the artist who has been abandoned by his ostensible subject. The artist we now see is one whose energies are largely lavished on defensive maneuver, on masquerade. The power she now exercises is a measure of the degree to which the masquerade is itself something American. It is a small power when compared with Whitman's, but it is, despite the shell-work of fictional convention, a power of the same kind which engages us in "Song of Myself": a delighted absorption in the capacity of the self to embrace the world. In Whitman this play is overt; in Willa Cather it is masked. . . . Whitman's acceptance of his role was not open to a woman; instead Willa Cather carried on a masquerade which made it appear that she was accepting the conditions of adulthood while actually rejecting them. It was a shrewd woman of 40 who published *O Pioneers!*, and discovered the terms of her disguise.

> Quentin Anderson. *New Republic*. Nov. 27, 1965. pp. 28, 31

All of what Willa Cather wrote, it seems to me, is ultimately a metaphor of the conflict which Miguel de Unamuno referred to as an "inward tragedy," the conflict "between what the world is as scientific reason shows it to be, and what we wish it might be, as our religious faith affirms it to be." For Willa Cather, this conflict was most broadly expressed in terms of the world she knew in her childhood—the pioneer era which she clearly idealized and ennobled in her fictional re-creation of it—and the post–World War I wasteland she so thoroughly repudiated. It is easy to lose sight of the essentially symbolic nature of this conflict and to read it too

narrowly in terms of literal past versus literal present. Her theme was not the superiority of the past over the present, but, as Henry Steele Commager has observed, "the supremacy of moral and spiritual over material values, the ever recurrent but inexhaustible theme of gaining the whole world and losing one's soul."

Rather than being irrelevant to the modern world, the moral thrust of Willa Cather's art, her concern with pioneers and artists as symbolic figures representing the unending human quest for beauty and truth, places her among the number, not of the backward-looking (which she saw herself as being one of), but of the true spiritual pioneers of all ages in whose lives or work other men continue to find inspiration.

> Dorothy Tuck McFarland. *Willa Cather* (Ungar). 1972. pp. 4–5

It is love's partner, affection, that warms the life in [Cather's] work, and love's opposite, hate, that chills it. We meet pity and reconcilement there, and we meet obsession, and the hunger for something impossible. But what her characters are most truly meant for, it seems to me, is to rebel. For her heroines in particular, this is the strong, clear, undeniable impulse; it is the fateful drive. It is rebelling not for its own sake so much as for the sake of something a great deal bigger—that of integrity, of truth. It is the other face of aspiration. . . .

The desire to make a work of art and the making of it—which is love accomplished without help or need of help from another, and not without tragic cost—is what is deepest and realest, so I believe, in what she has written of human beings. Willa Cather used her own terms; and she left nothing out.

> Eudora Welty. *New York Times Book Section*. Jan. 27, 1974. p. 20

In . . . much of her fiction, Cather connects sexual passion with self-destruction; this remark suggests that the creator's passion, by contrast, thwarts death. The artist may "die of love" in the process of creation, but he is "born again." Cather's romantic apostrophe to the Nebraska soil in the concluding paragraph of *O Pioneers!* also promises rebirth for Alexandra, the novel's artist, after she has "faded away" into the land: "Fortunate country, that is one day to receive hearts like Alexandra's into its bosom, to give them out again in the yellow wheat, in the rustling corn, in the shining eyes of youth!". . .

In speaking of *O Pioneers!* Willa Cather provided support for those critics who have found the novel's structure loose, insisting that she made no effort to impose form on her material: the book formed itself without her conscious intervention. The "cold Swedish story" had simply "entwined itself" with the Bohemian story, she told Elizabeth Sergeant, and "somehow she had on her hands a two-part pastoral." She struck a similar note in her preface to the second edition of *Alexander's Bridge* (1922), explaining that when the artist found "his own material" (as she had in *O Pioneers!*) he would have "less and less power of choice about the molding of it. It seems to be there of itself, already molded." But to trust the tale rather than the teller is to find that the two parts of Willa Cather's pastoral are carefully intertwined; these contrasting and counterpointed explorations of creative and sexual passion with their opposed heroines give the novel both thematic and structural unity. Willa

Cather quite likely believed her statement that she did not consciously shape *O Pioneers!*, but in drawing on creative and psychological energies beneath consciousness she produced a novel whose structure may even seem overly controlled and balanced.

Sharon O'Brien. *Studies in American Fiction.* Autumn, 1978, pp. 168–69

My Ántonia (1918), Willa Cather's celebration of the American frontier experience, is marred by many strange flaws and omissions. It is, for instance, difficult to determine who is the novel's central character. If it is Ántonia, as we might reasonably assume, why does she entirely disappear for two of the novel's five books? If, on the other hand, we decide that Jim Burden, the narrator, is the central figure, we find that the novel explores neither his consciousness nor his development. Similarly, although the narrator overtly claims that the relationship between Ántonia and Jim is the heart of the matter, their friendship actually fades soon after childhood: between these two characters there is only, as E.K. Brown said, "an emptiness where the strongest emotion might have been expected to gather." Other inconsistencies and contradictions pervade the text—Cather's ambivalent treatment of Lena Lingard and Tiny Soderball, for example—and all are in some way related to sex roles and to sexuality.

This emphasis is not surprising: as a writer who was also a woman, Willa Cather faced the difficulties that confronted, and still do confront, accomplished and ambitious women. As a professional writer, Cather began, after a certain point in her career, to see the world and other women, including her own female characters, from a male point of view. Further, Cather was a lesbian who could not, or did not, acknowledge her homosexuality and who, in her fiction, transformed her emotional life and experiences into acceptable, heterosexual forms and guises. In her society it was difficult to be a woman and achieve professionally, and she could certainly not be a woman who loved women; she responded by denying, on the one hand, her womanhood and, on the other, her lesbianism. These painful denials are manifest in her fiction. After certain early work, in which she created strong and achieving women, like herself, she abandoned her female characters to the most conventional and traditional roles; analogously, she began to deny or distort the sexuality of her principal characters. *My Ántonia*, written at a time of great stress in her life, is a crucial and revealing work, for in it we can discern the consequences of Cather's dilemma as a lesbian writer in a patriarchal society. . . .

In order to create independent and heroic women, women who are like herself, the woman writer must avoid male identification, the likelihood of which is enhanced by being a writer who is unmarried, childless, and a lesbian. In the case of *My Ántonia*, Cather had to contend not only with the anxiety of creating a strong woman character, but also with the fear of a homosexual attraction to Annie/Ántonia. The novel's defensive narrative structure, the absence of thematic and structural unity that readers have noted, these are the results of such anxieties. Yet, because it has been difficult for readers to recognize the betrayal of female independence and female sexuality in fiction—their absence is customary—it has also been difficult to penetrate the ambiguities of *My Ántonia*, a crucial novel in Cather's long writing career.

Deborah G. Lambert. *American Literature.* Jan., 1982, pp. 676–77, 690

Blithe appropriations of Cather as a lesbian-feminist are anomalous and inappropriate—as here:

Thirty years after her death, . . . at a public hearing on gay rights, a speaker would cite Willa Cather as one of the homosexuals whose presence in New York had enriched the city's cultural and intellectual life.

Cather looks uncomfortable under this banner. She did not call herself a lesbian, would not have thought of herself as such, wrote disapprovingly of Oscar Wilde's "infamy" even when she was enthusiastic for 1890s decadence, obscured her sexual feelings in her fictions, and may not have had sexual relationships with the women she loved. Nor did she have the slightest interest in political support among women, or in what Adrienne Rich, in her attempt to extend the definition of the word lesbian, calls "the bonding against male tyranny."

None of this means, of course, that we are not allowed to describe her, now, as a lesbian writer. If we can't say anything about writers which they would not have said about themselves, then there is no use in writing about them. But it is important not to collapse Cather's imaginative life into a simple matter of repression, nor to condescend to her for her lack of "openness.". . .

Though she is best known, I suppose, for the strong immigrant women heroes of her earlier novels, these semimythical figures are in sharp contrast to her dangerously seductive, theatrical "ladies," and to the obstructive matriarchs who play such persistent and alarming roles in her writing. (At the same time that she gives her female characters such various power, allure, and force, she invents male "heroes" who are contemplative, passive, sensitive, and withdrawn.) From the first, too, Cather is interested in groups of women whose stoical domestic labor is a form of narration, and who provide inspiration for an American writing which can be at once heroic and female. . . .

But this is not her only kind of writing, nor her only subject matter. Cather's work gets its energy from contraries. She is pulled between the natural and the artificial, the native and the European. She is a democrat and an elitist. She relishes troll-like energy and primitivism as much as delicacy and culture. She is religious, and fatalistic. She is equally interested in renunciation and possessiveness, in impersonality and obsession. Her fictions are of split selves and doublings. Above all, there is a paradox for Cather in the act of writing itself.

Hermione Lee. *Willa Cather: A Life Saved Up* (London: Virago, 1989), pp. 10–12, 15–16

Willa Cather's fiction responds to the secularization of American space after the Darwinian revolution and to the threat it represents to the moral and spiritual moorings of Americans. Before Darwin, Americans considered themselves as the chosen of the universe; after Darwin, they were no longer the pinnacle of God's creation—they no longer could claim the benevolent garden as their home. As a result, Americans were forced to come to grips with new notions concerning the space that surrounded them, and Cather's fiction demonstrates how a person's world influences the direction of that person's life. Nevertheless, Cather's redefinition of American space goes beyond a mere acceptance of the Darwinian deterministic scenario. While the natural environment of Willa Cather's characters is antagonistic, it is not deterministic. She redefines the Darwinian world by rejecting the Darwinian laws of survival and by affirming the natural environment as an enabling context for proper human relationships. Yet Willa Cather's fiction also counters a romantic view of natural space by painting a picture of nature as hostile, by reducing the centrality of characters in the created order, by stripping those characters of their sense of "home," and by picturing the land itself as "other." Nature is no longer simply a means to transcendent reality, but nature is also not simply a means toward the human goals of success and domination. Rather, nature is otherness itself, and it participates in satisfying the human longing for an existence legitimated by, or grounded in, something greater than human design or control. . . .

What are the positive contributions of nature to human life in Cather's fiction then? First, nature is unpredictable and large enough to strike awe in those able to acknowledge its power; second, nature is a stabilizing force because it grants humanity a sense of limitation; third, nature is capacious enough to provide the room for understanding and reconciliation between differing cultural groups (on the frontier, many cultural groups can live and work together in a common effort to survive the harshness of the natural world); fourth, nature is both beneficent and forbidding, and this ambiguous quality, along with awesome power, grants it a sense of otherness; and finally, nature makes constructive human relationships possible, for while the natural life alone is not sufficient, it is necessary for the emergence of personal fulfillment and wholesome relationships.

The principal belief advocated by Cather's fiction, then, is in the paradigm for human relationships that it implies: (1) harmonious communion with nature is the context for the peaceful existence with one's neighbor; (2) natural and cultural communion establishes harmony within the (at times) antagonistic natural settings; (3) such harmony reinvests human life with a significance that the constraints of a Darwinian universe prevents; (4) finally, the human element overcomes the secularizing impulses of American life—impulses that fail to recognize the potential for sacrality in a person's relation to natural environments and to personal relationships. In other words, in Cather's secular world, human relationships replace what one loses from the destruction of the sacred environment, namely a relationship with deity.

> Conrad Eugene Ostwalt. *After Eden: The Secularization of American Space in the Fiction of Willa Cather and Theodore Dreiser* (Lewisburg: Bucknell Univ. Pr., 1990), pp. 73–74

[Willa Cather] was a very intense woman. She herself said that she always wanted to hang garlands on people or else put them to torture, and this tendency was so strong in her that it evidently rubbed off on those whose paths crossed hers, for all her life people seem either to have liked her greatly or else felt repelled by her. She made Thea Kronborg say that there was such a thing as "creative hate"; a good example of this in her own writing is her review of D'Annunzio's *Il Fuoco*, which she resented for its treatment of Eleonora Duse. . . .

[Cather] liked what was "real," honest, straightforward, clean by the standards of common, decent humanity. As early as her first trip to Europe in 1902, she turned with relief from Monte Carlo, where she even felt that the artificial activities carried on corrupted nature herself. In the *Archbishop* she would deplore the replacement in the churches of the Southwest of the original, crude, handmade art created by the people themselves with cheap purchased images, factory-made, and imported from the East. Even in Nebraska itself, once the generation of the pioneers had passed, a new breed came in that was more interested in driving into town in an automobile to buy something instead of staying on the farm and making it.

> Edward Wagenknecht. *Willa Cather* (New York: Continuum, 1993), pp. 139, 143–44

The new political readings of Cather are presumably being put forth in the service of political causes. Will they help those causes? Will it be useful if we argue that, while heterosexual men can write about anything they want, women can write only about gender, homosexuals only about sexuality? . . . Such a restriction, Cather decided, would not be placed on her. She wrote novels showing that women could do something important besides have sex. Then she wrote novels about history and exile and the life of the mind in relation to the world—in other words, all the things that women were not supposed to write about, though today they do, partly because Cather did. If we now argue that those subjects of hers were just covers, that what she was really writing about was the very things she chose not to write about, sex and gender, is this a vote for the rights of women and homosexuals? Or is it, however unwittingly, another attack on them?

Reading Cather criticism has taught me one thing. If it is not realistic to expect a nonpolitical criticism, one can still wish for and sometimes get a *sophisticated* criticism—one that, while indebted to a certain politics, can balance that concern with a sustained attention to what the artist is saying. . . .

I should add that feminism is no longer the cutting edge of Cather criticism. Multiculturalism is, though most of the work in this area is being done by feminists. These critics, probably born, on the average, in 1950, attempt to cope with the amazing fact that Ulysses S. Grant, sometimes betrays views different from theirs about blacks, Mexicans, and American Indians. Now and then, someone notices that Cather's opinions were typical of her generation—indeed, that they were also expressed by good feminists of the time. . . .

The parade of American literature goes by, float after float: realism, naturalism, psychological novel, social novel, political novel. Cather belongs with none of them, which means either that she is left out or, if she is desperately needed, that she is forced at gunpoint to put on a paper hat and join a group in which she has no place. Hence her uneasy standing with the feminists. She is not one of them, and they know it. That's why they don't like her.

> Joan Acocella. "Cather and the Academy." *TNY*. Nov. 27, 1995, pp. 70–71

BIBLIOGRAPHY

April Twilights, 1903 (p); *The Troll Garden*, 1905 (s); *Alexander's Bridge*, 1912 (n); *O Pioneers!* 1913 (n); *The Song of the Lark*, 1915 (n); *My Ántonia*, 1918 (n); *Youth and the Bright Medusa*, 1920 (s); *One of Ours*, 1922 (n); *April Twilights and Other Poems*, 1923; *A Lost Lady*, 1923 (n); *The Professor's House*, 1925 (n); *My Mortal Enemy*, 1926 (n); *Death Comes for the Archbishop*, 1927 (n); *The Fear That Walks by Noonday*, 1931 (misc); *Shadows on the Rock*, 1931 (n); *Obscure Destinies*, 1931 (s); *Lucy Gayheart*, 1935 (n); *Not under Forty*, 1936 (e); *The Novels and Stories of Willa Cather*,

1937–38; *Sapphira and the Slave Girl*, 1940 (n); *The Old Beauty*, 1948 (s); *Writings from Willa Cather's Campus Years*, 1950; *Willa Cather in Europe: Her Own Story of the First Journey*, 1956 (t, newsletters of 1902); *Collected Short Fiction*, 1965; *The Kingdom of Art*, 1967 (c); *April Twilights*, newly edited, 1968 (p); *The World and the Parish*, ed. William M. Curtin, 1971 (e); *Uncle Valentine, and Other Stories*, ed. Bernice Slote, 1973; *Willa Cather in Person: Interviews, Speeches, and Letters*, 1987 (misc); *Early Novels and Stories*, 1987 [Library of America ed.]; *Great Short Works*, 1989; *Later Novels*, 1990 [Library of America ed.]; *Stories, Poems, and Other Writings*, 1992 (misc); *My Ántonia*, 1994 (annotated ed.); *The Enchanted Bluff*, 1996; *Paul's Case and Other Stories*, 1996; *The Autobiography of S. S. McClure*, 1997; *Willa Cather Reader*, 1997

CHABON, Michael (1965–)

[In *A Modern World: And Other Stories*] each of the stories concerns an individual's adaptation to a changed relationship, be it with wife (or ex-wife), friend, lover, or parent. Particularly evocative are the five final stories which fall under the rubric "The Lost World." They deal with a boy's response to his parent's divorce and their subsequent attempts to establish new partnerships. [Michael] Chabon writes with intelligence, humor, and an obvious love of language. In the first story's marvelous opening paragraph, the protagonist goes from performing his toilet "with patience, hope, and a ruthless punctilic" to sitting in the back at his cousin's wedding "awash in a nostalgic tedium . . . wishing for irretrievable things." It leaves one hoping that like Dr. Shapiro in "More Than Human." Chabon never surrenders his love for "the soothing foolishness of words."

> David W. Henderson. *Library Journal.* February 15, 1991, p. 219

When Michael Chabon published his first (and so far only) novel at the age of twenty-three, responses tended to concentrate on its youthful decadence and sexual precocity. His fey charm and classic good looks seemed to merge with the novel's eloquent unease; writer and text were projected as one, the "brat-pack" had at last found their dandy. In place of [Bret Easton] Ellis's sparse postmodernity or McInerney's apocalyptic quest for selfhood, Chabon offered a prose rich with promiscuous abandon and articulate sensitivity. *The Mysteries of Pittsburgh* follows Art Bechstein through the summer of his graduation year—his ambiguous detachment from his gangster-father, his entanglement in a web of homo- and heterosexual friendships, and the eventual collision between these two apparently mutually exclusive worlds. Art's heroic drive is to reject the corrupt acquisition of money as represented by his father, and embrace instead the sublimated currency of his contemporaries—the language of learning, the veneer of social bohemianism, the alternative realm of righteous possession. As the very pun on his name suggests, Art opposes the laundered money of his family with the purity of the aesthete—a projection of himself whose value is measured by its distance from utility. In short, Art is not for sale.

From this brief synopsis, it is easy to see why [F. Scott] Fitzgerald provided the most common reference point for Chabon's readers and reviewers. Indeed, the novel's very first line evokes a conscious echo of the opening of *The Great Gatsby*. . . .

Similarly, the network of relations with which Art becomes involved all playfully invite their Fitzgeraldian equivalents. The hoodlum chic of Cleveland and the corrupt gentility of his girlfriend Jane both offer comparison with Tom and Daisy Buchanan. . . .

What seems to be emerging then is an unproblematic inheritance by Chabon of Fitzgerald's oeuvre—both writers standing side by side at the junction of propriety and transgression, the reserved and the renegade, the flavor of Europe and the freshness of America. Certain critics have even gone so far as to translate the last of these oppositions—Europe and America—into a paradigm for Art's bisexuality. . . .

Relationships through recall, discourse and desire, Chabon's trajectory is towards the histories of mystery, rather than the peculiarities of Pittsburgh. As with his collection of short stories, *A Model World*, the ironies that underpin his prose are implicit in his titles. The Euro-American may regard herself as exemplary, as the perfect model, yet behaves with the static all-consuming commerciality of the fashion model. From paradigm to mannequin, from the Art of speech to the (f)act of silence, Chabon presents us with an America torn between the ideal and insubstantial. His work testifies to the double-edged demands of appearance, the emotional *double entendres* of utterance. Chabon's achievement is to maintain the pose of the dandy while seeking to explode the foundations of that fiction.

In his novel and short stories, Chabon exists at the junction where his posture and imposture converge and do battle, where decorum and desire merge into the deceptive world of masquerade. Chabon's world is a model one, and therein lies its problem. For behind the model lurks the exposé, the expired, the self-destructive exhibition of never-ending desire.

> Graham Caveney. "French Kissing in the U.S.A." In Elizabeth Young and Graham Caveney, eds. *Shopping in Space: Essays on America's Blank Generation Fiction* (Boston: Atlantic Monthly Press, 1992), pp. 75–76, 83–84

Much of *Wonder Boys* possesses [a] fever-dream quality of narration, as the perpetually drugged, failed author Tripp stumbles through a weekend that would be much better lost, but refuses to go away.

Tripp's problem is not writer's block but writer's bloat; he is a former *Wunderkind* whose fourth novel, *Wonder Boys*, is clearly turning into a monster as flabby and directionless as its author. It is hard to avoid making ironic parallels between Tripp's work and Chabon's novel of the same title: indeed, the dust-jacket photograph (of Chabon's manuscript) and the blurb positively encourage such thoughts. Since his first novel, the much-hyped *The Mysteries of Pittsburgh*, was published in 1987, Chabon has produced only one book of short stories, while his more prolific contemporaries, Jay McInerney and Bret Easton Ellis, have seen their celebrity turned against them. But he has managed to make out of the stuff of novelist's nightmares a winningly cynical comedy of literary fame. *Pittsburgh* was praised for its transformation of the rite-of-passage genre; here, Chabon opts for a mixture of campus novel, *Sunset Boulevard*, and picaresque Gonzo-monologue. . . .

Perhaps inevitably, Tripp's story runs out of steam; and the novel ends up too much like *Fear and Loathing in the Creative Writing Faculty*. Nevertheless *Wonder Boys* has been worth the wait, although it may well prove a disappointment to devotees of Chabon's earlier work. The book provides a great deal of fun, partly because it stubbornly refuses to be the Great American Novel that Tripp's *Wonder Boys* fails to be. Chabon offers us a sobering suggestion that writers are destined to become the losers they love to portray; and an ounce of self-parody is worth several volumes of portentousness. Even so, one can't help feeling that he is gnawing a little too gleefully at the hand that feeds him.

Bharat Tandon. *TLS: The Times Literary Supplement*. April 21, 1995, p. 20

BIBLIOGRAPHY
The Mysteries of Pittsburgh, 1988 (n); *A Model World*, 1991 (s); *Wonder Boys*, 1995 (n); *Werewolves in Their Youth*, 1999 (n)

CHANDLER, Raymond (1888–1959)

Most of the characters in this story [*The Big Sleep*] are tough, many of them are nasty and some of them are both. . . . The language used in this book is often vile—at times so filthy that the publishers have been compelled to resort to the dash, a device seldom employed in these unsqueamish days. As a study in depravity, the story is excellent, with Marlowe standing out as almost the only fundamentally decent person in it.

Isaac Anderson. *New York Times Book Section*. Feb. 12, 1939. p. 20

After a long and notable career in the pulp magazines, Raymond Chandler made his mark in books with four novels published between 1939 and 1943. Most critics and almost all readers recognized in him the legitimate successor of Dashiell Hammett. . . . His new novel, *The Little Sister*, has been awaited with as much eagerness as Hammett's ten-year promised novel—especially by those critics and readers who have felt that Hammett and Chandler are significant exponents not merely of the detective story, but of the American novel. It is partly, of course, the heightened expectation which makes *The Little Sister* seem unsatisfactory. But partly, too, dissatisfaction comes from the revelation of an abyss of emptiness.

Plot and characters are the stuff of any run-of-the-mill toughie. Chandler's treatment differs from the routine in his prose, which is still vigorous, clean, distinctive. . . . But the great distinction dividing this from all other detective stories is its scathing hatred of the human race. The characters, aside from the little sister, are reasonably well-painted cardboard, brought to life only by the sheer force of their viciousness.

Anthony Boucher. *New York Times Book Section*. Sept. 25, 1949. p. 24

I pulled his leg about his plots, which always seem to me to go wildly astray. What holds the books together and makes them so compulsively readable, even to alpha minds who would not normally think of reading a thriller, is the dialogue. There is a throwaway, down-beat quality about Chandler's dialogue, whether wisecracking or not, that takes one happily through chapter after chapter in which there is no more action than Philip Marlowe driving his car and talking to his girl, or a rich old woman consulting her lawyer on the sun porch. His aphorisms were always his own.

Ian Fleming. *London Magazine*. Dec., 1959. p. 50

The writer of mystery novels, if he takes his work seriously, must find his situation maddening. His books may be relished by highly cultivated people and his literary skills widely admired, but through all the praise there will run a streak of condescension. Even his most ardent fans will never take him quite seriously, and their loftiest compliment is only too likely to be the suggestion that he ought to be writing ''real'' novels.

The frustrations this situation can provoke are vividly demonstrated in the letters of Raymond Chandler [*Raymond Chandler Speaking*] which have now been published, together with some essays, notes on writing, and scraps of fiction, three years after his death. . . . They differ from most letters in that they are as gripping as any novel. They are cantankerous, forthright, and often hilarious. . . . But what they reveal most clearly is the anguish of a man who considered himself an artist but knew that he was generally regarded as merely a brilliant hack. . . .

Sarel Eimerl. *The Reporter*. May 10, 1962. pp. 54–5

Mr. Raymond Chandler has written that he intends to take the body out of the vicarage garden and give the murder back to those who are good at it. If he wishes to write detective stories, i.e., stories where the reader's principal interest is to learn who did it, he could not be more mistaken, for in a society of professional criminals, the only possible motives for desiring to identify the murderer are blackmail or revenge, which both apply to individuals, not to the group as a whole, and can equally well inspire murder. Actually, whatever he may say, I think Mr. Chandler is interested in writing, not detective stories, but serious studies of a criminal milieu, the Great Wrong Place, and his powerful but extremely depressing books should be read and judged, not as escape literature, but as works of art.

W.H. Auden. *The Dyer's Hand* (Random). 1962. p. 151

Chandler's hero is the all-American boy with whom the reader easily identifies himself, the rough man of action who would never harm a fly but would stamp out injustice with a vigorous passion. Thematically, Chandler's work is in one of the mainstreams of American literature, not the nineteenth-century New England one of concern for the brooding thoughts of the introvert, but the broad stream of frontier literature that moved from Georgia of the 1830's to the California of the 1950's—enveloping as it traveled westward the simple problems of the extrovert who, by knowing right from wrong, had only to exert a courageous amount of rugged individualism in order to end up a hardened but virtuous hero. This mainstream of American literature contributed thousands of modern morality plays, of which Chandler's are excellently written examples.

T.S. Eliot discovered his poetic home in England; Eugene O'Neill rarely strayed from the Atlantic or its seaboard; Raymond Chandler found Los Angeles to be the natural milieu for his hero's efforts to untangle the messy web into which the American man had naively wandered.

> Philip Durham. *Down These Mean Streets a Man Must Go: Raymond Chandler's Knight* (North Carolina). 1963. pp. 5–6

The obvious accomplishment of his thrillers is to generate a sort of nervous tension which is the literary analogue to the tension generated by being an American. . . . Chandler's attitude is to look at what's there in the expectation that good and evil are all mixed together. . . . It is a stoic vision. In his novels Chandler did not quite sustain it, being much too romantic and not quite courageous enough to bear the full bitterness of that vision. . . . If you say that all this provides somewhat meager fare for romance, I must agree. But if you say that this distorts life beyond recognition, I must object that you do not know that meager region, Southern California, as well as Chandler did. His chief accomplishment, it seems to me, is to create for the place a fictional image which corresponds to the actuality more vividly and more accurately than anything written by anyone else. . . . Still, Chandler's version is not *the* version of Southern California. He, rather more than is strategic in a writer, puts himself at the mercy of the place's notion of itself; for this notion is self-deceiving, somewhat inaccurate and confused.

> George P. Elliott. *A Piece of Lettuce* (Random). 1964. pp. 54–5, 58, 63

There are all gradations of class and milieu and speech and diction in Chandler's novels. For these reasons, Chandler, through Marlowe, succeeds as no one else has succeeded in portraying Los Angeles, including Hollywood, and it seems at times that it is neither the violence nor the solution of the mystery Chandler is interested in as it is the city and the people, through the whole range of which, in the solution of the crime, Marlowe moves. . . . Emphasis is usually placed on the portrayal of Southern California, including Hollywood, and on the interrelation in this society between power and crime; and the unexpected relation of one segment to another, from the bottom (the little, helpless, incompetent, and hurt), to the top (usually the ruthless, rich, and spoiled). . . . In Marlowe's world, disunity, disruption, mobility, immorality, rootlessness and ruthlessness provide the constant motif. Marlowe himself is an old-fashioned character, chivalrous, with an individual sense of conduct and of justice; he judges his world, implicitly at least, from a point of view as conservative as Chandler's upperclass English education and his own cheerful admission that he was a snob would suggest.

> Herbert Ruhm in *Tough Guy Writers of the Thirties*, ed. David Madden (Southern Illinois). 1968. pp. 178–9

The action of Chandler's books takes place inside the microcosm, in the darkness of a local world without the benefit of the federal Constitution, as in a world without God. The literary shock is dependent on the habit of the political double standard in the mind of the reader: it is only because we are used to thinking of the nation as a whole in terms of justice that we are struck by these images of people caught in the power of a local county authority as though they were in a foreign country. The local power apparatus is beyond appeal, in this other face of federalism; the rule of naked force and money is complete and undisguised by any embellishments of theory. . . .

In this sense the honesty of the detective can be understood as an organ of perception, a membrane which, irritated, serves to indicate in its sensitivity the nature of the world around it. For if the detective is dishonest, his job boils down to the technical problem of how to succeed on a given assignment. If he is honest, he is able to feel the resistance of things, to permit an intellectual vision of what he goes through on the level of action. And Chandler's sentimentalism, which attaches to occasional honest characters in the earlier books, but which is perhaps strongest in *The Long Goodbye*, is the reverse and complement of this vision, a momentary relief from it, a compensation for it. . . .

The detective's journey is episodic because of the fragmentary atomistic nature of the society he moves through. . . . The form of Chandler's books reflects an initial American separation of people from each other, their need to be linked by some external force (in this case the detective) if they are ever to be fitted together as parts of the same picture puzzle.

> Fredric Jameson. *Southern Review*. Summer, 1970. pp. 632–3

Chandler had a fine feeling for the sound and value of words, and he added to it a very sharp eye for places, things, people, and the wisecracks (this out-of-date word seems still the right one) that in their tone and timing are almost always perfect. . . . It is impossible to convey in a single quotation Chandler's almost perfect ear for dialogue, but it comes through in all the later books whether the people talking are film stars or publicity agents, rich men, gangsters, or policemen. To this is joined a generous indignation roused in him by meanness and corruption, and a basic seriousness about his violent entertainments.

> Julian Symons. *Mortal Consequences* (Harper). 1972. p. 142

[*The Big Sleep*], and the six other novels by Chandler, are in the tradition of a negative romanticism which is perhaps the dominant mode of American literature from Hawthorne to our contemporary black humorists—that power of darkness which Hawthorne, Poe and Melville explored, which Mark Twain could not laugh away, and which created a mythical landscape in Faulkner. Poe's "The Fall of the House of Usher" can be regarded as the rehearsal for the saga of the Sartoris-Compson-Sutpen families in Yoknapatawpha County. And the predecessor of Chandler's Californian nightmare had his hero Dupin "be enamored of the night for her own sake." But where Poe brought inductive light to moral darkness, Chandler refuses to cheat his vision in like manner. When Marlowe has solved a dilemma, he has not explained the enigma. All of Chandler's books end on a note of dissatisfaction. The purported solution does not tidy things up since there is no end to a waking nightmare.

This dark vision has lost none of its power today. The excess of violence of which Chandler has been needlessly accused is now hardly noticeable, nor was it lovingly attended to for shock effect, but rather described because life is simply that cheap in this truly egalitarian society: literally, a matter of fact. And so Chandler does not laud death with the lyrical mesmerism of Hemingway, nor does he play metaphysical games with it in Sartrean ingenuity. A death is a waste of life.

E.M. Beekman. *Massachusetts Review*. Winter, 1973. p. 164

Now if in comparing the tender and the tough conventions one is looking for "real life" in the verifiable sense, one must conclude that although the first kind of story will not bear sceptical examination, the second is—as Shakespeare says apropos of two liars— "an even more wonderful song than the other." Nor is this all that Raymond Chandler's essay ["The Simple Art of Murder"] brings to mind. The tender school aims at producing a denouement having the force of necessity, as in Greek tragedy. All the facts (clues, words, motives) must converge to give the mystery one solution and one only. That by itself is a good reason for making the crime occur in a law-abiding circle, where the habits of the *dramatis personae* are by hypothesis regular and reasonable. In such a setting the violence of murder is the more striking, and stronger also the desire to manacle the offender. Murder among thugs and drug addicts is hardly unexpected, and the feeling that in this milieu anything can happen does not increase but rather lessens the interest. Hence the artistic need for the tough writer to involve some innocent, whose ways *are* peaceable, and to put steadily in peril the detective-defender of that lump of virtue. In short, in murder à la Chandler, murder is not enough to keep us going—and neither is detection, since it is never a feature of the foreground.

Chandler as artist is so aware of these lacks that he reinforces the damsel-in-distress motive with what is nothing less than a political motive. He makes it clear in his essay that the hero of the new and improved genre is fighting society. Except for the favoured victim, he alone is pure in heart, a C-green incorruptible. The rich are all crooked or "phonies," and cowards in the end. Since the police, the mayor, the whole Establishment are soon shown as a conspiracy to pervert justice and kill off troublemakers, we naturally share the detective's smothered indignation and are powerfully driven, like him, to see the right vindicated.

Jacques Barzun. In *The World of Raymond Chandler*, ed. Miriam Gross (A & W, 1977), pp. 161–62

Chandler's uniqueness—and the source of his popularity—is the product of a wide variety of personal traits and talents, circumstances and coincidences. He brought to his work a European sensibility and education supported by a bedrock of childhood experiences in the American Great Plains of the late nineteenth century. He arrived in California while the pioneering spirit still thrived and witnessed the rise of the movie studios and the attendant exploitation of glamour and illusion. He barely survived the First World War and was just achieving the peak of his writing career as Western civilization threatened to fall apart in the Second.

Given his far-ranging experience, it is perhaps remarkable that he maintained the conviction throughout it all that "the best way to comment on large things is to comment on small things." The "small things" that preoccupied him were character and language. By concentrating on the motives of individual characters, he approaches such larger themes as the unpredictability of human emotion under pressure and the manner in which changing times appear to alter one's ethical possibilities. He illuminates the way in

which characters are alternately responsible for the world in which they live and trapped by that world. As Dostoevsky reminded us in *Crime and Punishment*, "this damnable psychology cuts both ways." The reactions of Chandler's characters to their psychic binds imply the pervasive instability at the core of modern society. And the language by which these characters reveal themselves allows the author to convey a sense of the delicate web by which we are all bound together.

The most significant "small things" that occupy Chandler are the mind and actions of his detective, Philip Marlowe. Marlowe is a microcosm of both Chandler's concern for character and his concern for the language by which that character is expressed. It is Marlowe's voice, of course, that is the constant ground of Chandler's stories. It is the detached, ironic, frequently alienated tone of that voice that holds our attention and provides an interpretive framework for the tales.

But while we may feel we know Marlowe's voice almost instinctively, a close examination of the novels reveals very little of a "factual" nature about the detective. We know a few details about his surroundings, almost nothing about his past, and very little about his personal motives. We almost never see his mind working, except as that mental activity is translated into dramatic action. And yet, we identify with him.

Understanding that identification may be as close as we can come to appreciating Chandler's power and uniqueness as a writer. And comprehending what Chandler called his "objective method" is essential to that appreciation.

Jerry Speir. *Raymond Chandler* (Ungar, 1981), pp. vii–viii

BIBLIOGRAPHY

The Big Sleep, 1939 (n); *Farewell, My Lovely*, 1940 (n); *The High Window*, 1942 (n); *The Lady in the Lake*, 1943 (n); *Five Murderers*, 1944 (s); *Five Sinister Characters*, 1945 (s); *Finger Man and Other Stories*, 1946 (s); *Red Wind*, 1946 (s); *Spanish Blood*, 1946 (s); *The Little Sister*, 1949 (n); *The Simple Art of Murder*, 1950 (e, s); *The Raymond Chandler Omnibus* (*The Big Sleep, Farewell, My Lovely, The High Window, The Lady in the Lake*), 1953 (n) (England); *The Long Goodbye*, 1954 (n); *Playback*, 1958 (n); *Smart-Aleck Kill* (from *The Simple Art of Murder*), 1958 (s); *Pearls Are a Nuisance* (from *The Simple Art of Murder, The Little Sister, The Long Goodbye, Playback*), 1962 (n) (England); *Raymond Chandler Speaking*, 1962 (letters and previously unpublished fiction); *The Midnight Raymond Chandler*, 1971 (misc); *Chandler before Marlowe: Raymond Chandler's Early Prose and Poetry, 1908–1912* 1973; *Notebooks*, 1974; *The Blue Dahlia: A Screenplay*, 1976; *Selected Letters*, 1984; *Raymond Chandler's Unknown Thriller: The Screenplay of Playback*, 1985; *Four Complete Philip Marlowe Novels*, 1986; *Selections*, 1987; *Killer in the Rain*, 1988 (s); *Pickup on Noon Street*, 1988 (s); *Poodle Springs* (with Robert B. Parker), 1989; *Later Novels and Other Writings*, 1995; *Stories and Early Novels*, 1995

CHAVEZ, Denise (1948–)

With the publication of *The Last of the Menu Girls*, Denise Chavez joins the ranks of writers who are rounding out the parameters of

Chicano literature. The feminine voice adds a new vision and dimension to the literature of this community. Clearly, a new vanguard is here, and its name is woman.

In this collection, the reader will savor the poignant experiences and dreams of Rocio, a young girl whose rites of passage into womanhood give unity to the collage of stories. At the beginning of the novel Rocio cries out against the traditional serving roles which society has prescribed for women, and she opts for the life of the artist. By the novel's end she has found her calling, and that is to give meaning to the emotionally turbulent lives of the people she has known. It is Rocio's mother who wisely counsels and dares her daughter to write the story of their lives.

Denise's novel reflects her particular sense of place, revealing the depths of the world of women and the flavor of southern New Mexico. The central metaphor of the novel is the home. The family, the known neighborhood and the role of women in this context are Denise's concern as a writer. Her eye for detail is sharp; the interior monologues of her characters are revealing; and Denise's long training as a dramatist serves her well in creating intriguing plot and dialogue. In short, all the strengths of a writer are here.

Rocio's yearning is to write a great novel from the lives of those people she knows best. It is the same dream Denise Chavez has followed, challenging us to let go of familiar patterns and to enter the rich and imaginative world which she portrays with such feeling and insight.

Rudolfo A. Anaya.In the *The Last of the Menu Girls*, by Denise Chavez (Arte Publico Press, 1986), p. ix.

At this time, Chavez must be considered *the* chicana play-wright from New Mexico. Consistently active in the theater since the early seventies, she has written more plays and had more plays produced than any other Hispanic playwright. Her plays reflect different segments of New Mexican society; her characters talk and act like people familiar to all Hispanic New Mexicans. She celebrates the traditions and customs of Hispanic New Mexico. The *Sabor nuevomexicano* serves to root the plays in time and place. Yet there is a universal quality which makes these plays produceable outside of New Mexico. *Plaza* was a success at the Edinburgh Festival in Scotland). The inner conflicts of the characters are common to all humanity; so are their triumphs and defeats. Chavez' characters are masterful conceptions. They live on after the curtain has come down. For this reason, above all, Chavez is on her way to becoming an outstanding and original playwright. She is someone whose works are worth seeing and therefore deserves more recognition and support.

Martha E. Heard. *The Americas Review.* Summer 1988, pp. 83–91.

In the introduction to Denise Chávez's *The Last of the Menu Girls* (1986), novelist Rudolfo Anaya states: ''With the publication of *The Last of the Menu Girls*, Denise Chávez joins the ranks of writers who are rounding out the parameters of Chicano literature. The feminine voice adds a new vision and dimension to the literature of this community. Clearly, a new vanguard is here, and its name is woman.'' With these words Anaya alludes to the fact that Chicano literature written in the 1960s and 1970s, a literature that largely promoted the political agenda and ideals of a sociopolitical movement, was written primarily by men and manifested a male world view. This characteristic of the early stages of Chicano literature was to change drastically in the 1980s as the voices of Chicanas began to be heard and heeded as part of the corpus of Chicano literature. Denise Chávez's is one of the strongest female voices to speak with vigor and authority about the lives of Hispanic women, thereby contributing the missing brush strokes in the collective literary portrait of the Mexican American community. Of special importance is the fact that she writes about a region of the United States, Southern New Mexico, that has been virtually ignored at the national level. Its proximity to the Mexican–United States border makes this an area where two cultures meet, sometimes in violent confrontation but more often in an interdependent relationship. The use of Spanish in her English text brings to readers of American literature an acute reminder that ours is a nation comprised of racial, ethnic and linguistic diversity. . . .

Chávez's theater focuses on the quotidian aspects of life in small New Mexico towns. She blends Hispanic cultural imagery and folk traditions with motifs from mainstream popular culture to show the New Mexican Hispanic community struggling to maintain its ethnic identity vis-a-vis the swift and powerful currents of the dominant culture. But even as Hispanics resist the temptation, a process of cultural hybridization is apparent in Chávez's work. A sharp observing eye and a keen ear for colloquial speech allow Chávez to capture the richness that results from the clash and mingling of cultures that occur in the border contact zone where her stories and dramas unfold. While her dramatic themes are broad and encompass many aspects of Chicano culture, Chávez privileges female characters in her dramatic work, particularly in pieces such as *Novena Narratives y Ofrendas Nuevomexicanas* and *Hecho en México*. In this sense, her plays are the literary antecedents to her better-known work, *The Last of the Menu Girls*. . . .

Chávez's style, in both her drama and her narrative, is characterized by a persistent movement from exterior to interior reality. The poetic description of landscapes, for example, lead her to interior spaces where critical self-examination takes place. She explores the physical attributes of her characters as a means of revealing their psychological profiles. The enumeration and cataloging of cultural artifacts can turn abruptly to musings of a spiritual nature. Humor is also a mark of Chávez's work. The latter is most often achieved through the blending of Spanish and English and through the use of colloquial folk expressions intended as satirical barbs.

Memory is an important ingredient in Chávez's writing. In *The Last of the Menu Girls,* what Rocío Esquivel remembers most vividly from her past are family, place, and the many women who had an impact on her life. She recalls transcultural and cross-class relationships but she focuses most sharply on the intimate relationships between sisters and between mothers and daughters. The absence of the divorced father calls attention to the aching desire to fill the gap that he leaves in the family. But the presence of a bountiful and take-control mother, of aunts and Mexican maids, creates security for the growing daughters. This work fits well within the tradition of coming-of-age fiction in America. In keeping with this tradition, the text takes the reader on a journey to the narrator-protagonist's past to reveal gradually the discovery of selfhood. Those moments, events, places, objects and persons that imprinted themselves upon the narrator's psyche become significant in the present not only through the act of remembering but, more important, through the act in inscription. As is commonly the case with coming-of-age narrative, the final pages reveal the remembering self as writing self as well. It is thus at the crossroads of memory and inscription that the possibility of self-discovery and self-construction lies.

A sense of place is central to all of Chávez's work, and in *The Last of the Menu Girls* it is the crucial organizing metaphor. In the broader geophysical sense, the space that Rocío remembers is the desert of Southwestern New Mexico, or what she calls "the arid tension of the desert's balance." The balance brings spiritual solace to Rocío Esquivel; the arid tension stirs desire. Female desire thus becomes another theme that Chávez explores as an important facet of the young girl's journey to maturation. The neighborhood is a special place where children begin to learn the intricacies of social interaction. As Rocío recalls the ditch bank of her neighborhood and the special trees of her yard, she is able to reconstruct those first social encounters that structured the early configuration of her gendered self. And finally, Chávez's sense of place can be private. Rocío Esquivel spends hours in her mother's closet, scrutinizing family photos, forgotten Christmas gifts, old wedding dresses, bottles of perfume as she searches for clues to the meaning of womanhood. The home, with all its secret niches, thus becomes a key to the unfolding of the self within the circle of family.

While it is her fiction that has brought Chávez national recognition, there is no doubt that she continues to see theater as an essential part of her life. The recent tour in the United States of her one-woman performance piece, *Women in This State of Grace,* is a dramatization of scenes from her narrative works. In this performance, the talents of writer and actor blend as the characters come alive to share with the viewers their profoundly human qualities, their strong belief in the primacy of human relationships— especially relationships between women—and their ability to survive social pressures with dignity.

> Erlinda Gonzales-Berry. In *Reference Guide to American Literature, 3rd edition,* ed. Jim Kamp (St. James Press, 1994.)

In *Face of an Angel,* Soveida Dosamantes, the narrator and protagonist, unravels the lives of her family, her coworkers, her husbands, and her lovers. Agua Oscura (Dark Water), New Mexico, is one of those small towns where everyone knows everybody's ancestry, as well as their darkest secrets. "What stories I know about these people I will share with you. The stories begin with the men and always end with the women; that's the way it is in our family." Soveida views her world with a woman's eye, and the objectivity of a goddess. Rich in family gossip, the book is engrossing, amusing, and definitely one to be savored. The author's mordant wit is pervasive, the language is pithy, blunt, and explicit.

The novel's many characters are deeply flawed human beings who enmesh the reader in their complex lives. Soveida's Grandmother Lupita and her lifelong maid, Oralia, are the strong influences in this young woman's life. Her mother, Dolores, a seemingly weak woman, has been beaten down by Trancha, her strange and domineering mother.

Her Grandmother Trancha, until the day she died, remained a bitter woman whose words were "hard as a fist and painful as flesh doubled over." It was her Grandmother Lupita that Soveida called Mamá. Her mother was always Dolores or Dolly. Her father, whom she called by his first name, Luardo, had shown much promise: "If it hadn't been for his two loves—drinking and screwing—Luardo Dosamantes would probably have been a great man, maybe even governor of New Mexico." Soveida falls in love with good-looking men whom she marries. The first marriage ends in divorce; the second leaves her a widow. She then gets pregnant by her lover's brother.

For more than 25 years, Soveida works at El Farol Mexican Restaurant in Agua Oscura. The intimate details of the restaurant's life are related with humor and irony. The staff—chef Eloisa, "the Queen of Mexican food in Agua Oscura"; Larry Larragoite, the hard-working, anxiety-ridden owner of El Farol; Petra, the old waitress who could not add; and an odd assortment of busboys, salad chefs, and waitresses—delight the reader with their daily affairs. The funniest restaurant episode concerns the "the night of the cucas," when Chuy, the elderly custodian, decides to spray for roaches in the middle of the day rather than after the late evening closing: "Clumps of stunned and writhing roaches lay on the floor, or leapt from the moist walls, throwing their agitated bodies wherever they could. Others bounded past, feverishly driven, and under siege."

Soveida's legacy to her profession is *The Book of Service: A Handbook for Servers,* a 14-chapter handbook for waitresses. The theme of service is pervasive in the lives of Soveida and her female relatives, and is revisited throughout the novel through excerpts from Soveida's handbook. In the first chapter of her handbook, Soveida writes: "As a child, I was imbued with the idea that the purpose of life was service. Service to God. Country. Men. Not necessarily in that order, but lumped together like that. For God is a family man. . . . Life was, and is, service, no matter what our station in it."

The densely packed pages of this long novel made me laugh and nod in agreement. It left me wanting to read it again to catch the nuances I might have missed. Chavez has become a fine writer and a great storyteller. With *Face of an Angel,* her second book, her name can be added to the growing list of Chicana authors making their mark in contemporary American fiction.

> Irene Campos Carr. *Belles Lettres.* Spring 1995, pp. 35.

BIBLIOGRAPHY
Novitiates, 1973 (d); *The Mask of November,* 1975 (d); *The Flying Tortilla Man,* 1975 (d); *Elevators,* 1977 (d); *The Adobe Rabbit,* 1980 (d); *Nacimiento,* 1980 (d); *Santa Fe Charme,* 1980 (d); *An Evening of Theatre,* 1981 (d); *How Junior Got Throwed in the Joint,* 1981 (d); *Si, Hay Posada,* 1981 (d); *El Santero de Cordova,* 1981 (d); *The Green Madonna,* 1982 (d); *Hecho en Mexico,* with Nita Luna, 1983 (d); *La Morenita,* 1983 (d); *Francis!,* 1983 (d); *Plaza,* 1984 (d); *Plague-Time,* 1985 (d); *The Last of the Menu Girls,* 1986 (s); *Novena Narrativas,* 1987 (d); *The Step,* 1987 (d); *Language of Vision,* 1988 (d); *Women in the State of Grace,* 1989 (d); *The Woman Who Knew the Language of Animals/La Mujer que sabi̧ el idioma de los animales,* 1992 (ch); *Face of an Angel,* 1994 (n)

CHEEVER, John (1912–1982)

As examples of fiction from *The New Yorker*, these stories of Mr. Cheever's [*The Way Some People Live*] are among the best that have appeared there recently, and this is particularly true of those which exploit a cool and narrow-eyed treatment of tensions arising from the war. Mr. Cheever's drunken draft-dodger and his young draftee are particularly well managed, and the sketches in which they appear are quite unblemished by the pieties and embarrassments which ordinarily mark war fiction published while a war is on. Many of the other stories—and if my count is right, all but six of the thirty included here are from *The New Yorker*—have not improved by their being collected in a book. As individual magazine stories they seemed better than they are; read one after another, there nearly identical lengths, similarities of tone and situation, and their somehow remote and unambitious style, produce an effect of sameness and eventually of tedium. The formula has been flourished too obviously and too often.

> Weldon Kees. *New Republic*. April 19, 1943. p. 576

He does not so much imagine experience as have clever ideas for stories. There are [in *The Enormous Radio and Other Stories*] the ingenious camera-angles, the elevator operators (two of these) and the apartment-house superintendents, very cute and innocent and staring wide-eyed at quality folk. There are the neat discoveries of commonplace morals in sophisticated lives. When Mr. Cheever tries for the big idea, his stories waver toward a formally—and therefore morally—ambiguous melodrama. . . . These are the stories of a clever short-story manufacturer, a man who has ideas about experience but has never known these ideas in experience. Their language and technique are highly refined; their feeling is crude.

> Arthur Mizener. *New Republic*. May 25, 1953. pp. 19–20

The Wapshot Chronicle is an antique bureau filled with everything and apparently everybody under the sun. . . .

Roughly the first third of the book is devoted to life in this charming old river town. Most of the rest is about the fortunes and misfortunes of the two sons, Moses and Coverly, in Washington, New York, San Francisco, Island 93 in the South Pacific, a rocket launching settlement in the West, and an imported castle inhabited by an ancient Wapshot cousin named Justina and her toothsome ward, Melissa.

As readers of Cheever's short stories know, he is a wonder with the limited scene, the separate episode, the overheard conversation, the crucial confrontation. *The Wapshot Chronicle* reflects these powers with immense vitality, largesse, and profusion. But it is held together largely by spit and wire. It shows that while John Cheever's fortes are many, amusing, touching, and admirable, one of them is not architectonics.

> Carlos Baker. *Saturday Review*. March 23, 1957. p. 14

This is . . . a central theme in Mr. Cheever's work: the power of human love and desire, which turns out to be a shield for human loneliness and melancholy—along with a note of broad farce, or of downright burlesque at times, which accompanies the tragicomedy of sex. It is at this point that [*The Wapshot Chronicle*] breaks through the proper confines of "sensibility" in the typical *New Yorker* story. The depth of the narrative lies in the accent on human "unrequital" and in the lyrical apostrophes to the sea-born Venus, to love and women. The ironic twist lies in the antics of lovers. . . . The last half of the book is a picaresque of modern times set against the earlier, nostalgic background of the New England past. The two parts don't quite hang together, and the story as a whole becomes rather fragmentary and episodic. One has the final impression of a series of related "sketches," which do not quite achieve either the impact of the short story proper or the inner growth and development of a novel.

> Maxwell Geismar. *New York Times Book Section*. March 24, 1957. p. 5

For years every discussion of what constitutes a typical *New Yorker* short story has got around to Cheever, the common view being that he is quite representative and yet a good deal better than average. . . . He is one of the sharpest of observers, and some of his descriptions of suburban scenes are a pure joy. He has also developed an admirable technique for handling a complex series of incidents, so that such a story as "The Trouble of Marcie Flint" has a remarkable density. But his great gift is for entering into the minds of men and women at crucial moments. . . . Cheever knows where drama is to be found, and he has taught himself how to make the most of it.

> Granville Hicks. *Saturday Review*. Sept. 13, 1958. pp. 33, 47

What Cheever's well-heeled admirers want is what, by an ultimate failure of sensibility, he recedes into giving them: an exercise in sophisticated self-criticism, together with a way back into the situation as before. This isn't to say that he has nothing else to give; only that the extravagance of esteem for him has psychological, not esthetic origins . . . For Cheever, with all his wit and sophistication and his coldness of eye, is essentially a sentimentalist and usually contrives to let his fish off the hook. It is never clearer than when he is opposing something to the toreador pants and sterile parties and waspishness of suburban marriages. The land of deliverance he prays for is wholesome and American: "the trout streams of our youth," a lighthearted game of softball, bright welcoming lights behind the picture window. Or else it is romantic and "deep"—the "churches of Venice" or islands in the "purple autumn sea."

> Richard Gilman. *Commonweal*. Dec. 19, 1958. p. 320

His first novel and best book, *The Wapshot Chronicle* (1957), was decorated with lively quotations from an old New Englander's autobiography, but its hero was a rocket technician. His four volumes of short stories tell of marital agonies and failures of love not wholly unheard-of in the past, but invariably these agonies have a spot news quality. . . . Cheever is never angry, merely sad; his own range of feeling extends only to a generalizing pity for human helplessness; he neither claims nor possesses a massive power of intellect. And as should be added, unrelenting contemporaneousness is, in his fiction, a form of built-in obsolescence. (The march of events is already overtaking some of Cheever's newsy tales—"The Enormous Radio" for one.) But if this writer is what is called a minor figure, he is also an American original: witty, suggestive, intelligent, aware of the endless fascination of the junk with which his world and ours is furnished, and able almost at will to make his audience laugh out loud. There are fewer than half a dozen living American writers of fiction for whom more than this can be said.

Benjamin DeMott. *Harper's Magazine.* Feb., 1964. pp. 111–12

It is the peculiar and original genius of novelist John Cheever to see his chosen subject—the American middle class entering the second decade of the Affluent Society—as figures in an Ovidian netherworld of demons. Commuterland, derided by cartoonists and deplored by sociologists as the preserve of the dull-spirited status seeker, is given by Cheever's fables the dignity of the classical theater. . . .

Cheever's art deals less with what is called character and idiosyncrasy than with archetypes: father, son, brother, husband, wife, lover, seen in situations so intensely felt as to claim universality. His people move like characters in classic drama; the actors wear their fixed masks and are not expected to change one mask for another in the course of the action. Over the formal masks are fitted others modeled in the naturalistic detail required by the conventions of realism. He is able to give to the abstract personalia of this theater a local habitation and a name—a habitation so truly seen in detail that it becomes more real than the town's tax rolls. But the easygoing realism that accepts wife-swapping or any impiety of evaded obligation with a sociological shrug enrages him, for at bottom he is a New England moralist.

Time. March 27, 1964. p. 66

Most of John Cheever's people, even the wicked ones, are wistful secret angels—like seraphim they have their errands and burdens, only nobody notices. That nobody ever notices is the real scandal of *The Wapshot Scandal.* It is, also, in a way, Cheever's own scandal as a writer. . . . [In] the latest Wapshot novel the chief character is the 20th century, and now everything but Cheever's prose has deteriorated and grown corrupt. . . . Confronted by vulgarity and evil, Cheever takes a cautious step backward, shuts his eyes, waves his fastidious wand, and ping! vulgarity and evil are all at once redeemed by a secret beauty—"the abandoned buildings with the gantries above them had a nostalgic charm," he writes of the weapons site. Ping!

And exactly this sentimental disposition in the Wapshots and in his rendering of them is what Cheever himself seems not to have noticed. His ironic exposures add up only to a lightweight comic deceptiveness. . . . The larger deception implicit in his novel—the victory of supermarket and hardware culture over our better hopes—is lost finally in Cheever's hesitancy to push his irony to the hurting point, and to push right through the shield of his fantasy.

Cynthia Ozick. *Commentary.* July, 1964. pp. 66–7

Cheever writes in a relaxed, seemingly casual but thoroughly disciplined manner; his general mood is a compound of skepticism,

compassion, and wry humor; he is concerned with the complexities, tensions, and disappointments of life in a strictly contemporary world, a world of little men and women, non-heroic, nonspectacular, non-exceptional. . . . He is concerned with the loneliness which festers beneath the facade of apparently "happy" or "successful" individuals; he suggests the potential terror or violence inherent in the metropolitan apartment-dweller's condition. Beneath the often placid, impeccably depicted surfaces of his stories there is a reservoir of excitement or unrest which is capable or erupting into violence; his well-mannered characters walk a tightrope which at any moment may break; the vast, shining city masks cruelty, injustice, and evil.

William Peden. *The American Short Story* (Houghton). 1964. pp. 47–8

The novel [*Bullet Park*] is bleak, full of danger and offense, like a poisoned apple in the playpen. Good and evil are real, but are effects of mindless chance—or heartless grace. The demonology of Calvin, or Cotton Mather. Disturbing or not, the book towers high above the many recent novels that wail and feed on Sartre. A religious book, affirmation out of ashes. *Bullet Park* is a novel to pore over, move around in, live with. The image repetitions, the stark and subtle correspondences that create the book's ambiguous meaning, its uneasy courage and compassion, sink in and in, like a curative spell.

John Gardner. *New York Times Book Section.* Oct. 24, 1971. p. 24

Now, because Mr. Cheever has written a volume of stories [*The World of Apples*] which tend to show people as being motivated by old-style feelings like love and loyalty and kindness and consideration for others and protectiveness toward the weak (e.g., children), one doesn't want to represent him as preaching. It is merely that every work of art, like every creation of any kind, comes out of a system of values and preferences, and this is a book by a gifted and established writer which doesn't, for once, seem to come out of negativism, alienation, despair of the human condition and frantic self-gratification in whatever horrifying ways suggest themselves. One meets people in everyday life who have these old-fashioned values, and perhaps the shortest way to convey the rare quality of Mr. Cheever's book is to say that here, for a wonder, we have a modern work of literature in which people behave as decently as they generally do in real life, rather than behaving like sick fiends.

John Wain. *New Republic.* May 26, 1973. p. 26

With one or two exceptions, these stories [in *The World of Apples*] chronicle the sadness and futility of suburban and moneyed existences. In several the sound of the rain is intended as a balm for the bruised spirits of those grown more accustomed to the sounds of traffic. And perhaps this is one of Cheever's shortcomings. Writing strictly of one class, his books cannot compare with those attempting a Balzacian cross-section of humanity. . . . Cheever's humor and irony make him a greater writer than, say, Louis Auchincloss, whose humorless novels also examine the professional classes to the exclusion of all others. But the limitation is there.

The fictional landscape of Cheever's art includes the social pretensions and moral implications of modern suburbia, the larger patterns of human experience, such as the loss of innocence and the deep spiritual hunger for a golden simpler past, and the discovery of beautiful moments to celebrate within the contemporary wasteland. These themes and ideas occur again and again in the short stories and novels. The way they are organized and detailed reveals the form in which Cheever's fictional landscape is created. . . .

The emotional center or vision of Cheever's fiction remains somewhat elusive. His light, ironic style can cut both ways. On the one hand, he seems to be a romantic, yearning for the good old days of yesteryear, far from the madding crowds of the aimless, tasteless contemporary world. On the other hand, he seems to realize the essential futility and unreality of such romantic notions and seems determined to find moments of beauty within the chaotic and graceless contemporary world. . . . In either case Cheever's style can both illuminate and avoid the implications of the situations he writes about. He seems to want his style to be both disarming and protective at once. He seems, finally, to be celebrating his own ability to find delight in both the romantic past, however false, and the contemporary present, however chaotic. . . .

Cheever is neither concerned with uncovering the complexities within a particular moment of experience nor interested in sounding the depths of an episode. His is more an attempt to translate that immediate experience into the artistic opportunity to display the lyric gracefulness of his style, to focus the reader's attention primarily upon the encounter between the artist and his material.

Samuel Coale. *John Cheever* (Ungar, 1977), pp. 115–17

My father was always a storyteller. His homeroom teacher at Thayer Academy used to promise her class that John [Cheever] would tell a story if they behaved. With luck, and increasing skill, he could spin the story out over two or three class periods so that the teacher and his classmates forgot all about arithmetic and geography and social studies. . . .

My father told these stories over and over again all his life. He wrote them into short stories and novels, and he passed them on to his children. He won the National Book Award, and the Howells Medal from the American Academy of Arts and Letters, and the Pulitzer Prize, and the National Book Critics Circle Award, and the National Medal for Literature. He also kept us amused. Still, he never got the stories quite right. Otherwise, how can you explain the way he kept changing them, embroidering some anecdotes and shifting the emphasis in others, adding sequences and even characters, as if he was searching for some ideal balance that might set him free?

As he grew older, my father became increasingly reluctant to talk about his early years, especially to psychiatrists, who invariably zeroed in on his anger at his dominating mother and identification with his weak father. Later, when he became famous and journalists' questions forced him to talk about his childhood, he patched together a background of suggestions and half-truths that implied a happy youth and a slow but steady progress in his chosen career. It wasn't so. . . .

My father's certainty as a writer was never more apparent than during the year he was writing *Falconer*. When he read from it aloud to us, his voice vibrating with authority and pleasure in his own skill and imagination, it seemed to generate an electricity and excitement that reached outside the circle of listeners slumped in chairs in the library or the living room of the house in Ossining. I think I knew then that the book would be a best seller, and that my parents wouldn't have to worry about money anymore, and that my father was going to be successful and famous in a different way than he had ever been before.

Not only did my father have the energy to write at the top of his talent that year but the timing and the subject were ideal. Each chapter and scene seemed to stream from his imagination already written. These were the things he had been longing to say—the joys and anxieties he had not been able to write about before. *Falconer* is a novel about a man imprisoned for the murder of his brother. He is a heroin addict, and his marriage is a travesty of marriage vows. The center of the book is a tender homosexual love affair. The book's hero, Ezekiel Farragut, is in jail for violating the laws of society. In the end, he is freed from prison and from his addictions by a triumph of love and ingenuity. All these themes were deep in my father's consciousness, and they were to dominate the remaining years of his life. . . .

[T]he last half of the decade was as much a turning point for my father as the mid-fifties had been for the family. Once again, the miserable anxieties of failure and poverty gave way to a glorious success. In June of 1978, he was awarded an honorary degree from Harvard—a triumphant moment for a boy who had dropped out of Thayer Academy. And after the success of *The Stories of John Cheever* that same year, Knopf contracted to pay a $500,000 advance for his next novel. This was not a fortune by famous writers' standards—some authors command advances in the millions—but for my father it was a guarantee of financial security for the foreseeable future, and for the first time in his life he made a few conservative investments.

Susan Cheever. *Home before Dark* (Boston: Houghton Mifflin, 1984), pp. 1, 2, 202–3, 206

By 1979, John Cheever had become a literary elder statesman. "I'm a brand name," he used to say, "like corn flakes, or shredded wheat." He seemed to enjoy this status. He must have suspected that the publication of the journals would alter it. His public image was that of a courtly English gentleman who lived in an antique farmhouse and raised bird dogs. His later books had expressed a candid interest in other facets of his life, but it was certainly conceivable that this interest was purely intellectual. Few people knew of his bisexuality. Very few people knew the extent of his infidelities. And almost nobody could have anticipated the apparent desperation of his inner life, or the caustic nature of his vision. But I don't think he cared terribly about being corn flakes. He was a writer before he was a breakfast food. He was a writer before he was a man.

In notes and letters many writers of astonishing talent will let down their guard, and one can see them blundering along like the rest of us, seeking clumsily for the cliche. This didn't happen to my father. "I know there are some people who are afraid to write a business letter because they will encounter and reveal themselves," he used to say with disdain. I can see now that the person he was disdaining was himself. He didn't write a postcard without encountering himself. But he'd write the postcard anyway. He'd encounter himself, transform himself, and you'd have a hell of a postcard.

He saw the role of the serious writer as both lofty and practical in the same instant. He used to say that literature was one of the first indications of civilization. He used to say that a fine piece of prose could not only cure a depression, it could clear up a sinus headache. Like many great healers, he meant to heal himself.

> Benjamin Cheever. Introduction. *The Journals of John Cheever* (New York: Alfred A. Knopf, 1991), pp. ix–x

This present collection of thirteen hitherto uncollected stories allows us to watch. . . [Cheever's] stories take shape. But not that only: to watch a career take shape as well. For these stories provide a synoptic glimpse of his formative years, those efforts (as he called them) to discover his "singing voice," that assured, expansive, intensely personal style we associate with the mature Cheever of the 1950s and the 1960s. . . .

I insert. . .biographical parallels with some trepidation, because Cheever himself was vehement about the oft-noted confusion between fiction and autobiography. In a 1976 interview, later published in the Stanford University literary review, *Sequoia*, he reiterated this objection by saying: "What I usually say is, fiction is not crypto-autobiography: its *splendor* is that it is not autobiographical. Nor is it biographical."

> George W. Hunt, S.J. Introduction. In Franklin H. Dennis, ed. *Thirteen Uncollected Stories* (Chicago: Academy Chicago Publishers, 1994), pp. v–vi, vii

From the utter despair of *The Journals*'s opening paragraph to the cancer-driven agonies of his final pages, Cheever's command of language stuns with its eloquence, incisive scrutiny of both the author's depravity and his nobility, and its absolute, searing honesty.

You may be annoyed or disgusted by this book, but you won't be bored. *The Journals* seem to have functioned partly as notebooks for Cheever's fiction—he often writes about ideas for new stories or revisions of old ones—partly as therapy. . . . The entries, organized by year, focus most consistently on his family troubles, mainly his constant pleading for affection and/or sex from his wife, Mary, who responds with apathy or vicious denial. . . that prompt comments that range from homicidal . . . to sarcastic ("Can I do anything to help you," he asks her once, "short of dropping dead?")

The picture that slowly emerges, page by page, is one of a marriage that is a sort of mutual nervous breakdown over three decades, an infected relationship sadly indissoluble because of Cheever's insatiable need for both sex and tenderness and because, as he wryly observes, "people named John and Mary never divorce."

When he is not lamenting his wretched married life, Cheever writes most often of the war that went on without surcease inside him: the tension between desire and fear of his homosexual relationships, and his fragile control over his urges. "If I followed my instincts," he writes, "I would be strangled by some hairy sailor in a public urinal."

Cheever's bisexual and throbbing erotic hunger made a normal, satisfying sex life impossible, leaving him alternately ravenous or raw. . . . And it is fascinating, as you read his journals, to chart the progress of Cheever's coming out of the closet—at least on paper: he never openly avowed his homosexuality. . . .

Perhaps, in the last year of his life, wasting away from chemotherapy and talking to his dogs of the first snowfall that he would not be able to walk them in, Cheever realized that, at least in death, he could lead a truthful life.

> Doug Rennie. *Plant's Review of Books*. Winter, 1994, p. 17

BIBLIOGRAPHY

The Way Some People Live, 1943 (s); *The Enormous Radio*, 1953 (s); *The Wapshot Chronicle*, 1957 (n); *The Housebreaker of Shady Hill*, 1958 (s); *Some People, Places and Things That Will Not Appear in My Next Novel*, 1961 (s); *The Wapshot Scandal*, 1964 (n); *The Brigadier and the Golf Widow*, 1964 (s); *Bullet Park*, 1969 (n); *The World of Apples*, 1973 (s); *Falconer*, 1977 (n); *The Stories of John Cheever*, 1978; *Oh What a Paradise It Seems*, 1982 (n); *Glad Tidings: A Friendship in Letters* [correspondence with John D. Weaver, 1945–1982], 1983; *Conversations*, 1987 (r, i.e., interviews); *Letters*, 1988; *Journals*, 1991 (m); *Thirteen Uncollected Stories*, 1994

CHESNUTT, Charles W. (1858–1932)

The keynote of the [seven stories in *The Conjure Woman*] is the blind superstition and duplicity of character fostered by the life of servility and cringing to the master. These stories stand out as an impartial picture of the life of the slave in the Southern States. Uncle Julius is a fine type of the old slave devoted to his master, never lacking in dignity and courage, but withal possessing an indifferent code of morals, the result, most likely, of his close association with the white man whose ethics were, to say the least, pliant. All the wrongs of the race are in these simple tales unfolded, but with never a complaint, a strict justice being displayed in the drawing of the good and bad master, the good and bad slave, each having a fair showing. Mr. Chesnutt does not strive for any dramatic effects, nor does he ever introduce any unnecessary harrowing situations; there is a surprising absence of false sentiment. Love, hate, jealousy and cruelty are dealt with in a thoroughly sane, good-natured, sensible manner. No hysterics, no posing, mar the simple recitals of Uncle Julius as he happens to talk to the Northern man and his wife who have come to North Carolina. . . .

Between the introduction of slavery into the South and the Civil War lies a picturesque period, something more than dramatic and less than tragic, fraught with wonderful possibilities for just such a facile, discriminating pen as Mr. Chesnutt's. As we of this day look back over that shadowed bit of history, such a transaction as is set forth in "Sis' Becky's Pickaninny" seems absolutely incredible, and moves our hearts to an outspoken rebellion that such things could ever have been, and yet the author does justice to every one in the tale. . . . In this story more than in any other of the group does Mr. Chesnutt place before his readers the two kinds of masters, and a strong wave of irrepressible compassion sweeps over us as we grasp the tragical undercurrent of those lives bowed down with ignominy and shame. Through the medium of "The Gray Wolf's Ha'nt" and "Po' Sandy" the author pictures the every-day, pathetic side of the negro's life, and forcibly brings out that peculiar mysticism which may be the black man's inheritance from the Orient; the beliefs and superstitions which have been transplanted along with the race. But across the darkest phase of the slave's life there flashes that quaint humour which saves even the most tragic scenes from too heavy a shadow of horror. So clever a master of literary skill, so keen a student of human nature is Mr. Chesnutt, that he never allows himself to drift into too great gloom, but plays with an artistic touch on our emotions and our sense of humour in an equal degree. . . .

The Conjure Woman is a collection of quaint tales, with an admirable Southern setting, replete with the humour and tragedy of slavery, so skilfully blended that often one does not know where the one begins and the other ends. The dialect in which the storyteller speaks is smooth and readable, evidently a means and not an end, and Mr. Chesnutt's English is remarkable for its literary style and quality.

> Florence A.H. Morgan. *The Bookman,* New York Company. May, 1899, pp. 372–73.

[To Mr. Chesnutt] may perhaps be given the credit of the first publication of a subtle psychological study of the negro's spiritual nature, the first actual revelation of those secret depths of the dusky soul which no white writer might hope to approach through his own intuition.

The depth of the revelation [in "The Wife of His Youth"]—its width and completeness—are scarcely apparent at a glance, the little story is so short and so simply and quietly told. The author extenuates nothing. The man is drawn as he is—vain, conceited, puffed up over his small measure of success, thinking, over-much of his white blood, and looking forward to an ambitious second marriage, without troubling himself as to whether the wife of his youth be living or dead. The woman also stands in full light, a mere withered atom of old plantation life—ignorant, bent and black—"so black that her toothless gums, revealed when she opened her mouth to speak, were not red, but blue"—with tufts of wool, instead of hair, protruding around her ancient bonnet. Such are the actors in the humble tragedy that Mr. Chesnutt has written, yet neither they nor their lowly environment ever touch the absurd or even the commonplace. There may be a smile at the sidelights of the quiet beginning, but the long shadow of slavery still stretches too far across the lives of the emancipated for the smile to last. From its very simplicity, its quiet, its reserve, comes the force of its great appeal.

All this and more may be said in praise of the first and the shortest of the nine stories forming the volume. The others are hardly worthy of mention in comparison with the first. The single partial exception is "Uncle Wellington's Wives," but even this is readable chiefly because of its kind, mellow humour and its photographic portrayal of a familiar type of the negro. As fiction it has little if any claim to consideration, and a graver fault than its lack of literary quality is its careless approach to the all but unapproachable ground of sentimental relations between the black race and the white race. Touching this and still more dangerous and darker race problems, Mr. Chesnutt shows a lamentable lack of tact of a kindred sort, an incomprehensible want of the good taste and dignified reserve which characterises his first beautiful story and the greater part of all his work. "The Sheriff's Children" furnishes, perhaps, the most shocking instance of his reckless disregard of matters respected by more experienced writers. In saying this there is no intention to deny the too probable truth of the untellable story, nor any wish to dispute its tragic importance as legitimate literary material. On the contrary, it is the recognition of that terrible truth and its mighty weight which cause the protest. Had the author

recognised these things, it would seem that he must either have left them alone or have approached them more carefully, and with greater strenuousness; that he must have felt the need of laying hold of them with far surer, firmer, larger grasp, if he touched them at all. It may be, however, that Mr. Chesnutt earnestly tried to reach beyond his grasp, and failed.

Be that as it may, it is much to be regretted that he has not held to the themes well within his scope, where the surety and strength of his touch needs no better proof than the faithfulness and beauty of *The Wife of His Youth.*

> Nancy Huston Banks. *The Bookman*, New York. February, 1900, pp. 597–98.

The critical reader of the story called "*The Wife of his Youth*" . . . must have noticed uncommon traits in what was altogether a remarkable piece of work. The first was the novelty of the material; for the writer dealt not only with people who were not white, but with people who were not black enough to contrast grotesquely with white people,—who in fact were of that near approach to the ordinary American in race and color which leaves, at the last degree, every one but the connoisseur in doubt whether they are Anglo-Saxon or Anglo-African. Quite as striking as this novelty of the material was the author's thorough mastery of it, and his unerring knowledge of the life he had chosen in its peculiar racial characteristics. But above all, the story was notable for the passionless handling of a phase of our common life which is tense with potential tragedy; for the attitude, almost ironical, in which the artist observes the play of contesting emotions in the drama under his eyes; and for his apparently reluctant, apparently helpless consent to let the spectator know his real feeling in the matter. Any one accustomed to study methods in fiction, to distinguish between good and bad art, to feel the joy which the delicate skill possible only from a love of truth can give, must have known a high pleasure in the quiet self-restraint of the performance; and such a reader would probably have decided that the social situation in the piece was studied wholly from the outside, by an observer with special opportunities for knowing it, who was, as it were, surprised into final sympathy.

Now, however, it is known that the author of this story is of negro blood,—diluted, indeed, in such measure that if he did not admit this descent few would imagine it, but still quite of that middle world which lies next, though wholly outside, our own. Since his first story appeared he has contributed several others to these pages, and he now makes a showing palpable to criticism in a volume called *The Wife of his Youth, and Other Stories of the Color Line*; a volume of Southern sketches called *The Conjure Woman*; and a short life of Frederick Douglass, in the Beacon Series of biographies. The last is a simple, solid, straight piece of work, not remarkable above many other biographical studies by people entirely white, and yet important as the work of a man not entirely white treating of a great man of his inalienable race. But the volumes of fiction are remarkable above many, above most short stories by people entirely white, and would be worthy of unusual notice if they were not the work of a man not entirely white.

It is not from their racial interest that we could first wish to speak of them, though that must have a very great and very just claim upon the critic. It is much more simply and directly, as works of art, that they make their appeal, and we must allow the force of this quite independently of the other interest. Yet it cannot always be allowed. There are times in each of the stories of the first volume when the simplicity lapses, and the effect is as of a weak and uninstructed touch. There are other times when the attitude, severely impartial and studiously aloof, accuses itself of a little pompousness. There are still other times when the literature is a little too ornate for beauty, and the diction is journalistic, reporteristic. But it is right to add that these are the exceptional times, and that for far the greatest part Mr. Chesnutt seems to know quite as well what he wants to do in a given case as Maupassant, or Tourguenief, or Mr. James, or Miss Jewett, or Miss Wilkins, in other given cases, and has done it with an art of kindred quiet and force. He belongs, in other words, to the good school, the only school, all aberrations from nature being so much truancy and anarchy. He sees his people very clearly, very justly, and he shows them as he sees them, leaving the reader to divine the depth of his feeling for them. He touches all the stops, and with equal delicacy in stories of real tragedy and comedy and pathos, so that it would be hard to say which is the finest in such admirably rendered effects as ''The Web of Circumstance'', ''The Bouquet'', and ''Uncle Wellington's Wives.'' In some others the comedy degenerates into satire, with a look in the reader's direction which the author's friend must deplore.

As these stories are of our own time and country, and as there is not a swash-buckler of the seventeenth century, or a sentimentalist of this, or a princess of an imaginary kingdom, in any of them, they will possibly not reach half a million readers in six months, but in twelve months possibly more readers will remember them than if they had reached the half million. They are new and fresh and strong, as life always is, and fable never is; and the stories of *The Conjure Woman* have a wild, indigenous poetry, the creation of sincere and original imagination, which is imparted with a tender humorousness and a very artistic reticence. As far as his race is concerned, or his sixteenth part of a race, it does not greatly matter whether Mr. Chesnutt invented their motives, or found them, as he feigns, among his distant cousins of the Southern cabins. In either case, the wonder of their beauty is the same; and whatever is primitive and sylvan or campestral in the reader's heart is touched by the spells thrown on the simple black lives in these enchanting tales. Character, the most precious thing in fiction, is as faithfully portrayed against the poetic background as in the setting of the *Stories of the Color Line*.

Yet these stories, after all, are Mr. Chesnutt's most important work, whether we consider them merely as realistic fiction, apart from their author, or as studies of that middle world of which he is naturally and voluntarily a citizen. We had known the nethermost world of the grotesque and comical negro and the terrible and tragic negro through the white observer on the outside, and black character in its lyrical moods we had known from such an inside witness as Mr. Paul Dunbar; but it had remained for Mr. Chesnutt to acquaint us with those regions where the paler shades dwell as hopelessly, with relation to ourselves, as the blackest negro. He has not shown the dwellers there as very different from ourselves. They have within their own circles the same social ambitions and prejudices; they intrigue and truckle and crawl, and are snobs, like ourselves, both of the snobs that snub and the snobs that are snubbed. We may choose to think them droll in their parody of pure white society, but perhaps it would be wiser to recognize that they are like us because they are of our blood by more than a half, or three quarters, or nine tenths. It is not, in such cases, their negro blood that characterizes them; but it is their negro blood that excludes them, and that will imaginably fortify them and exalt

them. Bound in that sad solidarity from which there is no hope of entrance into polite white society for them, they may create a civilization of their own, which need not lack the highest quality. They need not be ashamed of the race from which they have sprung, and whose exile they share; for in many of the arts it has already shown, during a single generation of freedom, gifts which slavery apparently only obscured. With Mr. Booker Washington the first American orator of our time, fresh upon the time of Frederick Douglass; with Mr. Dunbar among the truest of our poets; with Mr. Tanner, a black American, among the only three Americans from whom the French government ever bought a picture, Mr. Chesnutt may well be willing to own his color.

But that is his personal affair. Our own more universal interest in him arises from the more than promise he has given in a department of literature where Americans hold the foremost place. In this there is, happily, no color line; and if he has it in him to go forward on the way which he has traced for himself, to be true to life as he has known it, to deny himself the glories of the cheap success which awaits the charlatan in fiction, one of the places at the top is open to him. He has sounded a fresh note, boldly, not blatantly, and he has won the ear of the more intelligent public.

William Dean Howells. *Atlantic Monthly*. May, 1900, pp. 699–701.

Mr. Chesnutt, it seems to me, has lost literary quality in acquiring literary quantity, and though his book, *The Marrow of Tradition*, is of the same strong material as his earlier books, it is less simple throughout, and therefore less excellent in manner. At his worst, he is no worse than the higher average of the ordinary novelist, but he ought always to be very much better, for he began better, and he is of that race which has, first of all, to get rid of the cake-walk, if it will not suffer from a smile far more blighting than any frown. He is fighting a battle, and it is not for him to pick up the cheap graces and poses of the jouster. He does, indeed, cast them all from him when he gets down to his work, and in the dramatic climaxes and closes of his story he shortens his weapons and deals his blows so absolutely without flourish that I have nothing but admiration for him. *The Marrow of Tradition*, like everything else he has written, has to do with the relations of the blacks and whites, and in that republic of letters where all men are free and equal he stands up for his own people with a courage which has more justice than mercy in it. The book is, in fact, bitter, bitter. There is no reason in history why it should not be so, if wrong is to be repaid with hate, and yet it would be better if it was not so bitter. I am not saying that he is so inartistic as to play the advocate; whatever his minor foibles may be, he is an artist whom his stepbrother Americans may well be proud of; but while he recognizes pretty well all the facts in the case, he is too clearly of a judgement that is made up. One cannot blame him for that; what would one be one's self? If the tables could once be turned, and it could be that it was the black race which violently and lastingly triumphed in the bloody revolution at Wilmington, North Carolina, a few years ago, what would not we excuse to the white man who made the atrocity the argument of his fiction?

Mr. Chesnutt goes far back of the historic event in his novel, and shows us the sources of the cataclysm which swept away a legal government and perpetuated an insurrection, but he does not paint the blacks all good, or the whites all bad. He paints them as slavery made them on both sides, and if in the very end he gives the moral

victory to the blacks—if he suffers the daughter of the black wife to
have pity on her father's daughter by his white wife, and while her
own child lies dead from a shot fired in the revolt, gives her
husband's skill to save the life of her sister's child—it cannot be
said that either his æsthetics or ethics are false. Those who would
question either must avow, at least, that the negroes have had the
greater practice in forgiveness, and that there are many probabilities to favor his interpretation of the fact. No one who reads the
book can deny that the case is presented with great power, or fail to
recognize in the writer a portent of the sort of negro equality against
which no series of hangings and burnings will finally avail.

W. D. Howells. *The North American Review*. December,
1901, pp. 872–88.

Paul Dunbar's undoing was his willingness to fulfill the expectations of the white world. Charles Chesnutt, a man of tougher moral
fiber, was uncompromising in his opposition to anything that
threatened his essential dignity. From the outset he refused to lie in
the Procrustean bed prepared for him by partisans of the Plantation
School. In a letter to George Washington Cable, he denounced the
current literary portraiture of Negroes: ". . .their chief virtues have
been their dog-like fidelity to their old masters, for whom they have
been willing to sacrifice almost life itself. Such characters exist. . . .
But I can't write about those people, or rather I won't write
about them."

In rejecting the myth of the faithful black retainer, Chesnutt was
striking at the heart of Southern pastoral. For the pastoral ideal,
according to Empson, assumes "a proper or beautiful relation
between rich and poor" [*Some Versions of Pastoral*, 1935]. If the
master-servant relation is portrayed as other than idyllic, the effect
is antipastoral. Chesnutt's antipastoral intentions are most explicit
in a story called "The Passing of Grandison", which is best
described as a loyalty tale turned inside out. Here Chesnutt pushes
the stereotype of the loyal slave to the point of absurdity, whereup-
on the tale, yielding to ironic pressure, is transformed into
mock-pastoral.

Chesnutt's masterpiece of antipastoral is *The Conjure Woman*.
Set in rural North Carolina, and dealing ostensibly with grape
cultivation, this book of stories is designed to expose the serpent in
the Southern garden. It constitutes, in fact, a devastating parody of
Southern pastoral. Arcadia lies in ruins in the aftermath of civil
war. Hence the images of dilapidation and decay that permeate
these tales. The author's aim is to force us to confront the
destruction of the Garden, ponder its fundamental cause, and trace
it in the end to chattel slavery, the fatal flaw in the ancien regime.

Enough has perhaps been said to indicate that Chesnutt's art is
rooted in antithesis and opposition. If the Plantation School inclines toward pastoral, he employs the counter-genre. If white
audiences object to mulatto characters, he devotes a whole volume
to stories of the color line. Nor is Chesnutt's contrariety exclusively
a racial stance. In "The Wife of His Youth" and "A Matter of
Principle", he satirizes the color prejudices of the Negro middle
class. In "The Web of Circumstance", he challenges the Washington formula of education and property as a panacea for racial ills.
Chesnutt chose, in short, to work against the grain.

This cantankerous streak is the mark of a born satirist. A gift for
satire was in fact Chesnutt's major contribution to Afro-American
letters. Drawing on the satirical resources of the black folktale, he
founded a tradition that descends through Langston Hughes and

George Schuyler to William Melvin Kelley and Ishmael Reed. As a
writer of satirical tales, Chesnutt was by far the most accomplished
literary artist of the Age of Washington. His chef d'oeuvre, *The
Conjure Woman*, is a tart confection of sly derision and purgatorial
laughter. Unmatched for subtlety, sophistication, and depth of
moral vision, this book is the most important product of the black
imagination prior to the First World War. . . .

The moral atmosphere of slavery, as Chesnutt re-creates it, is
one of mutual deception, slyness, and intrigue. It is a world of
masking jokers in which everyone—white and black alike—is
trying to outsmart or swindle everybody else. It is in short the world
of Brer Rabbit, where the devil takes the hindmost and the height of
folly is to trust your neighbor. A secondary theme, which will
reverberate throughout *The Conjure Woman*, is the deceitfulness of
appearances and the necessity of a certain skepticism where human
motives are concerned. Thus the white narrator discovers that
Julius has been exercising squatter's rights on the ruined plantation
and deriving a substantial profit from the goophered grapevine. . . .

"The Gray Wolf's Ha'nt" is Chesnutt's finest conjure tale; in it
he comes closest to defining his essential theme. His intent throughout
The Conjure Woman is to penetrate the disguises of the demon,
Slavery. His assumption is that evil presents itself to men in the
guise of innocence. The Plantation School, for example, was
concerned entirely with the innocent surfaces of slavery. But the
Brer Rabbit tales, which formed so crucial a part of Chesnutt's
heritage, penetrated to the essence of the crime. Like the anonymous creators of the slave tales, Chesnutt was determined to strike
through the mask. In pursuing this objective he developed a
technique that made him an impressive master of the short-
story form.

Robert Bone. *Down Home: A History of Afro-American
Short Fiction from Its Beginnings to the End of the Harlem
Renaissance*. G. P. Putnam, 1975 pp. 74–93.

Charles Waddell Chesnutt, a "voluntary Negro," reflects in his
writings major inter- and intraracial tensions of the 19th-century
United States. Beginning and ending his life in Cleveland, Ohio,
and from age seven to 25 living in North Carolina, he found the
major motivations and materials of his works in his own life and
that of contemporaries or immediate forebears on both sides of the
Mason-Dixon line. Chesnutt's preoccupations with the problems
of powerless blacks and poor whites is doubtless a reflection not
only of the trauma which marked his own poverty-stricken youth
but also of the resultant resolve to improve the quality of life for all
those denied access to the fullness of American life because of
color and/or class.

Chesnutt's fiction ranges in form from simple tale to highly
plotted novel, in mood from comic to tragic. The subject matter
reflects the major contemporary concerns of black Americans.
However, the general reading public, primarily white, rejected
Chesnutt's increasingly explicit advocacy of equal rights for blacks
and other under-privileged citizens. Consequently, after *The Colonel's Dream* in 1905, Chesnutt terminated his writing career.

By that time, however, Chesnutt had won a permanent place in
American literary history, especially for his short fiction. His
serious consideration as a conscious, accomplished author by
critics such as William Dean Howells and George Washington
Cable was unprecedented for a black American prose writer. His
works, usually presented from a black perspective, are historically

and sociologically accurate as well as aesthetically satisfying and ethically admirable. Chesnutt is recognized as ''the first real Negro novelist,'' ''the pioneer of the color line,'' and the first American writer not only to use the folk tale for social protest but also extensively to characterize black Americans.

After he stopped writing Chesnutt used in other ways his increasing influence to improve the status of his fellow blacks. In recognition of his achievements, the National Association for the Advancement of Colored People awarded him its annual Spingarn Medal in 1928. Upon Chesnutt's death in 1932, a friend summed up accurately: ''His great contribution in letters is a monument to our race and . . . to our national life.''

Sylvia Lyons Render. In *Reference Guide to American Literature, 3rd edition*, ed. Jim Kamp (St. James Press, 1994).

BIBLIOGRAPHY
The Conjure Woman, 1899 (s); *Frederick Douglass*, 1899 (b); *The Wife of His Youth and Other Stories of the Color Line*, 1899 (s); *The House behind the Cedars*, 1900 (n); *The Marrow of Tradition*, 1901 (n); *The Colonel's Dream*, 1905 (n); *The Short Fiction of Charles W. Chesnutt*, 1974 (s), revised edition, 1981

CHESTER, Alfred (1928–1971)

Except for the juvenilia of his Paris years, most of [Alfred Chester's] reviews and literary essays were written between 1962 and 1964, a period when he was one of the most sought after and talked about writers on the New York literary scene. This was in sharp contrast to the neglect a few years later, after his virtual ''disappearance,'' when he had rejected writing criticism as a betrayal of his talents, and after his book of short stories, *Behold Goliath* (1964) and the novel *The Exquisite Corpse* (1967), failed to get more than cursory critical attention. . . .

The irony was that the minute he turned to criticism, the editors started pursuing him, and he was faced with the shocking but undeniable fact that as a critic he was a hot number on the scene. This was very hard for him to swallow. Alfred's critical prose was high-powered, racy, and iconoclastic. He was called a ''sport'' in the critical field, for his original, off-center, ruthless, and devastating analysis. But beyond that, he turned literary criticism into entertainment, much as he insisted that fiction should be entertaining.

Editors started asking him for more than book reviews, they wanted controversial reassessments. . . . He was willing to oblige them, and produced, one after another in the next two years, essays on Updike (a famous roasting), Nabokov, Burroughs, Rechy, Albee, Salinger, Genet, and others. He worked with great intensity, laboring for long hours through draft after draft. . . .

Writing a column aimed at a mass readership was at variance with Alfred's image of himself as writer for the literary few, but he could not ignore the fact that he was being widely read for the first time. It disturbed him. . . .

When he returned from Morocco to New York, in the winter of '65–'66, he began his novel, *The Foot*, much of which has been lost. And as his mental state deteriorated and he disappeared, for

real this time, his literary production became sporadic. There is firm evidence that he wrote a story called ''Trois Corsages,'' about his three friends, Harriet (Sohmers) Zwerling, Susan Sontag, and Irene Fornes, but this too has been lost, along with most of his unfinished and unpublished works. In his madness, I believe he destroyed much correspondence and many letters. . . .

After much erratic wandering, Alfred Chester settled in Israel sometime in 1970, where he wrote a final essay, ''Letter from the Wandering Jew,'' that was never published. (It exists thanks to Theodore Solotaroff who photocopied it when it was submitted to him. . . .) If his charm has disappeared, and his sense of humor (either due to a state of mental deterioration or on his way to death), it reveals a new identity, no longer worried about who he was. . . .

In a commentary in the *New York Review of Books*, Gore Vidal wrote that he ''was a glorious writer, tough as nails, with an exquisite ear for the false note; his review of [John] Rechy's *City of Night* is murderously funny, absolutely unfair, and totally true, a trick that only a high critic knows how to pull off.''

Edward Field. Foreword. In Alfred Chester, *Looking for Genet* (Santa Rosa: Black Sparrow Pr., 1992), pp. 7, 9, 15, 16–17

Chester was frequently an enthusiastic and generous reader, who . . . recognized the virtues of writers such as Updike and Sarraute before elucidating why he found them irksome. He was particularly fond of the work of Jean Genet, Christopher Isherwood, Mary McCarthy, and the early and late writings of Truman Capote.

The columns Chester wrote for *Book Week* are more informal and chatty than his book reviews. Frequently he begins with anecdotes of his life in Morocco, then moves on to some literary topic such as the relation of the author's life to the work. Like his acquaintances Baldwin, Mailer, and Sontag, Chester may have been most suited to this form: the literary essay that builds on autobiography and applies the same critical eye to life and books. Some of his finest fiction is thinly disguised autobiography (in which, for example, Paul Bowles appears as Peter Plate). The columns parade his variety and range. Though his literary musings could never be called disinterested, the remote vantage of Morocco provided him with added perspective on the literary questions that continued to obsess him. . . .

The third section of *Looking for Genet: Literary Essays & Reviews* [an anthology of Chester's writings, edited by Edward Field] is a true miscellany, tracking the parabola of Chester's career by collecting writings from the young unformed novelist in Europe through those of the sad teetering crank on the verge of oblivion, insanely attempting to substitute Israel for his beloved Morocco, from which he had been suddenly expelled without explanation. The earliest piece, ''Silence in Heaven,'' was published in *Botteghe Oscure* when Chester was twenty-three years old. Reading it, one understands why the magazine's publisher, the Princess Caetani, thought so highly of Chester that she not only solicited on his behalf a recommendation for a Guggenheim grant from Lionel Trilling, but sent Trilling's first recommendation back to its author for not being enthusiastic enough. . . . The last published essay, ''Letter from a Wandering Jew,'' chronicles Chester's hapless last days in Jerusalem. I agree with Edward Field that the letter reminds one of Celine, but I never wanted to weep for Celine the way I feel like weeping for Chester. Sadly, the substance abuse that is so much a part of Chester's descent into hell has become too familiar; we know whence some of the madness comes.

Gary Lenhart. *American Book Review*. June–July, 1994, pp. 9, 14

BIBLIOGRAPHY
Here Be Dragons, 1955 (s); *Jamie Is My Heart's Desire*, 1956 (n); *The Exquisite Corpse*, 1967 (n); *Head of a Sad Angel: Stories 1953–1966*, ed. Edward Field, 1990; *Looking for Genet: Literary Essays and Reviews*, ed. Edward Field, 1992

CHILDRESS, Alice (1920–)

Alice Childress, a serious contemporary playwright whose work has received little scholarly recognition, has been working in American theater for four decades. Born a decade before Lorraine Hansberry, Alice Childress produced her first play, *Florence*, ten years before Hansberry's *A Raisin in the Sun*. Childress was, in fact, the first black woman to have a play produced on the professional American stage, and she is still writing successful drama in the 1980s. . . .

Like Hansberry, Childress has affirmed a deep commitment to social and political causes that promote human rights for black people and women. Unlike Hansberry, however, Childress features black women as protagonists in her fiction and drama.

Although all of Childress's published work deserves to be read, *Wedding Band* is her finest and most serious piece of literature and deserves comparison with the most celebrated American tragedies. Like Childress's other plays, it features an ordinary black woman past her prime. What we have here is that Julia's soul-searching in the midst of her moral dilemmas takes place on stage; her confusion is fully dramatized. The problems which face Julia are complicated by a convergence of historical and political dilemmas with which a woman of her education and conditioning is ill prepared to cope. That she and the other flawed women in *Wedding Band* survive is tenuous but believable.

Childress's mode of characterization is unflinching realism. Earthy dialogue and crude figurative language characterize the "nitty-gritty" characters who populate her plays as bursting with vitality and a fully realized sensuality. No saints or villains clutter Childress's dramatis personae. In *Wedding Band*, racism and the desire for respectability obsess both black and white characters. Every ethnic minority suffers insults. . . .

Name-calling and racist insults bolster the fragile dignity of the member of any ethnic minority desperate to be thought respectable or at least higher on the ladder of social respectability than someone else. Clinging to symbols of respectability is the only way to survive the rejection of the larger society. In a similar way, Fanny brags about her silver tea service, her English china, and her Belgian linen; Julia keeps her hope chest. In an absurd attempt to conceal Julia's indiscretion from the children, Mattie tells them that Herman is Julia's husband—"a light colored man."

The antagonist of *Wedding Band*, seems to be the whole system of government-sanctioned oppression and the conservative status quo fearful of change. However, Childress's uneducated characters lack the ability to understand the nature of the enemy or to articulate their own victimization. Herman and Julia are not presented as the American version of Romeo and Juliet, although their plight invites comparison. They lack the requisite youth and beauty, social prominence and wealth, romantic perfection. They are weak, confused, superstitious, lonely, and impatient; no empires crumble when catastrophe strikes them. Herman's death and Julia's madness create nothing to nurture the healing of racial hatred. However, despite their insignificance, they are brave and honest enough to carry on a love affair threatened by criminal penalties because they know instinctively that love is stronger than unjust laws.

Wedding Band dramatizes more than a tragic love affair. It presents the social, economic, moral, religious, legal, political, historical, psychological context in which a black woman like Julia Augustine makes independent decisions that affect her life and the lives of everyone she touches.

Rosemary Curb. *Multi-Ethnic Literature of the U.S.* Winter, 1980, pp. 57–67.

Alice Childress has written a remarkable book [*A Short Walk*] that takes its title from the answer given by protagonist Cora James' father to the question "What is life?"—which she asks him at age five while watching a minstrel show. Life, he responds, is "a short walk from the cradle to the grave . . . and it sure behooves us to be kind to one another along the way." On the same occasion, when a storm threatens to erupt out of a black performer's impromptu musical discourse on oppression, Cora's father counsels, "Let all run that wants to run, Cora. We stay put where we are, so's not to get trampled."

Deeply influenced by her relationship with her father (which relationship, incidentally, displays our child-rearing system in one of its most satisfactory variations), Cora develops into a kind, loving adult who stays put a good deal and is adept at dealing with those problems that present themselves. From her father she has taken a strong will, a deep love for her people and their culture, a critical eye and a strong sense of responsibility for herself and those close to her.

In Cora James' odyssey from the Low Country of South Carolina to the Big Apple, we see reflected those legions of black folk who made the journey and poured their energies into creating Harlem, U.S.A. Thoughtful, womanly, strong, responsible, tough, resilient and stubborn, Cora is at once uniquely herself and every black woman "that's ever had to stand squarefooted and make her own way." Author Childress sees to it that we come to know and understand the whole Cora and that we take special note of her solitariness, that pronounced aloneness which often goes unrecognized in the lives of so many black women. Cora's blood mother, we learn, had suffered such aloneness to a tragic degree at a very young age.

We also realize, after reading what it was like for Cora to come to a big city and survive, that her struggle is the same forty or fifty years later and will probably be the same forty years from now. So you check back through the pages of *A Short Walk* to note again just what it was that kept her going.

In her relationships with men, Cora seeks some justice, comfort and understanding, *and she struggles for them*. The man, Cecil, whom she deeply loves, she loves through the long haul though she is pained because "he cannot see himself at all as I see him." She realizes that the reverse is also true. The male characters are dramatic and memorable, each for different reasons; and though not all are strong, entirely admirable people, none is caricatured.

Perhaps it is the author's playwrighting skills which account for the novel's superb dialogue—a veritable celebration of the black community's use of language. And not only the dialogue but the descriptive passages as well are rich, both in imagery and adroitly used proverbs.

Through the author's masterful juxtapositions of tragedy and humor, sorrow and joy, cruelty and kindness (sometimes in the same person), readers are led to deal with her juxtaposition of African/African-American culture and cultural repression in stunning ways. There are political elements which invite family discussion—you will recognize them. You will be energized by this book, and you will be surprised from time to time—nobody's predictable, certainly not Cora. You will remember *A Short Walk* and think about your own.

Geraldine L. Wilson. *Freedomways*. 1980, pp. 101–02.

[Childress's *A Hero Ain't Nothin' But a Sandwich*, which has been adapted for film,] is the story of Benjie, a thirteen-year-old drug addict. There are some awesomely beautiful and powerful moments in this novel. One that comes immediately and vividly to mind is the poignant scene in which Butler Craig, the "stepfather," saves spaced-out Benjie from falling from a Harlem rooftop, even as the boy begs his stepfather to let him go. "'Let go, Butler . . . let me die. Drop me, man!' He's flailing his legs, trying to work loose my hold, hollerin and fighting to die. 'Let me be dead!'"

There are times in the book, however, when the characters, the victims, in this novel are their worst enemies. They appear unable to get out of their own way. Perhaps life is a treadmill, but the enemy of the people, the hand of the oppressor, is not clearly delineated in this one. Mari Evans says: "To identify the enemy is to free the people." Which just goes to prove that no one is perfect. Even an expert marksperson like Alice Childress does not hit the bull's-eye every time she picks up the rifle.

Alice Childress's latest and most rewarding novel is *A Short Walk*. "Life is just a short walk from the cradle to the grave—and it sure behooves us to be kind to one another along the way." This is the saga of Cora James from just before her fifth birthday in a racist Charleston, South Carolina.

Alice Childress brings the history of the times alive, as we, along with Cora James, join the Garvey movement, the U.N.I.A. (Universal Negro Improvement Association), the fabulous pomp, the militant pageantry, the grand and colorful parades through Harlem, the African Orthodox Church. It's all here, along with the struggle for race pride and identification with Africa. "Back to Africa!"—"Africa for the Africans! At home and abroad!" You've seen it written about many times before, but never has it come alive like this. It is history relived. We go with the Movement's ship, the Black Star Line's S.S. *Frederick Douglass* (Yarmouth) on its maiden voyage to Cuba. The writer's genius, her artistry, is her ability to totally involve you in the happenings, as you, the reader, happen along with them. You emerge from the spell of her writing with the feeling of a lived experience.

Alice Childress is a tremendously gifted artist who has consistently used her genius to effect change in the world: to change the image we have of ourselves as human beings, Black and white. Her primary and special concern has been the African image. She knew that Black was beautiful when so many of us thought that Black Beauty was the name of a storybook horse, a figment of a writer's fantasy. Her gift has been used as an instrument against oppression; notwithstanding, she is always the consummate artist, telling her story powerfully and artistically. Her writing is always realistic, avoiding somehow the indulgence of wallowing in quagmires of despair and pessimism. After all, life *is* a short walk. There is so little time and so much living to achieve. Perhaps her greatest gift, along with her satiric bent and the thematic accent on struggle, is the leitmotif of love for people, particularly her own people. I have come away from most of her writing feeling mighty damn proud of the human race, especially the African aspect of it. Portraying it with great fidelity in all of its meanness, its pettiness, its prejudices, its superstitions, Childress captures most of all its capacity to overcome, to be better than it is, or ever could be, its monumental capacity for change.

At a writers' conference sponsored in 1974 at Howard University by Dr. Stephen Henderson and the Institute for the Arts and Humanities, writer Toni Cade Bambara said: "The responsibility of an artist representing an oppressed people is to make revolution irresistible." At the same time, when so many Black writers have decided that the thing to do is to "get over" with the great white racist publishing establishment, despite the price one may be forced to pay in terms of self-esteem, human dignity, and artistic integrity, Childress has made a deliberate choice of weapons; she has chosen the weapon of creative struggle. Black blessings on you, Alice Childress.

John O. Killens. *Black Women Writers (1950–1980): A Critical Evaluation*, Mari Evans, ed. (Anchor Press/Doubleday) 1984, pp. 129–33.

Most of the plays of Alice Childress are about common people. Avoiding racial stereotypes found in much of contemporary literature and drama, her works present deftly drawn and realistic portraits of human beings attempting to find a sense of dignity in a world which seems rather to appreciate less noble values. Through her dramas, Ms. Childress exposes racism in the United States and challenges each of us to redress our racial problems. Her dynamic, poignant plays prepared the commercial stage for the works of other African-American playwrights, including Lorraine Hansberry, Amiri Baraka, and Ed Bullins.

Set during the rehearsal of a melodrama about lynching in the South, *Trouble in Mind* concerns black and white cast members who become involved in a real-life drama of racial tensions arising from the portrayal of black stereotypes. The drama skillfully mirrors a world where racist and sexist problems are initially hidden under "masks," but are forced to surface. The play centers on Wiletta Mayer, a veteran actor. She is an attractive middle-aged black woman, with an outgoing personality. She has made a career out of playing stereotypical black roles, but aspires to be cast in parts more deserving of her rich talents. Initially, she readily gives advice to a novice black actor on how to ingratiate oneself; to stay on good terms with the management no matter how loathsome the production may be. When rehearsals begin, however, she cannot adhere to such a strategy when the white director uses tactics that humiliate her and the script calls for the black characters to make statements and perform actions that offend her racial pride. Consequently, by the play's end, Wiletta removes her "mask" and becomes an outspoken critic of the production even though this action puts this job and, possibly, her career in jeopardy. It is a courageous choice, but a lonely one. None of the other cast members are willing to support her.

Wine in the Wilderness, set in Harlem in 1964, examines the arrogance of the black middle class in their relations with lower income African-Americans. Bill Jameson, an artist with a privileged background, seeks a model for his painting characterizing the average African-American woman as coarse, poorly educated, and culturally illiterate. The artist's married friends, Sonny-man and Cynthia, bring to Bill the person they believe best represents this ideal—Tommy, a thirty-year-old factory worker. Despite their dubious intent, by the play's end it is Tommy who teaches the others how they are merely dilettantes masquerading as blacks. Tommy's speech and behavior communicates that being black demands a sense of unity and respect for all members of the race, no matter how different their backgrounds and lifestyles might be. Tommy's actions exemplify her philosophy as, unlike the others, she shows respect to the character Oldtimer, by asking about and calling him by his birth name. Tommy recognizes the role of black organizations in the socio-political progress of African-Americans. Like her birth name, Tomorrow, she is forward-looking, while the others are mired in the past. She identifies with current black leaders, whereas Bill talks only of dead heroes. Through Tommy, the once pretentious characters are humbled as they learn being black lies not in the way one looks, but in the way one thinks and relates to the world.

Wedding Band deals with the subject of interracial romance in an insightful, unsentimental manner unlike the usual depiction of this subject on the stage and in popular media. The drama is set in 1918 in South Carolina when it was illegal for blacks and whites to marry or cohabit. For ten years Julia, a black woman, and Herman, a white man, have nurtured a clandestine relationship held together with the promise that they will one day move to the North to marry as soon as Herman has fulfilled his financial obligations to his mother. However, Julia comes to the painful realization that marriage to Herman is nothing more than a pipe dream. She learns that Herman harbors many of the same prejudices as other whites; and he is unwilling to endure the racial taunts of others who would object to their relationship once out in the open. The recognition of the futility of their relationship also awakens a sense of racial pride within Julia. Once a passive woman, by the play's end Julia asserts her right to live the way she chooses in a country cultivated and sustained by the labors and lives of her African ancestors.

A more recent work—*Moms*—is based on the life of the famed comedienne Jackie "Moms" Mabley. A series of scenes with music and dance depict her public and private life from her performances on a early-20th century black theatre touring circuit to her death in 1975. The play pays tribute to the comedienne's impeccable comic timing and strong rapport with the audience. However, the author does not gloss over the comedienne's more ignoble traits. The play mentions her overbearing personality, miserly disposition, portrayal of degrading stereotypes, ambivalence concerning her sexual preference, and lack of personal

attention to the care of her children. Still, *Moms* is a fitting, even-handed tribute and a fine tour-de-force for the appropriate black actress.

Addell Austin Anderson. In *Contemporary Dramatists, 5th edition.*, ed. K. A. Berney (St. James Press, 1993).

Although Alice Childress is known for her participation in theater arts, the impact she has had upon the theater far exceeds the recognition she has received. Childress began her career as an actress and director with the American Negro Theater in New York. Her first performance was in *On Strivers Row* (1940), but within nine years Childress had written and directed her own play *Florence* (1949). In 1952, Childress became the first black woman to write a play and have it professionally produced on the New York stage. *Florence* went on to be performed on Broadway. Along with several of her other works, including *Wine in the Wilderness: A Comedy-Drama* (1969), *Wedding Band: A Love/Hate Story in Black and White* (1973), *A Hero Ain't Nothin' but a Sandwich* (1978), and *String* (1979), for which Childress wrote screenplays, *Florence* was produced for television.

At a time when the country found itself embroiled in many racial conflicts, Childress chose to explore racial concerns through her art. Due to her frank representations of racial issues, however, her work often received unfair treatment. *Wine in the Wilderness,* for example, was banned by the state of Alabama and *A Hero Ain't Nothin' but a Sandwich* was barred from the school library system of Savannah, Georgia. And some affiliate television stations refused to air her plays. Childress has been characterized as a forerunner of her time because her choice of subject matter challenged audiences to establish new ways of understanding race in America. By refusing to accept race and gender concerns as binary oppositions she positioned herself as more than an artist, playwright, or novelist by laying the groundwork for valuable social critiques.

Childress' writings dismiss much of the negative imagery so common in representations of the black community and replace stereotypical characters with vibrant themes that celebrate black experiences. Unlike the psychological characterizations prevalent in contemporary theater, in the plays of Eugene O'Neill, Tennessee Williams, and Arthur Miller for instance, Childress emphasizes theme rather than character. In her essay, "A Candle in a Gale Wind," Childress explains: "My writing attempts to interpret the 'ordinary' because they are not ordinary. Each human is uniquely different. Like snowflakes, the human pattern is never cast twice. We are uncommonly and marvelously intricate in thought and action, our problems are most complex and, too often, silently borne." In her exploration of the particularities of individuals and their specific situations, Childress finds the content of her work.

Childress' writings depict the heroic nature of the struggle to do more than simply survive the racist institutions which circumscribe the lives of her characters. Whether through the use of fiction, television, or the stage, Childress' work seeks to be a vehicle of transformation for social concerns. In her novel *A Hero Ain't Nothin' but a Sandwich,* as well as the television production by the same name, to give one example, she explores the potential of human relationships to impact the life of a teenaged heroine addict either positively or negatively. The novel ends without a resolution but Childress invests a tremendous amount of hope in man's ability to reach out to his stepson. It is the "human" part which most interests Childress in her work because it is the part that is most unwilling to be defeated and the most likely to overcome.

Valerie Sweeney Prince. In *Reference Guide to American Literature, 3rd edition,* ed. Jim Kamp (St. James Press, 1994).

BIBLIOGRAPHY
Florence, 1949 (d); *Just a Little Simple,* 1950 (d); *Gold through the Trees,* 1952 (d); *Trouble in Mind,* 1955 (d); *Wedding Band: A Love/ Hate Story in Black and White,* 1966 (d); *String,* 1969 (d); *Young Martin Luther King,* 1969 (d); *Wine in the Wilderness: A Comedy-Drama,* 1969 (d); *Mojo: A Black Love Story,* 1970 (d); *A Hero Ain't Nothin' but a Sandwich,* 1973 (yn); *Sea Island Song,* 1977 (d); *A Short Walk,* 1979 (n); *Rainbow Jordan,* 1981 (yn); *Gullah,* 1984 (d); *Moms: A Praise Play for a Black Comedienne,* 1987 (d); *Many Closets,* 1987 (e); *Those Other People,* 1989 (yn)

CHOPIN, Kate (1851–1904)

Kate Chopin belongs to the artistic realism of today, as well as to her own generation. This generation sees life, or reality, differently from any generation before it. The literary artist in his absorbing process is no longer a discoverer, no longer a refiner, still less a dictator, but an observer at best, with an impulse to state his impressions clearly. And if one were to ask in what way after all Kate Chopin differs from a pastmaster in the short story art, say, de Maupassant, the answer may be that she blesses while he bewailed the terrible clearsightedness which is the strength and the anguish of every good writer. . . .

The Awakening follows the current of erotic morbidity that flowed strongly through the literature of the last two decades of the nineteenth century. The end of the century became a momentary dizziness over an abyss of voluptuousness, and Kate Chopin in St. Louis experienced a partial attack of the prevailing artistic vertigo. The philosophy of Schopenhauer, the music of Wagner, the Russian novel, Maeterlinck's plays—all this she absorbed. *The Awakening* in her case is the result—an impression of life as a delicious agony of longing.

In *The Awakening* under her touch the Creole life of Louisiana glowed with a rich exotic beauty. The very atmosphere of the book is voluptuous, the atmosphere of the Gulf Coast, a place of strange and passionate moods.

Daniel Rankin. *Kate Chopin and Her Creole Stories* (Pennsylvania). 1932. pp. 170, 175

But there was one novel of the nineties in the South that should have been remembered, one small perfect book that mattered more than the whole life-work of many a prolific writer, a novel of Kate Chopin, who wrote Creole stories, like one or two others in New Orleans who carried on the vein of George W. Cable. *The Awakening* was more mature than even the best of Cable's work, so effortless it seemed, so composed in its naturalness and grace was

this tragic tale of Grand Isle, the fashionable New Orleans summer resort where the richer merchants deposited their wives and children. There, with the carelessness and lightness of a boy, the young Creole idler Robert awakened, with sorrowful results, from the dull dream of her existence the charming young woman whose husband adored her while he made the sad mistake of leaving her alone with her reveries and vague desires.

Van Wyck Brooks. *The Confident Years: 1885–1915* (Dutton). 1952. p. 341

There is a good deal of marital instability in the fiction of Kate Chopin, whether she writes of Acadians or New Orleans Creoles. She was bilingual and translated Maupassant. The situations in her first novel [*Atlantic Monthly Fault*] were already rather uncomfortable from the point of view of conventional morality; but in the central one she followed the then standard procedure of getting rid of an undesirable wife by having her accidentally drowned so that the lovers might be finally united. In 1899, however, she published a novel, *The Awakening,* quite uninhibited and beautifully written, which anticipates D.H. Lawrence in its treatment of infidelity.

Edmund Wilson. *Patriotic Gore* (Oxford). 1962. p. 590

In detail, *The Awakening* has the easy candor and freedom appropriate to its theme. It admits that human beings are physical bodies as well as moral and social integers and that spirit acts not only by sublimation but directly through the body's life. Not many English or American novels of the period had come so far. And its successive scenes—of household, country place, cafe garden, dinner party, and race track—are vividly realized. Kate Chopin seems to have paid some attention to the recently translated *Anna Karenina* and its extraordinary clairvoyance of observation. (Her short stories . . . are less successful, relying excessively on Maupassantesque twists of ironic revelation on the last page. But the people in them are real physical presences; invariably they strike us as having actual body, breath, color and temperature.)

Warner Berthoff. *The Ferment of Realism: American Literature, 1884–1919* (Free). 1965. p. 89

. . .there are two respects in which Mrs. Chopin's novel [*The Awakening*] is *harder* than Flaubert's [*Madame Bovary*], more ruthless, more insistent on truth of inner and social life as sole motivation. Edna Pontellier has her first affair out of sexual hunger, without romantic furbelow. . . . And, second, Mrs. Chopin uses no equivalent of the complicated financial maneuvers with which Flaubert finally corners his heroine. Edna kills herself solely because of the foredoomed emptiness of life stretching ahead of her. It is purely a psychological motive, untouched by plot contrivance.

The patent theme is in its title (a remarkably simple one for its day): the awakening of a conventional young woman to what is missing in her marriage, and her refusal to be content. Below that theme is the still-pertinent theme of the disparity between woman's sexual being and the rules of marriage. And below *that* is the perennial theme of nature versus civilization.

Stanley Kauffmann. *New Republic.* Dec. 3, 1966. p. 38

Greater attention, it seems to me, has to be given to the integral relationship between local color in [*The Awakening*] and the development of its theme, as well as to Kate Chopin's use of related symbolism. There is no doubt a certain irony in suggesting a new reading of *The Awakening* in terms of its local color. It was precisely because of diminished interest in regional literature that many commentators feel it was so long ignored; there is the obvious implication that regional literature is somehow incompatible with universal appeal. In exploring both local color and related symbolism more fully though, it seems to me that critics will do greater justice to the profundity of Kate Chopin's theme. For the novel is not simply about a woman's awakening need for sexual satisfaction that her marriage cannot provide; sexuality in the novel represents a more universal human longing for freedom, and the frustration that Edna experiences is a poignant statement about the agony of human limitations. . . .

There is a wealth of sensuous imagery in the novel, and this has been noted consistently by the critics; but what has not been noticed . . . is that sensuousness is a characteristic feature of the setting, a product of climate and the Creole temperament. And thus it must be considered primarily as constituting the new environment that Edna marries into, and not as directly supporting a preoccupation with sexual freedom. It is this environment that becomes the undoing of the American woman.

John R. May. *Southern Review*. Fall, 1970. pp. 1032–3

It does not seem probable that [Kate Chopin] will burst into glory with the reissue of her complete works . . . but she is deserving of a good deal more attention than she has received, partly because she was long before her time in dealing with sexual passion and the intricate familial and personal emotions of women, and partly because she is an uncommonly entertaining writer. The stories, a good many of them only a page or two long, are frequently no more than anecdotes or episodes or even tricks; but, like Maupassant, whom she translated and by whom she was much influenced, she usually embedded her skeleton in sufficient flesh and musculature to conceal the joints. . . .

Mrs. Chopin's landscapes and her interiors, metropolitan or rural, are animate and immediately perceived; there is no self-indulgent clutter in them, just as her characters rarely are cartoons, generally recognizable as they may be. She is sparing and precise whether she is dealing with simple folk or people of elaborate construction, and she seems to have known and to have comprehended fully a great variety of people in a variety of strata.

Jean Stafford. *New York Review of Books*. Sept. 23, 1971. pp. 33, 35

BIBLIOGRAPHY

Atlantic Monthly Fault, 1890 (n); *Bayou Folk*, 1894 (s); *A Night in Acadie*, 1897 (s); *The Awakening*, 1899 (n); *The Complete Works*, 1969; *The Storm and Other Stories: With "The Awakening,"* 1974; *The Awakening and Selected Stories of Kate Chopin*, 1976; *A Kate Chopin Miscellany*, 1979; *Portraits: Short Stories*, 1979; *A Vocation and a Voice: Stories*, 1991; *The Awakening: An Authoritative Text, Biographical and Historical Contexts, Criticism*, 1994; *Beyond the Bayou*, 1996 (s); *A Pair of Silk Stockings and Other Stories*, 1996; *Kate Chopin's Private Papers*, 1998

CIARDI, John (1916–1986)

Evidently of immigrant family, Ciardi searches out for himself the meaning of America for his own generation. Undoubtedly he is well acquainted with the English poet, Auden. His technique, at best, stems from Auden. Weaker passages hint MacLeish. But, more important, he proves that for the young American poets as for the English, the personal themes of love, friendship and family relationships cannot be divorced from the social theme. . . . He can write. . . the symbolic lyric—and beautifully. But for his purposes—the precise representation of the American scene without utopian thinking, and of the growing psychology of general apprehension—his poetry of statement rather more than that of song or of violent image is successful.

Eda Lou Walton. *New York Times Book Section*. Feb. 25, 1940. p. 5

The poems have a youthful ring which it is pleasant to come upon, and it is a tone not obscured by echoes. That Ciardi seems fresher than most poets is probably due to the fact that he is content with getting a scene down on paper, sometimes sprawlingly, but with care for the truth of it. He is not yet concerned to any great extent with interpretation.

Coleman Rosenberger. *New Republic*. July, 1940. p. 36

Unlike Eliot, who is only one of his "ancestors," Ciardi likes humanity well enough to satirize with warm wit, rather than with cold distaste. There is throughout his work a personality that expands to encompass the experiences of his fellows.

His considerable wit shows itself not only in the surprising juxtaposition of images, ideas, and language. . . but also in the rhythms and stanzaic forms. . . . But make no mistake—he deals in serious matters. His sense of the ironic gives him that authority (only the humorous should be allowed to be serious).

Gerard Previn Meyer. *Saturday Review*. Dec. 6, 1947. p. 60

John Ciardi is a poet of genuine if unequal gifts, whose best poetry has wit, perception and humanity. His greatest fault is lack of poetic liveliness, which derives not from any dullness of imagery or conventionality of vision but from rhythmic monotony. . . . But this fault Mr. Ciardi shares with many distinguished modern poets, including, in some degree, Eliot himself. His virtues are more individual and more interesting. . . . Ciardi produc(es) poetry both intelligible and mature, poetry which draws upon all the resources which the modern tradition has made available to the poet without losing touch with the reader.

David Daiches. *New York Herald Tribune Book Section*. Jan. 1, 1950. p. 6

Mr. Ciardi's poetry depends on the world of his imagination as much as it does on the world in which he is living, and, they are not discrete but interdependent essences. Therefore, he writes a poetry that is psychologically sound as he exercises his wit, satire, and compassion with precise control. He may be acidulous, but he is genuinely humane.

I.L. Salomon. *Saturday Review*. Jan. 28, 1956. p. 24

The most notable thing about John Ciardi's *As If* is a kind of crude power. The hesitations, reticences, and inabilities of the poetic nature—for to be able to say what it does say is to be unable to say everything else—are unknown to natures of such ready force, natures more akin to those of born executives, men ripe for running things. This writer uses Stevens's, or Shapiro's, or half a dozen other poets' tricks and techniques as easily, and with as much justification as a salesman would use a competitor's sales-talk—it works, doesn't it? But he doesn't use the styles as delicately and helplessly as these poets used them—after all, he *can* help himself, has helped himself. . . . He is much at his best as a translator where his native force can put on a more sensitive and individual mask—his translation of the *Inferno* has more narrative power, strength of action, than any other I know.

Randall Jarrell. *The Yale Review*. Spring, 1956. p. 479

The one theme which stands out above others which could be cited in Mr. Ciardi's variously paced poetry is a concern with time, a concern which shows itself in the birthday poems, the elegies, the family poems . . . and those poems in which the poet meditates on the history and meaning of man. . . . Several of these poems which explore history and childhood are, at bottom, the signs of the poet's encounter with the hard old fact of death. The transiency of human life and all human things is a theme as old as poetry but Mr. Ciardi's version is so modern as to be almost fashionable. He faces time, death and change under the contemporary shadow of man's existential nothingness. . . . Yet the sweat of the engagement is real and is his own.

Ernest Sandeen. *Poetry* July, 1956. p. 267

The best thing about John Ciardi is his personality. He is singularly unlike most American poets with their narrow lives and feuds. He is more like a very literate, gently appetitive, Italo-American airplane pilot, fond of deep simple things like his wife and kids, his friends and students, Dante's verse and good food and wine. The next best thing about John Ciardi is his poetry. It is truly refreshing. It is singularly free from the vices that beset most American poets nowadays, with their provincial imitations of English-Baroque verse and their trivial ambiguities. . . . These are good poems—clear, intimate and living.

Kenneth Rexroth. *New York Times Book Section*. Aug. 3, 1958. p. 6

His poems show the same lack of subterfuge, perhaps even of nuance, as his editorial deeds. Everything is stated as it arises, with a curbed vigor rather than with mystery or subtlety. This poetry is the spectrum of a whole man who, however antic he may be in life, feels in his art no need to strike literary poses. . . . He is at times as good a phrasemaker as Dylan Thomas, but more sparing in his

effects. . . . His phrases are the body, often the naked body, and not the clothing of his thought.

Dilys Laing. *The Nation*. Sept. 13, 1958. p. 138

Most of the pieces in this book [*Dialogue with an Audience*] will be familiar to librarians, having first appeared in *The Saturday Review* where the author has been poetry editor since 1955. The book is composed of five general sections: "Dialogues," "Controversies," "Robert Frost", "On Reading and Writing," and "The Situation of Poetry." Included is the celebrated review of Anne Morrow Lindbergh's *The Unicorn and Other Poems* which precipitated such a wrath of indignation on the poor poetry editor's head. As interesting as that article is, it is not nearly so interesting as the reaction it provoked. Here are the letters that constituted "the biggest storm of reader protest in the thirty-three-year history of *The Saturday Review*." If "Controversies" is the most sensational part of *Dialogue with an Audience* (is this what makes the book so heavy?), this reviewer preferred the quieter pieces on Dante, Robert Frost, and poetry in general. Although Mr. Ciardi's style is marred by repetition and the relentless underlining of the obvious (e.g., "On Writing and Bad Writing"), he is a passionate partisan of poetry, a veritable Roman candle who strikes sparks.

John C. Pine. *Library Journal*. Jan. 1, 1964. p. 108

He has not God's loveliest gift to poets, the gift of breathing in impressions and letting them gather in silence into a perfect richness. He is a controversialist, a banger-together of arguments, an anecdotalist of sorts, full of memories of his childhood in an Italian immigrant family. He likes to make loud noises, sometimes to impress a political point, sometimes in wryly comic deference to the family life he remembers, sometimes out of sheer exuberance and a purely technical interest in being noisy like Ezra Pound's when he was writing "Sestina: Altaforte." . . .And yet the quieter sensitivity that links him at times with Mr. [Richard] Wilbur is never altogether absent. . . . It is precisely this felt sensitivity, present but neglected in so many poems that leap about and shout and run as fast as their impatient metric can carry them, that is irritating in his poetry.

M. L. Rosenthal. *The Reporter*. Feb. 15, 1962. p. 50

The pressure of imagination is very low. Sometimes he rises above the dead level, with tenderness or good humor, but never does he surprise us. Now and then he remembers that he is a poet, and uses a word that has poetic pretensions. . . . But poetry is not a matter of mechanics, it is a vision; and vision Mr. Ciardi has not got.

Louis Simpson. *Hudson Review*. Spring, 1963. p. 134

BIBLIOGRAPHY

Homeward to America, 1940 (p); *Other Skies*, 1947 (p); *Live Another Day*, 1949 (p); *From Time to Time*, 1951 (p); *The Inferno*, 1954 (tr); *As If*, 1955 (p); *I Marry You*, 1958 (p); *39 Poems*, 1959; *How Does a Poem Mean?* 1960 (c); *The Purgatorio*, 1961 (tr); *In the Stoneworks*, 1961 (p); *In Fact*, 1962 (p); *Dialogue with an Audience*, 1963 (j); *Person to Person*, 1964 (p); *This Strangest Everything*, 1966 (p); *An Alphabestiary*, 1967 (p); *The Monster*

Den; or, Look What Happened at My House—and to It, 1966 (juv p); *A Genesis*, 1967 (p, with etchings by Gabor Peterdi); *The Achievement of John Ciardi*, ed. Miller Williams, 1969 (p coll); *Lives of X*, 1970 (p); *Someone Could Win a Polar Bear*, 1970 (p); *Manner of Speaking*, 1972 (e); *The Little That Is All*, 1974 (p); *Fast and Slow: Poems for Advanced Children and Beginning Parents*, 1975; *The Divine Comedy, by Dante Alighieri*, 1977 (tr); (with Isaac Asimov) *Limericks, Too Gross*, 1978 (p); *For Instance*, 1979; *A Browser's Dictionary, and Native's Guide to the Unknown American Language*, 1980; (with Isaac Asimov) *A Grossery of Limericks*, 1981 (p); *Saipan: The War Diary*, 1988 (m); *Poems of Love and Marriage*, 1988 (p); *The Complete Browser's Dictionary*, 1988; *The Hopeful Trout and Other Limericks*, 1989 (p); *Echoes: Poems Left Behind*, 1989 (p); *Ciardi Himself: Fifteen Essays in the Reading, Writing, and Teaching of Poetry*, 1989; *Mummy Took Cooking Lessons and Other Poems*, 1990; *The Selected Letters*, ed. Edward M. Cifelli, 1991; *The Collected Poems*, ed. Edward M. Cifelli, 1997

CISNEROS, Sandra (1954–)

In some recent essays collectively titled "From a Writer's Notebook," Sandra Cisneros talks about her development as a writer, making particular references to her award-winning book, *The House on Mango Street*. She states that the nostalgia for the perfect house was impressed on her at an early age from reading many times Virginia Lee Burton's *The Little House*. It was not until her tenure at the Iowa Writers Workshop, however, that it dawned on her that a house, her childhood home, could be the subject of a book. In a class discussion of Gaston Bachelard's *The Poetics of Space*, she came to this realization: "the metaphor of a house, *a house, a house*, it hit me. What did I know except third-floor flats. Surely my classmates knew nothing about that." Yet Cisneros's reverie and depiction of house differ markedly from Bachelard's poetic space of house. With Bachelard we note a house conceived in terms of a male-centered ideology. A man born in the upper crust family house, probably never having to do "female" housework and probably never having been confined to the house for reason of his sex, can easily contrive states of reverie and images of a house that a woman might not have, especially an impoverished woman raised in a ghetto. . . . Cisneros inverts Bachelard's nostalgic and privileged utopia, for hers is a different reality: "That's precisely what I chose to write: about third-floor flats, and fear of rats, and drunk husbands sending rocks through windows, anything as far from the poetic as possible. And this is when I discovered the voice I'd been suppressing all along without realizing it."

The determination of genre for *Mango Street* has posed a problem for some critics. Is *Mango Street* a novel, short stories, prose poems, vignettes? . . .

The focus. . . on compression and lyricism contributes to the brevity of the narratives. With regard to this generic classification, Cisneros states:

> I said once that I wrote *Mango Street* naively, that they were "lazy poems." In other words, for me each of the stories could've developed into poems, but they were not poems. They were stories, albeit hovering in that grey area between two genres. My newer work is still exploring this terrain.

On a different occasion, Cisneros had called the stories "vignettes." I would affirm that, although some of the narratives of *Mango Street* are "short stories," most are vignettes, that is, literary sketches, like small illustrations nonetheless "hovering in that grey area between two genres.". . .

Mango Street is a street sign, a marker, that circumscribes the neighborhood to its latino population of Puerto Ricans, Chicanos and Mexican immigrants. This house is not the young protagonist's dream house; it is only a temporary house. The *semes* that we ordinarily perceive in house, and the ones that Bachelard assumes—such as comfort security tranquility esteem—are lacking. This is a house that constrains, one that she wants to leave; consequently, the house sets up a dialectic of inside and outside of living *here* and wishing to leave for *there*. . . .

The realization of the possibility of escape through the space of writing, as well as the determination to move away from Mango Street, are expressed in "Mango Says Goodbye Sometimes." . . .

I do not hold with Juan Rodríguez that Cisneros's book ultimately sets forth the traditional ideology that happiness, for example, comes with the realization of the "American Dream," a house of one's own. In his review of *Mango Street*, Rodríguez states:

> That Esperanza chooses to leave Mango St., chooses to move away from her social/cultural base to become more "Anglicized," more individualistic; that she chooses to move from the real to the fantasy plane of the world as the only means of accepting and surviving the limited and limiting social conditions of her barrio becomes problematic to the more serious reader.

This insistence on the preference for a comforting and materialistic life ignores the ideology of a social class's liberation, particularly that of its women, to whom the book is dedicated. The house the protagonist longs for, certainly, is a house where she can have her own room and one that she can point to in pride, but, . . . it is fundamentally a metaphor for the house of storytelling. Neither here in the house on Mango Street nor in the "fantasy plane of the world"—as Rodríguez states, does the protagonist indulge in escapism.

We can agree, and probably Cisneros on this occasion does, with Bachelard's observation on the house as the space of daydreaming: "the places in which we have experienced daydreaming reconstitute themselves in a new daydream, and it is because our memories of former dwelling places are relived as daydreams that these dwelling places of the past remain in us for all time." The house that Esperanza lives and lived in will always be associated with the house of story-telling—"What I remember most is Mango Street"; because of it she became a writer. Esperanza will leave Mango Street but take it with her for always, for it is inscribed within her.

> Julián Olivares. In María Herrera-Sobek and Helena María Viramontes, eds. *Chicana Creativity and Criticism* (Houston: Arte Publico, 1988), pp. 167–69

Writing is central in Sandra Cisneros's work of fiction *The House on Mango Street*, [which is characterized] by a deceptively simple, accessible style and structure. The short sections that make up this slim novel, . . . are marvels of poetic language that capture a young girl's vision of herself and the world she lives in. Though young, Esperanza is painfully aware of the racial and economic oppression her community suffers, but it is the fate of the women in her *barrio* that has the most profound impact on her, especially as she begins to develop sexually and learns that the same fate might be hers. Esperanza gathers strength from the experiences of these women to reject the imposition of rigid gender roles predetermined for her by her culture. Her escape is linked in the text to education and above all to writing. Besides finding her path to self-definition through the women she sees victimized, Esperanza also has positive models who encourage her interest in studying and writing. At the end of the book, Esperanza's journey towards independence merges two central themes, that of writing and a house of her own: "a house as quiet as snow, a space for myself to go, clean as paper before the poem."

Esperanza's rejection of woman's place in the culture involves not only writing but leaving the barrio, raising problematic issues of changing class:

> I put it down on paper and then the ghost does not ache so much. I write it down and Mango says goodbye sometimes. She does not hold me with both arms. She sets me free. One day I will pack my bags of books and paper. One day I will say good-bye to Mango. I am too strong for her to keep me here forever. One day I will go away. Friends and neighbors will say, what happened to Esperanza? Where did she go with all those books and paper? Why did she march so far away?

But Esperanza ends the book with the promise to return: "They will not know I have gone away to come back. For the ones I left behind. For the ones who cannot get out."

The House on Mango St. captures the dialectic between self and community in Chicana writing. Esperanza finds her literary voice through her own cultural experience and that of other Chicanas. She seeks self-empowerment through writing, while recognizing her commitment to a community of Chicanas. Writing has been essential in connecting her with the power of women and her promise to pass down that power to other women is fulfilled by the writing and publication of the text itself.

Yvonne Yarbro-Bejarano. In María Herrera-Sobek and Helena María Viramontes, eds. *Chicana Creativity and Criticism* (Houston: Arte Publico, 1988), pp. 142–43

If ideological and economic considerations structure Moraga's and Lizárraga's rape narratives, it is the theme of loss of innocence that predominates in Sandra Cisneros's short story "Red Clowns." In this vignette we encounter Esperanza, the innocent and naive protagonist who is accompanying her older and street savvy friend Sally to the carnival. Sally disappears with her boyfriend and Esperanza, alone in the amusement park, is attacked by a group of boys. The narrative begins with the bitter recriminations of a disillusioned and traumatized Esperanza after the sexual transgression has occurred where, in a monologue full of hurt and despair, she mourns her loss of innocence: "Sally, you lied. It wasn't what you said at all. What he did. Where he touched me. I didn't want it, Sally. The way they said it, the way it's supposed to be, all the storybooks and movies, why did you lie to me?" The diatribe is directed not only at Sally the silent interlocutor but at the community of women who keep the truth from the younger generation of women in a conspiracy of silence. The protagonist discovers a conspiracy of two forms of silence: silence in not *denouncing* the "real" facts of life about sex and its negative aspects in violent

sexual encounters, and *complicity* in embroidering a fairy-tale-like mist around sex, and romanticizing and idealizing unrealistical sexual relations. . . .

The theme of the silent, voiceless victim, the woman that is afraid to denounce her attackers, is reiterated in Cisneros's story: "Sally, make him stop. I couldn't make them go away. I couldn't do anything but cry. I don't remember. It was dark. I don't remember. I don't remember. Please don't make me tell it all." This response to block out the rape scene and to become silent and withdrawn is common in victims of sexual assault.

María Herrera-Sobek. In María Herrera-Sobek and Helena María Viramontes, eds. *Chicana Creativity and Criticism* (Houston: Arte Publico, 1988), pp. 177–78

Besides the double marginalization that stems from gender and ethnicity, Cisneros transgresses the dominant discourse of canonical standards ideologically and linguistically. In bold contrast to the individualistic introspection of many canonical texts, Cisneros writes a modified autobiographical novel, or *Bildungsroman*, that roots the individual self in the broader socio-political reality of the Chicano community. As we will see, the story of individual development is oriented outwardly here, away from the bourgeois individualism of many standard texts. Cisneros's language also contributes to the text's otherness. In opposition to the complex, hermetic language of many canonical works, *The House on Mango Street* recuperates the simplicity of children's speech, paralleling the autobiographical protagonist's chronological age in the book. Although making the text accessible to people with a wider range of reading abilities, such simple and well-crafted prose is not currently in canonical vogue.

The volume falls between traditional genre distinctions as well. Containing a group of forty-four short and interrelated stories, the book has been classified as a novel by some because, as occurs in Tomas Rivera's *. . .y no se lo tragó la tierra*, there is character and plot development throughout the episodes. I prefer to classify Cisneros's text as a collection, a hybrid genre midway between the novel and the short story. Like Sherwood Anderson's *Winesburg, Ohio*, Pedro Juan Soto's *Spiks*, Gloria Naylor's *The Women of Brewster Place*, and Rivera's text, Cisneros's collection represents the writer's attempt to achieve both the intensity of the short story and the discursive length of the novel within a single volume. Unlike the chapters of most novels, each story in the collection could stand on its own if it were to be excerpted but each attains additional important meaning when interacting with the other stories in the volume. A number of structural and thematic elements link the stories of each collection together. . . .

On the surface the compelling desire for a house of one's own appears individualistic rather than community oriented, but Cisneros socializes the motif of the house, showing it to be a basic human need left unsatisfied for many of the minority population under capitalism. It is precisely the lack of housing stability that motivates the image's centrality in works by writers like Cisneros and Rivera. For the migrant worker who has moved continuously because of job exigencies and who, like many others in the Chicano community, has been deprived of an adequate place to live because of the inequities of income distribution in U.S. society, the desire for a house is not a sign of individualistic acquisitiveness but rather represents the satisfaction of a basic human need. . . .

Unlike many introspective writers, Cisneros links both the process of artistic creation and the dream of a house that will enable this art to social rather than individualistic issues. . . . She conceives of a house as communal rather than private property; such sharing runs counter to the dominant ideological discourse that strongly affects consciousness in capitalist societies. Cisneros's social motifs undermine rather than support the widespread messages of individualized consumption that facilitate sales of goods and services under consumer capitalism.

Cisneros touches on several other important women's issues in this volume, including media images of ideal female beauty, the reifying stare of male surveyors of women, and sex roles within the family. In an effort to counter the sexual division of labor in the home, for example, Esperanza refuses one instance of women's work: "I have begun my own quiet war. Simple, Sure. I am the one who leaves the table like a man, without pulling back the chair or picking up the plate." Although this gesture calls critical attention to gender inequities in the family, Cisneros avoids the issue of who, in fact, will end up performing the household labor that Esperanza refuses here. This important and symbolic, yet somewhat adolescent gesture merely touches on the surface of the problem and is likely, in fact, to increase the work for another woman in Esperanza's household.

The majority of stories in *The House on Mango Street*, however, face important social issues head-on. The volume's simple, poetic language, with its insistence that the individual develops within a social community rather than in isolation, distances it from many accepted canonical texts. Its deceptively simple, childlike prose and its emphasis on the unromanticized, non-mainstream issues of patriarchal violence and ethnic poverty, however, should serve precisely to accord it canonical status. We must work toward a broader understanding among literary critics of the importance of such issues to art in order to attain a richer, more diverse canon and to avoid the undervaluation and oversight of such valuable texts as *The House on Mango Street*.

Ellen McCracken. In Asunción Horno-Delgado et al, eds. *Breaking Boundaries: Latina Writings and Critical Readings* (Amherst: University of Massachusetts Press, 1989), pp. 63–64, 66, 70–71

From the moment of its publication, *The House on Mango Street*, by Sandra Cisneros, has attracted critical interest for various reasons. Some critics do a feminist reading of the work, as do Erlinda Gonzalez-Berry and Tey Diana Rebolloedo or Julián S. Olivares; others deal with the problem of literary genre, as does Pedro Gutierrez-Revuelta; and others are concerned with ideology, like Gutierrez-Revuelta, again, or Juan Rodriguez. . . . I am going to analyze the work as an act of discourse, a speech act, inscribed in a communicative literary situation, through which its author narrates a series of real or imaginary experiences with the intention of establishing a dialogue with an unknown audience and creating certain effects with her communication.

From this point of view, the change in the book's title that I suggest *The Book on Mango Street* is justified in two ways. First, externally, because as readers we confront The Book of Mango Street, that is, the literary text that creates the fictional space that is Mango Street. The other, internal, because in one of its symbolic possibilities, the house represents the book. . . . Moreover, the book

is one of the preoccupations that Sandra Cisneros reveals in her critical essays. . . .

As a writer, Sandra Cisneros approaches the writing of *The House on Mango Street* as a cross between poetry and fiction: she wants to write narratives that individually have a unity in themselves but that, at the same time, could be brought together to form a larger work. . . .

As an act of discourse, *The House on Mango Street* must be understood in two ways: one, on the level of the characters' discourse, the other as a connection between the author and the group of readers who receive the work. In the first case, we encounter a multiplicity of voices coming, for the most part, from the barrio in which Esperanza, the narrator, lives. In the second, it is the voice of the author that we perceive through the text as we apprehend the work, which makes us conscious that we are dealing with a literary text produced by the author as such. . . .

Nonetheless, the representation of the community's voice should not be confused with the community's own voice expressing itself. In this sense, *The House on Mango Street* is an individual speech act, product of a concrete author. This author's intention, as she indicates in "Notes to a Young(er) Writer" was to speak about what others barely mention, the reality of the barrio and of the women without voice and without access to the world of books. . . .

The book thus takes on the importance of an object capable of achieving certain effects, particularly in recording the voices of those silenced beings or, at least, channeling their stories through the voice of a central narrator. In this sense, it belongs to the category of speech acts that J.L. Austin has called illocutionary.

Manuel M. Martín Rodriquez. In Aralia López Gonzalez et al, eds. *Mujer y literatura mexicana y chicana*, vol. 2 (Mexico City: Colegio de Mexico; Tijuana: Colegio de la Frontera del Norte, 1990), pp. 249–50, 252–53

In Sandra Cisneros's autobiographical prose poems, *The House on Mango Street*, the child protagonist Esperanza has a mystical experience of solidarity. Three elusive aunts, like fairy godmothers, admonish the aspiring young writer, "You will always be Mango Street. . . . You must remember to come back. . . . For the ones who cannot leave as easily as you." Although Esperanza dreams of "a house quiet as snow, a space for myself to go, clean as paper before the poem," her girlfriends reiterate, "Like it or not you are Mango Street and one day you'll come back too." Cisneros, the "About the Author" tells the reader, "reaffirms our belief that art and talent can survive even under the most adverse conditions."

This meeting of a history, in this case a multiethnic history, that will not be past and the distinction of the writer who nonetheless sees herself as somehow different, separate, from it, is one of the most sensitive issues of feminist autobiography. For students of autobiography per se, it has historical resonances. In nineteenth-century working-class writers, one often sees a similar struggle to distinguish oneself from the anonymous, unindividuated "masses" in order to establish a position from which to present oneself as a distinctive "I." Yet, like Cisneros, these workers separated themselves from history only the better to objectify and ultimately reclaim it: "What I remember most is Mango Street, sad red house, the house I belong but do not belong to."

Cisneros's artistic distinction, although similar in some respects to that of earlier working-class writers, echoes another tradition about which feminists might be more ambivalent. . . . Cisneros's autobiography gives rise to a tension between an ethos of artistic distinction (the privileged creative imagination) and the kind of gender and ethnic solidarity Cisneros seeks.

> Regenia Gagnier. *Feminist Studies*. 17:1, Spring, 1991, p. 137

In *House on Mango Street*, Esperanza herself is the narrative medium and the bridge. The narrative itself is a series of vignettes joined by the consciousness of Esperanza, whose role as medium and go-between is signaled by her doubled name: "In English it means hope. In Spanish it means too many letters. It means sadness, it means waiting." The very titles of the vignettes suggest the conversation of voices the narrative represents: "Cathy Queen of Cats"; "Alicia Who Sees Mice"; "Edna's Ruthie"; "Elenita, Cards, Palms, Water"; "Rafaela Who Drinks Coconut and Papaya Juice on Tuesdays." Esperanza becomes a writer who will tell these stories: "I put it down on paper and then the ghost does not ache so much." Esperanza can tell these stories because she is the one between, the one who has "gone away to come back. For the ones I left behind. For the ones who cannot get out."

In *The House on Mango Street*, "los espiritus" visit the kitchen of the wise woman Elenita. Holy candles burn on the top of her refrigerator; "a plaster saint and a dusty Palm Sunday cross" adorn the kitchen walls along with a "picture of a voodoo hand." Elenita, the "witch woman" who "knows many thing" tells the protagonist's fortune with the tarot, while in the next room Elenita's children watch Bugs Bunny cartoons and drink Kool-Aid on the plastic slipcovered furniture. Esperanza sees her "whole life on that kitchen table: past, present, future" and tries to feel on her hand the cold of the spirits, while a part of her mind is turned to the favorite cartoon she hears from the other room. Waiting for the spirits at the kitchen table is made no stranger nor more unfamiliar here than sitting in the living room drinking Kool-Aid.

> Wendy K. Kolmar. In Lynette Carpenter and Wendy K. Kolmar, eds. *Haunting the House of Fiction* (Knoxville: University of Tennessee Press, 1991), pp. 245, 239

BIBLIOGRAPHY

Bad Boys, 1980 (p); *The House on Mango Street*, 1983 (s); *The Rodrigo Poems*, 1985 (p); *My Wicked, Wicked Ways*, 1987 (p); *Woman Hollering Creek and Other Stories*, 1991 (s); *Loose Woman: Poems*, 1994 (p); *Hairs = Pelitos*, 1994 (p)

CLAMPITT, Amy (1920–1994)

Like the tornadoes that occasionally rip across the flatlands of her native Iowa. Amy Clampitt seizes upon whatever lies in her path. No living poet writes with fiercer energy, or is able to transform the diversity of life into such a variegated unity. In her fourth collection, *Westward*, there is a poem that contains descriptions of landscapes from turn-of-the-century Pasadena to present-day Manhattan, and takes us on side trips to the Caucasian steppes. This "travelogue," full of philosophical overtones, is spiced with

quotations from Homer, George Eliot, Emerson, Simone Weil, and Joseph Brodsky. Its cast of characters includes Anton Chekhov, New York bag ladies, native Americans, the writer herself, and her pioneering grandfather as a young man. The poem's very title, "The Prairie," suggests the vastness of Clampitt's concerns.

Clampitt stormed the poetry scene in 1983 with her first book, *The Kingfisher*. Before that her only published work had been a few poems in magazines, and two minor chapbooks. Nevertheless, readers of the initial collection encountered not a "promising talent" but a mature voice, as authoritative as those of her most distinguished contemporaries. Already middle-aged, Clampitt had formed her style on the icons of her college days: John Donne, Gerard Manley Hopkins, and Marianne Moore. Her themes, however, were intensely of her time. Allen Ginsberg in his prime never chose more topical subjects. Ecology, feminism, Eastern European politics, modern education, and many other similar issues have been examined by her. Over the past seven years she has broken new ground with each volume.

Since her ideas are of great complexity and need space in order to be worked out, Clampitt favors long poems. (Her allusions also require her to append explanatory notes to each book, and these make a fascinating study in themselves.). . . .

The new collection's title poem is a meditation on Clampitt's most abiding preoccupation—human culture. "Distance is dead," the poet affirms as she lands at London's Heathrow Airport in a jet—one of those "overleapers of the old silk route." Soon she boards a creeping train for western Scotland. She is making a pilgrimage to the isle of Iona, where, in 534, St. Columba led his educated monks to "the raw edge of Europe" (an apt image for the jagged coastline, as well as this distant outpost of human habitation). . . .

Indeed, the poet envisions our civilization as a web of migrations, splayed and tangled like so many spun-out threads. . . . Clampitt believes "it's there in all of us," this impulse to project our inner turmoil onto natural forces, or to imagine that our private conflicts echo historical ones. Whether or not that is the case, her obsession with pilgrims and pioneers seems an appropriate metaphor for her poetic adventurousness—her ambitious wrestling with large, complicated subjects. Her knapsack is crammed with the most sophisticated tools of traditional—even old-fashioned—poetry. What she makes with them, however, becomes as surprising as a tall building rising out of the buffalo grass in the midst of an otherwise uninhabited plain. From her farmer grand-parents, she has learned how to cultivate unplowed territory.

> Phoebe Pettingell. *New Leader*. April 16, 1990, pp. 16–17

If James Merrill was a father figure in poetry, Amy Clampitt was even more definitively my mother. (In this, too, I was not alone: many younger poets sought her generous guidance.) For fifteen years she and I shared drafts of nearly every poem we wrote, though in receiving her criticisms, I got the much better deal. Her death at the age of seventy-four last September seemed impossible, even if one had seen her slender frame starved to nearly nothing from cancer. Never have I met anyone who combined such seriousness of purpose with such dizzying, childlike vivacity. Having discovered her vocation late—her first book, *The Kingfisher*, was published when she was sixty-three—she had taken in her rapid stride the overwhelming acclaim our culture usually reserves for novelists. As if hardly pausing to look up, she wrote in the next eleven years a book of essays and a play, and four more volumes of poems, densely musical and fiercely original.

But she did look up, to watch birds—all of which the Iowa farmer's daughter seemed to know personally, by their colorful names. She peered down at wildflowers and derived morals from moss. Her first published poem in *The New Yorker*, "The Sun Underfoot among the Sundews," heralded all the traits we would come to think of as distinctively Clampitt: a microscopically detailed vision, . . . a wry refusal to believe in a First Cause, . . . and an abandonment of pure sensation. . . .

In her final weeks she had little strength to speak but, fittingly, her last really animated conversation had to do with a book. It was the advance galley of Alice Munro's *Open Secrets*. . . . Her words came out breathlessly, with spaces between them: "Trees. Rivers. Rain. And the names of things that grow." It's a parent's job to teach us to name things. For a generation of younger writers, Amy Clampitt and James Merrill taught by example—and made it clear that we're never too old to need someone to look up to.

Mary Jo Salter. *New Republic*. March 9, 1995, p. 46

What an antidote to youthful ambition she [Clampitt] was! She had decided from the beginning that she would not marry and have children—but as time went on the identity of her true vocation remained stubbornly beyond her ken. Amy spent her first thirty years patiently groping toward the thing she felt called to produce, and then, having committed herself to writing, she spent the next twenty years slowly reorienting herself from fiction to poetry. Along the way she wrote three novels which no editor was interested in publishing, while supporting herself in New York as a secretary for Oxford University Press, a librarian for the Audubon Society, and an editor for E.P. Dutton. Periodically she returned home to her native Midwest to wonder if she was really making the best of her life. . . .

If she'd been able to look into the future, she wouldn't have worried. From the moment her first poem was accepted by *The New Yorker*, Amy's ascension was both sure and swift. She wrote with the awareness of having to produce a lifetime's length, a challenge she met with grace. *The Kingfisher* was followed by *What the Light Was Like* (1985), *Archaic Figure* (1987), *Westward* (1990), and *A Silence Opens* (1994), as well as *Predecessors, Et Cetera* (1991), a collection of essays. And there was acclaim. The Academy of American Poets awarded her a fellowship for distinguished achievement, and a MacArthur Fellowship enabled her to purchase the small cottage she loved, in the Berkshire Mountains of Western Massachusetts.

Amy's funeral, held in the backyard of the cottage only a few days after her death on September 10 from ovarian cancer, was—fittingly—infused with a strange but ultimately transcendent happiness.

Jean Hanff Korelitz. *Poetry Society of America Newsletter*. Spring, 1995, p. 5

BIBLIOGRAPHY

The Kingfisher, 1983 (p); *The Summer Solstice*, 1983 (p); *What the Light Was Like*, 1985 (p); *Archaic Figure*, 1987 (p); *Westward*, 1990 (p); *Manhattan: An Elegy, and Other Poems*, 1990; *Predecessors, et cetera*, 1991 (e); *A Silence Opens*, 1994 (p); *The Collected Poems*, 1997 (p)

CLARK, Walter Van Tilburg (1909–)

The tendency to explain, to probe, to analyze, is certainly more characteristic of the people of the eastern half of this country than it is of Westerners. Though born in the East, Walter Van Tilburg Clark is a Westerner in sympathy and spirit. Like the large landscapes with which the book is filled, his style is ample and spacious rather than compact. The reader whose life is not leisurely may find himself skipping paragraphs. . . . The dialogue is never false but it lacks the impact of character, and there is no humor.

William Maxwell. *Saturday Review*. June 2, 1945. p. 13

He is a storyteller before he is a moralist, a writer before he is a philosopher. . . . What makes him a serious writer, to my mind, is that he can write with parables which are as absorbing for their telling as for their moral. . . . It may just be that Walter Van Tilburg Clark is a Young Lochinvar coming riding out of the West to the American novel's rescue.

Hilary H. Lyons. *Holiday*. Oct. 1949. p. 20

(*The Watchful Gods*) reinforces our awareness of that combination of personal integrity and artful concentration which, aside from his Western settings, is the trade-mark of Mr. Clark's talent. . . . The activities of the Western setting seem always to be under examination, as though the author recognized the challenge to investigate the relationship of the human being to an environment which has too often frustrated the attempts of the writer to subdue it.

Mr. Clark's nature is not the idyllic world of nineteenth-century romanticism; neither is it a world of irrational malevolence such as that portrayed by our literary naturalists. Nature represents, rather, a stage whereon man's actions of necessity become more clearly defined.

Ray B. West, Jr. *Saturday Review*. Sept. 30, 1950. pp. 17–8

The difficulty is not that Mr. Clark is too much preoccupied with man's relation to the forces of nature but rather that he is apparently so little interested in the relations that exist between men, except in those limited areas where people have differing conceptions of their connection with the natural world. . . . When in 306 pages of short stories (*The Watchful Gods*) perhaps only 15 contain any dialogue, aside from people talking to animals, one must inevitably consider the extent of their relevance to the human situation, and one must wonder whether the writer's horizons are not bounded on the one hand by the hawk and on the other by the boy with the twenty-two.

Harvey Swados. *The Nation*. Oct. 7, 1950. p. 318

Clark's world is spiritually the world of the rural American, consisting of Nature, on the one hand, and Man on the other. . . . In all of Clark's fiction his exceptionally acute observations of outdoor sound, light, smell, mass, texture, and relationship are superior to his understanding of the human psyche in any but a decivilised area of operation. There is no living American writer of fiction who can type a richer page of landscape but no writer of equal talent is more endangered by the inability to enrich his human types.

Vernon Young. *AQ.* Summer, 1951. pp. 110–1

The Track of the Cat deals with a great theme in American fiction, perhaps the greatest: the pursuit of an enemy in nature. . . . Clark localizes his theme in the attempt by a family of brothers to track down a great black panther during a mountain blizzard. His story is continuously and wonderfully exciting. He is able to bring before the reader with extraordinary vividness the clash of stubborn wills in the snow-bound ranchhouse, the unpopulated mountain landscape, the snow and cold, and above all, the hunt itself.

Paul Pickrel. *The Yale Review.* Autumn, 1949. pp. 190–1

There is an artistic unity and simplicity in *The Track of the Cat*, but there is also some of the looseness and apparent capriciousness of events which are in life. The actions have implications that go far beyond their limited context. . . . You can take *The Track of the Cat* as a symbolic, universal drama of Man against an implacable Evil Principle, forever stalking him, and you can ponder its implied question: If humility and violence meet the same end, is it a stalemate? Or you may enjoy it, without mysticism, as a stark story of man struggling with elemental antagonists in nature.

Edmund Fuller. *Saturday Review.* June 4, 1949. pp. 9–10

The Track of the Cat is one of the great American novels of ''place.'' Something of its nobility should be suggested by the fact that one cannot bring to mind a similar novel of its kind that is quite worthy of comparison. One thinks of the best in the genre, even of such work as Elisabeth Madox Roberts' *The Tree of Man* and Willa Cather's *My Antonia*, and they come to seem, by comparison, more than ever like miniature studies of special manners, more than graceful surely, yet without grandeur. Mr. Clark's new novel likewise transcends his own earlier books. . . . *The Track of the Cat* may well be the achievement that twentieth-century American regionalism has needed to justify itself.

Mark Schorer. *New York Times Book Section.* June 5, 1949. p. 1

BIBLIOGRAPHY
The Ox-Bow Incident, 1940 (n); *The City of Trembling Leaves*, 1945 (n); *The Track of the Cat*, 1949 (n); *The Watchful Gods*, 1950 (s)

CODRESCU, Andrei (1946–)

At first glance Andrei Codrescu seems to be an anti-traditional poet. Nothing happened until I was here, he says [in *The History of the Growth of Heaven*]:

allowing for the thousand distortions
that make us laugh, tell me,

has anyone ever said anything?

Like the Dadaists he denies the existence of tradition, although this itself has become a well-known tradition. He treats the world as a newly created *tabula rasa* for his imagination. This is brash, but it has advantages. Perceptions are fresh, and there is genuine psychological realism; when experiences occur in life they often seem totally unique and the comparing process occurs only after the event. It is hard to be true to the experience and to the intellect at the same time.

Many actions in the poems are stated rather than evoked. Often the language is rather flat, without nuances, and there are some mistakes in English. After an interesting description of sex in New York and thousands of intertwined limbs, tongues, and genitals, the poet concludes: ''A ball of flame floats permanently around the city.'' This is a disappointing stock image. Or: ''things look real/ they freak me out''. Or: ''All resurrection must begin right away.'' Miraculous things occur and the poet presents many metaphors which are quite original but usually directly stated, with only a dime-store finish, and not evoked. There is freshness and magic in these poems; there is little intense feeling, but I think this is the intention of the author. He assumes that the world makes no sense, and because he believes each of his experiences is totally new he refuses to put himself in anyone else's shoes. He cannot speak for other, nor for what has happened in the past; he cannot compare. He gains in spontaneity, but loses in participation; the freshness is specialized. There are many good poems in this book: ''To the Virgin as She Now Stands'' and ''Late Night, San Francisco'' are strong poems with powerful endings. . . .

John R. Carpenter. *Poetry.* December, 1974, pp. 166–73.

[Andrei Codrescu is] considered by many writers to be one of this country's most imaginative poets, with talents similar to those of Walt Whitman and William Carlos Williams. . . . Collections of [Codrescu's] poetry have appeared in numerous small press chapbooks and in two full-length books: *License To Carry a Gun* and *The History of the Growth of Heaven*. His poetry has been characterized as a ''magnificent clash of words,'' touched by an imagination that is magical, a clearer penetration into the soul of America by a foreigner than any by a native American poet.

All of these tributes are made to his poetry and it would be overly generous to extend these same characterizations to all of his prose writing. This autobiographical account [*The Life and Times of an Involuntary Genius*] is a procession of short jerky sentences that tell the story of the poet's childhood spent in a haunted castle in the dark hills of Transylvania. His grandmother lived in just two rooms on the lower floor which were the former servants' kitchen next to the big old kitchen. The other inhabitants of this dreary place were spiders, bats, ghosts, and various astral species. Andrei would see his mother on occasions whenever ''her men left her'' and then ''she would go into unending fits of despair and would threaten to wash the world away with her tears.'' Bursts of his poetic powers appear in almost every description of his parents, his grandmother, his young associates. . . .

The autobiography races rapidly through early adulthood and the worthless struggles with communist power which the poet experienced as an unbearable burden because of his scorn for authority. His early attempts at writing were belittled by the critics and he was expelled from the university and served notice for military conscription. He decided to escape from his country without money, friends, or any knowledge of other languages and he wandered through the ghettos of Paris, Rome, Detroit, and New York's Lower East Side, and finally reached California. These accounts are full of adventure and colorful experiences with many bizarre characters and they move with spirit and brio. America becomes a place for him where the people "smile dazzlingly and bang their Cadillacs into one another." Two Frenchmen whom he meets there at the corner of Bleecker and MacDougal in the Village had the ingenious way of making money by working with a Sperm Bank. Andrei worked at the famous 8th Street Bookstore before he finally migrated to San Francisco "that wicked town filled with the most marvelous Mediterranean air and suicidal fog."

The imagery and the freshness of the descriptions never cease to come, one after the other. It may be the greatest tribute to Codrescu that his prose drives a reader to the magical language of his poetry....

Thomas A. Wassmer. *Best Sellers* June, 1975, pp. 69–70.

The typical Codrescu text throughout *Selected Poems* is short, quickly paced rather than discursive or meditative, surreal, erotic, intermittently violent, full of surprising turns of phrase and image—images and phrases enigmatic enough to invite more than one reading—and pervaded by a playful sense of humor. For Codrescu, even the most serious poetic utterance is a kind of joke, often a joke on the poet, told with the glee of a naughty little boy, which he clearly enjoys being. He revels in the shifting identities of the creator's role....

The writer is having a good time, engaging in mischievous and ironic activity even when writing from the depths of sadness and depression, but not in a manner to set him brooding on the artist's tragic fate. No, the poet's art is magical, miraculous, and therefore comic for Codrescu: it can turn grief into fun simply by a twist of the sinewy mind, a turn of the tongue, his tongue, which is all the more amazing because it speaks in a second language, American English, which he wields with remarkable facility, felicity and fire.

Selected Poems is a sprightly book, light and smart like the banter of streetwise city boys after a horror movie, charged with a nervous youthful energy, sexy, a little menacing at times and clever in the best and worst of ways. At worst Codrescu's work comes off as evasive, cute or frivolous—"Creative Jive"—but at least these pieces make no pretense of their own importance. Most of the poems have a refreshing gleam in their eyes, a good-natured slash at the sensitive ego so often wounded by delusions of significance. At best they resonate very mysteriously, offering lively proof of the power of imaginative play....

In America's Shoes is a parallel tale in prose which documents the period during which the poems were written, a warmly humorous narrative account of the poet's emergence as an American. It is a sequel to Codrescu's earlier "autobiography," *The Life and Times of an Involuntary Genius*. While continuing with what purports to be his own life story—a sometimes fanciful mixture of legend and confession—he focuses on several of his friends of the 1960s and '70s, portraying them not only as interesting characters but also as cultural archetypes, poets and hippies and borderline bohemians with whom he shared various adventures, tragedies and revelations in the course of coming of age, marrying, and fathering two children.

The book opens with a very funny account of the author's induction into American citizenship. His perspective as an immigrant with a wickedly sardonic sense of the oppressive stupidity of all governments makes his testimony deliciously disillusioned yet cheerful. There is much shrewd, cynical insight into the workings of bureaucracy, and at the same time a tender appreciation of the sweetness and solidarity of friendship in the land of the free, where he now writes within earshot of a baseball stadium.

Because of his East European Jewish background, Codrescu becomes a kind of grandfather figure to many of his American contemporaries. He has an almost protective understanding of the fragility of yankee innocence and rootlessness while relishing the freshness of that innocence and mobility, enthusiastically cultivating those qualities in himself. Like any wandering rascal poet he experiments with experience, making assorted urban and rural scenes from coast to coast, meeting eccentric people, taking drugs, making love, and writing it all down.

What makes Codrescu's story more than just another personal tale of the life and loves of a roving rogue is his keen apprehension of American culture as only an outsider can see it. He claims, paradoxically, "I've always been an American," and he is, in some ways even more profoundly than his native friends. The restlessness of his energy, his optimism, his refusal to be a sober adult—these are a few of his typically American traits. The book is an essay on US cultural history in the '70s, informally chronicling the massive turn toward guru-worship and the marketing of the psyche as suffered by some of his dearest comrades from the counter-culture.

In America's Shoes is also an interesting glimpse, or kaleidoscope of glimpses, into various poetry "scenes"—especially of the San Francisco Bay area—of the '60s and '70s whose participants continue to make waves, or stagnant pools, in the swamps of American writing.

Codrescu is gossipy, alive to what's happening, young but seasoned enough to discount cultural icons or joyfully skewer their presumed authority. Kenneth Rexroth, Robert Bly, Jack Hirschman, and Bob Dylan are among the figures he sketches with delightful insight and irreverence. He seems an unusually happy person and his happiness radiates from the pages of his prose even more generously than from the poetry. The writing is a celebration, a festive song of gratitude for his good luck in the New World, and is pleasantly free of literary pretense even though he moves in literary realms.

In Baltimore, where he now lives, Codrescu writes a column for the Sunday Sun and co-edits the new journal *Exquisite Corpse*, "a monthly of books and ideas," whose first few issues have been a dynamic mixture of opinion, polemic, satire and otherwise stinging commentary on current events in contemporary culture. If the *Corpse* survives, it promises to be a notable contribution to the country's maelstrom of little magazines. The wit and energy of his efforts give me the impression that Codrescu's presence as a poet and all-around cultural agitator will matter more and more. *Selected Poems* and *In America's Shoes* are suggestive evidence of a versatile writer whose gifts are swiftly evolving....

Stephen Kessler. *San Francisco Review of Books* Winter, 1983–84, pp. 5–6.

When one reads the young Codrescu, one imagines an artist who wants to burn the museums. But he has written 15 volumes of poetry and two autobiographical prose works. Today he teaches at

Louisiana State University after a stint at Johns Hopkins and is a regular commentator on National Public Radio's "All Things Considered." In the contemporary world of accelerated pace and dislocation, his expatriate sensibilities of wonder and detachment seem ever more timely.

In *Comrade Past & Mister Present*, his splendid new collection of poetry, prose and journal entries, this perpetual outsider offers ample evidence that even as his life grows more settled, he continues to push at his own outer limits, all the while treating the derangement of his senses with uncommon spontaneity and wit. Perhaps Flaubert was right when he suggested in his letters that one should live as a bourgeois, so that one can be wild and free in one's art. In [*Comrade Past & Mister Present*], he has successfully found a meeting place for his prose and poetry. He has left the characteristic movement of his earlier work, which was posing questions, taking them out of context and then allowing his diabolically dialectical mind to eat up the question itself. "Comrade Past" is an elliptical, extended poem with longer lines, designed like a series of opening doors or peeled-off layers. . . .

For Mr. Codrescu, images are embedded in language "like anchovies in a pizza," as he puts it. He may play games, but if his intent is to take the reader's head off, he gently unscrews it and places it in one's lap. He shifts effortlessly from comic surrealist to naturalist, philosopher to saint to madman, but he is always the seeker after transcendence, in thrall to the unknown. . . .

In Mr. Codrescu's native Transylvania, poets are social spokesmen, and that perhaps explains his fearlessness of treading on the languages of philosophy, religion, politics, science or popular culture. His focus on a pet theme, oppression, is as much concerned with the private as with the public. He ominously begins the poem "Momentary Bafflement with Return Home at Dawn": "Extremely logical circumstances are in effect / we are in danger of behaving as expected." Mr. Codrescu has a knack for bringing out dichotomies in matters moral, sexual and political, as when asking the perplexing question in the poem "Dear Masoch": "What do you do if you're a masochist but have been placed / in a position of power?"

His journal entries, entitled "The Juniata Diary: With Timely Repartees," range from remembrances of losing his virginity at the Museum of the Communist Party to explorations of "sleep linguistics" for a university of the future and reflections on those who have influenced his work (he eulogizes the late poet Ted Berrigan, much venerated as the "Gulf Stream of Consciousness," as a mentor and a father). In this diary Mr. Codrescu also includes some of the rigorous intellectual gymnastics that find lyrical expression in the poems. Even when his sharp observations yield little more than dime store philosophy, it is a most interesting and frequently dazzling dime store presided over by one of our most prodigiously talented and magical writers.

Bruce Shlain. *The New York Times Book Review.* January 25, 1987, p. 15.

"America can be taken for granted," counsels Andrei Codrescu near the outset of his latest prose flight. "The obvious is very serious about itself here." The point can hardly be argued in a country where morning papers carry headlines like "Study Reveals Unreality May Be Good for You." It is with healthy doses of such medicine that the Romanian-born poet seeks to treat his adopted homeland. If these stories are termed "instances of realism" that's

only because this eternal emigre views American reality as the outdated passport each new arrival carries in his vest pocket. As in his weekly musings for National Public Radio's "All Things Considered," Mr. Codrescu succeeds in carving out his place as an American voice by failing to heed his own advice. In his work, not a single advertising jingle is taken for granted, the obvious is subverted through carefully aimed barrages of obscurity and no punditry is ever handled more seriously than a trip to the 7-Eleven.

Still, this volume [*Monsieur Teste in America*] will baffle a listening audience who have come to expect a cross between Andy Rooney and Andre Gide. Out of artistic integrity or self-indulgence, Mr. Codrescu chooses here to abandon mass taste, along with linear thought and most literary conventions. "He was irony, she was subjective mysticism" is about as much character development as we get. While *Monsieur Teste in America* offers copious servings of poetic observation, it skimps on the everyday detail that makes Mr. Codrescu's radio musings so affecting.

The title novella in this collection of short fiction offers an intriguing premise. On his 29th birthday, Mr. Codrescu summons Monsieur Teste, the Paul Valery creation who represents his intellectual conscience, to help him make sense—or better yet, nonsense—of American symbology. But premises are mere pretense, as is writing about how all writing is pretense, and Mr. Codrescu's dialogue soon makes the two alter egos sound like dueling Zen roshis: "'The point is that you can't trust the world with your understanding of it.' 'But how then . . . . can you entrust the world to your understanding?'" The story meanders off into the birth of a hermaphroditic love-child named Maximum, a discourse on "crypto-morons" and the cataloguing of American schools of poetry in the form of a luncheon menu. ("Aktup, Metabolism, the Bowel Movement and Syllogism. All have me as one of the founders.") It comes as no shock when the piece concludes about Mr. Codrescu's European shadow, "I had learned nothing from him and he who knew everything had taught nothing."

In "Samba de los Agentes," the ramblings and cadence of a Colombian immigrant named Jose sound suspiciously Slavic. Everyone in Mr. Codrescu's universe, including this ex-cop protagonist, is a poet and knows it. And all gain acceptance in America by sending some packaged piece of their souls to market. "I have an agent, therefore I am," seems to be one of many subtexts in this odd regurgitation of the crime story genre. The six shorter pieces in the collection are scattershot affairs united solely through the use of female narrators who are hip, sassy and, once again, familiarly literary in their obsessions. The only voice individuated from the author's is faint indeed, emanating from the disembodied spirit of a spacey grad student channeled through a Brooklynese medium named Madame Rosa.

Like Nabokov's, Mr. Codrescu's greatest strength lies in his outsider's appreciation for the succulence of American idioms. Where language is reinvented daily on billboards, it offers liberation from the chains of connotation. "Contagious words imbued with mass-market meanings like a sponge full of ink crowded my mind to dictate their grammar to me!" the narrator confesses. "The words of America's language brought me an incalculable dowry."

Unlike that strain of American writing that seeks authenticity through spareness, Mr. Codrescu proves he's comfortable with the American idiom by taking colloquialisms out for every possible spin. For him, English is not a tool chest but a toy box—and there is playing in every page here. By now, Mr. Codrescu has become a master at mixing ontological speculation with such random bits of

Americana as "flying K-Mart lawn chairs." But the author remains too enamored of purple prose for purpleness's sake. "My dreams are dotted with the dance of psychopatia sexualis in the graveyard of the planet," is one of many sentences that read like bad sendups of beatnik prosody. And Mr. Codrescu would do well to sign up for the 12-step recovery program at Simile Addicts Anonymous. A sampling: New York is said to lie "under the general strike like an actress under a Foreign Legionnaire"; "Vague regrets coursed through him like phosphorus through protozoa"; "'I'm stuffed up with thoughts like a swan with pomegranates'"; "Truth sits in an autobiography like a bird dog in an underground hospital."

At this rate, America will need Andrei Codrescu the way a cement mixer needs a parakeet. *Monsieur Teste in America* opens with the author's admission that he's "bored in heaven"—and what follows is both a celebration and a frantic evasion of that delicious fate that unites the assimilated and the lunatic. Perhaps Mr. Codrescu can't admit aloud that there's as little to becoming an American as he feared—or that, for all his wealth of associations, America may yet prove too small a subject.

John Krich. *The New York Times Book Review*. January 10, 1988, p. 17.

Like the panorama of life in post-revolutionary Romania, which the poet and essayist Andrei Codrescu describes with both awe and revulsion, *The Hole in the Flag* is a work of great complexity and subtlety. For everyone who watched as the Romanian revolution unfolded, Mr. Codrescu provides a gripping political detective story.

Mr. Codrescu, a regular commentator for National Public Radio who had been fiercely critical of the Ceausescu regime, arrived in Bucharest with a radio crew in the days of the December 1989 revolt. On one level, his book is a travelogue. In crisp, often humorous detail, he describes his experiences and reactions on returning to a land he had left as a teen-ager.

We learn a great deal about the harsh conditions in Romania that induced Mr. Codrescu and his mother to leave their homeland, and about the subtle and not-so-subtle changes brought about by 25 years of Ceausescu rule and a few days of revolution. These observations provide the background against which the other, more unsettling, themes of the book are woven. Foremost among these is the dark and still-unsolved mystery of what exactly did happen during those eight fateful days when Nicolae Ceausescu was toppled and a new Government took control.

Like most everyone else, Mr. Codrescu starts out convinced that the Romanian revolution was the result of a spontaneous popular uprising by an oppressed people against a tyrannical, narcissistic dictator. Early chapters describe the images of the revolution as portrayed in the media: a peaceful protest in Timisoara; machine guns firing into a crowd of unarmed civilians; the flight, capture and execution of the Ceausescus; a protracted battle between the Army and the shadowy forces of the Securitate; the deaths of tens of thousands and destruction reminiscent of World War II; the defeat of battalions of fanatical Ceausescu loyalists; and the final victory of the people under the benign leadership of a spontaneously created caretaker Government. A euphoric and ingenuous Mr. Codrescu—like much of the rest of the world—accepted this melodrama as the revealed truth.

Having skillfully carried us with him, he starts planting seeds of doubt by pointing out inconsistencies and improbabilities in the

official account of the revolution. He winds up dissecting it event by event, image by image, assumption by assumption. The glorious, pure, idealistic vision of the Romanian revolution gives way to an ugly and misshapen thing, the product of a grotesque masterpiece of deception, "a process of mass hypnosis."

Everyone, of course, recognizes tyranny in a monster like Ceausescu. But Mr. Codrescu explores the ways in which government can accomplish its tyrannical ends by misdirection, without need of force. He argues that the revolutionary Government bamboozled the Romanian people through its control over the country's only television station. By manipulating televised images, Mr. Codrescu believes, members of the new Government managed to etch themselves into the minds of the Romanian people so deeply that no other party stood a chance of dislodging them. Much of the evidence the author marshals to support his thesis consists of deduction and speculation; it will be up to the reader to decide which vision of the Romanian revolution to believe.

What seems unassailable, however, is Mr. Codrescu's touching, painstakingly accurate description of Romania and its people, the good and the bad, the pristine and the hideous. Romania is one of the most beautiful places on earth. With a loving eye, Mr. Codrescu fills his book with the rich texture of Romanian culture, from the noble, turn-of-the-century buildings of Bucharest to the peasant shrines of his Transylvanian birthplace. He contrasts these with the unsightly rows of boxcar apartments built by Ceausescu and the ghastly pollution generated by mindless industrialization.

The Romanian people, too, present a series of disquieting contrasts. They are portrayed as generous, friendly, cosmopolitan and politically savvy, and as mean-spirited, grim, ethnocentric and politically naive. Drawing from the country's violent and often tragic history, Mr. Codrescu explains how the contradictory images are both accurate. Indeed, one cannot understand Romanian society, or grasp the magnitude of the problems it faces on its way to a Western-style democracy, without understanding paradoxes such as these in a country that has guarded the gateway to Europe for two millennia.

The most significant lesson of the Romanian experience may be that he who controls the media controls the course of events. This underscores the conviction that the ultimate guarantee of our own freedom lies not in our system of checks and balances, nor in our constitutional protections against unreasonable searches and seizures, nor in many of the other protections afforded by the Constitution—important though they all be—but in the First Amendment, which puts private individuals, the Government, firmly in control of our political and social discourse. It is a lesson well worth keeping in mind.

Alex Kozinski. *The New York Times Book Review*. June 30, 1991, p. 16.

Mr. Codrescu, a poet who is best known as an essayist on National Public Radio, takes this drive-time script and turns it inside out into a fine trick bag of wit, discovery and self-deprecation in a book badly titled *Road Scholar: Coast to Coast Late in the Century*.

From the outset, he is smart enough to anticipate the main pothole in driving a 1968 red Cadillac and retracing his own racy immigrant roots (he was born in Romania and came to the United States in the 1960s) through the locales of Hippiedom. "I expected to find nothing in those places," he concedes, "partly because there would be little time to discover anything genuine, and partly because I never found anything of interest deliberately; the best discoveries of my life have beèn by accident.'' Fortunately, he changed his mind upon being advanced ''a ridiculously small amount of money that was, however, more than my poetry had earned me in a lifetime of practicing its dangerous pinturns.''

Mr. Codrescu takes off with a television documentary crew and a photographer, David Graham, who complements the author well in glimpsing the random nonsense and unreliable reality of things in general. It is a measure of Mr. Codrescu's talent that such an orchestrated mission manages to produce an unpretentious, wry journey in the art of essay writing, from light to sparsely serious. Once at the wheel of America's ''banal instrument of carnage,'' the writer buys fuzzy dice and a drink holder and begins driving from his New Orleans home to the Lower East Side digs of Allen Ginsberg. There they lightly agree to plot for the reburial of the poet Ted Berrigan's remains in the St. Mark's Church grave of Peter Stuyvesant, documented in passing from Mr. Codrescu's interesting store of American antihistory as a founding anti-Semite.

Thus does he putter in a kind of countertravelogue about the land, all the way to San Francisco, via the ''Kingdom of If,'' Las Vegas, with rarely a dull page in this simple book. It is mainly about the fun of writing and reading and meandering, rather than self-conscious synthesizing. Better for the reader to have Mr. Codrescu philosophically accepting a fax about the next city's lodgings from a cemetery attendant in Camden, N.J., who intrudes as the writer tries to have a special thought at the grave of Whitman, ''sexually manifold and optimistic, the spokesman of liberty in all its guises.''

Non sequitur, no harm. We're soon visiting the Burned-Over Patch region of surviving zealotries in a narrow swath of rural western New York. First, the Hutterians, the Christian communist and pacifist refugees who fled Hitler to live in Amish-like aloofness in a Bruderhof, or ''place of brotherhood.'' Then the descendants of the Oneida Perfectionists, who lived in a community conceived in free love, where the poet pines for the lost spirit of ''continual flirtation as in a medieval court of love.'' Mr. Codrescu is the sort of writer who feels obliged to satirize and interplay with reality and not just catalogue impressions. He can redeem flagging curiosity in a single sentence, as when, returning to Detroit haunts he loved as a student, he finds he must wax more Mad Maxish than Whitmanesque: ''I see that when a city becomes extinct, its last inhabitants go crazy.''

Mr. Codrescu is a reminder that locomotion is not the heart of the matter; a decent imagination is. Opinionated travelogue inventories of Americana won't do. Nor will serial compilations of unforgettable characters suffice, as Pete Davies proves in *Storm Country: A Journey Through the Heart of America*. Mr. Davies, a British novelist, is tireless as a lepidopterist in netting what feels like each and every flitting Midwesterner he spies in his travels (13 states, 1981 Ford pickup) in the heartland ''with its savage weather and its sentimental music.'' He packs his pages with characters, and the friends and relatives of these characters, each of them with a story to tell and each story pretty much told in his book to the point of Chaucerian overdrive. ''It's the nearest thing I know to going to the moon—and I love it! '' he exults as he wheels about, trying to document the withering of ''the whole mythic notion of what America is'' and capturing individual lives ''fresh out of a country song.'' It is the latter quality that intoxicates the book all too well. He concludes his 7,449 miles by comparing America to ''that girl you had that thing with when you were 20,'' an

experience ''bigger than good or bad, bolder than right or wrong.'' Well, I guess. . .

. . . .Like a traveling child, a reader needs road games in these wordy jaunts. Mr. Codrescu, one eye on the mirror to check on our attention span, takes care to detour to places like Sun City, Ariz., a retirement community of gray-haired bikers, so we can hear its punk rock band, One Foot in the Grave, play ''Menopause.'' It beats counting brindled cows from the back seat. His imagination even saves us, just barely, at the book's more extended side trips into the post-Hippie spiritual pranks and placebos of the New Age counterculture in Santa Fe, N.M. Mr. Codrescu cannot resist nostalgically sampling the latest distractions from life at the hands of a crystal healer who transports him to ''a profoundly tacky psychic gap.'' ''You better hurry,'' he advises voyeuristic America. ''Prices are going up as we speak.''

Mr. Codrescu does well by vicariousness. His trip, antic as it is, silly as it can get, is best as a selfish sample of a nation changing weirdly, wonderfully, in one of its liveliest, most valuable eras of new immigrants—those fresh life-and-death travelers who are instantly redefining the lay of the land. ''America is the place where you must deliberately forgo revenge if you are to go forward,'' is as close as Mr. Codrescu comes to prescribing from the wheel of the red Caddy. ''You can be born again here, but like a baby you must cancel the pain that brought you here.''

Francis X. Clines. *The New York Times Book Review*. May 9, 1993, p. 1.

In his buoyant 1993 film, *Road Scholar*, the Romanian expatriate Andrei Codrescu emulated the American odysseys of Walt Whitman and Jack Kerouac. Stopping along the way west to scrutinize quaint national divinities, from hamburgers to crystals, Mr. Codrescu, grinning in his red Cadillac, fulfilled his immigrant's pledge: ''We were done with the Old World; liberty was ours.''

In his new novel, *The Blood Countess*, a Hungarian emigrant goes back to his bloody Old World, with no red Cadillac in which to escape crazy faiths. Drake Bathory-Kereshtur, a journalist in America, returns to an ''anxious and unsettled'' Budapest swarming with skinhead fascism, anti-Semitism and medieval magic from the fairy tales—or horror stories—that Communist indoctrination had suppressed. He sees that ''the lightly settled soil of democracy and atheism was rapidly turning over, releasing dormant agents.''

Awakening after a burial that seems long only to mortals, these ancient agents of savagery overwhelm modernity and its representative, the bemused Drake. The most tenacious monster is a woman: the 16th-century Countess Elizabeth Bathory, Drake's ancestor and the personification of his national past, who is said to have preserved her youth by bathing in virgins' blood. Elizabeth erupts into the present when a monarchist coterie declares Drake King of Hungary.

At the climax of the novel, Drake travels with these motley believers to ancient Bathory castles. In this nightmare journey, characters and country revert to their haunted past. Elizabeth returns as various strange apparitions, instigating a murder, which Drake accuses himself of before a high-minded American judge.

This parable of atavism and possession is chilling, but unfortunately, it is not the only story; interwoven with Drake's journey is a historical novel about Countess Bathory herself. Though she does not bathe in maidens' blood, she showers in it with the help of an ingenious cage. Menstruating, marrying, studying herself in mirrors, biting little pieces out of her maids, experimenting with baroque sexual refreshments, Elizabeth Bathory supposedly embodies the demonic past.

Alas, she is too silly for that. On her wedding night she arouses herself with dreams of spurtings and spoutings and whippings fit to print only on the walls of a boys' locker room. As an incarnation of history, Elizabeth is closer to pornographic Victorian biters like Swinburne's pagan goddesses than she is to the cold hate at the heart of Mr. Codrescu's historical horror. Her supposed perversions distract from and diminish the authentic abominations of our own chilling times.

The Blood Countess is an ornate novel, thick with dense symbolism and decorative violence. It reveals a more ambitiously literary Andrei Codrescu than the popular commentator on National Public Radio, who is a wry and realistic political observer flaunting his dissociation from all countries, relishing quirks and denouncing all specimens of stupidity and tyranny. As a novelist, Mr. Codrescu borrows Kafka's enigmatic dream mode. He no longer aims to observe nations, but to create fantastic national allegories. His novel is so drenched in elaborate (if studiously metaphorical) sadism, in obscure fairy tales and legends, that I longed for his incisive radio voice to tell me what was going on.

The problem in this novel, as in its version of history, is women. They are virgins or vamps, victims or furies, who mess up an effective thriller. In the course of *The Blood Countess* the spirit of Elizabeth possesses all the modern characters, including a glamorous female professor who studies the Bathory archives, beats her adoring students and finally turns into a ridiculously overdrawn emanation of the Countess. Elizabeth also inhabits a comatose woman, allegorically named Eva, who prowls ominously around Hungary at the end, getting younger and younger. The arousal of women, this ending suggests, is the death of civilization.

I don't believe that, and I don't think Mr. Codrescu does either. *The Blood Countess* gets lost in lurid symbolism and bizarre sexual embellishments. Its operatic women become scapegoats for all social viciousness, but in the best parts of the book hatred is a pervasive, even casual motivation to everyone. I wish Mr. Codrescu had written a sparer, tighter novel about his bedeviled King of Hungary without trying to resurrect Elizabeth. As a specter, she is wonderful; as a character, she is ludicrous. Mr. Codrescu writes splendidly about women as remote agents of fear, but when he tries to depict them, campy posturing undermines political dread.

Nina Auerbach. *The New York Times Book Review*. July 30, 1995, p. 7.

BIBLIOGRAPHY
License to Carry a Gun, 1970 (p); *The History of the Growth of Heaven*, 1971 (p); *Why I Can't Talk on the Telephone*, 1971 (e); *The Here, What, Where*, 1972 (p); *How I Became Howard Johnson*, 1972 (e); *The Questionable Hell*, 1972 (e); *San Francisco*, with Aram Saroyan, 1972 (p); *Secret Training*, 1973 (p); *A Serious Morning*, 1973 (p); *& Grammar & Money*, 1973 (p); *The Life and Times of an Involuntary Genius*, 1975 (e); *Au bout du Monde*, 1977 (p); *The Lady Painter*, 1977 (p); *The Marriage of Insult and Injury*, 1977 (p); *The Repentance of Lorraine*, 1977 (n); *For the Love of a Coat*, 1978 (p); *Diapers on the Snow*, 1981 (p); *Necrocorrida*, 1982 (p); *In America's Shoes*, 1983 (e); *Comrade Past & Mister Present*, 1986 (p); *A Craving for Swan*, 1986 (e);

Monsieur Teste in America and Other Instances of Realism, 1987 (s); *Raised by Puppets: Only to Be Killed by Research*, 1989 (e); *The Disappearance of the Outside: A Manifesto for Escape*, 1990 (e); *Belligerence: New Poems*, 1991 (p); *The Hole in the Flag: A Romanian Exile's Story of Return and Revolution*, 1991 (e); *Road Scholar: Coast to Coast Late in the Century*, 1993 (e); *The Muse Is Always Half-Dressed in New Orleans and Other Essays*, 1993 (e); *Zombification: Stories from National Public Radio*, 1994 (s); *The Blood Countess*, 1995 (n); *The Dog with the Chip in His Neck*, 1996 (e)

CONDON, Richard (1915–1996)

Mr. Condon shows himself well able to construct an exciting tale of crime on traditional lines, with all the homey concomitants of violence, double-cross, and rubbings-out.... Mr. Condon has placed his story [*The Oldest Confession*] in a Spanish setting so wild as to interfere with this enjoyable reading. We are constantly breaking off to laugh aloud or to rub our eyes and wonder if we really see what we think we do.... Mr. Condon can also be funny when he means to be. But the unconscious efforts remain, for me, the best.

Honor Tracy. *Saturday Review*. June 14, 1958. pp. 39–40

Unlike most other first novels, Richard Condon's [*The Oldest Confession*] is a fully controlled job of writing rather than an ardent grope. Written throughout with painstaking grace, not one scene or description is ever thrown away or treated in a commonplace manner....

And yet the one thing its author is unable to convey is any feeling of depth, of real mortality unfolding before the reader. The deterioration of James Bourne, ivy-league master criminal, is singularly unmoving even as one stunningly dramatic scene or ingenious plot turn follows another.... If, the next time out, he can manage to open up and write more personally without marring his exceedingly refined sense of literary form, then we shall really be seeing a book. As things are now, no apologies are necessary to anyone for this is quite an impressive debut.

Gerald Walker. *New York Times Book Section*. June 22, 1958. p. 18

Richard Condon has found an original way of avoiding the second-novel problem. Last year he published his stimulating *The Oldest Confession*. Now in *The Manchurian Candidate* he comes up, simultaneously as it were, with his second, third, and fourth volumes. Within two covers he compresses (a) a breathlessly up-to-date thriller, gimmicked to the gills, from judo to narco-hypnosis; (b) a psychoanalytic horror tale about (what else?) a mother and a son; and (c) an irate socio-political satire that tries to flay our shibboleths alive.

Into all three stories Mr. Condon wades with the same brash, flat vim and with widely varying degrees of skill.... Mr. Condon is a fervently vivid, phrase-prone writer whose every sentence packs a compulsory punch. As soon as he becomes aware of an insight, he hits it home promptly with such might that the bang often drowns out the meaning. When it comes to the rendition of mental states his typewriter really stutters.

His verbal manner fits much more happily into the satirical portions of *The Manchurian Candidate*.... Here Mr. Condon brings into play his true gift: a villainous flair for the ribald anecdote. His account of the sexual misadventures of a Senator is a wonderfully mean little masterpiece. The ignition and confusion of Washington's publicity engines by a surly Medal winner makes a vignette of murderous hilarity. What Mr. Condon has done to political conventions has been done to them before by other writers, but not very much better.

> Frederic Morton. *New York Times Book Section*. April 26, 1959. p. 4

Richard Condon has concocted a smooth and palatable pousse-café of political satire, psychological speculation, pleasantly risqué antics a la Thorne Smith, and espionage maneuvering. His characters [in *The Manchurian Candidate*] are believable, if one-sided: Shaw remains an automaton, despite a rather dream-like love affair; his mother, the lovely and ambitious Mrs. Iselin, is by all odds the wickedest witch since Lady Macbeth, guilty of incest, adultery, pandering, betrayal and a host of other crimes, including nailing a puppy's paw to the floor; the Russian agents are superhumanly efficient; our own FBI and CIA only too fallible. Also, the basic assumptions of the plot do not withstand close examination. Happily, however, such examination is not necessary: this is a diversion, and a good one.

> Talliaferro Boatright. *New York Herald Tribune Book Section*. June 28, 1959. p. 8

Meanwhile, we have Mr. Condon's spectacular—a documentary novel that reads rather like a newsreel with action packed people scenes between. *An Infinity of Mirrors* also has what film people call a strong story line as well as plenty of hotsy scenes. In fact the basic plot, like too many TV salesmen's faces, could move any product. It fits a western as well as a thriller. In this case, it just happens to be intercut with the holocaust. . . .

All the same, it's only fair to add that *An Infinity of Mirrors* is very readable, fast-moving, and rich in romantic detail of the high life. In fact what Mr. Condon has succeeded in doing is to make the rise of Hitler seem glamorous and sexy. There is even a comic sub-plot about secret agents in the best British film tradition. My chief complaint, then, is not that Mr. Condon has written a bad novel, it is that he has written an immoral one.

> Mordecai Richler. *New York Herald Tribune Book Section*. Sept. 13, 1964. pp. 4, 19

In *The Vertical Smile* Richard Condon, like many of his compatriot writers, has much to offer in brimming energy and expertise while displaying a complex and varied background. He sub-titles this long comprehensive novel as an "entertainment" but not everyone will accept this as an accurate description of the provocative disclosures and sexual deviations, sufficiently "off-beat" to alert even the most "permissive" reader. Ada Harris and Osgood Noon, lovers who met fortuitously by night in a hotel corridor and embarked upon a passionate affair without the formality of an

introduction, are both in their "seventies." . . . This curious situation could have been sufficient content for the novel. In fact it is only the jumping off point for a commentary on the American manner of conducting national policies. . . .

Clearly, Richard Condon is genuinely concerned at the pace, the corruption and the general craziness of so much in the American way of life. Like James Hanley, he sees people as being irrevocably divided into separate camps, but his technique of putting this across is totally different, in that he draws outsize, self-obsessed characters and places them in exaggerated situations. He offers no solutions. The reader may be so appalled by the frankness and crudity that he will reject the jolting disturbance of reading *The Vertical Smile*. If he persists he will emerge from the experience shaken but wiser, having enjoyed quite a few laughs on the way.

> Rosalind Wade. *Contemporary Review*. July, 1972. p. 46

One has to piece together the Condon life—its details being inseparable from data about bathtubs in Indianapolis and zoning laws in Portugal—but the confusing evidence suggests that he got into writing late (except for an early monograph for *Esquire* on Mickey Finns) via a curious Hollywood route. He had been "chief braggart" for a number of films, then decided one day to leave press agentry, scribble up some scripts and thereby "be fitted for gold toenails"; but when he sat down to his Olivetti he slipped inadvertently into the past tense and so turned novelist.

Maybe some of the extravagance of such tales as *The Manchurian Candidate* and *The Vertical Smile* derives from his Hollywood braggart period, but more likely it goes further back; as he says somewhere in this crazy new book [*And Then We Moved to Rossenarra*] he was perfectly modest until he was six. Anyway you would think that in dealing with dear old reality rather than fiction he would slow down. He is not noveling in the new book—and he is nearer 60 than six—but it makes no difference; he is still a glorious verbal braggart.

> Reed Whittemore. *New Republic*. June 2, 1973. p. 26

Winter Kills is . . . a triumph of satire and knowledge, with a delicacy of style and a command of tone that puts Condon once again into the first rank of American novelists. Condon's hero is the lineal descendant of the ineffectual avengers who stalked the movie world of the 1950s. But while they were trying to hold onto a warped dream of individuality, Nick Thirkield is merely trying to find a fact. And Condon goes with him, less interested in facts than in nonfacts and superfacts, not historical truth but the Macy's parade of history, the overblown images from which we have all manufactured our own paranoid vision of the true connections of American society. . . .

Winter Kills, then, is "some kind of bummer through American mythology," in which almost all of Condon's characters, from highest to lowest, are driven by the American dream of being someone, making a difference, having power and control. *Winter Kills* isn't the world; it's the way we think about the world, the distortions and how they are created, "the application of the techniques of fiction playing like search-lights on a frenzied façade of truth." Condon has created a paranoid novel that does not leave us trapped inside its world, but functions instead as a liberation, exposing through the gentler orders of fiction the way we have been programmed to believe anything in print. By mingling historical reality with his own fabulous invention, Condon savagely satirizes a world in which fiction and reality are mingled to manipulate, exploit and kill.

Leo Braudy. *New York Times Book Section*. May 26, 1974. p. 5

BIBLIOGRAPHY

Men of Distinction, 1953 (d); *The Oldest Confession*, 1958 (n); *The Manchurian Candidate*, 1959 (n); *Some Angry Angel*, 1960 (n); *A Talent for Loving*, 1961 (n); *An Infinity of Mirrors*, 1964 (n); *Any God Will Do*, 1966 (n); *The Two-Headed Reader* (*The Oldest Confession* and *The Manchurian Candidate*), 1966 (n); *The Ecstasy Business*, 1967 (n); *Mile High*, 1969 (n); *The Vertical Smile*, 1971 (n); *Arigato*, 1972 (n); (with Wendy Bennett) *The Mexican Stove*, 1973 (t and cookbook); *And Then We Moved to Rossenarra*, 1973 (t); *Winter Kills*, 1974 (n); *The Star Spangled Crunch*, 1974 (t); *Money Is Love*, 1975 (n); *The Whisper of the Axe*, 1976 (n); *The Abandoned Woman*, 1977; *Bandicoot*, 1978 (n); *Death of a Politician*, 1978 (n); *The Entwining*, 1980; *Prizzi's Honor*, 1982 (n); *A Trembling upon Rome: A Work of Fiction*, 1983; *Prizzi's Family*, 1986 (n); *Prizzi's Glory*, 1988 (n); *Emperor of America*, 1990 (n); *The Final Addiction*, 1991 (n); *The Venerable Bead*, 1992 (n); *Prizzi's Money*, 1994 (n)

CONNELL, Evan S., Jr. (1924–)

The writer who tries to create art with the story must . . . take a position. He must feel deeply (passionately, I suspect) about why the human beings he is telling about operate as they do. It's not a matter of striking a pose or rising to a moral. It is a matter of finding motivation that prevails, getting at a piece of truth.

This is what makes Connell's short stories worth considering seriously. His people are captives within themselves. They are isolated—so isolated that we wonder whether Mr. Connell wouldn't like to make this isolation one of those "eternal verities" or whatever they are that William Faulkner insists on throwing at us. For when Mr. Connell's characters reach out from their isolation to make contact with the world and its inhabitants, they are either rebuffed, entangled in the debris of other lives, turned further inward or simply destroyed.

Webster Schott. *New Republic*. Oct. 14, 1957. p. 20

It seems to me that Evan Connell could become one of our best writers. . . . The Bridges [in *Mrs. Bridge*] are as vivid a family as I have encountered in modern fiction, and as individuals they are scarcely less immediate. But they are terribly, deliberately and predictably limited. . . . Mr. Connell knows so much more than he is willing to tell that he has failed us by remaining partially silent. . . .

But whether Evan Connell writes up, down or sideways he is a joy to read for he employs a prose style that is his own and yet not grotesque in its singularity nor dense in its idiosyncrasies. It is clear, it is clean, and it communicates. Finally, Mr. Connell is able

to do easily—so easily—the one thing that it has always seemed to me hardest and most important for a novelist to do. He can make his characters change.

Robert Gutwillig. *Commonweal*. Feb. 13, 1959. p. 525

[*Mrs. Bridge*] is a startling performance, one of brilliant wit and, despite a surface coldness of satire, a sympathetic one. Mr. Connell's characters are not notably depraved or wicked or even ungenerous, but they are small. They seem bent upon making spiritual midgets of themselves, or perhaps it is the thin air they breathe that makes them so small, so disappointing to themselves. . . . In spite of the superb technique many readers may find this a chilling book, but for others that very astringency will be part of its individuality and impact.

Riley Hughes. *Catholic World*. March, 1959. p. 509

Evan Connell has written a curious and original book about an American at war. Everybody knows the intensity with which American writers have studied the experience of the last war, but *The Patriot* avoids their inclination to regard the experience as somehow too big to be moralized over. Such novelists have concluded that the war was fearsome, that it was "real" in an unprecedented way and altered understanding and attitudes, but only the squarest characters in their fiction discuss it in terms of good and bad. Cadet Isaacs, by contrast, escapes with his moral faculty just intact. . . . Mr. Connell and his hero rend their innards in the effort to digest an experience conventionally indigestible.

Neal Ascherson. *New Statesman*. Feb. 16, 1962. p. 235

In a remarkable, long poem [*Notes from a Bottle Found on the Beach at Carmel*] written in prosaic lines chocked and often choked with facts, containing all manner of odd, bizarre and quaint information, Evan S. Connell, Jr. states the condition of our times. . . .

Evan Connell is a Spengler for declining the West. The speaker of the poem is a speculative protagonist, a meditative man, a philosopher who goes on a vast odyssey of seas, libraries, and histories to discover the meaning of life and final meaning. . . .

It is enjoyable to read the poem for its philosophy. The author never raises his voice as he traverses his fabulous seas, lands, histories, and life cycles. He poses no solutions. He is unprophetic. He warns and remonstrates, baring his calm, rational, all-observant wisdom throughout.

Richard Eberhart. *New York Times Book Section*. Nov. 10, 1963. p. 18

A recent and extraordinary book which has a growing underground reputation is *Notes from a Bottle Found on the Beach at Carmel* by Evan S. Connell, Jr. [It] is a long (238 pp.) beautifully executed narrative poem of the size and scope of Pound's *Cantos*. It is a learned and subtle poem, yet written in a style of great clarity and precision, all its virtuosity gracefully concealed. This poem could easily be the most important single poem of our period when we have enough perspective to see things clearly. That it has, so far, been ignored by most of the critics of poetry may charitably be attributed to the fact that Connell enjoys a considerable reputation as a prose writer and has published very little verse in the magazines. Meanwhile, strange as it seems, without fanfare or controversy, *Notes from a Bottle Found on the Beach at Carmel* has sold quite well in the bookstores.

> George Garrett in *American Poetry*, edited by John Russell Brown, Irvin Ehrenpreis, and Bernard Harris (St. Martin's). 1965. pp. 237–8

The sensational but truly descriptive title of Mr. Connell's fine new novel [*The Diary of a Rapist*] may lead readers who do not already know his work to expect a lurid sex adventure concocted for the best-seller and paperback trade. This is very far from the case. The diary is a low-keyed, pointillistic rendering of the needs and despairs of a young clerk working in a federal employment bureau, married to a woman who has rejected him, and seeking refuge in hopeless ambitions, fantasy, and petty violence. The quiet piecing together of incident recalls Mr. Connell's *Mrs. Bridge*; the jeremiads against civilization, *Notes from a Bottle Found on the Beach at Carmel*. On the whole, however, Mr. Connell's book is closer to Keith Waterhouse's *Jubb* than to any of his own previous books. The mood is British, restrained, melancholic; the prose highly polished, elegant even in its occasional inelegancies.

> Dorothy Nyren. *Library Journal*. April 15, 1966. p. 2084

Before attempting a novel, Connell mastered the short story. His first book was *The Anatomy Lesson, and Other Stories*. He has acknowledged debts to Proust, Mann, and Chekhov, has studied under Wallace Stegner and Walter van Tilburg Clark, and has expressed his admiration for the historical fiction of Janet Lewis. The tone of a Connell story is unmistakably American; the perception is European. He can evoke a heightened moment of experience, relying less on plot than on innuendo. With Joyce and Flaubert, he shares a predilection for epiphanic detail and "the ineluctable modality of the possible."

A Connell story is like the sieve of Eratosthenes: everything nonessential is filtered out until only what is prime remains. Grace and equipoise are properties of his work, and he is adept at rendering the ambiguity of an emotion or situation. Avoiding the beginning-middle-end artifice of narrative fiction, Connell creates the illusion that his stories are nothing more than textures or surfaces. Smooth overall, the narrative armature of a Connell story is oblique, helical, and sinusoidal. Here his affinities with Chekhov and Proust are apparent, particularly in his preference for the rough-edged story of mood. Shunning any realistic imitation of life, he unerringly achieves intense verisimilitude. With Joyce's godlike author, Connell remains aloof from his creations, completely outside them, in apotheosis, paring his fingernails.

> Gus Blaisdell. *New Mexico Quarterly*. Summer, 1966. p. 183

Ten years ago Evan S. Connell, Jr., published a first novel entitled *Mrs. Bridge*. It consisted of 117 related vignettes in which Connell, with great skill, laid bare the privileged yet empty life of his white Protestant, upper-middle-class heroine. . . .

Mrs. Bridge was a tour de force, a well-written, bittersweet book in which the author's despair for the fate of his people was nicely balanced by his love for them.

Now, ten years and several books later, Connell has returned to the materials of his early success. In *Mr. Bridge* the characters are the same, as is the technique, but this time the spotlight is trained on the husband. . . .

The vignettes in *Mr. Bridge* are readable, often insightful, sometimes brilliant; but they lack the consistent precision and dazzle of the earlier work. The story itself has less of a cumulative effect. . . .

Taken alone, *Mr. Bridge* is not a bad book, in spite of its defects. But it is not as good a novel as the one with which it will inevitably be compared.

> Peter L. Sandberg. *Saturday Review*. May 3, 1969. p. 32

Like many of his contemporaries, Connell is no storyteller. Writers like Roth and Bellow, however, find cunning facades for their jerry-built structures (through Portnoy's psychoanalysis or Herzog's letters), whereas Connell is ingenuous in disguising his inability to construct a tale. *Mrs. Bridge* is written in a series of very short chapters (some paragraph-long) that simply slice up the heroine's life, while *The Diary of a Rapist* employs the oldest and least convincing plot evasion known to literature.

Evan Connell, then, is a novelist who can't construct stories about uninteresting or remote people told in characterless prose. Why give him any attention? Because in everything he writes, he is admirably serious and painstaking and because, like a character actor who disappears into his role, Connell always has the potential for turning imitation into insight.

> Charles Thomas Samuels. *New Republic*. June 7, 1969. p. 21

Ten years ago, when everything was different, the novel *Mrs. Bridge* by Evan S. Connell, Jr. attracted attention as one of those few American books which succeed in telling us something about that mysterious realm, the American Middlewest of the middle classes. . . .

In *Mrs. Bridge* Connell named the artifacts of that place and that time, spoke the dialect, rehearsed its folkways, all with the inseparable mixture of love and horror we must each of us have had for our parents and for our own childhood. Its form was ingenious. A major part of the success of the book was that Connell had found a solution to the problem of making a whole book out of lives whose only story, whose entire theme and plot and texture, is simply that they have no story.

> John Thompson. *Commentary*. July, 1969. p. 63

[*Points for a Compass Rose*] is a book—plainly and simply that, gracefully written in fine ironic style expressing very well the moral tensions of the inner man who is the author. The work most like it, of course, is Connell's earlier *Notes from a Bottle Found on the Beach at Carmel*, for both of these must have found their origin in his journals. But *Points for a Compass Rose* also calls to mind J.G. Ballard's collection of grotesqueries, *The Atrocity Exhibition*, and William S. Burroughs's *Naked Lunch*.

His purpose is didactic—and now beware, for we are into the meaning of it all. Connell seems constantly to be adjuring us to "look" or "listen," or challenging us, "Do you understand?" Clearly, he wants us to understand, for this work which he calls "a gnomic book about America" has been written to show us what we have become. "Of what value is life," he asks, "if it's not woven on history's loom into other lives?" Well, in *Points for a Compass Rose*, Evan S. Connell, Jr., attempts to do just that. Our civilization, our culture, our lives are on his loom here. We may not like the pattern of moral disaster that emerges, but there is no denying a certain cruel accuracy in the lineaments of his design.

Bruce Cook. *Book World.* May 27, 1973. p. 10

When I first heard that Evan S. Connell, Jr. had brought out another epic-length poem [*Points for a Compass Rose*], I was exhilarated for days. We have here on the planet with us a man of such courage and strength of spirit that he has not lost what Alfred Adler calls "the nerve for excellence." He has kept it despite the burden of an awareness not only of the enormity of his project and of the limitations of his own human understanding, but also of the abject ignorance and indifference of his audience. . . .

It is time—past time—to approach Connell's poetry seriously, with meek heart and due reverence. . . .

[*Points for a Compass Rose* and *Notes from a Bottle Found on the Beach at Carmel*] are masterpieces. You could bend a lifetime of energy to their study, and have lived well. The fabric of their meaning is seamless, inexhaustible. . . .

Their language is steely and bladelike; from both of its surfaces flickering lights gleam. Each page sheds insight on every other page; understanding snaps back and forth, tacking like a sloop up the long fjord of mystery. Thinking about these poems, one at a time or both together, is a sweet and lasting pleasure to the mind.

Annie Dillard. *Harper's Magazine.* Jan., 1974. pp. 87, 90

A certain kind of novel has always reported on reality for us, told us things we didn't know; has let us into feelings and places we haven't had and haven't seen; and it is probably the current scarcity or ineptitude of this kind of novel which is driving us to biographies for a sense of how other people live (or used to live) their daily lives. *The Connoisseur* admits us into a man's mind, persuasively evokes the beginnings of a mild mania, takes us to Taos, brings us back to New York, propels us through a party, a museum, an art gallery, and a Mexican restaurant. But its major development is an extended description of an auction held in a motel in Queens. . . .

The effect is not that of a documentary, but it is that of a novel: an unfamiliar world is made present, real enough for us to feel that our experience of life has been extended by our reading. It doesn't matter whether Connell invented the auction or transcribed an actual event more or less faithfully. It is the business of many novels to make such distinctions seem trivial. . . .

Connell's writing . . . is discreet, efficient, sometimes flat, quite often verging on cliché. . . .

The Connoisseur seems to be asking whether this kind of fiction—the imaginative exploration of a moment of change in a none too representative life—has any future.

Michael Wood. *New York Review of Books.* Nov. 28, 1974. pp. 29–30

BIBLIOGRAPHY
The Anatomy Lesson, and Other Stories, 1957; *Mrs. Bridge*, 1959 (n); *The Patriot*, 1961 (n); *Notes from a Bottle Found on the Beach at Carmel*, 1963 (p); *Atlantic Monthly the Crossroads*, 1965 (s); *Diary of a Rapist*, 1966 (n); *Mr. Bridge*, 1969 (n); *Points for a Compass Rose*, 1973 (p); *The Connoisseur*, 1974 (n); *A Long Desire*, 1979 (nf); *The White Lantern*, 1980 (nf); *Son of the Morning Star*, 1984 (nf); *The Alchymist's Journal*, 1991 (n); *The Collected Stories*, 1995

CONNELLY, Marc (1890–1980)

George S. Kaufman and Marc Connelly, whose delectable comedies *Dulcy* and *To the Ladies* struck one more through their reserve than through any expression of ironic vision, have let themselves go at last. . . . I wish to praise the authors of *Beggar on Horseback* most heartily for this, that they laugh at fatuousness and gross materialism, at triviality of mind and soul, at stubborn stupidity and dishonor no longer conscious of itself, not as these qualities are contrasted with some specious moralistic idealism, but as they are contrasted with art, with the eternal creative spirit, with the quest of him who is driven despite himself to pursue that beauty which is also truth.

Ludwig Lewisohn. *The Nation.* Feb. 27, 1924. pp. 238–9

What would make *Beggar on Horseback*, agreeable as it is all through, into a play of importance, would be a continuation of the exact comment on life, and especially on middle-class American life, that appears in the first act. This satire, tinged with love and with the purity that arises in the young man through his desire for beauty and creation, might move to a slightly darker note now and again, but the comic simile and the wit of it would in the end arrive only through this exactitude and this patient study with delight. . . . In sum *Beggar on Horseback* starts sharply toward something that, if it were achieved, would be gayer by reason of its subtlety, more biting for its reckless satire and crude truth, and more unforgettable because of its long thought and because of the wistful, frank reserve that underlies so much of American self-expression. It does not arrive at this something, though the promise is there often enough, and in the first act almost always.

Stark Young. *New Republic.* March 5, 1924. p. 45

. . . Mr. Connelly does not go far into social philosophy; his play *The Wisdom Tooth* has only implications of social satire, only little hints about business men and boarders, and not many hints and implications at that. His hero is a single case and we are to watch his fortunes more, I gather, for the sentiment involved, the fantasy and the homely romance, than for any sting or theory about our society, our national or local characteristics, our blurred uniformity. And yet there are elements in *The Wisdom Tooth*, as there were in *Dulcy* and *To the Ladies*, and *Beggar on Horseback*, that stick in the mind and ramify.

Stark Young. *New Republic.* March 3, 1926. p. 45

Leading the play [*The Green Pastures*] thus, through numerous scenes and incidents that may sometimes appear merely casual and relaxed, on to a final summit, makes for the inclusion of many conceptions familiar in religious thought—that, for instance, of God needing man as man needs God—and by ending on that note of God's sacrifice through his own son, achieves a genuinely heroic and mystical level. And this is accomplished with no violation of the material in the book. . . . In Mr. Connelly's play, in Mr. [Roark] Bradford's book [*Ol' Man Adam an' His Chillun*] . . . this figure of God, with his kindness, his tricks, his patience, pleasures and human troubles and ups and downs, is a remarkable interpretation of the whole soul of the people in the play; it is, in the finest sense, a creation of an idea in dramatic terms.

Stark Young. *New Republic*. March 19, 1930. p. 129

Marc Connelly, to whom the play [*The Green Pastures*] was suggested by a series of stories in Negro dialect—Roark Bradford's *Ol' Man Adam an' His Chillun*—is the person most immediately responsible for the extraordinary performance, but neither he, the original author, nor even the fine cast of black actors can claim the largest share of the credit, since the fundamental creative work was done by the anonymous geniuses who composed the spirituals upon which the whole is based. Mr. Connelly and the rest have cooperated with great skill and delicacy; they seem, one and all, to have been gifted with a remarkable imaginative insight into the mood of the materials at hand. . . .

Joseph Wood Krutch. *The Nation*. March 26, 1930. p. 376

. . . *The Green Pastures* is not a dramatization. Distinctly this is an adaptation. The book of [Roark] Bradford's served as a springboard for the play of Connelly's. I am aware that there are a number of lines in the play which are taken literally from *Ol' Man Adam an' His Chillun*, but there is a vast change in mood. Mr. Bradford seems to have been interested almost exclusively in the humorous potentialities of Bible folklore told from a Negro point of view in Negro dialect. The agonizing, heartbreaking moments of the play are wholly Connelly.

I do not hold that pathos is of necessity a higher artistic expression than the merely comic, but Connelly's contribution is better rounded. He has taken black loam and breathed upon it. There is nothing in the book which lays hands upon my spine as does the march of the Children in the scene which pictures the road to *The Promised Land*.

But whether the play or the book is better makes a small difference for the purpose of this piece. It is enough to indicate that they are different.

Heywood Broun. *The Nation*. April 9, 1930. p. 415

In a sense *The Farmer Takes a Wife* is robustious enough and enlivened by a great deal of very picturesque speech, but I am led to wonder whether or not anyone has ever noted the fact that Mr. Connelly is distinguished from other Broadway playwrights with whom one might tend to think of him by the fact that he is not in the least "hard-boiled." Somehow or other he has managed to escape from the tough tradition which rules our stage in so far as it is dominated by that Broadway with which he is more or less

associated. His plays are never vulgar and never, like the typical product, somehow unpleasantly brassy. Below the surface of his sophistication is a delicate fancy, an essentially gentle spirit, something one would be inclined to call a kind of quaintness if it were not for the unfortunate associations of that word. It is that which in general makes the charm of his plays and that which contributes so much to *The Farmer Takes a Wife*. It is romantic with a romanticism which takes one unawares, charming with a charm which one does not resent because it is insidious without being obtrusive.

Joseph Wood Krutch. *The Nation*. Nov. 14, 1934. pp. 573–4

"Gangway! Gangway for de Lawd God Jehovah!" The modern theatre has produced no entrance cue better known or more affectionately remembered. These are words which even when read make the heart stand still. Heard again in the theatre, heard in the world as it now is, their impact is, if anything, greater than when they were spoken twenty-one years ago in that other simpler and comparatively civilized world in which *The Green Pastures* was first produced.

When Marc Connelly finished his script, he had written a far, far larger play than perhaps he realized he was writing. . . . *The Green Pastures* is a masterpiece. I came to realize this early during its initial run and only wish I had had the sense to do so on the night of its opening. But then, to my shame, I missed the boat, which was quite a boat to miss considering it was the Ark. Though back in 1930 I saluted *The Green Pastures* as being brave and meritorious, I felt that, in spite of its charms and delights, it somehow fell short of its ultimate goal. . . . Whatever my reasons may have been, this much I know: I was wrong.

John Mason Brown. *Saturday Review*. April 7, 1951. pp. 28–30

The Green Pastures has always seemed to me a deft, picture-book sort of play for big-city people who are nostalgic about a quality they believe their parents or grandparents once possessed and which they can only recapture in the form of "clever" fun—gay pigment and self-consciously cute drawing. I find no trace of genuine moral sentiment here, only the pseudo-religiosity of the Easter pageant in the larger movie houses—far more skillful and entertaining, of course, but only a little less hypocritical.

Harold Clurman. *New Republic*. April 16, 1951. p. 30

He says he is attempting [in *The Green Pastures*] to translate the religious conceptions of thousands of untutored Negroes as they have adapted the Bible stories to suit the experiences of their lives. Yet . . . he admits that he has used certain characters in his dramatization which are not in the Bible at all. His only justification for using such counterfeit characters is his belief that "persons like them have figured in the meditations of some of the old Negro preachers."

However, let us not hold this inconsistency against Mr. Connelly. Let us see whether or not he has achieved his main purpose, which is to present a genuine representation of the religious beliefs of thousands of untutored Negroes in the deep South.

I charge that Mr. Connelly has utterly failed to accomplish this purpose, and that his representation is counterfeit.

Nick Aaron Ford. *Phylon*. Spring, 1959. p. 68

BIBLIOGRAPHY

(with George S. Kaufman) *Dulcy*, 1921 (d); (with George S. Kaufman) *To the Ladies*, 1923 (d); (with George S. Kaufman) *The Deep Tangled Wildwood*, 1923 (d); (with George S. Kaufman) *Beggar on Horseback*, 1924 (d); (with George S. Kaufman) *Merton of the Movies*, 1925 (d); *The Wisdom Tooth*, 1927 (d); (with Herman J. Mankiewicz) *The Wild Man of Borneo*, 1927 (d); *The Green Pastures*, 1930 (d); (with Frank B. Elser) *The Farmer Takes a Wife*, 1934 (d); (with Arnold Sundgaard) *Everywhere I Roam*, 1938 (d); *The Traveler*, 1939 (d); *The Flowers of Virtue*, 1942 (d); *Story for Strangers*, 1948 (d); *Hunter's Moon*, 1958 (d); *A Souvenir from Qam*, 1965 (n); *Voices Offstage*, 1968 (m)

CONROY, Pat (1945–)

He's not much of a stylist and his sense of humor needs work, but Pat Conroy has a nice, wry perspective and a wholehearted commitment to his job. It's a hell of a job and *The Water Is Wide* is a hell of a good story. . . .

Why did Pat Conroy want to go to Yamacraw [Island]? Because he was young and ambitious and he loved teaching. Even more important, he was a do-gooder, enveloped in a "roseate, down-like and nauseating glow" at the masochistic prospect of accepting a job in which the odds were all against him. A former redneck and self-proclaimed racist, he brought to Yamacraw the supererogatory fervor of the recently converted. . . .

Mr. Conroy's first job was to prove to his pupils that learning could, and should, be fun. His theory of pedagogy held "that the teacher must always maintain an air of insanity, or of eccentricity out of control, if he is to catch and hold the attention of his students." He believed in "teacher dramatics, gross posturings and frenzied excesses to get a rise out of deadhead, thought-killed students. . . ." Two things he did not realize were that his students would take his antics literally and that they could hardly understand a word he said. Nor could he understand them at first, because they spoke a local version of the Gullah dialect. . . .

Mr. Conroy's modesty will not allow him to claim much for his year at Yamacraw, but he did get his pupils to listen to Beethoven and Brahms by alternating them with James Brown. He also opened their minds to an outer world they had never even conceived of. And, most memorable of all, he taught them to trust a white man and to believe that he cared about them.

After his first year, Mr. Conroy "desperately" wanted to return to Yamacraw, but he was fired on the grounds of insubordination, failure to respect the chain of command and lateness when his boat got lost in the fog or buffeted in heavy water. The real reason was never in doubt: He had tried to do too much too soon. If he had been more diplomatic, if he could have conquered his ego, the author says with commendable candor, he might have been allowed to continue.

He refuses to make a villain out of the school superintendent who fired him. Unlike many liberal do-gooders, Mr. Conroy does not see all conservatives, racists, reactionaries or rednecks as one-dimensional monsters. In his eyes, they are as much victims of their history—at least in their thinking—as the black people whose problems they haven't even begun to understand.

Anatole Broyard. *The New York Times Book Review*. July 13, 1972, p. 33.

"They gave me a boat, told me 'Good Luck,' and that was all they told me," Conroy recalls [in *The Water Is Wide*]. Apparently, however, he had a tape recorder in hand and photographers in tow. Conroy's brief sojourn into the life of Yamacraw Island seems to have been a planned "experience," one from which he was determined to garner a book.

This is not to negate the experiential value of Conroy's travels into the wilds of the Sea Islands, but it is to suggest that as educational literature *The Water Is Wide* offers nothing. Conroy does not provide any of the badly needed alternative suggestions for alleviating or controlling the stifling ignorance that is an ever-present part of the American education scene. Perhaps this was not his intent; if so, his writing style unfortunately belies it. . . .

When Conroy arrived at the little schoolhouse on Yamacraw, the average reading ability of the 17 students in grades five through eight was first grade level. We never really know if Conroy attempted to teach them to read as opposed to remembering information by rote, or if he tried to apply his call-answer technique to the teaching of information more fundamental to their Sea Islands existence.

Conroy's book is worth reading if only for the acknowledgments, which read like the Charleston and Columbia, South Carolina, social register. It is entertaining and very readable as a sympathetic view of the Sea Islands and as the story of a young white Southerner's awakening. It gives interesting insights and observations about the processes of black Southern rural education from a young white Southerner's point of view; but it would seem that while Conroy understood that the water is wide, he did not "keep the river on his right."

Jim Haskins. *The New York Times Book Review*. September 24, 1972, p. 10.

[With *The Lords of Discipline*], Mr. Conroy has found a great subject and has produced a book so superior to his other efforts that it might have been written by a different person. In fact, I read the first 200 pages thinking that this not only was a very good book but also one so memorable and well-executed that it would become the yardstick against which others of its kind would be measured. Alas, the next 300 pages proved this not so.

The Lords of Discipline deals with those beautiful, terrible years when a boy struggles toward manhood, when he must try to decide wherein honor lies, when he is faced with making the decision about what he wants and what he is willing to pay to get it. And he must, during this dreadfully uncertain time, bear the burden of what his parents want and expect of him, as well as the crushing pressure of his peers. Some fight their way through to their own truth; others bend or break during the ordeal.

Will McLean, the boy at the center of this story, makes the passage to manhood without breaking, but he is left with deep and permanent scars. . . .

In the second section of the book, the story that has been set into motion thus far stops and Will McLean relives his own nightmarish plebe year. This may seem an unlikely way for the novel to proceed, but to my mind it works and is natural and necessary. Here Pat Conroy lays open the barbaric nature of the human heart. Boys set upon other boys like packs of dogs. For the plebes, there is no recourse, no redress. They either bear it or break. Some break, and many who don't become sadists.

The story has more twists than a snake's back. There are reversals inside reversals. Mysteries sprout like mushrooms after a summer rain. The greatest plot reversal comes in the final 10 or so pages. But I was not surprised; I knew who the arch villain was long before he was revealed. Even if I had been surprised, I don't think I would have cared. It's that kind of book.

Simply put, after a very auspicious start, Pat Conroy's creative energies are sidetracked during the course of this book. Ultimately, he is more interested in posing and solving clever puzzles than in developing the character of the human beings inside those puzzles. Consequently, the reader remains unmoved ... by the ultimate betrayal that ends the novel.

Harry Crews. *The New York Times Book Review*. December 7, 1980, pp. 12, 43.

The Southern-boy protagonists of Pat Conroy's fiction have twin obsessions—oppressive fathers or father figures, and the South. Against both they fight furiously for selfhood and independence, yet they never manage to secede from their seductive entrappers. Some fatal combination of nostalgia and loyalty holds them back; they remain ambivalent sons of their families and their region, alternately railing against, then shamelessly romanticizing, the myths and strictures that imprison them.

After Bull Meecham, the self-aggrandizing hero of *The Great Santini*, crashes his F-7 and is buried with military honors, his oldest son, who has often prayed for his death, dons the father's flight jacket and is overwhelmed with love for him. In *The Lords of Discipline*, a corrosive fictional expose of racism and brutality in a Southern military college, the narrator, a graduate of the college, tells us: "I want you to understand why I hate the school with all my power and passion. Then I want you to forgive me for loving the school."

The same ambivalences are rife in *The Prince of Tides*. The Southern-boy narrator, Tom Wingo, is now in early middle age. A fired high school teacher and football coach, he describes himself as a Southern-made and Southern-broken failure, "the most dishonest person I've ever met. I never know exactly how I feel about something." But he also claims that it is the Southern part of him "which is most quintessentially and fiercely alive," and that his Southern memories "surround the lodestar of whatever authenticity I bring to light as a man."

In contrast, Tom's twin sister, Savannah, is "one of those southerners who were aware from an early age that the South could never be more for them than a fragrant prison administered by a collective of loving but treacherous relatives." Having fled the low country of South Carolina right after high school, she is now a famous poet, living in New York and writing poems that make the language "sing and bleed at the same time" about growing up as a shrimper's daughter. "The South kills women like me," she tells Tom. However, safe in Greenwich Village, she periodically tries to kill herself.

It is her latest suicide attempt, followed by a severe psychotic withdrawal, that lands her in Bellevue, summons Tom to New York and provides the novel's narrative device. Savannah's psychiatrist, Dr. Susan Lowenstein ("one of those go-to-hell New York women with the incorruptible carriage of lionesses"), asks Tom to stay in New York for an extended period and tell her "all he knows" about Wingo family life. "From beginning to end," he promises, over a candlelit dinner at Petite Marmite. For the rest of the book, the chapters alternate between Tom's narratives of "the grisly details of our epic childhood" and his increasing romantic involvement with his sister's psychiatrist.

The Wingo family configuration bears resemblances to previous parent-sibling setups in Mr. Conroy's work, but this time everything is bulging with symbol and jacked up to the lofty realm of myth. The bullying Henry Wingo is another Santini, with a shrimp boat instead of an F-7, but the negative aspects of fatherhood and manhood that he personally embodies now extend to the bigger Bad Daddies of business, politics and the narrow-minded authoritarianism of government. The beautiful Lila Wingo belongs to that species of Southern mothers described in *The Lords of Discipline* who "rule their families with a secret pact of steel," and whose sweetness, deadly as snakes, "has helped them survive the impervious tyranny of Southern men." But her beguiling, undermining poisons have now leached beyond the domain of a specific family and stand for treacherous womanhood in all its manifestations, as well as the Southern way of life.

In the Wingos' "grotesque family melodrama," as Tom calls it, each of the three children has been assigned an unchangeable role. Savannah is the gifted lunatic who bears the accumulated psychotic energy. Luke, the older brother, is the strong, simple man of action, "The Prince of Tides" in Savannah's book of poems by that name, who becomes a local martyred folk hero after waging a one-man guerrilla war against the heaviest father of them all, the Atomic Energy Commission, which appropriates his hometown and the family's island to make plutonium for hydrogen bombs. And Tom is "the neutral country, the family Switzerland," a go-between with "the soul of a collaborator," who has been "tamed by mortgages, car payments, lesson plans, children, and a wife with more compelling dreams and ambitions than my own."

The ambition, invention and sheer energy in this book are admirable. But many readers will be put off by the turgid, high-flown rhetoric that the author must have decided would best match his grandiose designs. And as the bizarre, hyperbolic episodes of Wingo family life mount up, other readers are likely to feel they are being bombarded by whoppers told by an overwrought boy eager to impress or shock.

But readers who have a high tolerance for the implausible, the sentimental and the florid will pad happily off to bed for a week or so with this hefty tale of a Southern family "that fate tested a thousand times" clasped cozily to their chests, and read about the birth of twins in a hurricane, and a boy shooting the last bald eagle (his father makes him eat it and wear the feathers to school), and dead siblings stored in the freezer with the shrimp until burial time, and the pet tiger that rips the faces off rapists; and, progressing parallel to all this Wingo memorabilia, the satisfying, present-time story of a sassy, middle-aged Southern boy who sweeps the "breathtakingly beautiful" New York psychiatrist off her feet, teaches her unhappy son to play football, and comes to better terms with "the beauty and fear of kinship, the ineffable ties of family," so he can return home to "try to make something beautiful out of the ruins,'' as his sister has done with her poems, and raise his children ''in a South stolen from me by my mother and father.''

''With all due respect,'' Dr. Lowenstein asks Tom in their first meeting, before she succumbs to his charm, ''why should we entertain the opinion of a white southern male?''

''Because, Doctor,'' Tom retorts provocatively, ''when I'm not eating roots and berries . . . and when I'm not slaughtering pigs out back at the still, I'm a very smart man.''

The thing is, beneath all his anguished ambivalence and excessiveness, Mr. Conroy is a smart man too. ''I have a need to bear witness,'' his narrator tells us in *The Lords of Discipline*. ''I want a murderous, stunning truthfulness. I want to find my own singular voice for the first time.'' In *The Prince of Tides*, the smart man and serious writer in Pat Conroy have been temporarily waylaid by the bullying monster of heavy-handed, inflated plot and the siren voice of Mother South at her treacherous worst—embroidered, sentimental, inexact, telling it over and over again as it never was.

Gail Godwin. *The New York Times Book Review*. October 12, 1986, p. 14.

BIBLIOGRAPHY
The Boo, 1970 (n); *The Water Is Wide*, 1972 (n); *The Great Santini*, 1976 (n); *The Lords of Discipline*, 1980 (n); *The Prince of Tides*, 1986 (n); *Beach Music*, 1995 (n)

COOVER, Robert (1932–)

[*The Origin of the Brunists*] is a remarkable effort of the imagination, concern, and a sheer creative force—sustained and elaborated from beginning to end. . . . Mr. Coover's characterizations are sharply wrought and remarkably multi-dimensional. . . . The handling of so many characters so masterfully is virtually unknown in first novels. In addition, Mr. Coover sustains the intensity and readability of his narrative joining and moving his people and their dilemmas toward a final effort that is compelling and lasting. . . . This is fiction as it should be, the product of high emotion and dedicated talent; real, hot with life in conflict, filled with the bizarre and the commonplace.

William Mathes. *Book Week*. Oct. 9, 1966. p. 14

A sense of metaphysics . . . pervades Robert Coover's book [*The Origin of the Brunists*]. . . . Coover's is a major work in the sense that it is long, dense, and alive to a degree that makes life outside the covers almost pallid. As a first novel it is extremely impressive in massive architecture, assurance, texture and invention. . . .

The chief merit of the novel is the reality of the characters. . . . There is much irony in the book, but it is never facile, and is made the deeper by the compassion with which the characters are felt and drawn. . . . If Coover can equal this book with his second novel he will be quite formidable. In fact he is formidable already.

Miles Burrows. *New Statesman*. April 14, 1967. p. 514

It would be a pity if the baseball buffs were put off by this mythology [in *The Universal Baseball Association, Inc.*] or the mythology rooters dismayed by the baseball. Coover has in fact written a fine baseball novel, the best I can remember in an admittedly thin field, and based obviously on a study of the texts. The atmosphere is turn-of-the-century early Lardner, when the game was in full swagger, but his averages are lively-ball 1930. The best of both worlds, in my opinion. The language is just right—colorful but not fancy. Take away the big metaphor in the middle, and the book still stands up. Conversely, not to read it because you don't like baseball is like not reading Balzac because you don't like boarding houses. Baseball provides as good a frame for dramatic encounter as any. The bat and ball are excuses. Baseball almost involves a real sub-culture, a tradition, a political history that were in some sense pre-ordained when the first diamond was laid out, that were implicit in the distance between bases, and that continue to make ball parks seem like unfrocked churches, places where even the boredom is of a finer quality. That the players and fans might be shadows in the mind of a Crazy Accountant up there is not only believable but curiously attractive.

Mr. Coover's admirable novel adds to our stock of benign legends. And how many books have you read lately that do that? [1968]

Wilfrid Sheed. *The Morning After* (Farrar). 1971. pp. 81–2

Robert Coover has published two novels. . . . What makes these books something more than rattling good tales is the fact that they treat in a loose, semi-allegorical way the origin and nature of religion. They say something about the meaning or lack of meaning of history. And they make a tentative statement about supernatural possibilities. The books are grounded in an impressive knowledge of religion, history, philosophy, theology, black arts and assorted crafts.

Though much of the factual detail in Coover's books appears to rest on Christian tradition, ritual and faith—on the Bible particularly—the books are in no way arguments for Christianity. They contain no pietistic strains, no gentle instruction, no comforting hope. A slangy, cocky, hip tone characterizes Coover's treatment of religious themes; the writer is above his subject, a kind of literary-theological folk-rock thing straight out of a hustler world that would rather not be conned. Perhaps Christians have consistently misunderstood human experience and its relationship to a creator: ''I'm afraid, Gringo, I must agree with our distinguished folklorist and foremost witness to the ontological revelation of the pattern of history,'' says one character towards the end of the baseball book, ''and have come to the conclusion that God exists and he is a nut.'' The flip and playful tone in no way diminishes the seriousness of the observation.

Lee J. Hertzel. *Critique*. 11, 3, 1969. pp. 12–3

Coover doesn't care what his characters feel about radical politics, not even what they did last summer; he is concerned with them only as types which put readers on, onto ''new modes of perception and fictional forms.'' To that end he reconstructs fairly tales—''The Ginger-Bread House,'' ''Jack and the Beanstalk'' and ''Little Red Riding Hood''—and Bible tales: Joseph and Mary, Noah's flood. All this is done to flow our minds out of their ruts of conventional responses to traditional formulations, demonstrates to our satisfaction that "anything can happen," in art if not in life. . . .

We are not asked to be concerned with resolutions in his characters' lives, but with resolutions in his technique. Coover has written fine fiction before . . . fiction which deals with people who create their own fictions (religion, baseball), they live and die in them. But these novels were located in the world, not in the anti-world of *Pricksongs and Descants* where, if anything can happen, anything and nothing happens and it all doesn't matter much anyway.

Shaun O'Connell. *The Nation.* Dec. 8, 1969. p. 640

John Barth looms behind the crude fatuities and linguistic boisterousness of Mr. Coover's "Morris in Chains," and Donald Barthelme is likely to be at once brightly attentive and slightly bored in the face of the whimsical-sinister tales which adapt Red Riding Hood and Hansel and Gretel. . . .

Fortunately there is the benign influence of Beckett. *Pricksongs and Descants* has affinities with *More Pricks than Kicks.* Sometimes the debt is a bad one, creating nothing but the pastiche of a tone of voice. . . . But Mr. Coover—who is manifestly very clever indeed, and very sensitive despite his decision that it is *de rigueur* to alternate between glowering and twinkling—has caught much more than mannerisms from Beckett or from the zeitgeist. . . .

"The Wayfarer," "The Marker," "The Babysitter," "The Hat Act": these are not vacant surrealisms, and even those who feel that the sick joke has been an unconscionable time dying may yet like Mr. Coover's bedside manner. The glacial hauteur is designed to ward off any possibility of finding out whether or not the words are heartfelt, but there can be no doubt as to their being headfelt.

Christopher Ricks. *New York Review of Books.* Feb. 12, 1970. p. 22

In his fictions, long and short, Coover has always been primarily concerned with the power of the imagination and its inextricable involvement with religious and sexual urgings, not in the argumentative chicken-egg primacy sense of Freud and Jung, but with an understanding of how they are all one, all manifestations of the principle of growth at the center of all being, the continual motion flowing from the universal's love of the particular. And he is as aware of the danger inherent in that power as of its creative and moral potential. In *The Origin of the Brunists*, he approaches the force of sex and the imagination in the birth of a religious sect; the blood and violence on the Mount of Redemption in a night of religious frenzy are as essential to the creative union of the lovers in the novel as the Beast's rage is to the curing of its poisonous head. In *The Universal Baseball Association, Inc.*, he celebrates the reality of the living moment in all its inscrutability even as he admits the danger of the imagination to the dwellers in that moment. In both books, he cares truly for the creation with all its madness and disaster.

R.H.W. Dillard. *Hollins Critic.* April, 1970. p. 3

Like a child who pats a pile of wet sand into turrets and crenelated ramparts, Robert Coover prods at our most banal distractions and vulgar obsessions, nudges them into surreal and alarming forms.

His fictions—novels, stories and . . . plays—sound at times like incantations which, as they progress, mount to frenzy. What began slowly, seemingly grounded in homely realistic details, lurches, reels a bit, becomes possessed by manic excitation; the characters' faces dissolve to reveal archetypal forms beneath; time and direction come unglued; the choices a writer makes to send his story one way or another are ignored so that simultaneously all possible alternatives occur and, at the end, as often as not, we find our laughter contracting in our throats because some of Coover's stories can be fearsome indeed.

Peter S. Prescott. *Newsweek.* May 15, 1972. p. 98

Robert Coover's fictions demonstrate how diverse perceptions combine and recombine to create meaning. His work, from the early *Origin of the Brunists* (1966) to the recent *The Public Burning* (1977), does not employ language to refer to a fixed set of meaning behind which lies a central, unifying order. Rather, his fictions suggest that meaning resides everywhere and nowhere. It can be located only by a fiction—perhaps the reader's, perhaps the narrator's—constructed in language. Of course, even there, new meanings accrue as we sally into the world of the imagination, a world where interpretation mounts on interpretation and perceptions can constantly shift.

Coover plays with the many possibilities and alternatives contained within language and narrative structures. At the same time, fictions which open a labyrinth of meanings do not therefore imply an absence of ethical strategy or even moral vision. The world of experience exists despite our fictions, and it is a world to which we must always return, even if it is fundamentally incomprehensible. Yet, the imagination gives us our sense of the world, and Coover enjoins us to become aware of the various relationships and perspectives in constant need of reformulation. To live, we choose whatever fictions best sort out our perceptions and sensations. Yet, we often and conveniently forget that our point of view, itself fictional, implies an element of choice. In our forgetfulness, we allow our fictions to overtake our lives. . . .

Coover does not, therefore, dispense with the notion of consciousness or imagination but rather underscores need for balance. Neither narrator nor character, writer nor reader, self nor environment create independently. On the other hand, he does not go as far as the French objectivist novel, for example, or Donald Barthelme, for another example, in the reduction of the self to the level of all other surfaces. Coover's stories present the mind at work, discovering the contiguous relations amidst a network of alternatives. . . .

[A] metaphor for the place of imagination—neither here nor there—appears in *The Universal Baseball Association.* Creative renewal occurs on the playing field. In this novel, Coover suggests that realms of the actual and of the imagination interpenetrate but must remain autonomous as well. For Coover, life bears on our fictions and fictions bear on our lives. The interdependence of imagination and actuality, however, assumes their separation. One realm must not be totally submerged by the other. Henry Waugh submerges himself so completely in his fiction that he not only becomes lost to life, but his invention fails him as well. We need our fictions to cope with life, and we need experience to keep our fictions vital.

Brenda Wineapple. *Iowa Review.* Summer, 1979, pp. 66, 68–69, 71

Coover's fictions clearly emphasize their author's interest in providing his readers with the kinds of metaphors that are necessary for a healthy imagination. Unfortunately, Coover says between the lines in every story he writes, people today have lost their desire for the thrill of discovery. They have become comfortable with having their conventional viewpoints confirmed through a limited range of artistic forms that have outlived their usefulness. Each of Cover's stories, then, invites its reader to relinquish one or more of his traditional approaches to art and participate with its author in an exercise of wit that frequently juxtaposes what is fantastic in life with the everyday.

The principal method through which Coover liberates readers from sensibilities that have been deadened by the familiar is irony. Irony enables Coover and his readers to distance themselves from traditional forms without isolating themselves from the human content of those forms. As a result, Coover's readers have the opportunity and pleasure of tearing down many of society's inherited approaches to art and life without losing their concern for humanity's condition. The result is a healthy sense of humor and the awareness of a developing consciousness. . . .

Reworking history, as he has done with myths, legends, and fairy tales, may represent a new arena in which Coover can explore further the interests that have been of primary concern to him since *The Origin of the Brunists*: "Like in the creation of myths, I sometimes transpose events for the sake of a kind of inner coherence, but there's a certain amount of condensation and so on, but mainly I accept that what I'm dealing with here is a society that is fascinated with real data, facts and figures, dates, newspaper stuff. I can't mess around too much with the data here lest I lose contact with that fascination." . . .

However Coover chooses to reinterpret history, his readers can be assured of accomplished and inventive stories that deal absurdly and metaphysically with the human condition without losing their sense of humor.

Richard Andersen. Robert Coover (Twayne, 1981), pp. 141–43

Robert Coover is one of the great innovators of contemporary American fiction. Primarily a novelist, Coover's first collection of short fiction, *Pricksongs & Descants*, published in 1969, had an immediate impact upon the writers and readers of the time. The novellas and two collections he has published since then have all had an influence on the writing and understanding of American short fiction and on American culture.

The short fiction of Robert Coover is an integrated part of the culture in which it appears. It would be difficult, for example, to read *P&D* with full appreciation without knowing something of Grimm fairy tales, the Bible, the TV game show format, American movies and movie houses of the 1940s and 1950s, and the art of fiction as practiced in the United States in the latter half of the twentieth century, the "wreck" of which Coover seeks "to intuit the enormity of."

To satisfactorily appreciate Coover's short fiction in context requires some preliminary consideration of the situation of American fiction of the past three decades and the attitude of publishers, writers, and readers toward realism and reality in American fiction. In the 1960s a curious thing happened in American fiction. Writers divided into two opposing groups: One moved toward what purported to be "real life," and the other engaged itself with reality as artifice, distancing itself from everyday perceptions of reality in

order to explore reality's greater dimensions as well as the dimensions of the art that defines reality.

Thomas Kennedy. Robert Coover (Twayne, 1992), p. 3

BIBLIOGRAPHY

The Origin of the Brunists, 1966 (n); *The Universal Baseball Association, Inc., J. Henry Waugh, Prop.*, 1968 (n); *Pricksongs and Descants*, 1969 (s); *A Theological Position*, 1972 (d); *The Public Burning*, 1977 (n); *Hair o' the Chine*, 1979 (scrp); *A Political Fable*, 1980 (n); *After Lazarus: A Filmscript*, 1980; *Spanking the Maid*, 1982 (n); *In Bed One Night, and Other Brief Encounters*, 1984 (s); *Gerald's Party*, 1986 (n); *Aesop's Forest*, 1986 (s); *A Night at the Movies; or, You Must Remember This*, 1987 (s); *Whatever Happened to Gloomy Gus of the Chicago Bears?*, 1987 (e); *Pinocchio in Venice*, 1991 (n); *John's Wife*, 1996 (n); *Briar Rose*, 1996 (n); *Ghost Town*, 1998 (n)

CORSO, Gregory (1930–)

Gregory Corso's an aphoristic poet, and a poet of ideas. What modern poets write with such terse clarity that their verses stick in the mind without effort? Certainly Yeats, Pound, Williams, Eliot, Kerouac, Creeley, Dylan & Corso have that quality.

Corso's handling of ideas is unique, as in various one-word title poems ("Power," "Bomb," "Marriage," "Army," "Police," "Hair," "Death," "Clown," and later "Friend"). He distills the essence of archetypal concepts, recycling them with humor to make them new, examining, contrasting, and alchemizing common vernacular notions into mind-blowing (deconstructive or deconditioning) insights. In this mode, his late 1950s poems (like Kerouac's 1951–52 scriptures on "Joan [Crawford] Rawshanks in the Fog" & "Neal and the Three Stooges") manifest a precursor Pop artistry, the realized notice of quotidian artifacts. . . .

As poetic craftsman, Corso is impeccable. His revision process, which he calls "tailoring," generally elision and condensation, yields gist-phrasing, extraordinary mind-jump humor. Clown sounds of circus, abstracted from plethora are reduced to perfect expression. "Tang-a-lang boom. Fife feef! Toot!: Quick sketch, sharp mind scissors." . . .

Corso also excels as political philosopher; his many years as classic artist wanderer dwelling in European hotels, castles, & streets give him perspective on North America. His crucial position in world cultural revolution mid-xx century as originator of the "Beat Generation" literary movement; along with Kerouac, Burroughs, Orlovsky & others, grants him an experience inside history few bards or politicians have known. Readers of the poem cluster "Elegiac Feelings American" will appreciate Corso's generational insight into Empire sickness. Earlier poems like "Power," "Bomb," "Army," & many brief expatriate lyrics prove Corso to be Shelley's natural prophet among "unacknowledged legislators of the world."

Corso is a poet's Poet, his verse pure velvet, close to John Keats for our time, exquisitely delicate in manners of the Muse. He has been and always will be a popular poet, awakener of youth, puzzlement & pleasure for sophisticated elder bibliophiles, "immortal" as immortal is, Captain Poetry exampling revolution of

Spirit, his "poetry the opposite of hypocrisy," a loner, laughably unlaureled by native prizes, divine Poet Maudit, rascal poet Villonesque and Rimbaudian whose wild fame's extended for decades around the world from France to China, World poet.

> Allen Ginsberg. Foreword. Gregory Corso. *Mindfield* (New York: Thunder's Mouth Press, 1989), pp. xiii–xv

The central concerns of Corso's work, the ideals which his writing consistently strives to affirm and to uphold are those which are most concisely summarized in a phrase from the poetry of William Wordsworth: "Delight and liberty, the simple creed of childhood."

The theme and the element of delight are manifest in virtually every poem, every play and prose piece that Corso has written. The droll humor, the astonishing imagery, the exuberant invention and the playful use of language which characterize his writing are all expressions of this quality. Delight is, for Corso, the natural condition of man, his original and final state; it is a natural force latent in every mind and spirit, but blocked, suppressed by blind negations, by distortive habits and conventions, by fear and resignation.

It is from such checks and limitations that Corso's work seeks to liberate us. His writing both urges and enacts that liberation, disrupting and denying conventional perceptions of reality, and affirming magic, joy, wonder, and beauty. Corso's work vehemently opposes all forms of tyranny and oppression, together with all agencies of repression and joylessness, as it celebrates the persistence and the irrepressibility of imagination, desire, and liberty. . . .

In an era of so many university-trained writers, so many professor-poets, Gregory Corso represents something of an anomaly: a drop-out with a sixth grade education, an ex-con, an autodidact, a natural singer-seer, a street bard. At a time when so many poets seem implicitly to have accepted W. H. Auden's dictum that "poetry makes nothing happen" and to have adjusted their vision and their verses accordingly, Corso has reaffirmed the Shelleyan role of the poet as prophet and catalyst, as "unacknowledged legislator of the world." In an age of American literary mandarinism, a critic-ridden period whose most characteristic poems are distinguished by pinched wit, learned allusion, and polite despair, all carefully structured and measured, all polished and ready for explication by graduate students of English, Corso stepped forth as an outlaw clown, "a word-slinger" determined to redeem the time.

> Gregory Stephenson. *Exiled Angel: A Study of the Work of Gregory Corso* (London: Hearing Eye, 1989), pp. 8–9, 97–98

BIBLIOGRAPHY
The Vestal Lady on Brattle and Other Poems, 1955; *The Happy Birthday of Death*, 1960 (p); *The American Express*, 1961 (n); *Herald of the Autochthonic Spirit*, 1981 (p); *Mindfield*, 1989 (p)

COWLEY, Malcolm (1898–1989)

By an ill adjustment Malcolm Cowley is best known as a critic and translator, whereas his verse is by far his most important contribution. . . . Cowley is not to be labeled the poet exclusively of this or

that. But the one note which appears most often is a kind of indefinite regret. Though willingly accepting this as the only possible of worlds, to the contemporary he supplies a Baudelairean corrective of nostalgia prior to the facts, a nostalgia which would prevail regardless of the environment. There is the frequent meditation upon death and upon that stagnation of the mind which may precede death by many years. There is the constant suggestion of a vague return. . . . There is the hankering after something native.

> Kenneth Burke. *New York Herald Tribune Book Section*. Aug. 18, 1929. p. 2

It would be difficult to find a single book of poems more symptomatic of the experiences of the post-war writers of America than Malcolm Cowley's. . . . *Blue Juniata* is important not only because it gives us the assembled verse of a new and definitely interesting poet, but because it sets itself up as a self-confessed logbook of literary youth in America during the ten years which followed the war. . . . Unlike many poets who at the present moment are being read and quoted with high favor, Mr. Cowley is not devising his tunes with gymnastic agility on a single string. He has obviously submitted to the charms of many influences, and he has managed to go through a period of high excitement in our cultural experience and yet realized a significance in the manifold distractions and vogues that crowded it.

> Morton Dauwen Zabel. *The Nation*. Aug. 21, 1929. pp. 200–1

His mind is basically concrete and unspeculative; he brings to facts and observations an even emotional tone that is the mark of a genuine style; but in criticism Cowley's instinct for exact definition is not strong; and the necessity for a certain amount of abstraction only violates the even tone of his style. It is in poetry, at least for the present, that Mr. Cowley may be seen at his best.

And yet the long discipline of prose has given to his poetry much of its distinction of form. . . . There are no great moments in Cowley, and there are no disconcerting lapses. There is subdued emotion; there are exact feelings and images; and over all, a subtle vision of the startling qualities of common things.

> Allen Tate. *New Republic*. Aug. 28, 1929. pp. 51–2

Cowley has the sense of a lyric poet (which he is) for the unique value of the individual. . . . Yet because he also has the social historian's sense that each life, besides having a pattern of its own, is a part of the pattern of the age, he can make you see how all these lives fitted the pattern of alienation which led a whole generation of intellectuals into exile. . . . *Exile's Return* is far and away the best book about this generation (of the 1920s) by a participant, and this is a generation that was crucial not only for American literature but for the whole of American culture.

> Arthur Mizener. *New York Times Book Section*. June 10, 1951. p. 9

Calmly ignoring those austere critics who claim it is the literary work that should concern us and not the private life of the creator, Malcolm Cowley has put together a fascinating account of the American writer as a human being (in *The Literary Situation*). A critic, editor, and poet who brings to his interest in writers' lives an *avant-garde* background, Mr. Cowley transforms literary anecdotage and journalism into a valuable analysis of what makes the American writer run. His approach is like that of the Lynds to Middletown, U.S.A., except that his conclusions are based on personal observation and inquiry rather than statistics and questionnaires, and that some of the best things in the book are purely—and maliciously—subjective.

Milton Rugoff. *New York Herald Tribune Book Section.* Oct. 24, 1954. p. 6

No other critic was more engaged in the *Kulturkampf* of the times or more strategically placed to observe the sorties of the warring intellectual platoons—Humanist, Communist, Technocrat, Agrarian, Liberal. And few writers identified with the left during this period managed better than Cowley did to remain on speaking terms with literary acquaintances to the right and left of him.

For more than ten years, beginning in 1930, Cowley ran the book section of *The New Republic.* Almost every week, from 1934 until the early 1940s, he reviewed a book that challenged his interest or provided him with a text. Through a newly acquired "Marxist" perspective he was able to arrange such diverse items as Yeats, the Bonus Marchers, Thomas Mann, revolutionary China, the Lynds' *Middletown*, Cummings's verse, Russian films, Trotsky's history and Faulkner's novels, in one ideological panorama. Each article or essay-review, composed under pressure, also served (Cowley tells us) as "my blank verse meditations, my sonnet sequence, my letter to distant friends, my private journal." Some of the men and events he dealt with now seem pretty remote, yet *Think Back On Us. . .* conveys the intellectual excitement and moral fervor of the period. Illuminating simply as social history, it can also be read as the public soliloquy of a man in the process of acquiring and shedding certain political convictions; the Cowley of 1940s is not the Cowley of 1930.

Daniel Aaron. *New York Times Book Section.* Feb. 12, 1967. p. 4

I wasn't altogether happy when I heard last fall that Henry Dan Piper of Southern Illinois University was publishing a selection of pieces that Cowley had written in the Thirties. I had read the pieces as they appeared, with great eagerness and usually with marked appreciation though sometimes with sharp disagreement; but I didn't look forward to rereading them thirty years later. In those three decades I had changed and Cowley had changed and the world had changed, and I thought that the pieces would be dated if not dead. In a sense they *are* dated, and that is why the book [*Think Back on Us. . .*] serves the purpose for which Professor Piper edited it—to give young people some idea of what the Thirties were like. But almost nothing seems merely old stuff, and the best of the pieces are alive today.

Granville Hicks. *Saturday Review.* March 11, 1967. p. 31

It is possible to approach a work like [*A Second Flowering*] with just a touch of resentment. We have read about the Lost Generation until our heads are water-logged with its self-congratulation, its

nostalgia. One broods over the gallons, the tuns, the tank cars of ink spilled out on the lives and work of these men—Hemingway's bibliography alone must be on its way to several volumes requiring sturdy book ends—and one thinks: enough. . . .

These are not just thrice-told tales, they seem by now to be so numbingly familiar as to be almost personal—tedious old gossip having to do with some fondly regarded but too often outrageous kinfolk. And if the work also affects a critical stance, do we look forward to still more commentary on "The Bear" or Cummings's love lyrics? Or another desolating inventory of the metaphors in *The Great Gatsby?* In *A Second Flowering* all of these matters are touched upon, yet it is testimony to Cowley's gifts both as a critic and a literary chronicler that the angle of vision seems new; that is, not only are his insights into these writers' works almost consistently arresting but so are his portraits of the men themselves.

William Styron. *New York Times Book Section.* May 6, 1973. p. 8

In a sense *A Second Flowering* represents a part of a long struggle on Cowley's part to redeem the American writer from his condition of alienation. It would be misleading to say that this struggle has dominated Cowley's wide-ranging work as a literary critic. It is hardly too much to say that it provides a strong unifying theme in his complex and varied achievement. But in the same breath we must observe that it is a struggle Cowley has never intended to win. When we add to his criticism Cowley's small but important body of poetry, we see running through the whole range of his work as a twentieth-century poet, critic, and literary and cultural historian a basic motive of alienation. As both a creator and an interpreter of the literature of the lost generation, Cowley is a contributor to one of its leading aspects: a myth or a legend of creativity which is definable as a poetics of exile.

Lewis P. Simpson. *Sewanee Review.* Spring, 1976, p. 225

What is perhaps most impressive about Cowley as a literary and cultural commentator is his ability—most clearly demonstrated in his earlier writings—to sense and report the psychic weather, the dominant moods and styles, the subtle forces that shape the collective state of mind of the historical moment very often while the moment is still in the process of being formed and he himself is being formed by it. This is what gave *Exile's Return* its special quality of seeming to be almost magically evocative of his generation's experience at the same time that it arranged that experience into a pattern of tonal and thematic development which was more fictive than historical. . . .

But although Cowley had something of Dos Passos' historical perspective and wrote a prose that at times uncannily resembled Hemingway's, he was most like Fitzgerald in seeing his personal experience as a sort of microcosmic version of what had happened to them all, as emblematic of their common fate and fortune. . . .

Cowley's literary contemporaries did indeed have a remarkable awareness of shared experience, and his own career is not only . . . representative but almost seismographically reflective of the changes that have occurred in the literary life of this country over the past sixty years. During that time he has lived through nearly all the evolutionary phases of the modernist movement in literature, and he has made his own significant contribution to each. More than any other historical critic except possibly Edmund Wilson, he has been persistently alert to the complex interplay of cultural and intellectual forces which have helped shape the character of modern literature even as they provided the collective history from which his generation of writers derived their strong sense of united creative purpose. . . .

If now in his old age Cowley cannot enjoy the satisfaction of spectacular triumph, great reputation, or large public accolade, he does have behind him more than half a century of working honorably and successfully at the writer's trade, retaining a devotion to the high calling of literature that is now very nearly extinct in the world, and keeping alive the works and days of his generation whom he now lives on to commemorate and represent.

John W. Aldridge. *Michigan Quarterly Review.* Summer, 1979, pp. 482–83, 489–90

That [Malcolm] Cowley is seen almost as two different persons by scholars of differing persuasions, backgrounds, and critical methods is evident in another published essay on his work. Citing an essay on Van Wyck Brooks that Cowley wrote in 1936, which Joseph Epstein used as evidence of Cowley's anti-Americanism, Lewis P. Simpson wrote in 1976 that when looked at as a whole, Cowley's published work is more complex than has generally been noticed. While apparently preoccupied with a "poetics of exile," the alienated aesthetic and social ideas that have dominated Western intellectual and artistic life for almost two hundred years, Cowley has, in fact, taken for his subject the role of the writer in the modern world. And Cowley's major theme in this enterprise has been to show the public, as well as writers themselves, the ways in which artists must recognize and come to terms with their human need for social community, even though social revolt and spiritual isolation have been the characteristic themes in modern art. Paradoxically, Simpson pointed out, the American literary tradition, which Cowley spent much of his career coming to terms with—and helping to define—was one of individual solitude, as indeed were Cowley's own life and work. For Simpson, then, Cowley's work could be said to deal with the central issue of a particular American tradition of literature.

All these conflicting assessments of Malcolm Cowley reveal, I believe, not only that Cowley is an interesting figure in his own right in modern American literary history but also that a study of his life permits one to focus on issues that have remained subjects of critical conflict for much of modern cultural history. These issues include a debate over what modern American art represents, why political and social rebellion by American artists has been so persistent, and what constitutes "Americanism" with respect to American writers and the American literary tradition. That Cowley's involvement with modern art and Communist politics has been sometimes vigorously attacked by polemicists from both the political left and the right may say less about Cowley than about the confusions of American cultural politics. The persistent misunderstanding of his views is, however, puzzling.

A further example of this misunderstanding is the assertion that Malcolm Cowley's work in the 1930s resulted only from a flirtation with radical Communist politics. This assertion obscures the more complex reality of his intellectual development and his actual

writing. Those who make it must ignore his persistent attempt in those years to clarify, counteract, and socialize the intellectual and aesthetic tradition of modern art, with which for almost a decade before 1930 he had been locked in personal struggle.

James Michael Kempf. *The Early Career of Malcolm Cowley: A Humanist among the Moderns* (Baton Rouge: Louisiana State Univ. Pr., 1985), pp. 6–7

Sharing Faulkner's "admiring and possessive" love of the land, as well as his "compulsive fear lest what he loves should be destroyed," Cowley remained a country boy at heart. All his life he was a devoted gardener and conservationist. Though he spent a substantial part of his professional life in the cosmopolitan company of big-city writers and intellectuals, particularly in New York and Paris, such a milieu filled him with feelings of uneasiness and distrust. How deeply country tastes and habits remained an ingrained part of his character is difficult to fathom. Although he may have exhibited a degree of posturing in his way of confronting city intellectuals and academics, some literary acquaintances have perhaps concluded too easily that Cowley was playing a plebeian part, construing a facade of sophisticated provincialism to hide his weaknesses. Such a feeling may have informed John Peale Bishop's condescending epithet: "the plowboy of the Western world who has been to Paris."

In a literary career spanning over seven active decades, Cowley combined an impressive multiplicity of functions: he was poet, critic, literary consultant to publishers, and, in general, "middleman" of letters. His awareness of the literary profession as "interdependent at all its levels" prompted him to speak up in its defense whenever he saw it threatened. On behalf of the "little American republic of letters" he took his own firm stand against the "Philistines" in the controversy over the Bollingen Award to Ezra Pound in 1949. At the same time he recurrently expressed his skepticism about the inroads made into the writing trade by commercialism and collectivization and voiced his fear that writers might lose their status as "independent craftsmen" to become officials in a bureaucratic structure, possessing technical virtuosity but paralyzed by timidity, conventionality, and lack of personal courage. During the McCarthy years he was disturbed by the pervasive mood of anti-intellectualism, by the decline of the reading habit, and by the potentially dangerous effects of an alliance between creative writing and academic careerism. At the same time, he worked within academe as a teacher, writer in residence, and lecturer at writers' conferences. Always, however, he felt slightly out of place among academic scholars. . . .

Few have had Cowley's talent for friendship and geniality of temperament to associate on terms of equality (and often intimacy) with a wide and varied circle of literary friends and acquaintances, from Faulkner, Hemingway, Crane, and Tate, to younger writers like John Cheever, Tillie Olsen, and Ken Kesey. . . . Though some of his literary friends must have strained his capacity for tolerance and compassion, Cowley, in his dealings with writers, often showed (in the words of George Core) "an uncommonly even disposition, a remarkable ability to forgive, and a wise but not uncritical acceptance of human fallibility."

Hans Bak. *Malcolm Cowley* (Athens: Univ. of Georgia Pr., 1993), pp. 16, 486–87

BIBLIOGRAPHY

(with others) *Eight More Harvard Poets*, 1923 (p); *Racine*, 1923 (c); *On Board the Morning Star*, by Pierre Mac Orlan, 1924 (tr); *Joan of Arc*, by Joseph Delteil, 1926 (tr); *Variety*, by Paul Valéry, 1927 (tr); *Catherine-Paris*, by Marthe Bibesco, 1928 (tr); *Blue Juniata*, 1929 (p); *The Count's Ball*, by Raymond Radiguet, 1929 (tr); *The Green Parrot*, by Marthe Bibesco, 1929 (tr); *The Sacred Hill*, by Maurice Barrés, 1929 (tr); *Exile's Return*, 1934, rev. ed., 1951 (r); (with Bernard Smith and others) *Books That Changed Our Minds*, 1939 (e); *The Dry Season*, 1941 (p); *Imaginary Interviews*, by Andre Gide, 1942 (tr); ed., *The Portable Hemingway*, 1944; ed., *The Portable Faulkner*, 1946; *The Literary Situation*, 1954 (c); (with Daniel Pratt Mannix) *Black Cargoes: A History of the Atlantic Slave Trade*, 1962 (h); *Letters and Memories* (of William Faulkner), 1966 (r); *Think Back on Us*, 1967 (h); *Blue Juniata* (enlarged edition), 1968 (p); *A Many-Windowed House*, 1970 (c); *A Second Flowering*, 1973 (r); *And I Worked at the Writer's Trade*, 1978 (m); *The View from Eighty*, 1980 (a); *The Dream of the Golden Mountains*, 1980 (h); *Unshaken Friend*, 1985 (b); *Conversations*, 1986 (r, i.e, interviews); *The Flower and the Leaf*, 1986 (c); *Selected Correspondence of Kenneth Burke and Malcolm Cowley 1915–1981*, 1988; *The Portable Malcolm Cowley*, 1990 (misc); *New England Writers and Writing*, 1996 (c)

COZZENS, James Gould (1903–1978)

There is no question but that Cozzens's work, except in regard to his larger dramatic frames, shows a steady progress toward greater mastery of his craft, increased consciousness of his effects, and constantly augmented scope. Except for *Castaway*, however, he has given us every ingredient of first-rate novels except the novels themselves. His faults, the prejudices and blockages that make his treatment of race and sex so unsatisfactory, and his constant dissipating of tragedy into irony and melodrama, seem to be the obverse of his virtues: his enormously representative quality and his uncompromising honesty. When Cozzens can write novels with the breadth and depth of *The Just and the Unjust* or *Guard of Honor* in as taut and satisfactory a dramatic frame as *Castaway* has, when he learns to combine the realism of his later work with the symbolism of his middle period and deepen both in the process, he should be a novelist to rank with the best America has produced.

> Stanley Edgar Hyman. *New Mexico Quarterly*. Winter, 1949. p. 497

He has nothing less than a passion for detachment.

This passionate detachment of his is closely associated with his great technical skill. I do not mean that he has acquired that skill merely by virtue of being detached, for obviously he has worked hard for it, but the basis on which his craftsmanship has developed is his objectivity. Deliberately standing apart from his material, he strives to see clearly and to render with perfect accuracy what he sees. His writing is always careful and never more careful than in the avoidance of pretentiousness.

> Granville Hicks. *English Journal*. Jan., 1950. p. 4

Mr. Cozzens's grasp of American life is not based upon long familiarity with a single region, . . . but upon his wisdom in the ways of the upper middle class, which is very much the same all over the country. He has profound respect for the responsible citizens who actually make our civilization work. Ibsen called them "pillars of society," and made the very term imply hypocrisy. Mr. Cozzens, on the other hand, likes to portray this class from the point of view of a member of one of the great professions, Law, the Church, Medicine, and by that means he brings out the humane values he sees in *his* pillars of society.

> Francis Fergusson. *Perspectives U.S.A.*. Winter, 1954. pp. 36–7

I know of no modern novelist who commands such a range of idiom, allusion, cadence, rhetorical radiation and vocabulary. It is a muscular, virile style with certain strong affinities to seventeenth-century prose—Cozzens is found of Bunyan, Milton, Defoe, among others. Yet one does not get the feeling of reading a literary novel. The ironic view alone prevents this. . . . In Cozzens's novels the world of types explored by Dickens and by Shaw and by Ben Jonson comes before us again in its unfamiliar shape—the shape of the local, urban, and workaday, qualities too trivial to most novelists in recent years to seem worthy of their attention. Cozzens forces our attention, concentrates it, makes us inescapably aware of the density of the lives we live.

> Louis O. Coxe. *American Literature*. May, 1955. pp. 163, 168–9

Cozzens would no more deform a character to meet the demands of his plot than he would steal from his Delaware Valley neighbors. Nevertheless, it *is* a pattern, almost a formula, and it has reappeared in one of his novels after another.

There is a lawyer, young or old, or a staff officer in the Air Force, or a clergyman deeply involved in the lives of his parishioners. There is a climax in his career, a period of two or three days during which hell breaks loose; men die in accidents, women commit suicide, friends of his family are charged with sexual crimes, his closest associates betray him through irresponsibility; and meanwhile the hero tries to do his best for everyone, succeeding in some cases, failing lamentably in others, yet somehow surviving by force of character.

> Malcolm Cowley. *New York Times Book Section*. Aug. 25, 1957. p. 1

The essential difference between Cozzens and his contemporaries lies in the character of his work. Here he is the complete nonconformist: a classic man, operating in a romantic period. This, I suspect, is the basic reason why he has missed both popular and critical appreciation. He puzzles ordinary readers whose palates have been dulled by the Gothic extravagance of most fiction; and he offends critics whose professional mission has been to exalt the romantic novel which has been in high fashion for the last thirty years. . . . Cozzens may, indeed, signal the turning of the tide. In his salad days, he too flirted with the romantic technique, but in his mature novels he has moved steadily away from it. Instead he has been attempting something far more difficult: to write an engrossing story about ordinary people, living ordinary lives, in ordinary circumstances.

John Fischer. *Harper's Magazine*. Sept., 1957. pp. 15–8

Cozzens's heroes are becoming steadily richer and more Protestant, while his upstarts—Catholics, Jews, or reformers—are something like caricatures and invariably obnoxious. (His Negroes now, because of spotless subservience, fare somewhat better. They *like* to take communion last.) He has, of course, like any author, the right to choose the class he will deal with—Jane Austen did as much—but this kind of limitation is doubled because of Cozzens's obvious distaste for the people into whose minds he will not choose or deign to enter. . . . His sympathy is husbanded too narrowly, and he lacks what Henry James called "the sacred rage." He walks away from us cool, disenchanted, a little superior, pleased to have kept his distance.

Richard Ellmann. *The Reporter*. Oct. 3, 1957. pp. 43–4

Like most of Mr. Cozzens novels (making some exceptions for *Castaway*) *By Love Possessed* suffers from a want of essential drama: though all the great rites of tragedy are prepared and invoked, the demonstration remains at last unmade; as though the author had some reservations—possibly about "real life" and "the way things really work out"—which protect his major actors from their ends. I cannot help thinking that the book, in this respect, functions as a kind of secular apologetics, the defense of an image of life, much idealized, which is regarded with so much reverence and nostalgia that its exemplars may not and must not be brought down from their high places. . . . The mere acknowledgement of the possibility will do instead, so that in the end honor, wealth, position, are saved at the expense of honesty, on the stated ground that considerations higher than honesty (charity, compassion, expediency) are involved, a shift of justifications not without its Jesuitical quality.

Howard Nemerov. *The Nation*. Nov. 2, 1957. p. 308

In his previous works there has always been a certain absence of primary feeling; he is a cold writer who has needed a recharge, say, of human sympathy. To a certain degree *By Love Possessed* is probably the attempt to get at just this issue in his own work and career—but an attempt which, rather than enlarging the writer's capacity to feel, simply confirms his prejudice against feeling. It is a treatise on the different kinds of love—parental, oedipal, sibling, self-love or vanity, religious, sexual. But why is it that all these types of love are only destructive and never even momentarily rewarding?. . . What Mr. Cozzens does not seem to understand for all his classical lore, is that the Goddess of Love, whatever her cruel demands on her afflicted subjects, is also the Goddess of Life.

Maxwell Geismar. *American Moderns* (Hill and Wang). 1958. pp. 148–50

He is writing about the individual in society, about the obligations, the hazards, the rebellious and painful accommodation of human beings to the way things—not *are* (this has been misunderstood)—but *work:* the way things work, the functioning of the world. His heroes are men who understand these functions, live with them, interpret them for others and in some part keep the machinery running. Able, responsible men, more burdened by duty than eager for power, learning in maturity that one never really knows enough, stoically bearing the weight of the world—these are the men Cozzens sets up as admirable. They are admirable. But they are also the Ruling Class, if only on the provincial level.

This being so, it is easy to see why he has been attacked for supporting the status quo and writing "Novels of Resignation."

Elizabeth Janeway. *New York Times Book Section*. Aug. 9, 1959. p. 1

His style is essentially eighteenth-century, like that of Swift or Steele, both of whom he admires. It is good for saying that whatever is, is right (or wrong, as the case may be), but it is not so good for saying that whatever is, is continually changing. He does not use the symbolic structure of death and rebirth which many romantics from Wordsworth to Hemingway have used to formulate the essence of change, nor does he use the kind of symbolic imagery with which they commonly reinforce that structure and that theme. As a result, his heroes tend to give an impression of stuffiness or priggishness instead of the vision of heroic maturity arising out of heroic struggle which they seem to be intended to give. They and the works they live in are, to a degree, intellectually abstract and emotionally thin.

R. P. Adams in *Essays in Modern American Literature*, ed. Richard E. Langford (Stetson). 1963. p. 110

The peculiar excellences or distinctions of Cozzens' art, more than anything else, justify critical study, for these distinctions reveal a complicated and deliberate novelist at work. No other writer of our time has dared to make such an extreme commitment to reason; and this commitment has led Cozzens into an attitude toward man which dares to be condescending, anti-democratic, and altogether dispassionate. To the rational principle Cozzens has remained firmly loyal, although his growing mastery of the technical aspects of literature has allowed him to dramatize his vision of reality with more and more impact and meaning. At the same time, Cozzens has persisted in standing apart from the literary fashions of his time: he has worked consistently within the framework of the traditional English novel, and has (with one exception) rejected any attempt at experimentation. And appropriately enough, a large part of his current significance lies in his ability to expand beyond the capacity of anyone else in his generation the scope and quality of the traditional.

Harry John Mooney. *James Gould Cozzens* (Pittsburgh). 1963. p. 3

Cozzens' respect for life as it is gives him an exceptional interest in the actual world. This interest ranges all the way from his pleasure in the ingenious organization of things like department stores and air force bases to his almost anthropological curiosity about the customary life of social institutions like the small town or of professions like the law and medicine. He has a deep respect for men who can function effectively in the world, whether they are skilled mechanics or talented pilots, able generals or smart judges, and this respect, because it is not dictated by a theory, is without condescension. Both *The Just and the Unjust* (1942) and *By Love Possessed* (1957) are legally impeccable novels about the law; the hero of *The Last Adam* (1933) is a doctor and the hero of *Men and Brethren* (1936) is a priest. Three of these four novels show a fascinated intimacy with the social life of the American small town. *Guard of Honor* (1948) is a novel about life on an Army Air Force base during the war; no one has ever been able to find a flaw in its minutely detailed account of that life. . . .

Cozzens confronts squarely the rawness of the deal that drives the subjective novelists to a defiance of life itself. He knows, as well as Melville and Faulkner, how strong the passions of the heart are. But, since he never loses sight of the simple, obvious fact that life is what life is, he is always conscious that it is not what these passions so often convince men it is, or may be. To him, their effect on men is a kind of possession—in the sense of being influenced to the point of madness.

Arthur Mizener. Kenyon Review. Nov., 1966. pp. 598–9

It is . . . harder to write about Cozzens than it is to write about the romancers who form the majority of our authors, whether Poe and Hawthorne back then, or Pynchon and Ellison and Updike now. . . .

Almost all of Cozzens's best work is laid in small towns or communities with urban values. . . . In each case you have a center which is yet a provincial center, which has firm traditions of its own, and which has little or not desire to drop its own values for those of the big city. On the contrary, representatives of big-city culture. . . . tend to be seen as threats and even as corrupters. In our prevailing literary view, they ought, of course, to be seen as bringers of enlightenment. . . .

But in his fiction what produces that sense is the difference in values between the provincial center and the metropolitan center. The metropolitan center is, of course, pluralistic. It is the place where roots matter least, and oneself now matters most. . . .

By contrast, both the pastoral milieu and the town milieu tend to carry a single set of standards, which express and contain the whole history of the place, which all accept. There is one network—and maybe one hierarchy—of which everybody is a part. . . .

To my taste, he is one of the supreme stylists in American literature. I mean, he writes well. But what he writes is the periodic sentence, the highly wrought paragraph, the book which is clearly the product of the whole history of English and American literature. Such a style is exclusionary. It's not difficult to read, in the way that almost any important work in social science is difficult, or in the way *The Sound and the Fury* is difficult. But it does withhold itself, at least in part, from the reader whose ear is not attuned to the cadences of language, and perhaps from the reader whose past has not included considerable reading of classical English literature—books in the high style. Perhaps a better way to put it would be that Cozzens seems to assume consistently that there still is a high style, and not merely a lot of different ways of writing, which there is no way to grade or rank or sort. As opposed to the ingratiating openness, the friendly looseness of the American casual style, which invites the reader in ("come as you are"), a chapter of Cozzens makes demands, puts the reader on his mettle, may even

shut doors in his face. You can do that in the pastoral milieu, as Frost did, but not so readily in the town milieu.

Noel Perrin. New Republic. Sept. 17, 1977, pp. 44–45

James Gould Cozzens is the least-read and least-taught of the major American novelists. It cannot be said that his work has suffered from inadequate exposure; but not even six Book-of-the-Month Club selections have attracted a broad readership. Except for *By Love Possessed*, no Cozzens novel has had a substantial mass-market paperback sale; and none has become a college classroom standard text. Although he has staunch admirers, one of the master American novelists is in some ways a cult-author. The resistance to Cozzens's work has been blamed on his refusal to make concessions to inattentive or unintelligent readers. Yet he is not difficult to read. His prose is precise; his meanings are clear; and, before *By Love Possessed*, his style is unembellished. The increasing dignity of style enforces Cozzens's objectivity. The "coldness" that critics have cited in Cozzens's observation of his characters is the stoical detachment of a writer trying to achieve "the stability of truth" in dealing with profound matters of human conduct. The periodic sentences and heavy subordination of *By Love Possessed* and *Morning Noon and Night* can intimidate only those who have not mastered the structure of the English sentence. The by-no-means overwhelming use of uncommon words achieves exactness of statement. Such words are intended to fix the reader's attention and, if necessary, send him to a dictionary. Cozzens's developed style is the natural expression for a highly literate writer with a traditionalist's respect for language. The complexity of sentence structure is appropriate to the complexity of his thinking. His use of open or concealed literary allusion in *Guard of Honor*, *By Love Possessed*, and *Morning Noon and Night* does not exclude the much-cherished general reader. The allusions are there for readers who recognize them; but the meanings of the books do not depend on that recognition. Cozzens is not a mandarin author; his work is far more accessible than that of many novelists currently in critical favor. He does not, in fact, make extraordinary demands on readers—beyond requiring them to pay attention.

The concept of vocation is central to Cozzens's representations of general nature, but he fully credits the determining factors in human conduct—education, social position, intelligence, training, luck, and what used to be called "character." The mark of Cozzens's people is that their values and behavior are developed in terms of their professions. You are what you do and how well you do it. This recognition may partly account for the denigration of his work among humanists who hold the job of teaching literature. Believing that success is a sign of corruption, they endeavor to persuade students that the real business of life is to live in accordance with one's feelings. Cozzens alarms proponents of the higher failure.

Cozzens has been called a conservative, an aristocrat, and a classicist. He rejects all of these identifications, insisting that he tries only to render life and people accurately as he sees them. He respects intelligence, moral firmness, and self-discipline. He rejects emotions as guides for conduct while recognizing the force of "Man's incurable wish to believe what he preferred to believe."

Matthew J. Bruccoli. Introduction to Just Representations:
A James Gould Cozzens Reader (Southern Illinois Univ. Pr.
and Harcourt Brace Jovanovich, 1978), pp. xviii–xix

The burden of Cozzens's fiction is that man must recognize and accept his condition and still bear the responsibility of action. . . . To act in the full awareness of the irony of the conditions within which he must act is, for Cozzens, the dignity of man.

If this is Cozzens's theme—and it is, I think, present in all the major novels—then he may now have found his own moment in time; until now Cozzens has been neglected, but there are signs that this neglect is about to end. History has finally prepared for him an audience that can share his angle of vision. Until it did, Cozzens went his solitary way, writing fine novels, pursuing his own sense of what life is about, undeterred by the almost total absence of recognition.

> John William Ward. In *James Gould Cozzens: New Acquist of True Experience*, ed. Matthew J. Bruccoli (Southern Illinois Univ. Pr., 1979), pp. 15–16

BIBLIOGRAPHY
Confusion, 1924 (n); *Michael Scarlett*, 1925 (n); *Cockpit*, 1928 (n); *The Son of Perdition*, 1929 (n); *S. S. San Pedro*, 1931 (n); *The Last Adam*, 1933 (n) (English edition, *A Cure of Flesh*; 1933); *Castaway*, 1934 (n); *Men and Brethren*, 1936 (n); *Ask Me Tomorrow*, 1940 (n); *The Just and the Unjust*, 1942 (n); *Guard of Honor*, 1948 (n); *By Love Possessed*, 1957 (n); *Children and Others*, 1964 (s); *Morning, Noon and Night*, 1968 (n); *Just Representations: A James Gould Cozzens Reader*, 1978 (misc); *Selected Notebooks, 1960–1967*, 1983; *A Time of War: Air Force Diaries and Pentagon Memos, 1943–45*, 1984

CRANE, Hart (1899–1932)

Mr. Crane has a most remarkable style, a style which is strikingly original—almost something like a great style, if there could be such a thing as a great style which was, not merely not applied to a great subject, but not, so far as one can see, applied to any subject at all. . . . One does not demand of poetry nowadays that it shall provide us with logical metaphors or with intelligible sequences of ideas. Rimbaud is inconsecutive and confused. Yet, with Rimbaud, whom Mr. Crane somewhat resembles, we experience intense emotional excitement and artistic satisfaction; we are dazzled by the eruption of his images, but we divine what it is that he is saying. But, with Mr. Crane, though he sometimes moves us, it is in a way curiously vague.

> Edmund Wilson. *New Republic*. May 11, 1927. p. 320

Crane labored to perfect both the strategy and the tactics of language so as to animate and maneuver his perceptions—and then fought the wrong war and against an enemy that displayed, to his weapons, no vulnerable target. He wrote in a language of which it was the virtue to accrete, modify, and interrelate moments of emotional vision—moments at which the sense of being gains its greatest access—moments at which, by the felt nature of the knowledge, the revealed thing is its own meaning; and he attempted to apply his language, in his major effort, to a theme that required a sweeping, discrete, indicative, anecdotal language, a

language in which, by force of movement, mere cataloging can replace and often surpass representation. He used the private lyric to write the cultural epic.

> R.P. Blackmur. *The Double Agent* (Arrow). 1935. p. 126

His world has no center, and the compensatory action that he took is responsible for the fragmentary quality of his most ambitious work. This action took two forms, the blind assertion of the will; and the blind desire for self-destruction. The poet did not face his first problem, which is to define the limits of his personality and to objectify its moral implications in an appropriate symbolism. Crane could only assert a quality of will against the world, and at each successive failure of the will he turned upon himself. . . . By attempting an extreme solution of the romantic problem, Crane proved that it cannot be solved.

> Allen Tate. *Reactionary Essays* (Scribner). 1936. pp. 40–3. Courtesy of Alan Swallow

Although Pound and Eliot had been largely responsible for reviving an interest in the poetry of the sixteenth and seventeenth centuries, they were themselves temperamentally incapable of doing more than adapting, imitating, and assimilating certain of its characteristics. . . . It remained for Crane, unschooled, unspoiled by scholastic nostalgia and self-consciousness, to use the medium in a completely modern way, easily and naturally combining in it rhetoric, conversation, and discursive thought, and sounding afresh the grand note so rarely heard in modern times. . . . In the process of renovating blank verse Crane also revivified the poetic language of his time. He was able to discover words, and use them, almost as things in themselves, prized their colors, sounds, and shapes as more meaningful than their strict definitions.

> Philip Horton. *Hart Crane* (Norton). 1937. pp. 309–10

Essentially Crane was a poet of ecstasy or frenzy or intoxication; you can choose your own word depending on how much you like his work. Essentially he was using rhyme and meter and fantastic images to convey the emotional states that were induced in him by alcohol, jazz, machinery, laughter, intellectual stimulation, the shape and sound of words and the madness of New York in the late Coolidge era. At their worst his poems are ineffective unless read in something approximating the same atmosphere, with a drink at your elbow, the phonograph blaring and somebody shouting into your ear, ''Isn't that great!'' At their best, however, the poems do their work unaided except by their proper glitter and violence.

> Malcolm Cowley. *Exile's Return* (Viking). 1951. pp. 230–1

Crane referred to *The Bridge* as his *Aeneid*, and his critics have generally taken the genre of the poem for granted. Yet what happens when the romantic poet becomes a culture hero, when the reference of the myth is shifted from the usual epic hero, who embodies the positive ideals of his world and is in tune with it, to a figure who stands outside society? When Crane interpreted the death of the voyager as the death of Everyman, he was doing no less than re-creating Everyman in the voyager's image, fashioning society in the image of himself; and it is here that the distinction between lyric and epic is wholly obscured.

Yet in another sense, Crane himself is representative, for his dilemma, establishing an imaginative vision in a society that no longer can believe in visions, is the dilemma of the twentieth-century man who finds himself alone and unimportant in the universe and will not accept his fate. Perhaps, after all, Crane was a kind of culture hero, appropriate to the times and in a way he never imagined: uneducated, alcoholic, homosexual, paranoic, suicidal—victimized by himself and by the world—he still wrote optimistic, visionary poetry. Indeed, Allen Tate has actually called him a hero, and it seems to me that those who believe in heroes would have to agree.

> L.S. Dembo. *Hart Crane's Sanskrit Charge* (Cornell). 1960. pp. 132–3

Many have justly criticized *The Bridge* as a "Myth of America" for its chaotic historical and chronological sense and for the apparent lack of continuity between several of its sections. Yet it is fair to look again at the poem with a little more of Crane's eye. In the first place, he considered his poem symphonic, a "mystical synthesis" of America in which history, fact, and location "all have to be transfigured into abstract form." It was not to be a narrative epic which would proceed in historical sequence but an evolution in which idea and motif would in recurrence construct the imaginative body of the poem as an "organic panorama." Thus one might dare to say that *The Bridge* is not the Myth of America in an historical sense at all, but a construction and ritual celebration of the spiritual consciousness and creative force possible to America. Because present and past are often simultaneous and chronology distorted (as in a Faulkner novel), *The Bridge* must rely on a psychological order that is more intuitive, emotional, and mystical than rational.

> Bernice Slote. *Start with the Sun* [with James E. Miller and Karl Shapiro] (Nebraska). 1960. p. 163

Mistakenly assuming that Crane's intention was oversimple—a total, indiscriminate affirmation—critics have then condemned it for its complex duality, its vacillation, its merely partial affirmation, its tension between "an over-simplified vision and a tortured awareness of realistic circumstance." In one breath Crane is charged with a mindless optimism or idealism; in the next he is charged with including ugly realities and negations that conflict with this idealism and "confuse" the poem.

A more consistent and, I believe, more accurate view will recognize that *the ugly realities are intended*. The tortured awareness of realistic circumstance is *an integral part of the vision*. The poem's vacillation, or dialectic (to give it an approved name), serves the clear purpose of keeping the vision from being oversimple—tempers it, ironically qualifies it, complicates it. In short, Crane is trying for a difficult rather than an easy beauty, a complex rather than a synthetic coherence.

> Gordon K. Grigsby. *College English*. April, 1963. pp. 518–19

Crane's poetry is important for several reasons. First, he possessed an extraordinary gift for metaphor. As stated earlier, the remembrance of single phrases or lines is the most widespread general response to Crane's work. His poems, of course, present a harmony embracing more than single images, but their greatest intensity—their brilliance—is located in particular phrases. His distinguishing trait is the pitch of eloquence that he often achieves several times in a single poem through the startling aptness of his imagery. . . .

His work is significant, too, because of its irresistibly moving theme: man's quest for enduring love and absolute beauty. He expresses moods varying from exultant trust that the fulfillment of his quest is imminent to a downcast premonition of continued failure, but his desire never deviates from the true north of his idealism. This preoccupation gives a dignity and a universality to his poetry.

> Vincent Quinn. *Hart Crane* (Twayne). 1963. p. 127

If one approaches *The Bridge* without a precommitment to Crane's own statement of its theme, it is possible to find in it a theme which provides a high degree of organic unity. The poem is a search or quest for a mythic vision, rather than the fixed, symbolic expression of a vision firmly held in the poet's mind. The vision sought is one that will be based on a knowledge of a glorious past, and will provide a bridge from that past to the hopeful future, in spite of the dearth of hopeful signs in the actual present. The poem is highly subjective in language and content, and understandably so, because the quest is a personal quest, the search of the poet for a vision that will satisfy his *own* needs. But Crane also saw the problem of the poet as reflecting the central problem of the society in which he lived, and the poet's solution to the problem—if he could achieve one—as having consequences far beyond the poet's own private life.

> Thomas A. Vogler. *Sewanee Review*. Summer, 1965. pp. 381–2

Hart Crane's six "Voyages" are one poem, the only one of his poems in which Crane manages to express a sense of being at peace with himself. "The Broken Tower" tries to do the same, but the experience is new and uncertain; the title belies the swelling tower of the last stanza. In "For the Marriage of Faustus and Helen" and *The Bridge*, the positive, transcendental conclusions are doctrinaire rather than personal; they are necessary responses to poems full of experienced despair. In other personal poems of the mid-Twenties, the aspiration toward transcendence is itself a desperate maneuver. Only in "Voyages" can the tone even remotely be called serene. . . .

In another, less finished poem, "Repose of Rivers," the sound of willows is made to represent what happiness Crane knew as a child. His adult search to rediscover that happiness culminates in hearing the sound of the sea. At the end of the "Voyages," however, the sound is hushed. The "imaged Word . . . unbetrayable reply" is completely apart from Crane's hello-and-goodbye adventures in real life. At the top of his power, Crane isolates the axle-pole of his best self, assured that his love has found poetry and that his poetry has found infinity.

> Maurice Kramer. *Sewanee Review*. Summer, 1965. pp. 410, 423

Finally, one must point to the fundamentally religious character of his outlook as another source of his comparative obscurity. By nature and nurture a transcendental idealist, he embraced no formal philosophy and no organized religion, despite his reading of Plato and Nietzsche and his exposure to Christian Science. His religion became the pursuit of the Absolute, conceived not as God but as the equivalent of God and experienced as a living ideal whose reality transcends space and time. His pursuit of this ideal is manifested in religious diction which may often appear Biblical or Neoplatonic yet has no specific traditional content, no reference to a text which would guide us to his meaning. It is not so much the confusion of his "vision" as the relative lack of a traditional vocabulary that leads to the charge of unintelligibility. In short, Crane is one of the many who, through no fault of their own, have been largely deprived of the common sources of the western tradition—the Bible and classical mythology and philosophy.

Hilton Landry in *The Twenties*, ed. Richard E. Langford and William E. Taylor (Everett Edwards). 1966. p. 24

Crane ends ["Passage"] characteristically, with questions rather than answers (when his poetry contains answers, they are usually silent ones, as in "At Melville's Tomb"). But it seems evident that the grasp of memory and everything associated with it—memory that is committed to the already written and established, memory escaped from, earlier, and then yielded to—has been broken; and that hearing, the ability to hear the voice of spirit, is about to be restored. The ceremonial action of "Passage"—its rhythm of gain, loss and potential recovery—is badly cramped in execution. But it is Crane's honest and accurate account of the continuing rhythm of his own poetic career.

R.W.B. Lewis. *Massachusetts Review*. Spring, 1966. p. 232

In one way perhaps Whitman's example, which seemed to offer [Crane] validation, did him more harm than good. Temperamentally, perhaps, especially in the final years of his short life, Crane had more in common with St. John of the Cross than with Whitman. If he had lived earlier and elsewhere, he might have trusted his mystic experiences, and interpreted them as "a flight of the alone to the alone." "The way down," into the depths of consciousness, was very possibly the only mystic way Crane had ever personally and strongly experienced. His life was too anguished, his experience too scarifying, to encourage frequent perceptions of "immanent divinity." But Whitman's "way up," his nature mysticism, was the only *example* Crane knew. He was forced to interpret his experiences of illumination in terms fundamentally alien to his temperament.

Hyatt H. Waggoner. *American Poets from the Puritans to the Present* (Houghton). 1968. p. 509

In modern American poetry the lyric customarily records the confessional impulses of a tormented sensibility, often in an overwrought rhetoric, in a poem of and about self-consciousness. In these journals of pain, the poet's forcing of feeling sometimes induces a forcing of syntax and a taxing of language. Each poem is an unfolding of contraries, a religious-erotic experience. In Crane's poems, the points of pressure are often the sublimated equivalents of the pressure of feeling in his life: the swings from hurt to joy and from exaltation to despair, the air of tense, distraught eagerness to will love into being and to war with death in the self. This drama of both unfulfillment and transfiguration is played out to a dazzling, driven music. The language sweeps along lyrical currents—jammed, excited, buoyant, involuted, majestic.

The immediacy and verve of Crane's poetry or its complicated verbal surface cannot be denied. Many of his readers feel that they are looking through a frosted window and are only dimly if tantalizingly aware of what is behind that window. But, as T.S. Eliot said, it is a test that "genuine poetry can communicate before it is understood." What is not sufficiently accepted is that Crane was a good poetic workman, devoted to his craft and continually refining his tools. He is not an unschooled rhapsode. There are pattern, sense, and method in his poems. . . .

Herbert Leibowitz. *Hart Crane* (Columbia). 1968. p. 21

The synesthesia, synergy and syncopation [Crane] so brilliantly mastered were the shifts of a peculiarly naked temperament supported by a first-rate intelligence.

In all the many willingly submissive acts he had to perform, acts of graceful homage to masters genuine and spurious, to Stieglitz, Stein, Whitman, Blake, Rimbaud, Hopkins, Dante and Eliot on the one hand (I've left out a dozen), to Ouspensky and Spengler on the other, his keen mother wit told him that he had arrived somehow just off the beat—by a hair. It had already cost him a mighty effort to break free of the myths laid down by the great Midwestern novelists. Once free, like Keats he seemed to embrace and swallow all his own time, releasing it only in a poetry so splendidly ambiguous about most of the things that harried his time-bound friends that to this day it guards its wisdom with a positively Delphic severity.

Not bridges, harbors, Manhattan or the Indians, not Columbus or Pocahontas or the tropics or jazz or the sea, were his private discoveries. But it was a measure of his genius that his finest verse in *The Bridge* dared to rival Twain on the Mississippi and Whitman on New York, achieving in his serviceable contracted iambic pentameter almost the same magnificence. No models, then, but the best and least widely understood.

R. W. Flint. *New York Times Book Section*. July 21, 1974. p. 5

Not only is *The Bridge* constructed according to Crane's theory of organic poetry, and hence to some extent explicable in terms of his poetics; but also, *The Bridge* is a poem about the creation of a poem, one that can embody the truth of the fictional poet's imagination in "one arc synoptic" ("Atlantis"). The poem, then, not only results from a process of organic creation, it also continually celebrates and re-enacts that process as its proper subject. Thus to propose a goal for, or a critical appreciation of, *The Bridge* which is based on categories or intentions not inherent in Crane's poetic purposes is to run that risk of a confusion of categories. In the American tradition of Emerson and Whitman, Crane was not concerned with society except insofar as it proceeded from the life of the individual, which for the poet means the life of the individual's imagination. Such poetry "teaches" society by evincing that life. . . .

There are three major aspects of Crane's poetic theory which bear on the nature and direction of *The Bridge*: the process by which a poem is created, the kind of poem resulting from this process, and the function of the poem in relation to the reader. The creative process is an organic one in which the poet submits to experience, assimilates and unifies it, then represents to the world the evidence of this unifying of experience within a poem. . . . Thus . . . the poem is . . . a celebration of the power of the imagination, the harp that engenders the chord, and hence a celebration of the life and act of the imagination. The dream of act is the dream that the poet-persona will, in the life of his particular imagination, be able to unite diverse materials, reach a state of unity and absolute innocence, symbolized by Atlantis, and then cast a "mythic spear," meaning write the poem, *The Bridge*, that will urge others (the audience) to the same kind of activity, the same kind of life, that engendered the poem. It is within this context that *The Bridge*, Crane's epic of the modern consciousness, must be described.

> Richard P. Sugg. *Hart Crane's "The Bridge"* (Univ. of Alabama Pr., 1976), pp. 4, 7

The Romantic tradition in which Crane is writing has been profoundly antidogmatic from the beginning. In Crane's poetry the balance between circumstantial or contingent truth and its dissolution in random occurrence is never given over in favor of some answer from Beyond. Crane celebrates the possibility of meaning, faith, and work in individual circumstances, while he demonstrates through the dramatic contexts of the poems that "meaning" is a temporary product of an always creative destructive mind. This is why seeing Crane as a "redeemer" must be seriously qualified. I do not believe that Crane's poems represent an attempt to reassert the religious consciousness in an unreligious age. Their honesty and skepticism continually see through the efforts of the mind to redeem the world. What Crane has discovered is that the power of the mind never has depended on the absolute truth of its beliefs. Instead, the flexibility of the mind, its genius for disagreeing with itself, is its greatest strength. . . .

Crane's poems work toward a revelation which could be characterized as seeing through an experience without surrendering or demeaning a naive sense of its reality. Absolute knowledge for him is a momentary recognition of what is naive about the experience *and* what is wonderful about it. Such a recognition is absolute in the sense that it is both undeniably real and free of the biases of the poet and of the reader. Crane accepts the problematical nature of its interpretation and the precarious state of its existence as challenges to expression. . . .

The special character of Crane's lyrics was produced from a sensibility passionate and simple, by a mind as brilliant as Eliot's. Crane could glean from a magazine article or an offhand conversation the essence of a current of thought too advanced for most to grasp with the best education. His poetry begins with the complete and honest indulgence of personal feelings; then a most penetrating introspection pushes these toward what I have called absolute knowledge. The result is an intensely personal lyricism cast in the light of an awareness of the deceiving nature of thought and feeling themselves. But neither the feeling nor the awareness is surrendered. Crane's difficult style is his solution to the problem of sustaining tension between the two. It involves exploiting the ambiguity of sense experience under the direction of the sense of value. His willingness to destroy the comfortable individuation and public aspect of experience results in a Dionysian art which rejects optimism but transcends pessimism. And it results in a uniquely Romantic lyric which celebrates life without pretending to correct existence. His poetry is thus unabashedly personal, confessional, proud, and relentlessly self-conscious.

> Robert Combs. *Vision of the Voyage: Hart Crane and the Psychology of Romanticism* (Memphis State Univ. Pr., 1978), pp. x–xi, 39, 106–7

The Bridge is a revolutionary breakthrough for [Hart] Crane, not just as a poet but as an individual; it is, in fact, the great extended moment in which he acts as an individual and as a poet.

But *The Bridge* was not supposed to be a personal epic. And everyone was ready with an idea of what it should be instead. Allen Tate pressed him hard to write a historical poem; Waldo Frank looked forward to one more voice added to his dialogue with the machine and its problems; and Yvor Winters cautioned him, as he cautioned everyone, to marshal his thoughts in a more rigorous and logical manner. There were others who could not be disappointed: his parents, his patron, influential friends. The extraordinary breakthrough of 1926 was reassembled almost as it was still assembling itself, and what emerged at last offered a bit of something for everyone. The 1930 *Bridge* offered history to Tate, the machine to Frank, a stronger narrative line to Winters, even a passage on the airplane for his new friend and patron, Harry Crosby.

In the process, all these extras crowded Crane out of his own poem. There are a number of reasons why Crane had so much difficulty bringing his epic to a conclusion and so much difficulty writing at all after 1927, but first among them must be his own intuition that the poems as he was presently shaping them somehow excluded him. Only in the letter-poems, where he almost stubbornly insisted upon directly addressing those who mattered to him, did he thoroughly include himself; and in those works, he is as modest as he can be.

Would the cycle have come around again, had Crane continued to live? Would he have been able, under some extraordinary or unique condition, to risk again writing as intimate and personal and vulnerable as in the 1926 *Bridge*? Possibly not for some time. As his new relationship with a woman suggests, he was at this moment compelled to change his own life rather than to accept his life as it was; the relationship appears as a desperate swerve, an effort to lose who he is by believing he can become someone new and different. Out of such pressures, suicide seems to be a familiar alternative; so many preceding decisions are, in effect, miniature suicides themselves, decisions to die to one's self, to adopt a mask, to play a role.

But twice in his life he had let himself be more open than ever before—once in *Voyages*, again in 1926 with *The Bridge*. He carried within himself the seeds of understanding what it was that he needed; both of his extended poems, as well as some shorter works, were acts of self-understanding and achievements of self-therapy: confrontations of the problems that were crushing him. The problems were immensely complex, and made even more so by his own integrity. So complex were they that a third try might perhaps have been beyond his reach. Yet if he had lived longer, his own compulsion to write might have carried him through, or led him at least to another work in which, once again, he broke through to matters of deepest importance to him.

Edward Brunner. *Splendid Failure: Hart Crane and the Making of "The Bridge"* (Urbana: Univ. of Illinois Pr., 1985), pp. 244–45

With Crane line and stanza are the primary expressive units, to the point frequently of putting at risk the larger structures meant to contain them; the effect of something "fragmentary" in his finished and published work that was noted early on by the English poet and critic D.S. Savage marks individual poems as well as the mass of his writing. His desire to make each such expressive strophe effectively autonomous and incontrovertible has about it something of the same willfulness and urgency, the same intemperate adventuring, to be felt—his closest friends all sensed this—in his private conduct and erotic life. ("Creative opportunism" was Philip Horton's critical phrase for it in 1937.) Hart Crane lived along the knife's edge in more ways than one. Technique for him, as Waldo Frank was not wrong in thinking, was more than a choice of means to a foreseen end. His verse stanzas—he seems to me as great a master of the formal lyric stanza as Yeats, Eliot, Wallace Stevens—work to advance thought and crystallize further apprehension as well as concentrating and intensifying the undertaken statement. Line and stanza became, for Crane, acts of life, and not only poetic life. Each one when completed served as a renewal, a vital self-justification. In some definite and self-acknowledging fashion the delivered words of each poem are meant, for this child of the Protestant sensibility's American diaspora, to realize anew the generative "Word" at the axis of all creation.

In any round estimate of Crane's place in American writing and in twentieth-century poetry, Yvor Winters's extreme ambivalence will remain a crux. Whatever we decide about its causes and reasons. But it was Winters himself who, years after dismissing Crane as a performative model, most memorably articulated what I think anyone who responds to Crane's imaginative and prosodic intelligence more than glancingly will be brought to feel. "So far as I am concerned," Winters wrote (in scorn of the homogenizing intelligence of an imaginary Professor X); "I would gladly emulate Odysseus, if I could, and go down to the shadows for another hour's conversation with Crane on the subject of poetry."

Warner Berthoff. *Hart Crane: A Re-Introduction* (Minneapolis: Univ. of Minnesota Pr., 1989), pp. x–xi

BIBLIOGRAPHY
White Buildings, 1926 (p); *The Bridge*, 1930 (p); *Collected Poems*, 1933; *Letters*, 1952; *Complete Poems and Selected Letters and Prose*, 1966; *Robber Rocks*, 1969 (letters); *Letters of Hart Crane and His Family*, 1974; *Hart Crane and Yvor Winters: Their Literary Correspondence*, 1978; *The Poems of Hart Crane*, 1986; *O, My Land, My Friends: The Selected Letters of Hart Crane*, 1997

CRANE, Stephen (1871–1900)

He sang, but his voice erred up and down the scale, with occasional flashes of brilliant melody, which could not redeem the errors. New York was essentially his inspiration, the New York of suffering and baffled and beaten life, of inarticulate or blasphemous life; and away from it he was not at home, with any theme, or any sort of character. It was the pity of his fate that he must quit New York, first as a theme, and then as a habitat; for he rested nowhere else, and wrought with nothing else as with the lurid depths which he gave proof of knowing better than anyone else.

William Dean Howells. *North American Review*. Dec., 1902. p. 771

In his art he is unique. Its certainty, its justness, its peculiar perfection of power arrived at its birth, or at least at that precise moment in its birth when other artists—and great artists too—were preparing themselves for the long and difficult conquest of their art. I cannot remember a parallel case in the literary history of fiction. . . . His art is just in itself, rhythmical, self-poising as is the art of a perfect dancer. There are no false steps, no excesses. And, of course, his art is strictly limited. We would define him by saying he is the perfect artist and interpreter of the surfaces of life. And that explains why he so swiftly attained his peculiar power and what is the realm his art commands and his limitations.

Edward Garnett. *Friday Nights* (Knopf). 1922. p. 205

He had a quiet smile that charmed and frightened one. It made you pause by something revelatory it cast over his whole physiognomy, not like a ray but like a shadow. . . . Contempt and indignation never broke the surface of his moderation simply because he had no surface. He was all through the same material, incapable of affectation of any kind, of any pitiful failure of generosity for the sake of personal advantage, or even from sheer exasperation which must find its relief. . . . Though the word is discredited now and may sound pretentious, I will say that there was in Crane a strain of chivalry which made him safe to trust with one's life.

Joseph Conrad. Introduction to Thomas Beer's *Stephen Crane* (Knopf). 1923. pp. 5, 7, 9–10

He is American literature's "marvelous boy." Like the Bowery, he was elemental and vital. He would sleep in a flop house to taste the bitter of experience. He loved living. And adventure enough was crowded into his eight sick years of manhood. He looked at life clearly and boldly, knew its irony, felt its mystery and beauty, and wrote about it with a sincerity and confidence that spring only from genius.

Vernon Loggins. *I Hear America* (Crowell) 1937. p. 23

Crane left on me an impression of supernaturalness that I still have. It was perhaps the aura of that youth that never deserted him—perhaps because of his aspect of frailty. He seemed to shine—and perhaps the November sun really did come out and cast on his figure, in the gloom of my entry, a ray of light. At any rate, there he stands . . . radiating brightness. But it was perhaps more than anything the avenging quality of his brows and the resentful frown of his dark blue eyes. He saw, that is to say, the folly and malignity of humanity—not in the individual but in committees.

Ford Madox Ford. *Portraits from Life* (Houghton). 1937. p. 24

For all its beauty, Crane's best work was curiously thin and, in one sense, even corrupt. His desperation exhausted him too quickly; his unique sense of tragedy was a monotone. No one in America had written like him before; but though his books precipitately gave the whole aesthetic movement of the nineties a sudden direction and a fresher impulse, he could contribute no more than the intensity of his spirit. Half of him was a consummate workman; the other half was not a writer at all. . . . His gift was a furious one, but barren; writing much, he repeated himself so joylessly that in the end he seemed to be mocking himself with the same quiet viciousness with which, even as a boy, he had mocked the universe.

Alfred Kazin. *On Native Grounds* (Reynal). 1942. pp. 71–2

Crane was one of the first post-impressionists. . . . He began it before the French painters began it or at least as early as the first of them. He simply knew from the beginning how to handle detail. He estimated it at its true worth—made it serve his purposes and felt no further responsibility about it. I doubt whether he ever spent a laborious half-hour in doing his duty by detail—in enumerating, like an honest, grubby auctioneer. If he saw one thing that engaged him in a room, he mentioned it. If he saw one thing in a landscape that thrilled him, he put it on paper, but he never tried to make a faithful report of everything else within his field of vision, as if he were a conscientious salesman making out an expense account.

Willa Cather. *On Writing* (Knopf). 1949. pp. 69–70

The immense power of the tacit . . . gives his work kinship rather with Chekhov and Maupassant than Poe. "I like my art"—said Crane—"straight"; and misquoted Emerson, "There should be a long logic beneath the story, but it should be carefully kept out of sight". How far Crane's effect of inevitability depends upon this *silence* it would be hard to say. Nowhere in "The Open Boat" is it mentioned that the situation of the men is symbolic, clear and awful though it is that this story opens into the universe. Poe in several great stories opens man's soul downwards, but his work has no relation with the natural and American world at all. If Crane's has, and is irreplaceable on this score, it is for an ironic inward and tragic vision outward that we value it most, when we can bear it. . . . Crane does really stand between us and something that we could not otherwise understand. It is not human; it is not either the waves and mountains who are among his major characters, but it acts in them, it acts in children and sometimes even in men, upon animals, upon boys above all, and men. Crane does not understand it fully. But he has been driven and has dragged himself nearer by much to it than we have, and he interprets for us.

John Berryman. *Stephen Crane* (Wm. Sloane Associates). 1950. pp. 291–2

Jean Julius Christian Sibelius (born six years before Stephen Crane) may or may not slink down the cellar stairs whenever

"Finlandia" is played, and Stephen Crane might have developed a comparable skin-crawl every time *The Red Badge of Courage* was mentioned. The fact that his other novels, all of them short for their day and rather shorter for ours, now go unread might not distress him, and toward his verse, with its conscious and even proclaimed echo of Emily Dickinson (an echo louder than the voice of origin), he might today be as patronizing and indulgent as the next man. (There is one great advantage to dying young—you can impute all your faults to your youth.) But he would, I am sure, take high pride in his competence with the short story, and it would be a proper pride. For Crane still has, and always will have, the capacity to teach by sterling example (as in "The Open Boat" and "The Blue Hotel") the fine art of narration.

John T. Winterich. *Saturday Review*. Feb. 3, 1951. p. 43

Irony is Crane's chief technical instrument. It is the key to our understanding of the man and of his works. He wrote with the intensity of a poet's emotion, the compressed emotion that bursts into symbol and paradox. . . .

Crane's style is prose pointillism. It is composed of disconnected paintings, which coalesce like the blobs of color in French impressionist paintings, every word-group having a cross-reference relationship, every seemingly disconnected detail having interrelationship to the configurated whole. The intensity of a Crane work is owing to this patterned coalescence of disconnected things, everything at once fluid and precise. A striking analogy is established between Crane's use of colors and the methods employed by the impressionists and neo-impressionists or divisionists, and it is as if he had known about their theory of contrasts and had composed his own prose paintings by the same principle.

Robert W. Stallman. *Stephen Crane. An Omnibus* (Knopf). 1952. pp. xxv, 185

. . .the Crane story again and again interprets the human situation in terms of the ironic tensions created in the contract between man as he idealizes himself in his inner thought and emotion and man as he actualizes himself in the stress of experience. In the meaning evoked by the ironic projection of the deflated man against the inflated man lives Crane's essential theme: the consequence of false pride, vanity, and blinding delusion.

James B. Colvert. *Modern Fiction Studies*. Autumn, 1959. p. 200

Any student can recall that Stephen Crane has been termed realist, romantic, naturalist, imagist, existentialist, symbolist, impressionist, expressionist, and *pointilliste*. (I may have overlooked some). That roaster becomes doubly formidable when one remembers that somebody has taken the trouble to deny the validity of almost every one of those labels—if only to make room for pasting on his own red wafer. Common sense suggests, therefore, that we are dealing with a vivid and significant writer who cannot be categorized simply—perhaps not at all. . . .

One conclusion suggested by these facts is that Crane never outlived his apprenticeship. He did not live to become any sort of "list." . . . Crane died a Seeker. . . .

His experience of sports brought Crane knowledge, and attitudes consequent on that knowledge, important to his point of view. It give him the experience of testing his courage and thence personal knowledge of pain and fear, victory and defeat. From what vantage point he commanded the cosmic gambler's stoic outlook: despising the petty, safe and comfortable; prizing the chance-taking, the enterprising, the seeking, aggressive and tough. In this he was at one with the prophets of the strenuous life. But he went beyond them in the depth of his forceful but ambivalent compassion for losers. He was anxious that their courage or at least their agony be defended against and registered upon the smug and ignorant. But he would not have defended them against the law, against the rules of the game of life.

> Edwin H. Cady. *English Literary History*. Dec., 1961. pp. 378, 381

Both Crane and Hemingway began with a sense of irony, a gift for understatement, an abhorrence of sentimentalism and a view of man that made war one of the important, inevitable metaphors for dramatizing their insights. Man under stress, at the center of powerful, irrational forces, man forging and tempering an answerable courage and code is the repetitive situation at the center of both writers' works. They both assert that in heaven there is *nada*, that nature is indifferent, that the unlimited, unwounded are ignorantly cruel and barbarously sentimental. Only the scarred can hope to offer even a tentative interpretation of man's dilemmas.

> Sy Kahn in *Essays in Modern American Literature*, edited by Richard E. Langford (Stetson University). 1963. pp. 36–7

Maggie

Maggie is not a story *about* people; it is primitive human nature itself set down with perfect spontaneity and grace of handling. For pure aesthetic beauty and truth no Russian, not Tchekhov himself, could have bettered this study which, as Howells remarks, has the quality of Greek tragedy.

> Edward Garnett. *Friday Nights* (Knopf). 1922. pp. 214–5

It is a short, a novelette. Yet it suggests more life than any American contemporary of Crane could have depicted in a thousand pages. In its every crowded phrase and metaphor it is reality. The little book breaks all traditions of fiction. Crane has no model for it—except possibly the page or two he had read from Zola. But it is not Zolaesque. Critics like to call it the first specimen of genuine realism produced by an American. Perhaps it is that. But it should be judged as a thing unique—just a faithful and vivid projection of the grim degradation and sordid beauty of the Bowery.

> Vernon Loggins. *I Hear America* (Crowell). 1937. pp. 25

The Red Badge of Courage

The deep artistic unity of *The Red Badge of Courage* is fused in its flaming, spiritual intensity, in the fiery ardour with which the shock of the Federal and Confederate armies is imaged. The torrential force and impetus, the check, sullen recoil and reforming of shattered regiments, and the renewed onslaught and obstinate resistance of brigades and divisions are visualized with extraordinary force and color. If the sordid grimness of carnage is partially screened, the feeling of war's cumulative rapacity, of its breaking pressure and fluctuating tension is caught with wonderful fervour and freshness of style.

> Edward Garnett. *Friday Nights* (Knopf). 1922. pp. 212–3

Intense, brutal, bloody, *The Red Badge of Courage* vitalizes the smoke, noise, stench dread, terror, agony, and death of the battlefield. Thrust into the horror, the reader identifies himself with Henry Fleming and feels with him the trepidation of fear and heroism. How a boy of twenty-two conceived the story and within a few days got it down on paper with such truthfulness to detail that no veteran soldier has ever been able to question its authenticity is one of the mysteries of artistic creation.

> Vernon Loggins. *I Hear America* (Crowell). 1937. p. 26

Suddenly there was *The Red Badge of Courage* showing us, to our absolute conviction, how the normal, absolutely undistinguished, essentially civilian man from the street had behaved in a terrible and prolonged war—without distinction, without military qualities, without special courage, without even any profound apprehension of, or passion as to, the causes of the struggle in which, almost without will, he was engaged. . . . With *The Red Badge of Courage* in the nineties, we were provided with a map showing us our own hearts. If before that date we had been asked how we should behave in a war, we should no doubt have answered that we should behave like demigods, with all the marmoreal attributes of war memorials. But, a minute after peeping into *The Red Badge* we knew that, at best, we should behave doggedly but with a weary non-comprehension, flinging away our chassepot rifles, our haversacks, and fleeing into the swamps of Shiloh.

> Ford Madox Ford. *Portraits from Life* (Houghton). 1937. pp. 22–3

Crane's hero is Everyman, the symbol made flesh upon which war plays its havoc and it is the deliberation of that intention which explains why the novel is so extraordinarily lacking, as H. L. Mencken puts it, in small talk. Scene follows scene in an accelerating rhythm of excitement, the hero becomes the ubiquitous man to whom, as Wyndham Lewis once wrote of the Hemingway man, things happen. With that cold, stricken fury that was so characteristic of Crane—all through the self-conscious deliberation of his work one can almost hear his nerves quiver—he impaled his hero on the ultimate issue, the ultimate pain and humiliation of war, where the whole universe, leering through the blindness and smoke of battle, became the incarnation of pure agony. The foreground was a series of commonplaces; the background was cosmological.

> Alfred Kazin. *On Native Grounds* (Reynal). 1942. pp. 71–2

The Red Badge of Courage probes a state of mind under the incessant pinpricks and bombardments of life. The theme is that man's salvation lies in change, in spiritual growth. It is only by immersion in the flux of experience that man becomes disciplined and develops in character, conscience, or soul. Potentialities for change are at their greatest in battle—a battle represents life at its most intense flux. Crane's book is not about the combat of armies; it is about the self-combat of a youth who fears and stubbornly resists change, and the actual battle is symbolic of this spiritual warfare against change and growth. Henry Fleming recognizes the necessity for change and development, but wars against it. The youth develops into the veteran: "So it came to pass. . . his soul changed." Significantly enough, in stating what the book is about Crane intones Biblical phrasing.

    Robert W. Stallman. *Stephen Crane. An Omnibus* (Knopf). 1952. p. 193

The achievement of Crane in *The Red Badge of Courage* may be likened, it seems to me, to Chaucer's in *Troilus and Criseyde*, despite the lesser stature of the novel. Both works are infused with an irony which neatly balances two major views of human life—in *Troilus and Criseyde*, the value of courtly love versus heavenly love; in *The Red Badge of Courage*, ethical motivation and behavior versus deterministic and naturalistic actions. Both pose the problem, "Is there care in Heaven?" One is concerned with human values in a caring Universe, the other in an indifferent Universe. . . . Crane's magnum opus shows up the nature and value of courage. The heroic ideal is not what it has been claimed to be: So largely is it the product of instinctive responses to biological and traditional forces. But man does have will, and he has the ability to reflect, and though these do not guarantee that he can effect his own density, they do enable him to become responsible to some degree for the honesty of his personal vision. It is the duality of view, like Chaucer's, that is the secret of the unmistakable Crane's art.

    Stanley B. Greenfield. *PMLA: Publications of the Modern Language Association of America*. Dec., 1958. pp. 571–2

Crane artistically rendered the raw experiences of war in a special, prismatic prose, in our color-shot imagery and elegant impressions. It is a world where each sound is amplified by human terror, each color made brilliant and blaring by the frightened, wary eye, and the enemy invested with one's deepest, primitive fears. All this Crane instinctively knew in *The Red Badge of Courage*. In the fictional world of war, Crane's ironic vision, his talent for bizarre imagery, his curious religious and biblical diction (by which he inflates the egoistic actions and poses of his characters for later puncturing by pointed, ironic understatement), and his impressionistic descriptions could find their most made ample expression. Crane's young soldier, Henry Fleming, like Hemingway's Nick Adams, finds himself thrust into a world that shocks him into new levels of feeling and perception; the two men are symbols of innocence blasted by violence, by what at worst seems an intelligent malevolence.

    Sy Kahn in *Essays in Modern American Literature*, edited by Richard E. Langford (Stetson University). 1963. p. 36

Poetry

The poems have an enigmatic air and yet they are desperately personal. The absence of the panoply of the Poet is striking. We remember that their author did not like to be called a poet nor did he call them poetry himself. How unusual this is, my readers will recognize: most writers of verse are merely dying to be called poets, tremblingly hopeful that what they write is real "poetry." There was no pose here in Crane. His reluctance was an inarticulate recognition of something strange in the pieces. They are not like literary compositions. They are like things just seen and said, *said for use*. . . . He has truths to tell. Everybody else in the 'nineties is chanting and reassuring and invoking the gods. So Crane just says, like a medicine man *before* chanting or poetry began. And what he says is savage: unprotected, forestlike.

    John Berryman. *Stephen Crane* (Wm. Sloane Associates). 1950. pp. 272–3

Crane's best poems. . . present the bare outlines of a narrative situation in which there is a tension between two opposed forces. The tension may be expressed in terms of antithetical statements, dialogue, descriptions, or the effect upon the observer of an action he witnesses. . . . By making his human figures faceless and nameless, by pitting them against elemental forces, by describing their ambitions and their plights in simple yet overwhelming metaphors, Crane created for his poetry a symbolical form which represented a great advance in subtlety and flexibility over its allegorical beginnings.

    Daniel Hoffman. *The Poetry of Stephen Crane* (Columbia). 1956. pp. 263–4

BIBLIOGRAPHY
Maggie: A Girl of the Streets, 1893 (n); *The Black Riders*, 1895 (p); *The Red Badge of Courage*, 1895 (n); *George's Mother*, 1896 (n); *The Little Regiment and Other Episodes of the American Civil War*, 1896 (s); *The Third Violet*, 1897 (n); *The Open Boat and Other Tales of Adventure*, 1898 (s); *War is Kind*, 1899 (p); *Active Service*, 1899 (n); *The Monster and Other Stories*, 1899 (enlarged edition, 1901); *Whilomville Stories*, 1900; *Wounds in the Rain*, 1900 (s); *Great Battles of the World*, 1901 (h); (with Robert Barr) *The O' Ruddy: A Romance*, 1903 (n); *The Work of Stephen Crane*, 1925–27; *The Collected Poems*, 1930; *The Blood of the Martyr*, 1940 (d); *The Sullivan County Sketches*, 1949 (s); *Stephen Crane: An Omnibus*, 1952; *Letters*, 1960; *Complete Short Stories and Sketches*, 1963; *The War Dispatches of Stephen Crane*, 1964 (j); *The New York City Sketches*, 1966; *The Poems of Stephen Crane: A Critical Edition*, 1968

CREELEY, Robert (1926–)

Robert Creeley . . . is a hit-or-miss poet; and, if he is satisfied, then so must I be—for he is a good poet. Intransigent, "engaged," he can perceive the apocalypse in almost any moment he chooses. His method has been from the first poems in *Le Fou* staccato, elliptical. The dramatic situation—almost all the poems entail one or reactions to one—is made clear to the reader by shreds of rhetoric which are the involvement in it and act like images in a cluster. In this latter connection, Creeley's poems are one of our stronger links with other literatures—the Spanish and French especially—where writing from image to image is at least as important and frequent as protracting a single image into a rational conceit.

David Galler. *Sewanee Review*. Winter, 1961. p. 171

[William Carlos] Williams also presides behind the work of Robert Creeley. Most of the poems are short, and it is often the movement quite as much as the words that does the work, as for example in one of the best early poems, "The Innocence." At the same time his plainness of language may on occasion become a baldness, and the resulting poems are sometimes more similar to the notes for poems than to completed poems. . . .

His effect is at best one of purity and elegance; "care" is a favorite word in his early poems, and his care in suggesting minutiae is close to a moral care. There is a fragility, however, to most of his work, and it is only seldom (notably in "The Figures") that one feels his concerns are as fully explored as they deserve.

Thom Gunn. *The Yale Review*. Autumn, 1962. pp. 130–1

Creeley seems not to like pattern, really to be afraid of it, whether it is intellectual, structural (as in parallels or antitheses), metrical (when metric patterns are set up it is only so that they may be abandoned, thus defeating the expectation of recurrence), or a matter of rhyme (which is sometimes forced into a parody of itself that denies it value). Creeley seems not to like excitement either, at least in the forms of sound and image, for he persistently reduces poems to language that is prosaic. . . . What I hope is happening in Creeley's poetry is that the reticences are diminishing, and that the individual, direct and effective features of language which have been there all along—brevity of development, short lines, simple diction with considerable colloquialism and a little useful profanity—are now more willing to be united with an explicit situation.

William Dickey. *Poetry*. March, 1963. pp. 421, 423

Robert Creeley does a simple but rare thing. In each form he uses—up to now poetry, criticism, and a huge amount of letter writing—he insists on being "personal." That is, he allows his own mind to dominate, to dictate, formal procedure. He is the man who said it: "Form is only an extension of content"; and in his own work it is *consciously* so. He is, for instance, the only writer I know in whom I cannot find one rhetorical instance, i.e., "fitting" a sound: Creeley insists the opposite. And the forms themselves are of course changed by this, in the sense that they are "re-formed" each time to his personal measures. Also as a consequence, Creeley may maintain a consistency this way as "person" that is "transformal." He is one of the minority of poets who write good prose, and is even rarer for writing prose that is "like" his poetry.

Aram Saroyan. *Poetry*. April, 1964. pp. 45–6

The subject of [*The Gold Diggers and Other Stories*] is that kind of relation between people which is penetration, a locking or growing together in which the life becomes not what each one has alone but what is between them—all the inseparable pains and pleasures, terrors and joys of that kind of relation, in its presence, or at times in

its absence. . . . In such an effort, the principled use of the conventional arts of fiction becomes a distraction. What takes their place, giving the stories the concrete texture of their substance and giving the reader his experience, are the kinesthetic rhythms of the utterance. These rhythms are the gestures of Creeley's apprehension of his characters, at the level where apprehension is itself response. . . .

It is because Creeley is so completely "in" these stories . . . that he has discarded conventional craft for utterance. It is for the same reason that in his poetry he has discarded the formal use of symbol and meter, again for utterance. He has minimized the differentia of poetry and fiction in his work, so that his stories take a position somewhere between the novel and the poems in a continuum, different not so much in kind from each other as in narrowness of focus. The stories are comparable in length to the chapters of the novel, but their intensity is much greater. The poems are at the other end of the range, straining articulation to its limits and approaching absolute intensity.

Samuel Moon. *Poetry*. August, 1966. pp. 341–2

Pieces is a very wise and very beautiful book of verse. It enacts the piecemeal achievement of a vision so scrupulous and catholic that what by method is merely muscular and aesthetic becomes in the end profoundly moral. . . . Ordinary objects . . . locate extraordinary experiences in Creeley's poetry because he is so careful about his words and the expressive possibilities of line length. . . .

The stunning quality of such spareness can perhaps only be fully appreciated in the context. This means, in the fullest sense, as part of the entire book, for Creeley has carefully constructed the whole thing as a unit of beautiful discretions: "My plan is/these little boxes/make sequences." Which is to say, every word, every line, every poem, is forced to absolute separateness, for Creeley believes that real unity can only come when the pieces possess their own radical integrity. . . . Language here is perfectly articulated—if the poem courts a danger it is that all the pieces will collapse and scatter, like a stack of blocks—yet the whole accumulates itself in a collective refusal to swallow up any of its parts. We see the pieces and the sequences with equal clarity, as Creeley planned us to do. Such a devotion to language is a double pleasure, of purpose, of result. One does not achieve this easily: a poet must know his place and see to it.

Jerome McGann. *Poetry*. Dec., 1970. pp. 201–3

The basic organizational plan [of *A Day Book*], the jacket explains, is of "a record of experience." The implicit aim is to embody poetic process, the way we get from our daily empirical consciousness into a self-transcendent art. Almost half the book's approximately 165 pages is made up of prose entries in a journal; the rest consists of poetic entries, often parallel or at least reciprocal to the prose. Since the book is unpaginated (an annoyance, given its size, whenever one wants to go back and find anything in it), and since no time divisions within its span of more than thirty months are specified, we have the impression of an almost undifferentiated drift of consciousness. Yet the sequence retains a fundamental, sometimes absorbing *promise*. Who can tell what will show up next in the float, partly confessional and partly atmospheric, of events, conversations, gossip, crumbs of literary or philosophical thought, introspective moments, *aperçus*, outbursts of erotic fantasy and memory, and moments of defeat by or triumph over depression that the drift carries along with it? If we take into consideration the poet's varied interests in jazz, drugs, varieties of sexual behavior, being on the move, and the confusions of love and family life, we have an ambience not unlike the television documentary *An American Family*, with modulations—would God that side were more consciously striven for!—toward Proustian recollection. When that Proustian effort does occur, as in the long poem "People," we see how moving the whole work might have been.

M.L. Rosenthal. *Parnassus*. Fall–Winter, 1973. pp. 205, 207

I believe that Creeley's major accomplishment will be technical and that he will be remembered primarily as a craftsman. Time and again I have been impressed with the total control he exerts over the rhythms, especially, of his prose and poetry. The line, the pauses, the hesitancies, the syntax and ellipses usually mirror precisely the statement of the poem; in fact, in his best poems and in his best short stories, these elements become the statement itself. What he says is relatively less important than how he says it, or at least I believe that that is what future generations will say. . . .

Creeley has chosen, or as he might say, it has been chosen for him, to write poetry that constricts itself to a small point of intensity, with the emphasis on small as well as intensity. His poetry and fiction avoid the grand statement and the grand method; in fact, they accept technical limitations in the same way that they accept thematic limitations. His work is minimal in that it functions more by what is excluded than by what is included. The question then is not so much whether Creeley is or will be known as a major writer, but rather whether minimal art itself can ever be major. In other words, has Creeley, by the course he runs, removed himself from consideration as a major writer? Although any answer to this question can be argued endlessly, I suspect that the answer is yes. So far in his career at least, Creeley's work lacks both the thematic and technical scope to qualify as major. Within the self-imposed limitations of his poetry and fiction, the achievement is impressive; however, those self-imposed limitations are still limitations. To the literary historian, that evaluation is both justifiable and understandable; however, to the poet such a statement remains fortunately irrelevant.

Arthur Ford. *Robert Creeley* (Twayne, 1978), pp. 137–38

Apart from [Charles] Olson. . .the most important poets connected with the Black Mountain group are Robert Creeley, Ed Dorn, and Robert Duncan. In Creeley's case, an interest in open forms and the belief that "words are things too" has combined with two quite disparate but in a way complementary influences. There is, first, his involvement with the free-flowing experiments of Abstract Expressionism and modern jazz. "To me," Creeley has said, "life is interesting insofar as it lacks intentional 'control,'" and it is clear that the example of painters like Jackson Pollock and musicians like Charlie Parker and Miles Davis has encouraged him to see the artist as someone immersed in the work he creates, experiencing its energy, involved in its movement, and limited in terms of how he expresses himself only by "the nature of the activity." Along with this, there is what Creeley has termed his "New England temper." New England has given Creeley many things, including a tendency to be "hung up," to suffer from pain ("I can / feel my eye

breaking") and tension ("I think I grow tensions / like flowers"). Above all, though, what it has given him is two things, one to do with perception, the other with expression. "Locate *I*," declares Creeley in one of his poems; elsewhere, he insists, "position is where you / put it, where it is." He is fascinated, in effect, by the perceptual position of the speaker, how the poem grows out of the active relationship between perceiver and perceived. The preoccupation with the limits of vision that earlier New Englanders demonstrated is consequently translated into cool, modernist terms: the aim being not an "ego-centered" verse but precisely its opposite, words that reveal how our eyes and minds "are not separate. . .from all other life forms." At the same time, New England habits have, Creeley says, given him a "sense of speech as a laconic, ironic, compressed way of saying something to someone," the inclination "to say as little as possible as often as possible." So the forms of his saying have become, as he believes they should, an extension of content. His purpose is "a realization, a reification of what is": "a process of discovery" that turns out to be a matter of vocabulary as well as vision. "What's the point of doing what we already know?" Creeley has asked, and his writing continually illustrates this belief in experiment. His poems evolve on both a sequential grammatical level and a cumulative linear level; each line reaffirms or modifies the sense of the sentence and the total argument, each word exists in contrapuntal tension with all the others. There is risk here, in fact, a taste for the edgy and subversive, of a kind that would be equally familiar to Thelonious Monk and Emily Dickinson.

Richard Gray. *American Poetry of the Twentieth Century* (Essex: Longman, 1990), pp. 285–86

BIBLIOGRAPHY
Le Fou, 1952 (p); *The Immoral Proposition*, 1953 (p); *The Kind of Act*, 1953 (p); *The Gold Diggers*, 1954, rev. ed., 1965 (s); *All That Is Lovely in Men*, 1955 (p); *If You*, 1956 (p); *The Whip*, 1957 (p); *A Form of Women*, 1959 (p); *For Love: Poems, 1950–1960*, 1962; *The Island*, 1963 (n); *Poems: 1950–1965*, 1966; *Words*, 1967 (p); *Mazatlan: Sea*, 1969 (p); *Pieces*, 1969 (p); *The Charm: Early and Uncollected Poems*, 1970; *A Quick Graph: Collected Notes and Essays*, 1970; *As Now It Would Be Snow*, 1971 (p); *St. Martin's*, 1971 (p); *A Day Book*, 1972 (p); *Listen*, 1972 (d); *Contexts of Poetry*, 1973 (interviews); *Thirty Things*, 1974 (p); *Away*, 1976 (p); *Selected Poems*, 1976; *Later*, 1978 (p); *Hello: A Journal, Feb. 29–May 3, 1976*, 1978; *Mabel: A Story, and Other Prose*, 1979 (s); *Was That a Real Poem? and Other Essays*, 1979; *Charles Olson and Robert Creeley: Complete Correspondence*, 5 vols., 1980–82; *Mirrors*, 1983 (p); *Collected Poems, 1945–1975*, 1983; *Collected Prose*, 1984 (n, s, rd); *Memory Gardens*, 1986 (p); *Collected Prose*, 1988; *Irving Layton and Robert Creeley: The Complete Correspondence*, 1990; *Windows*, 1990 (p); *Selected Poems*, 1991; *Echoes*, 1994 (p); *Daybook of a Virtual Poet*, 1998; *So There: Poems 1976–1983*, 1998

CULLEN, Countee (1903–1946)

There are numerous things which Mr. Cullen as a poet has not yet begun to do, and there are some which he will never do, but in this first volume (*Color*) he makes it clear that he has mastered a tune. Few recent books of poems have been so tuneful—at least so tuneful in the execution of significant themes. . . . Mr. Cullen's skill appears in the clarity and the certainty of his song. . . . If Mr. Cullen faces any danger it is this—that he shall call facility a virtue rather than the aspect of a virtue.

Mark Van Doren. *New York Herald Tribune Book Section.* Jan. 10, 1926. p. 3

Cullen is, it seems to me, just a little too much the product of our American colleges. His earlier work was more his own. This is true not only because his earlier poems had to do, often, with the emotions of the Negro race, but because they were more direct statements of the poet's own sensitivity. If the earlier poems were less perfect technically, they had more complete sincerity. Sincerity is not necessarily art, of course, but while a poet speaks his own language, however crudely, there is hope that he may develop the necessary skill of the true artist. When he speaks too often in literary phrase and image, he ceases to be significant. These last lyrics and sonnets of Cullen's have this defect.

Eda Lou Walton. *New York Herald Tribune Book Section.* Sept. 15, 1935. p. 17

Where Oxford dons have so often failed, an American Negro writer has succeeded. Mr. Cullen has rendered Euripides's best known tragedy (*The Medea*) into living and utterable English. He has made little attempt to convey the poetry of the original, preferring to concentrate on dramatic situation and realistic portrayal of character. The result is a very forceful and poignant re-creation of the story of the barbarian sorcerer. . . . Mr. Cullen's version is admirably suited to the exigencies of the contemporary stage. For an adaptation which does not pretend to be a literal translation, it follows the original closely, giving English equivalents for all but a few of the speeches in the Greek.

Philip Blair Rice. *The Nation.* Sept. 18, 1935. p. 336

Cullen's verses skip; those by Hughes glide. But in life Hughes is the merry one. Cullen was a worrier. . . . Equally evident . . . was Cullen's tendency to get his inspiration, his rhythms and patterns as well as much of his substance from books and the world's lore of scholarship. . . . Cullen was in many ways an old-fashioned poet. . . . About half of his "best poems" were written while he was a student of New York University, and it was during these years that he first came up for consideration as an authentic American writer, the goal to which he aspired. . . . Cullen did not live to see another springtime resurgence of his own creative powers comparable with the impulse that produced his first three books of poetry, the books which give his selected poems most of their lilt and brightness.

Arna Bontemps. *Saturday Review.* March 22, 1947. pp. 12–3, 44

As we read Cullen's racial poetry today, our feelings are mixed. Even though we understand and appreciate the larger implications

of the alien-and-exile theme, we recognize its basic fallacy just as Cullen himself seemed to recognize it in *The Black Christ*. We also recognize that protest poetry of every type has lost much of its former popularity. We realize too that in the age of "new criticism" and intellectual verse, Cullen's style and general approach to poetry are dated; the Pre-Raphaelite delicacy of his lyrics is lost upon a generation which can find value only in "metaphysical" poetry. And yet in spite of these drawbacks, I believe that Cullen's racial poems will live. They will live first of all because they are a record of and a monument to the New Negro Movement, and as such they will always be important to the literary historian. Second, they will live for the social historian because they have made articulate the agony of racial oppression during a dark period in our continuing struggle for democracy. And most important of all, a few of them will live because they are good poems—good enough to survive the ravages of time and changing taste.

Arthur P. Davis. *Phylon.* Sept., 1953. p. 400

[Cullen] was, and probably still is, considered the least race-conscious of the Negro poets. . . . Nevertheless, it was because of the color of his skin that Countee Cullen was more aware of the racial poetry and could not be at all times "sheer poet." This was clearly a problem for Cullen—wanting to write lyrics on love, death, and beauty—always so consciously aware of his race. This can be seen, for instance, in his poem "Uncle Jim," where the struggle is neatly portrayed through the young boy, thinking of Keats, and his uncle, bitter with thoughts of the difference between being a black man or a white man in our society. . . .

For Cullen, then, the racial problem was always there, even when one was thinking of odes by Keats, and he was impelled—*in spite of everything I can do*—to write about this subject. This was the cause of much weakness in his writing, as well as some strength; for there are poems about race which have an emotional intensity that most of his white peers could not have matched.

Margaret Perry. *A Bio-Bibliography of Countee P. Cullen* (Greenwood). 1971. pp. 26–8

Few of the notable Negro poets of the 1920s worked with the pagan primitive theme as much as Cullen (indeed, it appears in only a few of his poems). . . . And Cullen's efforts were confused as well, because they were not merely attempts to explore the source of African nativity, the wellsprings of Negro spirit and identity. But for that poet, Africa and "paganism" were instruments in his personal rebellion against the Christian church. His religious skepticism was always voiced as stemming from race consciousness: "Lord, I fashion dark gods, too." Cullen's attitudes about Africa and primitivism are enigmatic because they are only tools of this deeper revolt. "The Shroud of Color," which is free of primitivism, is a far more successful statement of his problem with Christianity than "Heritage." And while the latter is probably the author's best known work, the former is far the better poem for its clarity. Actually, even his struggle with faith was emblematic of a far deeper and more traumatic rebellion which his training in the genteel convention ill-equipped him to handle. Both as a person and a poet, Cullen tried to free himself of an unusually close relationship with his adoptive father, a minister. His personal rebellion was slight and genteel. Searching always—and futilely—for an adequate *persona*, Cullen toyed with the self-image of the pagan poet.

Nathan Irvin Huggins. *Harlem Renaissance* (Oxford—N.Y.). 1971. pp. 164–5

In his earliest poems, Cullen . . . wanted to believe that impulses of his African heritage surged past his censoring consciousness and forced him to repudiate the white gods of Western Civilization. Cullen's Africa, however, was a utopia in which to escape from the harsh actualities of America, and the heritage a myth on which he hoped to erect a new faith to comfort himself in a world seemingly dedicated to furthering the interests of white men. . . .

As the African impulse waned, Cullen knelt before the altar of love, but there also false gods demanded sacrifices he would not offer. Like a wanderer disconsolate after a worldwide search, Cullen turned back to Christ. But he still could not rely upon the white god who governed the Methodist Church in which he had been reared; he could not believe a white god capable of comprehending the depths of a black man's suffering. Therefore, he fashioned for himself a black Christ with ''dark, despairing features.'' This image, however, furnished scant comfort; Cullen knew that his own creation could not correct mankind's transgressions. Without faith, without vision, Cullen, whom Saunders Redding has compared with Shakespeare's ethereal Ariel, lost his power to sing and soar above the fleshly Calibans.

Darwin T. Turner. *In a Minor Chord: Three Afro-American Writers and Their Search for Identity* (Southern Illinois). 1971. p. 61

BIBLIOGRAPHY

Color, 1925 (p); *The Ballad of the Brown Girl*, 1927 (p); *Copper Sun*, 1927 (p); *The Black Christ*, 1929 (p); *One Way to Heaven*, 1932 (n); *The Medea*, 1935 (p); *The Lost Zoo*, 1940 (s, p); *My Lives and How I Lost Them*, 1942 (s); *St. Louis Woman*, 1946 (d); *On These I Stand* (selected poems), 1947; *My Soul's High Song: The Collected Writings of Countee Cullen, Voice of the Harlem Renaissance*, 1991

CUMMINGS, Edward Estlin (1894–1962)

I have heard two personal friends of E. E. Cummings debating as to whether his prosodical and punctuational gymnastics have not been a joke at the expense of the critics of poetry. One of them thinks Cummings will some day come out and announce that he has been joking; the other insists with fervent and faithful admiration that he is really as crazy as he seems.

Max Eastman. *The Literary Mind* (Scribner). 1932. p. 103

What Mr. Cummings likes or admires, what he holds dear in life, he very commonly calls flowers, or dolls, or candy—terms with which

he is astonishingly generous; as if he thought by making his terms general enough their vagueness could not matter, and never noticed that the words so used enervate themselves in a kind of hardened instinct.

R.P. Blackmur. *The Double Agent* (Arrow). 1935. p. 20

Leave him alone, and he will play in a corner for hours, with his fragilities, his colors, and his delight in the bright shapes of all the things he sees. . . . The important point about E.E. Cummings is, however, that he was not left alone. He was dumped out into the uninnocent and unlyrical world. . . . His lyricism, shy enough at best, ran completely for cover, and he turned upon the nightmare worlds of reality, partly with the assumed callousness and defensive self-mockery of the very sensitive, and partly with the white and terrible anger of the excessively shy.

S.I. Hayakawa. *Poetry*. Aug., 1938. pp. 285–6

No American poet of the twentieth century has ever shown so much implied respect for the conventions of his milieu through conscious blasphemy as E. E. Cummings. If Cummings's verse seemed ''revolutionary'' and radical (which it was in the sense that its wit was concerned with the roots of syntax and grammar) it was because its life was and still is so completely surrounded by conventions. . . . The entire question of Cummings's maturity in the writing of his poetry has been and still remains a private matter. In the light of Cummings's accomplishments and in the recognition of the boundaries or limits that they have circumscribed, it is very nearly an impertinence for anyone to tell him to ''grow up,'' for one must not forget that he is one of the finest lyric poets of all time.

Horace Gregory and Marya Zaturenska. *History of American Poetry* (Harcourt). 1947. pp. 337–47

The Enormous Room has the effect of making all but a very few comparable books that came out of the War look shoddy and worn. It has been possible to re-read it, as I have done . . . and always to find it undiminished. . . . Cummings . . . encountered, in that huge barracks at La Ferté-Macé which he calls the Enormous Room, a sad assortment of men. They from being his companions in misery become, whether they speak or not—and the most eloquent are those who have the smallest command of words—his counsellors in compassion. . . . The mind provides no answer to the problem of suffering. . . . The answer, even for a poet, is not in words. . . . For what can oppose the poverty of the spirit, but the pride of the body? . . . And in Cummings there is from now on, in all he writes, an exaltation of the lowly and lively. He is himself, and he accepts his common lot.

John Peale Bishop. *Collected Essays* (Scribner). 1948. pp. 89–91

If Cummings is undistinguished as a thinker, he is always surprising as a creative craftsman. He is simultaneously the skillful draftsman, the legpulling clown, the sensitive commentator and the ornery boy. The nosethumbing satirist is continually interrupted by the singer of brazenly tender lyrics. A modern of the moderns, he displays a seventeenth-century obsession with desire and death; part Cavalier, part metaphysician, he is a shrewd manipulator of language, and his style—gracefully erotic or downright indecent—is strictly his own.

Louis Untermeyer. *Modern American Poetry* (Harcourt). 1950. p. 509

We see him ever as an individual, liking and respecting other individuals, but hating the masses as masses, hating governments, hating war, hating propaganda (ours or anybody else's), hating machinery, hating science. Willing to settle for nothing less than perfection, he is a great hater, although he is also a great lover, perhaps the most ardent or at any rate the most convincing poet of love in our day. Whom and what he loves he loves deeply, but for him the existence of love demands the expression of anger, contempt, disgust for what is unworthy of love. That is what he is and what he has been since coming of age, though practice has refined him in the art of being nobody-but-himself.

Granville Hicks. *Saturday Review*. Nov. 22, 1958. p. 14

Cummings' concept of the individual did not emerge fully developed at the beginning of his career to be reaffirmed through successive volumes of poetry without any perceptible change or increase in significance, as has too often been stated. Rather, the early volumes primarily celebrate the simple joy of living through the senses, though they also contain some of Cummings' best satiric pieces.

The middle volumes, beginning approximately with *is 5* in 1926, reaching a culmination with *no thanks* in 1935, and showing evidence of a changing emphasis with *50 Poems* in 1940, reveal a heightened and defensively sensitive awareness of the individual in relation to his social environment. . . .

With the publication of *50 Poems* another important dimension becomes evident in Cummings' poetry. Beginning approximately with this volume and extending through *95 Poems* in 1958 and *73 Poems* in 1963, we find Cummings examining the positive impact that the individual exerts upon his fellow men. As we have seen, what the individual has to offer, what the pattern of his life illustrates, is love. He is a practitioner of love for life, for others, and for one particular beloved. In the latest poems the individual emerges as the only true exponent of love.

Robert E. Wegner. *The Poetry and Prose of E.E. Cummings* (Harcourt). 1965. pp. 80–1

. . . cummings' free style is exemplary in the sense that he seems never to imply, ''Exactly imitate me!'' but rather, ''Here is what one of us can do with the conventions and still communicate effectively (at least on a par with most attempts); so why not go and see what you can do in *your* way? Each of us is valuable to others chiefly as he is honestly himself.'' Together, the love-poems and the satires, the many pages of vital, maturing poetry from *Tulips and Chimneys* (1923) to *73 Poems* (1963), present a broad spectrum, from brutal irony against what he felt unworthy of human beings to pure lyricism, celebrating the love which he found inseparable from truth and beauty, and the best, even the noblest, human experience. If he shocks, it is not to lower standards but to raise them—invariably in the direction of valuing and respecting

individual worth and freedom, toward realizing and cherishing the dignity in each created soul.

Robert G. Tucker in *The Twenties*, edited by Richard E. Langford and William E. Taylor (Everett Edwards). 1966. p. 26

Although in so frankly a primitivistic ethos as Cummings', ideal perception and response are not really a matter of exotic vision, Cummings is inclined to make the same kind of distinctions that one would find in objectivist theory. There are the deluded rationalists (bourgeois society) and the enlightened irrationalists (poets). . . . Similarly, Cummings' ideas concerning the ''self'' and its relation to the external world, nature, follow a logic not remote from the objectivist's. To begin with, identity with ''Life'' means ''self-transcendence'' and what would be called by ''most people'' nonidentity, since to be ''most truly alive'' means to transcend the social self and to acquire the natural one (selflessness) that comes with response to the universe.

L.S. Dembo. *Conceptions of Reality in Modern American Poetry* (California). 1966. p. 119

Generally we may say that Cummings' typographical inventions are instruments for controlling the evocation of the poem in the mind of the reader; they are means of mitigating the temporal necessities of language with its falsification of the different, temporal rhythms of experience itself. Cummings is a painter, of course, and most of his poems are two things, auditory art and visual art, nonrepresentational pictures whose appearance on the page is essential to the artist's intention. (His correspondence with his publishers confirms this.) There is, typically, an intimate connection between the poem's appearance and the proper control of reading rate, emotional evocation, and aesthetic inflection. Indeed, one has the sense, reading these ''picture poems'' (his phrase) aloud, that one is translating inadequately from one language to another, with proportionate loss to the mere listener. This is an especially striking realization when one remembers that Cummings himself read his poems memorably, indeed read his own work better than any other living poet. One wonders what the greatness would be if he could hear in Cummings' voice what is added in the eye.

John Logan in *Modern American Poetry*, edited by Jerome Mazzaro (McKay). 1970. p. 260

I certainly don't think Cummings' reputation is helped by the persistent preservation, inviolate, of all 739 poems in the new edition [of *Complete Poems*]; for his was a narrow art; he repeated himself shamelessly and went through practically no development of theme or method once he had settled into a niche. If poems were paintings the 739 could be bought and sold and hung with joy in 739 individual parlors, but since they are not paintings they huddle together uncomfortably in this heavyweight volume and represent him as a heavyweight poet, which he was not: he was a gloriously special poet who could do what he could do.

Particularly since he prided himself on his uniqueness—and in fact thought of any act of creation as primarily an individual's assertion of uniqueness—it seems a mistake to have the 739 wandering around forever in a lump. He deserves a slimmer, brighter image, for he remains a delight for youth. It doesn't matter that while he tells youth not to pay any attention to the syntax of things he is himself infatuated by the syntax of things; he comes over loud and clear as an indefatigable promoter of spring, love and the private life, and an equally indefatigable condemner of most of our faceless modernity.

Reed Whittemore. *New Republic*. Oct. 21, 1972. p. 32

Where Emerson was essentially a Neoplatonist, Cummings was a scoffer in his youth, then more and more a Christian. He does not think of Christ as the most perfect man, in Emerson's way of speaking, but rather prays to him as a divine intercessor. In theological terms his God is less immanent than Emerson's and more transcendent. He says in a poem addressed to God—here I translate into prose—"How should any tasting, touching, hearing, seeing, breathing, merely human being—lifted from the no of all nothing—doubt unimaginable You?" As regards a future life, one of the subjects on which Emerson remained ambiguous, Cummings lets us infer that he believes in the resurrection of the flesh.

Malcolm Cowley. *The Yale Review*. Spring, 1973. p. 352

The mystery of E.E. Cummings's great aborted talent is not solved, only deepened, by his *Complete Poems*. His brave quixotry . . . has made him one of the poster gurus of a new generation: "one's not half two. It's two are halves of one," says the motto shining poignantly on a brilliant yellow-orange background, with a single flower as shy adornment of this revealed truth. In fact, Cummings's first and last lines are nearly always, as in this case, his memorable ones, and most of his poems sag in the middle. While we all go round remembering "nobody, not even the rain, has such small hands," or "the single secret will still be man," or "there's a hell of a good universe next door, let's go," we rarely recall what led up to these declarations. Something is wrong with the relation of parts to wholes in Cummings: we do not receive, as Coleridge thought we should, "such delight from the *whole*, as is compatible with a distinct gratification from each component *part*." Cummings was capable of stunning parts, and these parts glitter on the page like sparklers, float up like scraps of hurdy-gurdy music—but the sparks don't organize into constellations, the music falls apart into notes and remains unorchestrated. "Our genuine admiration of a great poet," says Coleridge, "is a continuous *under-current* of feeling; it is everywhere present, but seldom anywhere as a separate excitement." Whether this is true or not, it is certain that for the most part Cummings provides only separate excitements, and is for that reason beloved of the young, who vibrate to his local effects and ask no more.

Helen Vendler. *The Yale Review*. Spring, 1973. p. 412

The poetry of E.E. Cummings has made a lasting impact upon twentieth-century literature. For one thing he taught his audience how to read him. To date four editions of his *Complete Poems*, each with an expanded number of items, have been published, and many of his earlier volumes have been reissued. His poems continue to appear in anthologies, particularly those for literary study in college courses. The persona that the poems project has a special appeal for young, sensitive readers who are aware of the overwhelming forces, social and political, that surround them and whose emotions surge as they grope for ways to adjust to their world. Cummings's self-characterization as "i," the "non-hero," expresses for them their joy in life, their conflicts of desire, their push against authority, and their desire to grow. . . .

In addition Cummings showed the way in which he could choose ordinary scenes and experiences and make them become little myths of twentieth-century life whether they were the childhood activities of Cambridge, the street happenings of New York, or encounters with the features of rural life in New Hampshire.

As for his love poems and his treatments of natural phenomena, he was continuing the Romantic tradition in a time when the harsh realities of urbanization and the pervasive intrusions of technology were bruising the sensibilities of modern human beings and blunting the awareness of the essential self and the consciousness of individual feelings.

But the exploration of the possibilities of linguistic expression was his special contribution. His legacy to later writers was the spectacle of his pushing language to its extremes. Joyce, Eliot, Pound, Dos Passos, and Faulkner were the major innovators of his time, but Cummings did not imitate them. He responded in spirit to their work but he made his own innovations, inspired especially by the modern movements in the visual arts: Impressionism and Postimpressionism, Cubism and Futurism, Dada and Surrealism. His poetic practice shows continuing experiment and growth over a stretch of forty-five years so that like Eliot and Yeats he was a poet of two generations. Not all of his attempts were aesthetic successes, nor was he critically stringent in what he allowed himself to publish. But an extensive selection of his poetic output would yield a huge body of permanently valuable work. . . .

Richard S. Kennedy. *E.E. Cummings Revisited* (New York: Twayne, 1994), p. 137, 139–40

BIBLIOGRAPHY

The Enormous Room, 1922 (n, m); *Tulips and Chimneys*, 1923 (p); *& (And)*, 1925 (p); *XLI Poems*, 1925 (p); *Is 5*, 1926 (p); *Him*, 1927 (d); *The Village Voice (ViVa)*, 1931 (p); *Eimi*, 1933 (t); *No Thanks*, 1935 (p); *Collected Poems*, 1938; *1 x 1*, 1944 (p); *Anthropos: The Future of Art*, 1944 (e); *Santa Claus*, 1946 (d); *XAIPE*, 1950 (p); *i: Six Nonlectures*, 1953 (a); *Poems 1923–1954*, 1954; *E.E. Cummings: A Miscellany*, 1958, rev. ed., 1965; *95 Poems*, 1958; *73 Poems*, 1963; *Selected Letters*, 1969; *Complete Poems: 1913–1962*, 1972; *Complete Poems*, 1979; *Etcetera: The Unpublished Poems of E.E. Cummings*, 1983; *Complete Poems, 1904–1962*, 1991 [corrected and expanded ed.]; *Selected Poems*, 1994; *Pound/Cummings: The Correspondence of Ezra Pound and E. E. Cummings*, 1996

D

DAHLBERG, Edward (1900–1977)

The author of *Bottom Dogs* is . . . very close to us—he is closer to us, indeed, than we quite care to have literature be. *Bottom Dogs* is the backstreets of all our American cities and towns. . . . The prose of *Bottom Dogs* is derived partly from the American vernacular, but to say this may give a misleading impression—Dahlberg's prose is primarily a literary medium, hard, vivid, racy, exact, and with an odd kind of street-light glamor. I do not agree with D. H. Lawrence . . . that the dominating feeling of the book is repulsion—it would be quite easy for a writer of the harsh or satirical kind to make Dahlberg's material repulsive, but I do not feel that Dahlberg has done so: the temperament through which he has strained the barber-shops, the orphan homes, the bakeries and the dance-halls of his story is, though realistic and precise, rather a gentle and unassertive, and consequently an unembittered, one.

Edmund Wilson. *New Republic*. March 26, 1930. p. 157

Dahlberg's second novel [*From Flushing to Calvary*] emerges from his first—*Bottom Dogs*. Having laid his foundations there, he here uses cinematic photography of the life of Lorry and his mother, Lizzie, in their new environment, the suburban slums of Long Island. . . . Dahlberg's gift lies in his ability to re-create actuality, either by a process of building up detail; as in his story of the orphan days in *Bottom Dogs*, or swiftly, sharply, as in this novel. There is no character study here. There is neither psychology nor ideas nor meaning nor interpretation. When he gives the thoughts of his people, it is their immediate conscious thoughts which interest him. The thinking is merely a phase of the realism. And his people are moths that flit in and out of the path of an intense light until, singed and defeated, they fall away into darkness. But during the intervals of light he sets them forth with remarkable accuracy, and in the same way he sets forth their background with definitive sureness.

F. T. Marsh. *The Nation*. Nov. 16, 1932. pp. 483–4

Dahlberg is adept at taking grotesque, harried and abysmal characters, and prodding them to become more and more themselves. The persons of his books whom he has selected for particular dislike, he pursues with a corrosive brand of comment which constantly crashes through their own concepts of their lives, like a heckler who breaks a debater's sequence at every point by shouting out unwieldy questions. Dahlberg's style is highly mannered, with a distinctiveness that can readily alienate whenever it ceases to attract. . . . Dahlberg has obviously been under great strain in this ailing society, and in his writing he is settling a score.

Kenneth Burke. *New Republic*. Nov. 21, 1934. p. 53

Dahlberg and other writers of his ilk, together with their raving readers and other less studious camp-followers, are but the pseudo-intellectual auxiliaries, in our decadent civilization that they rightly revile, of the "garage proletariat" that they unjustifiably despise. Their claims to an intuitional omniscience are thus another expression of the unlettered "know-all" faith that also characterizes the modern gadget-maniac. The Dahlbergs and those whom they attack thus represent, together, the two elements of disruption that threaten our civilization most gravely: Practical reason and intuitional reason that both pose as pure reason.

Edouard Roditi. *Poetry*. Jan., 1951. p. 238

Not surprisingly, the best depression novels are those which were least mindful of the party line as this was being laid down in the *New Masses* by Michael Gold and Granville Hicks, and proselytized locally over the country by the John Reed Clubs. Edward Dahlberg's *Bottom Dogs*, published in 1930 with a rather inappropriate introduction by D. H. Lawrence, has hardly any overt political feeling at all. But this mordantly whimsical and grotesque book, with its echoes of Mark Twain and Sherwood Anderson, makes very good reading, especially if one had shared the dim image of Dahlberg that came down into the 1940s as some sort of Lawrencian apocalypticist who had once said something important about Melville. The picaresque story has to do with the adventures of Lorry Lewis, who as a young boy is put in an orphanage by his mother, a lady barber with a horrible pair or pince-nez glasses that are always slipping awry, so that she can take up with a Mississippi river-boat captain. There is much sordid realism and much sharp observation in the chapters dealing with the boy's early days in Kansas City and the years in the orphanage with such brilliantly caricatured companions as Herman Mush Tate and Bonehead-Star-Wolfe. The later scenes, in which Lorry Lewis, now a tramp on the eve of the depression, winds up in Los Angeles and gets involved with a group of vegetarian intellectuals and homosexuals in the Y.M.C.A. are very funny. And the chapter about Solomon's Dancepalace is a memorable picture of the underside of the Fitzgerald era.

Richard Chase. *Commentary*. Jan., 1957. p. 69

Mr. Edward Dahlberg's *Can These Bones Live* is an American classic, even if only a few people know it, but what kind of classic, it is difficult to say. Criticism as we write it at present has no place for it, and this means that I probably shall not be able to do justice to my own admiration. Mr. Dahlberg, like Thoreau whom he admires more than any other nineteenth-century American, eludes his contemporaries; he may have to wait for understanding until the historians of ideas of the next generation can place him historically. For we have at present neither literary nor historical standards which can guide us in to Mr. Dahlberg's books written since *Bottom Dogs*, which was published more than thirty years ago. It is significant that he has repudiated this early, naturalistic novel, in spite of the considerable admiration that it won and still retains among a few persons. *Can These Bones Live* may be seen as the summation of a three part visionary and prophetic work which includes *The Flea of Sodom* and *The Sorrows of Priapus*.

We shall get nowhere with Mr. Dahlberg if we begin with an inquiry into his influences and his philosophy; this kind of thinking would inevitably be reductive. We must return repeatedly to the text to ponder the hundreds of aphorisms, epigrams, and paradoxes which add up to an intuitive synthesis of insights which defies logical exposition. . . . His tragic vision of the human condition redeems what might otherwise appear to be a kind of romantic anarchism. . . .

Allen Tate. *Sewanee Review*. Spring, 1961. pp. 314–16

What appears at first to be no more than a rewrite of Dahlberg's *Bottom Dogs*, that expatriate log of a vernacular midwest childhood, a crapulous youth and a lady-barber mother, is in fact a performance of another order entirely—one of the rare examples in our letters of the self overtaken. For this new book *Because I Was Flesh* is the creative reflection (a reflexive as well as a reflective act) of a man upon his own life (autobiography and lyric) and his mother's (hagiography and demonology). By his metamorphosis of the first version of those lives, by what has happened to his prose since that version, we discover how *he* has been changed, what he has learned, lost, won. . . . It is only, at last, in this new book, a memorial instance "because a breath passeth away and cometh not again", that raw event is inspissated by myth and morality, transcending the limitations suggested by comparison with other great American autobiographies.

Richard Howard. *Poetry*. March, 1965. pp. 398–9

The fact is that in *Because I Was Flesh*, Dahlberg has given us a world of the kind we used to find in the great novels, and, that it casts a spell. One forgets that there were, and some still are, living people who walked the earth, for the book envelops us in so authentic an atmosphere that the actualities of time and space die down, and another existence, that of eternity, takes its place. Even the cobblestones of the old streets in Kansas City have their echoes, as does the very grass and sky, and the dinginess of the back-parlor, where Lizzie heats soup in a battered kettle for her squeamish, delicate but remarkably enduring son, is no more than the mirrored light of countless scenes which most modern fiction would have us forget. The very image of a whole woman, sensual, pining, mistaken and utterly appealing in her unworldly attempts to battle with the world is, by this time, a novel event. One even forgets that the son, who flees the mother to find himself, and returns to the mother to beseech for the unknown father, and who must invoke the dream for revelation, is the author, and not the fable. For the fable takes over, as the dream enlightens the author, and the magic of an experience that sought the dark to find the light, casts its mighty spell.

Because I Was Flesh is a great achievement, and, as the culmination of a long, arduous, dedicated, creative venture during which the contraries, the irascible, the didactic were finally reconciled with the *Amor Fati* of acceptance, it is also a triumph.

Josephine Herbst. *Southern Review*. Spring, 1965. p. 351

Edward Dahlberg's imagination is rich in history and myth; his style is fresh in allusion and muscular with verbs. The best of his

work, alive with incantatory rhythms and a prophetic tone, generates the power of psalm or prayer. In the title poem [*Cipango's Hinder Door*], celebrating the innocent antiquity of the western hemisphere, Mr. Dahlberg combines impeccably cadenced free verse with short prose paragraphs in a remarkably successful contrapuntal structure.

As these generalizations imply, this book transcends egocentricity. In a foreword, Allen Tate calls attention to the recurrent myth of Cain and Abel, which, he says, suggests "that the historical past (Abel) is dead and that it can live again only in the timeless intuition of the poet". That seems an oversimplification, partly because other mythological and historical symbols recur—Greek, Central American, North American Indian—and partly because Mr. Dahlberg invokes the past of the race for more specific reasons. Our slaughtered innocents lie there, but so does our lost innocence.

Donald W. Baker. *Poetry*. March, 1967. pp. 403–4

Dahlberg's early novels dealt with the theme of alienation, loneliness, separateness. They showed Lizzie clinging to society by the precarious handhold of other people's bunions, double chins, sagging breasts, stubby chins, and unwanted pregnancies, and her son forced by the hailstorms of the world into a relationship with her that was too close for comfort, so that he longed continually to be free; yet when circumstances did free him for a time, it was always into some hell like the Cleveland Jewish Orphans' Home. These disadvantages would have sunk an ungifted man, turned him permanently into a grumbling failure. In Dahlberg's case, the disadvantages became the title-deed to his own birthright. During his period of re-thinking, he rejected the dominant assumptions of the modern world, including its cultural assumptions, and by a paradox this catapulted him into the imaginative world of Yeats, Eliot, Joyce and Rilke. That he drew his own map of the world is owing to another important element in Dahlberg's character as an artist: his Jewishness.

John Wain. *New York Review of Books*. Jan. 2, 1969. p. 13

Dahlberg's "*Walden*" is his masterpiece, the autobiography *Because I Was Flesh*. In it the American of *The Carnal Myth* (and *The Sorrows of Priapus*) is personified as Dahlberg and his mother, who are mythologized as Ishmael and Hagar wandering in the American urban wilderness. Through the vision and style forged in *The Carnal Myth* (and other works) Dahlberg is able to assimilate their story into the universal aspects of man's nature and its embodiment in the western cultural tradition (especially its classical and Biblical aspects) and thus make of it a specific exemplification of that nature and that tradition. In so doing he overcomes that alienation from other men which all Americans suffer from he believes, but which he suffers more acutely and with more awareness because of his illegitimacy. The book is also an act of expiation, he says, through which he embraces in love the mother he could not fully accept in life. He calls the book "a memoir of my mother's body." In it she is both a human being and an image of the earth, that ultimate source which all of his adventurers in *The Carnal Myth* unknowingly were searching for. In making her such an image and in finally embracing her, Dahlberg has, again, implicitly achieved—in the work at least—release from the American fate; instead of a sterile "treeless ghost" he is a living man in vital connection with man's source, as well as with other men.

Melvin Lyon. *Prairie Schooner*. Spring, 1970. p. 83

BIBLIOGRAPHY

Bottom Dogs, 1930 (n); *From Flushing to Calvary*, 1932 (n); *Those Who Perish*, 1934 (n); *Do These Bones Live*, 1941 (e) (republished in 1960 as *Can These Bones Live*); *Sing, O Barren*, 1947 (e); *The Flea of Sodom*, 1950 (e); *The Sorrows of Priapus*, 1957, rev. ed., 1972 (e); (with Herbert Read) *Truth Is More Sacred*, 1961 (c); *Because I Was Flesh*, 1964 (a); *Alms for Oblivion*, 1964 (e); *Reasons of the Heart*, 1965 (maxims); *The Leafless American*, 1967 (e); *Epitaphs of Our Times*, 1967 (letters); *The Edward Dahlberg Reader*, 1967; *The Carnal Myth*, 1968 (e); *The Confessions of Edward Dahlberg*, 1971 (m); *The Gold of Ophir*, 1972 (e, anthol); *The Olive of Minerva, The Comedy of the Cuckold*, 1976 (n); *Bottom Dogs, From Flushing to Calvary, Those Who Perish, and Hitherto Unpublished and Uncollected Works*, 1976; *Samuel Beckett's Wake and Other Uncollected Prose*, 1989; *In Love, In Sorrow: The Complete Correspondence of Charles Olson and Edward Dahlberg*, 1990

DELANY, Samuel R. (1942–)

Delany's literary style is a combination of subtly derived linguistic techniques coupled with a disturbing liberation of certain structural elements. Within Delany's novels, time, logic, and point of view are cut loose from traditional literary positions, and function relativistically. Yet these free elements are rigidly controlled by the rules of a relativistic universe, thereby fulfilling Delany's comment that technical possibility actualizes metaphor in science fiction. . . .

In the relativistic universe, time is indeed not a constant, but is related to the velocity and frame of reference of the observer. This is dramatized in *Dhalgren*, and although it is a physical reality of the universe we all inhabit, we persist in viewing time as a universal and linear norm.

The uses of time in Delany's novels, here and more notably in *Empire Star* (1966), violate certain conventions of prose fiction. What seems to be a fantastic use of time is in fact a realistic use of time, because time is psychologically a function of the state of the observer and physically a function of the velocity of the observer. In more traditional fiction, the use of psychological time is well understood. But when Delany applies relativistic physical laws to time, the psychological metaphor of variable time becomes confusing, because the metaphor has been-transformed into fact. . . .

The handling of simultaneous material in a necessarily linear form is a good indication of the kind of word-by-word craftsmanship in Delany's prose. In resolving the problem of rendering a "fantastic" or science-fictional sequence realistically, he visualizes the subject matter completely, rather than retreating from it into vague cubist shapes or highly mannered prose. And remarkably, by striving to describe the seams of reality, he breaks through "reality" to describe the perceiving mind as much as the perceived experience. The parenthetical statement is a good example, for it is both a pause in the exposition and a gloss on the transcribed

experience without. Together, reality, observer, and language form a collage of meaning. It is like his concretizing of metaphor. The vaguely like becomes the solid is. Precision is what these two techniques share.

Delany's theoretical concern with the uses of prose appears frequently in his fiction, almost as if the work was a test-bed for linguistic theory. He considers the totality of the story, plot, character, language, etc. to be a *textus*, or web of meaning, within which the text proper resides. The manner in which *textus* translates into text he alludes to with the term metonymy, the concept of language as connotative rather than denotative. . . . It is therefore not unusual to find images of myths, meanings, and memories, as well as convoluted symbolism in Delany's fiction. His concept of language and literature implies this rich depth of layering. . . . That each major group of metonymic meanings has an analogue in the surface of the story is proof enough of that. What Delany does with this technique is to make the reader feel the weight of meaning and symbol around the text, i.e., invoke a *textus* for the story. This enriches the story, and charges the linear tale with alternative meanings, possibilities, and significance. It is another way of transcending the limitations of realism, of working in the subjective mind of the reader. . . .

For Delany, the process of artistic creation is an attempt to derive order from the chaos of experience. More precisely, it is an attempt to reconcile the contrary demands of the subjective perspective of the artist, who must admit to experiencing life from a biased point of view—the structural requirements of formal literary patterns, which can wrench meaning and order from randomness, and the restrictions inherent in language as a medium of transmitting vision. In Delany's prose, neither the subjective nor the objective—neither the chaos of the individual mind's perceiving, nor the artifice of literary device, is given primacy. Just as metaphor is solidified by fact, experience is ordered by the effect of art upon the raw material of the mind, which is able to translate the chaotic elements of life accurately into words. Delany's later novels, especially, are arenas in which life and language confront one another and come together to form a dialectic of literature. Delany's science fiction includes and capitalizes on the tension between scientific theory and linguistic potential.

Peter S. Alterman. *Science-Fiction Studies*. March, 1977, pp. 25–34.

Delany's career is a fascinating one in terms of the cultural development of science fiction. Born in Harlem in 1942, Delany's own transmigration took him into the nascent hippie culture, and in 1962, with the publication of his first novel, *The Jewels of Aptor* (he was 20 at the time), into a world of pulp science fiction then undergoing radical reorientation. In the early 1960s, Campbell's "Golden Age" was over, but it had generated a flood of writers and formulas that poured, from the mid-50s on, into the new medium of paperback novels. Out of this flow, however, a new kind of SF writer was emerging. Judith Merril's blurb on the cover of the Ace Books first edition of *Jewels of Aptor* sees in young Delany "a mythopoetic power comparable only to that of Sturgeon, Ballard, Vonnegut, and Cordwainer Smith." Here we have the emerging line: Sturgeon, link to the Golden Age; Ballard and Vonnegut, British and American surrealists respectively; the indescribable SF fantasist "Cordwainer Smith." Delany's early work, published in the (for the decade) garish and pulpy Ace paperback line, fits at once into this emergent ''mythopoetic'' SF tradition. His career, from this point on, is a voyage, via the ''New Wave'' SF, out of this pulp matrix, into first of all the world of ''literature,'' then (following perhaps the much-discussed exhaustion of that literature), into the academic world of postmodernism, and a university professorship.

From the beginning, it is clear Delany entered science fiction with the desire to be a ''literary'' writer. . . .

Of the early fiction, *The Fall of the Towers* is most interesting in its sense of design and scope; in terms of the intricate variational *system* Delany builds here, this large work looks forward to the labyrinthine complexities of *Dhalgren* (1975), and even those of the Nevèrÿon series (begun with *Tales of Nevèrÿon,* 1979). Already in this early trilogy, we have a textual web Derrida would be proud of. . . .

In 1966, still in Ace Books, Delany published two novels: *Empire Star* and *Babel-17.* The latter novel won the Nebula Award, given not by fans but by writers of SF, and is an homage to the craft of this novel, which in its tightness of construction and highly developed mythic resonances, ushers in what many believe the high period of Delany's art, set forth in two subsequent novels: *The Einstein Intersection* (1967) and *Nova* (1968), and in the short stories collected in *Driftglass.* . . .

Einstein is Delany's masterpiece of suggestive complexity. Like *Babel,* it is a tightly patterned work; yet in its greater mythopoetic suggestiveness, its structures resist analysis. This novel too approaches the human condition as enmeshed in a human *system.* Yet, if in *Babel* the system is engaged as primarily a grammatical or linguistic problem, *Einstein* operates less on the level of mankind's words than its myths—the patterns of behavior or codes of action that contain its system of values. . . .

The third great novel of this mid-60s period is *Nova* (1968). It is a longer work, and one in which the quest myth, the search for the grail, attains epic proportions as it extends across galaxies, taking as its decor the space-opera in the high Doc Smithian sense. Delany's full fascination for Romantic mythology is deployed in this work. . . .

A gap of seven years separates *Nova* from the publication of a very different novel, *Dhalgren* (1975). The very opposite of Delany's earlier concise and symbolically dense textures, *Dhalgren* is a long, loose exploration of a quite plausible American inner city in decay. The novel is science fictional only in the sense that two moons and a giant red sun have risen inexplicably over this urban landscape. Delany here for the first time is doing what his later fiction revels in: playing with the generic codes that he sees marking reader expectations. . . .

If *Dhalgren* is under the sign of Joycean metafiction, his next novel, *Triton* (1976), is under that of theoretician Michel Foucault. This novel, shifting decor from an isolated contemporary city on Earth to an equally ''alternate'' urban landscape on a moon of Neptune, is an extended, and often tedious, exploration of the Foucaultian theme of ''heterotopia'': sexual and gender power, and the multivalent nature of social systems in an experimental context. . . .

Perhaps the real ancestor of Nevèrÿon, pairing off with it as *Dhalgren* pairs with *Triton,* is the piece of literary pornography, *The Tides of Lust* (1973). We have a Gulf Coast contemporary setting, minimal evocation of SF codes (the Black Captain compares boats and ports with spaceships and stars), and a lush overlay of literary allusion—the Captain is on a Faustian quest, doomed to

come 24 times before the cock crows; Proctor the artist, ''doomed to restoring old work with the energy I want to put toward new,'' paints clocks ''whose long hand is a penis, the short, a hirsute sack.'' This preciosity covers, again in a world whose characters are free to explore society as system, what has become an ''ambiguous dystopia,'' an obsessive world of perversity, sexual violence, pederasty, and coprophagy. The same kind of curious ''experimentation'' marks the Nevèrÿon books, which begin in earnest with *Nevèrÿona* (1983, linked stories), and proceed through *Flight from Nevèrÿon* (1985, more stories), to *The Bridge of Lost Desire* (1987). These, along with the 1988 revision of the earlier *Tales of Nevèrÿon* (1979), comprise a vast set of ''fictions'' where, marked by open ''theoretical'' pleasure of manipulating codes, formulas, and signs, all sense of the fictional ''life'' of the story, however debased it might be in sword-and-sorcery fantasy, is gone. These works, filled with self-reflexive poses and disquisitions on the polyvalence of ethics, values, and, most notably, problems of economic systems (conceived in the semiotic-Marxian vein of a critic like Roland Barthes), are every bit as tedious as the didactic digressions of the late Heinlein, if more pretentious. What makes works like *Einstein Intersection* and *Nova* so powerful is Delany's ability to *deepen* and enrich SF formulas with the mythopoetic resonances that once belonged to their ''epic'' plotlines. To do so, however, a writer must in a sense suspend disbelief, and take the monomyth seriously, as a dominant cultural and human pattern. Delany's later fiction, following the ''theoretical'' deconstructive questionings of the same French thinkers who dominate academic criticism in U.S. universities today, loses itself in its own labyrinth of roles, codes, and system-building.

In the Nevèrÿon books, increasingly, Delany takes up such topics as bisexuality and the AIDS epidemic. Some have seen the switch in Delany's publishing venues, from mass market paperbacks to small press and university press editions, as a result of market censorship: these are forbidden themes for the SF market. I would argue however that Delany, writing more and more openly under the aegis of ''deconstructionism,'' and taking on issues of gender deviance and social guilt associated with the AIDS question, has simply shifted narratees. He is no longer writing for the science fiction fan world (whose generic codes he better than anybody else knows), but for the university graduate student and professor. This milieu is today caught up in theoretical debates over ''power'' in the Foucaultian sense; its pundits and students welcome a bisexual, African American writer who engages these debates, and who, as well as any academic critic, speaks the language of the French masters. Quite simply, Delany is not writing for the mass market SF reader any more.

This shift is more than clear in his most recent publications. *Nevèrÿona,* for example, has recently been reissued in a lavish university press edition (Wesleyan University Press, 1988), given a tasty non-generic cover, and adorned with obfuscating quotes from prominent critics: Fredric Jameson calls the series ''a major and unclassifiable achievement in contemporary American literature.'' Delany himself has played enough jokes on the unclassifiability of generic forms to make this statement a joke on the critics. More significant yet is the publication, 20 years after its being written, of Delany's *other* piece of pornography, *Hogg* (1994). Published by Black Ice Books, again with a classy abstract cover (and an x-rated warning on the back), *Hogg* is again hailed as a ''literary'' achievement. Norman Mailer (an authoritative voice when speaking for the criminal artist) tells us that ''there is no question *Hogg*

. . . is a serious book with literary merit.'' Another quote calls it ''a terrifying journey into the body and soul of a man who embodies all the nightmarish excesses of our century.'' The novel itself, from page one, is a spewing forth of sexual and bodily depravity, which makes it, like all pornography, eminently boring. If anything it is a symptom of our times, not a critical anatomy. Written in the early 70s as a literary exercise, it is lauded in the 1990s as a portrait of Jeffrey Dahmer.

Much of Delany's most recent work is either autobiography, or critical essays, the university scholar's main mode of writing. His exercise in literary autobiography, *The Motion of Light in Water: East Village Sex and Science Fiction Writing,* an attempt to capture the milieu of the 1960s hippie culture in New York, is for the most part anecdotal. Essays and articles include *Wagner/Artaud,* today an almost mainstream scholarly topic; *The Straits of Messina* (Serconia Press, 1989) features critical articles by Delany's alter ego Leslie K. Steiner, a composite of names of famous academic critics. Most recently, Delany has published (again in University Press of New England) *Silent Interviews: On Language, Race, Science Fiction, and Some Comics* (1994), where he talks again of reading codes for SF and other genre forms. The most recent fiction he has published fits these sophisticated semiotic analyses like its matching glove: *They Fly at Çiron* (Incunabula Press, 1993). It is another piece of meta-sword-and-sorcery in the Nevèrÿon vein (and complete with complex diacritics in the title).

In conclusion, Delany is following a career pattern analogous to that of fellow Ace Books author in the 1960s Ursula K. Le Guin. Le Guin has spoken of lifting herself, through the craft of fiction, out of the ''saurian ooze'' of her early pulp SF beginnings, into a world of literary and social high seriousness and ''relevance.'' What has occurred, however, is what happened to Antaeus when held up from touching his Earth roots—enfeeblement. Here the result is academic effeteness. Works like *The Left Hand of Darkness* and *The Einstein Intersections* or *Nova* are powerful because they fully engage the deep river of the science fiction culture. They are new works, because they work within, and out of, the old formulas and patterns that, in SF, cover even deeper mythic paradigms. To trade this for a literary or academic ivory tower means today what it has always meant—abandoning storytelling in its primal sense.

> George Slusser. In *St. James Guide to Science Fiction Writers, 4th edition,* ed. Jay P. Pederson (St. James Press, 1996).

BIBLIOGRAPHY
The Jewels of Aptor, 1962 (n); *Captives of the Flame*, 1963 (n), revised as *Out of the Dead City*, 1968; *The Towers of Toron*, 1964 (n); *City of a Thousand Suns*, 1965 (n); *The Ballad of Beta-2*, 1965 (n); *Empire Star*, 1966 (n); *Babel-17*, 1966 (n); *The Einstein Intersection*, 1967 (n); *Nova*, 1968 (n); *Driftglass: Ten Tales of Speculative Fiction*, 1971 (s); *The Tides of Lust*, 1973 (n), revised as *Equinox*, 1994; *Dhalgren*, 1975 (n); *Triton*, 1976 (n), published as *Trouble on Triton: An Ambiguous Heterotopia*, 1996; *The Jewel-Hinged Jaw: Notes on the Language of Science Fiction*, 1977 (c), revised edition, 1978; *The American Shore: Meditations on a Tale of Science Fiction by Thomas M. Disch*, 1978 (c); *Empire: A Visual Novel*, 1978 (n); *Heavenly Breakfast: An Essay on the Winter of Love*, 1979 (m); *Tales of Nevèrÿon*, 1979 (n); *Distant Stars*, 1981 (n); *Nevèrÿona, or, The Tale of Signs and Cities*, 1983 (n); *Starboard Wine: More Notes on the Language of Science Fiction*, 1984 (c); *Stars in My Pocket Like Grains of Sand*, 1984 (n); *Flight from Nevèrÿon*, 1985 (n); *The Bridge of Lost Desire*, 1987 (n), as Return to Nevèrÿon, 1994; *The Motion of Light in Water: Sex and Science Fiction Writing in the East Village, 1957-1965*, 1988 (m), unredacted edition, 1993; *Wagner/Artaud: A Play of Nineteenth and Twentieth Century Critical Fictions*, 1988 (c); *The Star Pits*, 1989 (n); *Straits of Messina*, 1989 (e); *They Fly at Çiron*, 1992 (n); *The Mad Man*, 1994 (n); *Hogg*, 1994 (n); *Atlantis: Three Tales*, 1995 (s); *Longer Views: Extended Essays*, 1996 (e); *Bread and Wine*, 1998 (m)

DELILLO, Don (1936–)

Although his eight novels have been widely and well reviewed, and although several—*End Zone, Americana,* and *Ratner's Star*—are formally innovative, [Don] DeLillo has received comparatively little academic attention. Although *End Zone* is a particularly explicit and perhaps Derrida-influenced deconstructive work, a novel in which DeLillo's intellectual and artistic sophistication is plainly evident, its subversions are largely ignored, whereas Coover's *Universal Baseball Association*, to which *End Zone* is similar, is explicated again and again. *End Zone* also has, as a ''sports novel,'' readerly interests that the more academic or militantly theoretical novelists exclude, interests or expectations that, once denied, create a wider play of internal differences than more narrow, writerly texts can offer. ''Midfiction'' is the term Alan Wilde has coined for recent writers, such as Barthelme, Stanley Elkin, and Max Apple, who have synthesized or compromised experimental and realistic techniques. *End Zone* and the best of DeLillo's other books are, rather than ''midfictions,'' polarfictions, combinations of unusual extremes, popular subgenres such as the detective story, disaster book, or science fiction mixed with profound ideas and forms from extraliterary sources—linguistics, anthropology, cybernetics, mathematics, and neurophysiology. Polarization, says Derrida in *Of Grammatology*, is the structure of language. DeLillo's polarizations in *End Zone*, as well as in *Americana, Ratner's Star, The Names,* and *White Noise*, create a plurality of orientations— inward to the processes of language and fiction, outward to psychological, social, and ecological relations, and outward as well to the readers solicited and confuted by DeLillo's rhetoric.

> Thomas Le Clair. ''Deconstructing the Logos: Don DeLillo's *End Zone*.'' *Modern Fiction Studies*. Spring, 1987, pp. 105–6

In general, DeLillo is haunted both by an attraction to pockets of cultural marginality, and by a dread that the currency of such marginality in contemporary political art is a trap—including, by the way, the marginality of contemporary art itself: ''How I would enjoy being told the novel is dead,'' he has one dreamily romantic character say, ''How liberating, to work in the margins, outside a central perception.'' It is important, though, to see his wavering *ressentiment* as the underside of a deep longing for some such discourse of opposition, and a despair at being denied such positions by his own—and postmodernism's—attitudes toward language. The ultimate lesson of DeLillo's novels, in political terms, is a warning that postmodernism badly needs a way of shaping a political discourse that is unified by something other than the position of its speakers. The most useful complaint of the novels is that the postmodern discourse of political opposition is dangerously built on a shallow mythology about social origins that limits its own political possibilities. Certainly, within such a discourse, the white male writer who seeks to discover his own political voice will necessarily find his desire for opposition to be unspeakable.

John Kucich. "Postmodern Politics: Don DeLillo and the Plight of the White Male Writers." *Michigan Quarterly Review*. Spring, 1988, p. 341

Given his diffidence toward his readers, and the games and puzzles he confronts them with, and given his inclination to dress his ideas in masquerade, it's no wonder that he has been misjudged. "The writer is working against the age," he told an interviewer in 1983, "and so he feels some satisfaction in not being widely read. He is diminished by an audience." Furthermore, DeLillo has taken pains to separate himself from his characters. He neither likes nor dislikes them, he says; he recognizes them and reports their attitudes, leaving it up to the reader to decide the degree to which he shares or rejects their sentiments. (I think he does care about their ideas, although he is professedly indifferent to them as "persons," and he isn't always so detached as he claims to be.)

Yet it so happens that a good many speakers in his novels from *Americana* to *Libra* roundly and eloquently savage American society and culture. In brief, their collective indictment might be summed up as follows: the country is "totally engulfed by all the so-called worst elements of our national life and character." It is populated with lonely, bored, empty, fearful people inured to abominations and complicit, whether they realize it or not, in the destruction of what they ostensibly revere—including the treasured beliefs and artifacts of the past. Perceived from abroad, America signifies ignorant, blind, and contemptuous corporate power, "the whole enormous rot and glut and glare" of its popular culture spreading across the world like a cancer. It is "big business, big army, and big government all visiting each other in company planes for the sole purpose of playing golf and talking money."

This hyperbolical indictment is usually voiced by wacky or disintegrating personalities launched on obsessional quests. They may serve as vents for DeLillo's own vagrant mediations, but there's no reason to assume that in unequivocally rejecting an "Amerika" devoid of "beauty, dignity, order, proportion" they are invariably speaking for him. DeLillo is no ideological Jeremiah. He thrives on "blaring" social imperfections and is fascinated by the one-dimensional, ruthless half-men, the single-minded system planners and management consultants and nuclear strategists who exhibit "distinctly modern" characteristics. The blackened America in which they flourish is less a historical place, a people with a history, than it is a premonition, a clue to the puzzle of what's to come, and a target of a universal grievance. America in DeLillo's fiction is objectified in the accents and tones of American language. It's a real place with its own colors and textures, not like the allegorical or abstracted settings of Kafka and Beckett. . . .

Don DeLillo is a writer of fiction but like Nicholas Branch his mind's eye fixes on the shadowy connections professional historians usually fail to see or dismiss as baseless supposition. All of his novels breathe a kind of historical essence. They catch what he has described as the "movements or feelings in the air and the culture around us" and (I should add) the reverberations from below. I like to read him for many reasons: for his intelligence and wit, his range

of reference, vocabulary, energy, and inventiveness, and not the least for the varieties of styles in which he couches his portentous bulletins to the world.

Daniel Aaron. "How to Read Don DeLillo." *South Atlantic Quarterly*. Spring. 1990, pp. 311–12, 319

In *Mao II*, I think more than in any of his previous novels, DeLillo extends himself into private and political languages that must ultimately escape compositional control: the language of crowds and street people, "the rag-speak of shopping carts and plastic bags," a television representing "everything that is not clear and sharp and bright." The resistance of these things to the writer's control is not a limitation of the novel, but rather a source of its political insight: "The experience of my own consciousness," says Grey, "tells me how autocracy fails, how total control wrecks the spirit, how my characters deny my efforts to own them completely, how I need internal dissent, self-argument, how the world squashes me the minute I think it's mine." DeLillo's recognition of both the power and the limits of language suggests that, as he himself comes to occupy a culturally central role, his art will continue to have a more than topical interest.

Joseph Tabbi. *The Review of Contemporary Fiction*. Fall, 1991, p. 270

BIBLIOGRAPHY
Americana, 1971 (n); *End Zone*, 1972 (n); *Ratner's Star*, 1976 (n); *Running Dog*, 1978 (n); *The Names*, 1982 (n); *White Noise*, 1985 (n); *The Day Room*, 1987 (d); *Libra*, 1988 (n); *Mao II*, 1991 (n); *Great Jones Street*, 1994 (n); *Underworld*, 1997 (n)

DELL, Floyd (1887–1969)

Moon-Calf, by Floyd Dell. . . , will have a sequel and will certainly be compared with *Jean-Christophe*, but it has its private merits in moments of unexpected loveliness, in the occasional presentation of relevant and illuminating truth. These are chiefly in the story of Felix Fay's childhood, after which the author writes carefully until adolescence with all its terrors sets in. The author has surprised his enemies by not writing à *thèse* and delighted his friends by a masquerade, but *Moon-Calf*, as it stands, has the importance of showing how serious and how well-composed an American novel can be without losing caste. It is an effective compromise, in manner, between the school of observation and the school of technique.

Dial. Jan., 1921. p. 106

Sherwood Anderson's *Poor White* and Floyd Dell's *Moon-Calf* are the latest important recruits in the ranks of realistic reporting, but, to a certain extent, they march backward, backward toward the gods of an elder day. True, they maintain the Underwood and Underwood photographic standard of descriptive writing, and their atmosphere is that of the same unimportant middle class which pervades *Miss Lulu Bett* and *Main Street*. But in their heroes they forsake the commonplace. They are both unusual men, however usual their surroundings may be. . . . Felix Fay is not a successful inventor. In fact, he is not a successful anything. But he is not an ordinary boy by any means. He is a hyper-sensitive, nervous lad, whose confinement to the prosaic surroundings of his home town constitutes much more of a tragedy than the confinement of Carol Kennicott to Gopher Prairie in *Main Street*, for Felix's aloofness was born of a genuine distinction, whereas Carol was at heart a Gopher Prairieite herself with a Sears-Roebuck education.

And Felix Fay grows up to use his brain, which would disqualify him forever from competition with a hero of real life. It is true, he uses his brain to bad advantage and flounders about in a maze of socialism, atheism, and free-love, bungling them all very badly, especially the free-love. But he is a superman mentally compared to the people in *Miss Lulu Bett* and *Main Street*, and whoever heard of a superman in a novel which is strictly truthful?

Both *Moon-Calf* and *Poor White* have a certain vein of poetry running through them which distinguishes them from the rest of the realistic novels, and it is probably this poetic sense which would not allow their authors to have ordinary men for their heroes.

Robert C. Benchley. *Bookman*. Feb., 1921. pp. 559–60

The spirit of revolt and the passion of poetic protest infuse this book [*Intellectual Vagabondage*] with a beauty and an eloquence that are more reminiscent than real. The May Days of yesterday rather than of today and tomorrow afford its inspiration. The vagabondage is of a generation of youth that already has begun to age, already has begun the prosaic task of adjustment, marrying realities instead of dreams, forced to live life instead of changing it. . . . Mr. Dell is really an essayist and not a critic. He polishes a thought so neatly that its most radical import would never excite or offend.

V.F. Calverton. *The Nation*. May 26, 1926. p. 585

The maladjustment of individuals to our modern society, so he tells us [in *Love in the Machine Age*], is caused by faults in their upbringing. These faults, in turn, are produced by lingering survivals of the patriarchal family system. Under this system, which was introduced by the aristocracy, but which spread through all classes of society, individuals were never permitted to become fully adult; especially they were prevented from making an adult choice of their life-mate. The results of this repression were public and private vices—prostitution, adultery, homosexuality, drunkenness— as well as celibacy, impotence, frigidity and neuroses of every sort. . . . Mr. Dell reveals the patent medicine he is vending. It is, in a word, liberty—the liberty of modern children to follow their own desires. He abandons other theories of education to preach the *laissez-faire* of the instincts.

Malcolm Cowley. *New Republic*. April 30, 1930. p. 304

Until now I have placed *Moon-Calf* well above Mr. Dell's other writings. My present judgment is that the autobiography belongs beside the autobiographical novel. Neither the one nor the other approaches greatness (even though I once called the earlier "a

masterpiece of fiction"); and, as regards the probable life of either, we all know how oblivion scattereth her poppy. But *Moon-Calf* did reveal a character, and *Homecoming* confirms and extends the revelation. The first is an interesting novel of adolescence, and the second is an interesting record; more interesting, I am afraid, than has been indicated here, with its sexual and psychological data that could provoke comment and argument running far beyond this review or a dozen like it. But it is never a scandalous record. As the author said, he had no intention of telling other people's secrets.

Ben Ray Redman. *Saturday Review*. Sept. 30, 1933. p. 145

A large part of the work of Floyd Dell, including most of this autobiography [*Homecoming*], is amazingly intelligent and much of it is fine and sensitive. It is doubtful if any other writer has covered so expertly and broadly the mental world of the "intellectuals" of our time, and as a result the autobiography is constantly entertaining, the pages full of half and quarter-thoughts, perceptions, complex mental reactions and points of view. It is readable, surprisingly lucid and, particularly in the opening chapters, which deal with his childhood and family, rich in concrete detail presented with literary art. Yet, as in Floyd Dell's early work, there seems no personality behind his writing; the problems of his life, however vividly and entertainingly told, are reflections from the mental life of his environment.

Hutchins Hapgood. *New Republic*. Nov. 29, 1933. p. 80

Floyd Dell has the rare felicity of being able to remember and re-create the experiences of childhood and by a flawless selection of significant detail to bring out a "clear emotional pattern." The very nature of his materials in *Moon-Calf* permitted him to work in a realistic manner and at the same time introduce the poetry as well as the humiliations to which youth is subject. The book was so autobiographical that when he wrote his excellent *Homecoming* . . . he incorporated into it pages and paragraphs from *Moon-Calf* without change. . . . The novels came along through the twenties, amplifying with unequal power the themes defined in the first two. *Janet March* . . . moved directly into Greenwich Village in search of the ideal of joy, companionship, freedom, self-giving love, picnic excursions to the beach by moonlight or to the woods, and a carefree, irresponsible existence in an attic studio. Floyd Dell has written beautifully about it all in *Homecoming* in a fine chapter entitled "Greenwich Village." In fact, the autobiography is done so capably that, in a sense, it supersedes the novels.

Harlan Hatcher. *Creating the Modern American Novel* (Farrar and Rinehart). 1935. pp. 77–8

If it was Francis Hackett who first brought the new light to Chicago, it was Dell who made plain the creative power of its rays, and his task by no means ended with its departure for New York in 1913. He moved on to Greenwich Village, the *Masses*, and a larger theater of operations, but the force he had acquired in Chicago and the Midwest remained fresh in his memory and operative in his life. In 1920 and 1921 he published two important novels, *The Moon Calf* [*sic*] and *The Briary Bush*, and wrote into them what must remain the classic account of the Chicago experience. The novels, written with the same lively and intelligent imagination Dell brought to all his work, caught up not only the details of his adventure but enlivened them with a high and dramatic sense of the whole movement.

> Bernard Duffey *The Chicago Renaissance in American Letters* (Michigan State). 1954. p. 180

This "Spiritual Autobiography" [*Intellectual Vagabondage*] is a description of the literary and social influences which had produced in his time, he believed, a generation of intellectual vagabonds, a deracinate group pushed to the boundaries of society by its inability to find a place in or come to terms with a machine civilization. . . . In his excellent first novel, *Moon-Calf. . .*, he had drawn an autobiographical character sketch of a very young man who happens, as part only of his intellectual development, to join the Socialist Party. It was not a radical novel at all, in the usual sense, but a shrewd psychological study of an intellectual vagabond. His later novels were likewise psychological studies, for he had become deeply interested in Freudian theories.

> Walter Rideout. *The Radical Novel in the United States* (Harvard). 1956. pp. 125–6

The assault against Dell as the disagreeable anti-hero, the radical corrupted, was carried on by [Michael] Gold and the spiritual sons of John Reed with increasing bitterness after 1926. Gold and Dell had sparred with each other in *The Liberator* days when Dell repudiated his anarchistic notions about love and marriage and came out for monogamy and babies. He had also poked barbed fun at Gold's proletarian imago. Yet Dell had not given up his socialist convictions, and in such books as *Intellectual Vagabondage*, in his biography of Upton Sinclair, and in occasional reviews and articles, he continued to voice his radical opinions.

But to the young radicals, Dell was merely paying lip service to ideas he once believed in, and had retired from the class struggle.

> Daniel Aaron. *Writers on the Left* (Harcourt). 1961. pp. 214–15

Few small-town lads ever had their high-school poems accepted by *Harper's* and *Century* and *McClure's*, as Floyd Dell's were. Nor had many been, like him, a card-carrying Socialist and religious freethinker at fifteen. Dell nevertheless fitted a certain pattern: the dreamy, sensitive boy or girl of impoverished family whose thoughts roamed to conquests of artistic worlds, the kind in whom a teacher or librarian saw the fire and felt the iron and urged, "Go try!"

Some time later Dell grew into the very picture of a gay, brave, poetically handsome city bohemian, indeed the acknowledged Prince of New York's Greenwich Village, lover of the haunting Edna St. Vincent Millay, his name a synonym for uninhibited, reckless love. He would sit nonchalantly in court as the Government sought his life for, so it claimed, treason in the first World War. He was to be, too, a well-known editor, a successful novelist, a Broadway playwright.

Yet his most important work was done in the first blush of young manhood, as a book critic on the one hand and on the other a personal leader among the young men and women of Chicago who

were assaulting old traditions on their way to making a literary Renaissance.

> Dale Kramer. *Chicago Renaissance* (Appleton-Century). 1966. p. 13

BIBLIOGRAPHY
Moon-Calf, 1920 (n); *The Briary-Bush*, 1921 (n); *King Arthur's Socks and Other Village Plays*, 1922 (d); *Janet March*, 1923 (n); *Looking at Life*, 1924 (e); *This Mad Ideal*, 1925 (n); *Runaway*, 1925 (n); *Intellectual Vagabondage*, 1926 (e); *Love in Greenwich Village*, 1926 (s, p); *An Old Man's Folly*, 1926 (n); *An Unmarried Father*, 1927 (n); *Souvenir*, 1929 (n); *Love in the Machine Age*, 1930 (e); *Love Without Money*, 1931 (n); *Homecoming*, 1933 (a)

DEVOTO, Bernard (1897–1955)

This book [*Mark Twain's America*] is a polemic, infused in many passages with the kind of exasperation which Mark Twain himself often exhibited; and its densely packed pages stir a crowd of responses. First of all, its importance as a "preface" for Mark Twain and also for an understanding of basic elements in American literature is unmistakeable. The book is not, strictly speaking, a biography; at the outset Mr. DeVoto declares that he has not tried to represent "the most engaging personality in American letters," and though he has not been able entirely to sustain this renunciation, the title is a true one. The major passages unroll Mark Twain's America, not with the obvious mileage of that great contemporary panorama which has sometimes been emulated by writers on the older American scene, but with a highly knowledgeable sense of those influences that bore upon Mark Twain during his youth and early years as a writer. . . .For critics *Mark Twain's America* should provide life-giving provender for many a long day. It is, above all, in many of its passages an eloquent book, with the warm eloquence of partisanship, lavishly evoking a whole mind and an era.

> Constance Rourke. *New York Herald Tribune Book Section.* Sept. 11, 1932. p. 3

On certain aspects of life on the frontier and on its edge, in Mark Twain's early days, Mr. DeVoto is informed and eloquent; on the purely literary derivation of Mark Twain's humor (the tall tale, frontier burlesque, etc.), he makes a valuable contribution to criticism. But, taken as a whole and as a portrait of a complex character, his book [*Mark Twain's America*] is almost worthless. In his eagerness to adorn himself with the scalps of [Van Wyck] Brooks and his followers, Mr. DeVoto has overstated or misstated everything, and he leaves us with a false and superficial impression of his subject.

> Newton Arvin. *New Republic.* Oct. 5, 1932. p. 211

Mr. DeVoto also belongs to the school of the gentlemanly essayist—though he might not like to be told so. "Tough guy's essays" might be his own term for these truculent and forthright papers, which range in subject from a study of the origin and evolution of the Mormon Utopia to appraisals of New England and culture and examinations of the theory of biography and criticism. In history, Mr. DeVoto wants us to remember—and very sensibly too—that we are dealing with a pluralistic world, about which it is dangerous to dogmatize on restricted evidence. In biography, he wants us to stick to facts, and nothing but facts—just the documents, no guesswork, no psychoanalytical reconstruction or re-creation or interpretation—which leaves just about nothing at all. . . . In criticism, he would like to see a sociological or functional check on esthetic and popular judgments, as on evolutions in taste or fashion—not an original idea, but worth saying often. In short, Mr. DeVoto is sensible, a lot of the time, but is inclined to be a little angry and repetitive about it, and a little too sure that nobody else is as sensible as himself.

Conrad Aiken. *New Republic*. Jan. 20, 1937. p. 364

This volume [*Mark Twain at Work*] contains the "Boy's manuscript," the *Huckleberry Finn* notes, and part of the most interesting manuscript preparatory for *The Mysterious Stranger*. It also contains three essays by Mr. DeVoto, one about the writing of each of the three books involved, in which he brilliantly records the results of his study of these and other relevant documents. He ponders all his evidence, reasons shrewdly, and unfolds the story of his deductions with skill comparable to that of a mystery novel writer. Consequently, this book sets forth information which hereafter will be indispensable to scholars, and sets it forth in such a way as to make it fascinating reading.

Walter Blair. *Saturday Review*. June 20, 1942. p. 11

On the whole I expect that Mr. DeVoto's conception of Mark Twain's development as a writer and of the partial disintegration of his talent after his bankruptcy and the deaths of his wife and daughter will gain more acceptance as time goes on. . . . Since Mr. DeVoto never forgets that he is dealing with an instinctive and great artist, his criticism of Mark Twain is the best that we are likely to have for some time to come.

George F. Whicher. *New York Herald Tribune Book Section*. July 12, 1942. p. 7

When DeVoto is not attempting to defend any thesis, either about Twain or the frontier or himself, he gives us some of the ripened insights that can come only through years of devoted attention to an author. . . . We can be grateful for these insights, even though DeVoto seems determined to prove through his tub-thumping exaggerations that he possesses every temper except the critical temper.

F.O. Matthiessen. *New Republic*. Aug. 10, 1942. p. 179

Written in the tradition of vivid narrative history, this volume [*The Year of Decision: 1846*] is in many ways a prime example of its kind. Conceive of a latter-day poet of Manifest Destiny with a sense of humor and you have an idea of Mr. DeVoto's work. He has the first requisite of a good narrative historian: an imagination lusty enough to reach out for the full body of life, and yet disciplined enough to stay within range of his sources. He has done a capital

job of research and he has a flair for getting a concrete image out of his documents. He has, moreover, a talent for cordial malice.

Richard Hofstadter. *New Republic*. May 3, 1943. p. 610

This complex narrative [*The Year of Decision: 1846*], managed with a firmness and vividness which can have proceeded only from an absolute steeping of the historian in his sources, is kept in perspective by constant reference to the endless political maneuvers in Washington . . . and by "Interludes" devoted to such aspects of mid-century American society as Stephen Foster's songs, the hints of the machine age in the National Fair of 1846, and William Morton's first public demonstration of anesthesia in Boston.

There can be no doubt that Mr. DeVoto has magnificently achieved his announced intention: "to realize the pre-Civil War, Far Western frontier as personal experience." This is, as he points out, a literary purpose, and he rather self-consciously adopts the fiction that he is only an amateur historian, half afraid to venture into the preserves of the professionals. It is a graceful pose; it would be less amusing and more convincing if Mr. DeVoto had not so resolutely disciplined himself to precisely those rigors of documentation, contempt for secondary sources, and thoroughness in detail which make up four-fifths of the academic guild. If he comports himself in any ways unlike those of the professionals, it is in the liveliness of his style, his willingness to state conclusions even though they might be open to some question, and the frankness with which he avows his preferences among the characters who people his stage.

Henry Nash Smith. *New England Quarterly*. Sept., 1943. pp. 499–500

When his *The Year of Decision* appeared last year and we found that if he would but gag his babbling ego he could still write remarkably sound and unhackneyed history, many of us believed, however, that he still had a soul to save, and that the salvation might require nothing beyond a couple of miracles and twenty years of patience. . . .

[*The Literary Fallacy*] certainly is not a complete account of the literary crimes of the 1920's. In fact, it is nothing at all but a long-winded confession of DeVoto's obsession about Van Wyck Brooks, plus a few envious references to other contemporaries, and two essays, one on the geologist John Wesley Powell and the other on the medical treatment of burns. These essays, which are as original and definitive as a high-school theme, are supposed to indicate how many things we others failed to know and write about in the 1920's and to show how our books would have been written if we had been so lucky as to have Mr. DeVoto write them for us.

Sinclair Lewis. *Saturday Review*. April 15, 1944. p. 10

The principal crime of which DeVoto accuses both generations together is that of indulging in what he calls "the literary fallacy." . . .There is also a critic's fallacy, however, and it is somewhat less innocent than the others we have mentioned. It consists in projecting an imaginary purpose for works of literature, quite different from the actual purposes of their authors, and then condemning the authors jointly and separately because they failed to achieve it. DeVoto writes as if to illustrate that fallacy. He takes for granted that the authors of the 1920's should all have been cultural historians and should all have depicted American civilization as DeVoto now sees it; then he charges them with offering only a false or fragmentary picture.

Malcolm Cowley. *New Republic*. April 24, 1944. p. 565

Bernard DeVoto's investigation of the origins and growth of what he calls the "continental mind" has been persistent and brilliant. *Mark Twain's America* displayed Manifest Destiny in its peak years, the period closed and symbolized by the meeting of the rails at Promontory. *The Year of Decision* went back in time to trace the complex lines of force that in 1846 made inevitable the pattern of western settlement, the war between the states, the eventual triumph of the continental idea. The present book *Across the Wide Missouri* goes still farther back, into the closing years of the mountain fur trade. In his next he will deal with Lewis and Clark, back in the years when the West was still Louisiana or Mexico, and the idea of a continental nation had just been born. . . . But because of its constant cross-references and its restless curiosity in a very wide context, it [*Across the Wide Missouri*] becomes something more: the kind of intelligent study of social dynamisms that not too many historians are capable of.

Wallace Stegner. *Atlantic Monthly*. Jan., 1948. p. 122

Mr. DeVoto makes a number of shrewd observations on the treatment of time, of character, of point of view ("means of perception" is the phrase he prefers), of conveying information, and of dramatizing ideas in novels. He returns again and again to the central truth that a novel is a story, a work of enchantment, a stay against boredom or confusion, whether it be by Margaret Mitchell or Marcel Proust. The novelist departs at his peril from the obligation to tell a story, and when new technical devices, new social sanctions, or new critical theory drive the novelist too far from this primitive but primary necessity, fiction reaches a dead end. The modern "revulsion against story" is, on the whole, a revulsion among a small group of persons who desire experience so far refined it cannot be recognized.

Howard Mumford Jones. *Saturday Review*. April 15, 1950. p. 46

The sustained poetic intensity of DeVoto's continental vision explains part of the success of *The Course of Empire*. Part lies too in his geographical intuition, which sharply indicates limitation and opportunity and places human striving in a specific background of land, water, forest and plain. And much of the success lies in his careful and exact knowledge and his inexhaustible curiosity—knowledge of the terrain, of the routes of trade, of the contemporary conditions of geographical understanding, curiosity about the human experience,—and in his style, a powerful weapon, more disciplined here, perhaps, than it has been before. . . .

Summary hardly does justice to this work. It brings the history of continental exploration into a new poetic perspective, and it

founds its poetry on the hard substratum of provable fact. Mr. DeVoto's old and robust confidence has not waned; and occasionally he may utter judgments more definite than the facts permit; but on most points he argues his case fairly, temperately and convincingly. It is a book which will freshen the vision of the historian and renew his insights; and, for the lay reader of history, it will prove an exciting and rewarding experience.

Arthur Schlesinger, Jr. *New England Quarterly*. June, 1953. pp. 259–60

. . .DeVoto spoke to his fellow Americans, off and on for twenty years. . . .He told them they needn't put up with either shoddy products or shoddy thinking, and, naming names, he attacked the purveyors of both with energy, zest, and skill. No doubt his responses . . . were somewhat disproportionate to the stimuli that evoked them. But considering the craven attitude of most of us in the face of the assorted impositions, shams, discomforts and uglinesses DeVoto denounced, we can only applaud his willingness to call for action against them in tones loud enough, frequently, to get it. . . .

DeVoto wanted the American past the way it was, not the way tendentious critics or historians thought it should have been, because he was deeply stirred by the drama and the greatness that it revealed to him and that he in turn revealed to an ever-growing number of readers. As for America today, he had a lover's quarrel with it. He could and did make frequent suggestions for its improvement, but that was because there was some practical point in doing so. He believed the improvements he advocated would enhance the American future, in which Bernard DeVoto never lost faith and in which, it seems both likely and fitting, he will be remembered for a long time to come.

L.H. Butterfield, *New England Quarterly*. Dec., 1956. pp. 436, 442

DeVoto's histories are an extension of his fiction in that as he grew older his writing moved progressively back into the past, probing for the distinctive causative factors of the present, for one's inheritance. They are in a very small degree an escape from the present. . . . The intuitive understanding in DeVoto came from his own Western boyhood; the intellectual grasp of his subject is, of course, the product of his years in the East—and there is a kind of a tension between the two which is the source of literature.

Robert Edson Lee. *From West to East* (Illinois). 1966. pp. 146–8

BIBLIOGRAPHY
The Crooked Mile, 1924 (n); (with others) *The Taming of the Frontier*, 1925 (e); *The Chariot of Fire*, 1926 (n); (with W.F. Bryan and Arthur H. Nethercot) *The Writer's Handbook*, 1927; *The House of Sun-Goes-Down*, 1928 (n); *Mark Twain's America*, 1932 (c); *We Accept with Pleasure*, 1934 (n); *Forays and Rebuttals*, 1936 (e); (with others) *Approaches to American Social History*, 1937 (h); *Troubled Star* [pseud. John August], 1939 (n); *Minority Report*, 1940 (e); *Essays on Mark Twain*, 1940 (c); (editor) *Mark*

Twain in Eruption, 1940; *Advance Agent* [pseud. John August], 1941 (n); *Mark Twain at Work*, 1942 (c); *Rain Before Seven* [pseud. John August], 1942 (n); *The Year of Decision: 1846*, 1943 (h); *The Literary Fallacy*, 1944 (c); *The Woman in the Picture* [pseud. John August], 1944 (n); *Across the Wide Missouri*, 1947 (h); *Mountain Time*, 1947 (n); *The World of Fiction*, 1950 (c); *The Hour*, 1951 (e); *The Course of Empire*, 1952 (h); *The Easy Chair*, 1955 (e); *Women and Children First* [pseud. Cady Hewes], 1956 (e)

DE VRIES, PETER (1910–1993)

Peter De Vries has pitched *The Tents of Wickedness*, his most recent novel, in the small city of Decency, Connecticut, not far from the large indecent city of New York. Decency, as readers of *Comfort Me with Apples*, an earlier novel of Mr. De Vries's, will remember, is lived in by the kinds of people who are picked upon and apart by sociologists and sociological-novelists as organization men, conformists, and most recently, "status seekers." Mr. De Vries, on the other hand, views them not as easily manipulated statistics but as uneasily struggling individuals trapped in a snare of clichés. . . .

But *The Tents of Wickedness* is only secondarily a novel; it is primarily a vehicle, a sort of circus wagon to transport and display Mr. De Vries's talents as a clown, a juggler, and a mimic. And very considerable talents they are. Mr. De Vries has an extraordinarily accurate ear for speech and for the nuances of literary style. His parodies of Marquand, Faulkner, Fitzgerald, Proust, James, and several other novelists are accurate to a fault. (The fault is that they are not always independently funny, which parody, I believe, should be.) But his verses . . . display not only acute understanding of the method and tone of voice of a variety of poets from Emily Dickinson to Dylan Thomas but the real comic spirit as well. His clowning is often pure boffola, but he also contrives comic situations that combine imaginative lunacy with considerable subtlety.

> Russell Lynes. *Saturday Review of Literature.* July 18, 1959. p. 14

In recent years the Peter De Vries novel has become almost a sub-genre of our fiction. Its archetype is written in an antic spirit, savagely and broadly satirical. Generally it portrays exurbia. Its stock-in-trade includes a miscellany of tricks, japeries, buffooneries and parodies, the net effect of which—even including his addiction to comic names—he manages to make sophisticated. It varies in quality but is invariably fun to read.

The Blood of the Lamb is not that familiar Peter De Vries novel. This could be much to his credit as a demonstration of range and versatility. I wish I could call it an unqualified success but cannot do so. It does not seem to be all of a piece, to have assimilated its many elements and found its own nature. It shifts erratically, being now one kind of book and now another, its narrative sometimes interrupted simply to tell jokes. It does not have the effect of steady flow and progression, but lurches along.

On the other hand, the book is interesting and frequently funny. It keeps the reader's attention (partly hanging on unfulfilled

hopes), and the closing section is painfully moving. . . . Questions of faith haunt the whole book.

> Edmund Fuller. *New York Times Book Section.* March 18, 1962. pp. 4, 37

Peter De Vries began as a *New Yorker* writer, a superior gagman whose comedy had an ambling and self-deprecating resemblance to the novel. His development has been steady and continuous; and in *Reuben, Reuben* . . . he is not only a very funny writer, but a serious novelist with very troubling themes behind all the laughter. . . . Mr. De Vries's title is taken from the old ballad in which Reuben and Rachel consider the prospect of transporting men and women as far from each other as they can get. Though sex is rampant all over the local landscape, men and women are unable to come to terms with each other. . . .

Mr. De Vries may have created a new genre of fiction, which could be labeled tragifarce. While he amuses us with his clowning, throwing away gags that a lesser writer would have to hoard, he is a disturbing moralist with a sharp and uncomfortable perception of things as they are.

> William Barrett. *Atlantic Monthly.* March, 1964. pp. 180–2

Next to Peter De Vries most of our comic writers look like bumpkins. . . . Yet there are stretches in this [*Let Me Count the Ways*], as in his other recent novels, which suggest De Vries is wearying of a routine brought to perfection so long ago and has since had nowhere to go but down. He has, for one thing, neutralized some of the off-characters and off-scenes, so that every police sergeant, every waitress, is not one more daffy bearer of the De Vries point of view. The surface is inching closer to reality and De Vries is inching closer to a straight novel. . . . This final sequence of the book has a kind of somber charm, as the author's two muses, low farce and a sort of dandified melancholy, sing in sustained harmony for once. . . . But in the sickroom he really comes to the edge of great tragicomedy: and one wonders whether here, in the freakish disorder and the farcically helpless patient, this admirably restless writer may not find the key that he has been looking for to the serious novel. *Let Me Count the Ways* seems to mark a step in that direction, as well as being the most stylishly funny novel since Mr. De Vries' last one.

> Wilfred Sheed. *New York Herald Tribune Book Section.* July 25, 1965. pp. 3, 13

De Vries is fun, and the humor is the most obvious element of his work. I have neglected this more obvious element to get at other sides of his characters, their individuality, sensitivity to human need, and moral self-consciousness. I have tried to point out that the atmosphere of his work changed so that these personal qualities in the second half of his corpus are grounded not on some transcendent power which supports human life but are established against transcendent powers which are impersonal and disruptive. . . .

In the later fictions, De Vries's characters see evil occurrences as not such singular, isolated events. They suffer so many losses that they give up God's world of deprivation and death and opt for the human world of joy and intimacy, a world which stands opposed to the world of change or decay. God is associated with evil; mirth and human beauty, holy moments which redeem life from sadness, are human creations.

Wesley A. Kort. *Shriven Selves* (Fortress). 1972. pp. 55, 61

Perhaps it is because [De Vries's] unrestrained use of outrageous puns and similar verbal low comedy is so dazzling that we tend to slight his other talents as a humorist. But the range of his performance is hard to equal.

His phrasing, for instance, can be as deft as Waugh, Benchley or any of the other great comic manipulators of English, where the fun lies principally in the precise choice of words and their precise order in a sentence. He is a master of booby-trapping paragraphs. He will come on in a style as elegant as Edward Villella in a *pas de deux* and shift abruptly into some verbal pratfall in the Groucho Marx manner. He strings together narrative sequences, novel length as well as short pieces, that are as happily zany as anything Wodehouse or Mack Sennett ever dreamed up. . . .

His parodies never miss a note of the originals, and they are funny as well as accurate, which is not always the case with well-wrought parodies. The samples in this book [*Without a Stitch in Time*] run from Faulkner and Waugh to Katherine Anne Porter and Ring Lardner. He long ago showed us how to turn out the classic short piece on a light subject, with the theme stated clearly in the first sentence or two and a snapper at the end echoing back to the beginning.

Yet with all this virtuoso clowing, De Vries produces something that is more than brilliant entertainment. Like the Elizabethan fool and like all great comic writers, he is continually presenting us with the sharpest, wholly unillusioned insights into the intricacies of human relationships.

Paul Showers. *New York Times Book Section.* Dec. 24, 1972. p. 3

Amongst most American novelists, even those who urgently foster a sense of the ridiculous, there exists an undermining inability to question the tenets of bastardized and expensive Freudianism. These writers, who occasionally and heroically manage to be funny in spite of it all, are in the situation of snobbish members of the English ruling classes who think to satirize the things they love and only make them shine. De Vries has evidently approached the knotty topic of analysis from the point of view of an outsider who knows that it has a certain amount in common with the devout notion of warfare between the flesh and the spirit, though it lacks the tetchily august presence of the Godhead, which is not replaced by journalism about dreams or by paperbacks about experiences on the couch. It is De Vries' Dutch Reformed background in the Christian form of the conflict, mixed with an exquisite knowledge of what everyone doesn't know about Freudian theory, that helpfully makes him an onlooker in this land.

Penelope Gilliatt. *New Yorker.* July 16, 1973. p. 78

The opening chapter of *Madder Music* . . . is as sustained a piece of comedy as anything De Vries has ever achieved. His effects cannot properly be conveyed by quotation since the dazzling edifice he

builds depends upon his unique capacity to pile on witticism precariously on top of another. Like Oscar Wilde he believes a good remark is worth repeating, but there is enough fresh material for the reader to overlook such lapses as "she was one of those women you don't give a book because they've already got one." Just occasionally he reveals too much of the stage machinery; a character called Betty Tingle remarks to the hero as he fondles her breasts "You're making Betty Tingle"—worth it for the triple entendre?

Madder Music is the story of the events that forced the hero to escape into the character of Groucho Marx. De Vries makes play with those reversals of the natural order of things that occurs so often in everyday life. In his own house, the hero chances upon his wife making love to someone else. He desperately tries to hide and to his everlasting shame is discovered by the lovers crouching in a cupboard: "He had been caught in the act of catching in the act lovers who were rendered thereby vastly less guilty than himself, since his offense was the pettier though theirs the graver." As in his previous novels, De Vries delivers numerous homespun insights of this sort into the curious workings of the human mind: they are always expressed with deft economy—"Nothing will make a man a model husband faster than infidelity."

De Vries's satire is as accurate as ever: he successfully derides many contemporary American institutions, including modern art, psychiatry, and real estate business and of course current sexual mores. But his satire lacks passion—and one suspects he would not really wish the world very different from the way it is for then there would be less to laugh at.

In some of the novels of his middle period, such as *Reuben, Reuben,* Peter De Vries combined a feeling for the comedy of the human situation with genuine feeling for its victims. *Madder Music* and its immediate predecessor, *I Hear America Swinging,* revert to the style of earlier novels such as *Mackerel Plaza.* The characters are mouthpieces for De Vries's own witticisms—a nice device for disclaiming a bad joke. He has moments of sympathizing with them, but even then he holds them at a considerable distance: his hero is "unfit for either marriage or adultery, being restless in the one and remorseful in the other." When De Vries's verbal inventiveness flags, his lack of serious interest in his characters makes for the occasional dull page, but he remains one of the most stylish of living novelists and much, much the funniest.

Stuart Sutherland. *TLS: The Times Literary Supplement.* March 24, 1978, p. 337

Nineteen eighty marks the publication of Peter De Vries' twenty-fifth book, *Consenting Adults,* and his seventieth birthday. A retrospective is in order for one of our most gifted but neglected comic writers. . . .

A little religion, a good deal of sexual warfare and then victory-making, a cast of unbelievable but effective satiric characters all go toward fleshing out *Consenting Adults.* De Vries' major theme remains constant too. One of the characters says "We must sooner or later be trundled into surgery for . . . an illusionectomy," and in investigating human relations and the relations the individual must have with those institutions around him, De Vries has composed his latest novelistic lesson on the text of growing up in modern America, on the necessity of separating workable illusions from those that defeat the individual. . . .

The book ends touchingly, perhaps forewarningly, as Peachum envisions his deathbed scene. The elegiac note here might remind us that De Vries is himself seventy years old, that perhaps here in Peachum's comic acceptance of the cosmos with all of its flux and paradox is also De Vries' own, that De Vries, like Prospero, may soon be ready to give up his particular brand of magic. Like the world of De Vries' early and masterful fictions, the world of Peachum is comic and positive rather than darkly absurd as in De Vries' later novels, a world that, with all its confusion and chaos, as Peachum learns, beckons commitment, not avoidance.

Taken together, the novels of Peter De Vries form a fascinating investigation into the mores of America over the last thirty years. We tend to neglect De Vries' artistry and insight because of the sheer wealth of his comic virtuosity—a typical De Vries novel contains enough wit for other authors to salt judiciously throughout their canons. But the exuberant comic display masks the unity of comic vision and technique. De Vries' most serious comic devices—fallible narrators, character role-playing, stylistic parody and burlesque, and word play—typically serve dual purposes. They entertain—at times almost overwhelmingly so—but they also reinforce and support his major theme of the illusion-making propensities of the individual, especially when rebelling against tradition or institution. There is a purposeful confluence, then, between idea and form in De Vries' work, a deft union of language, style, wit, and theme that creates an enduring comic vision of the way we live.

T. Jeff Evans. *American Humor.* Fall, 1980, pp. 13, 15–16

Peter De Vries . . . is a dedicated Puntheist, which is why he is rightly shameless. There is a character in this latest novel [*Slouching towards Kalamazoo*] who nudges his listener so violently every time the point of a joke comes looming up (''She was disappointed in love. She got married.'') that the hero is jested black and blue: I'm sure we are meant to notice that the author does the same. It will come as no surprise to De Vries's admirers to be told that in this novel someone does slouch to Kalamazoo, Michigan, and there is a birth there; the baby is named Ahab, after one of the rougher beasts in American Literature, which this novel continuously and joyously celebrates.

It isn't just a baby that gets born either. The baby is the product of a brief liaison between Maggie Doubloon, a spirited English teacher, and the eighth-grade, thirteen-year-old, hero, the ''star underachiever'' of the town they agree to call Ulalume, North Dakota. The lad, Tony Thrasher by name, has a rash which reveals not only that he is itching to get out of town but also that his mother is taking a prurient interest in a dermatologist.

Class has been studying Hawthorne's *Scarlet Letter*, and when Maggie discovers that she is pregnant with meaning (and Tony is unhelpful: sent off to the chemist to get hold of some pills to get a girl out of trouble, he comes back with the Pill, woefully confusing cause and effect) she defies the overly virtuous townsfolk by appearing on a public balcony wearing not a scarlet A, but a scarlet A+, the sexual grade her pupil has accorded her. She thereby gives birth, De Vries suggests, to additional offspring: the sexual revolution and the modern tee-shirt. . . .

There is a subplot, of course. Tony's father, a silver-tongued preacher, given to reading the great monuments of American literature at length to his cowering wife and son ('''If you just wouldn't read with expression,' she blurted out'') takes on in public debate the dermatologist, his rival and the town unbeliever, the subject the existence of God or sense in the universe. The

debate is a draw, each convinces the other, and they exchange extremisms. The Preacher leaves his church and takes up television commercials; the infidel becomes a born-again knocker-on-doors and utterer of texts. Concerned relatives manage to stage a rematch, after which both speakers are converted to Christian Atheism, which I take to be De Vries's own theological stand. If there is a meaning in the scheme of things it is a double meaning.

There is a certain quality of homogeneity in Peter De Vries which his fans welcome, though non-fans, and I can imagine with an effort that such people might exist, would regard it as a certain sameness. This is the reliable product once again, the real McCoy; and if it must be said—and it must—that the whisky is a little watered to make a longer drink (some of his neater books would have had a dozen subplots) there is still enough to quench one's thirst. And there's still an artesian outpouring of parodistic and mimetic felicities, of literary nudges and verbal and nominal wheezes.

Eric Korn. *TLS: The Times Literary Supplement.* Aug. 26, 1983, p. 898

BIBLIOGRAPHY
The Handsome Heart, 1943 (n); *No, But I Saw the Movie*, 1953 (s); *The Tunnel of Love*, 1954 (n); *Comfort Me with Apples*, 1956 (n); *The Mackerel Plaza*, 1958 (n); *The Tents of Wickedness*, 1959 (n); *Through the Fields of Clover*, 1961 (n); *The Blood of the Lamb*, 1962 (n); *Reuben, Reuben*, 1964 (n); *Let Me Count the Ways*, 1965 (n); *The Vale of Laughter*, 1967 (n); *The Cat's Pajamas and Witch's Milk*, 1968 (n); *Mrs. Wallop*, 1970 (n); *Into Your Tent I'll Creep*, 1971 (n); *Without a Stitch in Time*, 1972 (s, sk); *Forever Panting*, 1973 (n); *The Glory of the Hummingbird*, 1974 (n); *I Hear America Swinging*, 1976 (n); *Madder Music*, 1977 (n); *Consenting Adults; or The Duchess Will Be Furious*, 1980 (n); *Sauce for the Goose*, 1981 (n); *Slouching towards Kalamazoo*, 1983 (n); *The Prick of Noon*, 1985; *Peckham's Marbles*, 1986

DEXTER, Pete (1943–)

''A picture is the beginning of misstatement and misunderstanding. You got people looking at it with all different opinions, and they make up stories to go with them.'' These are the words of Pete Dexter's Wild Bill Hickok, who, like a good western hero, realizes that to be famous is to be public property and prefers to move along the trail ahead of his reputation. Historical figures from the Black Hills pioneer days people the novel; Dexter claims that the events and all the characters, save one, are ''real.'' The assassination of Wild Bill occurs halfway through the book, but the momentum of the narrative continues as those who loved him and thought they knew him—Charley Utter, Agnes Lake, Calamity Jane Cannary, and others—wrestle with their memories and learn about Bill from each other.

The tale unfolds mostly through the perceptions of Bill's best friend, ''Colorado Charley'' Utter. Like Gatsby's Nick Carraway, Charley judges people and considers events in a way that sets him apart from the rest of Deadwood's denizens. In a move that does *The Virginian*'s narrator one better, Charley is forced to confront his deep love for Bill when Bill saves his life, and the complexity of Charley's reaction reveals hitherto unexplored emotion beneath the surface of a macho gunman. Charley is pained that while he has to admit what he feels, Bill, because he has ''as much feelings as a hawk,'' is ''incomplete. One half of a perfect man.''

Throughout the novel run intertwining images of bottles and themes of drinking (people never eat, but they guzzle brown whiskey and pink gin all day in a quest to release the personality and alter perception) and the liberty of the human soul. As much as Charley wishes to preserve the Bill that he knew from fictionmongers in the press, he realizes that what's set in stone hereafter—his perceptions or anybody else's—is not Bill at all, and that Bill ultimately has his freedom. Thus Dexter releases himself from the onus of ''truth'' in a historical narrative, using fact to create a superbly entertaining and thoughtful novel about how fact necessarily becomes fiction.

Margaret A. Lukens. *Western American Literature*. Winter, 1987, p. 360.

[The title character of *Paris Trout*] was only taking care of business, trying to collect on Henry Ray Boxer's debt. That little black girl, Rosie Sayers, who got shot and killed in the scuffle, shouldn't have got in his way, or the woman with Rosie, who still walks around with Trout's bullet in her chest.

''I did what was right as rain,'' Trout tells his lawyer, and believes it. When the eye-for-an-eye rule is mentioned, Trout says, ''Those ain't the same kind of eyes and they ain't the same kind of rules.''

Mr. Dexter has created a character whose racism is a blunt, unregenerate fact, as primitive and willful as an earthquake or a rainstorm—and just as sealed off from argument, examination or questions of mercy. What the town's polite society takes care to disguise in Sunday-go-to-meeting euphemisms, Paris sets in defiant, ugly relief; he makes it easy for them to believe they are innocent of racism.

Trout's stubborn assumption that what he calls ''the real rules'' will eventually free him is, at first, simply an embarrassment to Cotton Point, an ostensibly enlightened Eisenhower-era Southern town. As Trout presses his claim more ominously, the townspeople come to fear him: he is dragging out into the air and light their own elaborately camouflaged prejudices. And still they excuse him because they have to excuse themselves.

Three years after a jury has found Trout guilty of second-degree murder, he remains free—but his inner corrosion has brought paranoia and derangement. When Mr. Dexter describes Trout's increasingly erratic behavior, he often comes perilously close to losing his bearing and turning the book into a thriller, using Trout's outcroppings of brutality and growing arsenal of guns to titillate rather than to advance the plot. It's as if he has to sell us on Trout's total depravity: being a racist killer isn't enough.

Mr. Dexter's strongest suit is his exquisite understanding of the finely meshed engines of greed, appetite and self-interest that drive a small town. . . . Mr. Dexter draws [Cotton Point's inhabitants] with precise and detailed conviction—their giddily adolescent parties and casual infidelities, their utterly utilitarian disparagement of blacks. When Trout's lawyer, Harry Seagraves, tells his wife that Trout has shot two black women, her first question is, ''Did they work for anyone we know?''

Mr. Dexter's characterization of Seagraves is particularly persuasive—no glib paraphrase of the all-purpose, rumpled, hard-drinking, conscience-torn Southern lawyer. True, Seagraves is rumpled and hard-drinking, but his steely assessment of his own interests when he takes on the case makes his slow, agonizing waking to the horror of Trout's actions and his own complicity all the more affecting.

The primary agent of Seagraves' conversion is Hanna Trout, Paris's wife, a plain-spoken, bluntly sensual middle-aged woman—a former schoolteacher. You sense that Mr. Dexter, who writes regularly for *Playboy* and *Esquire*, is at pains to show that he can create a strong, resonant female character. For the most part he succeeds, although Hanna's assigned role of primal woman and conscience of Cotton Point occasionally gets on your nerves.

Trout's private victimization of Hanna by sexual abuse and corrosive disregard is analogous to his public victimization of Rosie Sayers, and there are lingering suggestions that each woman asked for what she got from Trout. Rosie never gets the chance to defend herself against this accusation. But Hanna, as it turns out, is one of the few people in Cotton Point who refuses to yield to Trout. She is the only white person to go to Rosie's funeral; she later refuses to appear at her husband's trial. And Hanna is the only character to escape the grotesque outcome of Cotton Point's three-year collaboration with the killer of a 14-year-old child.

At a time when virulent racial incidents can no longer be conveniently fenced off in small Southern towns, Mr. Dexter's great accomplishment is to remind us, with lucidity and stinging frankness, the lengths to which we will go to deny our own racism and to reassure ourselves that we are innocent.

Deborah Mason. *The New York Times Book Review*. July 24, 1988, pp. 7–8.

Although he was born in Michigan and has subsequently lived in—and written about—other parts of the country, Pete Dexter spent part of his boyhood in Georgia and has been able to re-create convincingly [in *Paris Trout*] the mores of an era when blacks were still referred to (formally) as Negroes and when the notion that they deserved equal justice with whites in a court of law had barely begun to take root in the rural South.

We meet first a severely deprived and possibly retarded fourteen-year-old black girl, Rosie Sayers, who, in the opening pages, is bitten on the leg by a rabid fox. We also meet a harsh-mannered white man in his sixties, Paris Trout, who keeps a general store and lends money to the local blacks in the small, central Georgia town of Cotton Point. . . .

The novel moves back and forth between the major characters—poor Rosie, whose story is soon told; Seagraves, whose behavior and attitudes reflect the prevailing ethos of the town's establishment; Trout's pathetically abused wife, Hanna, who had once befriended Rosie; and the eager young lawyer, Carl Bonner, whom Hanna hires to help her get a divorce from Trout. It is through their eyes and the eyes of a great many minor characters that we see Trout as he pursues his obsessed and threatening course through the novel.

We watch with revulsion as he sodomizes Hanna with a bottle of mineral water, as he forces unwanted food into her mouth, as he holds her head under water in the bathtub. We follow him through his trial, hear his self-justifications (which never include a moment's remorse for the murder of Rosie) and his lies. To the surprise of nearly everyone, he is convicted and given a ridiculously short sentence. Then, three years later, after all his appeals have failed, we accompany Trout (still flagrantly carrying a pistol) and the wary sheriff to the state prison farm where he is supposed to begin serving his sentence—only to watch him bribe a local judge to free him on a writ of *habeas corpus*. By this time he has so intimidated Cotton Point that nothing is done to bring him back to jail—and the novel plunges ahead to an apocalyptic shoot-out involving most of the main characters that the reader will have anticipated many pages beforehand.

Only rarely are we told directly what Trout is thinking. The picture we get from Dexter's description of him is that of a full-blown paranoid case, a shabby, unkempt, violent man reeking of urine who thinks that his wife is poisoning him. . . . By making his central character an out-and-out psychotic, Pete Dexter has, I think, run afoul of what seems to approach being a literary axiom: that while neurosis may lend itself to fictional treatment, psychosis generally does not. A character wholly given over to mad obsessions and thus entirely cut off from other people tends to arouse in the reader only a clinical curiosity or—if the madman's deeds are horrific enough—a sensationalist thrill. The descent of a person into madness may be fascinating, moving—even tragic; but madness itself is essentially dull once all possibilities of interesting conflict with others or any sense of conscience have been removed.

The effect of madness upon others can of course be made interesting, and Dexter attempts to do so in the case of Seagraves and Hanna. The experienced, rather jaded lawyer who must defend a repellent client while nursing pity for his victim is a nicely conceived character. Similarly, one can respond with sympathy to the plight of the wife, who married late to escape spinsterhood only to find herself captive of a brute determined to terrorize, humiliate, and possibly murder her. When the lawyer and the abused wife are brought together, Seagraves urges Hanna to keep up the appearance of a normal marriage with Trout in order not to prejudice his coming trial. Hanna refuses, saying that her husband is an ''aberration'' and that she will not be a party to the shooting of children. . . .

[A] love affair soon develops between the two in the ominous shadow of Paris Trout, with much closely described activity in bed.

These characters and this relationship are convincing—up to a point. Unfortunately, Pete Dexter never takes his material beyond what is journalistically plausible. His characters stay on the surface, lacking distinctive voices or personalities. Where he is most successful is in evoking a southern community of that period, ranging from the blacks who live in such places as Damp Bottoms and Indian Heights to the substantial folk like Seagraves and his wife who live on Draft Street. There is a wonderfully funny account of the town's celebration of its sesquicentennial—in which every man in town is required to grow a beard and stocks are put up to punish those still beardless after a certain date.

Mr. Dexter's prose is lucid and efficient, but without much color or individuality. The story gets swiftly told; it is an interesting story, though not one that I found engrossing or of much moral weight. *Paris Trout*, . . . will, I expect, fade rather quickly in the memory of most of its readers. . . .

Robert Towers. *New York Review of Books*. February 16, 1989, pp. 18–19.

BIBLIOGRAPHY
God's Pocket, 1984 (n); *Deadwood*, 1986 (n); *Paris Trout*, 1988 (n); *Brotherly Love*, 1991 (n); *The Paperboy*, 1995 (n)

DICKEY, James (1923–1997)

Going into this book [*Helmets*] is like going into an experience in your own life that you know will change your mind. You either go in willing to let it happen, or you stay out. There are a lot of good poems here. . . . I realize to what an extent sympathy is the burden of this book, how much there is of seeing into the life of beings other than the poet. The reader is moved imaginatively and sympathetically into the minds of horses at nightfall, of farmer and animals divided and held together by fences, of a young girl scarred in a wreck, of bums waking up in places they never intended to come to. . . . But I think that Mr. Dickey is also capable of much less than his best. There are poems that seem to have been produced by the over-straining of method, ground out in accordance with what the poet has come to expect he'll do in a given situation. . . . But I want to end by turning back to the goodness of the book. There are poems here of such life that you don't believe they're possible until you read them the second time, and I've got no bone to pick with them.

Wendell Berry. *Poetry*. Nov., 1964. pp. 130–1

I have been drawn to the poetry of James Dickey by two poems, ''The Being'' and ''Drinking from a Helmet,'' which tell of seizures or psychic invasions—''as if kissed in the brain''—where the erotic and the spectral seem to advance an initiation, as if he had passed a shadow-line that gave him a secret commission in poetry. . . . Wherever the thought of the dead, of animal, human or demonic hauntings—the theme of popular spiritism—comes to him, James Dickey's imagination is stirred. . . . I am moved by the suggestion throughout of the mysteries of Orpheus, the poet as hero who would charm the dead and the animal world with his music. . . . In these *Two Poems of the Air*—''The Firebombing'' and ''Reincarnation''—James Dickey continues in his fascination with the spectral, but he has shifted from the tense verse and concentrated stanza sequence, the direct mode of a poetic experience and commitment, towards a more casual verse following a set story line, allowing even clichés of the supernatural tale. . . .

Robert Duncan. *Poetry*. Nov., 1964. pp. 131–2

Though Dickey will always retain, for strategic use, the rhythms he had early developed to be those in which he most naturally addresses himself, entrusts his consciousness to the language, it is evident that a formal metamorphosis must occur, after *Helmets*, to accommodate the other change, the transformation of ritual into romance, which Dickey has effected in his poetry. . . .

That metamorphosis has occurred in Dickey's latest book, *Buckdancer's Choice*, . . . and occurred with such a rush of impulse that the reader of the earlier collections, having come to expect the somnambulist forms of Dickey's imagination of recurrence, will be jarred by the immediacy, the brutality of disjunct actions, performed once and, however celebrated, done away with. . . . [F]or the most part, Dickey's universe, and the measures which accommodate and express his phenomenology of exchange, has ceased to be one of eternal return, of enchantment. Instead, once out of eternity, the poet confronts and laments (exults over) the outrage of individual death, of a linear movement within time—each event and each moment being unique, therefore lost. . . . Obsession, madness, excess: the burden of *Buckdancer's Choice* is altogether new in this poet, and crowned, or ballasted, by a pervasive terror of extinction.

Richard Howard. *Partisan Review*. Summer, 1966. pp. 480–1

An attempt to be guided by afflatus marks James Dickey's work. He is the most expansive and energetic of these poets, and his poetry is alive with fugitive notes of compassion, fantasy, empathy with personalities that sometimes hold, sometimes flicker in a poem and then disappear. He seems capable of great compression, of an economy that could hold within deliberately contrived limits diverse elements working together. But language for Dickey is a form of energetic action that does not necessarily allow him to work his materials into achieved formal shape and meaning. The poems tend to grow more than to be shaped; their expansion is a necessary aspect of his discovery of what he wishes to say and to release through them.

M. L. Rosenthal. *The New Poets*. (Oxford). 1967. pp. 325–6

The persona in James Dickey's new poems, those that appear in the final section ("Falling") of his new book [*Poems 1957–1967*], is a unique human personality. He is a worldly mystic. On the one hand, a joyous expansive personality—all candor, laughter and charm—in love with his fully conscious gestures, the grace and surety of moves of his body. An outgoing man. An extrovert. On the other hand, a chosen man. A man who has been picked by some mysterious intelligent agent in the universe to act out a secret destiny. . . . How does a man re-connect with common unchosen humanity when he has just returned from the abyss of nonhuman chosen otherness? That is the chief problem to which the final volume addresses itself. How to be a man who feels perfectly at home, and at his ease, in both worlds—the inner and outer. A man who can make of himself and his art a medium, a perfect conductor, through which the opposed worlds—both charged with intensity— can meet and connect, flow into each other. The worldly mystic. It is the vision of a man who for years has been just as committed to developing his potential for creative existence as for creative art. All discoveries and earnings, spiritual or worldly, must carry over from one universe to the other.

Laurence Lieberman. *Hudson Review*. Autumn, 1967. p. 513

At the core of James Dickey's *Deliverance* is a primal fable of intense power. The four unlikely city slickers who ride down the wild Cahulawassee River learn, in horrifying detail, what survival means and how cheap and expensive life can be. While it stays with these men and their journey, *Deliverance* partakes of the bardic magic that has held audiences in thrall for thousands of years, the magic of a narrative more insistent, while it lasts, than the concerns of life itself. When its battered canoe touches shore and civilization, though, Dickey's novel raises questions that cannot be ignored.

Chief among these is the retrospective attitude of the narrator, Ed Gentry, toward his experience. At the outset, the trip holds the brief promise of "another life, deliverance" from his soft urban life, from his job as art director of a commercial photography studio; it also promises Gentry another chance to study the challenge of Lewis Medlock, an intense, compelling fanatic who believes that "the whole thing is going to be reduced to the human body" and who lavishes a lover's care on his own body so as to "be ready." The disastrous journey downriver fulfills both of these promises, but it also introduces a new factor [the meaning of survival] that obliterates their importance. . . .

Paul Edward Gray. *The Yale Review*. Autumn, 1970. p. 104

For all his collections of poetry, James Dickey came closest to capturing his personal mythopoeic vision in the controversial novel *Deliverance*. That his vision was admittedly masculine seems unnecessary to justify, and that the novel was filled with violence, gore, and sport imagery is also defensible. For what Dickey was creating in his novel was a *Pilgrim's Progress* of male egoism, complete with all varieties of masculine fantasy—physical power and prowess, sexual expectation and satisfaction, and above all, contest, competition. What he achieved in the execution of the novel was a resolution far different from his characters' expectations—whether those of Lewis Medlock, the greatest achiever, or those of Ed Gentry, the follower. Dickey's resolution was an understanding beyond fantasy, an understanding of the reality of life, and an acceptance. . . .

Perhaps the chief weakness in *Deliverance* is the fact that all its parts do mesh so well. The explicit leads of the opening—with the charged dialogue between Ed and Lewis, even though it may be ironic dialogue, speech that we as readers understand as naive and indulgent—leave very little for the reader to come to alone. Once into the story, however, the demands of the plot keep Dickey from repeating his theme excessively; the movement of the book is apt for this twentieth-century river story. Dickey's is an incremental yet never leisurely rhythm, based on moderately long sentences which often branch with unexpected modifiers, and come up short in a simpler structure. . . .

Viewed as a masculine initiation story, set on a river, *Deliverance* can be considered a kind of gothic, even bitter, *Adventures of Huckleberry Finn*. That the story is no idyll is part of Dickey's theme: the simple tests, the primitive encounters, may be almost beyond civilized people—not out of their own deficiency, either physical or moral—but from the exigencies of common sense. Just as Dickey's comments on the seemingly pastoral life are scathing in their satire, and the doctor echoes them, so his notion that civilization *has* brought humanity pervades the "After" section. . . .

The three days of Dickey's *Deliverance* have seemed like an eternity, and in some ways they are. But they give Ed, and Lewis, and perhaps Dickey himself, the kind of freedom from the stereotyped male image, and from the pride, that blinds so many would-be powerful men. It is no simple journey; rather it is a contemporary descent into hell, modeled on the exploration-of-self through exploration-of-river that images a peculiarly American, masculine quest for identity. . . .

Linda Wagner. *South Carolina Review*. April, 1978, pp. 49, 52–55

[James] Dickey's treatment of the evolution of the Self has generated a set of repeated symbols, most of them associated with nature. Because the action of many of his poems occurs at night, the moon plays a special role in endowing his speakers—as in "The Owl King"—with unique visionary powers denied them during their rational, daylight hours. (Indeed, sight/blindness is a major motif throughout Dickey's work.) The urge toward celestial beings and powers also appears in "For the Nightly Ascent of the Hunter Orion" (and *The Zodiac*) and of magically endowed birds of prey (the sea bird in "Reincarnation (II)," the owls in "The Owl King" and *Deliverance*). Water, traditionally associated with rebirth, assumes additional complexity in Dickey's work. In *Deliverance* . . . it functions as both a renewing and a destructive element; in the latter capacity it shows some of the features of the shark and the snake, the poet's persistent emblems of impersonal, unyielding malevolence.

The most complex of Dickey's symbolic creations is his underworld of the dead, to which water often leads. For him the dead have a physical reality, and they involve themselves with the living as sometimes helpful, sometimes hostile intruders; the godlike specter of Eugene in "The Other," for instance, both inspires and intimidates the speaker. In his interview with William Heyen, Dickey states, "I tried to fathom what it [death] was, what death is essentially. I finally decided that it's being in the ultimate strange place, the thing that's most completely different from what you're accustomed to." In his underworld the dead reside in a Hades-like location "Below the surface of thought/Below the ground," as he describes it in "The Signs.". . . Because the dead embody the causes for a speaker's guilt, they serve as haunting presences impelling the poet's attempts to break away from or transform the Self. . . .

It should be apparent that in defining what is suspect from what is genuine in poetry, Dickey's criticism outlines his own poetic theory. His honesty may cause him to be perceived by some as a "hatchet man," but in fact it suggests the seriousness with which he approaches his task. He is a poet who cares deeply about his art, who consequently insists on the highest possible standards. Richard Kostelanetz's 1965 statement calling Dickey America's finest critic of poetry may be even more accurate now than it was over 20 years ago.

> Ronald Baughman. *Understanding James Dickey* (Univ. of South Carolina Pr., 1985), pp. 14–15, 153

We find in Dickey one of those hybrids that blooms from time to time. As in William Carlos Williams and Dannie Abse, in whom physician and poet converge to produce superior poetry (and, arguably, more humane medical care), Dickey's skills as a commercial writer combine with his poetic interests to make him, if not a better poet, then the particular kind of poet he is. In a profession sometimes noted for its detachment from the everyday world, Dickey stands out as a writer not content to let the poem survive "in the valley of its making," but chooses to carry it out into the world, even into the corridors of the busy executives.

During the years Dickey worked in the advertising business, he took a book of poetry to the office each day, carrying it or the manuscript of one of his own poems "as if it were a bomb" "through the acres of desks where typists typed five carbons of The Tony Bennett Record Promotion." His was a subversive act, taking what mattered most to him into a place where it mattered not at all. But when he left at day's end, with his poetry under his arm or

tucked away in his briefcase, Dickey may not have been aware of intrusions in the other direction. If poetry can help, however privately, to humanize the business office, how might the office operate on poetry and, in Dickey's case, on the poet?

I want to answer that question by considering James Dickey as a poetic "pitchman," but I do not intend that term to be pejorative. In particular, I do not suggest that Dickey's motives for writing poetry were not artistic. However, the same abilities that made him such a successful young advertising executive contributed to his success as a poet. He understood that to get ahead in the marketplace the poet must know how to promote his product, and he combined the businessman's pragmatic view of the world with the artist's sensibility. Dickey knew, better than his contemporaries, how to sell the things he had to offer: himself, the poem, and (in his own view) God.

> Neal Bowers. *James Dickey: The Poet as Pitchman* (Columbia: Univ. of Missouri Pr., 1985), pp. 5–6

BIBLIOGRAPHY
Into the Stone, 1957 (p); *Drowning with Others*, 1962 (p); *Interpreter's House*, 1963 (p); *Helmets*, 1964 (p); *The Suspect in Poetry*, 1964 (c); *Buckdancer's Choice*, 1965 (p); *Poems 1957–1967*, 1967; *Babel to Byzantium*, 1968 (c); *The Eye Beaters: Blood, Victory, Madness, Buckhead and Mercy*, 1970 (p); *Deliverance*, 1970 (n); *Self-Interviews* (recorded and ed. Barbara and James Reiss), 1970; *Sorties: Journals and New Essays*, 1971; *Jericho*, 1975 (t); *The Zodiac*, 1976 (p); *Poems, 1957–1967*, 1978; *God's Images: A New Vision*, 1978 (p); *The Strength of Fields*, 1979 (p); *Falling: May Day Sermon*, 1981 (p); *A Starry Place between the Antlers*, 1981 (t); *Puella*, 1982 (p); *Night Hurdling: Poems, Essays, Conversations, Commencements and Afterwords*, 1982 (p, e, interviews); *The Central Motion: Poems, 1968–1979*, 1984; *Bronwen, the Traw, and the Shape-Shifter*, 1986 (p); *Alnilam*, 1987 (n); *From the Green Horseshoe*, 1987 (p); *Wayfarer, a Voice from the Southern Mountains*, 1988 (p); *The Eagle's Mile*, 1990 (p); *The Whole Motion: Collected Poems 1945–1992*, 1992; *To the White Sea*, 1993 (n); *Striking In: The Early Notebooks*, 1996; *James Dickey: The Selected Poems*, 1998

DIDION, Joan (1934–)

First novels are the occasion of hope and prophecy. A new talent must be assessed, pigeonholed, labeled. Miss Didion [in *Run River*] writes superbly; her prose is her servant; she has an uncommon grasp of place and character. All is suavely understated, preventing melodrama, the pretense of epic dimensions, and tedious symbolism. The novel is reasonable and true. The landed gentry in California are like that. Yet—. . .

A big *yet* indeed. . . . The book is *too* even, *too* smooth. It sticks to its business with the determined regularity of minor art. All humor, all irony have been pared away. And where is invention? Must realism with all its sincerity be so flat? The English novel is eccentric, irregular, at once pathetic and ridiculous. Miss Didion has polished her prose too well for her own good. She should have put in some touches with her left hand, or attempted some little impossibilities here and there, so that we could appreciate the smudges.

Guy Davenport. *National Review*. May 7, 1963. p. 371

To read Joan Didion is to worry about her. There is in most of her work the terrible feeling that this latest pained and painful examination of whatever is on her mind right now is only the freshest installment in some epic suicide note to the world. The premonition of personal loss is apocalyptic. . . .

Here, in her second novel and first departure in almost a decade from the first-person reportage she does so excruciatingly well, are both disappointment and relief. Disappointment, because [*Play It as It Lays*] is nothing like the gorgeous caterwauling tour de force that might have been expected; relief, a personal relief, because at the end she explicitly rejects suicide as an alternative—for her—to the miserable goings-on so sparely chronicled. . . .

Familiarity with her autobiographical work makes it impossible to read this novel without recalling on almost every page the other memories, the real ones.

It doesn't seem important finally, whether this is a good book or not. Those who care about Joan Didion will have to read it. For one thing, it is a compelling exercise in literary pathology; but, most of all, it is a matter of devotion.

Nicholas A. Samstag. *Saturday Review*. Aug. 15, 1970. p. 27

Nullity, nothingness, human negation, *nil*—these are merely variants of the same phenomena, the essential emptiness of experience, that great hole at the middle of things. Single as the phenomena may be, the characters in novels can make varying approaches to it, as novelists themselves can have various feelings about it. It can be seized in a kind of hungry embrace, in the fashion of the moral idiots who people the world Miss Didion creates in [*Play It as It Lays*], a novel written with such bitter wit that the reader feels at the end that it must have been acid that he has been drinking. . . .

I am tempted to say that this novel is a triumph not of insight as such but of style, meaning by *style*, of course, the linguistic embodiment or, rather, actualization of imagination. . . . If Miss Didion had made one false move, the whole thing would have collapsed like a pricked balloon. But she didn't.

Mark Schorer. *American Scholar*. Winter, 1970–1. pp. 168, 174

Play It as It Lays depends upon an intimate connection between setting and theme; but also . . . its overriding thematic concern is man's relationship with himself and with existence in general. Didion's novel is neither primarily a sociological commentary on the values of contemporary American society nor a psychological case study of its heroine. It is, rather, a picture of personal dread and anxiety, of alienation and absurdity lurking within and without. For although Hollywood is her setting, nothingness is Didion's theme. . . .

The facts of Maria's life are the basic material of thousands of soap opera situations. What saves *Play It as It Lays* from degenerating into banality is Didion's control over her material, her skill in focusing attention not on the events in Maria's life so much as on her cumulative response to them. The real action of the novel takes place in the mind and heart of Maria as she is forced to deal with her experiences. Viewed from a medical point of view, she might well

be classified as a near schizoid personality whose experiences have precipitated a severe emotional crisis resulting in the loss of an integrated personality. In a more profound sense, however, her sickness is neither emotional nor psychological; it is ontological. She is suffering not from a nervous breakdown, but from the breakdown of a world around her which threatens to engulf her whole being with nothingness. . . .

With relentless attention to telling detail, a perceptive eye for sharply-etched characters, an unerring ear for the absurdities and non sequiturs that pass for daily conversation, and a diamond-hard unsentimental style, Joan Didion has fashioned a remarkable novel which never misses in its portrayal of a modern woman caught in a mid–twentieth-century crisis. She has cast anew, in her unique idiom, one of the prevailing concerns of modern literature: confrontation with the void. Despite its preoccupation with death, suffering, boredom and despair, *Play It as It Lays* is always fresh and alive. The novel not only touches the heart of its reader through its sensitive treatment of Maria Wyeth but also assaults the mind in its investigation of the heart of darkness too often discovered lurking behind the fundamental questions about existence in the modern world.

David J. Geherin. *Critique*. 16, 1, 1974. pp. 64–5, 78

[John Gregory] Dunne and his wife, Joan Didion, both best-sellers in a community that respects only the numbers, are the Lunts of the Los Angeles literary scene. Each in his own way celebrates the sights and symbols of California, a vacuum making its emptiness sensational. Their writing is typical of California insensibility.

As with the rest of the California middle class who jog, exercise, diet, sunbathe, and search for inner peace and self-awareness, Dunne and Didion are obsessed with themselves. . . .

"We tell ourselves stories in order to live," Joan Didion writes in the much-quoted first line of *The White Album*, essays that span the upheavals of the late 1960s and the becalmed 1970s. But the real story she is telling is that of her own suffering. She has the Brentwood Blues. She meditates on her desolation and makes it elegant. She puts herself in the vanguard of suffering and uses this to set herself apart from the rich, successful, and decadent Los Angeles life she enjoys. She needs the fiction to rationalize the fact that she is part of the problem she analyzes. . . .

In 1982, having exploited her private terror in print, Joan Didion was sent for two weeks to El Salvador to exploit other peoples'. Didion had used the fictional Central American country of Boca Grande as an exotic locale in her pretentiously arch novel *A Book of Common Prayer* (1973). But with the possibility of real and not imagined death in El Salvador. Didion finds new ways to make fear pay. It concentrates her mind wonderfully. . . .

Face to face with mayhem, Didion's detachment from life is dramatized as the inevitable, even essential way of negotiating the situation. With the adroit use of an impersonal pronoun, she can stage her affectlessness and the death she seems to abhor and make them both sensational.

John Lahr. *Automatic Vaudeville* (New York: Alfred A. Knopf, 1984), pp. 205–6, 213–14

"We tell ourselves stories in order to live," Joan Didion says. The stories she tells in *After Life*, her third book of collected essays, like those in *The White Album* and *Slouching towards Bethlehem*, are razor-sharp analyses of American popular and political culture that show American life to be contradictory, unsettling, and bizarre. Didion tells these stories in a deadpan, understated style that has the deadly impact of a concealed weapon. She could make a grocery list sound significant and sinister. And so she does in accounts of the press and politics in Washington, New York, and California—the exception being the title essay, "After Henry," a eulogy to Didion's editor and mentor, Henry Robbins, who died at fifty-one in 1979.

Her two most memorable pieces illustrate Poe's "poetic principle," that the most compelling narratives focus on the lingering death of a beautiful young woman. In Didion's version, dramatic interest is concentrated on the near death and lingering revival of Patty Hearst, in the essay "Girl of the Golden West," and on the unnamed 1989 Central Park rape victim in "Sentimental Journeys." Characteristically, Didion weights each victim, event, and context with portentous symbolism that assumes far greater significance than the individual to whom it is attached; each becomes the heroine of a significant story of America, past, present, and future. . . .

In calling attention to the narrative elements of the news, Didion is telling her story about their stories. We read these dozen pieces for Didion's story, sinister rather than sensational, and Didion's wry, dry style.

> Lynn Z. Bloom. *Belles Lettres*. Fall, 1992, p. 14

Didion can only be fully understood as a regional writer—more particularly, as a middle-class Anglo Californian who came of age in a place nobody recognized as having a legitimate culture of its own. . . .

This wasn't to say our culture [Northern California, Sacramento] lacked definition, even continuity. If there was less demonstrable commitment to ideas in Sacramento than in, say, Boston, there was at least a comparable and equally complacent order—racially prejudiced and oblivious to lives lived two and ten rungs below it. Filipinos, Japanese, and Latinos did not figure in this Anglo world except as household and garden workers.

This was the world Joan Didion grew up in. Scarcely altered, it continues to this day in East Sacramento and Old Land Park. . . .

To have grown up in such a world is to be more than ordinarily struck by the sea-changes that followed. Old Sacramento's outward fixity, its seeming timelessness, make encounters with the surrounding world almost traumatizing, a form of culture shock. It's not that life inside these purlieus isn't stifling: it's that the alternatives—so exciting, so foreign—are also clearly annihilating. . . .

To suggest, as Didion has repeatedly done, that "story" or "narrative" is nothing more than the imposition of the individual writer's self-interest on events creates a curiously hermetic universe—the moral equivalent of the Donner Party (to choose one of Didion's favorite bits of local history), which in fable at least survived only through autoingestion. In *Slouching towards Bethlehem* Didion remarked that her decision to keep a notebook was not motivated, as she had at first believed, by her interest in other people: "My stake is always, of course, in the unmentioned girl in the plaid silk dress [Didion]. *Remember what it was to be me*: that is always the point."

To take Didion at her own word here means recognizing that her often magnificent reportage, her "narratives," are in the end only her own. Their metanarrative—the story running like a river through all her essays and novels—is about a writer who grew up in a lost and irretrievable California, lived for a while after college in a New York just as lost, and who writes now about the cultural flashpoints lying at extremes from where she started. At bottom, Didion's metanarrative despairs of collective solutions to social problems, concentrates on incidental horrors at the expense of structural ones, selects grisly details that annihilate hope. . . .

Joan Didion [is] a self-professed outsider operating from within the heart of institutions but a lifelong Turnerian nonetheless, in perpetual mourning for the passing of an older West. Hanging over discovered landscape of public records in *After Henry*, *Miami* and "Eye on the Prize" [published in *New York Review of Books*, September 1992] is that old Westering metanarrative: action is deeply compromised, absurd, futile; politics is too corrupt to participate in, save as a "sensitive" observer; only the outsider can make a positive difference, and all such differences are too fine for politics. In these convictions, Didion strikes me as a peculiarly Western writer, depending on the authority of her own long suffering to confer meaning, make history. O, Pioneer!

> Jan Zita Grover. "Girl of the Golden West." *Women's Review of Books*. March, 1993, pp. 8–9

BIBLIOGRAPHY
Run River, 1963 (n); *Slouching towards Bethlehem*, 1968 (e); *Play It as It Lays*, 1970 (n); *Miami*, 1987 (e); *After Henry*, 1992 (n); (with John Gregory Dunne) *Up Close and Personal*, 1996 (scrp); *The Last Thing He Wanted*, 1996 (n)

DILLARD, Annie (1945–)

"I am no scientist," says Annie Dillard, "but a poet and a walker with a background in theology and a penchant for quirky facts." In *Pilgrim at Tinker Creek* she offers "what Thoreau called 'a meteorological journal of the mind.'"

The book is a form of meditation, written with headlong urgency, about *seeing*. A blind child the author happened to read about saw for the first time after cataracts had been removed from her eyes. "When her doctor took her bandages off and led her into the garden, the girl who was no longer blind saw 'the tree with lights in it.'" Annie Dillard had found the central metaphor for her book; it is the vision, the spiritual conception, that she will spend her days in solitude tramping the Roanoke creek banks and the Blue Ridge mountainside in search of herself.

A reader's heart must go out to a young writer with a sense of wonder so fearless and unbridled. It is this intensity of experience that she seems to live in order to declare.

There is an ambition about her book that I like, one that is deeper than the ambition to declare wonder aloud. It is the ambition to feel. This is a guess. But if this is what she has at heart, I am not quite sure that in writing this book she wholly accomplished it. I don't say this, though, to detract from her declared intention in laying herself open to the experience of seeing. It is a state she equates with innocence: "What I call innocence is the spirit's unself-conscious state at any moment of pure devotion to any object. It is at once a receptiveness and total concentration."

But apparently it is an unself-consciousness that can be consciously achieved and consciously declared. And part of her conception of seeing is that in the act of doing it she is herself, in turn, being seen.

"I walk out; I see something, some event that would otherwise have been utterly missed and lost; or something sees me, some enormous power brushes me with its clean wing, and I resound like a beaten bell. I am an explorer, then, and I am also a stalker, or the instrument of the hunt itself. . . . I am the arrow shaft, carved along my length by unexpected lights and gashes from the very sky, and this book is the straying trail of blood."

What happens to that paragraph is what happens to her book. As the episodes begin, we can imagine an appealing young woman standing alert in a meadow, dressed in shirt and pants, holding her field glasses and provided with a sandwich: she is waiting to see, being very patient and still. By the chapter's end, we realize or suspect we are watching a dervish dancing. Receptivity so high-strung and high-minded has phases of its own. The author shows us that it has its dark side too.

"The world has signed a pact with the devil; it had to. . . . The terms are clear: if you want to live, you have to die; you cannot have mountains and creeks without space, and space is a beauty married to a blind man. The blind man is Freedom, or Time, and he does not go anywhere without his great dog Death. The world came into being with the signing of the contract. . . . This is what we know. The rest is gravy."

I honestly do not know what she is talking about at such times. The only thing I could swear to is that the writing here leaves something to be desired. "What's going on here?" is one of the author's refrains. "The creator loves pizzazz," she answers herself.

She is better at stalking a muskrat: "Stalking is a pure form of skill, like pitching or playing chess. Rarely is luck involved. I do it right or I do it wrong; the muskrat will tell me, and that right early. Even more than baseball, stalking is a game played in the actual present. At every second, the muskrat comes, or stays, or goes, depending on my skill." This is admirable writing.

So is her account of the polyphemus moth—first in its cocoon, then emerging, then crawling away in the presence of a roomful of schoolchildren. It has been directly experienced at what I should say is eye-level. Her account of the migration of the monarch butterflies, which makes the reader see what they looked like coming, how they went over, what they left behind them, what the author learned from the whole event, is precise and memorable.

She can also write straight narrative, showing what the book would have gained in point, direction, and shape from being given a little more of it. . . .

Annie Dillard is the only person in her book, substantially the only one in her world; I recall no outside human speech coming to break the long soliloquy of the author. Speaking of the universe very often, she is yet self-surrounded, and, beyond that, book-surrounded. Her own book might have taken in more of human life without losing a bit of the wonder she was after. Might it not have gained more? Thoreau's wisdom had everything to do with the relationship he saw between nature and the community of man. She read Thoreau, including of course his own meteorological journal of the mind. . . .

[The] author is given to changing style or shifting moods with disconcerting frequency and abruptness. "Thanks. For the Memories." "This oft was thought, but ne'er so well expressed as by Pliny." "The cottage was Paradise enow." You might be reading

letters home from camp, where the moment before you might have thought you were deep in the Book of Leviticus.

The relationship between the writer and the reader is fully as peculiar and astonishing as the emergence of the polyphemus moth. It too has got to leave the cocoon, has got to draw breath and assume every risk of being alive before the next step, real understanding, can take place.

But a writer writes as a writer sees, and while the eyes are rolled up, what appears on paper may be exactly what it sounds like, invocation. "Mystery itself is as fringed and intricate as the shape of the air in time." This is a voice that is trying to speak to me out of a cloud instead of from a sociable, even answerable, distance on our same earth. . . .

She concludes her book by saying, "And then you walk fearlessly . . . like the monk on the road who knows precisely how vulnerable he is, who takes no comfort among death-forgetting men, and who carries his vision of vastness and might around in his tunic like a live coal which neither burns nor warms him, but with which he will not part. . . . The giant water bug ate the world. And like Billy Bray I go my way, and my left foot says 'Glory,' and my right foot says 'Amen': in and out of Shadow Creek, upstream and down, exultant, in a daze, dancing, to the twin silver trumpets of praise."

And that's the way Annie Dillard goes. Is the Pilgrim on her right road? That depends on what the Pilgrim's destination is.

But how much better, in any case, to wonder than not to wonder, to dance with astonishment and go spinning in praise, than not to know enough to dance or praise at all; to be blessed with more imagination than you might know at the given moment what to do with than to be cursed with too little to give you—and other people—any trouble.

Eudora Welty. *New York Times Book Review*. March 24, 1974.

Think, for a moment, of writing about your own early years—say from age 5 to 15—and consider the problem of getting, first, a grip on all that material, and then organizing and writing about it coherently and in such a way that readers will hang on every word. . . .

[*An American Childhood* does] this so consumately with Annie Dillard's '50s childhood in Pittsburgh that it more than takes the reader's breath away. It consumes you as you consume it, so that, when you have put down this book, you're a different person, one who has virtually experienced another childhood. You have been with this child on her summer visits to her grandparents' river house and on the boat trip she took (as an adolescent of the opposite sex did on the Mississippi) down the Ohio River with her dad. You have been inside her head as she watches her younger sister materialize. You have gotten a microscope on Christmas and discovered moving protozoa in a drop of water. You have gone to dancing class to learn, not just the fox trot, but a certain social ease. You also have discarded the ridiculous notion of religion in a fit of adolescent agnosticism.

Autobiography by definition would seem to require a singular subject. In *An American Childhood*, we get both more and less: Those people who figure large in her early life assume almost mythic proportions, but the author wisely spares her reader the undifferentiated, and what could be trivial, aspects of her childhood. Somehow, we experience the sensation of a summer's droning tedium without being bored for a second. . . .

Dillard follows a straightforward chronology in *An American Childhood*. This is not to say the writing is simple or unadorned. Like the river she uses as a unifying metaphor, each mile forward brings with it several more of meandering among serendipitous associations. In one, Dillard does the impossible: explaining the family private jokes without deadening their infectious good humor. There are meditations on the family's linguistics, on the portents of the nearby branch library, on the day of a huge snow, on the character of solid Presbyterianism, on an insect collection, on the dancing class's final exam.

In elaborations and playful, poetic digressions lie high stakes and heavy risks. Only a self-assured writer dare intentionally violate the commandment "Thou shalt not digress." Dillard does it, and manages to induce the reader not to get impatient. And to feel sad that it must come to an end.

An American Childhood is neither an adult's paean to romanticized memories nor the opposite sort of retributive memoir most readers would wish the writer never committed to paper. Dillard has not flinched at capturing the private fears alongside the rapturous joy, the humble alongside the grand the comforting rituals alongside the bedeviling puzzlements, the intellectual alongside the sensual. For an autobiographer to comprehend such a wealth of memory with such balance and understanding shows remarkable maturity, and for a writer to share it is an act of singular generosity.

> Catherine Petroski. *Chicago Tribune—Books*. September 13, 1987, pp. 1, 12.

[In] *Pilgrim at Tinker Creek*, Annie Dillard wrote that she had "no intention of inflicting all my childhood memories on anyone"; in her last book, *An American Childhood*, she did exactly that. She wasn't wrong, really, to break that promise—*Childhood* was a very good book, almost a great one—but still, it indicated how attenuated and self-obsessed her work was becoming. Now, in *The Writing Life*, Dillard has gone one step farther down that path: She has moved from writing about herself to writing about writing about herself.

The Writing Life isn't a bad book, exactly—I don't think Dillard is capable of writing anything awful—but it's thin and fragmented, and self-pitying. Nothing comes more easily to a writer than moaning about the creative agony of the artist, but Dillard has always had such perfect, poetic taste and such a fine sense of the ridiculous that I would never have expected it of her. Though her work has probably never sold in proportion to its merit, she does have a Pulitzer Prize and at least one best seller under her belt. So it's just plain embarrassing when she whines that writing is "work . . . so meaningless, so fully for yourself alone, and so worthless to the world, that no one except you cares whether you do it well, or ever." Ten minutes at a job that really is meaningless might change her mind. . . .

Even on a subject as barren as this one, though, Dillard's prose style remains amazing. Reviewers tend to use adjectives such as "luminous" and "radiant" in describing her writing. That usually means vague and sentimental and pseudopoetic—but she's not. Her prose is rich when it needs to be, but she never merely assembles conglomerations of syllables for their own sake. The nature writing in Dillard's *Pilgrim at Tinker Creek* can take the reader's breath away with its beauty, but she never yields to the temptation to be falsely pretty. . . . More important, everything in that book, and in most of her others, has a meaning beyond the literal. I sometimes believe that Dillard took Blake's "To see a world in a grain of sand/and a heaven in a wild flower" as her job description.

Most of Dillard's books have moments of immense beauty and power—that is why it is so jarring how silly some of the metaphors in *The Writing Life* are. Writing desks hover "thirty feet from the ground"; the writer, she says, must crank "the engine of belief that keeps you and your desk in midair." (Trust your feelings, Luke. The Force will be with you.) A two-page chapter is devoted to a typewriter that turns volcanic, "exploding with fire and ash." It shakes the walls and floor of her house in its fury; she grabs a bucket of water to douse it, but decides to leave it be, though the eruptions recur randomly through the night. A couple of days later, it works just fine. I know Dillard wants us to think deep mystical thoughts about creative fire, but the only deep thought I had was this: Could one of the most brilliant writers of our time be dumb enough to want to pour water in a burning electrical appliance?

One could be cynical and argue that there's a reason *The Writing Life* seems mostly self-obsessed: that Dillard has been navel-gazing so long that her chin has become permanently attached to her chest. But I don't really think that's the problem. Yes, most of her books are ultimately about herself, but they are really about how she transforms what she perceives. . . . Dillard's books, whatever their nominal subjects, constitute her spiritual autobiography, and that's the riskiest kind of writing—her books work only if every sentence is an epiphany. That's a word critics have debased beyond recognition, but Dillard's best work honestly provides something that can only be called revelation, and that something cannot be faked. So there may be a good reason that her last couple of books have been merely about the inside of her head: What else can you write when the epiphanies don't come?

> Michael Edens. *The Nation*. October 16, 1989, pp. 435–36.

BIBLIOGRAPHY
Tickets for a Prayer Wheel, 1974 (p); *Pilgrim at Tinker Creek*, 1976 (e); *Holy the Firm*, 1977 (e); *Living by Fiction*, 1982 (c); *Teaching a Stone to Talk*, 1982 (e); *Enounters with Chinese Writers*, 1984 (c); *An American Childhood*, 1987 (a); *The Writing Life*, 1989 (e); *The Living*, 1992 (n); *Mornings Like This*, 1995 (p)

DIXON, Stephen (1936–)

Conventionally realistic stories are *about* something. What makes Stephen Dixon's work so different is that it is that thing in itself, though not in the sense of stylistic opacity Samuel Beckett appreciated in James Joyce's fiction when he made this same formulation in 1929. *Finnegans Wake*, the work in progress Beckett had in mind, would be opaque nearly to the point of impenetrability. Dixon's novels and short stories are clear as a bell, with never a question about what's going on. His characters are familiar to the point of banality, and their actions never reach beyond the scope of what can happen to any American city dweller at any moment of any given day.

The difference is that these happenings are not reported by observing the outside world, but generated internally by the key elements set in place at the story's beginning. A social mannerist like John Updike will ask you to believe in not just his characters but the larger world they live in; their fortunes will be to interact with the sign system we all share (or at least can read), to the point that a protagonist introduced on page one may sharpen into focus as late as page ten or fifteen, when he or she interacts with a product taken down from the supermarket shelf. What happens in a Dixon story is predicated entirely by what's squarely before you on the first page; whatever follows must be created by the interaction of those elements fully apparent from the start. Dixon's genius is in generating so much action from so little initial material. Whereas conventional realists demand a literacy of the entire world, all Stephen Dixon asks is that we accept the flat statement of his story's first sentence. From there on, his narrative momentum will carry on virtually by itself.

Jerome Klinkowitz. *American Book Review*. September–October, 1989, p. 7

In spite of the fact that Stephen Dixon has published at last count 225 short stories, he is a terrific writer and *Garbage* is a superb novel.

Garbage is a story about a bar owner, Shaney, who goes one-on-one with a Mafia-style garbage hauler—Stovin's—because of a sense of loyalty to his present trash hauler, Eco. He is also concerned about what his deceased father would think if he were to cave in to Stovin's extortionate demands. But in the final analysis Shaney is simply a guy who doesn't like to get pushed around. Because of his commitments, he is obliged to endure a torched apartment, scorched parrot, busted head, jail, and general destitution. At this level, *Garbage* is like [the movie] *Prince of the City*, only funnier. One man's fight against all odds in the big city.

Curtis White. *American Book Review*. September–October 1989, p. 6

A Dixon story is almost immediately recognizable. . . . His prose has an edgy, jerky quality, reminiscent of, well, Dixon's own speech. Events are described minutely or telescoped alarmingly. And at the beginning of a Dixon story, you are plopped right into the middle of the action. For example, "The Parting," in *The Play and Other Stories* (1988) begins: "Then her new boyfriend showed up at the door, and I said, 'I guess it's time for me to go.'"

Recently, Dixon's distinctive style paid off. *Frog* (1991), his latest book, earned him long-deserved national attention. . . .

How did he develop his voice?

"Well, I started off the way I guess most writers start: I was writing a naturalistic story with good English and punctuation where it should be. Then I found that to be kind of dull after a while and that if I wanted writing to be as exciting as it had been when I first discovered writing fiction, I had to go off into something new. . . . That's why I think most other writers' work is so boring and dull, dead: because they're writing, rewriting, in the same way, usually the same stories. But if you're open to it, it'll come. Does that make any sense? See, even now I'm writing a new novel called *Interstate*, and it's very exciting because it sort of takes off where *Frog* left off, and I'm having a whole bunch of fun. . . . If it isn't exciting I don't see the point of writing."

It's this freshness of perspective, characterized by some as experimental realism, that is so engaging about Dixon's work.

Sono Motoyama. *Poets & Writers*. September–October, 1993, pp. 42, 43, 45

"What do you do the moment you know your kid's dead?" writes Stephen Dixon in *Interstate*, his first novel since *Frog*, a finalist for both the NBA and the PEN/Faulkner Award. It is a question that permeates *Interstate*. . . . The novel's eight sections retell, in eight different ways, the consequences of a drive-by shooting in which two men in a minivan pull up alongside a man driving with his two young daughters on an interstate highway and open fire, killing one of the girls.

For more than two decades, the prolific Dixon has published highly innovative novels and short stories, mostly with literary journals and small presses, exploring the frantic inner lives of ordinary individuals. Yet this novel's themes of memory, guilt, and trauma proved to be especially disquieting for him. "I have never written anything that possessed me so much," he says. . . .

Dixon has now published more than four hundred short stories in magazines from the *Atlantic* and *Esquire* to *TriQuarterly* and *Partisan Review*. His books comprise eleven story collections, including last year's *The Stories of Stephen Dixon*. . . .

Dixon began writing fiction in the 1960s, when he was a Wallace Stegner writing fellow at Stanford University. His first published story was taken by George Plimpton for the *Paris Review* in 1963. . . . Soon he was placing stories in *Confrontation*, *Carolina Quarterly*, *Mississippi Review* and many of the other little magazines in which he continues to publish to this day.

Joseph Barbato. *Publishers Weekly*. June 22, 1995, p. 40

BIBLIOGRAPHY
No Relief, 1976 (s); *Work*, 1977 (n); *Too Late*, 1978 (n); *Quite Contrary*, 1979 (s); *14 Stories*, 1980; *Movies*, 1983 (s); *Time to Go*, 1984 (s); *Fall and Rise*, 1985 (n); *Garbage*, 1988 (n); *Love and Will*, 1989 (s); *The Play*, 1989 (s); *All Gone*, 1990 (s); *Friends*, 1990 (s); *Frog*, 1991 (n); *Long Made Short*, 1993 (s); *The Stories of Stephen Dixon*, 1994; *Interstate*, 1995 (n); *Man on Stage: Playstories*, 1996 (s); *Gould*, 1997 (n); *30*, 1999 (n)

DOCTOROW, E.L. (1931–)

Doctorow [in *The Book of Daniel*] has written the political novel of our age, the best American work of its kind that I know since Lionel Trilling's *The Middle of the Journey*. . . . This is an artwork about the idea of the Rosenbergs and the people like them, how they came into being in this country, why their trial was needed, what their legacy is, and the intertexture of that legacy with the social-political climate today. I haven't looked up the facts of the Rosenberg case; it would be offensive to the quality of this novel to check it against those facts. This is a work of historic and psychic currents.

Stanley Kauffmann. *New Republic*. June 5, 1971, p. 25

[*The Book of Daniel*] seems to me extraordinarily sensitive both about the past that his narrator-protagonist, Daniel Isaacson, shared with his parents and about the present in which he searches for further clues to their true identities and his own. The book begins and ends in ambiguity, with Daniel refreshingly unsure about the meaning of anything. All we know for sure is the agony of his quest—and its importance. The book jumps madly, constantly from the first to the third person and back again, pauses for quiet, scholarly little dissertations on political and social questions, catching more truly than any fiction I have ever read the quality of the Stalinist mind, voice, and life-style, without sacrificing our human sympathy for the elder Isaacsons. . . .

[This] is the work of a novelist trying desperately to catch hold of at least a fragment of the truth of our time and succeeding in getting hold of more than most have lately managed to capture.

Richard Schickel. *Harper's Magazine*. Aug., 1971. p. 94

A method for giving us the *feel* of a historical moment—as distinct from information about it—is something that more and more of our novelists may soon be after, now that Thomas Pynchon and Doctorow have shown us how it is done, now that the millennial sixties are over and we are looking back to see what happened rather than forward to see what next. . . . The method of [Doctorow's] new novel [*Ragtime*] is dictated by the lives and times of America during that moment between the turn of the century and World War I, the moment of the arrival of the Model T, the assembly line, the moving picture, and Scott Joplin's rags. *Ragtime* succeeds entirely—as his three earlier books did not—in absorbing rather than annotating the images and rhythms of its subject, in measuring the shadows of myth cast by naturalistic detail, in rousing our senses and in treating us to some serious fun. . . .

It incorporates the fictions and realities of the era of ragtime while it rags our fictions about it. It is an anti-nostalgic novel that incorporates our nostalgia about its subject. It is cool, hard, controlled, utterly unsentimental, an art of sharp outlines and clipped phrases. Yet it implies all we could ask for in the way of texture, mood, character and despair.

George Stade. *New York Times Book Section*. July 6, 1975. pp. 1–2

Ragtime is blandly and confidently assertive, laying its short sentences like steps on the road to nowhere, so we can't see ahead, anticipate; the characters are rhetorical ploys, but splendid. Doctorow is never confused by life, though he is often dismayed, and his impudence is both witty and grave, so we can be pleasantly caught between feeling that he is only a novelist on holiday and that all other visions of the period before his may be the really irresponsible ones. Even the ironic juxtapositions that Doctorow loves almost sentimentally may be right, necessary. Because so many of the juxtapositions are of nasty rich and suffering poor, his politics tend to seem leftish, but Doctorow tells with amusement and affection the story of a radical starving Jewish artist on the Lower East Side who becomes Baron Ashkenazy, movie maker and millionaire. His vision is of the Seventies more than of the Sixties, and the juxtapositions themselves entrance him more than any political view of history. . . .

It's hard to make a whole book out of what Doctorow does best here; it's excellent in vignettes and short passages but unsuited for plots where we come to know the characters too well. . . . Still, no one has written a book quite like *Ragtime*, just as no one had written one quite like *The Book of Daniel*. Doctorow's restless and witty thoughtfulness seems like some combination of Pynchon, Edward Gorey, and William Appleman Williams, and certainly no one ever was *that* before.

Roger Sale. *New York Review of Books*. Aug. 7, 1975. pp. 21–2

Doctorow reminds us that writing history is a very creative activity, and that the professional historian would not claim that it is possible to write history *objectively*. . . . Doctorow's own brilliant imagination has given us not only some rather compelling—and disturbing—versions of America's past, but in addition his skillfully crafted narratives confront us with the terrible wisdom of great art, altering us in a manner that perhaps even the best historical discourse cannot do.

Doctorow points out that history exists for most of us as sets of images—the more remote in time, the fewer the images. The images in Doctorow's novels often clash violently with those that have seized the popular mind. *Welcome to Hard Times* demolishes the romantic view of the Wild West and its adulation of the "social bandit," reminding us that we have lionized individuals whose only mark of distinction was plunder and murder. In the nineteenth century the American West functioned as the nation's "safety valve," promising a new start for those fleeing from failure or personal tragedy in the East. Aggressively promoted as Arcadia, the frontier enticed many with its lure of "free land"; "the myth of the garden" even suggested that rainfall would follow the plow. Unfortunately the harsh and unrelenting climate of the arid Great Plains refused to yield to the myth, and many who journeyed West, faced with the lack of timber and water so bountiful in the East, found the American Dream a mere mirage, their hopes evaporating into disappointment, failure, or disaster.

No one who reads *The Book of Daniel* will succumb to the recent nostalgia for the "Fabulous Fifties." . . . Like Doctorow's earlier novels, *Ragtime* indicts our complacency and admonishes us that we continue to indulge in an uncritical nostalgia at our peril. Doctorow's novels suggest that by refusing to analyze our own responsibility for our past failures—not infrequently projecting evil outward onto other nations—we ensure that periods of mass hysteria like the McCarthy era or the burning of the nation's cities in the sixties will haunt us again.

Daniel L. Zins. *Hollins Critic*. Dec., 1979, pp. 2–3

The excitement caused by *Ragtime* five years ago was so great that, long before its European publication, we who live on the Mediterranean were itching to get hold of a copy. Summoned to Hollywood for a script conference, I made straight for a Los Angeles bookstore and bought one. Jet lag abetted my decision to read the book before even making amicable contact with my temporary masters at Universal. I was, of course, disappointed. Literary reality has never yet lived up to literary expectation. But that E.L. Doctorow was a genuine experimentalist I did not doubt. The aim of *Ragtime* was as purely aesthetic as that of *Ulysses*: The joy lay in the manipulation of the crass elements of history. Houdini and Scott Joplin and Freud and Jung and certain of their less reputable contemporaries were drawn into a kind of ballet. Bernard Shaw had done something similar in his *In Good King Charles's Golden Days*, but Doctorow's achievement didn't seem derivative.

Rereading *Ragtime*, I find that most of the initial impact has been blunted: Literary shocks are subject to the law of diminishing returns. I find, too, a certain vacuity of literary display. What once seemed verbally startling is now revealed as mostly tinsel. But that Doctorow was superior to most of his American fellow-novelists in his concentration on fiction as form, not as a vehicle for special or ethnic preaching, is made very clear. A rereading of *Welcome to Hard Times* and *The Book of Daniel* has confirmed Doctorow's special status. *Loon Lake* exhibits a new formal direction. It is a difficult book and I don't think it is a successful one. But it is a very honorable attempt at expanding the resources of the genre. . . .

I am happy to learn that *Loon Lake* is already a popular book, in that it is a Book of the Month Club choice and eighty-odd thousand copies have already been printed. Happy because, whatever the faults of the work (nearly always the admirable faults of the overreacher), serious students of the novel must recognize here a bracing technical liberation, and such a recognition is being forced upon a readership probably happier with *Princess Daisy*. The bulk of our popular fiction is the work of either cynics or simpletons. The serious novelist's problem is to be uncompromising and yet to find an audience. Doctorow has found an audience and nothing could be less of a fictional compromise than *Loon Lake*. Like most writers who consider the craft to be primarily an exploration of the nature of human consciousness, he is brought up against such damnable problems as the validity of memory, the truthfulness of the senses, and, more than anything, the ghastly dilemmas of style. And, behind the epistemological agonies, there rests that basic obligation of all but the French antinovelists—to invent living personages and a convincing space-time continuum to hold them. Doctorow's characters—Joe, Penfield, Clara, even the grotesque Fat Lady of the carney—are alive, unrefracted by the often wayward medium. That *Loon Lake* breaks new technical ground and yet possesses so many of the traditional virtues of fiction must be accounted its peculiar distinction.

Anthony Burgess. *Saturday Review*. Sept., 1980, pp. 66–67

BIBLIOGRAPHY
Welcome to Hard Times, 1960 (n); *Big as Life*, 1966 (n); *The Book of Daniel*, 1971 (n); *Ragtime*, 1975 (n); *Drinks before Dinner*, 1979 (d); *Loon Lake*, 1980 (n); *American Anthem*, 1982 (t); *Lives of the Poets: Six Stories and a Novella*, 1984; *World's Fair*, 1985 (n); *Billy Bathgate: A Novel*, 1989; *Jack London, Hemingway, and the Constitution: Selected Essays, 1977–1992*, 1993; *Three Complete Novels*, 1994; *The Waterworks*, 1994 (n)

DONLEAVY, J. P. (1926–)

Mr. Donleavy doesn't care in the least why Sebastian [*The Ginger Man*] is what he is, what disorders in the world or, for that matter, what frustrations in the nursery have shaped him; he simply gives us Sebastian, and we may take him or leave him. If we take him, if

we read about him with some pleasure, that can only be because we envy his arrogant self-indulgence even while we disapprove of it. We, of course, are far too civilized to behave in any such outrageous fashion, but perhaps we sometimes wish we weren't. . . . Mr. Donleavy's [writing] is distinguished by humor, often inelegant, even coarse, but explosive and irresistible. Humor and poetry are his weapons. The whole novel is a wild and unpredictable outburst. Yet Mr. Donleavy is anything but an artless writer. Observe, for instance, the adroitness with which he moves from outside Sebastian's mind to inside it, from writing in the third person to writing in the first, and you realize how much control has created this image of chaos. *The Ginger Man* is a disturbing book, not because of its occasional vulgarity but because of its fundamental nihilism; it is also a powerful and original one.

Granville Hicks. *Saturday Review*. May 10, 1958. p. 31

Portions of this book [*The Ginger Man*] are obscene and/or blasphemous; other portions may give offense to those who are Irish by birth or sentiment. . . . Mr. Donleavy, a New York Irishman now living in London, reads at first sight like Henry Miller turned loose in James Joyce's Dublin. Soon, however, we realize that he possesses what Miller lost long ago—a sense of humor. . . .

Mr. Donleavy has been classed with England's ''Angry Young Men,'' and his hero's revolt-against-society-without-social-revolution attitude certainly resembles that of Lucky Jim and his successors. But right there all resemblance stops. Mr. Donleavy's Irish eloquence and American drive make him a Don Juan among the eunuchs. . . . Sebastian Dangerfield may not fully realize what a prize s.o.b. he is, but his creator does—and yet Donleavy finally makes us feel affection for him.

Vivian Mercier. *The Nation*. May 24, 1958. p. 480

A novelist must not simply abandon himself to every mood and every crazy idea that occurs to him as he writes. This is exactly what Mr. Donleavy appears to have done. . . . There is a lot of Joyce in the style: indeed, the presentation of much of the story through the consciousness of the hero is done in short, jerky sentences, so that we begin to weary of them. The writing is, in fact, rather slovenly, with many sloppy sentences and some confused grammar which I don't think are meant to represent the hero's way of putting things but simply represent Mr. Donleavy's way of writing. They can be found in *The Ginger Man* too.

This is an amusing and intriguing novel [*A Singular Man*], and it lacks the aimless cruelty that I for one found offensive in *The Ginger Man*. Its exuberance, comic imagination and sheer inventiveness make it easy and pleasant reading. But it frustrates the reader at the same time as it amuses him. A writer who can do this can surely do more, we feel, if he would both deepen and discipline his imagination.

David Daiches. *New York Herald Tribune Book Section*. Nov. 17, 1963. p. 6

Where did mad Dangerfield go and madder Mac Doon? What happened to Cocklan, Malarkey and O'Keefe, that fantastic host of *The Ginger Man*? . . . Where a Joycean prose was so richly befitting to Dangerfield . . . the same device when employed by

George Smith [of *A Singular Man*] comes out in a voice flattened like a ventriloquist's. . . . Dangerfield, a tragic yet dangerous clown, asked questions worthy of a saint. . . . But Smith has no questions to ask. . . .

For such a falling-off only the author may account. Yet one wonders whether, in a civilization so affluent that it is no longer necessary to think, there may not be an indication here that, to be a writer, it has become equally inessential to write.

Nelson Algren. *The Nation*. Dec. 14, 1963. pp. 422–3

Nihilism is given its full head in . . . J.P. Donleavy's *The Ginger Man*. . . . it comes as a momentous shock when we begin to realize that Dangerfield is not an endearing "Rabelaisian" rascal. Not only does he treat his wife with appalling cruelty, but we learn that because he has been stealing their baby's milk money, the infant has developed a case of rickets. This is no joke, and it jolts us right out of the realm of pleasant fantasy into the most sordid of realities—which, of course, is exactly what Donleavy wants it to do. Why, then, do we continue to feel the attraction of Dangerfield? What claim does he exert on our sympathies? The decisive factor, I think, is his honesty. Unlike almost everyone else in the book (and incidentally unlike Kerouac's heroes, with whom he has been foolishly compared), he never simulates feelings that he does not in fact feel, he refuses to make excuses, and he will not hide behind empty pieties. He is not a burn and a scoundrel out of ill will or malice or insensitivity. On the contrary, he strikes us as a man who has looked into himself and found nothing, and then looked about the world and found no set of values (neither "traditional" nor "liberal") in sufficiently robust condition to exert any pull over his soul. Dangerfield, in short, is not exacting a fantasy of release, he is living by the truth of his times. Nor is he a rebel, for there is nothing to rebel against, everything gives way before him.

Norman Podhoretz. *Doings and Undoings* (Farrar). 1964. pp. 168–9

Compared to *The Ginger Man*, *A Singular Man* is an extremely neat presentation of the hero consenting to the trap of his society. For all of its incidental invention, however, it is a repetitive and finally rather dull book. *The Ginger Man* shows some of the same tendencies, but, in it, the style has not yet become mannered. The rhetoric, hovering between bathos and mockery, is suitable to Sebastian. The stylistic device—and a very clever one—which allows sudden shifts from first to third person within a paragraph suggests that Sebastian speaks as himself and then steps back to see himself, that he is always both sufferer and observer. The interplay between Sebastian's reality and his fantasies give a richness to the novel which is diluted only by the recognition that, in fact or in fancy, he is a somewhat tiresome man to spend much time with.

Gerald Weales in *Contemporary American Novelists*, edited by Harry T. Moore (Southern Illinois). 1964. p. 153

BIBLIOGRAPHY
The Ginger Man, 1958 (n); *The Ginger Man*, 1961 (d); *A Singular Man*, 1963 (n); *Meet My Maker the Mad Molecule*, 1964 (s); *The Saddest Summer of Samuel S.*, 1966 (n); *The Beastly Beatitudes of Balthazar B.*, 1968 (n); *The Onion Eaters*, 1971 (n); *The Plays*, 1972 (coll); *A Fairy Tale of New York*, 1973 (n); *The Unexpurgated Code: A Complete Manual of Survival and Manners*, 1975; *The Destinies of Darcy Dancer, Gentleman*, 1977 (n); *Schultz*, 1979 (n); *Leila: Further in the Destinies of Darcy Dancer, Gentleman*, 1983 (n); *De Alfonce Tennis: The Superlative Game of Eccentric Champions: Its History, Accoutrements, Rules, Conduct, and Regimen*, 1984 (misc); *J.P. Donleavy's Ireland: In All Her Sins and in Some of Her Graces*, 1986 (t); *Are You Listening Rabbi Löw?*, 1987 (n); *A Singular Country*, 1990; *That Darcy, That Dancer, That Gentleman*, 1991 (n); *The History of the Ginger Man*, 1994 (a); *The Lady Who Liked Clean Rest Rooms: The Chronicle of One of the Strangest Stories Ever to be Rumored about around New York*, 1997; *An Author and His Image: The Collected Shorter Pieces*, 1997; *Wrong Information Is Being Given out at Princeton*, 1998

DOOLITTLE, Hilda (H.D.) (1886–1961)

The poems of H.D. do not lend themselves to convenient classification, as Poems of Passion and Emotion, Poems of Reflection, Poems of the Imagination, and Poems Descriptive, and so on. In all of them, passion, emotion, reflection, and the image, the sharp, vivid image that does the work of description, are fused together in the burning unity of beauty. . . . H.D. invariably presents her subtlest, most metaphysical idea under some living sensuous image solid enough to carry the emotion. The air we are given to breathe may be rarefied to the last degree, yet we are moving always in a world of clear colours and clear forms.

May Sinclair. *Dial*. Feb., 1922. p. 203

H.D.'s thoughts were not often concerned with the world she lived in; another one, to her far more desirable, filled her mental vision almost completely. . . . She often sat with us, chatting of everyday things, when I am sure her spirit was somewhere near the shores of the Aegean. . . . I think a large part of her peculiar charm lay in the fact that she was always coming back to us; and she never came back reluctantly. . . . We had . . . the idea that she found us satisfying in our way and that her preoccupation with an ancient world only made her the more pleased with her own when she was in it. Her sudden entries into our talk and her effortless domination of it filled us with elation because she brought with her such disarming enthusiasms and delivered herself with such amazing speed and clarity on any subject that might be uppermost.

James Whitall. *English Years* (Harcourt). 1935. pp. 55–6

There was about her that which is found in wild animals at times, a breathless impatience, almost a silly unwillingness to come to the point. She had a young girl's giggle and shrug which somehow in one so tall and angular seemed a little absurd. She fascinated me, not for her beauty, which was unquestioned if bizarre to my sense, but for a provocative indifference to rule and order which I liked.

She dressed indifferently, almost sloppily and looked to a young man, not inviting—she had nothing of that—but irritating, with a smile.

William Carlos Williams. *Autobiography* (Random). 1951. pp. 67–8

Her special form of the mode of Imagism—cold, "Greek," fast, and enclosed—has become one of the ordinary resources of the poetic language; it is a regular means of putting down words so that they will keep; and readers are mistaken who confuse familiarity with flatness or who think facile imitation of the form emulates the perception that goes with the mode. She has herself made sharply varied use of her mode, but she has not exhausted it; she has only—for present changing purposes of a changing mind—partly broken it down into the older, perhaps primary mode of the distich. The relatively long uncoiling of a single spring of image, unpredictable in its completeness, now receives a regular series of impulses and arrests, of alternations and couplings.

R.P. Blackmur. *Language as Gesture* (Harcourt). 1952. p. 352

H.D. has herself abandoned the "Imagist" effects of her early poems, the best of which suggest the clean line of Greek vase-paintings and, for all the passion they assert, have a lapidary quality about them. In her later work the old vehemence, if subdued, is present, and the phrasing recalls the familiar cadences. Yet it differs from what went before in carrying a far heavier weight of symbolic meaning and in being overtly subjective. . . . Again and again, turning the pages of this quondam Imagist, the reader hears a melody not only in the lines themselves but suggested by them, as it were, hovering just beyond the expressed sounds for some musician, not a maker of verse, to capture and realize.

Babette Deutsch. *New York Times Book Section*. Sept. 22, 1957. p. 37.

"Invisible," "most proud," in love: these are the strength of the poet throughout the work of H.D. Ardent and clear, her lyrics show us that an everpresent devotion to the art of the poem sustains passion. The strength of the poem lies in her command of words so that they call up sensual immediacies (as images) and are themselves sensual immediacies (as elements of a most skilled tonal structure), and, increasingly in the later work, in her knowledge of words, their roots and histories, their lore and powers. Her trilogy written during the Second World War *The Walls Do Not Fall*, *Tribute to Angels*, and *The Flowering of the Rod* stands with Ezra Pound's *Cantos*, Eliot's *Four Quartets*, and William Carlos Williams' *Paterson* as a major work of the Imagist genius in its full.

Robert Duncan. *Poetry*. Jan., 1958. p. 256

H.D. in her perceptions of timelessness, and in her search for the "real," has always seemed to be writing in advance of her times. In that respect the present generation might well regard her as "a poets' poet."

To be "a poets' poet" has few tangible rewards, for this means that the poet who holds that title must often wait upon the future for true recognition. Yet the poems of H.D. have acquired a life, a being of their own; at this date one need not argue that they should be read. Of contemporary poets H.D. is among the few whose writings are likely to endure.

Horace Gregory. *Commonweal*. April 18, 1958. p. 83

H.D.'s strength lies in her rendition of detail: her weakness is in structuring those details into a poetic, characterological, or, still more acutely, fictional whole. Poems, fiction, even essays like *Tribute to Freud* or *By Avon River* become a series of isolated images or events linked by free associations, often through mythological themes. At the very sentence level, her boundaries tend to be ill-defined. A sentence modifier from one sentence will seem to apply to the next. Lists (of which H.D. uses many) will be oddly broken between sentences. The word to which a pronoun or adjective refers may be one or two sentences back; the reference itself may be twinned or multiple. Often, for structure, she will resort to a series of parallel structures to be summed into a totality. Sometimes she will use negations—a series of *not*'s or *nor*'s to strip off the extraneous and come to the final, finely rendered residue as a climax.

Doubtless no small part of H.D.'s propensity for myth is a quest for similar organizing structures. If one can see present people, events, and feelings as projections or continuations of a simpler, more structured mythic past, they become more manageable and, for H.D. at least, somehow more real. She uses for living people the image of a palimpsest or a series of old photographic negatives on top of one another; the sign one sees on the surface implies a deeper reality underneath. She seeks to turn herself, her very body, into an hieroglyph or emblem—as in the use of her initials for a seal or sign. Her poetry, like the myths she emulates, manifests that which is spiritual, abstract, and timeless by the hard, the real, the objective, the exact.

Norman Holland. *Contemporary Literature*. Autumn, 1969. p. 475

The poems in this new book [*Hermetic Definition*] date from circa 1960, when [H.D.] was 74. She had been inserted into literary history at 26, when Ezra Pound invented "Imagism" to supply a context for five poems of hers. A normal context would have been a book of poems, but Pound sensed that a book's worth would be a long time getting written. He had didactic uses for a "movement" anyhow, and "Hermes of the Ways," "Orchard," a few others might as well exemplify it as wait for an *oeuvre*.

Unhappily the invented movement that was meant to float her reputation encapsulated it, and though she lived many more decades and extended her self-definition through many volumes, she has remained totally identified with the very little she had done when she was first heard of. It is as though five of the shortest pieces in *Harmonium* were to stand for the life's work of Wallace Stevens.

Her psychic life was contorted. Freud himself analyzed her, and she lived her last years at Küsnacht on Lake Zurich under care that was partly psychiatric, partly directed toward the corporeal needs of an old woman who had broken her hip and walked only with difficulty. She kept resin and pine-cone burning in her room, and pondered books of hermetic symbolism. . . .

These poems are "about" her phantasmagoric self, in part her sense of having become a myth prematurely. . . .

Hugh Kenner. *New York Times Book Section*. Dec. 10, 1972. p. 55

In short, writing under the pressure of war in London, the bombs falling around her, H.D. brought together all her powers in one marvelous synthesis [*Trilogy*]: her verbal power in its superbly workable maturity, her spiritual and cognitive powers, the power of her concern for the humanity of the world. If she said things about the "holiness" of the "scribe" which I as a young man in that same war learned to distrust and fear, she nevertheless grounded them firmly in the actuality of the human condition; and in doing so she created one of the great works of her time in poetry. It has been out of print for many years. Now its publication in one volume is an event to be celebrated by us all.

Hayden Carruth. *Hudson Review*. Summer, 1974. p. 311

Why is her poetry not read? H.D. is part of the same literary tradition that produced the mature work of the "established" artists—T.S. Eliot, Ezra Pound, William Carlos Williams, D.H. Lawrence. She in fact knew these artists well; she had known and almost married Pound while the two were students in Philadelphia (H.D.'s intensely absorbing recreation of their lifetime friendship, *End to Torment*, is being prepared for publication); her friendship with Williams goes back to those student days; but most important, she was an active member of the London literary circle that spun out the dazzling succession of artistic "isms"—imagism, dadaism, vorticism, futurism—before the catastrophe of the First World War smashed this coterie into the confusion of a spiritual wasteland. Like these artists, H.D. began writing in the aestheticism and fascination for pure form characteristic of the imagists; and like them, she turned to epic form and to myth, religious tradition, and the dream as a way of giving meaning to the cataclysms and fragmentation of the twentieth century. Her epic poetry should be compared to the *Cantos*, *Paterson*, the *Four Quartets*, and *The Bridge*, for like these poems, her work is the kind of "cosmic poetry" the imagists swore they would never write.

The pattern of her poetic development not only paralleled that of more famous artists, but it was also permeated by major intellectual currents of the century. In 1933 and 1934 she was psychoanalyzed by Freud, an exploration deep within her own unconscious that ultimately linked for her the personal with the universal, the private myth with the "tribal" myths. At the same time that she studied with Freud, the convinced materialist, she was a student of comparative religion, of esoteric tradition, and, like Yeats, of the occult. The forces perpetually at work to bring a directionless century to war were a constant preoccupation in her work. Consciously rejecting the mechanistic, materialist conceptions of reality that formed the faith of the empirical modern age, H.D. affirmed a "spiritual realism" and the relevance of a quest for intangible meanings. Her growth into a poet exploring the psyche or soul of humanity and reaching out to confront the questions of history, tradition, and myth places her squarely in the mainstream of "established" modern literature. But still, outside of a few poets

like Denise Levertov, who wrote "An Appreciation" of H.D., Robert Duncan, and the aficionados who circulate a pirated edition of *Hermetic Definition*, few people read her poetry. . . . H.D. was a serious prolific poet exploring the same questions as her famous counterparts and thus inviting comparison with them. It is something of an understatement, I think, to say that in our profession artists do not have to wear the badge of greatness in order to have articles and books written about them. The simple relevance of her work to the issues and experiments of modern poetry demands that it be studied. . . .

The answer is simple enough, I think. It lies biographically and factually right in front of our critical noses—too close perhaps to be seen easily. It lies in what makes H.D. and her work different from a long string of more studied poets like Eliot, Pound, Crane, Williams, and Yeats. And it lies in the response of her critics. She was a woman, she wrote about women, and all the ever-questioning, artistic, intellectual heroes of her epic poetry and novels were women. In the quest poetry and fiction of the established literary tradition (particularly the poetic tradition), women as active, thinking, individual human beings rarely exist. They are instead the apocalyptic Pocahontas and the demonic prostitute of *The Bridge*, the goddess in the park sought by the poet Paterson, the superficial women walking to and fro talking of Michelangelo. They are the static, symbolic objects of quest, not the questors; they are "feminine principles," both threatening and life-giving, and not particularized human beings. Women are dehumanized, while the quest of the male poet is presented and understood as the anguished journey of the prophet-seer for the absolute on behalf of all humankind. For "mankind" they may be the spokesmen, but for "womenkind" they are not. As a woman writing about women, H.D. explored the untold half of the human story, and by that act she set herself outside of the established tradition.

Susan Friedman. *College English*. March, 1975, pp. 802–3

Helen in Egypt is an epic poem of great depth and beauty; it is H.D.'s finest achievement. . . . As an impersonal poem *Helen in Egypt* is a meditation upon the cause of war. War takes place, says H.D., because someone (or some group or culture) will not bend to the will of someone else (or some other group or culture).

H.D. sees the war between the sexes as primal and believes all wars follow the same logic. A person or culture attempts to enforce his will on another person or another culture. Who, then, is to be blamed? The one who attempts to force his will on another or the one who refuses to submit? In H.D.'s experience men had attempted to force their will upon her; resistance leads to strife. Do we then blame the woman for resisting? Or do we blame her for provoking the attack? Or, suggests H.D., is it not the case that men ought to take responsibility for war? They are, after all, the aggressors. Why should women be blamed for simply existing? These are some of the larger questions that prompt the strophes of *Helen in Egypt*. . . .

While it is true that H.D.'s vision was informed by far more than Aldington, Pound, and Lawrence, she was always deeply aware that the particular traumatic events involving them had precipitated her coming to consciousness. Her work with Freud enabled H.D. to bring these events into consciousness on an epic scale and to understand the transpersonal nature of her experience. The Helen-Iphigeneia realization is not a mere metaphor for a personal event; rather, the event was the efficient cause, the precipitating occurrence from which the conception was realized. But the efficient cause is not the sufficient cause. The conception was informed by the entire body of circumstances of the poet's life and mind.

> Janice S. Robinson. *H.D.: The Life and Work of an American Poet* (Houghton Mifflin, 1982), pp. 362, 369, 378–79

BIBLIOGRAPHY

Sea Garden, 1916 (p); *Choruses from Iphigeneia in Aulis*, 1916 (tr); *The Tribute and Circe*, 1917 (p); *Choruses from Iphigeneia in Aulis and Hippolytus*, 1919 (tr); *Hymen*, 1921 (p); *Heliodora*, 1924 (p); *Collected Poems*, 1925; *Palimpsest*, 1926 (s); *Hippolytus Temporizes*, 1927 (pd); *Hedylus*, 1928 (s); *Red Roses for Bronze*, 1931 (p); *The Hedgehog*, 1936 (s); *Ion*, 1937 (tr); *The Walls Do Not Fall*, 1944 (p); *Tribute to the Angels*, 1945 (p); *The Flowering of the Rod*, 1946 (p); *By Avon River*, 1949 (p); *Tribute to Freud*, 1956 (e); *Selected Poems*, 1957; *Bid Me to Live*, 1960 (n); *Helen in Egypt*, 1961 (p); *Hermetic Definitions*, 1972 (p); *Trilogy*, 1973 (p); *A Tribute to Freud, Writing on the Wall, and Advent*, 1974 (e); *An End to Torment: A Memoir of Ezra Pound*, 1979 (m); *HER-mione*, 1981 (n); *Notes on Thought and Vision, and The Wise Sappho*, 1982 (e); *The Gift*, 1982 (n); *Collected Poems, 1912–1944*, 1983; *Nights by H.D.*, 1986; *Ion: A Play after Euripides*, 1986; *Selected Poems*, 1988; *Between History and Poetry: The Letters of H.D. and Norman Holmes Pearson*, 1997; *The Gift: The Complete Text*, 1998

DOS PASSOS, John (1896–1970)

Dos Passos *may* be, more than Dreiser, Cather, Hergesheimer, Cabell, or Anderson the father of humanized and living fiction . . . not merely for America but for the world.

Just to rub it in, I regard *Manhattan Transfer* as more important in every way than anything by Gertrude Stein or Marcel Proust or even the great white boar, Mr. Joyce's *Ulysses*. For Mr. Dos Passos can use and deftly does use, all their experimental psychology and style, all their revolt against the molds of classic fiction. But the difference! Dos Passos is *interesting!*

> Sinclair Lewis. *Saturday Review*. Dec. 5, 1925. p. 361

If we compare Dos Passos with other of our leading novelists, we find no one who is his superior in range of awareness of American life. In his tone, he most nearly approaches Hemingway. He can be as ''hard-boiled'' as the latter, particularly when he is dealing with hard-boiled characters; his freedom of language is, if anything, greater; his viewpoint, also, is nearly as external and behavioristic. But he has a greater range of sympathy. . . . And his social sympathies, one might almost say his class passions, give a drive to his work that Hemingway's, with its comparatively sterile point of view lacks. In its social implications Dos Passos' work is more nearly akin to that of Dreiser and Sinclair Lewis, and still more to that of Upton Sinclair. But where Sinclair's people are wax dummies, Dos Passos' are alive and convincing.

> Henry Hazlitt. *The Nation*. March 23, 1932. p. 344

Dos Passos will perhaps be remembered more as the inventor or at least the early practitioner of a technique in fiction than for the lasting significance of his novels. . . . Dos Passos attempts to catch in fiction the inventions of the day, the camera eye, the movie, the newspaper headline. He conveys dates and the background by flashes of contemporary events. The effect on the unity of the novels is confusing but the representation of confusion is evidently one of the author's chief aims. The "hero" of the novels is the contemporary scene rather than any individual. He attempts to crowd an era, a whole cross-section of a city or a period of economic development into a novel.

> Halford E. Luccock. *Contemporary American Literature and Religion* (Willett). 1934. p. 148. Courtesy of Harper and Brothers

In Dos Passos. . . there is a beautiful imaginative sympathy which permits him to get under the skin of his characters, but there is no imagination, and no Don Quixote. Dos Passos testifies to all this by his use of newsreels, just as he seeks the full sensibility in the impressions of the camera eye and the heroic character in the biographies; but in his central narrative the standpoint is always narrowed to what the character himself knows as the quality of his existence, life as it appears to him. And this leveling drags with it and tends to make rather crude and sometimes commonplace the sensibility shown in the other panels. . . . The whole truth of experience (if past literature is not wholly nonsense) is more than the quality of most lives. One is sure that Dos Passos knows this, since it is the reason for his four forms and his discontinuity. His novel is perhaps the greatest monument of naturalism because it betrays so fully the poverty and disintegration inherent in that method. Dos Passos is the gifted victim of his own extraordinary grasp of the truth. He is a victim of the truth and the whole truth.

> Delmore Schwartz. *Southern Review*. Autumn, 1938. pp. 364–7

The philosophy of *U.S.A.* was taut, as the book itself was taut. Everything in it echoed its mass rumble, and the far-reaching tactile success of the book came out of that massed power, the heaping together of so many lives in symmetrical patterns of disaster. Dos Passos' effects have always depended on a violence of pace, on the quick flickering of the real, the sudden climaxes where every fresh word drives the wedge in. No scene can be held too long; no voice can be heard too clearly. Everything must come at us from a distance and bear its short ironic wail; the machine must get going again; nothing can wait.

> Alfred Kazin. *New Republic*. March 15, 1943. p. 353

Certainly he is not a Tolstoy or even a Zola, to mention two masters of the panoramic form. In America today he ranks below Hemingway and Faulkner for many reasons, but principally because he seldom feels his way deeply into his characters. As a novelist—and in life, too—he is always moving, always hurrying off to catch a taxi, a bus, a train, a plane or a transatlantic steamer; and he tells us as much about people as a sensitive and observing man can learn in a short visit. That leads to his writing a special type of novel, broad and wind-scarred into intricate patterns like the Aral Sea, not deep like Lake Baikal, that gash in the mountains which is said to contain more water than all the Great Lakes together.

There is, however, a converse to this statement. To achieve breadth in a novel is a difficult art in itself and it is one in which no other American writer—not even Frank Norris—has ever approached Dos Passos.

Malcolm Cowley. *New Republic*. Feb. 28, 1949. p. 21

Nothing is deeper in the man than his fear of power. To begin with, he feared the power of the military, as he had experienced it in the first World War, and the power of men of wealth. The hatred of war and exploitation grew so acute that he accepted for a time the tempting radical doctrine that only power can destroy power. But what he saw of communism in Russia, in Spain, and at home convinced him that the destroying power could be more dangerous than the power it overcame. . . . His sympathies are wholly with the people who get pushed around, whether it is Big Business or Big Government that does the pushing. His trouble is simply that he has not found the ''better than that,'' the alternative to both bignesses, and hence his growing fear of government can only be accompanied by a growing toleration of business. . . . He has allowed himself to be forced into choosing one horn of the dilemma, and he is nicely impaled.

Granville Hicks. *Antioch Review*. Spring, 1950. pp. 95–8

Dos Passos. . . knows the everyday world of the ordinary apprehension—in which the essential Dos Passos appears to be so self-consciously not at home—as the movement of whole groups and classes and the clash of group prejudices. He is so preoccupied with representing these movements by newspaper headlines, historical figures, and, above all, by type characters that he reduces the movement of awareness in his characters to the simplified pattern we ascribe to the imaginary average man. You do not know his people except as you know the journalist's average businessman, Vassar girl, or labor leader; nor can you believe that the drama of their lives represents Dos Passos' full awareness of experience; the stifling personal and sensory awareness of the ''Camera Eye,'' so completely isolated from any larger context, is the Dos Passos who is omitted from the narrative: it is his Mallarmé, as the narrative is his Lenin.

Arthur Mizener. *Kenyon Review*. Winter, 1950. pp. 16–7

Chronic remorse, most moralists agree, is an unsalutary sentiment—the sinner who has genuinely repented does not become any the cleaner by rolling interminably in the mud; and chronic remorse is peculiarly disastrous where novelists are concerned. The novelist obsessed with the errors of the past—John Dos Passos is a case in point, since his political switch from far left to far right—is irresistibly drawn to revenge himself on his past by rewriting it, by showing that what he found good was disgusting. And the literary results of such an enterprise are apt to resemble a dredging operation: the principal yield is mud.

Charles J. Rolo. *Atlantic Monthly*. Oct. 1954. p. 98

Dos Passos' hate, despair and lofty contempt are real. But that is precisely why his world is not real; it is a created object. I know of none—not even Faulkner's or Kafka's—in which the art is greater or better hidden. I know of none that is more precious, more touching or closer to us. This is because he takes his material from our world. And yet, there is no stranger or more distant world. Dos Passos has invented only one thing, an art of story-telling. But that is enough to create a universe. . . . Dos Passos' world—like those of Faulkner, Kafka, and Stendhal—is impossible because it is contradictory. But therein lies its beauty. Beauty is a veiled contradiction. I regard Dos Passos as the greatest writer of our time.

Jean-Paul Sartre. *Literary and Philosophical Essays* (Criterion). 1955. pp. 89, 96

In retrospect, the work of Dos Passos falls into three periods. There is first the expression of the lonely dissident, the esthetic recluse. . . . Almost alone among the high individualists of the 1920s, those gifted expatriates and exiles, Dos Passos had, by the end of the decade, found a cultural base for his literary work.

This base was a theoretical rather than strictly political Marxism. The product of the second period included *Manhattan Transfer* in 1925 and the major trilogy, *U.S.A.*, published from 1930 to 1936. These are still the core of Dos Passos' fiction; they are persuasive and penetrating novels; and their description of American civilization, which hardly applied in the 1930s, may seem all too prophetic in the 1950s. But the crux of the Dos Passos problem is right here, too. The collapse of his belief in the Russian Revolution, the disillusionment with the methods of the Communist Party, led not only to a major revision of his thinking, but, apparently, to a complete cessation of his creative energy and his human emotions. There was a psychic wound that has never stopped bleeding.

Maxwell Geismar. *The Nation*. April 14, 1956. p. 305

John Dos Passos writes with great ease and he is technically inventive. He has conceived various means to write the story of his times as he sees it. *The Great Days* is a well and even an ingeniously constructed book. It is remarkable to think of how much it takes in, because the novel is only of normal length. Dos Passos has always been best at establishing scenes, rather than in portraying characters with depth and strong individuality. The characters reflect a world that is constantly changing, bringing failure and defeat. . . . The broken hopes of youth and of the days when this century was young have never been repaired. The expectations of the Wilsonian period have never been recovered. The later disappointments of the New Deal and the Second World War and the post-war era arouse less anger and, in the end, there is resignation. This is the sense of Dos Passos' writing as I can gauge it. He has honestly recorded the play of hope and disappointment over four decades. He has done this with dignity and seriousness.

James T. Farrell. *New Republic*. April 28, 1958. p. 18

With the change in emphasis since *U.S.A.* from the novel to history, there has been a corresponding change in the content and stimulus of Dos Passos' writing: from the imaginative toward the intellectual, from the need to create toward the need to understand and to preserve, from synthesis toward analysis. Dos Passos has not lost sight of his original twin goals of life, art and thought, "the desire to create" and "the desire to fathom"; and the writing of history is still *an art*. But it is not art (no great historian has been accused of artistic genius), and Dos Passos has simply moved nearer one guidepost than the other. He has been less concerned to produce lasting works of the imagination—art—and more concerned to devote his efforts to maintaining a civilization in which art is possible.... In his recent novels and reportorial commentaries, Dos Passos is too oppressed by the immediate and also too conscious of the writer's duty to inform and to teach before it is too late. Only in the histories, in which he is looking back a century and more, does the reader feel the aesthetic distance of the artist from his materials: the possibility of a view broad enough to be comprehensive and meaningful, and of a serenity permitting him to be wise and undidactic.

John H. Wrenn. *John Dos Passos* (Twayne). 1961. pp. 170, 175

Dos Passos' external devices are so obtrusive as to make us suspect that they are a mechanical attempt to establish a unique style and language not otherwise forthcoming. Clearly Dos Passos has *wanted* to discover a language which would be *internal*, in the sense of being an organic quality of his fiction, informing the whole with its tonality and structure. This quest for a language is suggested in the prologue to *U.S.A.* Here we have the familiar theme of the homeless young man on the road, and after a Whitmanesque catalogue of the places he has been to, the young man muses "it was the speech that clung to the ears, the link that tingled in the blood; U.S.A. . . . mostly U.S.A. is the speech of the people." This may remind us of other writers who are in the Whitman tradition: Thomas Wolfe—"Remembering speechlessly we seek the great forgotten language"—and William Carlos Williams—"What common language to unravel?" And it reminds us of Whitman himself, the Whitman of *Democratic Vistas*, who says that it is the duty of American writers to find a language which is at once a personal style and an archetypal expression of the culture. Lacking the thaumaturgic power to turn this difficult trick, Dos Passos has manufactured over the years a style that is energetic, efficient, and mostly anonymous.

Richard Chase. *Commentary*. May, 1961. pp. 398–9

Dos Passos' theme might be described as the capture of the nation by "strangers" who have penetrated the American Eden as insidiously as the tribe of the Snopeses infiltrated into William Faulkner's Yoknapatawpha County. To the Puritan "Saints" of the seventeenth century, the "strangers" were merely the unsanctified or unregenerate portion of the community. To Dos Passos, who ferociously memorialized them in a famous passage in *U.S.A.,* the "strangers" are the subverters of the American dream, spiritual parricides of the Founding Fathers. They might be old-stock Americans—college presidents, judges, statesmen, clergymen, labor czars—anyone in short who, as Dos Passos once wrote, "turned our language inside out" and "took the clean words our fathers spoke and made them slimy and foul." They scored terribly in 1927 when they electrocuted two Italian anarchists, but during the intervening years, according to Dos Passos' novelistic history

of the Republic, they have infected the entire body politic, corrupted the labor movement, corrupted the values of the nation, and reduced the "Saints" to a tiny embattled minority of libertarians.

Daniel Aaron. *Harper's Magazine*. March, 1962. p. 55

. . . Dos Passos has always been a negative function of power; that is, one finds him always at the opposite pole of where he conceives power to be. In this sense, he is more an anarchist, and always was, than a socialist or a conservative.

What Dos Passos achieved in *U.S.A.* was the creation of a form appropriate to the theme of the overwhelming, impersonal force of society, a structure which would carry the meaning of the primacy of society and make the anonymous processes of society the very stuff of a fictional world. . . .

The ultimate despair we confront in *U.S.A.* relates closely to what happens to language in the book. From the preface where the voice of the Camera Eye sections first identifies the meaning of America with American speech and the meaning of words, there is a constant concern, dramatically as well as explicitly, with the corruption of language. As we have seen, the betrayal of the promise of America is that words have grown slimy in the mouths of the ruling classes who have perverted old ideals.... Power superpower finally overwhelms even the language which creates the identity of America and if Dos Passos could say "we stand defeated," the defeat was particularly keen for the writer, the man who depends on words and his belief in the efficacy of language to sustain his personal identity. I would even speculate wildly and suggest that the vision of society Dos Passos presents in *U.S.A.* was a defeat for him personally and that is perhaps why he seems, to me at least, less estimable a writer after *U.S.A.* than before it. He had ceased to believe in the power of words.

John William Ward. *Carleton Miscellany*. Summer, 1965. pp. 26–7

Critics who have written about Dos Passos's journey to Spain during the Civil War, and who point to his shocking discovery while there of how ruthlessly the Communists were undercutting their supposed allies within the Popular Front as the operative cause of his disillusionment with radicalism, miss the point; the central experience in Dos Passos's political education in the early 1930s was the titanic labor of creating *U.S.A.* The trilogy changed the man who wrote it, inducing in him a new respect for "the ground we stand on," a new awareness of historical continuity, a new appreciation of the complexities of human motivation. History was not escapable, after all, nor was it as simple as it had seemed.... The battle-cry of *U.S.A.*—"all right we are two nations"—evokes the certainty of the younger author's mind, while the title Dos Passos gives to his Midcentury sketch of J. Robert Oppenheimer—"The Uncertainty Principle"—indicates the older writer's state of mind.

Kenneth S. Lynn. Introduction to *World in a Glass*, by John Dos Passos (Houghton). 1966. p. xv

The heroines, lost girls all, as well as the heroes of *U.S.A.* rest on 19th century types and naturalistic techniques which culminate in our standard cinematic images. Inadequately individualized and lacking complex and subtle development, the stereotypes nonetheless merge into a revealing vision of this country. The sordid patterns of defeat and the harsh cadences of the style, with their hypervisuality of place, poeticize the U.S.A., providing us with an America as recognizable and painfully endearing as an old movie. The experience of reading *U.S.A.* represents just this poetic and cinematic image of America, and in this Don Passos does not fail.

> Eleanor Widmer in *The Thirties*, ed. Warren French (Everett Edwards). 1967. p. 19

In functioning as an ''architect of history'' and attempting by means of the work of art to mold the course of social history, Dos Passos turned his fiction into a series of critical documents on the age, confronting contemporary problems from the time of his attack upon war in *Three Soldiers* to that of his assault upon labor in *Mid-Century*. His ''documents'' have been based upon a firm set of principles, sustained from first to last. Contrary to popular opinion, which has labeled him a political apostate, a liberal-become-conservative, his values have remained constant. Simply put, they comprise a hatred of ''collectivisms,'' with their concomitant of centralized power, an admiration for the ''proletarian soul,'' and a persistent desire to protect this ''soul'' from the aggregates of power.

If Dos Passos were willing to accept any label for himself, it might be that of an ''independent seeker,'' a nebulous term, to be sure, but one that suggests his perpetual focus both on individualism and on searching, with its implications of change. The various stereotypes that have been attached to him—the lost-generation aesthete, the fellow traveler, the ex-radical—have fitted only for a time. Underlying the ''phases,'' however, has been an unflagging credo, a faith in the individual sturdiness of the plain people. ''Individuality is freedom lived'' (*Occasions and Protests*, p. 52).

> W. Gordon Milne in *The Politics of Twentieth-Century Novelists*, ed. George A. Panichas (Hawthorn). 1971. pp. 264–5

Dos Passos went on producing—many novels, reportage of the World War II period, and long semi-popular histories of the growth of American democracy. But he felt isolated; he had lost his faith in people. This is even more striking a change than the long swing to the political right that went with it. . . . At the same time that he had, so to speak, come back to ''The American Way'' politically, he lost the openness, inventiveness and optimism that had made him so American when he was still a rebel. . . .

Dos Passos was one of the key figures in a literary lost generation that found itself and then lost itself again. It is a story still not fully told or understood, but these letters [*The Fourteenth Chronicle*], with their glimpses of an entire man who was so much more complex than his political notions or even his fiction, take us imaginatively and morally closer to understanding it.

> Robert Gorham Davis. *New York Times Book Section*. Oct. 14, 1973. p. 4

By its intricacy and by its comprehensive sweep the trilogy *U.S.A.* comes close to being the great American novel which had been the aspiration of writers since the turn of the century. It is one of the

ironies of our times that when the great American novel did arrive, it turned out to be condemnatory and pessimistic rather than a celebration of the American way. Yet there is an underlying affirmation in Dos Passos' denial. The American dream, battered and corrupted by men of ill will, or little will, still manifests itself—though in anguish—not completely stifled by the trappings of empire and the machinations of self-interest that the author describes.

What first aroused the enthusiasm of readers and critics was the technical virtuosity of the work. Dos Passos was clearly the heir of Balzac, Zola, and Galdós in his attempt to mirror contemporary society—as he was the competitor of Jules Romains, whose *Hommes de bonne volonté* was appearing during the same span of years. It is equally evident that the idea of multiple perspectives is something he owed to *Ulysses*. But the techniques he employed and the balance of elements he achieved are his own and stamp him as the last of the great inventors in the field of the social novel. He welded together four separate, even disparate, types of material, each of which is necessary to the statement the novel ultimately makes.

> George J. Becker. *John Dos Passos* (Ungar). 1974. p. 58

Century's Ebb may be unfinished, or at least unpolished, but it deserves to be published. It contains some good Dos Passos writing: the first, moving lyric about Walt Whitman, several impressionistic passages like one entitled ''Turnpike'' and another about George Eastman and his Kodak camera, and parts of the long narratives. But, finally, whether *Century's Ebb* is complete and whether it stands with Dos Passos' best fiction are not the main points to be made about the book. It is the last work of one of the major American writers to emerge during the 1920s. Most important, it brings down the curtain on Dos Passos' remarkable effort throughout his literary career to convey the panorama of 20th century society. His later novels are partly right wing polemics, but anyone wanting to dismiss Dos Passos should remember that he was not a crank, a Westbrook Pegler, but an intelligent, thoughtful man of letters who agonized about his politics.

> Townsend Ludington. *New Republic*. Nov. 22, 1975. p. 24

After his long and controversial career, John Dos Passos's literary politics remain a matter of some dispute. Starting out on the far Left and ending on the far Right, he has been called everything from agrarian to radical republican, rebellious neurotic to arch conservative. But the term most often applied to his fiction is ''anarchist''. Dos Passos, numerous critics have argued, was faithful to the individual alone, defending him in the early novels against the army, big business, and liberals, and in his later novels against the New Deal, big labor, and communists. . . .

Yet the novels themselves cannot be so neatly classified, for it is difficult to find in them any radical individualist who thrives. From the early aesthetes like John Andrews, crushed by the senseless machine, to the noble failures like Jasper Milliron and Blackie Bowman of the later novels, Dos Passos's individuals fare badly indeed. Even during the writer's more militant phase, his characters never find that bliss in unrestricted freedom that an anarchist philosophy would suggest. Instead, Dos Passos seems to be doing something else in his fiction—portraying the world in the dark, ''acid'' manner he discovered in Pio Baroja, a manner that can only be called ''picaresque.''

Although critics have occasionally noted a picaresque element in Dos Passos's fiction, none has applied the term consistently. Often the term "picaresque" has been used to mean "tale of the road," as in Linda Wagner's study, or to describe, by implication, Dos Passos's desperate vagabonds. Most careful has been Arthur Mizener, who called attention to a "characteristic novel form" in which a lone hero experiences "a series of socially representative adventures" that expose "the institutionalized corruption" of industry and politics. In a word, Dos Passos was a satirist—his target, the manifold threats to individualism. But to leave the matter there is to miss the most subtle and difficult aspects of Dos Passos's art. For the picaresque form inherently suspects individualism: it ruthlessly detaches its protagonists from all communal support, and then punishes them for their sins. Solitude *is* the picaro's sin: he wanders through a fallen world without church, saints, or God. For Dos Passos, this was the twentieth-century world, with its devastating wars and state terror, its rejection of those communal values he found in Federalist America. And yet it was the Federalists who preached freedom, the unrestrained inventiveness of a Franklin, whose "full career" had been "enough . . . for four men," the stout populism of a Jefferson. All his life Dos Passos sought to balance these conflicting needs for unrestricted freedom and visionary community. That balance was impossible in modern America, for the nation that so cherished restless enterprise had found the means to crush its visionaries—had turned its idealists into picaros and its picaros into millionaires. In his fiction Dos Passos explored the paradox; only in his histories could he master it.

Joseph Fichtelberg. "The Picaros of John Dos Passos." *Twentieth Century Literature*. Winter, 1988, pp. 434–35

Like many twentieth-century fictional masterpieces—*Ulysses*, for example, or Faulkner's Yoknapatawpha saga—*U.S.A.* seeks to portray a culture in both historical depth and social breadth by means of modernistic techniques. There is thus a modern epic convention, to which *U.S.A.* belongs, in which the traditional aim of the epic to make manifest the history and values of a culture is achieved, not by conformity to a prescribed set of epic rules, but by the author's individual adaptation of the complex fictional devices that have arisen in the twentieth century for the depiction of the interaction of self and society. The success of works in this convention derives not only from the depth of the author's insight into his culture but from the appropriateness and effectiveness of the modernistic fictional forms that he has chosen to render his vision.

Which is to say that *U.S.A.* can be discussed meaningfully in a number of ways but that the final test of its value and centrality in twentieth-century art lies in its nature and quality as a modernistic epic American novel. Dos Passos's model for the epic was principally Whitman as *U.S.A.* seeks to depict in full detail the "varied strains" that are the American experience. To Whitman, too, can be attributed Dos Passos's belief in a semimystical oneness in the multiplicity of America, a oneness that to Dos Passos was above all the nation's history of democratic idealism. There is also of course a Whitmanesque element in the deep exploration of self in the Camera Eye, an exploration that, in the end, is an exploration of what America should be and isn't. Thus, one of the most pervasive and central sources of relatedness, of unity, in *U.S.A.* is in its character as a self-reflexive novel in which the Camera Eye persona's search for identity and role results simultaneously in a

vision of self and a vision of America that is the remainder of the trilogy.

As an epic novel, *U.S.A.* is also a historical work, with history—like autobiography—simultaneously both a subject matter and a source of experimental form. In the pseudochronicle modes of the Newsreels and biographies Dos Passos consciously shapes a documentary base, through impressionistic selection and surreal juxtaposition, into an indictment of twentieth-century American life. . . .

U.S.A. is a kind of cubistic portrait of America—one in which the effect is of a multiplicity of visions rendering a single object, with every angle of vision related both to the object and to every other angle of vision. It is Dos Passos's relentless pursuit of juxtapositional relationships in the seemingly disparate and fractured modal ordering of the trilogy that is largely responsible for the integral vision of American life in *U.S.A.*

Donald Pizer. *Don Passos's U.S.A.* (Charlottesville: Univ. Pr. of Virginia, 1988), pp. 184–85

BIBLIOGRAPHY

One Man's Initiation: 1917, 1920s (n) (republished as *First Encounter*, 1945); *Three Soldiers*, 1921 (n); *Rosinante to the Road Again*, 1922 (n); *A Pushcart at the Curb*, 1922 (n); *Streets of Night*, 1923 (n); *Manhattan Transfer*, 1925 (n); *The Garbage Man*, 1926 (d); *Orient Express*, 1927 (n); *Airways, Inc.*, 1928 (d); *42nd Parallel*, 1930s (n); *1919*, 1932 (n); *In All Countries*, 1934 (j); *Three Plays (The Garbage Man, Airways, Inc., Fortune Heights)*, 1934; *The Big Money*, 1936 (n); *U.S.A. (42nd Parallel, 1919, The Big Money)*, 1937; *The Villages Are the Heart of Spain*, 1937 (t); *Journeys between Wars*, 1938 (t); *Adventures of a Young Man*, 1939 (n); *The Ground We Stand On*, 1941 (h); *Number One*, 1943 (n); *State of the Nation*, 1944 (j); *Tour of Duty*, 1946 (j); *The Grand Design*, 1949 (n); *The Prospect before Us*, 1950s (e); *Chosen Country*, 1951 (n); *District of Columbia (Adventures of a Young Man, Number One, The Grand Design)*, 1952 (n); *The Head and Heart of Thomas Jefferson*, 1954 (b); *Most Likely to Succeed*, 1954 (n); *The Theme Is Freedom*, 1956 (e); *The Men Who Made the Nation*, 1957 (h); (with others) *Essays on Individuality*, 1958 (e); *The Great Days*, 1958 (n); *Prospects of a Golden Age*, 1959 (h); *Midcentury*, 1961 (n); *Mr. Wilson's War*, 1962 (h); *Brazil on the Move*, 1963 (t); *Occasions and Protests*, 1964 (e); *The Shackles of Power*, 1966 (h); *The Best Times*, 1966 (a); *World in a Glass: A View of Our Century Selected from the Novels of John Dos Passos*, 1966; *The Portugal Story: Three Centuries of Exploration and Discovery*, 1970 (h); *Easter Island: Island of Enigma*, 1971 (t); *The Fourteenth Chronicle*, 1973 (letters and diaries); *Century's Ebb*, 1975 (n); *John Dos Passos: The Major Nonfictional Prose*, 1988 (misc); *Streets of Night*, 1990 (annotated ed.); *John Dos Passos's Correspondence with Arthur K. McComb; or, "Learn to Sing the Carmagnole,"* 1991; *USA*, 1996 (3n [Library of America ed.])

DOVE, Rita (1952–)

Reading Rita Dove's first novel, *Through the Ivory Gate*, I get the sneaking suspicion that I'm back on my weekly fourth-grade trip to the library, this time with Ntozake Shange's "woman in yellow"—and she gets Toussaint L'Ouverture, adventure, resistance, and the Adult Reading Room, while I get Dove's puppeteer heroine, Virginia King, instead.

I group Dove and Shange together for more than the reference to the vignette from *for colored girls*. . . . They are both consummate poets in a line of African American women—Gwendolyn Brooks, Margaret Walker, June Jordan, Audre Lorde, and Alice Walker, for instance—who begin with verse and reach out to prose. Dove, Shange, Brooks, and Jordan belong to a smaller subset still: Jordan's *His Own Where* (1970) is an adolescent love story, while Brooks's *Maud Martha* (1952), Shange's two novels, *Sassafrass, Cypress, & Indigo* (1982) and *Betsey Brown* (1985), all are coming-of-age stories of memory, pain, and discovery with young Black girls at their centers.

Dove extends Brooks's legacy even further: *Thomas and Beulah* (1987) made Dove the second African American poet ever to win a Pulitzer Prize; Brooks was the first (1949). *Through the Ivory Gate* arches back to revise Brooks's *Maud Martha*, and to give its heroine more flexibility and independence, while at the same time it highlights their protagonists' surprisingly similar fluster and angst. Imploded, almost claustrophobic spaces, narrative snatches that show Black women dealing with regular, ordinary, everyday troubles of color, childhood, and romance—nothing magical, nothing loudly tragic or grand—this is what the two novels share.

Dove's story is the story of Virginia King as she rattles "around the emotional furniture of her childhood." With drama degree in hand and stint with a political troupe called "Puppets & People" just folded, she comes back to the Ohio city of her youth as "Miss Puppet Lady," a visiting artist in the Akron primary schools. Through flashbacks we get glances of Clayton, her college friend and lover, who turns out to be gay; her distanced and dehydrated parents Ernie and Belle, who move the family out to Arizona to save their marriage; selected family stories and secrets; her childhood racial and romantic traumas; her "majorette days" and her love of the cello and mime. In the narrative present Dove describes Virginia's interchanges with the fourth-grade class she teaches and their parents, including an affair with a too well-groomed and scented Black single father who, in her Grandma Evans's words, is "too good-looking to do good" but tries nonetheless.

Dove's strengths come through most forcefully when she describes, or when the narrative is in the mouths of, its older characters. Her father's impulsive, family-minus-mother jaunts out of the stultifying heat of his home, their drives to Hopi mesas and his lectures about Papago and Pima culture, bring him to life. . . .

One might argue that Dove patterns her narrative structure after a collage; she chooses bits and pieces that come together, not to make a whole but to make an impression. Flashes from present to past and vignettes made of memories (one could go on) work like pregnant pauses, inviting us to fill in gaps and become participatory readers. Yet most of her breaks act more like interruptions. . . .

Nineteen ninety-two was a rich year for African American women writers—*Jazz*, *Bailey's Cafe*, *Possessing the Secrets of Joy*—all deal with memory and highlight form; and God knows *Waiting to Exhale* adds pace to the everyday trials and tribulations of Black women not much older than Virginia King. Some might find *Through the Ivory Gate* charming, its structure challenging, its treatment of Black men unimportant or inoffensive, and its musings and memories the stuff of our literary tradition. Rather, I see

this as the first novel of an accomplished poet whose second novel might take off from *Through the Ivory Gate*'s stronger moments.

Gabrielle Foreman. *Women's Review of Books*. March 1993, p. 12

Mother Love is an unsparing book. It observes both the vanity of mother love ("duty bugles and we'll / climb out of exhaustion every time") and the cliché of its appeal ("Any woman knows the remedy for grief / is being needed"). These sardonic remarks appear in the title poem of the volume, which tells the story of Demeter's transmutation into a monster. What, Dove asks, must have happened inwardly to Demeter as a result of [her daughter] Persephone's abduction? . . . In Dove's poem, a woman, pitying the bereft Demeter, offers her a male child to nurse, thinking that it will console her. Instead, Demeter decides to "save" the baby from the vicissitudes of experience by burning him to death. This is Dove's gothic tale of maternal grief gone wrong. . . .

If this is mother love, it is a force that distorts personality like few others. A book taking on such a subject is not neat—for all Dove's wish to be neat—nor can it be, in an ordinary sense, beautiful. It is often harsh and often lurid. It is at times sentimental in wanting to be lurid. But it is an energetic book—one that throws motherhood into the arena of the mind and says, "Look at it."

It is typical of Dove's moral even-handedness that, having thought so much about the relation between mothers and daughters, she has also explored the subject of sons. In a play called *The Darker Face of the Earth*, which will have its premiere in 1996, she has moved the Oedipus myth into a Southern slave setting. And it is typical of Dove's literary restlessness that, after writing poems, stories, and a novel, she decided to try her hand at a play. She is not the first writer to refresh poetry at the wells of fiction and drama; but Rita Dove is first and foremost a poet, one whose laser glance exposes and cauterizes its subject in new and disturbing ways.

Helen Vendler. *New Yorker*. May 15, 1995, p. 92

BIBLIOGRAPHY
Ten Poems, 1977; *Mandolin*, 1982 (p); *Museum*, 1983 (p); *Fifth Sunday*, 1985 (s); *Thomas and Beulah*, 1986 (p); *Grace Notes*, 1989 (p); *The Yellow House on the Corner*, 1989 (p); *Through the Ivory Gate*, 1992 (n); *Selected Poems*, 1993; *The Darker Face of the Earth*, 1994 (pd); *Mother Love*, 1995 (p); *The Poet's World*, 1995 (lectures)

DREISER, Theodore (1871–1945)

In his muddled way, held back by the manacles of his race and time, and his steps made uncertain by a guiding theory which too often eludes his own comprehension, he yet manages to produces works of art of unquestionable beauty and authority, and to interpret life in a manner that is poignant and illuminating. There is vastly more intuition in him than intellectualism; his talent is essentially feminine, as Conrad's is masculine; his ideas always seem to be deducted from his feelings. . . . He gets his effects, one might almost say, not by designing them, but by living them.

But whatever the process, the power of the image evoked is not to be gainsaid. It is not only brilliant on the surface, but mysterious and appealing in its depths. One swiftly forgets his intolerable writing, his mirthless, sedulous, repellent manner, in the face of the Athenian tragedy he instills in his seduced and soul-sick servant girls, his barbaric pirates of finance, his conquered and hamstrung supermen, his wives who sit and wait.

H.L. Mencken. *A Book of Prefaces* (Knopf). 1917. pp. 95–6

I admired the things which he could do in writing which nobody else could do—the simple and poignant truths of life; and I thought his philosophic notions bosh and his historical truths mere uneducated ignorance. I found that he did not agree with those critics who praised him for the immense amount of bricks and mortar that were visible in his towering structure of fiction—the multiplicity of details which such critics called "realism." He was not especially interested in the details, but was using them, and perhaps over-using them, earnestly in trying to achieve beauty. He once told me with honest tears in his eyes that a novel had no excuse for existence unless it was beautiful. And by beautiful I knew that he meant true to the deep emotions of the human heart, not to the mere visible surface aspects of life.

Floyd Dell. *Homecoming* (Farrar and Rinehart). 1933. p. 268

It is because he has spoken for Americans with an emotion equivalent to their own emotion, in a speech as broken and blindingly searching as common speech, that we have responded to him with the dawning realization that he is stronger than all the others of his time, and at the same time more poignant; greater than the world he has described, but as significant as the people in it. To have accepted America as he has accepted it, to immerse oneself in something one can neither escape nor relinquish, to yield to what has been true and to yearn over what has seemed inexorable, has been Dreiser's fate and the secret of his victory.

Alfred Kazin. *On Native Grounds* (Reynal). 1942. pp. 89–90

Theodore Dreiser . . . suggested to me some large creature of the prime wandering on the marshy plains of a human foreworld. A prognathous man with an eye askew and a paleolithic face, he put me in mind of Polyhemus . . . a Rodinesque figure only half out from the block; and yet a remark that someone made caused him to blush even up to the roots of his thin grey hair. Dreiser was hypersensitive, strangely as one might have thought,—he was a living paradox in more than one way; but a lonelier man there never was.

Van Wyck Brooks. *Days of the Phoenix* (Dutton). 1957. p. 20

There is little question that Theodore Dreiser is the most distinguished member of the whole group of modern American novelists. . . . He was a realist. . . . Yes, he, partly through his own innocence, perhaps, and early origins, told the truth about life when he could discover it. Probably no one else in our literature has had such a direct and intimate feeling for the common forms of experience, pleasant or disgraceful. But he was also, like Balzac,

who is the closest European counterpart, one of the high romantics of literature.

What gave his work its remarkable texture, its glamour, really, was his simple sense of the variety and mystery of life on all its levels.

Maxwell Geismar. *American Moderns* (Hill and Wang). 1958. p. 50

He was not, by and large, an attractive figure, and the letters present his unattractive qualities more relentlessly than the books that have been written about him have done. One notes, for instance, his dependence on other persons, particularly women, and his offhand acceptance of their services to him. One notes his arrogance and his greed. But at the same time one feels in the letters, as in the novels, that this was a man who was utterly faithful to his own vision of life.

As he wrote Mencken, he was born with a bias, a bias not so much in favor of the common man as a bias in favor of men and women as victims—of the economic system, of their own impulses, of life itself. This bias led him into ridiculous contradictions, but it also gave him insights that have made his novels, with all their many faults, a permanent part of our literature.

Granville Hicks. *Saturday Review*. April 4, 1959. p. 16

Dreiser was the first American to portray with truth and power our modern world of commerce and mechanization, the first to portray the dismal depersonalization of the individual which results from urbanization and intensifying societal pressure to conform, the first to draw us frankly and grimly as a nation of status-seekers. . . . *Sister Carrie* of 1900 and *The Bulwark* of forty-five years later, aside from particulars, tell the same story about America. Man is a mechanism, his pitiful existence determined by factors of biology and social environment which Dreiser, for want of a better term, labels "chemisms." The cosmos operating in his stories is uncaring, unfeeling; at bottom it is an unfair universe, controlled by gods who disdain involvement in their creation. We can nod in agreement with the writer or cavil at the darkness of his pessimism, but we are forced above all to stop, to consider, to think. . . . Probably because of his philosophy—we are all companions in the same sinking ship—Dreiser feels keenly the plight of each individual human soul at the mercy of chance and of forces beyond his control. It is significant that, though failures abound in his novels, there are no villains, only human beings who are more or less fortunate than their neighbors. In the Dreiser world, each life, is necessarily a tragedy.

Philip L. Gerber. *Theodore Dreiser* (Twayne). 1964. pp. 173–5

I soon found that Dreiser did straddle two worlds of time, our own and the past. His first novel, *Sister Carrie*, was begun in the nineteenth century and finished in the twentieth—a fact of which Dreiser was highly conscious. His masterpiece, *An American Tragedy*, was published at the midpoint of the 1920s, the decade when American writing assumed an importance on the international scene that had been unimaginable when Dreiser began. He was one of those—in America, the most important of those—who put their shoulder to the wheel turning past into present; one of the great international company of *survivors*, men formed before the turn of the century but dominant after the First World War—among them Mann, Gide, Stravinsky, Joyce, Wright, Valéry, Yeats.

For someone like myself, brought up in New York, the world of Dreiser's fiction is immediately familiar, and for all of us his subject matter remains the most important. He wrote about the child who comes alive in the American city, that ugly, intoxicating center of the modern world. Yet when I first read Dreiser I found him quite unlike any American novelist before him (and most after), in his rooted urbanism first of all. He seemed to accept the American situation as the norm—an unusual state of affairs for an American writer—and his style was peculiar. He handled words, sometimes brilliantly, sometimes wretchedly, without the sound of pebbles in the mouth—the nervous rattle of insecurity that makes much American fiction, for me at least, a provincial phenomenon even at its most brilliant. The publication of *Sister Carrie* in 1900 marks the boundary line not only between the old and the new, but between the European and the American century.

Ellen Moers. *Two Dreisers* (Viking). 1969. p. viii

We have been speaking as though *Sister Carrie* were important primarily as an historical and social document and as a record of the psychology of Dreiser. But it is more than a document, it is a vivid and absorbing work of art. In dealing with a novel, the most obvious question is what kind of material the author has thought worth his treating, what kind of world stimulates his imagination. For Dreiser this was the world he lived in and the world he was, and by accepting as fully as possible this limitation, he enlarged, willynilly, by a kind of historical accident if you will, the range of American literature. The same kind of compulsive veracity that made him record such details of his own life as masturbation and theft, made him struggle to convert into fiction the substances of experience at both the social and personal level that had not been earlier absorbed. The kind of realism that is associated with William Dean Howells had little relation to the depths that Dreiser inhabited, and even if Frank Norris had shocked the country with the realism of *McTeague*, he had, in the end, gratified the moral sense of America by converting the novel of greed and violence into a cautionary fable. But *Sister Carrie* was different from anything by Howells or Norris. What was shocking here was not only Dreiser's shamed willingness to identify himself with morally undifferentiated experience or his failure to punish vice and reward virtue in his fiction, but the implication that vice and virtue were, in themselves, mere accidents, mere irrelevances in the process of human life, and that the world was a great machine, morally indifferent.

Robert Penn Warren. *Southern Review*. Spring, 1971. p. 359

Dreiser's basic tendency as a novelist was to establish a clear central structure (Hurstwood's fall and Carrie's rise; Cowperwood's alternating business and love affairs; Clyde's parallel life in Kansas City and Lycurgus; Solon's double life as businessman and Quaker), to pursue this structure to its seeming conclusion (death or an emotional stasis), yet to suggest both by authorial commentary and by a powerful symbol within the narrative (a rocking chair, deepsea fish, a street scene, a brook) that life is essentially circular, that it moves in endless repetitive patterns. Frequently this circular

pattern involves a seeker or quester—sometimes driven by desire, sometimes by other motives—who finds at the end of the novel that he has returned to where he started: Carrie still seeking beauty and happiness; Jennie once again alone despite her immense capacity to love; Cowperwood's millions gone; Clyde still walled in; Solon returning to the simplicity of absolute faith. It is possible to visualize Dreiser's novels as a graphic irony—the characters believe they are pushing forward but they are really moving in a circle. . . .

Another pervasive structure in Dreiser's novels is best illustrated by "Butcher Rogaum's Door." The three principal figures in the story—Rogaum, Theresa, and Almerting—can be characterized as a well-meaning but ignorant and authoritarian parent, a youth seeking the wonder and excitement of life, and a seducer who takes advantage of the conflict between parent and child. Rogaum, blind to the needs of youth, drives Theresa to rebellion, and she is almost seduced by Almerting. This triangle and the narrative which derives from it constitute an archetypal structure within the world of Dreiser's novels, though it is a structure which appears in increasingly complex and displaced forms. . . .

A third significant characteristic of the form of Dreiser's early stories is their tendency toward the parody of sentimental or hackneyed narrative patterns. . . . Throughout his career as a novelist Dreiser was to rely on similar formulas, particularly those of the seduced country girl in *Sister Carrie* and *Jennie Gerhardt* and the Horatio Alger myth of success in the Cowperwood trilogy, *The "Genius"*, and *An American Tragedy*. In most instances, he both used the myth and reversed some of its traditional assumptions. Carrie "rises" not only despite her seduction but also because of it, and Clyde finds neither luck nor pluck in his attempt to succeed. Like many major American novelists. Dreiser used the mythic center of American life as a base from which to remold myth into patterns more closely resembling experience as he knew it.

The various overlapping structures which I have been discussing constitute in their totality the formalistic expression of Dreiser's basic cast of mind, a cast which can best be called ironic. For though Dreiser seldom engages in verbal irony, he habitually relies in his fiction on an intricately interwoven series of narrative or structural ironies. That is, he constantly juxtaposes the true nature of a situation and a character's estimation of it in order to reveal the weaknesses either in the character's values or in ours, a revelation which is at once theme and form in his work. . . .

On the one hand, these are the conventional ironies of all fiction. Fiction—because it is a temporal rather than a spatial art, and because it dramatizes the difference between what characters believe and what the author knows—is inherently ironic. On the other hand, Dreiser's ironic formulas in his short stories look forward to a bolder and more intense reliance on this particular characteristic of fiction than is usual in most novels. Like Stephen Crane, Dreiser translated an uneasy mixture of iconoclasm and unconventional belief into a structural principle. But whereas for Crane this principle was a subtle and complex modulation in authorial tone, imagery, and diction, for Dreiser it was an equally sophisticated ordering of events within an extended narrative. Dreiser labored to perfect this technique throughout his career as a writer of fiction, and after some twenty-five years he achieved in *An American Tragedy* a novel whose structural approximation of his deeply ironic view of life results in a work of complex beauty.

Donald Pizer. *The Novels of Theodore Dreiser* (Univ. of Minnesota Pr., 1976), pp. 25–27

To the end, Dreiser made no compromises with popular taste, and wrote as honestly, if not as well, as he always had. But his search for philosophical answers and his advocacy of social change had carried him beyond the novel to a more urgent vision of science and politics. His style and his fictional imagination could not keep up with his speculations. The mysteries of character, the ironies of fate, and the hidden workings of the social system ceased to interest him, at a time when the social system's failure dominated literary consciousness. In the end he had moved beyond the passions that drove his characters and novels, beyond the gropings of individuals toward a higher realm of meaning; he had stepped out from behind the scrim of fiction and confronted the great questions directly.

He had an enormous influence on American literature during the first quarter of the century—and for a time he *was* American literature, the only writer worth talking about in the same breath with the European masters. Out of his passions, contradictions, and sufferings, he wrenched the art that was his salvation from the hungers and depressions that racked him. It was no wonder that he elevated the creative principle to a godhead and encouraged by word and example truthful expression in others. If one were to identify the central, unifying theme of his contradiction-riddled life it was that he was totally subsumed in the role of author. Like many novelists, he was a congeries of different selves, from Hurstwood and Carrie to Cowperwood and Clyde. Moreover, he saw himself and all human beings as characters in the great, shapeless novel of life manipulated by the Author/Creator behind the veil.

He was the most "American" of novelists. His hungry curiosity probed the nooks and crannies of the national life, as he sought to perform what he saw as his mission—understanding a large, youthful, dynamic country that had no deep roots in the past and that was in a perpetual state of change and becoming. He retained a deep compassion for the voiceless mass of individuals in this land: their tawdry dreams and desires had for him the beauty of prayers.

His journey ended, ironically, in Hollywood, a factory town of dreams, beneath the expensive soil of Forest Lawn. He had frequently written of the lure of illusion and how it betrays the seeker. But art and beauty and love were themselves illusions. Or were they? In the end, he discovered, perhaps, that they were part of the greater Reality.

Richard Lingeman. *Theodore Dreiser: An American Journey, 1908–1945* (New York: Putnam's Sons, 1990), pp. 481–82

One must wonder whether Dreiser, always hostile to orthodox Christianity, would have resorted to those thinkers whose primary concern was the defense of orthodoxy, even had he been aware of them. Instead, Dreiser, who considered himself "more of a romanticist than a realist," simply evolved independently a personal rationale for belief that paralleled the primary defense of belief of the Romantic Era. Like the thinkers of that earlier age who ironically transformed science from the cause of doubt into the bastion of faith, Dreiser utilized science to escape a hopeless conception of the universe as a godless, self-operating mechanism and to secure a spiritual vision of the cosmos as a divine creation. Both in exploiting the authority of science for spiritual purposes and in interpreting the complex processes and order of nature that science revealed as a proof of the deity's existence, Dreiser's philosophy was a curious twentieth-century reoccurrence, independently evolved, of eighteenth- and early nineteenth-century Romantic thought.

Secondly, one might be tempted to dismiss Dreiser's final philosophical beliefs as intellectually shallow. Perhaps the lack of scholarly attention to Dreiser's philosophical writings lies in his reaching a philosophical conclusion that was in vogue over two centuries earlier. There may be a lack of intellectual sophistication in Dreiser's inability to go beyond his factual knowledge of Darwinian evolution to realize that the philosophical implications of evolutionary theory undercut the use of design as a proof of a supernatural designer's existence. One should recall, however, that Dreiser's responses to life and nature were always more importantly emotional than intellectual, that his philosophy was built more on intuition and faith than on logic and reason, and that he was, after all, an artist and not a philosopher or scientist. The real value of his final philosophy lies not in its originality, its intellectual sophistication, or its contribution to the canon of American philosophy, but in the personally satisfying closure that it gave Dreiser's troubled and confused, lifelong quest to know the unknowable.

Louis J. Zanine. *Mechanism and Mysticism: The Influence of Science on the Thought and Work of Theodore Dreiser* (Philadelphia: Univ. of Pennsylvania Pr., 1993), p. 212

BIBLIOGRAPHY

Sister Carrie, 1900 (n); *Jennie Gerhardt*, 1911 (n); *The Financier*, 1912, rev. ed., 1927 (n); *A Traveler at Forty*, 1913 (a); *The Titan*, 1914 (n); *The Genius*, 1915 (n); *A Hoosier Holiday*, 1916 (a); *Plays of the Natural and the Supernatural*, 1916; *Free, and Other Stories*, 1918; *The Hand of the Potter*, 1918 (d); *Twelve Men*, 1919 (b); *Hey, Rub-A-Dub-Dub!* 1920 (e); *A Book about Myself*, 1922 (a); *The Color of a Great City*, 1923 (t); *An American Tragedy*, 1925 (n); *Chains*, 1927 (s); *Moods*, 1928, rev. ed., 1935 (p); *Dreiser Looks at Russia*, 1928 (e); *A Gallery of Women*, 1929 (b); *My City*, 1929 (t); *The Aspirant*, 1929 (p); *Epitaph*, 1929 (p); *Fine Furniture*, 1930 (s); *Dawn*, 1930 (a); *Tragic America*, 1931 (e); *America Is Worth Saving*, 1941 (e); *The Bulwark*, 1946 (n); *The Stoic*, 1947 (n); *The Best Short Stories*, ed. Howard Fast, 1947; *The Best Short Stories*, ed. James T. Farrell, 1956; *Letters*, 1959; *Letters of Louise*, 1959; *Notes on Life*, 1974 (e); *American Diaries, 1902–1926*, 1982; *An Amateur Laborer*, 1983 (n); *Sister Carrie*, definitive ed., 1983 (n); *Selected Magazine Articles, 2 vols.*, 1985, 1987 (j); *Dreiser-Mencken Letters 1907–1945*, 1986; "Heard in the Corridors," *Articles and Related Writings*, 1988 (j); *Journalism*, 1988; *Yvette Szekely Eastman: Dearest Wilding: A Memoir with Love Letters from Theodore Dreiser*, 1995; *Theodore Dreiser's Ev'ry Month*, 1996; *Dreiser's Russian Diary*, 1996

DREXLER, Rosalyn (1926–)

This vital, intense "diary" [*I America the Beautiful Stranger*] of one Selma Silver, who was growing from ages 13 to 16 in the 1930's, is swift, complete, individual, and universal. You can mock its occasional sillinesses, but you're left holding its truths. For Selma is wholly convincing even when you can hardly believe her. . . . Back then, when "teenager" hadn't yet been invented, I don't think anybody talked the way Selma sometimes does. But nobody back then (except maybe Saroyan) wrote as spiritedly as Mrs. Drexler does, either.

Maggie Rennert. *Book Week*. June 27, 1965. p. 22

Rosalyn Drexler's plays suggest, more than anything else, the early Marx Brothers. Wayward, full of lip, fantastic yet anchored in domesticity, they work at reordering all those matter-of-fact details, from the date on the calendar to the necessity of putting on one shoe after another, which obstruct us in our pursuit of significant whim and appetite. . . . All her dialogue issues from an imagination which has previously discovered the uses of language for new guise, for bluff, feint, decoy and red herring—all necessary properties and instrumentalities of the crucial game that goes on in most of her work. The game might be called "keep them guessing" or "never give a sucker an even break." For Mrs. Drexler's imagination holds that the world is forever trying to impose roles and identities upon us which it is our duty and pleasure to resist and repudiate by outwitting the identifiers and the casting directors.

Richard Gilman. Introduction to *The Line of Least Existence* by Rosalyn Drexler (Random). 1967. pp. ix–xi

In addition to writing plays, the libretto for *Home Movies* which won the off-Broadway award known as the "Obie," and two successful novels, Rosalyn Drexler is a successful painter. This visual orientation may explain her highly untraditional view of theatrical language, a quality evident in all her plays. Like Koch, she conceives of language as most engaging when least eloquent, and closest to a state of pure "flatness." In *Hot Buttered Roll* the dialogue is in the prose style of the girlie magazine. The play is about a certain Mr. Corrupt Savage, whose most passionate wish is to go on spending his days in contemplation of the supposedly inspiring pictures and text characteristic of this genre. . . . In Drexler's reality, the eternally flesh-contemplating Corrupt Savage is the nearest thing to a true saint, or hero. It is the cold calculators who surround him, those contemptuous of human fantasies however odd or pathetic, who are the real villains of the piece.

Michael Benedikt. *Theatre Experiment* (Doubleday). 1967. p. 197

The Line of Least Existence is a joy to read, as are all Rosalyn Drexler's plays in the collection recently published by Random House. Few contemporary playwrights can equal her verbal playfulness, fearless spontaneity, and boundless irreverence; few in fact, share her devotion to pure writing, preferring their language functional, meaningful, or psychologically "real." Whether her plays amount to anything, whatever that means, is hard to say: hers is obviously an up-to-date sensibility, and I read considerable off-hand, tough, supercool wisdom about human relationships into her fantastifications, knowing all the time that they may be as frivolous as they look.

Michael Smith. *The Village Voice*. March 28, 1968. p. 50

The new literary voice comes from some odd and perilous psychic area still being charted, some basic metabolic flashpoint where the self struggles to convert its recurrent breakdowns into new holds on life and reality. It is the voice of writers like Donald Barthelme, Thomas Pynchon, and Rosalyn Drexler. In her new book [*One or Another*], Mrs. Drexler monitors the voice of Melissa . . . married to Mark. . . . In these lives madness is no longer a possibility—it is a note in their chord of being that automatically sounds with every breath they draw. . . . What counts now is the delicate new apotheosis, a new transcendence that accepts the mad world as the only human habitat, while plotting shrewdly against its madness. Few writers have been able to suggest this new transcendence. Mrs. Drexler is one of them: funny, scary, preternaturally aware, she is at the exact center where the new sensibility is being put together cell by cell.

Jack Kroll. *Newsweek*. June 1, 1970. p. 87

One or Another is a very funny book; moreover, it is both funny "ha-ha" and funny "weird," an observation Melissa Johnson, the novel's heroine-narrator, would be likely to make herself. In *One or Another* reality and unreality are merged; the borderline between dreams and actual events has been erased; shadows are indistinguishable from substance. Obviously, a novel of the interior is not concerned with plot. Mere sequences of events hold no interest. Style alone sustains *One or Another*. With careful economy and wit (that rare commodity bludgeoned out of so much of contemporary literature), Miss Drexler guides the reader through the tortured dreamscape in which Melissa Johnson finds both refuge and exile.

William Hjortsberg. *New York Times Book Section*. June 28, 1970. p. 5

[In *To Smithereens*] the relaxed sleaziness and community of the lady wrestling world alternates with the frantic, tired chic of the plastic New York art scene, in which here-barely-disguised New York artists and hangers-on act out their own fantasies of power, success, and grandeur. Does it all sound slightly sick, weird, ugly/sad, and obsessed-with-violence? It's exactly the opposite. . . . [Rosalyn Drexler] has a marvelous talent for taking this kind of material and imbuing it with qualities of great warmth and wicked satire, pathos, and a haunting aura of nostalgia for a world most of us have never known. . . . She's an absolute original who can take all the ingredients that usually characterize "serious fiction" . . . and use them with inventiveness, playfulness, and even hilarity.

Sara Blackburn. *Book World*. March 19, 1972. p. 5

The scene of [*To Smithereens*] is less a time and a place—New York, mainly in the late Sixties and early Seventies—than a condition of consciousness. New York becomes a name for a brand of hysteria, for a circus of crazies, comically seen and perfectly human and manageable as it turns out. Paul and Rosa, individual and well-defined as they are, tend to disappear into this collective portrait. Paul is the twitchy, ruined modern male from an R. Crumb comic ("the *universal* Paul," Rosa thinks), and Rosa is the resurgent female, all immediacy, innocence, and half-nelsons.

"You're not as crazy as you seem, are you?" a character says in Rosalyn Drexler's play *The Line of Least Existence*. "None of us is. We're all rational people." The specific context of the words makes them sound like a desperate pleading lie; we are just as crazy as we seem, if not crazier, but please let's not admit it. But the play itself, and in particular the character of the woman speaking the lines, suggests that what the words say is literally, drably true. We are dull people, and any semblance of vivid craziness we may present is an illusion. Mrs. Drexler knows that we really are crazy, and in very bad shape; but she also knows that the forms of our craziness have a conformity, a banality all of their own. Between madness and grayness, or out of a gray madness, we have to put something together.

> Michael Wood. *New York Review of Books*. Aug. 10, 1972. p. 14

The raunchy and the ridiculous are Drexler's home territory—you feel she spends a lot of time in all-night cafeterias. Her word-play is like sword-play—with rubber swords that still deliver a stinging slap. Her set-pieces—newspaper clippings, radio interviews, beauty advice—are among the delights of [*The Cosmopolitan Girl*]; her one-liners are memorable. . . . She weaves a seamy web of parodies that covers the situation perfectly. Moving back and forth between the absurd and the everyday Drexler puts both in their place—on the same plane. *The Cosmopolitan Girl* is a send-up and send-off for the New Woman.

> Sara Sanborn. *New York Times Book Section*. March 30, 1975. p. 4

BIBLIOGRAPHY

I America the Beautiful Stranger, 1965 (n); *The Line of Least Existence*, 1967 (d); *One or Another*, 1970 (n); *To Smithereens*, 1972 (n); *The Cosmopolitan Girl*, 1975 (n); *Starburn: The Story of Jenni Love*, 1979 (n); *Bad Guy*, 1982 (n); *Rosalyn Drexler: Intimate Emotions*, 1986; *Dear*, 1997 (d)

DU BOIS, W.E.B. (1868–1963)

What Henry James wrote of Nathaniel Hawthorne is equally true of W.E.B. Du Bois: "our author," James wrote, "must accept the awkward as well as the graceful side of his fame; for he has the advantage of pointing a valuable moral." Hawthorne's moral was that "the flower of art blooms only where the soil is deep, that it takes a great deal of history to produce a little literature, that it needs a complex social machinery to set a writer in motion." Du Bois's reputation as a man of literature is surely the "awkward" side of such fame as he possesses, and one meaning of his awkward side is essentially the same as Hawthorne's (as James saw it), with an important difference. The flower of art will bloom only where there is liberty or the memory of liberty. Du Bois understood the need for justice in the growth of the flower of art: "The time has not yet come," he wrote in 1913, "for the great development of American Negro literature. The economic stress is too great and the racial persecution too bitter to allow the leisure and the poise for which literature calls." Or, as James went on in the famous passage about Hawthorne, "American civilization has hitherto had other things to do than to produce flowers. . . ."

The other, more graceful sides of Du Bois's reputation vary with the attitude of each observer but rest somewhere in his pioneering and persisting works of history and sociology and his decades of crusading journalism against neoslavery in the South and in some respects similar oppression in the North. Trained at Fisk, Harvard, and the University of Berlin, he produced essays, monographs, and books of history and sociology that gave him by themselves the most prominent place among black American thinkers, so that the NAACP could write with justification in 1934 that "he created, what never existed before, a Negro intelligentsia, and many who have not read a word of his writings are his spiritual disciples and descendants." Certainly of Afro-American writers and the Afro-American theme one may claim of Du Bois what has been written of the English sociologists Sidney and Beatrice Webb—that every creative writer who has touched on the field of sociology has, directly or indirectly, been influenced by them.

But Du Bois ventured into the field of belles-lettres. And not by accident but as part of the plan of his life. On his twenty-fifth birthnight (1893) he confided solemnly to his journal that "these are my plans: to make a name in science, to make a name in art and thus to raise my race."

A bibliography of his writings runs to some two thousand entries, out of which it is difficult to separate those completely untouched by his love of art. But there are poems enough for a slender volume, a multitude of partly personal, impressionistic essays, some verse drama, autobiographies, five novels—including a trilogy composed near his ninetieth birthday. Great reputations have been made of a smaller volume of writing, but most of this work has contributed little to Du Bois's fame. Indeed, his basic competence as a man of literature has been challenged. An angry Claude McKay, singed by a Du Bois review of his first novel, informed him that "nowhere in your writings do you reveal any comprehension of aesthetics." The poet, novelist, and critic Arna Bontemps thought Du Bois unimaginative in that he leaned toward "the tidy, the well-mannered, the Victorian" in his choice of literature. His first biographer Francis Broderick barely mentioned this belletristic writing and declared that Du Bois wanted "a literature of uplift in the genteel tradition." His second biographer, Elliott M. Rudwick, mentions the creative work not at all. And though Du Bois called his second novel "my favorite book" among the two dozen or more he published, a major historian of the black novel in America dismissed him as a "Philistine."

Du Bois himself did not show great pride in this aspect of his work; he was apologetic on the very few occasions he wrote of his efforts in literature. His first novel was "really an economic study of some merit"—the sum total of his commentary on the work; he was hesitant to write "mere" autobiography; *Dark Princess* was his favorite book but that remark is all he ever ventured about the novel; his poems were "tributes to Beauty, unworthy to stand alone." Nor was he always complimentary about actual achievement in black literature. In 1913 he saw the body as "large and creditable [though] only here and there work that could be called first-class." In 1915 a five-point plan for the future of the race included "a revival of art and literature," presumably moribund. In 1926, surveying the field for the *Encyclopaedia Brittanica* he judged that "all these things are beginnings rather than fulfillments," though they were certainly significant beginnings. In 1933 he mourned that the so-called "Harlem Renaissance" had "never taken real and lasting root" and that "on such an artificial basis no real literature can grow." Somewhere around 1960 one of his fictional characters looked in vain for recent work of major artistic quality: "In the last decade we have not produced a poem or a novel, a history or play of stature—nothing but gamblers, prizefighters and jazz. . . . Once we could hear Shakespeare in Harlem.''

But with these splashings of cold water there was an equally cool and lucid sense of the potential of black writing, so that Du Bois could write in April 1920 that ''a renaissance of American Negro literature is due,'' and observe in the decade that followed, almost from the day of his prediction, the accuracy of his insight. Nor is there any lack of evidence that Du Bois was highly regarded as a man of literature, from the early praise of William and Henry James and the reverence in which he was held by black poets such as James Weldon Johnson and Langston Hughes, to the radical socialist magazine *The Messenger*, which in 1919 damned Du Bois with praise of him as ''the leading litterateur of the race.'' But more important than testimonies is a survey of his somewhat motley collection of essays, poems, novels, and other work for the ways in which he helped to shape modern Afro-American writing. For Du Bois, maturing in the most repressive period of black American history, took unto himself the primary responsibility of the would-be mythmaker, applying a luminous imagination and intelligence to ''Adam's task, of giving names to things.'' It is only slight exaggeration to say that wherever the Afro-American subsequently went as a writer, Du Bois had been there before him, anticipating both the most vital ideas of later currency and the very tropes of their expression. Some of these anticipations are slighter than others, but none is trivial to anyone who knows black literature. Collectively they underscore Du Bois's significance and raise challenging questions about the relationship of politics, art, and the individual imagination. . . .

Arnold Rampersad. *American Literature*. March, 1979, pp. 50–68.

During the course of his long career, W.E.B. Du Bois produced superb work in many genres. His Harvard dissertation *The Suppression of the African Slave Trade* (1896) was a pioneering, minutely detailed analysis of the growth and eventual elimination of the slave trade to the Unites States; his absorbing rendering of African culture and African-American history *The Negro* (1915) served as ''the Bible of Pan-Africanism''; and his later historical book *Black Reconstruction* (1935) bitingly challenged the traditional view of the post-Civil-War period as a time of white suffering and Negro abuses and abominations. His studies of the black family and community, especially *The Philadelphia Negro* (1899), remain valuable; his countless essays and reviews, not only in *The Crisis* but in other academic journals and popular magazines and newspapers, are impressive in their scope and virtuosity; and his numerous articles on education, labor, and the Pan-African movement further testify to his national and international vision of the development of colored people. He also wrote novels, stories, and poetry, and invented mixed gênres of his own, as the sociologically acute and lyrical *The Souls of Black Folk* (1903) demonstrates.

Du Bois's many autobiographical writings, notably *Dusk of Dawn* (1940) and his posthumous *Autobiography* (1968), are also rewarding texts that situate the life of the writer within the complex trends of the late-nineteenth and twentieth centuries.

As a premier man of letters, Du Bois has few rivals in this century. Yet with the exception of *The Souls of Black Folk*, his writings are infrequently taught and rarely accorded in literary history the credit they deserve. In part this results from the fertile ways in which Du Bois's writings cross and exceed generic and disciplinary categories. Who should teach him? Where should he be taught? Du Bois's astonishing range has possibly worked to his disadvantage, particularly in the academy, leaving the majority of his books unstudied because it is unclear to whose departmental terrain they belong. ''His contribution,'' concludes Arnold Rampersad, ''has sunk to the status of a footnote in the long history of race relations in the United States.''

Another, more commanding reason for Du Bois's uneven and troubled reputation is that he wrote politically: He always perceived his writing, in whatever form or forum, as having political point and purpose. As he noted in a diary entry on his twenty-fifth birthday, '''I . . . take the world that the Unknown lay in my hands and work for the rise of the Negro people, taking for granted that their best development means the best development of the world''' (*Autobiography*). Du Bois assembled knowledge, fired off polemics, issued moral appeals, and preached international brotherhood and peace in the hope of effecting differences in the lives of the lowly and oppressed. He stood for equality and justice, for bringing all men and women into ''the kingdom of culture'' as co-workers (*Souls*). So much was this Du Bois's intention that he was willing to use the explosive word *propaganda* to accent it. Viewing himself as, in everything, a writer and an artist, he affirmed that ''all art is propaganda and ever must be, despite the wailing of the purists. I stand in utter shamelessness and say that whatever art I have for writing has been used always for propaganda for gaining the right of black folk to love and enjoy'' (''Criteria for Negro Art'').

Du Bois's blunt deployment of art as ''propaganda'' makes plain the reason that he has proved an awkward figure for literary historians, yet it still remains curious that he is undertaught and undervalued. William James, Nathaniel Shaler, Albert Bushnell Hart, George Santayana, and others praised Du Bois during his student days at Harvard. Hart later said that he counted him '''always among the ablest and keenest of our teacher-scholars, an American who viewed his country broadly''' (cited in *Autobiography*). Some of America's most gifted novelists, poets, and playwrights admired him. Eugene O'Neill once referred to Du Bois as ''ranking among the foremost writers of true importance in the country.'' Van Wyck Brooks commended him as ''an intellectual who was also an artist and a prophet,'' a man ''with a mind at once passionate, critical, humorous, and detached'' and ''a mental horizon as wide as the world.'' Even earlier, no less an eminence than Henry James termed him ''that most accomplished of members of the Negro race.'' It was William James who sent his brother a copy of *The Souls of Black Folk*, referring to it as ''a decidedly moving book.''

The Souls of Black Folk is indeed a landmark in African-American culture. James Weldon Johnson, in his autobiography, stated that the book ''had a greater effect upon and within the Negro race in America than any other single book published in this country since *Uncle Tom's Cabin*.'' Rampersad has summarized its significance even more dramatically: ''If all of the nation's literature may stem from one book, as Hemingway implied about *The Adventures of Huckleberry Finn*, then it can as accurately be said that all of Afro-American literature of a creative nature has proceeded from Du Bois's comprehensive statement on the nature of the people in *The Souls of Black Folk*.''

William E. Cain. *Black American Literature Forum*. Summer, 1990, pp. 299–313.

At the age of 35, in 1903, W.E.B. Du Bois took intellectual leadership of those within the Afro-American world who preferred liberal idealism to compensatory realism. Du Bois was prepared for his role by rigorous training in the traditional liberal arts as well as the newer empirical social sciences. But it was confidence in the moral absolute of truth and a poetic imagination that were to prove the sources of his effectiveness.

Souls of Black Folk, the book in which Du Bois publicly announced his differences with Booker T. Washington, is constructed from first-hand observation, historical research, and reasoned analysis. Its power, however, derives from the images of divided consciousness (souls), a culturally united black nation (folk), and the veil behind which black remained nearly invisible. In a time when Jim Crow shaped perception as much as policy, Du Bois's metaphors represented intellectual liberation, giving blacks a profoundly dignified way of conceiving their own lives and history. The cultural nationalism of *Souls of Black Folk* had been implicit in the earlier study *The Philadelphia Negro,* in which Du Bois documented class structure and shared institutions. It reappeared as motivation for the utopian vision of agricultural cooperatives in *The Quest of the Silver Fleece* and the romantic narrative of worldwide organization for colored people in *Dark Princess.*

Du Bois's well-known commitment to the idea of leadership by a talented tenth has its counterpart in the learned rhetoric of his essays and the grandiose design of his novels. It is no wonder that writing as a critic in *The Crisis* he was unsympathetic to the experimentation and modern realism of the younger generation in the Negro Renaissance. Still, he made his own characteristic contribution to the "new Negro." His book *The Negro,* anticipating anti-colonial conferences organized after World War I, corrected popular impressions that American blacks were without roots by celebrating the African past. Then *Black Reconstruction in America,* written out of Du Bois's new enthusiasm for Marxism in the 1930s, recovered the significance of black people in the history of the south. Despite limitations of style, these historical re-evaluations initiated a scholarly revisionism comparable to the re-direction of thought in the book *Souls of Black Folk.*

Nearing the end of his life, Du Bois published his most comprehensive treatment of America, *The Black Flame,* a trilogy binding into one narrative an historical account of the years corresponding roughly to his own life and a fictional account of Manuel Mansart. That the plots are meant to inter-relate goes without saying. More to the point is the observation that Du Bois's career, capped by the trilogy, was his most important dialectical demonstration. Seeking to write as truthfully as possible, he became not only a scribe of history but its maker.

John M. Reilly. In *Reference Guide to American Literature, 3rd edition,* ed. Jim Kamp (St. James Press, 1994).

BIBLIOGRAPHY

The Suppression of the African Slave-Trade to the United States of America, 1638-1870, 1896 (nf); *The Philadelphia Negro: A Social Study,* 1899 (e); *The Souls of Black Folk: Essays and Sketches,* 1903 (e); *The Negro in the South, His Economic Progress in Relation to His Moral and Religious Development; Being the William Levi Bull Lectures for the Year 1907,* with Booker T. Washington, 1907 (l); *John Brown,* 1909 (b); *The Quest of the Silver Fleece,* 1911 (n); *The Star of Ethiopia,* 1913 (d); *The Negro,* 1915 (h); *Darkwater: Voices from within the Veil,* 1920 (misc); *The Gift of Black Folk: The Negroes in the Making of America,* 1924 (h); *Dark Princess: A Romance,* 1928 (n); *Africa: Its Geography, People and Products,* 1930 (h); *Africa: Its Place in Modern History,* 1930 (h); *Black Reconstruction: An Essay Toward a History of the Part Which Black Folk Played in the Attempt to Reconstruct Democracy in America, 1860-1880,* 1935 (h); *Black Folk, Then and Now: An Essay in the History and Sociology of the Negro Race,* 1939 (h); *Dusk of Dawn: An Essay Toward an Autobiography of a Race Concept,* 1940 (a); *Color and Democracy: Colonies and Peace,* 1945 (e); *The World and Africa: An Inquiry into the Part Which Africa Has Played in World History,* 1947 (c); *In Battle for Peace: The Story of My 83rd Birthday,* 1952 (m); *The Ordeal of Mansart,* 1957 (n); *Mansart Builds a School,* 1959 (n); *Worlds of Color,* 1961 (n); *Selected Poems,* 1964 (p); *The Autobiography of W. E. B. Du Bois: A Soliloquy on Viewing My Life From the Last Decade of Its First Century,* 1968 (a); *W. E. B. Du Bois Speaks: Speeches and Addresses,* edited by Philip S. Foner, 1970 (misc); *The Emerging Thought of W. E. B. Du Bois: Essays and Editorials from "The Crisis,"* edited by Henry Lee Moon, 1972 (e); *W. E. B. Du Bois: The Crisis Writing,* edited by Daniel Walden, 1972 (e); *The Education of Black People: Ten Critiques, 1906-1960,* edited by Herbert Aptheker, 1973 (e)

DUGAN, Alan (1923–)

Alan Dugan in his *Poems* ... takes the role of a soldier, an infantryman, the dogface of Bill Mauldin's cartoons. So many of the controlling images in Dugan's first book emerge from the knowledge of the squalor and confusion of war, from the self-absorption of the captive, from the inner suffering of the tortured prisoner, that it is not, perhaps, surprising that the poems dealing with other themes often lapse into wordiness and contrivance. When Dugan is at work in his favorite role, the language simplifies itself, the verse takes on a crestfallen irony, and the lines speak in a straightforward earthy rhythm.

Peter Davison. *Atlantic Monthly.* Nov., 1961. p. 172

It isn't that you have to really throw away the usual poetic flap when discussing Alan Dugan's work, but it helps. Nothing is here "in the old combinations," and this second book of his isn't going to make him any more friends in some centers of literary orthodoxy south of the Ohio River. But then, he is a great gambler: he takes chances on variations of tone, on in-and-out relationships in his imagery, on rhetorical effects that double back on the structure of what he has written, on bald profanity and ludicrous irony....

I think the most exciting aspect of Alan Dugan's work is that all the gambles arise from his predisposition, his insistence, on portraying what he sees from a bluntly personal point of view, and Dugan has a sensibility a hemisphere removed from the involutions of American Calvinism: his is the immediacy and heat of a Celtic temperament, and some of his best poems are those in which he takes a classical subject and ignites it with his own acid diction.... [H]e is a riverboat gambler, a weather-cock, a gadfly, and a painfully honest moralist. What can one say? He is exactly what we need, but I am not sure we know what he is. He is good for us; I hope in the long run we will be good for him.

Bruce Cutler. *Poetry*. March, 1964. pp. 390–1

He is complex, cantankerous, and middle-aged. Also very American. Yet he seems to possess that true weather-beaten eye, that bardic appetite that looks for nothing, accepts nothing without a fissure in it, the "lewd scratches" which "mar design." Dugan has few themes and few variations, but all of his poems have a grudging pathos or jaunty comic eloquence, and all run true to form or character. His is the truth that there is nothing so tragic that someone somewhere will not think of as comic. What he has seen he gets down, and what he has experienced he lets you know about.... What is striking in the poetry of Alan Dugan—the rancorous insights, the self-mocking wit—is paramount in the literature of today, a literature of limitations, an all encompassing grinding down, one that knows you test the strength of a man's character less by what he denies himself, than by what he's been denied. "*'Be alive', they say, when I/ am so alive I ache with it . . .*" But the ache is energy struggling with emptiness.

Robert Mazzocco. *New York Review of Books*. Nov. 23, 1967. pp. 20, 22

The poems of Alan Dugan come nearer [than those of Howard Nemerov] to a deep bitterness. They are enormously skillful and terse, and have been carved out in an idiom which Dugan has made entirely and identifiably his own. It is a strange but effective juxtaposition of lofty poetic diction and straight, unpolished, low-down vernacular. When his aim is satiric, as, for example, in "Self-Exhortation on Military Themes," this double-tone can obviously be used ingeniously to exhibit the cheapness and transparency of Noble Postures. But this is not the only way he uses it, and this book [*Poems 3*] is by no means a simple confrontation of "poetic" shams and ugly truths. Dugan is at least as much attracted by the possibilities of grandeur as by the need to confess disappointment; and I would be willing to bet that there's not a poet writing today who uses the exclamatory "Oh" more frequently.

Anthony Hecht. *Hudson Review*. Spring, 1968. pp. 214–5

The poet Robert Graves in a memorable lecture series once criticized Ezra Pound's unabashed ambition of writing great poems. For Graves, it is more than enough simply to try to write good poetry. Such a view may perhaps be too easily explained by the fact that it represents the advice of a minor poet to a great poet. Alan Dugan is a good poet who has in his own peculiar way proven what Graves was getting at. By cultivating what is by any standard a confining style, and by exercising his caustic intelligence on a relatively narrow range of subjects, Dugan has created a significant body of work that speaks with authority to a variety of modern readers. One does not get terribly excited about Alan Dugan's work, but one nevertheless returns to it with increasing regularity, for it successfully inhabits that middle ground of experience which our best poets today seem loathe to admit, as though to do so would somehow in itself constitute a denigration of their talents and a disavowal of intensity....

His predictable low-keyed humor, so often remarked upon by others, does little to mitigate the stinging venom of self-contempt that courses through so much of Dugan's work. His is a bitter eloquence. If the cadence is austere, it is rarely impoverished, and the muscular flow of his terse diction is rarely purchased at the expense of complexity. Dugan invites us to witness with him, without any redemptive qualification, the sordid spectacle of our common humiliation.

Robert Boyers. *Salmagundi*. Spring, 1968. pp. 43, 52

Days like these, to take Alan Dugan from the shelf is like finding another grownup at a birthday party for kiddies. An intelligent being! You want to fall to your knees in gratitude. Warfare versus Peace, for example, is a major theme in *Collected Poems*; unlike other writers who have been to the wars, Dugan neither boasts nor sobs, but like a man suckled on Virgil, Horace and Tacitus, he is businesslike and undeluded: war is interesting, but it is still hell.... There are no hawklike or dovelike answers in Dugan. He merely pays grim and merry attention to basics, whether he sings of childhood, lust, liquor, the dusty life of offices, city streets, domestic tranquility, birth, as in "Coat of Arms."...

As a craftsman, Dugan is extraordinary. He loads every rift with concrete; he makes a hard, crunching music; and his control of momentum is peerless: the poems, one after another, come barreling down the alley like big black bowling balls and down you go.

Alicia Ostriker. *Partisan Review*. Spring, 1972. pp. 272–3

BIBLIOGRAPHY
Poems, 1961 (p); *Poems 2*, 1963 (p); *Poems 3*, 1967 (p); *Collected Poems*, 1969 (p); *Poems 4*, 1974 (p); *Sequence: [poems]*, 1976 (p); *New and Collected Poems, 1961–1983*, 1983 (p); *Poems Six*, 1989 (p)

DUNBAR, Paul Laurence (1872–1906)

[Mr. Dunbar] is a real poet whether he speaks a dialect or whether he writes a language. He calls his little book *Majors and Minors*, the Majors being in our American English, and the Minors being in dialect, the dialect of the middle-south negroes and the middle-south whites; for the poet's ear has been quick for the accent of his neighbors as well as for that of his kindred. I have no means of knowing whether he values his Majors more than his Minors; but I should not suppose it at all unlikely, and I am bound to say none of them are despicable. In very many I find the proofs of honest thinking and true feeling, and in some the record of experience, whose genuineness the reader can test by his own....

Most of these pieces, however, are like most of the pieces of most young poets, cries of passionate aspiration and disappointment, more or less personal or universal, which except for the negro face of the author one could not find specially notable. It is when we come to Mr. Dunbar's Minors that we feel ourselves in the presence of a man with a direct and a fresh authority to do the kind of thing he is doing....

One sees how the poet exults in his material, as the artist always does; it is not for him to blink its commonness, or to be ashamed of its rudeness; and in his treatment of it he has been able to bring us nearer to the heart of primitive human nature in his race than any one else has yet done. The range between appetite and emotion is not great, but it is here that his race has hitherto had its being, with a lift now and then far above and beyond it. A rich, humorous sense pervades his recognition of this fact, without excluding a fond sympathy, and it is the blending of these which delights me in all his dialect verse. . . .

Several of the pieces are pure sentiment, like ''The Deserted Plantation''; but these without lapsing into sentimentality recall the too easy pathos of the pseudonegro poetry of the minstrel show. . . .

Mr. Dunbar's race is nothing if not lyrical, and he comes by his rhythm honestly. But what is better, what is finer, what is of larger import, in his work is what is conscious and individual in it. He is, so far as I know, the first man of his color to study his race objectively, to analyze it to himself, and then to represent it in art as he felt it and found it to be; to represent it humorously, yet tenderly, and above all so faithfully that we know the portrait to be undeniably like. A race which has reached this effect in any of its members can no longer be held wholly uncivilized; and intellectually Mr. Dunbar makes a stronger claim for the negro than the negro yet has done. . . .

I am speaking of him as a black poet, when I should be speaking of him as a poet; but the notion of what he is insists too strongly for present impartiality. I hope I have not praised him too much, because he has surprised me so very much; for his excellences are positive and not comparative. If his Minors had been written by a white man, I should have been struck by their very uncommon quality; I should have said that they were wonderful divinations. But since they are expressions of a race-life from within the race, they seem to me indefinitely more valuable and significant. I have sometimes fancied that perhaps the negroes *thought* black, and *felt* black; that they were racially so utterly alien and distinct from ourselves that there never could be common intellectual and emotional ground between us, and that whatever eternity might do to reconcile us, the end of time would find us as far asunder as ever. But this little book has given me pause in my speculation. Here, in the artistic effect at least, is white thinking and white feeling in a black man, and perhaps the human unity, and not the race unity, is the precious thing, the divine thing, after all. God hath made of one blood all nations of men; perhaps the proof of this saying is to appear in the arts, and our hostilities and prejudices are to vanish in them.

Mr. Dunbar, at any rate, seems to have fathomed the souls of his simple white neighbors, as well as those of his own kindred; and certainly he has reported as faithfully what passes in them as any man of our race has yet done with respect to the souls of his. It would be very incomplete recognition of his work not to speak particularly of the non-negro dialect pieces, and it is to the lover of homely and tender poetry, as well as the student of tendencies, that I commend such charming sketches as ''Speakin o' Christmas,'' ''After a Visit,'' ''Lonesome,'' and ''The Spellin' Bee.'' They are good, very good. . . .

W. D. Howells. *Harper's Weekly.* June 20, 1896, p. 630.

[The] sparkling wit, the quaint and delightful humor, the individuality and charm of Dunbar's poetry are not excelled by any lines from the pen of a Negro. No person can read his verse without being forcibly impressed that he is a remarkable man, a genius demanding attention. The New World has not produced a bard like him. Although distinctively American by birth and education, as well as a Negro, yet his prototype is on the other side of the Atlantic. Robert Burns and Dunbar, in many important particulars, are parallel poets. They seem to have been cast in the same mould; with limited educational advantages, both struggled up through poverty, and each wrote largely in the dialect of his clan. He is strong and original, and like Burns, lyrical in inspiration. Probably there never were two men of opposite races, so widely separated by time and distance, and yet so much alike in soul-qualities. With no desire and no doubt unconsciously, he has walked complete in the footprints of the eminent Scottish bard; has the same infirmity, animated by the same hope, and blessed with the same success. . . .

In Dunbar there is no threnody, not even distant clouds arch the sky. Hope and joy are the dominant notes of his song. No poet more effectively warms the cold side of our life and sends sunshine into grief-stricken souls than he. He laughs sorrow away; he takes us into the huts of the lowly and oppressed. There we find, amidst poverty and illiteracy, unfeigned contentment and true happiness; a smile is on every face, and hope displays her brightest gifts. No matter how sorrowful, who can read without considerable emotion ''When de Co'n Pone's Hot,'' ''The Colored Band,'' ''The Visitor,'' ''The Old Front Gate,'' ''De Way Tings Come,'' and ''Philosophy.''

But not all his poetry bubbles with fun, at times he is a serious poet, and appeals strongly to the serious side of life, as does his ''Weltschmertz.'' It is full of tender sympathy; it touches chords which vibrate throughout the poles of our nature; he makes us feel that he takes our sorrows and makes them his own, and helps us to bear up when burdened with woe. ''The Fount of Tears,'' ''Life's Tragedy,'' ''The Haunted Oak,'' and the fifth lyric of ''Love and Sorrow'' reveal a high order of poetical genius; he reaches the deepest spiritual recesses of our being. . . .

I prefer ''The Rugged Way'' to Lowell's ''After the Burial.'' ''The Unsung Heroes'' has all the imagination and pathos of Bryant's ''Marion's Men''; ''The Black Sampson of Brandywine'' will live as long as his ''African Chief.'' Read Bryant's and Dunbar's ''Lincoln''—the black poet does not suffer by comparison. I do not in the least wish to convey the impression that Dunbar is a greater poet than Bryant; they move in different parts of the poetical firmament. Each is a master in his respective sphere. As a writer of blank verse Bryant has no equal in America; and as a lyrical poet with a large vein of rich humor Dunbar is without a peer in the Western Continent.

Joseph G. Bryant. *The Colored American Magazine.* May, 1905, pp. 254–57.

Paul Laurence Dunbar stands out as the first poet from the Negro race in the United States to show a combined mastery over poetic material and poetic technique, to reveal innate literary distinction in what he wrote, and to maintain a high level of performance. He was the first to rise to a height from which he could take a perspective view of his own race. He was the first to see objectively its humor, its superstitions, its shortcomings; the first to feel sympathetically its heart-wounds, its yearnings, its aspirations, and to voice them all in a purely literary form.

Dunbar's fame rests chiefly on his poems in Negro dialect. This appraisal of him is, no doubt, fair; for in these dialect poems he not only carried his art to the highest point of perfection, but he made a contribution to American literature unlike what any one else had made, a contribution which, perhaps, no one else could have made. Of course, Negro dialect poetry was written before Dunbar wrote, most of it by white writers; but the fact stands out that Dunbar was the first to use it as a medium for the true interpretation of Negro character and psychology. And, yet, dialect poetry does not constitute the whole or even the bulk of Dunbar's work. In addition to a large number of poems of a very high order done in literary English, he was the author of four novels and several volumes of short stories.

James Weldon Johnson. *The Book of American Negro Poetry*, Harcourt Brace Jovanovich, 1922.

How tenacious, demanding, and circumscribing the dialect tradition and its concomitants had become before the turn of the century is illustrated in the poet Paul Laurence Dunbar. No Negro of finer artistic spirit has been born in America, and none whose fierce, secret energies were more powerfully directed toward breaking down the vast wall of emotional and intellectual misunderstanding within which he, as poet, was immured. . . .

[Dunbar is often noted as a poet of dialect.] Not so well known is the fact that his most serious efforts in *Oak and Ivy* and *Majors and Minors*, his second book, are given to the pieces in pure English. Scarcely known at all is the fact that all of his life he fervently sought to win recognition as a master of the pure tongue. . . .

If there are times when his English pieces achieved only a sentimental pathos, there are other times when he wrought lyrics of delicate beauty. Primarily a lyrist, the music of words is one of his chief charms. . . .

Not only did Dunbar use pure English for more than half his poetry, he used it for all his novels and most of his short stories. Perhaps this was a mistake. It may have been that he could have done as fine a work in the dialect short tale as Charles Chesnutt was to do. "The Case of 'Ca'line," a story in the folk tradition, helps support this view. Excepting only a few of his short stories, Dunbar invariably falls short in prose fiction. His failure is twofold: he did not understand fully the extreme adaptability of folk material; and he did not study the art of prose fiction. The result of the first is that nearly all the folk stories are limited to burlesque, while the result of the second is that some very fine story stuff is hopelessly bungled.

It is, however, in his prose that Dunbar more nearly expressed the Negro, though rather as champion than as an artistically objective creator. . . .

But champions are notably more effective in poetry than in prose. . . . [When] propaganda enters into prose fiction it acquires necessarily some of the broad solidity of the prosaic medium, and this firm quality immediately puts the reader on the defensive. The reader's reaction is as of one being gulled, being shown a thing for the good of his soul. These are the things one comes to feel in too many of the stories of Dunbar. Like a leaden ghost, Purpose treads the print of "Silas Jackson," "The Ingrate," "One Man's Fortunes," and "Shaft II." Not only is the technique of the stories faulty, but plausible, character-derived motivation and convincing

situation are lacking. The story that brushes aside esthetic ends must be faultless in construction and style in order to succeed. It must captivate by sheer perfection of form. Dunbar was not aware of this. He brought to this difficult art only a zest in the message of his serious tales, and an instinctive sense of the humor inherent in certain situations in his burlesque stories. The latter are saved from failure; but a story representative of the former, "The Strength of Gideon," with its powerful theme and well-defined plot, boils off in the end to a watery pottage.

The gem of Dunbar's stories is "The Trustfulness of Polly." In it Dunbar did not seek to express the Negro, but to recreate him. It was written in 1899, five years before his writing career ended, but he never again found such perfect focus of characterization, motivation, theme, plot, and style. It is a story of the low-life school, a type that was not to become popular until twenty years after Dunbar's death. . . . "The Trustfulness of Polly" is the first story of Negro low-life in New York written by a Negro. Not only is it significant as the forerunner of the long list of low-life stories from *Home to Harlem to Beale Street*, but it presaged the courageous, if misled, objectivity with which the post-war Negro artist was to see the life of his people.

With the exception of *The Sport of the Gods*, Dunbar's novels are as different in tone, treatment, and ideas from his short stories as it is possible for them to be. In them he carried his rebellion against the minstrel tradition to the extreme of repudiating race. But he came face to face with bitter irony. He saw clearly that even his own life story—the unfolding of his youthful spiritual struggles, his yearnings and ambitions—would not seem true to a people who knew the Negro only as a buffoon. There had been Negroes generally known to America as anything but buffoons, but they were oddities, "exceptional because of their white blood." The story of a Negro boy living through Dunbar's experiences would not win credence. Negroes simply could not have certain emotional and spiritual things happen to them. So, in the novel *The Uncalled*, Dunbar, for the sake of plausibility (so little does realism have to do with truth), characterized himself as Frederick Brent, a white youth.

In two other novels, *The Love of Landry* and *The Fanatics*, he went even further. He drew white characters in typical white environment and sought to inspire the whole with the breath of living truth. He worked on an assumption which the minstrel tradition had consistently denied. He took forcibly the stand that Dumas and Pushkin, products of entirely different milieus [and both mulattoes], had come into naturally. Fundamentally, he said, there is no difference between Negro and white: the artist is free to work in whatever material he wishes. This was more than letting an imaginary white character stand for him; this was standing for white characters. This was exchange—and of a most equalizing kind. He did not say that he was looking at white characters from a colored point of view. He simply assumed inherent emotional, intellectual, and spiritual identity with his characters. It had not been done before: except for a few scattered instances it has not been done in exactly this way since. . . .

That Dunbar's white novels are faulty proves only what is suggested by the faults of *The Sport of the Gods*: Dunbar was not a novelist. Because it deals with Negro characters, and because it was written after the discipline of the three other novels, *The Sport of the Gods* might be expected to be his best novel. But it is not. It is only his most interesting. As a blood and thunder tale of crime and retribution and as an analysis of the elements in the urban life of the

Negro it does very well. As an artistic accomplishment it ranks below both *The Love of Landry* and *The Fanatics*.

But we must go back to Dunbar's verse, his dialect pieces, for though the necessity that drove him to dialect was bitter to him, he did his best work in this medium. His dialect pieces are not, however, most representative of his creative temper: they are merely what he had to do to win and hold his audience.

The comparison which is made so often between Paul Dunbar and Robert Burns, the Scottish poet, cannot fairly be taken further than to say that they were both singers. Burns's dialect was standard, a native tongue, understood by all the Scots, representative of them and, therefore, broad enough to give full expression to the people to whom it belonged. Burns's medium did not impose upon him the limitations to which the Negro poet was confined. On the other hand, Dunbar's dialect was not native. It was not even representative of a few Negro communities. Had he imitated the speech of the north Georgia Negro and uttered it among the Geechees of south Georgia or the Gullahs of South Carolina he would not have been understood. Dunbar, from scant knowledge of many dialects, made a language, a synthetic dialect that could be read with ease and pleasure by the northern whites to whom dialect meant only an amusing burlesque of Yankee English. Through such a bastard medium it was (and is) impossible to speak the whole heart of a people. . . .

At [dialect verse] Dunbar was a master. His sense of rhythm and harmony, evident in whatever he wrote, makes all the difference between his dialect pieces and the dialect of dozens of his imitators. While he was sentimental, they were vulgar and maudlin. While they bent at the knees with coarse laughter, he was content with a gentle and pathetic smile. While they blundered with dialect, he knew what could be done with it and how far it could be made to go as a poetic medium. He knew the subjects it would fit—the sweet delight of calf love, the thrill of simple music, the querulousness of old age, the satisfactions of a full stomach, the distractions of an empty one, the time-mellowed pain of bereavement. He brought to these subjects a childlike quality, a hushed wonder that is the secret of his charm in them. At times, though, something sterner crept into the dialect pieces. He was not above touches of satire, cries of reproach, and even weary resignation to a life that at its best was extremely hard.

More often, however, he reserved the firmer tone for his pure English, going the way of challenging comparison in poetry that William Wells Brown had gone in prose, but doing it more effectively. Ignored by contemporary critics as this work was, it is principally by virtue of it that Dunbar holds the place of reverence in the hearts of Negroes. . . .

Such a poem as "The Colored Soldiers" marks him as being in one sense the spiritual father of James Weldon Johnson, Claude McKay, and a number of younger poets. But in these, as in his dialect pieces, Dunbar did not feel that he had fulfilled his larger self. He did not marvel, as does Cullen, that God had made a poet black and bade him sing. He was more concerned with singing than with blackness. He wanted to be known and remembered not as a black poet, but as a *poet*. The price he paid made his popularity among whites as dross to him. The tribute he paid to his race was in kind no different from that paid by Tennyson as poet-laureate to his queen. Time and again he expresses his disappointment at "the world's disdain" of the work which he himself held in the highest estimation.

The best of these pieces show a morbid concern with failure and death. He could not have been concerned with failure as a dialect poet. His success in that line was assured. It was the other failure he feared—and foresaw. . . .

How right was Dunbar's judgment as to the worth of his own poems is only partly our concern. It may be said, however, that if the poet is to be judged by his hold on the consciousness of his audience, Dunbar must rest content with the appeal of his dialect to his white audience and the grip of his eulogies on the hearts and minds of his Negro audience. Though certain of his pure English lines are frequently quoted, in general they are overlooked; not because they are poor, but because they do not distinguish him from dozens of other poets. And a poet, to succeed, must be distinguishable. Such poems as "Life," "We Wear the Mask," "Who Knows," and a half dozen others must be excluded from this general criticism.

J. Saunders Redding. In *To Make a Poet Black* (University of North Carolina Press, 1939; reprinted by McGrath Publishing Company, 1968).

Paul Laurence Dunbar is a natural resource of our people. He, like all our old prophets and preachers, has been preserved by our little people. Those who could command words and images, those whose pens thundered across the pages, those whose voices boomed from lecterns, those who set policy for our great publications then, as now, were quite silent. Not ever quite knowing what to do about one of America's most famous poets, when they spoke his name it was generally to condemn his dialect poetry—as if black people aren't supposed to laugh, or more as if Dunbar's poems were not the best examples of our plantation speech. One gets recitation after explanation of Dunbar's poetry, his love of his "white poems," his hatred of his need to please the white critics, but something rings quite hollow to me. I refuse to believe Paul Dunbar was ashamed of "Little Brown Baby, come sit on my knee." The poem has brought too much happiness to me. I categorically reject a standard that says "A Negro Love Song" should not make me feel warm inside. If Dunbar is only a poet with a gift in jingle tongue then there is no need for a critique. He is clearly much more. . . .

Dunbar preserved a part of our history. And accurately. It would be as foolish to say all blacks struggled against slavery as it would to say all acquiesced to it. The truth lies somewhere in the blending. Perhaps Dunbar's greatest triumph is that he has survived all those who would use his gift for their own dead-end purposes.

Every artist, should he create long enough, will come full cycle again and again. The artist is a political animal as well as a sensitive being. Like any person the artist is a contradiction. Dunbar will speak of the good ole days, then say "We Wear the Mask." The message is clear and available to us if we invest in Dunbar the integrity we hope others will give us.

It seems somehow strange to me that critics are so colorless—despite claims to deeper insights should they share an ethnic or religious background with the subject. . . . [In] Dunbar's case, he was black enough for the white but not white enough for the blacks. . . .

Dunbar . . . is peerless. There is no poet, black or nonblack, who measures his achievement. Even today. He wanted to be a writer and he wrote. He survived, not always well, by his pen. He probably did not want to be hassled by his peers, who through Dunbar's efforts were enjoying greater attention. He probably was plagued by as many doubts as any other person. Yet he dared to persist in hope.

> Nikki Giovanni. In *A Singer in the Dawn: Reinterpretations of Paul Laurence Dunbar*, ed. Jay Martin (Dodd, Mead & Company, 1975); pp. 243–46.

There were, in truth, two Paul Laurence Dunbars. One was the writer supported by the interest of white Americans because some of his work was sufficiently faithful to black stereotypical images designed and demanded by white Americans. The other, in a sense the more ''real'' Dunbar, was the writer of genuine literary talent and dramatic sensibility, whose true literary worth could not be widely assessed until a wide range of his work was gathered and published as late as 1975 in *The Dunbar Reader*.

In his first manifestation, that of dialect poet, Dunbar was not so much pandering to the demands of white editors and a white reading public as indulging his own natural affinity for the rhythms of common speech and often for comedy; dialect in literature was, after all, very much *à la mode* with the interest in local color in late 19th-century America. That he had a gift as a dialect poet is undeniable, but it is rather too bad that his white audience could not accept him as anything more.

Much more he was, as William Dean Howells recognized early. As a writer of fiction and essays, he used the stuff of black lore to greater effect than any previous black writer, and at least as well as such whites as Joel Chandler Harris had done. Particularly noteworthy in his work is the reflection of religion in black American life and of the implications of the black migration to American cities. As a poet, Dunbar often superbly starched his ready lyricism with a keen sense of drama. It is a truism to say that while his material was mainly black, his insights were universal.

Dunbar did not choose to be the exemplar of the white view of black America in his time—but he was, and he made a sturdy pivot. He managed to entertain and enlighten whites while helping to imbue fellow blacks with a sense of history and importance, making him a close spiritual ancestor of Countée Cullen, Langston Hughes, James Baldwin, and the other powerful 20th-century black American voices.

> Alan R. Shucard. In *Reference Guide to American Literature, 3rd edition*, ed. Jim Kamp (St. James Press, 1994).

BIBLIOGRAPHY

Oak and Ivy, 1893 (p); *Majors and Minors*, 1895 (p); *Lyrics of Lowly Life*, 1896 (p); *Folks from Dixie*, 1898 (s); *The Uncalled*, 1898 (n); *Lyrics of the Hearthside*, 1899 (p); *Poems of Cabin and Field*, 1899 (p); *The Love of Landry*, 1900 (n); *The Strength of Gideon, and Other Stories*, 1900 (s); *Candle-Lightin' Time*, 1901 (p); *The Fanatics*, 1901 (n); *The Sport of the Gods*, 1902, also published as *The Jest of Fate*, 1903, (n); *In Old Plantation Days*, 1903 (s); *Lyrics of Love and Laughter*, 1903 (p); *The Heart of Happy Hollow*, 1904 (s); *Howdy, Honey, Howdy*, 1905 (p); *Lyrics of Sunshine and Shadow*, 1905 (p); *The Life and Works of Paul Laurence Dunbar*, 1907 (misc); *The Complete Poems of Paul Laurence Dunbar*, 1913 (p); *The Best Stories of Paul Laurence Dunbar*, 1938 (s); *The Paul Laurence Dunbar Reader*, 1975 (misc)

DUNCAN, Robert (Edward) (1919–1979)

His poems are illustrations, objectifications of the interchange between order and disorder, accompanied by appropriate emotions, which are more nearly suggested than realized, of amazement and love at the sight of perfect order, awe and fear at the possibilities of new forms (sometimes monstrous) arising from disorder, and grief at the processes of decay, disintegration, and return. Art—specifically, poetry—is a part of this large concern, and references to poetry or to the poet occur in nearly every poem. Duncan's relationship of poetry, to the creation of form, becomes the symbol of order and change operating in all aspects of reality. . . .

Every *possibility* of the outstanding poet exists in this work: development of the poem's total form (as opposed to a few flashy lines), excellent sonant quality and movement, conservation of statement, and intensity of rendered image, and a commanding point of view. It is because Mr. Duncan is already an accomplished poet that I ask more of him: more immediate experience, less comment and explanation.

> A.R. Ammons. *Poetry*. April, 1960. pp. 53–5

Robert Duncan is another excellent poet whose work is measured and spare, although many of his poems are long. The diction is uncluttered, like that of Mr. Creeley; but whereas the sound of the latter's verse is like that of a human voice speaking, Mr. Duncan's considerable talent most often assumes the form and measure of a human voice singing. He is a lyrical poet in the most traditional sense: that is, he is a musician. I do not mean that his poems, as such, need to be set to music. And I do not mean that they drip like Swinburne. At his best, he is a master of rhetoric in the Elizabethan sense of the word. Employing the simplest diction and rhythm, he can lead the reader to expect a certain pattern of sound, and then he varies it, so that the music of his verse produces a fusion of fulfillment and surprise which is one of the chief delights created by such a great lyric poet as, say, Thomas Campion.

> James Wright. *Minnesota Review*. Winter, 1961. p. 251

Robert Duncan has that special quality of temper which he shares with Edmund Wilson or Pandit Nehru. He is a Good European. Although Duncan has been singularly open to all the influences of all times and places, and has learned from all the Old Masters of Modernism, from Reubén Darío to Yves Bonnefoy, his distinguishing characteristic is not the breadth of his influences, but the depth and humanness of his heart. Now that he is approaching early middle age he has begun to take on something of the forgotten grandeur of the great nineteenth-century ''men of the world'' of letters—Monckton Milnes or Walter Bagehot. I can think of no other poet of my time of which anything like this could be said—with most, the very idea is ridiculous. As mentor and example, Duncan's influence on the younger men of the new New Poetry has been incalculable.

The now widely publicized San Francisco Renaissance owes more to Duncan than to any other one person.

Kenneth Rexroth. *Assays* (New Directions). 1961. p. 192.

All of this power has come to him only gradually. Reading his *Selected Poems* of 1942–1950, one felt at times that Duncan, though entitled to experiment, didn't have to print so many tentative jottings from his laboratory. As the fifties went on, his work grew firmer and more sure, resulting in the very good collection, *The Opening of the Field*, which the present book *Roots and Branches* surpasses. Containing his work of the past four years, it is a hefty book with little chaff in it.

In approaching Duncan's poems, the reader may find a bit of blind faith useful. With it, he may surmount a few private allusions, mysterious gaps in syntax and quirky spellings (meant to distinguish the sounds of -ed endings: *calld, many-brancht*). . . .

Duncan's themes are the changes that take place in the self, the search for love, the decline of faith in the supernatural. . . . One of that large clan of poets who emerged in the fifties from Black Mountain College and the cafes of San Francisco, Duncan in this book stands as the most serious of them all, the most capable.

X.J. Kennedy. *New York Times Book Section*. Dec. 20, 1964. pp. 4–5

Only Duncan will ever know why the words are arranged and spaced as they are or how precisely one can or should read an image like ''stars flew out into the deserted souls.'' No amount of sympathetic reading can dispel the overwhelming sense of arbitrariness. But after a while it is reassuring to discover that Duncan does not care how good his poems are. They follow the patterns of his mind, nothing else, and anyone who writes this way is cheerfully oblivious of all who are not kindred spirits. Nothing is more serious than a Duncan poem, yet little asks so completely to be read as a kind of sport. Every reader will probably be able to follow along his curious paths for a passage or even a whole poem, and then the shout becomes a kind of song. To read Duncan in bulk is to become oneself an action painter, and for that process to work, nothing can be very clear. To believe in him, I should think, is to be quite mad.

Roger Sale. *Hudson Review*. Summer, 1965. pp. 302–3

. . .Robert Duncan is probably the figure with the richest natural genius among the Black Mountain poets. His work lacks [Robert] Creeley's consistent surface simplicity and [Charles] Olson's familiar cluster of localist and radically critical attitudes, and is consequently less well known than their writings. Also, it is cluttered by certain 'interferences,' partly stylistic and willful, partly related to his mystical and private attitudinal assumptions. . . . Though it seems clear now that Duncan's art is to some

degree self-defeating, one has only to leaf through these books to find poems and passages that mark him as a modern romantic whose best work is instantly engaging by the standards of the purest lyrical traditions.

M.L. Rosenthal. *The New Poets* (Oxford). 1967. p. 174.

The publication of Duncan's book, *Bending the Bow*, is an event exceeding questions of quality. I cannot imagine my friends, the poets who gather to dismember each other, asking of this book, as they would of the others in this review, those narrower in scope, smaller in style, ''Is it good or is it bad?'' The question doesn't arise; not because Duncan is a good poet, though he is superb, but because the comprehensiveness of his imagination is too great for us. Here is an event; for the present our only question is, can we respond to it?—can we respond adequately to its most important feature, a new open sequence called *Passages*? We are given the first thirty sections of it, from which we see immediately resemblances to Pound's *Cantos*, but also differences, and the differences are the more salient. Duncan has learned from Pound's failures. . . . For the present I read the *Passages* not only with admiration and envy, and not only with a responsive depth of feeling, but with a wondering intuition that new force and clarity have come into the poetic imagination of America. When I reflect that Duncan, although he has already written a great deal, is only now, at age 49, riding the crest of his power, and that he still has years to go, the future of our poetry looks much more attractive to me than it has at any other time since the generation of the elders desisted.

Hayden Carruth. *Hudson Review*. Summer, 1968. pp. 402–3

The Opening of the Field had announced the birth of a surpassingly individual talent: a poet of mysticism, visionary terror, and high romance. Duncan's work is outstanding among his contemporaries' in having rehabilitated from three hundred years of relative disuse and stagnation the emblem—not the image, or the symbol—as the central vehicle of the poem's drama. Duncan's emblems are populated by flaring presences, who, like crucified angels, blazingly dance out of the ''black pit'' of blindness, and into ''the beginnings of love.'' But in his recent books he has produced numerous exercises—lacking all vividness—while he waits for the return of his demon. These many autotelic performances are like prayers to the absent spirits urging their return: they may serve, for us, as a record of soul-priming, the readying of fallow poetic ground for the next major theme, whenever it may strike.

Laurence Lieberman. *Poetry*. April, 1969. p. 43

Where most postmodern poets are content to render dramatic instances of the mind satisfied in process, Duncan has grander ambitions. His aim to reinterpret the aesthetics of presence in terms that can recover the contemporary significance of the Romance and hermetic imaginative traditions. . . .

When critics notice [Duncan] at all, they comment on his weaknesses as a lyric poet, for his verse is often diffuse, boring, and without vitality in language or imagery. Moreover, like Olson, his work is often difficult and apparently remote from contemporary concerns because his mythic enterprise requires that he incorporate a good deal of abstruse learning into his work. Yet once one accepts him as a poet whose primary task is to reflect on what others express directly, one can, I think forgive some of the lyric weaknesses and learn to read him for his intellectual interest and for those moments when he develops those interests into intense lyrical passages. Duncan is at the least a very important influence on other poets like Creeley and Levertov and at best he rivals his stylistic master, Pound, in integrating historical and mythic meditations with lyrical exaltation. . . .

Sympathetically read, Duncan's work then has greater imaginative scope than that of his peers. By reflecting on what other poets are reflections of, he achieves a generality and abstractness that articulates the value schemes shared by most postmodern visions of Romanticism. He makes self-reflexive and systematic the analogical nature of [much of his poetry] . . . , and he defines the analogical process in a rich restatement of the Romantic dialectic between creative mind and creative nature. But his ambitiousness creates serious aesthetic problems, exacerbated by the fact that he is more deductive and allegorical in his use of myth than the great moderns and consequently exhibits little doubt or struggle. One cannot simply read Duncan dramatically: one must understand and work to share the beliefs before one can really participate in the poetry. In this skeptical age. . . readers find it difficult to pursue abstractions they see as hard to understand and impossible to trust—especially when Duncan's immediate surfaces are so thoroughly conceptual and remote from ordinary existential problems and needs.

Charles Altieri. *Enlarging the Temple: New Directions in American Poetry during the 1960s* (Bucknell Univ. Pr., 1979), pp. 150–51, 163

In his poetry and prose, Duncan grapples (much as Whitman did) with the meaning of America, not as political entity alone, but as the generative source for poetic and personal endeavor. It is undoubtedly the native American literary line to seek the basis of poetry in antipoetic or unpoetic material and to redeem the creative potentiality of mundane subjects. Emerson had invited poetic expression equal to the qualities and characteristics of the evolving nation. Whitman answered the invitation repeatedly. In his essay "Slang in America" he found an inherent piquancy in socially nontraditional language which captured his imagination and provided intimations of a mythic past. . . .

Duncan holds a far less sanguine view of America than Whitman, but his desire to call up its presence, despite inherent contradictions, is equally imperative. At the political level Duncan can work less on faith than Whitman, and he is too honest to fool himself that Whitman's egalitarian optimism remains viable for *all* men in the twentieth-century. . . .

Whitman is as much a formative influence on Duncan's work as Dante or Blake, providing him with a special legacy that answers Duncan's imaginative needs. . . . Duncan has called the Romantic movement in poetry "the intellectual adventure of not knowing". . . and he is firmly grounded in that tradition. Striving to extend the thematic and formal boundaries of the poem, Duncan goes beyond a concern for the poem itself into a total and often mystical participation in the rites of the "evolving and continuing

work of poetry [he] could never complete—a poetry that had begun long before [he] was born and that extended beyond [his] own work in it." His most characteristic poem in this vein, "Passages," can end only with his life—the process of the entire venture more important than the product. Again we hear Whitman, this time from the 1872 preface to *Leaves of Grass*: "But what is life but an experiment? and mortality but an exercise? with reference to results beyond. And so shall my poems be. If incomplete here, and superfluous there, *n'importe*—the earnest trial and persistent exploration shall at least be mine, and other success failing, shall be success enough.". . . The premise of incompleteness, the weight of the "never achiev'd poem". . . is a heavy burden indeed, but one which Robert Duncan, of all our contemporary poets, is best able to carry to fruition.

Mark Johnson and Robert DeMott. *In Robert Duncan: Scales of the Marvelous*, ed. Robert J. Bertholf and Ian W. Reid (New Directions, 1979), pp. 228–29, 231, 239–40

If the sublime comes to be regarded as an increasingly less viable mode of poetic discourse in New York in the Fifties and Sixties, then an attempt to revive it takes place at the same time across the country in Berkeley. Robert [Edward] Duncan stands at the center of the so-called San Francisco Renaissance; and along with such firmly established figures as Charles Olson and Allen Ginsberg, he represents a deliberate return to the poet's vatic role, based on an unprecedented synthesis of Romantic and Modernist strategies. Duncan in particular has declared himself derivative in his craft, thus affording himself "permission" to create the frequently outrageous totalities that mark his poetry as one of the most ambitious bodies of work in our time. For Duncan's poetic is totalizing: to an even greater extent than Pound or Olson, he seeks to in-form the "orders" or "scales" of reality in an open-ended tapestry or collage of language. In this regard, he operates in exact antithesis to Ashbery and O'Hara: he seeks to establish, or rather, prove, that the interrelated networks of material, psychological, and spiritual realities are all coordinated hierarchies that function under the force of universal Law. Rather than level modes of perception, value systems, and forms of knowledge, Duncan would place them all within their proper contexts, so that an awareness of overarching Form allows the reader to perceive a previously hidden totality. Poetry, of course, is the most significant medium for such a process; hence the poet holds a privileged place within the orders of language. Duncan's thought is transparently utopian in regard to matters of creativity and tradition, as well as in relation to immediate political concerns; and while sometimes problematic in its applications, its insistence on infinite human potential within a communal identity is, as [Georg] Oppen would say, "ennobling."

Duncan's insistent metaphors are often so compelling that they seem to obviate criticism, and therefore it is important to observe that at the same time Duncan's totalizing project is getting under way, a related but in some ways radically dissimilar poetic is being formulated by his old friend—and critic—Jack Spicer. Cranky, admonitory, haunted, Spicer's work presents as unified a poetic as Duncan's, but carefully avoids sweeping gestures of order and coherence that have become the distinguishing mark of even the most open of Duncan's poetic fields. Spicer's sincere distrust of the totalizing impulse in both Romantic and Modernist poetry leads him to a poetic of disruption and difference, of radical otherness and possession, in which the poet is far less the willing spokesman for the sublime than its unsuspecting victim. Whereas Duncan celebrates the ''Lasting Sentence'' in his *Structure of Rime*, Spicer warns us, in *The Heads of the Town up to the Aether*, that ''words / Turn mysteriously against those who use them.'' In fact, it could be argued that Duncan and Spicer draw upon the same poetic precursors and philosophical systems and create complementary views of the poetic act. For Duncan, Romantic mythmaking and theosophical doctrine combine with Modernist explorations of history, anthropology and phenomenology to confirm Yeats's old dictum that ''The things below are as the things above.''

Norman Finklestein. *The Utopian Movement in Contemporary American Poetry* (Lewisburg: Bucknell Univ. Pr., Rev. Ed. 1993 [1988]), pp. 68–69

BIBLIOGRAPHY

Heavenly City, Heavenly Earth, 1945 (p); *Medieval Scenes*, 1947 (p); *Poems 1948–49*, 1950 (p); *Song of the Borderguard*, 1951 (p); *The Artist's View*, 1952; *Medea at Kolchis*, 1956 (pd); *Caesar's Gate*, 1956 (p); *Letters*, 1958 (p); *Selected Poems (1942–1950)*, 1959; *The Opening of the Field*, 1960 (p); *Roots and Branches*, 1964 (p); *Writing Writing*, 1964 (p, e); *As Testimony: The Poem and the Scene*, 1964 (e); *Wine*, 1964 (e); *The Years as Catches: First Poems (1939–1946)*, 1966; *The Sweetness and Greatness of Dante's Divine Comedy*, 1968 (c); *Bending the Bow*, 1968 (p); *Of the War: Passages 22–27*, 1968 (p); *Medea at Kolchis, The Maiden Head*, 1968 (pd); *Names of People*, 1968 (p); *The Truth & Life of Myth in Poetry*, 1968 (e); *Program Notes and Reminiscences*, 1970 (r); *Derivations: Selected Poems, 1950–1956*, 1970; *The First Decade: Selected Poems, 1940–1950*, 1970; *Passages 31–35*, 1970 (p); *Dragons at the Gate*, 1976 (n); *Kiss*, 1978 (e); *Catalyst*, 1981 (p); *Collected Plays, Vol. 1*, 1981; *Selected Poems*, 1981; *Unpopular Poems*, 1981; *Ground Work: Before the War*, 1984 (p); *Fictive Certainties*, 1985 (e); *Faust Foutu: A Comic Masque*, 1985; *A Paris Visit*, 1985 (p); *The Regulators*, 1986; *Ground Work II: In the Dark*, 1987; *Selected Poems*, 1993; *A Selected Prose*, 1995

E

EASTLAKE, William (1917–1997)

This witty, exhilarating novel [*Go in Beauty*] displays some remarkable powers. Perhaps its major achievement is that William Eastlake's hilarious sense of irony allows him successfully to bathe a story that is essentially tragic in a calmly majestic humor. In the book's course he illuminates in passing the problems of sibling psychology, expatriation, primitivism, the artist's fidelity to truth, distributive justice (Emerson on the mesa!), the nature of integrity and a few others. . . .

Since somebody is bound to point to Eastlake's debt to Hemingway, let us say the mimicry has been metamorphosed here into mastery. The story is coherent, readable and told with a precisely right sandpapered style.

> Lon Tinkle. *New York Times Book Section*. Oct. 21, 1956. p. 4

After reading [*Go in Beauty*] once, one is impressed and puzzled; after reading a second time, one is still impressed but less puzzled. I think this is an important first novel. The author has written distinguished short stories; he has a definite style; and if he is not yet at home with the novel, he is perfectly at ease with each chapter. Instead of hanging out a list of complimentary adjectives, let's say that he is a writer worthy of close reading. . . .

The action is powerful, the conception is serious and the prose is lean and clear. . . . The sad beauty of Mr. Eastlake's tale is that reality, whether of the world or of the self, may be ignored or defied, but never thwarted.

> Thomas F. Curley. *Commonweal*. Jan. 4, 1957. pp. 363–4

William Eastlake's second novel [*The Bronc People*] makes definite the arrival on the scene of a new, hard, dry, tender, very contemporary talent. Eastlake has been writing about cowboys and Indians and the Southwest for several years; a small group of readers has noticed him, some of them puzzled by the kidded debt to Hemingway and a subject matter which edges up against that beer-and-pretzels category, "the adult Western." Now, however, the Hemingway trick is bared for a joke and the proximity to the portentous teevee or movie Western is made a part of the comic action. A free-swinging playfulness and a deep nostalgia for the truths of sensual experience give us something we always need—a storyteller of wit, compassion and venturesomeness in both language and fantasy.

> Herbert Gold. *The Nation*. Sept. 20, 1958. p. 158

I do not really know how to describe Mr. Eastlake's new book [*Portrait of an Artist with Twenty-six Horses*]. . . . His characters seem to me small, remote, yet very clear, presented through a reversed telescope that yet brings them right to the reader. Their motives, on the other hand, are a trifle larger than life size. . . . The plot is developed into a masterpiece of the kind of suspense that makes the reader want to reach into the story and yell at the oblivious characters on whom the outcome depends. . . . At another level, we have a second story. . . . It develops almost surreptitiously. As the story ends its resolution and the young man's fate become parts of one another. This is technically a neat trick, a nice job of construction. . . . Discard any thought of realism and accept this book for what it is, and it will give you real pleasure.

> Oliver La Farge. *New York Times Book Section*. April 28, 1963. p. 5

In a sense, it is unfortunate that all three of William Eastlake's novels have been set in the West, more specifically the Southwest, even more specifically New Mexico and the surrounding areas. *Go in Beauty* and *The Bronc People* have gone the way of all "Westerns" and are at present out-of-print. Eastlake's most recent novel, *Portrait of an Artist with Twenty-six Horses*, also is set in New Mexico and unfortunately may follow the same pattern despite its delightful title—unfortunately, because Eastlake's novels are neither the stereotyped "Westerns," nor are they regional Southwestern novels any more than William Faulkner's novels are "Southern" or regional novels of the South.

Just as Faulkner created his Yoknapatawpha County out of the area surrounding Oxford, Mississippi, William Eastlake is creating a fictional area in the "Checkerboard" region of the Navajo reservation and its adjacent areas in northern New Mexico. His characters live and die in a physical setting that often has dominated the works of lesser writers, turning their expressions into regionalistic descriptions. . . .

Eastlake is a writer who, like the Ernest Hemingway of *The Sun Also Rises* and *A Farewell to Arms*, keeps a tight rein on his materials, using physical descriptions to suggest or enlarge ideological content. He *uses*, then, the New Mexico landscape, history, and people not for ornament but for the enhancement of meaning. Reading Eastlake, one is always aware of the desert, the mesa, the mountain, the sky, in all their color and beauty, their proudness and mercilessness, but one is also aware that they may be the symbol of "home," or of the "cradle" or the "coffin" of civilization.

> Delbert E. Wylder. *New Mexico Quarterly*. Summer, 1965. pp. 188–9

I find *Castle Keep* impressive, though sometimes difficult. William Eastlake tells his story of American soldiers, defending a castle in the Ardennes in 1944, with a multiplicity of narrators. Get used to one and it's time to change over. But there's something appropriate in this guard-duty approach; it also gives one a kind of castellar impression, as though each narrator were a wing or wall. The big question is: what are they all defending? Abandon the stronghold and you preserve the fragments of civilization it guards; hold it, and you risk a sort of destruction of history. The interweaving of opposed attitudes is intricate, and, for a tale which involves so much sheer waiting, there is an unfailing sense of movement. Mr. Eastlake is strong on the dialectic and, eventually, on the action, and he has a considerable mastery of diverse American speech-rhythms. I think this is one of the really good American war-books. Soldiers' talk is sweetened by tapestries.

Anthony Burgess. *The Listener*. March 3, 1966. p. 325

William Eastlake writes as though Vietnam could still be explained. *The Bamboo Bed* makes *Catch-22* look like a comic strip. One suspects that Vietnam, a war conceived and illustrated by Chester Gould, makes *The Bamboo Bed* look like a comic strip. But Eastlake went over there to see, and came back and wrote *The Bamboo Bed*. If he left anything out, it was because he didn't think our civilian credibilities could stand any more. He is one of the best American novelists writing today and if he thinks that we can't stand more absurdity than he has written into *The Bamboo Bed* he is probably right. Even though there was probably more to tell. He tells enough.

Richard Rhodes. *Book World*. Nov. 9, 1969. p. 5

The Bamboo Bed is not a political novel, hardly even a war novel. It is neither realistic nor (in the ordinary sense of the term) hard-hitting. A brilliant, strange, wondrous performance: it is the kind of feather that knocks you over. It has something of the black humor of *Catch-22* which it superficially resembles. But Eastlake has done something more than spawn a sequel to Joseph Heller's novel. *Catch-22* is set in World War II *set in*; any conflagration could have been used as the backdrop to its madness. *The Bamboo Bed* is the war in Vietnam. . . .

A myth is a fiction that makes it possible to deal with the ineffable. Some myths are pernicious, which is why, as Mailer tells us, we are in Vietnam. *The Bamboo Bed*, a mythic exercise in its own right, deflates the myth behind our involvement in Vietnam by mythologizing that war out of existence.

Beverly Gross. *The Nation*. Nov. 24, 1969. pp. 576, 578

Most of [the poems in *A Child's Garden of Verses for the Revolution*] are introduced by skillfully written prose passages that establish the contexts. Eastlake . . . is deeply concerned about our time of violence, hatred, ignorance, and war—foreign and domestic. . . . For observation, detail, scope, and shattering insight into social ills, his poetry is among the best. Yet I think he is a better prose writer than a poet; the brevity of his language, the sense of detail, and the rhythm of his narration have the impact of engrossing journalism, not poetry.

Jon M. Warner. *Library Journal*. Nov. 1, 1970. p. 3785

If Eastlake is—though he wastes no time making a show of it—a deeply intellectual writer in that he confronts serious ideas with both depth and wisdom, he is also a most unusual intellectual, for he actively applies a tempering modicum of myth and magic to his work, thus achieving a dimension of ken unusual midst the single-minded technological thought patterns so widely praised today. And all these things are manifest in an impressionist manner that suggests rather than gouges. Eastlake's major triumph as a writer has been, at his best, to instill in his readers his own unique sense of life, a sense just different enough from their own to create important questions concerning man and the direction of contemporary life. His reintroduction of myth and magic may seem a step into the past, but these aspects of human experience are perpetually modern; Eastlake differs from many contemporary thinkers in his rejection of an all-or-nothing philosophy—all reason or all magic—in favor of a balance of both.

By presenting unusual perspectives and stimulating questions, Eastlake has triggered new feelings and new insights. In exploring the fictive world of William Eastlake, one confronts a portrait of the artist as shaman.

Gerry Haslam. *Western Review*. Spring, 1971. p. 12

William Eastlake is the funniest, most profound, most musical writer I have read in years. He has the greatness of soul not only to kid the characters in his book [*Dancers in the Scalp House*] (Navajos, semi-Navajos, quasi-Navajos, lunatic-fringe Navajo-sympathizers and anti-Navajos) but also to kid himself and his own style and thought as a writer. He has the confidence, in other words, of a man half-bard and half-bum, yet undeceived as to the truth in all the confusion. Eastlake is wise: a poet in the best sense. . . .

His mind is tough, reasonable, and crawls simply everywhere in the connections he makes. Funniness, last resort of the Indian, he has aplenty. . . . Eastlake is a fine American humorist, and he is wise. The last beautiful passage strikes in no uncertain tones one of the finest dirges I've seen.

Barry Hannah. *New York Times Book Section*. Oct. 12, 1975. p. 43

BIBLIOGRAPHY
Go in Beauty, 1956 (n); *The Bronc People*, 1958 (n); *Portrait of an Artist with Twenty-Six Horses*, 1963 (n); *Castle Keep*, 1965 (n); *The Bamboo Bed*, 1969 (n); *A Child's Garden of Verses for the Revolution*, 1971 (misc); *Dancers in the Scalp House*, 1975 (n); *The Long, Naked Descent into Boston*, 1977 (n); *Jack Armstrong in Tangier and Other Escapes*, 1984 (s); *Lyric of the Circle Heart: The Bowman Family Trilogy*, 1996 (n)

EBERHART, Richard (1904–)

Mr. Eberhart, either because his ear is defective or because he is over-anxious to avoid the merely smooth, makes the not uncommon mistake of establishing violence and perversity as his norm, with the inevitable result that where everything shrieks and clashes, the uproar at last cancels itself out, and it is as if nothing had been heard at all. This is a great pity, for he has a wonderful energy of vision, together with a fine gusto in phrase and an enviable muscular capacity for compressed statement; if he could only be severe with himself, and canalize his gifts, instead of simply going hell-for-leather at his Idea, with capitals, he could be one of the very best of contemporary poets, as he is already one of the most exciting.

Conrad Aiken. *New Republic*. Apr. 2, 1945. p. 452

In the manufacture of malt whiskey the barley is soaked, then dried, and then the malt thus obtained is brewed into a beer-like liquid. This liquid, when distilled, produces the raw whiskey. It has to lie mellowing a long time in sherry casks. Mr. Eberhart is always a good brewer but he does not always bother with the further processes of distilling and maturing—or rather, he often matures without distilling, Let him distil his poetry more often: the finer, subtler, stronger and more profound flavor of pot-stilled malt whiskey (now almost unobtainable, alas) is more exciting to the discriminating palate than the pleasantest of beers.

David Daiches. *Poetry*. May, 1945. p. 95

His trouble has always been that his faults are very obvious and easy to feel superior to, because they are as unmodish as it is possible for fault to be; they are Victorian faults. That Mr. Eberhart has also the Victorian virtues is easy to overlook. . . . When Mr. Eberhart succeeds, he achieves kind of direct rightness of feeling towards central experiences which is about the rarest thing there is in contemporary verse; and he does it in a language as simple and perfect for its purpose as you could ask.

Arthur Mizener. *Poetry*. Jan., 1949. pp. 226–7

His mysticism is self-aware and a little humorous. He writes in a good grainy language that puts him squarely in the most attractive tradition of American verse, and he reveals, in some of his poems at least, a marvelous control of stress and pitch, the play of the spoken language within poetic forms. Moreover, like Emily Dickinson, he possesses the ability to hit sometimes upon the absolutely perfect image, startling and simple, lustrous against the setting of the poems.

Hayden Carruth. *Poetry*. Oct., 1954. pp. 55–6

Whatever it is that makes a "true" poet, in the old platonic or the new subliminal sense, Richard Eberhart has it. When the god's hand is on him, the language pours forth, powerfully channeled, alive without bombast, rhetorically true. . . . Too many of his poems do begin in brilliant fashion, then fade into some forced paradoxical turn, or into the thick, guttered out language of a conventional and semi-mystical piety, or even into tautology. . . . But though we should not quite forgive him his failures of self-criticism, it is quite likely that Eberhart needs to work as he does; that if he allowed himself certain kinds of "doubts," the greater successes, those poems in which we sense the god's presence at every moment would be impossible.

M.L. Rosenthal. *The Nation*. Dec. 21, 1957. p. 480

Eberhart is a romantic poet in the old style. I don't mean that he imitates particular poets or poems, but that his ideas of poetical structure, and of effective combinations of words resemble the ideas of poets in the early years of the last century. Often he tells an anecdote and follows it with an ecstatic moral. But where Wordsworth moved toward speech and away from poetic diction, Eberhart's direction is characteristically the reverse. Wordsworth's capitalized abstractions are involuntary survivals of the old style;

but Eberhart's predecessor was T. S. Eliot, and when Eberhart uses grammatical inversion he is in effect renovating poetic diction. His language is a rhetoric which constantly approaches rhapsody.

Donald Hall. *Saturday Review*. Feb. 11, 1961. p. 65

Richard Eberhart's poetry is excellent only when it is religious in theme and tone, and not always then. In an interview with Denis Donoghue (*Shenandoah*, Summer 1964) Eberhart says that over the years many of his most successful poems have been god-given. I believe him, for those poems have an elevation and intensity quite incommensurate with most of those he has published. When the god speaks through him, the words come out right; sometimes when he meditates on religious subjects, he entrances himself, as it were, and the words come out mostly right; but a lot of the time, when he is being occasional or playful, everything goes wrong. No highly self-critical craftsman would write, much less publish, poems as embarrassing as "Father and Son" and "Father and Daughter"; but then, highly self-critical craftsman are much less likely to be seized by the god, whose taste is not always impeccable; and what a poet gives the world importantly is his good poems, not the average of his good and fair and bad. None of the poems in *The Quarry* is of the high, inspired kind. The three best ones are meditative: a very long parable called "The kite," and the two long concluding Meditations. In these the poet talks himself up to a pitch such that the big abstract nouns and ideas which are a source of gas in his bad poems here become sources of elevation.

George P. Elliott. *Hudson Review*. Autumn, 1964. p. 459

Poetry as knowledge, poetry as power—between these two tendencies Eberhart has divided his art. The poems that capture in all their suddenness and gratuitousness moments of illumination do not in any way contradict those moral essays that call to account human motives and actions. Each aspect of his verse complements and enriches the other. What counts in both is the instantaneous, sharp, and piercing vision, and its expression: the words which create an experience because they are of its essence and are not an afterthought.

Ralph J. Mills. *Contemporary American Poetry* (Random). 1965. p. 29

[Eberhart] continues after forty years, two *Selected Poems* and one *Collected Poems*, to be the vigorous, idiosyncratic visionary his many admirers have come to cherish. As Kenneth Rexroth remarked, Eberhart always *appeared* to be a poet of the academies, perhaps because of his long teaching career, while his work has actually been the articulation of a quite independent intelligence and imagination, fascinated by physical nature and metaphysical speculation, by the contrariness of human behavior and the elusive traceries of the Divine. Stylistically, Eberhart has developed after his own fashion as well, early absorbing Hopkins, Donne, Blake and others, but always putting what he learned to his own uses. As a poet of inspiration, one who often relies on the moment of perception and its rapid dictation, he has taken risks which more polished poets would avoid, yet the uniqueness of his poetry resides in this visionary intensity that throws caution to the winds in order to seize the given insight.

Fields of Grace, his poems of the past four years, shows that Eberhart has lost none of his power and exuberance; his imagination ranges widely and with keen receptivity over the surfaces, declivities, the abrupt transitions between life and death in the natural world. . . .

Ralph J. Mills, Jr. *Parnassus*. Spring–Summer, 1973. pp. 215–6

Richard Eberhart . . . is perhaps the most distinguished survivor of a tradition that remained potent well into this century but that has been partially eclipsed by the nihilist tendencies of the day, the tradition of religious romanticism whose greatest modern exemplars are Yeats, D. H. Lawrence, Dylan Thomas, and Roethke. If Eberhart sometimes strikes readers as an anomalous figure, it may be because his closest affinities have been not with his contemporaries, whatever their stripe, but with earlier Romantics—Wordsworth, Blake, and Hopkins in particular. I shall seek . . . to indicate the direction of the poet's spiritual development and to probe critical stages of it as they become manifest in representative poems.

[Eberhart's] most impressive early meditation on mortality is "The Groundhog." . . . Indeed most of the verse initially collected in *Reading the Spirit* (1936) seems important now mainly as evidence of his struggle to find the voice and point of view perfected in that poem. The question he poses is whether the animal's demise represents, not just physically but also spiritually, a "senseless change." Eberhart treats death most effectively when he is able to gain a certain, though not too great, distance on it.

One finds a characteristic instance of Eberhart's recoil from transcendence in "I walked out to the graveyard to see the dead." . . . With a wryness not much evident in the earlier poems but fairly common in the later work, he rejects the golden pheasant's invitation to contemplate the mysteries.

Richard K. Cross. *Concerning Poetry*. Spring, 1979, pp. 13–15

At seventy-six Richard Eberhart stands apart, as ever, belonging to no school of poetry, going his own way without apology. An irrepressible voice in American poetry for more than five decades, in *Ways of Light* he remains ebullient, quirky, brilliant and uneven. Not counting his large *Collected Poems* of 1975, this is his first book of poems since *Fields of Grace* (1972); readers familiar with his work will find Eberhart reworking his usual themes: the fragility of existence, the finality of death, mutability in its various aspects and guises. These are subjects which found their classic expression in his early work: "The Groundhog," "The Fury of Aerial Bombardment," "For a Lamb," and "Cancer Cells" come to mind, all widely anthologized. What is new in this book, or freshly seen, is the central but intractable nature of love; Eberhart rejoices in his love, not only of humankind, but of the earth as well, "The wildness of the thicket, the order of the garden,/And the apples, O the red apples of the orchard." He writes with poignancy, and with the peculiar angle of vision characteristic of his work.

Eberhart is perhaps the last genuinely Romantic poet not to suffer unduly from what Harold Bloom calls "belatedness." He is unabashedly vatic, believing in "inspiration" as innocently as any poet ever has. His work contains little of the ironic distance so common in American poetry in the past decades. This allows him to confront his subjects with an oddly affecting naïveté. . . .

Eberhart sounds [an] astringent, elegiac note throughout the volume. The mood of a New England autumn, with its traditional associations of brilliance in decline, predominates, this "Season of bliss and yellow wistfulness,/The corn going down with the sun late afternoon." . . .

It would be wrong to suggest that *Ways of Light* is a gloomy book because of Eberhart's fascination with mutability and decline. The second elegy for Lowell, "Stone Words for Robert Lowell," ends with defiance in the face of Death, personified as Goliath. And in a central poem, "Survivors," the poet celebrates the ancient ladies of the Maine coast who, in their nineties, can still "Drive from Boston to Maine," and who are "clear/In mind and body," sharp-tongued, sporting, very much alive. . . .

To praise what remains mysterious, to fight back at death, and to acknowledge decay with a certain sorrow but no final bitterness, requires both an autumnal serenity and in indomitable spirit. Eberhart has come upon both honestly, and their mixture informs this late product of a life dedicated to the art of poetry.

Jay Parini *TLS: The Times Literary Supplement*. Sept. 26, 1980, p. 1060

BIBLIOGRAPHY

A Bravery of Earth, 1930 (p); *Reading the Spirit*, 1937 (p); *Song and Idea*, 1942 (p); *Poems, New and Selected*, 1944; *Burr Oaks*, 1947 (p); *Selected Poems*, 1951; *Undercliff: Poems 1946–1953*, 1953; *Great Praises*, 1957 (p); *Collected Poems, 1930–1960*, 1961; *Collected Verse Plays*, 1962; *The Quarry*, 1964 (p); *Selected Poems, 1930–1965*, 1966; *Thirty-One Sonnets*, 1967 (p); *Shifts of Being*, 1968 (p); *Fields of Grace*, 1972 (p); *Collected Poems, 1930–1976*, 1976; *Selected Prose*, 1978 (e, c); *Of Poetry and Poets*, 1979 (e, interviews); *Ways of Light*, 1980 (p); *Florida Poems*, 1981; *The Long Reach: New and Uncollected Poems, 1948–1983*, 1984; *Collected Poems, 1930–1986*, 1988; *Maine Poems*, 1989

EDMONDS, Walter (1903–1998)

Rome Haul would be a notable book in any season. As the first novel of a man born in 1903 it is extraordinary. There are men and women here, of course. But not one of them bulks so large, in the completed tapestry, as the Erie Canal on which they live. . . . Mr. Edmonds undoubtedly set forth to make this a chronicle of the Erie Canal. In this he has succeeded most admirably. . . . Great deeds were done and great lives lived along the canal, *Rome Haul* is a fitting, if somewhat belated, monument.

William Vogt. *New York Herald Tribune Book Section*. Feb. 17, 1929. p. 5

One need hardly say more than that *Erie Water* is as good an historical novel as was Mr. Edmonds's first, *Rome Haul*. It is full of accurate detail and incidents recreated with all the stress and drama of the moment. The conversations, the expletives, in fact, the complete scene of that period and region are utilized with a mastery which points to the author's special study and love of his subject. The romance with which he flavours his story has not the virtue of originality, but its sincere emotion and suspense adequately serve the purpose of narrative interest.

Archer Winsten. *Bookman*. March, 1933. pp. 295–6

Whether the mood is light or dark, you will find in these stories (*Mostly Canallers*) a freshness of characterization which goes far to explain their eminent readableness, and which itself calls for some explanation. It seems to be founded not merely on quick imagination and the shrewd sense of where one man differs from another but in the author's solid admiration for these rough people of his, on the humor and sympathy with which he draws them out. . . . He has. . . given them an idiom and a relation to environment which give them individuality as a group. When they are lounging or storming about in their own peculiar attitudes they are honest-to-God, and vary satisfying to know.

Otis C. Ferguson. *New York Herald Tribune Book Section*. Feb. 25, 1934. p. 2

Drums Along the Mohawk is crowded with people and with incidents. And they all. . . are convincing. Mr. Edmonds is obviously not a born novelist. He cannot create clearly individualized characters who dominate a book and walk away with the reader's emotions. But he can do very well in painting a society, a countryside full of people. He did it expertly enough in his stories of the building of the Erie Canal; he has done it still more expertly and vigorously in this full book of the Valley in the days of Tories and hostile armies.

Allan Nevins. *Saturday Review*. Aug. 1, 1936. p. 5

Because he is primarily an artist, the work of Walter D. Edmonds goes beyond a local realism. Beneath his faithful use of local color he attempts to express the essential truths of human experience. His novels and stories have been compared to the folk literature of a region, for he treats innocence, courage, the home, as the ancestral virtues of our national birthright. . . . In style as a device for literary experiment he is not at all interested; he holds firmly to the story-telling tradition of the Anglo-Saxon novel. He has a story to tell as well as characters to present, and from characters against a definite background come the outlines of plot.

Dayton Kohler. *English Journal*. Jan., 1938. pp. 10–11

Mr. Edmonds does not content himself with going up into the attic and fetching down a beaver hat and a hoop skirt. He fetches in a whole lost age and makes it so natural that soon one is living in it. He is almost as much at home in Northern New York in the Eighteen Thirties as Mark Twain was with life on the Mississippi. He catches the incidental things. . . . The reader need not look for social significance (in *Chad Hanna*), for this is a yarn of local color, romance, and adventure. . . . This book is a vacation. It is an escape book. It pictures a land and time in which one would like to be for a change, and experiences not too painful to live through—and certainly not too dull!

R. L. Duffus. *New York Times Book Section*. April 7, 1940. p. 1

His outlook is almost exclusively masculine; his best portraits of women are those of women who might as well have been men, and he shows little delicacy of insight regarding the other sex. Against this objection if it is one, we may set the fact that he has great delicacy of perception regarding natural beauty, animals of all sorts, and children. He has not yet exhibited the highest type of constructive imagination, and his invention is in general short-breathed. But on the other hand few writers can excel him in straight story-telling or in the brilliancy with which he can flash a scene. His historical perspective has seldom achieved grandeur and his portrayal of the past lacks both latitude and altitude. He has, however, chosen to cultivate a restricted field intensively and he may have no ambition to extend it.

Robert M. Gay. *Atlantic Monthly*. May, 1940. p. 658

Mr. Edmonds is a romantic realist, he enjoys spinning a yarn for the yarn's sake, but he likes people for themselves rather than—as is the way of so many yarn-spinners—for the function they may be made to perform in the unfolding of the story. So his characters, whom one gets to know slowly, and likes better and better as one knows them, are a refreshingly genuine collection of characters from an America that is gone.

The words that Mr. Edwards puts into their mouths are particularly admirable. This, one says to oneself, is the way Americans must have talked in those days.

Robert Littell. *The Yale Review*. Summer, 1940. p. vi—viii

Like all Mr. Edmond's historical novels, *In the Hands of the Senecas* plays tricks with your calendar. It projects a more dangerous, headier age plump in your living room, and for a few hours you find yourself battling flames and hostile savages with no aid available from fire department or police; none, either, from your immediate neighbors, for in all likelihood you have none. You have become a rugged individualist, not from choice but in order to survive. . . . Mr. Edmonds takes advantage of every opportunity offered by his material and often creates breathless suspense by such devices as escapes, pursuits, and the like. But a different, more organic type of suspense also pervades the story, one's natural anxiety to know what will happen next to a group of always believable characters.

Jennings Rice. *New York Herald Tribune Book Section*. Jan. 26, 1947. p. 8

BIBLIOGRAPHY
Rome Haul, 1929 (n); *The Big Barn*, 1930 (n); *Erie Water*, 1933 (n); *Mostly Canallers*, 1934 (s); *Drums along the Mohawk*, 1936 (n); *Chad Hanna*, 1940 (n); *The Matchlock Gun*, 1941 (juv); *Young Ames*, 1942 (n); *Tom Whipple*, 1942 (juv); *Two Logs Crossing*, 1943 (juv); *Wilderness Clearing*, 1944 (n); *In the Hands of the Senecas*, 1947 (n); *The Wedding Journey*,1947 (n); *The First Hundred Years*, 1948 (h); *They Fought with What They Had: The Story of the Army Air Forces in the Southwest Pacific, 1941–1942*, 1951 (h); *The Boyds of Black River*, 1953 (n); *Hound Dog Moses and the Promised Land*, 1954 (juv); *Uncle Ben's Whale*, 1955

(juv); *Three Stalwarts* (*Drums along the Mohawk, Rome Haul* and *Erie Water*), 1961 (n); *They Had a Horse*, 1962 (juv); *The Musket and the Cross*, 1968 (h); *Time to Go House*, 1969 (juv); *Seven American Stories*, 1970; *Wolf Hunt*, 1970 (n); *Beaver Valley*, 1971 (juv); *The Story of Richard Storm*, 1974 (juv); *Bert Breen's Barn*, 1975 (n); *The Night Raider and Other Stories*, 1980; *The South African Quirt*, 1985 (n); *Tales My Father Never Told*, 1995 (m)

ELDER, Lonne (1931–)

Anybody who is worried about the future of the American theatre, or of just the theatre, had better try to get tickets for *Ceremonies in Dark Old Men*, the second production this year of the Negro Ensemble Company, at the St. Marks. *Ceremonies* is the first play by Lonne Elder III to be done professionally, and if any American has written a finer one I can't think what it is. And the actors bring to life all its tragic power and beauty, its humanity and humor and wit.

In trying to describe plays that one has enjoyed or admired, one is often forced to say that it is the individual scenes, not the plot, that matter. The plot of *Ceremonies in Dark Old Men* matters a great deal, but the scenes, many of them very funny, give the play its richness and the tragedy its depth. The writing is beautifully controlled, without a trace of rhetoric.

Edith Oliver. *New Yorker*. 15 February 1969, pp. 90–3.

It is a difficult time for those of us who look forward to an America in which mutual respect, warm friendship, and socioeconomic justice will prevail in all relationships between those of differing racial ancestry. Therefore, it is most heartening to visit the Negro Ensemble Company at their small St. Mark's Playhouse and find a play such as *Ceremonies in Dark Old Men*. For this work by Lonne Elder, 3rd, deals most realistically yet unrancorously with today's Harlem.

Furthermore, it never lets fear of possibly contributing to the perpetuation of a racist-held stereotype force it into a well meaning but patently false distortion of the characters it has chosen to depict. It is as if Mr. Elder is trusting us to think of these characters as the understandable victims of a racist society that has deprived them of virility and the incentive to become educated or even industrious. They are what any of us might be, if we had faced the same negative conditions.

Henry Hewes. *Saturday Review*. 22 February 1969, p. 29.

The only new play which has genuinely interested me for some time is Lonne Elder's *Ceremonies in Dark Old Men*, as given by the Negro Ensemble Company. When I say "play" I refer to the whole phenomenon of stage presentation: "words" in the "music" of an acting team perceived as a single experience. (*Tango*, in contrast, contains a vital text damaged by inadequate acting.) With *Ceremonies in Dark Old Men* I did not think to evaluate any of its parts (script, acting, setting, direction) separately. That is *theatre*. With Elder's play the Negro Ensemble has achieved its own proper pitch.

One may note some repetitiousness in the text and there were overfacile strokes for comedy effect. The total impression, however, is without blemish. Even the crudities in the play's texture are of a kind which appear organic with the material, part of its reality.

There is no special pleading: it proclaims no thesis, espouses no cause, appeals for no largess. *Ceremonies* is a family play whose characters are foolish, fallible, sweet, stupid, lovable, always understandable folk. They are richly human and as such not easily subject to petty compromise in humdrum jobs at paltry wages.

Russell Parker was a pop dancer till one day he no longer had the strength. He became a barber, but without any aptitude for the work, earned little in his Harlem shop and allowed his faithful wife to support him till she died of the burden. Their daughter took over her mother's task; now she supports her father who spends most of his time playing checkers with a kindly friend and recounting tall tales to the delight of his two sons, who also find indolence more convenient than work. One day the hard-driven girl, fed up with the situation, announces that either they get jobs or she will refuse to contribute her earnings to their further maintenance. Crisis!

The younger brother has already begun to amuse himself by larceny; the older one has hit upon a scheme suggested by a local racketeer, Blue Haven. Since the young idler has a talent for making bootleg whisky on the premises, they will arrange to convert the barber shop into a speak-easy. Parker balks at the proposal but, faced with the alternative humiliation of finding work "downtown," agrees to the plan.

It all ends disastrously, though the play cannot be said to have an "end." We know at the last fade-out only that the family will abandon their illegal trade after (but not because) the young brother has been killed during a robbery which is one of the activities into which he had been led by Blue Haven.

None of this gives any idea of the humor, the oblique pathos, the unsentimental pain—affecting the racketeer himself—with which the story is told. If the play were to be summarized in a bald reduction of its theme, it might be stated as an account of how poverty and other wretched circumstances in the lives of a black family force them into a tragic mess, for which there is no base motive, but only the wish to enjoy life, freely and fully. But such a summation lacks the savor of what I felt while observing the characters through what, despite elements of violence, are really little more than casual happenings in a poor black neighborhood. There is no sensationalism, not even a "problem"—only the warp and woof of ordinary living: funny, crazy, frightening and somehow strangely innocent, heartwarming as much as heartbreaking. The play, the first by a writer of 30, is a "little" comedy—much more telling than many that are ambitiously "significant."

What makes it altogether delightful and arresting is the unadorned, exciting, joyous and entirely devoted nature of the acting— the kind which not only makes one believe that he is *there* (yet happily in the theatre), but that the actors have invented their own lines, on the spur of the moment. Speech and flesh are one. It all seems so artless as to constitute the truest art.

If only one member of the cast were to be singled out, it would have to be Douglas Turner in the central role. His passion, his raciness, his vigor, his total commitment to the essence of each moment make his performance one of the memorable occasions of the year: far more expressive and *useful* than some of those exuberantly touted elsewhere in town. There are few more hilarious scenes in recent days than the one in which Turner, as Parker, tells of his travail on a chain gang—a yarn which ain't necessarily so but which he makes more vividly to the point than truth itself.

It would be a critical misdemeanor to pass over Arthur French. Parker's companion in fun, games and sorrow; he is inescapably winning. And William Jay as the older son, David Downing as the younger, Rosalind Cash as their doughty sister, Samual Blue, Jr., as the racketeer, and sexy Judyann Jonsson as Parker's fling all contribute more than honorably to the evening's success.

Harold Clurman. *The Nation*, New York. February 24, 1969, p. 253.

[Compared to Ed Bullins's *Clara's Old Man* there is] a slight drop in the quality of working-class reality in *Ceremonies in Dark Old Men*. In Bullins it is as if he were using black working-class folk themselves as the brushes with which to paint his canvas, while in Elder there seems to be greater distance than in Bullins between the artist and his black working class. Bullins is the effortless artist, so total the artist that, in his best work, one rarely senses contrivance; the naturalness, the grimness are so complete that they do not seem to be plays at all but rather the rakings of life dropped down before our eyes and our ears by the hands of some black god of life whose woolly head brushes against the clouds. Aretha has this total naturalness and the seeming absence of effort, the absolute spontaneity, and Bobby Blue Bland and Stevie Wonder have it, and Bird, and Coltrane, Sidney Bechet. But though there is a drop in the quality of working-class reality in *Ceremonies in Dark Old Men* we still have magnificence, and there is a reason. The reason is that Elder is wise enough to do as Bullins has done: to focus on his own people—neither to sickly include nor to sickly exclude the white man. In Bullins and Elder there is no sick sense of an omnipotent and ubiquitous oppressor, and of course the fearful sense of an omnipotent and ubiquitous oppressor means that the writer himself then must be to a degree impotent. And inasmuch as any sense of the omnipotence of the oppressor is not in these works, the writer himself, a reflection of his people, suffers from no impotence. The writer himself is victor: there is the sense of the black people themselves, as a people, as implicit victors; their very vigor, the fire of their style, the pride of their poetry, the flow of the music and poetry of their language, their vigorous and unashamed sexuality: these are implicits of an undefeated people: and more: their thrust and vigor and poetry and violence are the implicit expression of the potentialities of Man to rise above his present condition and attain a godliness, for in certitude one thing that Bullins does is to express in the lives of the people of *Clara's Old Man* and *In the Wine Time*, a sense of secular holiness, and the primary function of literature above all is to reveal to man that in his complexity and confusion there exist his potentialities of godliness, his destiny of grandeur.

Lance Jeffers. *CLA Journal* 1, September, 1972, pp. 32–48.

BIBLIOGRAPHY

A Hysterical Turtle in a Rabbit Race, 1961 (d); *Ceremonies in Dark Old Men*, 1965 (d), revised 1969; *Kissing Rattlesnakes Can Be Fun*, 1966 (d); *Charades on East Fourth Street*, 1967 (d); *Seven Comes Up, Seven Comes Down*, 1977-78 (d); *Splendid Mummer*, 1988 (d); *King*, with Richard Blackford, Maya Angelou, and Alistair Beaton, 1990 (d)

ELIOT, T.S. (1888–1965)

By technique we . . . mean one thing: the alert hatred of normality which, through the lips of a tactile and cohesive adventure, asserts that nobody in general and some one in particular is incorrigibly and actually alive. This some one is, it would seem, the extremely great artist: or, he who prefers above everything the unique dimension of intensity, which it amuses him to substitute in us for the comforting and comfortable furniture of reality. If we examine the means through which this substitution is allowed by Mr. Eliot to happen in his reader, we find that they include: a vocabulary almost brutally tuned to attain distinction; an extraordinary tight orchestration of the shapes of sound; the delicate and careful murderings—almost invariably interpreted, internally as well as terminally, through near-rhyme and rhyme—of established tempos by oral rhythms.

E.E. Cummings. *Dial.* June, 1920. p. 783

It is true his poems seem the products of a constricted emotional experience and that he appears to have drawn rather heavily on books for the heat he could not derive from life. There is a certain grudging margin, to be sure, about all that Mr. Eliot writes—as if he were compensating himself for his limitations by a peevish assumption of superiority. But it is the very acuteness of his suffering from this starvation which gives such poignancy to his art. And, as I say, Mr. Eliot is a poet—that is, he feels intensely and with distinction and speaks naturally in beautiful verse—so that, no matter within what walls he lives, he belongs to the divine company. . . . These drops, though they be wrung from flint, are none the less authentic crystals.

Edmund Wilson. *Dial.* Dec., 1922. p. 615

The writer of "The Waste Land" and the other poems of that period appeals to us as one struck to the heart by the confusion and purposelessness and wastefulness of the world about him. . . . And to that world his verse will be held up as a ruthlessly faithful mirror. The confusion of life will be reflected in the disorganized flux of images; its lack of clear meaning in the obscurity of language. . . . And now against this lyric prophet of chaos must be set the critic who will judge the world from the creed of the classicist, the royalist, and the Anglo-Catholic. . . . I think . . . that a sensitive mind cannot read "Ash Wednesday" without an uneasy perception of something fundamentally amiss in employing for an experience born of Anglo-Catholic faith a metrical form and a freakishness of punctuation suitable for the presentation of life regarded as without form and void. . . . He is a leader and a very influential leader. Our difficulty is that he seems to be leading us in two directions at once.

Paul Elmer More. *Saturday Review.* Nov. 12, 1932. p. 235

Eliot not only follows the classical dogma because he cherishes classicism; he follows it also because he cherishes dogma. . . . He loses much by being fastidious. He loses much by having no humor whatever, but he is capable of something else by having splendid wit. And the presence of wit and the absence of humor in Eliot argue his possession of great intellect and egoism, his lack of humanity, his lack of modesty and unselfconsciousness. He rests with those men who have chosen to see life distantly, from a single vantage-point; and had he, in the absence of warmth and sinew, a great intensity, he might possess permanent value for us. . . . But he is not intense, he is merely correct.

> Louis Kronenberger. *The Nation.* Apr. 17, 1935. p. 453

Eliot's own opinions are not merely related to his poetry. They qualify his whole critical attitude, and they make him to some extent a preacher. His aim as a writer has been to be a traditionalist: the tradition which he has adopted, being derived from the Church, has also sociological and educative implications. It is his object to show that the application of these principles in social life is as just as it is correct to apply them to literature. He seems to feel that unless he can prove this, he is, in his work, an individualist: not a traditionalist radically connected with the historic process: but isolated, original, personal, in the sense that he is writing about his own beliefs which are "home-made," and so make him eccentric and different from the people around him.

> Stephen Spender. *The Destructive Element* (Houghton). 1936. pp. 164–5

When Eliot stood isolated and dispossessed amid the ruins of a familiar universe, every nerve and sensation quivered with its own life. The antennae of his intelligence were alive with nervous vitality. This resulted in images and allegories of great focal sharpness. In more recent years, approaching a stranger territory, this grip on identity is no longer held, and with its relaxation the nervous sensibility of his diction and cadence has lessened. He writes either a more relaxed and speculative verse, or a sort of argument which attempts to extend his intellectual problems beyond their own limits. He has become a poet of more public qualities, of religious responsibilities, and even (in *The Rock*) of social concerns. These have entailed a change from a style of cryptic historical reference and erudition to one of dialectic lucidity, or even of popular simplification.

> Morton Dauwen Zabel. *Southern Review.* Summer, 1936. p. 170

If there is a metaphysical distinction between the poetry and the prose of T.S. Eliot, it is this: that in the former he is sceptical of his own knowledge of truth, and in the latter he is indicating the path along which he hopes to find it. In the poetry he sees things through a glass darkly; in the prose he is proclaiming the truth that will make us free. Both these activities, however, are offshoots of a unified intelligence, of a man who is singularly whole in his conception of the dignity and importance of his art. There is no real divergence between his theory and practice, no matter how lucid he may contrive to make his criticism, or how obscure his poetry.

> A.C. Partridge. *T.S. Eliot* (Pretoria). 1937. p. 3

He will soon make ordinary drama look cheap because of its lack of metaphysical interest, just as he had part in making the ordinary shallow poetry of twenty years ago look the same way, and for the same reason. . . . On the realistic level Mr. Eliot is superb in his

mastery of characterization (both the satiric and the sympathetic), handling of plot sequence, exposition of background through dialogue, and, I imagine, such other techniques as belong to an oral form like drama. It is comforting to think that an intellectualist, so strict and unconceding that he has been accused of living in a tower, has picked up without any fuss the knack for the close structural effects of drama.

> John Crowe Ransom. *Poetry.* Aug., 1939. pp. 264–6

It is to him, together with Ezra Pound, that we can trace the awareness of the urban scene, the employment of anti-poetic imagery, conversational rhythms, cinematic transitions and close-ups, which make contemporary verse deserve the adjective. And even the most vigorous and provocative of the younger men have not shown an "auditory imagination" equal to Eliot's. . . . What his "feeling for syllable and rhythm" has brought back, in its curious workings, has been chiefly a sense of disorder, of frustration and waste, an intimate and horrifying vision of death.

> Babette Deutsch. *American Scholar.* Winter, 1939. p. 30

Eliot, in brief, has surrendered to the acedia which Baudelaire was able to judge; Eliot suffers from the delusion that he is judging it when he is merely exhibiting it. He has loosely thrown together a collection of disparate and fragmentary principles which fall roughly into two contradictory groups, the romantic on the one hand and on the other the classical and Christian; and being unaware of his own contradictions, he is able to make a virtue of what appears to be private spiritual laziness; he is able to enjoy at one and the same time the pleasure of indulgence and the dignity of disapproval.

> Yvor Winters. *Kenyon Review.* Spring, 1941. p. 238

Eliot seldom involves himself steadily with the world about him. Instead he makes brief and startling sallies into the world and hence his poetry sometimes strikes us either as a discontinuous anthology of images or as an imitation of involuted psychological or biological processes which remain purely verbal. . . . Another result of this nervous intermittence is that Eliot's criticism of other poets—such as Donne, Marvell, or Dryden—makes the excellence of their poetry depend too much on their surprising success in image-making and too little on their steady sense of life. Eliot tends to give us what is occasional and spasmodic in a poet, rather than the poet's normal excellence.

> Richard Chase. *Kenyon Review.* Spring, 1945. pp. 220–1

The reconciliation of opposites is as fundamental to Eliot as it was to Heraclitus. Only thus can he envisage a resolution of man's whole being. The "heart of light" that he glimpsed in the opening movement of "Burnt Norton" is at the opposite pole from the *Heart of Darkness* from which he took the epigraph for "The Hollow Men." Essential evil still constitutes more of Eliot's subject matter than essential good, but the magnificent orchestration of his themes has prepared for that paradisal glimpse at the close, and thereby makes it no decorative allusion, but an integrated climax to the content no less than to the form. Such spiritual release and reconciliation are the chief reality for which he strives in a world that has seemed to him increasingly threatened with new dark ages.

F.O. Matthiessen. *The Achievement of T.S. Eliot* (Oxford). 1947. p. 195

In spite of everything, Eliot *has*, in his critical essays, said many of the things that most needed to be said in our time. He has documented with appropriate *dicta* the final ebb of the romantic movement, the reversal of the trend which saw poetry as the expression of the poet's unique personality, the rediscovery of the glories of the metaphysical poets, and the parallel reintroduction into English and American poetry of wit *and* passion. In some of his best essays—those on Dante, for example—he is often rearranging (as Mario Praz has shown) the ideas of Ezra Pound or others; in some of his worst, he is merely perverse or pigheaded or exhibitionistic. But his critical ideas are in themselves full of interest and excitement, and have become part of the intellectual atmosphere of our time.

David Daiches. *The Yale Review.* Spring, 1949. pp. 466–7

To my notion T.S. Eliot is the greatest of all literary critics. . . . Eliot's merit lies almost equally in his ability to raise the pertinent problems and in the fineness of his taste. He gave himself a rule of cogency early on and has had the strength of mind to obey it without evasion. This is the first critic of whom we can feel sure that the most important question will always be answered—namely, how successful *as art* is the work of art in hand? Eliot is no philosopher of aesthetics or criticism; he is both more and less than that: his critical practice demonstrates the right principles in action and we recognize them by their fruits rather than their definition.

Clement Greenberg. *The Nation.* Dec. 9, 1950. p. 531

Eliot's mind, let us say, is a mind of contrasts which sharpen rather than soften the longer they are weighed. It is the last mind which, in this century, one would have expected to enter the Church in a lay capacity. The worldliness of its prose weapons, its security of posture, its wit, its ability for penetrating doubt and destructive definition, its eye for startling fact and talent for nailing it down in flight, hardly go with what we think of today as English or American religious feeling. . . . However that may be, within the Church or not, Mr. Eliot's mind has preserved its worldly qualities. His prose reflections remain elegant, hard (and in a sense easy—as in manners), controlled, urbane (without the dissimulation associated with ecclesiastical urbanity), and fool-proof.

R.P. Blackmur. *Language as Gesture* (Harcourt). 1952. pp. 176–7

More than one critic has remarked that in Eliot the over-all organization of the poem as a whole is not lyrical in any recognizable and traditional way; nor is the poem organized in terms of narrative; nor is it dramatic in the literal theatrical sense; and it is certainly not logical, argumentative, or expository. . . . Where poets in the past would have used a logical, emotional, dramatic, or narrative basis for the transition from part to part, Eliot uses some

one of these kinds of transition freely and alternatively and without committing himself to any one of them or to any systematic succession of them; or he omits the connection between one passage and the next, one part and the part which succeeds it. . . . The characteristic over-all organization of the poem—of which "The Waste Land" is the vividest example—can be called, for the lack of a better phrase, that of sibylline (or subliminal) listening.

Delmore Schwartz. *Poetry.* Jan., 1955. pp. 236–7

[F.H.] Bradley, of course, didn't solve Eliot's initial poetic problem; there is no evidence that Eliot paid him any attention until after he had written *Prufrock* and *Portrait of a Lady*. (He did not buy his own copy of *Appearance and Reality* until mid-1913.) The study of Bradley, however, may be said to have done three things for a poet who might otherwise not have passed beyond the phase of imitating Laforgue. It solved his *critical* problem, providing him with a point of view towards history and so with the scenario for his most comprehensive essay, "Tradition and the Individual Talent"; it freed him from the Laforguian posture of the ironist with his back to a wall, by affirming the artificiality of *all* personality including the one we intimately suppose to be our true one; not only the faces we prepare but the "we" that prepares; and it released him from any notion that the art his temperament bade him practice was an eccentric art, evading for personal and temporary reasons a more orderly, more "normal" unfolding from statement to statement.

Hugh Kenner. *The Invisible Poet* (McDowell, Obolensky). 1959. p. 55

What most critics of Mr. Eliot's plays seem to ignore is that he is writing a new kind of drama. Whereas most plays appeal to the passions—pity, terror, the glamor of love—or to the intellect, or would stir our zeal for political reform, his plays are based on an appeal to the conscience, or the consciousness of self. Here is this person, he says in effect, guilty of this or that; how far are you, dear spectator, in the like case? Our response comes from a different center. That is why some people do not applaud his plays; nobody likes to be made to think about his weakness, his failures, or his sins. Not that many of us have committed crimes: but then crimes, as we are told in this play (*The Elder Statesman*) are in relation to the law, sins in relation to the sinner. . . . In all the plays about conscience, from Sophocles to Ibsen, we are detached spectators. . . . Here, however, we are forced to ask ourselves: "Have I never run away from myself? Have I never tried to blot out incidents from my past?"

Bonamy Dobrée. *Sewanee Review.* Winter, 1959. pp. 109–10

Eliot's poetic craftsmanship has been praised by very diverse critics, who agree that everything that he has to say, he says extremely well. We never get the feeling that he cannot quite say what he means, or that the felt significance is too big for the poem which has been used to express it (a feeling we experience with some of Dylan Thomas's poetry). The limitation of Eliot's poetry is in the subject matter. Only a narrow range of human experience seems to be subjected to the poetic process, a range which deals almost entirely with states of mind and soul, and which looks over a lonely territory where the poetic protagonist stands isolated from other beings. To adopt an expression of Eliot's, which he uses to describe Dante's poetic power, this is a poetry which comprehends the height and the depth of experience but is limited in breadth. This leads in Eliot's poetry to that unity of development of which we have spoken, but it also leads to a very *personal* poetry, for the states of mind and soul which he deals with are *his own:* he is his own subject matter.

> Sean Lucy. *T.S. Eliot and the Idea of Tradition* (Barnes and Noble). 1960. p. 160

In poetic form and imagery Eliot avoids all kinds of overloading, unless he is out for very special effects. Generally he finds a middle way between intellectualism and lyricism, or he balances the two in alternate lines and stanzas. The difficult and involved is continually set off by the simple and translucent, a fact which immediately emerges if his poetry is compared with the far opaquer medium of W.H. Auden. And Eliot's symbolism is supported and made accessible by naturalistic imagery, as a comparison with Yeats will bring out.

Eliot is not the arch-intellectualist in poetry that many people think. But, of course, his intellectual habits are mirrored in his poetry, so that the latter presents the attitudes of one accustomed to reflection. He may have had good reasons for the anti-emotionalism expressed in "Tradition and the Individual Talent", but it is impossible to refine emotion out of poetry altogether; and this Eliot has recognized, for he has told us repeatedly that his poetry expresses what it *feels* like to believe in something.

> Kristian Smidt. *Poetry and Belief in the Work of T.S. Eliot* (Humanities Press). 1961. p. 233

The origin of his attempt to develop a new theater is to be seen in his view that, just as man's nature needs to be guided by discipline and order, so dramatic art needs to be given a form which can draw a circle of abstraction around experience in order to make drama conform to the standard of all art—the ordered relationship of the parts to the whole. Believing that of all literary forms drama has the greatest capacity for recreating a complete and ordered world, Eliot developed a dramatic structure which was intended to lead the audience to a sense of religious awareness by demonstrating the presence of the supernatural order in the natural world. His dramatic theme is also the product of his religious concern to integrate the real and the ideal. In each of his plays he has portrayed the plight of the individual who perceives the order of God but, forced to exist in the natural world, must somehow come to terms with both realms.

> Carol H. Smith. *T.S. Eliot's Dramatic Theory and Practice* (Princeton). 1963. p. 31

Eliot wrote the work [*The Waste Land*] under the stress of illness. Six years of strenuous double-living—wage-earning faithfully and efficiently pursued, intellectual conquests pursued at the same time—had exhausted him. But a poet's breakdown is often the moment of creation. To let slip his hold on the day is to slip free of the day's hold on him; he gathers all that he has experienced into an innovative act. . . .

The Waste Land is a work in which the poet, like some of his predecessors, writes simultaneously about his own illness and the world's illness, of which his own is a reflection. He records and condemns his own "despairing" state and prescribes a discipline for his cure and for the healing of the city civilization of which he is the representative.

> Herbert Howarth. *Notes on Some Figures behind T.S. Eliot* (Houghton). 1964. pp. 234, 237

The image of structural unity pervades Eliot's social and literary criticism. What of his own poetry? Is he able to reach his goal of organic unity and write poems which live because they share the life of the European mind?

Most of Eliot's poems depend on the assumption that the poet can enlarge his private consciousness to coincide with a collective consciousness. This assumption is so easily and persuasively sustained that it is easy to forget what an extraordinary arrogation of power it is. Only a few early poems, such as "Prufrock" or "Portrait of a Lady," are limited to the perspective of a single ego. In most poems the reader is placed within everybody's mind at once. An act of self-surrender has expanded the private mind of the poet into the universal sphere of the mind of Europe.

> J. Hillis Miller. *Poets of Reality* (Harvard). 1965. p. 172

In between his visits we used to call upon him in London—once on Good Friday, when his precision occupied itself much with the exactly right temperature at which hot cross buns should be served. What was peculiar to TSE in this sort was the delicately perceptible trace, the ghostly flavor of irony which hung about his manner as though he were preparing a parody. For example, when we went to Peking in 1929, we wrote pressing him to come to stay with us in that enchanting scene. His reply: "I do not care to visit any country which has no native cheese." Not too much, I think, should be made of these "deliberate disguises", but he did have a repertory of more or less confessed poses which his friends were not debarred from seeing through.

> I.A. Richards. *Sewanee Review.* Jan.-March, 1966. p. 26

Sir Herbert Read tells me that the English poet for whom Eliot felt a conscious affinity, and upon whom he perhaps in some degree modelled himself, was Johnson. All the same it seems to me that the more we see of the hidden side of Eliot the more he seems to resemble Milton, though he thought of Milton as a polar opposite. As we look at all the contraries reconciled in Eliot—his schismatic traditionalism, his romantic classicism, his highly personal impersonality—we are prepared for the surprise (which Eliot himself seems in some measure to have experienced) of finding in the dissenting Whig regicide a hazy mirror-image of the Anglo-Catholic royalist. Each, having prepared himself carefully for poetry, saw that he must also, living in such times, explore prose, the cooler element. From a consciously archaic standpoint each must characterize the activities of the sons of Belial. Each saw that fidelity to tradition is ensured by revolutionary action. (Eliot would hardly have dissented from the proposition that "a man may be a heretic in the truth".) Each knew the difficulty of finding "answerable style" in an age too late. With the Commonwealth an evident failure, Milton wrote one last book to restore it, and as the élites crumbled and reformed Eliot wrote his *Notes [toward the Definition of a Culture]*. If Milton killed a king, Eliot attacked vulgar democracy and shared with the "men of 1914" and with Yeats some extreme authoritarian opinions.

Frank Kermode. *Sewanee Review*. Jan.-March, 1966. pp. 228–9

It won't be easy to reclaim his work from the conceptual and scholarly currency already invested in it. It will mean forcing ourselves to forget most of what exegesis has burdened us with, and it will mean returning for help to those very few difficult critics I've mentioned [Leavis, Blackmur, Kenner], all of whom have insisted, to almost no effect, on Eliot's deliberate irrationality. In trying to release Eliot from schematizations contrived mostly for the clarification and boredom of undergraduates, these, and a few others, direct us away from the seductions of neatness and into the wonderful mystery at the center of Eliot's poetry and criticism. What we find there, if we stay long enough, is that for Eliot ideas have no more organizational power than do literary allusions and that neither is as preoccupying as are the furtive memories and hallucinations, the sensuous images that stimulate a poem like "Preludes" but which remain at the end as unassimilated to any design as they were at the beginning.

Richard Poirier. *New Republic*. May 20, 1967. pp. 19–20

For me, the poetry [of *Four Quartets*] is saved by the scruple. The way in which it is saved may be indicated, perhaps, in a passage from *Varieties of Religious Experience*, where [William] James discusses the character of sanctity, particularly its ascetic quality. He remarks that while it is normal and, apparently, instinctive for us to seek "the easy and the pleasant," at the same time it is also normal "in moderate degree" to seek the arduous: "Some men and women, indeed, there are who can live on smiles and the word 'yes' forever. But for others (indeed for most) this is too tepid and relaxed a moral climate. Passive happiness is slack and insipid, and soon grows mawkish and intolerable. Some austerity and wintry negativity, some roughness, danger, stringency, and effort, some 'no! no!' must be mixed in, to produce the sense of an existence with character and texture and power."

Perhaps this is how *Four Quartets* lives, and how it communicates with those readers who do not share its Christian belief; by giving us the sense of an existence with character and texture and power. This is the tone of its "approach." Eliot has always implied, incidentally, that the satisfactions of poetry are in this tone. The great poet helps to purify the dialect of the tribe by making our stupidity unendurable.

Denis Donoghue. *The Ordinary Universe* (Macmillan— N.Y.). 1968. pp. 265–6

Those who are put off by Eliot's religion unconsciously agree with the pharisaical among churchgoers, for they, too, adopt the heretical opinion that the faith is a set of lucid propositions and the God of the faithful fully known. Their objection is not really to Eliot's idea of reality but to his calling this reality "God." They have in this a confidence about the meaningfulness of words which Eliot is innocent of. He supposes that all languages are approximations,

imperfect versions of reality, so that words are proved true only pragmatically, by their power to order experience. His is the least dogmatic and the most skeptical of religious poetry. To judge it fairly, one must ask not whether in the abstract the Nicene Creed is a true statement, but whether the experiences Eliot depicts hang together as credibly consistent.

The conversational tone of most of Eliot's work invites the reader to accept the persona in a more or less equal relationship. The persona does not speak down to the reader—even in *Four Quartets* he addresses the reader as a friend except in a few falsely humble, rather patronizing lines that tend to weaken the equal relationship. But while the conversational base defines the rapport between reader and persona, within the conversational tone the persona reveals a pattern of emotional response appropriate to his role as questing man. The talk of *The Waste Land* reflects in turn the speaker's aspiration and despair, his capacity for ecstasy and humor, his union of sense and sensibility which makes him a representative man.

George T. Wright in *Modern American Poetry*, ed. Jerome Mazzaro (McKay). 1970. p. 237

In Eliot's "The Love Song of J. Alfred Prufrock" and *The Waste Land*, myth discloses the personal terror and the feelings of impotence and despair which the protagonist objectifies in relation to society and history. Like Yeats and Auden, Eliot is ever aware of the seeds of death within the experience of love, but for Eliot there is no contest between the two; in *The Waste Land*, love retreats before its enemy as the protagonist takes on the role of the passive and maimed mythical king. Perhaps the most significant disclosure of unconscious feelings lies not in the actual myths Eliot uses in *The Waste Land*, but in the way mythical figures merge into each other. Like creatures in a dream, they depict the conflict and suffering of the protagonist and his distaste for the self which is finally defined by all of them. No doubt Yeats was correct in placing Eliot among those who attempted to exclude "the personal dream" from their work; certainly Eliot avoided the deepest psychological revelations of the very myths he employed. The conflicts and terrors that dream reveals, however, and indeed its very methods of condensation and merging, of disguising the self in a variety of forms, are present in his use of myth.

Lillian Feder. *Ancient Myth in Modern Poetry* (Princeton). 1971. p. 347

From first to last in Eliot's poetic career, from the undersea vision of Prufrock through the Hyacinth garden of *The Waste Land* to the rose garden of "Burnt Norton," it is a quintessentially Jamesian experience which lies at the heart of his work. The tragedy is that of one who can perceive but cannot act, who can understand and remember but cannot communicate. "I could not/Speak, and my eyes failed, I was neither/ Living nor dead . . . /Looking into the heart of light, the silence." At one time Eliot thought of titling the second part of *The Waste Land* "In the Cage," an obvious reference to [Henry] James's novella where the little telegraph girl, shut into her wire cage, can only live vicariously through the communications that pass across her desk. She knows everything, and can act upon nothing: she is like Tiresias, who knows all, foresuffers all, and can prevent none of it.

This is the vision of personal isolation that Eliot shares with James, and that lies at the deepest reaches of all his works. And yet, like James, Eliot was possessed with the complementary "vision of an ideal society"; the result was an art aware at every turn of the "disparity between possibility and fact." In his later works Eliot does explore ways of breaking the "closed circle of consciousness," through discipline or through grace.

A. Walton Litz in *Eliot in His Time*, ed. A. Walton Litz (Princeton). 1973. p. 21

No other poet in the history of the language, with the possible exception of Pound, has revalued so many reputations, or domesticated so many foreign poets in English taste. In accepting Eliot as my generation did, wholesale, we accepted not only "The Love Song of J. Alfred Prufrock" and *The Sacred Wood*, but an attitude toward the entire European past, a modification of its "pastness," and a spirit of inquiry that seemed to us life-giving. Perhaps that was only one of his two or three ideas, but it was a big one—too big, the critics now seem to feel, to have been expressed with full success in Eliot's first go at expressing it ("Tradition and the Individual Talent"); but with the passing of the years, it has been worked out to really enriching and liberating conclusions.

Robert M. Adams in *Eliot in His Time*, ed. A. Walton Litz (Princeton). 1973. p. 135

Yeats and Eliot made opposite public uses of romanticism to define their own poetic stances. While Yeats projected himself as the last romantic, Eliot posed as an anti-romantic modern; and whereas Yeats strove to rescue romanticism from its own defects, Eliot worked to purge literature as a whole of the contamination of romanticism. Both these postures exaggerate, for Yeats' rescue meant transformation and Eliot's overt wreckage masked covert salvage. Like the speaker of Stevens' "Man and Bottle," Eliot destroyed romantic tenements only to clear the ground for new pleasure domes. To have been told this in his youth would have horrified him; by old age it might not even have surprised him.

In one important respect the patterns of Eliot's and Yeats' long careers share the same relation to the romantics: a tripartite division of strong initial attraction and identification (a theme little heard of among Eliot's more devout admirers), violent rejection in order to form an independent identity as poet, and final if incomplete reconciliation. But here the parallel ends, for three main reasons. First, Eliot's romantic phase stops with his teens rather than with the onset of middle age. . . . Second, Eliot's grasp of romanticism was superficial compared to Yeats'. He never studied Shelley or Blake as intensely as Yeats and never understood them as well. . . .Finally, Eliot did not reconcile himself to the romantics while still primarily a practicing poet. His rapprochement coincided with his emergence as dramatist, Christian sociologist, and institution; in none of these identities did the romantics threaten him, and in some of them Coleridge was a positive help. . . .

Eliot unmistakably adopted a world view not just dependent on unhuman powers but requiring repudiation of both nature and imagination, as *The Cocktail Party* elsewhere makes clear. Blake repudiated all hypostatizations, Shelley adhered to a visionary skepticism, Keats was certain of nothing but the holiness of the heart's affections and the truths of imagination, and even the more

orthodoxly religious Wordsworth and Coleridge saw both nature and imagination as positive. Eliot did not, and his refusal generated the conflict between the overt and covert mental action of his poems. Unlike Shelley, who equally recognized the dangers of imagination, Eliot could never see "all that faith creates, or love desires" as ultimately human, although he, too, perceived "Terrible, strange, sublime and beauteous shapes." He was romantic against the grain, illustrating in his own career the contention of his essay on Baudelaire that in a romantic age a poet could not be antiromantic except in tendency. The saint repudiated the swordsman, although not without subterranean vacillation.

George Bornstein. *Transformations of Romanticism in Yeats, Eliot, and Stevens* (Univ. of Chicago Pr., 1976), pp. 94–95, 161–62

The Waste Land has seemed to be from the beginning a kind of incredibly complicated ink blot designed for a Rorschach test, confirming whatever is already present in the eye of the beholder. Whether Marxist, Christian, or merely aesthete, readers could hail the poem as summing up the attitude of a generation. And the poem's "meaning" became embodied not only in criticism, sociology, and history, but also in other works of art. Take, for example, three American novels: F. Scott Fitzgerald's *The Great Gatsby* (1925) presents a waste land in miniature in the valley of ashes that lies between West Egg and New York; Ernest Hemingway's *The Sun Also Rises* (1926) presents an impotent hero as spokesman for a lost generation living meaningless lives; William Faulkner's *Sanctuary* (1931) presents still other impotent (both psychically and physically) characters living and dying in a world of purposeless, pointless violence. These are but three instances that could be multiplied endlessly of works directly or indirectly influenced by *The Waste Land*—and the very influence suggesting an interpretation of the poem.

Thus making *The Waste Land* mean has been a task pursued with determination over a half-century by critics, poets, and novelists, with a conspicuous lack of unanimity as to what that meaning is—and with the bemused dismay of the poem's author. It would be difficult to find in all literary history a poet whose poem appeared abandoned so completely to others for revision and interpretation. It is almost as though it were snatched from the author's hands and cut, shaped, and read to fit the needs of an ailing modern age. And before his very eyes, his poem was metamorphosed into another identity, another existence, with which he himself would eventually need to come to terms.

James E. Miller, Jr. *T. S. Eliot's Personal Waste Land: Exorcism of the Demons* (Pennsylvania State Univ. Pr., 1977), p. 159

The poetry concerns us all, not because it is true or false, but because Eliot's mastery of our language makes his life-work a potent fact in the culture of the English-speaking world. His poetry has a power in our minds, through the authority of its diction and rhythms and images, to enforce certain meanings and feelings, and to suppress others. It has this power, of course, only because it is drawing upon meanings, and habits of feeling and perception already established in the language, and so in our mentality. Its potency is for animating a deep-rooted tradition of the common mind. We may like to think that Eliot's Mind of Europe is not ours; but very few of us can call our minds altogether our own. When Eliot writes of "heaven and damnation/Which flesh cannot endure," we know immediately and inwardly what he is saying whether we share his beliefs or not. It is the same with his "spirit" which he would have enter "that refining fire/Where you must move in measure, like a dancer": we may prefer Yeats' (and Valéry's) vision of the unified being of the dancer; but I suspect that Eliot's lines impose themselves upon us with weightier authority. We can become free of him—free to accept his vision, or to seek another—only by seeing his poetry as in itself it really is. . . .

Because he was a master of the actual experience of the ideal, Eliot's poetry can speak for and to this civilization. His poetry articulates the woe that is in the marriage of alienated neurotic egos; the atrophy and perversions of spirit in the crowd that flows over London Bridge; the pitifulness of its recreations, and the depressed resignation of humble people who expect nothing; the waste of living and partly living, of loving and partly loving; the sense of life turning to dust and ashes in the mouth; the anxiety, and fear, and sick loathing; the conscious impotence of rage at human folly, and the consequent self-contempt; and the death-wish. He had a certain real knowledge of the world. . . .

The essential experience of Eliot's poetry is the essential experience of an actual state of civilization, but in an extraordinarily refined and intelligent form. The interpretation he put upon it, and the cure he recommended, may seem out of touch with the common way of thinking. Yet by thus connecting the current form of the drive for the absolute and ideal with its relatively recent origins, and with a traditional form, he has rendered it the more intelligible. He is a true voice of our Western world.

A. D. Moody. *Thomas Stearns Eliot, Poet* (Cambridge Univ. Pr., 1979), pp. xv, 298

The shape of Eliot's life is one of paring down, concentration. Much had to be discarded to make his life conform to the pattern of the pilgrim, and there is a constant tension between an idiosyncratic nature and an ideal biography. His early years turned on his acceptance of this pattern, his later years on the question of its fulfillment. Its drama lay in efforts to close the gap between nature and perfection at whatever personal cost, reveling to some degree in that cost, and inspecting his torment as the distinguishing brand of his election. To be chosen, he had to purify the very ambition that set him off. And so the moral drama of the later years, from *Murder in the Cathedral*, centers not on the earlier festering of primitive violence, epitomized by lust, but on the subtler taints of public dignitaries, epitomized by pride. Eliot always calls for judgment but, we can never forget, for divine not human judgment.

Eliot was an expert on election. Like the divines, his ancestors, no one knew better the stages and signs of salvation, but he had limited spiritual gifts. He had diagnostic self-insight, strength of will, endurance, and a readiness to recognize the reality of the unseen, but he had not much gift of vision. He craved a lifetime burning in every moment, but had to accept a lesser course of "trying." Yet it was this acceptance of the common lot that made his mature poetry more accessible than the merciless clairvoyance of the early verse. He strove to content himself with right action, and not to hope too hard that saving grace would come to fill the waiting vessel of perfected conduct. But Eliot's was a God of pain, whose punishment, until the last eight years, was almost the only sign of the absolute paternal care.

The irony of Eliot's life was that he was unsuited to the model life of saints. He was simply too self-conscious to be a saint. Yet his struggle to subdue intellectual pride, his almost savage intolerance, proved the fertile matter of his poetry. There remains the paradox of a man who wished to be saint above poet, but who became all the greater as poet for his failure to attain sainthood. He fell back on another goal, to be God's agent, and as public spokesman he achieved an extraordinary authority. His pronouncements are still repeated as truths from on high. The prophetic role, like the Puritan rigor of introspection, came most directly from America, as well as the challenge of a terrifying nature where man measures himself in the face of an immeasurable power that is and was from the beginning.

Eliot's career circled back so that the sources of his own life, the Mississippi and Cape Ann, became the source of all life. Despite his adaptation to England, his adoption of English religion, manners, and clothes, and despite his marriages to English women, his poetry led him back to "the source of the longest river," and to the silence the child heard between two waves of the sea.

Lyndall Gordon. *Eliot's New Life* (New York: Farrar, Straus & Giroux, 1988), pp. 268–69, 272

The unresolvable tension of *Four Quartets* is that Eliot, a reluctant experimentalist, who wanted to (but did not) inherit viable traditional form, who wanted to (but did not) bury isolate selfhood in a community ("which is more valuable"), who could not finally hide his life entirely in Christ, nevertheless committed himself in this poem to the most uncompromising implications of avant-garde aesthetic. Knowledge of the past, he tells us, imposes falsifying pattern onto the present. Knowledge of one's craft, likewise, imposes falsifying pattern. The triumph of literary form and language is its radical mimesis is of the new and shocking moment. It is a triumph over literary history, over the falsity of received pattern, over convention. What we have already perceived, yesterday's perception caught in yesterday's poem, yesterday's triumph—good only for yesterday and who we were yesterday. Today we are dumb, and every effort to write and live freshly is necessarily a "raid on the inarticulate/with shabby equipment always deteriorating."

Yesterday's equipment is shabby, and so is yesterday's self. Shabby but comfortable, comfortable but a lie. Old men, or older men, as he should have written (the *Quartets* were composed between his forty-seventh and fifty-fourth years), would rather not be explorers. They would rather repeat themselves as writers. repeat themselves as selves. They would rather repeat than create; rather not chance possession because they do not wish to bear any Reality, or be borne by it. The courage to "make it new" as a writer is not a metaphor: it is Eliot's path to regeneration.

The other side of Eliot is never avant-gardist, is the very antithesis of the spirit of the avant-garde. The two sides coexist, always uneasily but always through necessity, in Eliot's writing, life being a truncated travesty if imagined otherwise. I refer, of course, to his commitments to tradition, literary history, the past. The urgent way to put it is the best way: his life, and ours, with the dead. Not the dead letters of texts, but those familiar, compound ghosts haunting texts.

The Waste Land will remain the singular aesthetic event of modernist poetry in the English language; and its stance, however we construct it, seems one we can live with because, however we construct it, it seems one that suits our sense of ourselves. But Eliot after *The Waste Land* will continue to be another matter: an event unabsorbed because, in the context of advanced Western values, it is unabsorbable.

Frank Lentricchia. *Modernist Quartet* (Cambridge: Cambridge Univ. Pr., 1994), pp. 285–86

The past decade has seen Eliot's reputation recede to its lowest ebb of the century. The postmodern attack on the pillars of modernism has managed at times to spare Virginia Woolf for her blurring of traditional gender roles, Joyce for his delight in sheer wordplay, and even, in critical tours de force, the unlikely pair of Pound and Lewis on the shaky basis of their disruptive styles. Eliot, however, as the primary spokesman and symbol of that against which literary post modernism has defined itself—modernist high culture—has been refused almost all amnesty. His claim to establish enduring criteria of value was, to pose the complaint in the language of these antagonists, a futile attempt to legitimate his narrative by reference to a metadiscourse. Further, as one of the progenitors of the New Criticism, the primary theoretical whipping boy of deconstruction, he had been systematically indicted on the related charge of being a particularly unabashed advocate of ''logocentrism.'' Indeed, he seems at times to have been doubly annoying to such critics precisely because he is so obviously self-indicting. . . .

The case against an elitist, absolutist Eliot has been carried on most recently in the name of a multiculturalism that takes issue sharply with him as the chief modern apologist for a hereditary canon of Western literary classics. A growing cultural diversity in England and even more obviously in the United States, coupled with the perceived need to amplify the voices of long-standing marginalized groups, made Eliot's insistence on the tradition seem an obvious exercise in oppression. . . .

The one merit of the cases against Eliot, misguided and overstated as they often are, is that they at least are open to the idea that extraliterary concerns might have shaped his work in ways generally unacknowledged previously. Typically, almost all attempts to place the work of Eliot in a larger intellectual context have looked to the poetic tradition. In his immediate past, affinities are found with Laforgue, Baudelaire, and various other French symbolists; earlier, with the Metaphysicals, whom he revived, or with Dante, whom he regarded as Christian Europe's culmination. His critical writings are taken to be epiphenomenal of the poetry (Eliot himself, late in life, said they were no more than this), colored perhaps by his ambivalent relationship to Matthew Arnold's essays on poetry and culture. But such studies, even when valuable, as they often are, tend to obscure what I perceive to be the thoroughgoing nature of Eliot's political commitment.

Simply put, it seems to me that from beginning to end, Eliot's work, including both the poetry and the prose, was shaped by a political vision inherited from French reactionary thinkers, especially from Charles Maurras. . . .

Where, then, do these revaluations leave Eliot studies? How will his reputation endure the change in century? First of all, it seems to me that whatever we may think of Eliot's solutions, he merits continued attention for the fullness of his response to a central problem of modernity: what sort of commonwealth is possible in a society held together only by procedure? In this regard, his continual, pointed insistence that social laissez-faire

may be every bit as disastrous as economic laissez-faire was a salutary corrective to glib liberal pieties. No less than [D. H.] Lawrence, he was painfully aware of the thinness of modern life. The difficulty with Eliot, though, is that to create community he excludes too much. Those outside the Latin tradition, the lower social orders, and women whenever they dare display their sexual nature are all denied full participation. Though neither before nor after did he make the case as intemperately as he did in *After Strange Gods*, the call for homogeneity voiced there never ceased to be a given for his conception of the social whole. While Denis Donoghue is right to insist, as he recently did, that Eliot's reputation ought not to hang on the social criticism, he is wrong to claim that the criticism has nothing to do with the poetry. As I have tried to demonstrate, there is a systematic lack of generosity, finally, of humanity, in Eliot's work—both prose and poetry—and, in the last analysis, it is this that will exclude him from the classical company to which he devoted so much of his life.

Kenneth Asher. *T. S. Eliot and Ideology* (Cambridge: Cambridge Univ. Pr., 1995), pp. 1–3, 164–65

BIBLIOGRAPHY

Prufrock and Other Observations, 1917 (p); *Ezra Pound, His Metric and Poetry*, 1917 (c); *Poems*, 1919; *Ara Vos Prec*, 1920 (p); *The Sacred Wood*, 1920 (e); *The Waste Land*, 1922 (p); *Homage to John Dryden*, 1924 (e); *Poems, 1909–1925*, 1925; *Journey of the Magi*, 1927 (p); *Shakespeare and the Stoicism of Seneca*, 1927 (e); *A Song for Simeon*, 1928 (p); *For Lancelot Andrewes*, 1928 (e); *Animula*, 1929 (p); *Dante*, 1929 (e); *Ash-Wednesday*, 1930 (p); *Anabasis*, 1930, rev. ed., 1949 (tr); *Marina*, 1931 (p); *Thoughts after Lambeth*, 1931 (e); *Charles Whibley: A Memoir*, 1931; *Triumphal March*, 1931 (p); *Sweeney Agonistes*, 1932 (pd); *Selected Essays, 1917–1932*, 1932; *John Dryden*, 1932 (e); *The Use of Poetry and the Use of Criticism*, 1933 (e); *The Rock*, 1934 (pd); *After Strange Gods*, 1934 (e); *Elizabethan Essays*, 1934 (e); *Words for Music*, 1935 (p); *Two Poems*, 1935; *Murder in the Cathedral*, 1935 (pd); *Collected Poems, 1909–1935*, 1936; *Essays Ancient and Modern*, 1936; *Old Possum's Book of Practical Cats*, 1939 (p); *The Family Reunion*, 1939 (pd); *The Idea of a Christian Society*, 1939 (e); *East Coker*, 1940 (p); *Burnt Norton*, 1941 (p); *The Dry Salvages*, 1941 (p); *Points of View*, 1941 (e); *The Music of Poetry*, 1942 (e); *The Classics and the Man of Letters*, 1942 (e); *Little Gidding*, 1942 (p); *Reunion by Destruction*, 1943 (e); *Four Quartets*, 1943 (p); *What Is a Classic*, 1945 (e); *On Poetry*, 1947 (e); *Milton*, 1947 (e); *A Sermon*, 1948; *Notes towards the Definition of Culture*, 1948 (e); *From Poe to Valéry*, 1948 (c); *The Cocktail Party*, 1949 (pd); *The Undergraduate Poems*, 1949; *The Aims of Poetic Drama*, 1949 (e); *Selected Essays* (new edition), 1950; *Poems Written in Early Youth*, 1950; *Poetry and Drama*, 1951 (e); *The Confidential Clerk*, 1954 (pd); *On Poetry and Poets*, 1957 (e); *The Elder Statesman*, 1959 (pd); *Collected Plays*, 1962; *Collected Poems, 1909–1962*, 1963; *Knowledge and Experience in the Philosophy of F.H. Bradley*, 1964 (e); *To Criticize the Critic*, 1965 (e); *The Complete Poems and Plays*, 1969; *The Waste Land: A Facsimile and Transcript of the Original Drafts Including the Annotations of Ezra Pound*, 1971 (p); *Selected Prose*, 1975; *Letters 1898–1922*, ed. Valerie Eliot, 1988; *The Varieties of Metaphysical Poetry*, ed. Ronald Schuchard, 1994 (lectures); *Inventions of the March Hare: Poems 1909–1917*, ed. Christopher Ricks, 1996

ELKIN, Stanley (1930–1995)

Gutsiness, let me say, is just about all [*Boswell*] has in common with *Catch-22*. That, and a sense of satirical fantasy. In point of style and of intellectual grace, the author of *Boswell* is to the author of *Catch-22* as a jeweler to a primitive potter. Nor have I any basis other than happenstance on which to justify this ramble from the old master to the late arrival as if they did in fact belong in the same box. The thing about happenstance, however, is that it does happen. I did find myself thinking of the two together. And what I found myself thinking was that I remain at least as grateful to *Boswell* for its wacky satire as I am to the [John] O'Hara shelf for its memory banks. . . .

Boswell, as it turns out, is nothing less than a satirist's diary of the ego. Have we not all sat with kings and captains inside our own reveries?—sat with them and found them wanting? This world is the ego's oyster and Jim Boswell is time's shucker.

From Stanley Elkin, moreover, Jim Boswell has an intellect both learned and honed, a perception forever ready to burst into its own sort of wild and wacky poetry and a well-mastered pen with which to keep his diary. It is a mad fantasy that rises from the pages of that diary. But in *Boswell*'s world only fantasy can begin to describe reality.

As for the poetry, let me recommend to any reader that he turn first to pages 137–52, to the account of Boswell's wooing of William Lome, "a rich man." And especially to the final encounter with Lome, in which he turns pitchman and sells bits of colored clay on the sidewalk. Elkin, to be sure, does not maintain an equal altitude throughout. I suspect the reader would die of anoxia on such a sustained flight. But glory to the heights in such moments as we can reach them.

Or it may be that *Boswell* is the hoax of the year, though if it is, it would be so only as one more semblance of the world as Elkin sees it. For the essence of this world, as seen, is exactly in the fact that it is a contrivance. But it is still that sort of contrivance we all more than half suspect our own world may turn out to be. A city of paper dragons. But add, too, that at its best it crackles around those weaving and bobbing grotesques like a Chinese New Year.

John Ciardi. *Saturday Review*. Aug. 15, 1964, p. 6

After finishing this zany, experimental short-story collection [*Criers and Kibitzers, Kibitzers and Criers*], one will probably be able later to recall a few ticklishly funny lines. . . .

If Elkin has the good grace to avoid ritual dramas stressing the "need for love" and the "essential brotherhood of all mankind," he compensates for it by playing back to the reader another unconscionably overworked literary theme and such institutional-ized ideas as the downtrodden shopkeeper in his waning little store (the title story), tragedy at a New York mountain resort ("Among the Witnesses"), a teenage gang of mediocre misfits in the Bronx ("Cousin Poor Lesley and the Lousy People"), a petit bourgeois trying to cope with a terminal illness ("In the Alley"). Elkin, the dust jacket avers, is "a deadly serious satirist." Often, indeed, he actually seems ready to belittle the cant phrases and stances of our climby, commerce-ridden society, as only a Bruce Jay Friedman at his best is capable of doing. Then, like a driver's license candidate using someone else's car in heavy traffic, he loses control, and there's rather a nasty mess.

The Elkin protagonist is lonely and isolated because he is bereaved or abandoned and has nowhere to turn. Greenspahn, the desolate merchant in the title story, mourns his recently-dead son Harold, who had not yet even married or settled down; after a period of unappeasable grief for his beloved son, he discovers that Harold had stolen from the store's cash register. Ed Wolfe, a cruel, self-centered orphan ("I Look Out for Ed Wolfe"), withdraws entirely from society, hoarding all his money; one night he meets a Negro at a bar, forces him to be sociable, and winds up with him at a Negro key club, where he insults a girl and offends everyone else, finally throwing his remaining money away at the audience. The dying Mr. Feldman ("In the Alley"), who didn't know how to spend his last days, ends up annoying two women at a bar. In the weirdest, least successful story, "On a Field, Rampant," a fairy-tale prince of obscure origin tries vainly to establish his identity in the great world outside; finally even his talismanic medallion can't help him and the mob closes in for the kill.

Perhaps the most disappointing features of Elkin's tales are the monotony of his "inability to communicate" theme and his straining for effect by means of unreal, unsuitable settings and plots. Often the perverse protagonist winds up addressing an assembly so alien to him that his message is ludicrous and pointless. . . .

So pitifully ill is the ego of the Elkin protagonist that he must do or say some hideous thing just to compel the proper kind of attention from his ignorers. . . . To Elkin himself, one wants to shout: "Be more natural and stop speaking your own private language. What's the matter with you? The writer must serve!"

Samuel I. Bellman. *Saturday Review*. Jan. 15, 1966, p. 41

"Though hypocrisy can take you far, it can only take you *so* far," says Dick Gibson, the protean-enriched radio personality of Stan-ley Elkin's third novel [*The Dick Gibson Show*]. It is one of those ebullient statements that instantly sprouts provocative questions: How far do you want to go? Who will you be when you get there?

The Dick Gibson of the title, a seriocomic straight man in a burlesque mythology of mass culture, wants to go all the way. But not vertically (to a network presidency), or even horizontally to become one of those tympanic coast-to-coast voices that always "seem to speak from the frontiers of commitment." Instead, like the wrestler in Elkin's first novel (*Boswell*) and the department store owner in his second (*A Bad Man*), Gibson craves the all-points dimension of human need.

An itinerant early media man, he has worked for dozens of small-town radio stations. As the perpetual apprentice, whetting his skills and adopting names and accents to suit geography, he evolves into part of American folklore. As Dick Gibson, the paradox of his truest identity is that he is from Nowhere, U.S.A. . . .

Gibson hits his peak as the star of *Night Letters*, a telephone participation show. Audience feedback creates a web of involve-ment and expands radio to almost mythic proportions. Spinning his dials and monitoring the tape delay device that censors callers' obscenities, Gibson is a McLuhan obfuscation made flesh—a benevolent witch doctor in an electronic village of the lonely, the sick and screwed up.

The Dick Gibson Show, like *Portnoy's Complaint*, contains enough comic material for a dozen nightclub acts. Yet it is considerably more than an entertainment. The banal and the profound, the vulgar and the touching, are humanely juggled into a vital blur—a brilliant approximation of what it is like to live with one's eyes and ears constantly open.

R. Z. Sheppard. *Time*. March 1, 1971, p. 82

Elkin's protagonists are ordinary men with extraordinary purposes and singular dreams, men who become obsessed with the improbable possibilities of the self's expansion. Isolated by their obsessions, these manic heroes mount single-minded assaults upon the world and force themselves toward ultimate fulfillments. Although development is their end, plot becomes the compulsive repetition of action and complex situation is reduced to simplicity by their obsessions. Even setting is defined by the radical subjectivity of the obsessive inhabiting it. Sellers of singleness, pitchmen of transcendence, Elkin's narrators and heroes have a high-energy, repetitive rhetoric, an exclamatory prose that intensifies the ordinary, presses the impossible, and registers the urgency of their fixations. The result is a unity of effect, a Siamese connection of substance and style.

It is probably a truism that characters in contemporary American fiction are obsessional, but Elkin's heroes, unlike those, say, of Mailer, Hawkes, or O'Connor, develop their obsessions from natural authorities, common needs, or the promises of a popular culture rather than from some social, psychological, or religious ideology. Elkin's are not the exotic products of a subculture nor the constructs of an experimental theory but the distortions of the American almost-ordinary. Because their obsessions arise from areas of mass fascination and because they expend their energies within recognizable—if sometimes dislocated—systems of value, their private thoughts and public careers reveal truths particularly relevant and available to the American present. Theirs is the singleness that illuminates multiplicity, the focus that creates perspective, and Elkin uses them to examine both the normalities and aberrancies of our time. . . .

Elkin's favorite performances are oral—tales, reminiscences, speeches, harangues, directives, lectures, routines, jokes, patter— and singular, repartee and dialogue somewhat detracting from the rhetorical effect of monologue. Elkin loves to let his obsessed characters, major and minor, talk, and since the qualities of their voices carry over into the style he uses to describe, analyze, and narrate, this style may also be called obsessive. Although Elkin's narrational style has the individuality, exuberance, and extremity of his obsessives, it is not experimental (or obsessive) the way Beckett's or Burroughs' is. Because Elkin's purposes are the pressurized expansion of sense and the executed appeal to a felt audience—not the music of randomness or song of solipsism—he mixes high and low elements, vernacular and literary, to achieve a charged communication.

Thomas LeClair. *Contemporary Literature*. Spring, 1975, pp. 146–47, 156

All of Elkin's novels have dealt with the by-now familiar modern issues of isolation, alienation, and the existential construction of value systems to help fill the void, pass the time in the face of mortality and an absurd but potentially destructive exterior environment. Like many modern characters, Elkin's heroes all have the same primitive need to say, like Bellow's Henderson, *I want, I want*, but unlike Henderson or Huck or Hemingway's characters,

and unlike Nabokov's Kinbote and Humbert, Coover's J. Henry Waugh, or Kesey's McMurphy, Elkin's characters find their transcendence and freedom not in lighting out for some literal or imagined territory, but in seeking out the familiar, in filling themselves with the drek and ticky-tack of modern America. . . . Elkin's heroes are moved by these kinds of excesses because they are obsessively aware of death and because they are isolated in the midst of a world of plenty. . . .

Elkin's heroes are also outcasts and outsiders, men who typically operate on the fringes of society even as they control it, and who even prefer it that way for fear that they will have to share their bounty with others. Such basic selfishness may help explain why no truly significant women or satisfying love affairs occur in Elkin's fiction. . . .

Elkin's claims that his novels have a "well-defined structure" are rather misleading and were probably induced by his simply getting tired of critics blaming him for something that does not have anything to do with the success of what he is aiming for in his novels. When we examine the way his books work, they really *do not* have a tightly woven structure, at least not in any usual notion of plot. Oh, they have a development of a sort, although Elkin's books develop more by a principle of repetition than by subtle shifts in personal motivation or by the gradual introduction of narrative complexities; and they usually have a sense of progression . . . although even it is created more by accretion than anything else. If we really take Elkin's books apart paragraph by paragraph, we hardly find the carefully balanced blend of elements and subtle interrelationships among significant details that we would find, say, in Nabokov's novels. Quite the contrary, we find constant digression, tall tales, jokes, and descriptions, none of which seems to lead anywhere. Above all, we discover that Elkin loves to stop the action of his novels to present what is his most singular and successful stylistic feature: his catalogues and lists. These catalogues do not contribute to the action nor even directly assist in illuminating anything related to the plot except insofar as they demonstrate the incredible vitality of the characters' rhetoric and imaginations. If we complain that Elkin has stopped the action "merely" to create a catalogue, tell a joke, or make a sales pitch, we are missing the point.

Larry McCaffery. *Critique*. 21, 2, 1979, pp. 40–42, 47

The Living End is Stanley Elkin's comic fable of Heaven, Hell and the Last Days, a small book big in every way but length. And I should say at once that this "triptych," as Elkin calls it, composed of three sections entitled "The Conventional Wisdom," "The Bottom Line," and "The State of the Art," is the work of a master, a story eloquent in its gestures and amazing for the ease with which it moves from a liquor store hold-up in Minneapolis to the "wall-to-wall Wall" of damnation, from Heaven as a "theme park" to Hell as "the ultimate inner city." Half farce, half morality play, *The Living End* puts God himself on trial, the Lord faced off against the damned who in their countless number equal Everyman. Quite possibly only Stanley Elkin possesses the exact blend of irreverence and care, of hardcore realism and fabulous invention, to have pulled this off.

Elkin knows that clichés are the substance of our lives, the coinage of human intercourse, the ways and means that hold our messy selves and sprawling nation intact. To exploit their vigor and set them forth with unexpected force has been the basis of his success as a novelist; no writer has maneuvered life's shoddy stock-in-trade into more brilliantly funny forms. Long before he wrote *The Franchiser*, Elkin appropriated the notion of the franchise—the idea that we Americans borrow our being from the staples of quotidian culture, the banal, the vulgar, the cartoon like and mean, all our packaged dreams and gaudy perks, accumulating thereby some concoction of clichés which, for each of us, constitutes our "story."

But if our stories are private they are in no way new. Our predicament, as a nation dedicated to exploring frontiers and starting fresh, is not only our rising sense of limits, but our fear of predictability, of stuckness, of *old* wine in old bottles, as if sameness were inherently ridiculous. And maybe it is. Originality is at best displacement of the ordinary. Our most outlandish moments are the stuff of public domain. In *The Bailbondsman*, Elkin's protagonist judges the jailed, sizes up the risk of posting their bail, merely by listening to their stories. At the end of *The Dick Gibson Show* the MC of a late-night talk program cannot bear to listen to yet *another* "story of my life": he knows by heart their silly pathos, their ludicrous outcomes, the garbled grief of options foreclosed.

Something of this desperation, relieved by raucous humor, slips into *The Living End*, where Elkin takes on the ultimate cliché, death and the preposterous protocol of Hereafter. To see how the mighty are fallen, to bring high things low, is a comic ploy as old as Aristophanes, accomplished in Elkin's case by setting standard myths of immortality within the low-rent clutter of ordinary life. So the angel of death talks "like a cabbie with an out-of-town fare." The crowd around the Lord's throne looks like the snapshot of a summit conference. Christ and his Dad don't get along, and the Virgin Mother never liked sex in the first place. As for sudden death, "all that wrath, those terrible swift sword arrangements, that's the M.O. of God Himself!"'. . .

There is a kind of vulgate glory to Stanley Elkin's prose, and much of the power of *The Living End* depends on how things are worded. Elkin is the *magister ludi* of American vernacular, and for sheer stylistic brilliance no other writer can top him. The American novelist he most resembles is Nathanael West, but whereas West allowed us to feel superior to life's lunacy through savage irony, Elkin refuses us this distance, this illusion. And unlike others of his generation, Thomas Pynchon and William Gaddis for example, Elkin does not identify with the laughter of the gods, he does not dissociate himself from the human spectacle by taking out a franchise on the cosmic joke. Hard and unyielding as his comic vision becomes, Elkin's laughter is remission and reprieve, a gesture of willingness to join the human mess, to side with the damned, to laugh in momentary grace at whatever makes life Hell.

Terrence des Pres. *Book World*. July 1, 1979, pp. 1, 4

In seven volumes of fiction published since the mid-Sixties, Stanley Elkin has made clear claim, by reason of the quality inherent in his work, to consideration as a major contemporary American writer. Yet though his books have inspired a following of devoted readers—both in and outside of the academic community—Elkin can be said to have largely missed out on the recognition due him. I should like to make a gesture towards righting that wrong by attempting a necessarily brief survey of Elkin's fictional works, and by making some general observations about his style

and themes. For if Elkin seems to be some sort of spiritual descendant of Nathanael West in the ways in which he attaches out-loud, falling-on-the-floor humor to reflections on the human state as a steady downward plunge to death, he is nevertheless very much his own man in the manner in which he explores and develops that tradition. . . .

Stanley Elkin's characters' contemplations of their situations have always been informed by the inevitable facts of their own deaths and those of others, giving his fiction an eschatological emphasis uncommon in contemporary letters. In *The Living End* (1979), Elkin moves beyond the point of death in an assault on received notions of theological order. That a lonely author of the universe should find confirmed by the behavior of his creatures the notion that his ways are not our ways, nor ours his, seems the suggestion of this short volume described on its cover as a "triptych." The allusion to paintings in panels of three, particularly altar panels, is fitting. The book is as crowded with scenes from the far side of the grave as something by Bosch or Grünewald. . . .

What next for Elkin? He is nearly through with a novel to be called *George Mills*—from excerpts I have heard, another *Bildungsroman*—which is to be published in 1982. It promises to be long, perhaps the most ambitious product of Elkin's career. One wishes him well with it, expecting full well that like its predecessors, it will be wrought with extraordinary care and love for the unleashed English tongue, and that like them it will also confront the human species trying to fast-talk itself into an understanding in the face of pain and of mortality. Most certain of all is that it will be, like them, full of the sound of a savage and infectious laughter. "So grotesque," concludes a woman newly risen from the dead in *The Living End*; "death grotesque as life. All, all grotesque."

John Ditsky. *Hollins Critic*. June, 1982, pp. 1–2, 10–11

Elkin's taste . . . is not as lowbrow as he claims. His greatest strength is the ability to combine high art and pop culture without shortchanging either one. His frequent subject is the regular guy with an all-American dream of making it big, but his sentences are often convoluted enough to give a Jamesian pause. This density of language may have kept Elkin off the best-seller list, but his natural audience is the one that appreciates John Irving and Kurt Vonnegut.

George Mills is not his most affecting book, and certainly not his funniest, but it is quintessential Elkin in style and substance. His five previous novels and two story collections not only capture Middle America; they embrace it. . . . Elkin deflates intellectual pretensions by recognizing that most people are perfectly comfortable in a fast-food world.

The Living End, Elkin's last novel, sets us up for *George Mills*. God puts in an appearance, and even he turns out to be a regular guy—part storyteller, part stand-up comic, part practical joker. *George Mills* takes this idea even further: it is about 1000 years of guys who are so ordinary they hand it down from father to son as a family tradition. From the first George Mills, servant to a nobleman during the Crusades, to the last, a working stiff in contemporary St. Louis, these are men who live under the curse of their "blue collar blood," pass on to their sons the story of this heritage, and always seem to be the butts of God's practical jokes. . . .

George's rejection of history is not necessarily a triumph. Faulkner's stylistic influence on Elkin suggests their common concern with the power of history and myth. (Elkin's Faulknerian voice runs through the novel, at times overwhelming his characteri-zation of George. Learning that a brother and sister live in a car parked outside the Glazers' house, George thinks of "the poor's special charters and manumissions, their little license and acquit-tals, all law's exonerate laxity and stretched-point privilege.") Elkin substitutes Middle America for the South and one-liners for Gothic darkness; the Millses are ironic equivalents of the Compsons. George is like Quentin, reconciling himself to his family history by sifting through its legends. *George Mills* suggests that however inflated and distorted its history, the past cannot be dismissed. . . . For Stanley Elkin, the greatest curse is not having a sense of humor.

> Caryn James. *The Village Voice*. Oct. 26, 1982, p. 52

The argument that [Stanley Elkin's] work is marred by its episodic nature assumes that Elkin is trying—and failing—to write plot-centered fiction, that his attempts at conceiving consonant, reso-nant stories and novels possessed of beginning-middle-end sequentiality and solid, satisfying narrative-level resolutions are somehow con-stantly going awry. *The Franchiser* clearly demonstrates how little Elkin is concerned with cohesion of this narrative-level sort. The chapter [in this book] dealing with that novel sets out to show that it is rendered coherent more through metaphor and analogy than through plot, its consonance achieved through the convergence of parallel scenes and the intertwining of patterns of reduplicative imagery. Implicit in this book and informing its every page is my assumption . . . that, although his earlier work seems to align itself naturally with the plot-centered fiction of contemporaries like Philip Roth and Saul Bellow, there has always been an antirealist tendency in Elkin's work, a tendency that ties it more closely to the fiction of Thomas Pynchon, Robert Coover, and Donald Barthelme than to the tradition of social realism that underlies the American Jewish novel. To perceive the evolution of Elkin's fiction in any other way obliges one to declare *The Living End* an inexplicable divergence from Elkin's habitual mode, rather than to see it . . . as an extension and culmination of tendencies discernible in his work from *Boswell* and *Criers & Kibitzers, Kibitzers & Criers* forward.

> Peter J. Bailey. *Reading Stanley Elkin* (Urbana: Univ. of Illinois Pr.), 1985, p. x

It may appear that there are few connections to be made between the metaphor of writing Elkin constructs in [his essay] "What's in a Name?" and his own writing as I have described it. Yet there are, indeed, links between the allegory of writing and its productions, for all writing, Elkin concludes, is a form of "connection": "What I suppose I've been talking about is connection. Connection, invention, and all the enumerate, lovely links, synapses, and nexuses of fiction." There is some relation, Elkin suggests, be-tween historical events, the aesthetics of fiction, and the names of characters, just as there is the connection Elkin makes *in writing* between slavery in the North, an absurdist tale portraying a domestic revolt, and the name of Paul Louis Pelgas. Thematically, Elkin's work reveals a concern with "connection" as the sign of genetic determinism, or paranoia, or the labyrinthine intricacies of a system of communication. The elaborate descriptions of a dry-cleaning shop, a cosmetic counter, a pharaoh's tomb, a power grid,

or a radio network all convey the sense that "what Elkin is talking about" is connection—that his fiction assumes the task of making the connection between the manifestations of a disparate, heteroge-neous reality and the artful metaphors by which it may be assimilat-ed. Writing, then, is the tracing out of these connections, almost as if the pen strokes themselves (or the printed characters) signified the "synapses and nexuses." Yet the allegory of writing presented in "What's in a Name?" suggest the fragility of connections and suggests further that, even while making them, writing fractures "these lovely links," even as the "cat's cradle" construction of the wall in Norbiton is consumed by the act of arson in the thicket. "Detail," Elkin writes, can be seen "as a kind of noun, and a menu of proper names . . . a register of fact." So the "fact" of fiction resides in its assemblage of name and detail into recognizable shapes or venues. Yet the edifice of this fact is built on shaky ground, for it is equally the work of the language of fiction to skew the facts, pervert its own history, and rob its own treasury when it scatters names across texts, or becomes opaque, or breaks form. This is the dialectic of fiction which, I believe, Elkin finely perceives.

The caves of Marabar that Elkin refers to in the last line of "What's in a Name?" are, in Forster's novel, a place of defamiliarization, where the ordinary is converted into the strange. "Esmiss Esmoor" (the proper name of Mrs. Moore skewed and echoed) understands these caves only because she can accept them as utterly alien, then escape them, then die at sea. Elkin, too, hollows out the language of the commonplace—the jingo, the sales pitch, everyday speech in order to reveal the deformed estrangements that lie hidden beneath forms of convention. Just as often, Elkin's fiction reverses itself when the exotic is made into the ordinary. . . .

Ultimately, this movement of language is the sign of the comic writer, who uses his language to parody the forms and intonations of conventional discourse while, at the same time, preserving these altered forms and accents in metaphor, catalogue, and speech. But this characterization of Elkin's writing does it justice only in the most general sense, from the overview provided by the critic's place on the parapet. There remain the discontents of analysis that only a plunge into the thicket, itself, will absolve.

> Patrick O'Donnell. "The Thicket of Writing." In Heide Ziegler, ed. *Facing Texts: Encounters between Contempo-rary Writers and Critics* (Durham, N.C.: Duke Univ. Pr., 1988), pp. 42–43

Van Gogh's Room at Arles is, I think, Stanley Elkin's best book. It's certainly the easiest to read—it moves right along, it asks nothing. The title novella is so well constructed that when you realize (or *think* you realize) where it is going, you feel a shiver at the back of your neck that intensifies when you see what turn the book is *actually* taking: toward a sudden, illuminating glimpse of the accidental, visionary, and (for lack of a better word) religious nature of art. What Stanley Elkin has always done well he does even better here. No one is more deft at pacing a scene for comic timing, and these fictions include scenes (a foundation social event at which grantees describe their silly projects, Schiff's monster of a party) which build to stunning heights of comic humiliation. Throughout these novellas, everything builds; their cumulative power is astounding.

> Francine Prose. *The Yale Review*. July, 1993, pp. 123–24

BIBLIOGRAPHY
Boswell, 1964 (n); *Criers and Kibitzers, Kibitzers and Criers*, 1966
(s); *A Bad Man*, 1967 (n); *The Dick Gibson Show*, 1971 (n);
Searches and Seizures, 1973 (n); *The Franchiser*, 1976 (n); *The
Living End*, 1979 (n); *Stanley Elkin's Greatest Hits*, 1980 (s);
George Mills, 1982 (n); *Early Elkin*, 1985 (misc); *The Magic
Kingdom* 1985 (n); *The Coffee Room*, 1986 (rd); *The Rabbi of Lud*,
1987 (n); *The Six-Year-Old Man*, 1987 (scrp); *The MacGuffin*,
1991 (n); *Pieces of Soap*, 1992 (e); *Van Gogh's Room at Arles:
Three Novellas*, 1993; *Mrs. Ted Bliss*, 1995 (n)

ELLIOTT, George P. (1918–1980)

Mr. Elliott has published short stories that I greatly admire, and in his novel [*Parktilden Village*] there is much firm, perceptive writing of the kind I anticipated, but I feel I have been let down by the book as a whole. . . .

The situation suggests that this is to be a comedy of manners; so does the title; so, most emphatically, does the style. . . . His whole air is that of a man who hopes the reader will be as amused by what he is writing about as he himself is. . . . People are behaving rather badly, to be sure, but they are behaving no worse than people the reader knows, and he can afford to be amused by them.

Suddenly, however, . . . the tone changes. . . . One could say that there are precedents for so great an alteration of tone. T. S. Eliot's *The Cocktail Party*, for instance, begins as comedy but develops the most serious religious implications. The play, however, moves gradually from the trivial to the serious, and the comic framework is retained. *Parktilden Village*, on the other hand, promising one thing and delivering another, leaves a bad taste in the mouth.

Granville Hicks. *Saturday Review*. May 31, 1958. pp. 10, 26

Now the subject of *Parktilden Village* is a genuine one: surely there can be few more interesting matters these days than the terrifying distance between the generation born after 1940 and the rest of us. Mr. Elliott is a naturally gifted writer who keeps things moving nicely, cleverly. But in the end one feels cheated. The material has been set up to serve a case: it all seems too neat, everything bends too conveniently to the writer's preconceptions, and what should have been an imitation of life comes to read like a fictional gloss on an essay in *Sewanee Review*.

Irving Howe. *New Republic*. Nov. 10, 1958. p. 17

Within the confused contemporary American literary scene, in which many writers seem to strive for attention as the classical starlet strives for parts—by pan-fried personal lives immediately translated into the negotiable currency of the news item—George P. Elliott has managed to make his reputation in a curious way. As poet, critic, essayist, short-story writer, and novelist . . . he has quietly assumed the burden of the old-fashioned man of letters. The odd and effective method by which he has sent his name into the busy world is this one: Beneath all the demand for brilliance in a "young writer," he has kept his gaze upon the need for truth.

Among the Dangs, a collection of ten of his stories, shows a thickly questing imagination at work. Many of the stories have that density of feeling and character, and complexity of event, which only a generous mind dares to employ in the story form. . . . Increasingly, especially in the later stories, Elliott has learned to recognize the humor of his horrors, and with his wit, he has increased his powers.

Herbert Gold. *New Republic*. Jan. 16, 1961. p. 19

David Knudsen purports to be an autobiographical account of the hero's quest for meaning. . . . Elliott is good at portraying the horror beneath the skin of modern society. . . . It is part of the virtue of this novel that it can make us think about metaphysical questions without being heavy or pretentious; every question is adequately embodied. Elliott is clearly to be one of the important writers of this decade, and this is an example of the quest-novel that one can be thankful for.

Wayne C. Booth. *The Yale Review*. Spring, 1962. pp. 635–6

He writes with that air of cool judicious detachment that is now universally recognized as one of the signatures of serious fiction in this period, but after reading a few pages of *Parktilden Village*, you become pleasantly aware of the absence of portentous solemnity in the tone, and you begin to see that for once the cool judiciousness is doing something more than calling your attention to the author's subtlety and good taste: it is working to define a critical attitude toward the main character.

Norman Podhoretz. *Doings and Undoings* (Farrar). 1964. p. 166

Mr. Elliott's anecdotes [in *A Piece of Lettuce*] are all of seemingly inconsequential sort. . . . He insists upon his provinciality, using it as a kind of surprise weapon against those who would dictate what life and literature are supposed to be like. His hidden argument seems to run: if I can be loyal to my ordinary background, if I can be spontaneous and frank even when this entails saying nothing of importance, then I will mirror the truth of things; I will be dealing with reality.

Deliberately rejecting what he calls "the miniature art of the conscious essay," Mr. Elliott weaves together childhood impressions and miscellaneous current opinions, always stressing the way experience never quite comes up to the level of poetry. Correspondingly, his literary taste runs to unpretentious, imperfect, frankly minor works. . . .

Mr. Elliott's low-keyed style does have limitations. . . . I also suspect that his distrust of mere logic serves in part to cover an ambiguous flirtation with Christianity that runs through nearly all his fiction and retains its coyness here. Mr. Elliott would evidently like to believe some things he regards as factually untrue, and his non-rational style enables him to avert a showdown. Nevertheless, the general impression I get from *A Piece of Lettuce* is one of refreshing directness.

Frederick C. Crews. *New York Herald Tribune Book Section*. March 15, 1964. p. 13

But if there are matters upon which one wants to take issue with Mr. Elliott, it is chiefly for the sake of that greater portion of his work, as a novelist, poet, and essayist, for which one is honestly grateful. Of the fifteen essays in the present collection [*A Piece of Lettuce*], at least ten strike me as first-rate—by which I don't mean to suggest that they are unexceptionable, but rather that they are illuminating. Mr. Elliott's peculiar virtue is an inability to let anyone else do his thinking for him. The defects of that pre-industrial bent are obvious. The advantage is that mostly we get from Mr. Elliott his own opinions, and mostly they have the quality of something made by hand, for a specific purpose, and incorporating the vital force of the man who made them. That is particularly true of the autobiographical essays in this book, six of which figure in my private list of the ten elect. They further persuade me of something suggested already by Mr. Elliott's verse and by his fiction, that he is less interesting as a critic of literature than as the poet of his own experience.

Emile Capouya. *Saturday Review.* April 4, 1964. p. 26

... the novelistic virtues of George P. Elliott are precisely those which spring from a kind of equanimity.... His first novel, *Parktilden Village*, impressed some readers by the calmness with which it viewed the complexities of love and generation, and his second, *David Knudsen*, was not more objectionable. In these works, as in the essays of *A Piece of Lettuce* and the stories of *Among the Dangs*, one feels that Elliott needs to understand the changing values of our world, values by which he is puzzled and somewhat repelled. The need is honest, firm, consistent; its expression is often tactful if not elegant, and the resources of the moral and artistic imagination behind it are unpretentious.

The judgment, I think, is confirmed by his most ambitious work to date.... As for the theme, it's the Modern World.... Elliott's intention in this big book [*In the World*] is clear. He wants to portray the moribund world of liberal values and foreshadow another world which the young are still powerless to create. And he wants the portrait to include the jumble of private feeling and public action. How much does Elliott succeed?

Not very much. All the pressing issues are here: religion, marriage, money, eugenics, war, sex, social justice. Yet no issue is projected with the intensity that brings illumination; nothing obeys the original force of insight.... But if a kind of softness, a kind of banality really, cripples this work, one feels wonder and sympathy that it can still move so far, impelled by the spirit of human decency, by the conviction that somehow man matters.

Ihab Hassan. *New York Herald Tribune Book Section.* Oct. 24, 1965. pp. 5, 30

It is difficult to pin down with any precision the reasons for Elliott's exceptional independence of spirit, but my own guess is that he enjoys a kind of inward harmony that comes of knowing one's own nature and powers and limitations. Something very much like inward harmony, it seems to me, is reflected in the calm suavity of his prose style, his gentle humor, and his easy authority. Writing out of the center of his own experience, Elliott has become one of America's most engaging essayists; and his criticism, which he frequently blends with autobiographical fragments, is consistently excellent and never dull.

Yet how useful the maxim "know thyself" is to the novelist is by no means certain. Although Elliott has now published three novels—in addition to the already-mentioned collection of short stories—his fiction remains the product of a mind most interesting in its analytical and critical, rather than dramatic, aspects.

Joseph Epstein. *New Republic.* Nov. 27, 1965. p. 40

His latest novel, *In the World* ... is an interesting attempt to raise the novelist's ante by getting back to the nineteenth century. How refreshing it is to find a novelist who still has enough nerve and enough sense of past to take society for granted, to demand of life that it be meaningful. For ours is a time when hysteria and alienation have become as commonplace to novelists as brushing one's teeth.... *Who cares?* cries the existential chorus. I *do*, answers George P. Elliott. It is a very protestant refusal to take the world's chaos for granted, an insistence that people behave as if they are in this world by choice, not necessity....

George P. Elliott is almost the novelist the WASP world has been crying for—almost, but not quite. His deficiency, finally, is the other side of his strength, for if he has enough nerve to take society for granted, he does not seem quite able to artistically come to grips with the destructive instincts in modern life. This is not to say that he is unaware of those instincts.... But when he is faced with the problem of integrating that aspect of life with the other, his talent seems confused and short of the mark.

Leonard Kriegel. *Commonweal.* Dec. 3, 1965. p. 276

Even stranger is what happens in George P. Elliott's *In the World.* In its demeanor it is not different from his *Parktilden Village* and *David Knudsen*, novels which seemed to demonstrate that the flat heavy American style is even less valid than cool English intelligence. *In the World* is long, over two hundred thousand words. As befits Elliott's efforts to allow his characters all the room they need to make their decisions and to live with them, the book is in the usual sense plotless. It should have been a disaster, adequate reward for someone who really wants to be Tolstoi. But there is great strength in this novel, derived more from Thackeray, really, than from Tolstoi; Elliott is determined to make "the world" as resonant a metaphor as "Vanity Fair." Of course it does not work, for Elliott is far less interestingly baffled by his overriding idea than Thackeray was by his.

Roger Sale. *Hudson Review.* Spring, 1966. pp. 131–2

Elliott calls himself a writer-critic rather than a scholar-critic or philosopher-critic. He deserves the name, not only because he has published novels, stories and poems as well as another volume of essays [*Conversations*], but also because he writes well. His manner (when not oracular) is attractively informal, neat yet colorful, and he combines cultural-literary comment with a kind of personal reminiscence that offers us a few glimpses into the role his temperament played in the formation of his opinions. But a little more of the philosophic and scholarly spirit might have strengthened his reasoning, and impressed upon him the fact that his dissatisfaction with a present in which he feels alienated, and his idealization of a past in which the artist enjoyed more sense of community, are fundamental characteristics of the very modernist tradition he deplores. . . .

It is too bad these essays are shot through with an unconvincing social polemic because Elliott does some things especially well. His praise of the art he loves—Dante's, Chekhov's or Tolstoy's—is fine indeed. His comments on teaching, pornography and the novel—subjects on which a sensible position is lent force by radical fashion—are consistently engaging and nicely balanced. Radical fashion also helps to explain why his pages on such extremists as McLuhan, Robbe-Grillet and Genet are exceptionally satisfying.

David J. Gordon. *New York Times Book Section*. Feb. 6, 1972. p. 29

[*Muriel*] moves along so smoothly that its wisdom, quiet strength and range of inclusiveness pass unnoticed. *Muriel* is alive clear through. Whereas most sagas of farming life are long and burly, *Muriel* needs only 154 pages to release its force. Where, then, does its strength come form? It depicts a small world; its characters do not struggle dramatically; no argument is broached, let alone proved. Like the rich Kansas plains where much of it takes place, the novel epitomizes the archetypal female, who is both motionless and brimming with motion. . . .

The shortness of the novel, finally, reflects the haunting brevity of life; life slips past Muriel before she can make sense of it. And, as in all good primitive art, no authorial intrusion mutes dramatic immediacy. Each character has a mystery life beyond the one presented to his family and friends, a life that Elliott respects too much to codify. Thus the structure of the novel helps shape Elliott's view of life: human existence is both fixed and free; although the whole fits into a (four-part) pattern, the individual parts move at random.

Peter Wolfe. *The Nation*. June 5, 1972. pp. 730–1

BIBLIOGRAPHY
Parktilden Village, 1958 (n); *Among the Dangs*, 1961 (s); *Fever and Chills*, 1961 (p); *David Knudsen*, 1962 (n); *Fourteen Poems*, 1964; *A Piece of Lettuce*, 1964 (e); *In the World*, 1965 (n); *An Hour of Last Things*, 1968 (s); *From the Berkeley Hills*, 1969 (p); *Conversions: Literature and the Modernist Deviation*, 1971 (c); *Muriel*, 1972 (n); *Syracuse Poems*, 1974; *Reaching*, 1979 (p); *A George P. Elliott Reader: Selected Poetry and Prose*, 1992 (coll)

ELLISON, Ralph (1914–1994)

Many Negro writers of real distinction have emerged in our century. . . . But none of them except, sometimes, Richard Wright has been able to transcend the bitter way of life they are still (though diminishingly) condemned to, or to master patiently the intricacies of craftsmanship so that they become the peers of the best white writers of our day. Mr. Ellison has achieved this difficult

transcendence. *Invisible Man* is not a great Negro novel; it is a work of art any contemporary writer could point to with pride.

Harvey Curtis Webster. *Saturday Review*. April 12, 1952. p. 23

The reader who is familiar with the traumatic phase of the black man's rage in America, will find something more in Mr. Ellison's report. He will find the long anguished step toward its mastery. The author sells no phony forgiveness. He asks none himself. It is a resolutely honest, tormented, profoundly American book. . . . With this book the author maps a course from the underground world into the light. *Invisible Man* belongs on the shelf with the classical efforts man has made to chart the river Lethe from its mouth to its source.

Wright Morris. *New York Times Book Section*. April 13, 1952. p. 5

Ellison has an abundance of that primary talent without which neither craft nor intelligence can save a novelist; he is richly, wildly inventive; his scenes rise and dip with tension, his people bleed, his language stings. No other writer has captured so much of the confusion and agony, the hidden gloom and surface gaiety of Negro life. His ear for Negro speech is magnificent. . . . The rhythm of the prose is harsh and tensed, like a beat of harried alertness. The observation is expert. . . . For all his self-involvement, he is capable of extending himself toward his people, of accepting them as they are, in their blindness and hope.

Irving Howe. *The Nation*. May 10, 1952. p. 454.

Ralph Ellison's *Invisible Man* is a basically comic work in the picaresque tradition, influenced by the novels of Louis-Ferdinand Céline. The hero of *Invisible Man* just happens to be a Negro, and everything he is and does includes ultimately the experience of all modern men. But this is not accomplished by abstraction; Mr. Ellison has managed to realize the fact of his hero's being a Negro in exactly the same way as nineteenth-century novelists realized their characters being French or Russian or middle-class: by making it the chief fact of their lives, something they take for granted and would not think of denying. Mr. Ellison displays an unapologetic relish for the concrete richness of Negro living—the tremendous variety of its speech, its music, its food, even its perversities.

Steven Marcus. *Commentary*. Nov., 1953. p. 458

Many may find that *Invisible Man*, complex in its novelistic structure, many-sided in its interpretation of the race problem, is not fully satisfying either as narrative or as ideology. Unlike the novel which depends for its appeal chiefly on the staple elements of love or sex, suspense and the dynamics of action, *Invisible Man* dispenses with the individualized hero and his erotic involvements, the working out of his personal destiny. Here we have, subtly and sensitively presented, what amounts to an allegory of the pilgrimage of a people. . . . By means of the revealing master symbol of vision, Ralph Ellison has presented an aesthetically distanced and memorably vivid image of the life of the American Negro.

Charles I. Glicksberg. *Southwest Review.* Summer, 1954. pp. 264–5

Ellison is a writer of the first magnitude—one of those original talents who has created a personal idiom to convey his personal vision. It is an idiom compounded of fantasy, distortion, and burlesque, highly imaginative and generally surrealistic in effect. It possesses at bottom a certain mythic quality. . . . He was striving, he recounts, for a prose medium "with all the bright magic of the fairy tale."

Though not in the narrow sense a political novel, *Invisible Man* is based on a cultivated political understanding of the modern world. The first half of the novel portrays the disillusionment of the protagonist with the shibboleths of American capitalism—a social system which he apprehends through the institutional structure of the Southern Negro college. The latter half treats of his disillusionment with Stalinism, which he encounters through a revolutionary organization known as the Brotherhood. By means of this carefully controlled parallel development, Ellison penetrates to the heart of the two great illusions of his time.

Robert Bone. *The Negro Novel in America* (Yale). 1958. pp. 196–7

Ellison, who has the formal sense of a jazz musician and the instinct of a singer of blues, understands that anger or agony is transient without art. Turbulence, in private or political life, amounts to a denial of the dignity of man. To acknowledge the innate dignity of mankind is also to reconcile the idea of freedom prescribed in the founding political documents of America with the violence of a Harlem race riot. The act of reconciliation is an action of what Ellison calls Mind, a fact of *form.* The "Negro question" becomes a question of determining the essence of the human in a way that the questioning and tormented Mind can grasp. This, if any, is the artistic credo of Ellison. The credo is one that requires him to exploit the resources of irony. And it prompts him, as will become evident, to draw upon the healing powers of the American joke and Negro blues.

Ihab Hassan. *Radical Innocence* (Princeton). 1961. p. 169

In the course of these pages [of *Shadow and Act*], the portrait of a strong, reserved and honest man emerges. More, it is when he addresses his attention to his particular experience that what the writer says is of the greatest importance. It is not by means of conceptualizing and abstracting, as he tended to do in the essays written in the forties, that Mr. Ellison gets to the difficult statements; it is by reaching so far into himself that he reaches right through to the other side and fetches forth truths he could have got in no other way.

He accomplishes this by always remaining *a man who.* He refuses to be put into attributive categories, but subordinates the attributes to himself. He does not say, "I am a Negro, a writer, an American." He says, "I am a man who is a Negro, a writer, an

American." He is not egotistical; he does not dump personal confession on you, assuming that what happened to him is worth your reading about because he is eminent. He always speaks of his own experience in order to make a larger point; reciprocally, the larger point is valid only as it is supported by evidence from his own experience.

George P. Elliott. *New York Times Book Section.* Oct. 25, 1964. p. 4

Invisible Man . . . was published twelve years ago and Ellison's second novel has long since taken on that unreal quality that haunted the unpublished *Ship of Fools.* Ellison spent two years in Rome, attended writer's conferences, submitted to interviews, wrote journalism, taught at various universities, and almost inevitably admirers have felt that the second novel, when it did appear, would reflect damagingly the anguish that accrues to a brilliant writer who takes so long to publish a book that nothing less than a masterpiece will justify the years of work and waiting.

Now, perhaps in lieu of the novel, Ellison has published a collection of essays. Such books have a way of quietly announcing the temporary or permanent demise of a novelist's will to imagine, so when *Shadow and Act* was announced, it was hard not to fear the worst. But though it is certainly not a great book, it shows that the fears were groundless. Ellison is still with us—large, impressive, ironic, cumbersome in his own polished way—and he seems to have lost no more faith in himself than is natural in a proud and serious man who finds writing difficult.

Roger Sale. *Hudson Review.* Spring, 1965. p. 124

Ellison's hero [in *Invisible Man*] has nowhere to go once he tells us he is invisible. He does indeed, in the Epilogue, say that he intends to rise again and try his hand at life, that he has faith in democratic principles, and that life itself is its own excuse despite the blows it has dealt him. But there is no evidence in the text to fortify his beliefs. The blues singer has depths of feeling to begin with, but Ellison's hero has just begun to learn to feel as the novel ends.

One dwells on these issues because *Invisible Man* is so very nearly a great book. Perhaps Ellison himself, caught somewhere between Negro blues and the symphonic complexities of Western experience, has yet to find his footing. Or possibly his position as an American Negro, an invisible man, will make it impossible for him to find his way.

Edward Margolies. *Native Sons* (Lippincott). 1968. p. 148

Ellison makes greater use of the blues than Baldwin does; he finds them vital and authentic celebrations of Negro experience. More important, though, is the range of his language. No one since Mark Twain is so rich, so varied, or so comic in his re-creation of oral speech. Bracing peals of laughter echo on and under the surface of *Invisible Man.* The whole is an elaborate musical and verbal joke, celebrating love, sacrifice, and self-knowledge as our ultimate resources against the vicissitudes of life.

Richard H. Rupp. *Celebration in Postwar American Fiction* (Miami). 1970. pp. 163–4

If one is a black individual (as the central character [of *Invisible Man*] is, while at the same time emblematic of everyone) in a society whose people denigrate (the pun is intended) blackness, then the institutions, dedicated as they are to the preservation of the status quo, must of necessity be in large measure against him. What, then, does the black person do? Does he support that which thwarts the realization of his potential? Does he seek to destroy the institutions, the only protection from chaos? These are the questions which Ellison's novel poses and in its own way answers. There are no solutions to such questions. One can only withdraw, thus solving the problem privately. No action is possible, for there is no basis for action. This seems to be the implication of *Invisible Man*. He is as invisible at the end as he was at the beginning, and he is invisible because he *feels* he is. The conception of invisibility exists only as a response to a society which tells individuals they are invisible. There may be alternatives different from accepting as fact that one is invisible; at least many people think so, people who believe in the possibility of significant change.

It is in the area designated by the above considerations that *Invisible Man* makes a political statement. Insofar as it suggests that significant changes of a social nature are not possible and in many ways not even desirable, it is a vehicle for a particular political bias, for that sentiment happens to be held by large numbers of people who express it by means of political actions. Hence, despite Ellison's intentions, despite his professions about being an artist and that alone, he expresses ideas and attitudes which, once freed into the world, are likely to have political consequences.

Donald B. Gibson in *The Politics of Twentieth-Century Novelists*, edited by George A. Panichas (Hawthorn). 1971. p. 315

Ellison's artistic sense . . . was far more developed than [Richard] Wright's—he never conceived of his own fiction as a device for exclusively expressing social protest, although protest mars some of his early work. After 1943 he ceased to concern himself primarily with politics and turned to the theme that dominates all of his later work: the need of white Americans to recognize Negro identity in all of its diversity. "Mister Toussan" (1941), a short story published in *The New Masses*, had already explored that idea, and later stories approached it from various points of view. Within a few years he had published several stories: "That I Had the Wings" (reprinted as "Mr.Toussaint"), "In a Strange Country" (1944), "Flying Home" (1944), and "King of the Bingo Game" (1944). These stories, together with "A Coupla Scalped Indians" (1956), have not yet been collected, but they indicate that Ellison is an impressive short story writer as well as a novelist and essayist.

Theodore L. Gross. *The Heroic Ideal in American Literature* (Free). 1971. p. 159

A kind of critical commonplace has grown up around *Invisible Man* to the effect that it is a novel centering on "the problem of identity." Certainly this seems a valid observation, but too often it serves to terminate rather than to begin a discussion of the book's basic concerns. The result is a battery of statements that would lead one to believe that by the novel's end the narrator knows who he *is*, when in fact it is more accurate to say that at that point he only knows who he *isn't*. His "state of hibernation," we should recall, is simply "a covert preparation for a more overt action." It is by that action that he must finally achieve identity.

The book, then, may be said to deal most essentially with considerations which precede identification; that is, with ontology itself. In making this point Ellison has said that "*Invisible Man* is an attempt to describe reality as it really exists rather than in terms of what [the narrator] has assumed it to be. Because it was the clash between his assumptions, his illusions about reality, and its actual shape which made for his agony." What Ellison's protagonist finally comes to see is that the "actual shape" of reality is wholly protean, ambiguous, and chaotic. He realizes—even as his tormentors do not—that any attempt to deal with such essential dynamism in terms of fixed and static phenomena is not only to delude oneself but ultimately to deny the possibility of any genuinely meaningful existence. *Invisible Man* carries its hero to the point of such realization, but not beyond. He comes to grips with the nature of reality; identity will be achieved only when that understanding is put to active use. . . .

The [bulk] of the novel, I believe, is structured around a series of encounters in which that sense of certainty is repeatedly challenged, proven inadequate, and supplanted by yet another. In each case the terms of the encounter are basically the same; someone embodying a particular institution of tradition imposes his fixed and rigid vision of reality upon the usually acquiescent narrator, thereby rendering him at once "invisible" and ignorant of his invisibility. Chronically failing to apprehend the basic flux of reality which disqualifies all such prescriptive visions, he is tossed from one set of certainties to another, until his mounting disillusionment finally exposes him to a perception of fundamental chaos and to a recognition of the primary sources of his invisibility. He is helped toward this perception, moreover, by other encounters with individuals who provide—deliberately or otherwise—certain strategic "clues" regarding the true nature of reality. The novel can be seen, then, as a succession of episodes which finally strip the hero of his illusions, either through a painful process of trial and error or by providing strategic glimpses of that essential fluidity which erodes and distorts all static formalizations of experience.

Jeffrey Steinbrink. *Studies in Black Literature*. Autumn, 1976, pp. 1–2

Ellison is by no means the first writer to inlay his work with the silver and gold of Afro-American folklore. Mark Twain, Charles Chesnutt, James Weldon Johnson, William Faulkner, Zora Neale Hurston, Sterling A. Brown, and Langston Hughes used it before Ellison, often with supreme skill. But Ellison's case is special, because of the sheer virtuosity of *Invisible Man*, which, replete with its "inside" use of black folklore, is also very modern in its technique. In this contemporary novel, the vital transformation from folk item to written literature seems wonderfully complete. The language is consistently astir with actual Afro-American speech, as well as with the tales, songs, and games of folklore. What Ellington and Wagner achieved in music is here achieved in fiction: the transmutation of folk materials into a fully orchestrated masterpiece. . . .

Ellison's artistic vision is always ironical, complex, ambiguous. And easy answers prove troubling. He points out, for instance, that paradoxical as it may seem, blacks are in certain ways the freest of Americans. Living at the bottom of the American social hierarchy, blacks have been left alone to experiment with new styles of expression. Echoing James Weldon Johnson, Ellison has observed that much that the world knows as uniquely American (particularly with regard to language, music, and dance) was created by black slaves and their offspring. . . .

It is ironic that James Weldon Johnson's fictional character, the Ex-Colored Man, retreats from the black world into the white one, but nonetheless narrates one of the most affirmative novels about black life. It is odd that the Invisible Man, who ends by escaping into a dark hole, tells a tale full of hope. In Ellison's fiction, especially from the forties on, the portraits of such strong black characters as Jefferson, Mary Rambo, Trueblood, and Hickman have been diverse and affirming. Characters are cheated, tricked, left for dead, beaten, and even lynched. But certain powerful figures, aware of roots in a sustaining tradition, manage to persevere with heroism and high style. The insistence on the heroic impulse in black life has contributed to Ellison's influence.

He has had a lasting impact on many younger writers, notably Al Young, Ishmael Reed, Leon Forrest, Toni Morrison, Alice Walker, and James Alan McPherson. His special contribution to the new wave of black writing is his unceasing insistence upon connections between the contemporary writer, and not only the American realistic tradition, but the symbolist tradition that nourished Melville and Faulkner, and the vernacular tradition, rooted in American language and lore.

> Robert G. O'Meally. *The Craft of Ralph Ellison* (Harvard Univ. Pr., 1980). pp. 3–5

Although he does not write a historical novel in [any traditional] vein, he uses the career of his protagonist to suggest the history of the southern black who has moved from slavery to Booker T. Washingtonism, to the migrations north, to Marxism, to (it is hoped) a viable position as a free human individual. . . . *Invisible Man* suggests that these experiences offer understandable meanings if we will but see them. Like [Ellen] Glasgow or [Henry] James, Ellison creates a social history that, while not always narrowly realistic, certainly captures satirically—and frequently humorously—the social manners he wishes to attack; and like Faulkner, Warren, Styron, and other southern authors, Ellison uses contemporary novelistic techniques masterfully to body forth the symbolic meanings he sees in his protagonist's experiences. Moreover, he creates a cyclical structure for his novel that in itself is a comment on the nature of man's experience in time. Ellison's evidence of the past's continued presence is embodied in the shadow it casts through folk elements—the songs, the extravagant language, the tall-tale, the evangelical Protestantism—that make up the shared experience of the southerner, both black and white. In [Hugh] Holman's terms, his message is Hegelian. There is meaning in history: the past is revealed through process, not replication. His voice is southern. His *Invisible Man* is worthy indeed to claim a place among the great southern novels of this or any other century.

> Ladell Payne. *Black Novelists and the Southern Literary Tradition* (Univ. of Georgia Pr., 1981), p. 98

If folk artists are to turn a profit from their monumental creative energies (which are often counteractive, or inversive, vis-à-vis Anglo-American culture), they must take a lesson from the boss quail and move without moving. They must, in essence, sufficiently modify their folk forms (and amply advertise themselves) to merchandize such forms as commodities in the artistic market. To make their products commensurate with a capitalistic marketplace, folk artists may even have to don masks that distort their genuine selves. Ralph Ellison is a master of such strategies.

Ellison reconciles the trickster's manifestations as untrammeled creator and as god of the marketplace by providing critical advertisements for himself as a novelist that carefully bracket the impoverishing economics of Afro-America. For example, in ''Change the Joke and Slip the Yoke'' he writes, ''I use folklore in my work not because I am a Negro, but because writers like Eliot and Joyce made me conscious of the literary value of my folk inheritance. My cultural background, like that of most Americans, is dual (my middle name, sadly enough, is Waldo).'' What is designated in this quotation as ''literary value'' is in reality market value. Joyce and Eliot taught Ellison that if he were a skillful enough strategist and spokesman he could market his own folklore. What is bracketed, of course, is the economics that required Ellison, if he wished to be an Afro-American artist, to turn to Afro-American folklore as a traditional, authenticating source for his art. Like his sharecropper, Ellison is wont to make literary value out of socioeconomic necessity. But he is also an artist who recognizes that Afro-American folk forms have value *in themselves*; they ''have named human situations so well,'' he suggests in ''The Art of Fiction,'' ''that a whole corps of writers could not exhaust their universality'' (p. 173). What Ellison achieves in the Trueblood episode is a dizzying hall of mirrors, a redundancy of structure, that enables him to extend the value of Afro-American folk forms by combining them with an array of Western narrative forms and tropes. Written novel and sung blues, polysyllabic autobiography and vernacular personal narrative, a Christian Fall and an inversive triumph of the black trickster—all are magnificently interwoven.

It is in such creative instances that one discovers Ellison's artistic genius, a genius that links him inextricably and positively to his invented sharecropper. In the Trueblood episode conceived as a chapter in a novel, one finds not only the same kind of metaexpressive commentary that marks the character's narration to Norton but also the same type of self-reflexive artist that the sharecropper's recitation implies—an artist who is fully aware of the contours and limitations, the rewards and dilemmas, of the Afro-American's uniquely expressive craft.

In the expository, critical moment, by contrast, one often finds a quite different Ralph Ellison. Instead of the *reflexive* artist, one finds the *reflective* spokesman. . . .

Ralph Ellison's identity as a public critic, therefore, does not forestall his private artistic recognition he ''ain't nobody but himself,'' and it is out of this realization that a magnificent folk creation such as Trueblood emerges. Both the creator and his agrarian folk storyteller have the wisdom to know that they are resourceful ''whistlers'' for the tribe. They know that their primary matrix as artists is coextensive not with a capitalistic society but with material circumstances like those implied by the blues singer Howling Wolf.

> Houston A. Baker, Jr. *Blues, Ideology, and Afro-American Literature: A Vernacular Theory* (Chicago: Univ. of Chicago Pr., 1984), pp. 197–99

In his essay on Charlie Parker, "On Bird, Bird-Watching, and Jazz" (1962), Ellison discusses the satirical aspect of signifying as one aspect of riffing in jazz. . . . Here . . . the parody is twofold, involving a formal parody of the melody of "They Picked Poor Robin" as well as a ritual naming, and therefore a troping, of an action "observed from the bandstand." While *riffing* is a term that has several meanings, I prefer that told to Alan Lomax by Jelly Roll Morton. A riff, according to Morton, is "a *figure*, musically speaking." A riff functions as "something that gives any orchestra a great background," by which Morton means "what you would call a foundation," "something you walk on." J. L. Dillard's definition explains that this "figure" works "as short phrase repeated over the length of a chorus, more or less like an *ostinato* in classical European musical notation." . . .

Ellison, of course, is a complex Signifier, naming things by indirection and troping throughout his works. In his well-known review of LeRoi Jones's *Blues People*, Ellison defines Signifyin(g) in yet a third sense, then Signifies upon Jones's reading of Afro-American cultural history which he argues is misdirected and wrongheaded. "The tremendous burden of sociology which Jones would place upon this body of music," writes Ellison, "is enough to give the blues the blues." . . .

Ellison in his fictions Signifies upon [Richard] Wright by parodying Wright's literary structures through repetition and difference. One can readily suggest the complexities of the parodying. The play of language, the Signifying, starts with the titles. Wright's *Native Son* and *Black Boy*, titles connoting race, self, and presence, Ellison tropes with *Invisible Man*, with *invisibility* as an ironic response of absence to the would-be presence of blacks and natives. While *man* suggests a more mature and stronger status than either *son or boy*. Ellison Signifies upon Wright's distinctive version of naturalism with a complex rendering of modernism; Wright's reenacting protagonist, voiceless to the last, Ellison signifies upon with a nameless protagonist. Ellison's protagonist is nothing *but* voice, since it is he who shapes, edits, and narrates his own tale, thereby combining action with the representation of action and defining reality by its representation. This unity of presence and representation is perhaps Ellison's most subtle reversal of Wright's theory of the novel as exemplified in *Native Son*.

Henry Louis Gates, Jr. *The Signifying Monkey: A Theory of Afro-American Literary Criticism* (New York: Oxford Univ. Pr., 1988), pp. 104–5, 106

Ralph Ellison turned eighty on March 1[, 1994], and his peculiarly modern burden, the burden of a second act, grows heavier with age. The man is far too composed, too regal, to betray the weight of it, but the soul must weary of its persistence. So great was the celebration in 1952 for his first (and only) novel, *Invisible Man*, that the sound of critical applause, rattling medals, and whispered expectations took years to fade. Few novels have entered the canon so quickly. . . .

Ellison did not intend to distinguish his career with such an austerity of publication. By 1955, he had begun a novel set mainly in the South and in Washington, D.C. At the center of the story—as far as we know it from a few published extracts—are the community and the language of the black church and the relationship between a black preacher and a friend who eventually becomes a senator and a notorious racist. After a few years of writing, Ellison

was not shy about showing excerpts to friends like Saul Bellow and the novelist and cultural historian Albert Murray. He was not reluctant to publish a piece here and there in literary quarterlies. . . .

[As] he described a fire two decades ago at his old summer house, in Plainfield, Massachusetts, he slumped back in his chair, resigned, his voice lowering into a growling whisper. "There was, of course, a traumatic event involved with the book," he began. "We lost a summer house and, with it, a good part of the novel. It wasn't the entire manuscript, but it was over three hundred and sixty pages. There was no copy."

Ellison's friends say that it was years before he went back to work on the novel. . . .

Ellison's readers can be greedy and hope for more novels and essays—come to think of it, a memoir would be nice, too—but what's done is done and, in a sense, is more than enough. On the occasion of his eightieth birthday, it becomes clearer than ever that *Invisible Man* and his two collections of essays, *Shadow and Act* (1964) and *Going to the Territory* (1986) are the urtexts for a loose coalition of black American intellectuals who represent an integrationist vision of the country's history and culture. Ellison's books are a foundation for talents as various as the novelists Charles Johnson, John Edgar Wideman, Leon Forrest, and James Alan MacPherson; the critics Shelby Steele, Henry Louis Gates, Jr., and Stanley Crouch; the poet Michael S. Harper. . . .

In Ellison's view, America is not made up of separate, free-floating cultures but, rather of a constant interplay and exchange. . . . What Ellison has called the "interchange, appropriation, and integration" of American culture is evident in the music we hear, the games we play, the books we read, the clothes we wear, the food we eat. For him, integration is not merely an aspiration but a given, a fact of cultural and political life.

David Remnick. "Visible Man." *New Yorker*. March 14, 1994, pp. 34–36

Certainly his career is far from being over. In a *New Yorker* article in 1976 Jervis Anderson wrote: "It might . . . be said of Ellison . . . that his prestige seems to grow with every novel he doesn't write." Which is one way of remarking the extraordinary life that *Invisible Man* has had over the past forty-two years. In 1965 about two hundred writers and editors, in a poll taken by *Book Week* (then the literary supplement of the now defunct New York *Herald Tribune* but today the Sunday literary review of *The Washington Post*) registered the judgment that Ellison's was the most distinguished American novel that had appeared during the previous twenty years, and it is not at all unlikely that, were a similar group to be canvassed at the present time, nearly thirty years later, the same valuation would again be rendered. Through the various editions of *Invisible Man* that have been produced in well-nigh twenty languages millions of copies have been purchased across the world, and there is virtually no college or university campus on the American scene where at least one course will not be found in whose syllabus it forms an important element. So the question that is raised in its narrator's famous concluding sentence—"Who knows but that, on the lower frequencies, I speak for you?"—has been resoundingly answered in the affirmative by Ellison's countless readers, black and white, who continue to find in the profundity of his metaphor about "invisibility" a luminousness that powerfully clarifies the general human condition.

But it is not alone the remarkable continuing life of *Invisible Man* that tells us that Ellison's career is by no means over, for he also left nearly two thousand manuscript pages of the novel on which he had been working for decades and which he had told me a few weeks before his death was "just about to finished." It had been a long struggle, for more than 350 pages of the novel in progress were lost in the mid-1960s in a fire that destroyed the Ellisons' summer home in Plainfield, Massachusetts. And so disheartened was he by this misfortune that not for another few years was he able to resume the project with any real intensity of concentration. But gradually he recovered self-command, and over a long stretch of time prior to his death he, with his characteristic deliberateness, had been steadily working with great joy and with great energy. And I am confident that Joseph Fox, his Random House editor, when he begins really to tackle the manuscript, will find a novel so nearly complete as to be easily publishable.

So, with the two brilliant collections of his essays—*Shadow and Act* (1964) and *Going to the Territory* (1986)—and *Invisible Man* and the massive manuscript (as yet untitled) that remains to be posthumously issued, we may safely take it for granted that the career of this prodigiously gifted writer will be a vital part of the American literary scene over as much of its future as can now be foreseen.

Nathan A. Scott, Jr. *Callaloo*. Summer, 1994, p. 360

BIBLIOGRAPHY

Invisible Man, 1952 (n); *Shadow and Act*, 1964 (e); *Going to the Territory*, 1986 (a); *Speaking for You*, ed. Kimberly W. Benston, 1987 (e); *Collected Essays*, 1995; *Conversations with Ralph Ellison*, ed. Maryemma Graham and Amritjit Singh, 1995 (i); *Flying Home*, ed. John F. Callahan, 1996 (s)

ERDRICH, Louise (1954–)

Louise Erdrich is a contemporary writer of German-American and Chippewa heritage. Like many literary works by Native Americans, her novels, *Love Medicine* (1984), *The Beet Queen* (1986), and *Tracks* (1988), reflect the ambivalence and tension marking the lives of people, much like herself, from dual cultural backgrounds. Erdrich's novels feature Native Americans, mixed bloods, and other culturally and socially displaced characters whose marginal status is simultaneously an advantage and a disadvantage, a source of both power and powerlessness. In *Love Medicine*, for example, Lipsha Morrissey, born with the shaman's healing touch, grows up with both Native American and Roman Catholic religious beliefs. His knowledge of both religions is sometimes an advantage, but at other times he is merely paralyzed between contradictory systems of belief. In *The Beet Queen*, Wallace Pfef, marginal as a homosexual in a small Midwestern town, plays an ambivalent role as Karl Adair's lover and as husband-and-father substitute to Karl's wife and daughter. His liminal status is a source of both happiness and grief. In *Tracks*, Erdrich's two narrators likewise struggle with liminality in their efforts to leave behind early lives in favor of others they have chosen. Nanapush grows up Christian in a Jesuit school, but later chooses life in the woods and Chippewa tradition;

the other narrator, Pauline, is a mixed-blood raised in the Native American tradition, but she wishes to be white. . . .

All of these conflicting codes in Erdrich's text produce a state of marginality in the reader, who must at some point in the reading cease to apply the conventional expectations associated with ordinary narrativity. The reader must pause "between worlds" to discover the arbitrary structural principles of both. This primary value—epistemological insight—which Erdrich's text associates with marginality might then be adopted through a revision of narrativity. Stranded between conflicting codes—deprived of "a stable point of identification" within the world evoked by the text—the reader is temporarily disempowered. However, such disempowerment or "alienation" leads to another kind of power. The reader must consider a possibility forcefully posited in all of Erdrich's works (as well as in those of other contemporary Native Americans): the world takes on the shape of the stories we tell. Exposure to radically different stories as ways of structuring the world brings the reader to see what Lipsha Morrissey understands when he says, "You see how instantly the ground can shift you thought was solid. . . . You see how all the everyday things you counted on was just a dream you had been having by which you run your whole life. . . . So I had perspective on it all" (*London Mercury*, pp. 209, 211).

Catherine Rainwater. "Reading between Words: Narrativity in the Fiction of Louise Erdrich." *American Literature*. December 1990, pp. 405, 422

Erdrich's second novel, *The Beet Queen* (1986), is a tighter and more polished work than *Love Medicine*, with a smooth style that led Leslie Silko to write: "Erdrich's prose is dazzling and sleek. Each sentence has been carefully wrought, pared lean and then polished." In this novel, six narrators share the episodic narrative with a third-person narrator in a chronological sequence shifting over time from 1932 to 1972. The story is one of men and women without reservations, hung out to dry on the flat, dull edge of the Minnesota–North Dakota heartland in a small town that could be anywhere or nowhere. The story is told in a triangulation that zeros in on Argus, a town that seems almost an empty place on the map. Just as water was the primary natural element in *Love Medicine*, in *The Beet Queen* the unifying element is air.

At first or perhaps even second glance, "Indian" seems to mean very little in this novel. In the same review in which she praised the style of *The Beet Queen*, Silko criticized the novel for this very point, writing: "What Erdrich, who is half-Indian and grew up in North Dakota, attempts to pass off as North Dakota may be the only North Dakota she knows. But hers is an oddly rarified place in which the individual's own psyche, not racism or poverty, accounts for all conflict and tension. In this pristine world all misery, suffering and loss are self-generated, just as conservative Republicans have been telling us for years." Silko concludes that "*The Beet Queen* is a strange artifact, an eloquent example of the political climate in America in 1986."

Oddly, in attacking the book for its refusal to foreground the undeniably bitter racism toward Indians in America's heartland, Silko seems to be demanding that writers who identify as Indian, or mixed blood, must write rhetorically and polemically, a posture that leaves little room for the kind of heterogeneous literature that would reflect the rich diversity of Indian experiences, lives and cultures—and a posture Silko certainly does not assume in her own fiction.

Louis Owens. *Other Destinies: Understanding the American Indian Novel* (Norman: Univ. of Oklahoma Pr., 1992), pp. 205–6

Although she has described herself in *Contemporary Authors* as "anti religion," Erdrich in four of her novels explores the family sagas of Native Americans and whites caught in the erosion of both Christian and Native American religious traditions. Her Native Americans suffer the loss doubly: they are alienated from the dogmatic "Christianity" imposed on them by the whites who subjugated them, and they are increasingly estranged from the shamanic religion of their ancestors as they struggle to preserve their identity in a secularized America. Erdrich is sharply critical of institutional Catholicism as a force that warps her Chippewa men and women. At the same time, she reveals how many of her own people abandon their native religion for the baubles of a materialistic culture—money, alcohol, cars, and commercial success.

Erdrich, nevertheless, counteracts these destructive forces by using mystical realism to create a world infused with supernatural mystery. Through her lyrical prose and the prophetic voices of her narrators, she breaks down the barriers between the material and spiritual worlds, between linear time and mythic reenactment, between "real" and imaginary events. By the power of the word, she affirms an enduring supernatural reality against the soulless liberalism of the hyperrational dominant culture.

John F. Desmond. *America*. May 14, 1994, p. 9

BIBLIOGRAPHY

Love Medicine, 1985 (n); *The Beet Queen*, 1986 (n); *Tracks*, 1988 (n); *Baptism of Desire*, 1989 (p); (with Michael Dorris) *The Crown of Columbus*, 1991 (n); *The Bingo Palace*, 1994 (n); *Conversations*, 1994 (r, i.e., interviews); *The Blue Jay's Dance: A Birth Year*, 1996 (e); *Tales of Burning Love*, 1996 (s); *Grandmother's Pigeon*, 1996 (juv); *The Antelope Wife*, 1998 (n)

ESPADA, Martín (1957–)

[Martín] Espada spent most of his childhood in Brooklyn, where he was born in 1957. When he was about thirteen, his family moved to Long Island, which he calls "my own private Mississippi," because of the difficulties he encountered as a Puerto Rican in a white suburb. When he first started writing poetry at sixteen, he did so partially to search for a positive identity in a negative atmosphere. . . .

When he dropped out [of college] after a year, he began what he calls an "odyssey." Many of the poems in Espada's books mention the myriad jobs he has encountered in his life, and this period, when he was between colleges, was rich in poetic material, if not in material gain. He worked as a door-to-door encyclopedia salesman, a clerk, a telephone solicitor for Time-Life Books, a gas station attendant, a bouncer, and a bindery worker in a printing plant. . . .

Espada began to suspect he was able to work as a poet when, in 1984, he received a five thousand dollar grant from the Massachusetts Artists Foundation, while he was still in law school. . . . His first book, *The Immigrant Iceboy's Bolero*, came out in 1982. . . .

Another turning point came when his second book, *Trumpets from the Islands of Their Eviction*, came out in 1987. . . . But it took until his third book. *Rebellion Is the Circle of a Lover's Hands*, published in 1989 . . . for him to feel that his poetry was really taking off. . . .

Over the course of eleven years and four books, Espada says he's become much more critical about his poetry, and much more disciplined and consistent in terms of language. "My central preoccupations remain the same," he says. "The themes, the identities, the sympathies are essentially the same but I think my ability to use the language and my vocabulary has evolved in a certain direction. For example, I'm much more aware of certain literary devices, and I'm more grounded in the senses than when I first started writing." His language may have evolved, but many things remain the same, such as his reliance on imagery.

"My father is a documentary photographer and I think there's a documentary sensibility in my poetry. . . . I think a lot of my imagery is derived from foregrounding and shadow, and there is a starkness in my poetry, a rawness that comes through in the documentary grounding there." . . .

Classifications have always been pushed on Espada . . . labeling him a "Latino poet," or an "advocate," or a "political poet."

"There are classifications which restrict, which stereotype, and there are classifications that define. I don't mind being defined. I don't mind someone saying I'm a *Latino* poet, I don't mind *political poet*. Those are definitions, they help a reader understand what it is you're about to get. I just wouldn't want to be stereotyped, called a *street poet*. Part of the dilemma we face as Latino writers, Puerto Rican writers, is how do we declare our independence as individuals and still be part of this community?"

Elizabeth Gunderson. *Poets & Writers*. March–April, 1995, pp. 51–52, 53, 54–55

BIBLIOGRAPHY

The Immigrant Iceboy's Bolero, 1982 (p); *Trumpets from the Islands of Their Eviction*, 1987 (p); *Rebellion Is the Circle of a Lover's Hands*, 1990 (p); *Clemente Soto Velez: The Blood That Keeps Singing*, 1991 (tr); ed., *Poetry Like Bread: Poets of the Political Imagination*, 1994 (anthol); *City of Coughing and Dead Radiators*, 1994 (p); *Imagine the Angels of Bread*, 1996 (p); ed., *El Coro: A Chorus of Latino and Latina Poetry*, 1997 (anthol); *Zapata's Disciple*, 1998 (p)

FARRELL, James Thomas (1904–1979)

Like Proust, Farrell seems to have endured certain personal experiences for the sole purpose of recording them; but he also desired to avenge them, and he charged his works with so unflagging a hatred of the characters in them, and wrote at so shrill a pitch, that their ferocity seemed almost an incidental representation of his own. Like Caldwell, he wrote with his hands and feet and any bludgeon within reach; but where Caldwell's grossness seemed merely ingenuous or slick, Farrell wrote under the pressure of certain moral compulsives that were part of the very design of his work and gave it a kind of dreary grandeur.

> Alfred Kazin. *On Native Grounds* (Reynal). 1942. p. 380

Farrell the moralist is all-of-a-piece with Farrell the fiction writer. The one reflects upon the experience the other records. The fiction writer composes canvases depicting frustrated petty hopes and mean defeats, prolix obituaries of the spiritually impoverished, of greenhorns and other outsiders, the anonymous integers that go only to swell the population figures, the devalued people of his time whose fruitless dignity and courage (when these they have) are eternally betrayed by what Thomas Hardy called "circumstances." . . . The writer of fiction may leave us with the impression that his vision is of the drabness and tawdriness of life; and Farrell has indeed been beaten over the head innumerable times for precisely that crime, but the moralist takes a different tack and from the same data draws the conclusion that these things need not be.

> C. Hartley Grattan. *Harper's Magazine*. Oct., 1954. p. 93

Mr. Farrell's stories are painful, awful and wonderful.

How can he commute so easily between such extremes? I think the answer proceeds from the fact that Mr. Farrell dispenses with art as well as with artifice. . . . Mr. Farrell is innocent of all the invisible but complicated apparatus now fashionable with the short-story writer—the subtleties of form, the casual but cunning clues for motivation, the deployment of symbol and the planned ambiguities. His language is humble, but never studiedly so. He doesn't make an *outré* elegance out of plainness, as Hemingway sometimes does, or Steinbeck in his portraits of the primitive. Mr. Farrell's simplicity is helpless and genuine. . . . Yet who is better— the slide-rule fictioneer of our day, who frequently refines his short story into a weary and well-tailored void, or Jim Farrell, who reaches out with a rough hand and comes up, quite often, with an authentic fistful of human truth?

> Frederic Morton. *New York Times Book Section*. Feb. 10, 1957. p. 30

The critics are usually bored by his dogged, humorless methods, but they are also surprised by his quality. Farrell has not only gone

on doing his chosen job as well as he did in his early years—they keep saying—but does it with deepened insight and humanity. *The Face of Time*, published in 1953, for instance, received the sort of respect which would have stirred general excitement about a new author. Yet even though living writers are being given intensive treatment in a steady stream of studies pouring from the academic presses, Farrell is virtually ignored. Inevitably, by the mysterious laws of literary favor, he will be rediscovered, though not perhaps until one or two books from now. . . .

Sooner or later Farrell will be given his place as a sort of William Dean Howells of Jackson Park in recognition of the scope and faithfulness with which he recorded the day-to-day, almost hour-by-hour suffering, sentimentality, dignity, coarseness and despair of an important part of the nation's population at a time of decisive change in its psyche.

> Robert Gorham Davis. *New York Times Book Section*. May 12, 1963. pp. 1, 43

In the midst of a long-overdue assessment of his contribution to American fiction, it is not generally recognized that Farrell's critical writing forms in itself a body of searching and incisive judgments much richer and of wider range than those of his novelist contemporaries. To read this criticism is not only to probe in retrospect the dilemmas of the artist in American life over the past three decades; it is also to visualize Farrell's deliberate involvement in social and political agitation at the cost of precious time taken from his art. In this choice Farrell has nothing in common with Hemingway and Faulkner. Both as writer and social critic he has felt closer to Dreiser and Anderson than to writers born in this century. A refreshing thing about Farrell is that he rejects no vision as alien to his art or his thought. Thus he was profoundly influenced simultaneously by Joyce and Tolstoy, Dreiser and Dostoievsky, Trotsky and Pater. Such a catholic openness to the thought of his great predecessors has given Farrell's critical outlook a richness and perspective unique on the American scene of our generation.

> Don M. Wolfe. Introduction to *Selected Essays*, by James T. Farrell, ed. Luna Wolfe (McGraw). 1964. pp. ix–x

If he would persist in his folly, it has been said, the fool would be wise. I am not saying James T. Farrell has been foolish in his persistent and repeated explorations of what is by now his own terrain. But persistent he certainly has been. And that in the face of continued critical and, in recent years, popular neglect. What is interesting in reading his new novel, *Lonely for the Future*, is to realize that with persistence has come distance. The magic of time has transformed Farrell into a historical novelist: his period, the Twenties and early Thirties; his place, Chicago. Now, as a profoundly probing recording angel of the social scene, as exemplified by the lower middle classes (Irish-Catholic variety), Farrell is not the American Balzac he would like to be. However, as a fairly accurate painter of the social and sexual agonies of the young of a more naïve time, he is quite good. . . .

. . .what prevents this book [*Lonely for the Future*], like most of Farrell's work, from having any great substance is that he is perhaps too closely identified with his characters. Their naïveté seems to be his; their awakenings to the possibilities of life that lie beyond the middle-class home seem to be his own awakening of many years ago, obsessively re-enacted over and over again. Just that—and no more.

Daniel Stern. *Saturday Review*. Jan. 22, 1966. pp. 43–4

Farrell's work, like that of other writers, is uneven from book to book and exhibits both weaknesses and strengths, the weaknesses sometimes being the defects of the strengths. For example, it may be said that at times Farrell depends too exclusively on dialogue for characterization, yet that technique dramatically reveals the mentality behind the words and thus carries and verifies the thematic indictment of what city life does to people. His writing can be doggedly repetitive and wordy, but again it is often so for thematic purposes—just as Walt Whitman, Henry James, and William Faulkner can be repetitive and wordy in their ways to achieve their effects. Such flaws of his style, if that is what they are, are in any case minor compared to its virtues in his best work: its overall thematic suitability, its expressive adaptability to the speech patterns of many characters, its frequent attainment of a natural eloquence. . . .

Farrell has not realized the full potential in his vision. But his vision is large and single, and step by step he has created a single world of ample proportions. His cycles of novels with his other fiction approximate a sequence, a rarity in American literature. At its best, the American past he creates is deeply authentic as art and as social history, like Faulkner's South. Farrell's re-created and recorded past is especially meaningful to us because, through its rich details of urban manners, it shows the heavy cost exacted of people and institutions by the modern city. His characters' lives expose social process; time slowly brings change, and the making of personality and the formation of society merge. His Lonigans, O'Flahertys, and O'Neills are deeply immersed in their time and place—interesting contrasts to Hemingway's disengaged Americans—and his work is exceptional in our fiction for the number of its living characters. The contrast between their often blind groping for a better future and the grimness of their present, flowing inevitably out of their past, is a subject with tragic power.

Edgar M. Branch. *James T. Farrell* (Twayne, 1971), pp. 169, 171

If Farrell had not possessed a major talent and a major subject, his feat of endurance would be less interesting if still significant. The inheritor of a largely unscrutinized American literary tradition represented by Dreiser, Anderson, and Lewis, Farrell had both the talent and the subject. He was a master in the creation of mass scenes: raging, hilarious, bitter family quarrels with a cast of dozens, piously organized civic and religious festivities, violent, protracted New Year's Eve parties. Few have been better chroniclers than Farrell of that particularly American experience and subject, the mood: the endless series of frightened adjustments called living, the lunging and inching toward attention by each individual psyche within a hopelessly blurred crowd, the troubled intimacy with which one tentatively fixes and appropriates one's

alien *persona*, the confusion in which one haphazardly sorts the fragmented hurtful thoughts one wakes up to and goes to sleep with. No one has equalled Farrell's sustained delineation of second- and third-generation Americans: women who must live too often as stereotypes within the minds of would-be stereotypes, men who are fans and outsiders in their adopted land, incarnations of social anxiety.

With Farrell's death, we have lost our finest literary perspective on the meaning of assimilation and ambition in American life, and a writer uniquely and admirably free from that most malignant form of cultural life: audience dependency. Farrell was always ready to fulminate about the critics' neglect and misunderstanding of him, but in the last analysis, he wrote for himself. Writing for Farrell was only the postponement of the inevitable, a definition that covers most of life as Farrell portrays it that admits what it postpones, and thus genuinely *happens*. For Farrell, writing was still a synonym for self-sufficiency; and this was the most radical self-definition possible to one who believed that America was becoming a nation of consumers and spectators. We possess, as he meant us to, his example and his books. Farrell's work constitutes the last important experiment to date in American literature with what can be viewed as deliberately unedited material. The malice he drew from censors and critics was out of proportion to the boldness, or the awkwardness, of his enterprise. The censorship battle is over; the critical one has barely begun. Others will honor James Farrell; they will read and sort and care for his works if we do not.

Ann Douglas. *Dissent*. Spring, 1980, p. 216

Reading [James T.] Farrell's novels, one is always struck by the persistence of their themes. The making of a self within the story of America as he knew it depends, of course, upon the self he wrote about and the *Americas* he knew. Chicago and New York? Perhaps the obsession he had for his subject and theses should remind us of what used to be called the obligations of the novelist. His insistence upon reinterpreting the past from his changing present circumstances (and what he believed were changing national occasions as well) is part of his distinct perspective. Yet Farrell's major works, and even his later ones that are embarrassing palimpsests to an apparently uncapturable past, transcend their minute fidelity to an area and age of the city. They remain anatomies of freedom made possible by the city itself: Farrell's aspiration that a rational, democratic urban life is shared human history and a commitment to face the contingency of experience.

Farrell's allegiances to the naturalism of [George Herbert] Mead and [John] Dewey, and his exploration of urban ecology could have made his writing more arid and even less contemporaneous. After the Second World War, what novelist acknowledged these thinkers as shaping the literary imagination? In an age in which the concepts of alienation and dread guided American letters, Farrell's intellectual heritage seemed out of place and old-fashioned. Yet he would not turn away from his hope for the democratic community. He did not invert, as did many postwar writers, the liberal, communalizing nature of the city to produce new fables of alienation.

Judging from his critical discussions of [Lev] Tolstoy, of [Theodore] Dreiser, of [Fyodor] Dostoevsky, and of realism,

Farrell would have been at home with a distinctly nineteenth-century audience, one concerned with having the novelist dramatize a new subject or idea. And for him, this subject was, of course, the city as he understood it. His attention to the mundane and seemingly pedestrian is his presentation of how the self grows within the city. His fiction insists that his readers understand this often tedious portraiture as a clue to their own individuality and its *pasts*. In this ethical sense, he is akin to the writers he admired.

Lewis F. Fried. *Makers of the City* (Amherst: Univ. of Massachusetts Pr., 1990), pp. 156–57

BIBLIOGRAPHY
Young Lonigan, 1932 (n); *Gas-House McGinty*, 1933 (n); *The Young Manhood of Studs Lonigan*, 1934 (n); *Calico Shoes*, 1934 (s); *Judgment Day*, 1935 (n); *Studs Lonigan (Young Lonigan, The Young Manhood of Studs Lonigan, Judgment Day)*, 1935 (n); *Guillotine Party*, 1935 (s); *A World I Never Made*, 1936 (n); *Can All This Grandeur Perish?* 1937 (s); *The Short Stories of James T. Farrell*, 1937; *No Star Is Lost*, 1938 (n); *Tommy Gallagher's Crusade*, 1939 (n); *Father and Son*, 1940 (n); *Ellen Rogers*, 1941 (n); *$1000 a Week*, 1942 (s); *My Days of Anger*, 1943 (n); *Fifteen Selected Short Stories*, 1943; *To Whom It May Concern*, 1944 (s); *The League of Frightened Philistines*, 1945 (c); *Bernard Clare*, 1946 (n) (republished as *Bernard Carr*); *When Boyhood Dreams Come True*, 1946 (s); *Literature and Morality*, 1947 (c); *The Life Adventurous*, 1947 (s); *The Road Between*, 1949 (n); *An American Dream Girl*, 1950 (s); *This Man and This Woman*, 1951 (n); *Yet Other Waters*, 1952 (n); *The Face of Time*, 1953 (n); *Reflections at Fifty*, 1954 (e); *French Girls Are Vicious*, 1955 (s); *An Omnibus of Short Stories*, 1956; *My Baseball Diary*, 1957 (e); *A Dangerous Woman*, 1957 (s); *Saturday Night*, 1958 (s); *It Has Come to Pass*, 1958 (t); *Short Stories*, 1961 (coll); *The Silence of History*, 1963 (n); *What Time Collects*, 1964 (n); *Selected Essays*, 1964; *Collected Poems*, 1965; *Lonely for the Future*, 1966 (n); *When Time Was Born*, 1966 (p); *A Brand New Life*, 1968 (n); *The Dunne Family*, 1976 (n); *Literary Essays, 1954–1974*, 1976; *Olive and Mary Anne*, 1977 (s); *The Death of Nora Ryan*, 1978 (n); *Eight Short, Short Stories and Sketches*, 1981; *On Irish Themes*, 1982 (e); *Sam Holman*, 1983 (n); *Hearing out James T. Farrell: Selected Lectures*, 1985; *A Note on Literary Criticism*, 1992; *Chicago Stories*, 1998

FAST, Howard (1914–)

Place in the City is an astonishing novel for a boy of twenty three to have written; but it is astonishing not because it is so good, for most of it is not good at all, but because it is so exasperatingly soft. . . . Despite the superficial toughness the book is really a study in innocence, full of garlands and tears and sighs, and there are passages, in fact, where it reads like a cross between Fannie Hurst and Sherwood Anderson. . . . Mr. Fast has talent and that talent bubbles in this book; but he has not learned that second-hand pathos is the easy refuge of second-hand thoughts.

Alfred Kazin. *New York Times Book Section*. Aug. 8, 1937. p. 7

Mr. Fast writes with a catch in his breath and sometimes brings tears to his own eyes instead of the readers'. Sometimes his words are less an echo of history than they are of Hemingway. . . . Sometimes he takes his characters from the same casting agencies that are used by other historical novelists. . . . If his book does not belong to the history of American literature, at least it will be important in the history of the popular mind.

Malcolm Cowley. *New Republic*. Aug. 17, 1942. p. 203

Once again Howard Fast has taken a figure out of American history and by the intensity of his emotional sympathy and intellectual respect had made him into a living man. Just as in *The Unvanquished* George Washington became under Mr. Fast's austerely glowing art an individual of flesh and blood, beset by doubts and fears of personal inadequacy in the role he had to play, so does Thomas Paine in the novel *Citizen Tom Paine* become a creature known and knowable in his moments of grandeur and his moments of degradation. . . . Mr. Fast's story of this unique character in history is a brilliant piece of fictional biography.

Rose Feld. *New York Herald Tribune Book Section*. April 25, 1943. p. 3

When a writer of historical fiction is in top form he somehow can suggest that he does not merely re-create the past but rather that he lives there and is reporting on the life around him. Sometimes the author of *Citizen Tom Paine* and *Freedom Road* does this . . . when he is writing well and effectively, in a minor key, and you follow along with him and belong to the world he evokes. . . . His gift in his best work is for a certain reticence—and this is no negative virtue in the historical school, many of whose practitioners would dazzle you by piling up of theatrical "props" and are concerned with character only secondarily, if at all.

John K. Hutchens. *New York Times Book Section*. Apr. 8, 1945. p. 6

In half a dozen novels this popular author has dealt with various critical periods in the American past and the last three of his books—*Citizen Tom Paine*, *Freedom Road*, and now *The American*—fit the same pattern. A society full of class tyranny, economic exploitation and political corruption; a proletariat, dumb, yearning, struggling, that plainly waits for a great leader; a hero who rises to struggle against the entrenched forces of Mammon and the dead weight of middle-class complacency; a defeat that gloriously points the way to future victories—this is the general scheme that Mr. Fast uses.

Allan Nevins. *New York Times Book Section*. July 21, 1946. p. 4

In the writing career of Howard Fast we trace the unusually rapid decline of a pleasant fictional talent into dull political servitude. . . . His eye (has) been ever more tightly shutting itself to the kind of truth with which fiction is properly concerned, his heart increasingly hardening under the strain of pumping such a steady stream of practical benevolences until now . . . all that remains of any original creative gift is some kind of crude energy of intention, a shallow but complex urge to pedagogic power. Mr. Fast has come of literary age in a period in which to be a radical or even a liberal is to feel no need to smile when one says patriotism.

> Diana Trilling *The Nation*. Aug. 3, 1946. p. 134

Howard Fast is a historical novelist with a difference. He has always shunned the standard ingredients of that art—sex, saber, and swash-buckling—and he has never permitted the drama on the stage to be obscured by the opulence of the setting. Nor has he tried to retell our history or ancient legends with our modern vision, pouring in (as Thomas Mann has done in the Joseph cycle) the intellectual resources of the twentieth century. Rather has he always been fascinated by the spectacle of those who either singly or in groups gave their powers and their lives for a cause, for the extension of human dignity and for what is perhaps the greatest of all rights, the right to be let alone.

> Thomas Lask. *New York Times Book Section*. Oct. 10, 1948. p. 4

Fast was long considered to be a diabolical Communist, hardly even human; now, as he presents himself as a disillusioned idealist, he seems sincere and very human. If we trust his motive and listen to what he has to say, we must grant his idealism and humanity even while a Communist. . . . It is far better when a man like Fast leaves his party for the reasons he did than because of fear or other opportunistic reasons.

> Paul Knopf. *New York Times Magazine*. June 30, 1957. p. 2

BIBLIOGRAPHY

Two Valleys, 1933 (n); *Strange Yesterday*, 1934 (n); *Place in the City*, 1937 (n); *Conceived in Liberty*, 1939 (n); *The Last Frontier*, 1941 (n); *Haym Solomon*, 1941 (juv); *The Unvanquished*, 1942 (n); *Goethals and the Panama Canal*, 1942 (juv); *Citizen Tom Paine*, 1943 (n); *Freedom Road*, 1944 (n); *Patrick Henry and the Frigate's Keel*, 1945 (s); *The American*, 1946 (n); *Clarkton*, 1947 (n); *The Children*, 1947 (n); *My Glorious Brothers*, 1948 (n); *Departure*, 1949 (s); *The Proud and the Free*, 1950 (n); *Literature and Reality*, 1950 (c); *Spartacus*, 1951 (n); *Peekskill, USA*, 1951 (j); *The Passion of Sacco and Vanzetti*, 1953 (n); *Silas Timberman*, 1954 (n); *The Last Supper*, 1955 (s); *The Story of Lola Gregg*, 1956 (n); *The Naked God*, 1957 (e); *Moses, Prince of Egypt*, 1958 (n); *The Winston Affair*, 1959 (n); *The Howard Fast Reader*, 1960 (n, s); (as E. V. Cunningham) *Sylvia*, 1960 (n); *April Morning*, 1961 (n); *The Edge of Tomorrow*, 1961 (s); *Power*, 1962 (n); (as E. V. Cunningham) *Phyllis*, 1962 (n); (as E. V. Cunningham) *Alice*, 1963 (n); (as E. V. Cunningham) *Shirley*, 1963 (n); *Agrippa's Daughter* 1964 (n); *The Hill*, 1964 (scrp); (as E. V. Cunningham) *Lydia*, 1964 (n); (as E. V. Cunningham) *Penelope*, 1965 (n); (as E. V. Cunningham) *Helen*, 1966 (n); *Torquemada*, 1966 (n); (as E. V. Cunningham) *Margie*, 1966 (n); (as E. V. Cunningham) *Sally*, 1967 (n); *The Hunter and the Trap*, 1967 (n); *The Jews*, 1968 (h); *The General Zapped an Angel: New Stories of Fantasy and Science Fiction*, 1970; *The Crossing*, 1971 (n); *The Hessian*, 1972 (n); *A Touch of Infinity: Thirteen New Stories of Fantasy and Science Fiction*, 1973; *Time and the Riddle: Thirty-One Zen Stories*, 1975; *The Art of Zen Meditation*, 1977 (e); *The Immigrants*, 1977 (n); *Second Generation*, 1978 (n); *The Establishment*, 1979 (n); *Departure, and Other Stories*, 1980; *The Legacy*, 1981 (n); *Max*, 1982 (n); *The Outsider*, 1984 (n); *The Immigrant's Daughter*, 1985 (n); *Citizen Tom Paine: A Play in Two Acts*, 1986; *The Dinner Party*, 1987 (n); *The Call of Fife and Drum: Three Novels of the Revolution*, 1987; *The Pledge*, 1988 (n); *The Confession of Joe Cullen*, 1989 (n); *Being Red*, 1990 (m); *The Novelist: A Romantic Portrait of Jane Austen*, 1992 (b); *War and Peace: Observations on Our Times*, 1993 (r); *The Trial of Abigail Goodman*, 1993 (n); *Seven Days in June: A Novel of the American Revolution*, 1994; *The Bridge Builder's Story*, 1995 (n); *An Independent Woman*, 1997 (n)

FAULKNER, William (1897–1962)

Faulkner seems to me to be melodramatic, distinctly. All the skies are inky black. He deals in horror as in a cherished material. Coincidence, what he would call "fate," does not stand on ceremony, or seek to cover itself in any fussy "realistic" plausibility, with him. . . . A man like William Faulkner discovers fatalism, or whatever you like to call it: it at once gives his characters something to live for—namely a great deal of undeserved tribulation culminating in *a violent death*. That simplifies the plot enormously—it is, in fact, the great "classical" simplification, banishing expectation.

> Wyndham Lewis. *Men without Art* (Cassell). 1934. pp. 54–5

As a thinker, as a participant in the communal myth of the South's tradition and decline, Faulkner was curiously dull, furiously commonplace, and often meaningless, suggesting some ambiguous irresponsibility and exasperated sullenness of mind, some distant atrophy of indifference. Technically he soon proved himself almost inordinately subtle and ambitious, the one modern American novelist whose devotion to form has earned him a place among the great experimentalists in modern poetry. Yet this remarkable imaginative energy, so lividly and almost painfully impressed upon all his work, did not spring from a conscious and procreative criticism of society or conduct or tradition, from some absolute knowledge; it was the expression of that psychic tension in Faulkner . . . which, as his almost monstrous overwriting proves, was a psychological tic, a need to invest everything he wrote with a wild, exhilarated, and disproportionate intensity—an intensity that was brilliant and devastatingly inconclusive in its energy, but seemed to come from nowhere.

> Alfred Kazin. *On Native Grounds* (Reynal). 1942. pp. 456–7

Faulkner believes that individual responsibility is the most important goal for man. Here is his positive answer to his own negative despair. . . . Thoreau based his personal individualism upon his tremendous love of nature. In Faulkner the love of nature is replaced by the love of the land. How much one would want to distinguish between land and nature I don't know. Basically the only difference is . . . the transcendental ideas in Thoreau's concept of nature. . . . Instead of having Thoreau's leaven of transcendentalism, he has Hawthorne's leaven of the brotherhood of man. Man must love the land that God has supplied to him for his well-being. Through the intimate association with the land, man acquires a sense of loyalty to his family, his immediate social environment, and the all-encompassing land itself. Loyalties, as with so much of man's activities, are governed by what is inherited from the past. By accepting these loyalties and the force of the past, man develops his individuality—the end for which all the other things of man's existence are means.

Ward L. Miner. *The World of William Faulkner* (Duke). 1952. pp. 153–4

Faulkner had what (giving up the attempt to define it more closely) we call genius. It is what Herman Melville had when he wrote *Moby Dick* and rarely manifested thereafter. We know that genius seldom lasts, but we are always saddened when it goes.

On the other hand, if something has been lost (in *The Mansion*), something has been gained. In his note Faulkner says that "the author has learned, he believes, more about the human heart and its dilemma than he knew thirty-four years ago." Indeed he has. He has learned, for one thing, to respect deeply the human capacity for sheer endurance. He has also acquired compassion. . . . The Snopeses, it turns out, are not personifications of greed or anything of the sort; they are poor sons of bitches like the rest of us.

Granville Hicks. *Saturday Review*. Nov. 14, 1959. p. 21

Faulkner is right in assuming that the hope in man's will to endure and prevail has been the subject of his fiction all along; but this will is variously represented, and the degree and quality of context in which we see it vary considerably from the beginning of his career to the present. He moves from what is almost a total lack of awareness to a vague and fleeting insight into human beings—to the point where the meaning of existence is not only seen but overtly defined. Throughout this progress, however, there are many uncertainties which upset the calculation, and his characters are frequently seen missing their chances and blundering badly despite their sense of dedication. This is one among many reasons for the value of Faulkner's work; it appears an endless variety of new experiments in the means to express not only man's worth but the elaborate stratagems he is guilty of using to conceal it.

Frederick J. Hoffman. *William Faulkner* (Twayne). 1961. pp. 117–8

The European reader finds something uniquely American in Faulkner, and obviously no European could have written his books; the few European commentators that I have read seem to me to glorify William Faulkner in a provincial American (or Southern) vacuum. I believe that as his personality fades from view he will be recognized as one of the great craftsmen of the art of fiction which Ford Madox Ford called the Impressionistic Novel. From Stendhal through Flaubert and Joyce there is a direct line to Faulkner, and it is not a mere question of influence. Faulkner's great subject, as it was Flaubert's and Proust's, is passive suffering, the victim being destroyed either by society or by dark forces within himself.

Faulkner is one of the great examples of the international school of fiction which for more than a century has reversed the Aristotelian doctrine that tragedy is an action, not a quality.

Allen Tate. *Sewanee Review*. Winter, 1963. p. 162

To the neophyte Faulkner reader, the prose may seem a continual flow of words that obscures the story action rather than developing it. The difficulties should not be minimized. The diction, the syntax, seem designed to obfuscate, not communicate. Faulkner sometimes deliberately withholds important details, and the narrators frequently refer to people or events that the reader will not learn about until much later, making the style seem even more opaque than it actually is. And the long sentences are difficult to follow, with clauses that proliferate, developing not from the main subject or verb of the sentence, but growing out of preceding clauses. As a result, the main thought is often lost in the mass of amplifying or qualifying ideas. Antecedents of personal pronouns are frequently not clear. Faulkner's style does not provide relaxing reading, but forces the reader to participate in the search for understanding and truth. . . . Had Faulkner been a U. S. senator, his speeches would have been squarely in the tradition of Southern oratory. Some of his sentences sound almost like selected passages from a filibuster. Rather than run the risk of interruption and lose the floor, he does not pause; he rolls on, using all the rhetorical devices of the speechmaker: colorful, grandiloquent and emotive words, repetition, parallel structure, a series of negative clauses preceding a positive, delayed climax.

Edmund L. Volpe. *A Reader's Guide to William Faulkner* (Farrar, Straus). 1963. pp. 38–9

If Faulkner feels the past as the repository of great images of human effort and integrity, he also sees it as the source of a dynamic evil. If he is aware of the romantic pull of the past, he is also aware that submission to romance of the past is a form of death. If he finds in modernity a violation of the dream of the "communal anonymity of brotherhood," of nature, and of honor, he does not see it as the barred end of history; it is also the instant in which action is possible, with a choice between action as "doom" from the past and action as affirmation. If the Flems and the Jasons drive hard to define a dehumanized future, there are the Dilseys and the Ratliffs who see the future as part of the vital human continuity. In other words, Faulkner's dialectic of time is inclusive, dynamic—and painful.

Robert Penn Warren. *Southern Review*. Summer, 1965. p. 526

And Faulkner himself: did he find the right answers to his problems in life and in the continued production of his works? There are no completely right answers. It had better be said that his later books, in general, had not the freshness and power of the early ones. That is the common fate of imaginative writers (except for a few poets); some original force goes out of them. The books they write after the age of fifty most often lose in genius what they may possibly gain in talent.

Faulkner lost substantially less than others. Though none of his later books was on a level with *The Sound and the Fury* or *Go*

Down, Moses, none of them made concessions to other people's tastes. One hears a person speaking in each of them, not an institution, and a person with reserves of power who may surprise us on any page. Some of Faulkner's best writing is in passages of *Requiem for a Nun*, and *Intruder in the Dust*, and especially—almost at the end—in the Mink Snopes chapters of *The Mansion*. In retrospect I should judge that he solved the problem of keeping alive his genius better than any other American novelist of our century.

Malcolm Cowley. *Saturday Review*. June 11, 1966. p. 26

To speak of greatness with regard to one's contemporaries is dangerous. But if there are any American novels of the present century which may be called great, which bear comparison—serious if not favorable—with the achievements of twentieth-century European literature, then surely *The Sound and the Fury* is among them. It is one of the three or four American works of prose fiction written since the turn of the century in which the impact of tragedy is felt and sustained. Seized by his materials, Faulkner keeps, for once, within his esthetic means, rarely trying to say more than he can or needs to. *The Sound and the Fury* is the one novel in which his vision and technique are almost in complete harmony, and the vision itself whole and major. Whether taken as a study of the potential for human self-destruction, or as a rendering of the social disorder particular to our time, the novel projects a radical image of man against the wall. Embodied and justified, this is an image of great writing.

Irving Howe. *William Faulkner* (Random). 1952. pp. 126–7

If Faulkner was "a perfect case of split personality," it was not as he intended; Faulkner the writer and Faulkner the "denizen of the world" were never very far apart. His "polar" imagination empathized with the Negro and liberal as he criticized the segregationist, with the Southerner as he criticized the Negro and liberal, maintaining all too often, instead of a firm middle-of-the-road position, a mere political schizophrenia. Faulkner was not the hero who can successfully say, "This stinks and I'm going to do something about it"—he was no Chick Mallison or Nancy Mannigoe, daring existential action in the face of blind unreason and failed communication. He was not even an Isaac McCaslin, swearing "at least I will not participate in it myself." He was still very much the author of *Go Down, Moses* who found Isaac's stand painfully ambivalent; the author of *Intruder in the Dust* and *Requiem for a Nun* unable to portray heroism except in terms of fantasy and sensationalism. The same endowments which insured his success as a novelist insured his failure as a political voice.

Walter Taylor. *Southern Review*. Fall, 1970. p. 1092

In his prefatory note to *The Mansion* Faulkner comments that "'living' is motion, and 'motion' is change and alteration and therefore the only alternative to motion is un-motion, stasis, death." Man must act conditionally, must be adaptive. In the language of "The Bear," man must examine the Grecian urn, acknowledge the truth and beauty of its depictions, and then transcend the static moments captured there. He cannot transport himself into a bygone frieze, into an historic moment like the past

hunt for Old Ben or into an artistic design like the Nazarene of messianic teaching. It is important that Old Ben in death "almost resembled a piece of statuary" for he resembles both beauty and non-life. Any fixed moment or grand design is contrived, a kind of death; life for Faulkner is in becoming rather than being; ripeness is all. That is why truth for Faulkner embodies intuition as well as intellect and why conceptualization must ultimately give way to the primacy of the heart. . . . Ike McCaslin illustrates that for Faulkner heroism lies not in the vision of a new Canaan nor even in the sacrifice of a corrupted heritage, but in an ability to suffer, in Ike's remarkable capacity to grieve.

Arthur F. Kinney. *Southern Review*. Fall, 1970. p. 1124

In *Light in August* Faulkner had presented individuals who were victimized by history largely without knowing it. But in *Absalom, Absalom!* he advances to a much more complex presentation of history. Before, history had been treated as a static, simple, essentially known quality which finally weighted down its unalert human vehicle. Now, however, history becomes a dynamic, highly volatile quality that presents first an aspect of startling clarity, then an aspect of shadowed obscurity, teasing and confusing the mind it penetrates while at the same time demanding that the mind subdue it. . . . It is the confrontation that is significant in the novel; neither the legend of Thomas Sutpen, which is really a capsule history of the South, nor the meager account of Quentin Compson hearing and then telling the story of Thomas Sutpen provides the final significance of the work; it is the rendering of the process of historical interaction between myth and recipient, a process now vivid and dramatic, now obscure and ambiguous, which causes many readers to regard the novel as Faulkner's best.

Lewis A. Lawson in *The Politics of Twentieth-Century Novelists*, edited by George A. Panichas (Hawthorn). 1971. pp. 288–9

It appears that in his last two novels Faulkner's comedy has lost its satiric edge. His miser, Flem Snopes, was murdered almost gratuitously in *The Mansion*, long after he had been turned from an incarnation of Mammon into the country boy who made good. It is a measure of Faulkner's final reconciliation to human frailty that the most apt exemplars of Snopesism we can find in *The Reivers* are a country farmer who plows mudholes in the Memphis road so that he can use his mule team to pull out mired automobiles for a fee, and a depraved little boy, Otis—Ned calls him "Whistle-britches"—whose greatest feat is to steal the gold tooth from a sleeping Negro maid in a whorehouse. It's all good fun, but for great satiric comedy, with a Swiftian bite and Rabelaisian pungency, we must still turn back to *The Hamlet*, surely one of the great comic creations of our time. In it Faulkner proved himself a master of the comic mode, as *Absalom, Absalom!* had proved him a master of the tragic.

Robert D. Jacobs in *The Comic Imagination in American Literature*, edited by Louis D. Rubin, Jr. (Rutgers). 1973. p. 318

[Faulkner] had been advised . . . by his mentor Sherwood Anderson, to write about his own Mississippi, and in 1926 he set out to do that. He wrote *Flags in the Dust*, but the finished manuscript was rejected left and right. Finally Harcourt Brace agreed to publish it on the condition that it be severely cut, a task Faulkner could not bring himself to do; the cuts were made by his agent, Ben Wasson, and the novel was published as *Sartoris*. Faulkner's affection for the original never faded, however, and he preserved the manuscript and typescript; we have it now in an edition edited by Douglas Day and, though he is credited only in the introduction, Albert Erskine.

Obviously *Flags in the Dust* will be of great value to Faulkner scholars (though presumably many of them have already had access to the manuscript), but the book is of broader value. It offers the opportunity to observe, by comparing it with *Sartoris*, what happens to a manuscript when it comes into the hands of an intelligent and demanding editor. Of far more importance, *Flags in the Dust*, because it is much more intricate than *Sartoris*, makes clear that everything that would engage Faulkner for three and a half decades had formed in his imagination at the outset.

Jonathan Yardley. *New Republic.* Sept. 8, 1973. p. 32

Passages of [Faulkner's] prose bubble up in [Joseph Blotner's biography] to frighten and amaze us . . . the sonorous opening chords of *Absalom, Absalom!*, for instance, with their impressive adjectival orchestration, the careful fastening of consciousness to its object, and Faulkner's characteristically increasing rhetorical beat, a precise local observation blown through a metaphor like a herald announcing . . . what? always . . . the palpable appearance of Time. . . .

It is as if remembered things themselves had memories, as if matter *were* memory. The muscles that hoed the garden remember the moves they made. To *see into*—for Faulkner—is to *think back*. . . .

He was rarely among people who understood his achievement, not that this might have lifted his loneliness very much (solitude was the space of more than his imagination), and the needs, sensations, and feelings—the pity, the pure fury—which one time had created those incredible lengths of language, those new and powerful forms, became themselves rhetorical habits, last rites, passionless gestures of passion. . . .

William Gass. *New York Review of Books.* June 27, 1974. pp. 4–5

I interpret Faulkner to be saying that time does not exist apart from the consciousness of some human being. Apart from that stream of living consciousness, time is merely an abstraction. Thus, as *actually experienced*, time has little to do with the time that is measured off by the ticking of a chronometer. Such a conception of time, however, did not impel Faulkner to destroy his own watch as Quentin Compson did (in *The Sound and the Fury*). Though clock time, as an abstraction, might be deemed to be in some sense unreal, Faulkner, like Henri Bergson himself, conceded that clock-and-calendar time had its uses and that no human life of the slightest complexity could get along without constant reference to it. . . .

To come at the problem from another direction: in spite of Faulkner's acceptance of Bergson's conception of time as fluid and continuous (time as "duration"), it is hard to think of a novelist who exceeds Faulkner in his careful attention to the details of clock time and calendar time. I am thinking here particularly of the chronology of his novels. Each conforms not only to a generally consistent time scheme; the details of the time scheme are often very precise. Indeed, it is a revelation to go through a Faulkner novel, giving special attention to its chronology, and so discover how many unobtrusive but specific time-clues Faulkner has planted. Though such clues often do not call attention to themselves, yet when noted and put together, the chronology that they plot is much too consistent to be unpurposed. Even if Faulkner did not mean for every reader to be aware of these buried chronologies, we may be sure that he was himself in command of the sequence of events. . . .

To sum up, though Bergson may have confirmed some of Faulkner's notions about time and about the ways in which human beings can know reality, and though Bergson may have stimulated Faulkner to experiment with the verbal presentation of motion and action, I find little in Faulkner's narrative treatment that can be certainly attributed to Bergson's influence. Many of Faulkner's techniques turn out to be simply skillful and imaginative adaptations of traditional narrative methods, but if one were to specify particular influences it would not be Bergson's so much as Conrad's, the early Eliot's, and Joyce's. Whatever Faulkner's indebtedness, his handling of time reached perhaps its most brilliant achievement in *Absalom, Absalom!*

Cleanth Brooks. *William Faulkner: Toward Yoknapatawpha and Beyond* (Yale Univ. Pr., 1978), pp. 254, 258, 264–65

Like Thomas Hardy's Wessex, William Faulkner's Yoknapatawpha County originated in the imagination of a young writer reared in a provincial community. In both instances a youthful mind, endowed with literary genius, discovered that the small, remote world of his nativity embodied the major experience of modern Western civilization: the world historical differentiation of a novel society of history and science from a sacramental order of myth and tradition. In either case a youthful writer entered into the knowledge of this phenomenon through an unacademic but intense and sustained process of reading in varied literary and philosophical works; and in either case, during the struggles of his self-education, a youthful writer began to conceive of himself as a member of the cosmopolitan realm of poets and literary prophets that for five hundred years or more has sought to give moral and spiritual guidance to the long process of societal differentiation in Western civilization. . . .

Implied in Faulkner's serene, retrospective vision of Yoknapatawpha as a transcendent autonomy of the artist is all the pathos of the literary myth of modern history—of the drama of the artist and the historical differentiation of the self. The vision reveals what it denies: the unremitting tension between self and history. Yoknapatawpha is in truth no sublimation of the actual but the embodiment of the profoundest reality: the terrifying modern internalization of history—which in its ineffable and pervasive dominion comprises man and nature, God, world, and universe—in the self. Faulkner hid the truth of Yoknapatawpha from himself at times, particularly in his later career. But he acknowledged it all the same—in the term that he used to describe Yoknapatawpha: "my apocryphal county." Sometimes he called the Yoknapatawpha stories "my apocrypha." He meant more than "my fictions." He meant my stories in which there are "hidden things," and notable among the things he hid in the tales is the story of the artist and his struggle against modern history. In this struggle Faulkner followed the defiant Joycean dream of sacramentalizing the role of the artist by means of grace self-bestowed. But Faulkner knew, perhaps more surely than Joyce knew, that dreaming his biography was only a part of his being as a creature of history. He understood this irony as an American, and especially as a southerner. He grasped it so well that in his final novel, *The Reivers*, subtitled *A Reminiscence*, though trying not to do so, he virtually surrenders to the pathos of history: creating a Yoknapatawpha existing neither in the *was* of Quentin Compson nor in the *is* of Gavin Stevens but in a mingled *is-was* that, transcending all tense, is yet the truest tense for Americans, the tense of nostalgia—the tense Americans use when they speak of America as "home sweet home," the place beyond all grief and sorrow.

Lewis P. Simpson. In *The American South: Portrait of a Culture*, ed. Louis B. Rubin, Jr. (Louisiana State Univ. Pr., 1980), pp. 227, 244

Faulkner's fondness for the tall tale or anecdote, humorous or otherwise, has a bearing upon the form of his fiction. Throughout his fiction, the basis of his art is the single episode. As a result, his books seem to divide into brilliant but very loosely unified stories at times ingeniously yoked together. For example, after reading *The Sound and the Fury*, the reader is likely to remember the work not as a single story but as at least four separate stories relating to the Compson family. Such works as *Sartoris*, *Sanctuary*, *Light in August*, and *Absalom, Absalom!* similarly contain multiple plots, while there is serious question if *The Unvanquished*, *The Hamlet*, and *Go Down, Moses* may not be more properly called volumes of short stories than novels. In Faulkner's great outpouring of superb fiction during the 1930s, perhaps only *As I Lay Dying* was conceived and written as a single story. . . .

The perspective of literary history today helps Faulkner's reader to grasp the implications of his work far more clearly than they could have been understood in the author's lifetime. Presently, Faulkner's fiction seems more a continuation or logical development from the American nineteenth century than the outpouring of a radical innovator or experimenter. Currently, as in the future his contribution to American literature rests not so much upon his ideas about artistic form, his narrative skills, the devices of his fiction, or even his stylistic accomplishments—important though these matters are—as it does upon the intensity and sincerity with which he has depicted the complexities of human experience measured by the progression of history. No other writer since Henry James has identified so directly and expressed so forcefully as Faulkner the truths that govern man's success or failure in right living.

Like many other Southerners of the 1930s, Faulkner held the Southern economic system based upon tenant farming and sharecropping, legacies of the Civil War and its aftermath, responsible for much of the unhappiness and poverty of the South. When administered by dishonest and unscrupulous landowners, the "economic edifice" locked both races into bondage to the land, depressed their living standards, and stifled ambition. Although nominally free, the Negroes (and poor whites) were still bound in a vicious round of debt from which they might never be free. Although Faulkner had great admiration for the endurance and strength of the Negro race, in the 1930s, the decade of the Great Depression, he saw little evidence of immediate change in their prospects for the better.

Harsh and oppressive as the economic system of the South seemed to him and regardless of his awareness of the depths of

man's folly and his propensity for evil, Faulkner yet asserted that man could "prevail." Like millions of his countrymen, past and present, Faulkner believed in the possibility of reform and progress. One has only to consider the lives of Jason Compson, Temple Drake, Gail Hightower, Thomas Sutpen, Flem Snopes, and others to understand that Faulkner believed that man's greatest enemy lay within himself and that man must reform himself from within before he can defeat those forces that undermine the quality of his life. Man's pride, hate, self-interest, greed, and willingness to purchase material possessions at the cost of private integrity inhibit his enjoyment of the good life. Insofar as he can, man must replace these traits with the virtues Faulkner names in his Nobel Prize Speech of Acceptance, "the courage and honor and hope and pride and compassion and pity and sacrifice which have been the glory of his past." To Faulkner, these are the verities of human experience. More and more, as time passes, Faulkner emerges as an advocate of traditional humanistic values. At the heart of Yoknapatawpha lies Faulkner's vision of man in a moral universe.

John Pilkington. *The Heart of Yoknapatawpha* (Univ. Pr. of Mississippi, 1981), pp. 293, 295–97

The problem of trying to come to terms with [William] Faulkner's female characters has caused a number of critics to seek categories by which to analyze them. Miller finds two categories: earth mothers and ghosts. Kerr concludes that Faulkner's rejection of the southern ideal or what she calls southern gyneolatry accounts for his two attitudes toward women: rejection of those who personify it and sympathy for those who rebel against it or live naturally outside it. Jackson's categories are "demon-nun and angel-witch."

Obviously, the question of how Faulkner viewed women will not be answered by arriving at any number of categories, no matter how useful and interesting those approaches might be. Nor is the type of the indestructible woman meant to be used as a touchstone by which to judge Faulkner's attitude toward all women. The women in his works are diverse and his attitudes toward them are by no means monotypic. The delineation of such a type in his works is meant, among other things, to suggest one way in which the articulated optimism of Faulkner's Nobel Prize speech is communicated in his fiction, to identify a type which personifies one of Faulkner's dominant attitudes toward women and to suggest the similarities between his attitudes and those of two of his distinguished peers [Steinbeck and Hemingway].

The character type of an indestructible woman transcends most categories based on antipathies because of the mythic paradigm that underlies her development. It is also derived from the combination of Faulkner's philosophical primitivism and subjective masculinism, an inability to see woman as anything but a different species. The primitivism in Faulkner concludes that that which is simple and natural will survive; those who are more attuned to life's processes will endure. Woman as *other*, as matter instead of mind, as manifestation of the Earth Goddess instead of the individual being, is organically attuned with the motion of life and thereby more enduring. But this primitive being is also of an earthiness and physicality which may offend the fastidiousness of the more spiritually inclined male. The way Faulkner's indestructible females are often characterized reflects an awe that is born of reaction to their awfulness, in both senses of the word. Traditional morality has nothing to do with it, nor has a sense of what is customarily regarded as normal or abnormal. The characterizations are born of the same kind of fascination and repugnance that one experiences in the presence of many examples of the way that nature insures survival, such as the black widow devouring her mate or larvae feeding off of the bodies of their parents. . . .

Though Faulkner's world is inhabited by men, women, and children, blacks and whites, aristocrats and poor whites, the prevailing perception is that of the white male. The problems of dealing with the past, with race, with the "slings and arrows of outrageous fortune" seem essentially his. Other types may be part of his problem or may have already come to terms with life and thereby serve as models. Women play a significant role in the mythic overstructure that the men are trying to cope with, but large as that role might be it is generally presented by a subjective viewer. Often the parts women play in these tales of sound and fury are primarily assigned on the basis of what Faulkner perceived to be an essential characteristic of their womanhood, their ability to endure and prevail, their indestructibility.

> Mimi Reisel Gladstein. *The Indestructible Woman in Faulkner, Hemingway, and Steinbeck* (Ann Arbor, Mich.: UMI Research Pr., 1986), pp. 38–39, 45

William Faulkner's major novels, written between 1929 and 1942, explored, earlier than most critics did, the systematic paradoxes within the fabric of literary discourse, and exposed, earlier than many Americans, related paradoxes in the institution of American racial segregation, whose statutory divisions began slowly to be dismantled just before Faulkner's death in 1962. In this study, I take up Warren's forty-year-old observation that Faulkner's words scrutinize apparent social polarities, an enterprise that shows conventional oppositions to be a kind of willful linguistic and social error. In Faulkner's novels, "polarity" means racial division, racial segregation, and the mythologies surrounding it, which collectively try to outlaw interracial contiguity, cohabitation, and consanguinity. Faulkner's characters, black and white, live under a body of racial barriers and prohibitions that structure the self-understanding of Yoknapatawpha County. The futility of applying strictly binary categories to human affairs is the main lesson of Faulkner's novels, which dramatize the problematics of division through sensitive white characters such as Quentin Compson, Darl and Addie, and Ike McCaslin. By accident, intelligence, or pure stubbornness, these Faulknerian protagonists reject division, discovering instead those social and psychological margins where merging, opposition's opposite, may exist unassailed. Faulkner's narratives utter a truth of merging across social boundaries that his contemporaries found unspeakable. Faulkner himself set this truth in an elusive, complex discourse of indirection, a literary disfigurement of divisive social figures. . . .

Since figures of division are at the same time social and linguistic, Faulkner's novels, as literary texts, can examine their invention and demise on both thematic and stylistic levels of analysis. Particularly germane to Faulkner's novels as an instance of actual and stylistic merging is the issue of *miscegenation*. The system of racial division elicits the desire for racial mixing or miscegenation, the South's feared, forbidden, denied, yet pervasive release from societal division. Notions such as "white racial purity," aimed at underpinning the economic order, underlie figures of division. Southern society typically and publicly abhorred racial mergings by integration, cohabitation, and miscegenation. Yet Faulkner's narratives repeatedly present a world in which blacks and whites eat, live, and often sleep together, despite written Jim Crow laws and spoken categories of racial differentiation. Faulkner's narratives dismember figures of division at their weakest joint, the "purity" notion that seems the requirement for white supremacist logic. White skin could never be the certain signifier of the absence of "black" blood (white racial purity), because white skin, as Faulkner amply demonstrates, can also signify "mixed" blood.

Faulkner's most compelling protagonists do not seek division, but rather its often nonconventional remedies: miscegenation, incest, Edenic refuge in the Big Woods, or schizoid mental mergings. Absolutisms, facing the test of experience, break down under the pressure of the unsystematic real. Faulkner's major novels—*The Sound and the Fury; As I Lay Dying; Light in August; Absalom, Absalom!; The Hamlet*; and *Go Down, Moses*—primarily concern the white mind and its struggles with the systems of division it has created. The stylistic strangeness of Faulkner's novels is not purely post-Joycean experimentalism, as often suggested, nor even a residue of his infatuation with Romanticism and French symbolism. Instead, Faulkner's narratives are accurate reconstructions and dismantlings of linguistic and social classifications, proving that some extraordinary human beings struggle, against overwhelming odds, to reverse a separation that rhetoric has tried to make into a permanent reality.

> James A. Snead. *Figures of Division: William Faulkner's Major Novels* (New York: Methuen, 1986), pp. ix-x, xiii-xiv

Much has been written about [the early] period in Faulkner's development, about his decadent, dilettantish persona, and about the pervasive influence of the Symbolists on all of his later verse; but not enough attention seems to have been paid to the remarkable imprint left on the *poète manqué*, to the manifestations of this Symbolist apprenticeship in the body of prose fiction comprising Faulkner's major literary contribution. It is both interesting and illuminating to see just how their aesthetics thrive and evolve when transplanted from the exotic realm of French *poésie* to Faulkner's "own little postage stamp of native soil.". . .

Through [Arthur] Symons's [*The Symbolist Movement in Literature*] and the poems themselves Faulkner had full access to the theories and practices of Symbolist aesthetics, the lyrical, elaborate, often synaesthetic verbal imagery designed to evoke and suggest rather than directly state, to capture the mystery and evanescence of experience in language seeking the purity and expressiveness of music. He was a good student. We can see these ideas incorporated in his novelistic style and vision, providing those elements H. E. Richardson refers to in calling Faulkner "a regional writer with a difference." This difference permeates his major work, manifesting itself not only in language but also in content and theme. . . .

Symbolist indirection . . . is much more than a method of handling indelicate matters: the aesthetic of suggestion and intimation is at the very heart of Symbolism; it is the foundation upon which the superstructure of lyricism, symbolism, and synesthesia is built. If any one statement could be called the Symbolist manifesto, it would certainly be Mallarmé's famous dictum: "To name an object . . . is to suppress three-quarters of the enjoyment of the poem . . . to suggest it, there's the dream. The perfect use of this mystery constitutes the symbol; to evoke little by little a mood, or, inversely, to choose an object and to disengage from it a mood, through a series of decipherings.'' If Faulkner did not read Mallarmé's *Oeuvres Completes*, he had a distillation of this aesthetic in Symons's book: ''to name is to destroy, to suggest is to create.'' It is a concept he took to heart. . . .

Intimation places strenuous demands upon the reader, forcing participation in the creative processes. In Faulkner these demands are in parallel layers or strata, ranging from the word and phrase to the long, involved, often periodic sentences to the frequently unresolved conclusions, with the reader forced to decipher and contribute each step of the way. It is this complex interaction that renders the novels so inaccessible yet so ultimately rewarding. Irresolution and paradoxical suspensions of meaning tend to deny or subvert interpretation, but the result is the delegation of hermeneutic responsibility to its rightful province: the individual subjective consciousness. The elusive, subjective nature of truth could arguably be called *the* theme of Faulkner's major work, and it is certainly the central concern of *Absalom, Absalom!*, perhaps his greatest achievement. After hearing various and often contradictory versions of ''truth,'' Quentin and Shreve must create their own, a poetic, mythic truth animated by their individual needs and obsessions. Ultimately, however, it is the reader who must sort out, evaluate, and create the final version—it is the perfect achievement of the Symbolists' desire for direct reader experience.

Alexander Marshall III, ''William Faulkner: The Symbolist Connection.'' *American Literature*. October 1987, pp. 389–90, 400

Faulkner's reputation in this country was created by the academics and literary critics who integrated him into the modernist tradition, who found in his vast, complex, and difficult work the kind of demanding literature that they had been trained to explicate, and who operated in a closed community of enforced conformity where dissent was suppressed and oppositionist literature and criticism were displaced. Given the cultural politics of the Cold War, which worked to eclipse the rebellious tradition of realism/naturalism, there was a general revival of interest in the classic American writers—Hawthorne, Poe, Melville, and James. After 1945, Faulkner quickly became the modernist representative of that tradition, and the quintessential technical and stylistic revolutionary. In short, he was, I believe, perfectly suited to represent the new conservative liberalism and humanitarianism of American democracy. And analogously, Cowley's rediscovery of Faulkner's ''greatness'' was perfectly suited to the prevailing formalist aesthetics of the postwar era which claimed, in part, that literature in its fully realized form was universal and apolitical.

Within a few years of the end of World War II the definition of social responsibility in art was radically transformed. The liberal aesthetics traditionally associated with naturalism and socially conscious literature came to be identified with the ''totalitarianism'' of the Soviet Union and Stalinist politics. Ahistorical art-for-art's-sake formalism was adopted as the aesthetics of postwar America and became redefined as cultural liberalism. Certainly, there were tensions and disagreements within this coalition, but the coalition itself was evidence of the supposed openness and pluralism of American culture.

Once the United States government assumed much of the responsibility for the costs of the Cold War, Faulkner, always the

patriot, was enlisted as a state department cultural ambassador and one of Eisenhower's leaders for the ''People to People'' program. However, much of the intellectual ground-work for this public affirmation of American culture was laid in the period immediately after the war.

In sum, the renewed interest in Faulkner coincided with and was related to the heightened Cold War. The Nobel Prize for Literature, which Faulkner won in 1950, was the keystone of this process. But his reemergence had its origins in the cultural upheaval immediately after the war, which required a great new American novelist to represent the dominance of Western humanist values. Ultimately, Faulkner's work was championed and canonized because his often supremely individualist themes and technically difficult prose served an ideological cause. Unintentionally, he produced a commodity of enormous value as a cultural weapon in the early years of the Cold War.

Lawrence H. Schwartz. *Creating Faulkner's Reputation: The Politics of Modern Literary Criticism* (Knoxville: Univ. of Tennessee Pr., 1988), pp. 202–3, 209–10

What needs to be stressed . . . is that, no matter how massive and inscrutable, the forces we watch at work on [Faulkner's] people are always forces of this world. Whatever his debt to Christianity and his private beliefs, no twentieth-century novelist is in the last analysis less other-worldly than Faulkner; his language presses at the edge of the knowable but never hints at any metaphysical *hinterwelt* beyond the private fantasies or common myths of his characters. We need only to think of his fellow Southerner, Flannery O'Connor, to realize at once how thoroughly secular a writer Faulkner was. Heroism and art were the only possibilities of transcendence he cared about as a novelist, and in his greatest books the stress falls invariably on the limitations and failures of the human mind, not on its powers and achievements. Indeed, nearly all of his work could be read as an illustration of Marx's statement that ''it is not the consciousness of men that determines their existence, but on the contrary their social existence that determines their consciousness.'' Not that Faulkner can be easily fitted into the realist-naturalist tradition and its mechanistic explanation patterns. His involvement with his creatures was far too intense, his feelings about the South, past and present, too much of a passionate love-hate relationship to permit the detached, objective stance of an outside observer, and his ''private cosmos'' is too fiercely idiosyncratic ever to be reduced to a sociological document. Writing the South was Faulkner's way of reading the South, but like the telling of the Sutpen story by Quentin and Shreve in *Absalom, Absalom!* it was always also a vehement imaginative (re)enactment.

Andre Bleikasten. *The Ink of Melancholy: Faulkner's Novels from ''The Sound and the Fury'' to ''Light in August''* (Bloomington: Univ. of Indiana Pr., 1990), pp. 354-55

There are, of course, moments in Faulkner's fiction in which a character or a narrator (and sometimes a narrator that one strongly suspects reproduces a subject position that Faulkner at a certain moment also occupied) says things that are racist or sexist. It would, I think, be more surprising if such moments did not appear in the writing of a white male who grew up in rural Mississippi during the first quarter of the twentieth century. What is striking in Faulkner's fiction of the 1930s is the way it confronts racism and misogyny. And although Faulkner's texts operate in a horizon of misogyny, the alternative communities created by marginal couples in those texts provide alternate narratives for rethinking hegemonic myths of love and bourgeois marriage. At any rate, it is not the job of critics to reproduce the racism or sexism of the texts with which they work but rather to think such issues further. . . .

Despite the power of certain of Faulkner's texts to destabilize cultural polarizations of masculinity and femininity, there are limits to the usefulness of his fiction for feminist thinking. Woman often remains the object of male discourse and of the male voyeuristic gaze. . . . If we wish to speak of a failure of vision in Faulkner's fiction, it might be that, while his narratives reconceptualize masculinity rather thoroughly in figures such as Byron Bunch and Roger Schumann, the partner for this new man is less fully developed because she is still viewed externally. Moreover, in Faulkner's later fiction, his alternative communities seem to shift from heterosocial to homosocial bonds, as the all-male world of the hunting camp or the friendship between Gavin Stevens and V. K. Ratliff suggest. The notion of female bonding as an alternative community seems outside Faulkner's imaginative grasp, so that the later texts are more implicated in a significant aspect of patriarchal ideology (i.e., that it is men who matter); thus any critique of the hegemony after *The Wild Palms* proceeds from well within that same hegemony and is of a piece with Ishmael's whaling ship or Huck Finn's lighting out for the territory to escape feminine culture.

Another limitation is that Faulkner seems unable to conceive of subjectivity's genesis outside recurring Oedipal triangles that privilege the role of the father or father surrogate. Does this limitation, then, make Faulkner's texts hopelessly retrograde? Perhaps we are confronted here with the problem of what we can legitimately expect texts to do. If we wish to think about the role of the mother in the formation of the subject, we undoubtedly do better to turn to Nancy Chodorow than to William Faulkner. But this very weakness—the failure of his texts to explore pre-Symbolic subjectivity—returns us to what is available in Faulkner, namely, a recurring scrutiny of the uses and abuses of patriarchal authority through characters warped by the will of the father.

> John N. Duvall. *Faulkner's Marginal Couple: Invisible, Outlaw, and Unspeakable Communities* (Austin: Univ. of Texas Pr, 1990), pp. 17, 131–32

Operating by extremes permitted Faulkner to suggest the whole range of human experience—the realism modernists sought—while he worked with some fairly stock characters: the Earth Mother, the hot spinster, the prostitute with the heart of gold, the weak-kneed intellectual, the mean half-breed. They are not stereotypes: they present too many surprises for that. Like many modernist characters, conceived out of their underlying form, they are archetypal, with reinforcing quirks and oddities. But the fact that Faulkner animated these lumps of rage and jest under secret wraps suggests that they were shaped by a fierce sentimentality, an expression of unfulfilled longings. Apparently one of Faulkner's engines was a treacherous tenderness toward his characters, glaringly evident in *The Reivers*. To protect himself from his own pathos, he permitted his characters brutal or ludicrous behavior—behavior which he alone (like the Creator) could explain. . . .

When Milton wrote *Paradise Lost*, . . . his edifice was the transformation of all those bits of glass and stone and mortar into a cathedral. So it is with Faulkner's art. Having studied the principles of giving evidence in a trial in equity, he worked out his ironic nine-part structure for *Absalom, Absalom!* Having fully stocked the lumber room of his brain-attic with John and Frazer, he demonstrated that he could fashion every element—word, metaphor, description, and incident—to fit the grand design of *Light in August*.

> Virginia V. James Hlavsa. *Faulkner and the Thoroughly Modern Novel* (Charlottesville: Univ. Pr. of Virginia, 1991), pp. 17–19

Like other writers in the United States during the early twentieth century, Faulkner was an heir less of the dominant culture of the nineteenth century than of its great rebels. Much of the daring, even the headiness, of the assaults that Darwin, Marx, Nietzsche, and Freud—to name only four—mounted against accepted beliefs found expression in the brashness of writers like Faulkner, as they set out to invent literature anew. Faulkner's almost fierce determination to deal with the past on his own terms not only marked him as a rebel; it also shaped his art. Like much modern fiction, his is often pessimistic and violent, even brutal and despairing. He is a poet of deprivation and loss. Affluence and plenty mark his work only in style and imagination. Yet we find other things there: remnants of the good hope of the Lyric Years, which was political as well as aesthetic; the persistence of the exuberance of the twenties, which was experimental as well as escapist; and the difficult hope against hope that sprang to life during the Great Depression, of creating anew an imperfect community, knit together by imperfectly possessed and painfully held memories and by imperfectly shared and practiced values. These things he infused with the same boldness of spirit and moral courage that we see in the striking formal experiments that give his fiction its special place in a great and varied outpouring of innovative, conflicted, and often self-critical expression.

> David L. Minter. *A Cultural History of the American Novel: Henry James to William Faulkner* (Cambridge: Cambridge University Pr., 1994), p. 229

BIBLIOGRAPHY

The Marble Faun, 1924 (p); *Soldiers' Pay*, 1926 (n); *Mosquitos*, 1927 (n); *Sartoris*, 1929 (n); *The Sound and the Fury*, 1929 (n); *As I Lay Dying*, 1930 (n); *Sanctuary*, 1931 (n); *These Thirteen*, 1931 (s); *Salmagundi*, 1932 (e, p); *Light in August*, 1932 (n); *A Green Bough*, 1933 (p); *Doctor Martino and Other Stories*, 1934; *Pylon*, 1935 (n); *Absalom, Absalom!*, 1936 (n); *The Unvanquished*, 1938 (n); *The Wild Palms*, 1939 (n); *The Hamlet*, 1940 (n); *Go Down, Moses and Other Stories*, 1942 (s, also *The Bear*, n); *The Portable Faulkner*, 1946; *Intruder in the Dust*, 1948 (n); *Knight's Gambit*, 1949 (n); *Collected Stories*, 1950; *Requiem for a Nun*, 1951 (n); *Requiem for a Nun*, 1951 (d); *A Fable*, 1954 (n); *The Faulkner Reader*, 1954; *Big Woods*, 1955 (s); *Faulkner at Nagano*, 1956 (interviews); *The Town*, 1957 (n); *New Orleans Sketches*, 1958 (sk); *The Mansion*, 1959 (n); *Faulkner in the University*, 1959 (i); *The Reivers*, 1962 (n); *Early Prose and Poetry*, 1962; *Essays, Speeches and Public Letters*, 1966; *Lion in the Garden*, 1968 (i); *Flags in the Dust*, 1973 (n); *The Marionettes: A Play in One Act*,

1975; *Selected Letters*, 1977; *Jealousy and Episode*, 1977 (s); *Uncollected Stories*, 1979; *Mayday*, 1980 (juv); *Helen: A Courtship, and Mississippi Poems*, 1981 (p); *Sanctuary: The Original Text*, 1981 (n); *Faulkner's MGM Screenplays*, 1983; *Father Abraham*, 1983 (s); *Vision in Spring*, 1984 (p); *The Sound and the Fury*, new and corrected ed., 1984 (n); *Novels, 1930–1935*, 1985 [Library of America ed.]; *Tomorrow and Tomorrow and Tomorrow*, 1985 (s, scrp, tv); *Country Lawyer and Other Stories for the Screen*, 1986 (s, scrp); *Absalom, Absalom*, 1987 [corrected text]; *The Sound and the Fury*, 1987 [critical ed.]; *Stallion Road: A Screenplay*, 1989; *Novels 1936–1940*, 1990 [Library of America ed.]; *As I Lay Dying*, 1990 [corrected text]; *Sanctuary*, 1990 [corrected first ed.]; *Thinking of Home: Letters to His Mother and Father*, 1992; *Collected Stories*, 1995

FAUSET, Jessie Redmon (1886–1961)

This novel [*There Is Confusion*] is significant because it is the first work of fiction to come from the pen of a colored woman in these United States. It is evidence that we can with assurance look forward in the near future to having our fiction dealing with life among the Negroes written by the Negroes themselves. And this is as it should be. Long the object of burlesque and pitiless satire, it is natural that the Negro in his upward plunge should want to strike back, to write out of his own rich and varied experience, not for the delectation of the whites, but for the edification and enjoyment of his own people.

The mushroom growth of magazines published by the Negroes and the fiction to be found in them, the serialization of stories of obscure colored authors in Negro newspapers, the establishment, even, of reputable Negro publishing houses—all point to this new, up and pushing spirit.

Having as its motif the futility that must not arrest the conquering progress of the Negroes, Miss Fauset's book, however, is not really "younger generation Negro" stuff. Toomer's insouciant *Cane* in this respect is miles beyond it. Indeed, it is a sort of bridge between the old and the new Negro generations. For the literature of these strident neophytes is of a shockingly esoteric nature—full of beauty and passion and blackly steering clear of the inferiority complex. Mediocre, a work of puny, painstaking labor, *There Is Confusion* is not meant for people who know anything about the Negro and his problems. It is aimed with unpardonable naiveté at the very young or the pertinently old.

E.D.W. *The New Republic*. July 9, 1924, p. 192

Sir: Your review of Jessie Fauset's *There Is Confusion* is really not worthy of the *New Republic*. It is not a review or even a comment, but a quite gratuitous slur upon a work which, whatever its merits, is at least a sincere and unusual product.

W.E.B. DuBois. *The New Republic*. July 30, 1924, p. 274

For once, a book has been advertised too modestly. *The Chinaberry Tree* has been recommended by its publishers, and by Miss Gale, its

sponsor, as a revelation of the life led by educated Negroes. But it is considerably more than that. Though faulty, it is the work of a remarkable psychologist who can be congratulated not simply because her material is interesting but because she has understood so well the human factors involved in it.

The greater portion of *The Chinaberry Tree* is devoted to the love affair of two colored high-school students who do not know that they are brother and sister. This dramatic theme, singularly enough, is the least exciting part of the story. We learn most about Miss Fauset's book as a whole not through Melissa and Malory, or their narrowly averted incestuous marriage; but through Laurentine, the beautiful apricot-colored dressmaker who is the book's real heroine and symbol of the world it depicts; Laurentine, who sat as a child under the Chinaberry Tree and wondered why other children, either white or black, wouldn't play with her.

The best part of the story lies in the background. Colonel Halloway, a wealthy white factory-owner, while still a college student falls in love with his mother's Negro maid. He marries a white woman, but his real love is given to the colored girl, whom he handsomely establishes in a white house with green shutters, a well-kept garden, and the Chinaberry Tree. His daily visits to her are concealed from no one. Their love is a scandal to both black and white inhabitants of the New Jersey town. And Laurentine is their child. She is brought up in comparative luxury, but is a double outcast. And the passion which animates her is closely allied to the passion which animates the book. What does the illegitimate mulatto grow up to want? Respectability. Once she cries: "Oh God, you know all I want is a chance to show them how decent I am." This might serve as the motto for *The Chinaberry Tree*. It is so much the book's real theme that once recognized it helps to explain the striking gentility of certain passages, as well as the exceptional importance attached to small material comforts that most white people would take for granted. . . .

It is a world in which such little things mean much, a touching world, its humility displayed through its pride. The book attempts to idealize this polite colored world in terms of the white standards that it has adopted. And here lies the root of Miss Fauset's artistic errors. When she parades the possessions of her upper classes and when she puts her lovers through their Fauntleroy courtesies, she is not only stressing the white standards that they have adopted: she is . . . minimizing the colored blood in them. This is a decided weakness, for it steals truth and life from the book. Is not the most precious part of a Negro work of art that which is specifically Negroid, which none but a Negro could contribute?

We need not look for the reason for Miss Fauset's idealization. It is pride, the pride of a genuine aristocrat, and it is pride also that makes her such a remarkable psychologist. However many her artistic errors, Miss Fauset has an understanding of people and their motives. I suppose there is no better way to come to understand other than to be extraordinarily sensitive to one's self. . . . Considering the position of [the] educated Negro in America, it is no wonder then that an aristocrat like Miss Fauset has idealized her little world, has made it over-elegant! Inspired by the religious motive which so many Negro writers seem to feel, she has simply been trying to justify her world to the world at large. Her mistake has consisted in trying to do this in terms of the white standard.

"To be Negro in America posits a dramatic situation." Yes, and to be one of Miss Fauset's amber-tinted . . . refined Negroes—not having to deal much with whites, but surrounded on all sides by the white standard—posits a delicate psychological situation. It is for this reason that few white novels have anything like the shades of feeling to be found in *The Chinaberry Tree*. Every moment speaks of yearning. That is why, once it is seen as a whole, even its faults are charming, for the story they tell is poignant and beautiful.

Gerald Sykes. *The Nation.* July 27, 1932, p. 88

Viewing the Negro Renaissance in retrospect, Richard Wright has written caustically of "the prim and decorous ambassadors who went a-begging to white America, dressed in the knee-pants of servility, curtsying to show that the Negro was not inferior, that he was human, and that he had a life comparable to that of other people." Without a doubt one of the prime offenders whom Wright had in mind was Jessie Fauset. Yet with all her primness, Miss Fauset presents something of a paradox, for in her editorial work on the *The Crisis* she often championed the young rebels of the Harlem School. . . .

Claude McKay writes of Jessie Fauset in his autobiography, "All the radicals liked her, although in her social viewpoint she was away over on the other side of the fence." But if Miss Fauset won personal acceptance among Harlem's colorful Bohemians, in her novels she maintained an irreproachable decorum. . . .From the first. . . .her literary aspirations were circumscribed by her desire to convey a flattering image of respectable Negro society.

Jessie Fauset was the most prolific of the Renaissance novelists, publishing four novels during a ten-year period from 1924 to 1933. But in spite of an admirable persistence, her novels are uniformly sophomoric, trivial, and dull. *There is Confusion* (1924) is nothing if not well titled, for it is burdened with a plethora of characters whose complex genealogy leaves the most conscientious reader exhausted. *Plum Bun* (1928) is a typical novel of passing. . . . *The Chinaberry Tree* (1931) seems to be a novel about the first colored woman in New Jersey to wear lounging pajamas. *Comedy American Style* (1933) is an account of a colored woman's obsessive desire to be white, not unlike the novels which condemn passing in its nationalist implications.

Undoubtedly the most important formative influence on Miss Fauset's work was her family background. An authentic old Philadelphian (known as "O.P.'s" in the colored society of that day), she was never able to transcend the narrow limits of this sheltered world. It accounts for her gentility, her emphasis on heredity and genealogy, and her attitude toward race. Miss Fauset's characters are bred to "rise above" racial discrimination, to regard it merely as "an extra complication of living." Yet "the artificial dilemma," as she calls it, is always present as an obstacle to gracious living, and is the real antagonist of her novels. Racial protest, be it ever so genteel, is an irrepressible feature of bourgeois nationalism.

Robert Bone. *The Negro Novel in America* (New Haven: Yale University Press, 1958, rev. 1963), pp. 101–2

Bone, Littlejohn, and Gayle, in three of the most popular and simultaneously distorted, partisan and inaccurate critical works on Afro-American literature, have consigned Fauset's work to a very narrow groove and have failed to probe beneath its surface realities. In their disproportionate emphasis on her literary traditionalism, for example, they draw hasty and not totally accurate conclusions about her fictional intentions. To be sure, she was traditional to

some extent, both in form and content, but as Gary de Cordova Wintz rightly observes, "in spite of her conservative, almost Victorian literary habits," Fauset "introduced several subjects into her novels that were hardly typical drawing room conversation topics in the mid-1920s. Promiscuity, exploitative sexual affairs, miscegenation, even incest appear in her novels. In fact prim and proper Jessie Fauset included a far greater range of sexual activity than did most of DuBois's debauched tenth."

When attention is given Fauset's introduction of these challenging themes, it becomes possible to regard her "novels of manners" less as an indication of her literary "backwardness" and more as a self-conscious artistic strategem pressed to the service of her central fictional preoccupations. Since many of Fauset's concerns were unpalatable to the average reader of her day and hence unmarketable in the publishing arena, the convention of the novel of manners can be seen as protective mimicry, a kind of deflecting mask for her more challenging concerns. Fauset uses classic fairy tale patterns and nursery rhymes in a similar fashion; however, although these strategems are consciously employed, they are often clumsily executed.

In addition to the protective coloration which the conventional medium afforded, the novel of manners suited Fauset's works in that the tradition "is primarily concerned with social conventions as they impinge upon character." Both social convention and character—particularly the black female character—jointly form the nucleus of Fauset's literary concerns. The protagonists of all of her novels are black women, and she makes clear in each novel that social conventions have not sided well with them but, rather, have been antagonistic.

Without polemicizing, Fauset examines that antagonism, criticizing the American society which has institutionalized prejudice, safeguarded it by law and public attitude, and in general, denied the freedom of development, the right to well-being, and the pursuit of happiness to the black woman. In short, Fauset explores the black woman's struggle for democratic ideals in a society whose sexist conventions assiduously work to thwart that struggle. Critics have usually ignored this important theme which even a cursory reading of her novels reveals. This concern with exploring female consciousness and exposing the unduly limited possibilities for female development is, in a loose sense, feminist in impulse, placing Fauset squarely among the early black feminists in Afro-American literary history. . . .

The idea of Fauset, a black woman, daring to write—even timidly so—about women taking charge of their own lives and declaring themselves independent of social conventions, was far more progressive than critics have either observed or admitted. Although what Fauset attempted in her depictions of black women was not uniformly commensurate with what she achieved, she has to be credited with both presenting an alternative view of womanhood and a facet of black life which publishers, critics, and audiences stubbornly discouraged if not vehemently opposed. Despite that discouragement and opposition, Fauset persisted in her attempt to correct the distorted but established images of black life and culture and to portray women and blacks with more complexity and authenticity than was popular at the time. In so doing, she was simultaneously challenging established assumptions about the nature and function of Afro-American literature. Those who persist, then, in regarding her as a prim and proper Victorian writer, an eddy in a revolutionary literary current, would do well to read Fauset's work more carefully, to give it a more fair and complete appraisal, one that takes into account the important and complex relationship between circumstances and artistic creation. Then her fiction might finally be accorded the recognition and attention that it deserves and Fauset, her rightful place in the Afro-American literary tradition.

> Deborah E. McDowell. In Marjorie Pryse and Hortense J. Spillers, eds. *Conjuring: Black Women, Fiction, and Literary Tradition* (Bloomington: Indiana University Press, 1985), pp. 87–88, 100

Audience was a consideration ... for Jessie Fauset, the most published Afro-American woman novelist of the Harlem Renaissance. She, together with Nella Larsen, wanted to correct the impression most white people had that all black people lived in Harlem dives or in picturesque, abject poverty. In her preface to *The Chinaberry Tree* (1931) she tells us why she chose to create the heroines she did. Beginning with the disclaimer that she does not write to establish a thesis, she goes on to point out that the novel is about "those breathing spells, in-between spaces where colored men and women work and live and go their ways in no thought of the problem. What are they like then? So few of the other Americans know." And she concludes her preface by identifying the class to which her characters belong: the Negro who speaks of "his old Boston families," "old Philadelphians," "old Charlestonians."

Both [Frances E. W.] Harper and Fauset were certainly aware of the images, primarily negative, of black people that predominated in the minds of white Americans. They constructed their heroines to refute those images, as their way of contributing to the struggle of black people for full citizenship in this country. Of necessity their language was outer-directed rather than inwardly searching, for their characters were addressed to "the other Americans" who blocked group development. To white American readers, self-understanding for black characters might have seemed a luxury. To the extent that their writers emphasized the gender as well as the race of their heroines they were appealing to a white female audience that understood the universal trials of womanhood. These writers' creations, then, were conditioned by the need to establish "positive" images of black people; hence, the exploration of self, in all its complexity, could hardly be attempted.

> Barbara Christian. In Marjorie Pryse and Hortense J. Spillers, eds. *Conjuring: Black Women, Fiction, and Literary Tradition* (Bloomington: Indiana University Press, 1985), pp. 234–35

Jessie Fauset, whose fiction falls to some extent within the romance genre, makes ... use of the Cinderella Line as narrative strategy.... Olivia Cary, the unpleasant central character of *Comedy: American Style*, resembles the "typical mother" in marriage novels—Mrs. Bennett in *Pride and Prejudice*, for example. The subtext of Fauset's novel follows the Cinderella Line: Olivia dreams her lightskinned daughter Teresa marries a princely (white, rich) husband. The achievement of Olivia's dream, however, is thwarted by the larger racial issue which informs the novel, the issue of passing. Jessie Fauset, whose novels espouse essentially middle-class values, nevertheless offers, particularly in *Comedy: American Style*, a critical perspective of these very values. This

ambivalence results in a subversions of the Cinderella Line. Teresa, who has passed at her mother's insistence, marries not a prince but a pauper. At the end of the novel both mother and daughter, defeated in the marriage quest, are left without a culture and without a language, in the threadbare clothing which signifies an unhappy ending.

Clothing and skin are meticulously described throughout *Comedy: American Style*, mirroring as they do the values and attitudes of the various characters ... [Fauset's] deftness and attention to shades of skin are evident also in her many descriptions of clothing. One might say that, for Fauset's characters, clothing often becomes a second skin, at times meant to enhance the complexion, at other times meant to disguise, to be used as a vehicle for passing.

> Mary Jane Lupton. *Black American Literature Forum*. 20, 1986, pp. 410–11

Issues of race and gender are major concerns in Fauset's fiction. Adhering to principles she adumbrated in her reviews, she claimed that her novels were not propagandistic. Neither, she averred, were they constrained by issues of race. Both claims are false in precisely the same way her observation that McKay did not write propaganda was false. Fauset believed that Afro-American writers had a role to play in the political struggle; they had a duty, as she put it in a wide-ranging interview in 1932, to "tell the truth about us." But she thought Afro-American writers discharged this duty best when they wrote skillfully and truthfully.

Fauset did not find a fictional form conducive to the truth she wanted to tell. *There Is Confusion* (1924), *Plum Bun* (1929), *The Chinaberry Tree* (1931), and *Comedy: American Style* (1933) are all sentimental novels. The plots often strain credulity, and their resolutions are uniformly happy: the still courageous but chastened heroine finds happiness with a protective yet more understanding hero. Yet, as McDowell has noted, Fauset's novels use literary and social conventions partly as a "deflecting mask for her more challenging concerns." The clichés of the marriage plot and the "passing" novel notwithstanding, *Plum Bun* reveals a sophisticated understanding about the politics of race and gender. Fauset's protagonist, Angela Murray, is aware of the hierarchical arrangement of race and gender relations, but she is naive about their implications. Her creator was not.

The foreword to *The Chinaberry Tree*, the most cogent statement of Fauset's personal aesthetic, has often been cited and frequently censured as a betrayal of a racial birthright. The weaknesses inherent in Fauset's position are clear; the racial defensiveness is palpable. Yet Fauset's "breathing-spells, in-between spaces where colored men and women work and love," may in fact be comparable to Hurston's renderings of the Eatonville store porch whose "sitters had been tongueless, earless, eyeless conveniences all day long." On the porch Hurston's characters cease to be mules and become men and women. For Hurston such "in-between spaces" are inscribed by cultural differences; Fauset emphasizes commonality. Taken in tandem, the fiction of these two women explores the multidimensional experiences of Afro-Americans.

In this regard, Fauset's refusal to write about the kinds of characters and situations white readers expected and her insistence that all the drama in Afro-American life did not revolve around interracial conflict are important. Indeed, they are part of a larger effort waged by black women writers collectively to create a space in which they could tell their own stories.

Cheryl A. Wall. In Bonnie Kime Scott, ed. *The Gender of Modernism* (Bloomington: Indiana University Press, 1990), pp. 158–59

BIBLIOGRAPHY
There Is Confusion, 1924 (n); *Plum Bun,* 1929 (n); *The Chinaberry Tree: A Novel of American Life,* 1932 (n); *Comedy: American Style,* 1933 (n)

FEARING, Kenneth (1902–1961)

The world of Fearing is nothing if not metropolitan. He is as involved in, and fascinated by, metropolitan existence (with its "touch of vomitgas in the evening air") as Frost with his New England landscape, decorated with commonplaces, and Jeffers with his prop boulders and gulls. . . . Held by this life in futile ambivalence that has persisted for fifteen years, Fearing's mood appears to have changed little. . . . although the tone has become increasingly harsh. In the ticker tape, the radio, the tabloid, the pulp magazine and the advertisement he has found an objective correlative that has never deserted him.

Weldon Kees. *Poetry.* Jan., 1941. p. 265

He wants as many people as possible to react with immediate horror or delight; consequently he has dramatized the most ordinary sights and happenings of everyday living. What, then, is added to make it poetry and not mere reporting? Principally, it is Fearing's imaginative viewpoint. He has the double vision of the poet who sees the object we all see and sees at the same time its universal shadow.

Ruth Stephan. *Poetry.* Dec., 1943. p. 164

Mr. Fearing is a poet who can compete in excitement with the journalists and surpass them in that his words have a speed equal to his impressions. He at times seems too closely in competition with them, so rapidly does he pass from a personal anguish to a cold impersonal dismay. What saves him is that, in his approach to what he sees, "hatred and pity are exactly mixed." He is a product of the depression and somewhat limited to its mood. In his America is more despair than hope, and even hope is ominous. But it is a country in which, while he disclaims his ability to bring miracles to pass, he knows that miracles still occur.

John Peale Bishop. *Collected Essays.* (Scribner). 1948. pp. 319–20

Kenneth Fearing has sought and found his permanent level in the range of modern verse, and . . . it lies somewhere between Auden and Ogden Nash, with something of the former's surrealist imagination and a good deal of the latter's urban ability to pillory suburban mediocrity. Fearing does not, of course, derive his style from either. His style (it is a very good one, and by this time wholly his own) originated in Walt Whitman's long and casual line.

Selden Rodman. *New York Times Book Section.* Oct. 24, 1948. p. 18

Kenneth Fearing's poems are less prosy, more formal, than their appearance on the page would indicate. The long line, the irregular, or not particularly anything stanza pattern invite the risk of sagging; Mr. Fearing is a master of not letting the line down, and he can, with a very slight and deft touch indeed, point up his ironic effects with a brief parenthesis, an apparent afterthought, a single adverb or adjective. . . .Mr. Fearing does what he does so very well that it is all a little exasperating; you wish that he would be a bit more venturesome, inventive, experimental.

Rolfe Humphries. *The Nation.* Nov. 13, 1948. p. 557

As a practiced writer, Mr. Fearing can do a great deal with repeated words that would sound like material for nursery rhymes were it not for the grown-up ideas of change and decay that accompany them. It is readable, often brilliant writing of innuendo, of things seen out of the corner of his eye, of fears and doubts and strange characters in the background.

Eugene Davidson, *Yale Review.* Summer, 1949. pp. 725–6

I don't think a poet can be much more American, in the psychological if not the Fourth-of-July sense, than Kenneth Fearing. He talks the lingo straight, simple, and sardonic and knows the native panic at being lost in the shuffle which has created it. . . .In Fearing's writing, the "enemy" gradually becomes the Mob, official and unofficial, that thrives on the regimentation of individual thought and feeling through ever-greater control of the avenues of communication. . . .Fearing is an original, a canny Quixote and—more to the point—a kind of melancholy Jacques of the age, whose writing has often a topical surface that belies its depth of wry compassion and its stylistic purity. Edward Dahlberg once compared him with Corbiére, and the comparison was apt. But there are also American comparisons: He is one of the harder-bitten sons of Walt Whitman, a more mordant Masters or Sandburg, a poetic Lardner of wider scope.

M.L. Rosenthal. *The Nation.* Jan. 19, 1957. pp. 64–5

It is a fighting poetry, thank God, a poetry of angry conviction, few manners and no winsome graces. It is stubborn in its Old Guard attitude, stubborn in its technique: so unfashionable, indeed, in its resistance to the prevalent obsession with metrical vacuity, that a well-bred young neoclassicist might regard it as almost theatrically conservative.

Dudley Fitts. *New York Times Book Section.* Feb. 17, 1957. p. 4

His tone, for the most part, remains ironic. If he is a revolutionary poet, out of the proletarian tradition of the Thirties, and the best survivor of that tradition, he is one without a revolution to propose. . . . His art of brilliant surfaces and quick contemporaneity seemed more daring once, as a poetic configuration, than it does today, though the best poems keep their early lustre.

Stanley Kunitz. *Saturday Review.* June 29, 1957. pp. 25–6

The irony sometimes seems dated and callow, despite its honesty and technically accomplished presentation. It is as if Fearing's habitual irony only permitted him to see things by the gross or in generalities (as conventional as the "finny tribes" of earlier mannerists). Often, the consequence is too insufficient a discrimination to see a world behind the old stereotypes. For thirty years Fearing has fought the dragons of commercialism and conformity; the effects of the struggle on his poetry have not been altogether good. But there are those poems like "Five A.M.," "Continuous Performance," and "The Face in the Bar Room Mirror" that transcend the struggle and comment on it with the ominous and witty power Fearing can achieve at his best.

Leonard Nathan. *Poetry.* Aug., 1957. p. 328

The sense of the ominous is a dominant feature in all of Fearing's books of poems, though the face and shape of the threatening spectres shift. In the 20s his men and women are spooked by the fear that the affluence of the decade, the quick fortunes built on inflated stocks, merely gilded a life that had no moral center or stability. When the great bull market died in 1929, and the era of depression began, the characters of Fearing's poems not only still shake from the reverberations of the economic collapse that toppled both fortunes and the dream of eternal security but also they quake because in some subterranean way they sense the shaping of a new disaster, some second coming of a world war. For those who survived the 1929 crash, as well as the decade of the great depression and World War II, there are still new spectres to threaten them. In the poems of the 40s Fearing makes us aware of brutal and coercive forces and devices: the secret police, the informers and intriguers, the listening devices that monitor the individual man and the society with the purpose of rendering each man faceless and efficient. Any eccentricity of the human mind and heart are corrected or erased in order to make the person smoothly fit and remain faithful to a new totalitarian social order; if the customer proves too tough, he can be eliminated altogether. There is little relief for the Fearing man, haunted by the old disasters of the past and threatened by a new conspiracy of ruthless forces dedicated to the principles of subservience and conformity to the will of the state. For the Fearing man, as the books of poetry define his cosmos, every horizon is ominous, and the big clock strikes the hour of doom twenty-four times a day.

Sy Kahn, in *The Thirties*, edited by Warren French (Everett Edwards). 1967. pp. 134–5

BIBLIOGRAPHY
Angel Arms, 1929 (p); *Poems*, 1935; *Dead Reckoning*, 1938 (n); *The Hospital*, 1939 (n); *Collected Poems*, 1940; *The Dagger in the Mind*, 1941 (n); *Clark Gifford's Body*, 1942 (n); *Afternoon of a Pawnbroker*, 1943 (p); *The Big Clock*, 1946 (n); (as Donald F. Bedford, with D. Friede and H. Bedford-Jones) *John Barry*, 1947 (n); *Stranger at Coney Island*, 1948 (p); *The Loneliest Girl in the World*, 1951 (n); *The Generous Heart*, 1954 (n); *New and Selected Poems*, 1956; *The Crozart Story*, 1960 (n)

FERBER, Edna (1887–1968)

. . . although [*Dawn O'Hara*] deals in tragedy, it is a fabric woven from threads of sheer light heartedness, unquenchable courage, warm-hearted understanding of the things which go to make the essential joy of living. There are, for instance, certain chapters in the book picturing a delightful, unique, inimitable German boarding-house in Milwaukee that makes one sigh while reading them, partly from a vague nostalgia for happy bygone days in German pensions, partly also from sheer envy of the subtle touch that penned them. And then, too, there is one portrait of a broken-down sporting editor, a man whose days are numbered, a man vulgar in speech and with many sins upon his conscience, but who, nevertheless, is rich in some of the rarest gifts that human nature knows and whose final tragedy leaves a vacant spot in the heart akin to that of a personal bereavement. For these reasons it seems the part of wisdom to inscribe the name of Edna Ferber in some easily accessible part of our memory whereby there shall be no danger in the future of missing anything that may come from her pen.

F.T. Cooper. *Bookman.* July, 1911. p. 534

Any reader who has hoped that sometime he might have the opportunity to make the *amende honorable* to Edna Ferber has it now. If your have found yourself led along protestingly, however divertingly, through Miss Ferber's previous writings; if you have had an uncomfortable feeling that perhaps your author did not quite respect her reader, her art, or herself, here comes the chance to change your mind, to alter your attitude toward one of the most up-and-coming of our present-day fictionists. *Fanny Herself* . . . is the most serious, extended, and dignified of Miss Ferber's books. . . . *Fanny Herself* is a vivid, vital, full-blooded book; dealing with "big business" and the ascent of a forceful and persistent race, it is more successful than some of its kind in avoiding offences of ideality and taste.

Dial. Nov. 8, 1917. p. 463

The stiff plan of her story is forgotten once she begins to let her characters shift for themselves without regard to arriving at any definite point at a given time. There is emotion in *The Girls* and with it a persuasive clear-headedness. It is eloquent in its appeal for the right which the new generation seems to insist upon before all others—the right to be wrong. The book follows the development of a female line from its place in the home out to sunlight. Before we are done we know the chief figures of the novel intimately. Some of the minor sketches are meagre. Miss Ferber has not quite forgotten that she is a writer of short stories and she is inclined to be satisfied at times with fast blocking in of two-dimensional folk. She tries occasionally to make a sentence or so do the work of a paragraph.

Heywood Broun. *Bookman.* Dec., 1921. p. 393

At a time when realism is all but monopolizing literature, one experiences a sensation of delighted relief in encountering *Show Boat*. It is gorgeously romantic . . . romantic because it is too alive to be what the realists call real; because it bears within itself a spirit of life which we seek rather than have; because it makes a period and mode of existence live again, not actually different from what they were, but more alluring than they could have been. *Show Boat* is romantic not because its people and events violate any principle of possibility, but because they express a principle of selection. Miss Ferber has chosen the brightest colors and let the dull ones go. . . . With *Show Boat* Miss Ferber establishes herself not as one of those who are inaugurating first-rate literature, but as one of those who are reviving first-rate story telling. This is little else but an irresistible story; but that, surely, is enough.

Louis Kronenberger. *New York Times Book Section*. Aug. 22, 1926. p. 5

Miss Ferber's talent, this reviewer is irrevocably convinced, does not lie in the way of the novel at all. She writes a novel as a modern athletic girl might wear a crinoline and a bustle. She manages the trick, but she is self-conscious and filled with secret amusement over the masquerade. Why so many words? Why such a portentous enclosure for a mere story? So I imagine Miss Ferber secretly regarding the novel form. Her forte, I humbly submit, is the short story. She has the gift, and it is my belief she has the predilection, for that form of literary art. But editors and publishers demand novels spun out to serial length and Miss Ferber, who can do it, supplies the demand. That does not vitiate the argument that her short stories are remarkably good stories, while are novels are only remarkably good short stories spun out to novel length and thereby largely spoiled.

William McFee. *New Republic*. Sept. 15, 1926. pp. 101–2

. . . Miss Ferber, practiced writer that she is, could not fail to make a tale [*Cimarron*] that would fire the imagination of a great many thousand readers. But she has done more than draw a brilliant picture of Oklahoma. She has created men and women who go there to live—and in a measure do live there in the pages of her book. I say in a measure because I think Sabra and Yancey Cravat, and certainly Sol Levy and Dixie Lee and Cim and Donna and Felice, have a tendency to be gorgeous painted figures on the back drop of the West. . . . It turns out to be a fairy story. No matter if it really happened. It is the Fairy Story of the Pioneer and the Indian. It delights my eye but, like most fairy stories, it does nothing to my heart.

Dorothy Van Doren. *The Nation*. April 23, 1930. p. 494

Warm, alive, observant, her short stories skim the cream from the surface of modern life and preserve it in all its richness. That is all they do. Depth, subtlety, intensity are beyond Miss Ferber and with the possible exception of *The Girls*, that is as true of her novels as of her short stories.

Edith H. Walton. *New York Times Book Section*. May 14, 1933. p. 7

Reading one of her books gives you the pleasant sense of toil vicariously accomplished. And her novels are always success stories, in spite of the threatening implications she turns up and pats neatly back into place—which makes her popular reading. She squares off at her job in work-manlike fashion and turns out a nationally advertised product that looks as sound as this year's model always does, until next year's model comes along.

T.S. Matthews. *New Republic*. March 6, 1935. p. 107

The public will rush toward the book [*A Peculiar Treasure*] from many directions. Fiction writers will read it like gospel—and well they may for the frank story of developing craftsmanship, for authentic description of ways of writing, moods of writing, rewards of writing, fatigues of writing. They will find that, for all her frankness, she can no more put down the complete reason for her own success than she could give them a recipe for success of their own. Dramatists will read the book. Jews will read it, to uphold their faith and pride in their race, to revive memories of Jewish life in America, to share the exciting courage and warmth and devotion to family and race and work which is so true and apparent. It will be a very tonic book in that respect alone, and its title, with the verse from which it comes, will be quoted widely. The title is a little too heavy, a fine Scriptural phrase which is somehow not quite suited to the modern story of this successful, non-churchgoing writer.

Margaret Culkin Banning. *Saturday Review*. Feb. 4, 1939. p. 5

In *Show Boat* (from which, with the help of Jerome Kern, came the most appealing American opera in existence), in *So Big*, and in *Cimarron*, Miss Ferber has stressed with genuine feeling the exuberance, the fearlessness, and the roving instinct which make us what we are. . . .

The theme [of *Saratoga Trunk*]—as Colonel Maroon, now a millionaire, proclaims it in his opening interview with the press—is honestly American. For he has no false pride about how he got his millions and doesn't forget the scars his kind left on this country. But it is the development of this story that troubles me: in it I miss Edna Ferber's homely knowledge of city and country; I think she lost the chance to play up our special brand to integrity, and at the end I am left wondering if the author really cares deeply for any of the people in this book.

Edward Weeks. *Atlantic Monthly*. Dec., 1941. n. p.

. . . Miss Ferber is at her best when she stays closest to the milieu of her formative years—when she was carving out the raw material of her art as a reporter in the Middle West. Her back-street Chicago is more convincing than her Riviera romances; her prairie mornings will stay in your memory long after you've forgotten her station-wagon repartee. But even the most severely hand-tailored of her stories is much more than merely entertaining; if her matriarchs are terrifying and completely real, her star-crossed women executives, faded ingenues, and freshly lacqered adolescents are no less human under their patter. Sometimes, as in her novels, Miss Ferber's sheer, exuberant talent, her flair for the theatrical, outruns her material—with a consequent loss of realism. But even here, the emotion is honest. Her effective range is much narrower than these titles would indicate—yet every story is written from her heart.

> James MacBride. *New York Times Book Section*. Feb. 16, 1947. p. 3

Miss Ferber makes it very clear that she doesn't like the Texas she writes about, and it's a cinch that when Texans read what she has written about them they won't like Miss Ferber either. Almost everyone else is going to revel in these pages. . . . *Giant* makes marvelous reading—wealth piled on wealth, wonder on wonder in a stunning splendiferous pyramid of ostentation. . . . This is the Texas Miss Ferber has put into her bitter, brilliant, corrosive, excoriating novel. . . . It requires courage to take all this apart as scathingly as Miss Ferber has done; and in the process of so doing she paints a memorable portrait of that new American, *Texicanus vulgaris*, which is all warts and wampum. . . . For all the slickness of its writing (and Miss Ferber is a past mistress of best seller style), *Giant* carries the kind of message that seldom finds expression in such chromium-plated prose. What's more, Miss Ferber states it with a conviction that carries the ring of sincerity. All this may make it impossible for her to revisit the great Commonwealth without the law at her hip, but at least she has written a book that sets the seal on her career.

> John Barkham. *New York Times Book Section*. Sept. 28, 1952. pp. 4–5

It was inevitable that Edna Ferber should write a novel about Alaska. The magnetic northern land has all the qualities that draw her to a scene—robustness, magnitude, epic tradition, the clash of strong-willed men and their stubborn duel with Nature. In her novel *Ice Palace* she has put more of Alaska between covers than any other writer in its short and crowded history. . . . Here is the difference between Miss Ferber and the ''modern'' novelists, and a reason for the multitude of her readers. She still sees people in large dimensions, strong enough to be actors rather than to be acted upon. This novel contains a whole gallery of them, with Christine Storm in the center. Frankly heightened and exaggerated, they are men and women to match the seas and skies and mountains of the big North Country.

> Walter Havighurst. *Saturday Review*. March 29, 1958. p. 26

. . . her accounts [in *A Kind of Magic*] of the slave laborer's crematories at Nordhausen, of her visit to Buchenwald, and of VJ Day in New York City are first-class reportage.

A seasoned, hard-working, and dedicated writer, Edna Ferber is similarly interesting when she tells of the trials and delights of her trade. Moreover, apart from a tendency to overvalue her own fiction, she is worth listening to.

> William Peden. *Saturday Review*. Oct. 19, 1963, p. 38

BIBLIOGRAPHY

Dawn O'Hara, 1911 (n); *Buttered Side Down*, 1912 (s); *Roast Beef, Medium*, 1913 (s); *Personality Plus*, 1914 (s); *Emma McChesney and Co.*, 1915 (s); *Our Mrs. McChesney*, 1916 (d); *Fanny Herself*, 1917 (n); *Cheerful—By Request*, 1918 (s); (with Newman Levy) *$1200 a Year*, 1920 (d); *Half Portions*, 1920 (s); *The Girls*, 1921 (n); *Gigolo*, 1922 (s); (with George S. Kaufman) *Minick*, 1924 (d); *So Big*, 1924 (n); *Show Boat*, 1926 (n); *Mother Knows Best*, 1927 (s); (with George S. Kaufman) *The Royal Family*, 1928 (d); *Cimarron*, 1930 (n); *American Beauty*, 1931 (n); (with George S. Kaufman) *Dinner at Eight*, 1932 (d); *They Brought Their Women*, 1933 (n); *A Peculiar Treasure*, 1933 (a) (revised edition, 1960); *Come and Get It*, 1935 (n); (with George S. Kaufman) *Stage Door*, 1938 (d); *Nobody's in Town*, 1938 (n); (with George S. Kaufman) *The Land Is Bright*, 1941 (d); *Saratoga Trunk*, 1941 (n); *Great Son*, 1945 (n); *One Basket*, 1947 (collected stories); *Giant*, 1952 (n); *Ice Palace*, 1958 (n); *A Kind of Magic*, 1963 (a)

FERLINGHETTI, Lawrence (1919–)

Owner of the City Lights bookshop (headquarters for the San Francisco literary movement) and publisher of the Pocket Poets Series (most notable entry, Allen Ginsberg's *Howl*), Lawrence Ferlinghetti has been a leader in all that Jazz about poetry on the West Coast. He now appears with some verse [*A Coney Island of the Mind*] of his own, which I find highly readable and often very funny. . . . like many writers who keep pointing to their bare feet, Ferlinghetti is a very bookish boy: his hipster verse frequently hangs on a literary reference. His book is a grab bag of undergraduate musings about love and art, much hackneyed satire of American life and some real and wry perceptions of it.

> Harvey Shapiro. *New York Times Book Section*. Sept. 7, 1958. p. 10

Lawrence Ferlinghetti is certainly one of those advocates of universal nakedness, etc. . . . but he differs from most of the others in his high-flying joyousness of spirit and in his stylistic sophistication. He knows he is not the first man to take a peek at Darien and he has learned some useful things, and gladly, from various European and American experimenters. The religion of sex-and-anarchy, like other religions and creeds, starts off with certain simplicities but does not require its communicants to reiterate them monotonously and mechanically. Ferlinghetti can preach a little tiresomely; he proves he can in the seven ''Oral Messages,'' written ''specifically for jazz accompaniment,'' in which he tries to rival the worst of Ginsberg, Corso, et al. . . . Apart from the ''Oral Messages,'' however, and from a few other preachy pieces, Ferlinghetti is a deft, rapid-paced, whirling performer.

> M.L. Rosenthal. *The Nation*. Oct. 11, 1958. p. 215

This regional activity had been going full swing for many years when suddenly it received a number of spectacular recruits. First was Lawrence Ferlinghetti. He is a successful book dealer, secretly the possessor of three degrees, one from the Sorbonne, a most imaginative editor and publisher, whose ''Pocket Poets'' series has sold hundreds of thousands of copies, and a genuinely popular poet. His own *A Coney Island of the Mind* nudges *Howl* for first place as the most popular poetry book of the decade, and without the latter's somewhat dubious publicity. Resident for many years in France, he "thinks in French"; his verse bears strong resemblance to that of Raymond Queneau, Jacques Prévert and Paul Éluard. Its nearest American analogues are the work of e.e cummings and James Laughlin.

Kenneth Rexroth. *Assays* (New Directions). 1961. p. 193

Reality in this novel [*Her*] is all a fluid jumble and has no center other than the mind of the male protagonist as he searches for his completion, for his Sunday wife, for his Jungian "anima." Paradoxically, the very fact that the censor of this mind has been removed seems of produce a monotonously repetitive sequence of babbling rhyme associations which invariably lead to the hero's affirmation of self through protest and erection. As the protagonist blunders along "looking for the main character of my life," the sustaining image becomes that of the darkened movie house in which the "celluloid sequence" seems to be coiling and recoiling both image and existence, and this vision of reality may in part explain the technique with its flowing sentences, its merging of objects and its fuddling of time and space.

Daniel Leary. *Minnesota Review.* Summer, 1961. p. 505

. . . there seems to be nothing in Ferlinghetti's new narrative method that James Joyce didn't discover some time ago, while there is obviously a great deal that Joyce found out and which Ferlinghetti has evidently not yet discovered, such as the use of humor and understatement and irony. What is it that *Her* has to tell us? I have only read it twice, so I am not sure, but it seems to be that the short, fat man wishes he could be like Leda and couple with the godhead, except that the swan would have to be Hera and not Zeus because he, the short, fat man, is obviously not himself divine.

Louis D. Rubin. *Sewanee Review.* Summer, 1962. p. 505

Mr. Ferlinghetti documents his claim to being an oral poet by including, flipped in the back cover of his new book [*Starting from San Francisco*], a 7-minute LP record of himself reading his own poems. . . . Mr. Ferlinghetti's verse is perfectly suited to his style of delivery, and his style of delivery is effective and engaging. Free verse such as his needs plenty of room for its organizational necessities: repetition, listings, a long looping flow that goes back to its beginnings so as to make a rounded form. . . . He has the usual American obsession, asking, "What is going on in America and how does one survive it?" His answer might be: By being half a committed outsider and half an innocent fool. He makes jokes and chants seriously with equal gusto and surreal inventiveness, using spoken American in a romantic, flamboyant manner.

Alan Dugan. *Poetry.* Aug., 1962. pp. 314–15

The Beats made a great mistake in permitting a label to be glued on them, especially after they started believing what it said. Every moment Ferlinghetti expends on the hairs of Fidel's "beat beard" is snatched from the service of an underdeveloped gift. He is, or could be, a *comic* writer with a curiously neutral idiom. . . . On the predictable themes—Castro, Euphoria, Pot dreams, Journeys across the continent, nausea, Negative sanctity . . . he is portentously dull. But no stereotyped Beat has the wit for "The Great Chinese

Dragon," exalting it into the type of the orgiastic apocalypse, but not failing to note that the feet walking beneath it wear Keds.

Hugh Kenner. *National Review.* Aug. 14, 1962. p. 110

Neither Ferlinghetti's plays [*Unfair Arguments with Existence*] nor the hypothetical theater for which he intends them are new. In techniques and the themes of isolation and absurdity, he identifies himself with obvious antecedents: Sartre, Albee, Beckett, Genet, Camus. Most of the time he sounds as though he were giving back to his mentors, in a different idiom, what they have given him.

They would be pleased. Generally, these plays turn back upon and within themselves in miniature labyrinths of irony and pun, at the ends of which squats the same patient, grinning Minotaur. The paraphernalia of waste, the perplexing similarity between waking and dreaming, the potential dead-end of men's use of atomic energy, the tricks and masks of desire are the stuff the inhabitants of Ferlinghetti's insidious sewers grovel through.

Dabney Stuart. *Poetry.* July, 1964. p. 260

Routines comprises twelve "plays" which are closer to formalized "happenings," a genre which was given the hipster's kiss of death. I don't know what to make of them. They are not enough. Most of them deal with the miasmal condition of the current culture, but at the same time, they avoid coming to grips with that culture. They are against war, fascism, the bomb, witch hunts, and so forth— Ferlinghetti's heart is in the right place. But again, it's not enough. . . . It is a book which tells the truth, but which skates over the wellsprings of that truth.

Gilbert Sorrentino. *New York Herald Tribune Book Section.* Aug. 8, 1965. p. 15

At the end of "The Sleeper," one of twelve brief plays making up *Routines*, Ferlinghetti quotes the etymology of the word, *jazz*: "jas: jass: jasm: gism." Jazz carried back to gism is a lovely analogy for a way of writing plays that wants to get behind established drama, to re-see the beginning, radically, as form, exactly as that etymology lets us re-see jazz. . . . Though Ferlinghetti writes at a secondary intensity, he is, after all, professionally oriented, always with his ear to the ground, listening, smart and talented. He is, I think, clearly a good playwright. The form is proper to him. Additionally, for whatever it's worth, I cannot help feeling—after reading the last piece, "Bore"—how extraordinarily effective a politician he could be. Whatever he does it is always with, or from, the whole man. And that man is smart.

Richard Duerden. *Poetry.* May, 1966. pp. 125–6

[Lawrence] Ferlinghetti's poetics are functional. Directed toward a "resocialization" of art, he creates lasting work that combines realism and revelation in a cry for conscience and change. . . .

It is time to fill the critical gap surrounding his writing. Such an endeavor must, however, be based on the broad foundation of his work, one that goes beyond his associations with movements, writers, or locales and recognizes the poet's originality, diversity, and firm commitment to an international vision of writing as a cultural force, authentically engaged and engaging. Lawrence

Ferlinghetti has produced some of the most powerful and popular writing of our time. As one of the great artistic borrowers of our time (Eliot and Pound being others), he has taken his influences from the gamut of world literature, philosophy, art, and affairs, and yet integrated it all into his own personal vision—genuine and aware. Beyond his function as a literary figure or catalyst in the beat movement and San Francisco Renaissance in poetry he is a truly international artist and publisher, and is a contemporary model of the poet of revolt and affirmation. Exclaiming the injustices and suppression of life and propounding the compassionate unity of all life—earth to man to creature—he is forever that personal and public poet-at-large.

Ferlinghetti's achievement as an artist cannot be separated from his work as a man. Yet, it is essential to recognize both planes of this overlapping development. He has recreated a popular oral poetry, integrated open-form poetics with abstract expressionist theory, created a vital poetry of the streets, molded a rhetorical poetics that embraces the methods of surrealism, filmmaking, satire, and has developed diverse forms and applications of the prose poem. He is a poet of genuine humor and hard-won lyricism. His theater is provocative and engaging, a contemporary amalgam of expressionist, absurdist, existentialist, and surrealist theater. In his journal writing he has developed the poet-journalist perspective and brought about a further synthesis of poetry and prose. For some time he has been America's most outspoken and adept poet of political satire, and his antinovel *Her* stands as a major achievement for its expansion of the fiction techniques of narrative perspective, structural and stylistic devices, deep imagery and symbolism—all directed toward an open exploration of the nature of reality. While his artistic faults are invariably those of daring excess, his most stunning achievements are those of innovation and synthesis within his functional life-art dynamics. Repeatedly he has shown himself to be a craftsman with a broad artistic comprehension, a fine inner ear, and an unfailingly open eye and heart.

Larry Smith. *Lawrence Ferlinghetti, Poet-at-Large* (Carbondale: Southern Illinois Univ. Pr., 1983), pp. 196–98

Among the radical changes of technique and perspective in the art of the twentieth century, one that is frequently overlooked is the sociological fact that the situation of the artist has been altered by the proliferation of the mass media. Artists have become public to such an extent that their roles and reputations may easily become their major concerns—and their primary themes. The use of the first person in poetry traditionally becomes a device for universalization: an experience or sensation is employed to speak to or reveal a generalized point, embodying Lautréamont's tenet that "Whoever considers the life of a man finds therein the history of the species." However, in much of the poetry of the Beat Generation writers, the personal and subjective elements become distressingly autistic: everyday trivia and personal experiences are described, as is frequently the case in Lawrence Ferlinghetti's poems, to portray and congratulate the writer himself. A chief subject of Ferlinghetti's poetry is often Ferlinghetti himself. The subjective element in the poems seems calculated to reveal the poet to the reader rather than to illuminate the reader. The success of his subjective poems is compromised when Ferlinghetti focuses self-consciously on his role as poet or on nugatory occasions and indulges in mock self-deprecation, but more frequently the genuine wit and comfortable

presence of his speakers transform personal observations into significant images of the human condition. . . .

Ferlinghetti is one of the most conspicuous practitioners of a new type of poetry designed as an intentional rebuke to what the Beats considered the sterility of academic poetry. . . . The new poetry demands that the reader engage it, interact with it, rather than study it. . . . Together with the development of a fresh poetics, a new type of subject matter arrives which is intensely personal and which often focuses sharply and clearly on the poet's sensibilities, what Leslie Fielder calls "the reemergence of the 'I' at the center of the poem." However, this poetry is not confessional in the conventional sense. The poet details his everyday actions and reactions so that the poems become a record of his existence.

Michael Skau. "The Poet as Poem: Ferlinghetti's Songs of Myself." *Concerning Poetry.* 1987, pp. 57–60, 69

BIBLIOGRAPHY
Pictures of the Gone World, 1955 (p); *A Coney Island of the Mind*, 1958 (p); *Her*, 1960 (n); *Starting from San Francisco*, 1961 (p); *Unfair Arguments with Existence*, 1963 (pd); *An Eye on the World: Selected Poems*, 1967; *The Secret Meaning of Things*, 1969 (p); *Tyrannus Nix?*, 1969 (p); *The Mexican Night*, 1970 (t); *Back Roads to Far Places*, 1971 (p); *The Illustrated Wilfred Funk*, 1971 (p); *Open Eye, Open Heart*, 1973 (p); *Who Are We Now?*, 1976 (p); *Northwest Ecolog*, 1978 (misc); *Landscapes of Living and Dying*, 1979 (p); *Endless Life: Selected Poems*, 1981; *The Populist Manifestos*, 1981 (misc); *Over All the Obscene Boundaries*, 1984 (p); *Seven Days in Nicaragua Libre*, 1984 (t); *Pier Paolo Pasolini: Roman Poems*, 1986 (tr); *Inside the Trojan Horse*, 1987 (lectures, p); *Love in the Days of Rage*, 1988 (n); *When I Look at Pictures*, 1990 (p); *These Are My Rivers: New and Selected Poems 1955–1993*, 1993 (p); *A Far Rockaway of the Heart*, 1997 (p)

FIEDLER, Leslie (1917–)

Mr. Fiedler is a very clever writer; he has an engaging gift of candor, and he learned long ago not merely to accept himself as a Jew, an intellectual, a writer passionately interested in political events and a political critic essentially dedicated to literature, but, wherever possible, to throw his "tragic" knowledge at people in such a way as to embarrass them. He tells us that his essay on *Huckleberry Finn* has outraged the homosexuals, and adds— "This, I suspect, is success." This may be success, but I'm afraid that it is the only kind of success that can come from such deliberate provocativeness—this air of talking, talking brightly, brashly, penetratingly, all the time, no matter what the subject or whom he embarrasses.

Alfred Kazin. *New Republic.* Aug. 29, 1955. p. 20

A great deal of American fiction, Fiedler says, has been an escape from a society under female domination into an imagined world of male companionship. Much of it has revealed a fear of darker races, which represent wild Nature; and the hero of the novel is often involved in some close relation with an Indian, a Polynesian or a

Negro (Chingachgook in *The Last of the Mohicans*, Queequeg in *Moby Dick*, Nigger Jim in *Huckleberry Finn* and Sam Fathers in the *The Bear*). Fiedler wants us to believe that this relation is "a homoerotic fable," and he adduces a great deal of evidence—sometimes persuasive, sometimes based on a misreading of the text—in favor of his special interpretation. . . . It works pretty well with some of our best authors, including Hawthorne, Melville and Faulkner, but not necessarily with their best novels; for example, Fiedler has fresher things to say about Melville's deplorable nightmare, *Pierre*, than about *Moby Dick*; nightmares are more Freudian. It doesn't work at all with a whole galaxy of novelists whom Fiedler dismisses as "middlebrow": William Dean Howells, Edith Wharton, Willa Cather, Sinclair Lewis, James Gould Cozzens, or anyone else who tries to present normal Americans.

> Malcolm Cowley. *New York Times Book Section*. March 27, 1960. p. 1

It is an occasion for very considerable, if wary, satisfaction to have those ideas and countless more like them, jostling one another with a kind of cheery, subversive vigor within the covers of a single text. *Love and Death in the American Novel* is, at the least, an immensely valuable corrective to what, despite everything that has been said, is a continuing misapprehension about our literature and ourselves. But it is a good deal more than that, too. . . .

But the perspective *is* fresh, and what Mr. Fiedler says by means of it is memorable. He is one of the very few literary critics of his generation whose ideas one can actually remember from one day to the next. And if so, it is because his deliberately disturbing habit of seizing literature from the side or from below has not simply wrenched the works he studies into unnatural shapes. It is because, by yanking and pulling, he has also forced some of them back toward their proper shape. It is because this fresh viewpoint has managed to take hold of a serious portion of the truth about the motivations that inform the American novel. "Truth" is a strong word, and it is here intended as such.

> R. W. B. Lewis. *The Yale Review*. June, 1960. pp. 611, 614

One side of Fiedler's mind seems honestly drawn to Melville's commitment to "No! in thunder." The other side is satisfied only when he can show he's the sharpest and wittiest guy in class. "I'm Oliver Cool, the cleverest body in school." Fiedler has a good eye for pretense, he can worry an idea like a cat toying with a mouse, but he has a terrible need to be a show-off.

The various Fiedlers appear to write in different tones. The treatment of Warren is quite deferential until near the end, that of Faulkner is patronizing, and the article on Kingsley Amis and his contemporaries is fairly sober and well considered. One is never sure what the tone is going to be. But one is never surprised to see Fiedler sitting astride his subject, pressing its nose in the dirt, and saying grimly and gleefully, "Say Uncle!"

> William Van O'Connor. *Saturday Review*. Nov. 19, 1960. p. 46

Leslie Fiedler, a man of learning and intelligence, has composed another of those fascinating catastrophes with which our literary scholarship is strewn. *Love and Death in the American Novel*

seems to me destined to become a classical instance of sophisticated crankiness; it rides a one-track thesis about American literature through 600 pages of assertion, never relenting into doubt or qualification, and simply ignoring those writers and books that might call the thesis into question. . . . Most American fiction, suggests Fiedler, falls either into the gothic or sentimental category, neither of which allows a confrontation with the needs of maturity. . . .

In such essays [as *No! In Thunder*] the appearance of Fiedler's writing is all energy and verve, but what lies beneath it is a corrosive knowingness, a void of nihilism. Opinion, the clash of interest, the confrontations of belief—all give way under the pressure of his need to dazzle and display, to thrust his ego between the reader and his ostensible subject, to remain—all else failing—brilliant, brilliant, brilliant to the last bitter and anxious word.

> Irving Howe. *New Republic*. Dec. 5, 1960. pp. 17–19

Some of the verbal horseplay is funny, and some of the ideas being mocked deserve Menippean or Huxleyan satire. But the satirist has no position of his own, the exaggerated phrases cancel each other out, and all meaning or possibility of it soon disappears down a particular and often invoked drain. . . . Only four or five paragraphs in the whole novel *The Second Stone*, one of them on Michelangelo's *Pieta*, suggest how much has been omitted in the way of beauty, history, magnanimity, myth and a dozen other elements one might name.

> Robert Gorham Davis. *Hudson Review*. Summer, 1963. pp. 284–5

In the good old days, Jewish sons faced their fathers and verbally slapped them in order to be men. In these post–D. H. Lawrence times the hero smirks in his Buddha-like shell till he shrieks at the woman beside him he both needs and despises. Fiedler, who as a critic can comment so brilliantly on the psychological inadequacies of American writers, reads here *Back to China* like one of his targets in *Love and Death in the American Novel*.

The reaction to *Back to China* is likely to be intense, if only because one justly expects a great deal from Fiedler. Like Mailer, however, Fiedler is so immersed in his associations that he has not created a whole world, but has presented the undigested world of his vital imagination. Like Bellow, he has not created a structure, or at least a structure that is compelling enough to make the reader forget the constant appearances of literary gratuitousness and autobiographical reminiscences. . . .

Having said all these things, it may seem odd that I also want to praise the book. *Back to China* attempts a large view of society and it is not afraid to reveal its author's feelings. Fiedler grasps for the heavens and stumbles; but the space travelled has been through meaningful places.

> Martin Tucker. *Commonweal*. June 11, 1965. p. 388

. . . *Love and Death in the American Novel* is to my mind probably the best single book on American fiction ever written, and it is surely unsurpassed in its definition of Gothicism as a characteristic of that fiction. The book has been most resented for its purported emphasis on sexual perversity in American literature and in its use of this as an index to certain historical and cultural tensions. Actually Fiedler is altogether less daring and less insistent on this aspect of our literature than was Lawrence in his much earlier study, and he is in no sense as moralistic about sex as a literary component. . . . Fiedler's methods are not essentially different from those of other commentators who are concerned with recurrences of literary motifs and with the elaboration of these into archetypes or myths. It may be more provocative but it is not more or less valid to reduce American literature to certain versions of sexual dislocation than to reduce it to versions of Eden, Christ or the Frontier.

Richard Poirier. *Partisan Review*. Fall, 1966. pp. 636–7

I don't think that Fiedler's way of treating myth is as easily transferable into prescriptive program as he wants it to be. His methods do damage not just to literature, by breaking up whole works to salvage the "authentic" fragment, but to life, making it only a kind of *materia mythica* to be arranged and manipulated without entering very deeply into the particular experiences that compose it. He doesn't mean to do this, and his career is a deserved and salutary rebuke to those who would insulate art from its human motives and consequences; but *The Return of the Vanishing American*, for all its admirable intentions and its achieved pleasures and illuminations, is finally bad medicine.

Thomas P. Edwards. *Partisan Review*. Fall, 1968. p. 610

Fiedler has certain subjects—being a Jew in America, American Jewish writers, liberal politics and taste, the mythology of chaste homosexual relations at the center of classic American literature—to which he returns over and over, and about which he has had, essentially, one idea. He has gone on liking the idea, and gone on giving himself contexts in which it can be used. . . .

The real point about Fiedler, which we can make praise or blame as we choose, is that he is always a political writer, always putting himself into situations where he is speaking against this fashion or that obsolescence, deriding some official line, jockeying for some new position. He always acts as though we might be deceived by some other hawker of myths and contexts if he did not set us straight, and he loves doing this so much that he will take any opportunity that presents itself to keep us informed, protected, reminded. But he also just plain loves to hear himself talk, too, and as long as he is excited by an idea he will go on saying it.

Roger Sale. *New York Times Book Section*. Oct. 10, 1971. p. 10

BIBLIOGRAPHY

An End to Innocence, 1955 (e); *Love and Death in the American Novel*, 1960, rev. ed., 1967 (c); *No! In Thunder*, 1960 (e); *Pull Down Vanity*, 1962 (s); *The Second Stone*, 1963 (n); *Waiting for the End*, 1964 (e); *Back to China*, 1965 (n); *The Last Jew in America*, 1966 (n); *The Return of the Vanishing American*, 1968 (e); *Nude Croquet*, 1969 (coll s); *Being Busted*, 1970 (m); *Cross the Border—Close the Gap*, 1971 (art c); *Collected Essays*, Vols. I and II, 1971; *To the Gentiles*, 1971 (c); *The Stranger in Shakespeare*, 1972 (c); *The Messengers Will Come No More*, 1974 (n); *A Fiedler Reader*, 1977 (misc)

FIERSTEIN, Harvey (1954–)

Arnold Beckoff, the lonely but far-from-forlorn hero of Harvey Fierstein's *Torch Song Trilogy*, is a die-hard romantic who takes his heart, soul and fatalism from the 1920's ballads that give the work its title and its tone. At the end of a long, infinitely rewarding evening in the company of . . . his family and friends, [Arnold] confesses with a sigh that he has always wanted exactly the life that his mother has had— "with certain minor alterations."

Those alterations—Arnold is a homosexual and a professional "drag queen"—are the substance but not the sum of Mr. Fierstein's work, three plays that give us a progressively dramatic and illuminating portrait of a man who laughs, and makes us laugh, to keep from collapsing. The evening is a double tour de force for Mr. Fierstein, who, with his throaty Tallulah voice and manner, stars in his own touching triptych.

We first met Arnold in *The International Stud*, produced Off Broadway in 1978. At the time, I felt it was a sincere but sentimentalized view of a transvestite in extremis. Seeing the play again, in a carefully abridged version in a vastly superior staging by Peter Pope, I found myself enjoying Arnold's wit—he has the pithy humor of a Fran Lebowitz—at the same time that I was moved by his dilemma. He is a man of principle who compulsively plays the fool.

[In *Torch Song Trilogy*], *The International Stud* becomes the first chapter in a cycle of tales about Arnold. . . .

The current evening is designed as a trilogy of related plays, but it turns out to be one cohesive three-act play.

Each succeeding "act" adds to our understanding and fully justifies what has gone before. Instead of reiterating positions, Arnold's story becomes richer as it unfolds. There are still flashes of sentimentality in Mr. Fierstein's performance as well as in the text. The author is so accomplished at playing Arnold that he cannot resist an extra flourish or an easy wisecrack, and the ending is too neatly symbolic. But the cumulative event is one to be experienced and savored.

Among other things, it deals fairly—without any attempt at exploiting the situation or manipulating our emotions—with varieties of sexual orientation. For example, Arnold's lover is a bisexual who is caught between two magnets: what he thinks he needs and what he feels. The evening studies self-love and self-hate, headstrong passion and heartfelt compassion.

In the first part, the two men meet—to a counterpoint of torch songs, sung pensively—and after a sequence of on-again, off-again encounters, many of them humorous, they separate. In the second part, *Fugue in a Nursery*, Arnold and his new lover, a male model, visit Arnold's "ex" and his new girlfriend at their farmhouse. The tinseled cynicism of the first play sweetens as the quartet conducts a roundelay that is both fanciful and immensely civilized. The four switch partners, conversationally as well as romantically, with the irrepressibly sympathetic Arnold trying, but not succeeding, in turning a deaf ear to the problems of others.

In the third and best play, *Widows and Children First!* we meet Arnold's past and present family. First there is his Jewish mother, fresh from Miami with an archetypal self-salute, "I'm the mother," and an unextinguishable hope that her son may yet blossom into heterosexuality. The final addition is a troubled teenager whom Arnold has rescued from the streets and wants to adopt. The sociological implications are complex and the author treats them with equanimity, demonstrating that the flamboyant Arnold is truly a reflection of his assertive mother, which is why they are destined to spend their lives at logger-heads. . . .

All of the characters are of course subsidiary to Arnold's dominant personality. He is his own torch song, and the role is inseparable from the actor-author. Mr. Fierstein's self- incarnation is an act of compelling virtuosity.

Mel Gussow. *The New York Times.* November 1, 1981, p. 81.

[In *Torch Song Trilogy,* the] rambling and, because it can only move in circles, repetitive plot might do well enough. . . . But that self-mockery Mr. Fierstein delights in begins to pose problems as the performance now stands. It tends to become a permanent shield, concealing the man beneath it. Sometimes it is simply playful: two men on a telephone cooking up names for female singers, Kitty Litter, Bertha Vanation. Sometimes it is waspishly knowing: "I'm aging about as well as a Beach Party movie." Sometimes it makes "in" use of its homosexual background: "What's the matter—you catch your tongue on the closet door?" And sometimes it collapses of its own effort: speaking boastfully of all the "Hims" he knows well, Mr. Fierstein includes "The Battle Him of the Republic."

The quality of the jokes varies, but that's not the point. The point is that there's no knowing the joker. His defenses are, and remain, impenetrable. The author-actor is adding to this . . . by making certain of his gestures and reactions Road-Runner-broad: trying to arrange a date by telephone, he squirms in the armchair as though it had been invaded by red ants. Since none of the evening's other characters behave in this fashion (including two homosexuals and one bisexual), the excesses cannot be ascribed to his sexual patterns; neither can they be fitted into an over-all style that legitimately embraces the balance of the company. . . .

"I feel like freeze-dried death" isn't an unimaginative phrase; yet it is too self-conscious to make us think about, or feel for, the man uttering it. The phrase seems to be listening to itself, which makes it quite impersonal. Does this matter? I think it does. I found the constant tattoo of attempted left-field laughs ultimately wearing; and the barrage did get between the actor and any feelings I might have had for him. How much of this, I wondered, has come about during the weeks since the play opened downtown? Has that hard, ready-made laughter from out front hurt the complexity of the leading performances, helped turn it into a grab for the next guffaw?

The laughter—at least at the performance I saw—is peculiar because it is so unvaried and so unselective. Normally, audiences like to choose what they will laugh at. Perhaps a little laugh, a kind of chuckle of recognition. Or a medium size one, to indicate that the friendship is growing but the commitment is not yet permanent. Then, when surrender does come, the boffs. Here it's all boffs, which means that some of them simply cannot be genuine. For instance, I doubt that Mr. Fierstein makes a single campy gesture— or what a straight parodist would consider a homosexual gesture— that isn't greeted with instant hilarity. But this surely cannot be what Mr. Fierstein, as playwright, must once have had in mind. *Torch Song Trilogy* is certainly not a play meant to poke fun at homosexuals minute by minute. Laughter is legitimate, but other responses are called for. . . .

It's strictly gag-time as things now stand. Has playing the show for some weeks or more, and finding new ways to nudge the audience's funny-bone nightly, finally hollowed out the play,

erased variety and nuance, robbed it of its possible range of moods? The play's director, Peter Pope, might be well advised to take another, sterner look at it.

Walter Kerr. *The New York Times.* June 27, 1982, pp. H3, H16.

"La Cage aux Folles" is the first Broadway musical ever to give center stage to a homosexual love affair—but don't go expecting an earthquake. The show . . . is the schmaltziest, most old-fashioned major musical Broadway has seen since "Annie," and it's likely to be just as popular with children of all ages. Were you hoping for a little more? I must confess that I was. The glitz, showmanship, good cheer and almost unflagging tunefulness of "La Cage aux Folles" are all highly enjoyable and welcome, but, in its eagerness to please all comers, this musical is sometimes as shamelessly calculating as a candidate for public office.

Sometimes, but, happily, not always. There are more than a few startling occasions in this rapaciously busy extravaganza when the vast machinery comes to a halt—when David Mitchell's glorious pastel-hued scenic visions of St.-Tropez stop flying, when the transvestite dancing girls vanish, when the running gags about whips and wigs limp away. . . .

[Albin], as Zaza, is the headline attraction at the nightclub that gives the musical its title. For 20 years, Albin has had a tranquil domestic life with Georges . . . , the club's impresario. Albin is the more flamboyant of the pair. It is he who must dress up in drag every night to entertain the customers and who has the most to fear from growing old. . . .

Whether in his female impersonations or in civilian guise, [Albin] is neither campy nor macho here: he could be any run-of-the-mill nightclub entertainer in midlife crisis. But it is precisely his ordinariness that makes him so moving. When [Albin] sits in front of his dressing-room mirror to sing plaintively of how he applies "a little more mascara" to make himself feel beautiful, we care much more about what the illusion of feminine glamour means to the otherwise humdrum Albin than we do about the rather routine illusion itself.

That's how it should be. By making us see so clearly how precariously his self-esteem is maintained, [Albin] makes it all the more upsetting to watch what happens when that identity is attacked. And, as in the French film of "La Cage aux Folles" . . . , that shock quickly arrives. Albin and Georges's "son"—fathered by Georges in a long-ago, one-night heterosexual fling—announces his intention to marry the daughter of a bigoted politician. To help the young man perpetuate the fiction that he had a standard upbringing, Georges cruelly asks Albin to disappear when the prospective in-laws come to call.

What follows, at the end of Act I, is the evening's moment of triumph. [Albin] rushes on the stage of La Cage to perform as Zaza—only to stop in midstride and let loose with his real feelings of rejection and betrayal. In drag though he may be, the actor sings in a full-throttle baritone—with a pulsating force that induces shivers. The song, titled "I Am What I Am," is full of rage but, better still, of pride: even as Albin defends his right to live as he wishes, he pointedly asks not for either "praise" or "pity." . . .

When the stars aren't delivering . . . [their] songs, "La Cage aux Folles" can be as synthetic and padded as the transvestites' cleavage. . . . Harvey Fierstein, writer of the book, has misplaced his craftsmanship and bite on this outing; he's exercised few of his

361

options to bolster a property that was thin and coarse to begin with. The tiny plot of "La Cage" is dribbled out with painful lethargy in Act I, then resolved chaotically (and confusingly) for the final curtain. Worse, there is a homogenized, sit-com tone to the script, which suggests that Mr. Fierstein is pandering to what he apparently regards as a squeamish Broad-way-musical audience.

The ostensibly tart backstage wisecracks of Zaza's fellow transvestites are so tame and tired that they make the equivalent jokes of, say, "Victor/Victoria" or Mr. Fierstein's own "Torch Song Trilogy" sound like hardcore porn. . . . In the book scenes, unlike the songs, Georges and Albin are so relentlessly square that they become homogenized homosexuals in the manner of the scrupulously genteel black people of Hollywood's "Guess Who's Coming to Dinner" era. The lovers' turncoat son . . . is too wanly characterized for us to understand his casual callousness; the parents of the bride are such caricatured villains that even the more zealous homophobes in the audience can feel morally superior to them—and thereby escape the reach of the show's plea for tolerance. . . .

[Even when Fierstein and lyricist Jerry Herman] are cautiously watering down their material, their splashy entertainment usually hums along in its unabashedly conventional way. Wait for those privileged occasions when [the actors and] Mr. Herman summon up the full courage of the show's convictions, and you'll hear "La Cage aux Folles" stop humming and sing.

Frank Rich. *The New York Times*. August 22, 1983, p. C13.

Two recent plays about AIDS point up, by their failings, the delicate balance that [William] Hoffman's play [*As Is*] achieves. Harvey Fierstein's *Safe Sex*, the more ambitious of the two, at least in terms of its physical production, is also the more flawed, and has closed after a week on Broadway and an earlier trial run at La MaMa E.T.C. *Safe Sex* comprises three one-acters, two of which allow Fierstein to repeat the role he had such success with in *Torch Song Trilogy*: himself. The Fierstein persona combines the bitchiness of Truman Capote with the self-delighting self-parody of Liberace, and adds to that a smear of schmaltz as though he were for the moment possessed by the dybbuk of the supreme Jewish mother. With the recent demise of the above-named gay archetypes, Fierstein has probably inherited the title they once contested, as the homosexual Middle America most enjoys condescending to. My own reaction to Fierstein doing Fierstein is antipathetic to a degree that is probably out of proportion to any real thespic sins he may commit. As a gay myself, I felt like a black attending a Stepin Fetchit festival. Even if the jokes had been funny . . .

Applied to the AIDS crisis, the Fierstein persona is like a smiling-face, Have-a-Nice-Day sticker offered in lieu of medical treatment. In the first, mercifully brief playlet, *Manny and Jake*, Fierstein delegates his persona to a younger actor, John Mulkeen, deleting the camp humor and delivering instead gallons of mushy, McKuenesque prose-poesy. The theme of this mush, and of all the humor in the title one-acter that follows, is regret, not for the fallen but for the loss of promiscuous sex—a lament that doesn't ring true from Mulkeen or Fierstein, who both give off such auras of self-adoration that one can't imagine enforced celibacy posing either much of a problem. Through much of his monologue, Mulkeen must fondle his co-star John Wesley Shipp, which he does with all the erotic intensity of someone vacuuming a rug. When Fierstein comes to deal with the same unfortunate Mr. Shipp, they are placed at opposite ends of a symbolic seesaw, a contrivance that spares the

audience the distress of witnessing any gratuitous physical contact. The play was designed very much with a crossover (i.e., straight) audience in mind, and the laughter it generated the night I attended suggested that the target audience had been reached: there were hearty Har! Hars! and soprano titters whenever Fierstein called his partner by a feminine name or otherwise implied that boys will be girls.

And what did AIDS have to do with this? Very little, except to provide Fierstein with a convenient pretext for avoiding a subject that is uncongenial to him: physical (forgive the expression) sex. The Liberace side of the Fierstein persona requires him to treat that subject with prophylactic euphemism, so that even AIDS is never mentioned by its nasty name. Nor do the characters ever deal with a single practicality of the stated theme, safe sex, such as whether they can kiss. Nor does it occur to them that they might be tested to see if they've been exposed to the virus, and thus be spared much mutual suspicion and uncertainty. No doubt the theater has other purposes than offering instruction in sexual hygiene, but Fierstein's play simply sounds like someone dithering on the subject.

Thomas M. Disch. *The Nation*. May 16, 1987, pp. 656, 658.

BIBLIOGRAPHY
In Search of the Cobra Jewels, 1972 (d); *Freaky Pussy*, 1973 (d); *Flatbush Tosca*, 1975 (d); *Torch Song Trilogy*, 1981 (d); *Spookhouse*, 1982 (d); *Manny and Jake*, 1987 (d); *Safe Sex*, 1987 (d); *Forget Him*, 1988 (d)

FISHER, Dorothy Canfield (1879–1958)

Miss Canfield wants the whole of the psychic life to be carried on under the spot-light of the attention. It follows that she is opposed to the creation of instinct; that she desires, in fact, that the psyche should be like a country that refers all its business to a central government. That is a system that leads in the end to a tyrannous and inefficient bureaucracy and the decay of provincial life. . . . The fact is that Miss Canfield's mind is a stranger to the idea of "the thing in itself"; and that makes her very little of a poet and rather less of a moralist.

Rebecca West. *New Statesman and Nation*. July 28, 1921. p. 444

To satisfy . . . worried, but conscientious souls, and perhaps to satisfy herself, Dorothy Canfield has written an earnest and serious vindication of marriage. . . . She has evidently tried to be honest. . . . Dorothy Canfield makes marriage a real thing—a thing of substance and color—but she makes its alternative weak and pitiful. . . . If Dorothy Canfield would face the intensity of love and the lure of freedom as willingly as she faces the reality and depths of family life, she could make a memorable contribution to current thought.

Freda Kirchwey. *The Nation*. Dec. 7, 1921. pp. 676–7

Mrs. Fisher has taken issue with the indictment of the American scene which has colored the writing of many of our most significant contemporary novelists. Her loyalties are the old ones of the New England school; she finds neither malice nor stagnation nor dulless in the village. Her New Hampshire landscape glows with the veritable color of the hills; her village folk are kindly and simple and human; for her rural life still has the atmosphere of contentment and of a large peace. These contacts are notable because, in a sense, they place her definitely among the conservative in her outlook on life.

Lloyd Morris. *New York Times Book Section*. Oct. 15, 1922. p. 25

Dorothy Canfield's sense of humor is keen but she has not wit. Neither does she indulge in epigram. She has done very effective scenes but she is not a quotable novelist. It comes back, I should say, to the fact that with her the story is the thing. Very earnest people are seldom witty.... Dorothy Canfield is concerned with ideas and with people. She has chapters of passion and beauty, but you must take them as a whole.

Dorothea Lawrence Mann. *Bookman*. Aug., 1927. p. 700

Her stories seem to be verifiably true, because they are never written with scorn or with the endeavor to prove anything; unless it be to prove that ordinary day-by-day life may be filled with excitement, that love may grow in the intimacy of marriage stronger instead of weaker; that there are just as many Main Streets in Europe as in America; that the society of one's own children is more diverting than the average crowd at a Night Club.... I sometimes think that Dorothy Canfield, who has a deservedly international reputation, would be even a greater novelist if she did not possess so much common sense. She knows actual life so well, her ideas are so rational, so sound, and so sensible that her love of truth and reality may actually stand in the way of her reaching the highest altitudes.

William Lyon Phelps. *Saturday Review*. Oct. 11, 1930. p. 199

Despite an imperfect mastery of the art of compression and terseness, Dorothy Canfield is foremost today among those novelists who stand for same perspective rather than sensationalism, for verity rather than realism, for selection of facts focused upon an indwelling universal law rather than a chaos of facts-for-facts'-sake, for limited free will rather than complete determinism. Thus, amidst the stultifying and stale conventions of naturalism, Dorothy Canfield is radiantly and dynamically unconventional.

H.H. Clark. *Bookman*. Nov., 1930. p. 300

Because she has been popular from the beginning of her career, because her shrewd common sense and understanding of the conditions of everyday life, even more than her emotional power, make her the "favourite author" of enormous numbers of unanalytical women who find in every story some illumination for

their own lives, she has never had the recognition which her work deserves. She is journalistic to the extent that she produces constantly. She is unliterary partly because she is completely unselfconscious. If she achieves a beautiful passage it is because the words and sentences express what she has to say, and not because she is interested in beautiful writing except as a tool.

Elizabeth Wyckoff. *Bookman*. Sept., 1931. p. 44

Like Miss Cather, her wide knowledge at first hand of many sections of the United States and of some of Europe, prevented her from making those superficial generalizations which weaken the work of the satirists like Lewis, Dreiser, and Sinclair, and her knowledge of adolescence gained through her experience as a teacher, spared her from the errors of those novelists like Anderson who picture youth as a quagmire of evil. If her material seems at times to overwhelm her power of artistic assimilation and expression, her best fiction has an acuteness of insight which will keep her place secure.

Arthur Hobson Quinn. *American Fiction* (Appleton-Century) 1936. p. 714

It's always illuminating to see Dorothy in process of stabilizing all she writes by her constant re-pinning it fast to the common lot, to generic human experience. Her greatest achievement, to my way of thinking, lies in her power to stand firmly on this realistic ground, while at the same time she pulls a possible future through the present. It's a thing teachers sometimes do, but they seldom know how they do it, and I'm fairly sure Dorothy doesn't know how she does it. Teachers do it for individual children, whom they know fairly well; Dorothy does it for an unknown multitude.... Nobody could single out the influences strongly affecting American life for the first quarter of this century without including Dorothy's novels. They seize the reader by an intimate hand and take him at once on an incursion and an excursion.

Sarah N. Cleghorn. *Threescore* (H. Smith). 1936. pp. 132–3

Miss Canfield has had an accumulated mass of experience and anecdote from which to build her tales, and a birthright understanding of the persons of whom she writes.... Miss Canfield writes from the inside, looking out.... It is the ageless and universal striving of the human spirit of which she writes, and the material she has chosen is less noteworthy than the way she uses it.

All of us who are still learning to write should mark and envy the transparent simplicity, the quiet fluency of these tales.... Even more than these inestimable, warm tenderness that doesn't grow mawkish and sentiment that never sugars-off into sentimentality make the pretty everyday raw substances of Miss Canfield's tales beautiful and memorable.

Frederic F. Van de Water. *New York Times Book Section*. Oct. 23, 1949. p. 4

BIBLIOGRAPHY
Corneille and Racine in England, 1904 (c); *Gunhild*, 1907 (n); *What Shall We Do Now?*, 1907 (e); *The Squirrel Cage*, 1912 (n); *A*

Montessori Mother, 1912 (e) (published as *Montessori for Parents*, 1940); *The Montessori Manual*, 1913 (e); *Mothers and Children*, 1914 (e); *The Bent Twig*, 1915 (n); *Self-Reliance*, 1916 (e); (with Sarah N. Cleghorn) *Fellow Captains*, 1916 (e); *The Real Motive*, 1916 (misc); *Understood Betsy*, 1917 (n); *Home Fires in France*, 1918 (s); *The Day of Glory*, 1919 (s); *The Brimming Cup*, 1921 (n); *Raw Material*, 1921 (s); *The Life of Christ* (by Giovanni Papini), 1921 (tr); *Rough Hewn*, 1922 (n); *What Grandmother Did Not Know*, 1922 (e); *The French School at Middlebury*, 1923 (e); *The Home-Maker*, 1924 (n); *Made-to-Order Stories*, 1925 (s); *Her Son's Wife*, 1926 (n); *Why Stop Learning?* 1927 (e); *Learn or Perish*, 1930 (e); *The Deepening Stream*, 1930 (n); *Basque People*, 1931 (s); *Bonfire*, 1933 (n); *Tourists Accommodated*, 1934 (sk); *Fables for Parents*, 1937 (s); *Seasoned Timber*, 1939 (n); *Tell Me a Story*, 1940 (juvenile); (with Sarah N. Cleghorn) *Nothing Ever Happens* and *How It Does* 1940 (s); *The Knot Hole*, 1943 (n); *Our Young Folks*, 1943 (e); *American Portraits*, 1946 (b); *Four-Square*, 1949 (s); *Something Old, Something New*, 1949 (juvenile); *A Fair World for All*, 1952 (e); *Vermont Tradition*, 1953 (e); *A Harvest of Stories*, 1956; *Memories of Arlington, Vermont*, 1957 (m); *And Long Remember*, 1959 (m)

FISHER, Vardis (1895–1968)

Mr. Fisher has written strikingly of a great subject, of the appalling and beautiful Wilderness and of the men and women who conquered it. He has remembered them, the way they talked and moved, the loneliness in their faces as winter came on, their astonishing adaptability in difficulty, the grim laconic quality of their heroism, their coarseness and lewdness and wildness. . . . In *Tragic Life* . . . ranks with the best work of our young writers. It is strong and vital and holds forth great promise for its sequels.

John Bronson. *Bookman*. Jan., 1933. p. 91

The novels of Vardis Fisher, emerging from the last stronghold of the American frontier tradition, the Rocky Mountain West, belong in the main stream of American letters. These are not mere regional novels. In their courage and rigorous honesty they are kin to the great works of confessional literature which know no national boundaries. But just as surely they grow out of the heroic, tragic, building and destroying conquests and aspirations of the pioneers—the fruits of which are now visited on the sons unto the third and fourth generation. . . . Vardis Fisher, single-handed, as he sees it, is conducting a revolution against the pioneer tradition. . . . Like Rousseau, he is intent on showing, without modesty, his hero's courage and nobility; and, without shame, his hero's sins and silliness, ineptitudes and secret mortifications.

Fred T. Marsh. *New York Times Book Section*. Jan. 20, 1935. p. 4

A tetralogy concerned with present-day life in the United States, which remains to the end a puzzling combination of obvious talent for fiction, extreme egocentricity, an honest search for the meaning

of life and loose thinking, comes to an end with Vardis Fisher's *No Villain Need Be*. Like its three predecessors, *In Tragic Life*, *Passions Spin the Plot*, and *We are Betrayed*, it takes its title from a poem of George Meredith's. . . . There is no justification whatever for the loose and scattered ending of the work. . . . Nothing could be more fatal to an author's attempt to communicate his meaning to others than this deliberate failure to take into account the obligation to give his work as much coherence as possible, to use form as a means of communication, and not to deceive himself into thinking that he is being more honest than anybody else merely by discarding the conventions of the novel.

Herschel Brickell. *North American Review*. June, 1936. pp. 358–9

With all its faults—its sprawling formlessness, its monotony of tone, its occasional pomposity, and the didacticism and loss of story interest consequent upon the eventual absorption of Vridar Hunter in Mr. Fisher himself—the tetralogy had moments of power and passion. The naked spectacle of the awful secret agonies of childhood and adolescence dominated by terror and shame compelled emotional response; and there was conviction and trenchancy in the unsparing portrayal of the pettiness and pusillaminity of certain aspects of academic life.

Lucy Ingram Morgan. *Canadian Forum*. April, 1937. p. 30

A novelist can make no more serious demand on his art than that it tell us this: Granted such and such circumstances—and they will probably be those which the unsought experience of his own life has led him to consider—how shall a man conduct himself so that his soul may not sicken and die? It is because Vardis Fisher makes this demand that he commends himself to our interest. His resources as an artist are limited, his taste is uncertain, and his sense of form is not strong enough to allow him with impunity to discard the common conventions of the novel. But no one could doubt the earnestness of his moral purpose. His effort has been extreme to set down his conclusions honestly.

John Peale Bishop. *Southern Review*. Oct., 1937. p. 350

Placing Vardis Fisher is one of the sharpest problems offered by recent American fiction. Fisher's sincerity is so marked and his refusal to be beaten down is so gamely stubborn that he may seem at times to be a more significant novelist than he really is. . . . It is not a pleasant duty to list the faults of an author with so much talent and honesty and sense of human justice. . . . Perhaps Fisher could probe deeper into the current evasions if he also had a social scalpel, and his work might be given a logic and balance it now lacks. But the whole situation isn't so simple. Because Fisher has fallen into the trap of writing novelese, part of the answer to his problem would have to be technical.

Harry T. Moore. *New Republic*. July 27, 1938. p. 342

Vardis Fisher has chosen for his very considerable literary talents a very considerable fictional task. He has decided to write a family saga encompassing the history of man, beginning with prehistoric nomads and ending with whatever is left of contemporary humanity after the present military engagement. . . . It is his contention that the great discoveries which modern science has made concerning the origin and early experiences of man are locked away from the average citizen in text books and technical studies. Pondering this, he concluded that if such knowledge were put into the most popular form of literature, i.e., the novel, it would reach a general audience, and be absorbed into the national consciousness, where it might do some good by giving the voters in a democracy better knowledge of themselves and their problems.

Thomas Sugrue. *Saturday Review*. March 27, 1943. p. 22

(He) is, in part, fascinating, in part tedious and, throughout, plethoric. . . . No one can quarrel with (him) for being a novelist and wanting to be an anthropologist. One can only wish that he would keep his ambivalences to himself and be one or the other, for what emerges from his efforts is certainly not a novel and even less a reliable source-book. It is, rather, a kind of cross-pollination of the two and the resulting hybrid, defying classification, tends unpleasantly to baffle the reader.

R.J. Bender. *Chicago Sun Book Week*. Aug. 10, 1947. p. 6

In Fisher's case (as opposed to that of Erskine Caldwell) we have none of (the) sense of removal; he insists that we identify ourselves with his people. His characters' ignoble patterns of thought and pretenses of superiority are presented as the norm for humanity. Our self-love is affronted, and we read insults into these books. That is exactly the trouble: we feel that this is precisely how Fisher wants us to react. It is as if he has a perverse wish to outrage us, as if in his desire to publish discoveries of our common fraility he stands in the position of prosecutor and accuses us of crimes.

George Snell. *Shapers of American Fiction* (Dutton). 1947. p. 278

In each of the first four volumes (of the *Testament of Man* series) he has examined the deep motives and the major contrivings of early men and women, adroitly deployed in the various fateful circumstances of the misty dawn of humanity. Each book is self-sufficient, an engrossing story of male and female, of man and the gods he dreamed, of the pains of man's writhing emergence from all that he once was. . . . Touching as it does the most tender sensitivities of our self-consciousness, it will enlighten, disturb and delight its readers in all the ways that their own age-old symbolic conditionings will allow and necessitate.

Wendell Johnson. *New York Times Book Section*. Sept. 19, 1948. p. 21

Mr. Fisher's interpretations of man's development are naturally personal and conjectural. It is easy to see that there is more of modern psychology than anthropology in his approach, and it is possible to feel that his ancient men and women, only just out of the caves, have a strangely modern quality of subtlety in their thinking.

Nevertheless, Mr. Fisher is creating his continuous fabric of man's mental history with considerable success and is bringing to bear upon it a powerful poetic imagination.

Nathan L. Rothman. *Saturday Review*. Oct. 2, 1948. p. 30

BIBLIOGRAPHY

Sonnets to an Imaginary Madonna, 1927 (p); *Toilers of the Hills*, 1928 (n); *Dark Bridwell*, 1931 (n); *In Tragic Life*, 1932 (n); *Passions Spin the Plot*, 1934 (n); *We Are Betrayed*, 1935 (n); *The Neurotic Nightingale*, 1935 (e); *No Villain Need Be*, 1936 (n); *In April*, 1937 (n); *Forgive Us Our Virtues*, 1938 (n); *Children of God*, 1939 (n); *City of Illusion*, 1941 (n); *The Mothers*, 1943 (n); *Darkness and the Deep*, 1943 (n); *The Golden Rooms*, 1944 (n); *The Caxton Printers in Idaho*, 1944 (h); *Intimations of Eve*, 1946 (n); *Adam and the Serpent*, 1947 (n); *The Divine Passion*, 1948 (n); *The Valley of Vision*, 1951 (n); *The Island of the Innocent*, 1952 (n); *God or Caesar?* 1953 (e); *A Goat for Azazel*, 1956 (n); *Jesus Came Again: A Parable*, 1956; *Pemmican*, 1956 (n); *Peace Like a River*, 1957 (n); *My Holy Satan*, 1958 (n); *Tale of Valor*, 1958 (n); *Love and Death*, 1959 (s); *Orphans in Gethsemane*, 1960 (n); *Suicide or Murder?* 1962 (h); *Thomas Wolfe as I Knew Him*, 1963 (m); *Mountain Man*, 1965 (n)

FITCH, Clyde (1865–1909)

In his early original plays such as *A Modern Match*, *The Moth and the Flame* and *Lover's Lane*, Fitch used many old-fashioned dramatic conventions, but there is already a well-defined promise of finer work. He abandoned hackneyed stage phrases, filled his work with technical innovations and touches of realism, gave evidences of keen insight into human motives and emotions, and of a remarkable instinct to chronicle the minutest detail and circumstances of the life he saw around him. . . .

In his latest work, however, Fitch has . . . made an advance on anything he has yet done. His powers are becoming more symmetrical, and [*The Truth*] is a fine example of his ability to invest a play with an air of sincerity. He has learned that sound logic and straightforwardness are not incompatible with effective threatrical situations. The fact is that the level of his recent original work is unquestionably high. . . .

Martin Birnbaum. *Independent*. July 15, 1909. pp. 125–7

In all apparent ways his career was a success; he made more money and achieved a wider reputation than any other American playwright, past or present; his work was popular and well rewarded with critical esteem, not only in his own country but in England, Germany, and Italy as well; and yet, looked at largely, this same career appears to be a failure, because Fitch has left behind him no single drama that seems destined to endure. . . .

His very best and most important characters, if we examine them critically, are seen to be amplifications of what, in essence, are "bit" parts. In the girl with the green eyes, Fitch achieved a very searching study of a young woman afflicted with ineradicable jealousy; and in the heroine of *The Truth* he rendered with very wonderful insight the character of a woman constitutionally doomed to telling fibs. Fitch's truest people are women rather than men; and they are nearly always women who are weakened by a flaw in character. They are, in any real sense, *little* people. Thus, even at his best, Fitch achieves his effect by amplifying the little instead of by imagining the large.

> Clayton Hamilton. *Bookman*. Oct., 1909. pp. 135–6

Great interest naturally attaches to Clyde Fitch's last play, and his posthumous triumph with *The City* adds a pathetic touch to the history of his career. The workmanship of this play is so fine that it would seem that he had reached the perfection of his artistic growth. The philosophical meaning of *The City* is less definite than its effective passages of tragedy. The scenes are abhorrent and appalling, but this laying bare of a vicious soul in such a way that its absolute truth is felt is an achievement. . . . The play is as abhorrent . . . as Ibsen's *Ghosts*—perhaps because it has as much of a lesson.

> *The Theatre Magazine*. Feb., 1910. p. 34

His letters reveal that he never outgrew his depressing reaction to unfavorable criticism of his plays; not that he resented being told wherein he had failed, but so often the spirit behind the public comment was heedless and personal. . . . A review of the attitude of the press toward him would indicate that there was a stereotyped approach toward everything he did; that is why he liked to read to his friends the foreign estimates of him, which approached his plays on their individual merits, and placed him high as a man of letters in the theatre. At home the papers praised his dexterity, his clever use of familiar detail, his feminism, which they put into a formula until answered by *The City*, his unerring choice of casts. They pigeonholed him without weighing his literary worth, which, at the time, was a rare exception in the American theater. But Italy, Germany, and France were more ready to place him high for such a play as *The Truth*.

> Montrose J. Moses. *Clyde Fitch and His Letters* (Little). 1924. p. ix

His public career covered exactly twenty years, from 1889 to 1909. When he began to write, American drama scarcely existed; when he died, it was a reality. He did more for the American stage than any other man in our history; when the chronicles of our original plays come to be written, he will fill a large space. He made a permanent impression on the modern theatre; for he was essentially a man of the theatre.

> William Lyon Phelps. *Essays on Modern Dramatists* (Macmillan). 1929. p. 152

Fitch's position in American dramatic literature has never been fairly settled. Among critics old enough to have seen his plays in their original production, and what is more important, with the surrounding atmosphere of American society of that day, they hold,

undoubtedly, a higher value than they deserve. . . . They reveal, it is true, a fidelity to detail, and an occasional sharp commentary on social manners and customs, but it is obvious that they are more concerned with personality than with character and that the comment goes no deeper than a smartly superficial humor.

> John Anderson. *The American Theatre* (Dial). 1938. pp. 63–4

The early work of Clyde Fitch was tentative, but when he produced *The Climbers* . . . he entered upon a more definite period of workmanship, and showed himself a master in delineation of the actions and motives of people moving in social relations. This social consciousness had been in his work from the first. . . . Fitch, however, did not limit himself to social satire; his greatest plays have in them a central idea, which unifies the drama and gives it body.

> Arthur Hobson Quinn. *Representative American Plays* (Appleton). 1938. p. 639

There was, in Fitch, a *grand couturier* of genius. He could, with equal success, either invent a mode or perfect an established one; the result was always certain to become the actress for whom he designed it. When historical romances and costume plays were in vogue, he produced the best. When taste shifted to drawing-room drama, he was quick to excel in that fashion also. . . . In some ways, Fitch understood women better than they understood themselves. This insight accounted for much of his success.

His best comedies framed a series of portraits of the American woman of fashion at the opening of the twentieth century. . . . Fitch's most memorable heroines, for all their presumptive elegance and fastidiousness, were apt to be deeply tainted. . . . The flower of native "good society," they were, fundamentally, what a later generation would describe as vulgar bitches.

All this the moralist in Fitch perceived and implied. The artist in him . . . sought to disguise it by sheer bravura, so that the "mist of shams" might seem to represent the solid substance of life. . . . For forty years afterwards, Fitch could still be reckoned a master of scenic illusion whose drawing rooms were peopled by women idly chattering, displaying their vacuous souls and their delightful gowns, whose "society" resembled a wilderness of apes and wantons. . . . This was as close as Fitch dared come to expressing his sober verdict on his social environment.

> Lloyd Morris. *Postscript to Yesterday* (Random). 1947. pp. 175–7

. . .the untimely death of Clyde Fitch was commonly said to have cut off the one writer who might have produced the "Great American Drama." Fitch had, it is true, worked zealously in many styles in his few years in the theater and scarcely a season passed in the early years of the century without at least two of his plays competing vigorously for the entertainment dollars of New Yorkers. He was acclaimed for the power of his characterization, the freshness of his themes, and the frankness of his dialogue. Indeed for the last he was not infrequently reproached. . . . The scene in *The Girl with the Green Eyes* attests Fitch's close observation of human behavior and only increases the regret that he could not shake off the collar of theatricalism in connection with his major characters and their problems.

Alan S. Downer. *Fifty Years of American Drama: 1900–1950* (Henry Regnery). 1951. pp. 8, 12

Clyde Fitch . . . began to write under the spell of the romantic theater, but ended his short career with a number of realistic character-problem plays. . . . Yet even the romantic social comedies, melodramas, and period plays which gave Fitch an international eminence during his first decade were decidedly in advance of their times. . . . Fitch surpassed his mid-century predecessors in such romantic or even melodramatic situations by his wit, and by the appeal of the characters whom he has projected upon scenes so obviously idealized or exotic. . . . The character-problem plays of his last decade no doubt constitute Fitch's more lasting contribution to the literature of the stage.

Sculley Bradley in *Literary History of the United States*, edited by Robert E. Spiller *et al* (Macmillan). 1953. p. 1012

BIBLIOGRAPHY
Beau Brummell, 1890 (d); *Frédérick LeMaître*, 1890 (d); *Betty's Finish*, 1890 (d); *Pamela's Prodigy*, 1891 (d); *A Modern Match*, 1892 (d) (produced in London as *Marriage 1892*); *The Masked Ball*, 1892; (d, tr); *The Social Swim*, 1893 (d, tr); *The Harvest*, 1893 (d) (revised as *The Moth and the Flame*, 1898); *April Weather*, 1893 (d); *A Shattered Idol*, 1893 (d); *An American Duchess*, 1893 (d, tr); *His Grace de Grammont*, 1894 (d); (with Leo Ditrichstein) *Gossip*, 1895 (d, tr); *Mistress Betty*, 1895 (d) (produced in 1905 as *The Toast of the Town*); *Bohemia*, 1896 (d); *The Liar*, 1896 (d, tr); (with Leo Ditrichstein) *The Superfluous Husband*, 1897 (d, tr); *Nathan Hale*, 1899 (d); (with Leo Ditrichstein) *The Head of the Family*, 1899 (d, tr); *The Cowboy and the Lady*, 1899 (d); *Barbara Frietchie*, 1899 (d); *Sapho*, 1899 (d, tr); *Captain Jinks of the Horse Marines*, 1901 (d); *The Climbers*, 1901 (d); *Lovers' Lane*, 1901 (d); *The Last of the Dandies*, 1901 (d); *The Marriage Game*, 1901 (d); *The Way of the World*, 1901 (d); *The Girl and the Judge*, 1901 (d); *The Stubbornness of Geraldine*, 1902 (d); *The Girl with the Green Eyes*, 1902 (d); *The Bird in the Cage*, 1903 (d, tr); *The Frisky Mrs. Johnson*, 1903 (d); *Her Own Way*, 1903 (d); *Major Andreé*, 1903 (d); *Glad of It*, 1903 (d); *The Coronet of a Duchess*, 1904 (d); *Granny*, 1904 (d, tr); *Cousin Billy*, 1905 (d, tr); *The Woman in the Case*, 1905 (d); *Her Great Match*, 1905 (d); (with Willis Steell) *Wolfville*, 1905 (d); *The Girl Who Has Everything*, 1906 (d); *Toddles*, 1906 (d, tr); (with Edith Wharton) *The House of Mirth*, 1906 (d); *The Truth*, 1906 (d); *The Straight Road*, 1906 (d); (with Cosmo Gordon Lennox) *Her Sister*, 1907 (d); *The Honor of the Family*, 1908 (d, tr); *Girls*, 1908 (d, tr); *The Blue Mouse*, 1908 (d, tr); *A Happy Marriage*, 1909 (d); *The Bachelor*, 1909 (d); *The City*, 1909 (d); *Plays*, 1915

FITTS, Dudley (1903–1968)

Mr. Dudley Fitts has a subtle mind, sensitivity to beauty, an esoteric sense of humor . . . , and a most elliptical manner. He is already known as a translator of the *Alcestis*, and another of his translations from the Greek will be forthcoming this fall. . . .Mr. Fitts seems to me, more than most, to possess authentically the kind of mind and temper that have contributed to the achievement of T. S. Eliot. . . . I admire the deftness of Mr. Fitts, but he does not recapture that first fine careless robustness. This is not meant to imply that he has not his own originallty.

William Rose Benet. *Saturday Review*. July 3, 1937. p. 18

Like these men [Pound and Eliot], many of whose stylistic traits he has taken over (as witness his falling cadences, esoteric allusions, and juxtaposition of classicism and slang), he voices an attitude of disillusionment and despair tempered by irony and wit. But because he is writing at a later point in time, that is, at a time when these sentiments have lost their *raison d'être*, he is unable to bring to them the same vigor and conviction. Whereas Pound was disgusted and Eliot agonized by contemporary brutality and anarchy, Fitts tends to exhibit boredom and polite cynicism. . . .

Mr. Fitts is least successful when his disillusionment is self-conscious rather than lyrically spontaneous, when it seems the result of an attitude rather than of assimilated experience. In most of the longer poems . . . the sentiment is offered as a quasi-philosophical commentary, is conveyed through abstract rather than sensory terms. In the short lyrics, however—and Mr. Fitts's talent is essentially a lyric one—the emotion is objectified; there is unity of sentiment and form. Here the poet contents himself with the presentation of conventional moods such as nostalgia and melancholy and achieves a coherent and convincing poetic statement. The poetic personality is not diffused through any contradiction between approach and expression.

T.C. Wilson. *Poetry*. Nov., 1937. pp. 108–9

The poet in Fitts was more often than not concealed behind his adaptations into English from the Greek and Latin, which he seemed to carry before him as a shield—to protect, perhaps, and to keep alive the sensibility and wit which never failed to delight the sensitive reader of poetry. Fitts's sensibility in poetry was not one of possessing a "melodic ear" but rather one of tonal propriety and grace; his verse . . . moved with formal elegance within the traditions that inspired it. . . . The clean diction, the sense of classical restraint, the finely balanced periods and rhythms place Fitts's adaptations of the Greek anthology in a world far removed from the far more clumsy, thickly worded, unrhymed verses of Edgar Lee Masters' *Spoon River Anthology*.

Horace Gregory and Marya Zaturenska. *A History of American Poetry, 1900–1940* (Harcourt). 1946. pp. 356–8

Dudley Fitts . . . has gone for "faithfulness" rather than "Strictness," with the result that his *Lysistrata* comes through as a powerful experience in English. As a non-reader of Greek I had previously known the *Lysistrata* only in two feeble translations that may have caught the words but certainly missed the force, the tragedy, and the great roaring bawdiness of Aristophanes. With this rendering by Fitts I have found the play for the first time, an experience in delight. . . .Aristophanes, after all, went for what *Variety* calls the "boff." He wrote for the theater. And what would his audience—holding its side at a good raucous piece of bladder-flailing—care for the derivation of the gag? What it wanted was a gag it could respond to. And Fitts delivers it with an assurance that would certainly have delighted the old goat himself.

John Ciardi. *The Nation*. June 14, 1954. p. 525

Spontaneous as his gaiety seems it is frequently also remarkably faithful, . . . and where his raciness seems labored, Aristophanes too seems to limp. The issues of the play *The Frogs* (poetry and politics, and not, as the jacket says, the nether world) and the jokes stemming from the incongruities of the situation, Mr. Fitts reproduces with admirable sharpness; where he (and every modern reading of Aristophanes) must fall short is in the marcurial play of literary wit and in lyrics. . . . Vitality is not Mr. Fitts' only merit. His divisions of the text clarify the articulation of what usually appears as a jumbled mass. His Introduction and Notes present essential information succinctly and with spirit.

Moses Hadas. *New York Times Book Section*. Sept. 11, 1955. p. 10

For Dudley Fitts, as for Aristophanes, *The Birds* is fun. This modern, colloquial translation is, of course, aimed at introducing the comic literary and dramatic genius of Aristophanes to the general reader, but the apparatus of scholarly and critical notes and the index of proper names have a fresh exuberance that Aristophanes would surely have enjoyed. Fitts, moreover, has the imaginative insight to meet the Greek dramatist on his own literary grounds. . . . These literary games are not precocious mannerisms, for Fitts makes them an integral part of Aristophanes's dramatic and thematic structure. Instead of finding a unifying base in some dubiously allegorical Utopia, Fitts molds a play, not of ideas, but of dramatic voices—human and not so human, bird-like, and divine. The beauty and excitement of this version arise out of his ability to counterpoint a wide variety of voices—gentle, buoyant, crude, arrogant.

Paul H. Cubeta. *Saturday Review*. June 22, 1957. p. 30

Until very recently we were unhappily dependent upon the dated Aristophanes of B. B. Rogers or the clumsy prose of the Anonymous translation as debowdlerized by O'Neill. But with the gradual appearance of Fitts' versions . . . and the complete Greek Comedy forthcoming from Michigan, the gap should be filled. At the moment Fitts stands alone, and he is very good indeed. His virtues are fine wit, style, readability and a keen sense of comic motion, marred only by occasional lapses into an owlish coyness and archness.

William Arrowsmith in *The Craft and Context of Translation*, edited by William Arrowsmith and Roger Shattuck (Texas). 1961. p. 180

Some 40 years ago, it was Ezra Pound who advised young poets to revitalize the classics; and if they enjoyed the work of an ancient writer, to "make it new." In this country, Pound's immediate successor was Dudley Fitts, who converted the chore of translating

Greek and Latin verse into one of the liveliest of modern arts. The brilliance of his new versions of the Greek Anthology is now well known, and in the effort to revive Aristophanes, no one has equalled Fitts's *Lysistrata* and *The Frogs*. What he has done has been to breathe new life into the comic spirit of Athens and of Rome. . . .

Some kind of critical moral may be drawn from the success of [his] new version of Martial's epigrams: throughout the course of his career as a maker of ancient verse into something new, Dudley Fitts has never compromised his wit, his taste, or his well-assured affinity with the work that inspired him to write. His version of *Sixty Poems of Martial* is a supreme example of light verse in the 20th-century manner.

Horace Gregory. *New York Times Book Section*. Oct. 29, 1967. p. 12

BIBLIOGRAPHY
Two Poems, 1932 (p); (with Genevieve Taggard) *Ten Introductions*, 1935 (c); (with Robert Fitzgerald) *Alcestis*, 1935 (tr); *Poems, 1929–1936*, 1937; *One Hundred Poems from the Palatine Anthology*, 1938 (tr); (with Robert Fitzgerald) *Antigone*, 1939 (tr); *More Poems from the Palatine Anthology*, 1941 (tr); (with Robert Fitzgerald) *King Oedipus*, 1949 (tr); (with Robert Fitzgerald) *The Oedipus Cycle*, 1949 (tr); *Lysistrata*, 1954 (tr); *The Frogs*, 1955 (tr); *The Birds*, 1956 (tr); *Poems from the Greek Anthology*, 1956 (tr); *Thesmophoriazusae*, 1958 (tr); *Ladies' Day*, 1959 (tr); *Sixty Poems of Martial*, 1967 (tr)

FITZGERALD, F. Scott (1896–1940)

The world of his subject matter is still too much within Fitzgerald himself for him to see it sustainedly against the universe. Its values obtain too strongly over him, and for that reason he cannot set them against those of high civilization and calmly judge them so. Hence, wanting philosophy, and a little overeager like the rest of America to arrive without having fully sweated, he falls victim to the favorite delusions of the society of which he is a part, tends to indulge it in its dreams of grandeur, and misses the fine flower of pathos. He seems to set out writing under the compulsion of vague feelings, and when his wonderfully revelatory passages appear, they come rather like volcanic islands thrown to the surface of a sea of fantasy. . . . He has seen his material from its own point of view, and he has seen it completely from without. But he has never done what the artist does: seen it simultaneously from within and without; and loved it and judged it too.

Paul Rosenfeld. *Men Seen* (Dail). 1925. pp. 222–3

And now it seems almost too contrived that Scott should have chosen this year in which to die. For it is altogether fitting that Scott's career should begin where one world war ends and end where another begins. He spoke for a new generation that was shell-shocked without ever going to the front. He was one of our better historians of the no-man's-time between wars. He was not meant, temperamentally, to be a cynic, in the same way that beggars who must wander through the cold night were not born to freeze. But Scott made cynicism beautiful, poetic, almost an ideal.

Budd Schulberg. *New Republic*. March 3, 1941. p. 312

There are novelists who find their material almost entirely outside themselves, and there are others who find it almost entirely within themselves. Scott Fitzgerald's talent lay in an unusual combination of these two modes. The basis of his work was self-scrutiny, but the actual product was an eloquent comment on the world. He was that rare kind of writer, a genuine microcosm with a real gift of objectivity. The combination explains his success. It is the reason that the force of his best work always transcends its subject matter.

Mark Schorer. *The Yale Review*. Autumn, 1945, p. 187

Fitzgerald's great accomplishment is to have realized in completely American terms the developed romantic attitude, in the end at least in the most responsible form in which all the romantic's sensuous and emotional responses are disciplined by his awareness of the goodness and evilness of human experience. He had a kind of instinct for the tragic view of life. . . . He had, moreover, with all its weakness and strength and in a time when the undivided understanding was rare, an almost exclusively creative kind of intelligence, the kind that understands things, not abstractly, but only concretely, in terms of people and situations and events.

Arthur Mizener. *Sewanee Review*. Jan., 1946. pp. 66–7

Let us mean by (a masterpiece) a work of the literary imagination which is consistent, engaging, and dramatic, in exceptional degrees; which exhibits largely mastered a human subject of the first importance; and which seems in retrospect to illuminate the whole physical and spiritual situation of which it was, by the strange paturition of art, an accidental product.

One easy test will be the rapidity with which, in the imagination of the good judge, other works of the period and kind will faint away under any suggested comparison with it. Now a small work may satisfy these demands as readily as a large one, and *The Great Gatsby* satisfies them, I believe, better than any other American work of fiction since *The Golden Bowl*.

John Berryman. *Kenyon Review*. Winter, 1946. pp. 103–4

The root of Fitzgerald's heroism is to be found, as it sometimes is in tragic heroes, in his power to love. Fitzgerald wrote much about love, he was preoccupied with it as between man and woman, but it is not merely where he is being explicit about it that his power appears. It is to be seen where eventually all a writer's qualities have their truest existence, in his style. Even in Fitzgerald's early, cruder books, or even in his commercial stories, and even when his style is careless, there is a tone and pitch to the sentences which suggest his warmth and tenderness and, what is rare nowadays and not likely to be admired, his gentleness without softness.

Lionel Trilling. *The Liberal Imagination* (Viking). 1950. p. 244

He is so familiar with the characters and their background, so absorbed in their fate, that the book has an admirable unity of texture; we can open it to any page and find another of the touches that illuminate the story. We end by feeling that *Gatsby* has a double virtue. Except for *The Sun Also Rises* it is the best picture we possess of the age in which it was written and it also achieves a sort of moral permanence. Fitzgerald's story of the innocent murdered suitor for wealth is a compendious fable of the 1920's that will survive as a legend for other times.

Malcolm Cowley. Introduction to *The Great Gatsby* (Scribner). 1953. p. xx

The odd, the haunting thing about F. Scott Fitzgerald himself is how close he always was to being a "fringe writer." Or a marginal writer, perhaps, always treading the edge of the abyss, following a narrow ledge between achievement and disaster. And perhaps it was this artist's original confusion about fame (or popularity or cash) and art which led him so swiftly to catastrophe. In any case Fitzgerald's work is split down the middle, between the "objective" novels like *The Great Gatsby*, which lacked somewhere a solid center, and the "confessional" novels like *The Beautiful and the Damned* which lacked a solid form.

Maxwell Geismar. *Saturday Review*. April 26, 1958. p. 17

More important than the nature of Fitzgerald's moralism, of course, is its quality. The most serious charge that must be leveled against him is that he never made a really searching inquiry into the sources of his moral ideas or of the reasons behind the situations that moved him to render moral judgment. His own specific references to his tendency to moralize were always oblique, as though he felt he should either get rid of this predilection or make light of it. Instead of trying to understand it, he tried to direct his reader's attention to something else. When this was no longer possible, he found himself in the midst of a tangle of sometimes adolescent, sometimes senile ways of coping with the moral issues raised in his fiction and in his life.

The absence of a mature, well-defined position of moral perception in a writer is important only if it damages the effectiveness of his writing. In Fitzgerald's case it is clear that his work was damaged, and seriously so. This deficiency kept him from realizing the brilliant potentialities of some of the characters he created. It meant that even the best of them must be only pathetic creatures lost in a world they never made, a world that was hopelessly bewildering.

Kent and Gretchen Kreuter. *Modern Fiction Studies*. Spring, 1961. p. 80

With success Hemingway's slight early diffidence was vanishing into the restrained bravado of a champ. Comparing him to Fitzgerald at this time would be like comparing a butterfly and a bull; the butterfly has beautiful colors on its wings, but the bull is *there*. Hemingway was a force. His personality overpowered you, making you do the things he wanted to do, making you enthusiastic about the things he was enthusiastic about. The world revolved around *him*, while Fitzgerald—off to one side—was subtler, more insidious, more sympathetic, more like light playing through clouds. Fitzgerald had the dangerous Athenian qualities of facility and grace as against Hemingway's Spartan virtues of ruggedness and perseverance. Both were accomplished artists, but perhaps the ultimate choice lay between Fitzgerald's more sensitive penetration of human lives and Hemingway's harder, more burnished style.

Andrew Turnbull. *Scott Fitzgerald* (Scribner). 1962. p. 188

The legend of Fitzgerald's disorderly romantic life answers, and with a better writer, the intense American need for a mythical artistic hero like Poe. An interest in Fitzgerald's work can scarcely escape entanglement in the Fitzgerald legend. Nevertheless, his work today seems to enjoy great favor, perhaps because he seems less mannered than Hemingway, less tortuous than Faulkner, and less clumsy than any of a dozen novelists in the naturalistic tradition. The excellence of his style tends to hold his reputation high while other reputations tumble. But at least two other matters operate in his favor. The first is the hard core of morality which makes him one with those writers of greatest strength in American fiction: Melville, Hawthorne, and James. Second, unlike a majority of modern American writers, he offers a fiction which is hard to imitate but from which much can be learned.

Kenneth Eble. *F. Scott Fitzgerald* (Twayne). 1963. p. 153

Fitzgerald accomplished more than a chronicle of Jazz Age belles and playboys, with whom he has been consistently associated. His repeated emphasis on the theme of corruptive wealth—present even in the notes for the unfinished parts of *The Last Tycoon*—and his depiction of the melancholy implications in the dream of the social aspirer—these represent the core of his commentary on our experience. His contribution was twofold: he distilled in beautiful prose the spirit of an age, and he urged a penetrating criticism of the values that formed its foundation.

William Goldhurst. *F. Scott Fitzgerald and His Contemporaries* (World). 1963. p. 228

In these ''crack-up'' pieces one becomes gradually aware that Fitzgerald is referring not to a brief period of only two or even five years, but to the span of his whole career. The moral sickness was always there, and in 1936 it erupts like an ugly boil for all to see; although painful, perhaps the discharge will aid the cure—or at least relieve the inflammation. Like Melville's Bartleby the scrivener, Fitzgerald seems ready to face the blank wall and stare in profound silence for the remainder of his life, for he seems to have withdrawn completely from the human scene, and to have lost even the sense of his own identity....The only element throughout these terrible revelations which suggests that Fitzgerald is not doomed by self-revulsion is his acute sense of time....Only a man haunted by possible achievement could possess such an obsessive awareness of time.

James E. Miller. *F. Scott Fitzgerald* (NYU). 1964. p. 129

Artistically, however, it was a long step from a sense of the tragic complexities that emerged in him about 1923 to the embodiment of that sense in a viable work of art. As a novelist he had yet to create a hero who was indeed tragic, who could command the reader's

admiration as well as his compassion. To this pursuit, from about 1923 onward, he devoted the rest of his life.

We can watch him struggling in this direction in the surviving drafts that we have of *The Great Gatsby*. But because the book has two half-heroes—Nick the thinker and Gatsby the doer—instead of a single tragic hero, its artistic power is divided and diffused and it fails as formal tragedy. *Tender Is the Night* was also intended to be tragedy and Dick Diver possessed the attributes of a truly tragic hero: a keen intellect and a fine sensibility. He was to be the modern middle-class American raised to heroic stature and then destroyed by an excess of virtue, by his fatal gift of charm. But Fitzgerald could not maintain the necessary aesthetic distance, and halfway through, Dick lost his heroic attributes. As a result this novel also fails to sustain the tragic vision.

In the fragmentary *Last Tycoon*, Fitzgerald most fully realized his desire to write a modern tragedy that would fit the traditional design. Monroe Stahr is the classic hero who compels our respect and admiration as neither Gatsby nor Dick Diver could. Stahr is one of the archetypal heroes of American society—the self-made man doomed to fulfill his tragic destiny as a successful man of affairs.

Henry Dan Piper. *F. Scott Fitzgerald* (Holt). 1965. p. 295

Into the figure of Gatsby he put much of what he admired in America.... There is something in Gatsby's generous, ideal aspirations which transcends their sordid base and survives their squalid destiny. His hopes are visionary, even though his end is coldly actual. . . .Fitzgerald is remarkable because he never blinks at the gaudiness and sentimentality, indeed the almost majestic vulgarity of Gatsby's imagination, yet he can catch what is truly lyrical and valuable and rare in the spirit behind it. He never fell into cynical disillusion even though he went on to show how inwardly fallible and outwardly foredoomed the wondering idealist was.

Tony Tanner. *The Reign of Wonder* (Cambridge). 1965. p. 360

The thing to be emphasized about *Paradise*, after the apologies, is that it sincerely wished to grapple with the ominous sense of fate which obsessed Fitzgerald's youthful ''philosophers.'' Today's critics usually point out that this fatalism was a period melancholy, neither authentic nor universal. It was, admittedly, subject to egregious sentimentalisms, as in *Paradise*, but the malaise running through art, for order and purpose and self-identity, tells us something about the age and Fitzgerald's central role in it—his early awareness that the gift of imagination was at once the American's fall and his possible redemption, that the self was the imagination and the imagination the self, to be used upon life's exchange as the medium of a very precarious purchase. Unfortunately for Fitzgerald, and for a great many of his contemporaries, there were no absolute economic laws governing the expenditure of self, only ones made up as you went along.

Joseph N. Riddel. *Modern Fiction Studies*. Winter, 1965–66. p. 339

Yet to recognize the lapses of form in *Tender Is the Night* should not detract from the novel's extraordinary achievements. In a way

Fitzgerald fulfilled the ambitions with which he had begun his new novel back in 1925. *The Great Gatsby* had placed him among the leaders of the modern movement in the arts, and yet he had wanted to move beyond, to write a novel that would be "the model for the age that Joyce and Stein are searching for, that Conrad didn't find." With *Tender Is the Night* he did move beyond the modern movement, moved away from universal myths and toward the pathos of history. This novel is a vision in art of an era in American history, of the failure of a society and of an individual who embodied its graces and its weaknesses. In *Tender Is the Night* Fitzgerald created a work of fiction rare in American literature, a novel uniting romantic beauty and also historical and social depth; and he proved by his creation that his art, and his identity as an artist, could survive the death of the society which had nurtured and sustained him.

> Robert Sklar. *F. Scott Fitzgerald: The Last Laocoön* (Oxford). 1967. pp. 291–2

Why does Gatsby exist . . . to a far greater degree than Joyce's Stephen? We know from *Tender Is the Night* and "The Diamond as Big as the Ritz" that Fitzgerald entertained his fantasies to a degree dangerous in anyone and peculiarly so in a writer; his daydreams of the beauty and style of wealth are not unlike Stephen's proud exertions. But in *The Great Gatsby* and again in *The Last Tycoon* the dream is rendered in all its beauty and "placed"—not discarded. A distinguished intelligence that yielded to the dream in *Tender Is the Night* now insisted upon its rights. But the real explanation is that for Fitzgerald the person existed; *The Last Tycoon* is all person.

> Denis Donoghue. *The Ordinary Universe* (Macmillan—N.Y.). 1968. p. 67

Even Nick's own wishful vision of beautiful futility [in *The Great Gatsby*] recognizes the continual phoenix-rebirth of dream and aspiration as the fountainhead of human history. It was Amory Blaine, the hero of Fitzgerald's first novel [*This Side of Paradise*], who discovered and accepted the moral philosophy that one must, after defeat and failure, pick up and go on to "the next thing." Putting behind him Nick Carraway's rendering of a blind-end world in *The Great Gatsby*, and taking with him that part of it which has value as usable human truth, Fitzgerald went on, as an artist, to the "next thing" in *Tender Is the Night*, which is the story of a man who, with much fuller knowledge of the inexorable laws of reality than innocent Gatsby had, nevertheless pitted his character, his integrity, his personal vision and energy, flawed and imperfect as they were, against the futility and despair that he knew were the ruling truths of his world.

> Richard Foster in *Sense and Sensibility in Twentieth-Century Writing*, ed. Brom Weber (Southern Illinois). 1970. p. 108

In all Fitzgerald's thinking there is a consistent pattern, a habit of mind which asserts itself in every situation. His ideas on any subject tend to arrange themselves into a system of opposed contraries. We have just seen how strongly this is reflected in his conception of the artist, but it is equally apparent in all the other matters discussed in this chapter: he regarded wealth and social status from both a middle-class and an aristocratic standpoint; he acted as spokesman for a new freedom in morals and manners and

yet possessed a puritan conscience; and the Jazz Age fascinated him because he saw in it a capacity for delirious excitement balanced by equally strong potentialities for disaster. He was fully conscious of this tendency in his thought and assigned a very high value to it: as he remarks in "The Crack-up," "the test of a first-rate intelligence is the ability to hold two opposed ideas in the mind at the same time, and still retain the ability to function." It is no exaggeration to say that this is the essential element in his gift as a social novelist, but it implies a creative tension which can only be maintained at the cost of an enormous and unremitting effort. It provides the ground for the most fruitful kind of complexity in art, but must often lead to uncertainty and disorder in actual living. . . .

His intense self-awareness and the complexity of his reactions made it almost impossible for him to be spontaneous and natural, and his social life had the character of a series of complicated manoeuvres or theatrical tableaux. Sometimes these were hasty improvisations like the bus incident: often they were contrived in advance with the forethought of an impresario or a film producer. . . . Fitzgerald's feeling for the right thing was matched by an uncannily precise instinct for the worst possible behaviour: the quality of insight which enabled him to charm and captivate, could also be used to devise peculiarly subtle punishments for people who bored or irritated him. . . .

What appears as confusion and error in his life is transformed into an ideal clarity of vision in his art. While this is the case with many great artists, it is true of Fitzgerald to an unusually marked degree. It is the main reason why the critics and biographers who see his life and his work as alternative, almost interchangeable, versions of the same story are so completely misled.

> Brian Way. *F. Scott Fitzgerald and the Art of Social Fiction* (St. Martin's, 1980), pp. 19–21

All of Fitzgerald's characters start off with romantic expectations, with a heightened sense of self that eventually comes into conflict with the outside world. Amory Blaine gives way to postwar cynicism; Anthony Patch to a sense of drift in a work-a-day world; Jay Gatsby to a world of established money that he never understands; Dick Diver to an emotionally sick and sterile society; and Monroe Stahr to a materialistic world that cannot accommodate the fated idealist and quickly exhausts him. Like Monroe Stahr, Fitzgerald's characters create a sense of the lavish and heighten it further through the vitality of imagination. But it is imagination that is severed from everything but its own vision. Alone, detached, aloof, their dreams are exhaustible because they feed on themselves and are cut off from the resources of a vital culture. In Fitzgerald's fiction, a sense of romantic possibility plays itself out in a cultural wasteland. Fitzgerald's sense of opportunity warred with a Spenglerian sense of destiny; and if Fitzgerald found in Spengler a historian whose idea of the modern augmented his own, as I believe he did, he also brought to Spengler a sense of romantic possibility that challenged these historical assumptions at the outset.

> Richard Lehan. *Twentieth Century Literature*. Summer, 1980, pp. 154–55

The Great Gatsby's image patterns and even the workings of its plot show more than a general family resemblance to classical tales of flying men. The legend of Phaeton is the one which echoes in this novel most persistently and strongly—so strongly that there is cause for wondering whether Phaeton isn't as deliberately called up here as Odysseus is in Leopold Bloom's wanderings around Dublin. . . .

There is no proving that Fitzgerald consciously turned to Ovid in designing *The Great Gatsby*. He apparently never said a word about doing so; and we can be sure that if Phaeton was on Fitzgerald's mind, other tales were haunting him too. One of his working titles for the novel, *Trimalchio in West Egg*, certainly makes the case for *The Satyricon*, but there are also shadows of *The Waste Land*, and recently some interesting parallels have been turned up between passages in *Gatsby* and lines in *The Golden Bough*. The point, then, of looking at the Phaeton tale in *The Great Gatsby* is not to make an argument for one literary debt and one alone, or to arrive at one pat explanation of how the novel works and what Fitzgerald meant by it. If *Gatsby* borrows something from Phaeton, it might very well be an unconscious borrowing. But one way or the other we are left with the fact that parallels between the stories turn up in uncanny profusion, that the implications of those parallels need to be followed out, and that the closeness of the new myth to the old one helps us understand better how Gatsby's story is a myth, how the rise and fall of a deluded and childlike gangster turns into a vital classic of *our* time. . . .

At the end of the novel the "American Dream" is alive because Nick's imagination is still under its spell. If Gatsby has lived that dream to an inevitable, disastrous conclusion, he has done so in a fashion as much classic as American, and Nick has been classic in telling of it, not simply in allusion and metaphor but in condition of mind. Phaeton may be here in Gatsby by contrivance, or he may not; but *Gatsby* is certainly more akin to Ovid than it is to the Fuller-Magee case or Ben Franklin's *Autobiography* or *Hopalong Cassidy* or the Alger stories or any other rise or rise-and-fall tales that Fitzgerald ever knew of. The story is ancient in more than one way, and that is precisely why it stays with us, not only powerful, but invincibly new.

> Bruce Michelson. *Modern Fiction Studies*. Winter, 1980–81, pp. 566–67, 577

It should be clear that there is a curious unanimity about the critical approach to [F. Scott] Fitzgerald. The reason for this being that for some forty years all criticism has started from the unquestioned premise that he was an emotional rather than a conceptual thinker. This belief has led to a special interest in his life story because it is felt that life and art must be taken together in order to see him clearly. Whether he is seen as the tragic or the pathetic exemplar, the method of his critics is the same: they proceed from the assumption that his whole life was a struggle for personal understanding and artistic control. Even those critics who have sought to establish the idea of Fitzgerald as a careful craftsman have done so while maintaining the notion of the precarious subjectivity/objectivity balance. . . .

What has never been seriously considered is the possibility that everything Fitzgerald wrote was drawn from a firm intellectual center; that he had a consistent point of view which determined all the fiction. The curious fact is that this point of view is easily apparent. Although it operates in the manner of James's celebrated image of the figure in the carpet, it is not the expression of an arcane

philosophy. It has been passed over simply because the notion that Fitzgerald lacked a conceptualizing intelligence has determined that his critics have searched for an emotional "primal plan" rather than an intellectual plan. Far from stemming from a vaguely romantic predisposition toward subjective melancholia, the sad note in his later fiction had its origin in the same comprehensive and rational view of life which controlled the first novel. . . .

From the first attempts to achieve the correct form in "The Romantic Egotist" to the mature complete expression of *Tender Is the Night*, there is a remarkable consistency in Fitzgerald's thought. Even if his "philosophic concept" is not thought to be startlingly innovative, it did give his work intellectual coherence and its presence at the heart of all his artistic concerns should have obviated any suggestion of a lack of control.

> John B. Chambers. *The Novels of F. Scott Fitzgerald* (Basingstoke, England: Macmillan, 1989), pp. 9–10, 188–89

Overwhelmingly, the critical consensus on [*The Great Gatsby*] has asserted that its greatness as fiction resides in its totally successful disposition of particularities to attain artistic ends. The integration of its narrative details has been claimed to be nearly flawless, certainly exquisitely well performed. As I have indicated, the novel's chronology has previously been almost completely unexamined, but, within this critical context, surely an intricate and successful patterning of temporal details would seem a necessary corollary, and has in fact been categorically asserted by [Robert E.] Long: "Fitzgerald's handling of time may deservedly be called masterful; time broken up and scattered through the work has been used in every instance with maximum aesthetic effect."

It is most surprising that there is no recognition in the work of Matthew J. Bruccoli of how frequently chronological incoherence occurs in *Gatsby*. Bruccoli's admirable *Apparatus* for a definitive edition will be cited here repeatedly for matters of factual background, and its explanatory notes do concern themselves with chronological errors. However, only two of the literally dozens that occur are noted—the contradiction about the time of Nick's narration and the error in Pammy's age. . . . It should be unnecessary to state that I do not write in disparagement of these investigators of *Gatsby*. Quite to the contrary, my point is that the novel's chronological inconsistencies have passed unnoticed by even the best of its critics. Whether or not one agrees with the significances I will attach to those inconsistencies, it must, I think, be allowed that the fact of their existence should be noted. . . .

The temporal failings in *Gatsby* are failings in verisimilitude, and it is on the quality of fiction that thematic or symbolic meanings depend for their validity. If Daisy looked like Catherine or if Gatsby's house looked like Nick's, his "following of a grail" would be absurd. To repeat [Kenneth] Eble's dictum, "It is however, only because of the excellence of the particulars that general meanings suggest themselves." If in *Gatsby*, "five years" or "three months" or "several weeks" or "spring" or "just after the war" or "nine thirty" do not mean consistently and coherently what they should mean, then the particulars are somewhat less than excellent and the general meanings somewhat less than validly established.

There is beyond any argument a great deal to admire and appreciate in *Gatsby*—elegant language, powerful evocation, great energy, excellent dialogue, fascinating characterizations, marvelously well-rendered scenes. But as for its being a perfectly executed fiction—as Thomas Wolfe once told Fitzgerald—''Flaubert me no Flauberts, Bovary me no Bovarys.''

> Thomas A. Pendleton. *I'm Sorry About the Clock: Chronology, Composition, and Narrative Technique in The Great Gatsby* (Selingsgrove, Pa: Susquehanna Univ. Pr., 1993), pp. 13, 138

In ''F. Scott Fitzgerald and Fashionable Literary Antisemitism'' (the only essay on this subject, published in *Commentary* nearly fifty years ago), Milton Hindus attributed Fitzgerald's hostile attitude toward the Jews to ''the fashionable anti-Semitism of the 1920s, of the sort we find in T.S. Eliot at the same period.'' But Hindus based his argument solely on *The Great Gatsby* and *The Last Tycoon*; he ignored the evidence from Fitzgerald's two early novels, letters, notebooks, poems, essays, and stories, as well as memoirs about him; and he both obscured and oversimplified the origins of his anti-Semitism.

Fitzgerald's antipathy to Jews developed during his youthful years in St. Paul at the Newman School and Princeton—well before the 1920s. But in the 1930s—after Fitzgerald had formed a number of important friendships with Jewish writers, developed personal and professional contacts with many Jews in Hollywood during the last three years of his life and became increasingly aware of the Nazi threat to the very existence of the Jews—his attitude changed from bigotry to sympathy. In the Jewish hero of *The Last Tycoon*, he created his most impressive and appealing character.

Anti-Semitism was endemic among middle-class white Americans at the turn of the century. Fitzgerald—who came from a provincial, midwestern, socially insecure, Irish-Catholic background—was particularly susceptible to this kind of racial prejudice. His father was a genteel failure, his mother the eccentric daughter of a self-made immigrant, and the family clung precariously to the fringes of ''good society.'' As he told Sheila Graham, his companion at the end of his life: ''My mother went to mass every day. I'm sure she believed that Christian boys were killed at Easter and the Jews drank the blood. She was a bigot.'' . . .

Fitzgerald's attitude toward the Jews, however deplorable in its earlier manifestations, transcended the fashionable literary anti-Semitism of the 1920s and was, in the end, quite admirable. He was sufficiently open-minded and generous-spirited to reject the bigotry engendered by his background and education, and to follow the sound advice of Nick Carraway's father: ''Whenever you feel like criticizing anyone . . . just remember that all the people in this world haven't had the advantages that you've had.''

After meeting a number of sympathetic Jews, Fitzgerald was able to accept them, despite his former prejudice, and to form close friendships.

> Jeffrey Meyers. *Midstream*. January, 1993, pp. 31, 34

In a letter to Scribner's great editor, Maxwell Perkins, the impoverished Scott Fitzgerald pleaded for the possibility of a reprinting of *The Great Gatsby* as one more title in a series of twenty-five-cent paperbacks. ''Would a popular reissue,'' he asked, ''with a preface

not by me but by one of my admirers—I can maybe pick one—make it a favorite with classrooms, profs, lovers of English prose—anybody? But to die, so completely and unjustly after having given so much! Even now there is little published in American fiction that doesn't slightly bear my stamp—in a *small* way I was an original.''

The pathos of such pleading is equaled only by the painfulness of a vision of F. Scott Fitzgerald reduced to such a diminished view of himself by adversity and literary oblivion, for he was certainly an original. He introduced the idea of an entire generation in recoil and rebellion, a theme and a set of materials that since his focus on them in American fiction have been echoed again and again by the antiheroes of post-World War II fiction of the 1940s and 1950s, by the beat generation of the 1950s and 1960s, by the hip generation of the 1960s and 1970s, and by every dissenting generational sense that has transcribed itself in American fiction from Norman Mailer to J.D. Salinger to Ken Kesey to the present moment. Before Fitzgerald the literature of dissent was not so much an identification of generations as it was a struggle of the individual against self, society, and the universe. The pioneering experimentalists in realism and naturalism and literary impressionism—Fitzgerald's literary predecessors—were concerned more with universal types of the human psyche alone amid forces than with the historical identification of generations.

Fitzgerald changed that. In a *large* way he was an original. Not only in his marriage of Romanticism, realism, and modernism, but also in his subject matter he introduced new directions in American literature (for instance, he was one of the first to see Hollywood as archetypal American material), discovering that by turning his characters into generations, in effect, he could articulate his moral and historical vision of the meaning of American experience in the changes of time. And nowhere more than in *Tender Is the Night* did Fitzgerald successfully adapt his prose style to the metaphoric creation of the moral history of America. No other book so fully as *Tender Is the Night* becomes *the* American historical novel, in which the *idea* of America, the idealized and idealizing promises of the past, and its loss are identified and defined against the background of the disillusioning actualities of the present generation.

> Milton R. Stern. *''Tender Is the Night'': The Broken Universe* (New York: Twayne, 1994), pp. 11–13

BIBLIOGRAPHY

The Evil Eye, 1915 (lyrics for Triangle Club show); *Safety First*, 1916 (lyrics for Triangle Club show); *This Side of Paradise*, 1920 (n); *Flappers and Philosophers*, 1920 (s); *The Beautiful and Damned*, 1922 (n); *Tales of the Jazz Age*, 1922 (s); *The Vegetable*, 1923 (d); *The Great Gatsby*, 1925 (n); *All the Sad Young Men*, 1926 (s); *Tender Is the Night*, 1934 (n); *Taps at Reveille*, 1935 (s); *The Last Tycoon*, 1941 (n); *The Crack-Up*, 1945 (e, m); *The Stories of F. Scott Fitzgerald*, 1951; *Three Novels of F. Scott Fitzgerald* (*The Great Gatsby, Tender Is the Night* (revised version), *The Last Tycoon*), 1951; *Afternoon of an Author*, 1958 (s, e); *The Pat Hobby Stories*, 1962; *The Fitzgerald Reader*, 1963; *Letters*, 1963; *The Apprentice Fiction of F. Scott Fitzgerald, 1909–1917*, 1965; *Letters to His Daughter*, 1965; *F. Scott Fitzgerald in His Own Time*, 1971 (misc); *Dear Scott/Dear Max: The Fitzgerald-Perkins Correspondence*, 1971; *As Ever, Scott Fitz—: Letters between F. Scott Fitzgerald and His Literary Agent, Harold Ober, 1919–1940*, 1972; *The Basil and Josephine Stories*, 1973; (with Zelda Fitzgerald) *Bits of Paradise*, 1974 (s); *The Cruise of the Rolling Junk*, 1976 (s); *Notebooks*, 1978; *F. Scott Fitzgerald's St. Paul Plays: 1911–1914*, 1978; *Screenplay for "Three Comrades" by Erich Maria Remarque*, 1978; *The Price Was High: The Last Uncollected Stories of F. Scott Fitzgerald*, 1979; *Correspondence*, 1980; *Poems*, 1981; *F. Scott Fitzgerald on Writing*, ed. Larry W. Phillips, 1985 (misc); *The Short Stories*, ed. Matthew J. Bruccoli, 1989 (new Cambridge ed.); *The Love of "The Last Tycoon,"* ed. Matthew J. Bruccoli, 1993 (n, new Cambridge ed.); *A Life in Letters*, ed. Matthew J. Bruccoli, 1994 (l); *Jazz Age Stories*, ed. Patrick O'Donnell, 1999

FITZGERALD, Robert (1910–1985)

Robert Fitzgerald is one of the many young poets who have learned a great deal from the school of Eliot. His poetry is obviously influenced in technique and in philosophy by those figures in poetry who since 1925 have dominated the scene. This is both good and bad. He writes exceedingly well, with a fine command of form, of phrase and with a careful selection of imagery. He understands the use of the heightened statement. But he has not, as yet, a great deal to say that has not already been said.

> Eda Lou Walton. *New York Herald Tribune Book Section.* Jan. 26, 1936. p. 4

"Craftsman" is by a shade too earthy a word for Mr. Fitzgerald; "artificer," which suggests the silver-smith, the lace-maker, and the illusionist, is better. His first volume reveals a technique that is not equaled in subtlety and polish by any other of our younger poets. The magic of these poems springs from precision in the descriptive use of language, brilliance and intricacy of metaphor, and a mastery of elaborate patterns of sound. . . . This poetry has both the merits and the limitations of a mind that seems to be an isolated and a highly introspective one.

> Philip Blair Rice. *The Nation.* Feb. 19, 1936. pp. 227–8

A follower of Eliot and Pound, Mr. Fitzgerald is at present notable chiefly for the intelligent use he has made of his models and for his scrupulous craftsmanship. There is here little of the uncertainty or crudity of statement common to first books of verse—even when most derivative, these poems evince a skillful manipulation of cadence and phrasing that must command our respect.

In absorbing the stylistic virtues of his masters, however, this poet seems to have been obliged also to accept their philosophic and emotional attitudes. Loneliness, nostalgia, despair and bitter resignation are ghosts Mr. Fitzgerald seems unable to rout from his pages.

> T.C. Wilson. *New Republic.* June 10, 1936. p. 138

At every turn Fitzgerald gives the impression of knowing what he is doing and where he is going. He has devoted himself to a definite method with an admirable but perhaps needlessly exclusive single-mindedness. . . . Here is none of the nibbling at many uncongenial stylistic foods, none of the purblind groping that goes so far to

damage most initial efforts. Here, instead, is the work of a man who is sensitively aware of his method and of his own temperament and who speaks with the tone of authority that is characteristic of the practiced.

> C.A. Millspaugh. *Poetry.* June, 1936. p. 166

How good it is to read a book of poems not frantic with a message, not fancy with frilly fashions, using words gravely, for music's sake, or brightly, for that of image; literate without pedantry or affectation; sensitive without being neurotic or too full of nostalgia; moved but not excited; if not quite up to a pitch of high and joyous serenity, yet contemplative and calm, without complacence! How good, how rare; but these blessings are vouchsafed to us in Robert Fitzgerald's collection of poems, entitled *A Wreath for the Sea*.

> Rolfe Humphries. *New Republic.* March 6, 1944. p. 324

Today we are more ready (than in 1936) to appreciate his remarkable modulation and poise. The absence of trickiness, fever and "drama" is a relief. The poems have color and vigor, a spry, confident intelligence constantly at work fusing picture, metaphor, emotion, reflection into deeply satisfying utterance. At times there is a touch of artificially or superrefinement, but not often.

> Kerker Quinn. *New York Herald Tribune Book Section.* April 30, 1944. p. 10

Beyond any poet of my own generation, Fitzgerald seems to me to command the magic of evocative poetry; now in a phrase or line, now in a stanza, sometimes in an entire poem, scene and emotion are called up with a swiftness, an exactness, a poignancy so sharp and lovely and strong, that one is lifted past response to participation. . . . Fitzgerald seems to me a descendent of imagism, yet almost unrecognizably so since remarkably crossed with classicism. . . . It is the balance of emotion and intellect which so distinguishes these poems.

> Winfield Townley Scott. *Poetry.* May, 1944. pp. 111–2

The poetry, the lyric gift of Robert Fitzgerald are probably best known in the fine translations, with Dudley Fitts as his collaborator, of *Oedipus Rex* and *The Antigone* of Sophocles. As reinterpreters of Greek drama in terms of twentieth-century poetry and wit, Fitts and Fitzgerald made a rare, an almost priceless combination. The wit of Dudley Fitts counterbalanced Fitzgerald's lyricism—and the brilliance of their collaboration has already withstood the test of time. . . . It would seem that for some undiscovered cause behind the poems Fitzgerald is at his best in his translations from the Greek. There is no question of his seriousness, or his fine temper; yet a paradox remains: he is most at liberty, and most profoundly his "own man" behind the mask of Sophocles.

> Horace Gregory. *New York Times Book Section.* Feb. 17, 1957. p. 5

Fitzgerald's material ranges through graceful lyrics to long, autobiographical recitatives, taking in translations from the Latin on the way. Among the most amiable qualities of Fitzgerald's writing are calm and lucidity. . . . Fitzgerald's lines are clean; and despite their often personal character, cooly objective. . . . Here is none of the pseudo-elegance of dependence on superficialities of form, like wearing borrowed clothes, but an authentic grace implicit in the nature of the poems. It is a genuine poetry developing from an inner organic need which, after all, is the hallmark of good things at all times. Its classic qualities geometrically balance form and content, the realities of existence with poetic imagination.

Byron Vazakis. *Saturday Review*. April 13, 1957. p. 20

While he has been little favored by the popular anthologists and curiously neglected by the critics, the new volume of selected poems by Robert Fitzgerald makes it clear that he has never belonged anywhere but in the first rank of contemporary poetry. There is so much to commend in his book, that, in fear of shading work that deserves only praise, one hesitates to make a preference or lay an emphasis. Here is a poet, rare in the era of the one-shot chance and the jazzy push to "make it", who begins in a spirit of apprenticeship to form, and to a twenty-five hundred year old heritage which, in his case, is assumed as lightly as though it were a personal endowment. Under hard taskmasters—the Greek and Latin poets and the English poets of the seventeenth century—he proceeds at his own pace toward refinement of technique and attitude the outcome of which must either be self-determination or self-exemption.

John Malcolm Brinnin. *The Yale Review*. Spring, 1957. p. 455

BIBLIOGRAPHY
Poems, 1935; (with Dudley Fitts) *Alcestis*, 1936 (tr); (with Dudley Fitts) *Antigone*, 1939 (tr); *Oedipus at Colonus*, 1941 (tr); *A Wreath for the Sea*, 1943 (p); (with Dudley Fitts) *Oedipus Rex*, 1949 (tr); *In the Rose of Time*, 1956 (p); *Chronique*, by St. John Perse, 1960 (tr); *The Odyssey*, 1961 (tr); *Birds*, by St. John Perse, 1966 (tr); *Deathwatch on the Southside*, by Jorge Luis Borges, 1968 (tr); *Spring Shade: Poems, 1931–1970.*, 1971; ed., *The Collected Short Prose of James Agee*, 1972 (anthol); *The Iliad*, by Homer, 1974 (tr); *The Aeneid*, by Virgil, 1983 (tr); *Enlarging the Change: The Princeton Seminars in Literary Criticism, 1949–1951*, 1985; *The Third Kind of Knowledge: Memoirs and Selected Writings*, ed. Penelope Laurans Fitzgerald, 1993 (tr)

FLETCHER, John Gould (1886–1950)

In the idea of a series of symphonies in which the sole unity was to be a harmony of color, in which form and emotional tone could follow the lead of coloristic word-associations no matter how far afield, Mr. Fletcher discovered an "Open Sesame!" so ideal to his nature, and so powerful as to not merely open the door, but at one stroke to lay bare his treasure entire. . . .The result was, naturally, the most brilliant and powerful work which Mr. Fletcher has yet given us—a poetry of detached waver and brilliance, a beautiful

flowering of language alone, a parthenogenesis, as if language were fertilized by itself rather than by thought or feeling.

Conrad Aiken. *Dial*. Feb. 22, 1919. p. 190

He has yet to learn the restraint of the Greeks, whose exuberance was always proportioned and controlled. But since the first naïve blossoming of Imagism he has grown steadily. He has thought and felt deeply and sincerely. . . . Even when Mr. Fletcher describes what is dead or dying, he keeps his own vitality; even when he presents the grotesque, he sees it in relation to beauty. . . . He has not accepted the doom of an echoing discipleship. He realizes that to go alone is to arrive.

Marguerite Wilkinson. *New York Times Book Section*. March 13, 1921. p. 6

What Mr. Fletcher has not is patent enough; he has no instinct for telling a story, he employs neither wit nor satire, he is dramatic only in the large. What he has are his own unique perceptions and impressions, great knowledge, love of colour, form, and significance, and understanding to interpret the forces behind the actions of men.

Amy Lowell. *Literary Review*. April 16, 1921. p. 1

It is a question how far deliberation is creative. One rarely feels in Mr. Fletcher's art the true lyric rapture, the emotion that seizes the singer and carries him away. But one does feel something only a little less impassioned—the absorption of the contemplative spirit in its object, the self uplifted, and transcended into ecstasy. This latter mood or method, while more conscious than the other, while invoked rather than inspired, is but a little less authoritative in all the arts. It implies an imagination sensitive and worshipful, keen to accept and reflect all of this world's varied manifestations of beauty.

Harriet Monroe. *Poetry*. Jan., 1926. p. 206

His work would be important, if for no other reason, on account of the extension of rhythmical possibilities of the language and the peculiar care bestowed upon the richness and variety of verse texture. In the verse of both Swinburne and Hopkins there is a great intricacy and richness of texture, but a certain monotony. In his "highly-orchestrated and colored words" Fletcher has exploited surprise and resolution in a fashion not dissimilar to the verse of "Ash Wednesday". . . . And Fletcher was the first, or one of the first, to develop in English a type of imagery which Edith Sitwell has since erected into something like an oblique technique of vision.

Robert Penn Warren. *Poetry*. May, 1932. pp. 106–7

His imagery, curiously delicate, pale-tinted, often vague, is now accompanied by an echo of formal music, as though it were something made precious by distance and imperfect hearing. Like Shelley, like Whitman, his verse contains air-pockets: there is a frequent decline into soft, blurred phrasing, but at this point we must recall again that Fletcher's work also retains the imprint of the lesser Symbolists, whose poetry reveals the flaws as well as the sensibilities of their master, Paul Verlaine.

Horace Gregory. *New York Herald Tribune Book Section.* Dec. 29, 1935. p. 6

There is nothing to burrow in to find and feel the meaning out. There is more meaning immediately, at first glance, than can ever be found on subsequent intimacy; that is because the general intent, not the specific datum, is viable. You do not anywhere weigh these poems: you run through them. If you run through a lot of them, you will get quite a lot of Mr. Fletcher himself, a generous, brilliant, prodigal lot. . . . Mr. Fletcher is a personal poet in that it is the prevalent sense of his personality that animates his poems and alone gives them form.

R.P. Blackmur. *Poetry.* March, 1936. pp. 346–7

I think it is fair to say that Mr. Fletcher's noticeable defects as a poet have been these: his sense of humor sometimes fails to come to his rescue, he often seems to lack a real centre, whether geographical or emotional or both, he has diffused his effort into much experimentation, and his disillusionment, though understandable, is tiresome because it seems to have no beginning, no middle and no end. But these faults are occasional, and even if he had not outgrown them he would still be one of the three or four greatest living-American poets.

Baucum Fulkerson. *Sewanee Review.* July, 1938. pp. 286–7

The early work of John Gould Fletcher illustrates the weaknesses intrinsic in a strict application of the Imagist creed. The most memorable parts of his early poetry are the eleven color-symphonies in *Goblins and Pagodas.* These remarkable sequences of beautiful images are a practical demonstration of the inability of the human mind to live by images alone. It is not enough to string bright images on the thread of a single color; the reader demands the dynamic allurements of emotion or thought or action. But Imagism was merely a stage in Fletcher's complex development; in succeeding volumes, emotion and thought were not absent.

Fred B. Millett. *Contemporary American Authors* (Harcourt). 1940. p. 142

Although he shared in many group enterprises, he was never truly of any group or coterie, never had the support of any claque or organization, cultural, commercial, or political, never was the darling of any publisher, never enjoyed a real popular success. He is an extraordinary, almost unique example of the isolated artist. Independent to the last degree, outspoken and frank, uncompromising where his principles were involved, yet wholly without guile, he won all that he won by the test of merit alone. . . . He gave his strength to the cause of art and to those who were enlisted in that cause. To Fletcher, this was a chivalric pursuit, the only chivalric pursuit left to modern man to cherish. For this, and for much more, he will be remembered and honored.

Donald Davidson. *Poetry.* Dec., 1950. pp. 160–1

When he is compared with his contemporaries, his stature is not lessened. His range is greater than that of Frost; he takes into account nations and not alone individuals. His literary background is as rich as that of Amy Lowell, and his sympathies are broader. He is as philosophic as Robinson, and though he lacks the Maine poet's sense of narrative, his verse has greater clarity and equal lyric dexterity. . . . Through his residence abroad, his Americanism was thrown into sharper relief. Because of his prolific output, his technical abilities, his breadth of sympathy and experience, he may eventually come to be considered the poet most representative of his generation.

Norreys Jephson O'Conor. *Southwest Review.* Summer, 1953. p. 243

BIBLIOGRAPHY
The Book of Nature, 1913 (p); *The Dominant City*, 1913 (p); *Fire and Wine*, 1913 (p); *Fool's Gold*, 1913 (p); *Visions of the Evening*, 1913 (p); *Irradiations, Sand and Spray*, 1915 (p); *Goblins and Pagodas*, 1916 (p); *Japanese Prints*, 1918 (p); *The Tree of Life*, 1918 (p); *Some Contemporary American Poets*, 1920 (c); *Breakers and Granite*, 1921 (p); *Paul Gauguin*, 1921 (b); *Preludes and Symphonies*, 1922 (p); *Parables*, 1925 (p); *Branches of Adam*, 1926 (p); *The Dance over Fire and Water* (by Elie Faure), 1926 (tr); *The Reveries of a Solitary* (by Jean Jacques Rousseau), 1927 (tr); *The Black Rock*, 1928 (p); *John Smith—Also Pocohantas*, 1928 (b); *The Crisis of the Film*, 1929 (e); (with others) *I'll Take My Stand*, 1930 (e); *The Two Frontiers*, 1930 (e) (English edition, *Europe's Two Frontiers*); *XXIV Elegies*, 1935 (p); *The Epic of Arkansas*, 1936 (p); *Life Is My Song*, 1937 (a); *Selected Poems*, 1938; *South Star*, 1941 (p); *Burning Mountain*, 1946 (p); *Arkansas*, 1947 (t)

FOOTE, Shelby (1916–)

Of all the Civil War writings in the centennial harvest now coming, Shelby Foote's projected three-volume work [*The Civil War: A Narrative*] is one of the most ambitious in scope. The first volume, now published, opens with Jefferson Davis' resignation from the Senate and Abraham Lincoln's departure from Springfield, Illinois. It closes—nearly two years and more than 400,000 words later—with Lincoln's "We cannot escape history" message to Congress in December 1862.

In between, the reader is treated to a grand, sweeping narrative made up of many narratives. It includes the course of battle along the entire front, from Chesapeake Bay and the Carolina coast to the Mississippi Valley and the desert of New Mexico. It includes also the political events that bear most pertinently upon the fighting. All the themes are carried forward together, clearly and without confusion, by means of marvelously skillful transitions.

Throughout, the characters and careers of Davis and Lincoln provide a kind of unity in duality.

Both of the Presidents are viewed with sympathy and understanding. Davis being pictured as a man of courage and consistency, one who was loyal to those who were loyal to him, one who "sustained them through adversity and unpopularity." Viewed with sympathy also are the officers and men on both sides. The author, a Mississippian, by birth and upbringing, is no biased partisan of the Lost Cause.

Politicians, generals, soldiers—all appear in these pages as unique, living individuals, their appearance and personality convincingly suggested with an economy of descriptive detail. . . .

The reader puts down the book with the feeling that he actually has met and known the actors in it. He feels, too, that he has experienced the events they took part in. He has been in battle with them, seen the fire and smoke, felt the shock, heard the shouts and the moans, smelled the dust and afterwards the stench, sensed the exultation, the terror, and the weariness.

This sounds like history written by a novelist, and in fact it is. ''Accepting the historian's standards without his paraphernalia''— such as footnotes—''I have employed the novelist's method without his license,'' Foote explains. ''Instead of inventing characters and incidents, I searched them out, and having found them, I took them as they were. Nothing is included here . . . without the authority of documentary evidence which I consider sound.'' After all, he says, the novelist and the historian are seeking the same truth.

And Foote is as good as his word, or almost as good. Certainly he makes up no conversations, presents no stream-of-consciousness stuff, indulges in no empty ''poetic'' prose. He writes with transparent honesty.

Yet one may question whether the novelist and the historian, even when both are writing history, are always after quite the same kind of truth. The novelist is interested in the lifelike detail, which often is derived from a single, unsupported source. The historian insists upon the verifiable fact, which usually lacks sharp outlines and specific color, because it has to be somewhat generalized; it has to be reduced to the lowest common denominator of several more or less conflicting sources. The novelist, confronted with various bits of evidence, chooses the one that gives a realistic touch. Then he goes boldly ahead and makes the most of it. For him to hem and haw, as the historian often must, would destroy for the reader the precious sense of verisimilitude.

Choosing his sources by a storyteller's instinct as well as the historian's standard, Foote relates as accepted truth a number of things that historians question or dispute. At Lincoln's inauguration, he says, Stephen A. Douglas took and held the President's tall hat. Once in office, Lincoln knew he must unite the North, ''and he knew, too, that the most effective way to do this was to await an act of aggression by the South, exerting in the interim just enough pressure to provoke such an action.'' During the Sumter crisis he agreed to give up the fort if Virginia would adjourn its secession convention. And after the war Robert E. Lee, when asked who was the ablest Federal general he had opposed, replied: ''McClellan, by all odds.''

Now, all those propositions are dubious at best, and so are a number of others like them in Foote's narrative. Down-right misstatements of fact, however, are few. One of these concerns the Second Confiscation Act, of 1862, regarding which Foote says: ''No slave was to be freed by it until the master had been convicted of treason in a Federal court.'' In fact, as Lincoln himself remarked in objecting to the measure, it would forfeit property, including slave property, ''without a conviction of the supposed criminal or a hearing given him in any proceedings.''

On the main points Foote probably is as accurate as most historians writing a book of comparable coverage. Certainly he is more interesting. Any one who wants to relive the Civil War, as thousands of Americans apparently do, will go through this volume with pleasure and then await the next one with impatience. And, years from now, when the centennial ephemera have been forgotten, Foote's monumental narrative most likely will continue to be read and remembered as a classic of its kind.

Richard N. Current. *New York Herald Tribune Book Review*. November 23, 1958, p. 5.

Professionals do well to apply the term ''amateur'' with caution to the historian outside their ranks. The word does have deprecatory and patronizing connotations that occasionally backfire. This is especially true of narrative history, which nonprofessionals have all but taken over. The gradual withering of the narrative impulse in favor of the analytical urge among professional academic historians has resulted in a virtual abdication of the oldest and most honored role of the historian, that of storyteller. Having abdicated—save in the diminishing proportion of biographies in which analysis does not swamp narrative—the professional is in a poor position to patronize amateurs who fulfill the needed function he has abandoned.

In no field is the abdication of the professionals more evident than in military history, the strictly martial, guns-and-battle aspect of war, the most essential aspect. The burden of this kind of history has to be borne by narrative. The academic professionals are prolific with books on the political, diplomatic, economic, ideological, and psychological history of wars, but not on the purely military history. The leading chroniclers of the most important American military experience, that of the Civil War, have been Douglas Southall Freeman, Bruce Catton, Kenneth P. Williams, and Shelby Foote—none of them trained academicians. Allan Nevins did become a professor, but he was jealous of his amateur standing as a military historian.

Shelby Foote is the author of five novels, yet most of his writing has gone into his huge history of the Civil War, which he unabashedly describes as ''A Narrative.'' [''Red River to Appomattox''] is the third, the largest, and the final volume of a work that has been twenty years in the writing. Like his predecessors named above (with the exception of Nevins) his subject has been military history in the strictest sense. Within these limits, however, he has attempted a more comprehensive treatment than the others. Freeman viewed the war from the standpoint of the Confederate Army of Northern Virginia and was concerned primarily with the eastern theater. Catton treated the western theater as well as the eastern, but from the stand-point of the Union Army. Williams also covered both theaters, but from the outlook of the Union command. When one of these writers calls a chapter ''A Season of Reverses,'' you know whose reverses he is talking about. Save for river gunboat actions, they do their fighting ashore.

Foote undertakes to cover it all, all the military history—Union and Confederate, east and west, afloat and ashore. As narrator he is omnipresent, shifting from Grant's headquarters to Lee's, from Sherman's to Johnston's, from the eastern theater to the western and back again, and from dry land to blue water. Disavowing any ''thesis to argue or maintain,'' he does profess a desire ''to restore a balance,'' lacking in previous accounts, between the eastern and western theaters, and to correct the impression of the war in the West as ''a sort of running skirmish [that] wobbled back and forth, presumably as a way for its participants, faceless men with unfamiliar names, to pass the time while waiting for the issues to be settled in the East.'' In spite of his Mississippi origins, Foote also attempts to keep an even hand in giving North and South their due measure of praise and blame. Yet somehow a bit more adrenalin goes into his accounts of campaigns west of the mountains; there is more dash in a cavalry charge of Forrest's than in one of Sheridan's, and the heroes in gray were a bit more heroic than those in blue. And maybe that was the way it was.

It is the last year of the war—from the Red River Campaign in Louisiana in April, 1864, to Appomattox in April, 1865—that is covered in this volume. The conventional view is that by this time the Rebels had lost their will to win and that the action was essentially reduced to mopping-up operations. It did not seem that way to General Sherman, who was in a position to know. At the beginning of that last year he wrote his wife that ''no amount of poverty or adversity seems to shake their faith, . . . niggers gone, wealth and luxury gone, money worthless, starvation in view, . . . yet I see no sign of let up—some few deserters, plenty tired of war, but the masses determined to fight it out.'' They needed more persuasion, and he was prepared to give them all that was required, and more. ''All that has gone before is mere skirmishing,'' he told his wife as he set forth on the task—his knock-out blow to Georgia and his rape of South Carolina.

General Grant opened his Virginia campaign of that horrible last year with the same relentless savagery. Within one month after it crossed the Rapidan River the Army of the Potomac under Grant had lost no less than half as many men as it had lost in the previous three years of bloody fighting in Virginia. ''For thirty days it has been one funeral procession past me,'' protested one of Grant's generals, ''and it has been too much.'' Yet it was only the beginning. By the time he had crossed the James and besieged Petersburg, Grant's losses came to nearly 75,000 men—more than Lee and Beauregard had had in both their armies at the start of the campaign a month and a half before. In one charge before Petersburg a Maine regiment of 850 lost 632 men, more than 74 percent, in less than half an hour. Casualties among the graybacks were nearly always much smaller in numbers but larger in proportion to their available manpower and therefore more costly in military terms. With that fateful knowledge, Grant ruthlessly swapped casualties on unequal terms and never abandoned his meat-grinder tactics, pouring black meat after the white into the grinder.

While he is willing to admit that there is ''a good deal more to war than killing and maiming,'' Foote has little space for the other aspects. We are admitted to a few of Lincoln's cabinet meetings and some of the president's public speeches and private conversations. We are taken backstage occasionally in the Richmond theater of politics. We are permitted a passing glance at an election, a diplomatic exchange, and (particularly in the South) an economic crisis that had immediate military consequences. The politics of command in both armies—personal rivalries, political animosities, and power plays among the brass—are adequately kept before the reader. But always the main matter before us is the ''killing and maiming.''

To the predominantly analytical historians of the schools, this flood of action provides little of what they call ''insight.'' That means clues to mass motivation, keys to puzzles of grand strategy and policy, and answers to large questions of ''why''—why the North won and the South lost, for example. I suppose the narrative historian's answer might be that there is something to be said for knowing how a cataclysm was experienced as well as explaining why it happened. Problems of motive and explanation acquire a

new dimension in the presence of surviving veterans of the battle of Spotsylvania. . . .

The intimacy of combat in that age of warfare lends itself to Shelby Foote's impressive narrative gifts and to his dramatic purposes. In World War II, battleships opened fire at a range of thirteen miles or more—beyond sight of their targets. In the Battle of Mobile Bay the opposing flagships rammed each other head-on, and the *Tennessee's* guns were so close to the *Hartford* that the powder blackened her side. In the latter ship, Admiral Farragut had himself lashed to her rigging the better to command, and his opponent and friend Admiral Buchanan attacked Farragut's fleet of seventeen vessels with his one surviving ship out-gunned twenty to one. Rebel taste for histrionics supplies embarrassing riches of color. The duel between the *Alabama* and the *Kearsarge* in the English Channel is right out of Scott, with Admiral Semmes flinging his glittering sword into the sea as his ship sinks. Jeb Stuart whirls through cavalry actions in red-lined cape, bright yellow sash, black ostrich plume, and golden spurs—no less dangerous for it all.

Where possible, however, Foote tends to let his beloved Army of Tennessee upstage the easterners. The western spirit of desperate improvisation best typified the expiring rebelion. General Joe Johnston, the Virginian, whom Sherman described as ''a sensible man who only did sensible things,'' yielded command to General Hood, the Texan, an unsensible man who did desperate and unsensible things. One leg missing, one arm paralyzed, strapped to his saddle, he led his army of barefoot scarecrows to their doom. Three regiments that started the war with an average of 1,250 effective troops fought on with sixty-five, fifty, and sixty-four present for duty. In five weeks Hood lost 20,000 veterans in casualties, including sixteen generals. He was loyally supported by that genius of improvisation, General Forrest, whose engineers constructed bridges out of grapevines—literally.

For all this ''the butcher's bill'' was a North-South total of 623,026 dead from all causes and 471,427 wounded, or a total of 1,094,453 for both sides, in and out of more than 10,000 military actions. Another historian, Eric McKitrick, has calculated that a casualty rate in World War II comparable to Union deaths in the Civil War would have required nearly 2.5 million deaths as against actual losses of 384,000. Southern losses in dead or incapacitated were fewer in number but greater in proportion to the number available for service—one out of four (including noncombatant Negroes) as against one out of ten in the North. Of generals the Unions lost one out of twelve killed in action, the Confederates one out of five.

But what has all this to teach our ''psychohistorians,'' our ''cliometricians,'' and our crypto-analysts busy with their neat models, parameters, and hypotheses? It is hard to say for sure. It is possible, however, that the 1,100 pages of this raw narrative, bereft as it is of ''insight,'' might serve to expose them to the terrifying chaos and mystery of their intractable subject and disabuse them of some of their illusions of mastery.

C. Vann Woodward. *New York Review of Books.* March 6, 1975, p. 12.

Our historical profession of late has come under widespread attack because of a simple, growing and potentially fatal weakness. Historians, it is charged, have abandoned popular history. Turned around, the criticism is more biting. Professional scholars seemingly devote too much time to studies with limited readability. Too often historical works are ponderous if not pontifical; too often rebuttal and revision prevail at the expense of revelation; too often ''scholarly studies'' are designed for fellow historians and graduate students rather than for interested laymen and the buying public. In other words, a feeling persists that the study of history is slipping into a closed shop exclusively for the professionals. Such an occurrence would be disastrous for all concerned.

The possibility of that transpiring in the Civil War field is unlikely, thanks in great part to a corps of writers who have so popularized the conflict between North and South as to make it far and above the nation's favorite historical period. For example, Carl Sandburg, Clifford Dowdey, V.C. Jones and—especially—Bruce Catton have shown through numerous studies that history can be human, appealing at all levels, and enjoyable if the narrator can use a broad base and a gifted pen. These attributes have rarely been wielded in more brilliant fashion than by Shelby Foote; and now, with the completion of . . .[*The Civil War: A Narrative*] encompassing decades of labor, Foote hereby surges forth as one of the half-dozen major figures in Civil War writing. His trilogy is at once important and imposing. It offers a direct and competent challenge to Catton's *Centennial History of the Civil War*.

Foote is a native of Mississippi who long ago adopted Memphis as his home. His literary fame first developed with five novels. Two of them—*Follow Me Down* and *Shiloh*—had Civil War themes. Then, in 1954, he was persuaded to embark on a full-scale narrative history of the war. Neither Foote nor the publisher realized at the time the dimensions that the project would ultimately take: twenty years of work on three widely spaced volumes containing a total of 1,500,000 words.

Volume I, first published in 1958, begins the story with secession and preparations for war, skillfully carries the reader through the early crises, and concludes with the autumn, 1862, campaigns at Perryville and Antietam. Volume II, released in 1963, opens with preludes for battle at Prairie Grove, Stone's River and Fredericksburg. It provides an in-depth study of the major and awesome 1863 contests: Vicksburg and Chattanooga in the West, Chancellorsville and Gettysburg in the East. Some 900 pages later, it is March, 1864, and U.S. Grant arrives in Washington to take supreme command of the Union armies.

Now the long-awaited and concluding third volume is at hand. It fulfills every expectation. Certainly it is the most dramatically written of the three installments, in part because it treats of the war's most dramatic months. Sherman slashes his way across the Deep South, and Sheridan blackens the Shenandoah, while Grant methodically pounds Lee into the immobility of the Richmond-Petersburg defenses. A short series of blows in the spring of 1865 and, for the South, a dream ends but a heritage begins.

Comparing Foote with Catton is inevitable, and not merely because each is the author of a three-volume narrative history. The two men possess such writing talent as to put them in a special category to themselves. Both rely on printed sources—although Catton came to depend on research assistant E. B. Long for a wealth of manuscript material. Catton uses documentation; Foote disdains footnotes. Catton is a Northerner and Eastern-oriented. He concentrates on military matters and gives excellent discussions of a selected number of Civil War subjects. He writes in a moving, poignant prose style unequalled by any other current historian. Foote is a Southerner and Western-oriented. He is also interested

primarily in army actions, and he is given to a far broader but somewhat more shallow coverage of the struggle. His prose is powerful, tending more toward the overwhelming than toward the incisive.

Punctilious scholars will charge that historian Foote is assailable on at least four separate counts. First is his total reliance on printed sources. That is not as serious as it might seem. Indeed, it is difficult to criticize Foote's research because the literature of the Civil War is so immense that it is actually a compliment to any writer who can wade through thousands of volumes and glean informational nuggets to the successful degree demonstrated by Foote. He has carefully digested a mass of printed material and then rewritten the story to suit the tenets of his own presentation. This can hardly be branded as slipshod work. In fact, Foote regularly presents little human-interest stories that give personality to history. A Johnny Reb once shouted across no-man's land to a Billy Yank: ''Why don't you come over to our side? We're fighting for honor and you're fighting for money.'' The Union soldier hollered back: ''Well, I reckon each of us is fighting for what we need the most.''

The absence of documentation is a more serious flaw in this study. No one will challenge the authenticity of statements made by Foote, but it would have been extremely helpful to serious readers and working historians to know the sources for some of his facts. One case in point will suffice. At Gettysburg, Foote states, all Confederate corps and division commanders were West Point graduates save one—and he had attended Virginia Military Institute. Foote then points out that only 14 of 26 corps and division leaders in the Army of the Potomac had attended the Military Academy. The majority of Meade's generals were non-professionals who suddenly found themselves immersed in the most professional war then known to man. Such contrasting situations would be worth pondering further, if one only knew where to start the search for additional information. With no leads provided, frustration results.

Foote's stated aversion to making interpretations would seem to violate one of the historian's most basic obligations. He refuses to pause to render judgments or to argue conclusions. He makes no judicious observations, predictions or the like, he asserts, because in his mind this would be a gross encroachment on what he is primarily interested in producing: a narrative history in which he puts the action before the reader and the reader before the action and then allows no intrusion on his presentation. Foote takes pride in keeping the story free from opinion.

The irony of it all is that, in spite of Foote's efforts, interpretations abound throughout the text. Braxton Bragg is repeatedly portrayed as a general too narrow-minded for the intricacies of battle. William T. Sherman is ''a violent-talking man whose bite at times measured up to his bark, and whose commitment was to total war.'' Following Gettysburg, Lee's army ''had slipped back to the disorganization of the Seven Days'' because it ''could not make up for the crippling lack of direction from above and the equally disadvantageous lack of initiative just below the top.'' Foote's evaluation of Joseph E. Johnston is especially barbed. ''On the evidence, Old Joe's talent seemed primarily for retreat; so much so, indeed, that if left to his own devices he might be expected to wind up gingerly defending Key West and complaining that he lacked transportation to Cuba in the event that something threatened one of his flanks.''

Whether Foote admits it or not, these are interpretations—not facts.

Finally, some purists will allege that Foote says little not already well-known and readily accessible in other works. This is only half-true. Foote does present the usual stereotypes of the war's leading figures, and he sometimes displays an equalitarian tendency to lower or raise men to the same level. However, what sustains these three volumes—what Foote utilizes that others missed—is a prose ranging from powerful to adroit.

It alternately brims with natural movement, constructed excitement, allegory, color and force. On a few occasions, it overflows badly when Foote's sentences become hopelessly long and sometimes end with a damaging, dangling participle. Yet practically every page in this set contains at least one quotable passage. It might be a battle description such as Foote's statement after ''Stonewall'' Jackson's men delivered a point-blank volley into an assaulting Federal column at Fredericksburg: ''The blue line stopped, flailed ragged along its forward edge, and then reversed its flow.''

Or it might be a succinct assessment of one man, such as this comment on the Northern president: ''Nothing pleased Lincoln more than to have an opponent think he was an idiot. It was like swiping somebody with a razor and then telling them to shake their head.'' Or the prose could be a simple rendition of one human story. Foote has obvious (and commendable) admiration for Jefferson Davis. Volume I begins with Davis' farewell speech in the Senate on the eve of war. Volume II opens with his 1862 inaugural address in Richmond. Foote fittingly ends Volume III—and the study—with a statement Davis made just before he died: ''Tell the world I only loved America.''

Whether from a publisher's stinginess with review copies or from editors' apathy with widely spaced installments of an undocumented history, America's major historical journals largely ignored the first two volumes of Foote's study. The set is now complete. Foote no longer can be, or will be, ignored. He has provided a superb view of the forest rather than the usual and tiring look at a few trees; and he has done so in a writing style both fluid and appealing. The inclusion in this set of no less than 140 maps, each placed just where it is needed, is but a dividend to a sweeping history impressive to read and impossible to forget.

> James I. Robertson, Jr.. *Civil War History*. June, 1975, pp. 172–75.

BIBLIOGRAPHY
Tournament, 1949 (n); *Follow Me Down*, 1950 (n); *Love in a Dry Season*, 1951 (n); *Shiloh*, 1952 (n); *Jordan County: A Landscape in Narrative*, 1954 (s); *The Civil War: Fort Sumter to Perryville*, 1958 (h); *The Civil War:Fredericksburg to Meridian*, 1963 (h); *Jordan County: A Landscape in the Round*, 1964 (d); *The Civil War: Red River to Appomattox*, 1974 (h); *September September*, 1978 (n); *The Novelist's View of History*, 1981 (nf); *Stars in Their Courses*, 1994 (n); *The Beleaguered City*, 1995 (n); *Ride Out*, 1996 (n)

FORCHÉ, Carolyn (1950–)

Kinship is the theme that preoccupies Carolyn Forché. Although she belongs to a generation that is reputed to be rootless and disaffiliated, you would never guess it from reading her poems. Her imagination, animated by a generous life-force, is at once passionate and tribal. Narrative is her preferred mode, leavened by meditation. She remembers her childhood in rural Michigan, evokes her Slovak ancestors, immerses herself in the American Indian culture of the Southwest, explores the mysteries of flesh, tries to understand the bonds of family, race, and sex. In the course of her adventures she dares to confront, as a sentient being, the overwhelming questions by which reason itself is confounded: Who am I? Why am I here? Where am I going?. . .

Carolyn Forché's poems give an illusion of artlessness because they spring from the simplest and deepest human feelings, from an earthling's awareness of the systemic pulse of creation. The poems tell us she is at home anyplace under the stars, wherever there are fields or mountains, lakes or rivers, persons who stir her atavistic bond-sense. . . .

She listens. At Justin Morrill College, an experimental residential branch of Michigan State University, where five years ago the earliest parts of *Gathering the Tribes* were conceived, she began her avid consumption of languages. Now she studies Russian, Spanish, Serbo-Croatian, French and Tewa (Pueblo Indian), listening beyond grammar for the secret texts. She acknowledges a primal sense of the power of words. The power to ''make words''—in the mouth, in the heart, on the page—is the same to her as to give substance. Aiming at wholeness, strength, and clarity, she works at language as if it were a lump of clay or dough in her hands. In her search for poetry, in her effort to understand it, she has bent over the potter's wheel, climbed mountain ranges, ventured into the Mojave Desert. . . .

The places dearest to her include the south Michigan heartland where she was raised, Truchas and the Pueblo village of Taos in New Mexico, the Washington coast, and the Okanogan region of southern British Columbia. Anna, Alfansa, Teles Goodmorning, the dulcimer maker, Rosita, Jacynthe, the child born in the Okanogan, the monks of the mountain abbey, and Joey, a first love, who went off to study for the priesthood, are all characters clearly drawn from life and attached to specific locations. One might say that they are embodiments of the reality of their settings.

If I am right in supposing that ''Year at Mudstraw,'' ''Taking Off My Clothes,'' and ''Kalaloch'' are among the last poems written for this book, it would appear that Forché is moving toward a tauter line, packed with incisive detail, and a firmer dramatic structure than is evident in her earlier narratives. . . .

I have little doubt that the poem in *Gathering the Tribes* that will be most discussed, quoted, and anthologized is ''Kalaloch'' (pronounced ka-låĺok), an almost faultlessly controlled erotic narrative of 101 lines. In its boldness and innocence and tender, sensuous delight it may very well prove to be the outstanding Sapphic poem of an era.

> Stanley Kunitz. Foreword to Carolyn Forché. *Gathering the Tribes* (New Haven: Yale University Press, 1976), pp. xi–xiv

Carolyn Forché's second book of poems is interesting both because Forché is a talented poet—her first book, *Gathering the Tribes*, was a Yale Younger Poets selection—and because it tackles the political subject matter I [have been] arguing is so uncongenial to young poets. The first section, dedicated to the memory of Oscar Romero, the murdered archbishop of San Salvador, is set in EI Salvador, where Forché lived for two years and worked as a journalist. Other poems are addressed to old friends from the working-class Detroit neighborhood of Forché's childhood: one has become a steelworker haunted by memories of Vietnam; another, with whom Forché had shared adolescent dreams of travel and romance, lives with her husband and kids in a trailer. Elsewhere in the poems we meet a jailed Czech dissident, the wife of a "disappeared" Argentine and Terrence Des Pres, author of *The Survivor*, a study of the death camps. This is strong stuff, and the excited response *The Country Between Us* has already provoked shows, I think, how eager people are for poetry that acknowledges the grim political realities of our time.

At their best, Forché's poems have the immediacy of war correspondence, postcards from the volcano of twentieth-century barbarism. . .

Testicles are "crushed like eggs," rats are introduced into vaginas, José waves his bloody stumps in the air, Lil Milagro is raped and forced to defecate in public. "There is nothing one man will not do to another," Forché tells us. So shocking are the incidents reported here—so automatic is our horror at a mere list of places where atrocities have occurred ("Belsen, Dachau, Saigon, Phnom Penh")—that one feels almost guilty discussing these poems as poems, as though by doing so one were saying that style and tone and diction mattered more than bloody stumps and murdered peasants and the Holocaust.

This unease, though, should not have arisen in the first place, and it points to an underlying problem: the incongruity between Forché's themes and her poetic strategies. Forché's topics could not be more urgent, more extreme or more public, and at least one of her stated intentions is to make us look at them squarely. And yet, she uses a language designed for quite other purposes, the misty "poetic" language of the isolated, private self. She gives us bloody stumps, but she also gives us snow, light and angels. You have to read "The Island" several times, for instance, to get past the exotic tropical scenery, the white dresses, the "seven different shawls of wind," the mist that is like bread and so forth, and realize that this is a poem of homage to Claribel Alegría, a heroic woman whom Forché would like to resemble, and that Claribel is telling Forché not to give up hope for El Salvador. At least, I think that's what it's about. . . .

Whether or not one admires Forché for stressing the intensity of her responses to the sufferings of others—many readers, I should point out, do not share my discomfort with this emphasis—the intensity is vitiated by the inadequate means by which it is conveyed. It is embarrassing to read that Forché goes "mad, for example, /in the Safeway, at the many heads/of lettuce, papayas and sugar, pineapples/and coffee, especially the coffee." It trivializes torture to present it in terms of lunch:

> The *paella* comes, a bed of rice
> and *camarones*, fingers and shells,
> the lips of those whose lips
> have been removed, mussel
> the soft blue of a leg socket.
> ("In Memory of Elena")

It is wildly histrionic—and slanderous, too—to accuse politically moderate human-rights activists of deriving masturbatory pleasure from torture reports:

> they cup their own parts
> with their bedsheets and move

themselves
slowly, imagining bracelets
affixing their wrists to a wall
("The Return")

Does Forché think we read her poems as pornography?

It is not enough—this too may be a minority opinion—to dedicate one's poetry to the defeat of the torturers, to swear that

> I will live
> and living cry out until my voice is
> gone
> to its hollow of earth, where with our
> hands and by the lives we have
> chosen
> we will dig deep into our deaths.
> ("Message")

The boldness of the promise is undermined by the commonplace rhetoric ("hollow of earth" for "grave") and woolly syntax (the hands and lives dig into our deaths *after* the voice is dead?).

On the other hand, to make such a promise is not nothing, either. If poetry is to be more than a genteel and minor art form, it needs to encompass the material Forché presents. Much credit, then, belongs to Forché for her brave and impassioned attempt to make a place in her poems for starving children and bullet factories, for torturers and victims, for Margarita with her plastique bombs and José with his bloody stumps. What she needs now is language and imagery equal to her subjects and her convictions. The mists and angels of contemporary magazine verse are beneath her: she *has* seen too much, she has too much to say. Of how many poets today, I wonder, could that be said?

Katha Pollitt. *The Nation*. May 8, 1982, pp. 562–64

Is the country between us a medieval sword laid down between sleeping lovers on a soft pine forest floor like a steely oath of obdurate sublimation? Is it a country you would have to visit in order to be where I now am on the other side of the frontier? (Until you understand the horror, the horror, the cold chills, the sweat and oil, all that I saw, that I went through, we'll never be able to communicate with each other again.) Or, is it by any chance a country we implicitly share—roads groping from your flesh to my flesh? Or perhaps our territory. . .both. . .and. . .the sacramental conjunction of bread?

Whatever, between *us*. It is not only the lyric plurality of the pronoun that is important here, where two or three are gathered together, but its objective case—implying a sort of paralysis of the communal will, a screen (like that between the living and the dead) through which we (whoever we are) would have to burst with enormous energy in order to come out into the nominative light of existential affirmation. And were we fully to become it, whatever country (including the pun embedded there) formerly kept us apart would contain us whole, all of us, leaven of a deeper plenitude than want could possibly be aware of.

At this particular moment in history the country between us happens to have an incredibly suggestive name: El Salvador, where these bones and this flesh (as Aquinas said)—that body, hers, his— are being continuously broken and blood shed beyond the power of the outraged earth to absorb it. El Salvador, that is, where masses are hourly said over massacred fragments of our common humanity.

Those who commit themselves to the poor have to be open to the same destiny as the poor; and in El Salvador we already know the destiny of the poor: to disappear, to be captured, to be tortured, to reappear as corpses.

The man who said these words out loud above a whisper, who lived to be himself the language of truth incarnate, was shot saying mass on March 31, 1980. It is to him, Monsignor Oscar Romero, that Carolyn Forché dedicates the first section of this, her second book. A section of her life for the first time publicly located in time and space: "In Salvador, 1978–80," she calls it. . . .

We waited decades to hear how Akmatova waited outside Leningrad Prison for months during the Yezhov terror. Carolyn Forché's poems from El Salvador reach us while events duplicate to those she describes are still taking place. It's not as though we were waiting for faded or blurred records of ignominious naked genocide to be salvaged from history and released like a nightmarish family album. The film these days is smuggled out, processed, and wired almost immediately. Those maimed, violated bodies seem to be falling and decomposing before our very eyes, severed heads of youths falling, as it were, on our breakfast plates. With words alone Carolyn Forché brilliantly records such characteristic dismemberments.

Judith Gleason. *Parnassus*. 10, Spring–Summer, 1982, pp. 9–12

The Spring 1982 publication of *The Country between Us* by Carolyn Forché has stirred the old cauldron, painstakingly labeled in our culture, "political poetry." The book has already made literary history, winning the di Castagnola and Lamont prizes, going into its second printing in six weeks, with reviews in *Time* and *People Magazine* and other non-literary "mainstream" publications. As one poet put it, *The Country between Us* is close to becoming, unlike any poetry book of our times, a bestseller. In a culture noted for its disdain of poetry, and, among its poets, a disdain (in regards to subject matter) of the political, this is a phenomenon that cannot be readily dismissed. . . .

It is against [her] brilliantly perceptive description of contemporary poetry's dominant aesthetic that Pollit. . .discusses *The Country between Us*. But in doing so I think she misses a great point of the book. Forché's book is not a book of "political poetry," at least not in the way that concept is normally held. As Forché herself has said, "My poetry is no more political than that of a poet who is celebrating an afternoon as the sun sets in the Mediterranean. It's foolish to say because you're talking about poor people, or because your poetry celebrates or gives witness to the plight of the poor, that it's political. That is the perception of the right. The *status quo* never views itself as political, so it's only others, others in opposition or in striking contrast, who are viewed as political." And she has said it the other way: "'Political poetry' often means the poetry of protest, accused of polemical didacticism, and not the poetry which implicitly celebrates politically acceptable values. . . .There is no such thing as a nonpolitical poetry.'". . .

As everyone knows poetry *matters* in Latin America; it is the voice, or one of them, of the people. Were Forché's Salvadorean "educators" ignorant of the impoverished status of poets in the States, or is this book not, in fact, a message to us about the only path our culture grandly opens to poets: that city walk-up in dead of winter where personal redemption from our corrupt and evil country is silence, insanity, suicide.

I am taking liberties. The book, in our tradition at least, must stand on its own. Hints of the turmoil and sense of inadequacy of being "just a poet" in witness to such a place and ordeal *are* strewn throughout the poems—that is, the story continues, even in Salvador, of the Northamerican wanderer seeking her work, her words, her world. "The Colonel," the most oft-quoted and reprinted poem of the book is, interestingly, set in prose and the witness breaks down midpoint when the Colonel spills a sack of human ears onto the dinner table: "There is no other way to say this." Who is it that is breaking down here? Not the witness, but the poet with the burden of her U.S. aesthetics. Who is she apologizing to? First and foremost, to us, her fellow poets (or is it to her teachers and critics who will disapprove?). The opening lines of the piece are also addressed to us, I think. "What you have heard is true. I was in his house," as if a poet should not have been, as if to answer her poet friends who warned her about this. The ears "are like dried peach halves," the poet's only simile here and one I think that undeniably authenticates her experience. *We* need this simile, for how many of us have had the experience? It brings the ears alive for us, just as the one dropped in the glass of water by the Colonel "came alive." And even he addresses the poet's "problem" as he performs his heinous act. "Something for your poetry, no?". . .

For me, Forché's book is "political"—to try here to understand, to perhaps even claim the word—in that it is the female voice in many ways of my generation, representative of a vast number of women who are living outside of, and have been for some time now, the lives we were programmed for, the lives of our mothers. This is a poetic voice from which we have not heard much yet. The powerful, revolutionary female voice of our generation, besides that of popular music, has been the inestimably important lesbian-separatist one. (The majority of other well-published women poets write from the conservative, domestic stance Pollit describes.) Forché is clearly a nonseparatist feminist, the one we are familiar with in our music, though strangely, not our poetry: very female, erotic, sexual, mobile, independent, exploratory, nondomestic, childless (a nagging awareness in the book typical of the many still childless women who came to puberty with the advent of the Pill). "In what time do we live that it is too late to have children?" ("Selective Service"), a woman traveling alone, the hunter rather than the hunted, a very lonely *caminante*—but not a loner and not a separatist. . . .

The Country between Us is the work of a late-twentieth-century-educated-and-trained Midwest poet. The work does contain many of the characteristics and values Pollit describes of our contemporary literary form. Forché is working within the current "tradition," except perhaps for subject matter. And perhaps it is that subject matter—in both of her books—along with her wonderfully wild sensuous energy, her commitment to the present rather than the past, her subliminal ethic of action, that causes her always to transcend the static, "fascist" form. How true her language is to the "real" voice and the land and experience from which she comes is a question perhaps time will help to answer (though time is not necessarily free of the coercion of culture). But this poet, this extraordinary woman has already gone further than most ever will in trying to authenticate her voice, immersing herself and her language in the "real" and very dangerous world. She has used her verbal training like a guerrilla uses intimate knowledge of the land, taking the aesthetic jammed into her as a young working class woman gone to college and jamming it right back into the real, the political. This is a poetry of terrible witness, the strains of our villainies on the language and ethical constructs undoubtedly show. Thus the phrase, "the country between us."

Sharon Doubiago, *American Poetry Review*. January–February 1983, pp. 35–36, 39

What is. . . "allegiance to Art?" And what, given the circumstances, is sensationalism? I think, in the case of Carolyn Forché's second book, *The Country between Us*, the poet undergoes and records a journey that reconciles the political with the artistic rather than severs that vital connection—for, finally, there is nothing sensationalistic about setting down the facts of a dinner party. If one argues that such facts remain sensationalistic in the context of poetry it may be because readers no longer expect facts from poems. . . . And if this is so isn't one really arguing for that "inward" aesthetic that Hans Magnus Enzensberger criticizes? And isn't. . .such an aesthetic designed to limit poetry in its subjects? Therefore, isn't it, really and finally, another kind of censorship?. . .

Forché's position in the poems about El Salvador is admittedly partisan. She is, as are many of the people *in* El Salvador, against the military, against the government, the landowners, the mockery of "land-reform," and against all U.S. aid, especially military aid. But such partisanship seems, under the conditions now apparent in that country, not Leftist so much as simply decent and human, and describable in many ways as a concern for the poet's friends in El Salvador. . . .

Forché, in discovering another country, discovers herself—discovers, too, how American she is ("a country you never left"). Part of that discovery is the discovery of limits. It is a mature and brilliant act when Forché relinquishes her poem and allows Josephine to speak, when the poet becomes a listener as well as a speaker. For one of the ironies about the poems is the learning process, a reciprocal or dialectical process that resembles and actualizes the paradigm of Paulo Freire's in *Pedagogy of the Oppressed*, a book that Forché acknowledges as an influence on her work and on her life. Moreover, the irony of learning in the poem is positive just as the poet learns to be more human from Josephine. Josephine herself, in speaking of what most torments her, becomes a poet. The poem's relationships are unshakably egalitarian. And so it is proper that Forché listens, for the duty of a poem like this is to witness and report, to detail a particular misery, to try to rescue some of the dead from an almost certain oblivion.

Larry Levis. *American Poetry Review*. January–February 1983, pp. 10–11

Forché had already created a sensation among poets by describing her experience in war-torn El Salvador and calling for "a poetry of witness" more accountable than ever before to "the twentieth century human condition." *The Country between Us*, Forché's second volume of poetry, has reached a surprisingly large audience, and apart from the book's topical interest, one can sense in its powerful impact on readers and hearers an important argument for poetry. Initial commentary on the book evokes an old fear, the New Critics' fear of the corrupting influence of politics on the purity of the poem's language. Actually, Forcheé's book goes beyond the question "Can a good poem be political?" to some far more significant and fearful ones: Is poetry adequate to a century of holocaust? Can an intensely personal language and vision of things suffice? Can poetry help us? (*Are* we still human? some have asked.) *The Country between Us* possesses one of the severest orderings of poems of any collection in recent memory, and an examination of its three-part structure will help us ponder some of these questions. The book embodies the process by which Forché became a survivor who somehow found the courage and honesty to make of the atrocities she witnessed the test and education of her moral will. Her personal transformation becomes in the reading of the book an exemplar for our collective response. Above all, the book will suggest what a poetry of witness might involve in a time such as ours. *The Country between Us* enacts with intense drama and sensuous immediacy the agony of human survival in an age of mass death, and as such it is the compelling story for our century's ninth decade.

John Mann. *American Poetry* 3, Spring, 1986, pp. 51–52

In the four years since their publication, the poems of Carolyn Forché's *The Country between Us* have been identified with a renewed debate concerning the claims, the merits, and the possibilities for "political poetry" in contemporary America. They have been taken as an occasion for critical pronouncements on the question of "mixing art and politics" and have been widely praised as well as strenuously criticized. The apparent plurality of critical opinion surrounding *The Country between Us* would seem to suggest that the question of poetry's relationship to politics is once again productively open, but in fact it masks a more disturbing consensus: whatever their merit, these poems belong to a specialized genre—"political poetry." They are to be evaluated for their ability to "reconcile" or "balance" impulses generally regarded as contradictory: the personal or lyrical on the one hand, the political or engaged on the other. I see several problems with such a notion of political poetry. First, it implies that certain poems are political while others (the majority) are not, and it thus functions to marginalize those poems regarded as political without yet having explored the social and political constitution of all literary discourse. More importantly, such a notion of political poetry adopts unquestioningly an already reified conception of the social; it is incapable of helping us to think of relationships between individuals and society in terms other than those of opposition. As a result, it replicates the split in contemporary ideology between private and public. That subjects may be socially constituted is a question usually not asked. Finally, this taken-for-granted definition of political poetry is not a *historical* definition: it fails to consider the ways in which lyric poetry, since the Romantics at least, has been constituted *in opposition* or reaction to dominant modes of social and political discourse. Severed from history, the lyric poet becomes an isolated voice crying out in the empty wasteland of modernist despair: politics becomes mere psychologism and the struggle to wrest freedom from necessity is rewritten as a purely individual quest. The compulsion to read Forché's poetry as political in this narrower sense, then, has resulted in readings that distort and diminish the real accomplishments of the poems while undermining any claim they, or any contemporary poems, have to be political in any deeper sense.

In the autobiographical "El Salvador: An Aide-Memoire," Forché herself has provided us with a text that asks to be read as both a preface to and a theoretical defense of the project undertaken in *The Country between Us*. "Aide-Memoire" is pervaded by an uneasiness regarding the critical terms in which the poems have been received and discussed. In response to critics' classification of the poems as "political poetry," Forché writes: "I suspect that underlying this. . . is a naive assumption: that to locate a poem in an area associated with political trouble automatically renders it political." The essay, in fact, concludes with an enumeration of several of the more problematic questions concerning the theoretical status of poetry as political—suggestions, perhaps, of ways in which the political constitution of all poetry might more productively be explored. What emerges is the notion that there are really two different senses of the term "political." The first, more limited sense sees "politics" as the largely institutionalized, two-dimensional discourse of political programs and "ideologies" in the official sense; the second, invoked in response to the confinement of the first, defines politics far more broadly and flexibly as any action or discourse carried out in a social world. These two competing definitions are made dramatically clear in the juxtaposition, on the final pages of "Aide-Memoire," of the following two statements. First, Forché's own allegation that "there is no such thing as nonpolitical poetry"; second, a statement from Hans Magnus Enzensberger's "Poetry and Politics": "The poem expresses in an exemplary way the fact that it is not at the disposal of politics: this is its political content." Where most American readers of Forché seek to reduce the political to the more limited of these two senses, Forché and Enzensberger attempt to open up the notion, to make "the political" again the site of an ongoing, daily contestation.

Michael Greer. *Centennial Review*. 30, 1986, pp. 160–62

BIBLIOGRAPHY
Gathering the Tribes, 1976 (p); *The Country Between Us*, 1981 (p); *The Angel of History*, 1994 (p)

FORD, Richard (1944–)

Richard Ford's fourth novel [*Wildlife*] is a perfectly executed narration of one's childhood world as seen by an adult reliving those childhood experiences. The many appearances of such works in which viewpoint becomes a layered text of irony about the real content of observation make up almost a subgenre of contemporary American fiction. It is not that such fiction takes as its subject the growing up of a child, but that the tellers of the tales are adults attempting to regain their child's voice and eyes in order to capture truth in their telling; at the same time the writers-narrators admit the impossibility of doing so. Knowing the inevitability of their profound but enriching failure in recreating such a warp of time, the tellers rely on differences in tone from their present voice (and eyes) and their past ones, and yet as they end their tales, the persona's voice has become the narrator's voice. What the persona/protagonist all along was moving to is the narrator who all along has been struggling to capture the present of a time past and not passed through it. Still another inevitability of irony lies in these reflections recollected in modern ironic tranquility; the child persona and the narrator-adult become one locked in their identity

of loneliness and yet distinct from each other in the figments of the author's voice. Indeed, the author becomes still another presence, a third outpost, to tease the reader into layers of speculation.

Ford may be compared to E.L. Doctorow (particularly *Billy Bathgate*, in which the child and narrator are one, and all the difference in two worlds), and to John Irving's Owen Meany. His work also has associations with the classic texture of recollection as Wordsworth saw it, and of the terror lying beyond everyday life as Coleridge envisioned it. Yet Ford's novel stands as well on its own as an affecting story of a boy who watches the marriage of his mother and father fall apart and then come together again. In the process it is the boy who learns he must leave home while his parents learn their separation from each other is a greater void than the imperfection of their union. In Ford's understated style and in the minimalist literary techniques he uses, the shift of urgency is somewhat slowed, but the lyric power he evokes is enhanced. Ford's story of breakdown, recovery, and mystery of human character is effected by his spareness of approach; he creates reality and emotion by the purest flint of words. This newest novel is likely to gather him many readers.

Martin Tucker. *Confrontation*. Fall, 1990–Winter, 1991, pp. 217–18

Ford's achievement in *Independence Day*—and it is a considerable one—is to reclaim the strangeness of a country which he knows is at least as beguiling as it is wretched, and to rescue it from his worst own image. Amazingly, this late in the American century, he gives every impression of cruising through a territory nobody has laid claim to, nailing it with such a devouring—such an undeceived—eye that it begins to seem new again and in need of a writer of Ford's marvelous talents to explain and translate it. It needs a path to cut through its potentially murderous complexities with what Ford is not embarrassed to call "a hungrified wonder."

Edmund Wilson once praised Scott Fitzgerald's wonderfully clear judgment about Americans and American life—a judgment, Wilson said, "saturated with twentieth-century America." *Independence Day* is a book written in that exalted tradition.

Gordon Burn. *TLS: The Times Literary Supplement*. July 14, 1995, p. 21

Before he went West, so to speak, in his stories and in the novel *Wildlife*, Richard Ford had published three books of fiction: *A Piece of My Heart* (1970), *The Ultimate Good Luck* (1981), and *The Sportswriter* (1980). *A Piece of My Heart*, the first, is an elaborate, stylistically ambitious, and complex novel, somewhat in the Southern Gothic vein. . . .

Ford's second novel, *The Ultimate Good Luck*, is another trip altogether, this time to Mexico, around Oaxaca. It is a steamy ride through the south of the border labyrinth, with characters who are defined by situation, plot, intrigue, and denouement. They have a certain brittleness as they act out their roles; and there is a cinema noir aspect to the landscape of drug smuggling, prisons, bribery, disappearances, threats of murder, and actual murder. . . .

The Sportswriter followed the first two novels and preceded the Western stories and the novel *Wildlife*. Frank Bascombe is the sportswriter, living by choice in Haddam, New Jersey, a pleasant suburban town. . . .

Independence Day, Ford's new novel, returns to Frank Bascombe. *Rabbit Redux?* Not quite. Bascombe is an upscale ruminant, now in his forties, with opinions about everything and Emerson's *Self-Reliance* in the glove compartment. There is no outstanding typicality in him; instead he has the mysteriousness of the agreeable, nice person, harder to describe than the rake, the miser, or the snob. As a professional, or a working man, his resume is unsteady—short-story writer, sportswriter, and now a "realtor." . . . .

Independence Day, if you're taking measurements like the nurse in a doctor's office, might be judged longer than it need be. But longer for whom? Every rumination, each flash of magical dialogue or unexpected mile on the road with a stop at the pay phone, is a wild surprise tossed off as if it were just a bit of cigarette ash by Richard Ford's profligate imagination. *The Sportswriter* and *Independence Day* are comedies—not farces, but realistic, good-natured adventures, sunny, yes. . . . The new work, *Independence Day*, is the confirmation of a talent as strong and varied as American fiction has to offer.

Elizabeth Hardwick. *New York Review of Books.* Aug. 10, 1995, pp. 11, 12, 13, 14

BIBLIOGRAPHY

A Piece of My Heart, 1976 (n); *The Sportswriter*, 1986 (n); *Rock Springs*, 1987 (s); *The Ultimate Good Luck*, 1989 (n); *Wildlife*, 1990 (s); *Bright Angel*, 1991 (scrp); *Independence Day*, 1995 (n); *Women with Men*, 1997

FORNÉS, María Irene (1931–)

Despite the sharp differences between her early and her later plays, all of [María Irene] Fornés's work can be seen as a relentless search for a new theatrical language to explore what theater has always been about: the difference between text and subtext, between the mask and the naked face beneath it, between the quotidian and the secret, between love and the fear and violence always threatening its fragile dominion. Fornés's early plays are filled with a slightly melancholic cheer, the result of an interplay between a sequence of fantastic and whimsical interactions and the underlying knowledge of unrequited desire and unfulfilled hopes—or in the words of her Dr. Kheal, "Contradictions compressed so that you don't know where one stops and the other begins." *Promenade*, for example, is peopled by a variety of symbiotic pairs, escaped convicts and a jailer, rich socialites and servants, ladies and gentlemen, a mother and her children. It is a comedy about the failure to make connections, searching for its plot in the same way that the jailer searches for his prisoners or the mother for her lost children. Throughout the play the pairs keep missing each other and although they delight in the unexpected turns, there is an intimation of a darker reality always held at bay. At the end the mother asks the two convicts, "Did you find evil?" And when they tell her "No," she assures them, "Good night, then. Sleep well. You'll find it some other time."

Even in these early works, Fornés's revolutionary use of language is evident. From the first, she has honed speech to a simple, concrete and supple essence, whether in dialogue or . . . in the song of the convicts from *Promenade*. . . . This is language surprisingly capable of expressing complex shades of emotion and mobilizing a rich and understated irony. . . .

Fornés's plays differ from those of most of her contemporaries in that almost all are set either in a preindustrial society or on the far edge of middle-class culture. They are filled with a deep compassion for the disenfranchised, for whom survival—rather than the typically bourgeois obsession with individual happiness and freedom—is the bottom line. They do not delight, even covertly, in suffering but take a stand unequivocally against dehumanization and violence in its myriad forms. Perhaps it is in this context that her revolutionary use of language is best understood, its simplicity and beauty signaling, in the midst of violence and decay, a verbal utopia in which things are called by their proper names and brutality is so embarrassingly evident that it can no longer hold sway.

David Savran. *In Their Own Words* (New York: Theatre Communications, 1988), pp. 52–53

If *Promenade* brought Fornés a momentary commercial esteem in the late 1960s. *Fefu* brought critical recognition in the late 1970s. . . .

The uptown and downtown reviewers are almost perfectly split in their respective dismissal and praise of Fornés's work. The key issue seems to be the challenge that a Fornés play presents to the audience's understanding. The uptowners do not mind riddles as long as they get the answers by the end. The downtowners value the puzzle itself in its ineffable splendor. This is partly a matter of taste, but it is also a matter of Fornés's aesthetic strategy. Her plays do not provide tidy messages in either domestic homilies or zealous politics; they provoke thought in an open-ended, often haunting way. If the plays are hollow, it is because they carve out a cavernous space in which those thoughts can resonate after the final curtain. They are the audience's thought, though, not Fornés's; she has only instigated them, allowed them, to bubble up to the surface and pop as they hit the hostile air of consciousness.

The period since *Fefu* has been a prolific one for Fornés. She has written and directed at the rate of more than one play a year. *Eyes on the Harem* (INTAR, 1979) and *A Visit* (1981) suggest a return to the polymorphous perversity and satirical thrust of the earlier off-off-Broadway plays. . . . Both plays reflect Fornés's interest in sexual politics, this time using historical settings and source materials.

Scott T. Cummings. In Philip C. Kolin, ed. *American Playwrights since 1945*, (Westport, Ct.: Greenwood Press, 1989), pp. 116–17

Fornés's plays provide a striking opportunity for illustrating the nature of gestic language, especially gestic monologue, in feminist drama. Her works emphasize the creation of embodied characters—that is, characters who enact the movements toward and away from female subjectivity in which corporeality locates itself as the site of culturally conditioned "meanings." While these characters may reflect the "broken"-ness and isolation that are inevitable in their repressive environments (see, e.g., Julia in *Fefu and Her Friends* [1977], Sarita in the play by that name [1984], or

Marion in Abingdon Square [1987]), the fact that their "impulses" as such are communicated in the gestic, self-narrated discourse of Brechtianism allows a partial recuperation of this fragmentation. . . .

Fornés, then, presents what Catherine Belsey calls the "crisis of subjectivity," a crisis set in motion at the moment of entry into the symbolic order embodied in the mode of performance. A reclamation of the speaking body's ability to act (in its dual theatrical/existential senses) comes through recodifying this symbolic order; as Belsey says, "in the fact that the subject is a *process* lies the possibility of transformation." The *Gestus*, with its multivalent moments of highlighting the competition of logos and gestuality, insists on an attention to this process. The female bodies on stage in Fornés's plays may not "speak" with the comic literalness of [Carolee] Schneemann's interior scroll, but her theatricalization of the subject-in-process through the use of gestic monologues suggests a similar preoccupation with the scripting/inscription/conscription of a textualized voice, playing ironically, like Schneemann, off the notion that language "originates from" the body of the speaking subject.

> Deborah R. Geis. *Postmodern Theatric(k)s: Monologue in Contemporary American Drama.* (Ann Arbor: Univ. of Michigan Pr., 1993). pp. 119, 134

BIBLIOGRAPHY
Promenade and Other Plays, 1971 (includes *Tango Palace*, 1964; *The Successful Life of Three: A Skit for Vaudeville*, 1965; *A Vietnamese Wedding*, 1967; *Dr. Kheal*, 1971; *The Red Burning Light*, 1968); *Molly's Dream*, 1971, rev. ed., 1987 (d); *Fefu and Her Friends*, produced 1977, published in *Wordplays I*, 1980; *Orchards*, 1986 (d); *Plays*, 1986 (includes *Mud*, 1983; *The Conduct of Life*, 1986)

FOWLIE, Wallace (1908–)

There is something lofty, elegant and austere in the style Wallace Fowlie has made his own. Capable of tremendous absorption, condensation, sifting and synthesis, he imparts his profound erudition lightly. He is at home amidst the most antagonistic elements, directing his frail bark with the skill of a born mariner. . . . His certitude is never arrogant or pedantic. Woven into his skill, his grace, his dexterity there is always the element of risk, of daring, known alike by the acrobat and the poet. His moments of suspense are those same moments known to the performer and the man of solitude—when he takes flight with his whole being and emerges from the experience a new man, a man dedicated to still greater flights of daring, whether in the air or in the mind.

> Henry Miller. *Chimera.* Autumn, 1944. pp. 47–8

Repeatedly he insists that "all great poetry is knowledge of the occult." But Dante's poem, to which greatness cannot be denied, offers the knowledge that comes of a journey through the moral universe, which is not quite the same thing as "knowledge of the occult," and Homer's epics, even when they take us in the realms of the dead, are wonderfully lacking in mystery, except that mystery to which all being is inescapably knit. There are more kinds of poetry than the kind that Rimbaud wrote, and to take cognizance of their value is not to destroy or impair his greatness. One wishes that Mr. Fowlie had shown his appreciation of this fact. . . . His hierophantic air detracts from his most acceptable pronouncements.

> Babette Deutsch. *New York Herald Tribune Book Section.* Oct. 27, 1946. p. 30

Two outstanding gifts distinguish Wallace Fowlie as a critic. First, in the Bergsonian sense he understands "duration," the curve which is both art and philosophy and which marks a configuration in time. . . . His second gift is his reduction of multiple details to key symbols and categories. Fowlie's successors will be his debtors. They will borrow and debate his key signs. . . . Maritain characterizes Thomas Aquinas as a theocentric humanist. Fowlie extends the terms to Maritain. It is also applicable to Fowlie himself. His range of vision saves him many stumbles.

> Jeremy Ingals. *Saturday Review.* Sept. 20, 1947. p. 34

The author fell in love with the French language at school. He mastered the language as well as any American ever has, wrote several books of criticism . . . and became one of the most inspired teachers in the country. . . . Some of the sketches (in *Pantomime*) . . . are drawn with a delicate pen and reveal a sensibility which rarely coexists with scholarly knowledge or survives an academic career. . . . Behind the delicate and discreet touch of the author one gradually perceives a tragic obsession with the problem of the artist in the world and especially in America.

> Henri Peyre. *New York Times Book Section.* June 3, 1951. p. 5

He considers himself a spectator, a person playing different parts throughout life. He feels himself strongly attracted to the clown, "unashamedly awkward, exalted by the noblest dreams, and always tricked in some way before touching his dream."

And his reminiscences, like his interpretation of the clown, completely lack irresponsible spontaneity, a healthy sense of malice, and a reassuring arrogance: traits indispensable to the true clown. If Mr. Fowlie were the least bit fairer or more poised and gentle, he would be dull.

> Serge Hughes. *Commonweal.* July 13, 1951. p. 338

Fowlie can write with equal ease about people and places and ideas, he can be intimate and general, poetic and grave: and yet one has the feeling that it is all of a piece. It might be added, too, that this writing is in the French tradition of the journal; and this is not at all surprising coming from one who has so thoroughly adopted his beloved country that his work has sometimes been more generally appreciated abroad than at home. . . . Fowlie—in making his own the great French tradition—has brought to his prose-writing something of the penetration and sweep which he had found in his French masters.

Robert Heywood. *Renascence*. Autumn, 1951. p. 110

Before visiting a foreign city or foreign country, we often avoid dull Baedekers and consult friends who have been there. . . . In dealing with the foreign domain of contemporary French letters, Wallace Fowlie offers just such informal advice to the prospective traveler. His *causeries* are lively, personal, and stimulating. . . . If Mr. Fowlie frequently remains superficial and spends space in anecdotes, this is inherent in his conversational manner which is at the opposite extreme from the academic monograph.

Justin O'Brien. *New York Times Book Section*. Nov. 17, 1957. p. 56

BIBLIOGRAPHY
Matines et Vers, 1937 (p); *From Chartered Land*, 1938 (p); *Ernst Psichari*, 1939 (c); *Intervalles*, 1939 (p); *La Pureté dans l'art*, 1941 (c); *Clowns and Angels*, 1943 (c); *De Villon á Péguy*, 1944 (c); *Rimbaud*, 1946, rev. ed., 1966 (c); *Jacob's Night*, 1947 (c); *The Clown's Grail*, 1948 (c); *Sleep of the Pigeon*, 1948 (n); *Sixty Poems of Sceve*, 1949 (tr); *The Age of Surrealism*, 1950 (c); *Pantomime*, 1951 (a); *Mallarmé*, 1953 (c); *Rimbaud's Illuminations*, 1953 (c); *Mid-Century French Poets*, 1955 (tr); *The Journals of Jean Cocteau*, 1956 (tr); *Seamarks*, by St. John Perse, 1957 (tr); *Studies in Modern Literature and Thought*, 1957 (c); *A Poet before the Cross*, by Paul Claudel, 1958 (tr); *French Stories*, 1960 (tr); *Dionysus in Paris*, 1960 (c); *Break of Noon*, by Paul Claudel, 1960 (tr); *Tidings Brought to Mary*, by Paul Claudel, 1960 (tr); *A Reading of Proust*, 1964 (c); *André Gide*, 1965 (b); *Love in Literature*, 1965 (c); *Jean Cocteau*, 1966 (c); *Climate of Violence*, 1967 (c); *Works of Rimbaud*, 1968 (tr); *The French Critic, 1549–1967*, 1968 (c, h); *Stendhal*, 1969 (c); *French Literature: Its History and Its Meaning*, 1973 (c); *Lautréamont*, 1973 (b, c); ed., *The Major Texts of French Literature*, 2 vols., 1973 (anthol); (with Henry Miller) *Letters of Henry Miller and Wallace Fowlie,1943–1972*, 1975; *Journal of Rehearsals: A Memoir*, 1977; *A Reading of Dante's Inferno*, 1981 (c); *Aubade: A Teacher's Notebook*, 1983 (e); *Characters from Proust*, 1983 (p); *Sites*, 1987 (m); *Memory*, 1990 (m); *Poem and Symbol: A Brief History of French Symbolism*, 1990 (c); *Rimbaud and Jim Morrison: The Rebel as Poet*, 1993 (c)

FRANK, Waldo (1889–1967)

Waldo Frank's book [*Our America*] is a pessimistic analysis! The worst of it is, he has hit on the truth so many times. I am glad to see such justice done to Sherwood Anderson, but this extreme national consciousness troubles me. I cannot make myself think that these men like Dreiser, Anderson, Frost, etc., could have gone so far creatively had they read this book in their early days. After all, has not their success been achieved more through natural unconsciousness combined with great sensitiveness than with a mind so

thoroughly propagandistic (is the word right?) as Frank's? But Frank has done a wonderful thing to limn the characters of Lincoln and Mark Twain as he has,—the first satisfactory words I have heard about either of them. The book will never be allowed to get dusty on the library shelves unless he has failed to give us the darkest shadows in his book,—and I don't think he has.

Hart Crane. Letter to Gorham Munson, Dec. 13, 1919, in *The Letters of Hart Crane*, edited by Brom Weber (Hermitage House). 1952. pp. 26–7

Both the novels of Waldo Frank, *The Dark Mother*, as well as the earlier *The Unwelcome Man*, are large and remarkable conflagrations. But they are conflagrations which pour forth less clear orange flame than choking black smoke. The presence of a literary force, a force potentially richer and more abundant than that of perhaps any other of the young American prosemen, is most indubitably announced in them. The traits of the man who could cast up the many deposits of bulky, energetic, and hot-blooded prose to be found in both, who could agglutinate words into the arresting forms scattered through them, entertain such piercingly personal visions, and construct, even theoretically, a complicated pattern of human relationships like that in *The Dark Mother*, must appear well-nigh grandiose to any clear-sighted person. In his most confused, most jejune moments one knows, always, that Frank is a passionate and powerful and living creature, a man who has something to express, and who is driven by a veritable need of expression. But, unfortunately, the immense narrative power of Frank is still intimated rather than revealed. His force is still a force tangled and uneducated.

Paul Rosenfeld. *Dial*. Jan., 1921. p. 95

Rahab . . . is a good deal more confused than profound. . . . the doctrine seems to be that what the vulgar call salvation comes through what the vulgar call sin. Both story and doctrine call for careful statement, but both instead are clapper clawed and mauled and dragged through keyholes and kept in the cellar until only God and Waldo Frank can guess what the row is all about. It is a pity, for Mr. Frank has at times a quite uncanny perception and a quite arresting candor. Where in fiction has the leaping flame of a man's jealousy been hinted at with a more fiery accuracy than on page 64 of this novel? And there is a vividness in a method which, eschewing narrative, darts from mood to mood, seen always from within the consciousness. But the total effect is not that of clear light; it is that of lights tangled and blinding; it is that of several films projected all at once upon the same sheet, and all flickering.

Carl Van Doren. *The Nation*. April 26, 1922. p. 497

One goes into a park and sits down, and immediately, if one is an artist, the park becomes a problem. It lies there. The individual feels his edges knocking improperly against it. He is sitting in somebody else's park. Then, if he is Waldo Frank, he starts remaking that park. Exorbitant characters appear, the skyline begins to churn, mad speeches are ground out. And we have "John the Baptist," one of the most interesting stories of *City Block*. But such a park is a personal creation, and is statistically false; it is true as a reflection of Waldo Frank's temperament, true in a sense that Mallarmé's fauns are true, but completely erroneous as a gauge of our environment.

My reason for pointing this out is a somewhat complicated one. But first of all, I feel that it provides us with a criterion for approaching Mr. Frank. Thus, we have the two possibilities: a book must be statistically true, a whole and proper valuation of life; or it must be true in the sense that Mallarmé's fauns are true, must be a beautiful possibility created in the mind of the artist. I have consistently objected that Mr. Frank does not qualify on condition one; life as he presents it is assiduously culled, the volitional element of the artist is over-emphasized. Or, to borrow from a colleague, M. Cowley, I should say that he has stacked the cards. However, if we admit this cheating, take it as a basis of our calculations, we must next inquire as to whether Mr Frank cheats dextrously; we shall not ask if he is false, but if he is *superbly* false. On the whole, I think he is not, for the two books under consideration are not *finally* beautiful. They lack just that element of cold carving, that bloodless autopsy of the emotions, which allows Mallarmé so near an approach to perfection.

Kenneth Burke. *Dial.* Oct. 22, 1922. pp. 450–1

It is about time that the truth was told about this kind of thing. Critics for the most part, while they are eager to stop real progress and the development of literature, are afraid to tell the truth when they are brought face to face with anything as noisy as this book, for fear ''there should be something in it.'' Any one who foams at the mouth may be gifted with prophecy. They need not be afraid in this case. Mr Frank is not a writer of genius. He has, however, talent and is interested in things, and if he would stop thinking about genius, and would try to exercise restraint and develop his talent, he would give us writing as admirable as the chapter from ''The Will of Saint and Sinner.'' In this chapter [in *Virgin Spain*] he discards all his faults and develops all his virtues. . . . It is a great pity that Mr Frank is not content to restrain himself and give us writing like this more often. He would deepen and widen his talent and develop his powers, which are real. His admirers are doing this writer the worst disservice in bolstering him up to works of noisy bombast. No amount of shouting will bring fire down from heaven; but a beautiful household fire is within the reach of this writer of talent, if he cares to work for it.

Sacheverell Sitwell. *Dial.* Jan. 27, 1926. pp. 64–5

. . . Frank wishes passionately to communicate his world view, his sense of the Whole, his religious vision, to an audience. Yet his paradox is that he writes in such a way that most of his readers cannot see his form for the style, cannot, this is to say, grasp his message, that of a human being valiantly striving to solve the meaning and aim of existence, because of the intrusion of his personality. He does not wish to be simply a writer's writer nor a self-communer who happens to please a coterie: yet he does not pay the price of consciously manipulating the reader's psychology and so conducting him *through* his ordinary impressions, associations, and prejudices to a new insight. . . . Frank has a less naive view of man in relation to the cosmos than the majority of his contemporaries, and he strives to formulate this view, to become aware of it. As an artist, he is distinguished in his conceptions of form: all his

books have an astutely planned unity of larger organization. The two are related. Equally related are one's personality (a product mainly of education, taking that word in its widest sense) and style. And Frank's style shows so markedly the effects of artistic theories current to-day that it defeats his more profound intentions.

Gorham B. Munson. *Style and Form in American Prose* (Doubleday). 1929. pp. 184–5

Waldo David Frank's chosen method of writing, expressionism, is, after all is said, a way natural to him, at least in his rhapsodic moods—and they are frequent. It is failure to recognize this fact that is at the bottom of the frequent misunderstanding of the man and his purposes by the critics whose dislike for the mode prevents their getting at the matter of his work. It is a pity that this is so, because Frank's basic philosophy and ideas are good for all of us, especially now when any self-hood worth the keeping is in danger of being lost in the leveling process of standardization of thinking as well as of living.

John Jocelyn. *Sewanee Review.* Oct., 1932. p. 405

The strange career of Waldo Frank offers an instructive symbol of the intellectual fog through which America has blundered during the last two decades. A brilliant and ambitious critic, he has not been content merely to appraise books and literary forms; he has been driven by a nostalgia for the absolute to seek cosmic and abiding values, to frame a philosophy of life so comprehensive and organic that it would serve both as a religion and a *Weltanschauung*. What he sought in culture was not knowledge, but light and faith. He became a God-seeker, a passionate mystic who turned from the quest for a personal deity to embrace Humanity as God. Whatever he writes is permeated by the peculiar character of the man; everything that comes from his pen, be it impressions of travel, literary criticism, discussions of the drama or dance, is stamped with the same personal quality. No American writer today, not even Gertrude Stein, has a more individualized style and manner of thought. He is the most metaphysical of native critics—a strange mixture of mysticism rooted in the culture of the west, science employed against the pretensions of science, Marxism combined with a romantic conception of cosmic mystery. He is a visionary gifted with a turbid style which occasionally emits prophetic flashes of insight.

Charles I. Glicksberg. *South Atlantic Quarterly.* Jan., 1936. p. 13

Mr. Frank is one of those writers who tries to say more than he can. But no one can afford to dismiss the body of his thought smugly because the whole of it has been an attack on American smugness.

Max Lerner. *Saturday Review.* May 25, 1940. p. 3

. . .it is not only that Frank's poetic world—in which virtue and ''wholeness'' are achieved through naivety and ''darkness,'' through philosophical sexual raptures, metaphysical breasts and teleological wombs—is poetically inadmissible; practically and politically it is even to be feared. If Frank criticizes the Marxian determinism as but a niggardly conception of man and the world, what he offers for its enrichment is a Marxian Rosicrucianism. His creation of "higher" realities leaves no reality whatsoever; he can play with radical politics, for example, until it ceases to be politics and becomes a kind of activistic Nirvana in which all spiritual burdens are laid down. . . .In short, Frank makes the familiar leap from the frying-pan of rationalistic determinism into the fire of mystic authoritarianism; it is a feat that will, I think, be emulated with increasing frequency in our time of political irrationalism, easy feeling and undisciplined moral fervor.

Lionel Trilling. *Kenyon Review*. Winter, 1940. pp. 96–7

Before passing from Frank's fiction to his cultural studies, one should note that Frank's experiments with form in the novel make him one of the important innovators of the American Renaissance. The studied imitation of the rhythms of Whitman and of the Song of Solomon in *Rahab*, which become free verse in *Holiday* and *Chalk Face*, have undeniably affected the prose of several novelists, notably Sherwood Anderson in *Many Marriages* and *Dark Laughter*. The expressionism of Frank, best exemplified in *City Block*, is alleged to have exerted an influence on O'Neill and Dos Passos, while it is apparent the pattern of the book has a genetic relationship to Elmer Rice's *Street Scene*. Frank's influence will keep him alive long after any legitimate interest in his ideas is dead. He has been a fountain of power—for others—in our time.

Oscar Cargill. *Intellectual America* (Macmillan). 1941. p. 674

Indeed, many of the now mature and middle-aged literary men of the present day were as profoundly impressed with *Our America* as [Hart] Crane confessed himself to be. There was one important exception, however. Frank stressed the importance of spiritual components in the new pioneering. When he called for realism in literature, it was a realism controlled by spiritual realities and inner searching and not by material factors. Only upon Crane of all his contemporaries did this spiritual necessity postulated by Frank exert a compelling force of its own, and only in his work do we see its flowering to any considerable degree.

Brom Weber. *Hart Crane* (Bodley). 1948. pp. 166–7

In Frank's early novels one observes the materials of the artist, scarcely integrated, just as they appear in his early critical evaluations of American culture. One discovers that Frank is, after all, going beyond his materials, imposing a philosophy of his own upon his ideal hero, a fictional archetype whom he has sought for in vain in his studies of historical and contemporary characters. This ideal man is in some way or other a rebel against the world of statistics and profits. . . . Waldo Frank's debt to Freud is extensive. We discover it at first in the early works, which, though sincere in intention, are immature in form. Their mass of inadequately assimilated facts are the raw materials which he is to use later in subtler form. In the course of his development several clues suggest that he has not thrown off the influence of Freud: his preoccupation with the unconscious life of his later characters is not merely a deeper study of motivation; for the unconscious of his central

character is always the point to which events are referred. What Frank *does* furnish is the creative means of victory over death—the "mystic x" which Freud hesitates to allow.

Frederick J. Hoffman. *Freudianism and the Literary Mind* (Louisiana State). 1957. pp. 257,263

The basis of all of Frank's writing is his sense of the unity of all things: this unifying force in the multiverse he calls God; not a being or an object, but an action, expressing itself through its parts, among which are persons, peoples, and the total dynamics of creation. Philosophically, he fits in with Emerson, Thoreau, and Whitman. He continues Emerson's concept of the Whole Man and Whitman's "I" who is both Walt Whitman and mankind. To Frank, achievement of the self, becoming a Person, conscious of oneself as a part of the Whole, involves recognition of being partial—existing only in relation to all other persons and all other things—and at the same time involves recognition of God—not fragmented, but entire—within oneself. The Person aware of God within him does not live "in terms of the part as if it were the whole," but "in terms of the Whole expressed through its parts." If God is within the Person, God can be within the People, and achievement of harmony in a society—harmony within itself and harmony with other societies—involves the same awareness on the part of a people. . . .In his later fiction, Frank has been engaged in demonstrating the analogy between a healthy society—a People— and a whole Person. In this too, he has been unconventional.

William Bittner. *The Novels of Waldo Frank* (Pennsylvania). 1958. pp. 16–17

BIBLIOGRAPHY
The Unwelcome Man, 1917 (n); *The Art of the Vieux Colombier*, 1918 (c); *Our America*, 1919 (e); *The Dark Mother*, 1920 (n); *City Block*, 1922 (n); *Rahab*, 1922 (n); *Holiday*, 1923 (n); *Salvos*, 1924 (e); *Chalk Face*, 1924 (n); *Virgin Spain*, 1926 (t) (revised edition, 1942); *Time Exposures* [pseud. Search-Light], 1926 (b); *The Rediscovery of America*, 1929 (e); *New Year's Eve*, 1929 (d); *America Hispana*, 1931 (t); *Dawn in Russia*, 1932 (t); *The Death and Birth of David Markand*, 1934 (n); *In the American Jungle*, 1937 (e); *The Bridegroom Cometh*, 1938 (n); *Chart for Rough Water*, 1940 (e); *Summer Never Ends*, 1941 (n); *South American Journey*, 1943 (t); *The Jew in Our Day*, 1944 (e); *Island in the Atlantic*, 1946 (n); *The Invaders*, 1948 (n); *Birth of a World*, 1951 (b); *Not Heaven*, 1953 (n); *Bridgehead*, 1957 (j); *The Rediscovery of Man*, 1958 (m,e); *Cuba, Prophetic Island*, 1962 (t).

FREDERIC, Harold (1856–1898)

Frederic's understanding of racial and theological ideas is at times penetrating; for example, his analysis of the conflicting elements in the Irish character and his contrast of the Greek and the Hebrew ideal of life in Christianity. Frederic's picture of the Catholic Church is very interesting, but he is drawing with sympathy only one element in it, that of the man who loves its artistic side and is not concerned with dogma. . . . The general effect of this book [*The Damnation of Theron Ware*] is to paint religions as necessary concessions to human weakness. But, being an artist, he does this without descending into crude caricature as Sinclair Lewis does in *Elmer Gantry*. His people are real, and he never allows them to become shrill or disgusting, however he may be turning their souls inside out. His satire is therefore all the more effective.

> Arthur Hobson Quinn. *American Fiction* (Appleton). 1936. p. 452

In one of his most passionate novels, *Seth's Brother's Wife*, Frederic commented on the fact that American humor grew out of "the grim, fatalist habit of seizing upon the grotesque side," and his bitterness made the most of it. His most famous novel, *The Damnation of Theron Ware*, is a mischievously written museum piece, persistently overrated because it was among the first American novels to portray an unfrocked clergyman and to suggest the disintegration of religious orthodoxy. But the unfrocked clergyman was to become as useful a symbol of the new era as the businessman. . . .

> Alfred Kazin. *On Native Grounds* (Reynal). 1942. pp. 35–6

Frederic could agree with the age of Howells that the application of reason to passion could save; and *Seth's Brother's Wife* has a happy ending. When he came to investigate the growing complexities of other realms of the human mind, however, Frederic wrote not a comedy, but a tragedy: the story of the fall of a man, rather than his salvation, through illumination and knowledge: *The Damnation of Theron Ware*. . . . The really extraordinary objectivity of the author—the story was told strictly from the minister's point of view—involved the reader completely with the protagonist, so that he was unaware that the education of Theron Ware was anything but good; he was shown "expanding, growing in all directions," and only gradually was it realized that what seemed improvement was, instead, moral degeneration.

> Everett Carter. *Howells and the Age of Realism* (Lippincott). 1954. pp. 243–4

Many elements of the American Dream appear in this strong novel [*The Damnation of Theron Ware*] and participate in its vitality. There is the flouting of mere conventional morality, the belief in a scientific or rationalistic view of man and his relations, and the earnest faith in intelligence, human dignity, and freedom. There is also, initially, a firmly monistic sense of the interdependency of nature and spirit: both the rasping piety of the community and the personal inadequacy of Theron are introduced as functions of the environment. But, just as in *Seth's Brother's Wife*, the stream of moral earnestness separates from the stream of scientific analysis, and presently it appears that Frederic has slipped back into the simple formula of orthodoxy which says that a person who displays moral weakness is one of the damned. . . . What appears in the novel as the indignant condemnation of Theron for his moral deterioration began as Frederic's moral indignation with the small town. Because he did not have the technique to lay out the whole spiritual landscape, he funneled his passion into the study of

Theron—and there it appears, transformed but still providing the novel's vitality and interest.

> Charles C. Walcutt. *American Literary Naturalism, a Divided Stream* (Minnesota). 1956. p. 52

Satirical humor of a broader sort is the main virtue of . . . *The Damnation of Theron Ware*. . . . This interesting but recently overrated novel is at once an effort of critical realism—dealing as had Frederic's first novel, *Seth's Brother's Wife* . . . , with the decadence of village life and faith—and a problem novel. . . . Frederic is justly remembered as a forerunner in provincial satire of Sinclair Lewis.

> Warner Berthoff. *The Ferment of Realism: American Literature, 1884–1919* (Free). 1965. pp. 131–2

Possessed of an imaginative knowledge of his home county, in which character was inseparable from ethnic, religious, historical, political, and social conditions, he was able to follow Howells' lead in producing a fiction of the commonplace, yet to surpass the dean in rendering a sense of communal density. Not until Faulkner's Yoknapatawpha County did American literature have a region so fully and intimately explored as Frederic's fictionalization of his native area—the land around the invented cities of Tyre, Tecumseh, and Thessaly. In *Seth's Brother's Wife* (1887); *The Lawton Girl* (1890); *In the Valley* (1890), a historical romance about the region in colonial times; *The Damnation of Theron Ware* (1896); and several collections of short stories, Harold Frederic, sitting in London, detached from the immediate political maneuverings of upstate New York, brought into existence a fully articulated human community. The peculiar quality of rural brutality as well as rural speech, the way the political boss Beekman rules the countryside as well as the town, the relation of the best families to the processes of making public policy, the aldermanic view of responsibility, the contrasting social roles played by the Methodist and the Episcopal Churches, the Dutch resentment of the English settlers who had migrated from Massachusetts, and the code of the masculine small-town world as opposed to the public code of sexual morality, all emerge dynamically; they are, in Frederic's pages, so rich a context of action that the American would appear to be comprehensible only in terms of his dwelling place and the multifold allegiances and enmities that he has inherited with it.

> Larzer Ziff. *The American 1890s* (Viking). 1966. p. 209

In literary quality, the stories [*Stories of York State*] are competently handled for their time, with a surprising lack of mannered extremities: the clichés of feeling and expression, the incredible manipulations of plot and motivation, and the frequent sentimentality strike one as much less offensive than they might be. Although these seem to be negative virtues, the relative unobtrusiveness of the "period" features gives the stories a durability certainly not evident in the minor works of Mark Twain, for example.

The positive value of the stories lies in their appeal to Civil War enthusiasts, to antiquarians of the area, and to those who enjoy regional literature in general (if such readers exist at all). . . .

The stories possess two particular features which we often have assumed either the invention or the personal property of one or another contemporary writer; but this ghost, when he hears boasts of newfangled inventions, replies, "Oh, we had the same thing when I was young." For example, the persistence of the naïve, usually orphan, adolescent narrator . . . suggests that Hemingway and Salinger are a bit later in the field than is often realized. In addition, Frederic's treatment of a semi-imaginary county and its towns in these stories as well as in three of his novels, where place and family names recur, takes a bit of the edge off enthusiastic claims for Faulkner's giant achievement in the same kind of effort.

Frank Baldanza. *Southern Review*. Winter, 1969. pp. 250–1

The novels of Harold Frederic have a breadth that clearly goes beyond what the epithet "pioneer realist" suggests. Although much of his fiction was set in the same small area of upper New York State, his concerns were far from regional. He often returned to the hills and valleys of his home, but he always looked beyond them. His reputation must rest most heavily on *The Damnation of Theron Ware*, a work whose greatness has yet to be fully appreciated, despite the current revival of interest. As long as it is commonly thought to be what Van Wyck Brooks' edition proclaims it, a classic of realism "which exposes the cultural barrenness of the small town," the novel will probably never attract the kind of reader who would most appreciate its fine and subtle ironies, its complex and original treatment of the most American of themes—the ambiguous relationship between innocence and experience.

The other novels deserve wider attention too. Not all of them, to be sure, not *In the Valley*, *The Return of the O'Mahoney*, and *March Hares*. But the remaining works have in rewarding measure the artistry and intelligence which distinguish *The Damnation of Theron Ware*. From *Seth's Brother's Wife* through *The Market-Place* they tell a story worth telling, a paradoxical tale of an innocence that discovers itself endowed with new ideas, new opportunities, new powers, only to discover itself as still innocent, still limited, still banal.

Austin Briggs, Jr. *The Novels of Harold Frederic* (Cornell). 1969. pp. 211–2

Frederic tended on occasion to write dramatized essays rather than novels. Not only that, but he was curiously inept with essay materials and in these novels he was often betrayed by the unresolved conflict between his ideology and the dramatic reality which embodied most faithfully his deepest understanding of the nature of men. It was only in his last three years that this conflict was resolved and his mature genius found expression. When it did, his achievement was too far in advance of current attitudes to be comprehensible to his public. . . .

Frederic's achievement lies in the sensitivity and power with which he probed the naïveté and inconsistency of the American Dream and announced its inevitable collapse in the face of the new order of complexity of the twentieth century. In this he surpassed all his contemporaries in his ability to dramatize, allegorize, and mythicize the coming fall from innocence. In addition, testing his vision against his own experience, he understood that a loss of innocence might not bring a dignified, saddened wisdom, but might transform youthful egotism into debased cynicism, and ultimately into predatory rapacity. Thus Frederic wrote for the twentieth century, not his own, and in his greatest works achieved a vigorous

and alarming vision of the civilization to come which has, as we can now see, verified his worst fears and proved him to be one of the most perceptive and important novelists of his time.

Stanton Garner. *Harold Frederic* (Minnesota). 1969. p. 45

My own view is that *Gloria Mundi* illustrates an unresolved ambivalence toward the issue posed by all three of the principal women—and especially by Frances Bailey—that of female emancipation, and also a self-contradictory attitude in Frederic between his observations of human behavior and his will to believe in the possibility of human fulfillment. Furthermore, these problems of ambivalence as regards both topics are characteristic of his work more generally, and they account both for certain cruxes in individual works and for much of the intellectual interest and tension of the novels. An instance is Frederic's shifting moral attitude toward Celia Madden between *The Damnation of Theron Ware* and *The Market-Place*. The structure of *Gloria Mundi* is a negative example. We have here a portrait of human frustration upon which the will to be happy, to believe that love conquers or resolves all, is super-imposed in the form of the fairy tale. The traditional resolution of the romance (with the inheritance, the title, and the marriage) partially obscures both the architectonic structure, the dialectical character, and the irresolution of the novel of ideas.

Jean Frantz Blackall. *Markham Review*. May, 1972. p. 46

Frederic's War stories expressed all that [Stephen] Crane said they did. They also reflected a tacit bias that Crane left unmentioned. Far from celebrating the War as a holy cause, Frederic treated it as unmitigated disaster, and his stories are probably among the earliest examples of fiction written by a Northern writer of distinction which was not simply against war, as Crane's was, but against *the* War. . . .

Frederic is at his best in depicting the confused reactions of the villagers to the distant savagery. The ferocious casualties suffered by Oneida County contingents in the Peninsular campaigns alone stunned their families and friends. How much of these times Frederic actually remembered and how much he simply reconstructed from latter-day recollections of others it is hard to say, but he recreates as few writers have ever managed to do the atmosphere of a bereft community mourning its dead and swept up "in a hysterical whirl of emotions—now pride, now horror, now bitter wrath on top."

Daniel Aaron. *The Unwritten War* (Knopf). 1973. pp. 220–1

BIBLIOGRAPHY

Seth's Brother's Wife, 1887 (n); *In the Valley*, 1890 (n); *The Lawton Girl*, 1890 (n); *The Return of the O'Mahoney*, 1892 (n); *The Copperhead*, 1893 (n); *Marsena and Other Stories of the Wartime*, 1894; *The Damnation of Theron Ware*, 1896 (n); *March Hares*, 1896 (n); *Gloria Mundi*, 1898 (n); *The Market Place*, 1899 (n); *Stories of York State*, 1966; *The Major Works*, 1969; *The New Exodus: A Study of Israel in Russia*, 1970; *The Copperhead and Other Stories of the North during the American War*, 1972; *The*

Correspondence of Harold Frederic, 1977; *The Civil War Stories of Harold Frederic*, 1992

FRIEDMAN, Bruce Jay (1930–)

The peculiar pressure that inflates this book [*Stern*] to the bursting point is created by the author's relentless juxtaposition of the inadequacy of the common notion of manliness with the unavoidable compulsion of the hero to judge himself by it. The texture of the book is essentially poetic; it is the poetry of the feminine, accepting, creative personality challenged from without and within by the necessity to be a man and defend one's home and family against forces which are probably insuperable. . . . The terrible thing about Stern's fantasies—the quality which makes them grip and hurt—is that they have a large foundation in fact. Could Stern use the history of this century to soothe away his nightmares? The fact of the program shadows every page of the book. But of course Stern's Jewishness is just a special instance of a general fear and trembling. . . . Friedman is nervously alive to every bit of brutality that men grab to get through their lives untouched; he is wide open to the comedy and sadness that attend a man who will be touched.

Jeremy Larner. *The Nation*. Dec. 1, 1962. pp. 380–1

Stern was a small but brilliant book, kept from an absolute triumph only by a late flagging of impulse and decisiveness, but wonderfully consistent and revelatory for most of its length. Friedman's second novel is brilliant, too, largely in ways that its predecessor broke ground for. It confirms the feeling that his comic gifts are almost unique among writers of his generation, since they do not depend, as nearly everyone else's do, on contrivance or exaggeration; they do not press reality to yield up arbitrary and exotic charades but release it, through purely verbal agencies, into its inherent sense of displacement and sad, domestic absurdity.

Yet something is wrong with *A Mother's Kisses*—on a very high level, but wrong. It is a much less imagined and considered work than *Stern*, having clearly been appropriated from what one assumes is Friedman's own past. And this results in a failure of *transformation*, a failure to metamorphosize personal history into present vision.

Richard Gilman. *New York Herald Tribune Book Section*. Aug. 23, 1964. p. 5

Friedman has nothing of the cleverness of [Philip] Roth; he lacks Bellow's intellectualism altogether. Unlike Malamud, his people don't even have connections to a life of the past. . . . Friedman uses no props: his people simply lead ash-can lives. . . . What makes Friedman more interesting than most of Malamud, Roth and Bellow is the sense he affords of possibilities larger than the doings and undoings of the Jewish urban bourgeois, which, after all, comprises but an infinitesimal aspect of American life. What makes him more important is that he writes out of the viscera instead of the cerebrum. What makes him more dangerous is that while they distribute prose designed by careful planning for careful living, Friedman really doesn't know what he's doing. . . . Bruce Jay Friedman is that rarity, a compulsive writer whose innocence makes his flaws of greater value, ultimately, than the perfections of skilled mechanics.

Nelson Algren. *The Nation*. Sept. 21, 1964. pp. 142–3

Stern, it seemed to me, was nothing more than promising because its situation and tone were so totally conventional. It was good because intelligent and unpretentious, but I think his second book [*A Mother's Kisses*] shows more encouraging signs. Here mama dominates, primarily her son Joseph, who wants to go to college and ends up at Kansas Land, and though mama is drawn strictly within the confines of the type, any book that ends up at Kansas Land cannot be accused of having been written before, not even by Malamud. Besides, Friedman is trying to whoop up his style, not in itself a good thing, but it shows he is aiming at more than simple jokes and tears.

Roger Sale. *Hudson Review*. Winter, 1964–1965. p. 615

No young writer is more frightened than Bruce Jay Friedman. From the first pages of his first novel, *Stern*, he has been using fiction as juju—to control or appease or amuse the pressing uglinesses of modern life. Superfluously, I note that his work is such good art that it also functions for us or else he would be a mere autistic diarist. . . . *Stern*, movingly and bitterly, fixes—one may say, immobilizes—the ridiculousness of anti-Semitism and the way it can make Jews ridiculous. In his first book of stories, *Far from the City of Class*, assorted fears and fallacies are tickled into momentary lulls. In his second novel, *A Mother's Kisses*, he depicts the possessiveness of motherhood as a hilarious horror, with the Bosch-like image of a young man tied by an umbilical cord to a gaping womb that he drags after him as he flees it.

Now Friedman publishes a book of stories, *Black Angels*, in which he pushes, or is pushed, past black humor into black fantasy. In the past, like other black humorists, he has had fantastic visions of reality; most of these new stories are realistic visions of fantasy.

Stanley Kauffmann. *New Republic*. Oct. 8, 1966. p. 20

Friedman's humor is more reductionist than [Saul] Bellow's or [Isaac] Rosenfeld's; that is to say, it is less humane. In works of complex irony, like Italo Svevo's *Confessions of Zeno*, the narrator offers several alternative explanations for his actions, contrasting his motives with others' interpretations of those motives, and with the unanticipated end results. The idea emerges of man as an intricate, irreducible being who is both funnier and more precious than he ordinarily appears. But the black humor of *Stern* explains away all motives, presenting a view of man that is necessarily meaner and more circumscribed. The final pages of the book show Stern's overflowing sympathy, which is *almost* recognized as the manifestation of a great soul. . . . Stern's capacity to admit the humanity of his adversary, his vision of the enemy as just another ''refugee,'' could have made him a moral hero. Instead he is cut down to size in the final paragraph where all this emotion is exposed for the theatrical extravagance the author finds it to be.

The book remains critical of the protagonist and uses the weapons of satire to deflate him. Nevertheless, even Stern's ineffectual sensitivity is healing. If at the end he is still not at home in the world, he is at least more at home in his home, as husband and father and man.

> Ruth R. Wisse. *The Schlemiel as Modern Hero* (Chicago). 1971. pp. 89–90

Friedman's world is ominously dependent on chance, a world of inconsequential meetings and partings. The future ceases to exist as an estimable series of actions. The categories of time and space fail to define the limits of perception, leaving Stern and Joseph forever vulnerable to the indefinites of unfolding experience. As in the involved world of television defined by Marshall McLuhan, so in the would-be conformist worlds of *Stern* and *A Mother's Kisses* discontinuity and simultaneity have displaced uniformity and consecutiveness. Hence the absence in Friedman's stories of family history, of sense of place, of names (what is Stern's first name? Joseph's last? Joseph's father's?), of anything other than the rudiments of narrative succession; and contrariwise an emphasis on the terrifying involutions of the moment. Under the circumstances not to feel anxiety is not to be human.

> Max F. Schulz. *Black Humor Fiction of the Sixties* (Ohio Univ. Pr.). 1973. pp. 107–8

A number of our toughest novelists have gone so far in the direction of comprehensive in-joking, cosmic cynicism, urbane oversoul that they've out-toughed themselves, out-orbited modernity, and checked themselves back in with the basics—parents, children, marriage, friendship, gutted tradition. Their over-experienced, flailing heroes have reeled through all the circles of our hip Inferno and are now ready to retest their reactions to certain establishment values even if the retesting process hurts. And it does hurt.

Case in point: Bruce Jay Friedman's unheroic but swinging compendium of vulnerabilities named Harry Towns [in *About Harry Towns*]. . . .

A book . . . of brilliant chapters, a series of episodes with little development, change that is no real change, irresolute resolution. Harry writes scripts for Hollywood and scripts for the lives of himself and everyone else. The professional scripts sell and are evidently successful; the others are aborted by flaky circumstances. Friedman solves nothing for his well-meaning protagonist, who, on the last page, senses that maybe he ought to go to Sofia and knows that he must "try like hell not to get hit with a brick." Even Ulysses might settle for that in 1974.

> James R. Frakes. *New York Times Book Section*. June 23, 1974. p. 32

About halfway through the first act of Bruce Jay Friedman's newest fever dream of a comedy, *Have You Spoken to Any Jews Lately?* a man in the audience explodes with, more or less metaphorically speaking, words supplied by the playwright. "This is a cheap commercialization of this century's most barbarous act," the man shouts to the actors. "Have you no shame?" . . .

Not really.

Shame isn't much in evidence on the stage of the American Jewish Theater, where *Have You Spoken to Any Jews Lately?*

opened last night. Yet there's a lot of anger, fear, and compassion, sometimes expressed in terms that are as horrific as they are funny. Mr. Friedman is a novelist with sterling credits (*Stern, A Mother's Kisses*), and playwright (*Scuba Duba* and *Steam-bath*), who has recently been working in movies. Maybe that's why he likes to push his luck when he finds himself in the comparative freedom of the Off Off Broadway theater.

Have You Spoken to Any Jews Lately? is about Jack Horowitz, born and bred in the Bronx of devout Jewish parents. He's married to a beautiful, blond Roman Catholic, Flannery O'Halloran, and the father of an off-stage daughter. Chrissy, who has begun to bug him with questions about who she is. What, exactly, are her roots? Her ethnic obligations? . . .

Though *Have You Spoken to Any Jews Lately?* is loaded with Jewish manners, lore, figures of speech and history, it would be a mistake to consider the play as narrowly ethnic as it sounds. Beneath its engagingly disreputable particulars, the play is another consideration of the same kind of moral aimlessness Sam Shepard examined in *Simpatico*.

When American social and economic life was dominated by people sharing the same northern European heritage, one could speak of this country as a great melting pot. Today, it's apparent that we don't all melt down at the same speed and to the same consistency. Somehow we have to learn to accommodate that fact, Mr. Friedman seems to say. Otherwise, chaos.

> Vincent Canby. *New York Times Book Section*. Jan. 14, 1995, pp. C13, 18

There are 47 [stories] in this collection [*The Collected Short Fiction of Bruce Jay Friedman*], published between 1953 and 1995. . . . Mr. Friedman's stories with their whammo endings, tend to divide into two kinds: the first leave you whispering, "Wow"; the second go whistling over your head like an artillery round and leave you muttering "Huh?" . . . Out of nearly 50 stories, my "Wow" count came to 12, the "Huh?" to only a very few, leaving many pleasurable others in between (as well as one or two clunkers). . . .

Mr. Friedman's stories are about psychiatrists, Jewish mothers, Hollywood, death, the Air Force, cocaine, sex, getting cheated on, suicide, guilt, and exquisitely bizarre situations. . . . Mr. Friedman's absurdities amount to a kind of Jobian—as in Job, he of the dunghill—querulousness in the face of higher universal incomprehensibilities. . . .

Mr. Friedman has been likened to everyone from J. D. Salinger to Woody Allen. This collection should finally establish him for what he is: Bruce Jay Friedman, sui generis and no mean thing. No further comparisons are necessary.

> Christopher Buckley. *New York Times Book Review*. Nov. 5, 1995, p. 9

BIBLIOGRAPHY

Stern, 1962 (n); *Far from the City of Class*, 1963 (s); ed., *Black Humor* (coll); *A Mother's Kisses*, 1965 (n); *Black Angels*, 1966 (s); *Scuba Duba*, 1968 (d); *Steambath*, 1971 (d); *The Dick*, 1971 (n); *About Harry Towns*, 1975 (n); *The Lonely Guy's Book of Life*, 1978 (e); *Stir Crazy*, 1980 (scrp); (with others) *Splash!*, 1984 (scrp); *Let's Hear It from a Beautiful Guy*, 1984 (s); *Tokyo Woes*, 1985 (n);

The Current Climate, 1989 (n); *The Slightly Older Guy*, 1995 (coll, humor); *A Father's Kisses*, 1996 (m); *The Collected Short Stories*, 1997

FROST, Robert (1875–1963)

Mr. Frost's book (*A Boy's Will*) is a little raw, and has in it a number of infelicities; underneath them it has the tang of the New Hampshire woods, and it has just this utter sincerity. It is not post-Miltonic or post-Swinburnian or post-Kiplonian. This man has the good sense to speak naturally and to paint the thing, the thing as he sees it. And to do this is a very different matter from gunning about for the circumplectious polysyllable. . . . One reads the book for the "tone," which is homely, by intent, and pleasing, never doubting that it comes direct from his own life, and that no two lives are the same.

> Ezra Pound. *Poetry*. May, 1913. pp. 72–4

"Yankees is what they always were," sings Mr. Frost. His New England is the same old New England of the pilgrim fathers—a harsh, austere, velvet-coated-granite earth. . . . To present this earth, these people, the poet employs usually a blank verse as massive as they, as stript of all apologies and adornments. His poetry is sparing, austere, even a bit crabbed at times; but now and then it lights up with a sudden and intimate beauty; a beauty springing from life-long love and intuition.

> Harriet Monroe. *Poetry*. Jan., 1917. pp. 203–4

The Frostian humour is peculiarly important for America. No other of our poets has shown a mood at once so individual and so neighborly. Moreover, the comparative thinness of American literature, its lack of full social body and flavor, is due to the extraordinary interval between our artistry and our national life. Our nation is widespreading and unformed, tangled in raw freedom and archaic conventionalities. Our poetry, now responding to and now reacting from our national life, tends to be rather banal, or rather esoteric—in either case, thin. Mr. Frost's work is notably free from that double and wasting tendency. His own ambiguity is vital: it comes from artistic integrity in rare union with fluent sympathy. His poetic humour is on the highway toward the richer American poetry of the future, if that is to be.

> G. R. Elliott. *The Virginia Quarterly Review*. July, 1925. pp. 214–5

Mr. Frost's poetry was first awarded critical approval because it was thought to be in revolt against something at a time when poetry must be in revolt. . . . Poetry must now not be anything like Imagism and must not even revolt, but must be the kind of poetry that Mr. Pound or, more purely and quintessentially, Mr. Eliot wrote. . . . It is quite true that Frost does not write like Eliot, Pound, Auden, or Spender. Fools may conclude that he is therefore a bad or an unimportant poet, but intelligent people look at the poetry he has written. When you do that, unless your nerves are sealed with wax,

you immediately and overwhelmingly perceive that it is the work of an individual and integrated poet, a poet who is like no one else, a major poet not only in regard to this age but in regard to our whole literature, a great American poet.

> Bernard DeVoto. *Saturday Review*. Jan. 1, 1938. pp. 4, 14

If he does not strike far inward, neither does he follow the great American tradition (extending from Whitman through Dos Passos) of standing on a height to observe the panorama of nature and society. Let us say that he is a poet neither of the mountains nor of the woods, although he lives among both, but rather of the hill pastures, the intervales, the dooryard in autumn with the leaves swirling, the closed house shaking in the winter storms (and who else has described these scenes more accurately, in more lasting colors?). In the same way, he is not the poet of New England in its great days, or in its late-nineteenth-century decline (except in some of his earlier poems); he is rather a poet who celebrates the diminished but prosperous and self-respecting New England of the tourist home and the antique shop in the abandoned gristmill. And the praise heaped on Frost in recent years is somehow connected in one's mind with the search for ancestors and authentic old furniture.

> Malcolm Cowley. *New Republic*. Sept. 18, 1944. pp. 346–7

Frost . . . may be described as a good poet in so far as he may be said to exist, but a dangerous influence in so far as his existence is incomplete. He is in no sense a great poet, but he is at times a distinguished and valuable poet. . . . He is the nearest thing we have to a poet laureate, a national poet; and this fact is evidence of the community of thought and feeling between Frost and a very large part of the American literary public. . . . The principles which have hampered Frost's development, the principles of Emersonian and Thoreauistic Romanticism, are the principles which he has openly espoused, and they are widespread in our culture. Until we abandon them in favor of better, we are unlikely to produce many poets greater than Frost.

> Yvor Winters. *Sewanee Review*. Autumn, 1948. p. 596

Creatively, there are at least three Frosts—the actual artist, the legendary public character, posed and professed, and the latent, potential poet that might have been. . . . Frost himself all through his work, more or less, offers clues as to the kind of thing he might have done, the line of a frightful and fascinating interest that he almost dared to follow. The road not taken. . . . One wishes he had been a little less fearful of evil tidings, less scared of his own desert places. One wishes he had wasted less time being sane and wholesome, and gone really all out, farther than he did beyond the boundaries of New England's quaintness into its areas of violence, madness, murder, rape, and incest. . . . It is this night side of life and nature that Frost's art has, I think, scamped reporting, and not because he did not know it; no American poet, nor Poe in his stories, has come closer to Baudelaire.

> Rolfe Humphries. *The Nation*. July 23, 1949. pp. 92–3

The controlled development of his talent, and the finality and grace of statement in his best poems, are of moral no less than artistic value, exemplary for all who practice this art.... His vein of romantic triviality and perversity is not hard to distinguish, and it may be indulged.

That stern critic, Yvor Winters, considers Frost an Emersonian and therefore untrustworthy sage; but he would probably concede that on occasion Frost has had a harder edge and eye than Emerson, more humor, and more of the fear of God. It would be going too far to think of him as a religious poet, but his work tends towards wholeness, and thus towards a catholicism of the heart.

Robert Fitzgerald. *New Republic.* Aug. 8, 1949. p. 18

His cheerfulness is the direct opposite of Mr. Babbitt's or even of Mr. Pickwick's. It is a Greek cheerfulness. And the apparent blandness of the Greeks was, as Nietzsche showed in his *Birth of Tragedy* the result of their having looked so deeply into life's tragic meaning that they had to protect themselves by cultivating a deliberately superficial jolliness in order to bear the unbearable. Frost's benign calm, the comic mask of a whittling rustic, is designed for gazing—without dizziness—into a tragic abyss of desperation.... In the case of this great New England tragic poet, the desperation is no less real for being a quiet one, as befits a master of overwhelming understatements.

Peter Viereck. *Atlantic Monthly.* Oct., 1949. p. 68

Frost is that rare thing, a complete or representative poet, and not one of the brilliant partial poets who do justice, far more than justice, to a portion of reality, and leave the rest of things forlorn. When you know Frost's poems you know surprisingly well how the world seemed to one man, and what it was to seem that way: the great Gestalt that each of us makes from himself and all that isn't himself is very clear, very complicated, very contradictory in the poetry. The grimness and awfulness and untouchable sadness of things, both in the world and in the self, have justice done to them in the poems, but no more justice than is done to the tenderness and love and delight; and everything in between is represented somewhere too, some things willingly and often and other things only as much—in Marianne Moore's delicate phrase—''as one's natural reticence will allow.''

Randall Jarrell. *Kenyon Review.* Autumn, 1952. pp. 560–1

I think of Robert Frost as a terrifying poet. Call him, if it makes things any easier, a tragic poet, but it might be useful every now and then to come out from under the shelter of that literary word. The universe that he conceives is a terrifying universe.... But the *people*, it will be objected, the *people* who inhabit this possibly terrifying universe! About them there is nothing that can terrify; surely the people in Mr. Frost's poems can only reassure us by their integrity and solidity.... They affirm *this* of themselves: that they are what they are, that this is their truth, and that if the truth be bare, as truth often is, it is far better than a lie. For me the process by which they arrive at that truth is always terrifying. The manifest America of Mr. Frost's poems may be pastoral; the actual America is tragic.

Lionel Trilling. *Partisan Review.* Summer, 1959. pp. 451–2

The conditions which circumscribe Frost's poems are those of a world not yet dominated by urban, industrialized, bureaucratized culture—the very world which, seeing its inevitable coming, Emerson and his kind strove to confront and save for man before it would be too late. Frost glances at this world, only to turn to a one he knows better. In that world the proper life style—which in turn generates the literary style—is that of Frost's characteristic protagonists: individuals who again and again are made to face up to the fact of their individualism as such; who can believe that a community is no more than the sum of the individuals who make it up; who are situated so as to have only a dim sense, even that resisted mightily, of the transformations which the individual might have to undergo if he is to live fully in the modern world and still retain his identity as an individual. But, of course, Frost's protagonists refuse to live fully in the modern world and will have little or nothing to do with such transformations. Frost's work is in the end a series of expressions of that refusal and assessments of its cost.

Roy Harvey Pearce. *Kenyon Review.* Spring, 1961. pp. 261–2

Let the School System make a whited saint of Mr. Frost if it must; and as, alas, it will. The man himself remains an *hombre*. If he is half radiance he is also half brimstone, and praise be. His best poems will endure precisely because they are terrible—and holy. All primal fire is terrible—and holy. Mr. Frost could climb to heaven and hear the angels call him brother—*frater*, they would probably say—but he could as well climb Vesuvius and equally hear every rumble under his feet call out to him. The darkness in his poems is as profound as the light in them is long. They are terrible because they are from life at a depth into which we cannot look unshaken.

John Ciardi. *Saturday Review.* March 24, 1962. pp. 15–6

A question arises from Frost's *Collected Poems* . . . : what are the possibilities for a poetry based upon nothing more than a shared sense of human fact? Is this enough? Will it serve instead of those other ''certainties'' which are, for many readers, insecure?

Frost would seem to answer ''Yes.'' Yeats relied on nervous improvisations or religious patterns hired for the occasion of the poem.... Frost committed himself to the common ground he *knew* existed between himself and his putative reader. He knew that if he were to tell a pathetic story in a few common words whose weightings were part of our blood, we would respond feelingly. And that was something. Frost has spent a lifetime seeing how much he could say on those terms. He is the poet most devoted to bare human gesture.

Denis Donoghue. *The Yale Review.* Winter, 1963. p. 216

Both poets [Frost and Wallace Stevens] accept the physical world of positive, scientific, fact; both put aside comforting myths that deny the evidence of the senses, and for both truth is many observable truths. But both have experienced transforming moments in which the imagination creates undeniable reality of another sort. Both Frost and Stevens have given up Romantic metaphysics, but they are engaged in a sophisticated balancing act of enjoying the Romantic dream while 'having just escaped from the truth,' from 'the doctrine of this landscape.' (Stevens: 'The Latest Freed Man.') The poems also offer a clear index to the difference between the two writers, in that Frost concludes with 'parts of a world' as 'measured by eye'; Stevens, with a 'supreme fiction.' Stevens being closer to the Romantics leaves us in the 'strange world' of illusion (though we know from the start that it is one), and Frost takes us out of it (though we know what the illusion is like).

Reuben Brower. *The Poetry of Robert Frost* (Oxford). 1963. pp. 94–5

And here, in the abrasive play among the poems, there emerges, at least as a personal solution, a rather whimsical figure, the "literate farmer." (I take the term from the poem "The Literate Farmer and the Planet Venus.") This figure reveals himself at times as the clown, at times as the grotesque sage ("the tramp astrologer"), but eventually we see him as the fallible yet fulfilled man in "West Running Brook." His essential quality is that of a kinetic mind always in motion: the humorist yielding to fantasist in turn yielding to thinker. He is always in part the bright schoolboy—some patient soul ought to count Frost's references to schoolboys, college boys—the mercurial tease, the enquirer. The most notable facet of the personality, however, is the erudition, all the outdoor table talk, which seems at first glance at odds with probability. . . . when the literate farmer sends out his thought like a sonic signal and awaits the echo, he waits for the abstract to touch the enduring surface of nature—and to return; to return transformed. And this transformation buys a lyric intensity which perhaps diminishes the claims of realism or appropriateness. But the literate farmer has a stronger claim for acceptability. There is, after all, a tradition of the thoughtful country man in New England.

Radcliffe Squires. *The Major Themes of Robert Frost* (Michigan). 1963. pp. 67–8

In some quarters, even his acknowledged masterpieces have been tried and found wanting, at least in the light of his apparent self-indulgence in the role of national cultural hero. Yet the facts, the poetic facts, speak for themselves; the poems must be left to survive the spate of memoirs, commentary, letters, juvenilia, and appreciations, that has already swelled to something more than a spring freshet. Much of this material will prove valuable in the long run; but it will take a scholar of extraordinary gifts—one who is an acute reader of the poetry as well as a disinterested observer of the 20th century literary scene—to separate the trivia from the essentials, the useless from the useful. And because the trivial is sometimes useful, his task will be all the more difficult.

Samuel French Morse. *Poetry*. July, 1964. p. 254

If these letters are used initially to clarify discrepancies between the mythic and actual Robert Frost, as is hoped, certain warnings are in order lest the general public jump from one false extreme of assumption to another. Those who knew the poet largely from his poetry and his public appearances—and who take pleasure in remembering the evidence of his affirmations, encouragements, cherishings, tenderness, humor, wit, playfulness, and joviality—may not be prepared to see how often his private correspondence reveals periods of gloom, jealousies, obsessive resentments, sulking, displays of temper, nervous rages, and vindictive retaliations. Partly because he lacked confidence in himself, he suspected the presence of enemies everywhere, and he frequently indulged his passion for hurting even those he loved. "I'm a mere selfish artist most of the time," he admitted to one correspondent.

All of his self-deprecations complicate rather than simplify the problem of understanding Robert Frost. They suggest, through a mingling of frankness and guilt, his own constant awareness of the tension between his commitments as an artist and as a human being. If the artist in him demanded priority, as it almost always did, he never forgot that he had made two different kinds of promises and that he wanted to keep them both.

Lawrance Thompson. Introduction to *The Selected Letters of Robert Frost* (Holt). 1965. pp. viii–ix

The aim in Frost's poetry is to develop a human act which has meaning in terms of the world man really lives in. The first step is to find out what kind of world it really is. The world Frost discovers, and he depicts the making of this discovery in many nature lyrics, is not friendly to man's great hopes, dreams and needs. But to despair in it is *not* the human answer to the grim world discovered. . . .

On the other hand, grandiose, sustained or programmatic actions are not the answer either, for this is a world in which such actions can be initiated only through blindness or willful self-deception, neither of which states accords with Frost's picture of "mind." What is possible is the small gesture, which, however, must be unremittingly repeated. The human life is not heroic in an epic sense. It is a life of staying.

This solution is certainly not transcendental. This is not a life in conformity with nature, nor a life striving to be merged into nature. On the contrary, it is rather an endless battle against the decaying flux which nature, lacking mind, is continually victim to and therefore continually illustrates. Because the flux endures as long as existence endures, the battle against it is endless.

Nina Baym. *American Quarterly*. Winter, 1965. pp. 722–3

Frost's innate Emersonianism never showed as plainly as when he observed Emerson's directive to "feel all confidence in himself, and never to defer to the popular cry." When some act of government, or fashion, or personality was being cried up by half the populace and cried down by the rest, and the impression was left that all history depended upon the moment, the resultant crisis provided the test of the self-reliant individual. "Let him not quit his belief," advised Emerson, "That a popgun is a popgun, though the ancient and honorable of the earth affirm it to be the crack of doom." Thus it was for Frost with the Imagism of the World War I years, the art-for-art's sake of the 1920's, the social consciousness of the 1930's, the superpatriotism of the forties. In none of these seductive pools did Frost more than wet his toes.

Philip L. Gerber. *Robert Frost* (Twayne). 1966. p. 69

Throughout Frost's poetry the reader senses a struggle between the natural and human realms that is demarcated by a host of familiar emblems—walls, brooks, bridges, ice—which simultaneously separate and link the combatants. The oft-noticed conservatism of

Frost's statements—the refusal to tread either out far or in deep, or the fact that the swinging birches never swing out too far but always return to a middle range—is in fact a kind of phenomenological "trimming." For the problem of defining a poetic "self," with all its attendant vocational questions, while simultaneously exploring the contours of the self-in-the-world, provides the charm for so much of Frost's personal and artistic reminiscence, while simultaneously giving his poetry a unique spatial configuration.

Jan B. Gordon in *Modern American Poetry*, ed. Jerome Mazzaro (McKay). 1970. pp. 61–2

"Humor is the most engaging cowardice." Although Frost's manner is not always humorous, and although much of his ironic defensiveness represents . . . a conscious pragmatism, an awareness of the moral and psychological value of a humorous perspective, this statement perhaps sums up best of all why Frost is not among the great poets, though he is among the very good ones. We reserve greatness for "believers"—in no matter what. Frost's concern "not to set down an idea that is of [his] own thinking," but rather "to give it as in character" certainly made for liveliness, immediacy, and variety in his work. He greatly extended the "sound" of poetry. But all too often the "voice" of a poem acts as a mask, "simply a kind of guardedness," shielding the poet from the full implications of his serious subjects and preventing any real intellectual grappling with them. . . .

Apart from the interpretation of individual poems, a proper attention to the tones of voice in his poetry enables us to appreciate more exactly the nature of Frost's distinctive contribution to American literature. The sheer variety of sound in Frost's poetry makes most other poets seem one-dimensional. Working with the cadences of New England speech, and declining "music" in favor of "the sound of the talking voice," Frost ranged in tone from the lyric to the narrative, from the dramatic to the meditative, from the "terrifying" to the humorous. All the fun's in how you say a thing.

Elaine Barry. *Robert Frost* (Ungar). 1973. pp. 15–7

Let there be no confusion about the particular relationship that I claim for Frost and the modern tradition. Though Frost read William James, and through James came into contact with a number of the salient themes of modernist philosophy and aesthetics, I doubt that Frost was "influenced" in the sense that historicists used to say that imaginative writers were influenced or "shaped" by the "intellectual backgrounds of the times." My understanding is that writers are rarely influenced in that way; they learn almost nothing from philosophers, aestheticians, and literary critics. What happens is that they sometimes read a philosopher (or even a literary critic) and find their own intuitions about things reflected discursively, and hence in that sense confirmed. Modernism becomes the historical ambience of Frost's work in the sense that it is what one comes to conceptually if one moves outward from his poems in an attempt to define the intellectual milieu of the kinds of experience found there.

Frost is not modernist because he holds self-consciously to certain ideas which we identify with this or that modern philosopher because there are few ideas as such in his poetry (modernist or otherwise). Properly speaking his poems do not "belong" to the intellectual environment we call "the modern mind" because "the

modern mind" does not have independent, Platonic existence. It is a thing that the poems themselves have helped to create. The perspectives of modern philosophy and aesthetics are conceptual abstractions from that dense, pre-ideational, primary data of human experience which Frost renders from the inside, as lived.

More than most modern poets Frost needs to have some sort of historical context deliberately constructed for him. Unlike Wallace Stevens, Frost rarely deals directly with the issues of post-Kantian epistemology; unlike Hart Crane, William Carlos Williams, and W.H. Auden, he rarely situates us in the modern urban environment; unlike Ezra Pound and T.S. Eliot he does not measure in any richly allusive way the modern moment against tradition and the past. And, from the point of view of language and metrical experiment, Frost looks very traditional. In two of the best books about him, he is presented as inhabiting a sort of timeless world. John Lynen sees Frost in the venerable tradition of pastoralism. Reuben Brower, drawing his comparisons from the range of world literature, relates him to the tradition of tough-minded, unflinching writers who see things as they are and do not hesitate to tell the score. Lynen and Brower are both persuasive. Frost inhabits a timeless world as do all poets of high quality. Yet Frost did not exist in a vacuum, and his poems do not present an ahistorical consciousness. What I would call his "implicit poetics" is a regulative principle which does not help much in explicating the poems, but which does help us to "generalize" the experiential patterns of those poems, and hence to extend their significance for our times.

Frank Lentricchia. *Robert Frost: Modern Poetics and the Landscapes of Self* (Duke Univ. Pr., 1975), pp. 18–19

Frost is a poet of genius because he could so often make his subtleties inextricable from an apparent availability. The assumption that he is more easily read than are his contemporaries, like Yeats and Eliot, persists only in ignorance of the unique but equally strenuous kinds of difficulty which inform his best work. He is likely to be most evasive when his idioms are so ordinary as to relax rather than stimulate attention; he is an allusive poet, but in a hedging and off-hand way, the allusions being often perceptible only to the ear, and then just barely—in echoings of earlier poets like Herbert or Rossetti, or in metrical patternings traceable to Milton; he will wrap central implications, especially of a sexual kind, within phraseologies that seem innocent of what they carry. . . .

Frost seems to me of vital interest and consequence because his ultimate subject is the interpretive process itself. He "plays" with possibilities for interpretation in a poetry that seems "obvious" only because it is all the while also concerned with the interpretations of what, in the most ordinary sense, are the "signs" of life itself, particular and mundane signs which nonetheless hint at possibilities that continually elude us. . . .

His poetry is especially exciting when it makes of the "obvious" something problematic, or when it lets us discover, by casual inflections or hesitations of movement, that the "obvious" by nature is problematic.

Richard Poirier. *Robert Frost: The Work of Knowing* (Oxford Univ. Pr., 1977), pp. x–xi

Frost's most powerful inspiration seemed to take shape in visions of struggle. The speakers in his three score greatest poems, regional and nonregional alike, are explorers, seekers, questioners. What they long for is understanding, confidence, and a sense of form or order: what he called a "momentary stay against confusion." All his great works draw on this vision. As a young man (in fact, until he was approaching forty), his personal lack of confidence was so great and his sense of uncertainty and aberrancy so strong that he could hardly find effective ways to express his imaginative impulses. His quest for an attractive and imposing vantage point led him to adopt a variety of essentially Romantic poses; yet they elicited no sincere commitment and provided no satisfactory stance from which he could objectify his visions and give voice to his inspiration. . . .

To read or hear or recite Frost's great poetry is to share in the pursuit of a profound vision of human life. As we observe his speakers undertake physical, intellectual, and imaginative exploration, the power of their words and the beauty of their song persuades us that they deserve not only our attention, but also our commitment and fullest appreciation. Few modern American authors have more to offer us. Whether in America, or around the world in Europe, Africa, or Asia, we may find rewarding fields for our own exploration as we turn and turn again with increased understanding and enjoyment to those poems in which Frost made best use of his literary gifts and his extraordinary imagination, his special sensitivity to life in New England and his insight into human nature.

John C. Kemp. *Robert Frost and New England: The Poet as Regionalist* (Princeton Univ. Pr., 1979), pp. 230, 235

A number of Frost's best-known early lyrics are made of a language from which distinctively formal words are largely excluded. But it is equally true and important—although for this, etymological breakdowns cannot provide objective corroboration—that the language of these poems is lacking in words and expressions of distinctively colloquial quality. . . . The regionalisms so paradoxically lacking in poems so thoroughly regional are but one subclass of the distinctively literary elements, are by and large excluded. Frost's elected norm of discourse here, and the key to his verbal artistry, is the common level of style, which represents a selection from the spoken language rather than a reproduction of it. . . .

In setting himself up as the exclusive "guide" ("And put a sign up CLOSED to all but me") to a truth he has hedged about with verbal and symbolic obscurities, and in proceeding to imply that only those who can interpret this poetically mediated truth are worthy to be saved, Frost, one may well think, has his nerve. The teasing and testing, the archness and complacent whimsy, will always alienate a certain number of readers, and long familiarity will not render them any less irritating. But though "Directive" is flawed in part by the arch-avuncular pose of the elderly Frost, it is not seriously damaged. The ideal it upholds—the encompassing of Puritanical grimness and strength by a saving joy and imagination—is powerful and viable in this as in the other poems which make up Frost's New Testament. And, in "Directive" particularly, we must admire the brilliance with which so great a range of resources—rural Americana, American-style humorous understatement, legend, history and fairy tale, the literary past, the chivalric and Christian traditions—has been drawn upon and forged into a stylistic whole. Here, as in all Frost's best poems, what is literary and elevated seems not to impose itself upon, but to rise naturally

from, basic simplicity—the everyday things of country life, lucidly and concretely rendered in common language—which is Frost's primary and most memorable poetic world.

Marie Borroff. *Language and the Poet: Verbal Artistry in Frost, Stevens, and Moore* (Univ. of Chicago Pr., 1979), pp. 29, 40–41

Although Frost is reported to have joked once that "Directive" is his "Eliot poem" because it mentions the Holy Grail, the religious trappings are not throw-aways. Allusions to the Crucifixion ("tatters hung on barb and thorn") and to God as the final source ("Too lofty and original to rage") are offered seriously to those readers who would experience the poem as a religious statement. Frost himself pointed to the word "source" as the center of "Directive": "the key lines, if you want to know, are 'Cold as a spring as yet so near its source,/Too lofty and original to rage.'. . . But the key word in the whole poem is source—whatever source it is."

Despite the importance of the religious tone, the poem is indispensable because it nudges the reader to consider sources beyond religion. Frost hints as much when he comments on "whatever source it is," thus suggesting an extra-religious dimension. . . .

"Directive" ends with the word "confusion": "Here are your waters and your watering place./Drink and be whole again beyond confusion." A significant word in the Frost canon, "confusion" is probably best known as part of the memorable phrase in his essay "The Figure a Poem Makes" when he talks about "a momentary stay against confusion." Although the literal meaning of the phrase is that the completed poem stays the confusion which the poet experiences when he first begins to write, the context of the entire essay suggests that any consciously created form, but especially poetry, is a momentary stay against the permanence of confusion. Form stay chaos, but only for a while. Poems must be written again and again.

If this suggestion has merit, then the last great poem of Frost's career is as much about poetry as it is about religion. The source that helps mankind to be "whole again beyond confusion" will be different things to different people, but for Frost himself the source is poetry—it always was. The technique of "Directive" testifies to his artistic prowess in old age; he was seventy-three when *Steeple Bush* was published. One can only marvel at the stately blank verse, the sudden opening line of monosyllables, the metaphors of quest and home and child. But "Directive" is a major poem by any standard because it insists on the close relationship between artistic creation and religious faith. Those familiar with the Frost biography know how his commitment to poetry clashed with his commitment to family. Frost was a survivor. He would not be beaten down by anyone's death but his own. When pressure threatened and chaos called, he always had poetry to go on with. Art was his source. To create it was to affirm wholeness.

Affirmation of creativity is the heart of Frost's canon. Even in his darkest verse, those lyrics and dialogue poems that unsettle the reader with glimpses of universal terror and portrayals of domestic fear, the affirmation of technique balances the pessimistic theme. He lodged so many poems in American literature that his best work will be forever necessary to the cultural health of the nation. The phrase "the indispensable Robert Frost" thus cuts two ways: it describes the stature of a major author, and it invites a discussion of those parts of his canon that the reader who would understand his work should know. Frost himself might not have agreed with the

choices examined here, but eager to hold the spotlight he would
have been pleased that the examination was taking place.

Donald J. Greiner. In *Critical Essays on Robert Frost.* ed.
Philip L. Gerber (G.K. Hall. 1982), pp. 237–38

What [Robert] Frost valued, of course, were the ever-recurrent
occasions to discover something or make "a new start." Nor
would it matter when searching brought back only pieces,
glimmerings: "If you see the little truths with sharp delight or pain,
you will not be anxiously straining to do final justice to the whole of
reality." And if wisdom consists of enduring the world and our
limits just as they are, our ability to know the whole of reality
demands our trust in ultimates out of our reach. It also insists on
less-than-final statements, partial insights which can seem to deny
others. Frost so often spoke in terms of "as if" that its bearing on
contrarieties in some of his poems may be lost on readers. Radcliffe
Squires remarks in this regard on Melville's complaint: it was
unfair to hold a poet answerable forever for what was true for him
only in the moment.

Stanley Burnshaw. *Robert Frost Himself* (New York: George
Braziller, 1986), p. 303

Among major poets of the English language in this century, Robert
Frost is the one who takes the most punishment. "Like a chimpan-
zee" is how one friend of mine remembers him in the flesh, but in
the afterlife of the text he has been consigned to a far less amiable
sector of the bestiary, among the stoats perhaps, or the weasels.
Calculating self-publicist, reprehensible egotist, oppressive parent—theories of the death of the author have failed to lay the ghost
of this vigorous old contender who beats along undauntedly at the
reader's elbow. His immense popular acclaim during his own
lifetime; his apotheosis into an idol mutually acceptable to his own
and his country's self-esteem, and greatly inflationary of both; his
constantly resourceful acclimatization of himself to this condition,
as writer and performer—it all generated a critical resistance and
fed a punitive strain which is never far to seek in literary
circles anyhow.

Still, it would be wrong to see this poet as the unwitting victim
of the fashion which he surfed upon for decades. Demonically
intelligent, as acute about his own masquerades as he was about
other's, Frost obeyed the ancient command to know himself. Like
Yeats at the end of "Dialogue of Self and Soul," Frost would be
"content to live it all again," and be content also to "cast out
remorse." Unlike Yeats, however, he would expect neither a flow
of sweetness into his breast nor a flash of beatitude upon the world
to ensue from any such bout of self-exculpation. He made no secret
of the prejudice and contrariness at the center of his nature, and
never shirked the bleakness of that last place in himself. He was
well aware of the abrasiveness of many of his convictions and their
unpopular implications in the context of New Deal politics, yet for
all his archness, he did not hide those convictions or retreat
from them.

Frost's appetite for his own independence was fierce and
expressed itself in a reiterated belief in his right to limits: his
defenses, his fences, and his freedom, were all interdependent. Yet
he also recognized that his compulsion to shape his own destiny
and to proclaim the virtues of self-containment arose from a terror
of immense, unlimited and undefined chaos. This terror gets
expressed melodramatically in a poem like "Design," and obliquely in a poem like "Provide, Provide," but it is also there in
many of his more casual pronouncements.

Seamus Heaney, "Above the Brim: On Robert Frost."
Salmagundi. Fall–Winter, 1990–91, pp. 275–76

For many, [Frost] was the plain, popular, rural sage, a moral
sentimentalist, a poet of the rural heartland, an individualistic
democrat who spoke publicly for private values and was admired
by President Kennedy. But for others, like the critic Lionel Trilling,
he was the great poet of contemporary tragic vision, evoking a
"terrifying universe" of exposure and emptiness, the romantic
vacancies of modern secular life.

If Frost is a major Modernist poet, it is precisely because of this
latter dimension of his work. An essential development in the
history of twentieth-century poetry has been a coming to terms with
the withdrawn legacy of Romanticism, the fading traditional claims of
pantheism and transcendence. The poet is thus returned to him- or
herself, the word to vacancy, the symbol to disconnectedness. Frost
often seems to suggest that the old tradition of nature poetry is
recoverable; a major part of his verse is, after all, based on seasonal
or natural lessons drawn from a natural world that seems to contain
human significance. Frost strikes this pose, yet what he finds in
nature—the harsh lives, the rugged New Hampshire settings, the
relation of farmer to neighbor—breeds skepticism about ideas of
wholeness or fulfillment. Nature's mystery is present, but it is not
Emersonian. As in the poem "Design," it may be "the design of
darkness to appal" or there may be no design at all. The famous
"Stopping by Woods on a Snowy Evening," from the volume *New
Hampshire* (1923), is a poem of division between human promises
and obligations and the white mystery of nature. Yet the whiteness
is itself ambiguous in its meaning, as is apparent in another poem
from the same volume, "For Once, Then, Something.". . .

The vernacular roughness of Frost's lines is more than pure
populism; it is a skepticism of vision that gives him the curious and
distinctive metaphysical control of his best poems. An image,
word, or construction is turned and teased, as he as speaker tests
and retests himself. One of the key questions for the poets of Frost's
generation was whether a Whitmanian or Emersonian Romantic
posture was recoverable in the modern urban and secular world.
Frost gives us little of that world as a place, but he responds to its
poetic condition. Like Wallace Stevens, though with demotic
skepticism rather than philosophical abstractness, he is concerned
both with the difficulty of finding meaning in the thing perceived
and the danger of unacknowledged self-shaped perception.

Richard Ruland and Malcolm Bradbury. *From Puritanism
to Postmodernism: A History of American Literature* (New
York: Viking Penguin, 1991), pp. 282–84

I have been emphasizing Frost's distrust of too much form, his
awareness that metaphors ridden too far or taken as truth can betray
and oppress us. Frost also considers the making of metaphors, the
search for truth, or at least for trueness, to be essentially human. ("I
always think trueness better than truth. Trueness has a warmth
about it. It's human.") Frost's thinking, and his poems, occur
between complementary views, at the border where metaphors are

constantly building up and breaking down. Frost's commitment to the implications of that position was remarkably thorough. He mocked monism as ''moanism,'' for instance, yet with a characteristic gesture of ''bothering'' reconsideration he also recalled that we can ''take too much satisfaction in having once more remarked the two-endedness of things.'' ''A melancholy dualism is the only soundness. The question is: is soundness of the essence.'' Similarly, Frost's awareness of the dangers of too much commitment is countered by his complementary admiration for ''definiteness of position,'' his belief that, while ''every act is a great simplification,'' ''You should go ahead on insufficient information.'' He counted as one of the freedoms ''the wit to make unexpected connections''; he also said that the world is in parts, and that the separation of the parts is as important as the connection: the demand is for ''good spacing.'' Some readers find this ''shiftiness'' in Frost, his mixing of a heroic sense of the risks incurred in asserting form with a ''diminishing'' sense that it is all some interminable game, rather hard to take. (Asked if poets are born or made, Frost said, ''Most people can't bear poets.'') Frost's ''duplicity'' caused Yvor Winters to label him a ''spiritual drifter.'' Frost's own summations put the matter better: ''My ironies don't seem to iron out anything''; ''I'm not confused; I'm only well-mixed''; ''My motto for yesterday was, Don't let being mixed make you feel confused.... Keep moving. Keep changing your motto.''

Having said all this, it is tempting to skip over the vexed question of Frost's modernity and make him out a postmodernist, aware that human systems of order are the only orders we have and that those orders, carried so far that they are taken to be inevitable or natural, become modes of oppression that limit our freedom; aware, too, that we are all inevitably implicated in the making and consecrating of systems of order. But as radically provisional as Frost's poetry is, his differences from the postmodernists are many. His urge to form, however richly qualified it is, is never finally distrusted or despised. So, too, with his sense of authorship and authority. And Frost incorporates the past by other means than appropriation. He is too content with the rules of the game as laid down to fit postmodernist norms, too filled with ''vulgar'' vitality—with confidence that playing well is sufficient satisfaction and that no government or god could change the rules, too certain of the priority, presence, and continuity of the individual person and of his or her power to work successfully within given limits. Anticipating, say, Thomas Kuhn's *The Structure of Scientific Revolutions*, Frost drew a parallel between the methods of poetry and those of science: both, he thought, are ever in motion, building metaphors up and breaking them down in response to the ''antifictive of the given environment.'' That motion, expansion *and* contraction, is our life.

Guy L. Rotella. *Reading and Writing Nature: The Poetry of Robert Frost, Wallace Stevens, Marianne Moore, and Elizabeth Bishop* (Boston: Northeastern Univ. Pr., 1991), pp. 66–67

One key to Frost—both the poems and the poet—is his assertion that ''every poem is an epitome of the great predicament, a figure of the will braving alien entanglements.'' ... In comparing a poem to the will braving alien entanglement, Frost suggests that a poem contains within it the history of its making—the desires, struggles,

conflicts, *and* results. But we know it also contains seeds of its future—the alien entanglement of its reader. . . .

Reading Frost, of course, is . . . a ''braving [of] alien entanglements.'' An encounter with one of his poems can be seen as an engagement, perhaps a battlefield, perhaps a communion, where reader and writer meet, risk their ''wills,'' brave entanglement with one another. And in the potential encounter, each is risking his wholeness, his perception of self. The writer risks being misunderstood, or understood and appropriated at best. He risks being rejected or ridiculed at worst. He risks sharing ownership of his text. Sometimes Frost would say there is only one right way to read any text; at other times, he said, ''The poet is entitled to anything the reader can find in his poem,'' and at still other times, he wanted his texts to invite in only the right readers and leave out those who were not. As he implied in ''Directive,'' and later said of the cryptic phrase on parables in Mark, he did not want the wrong ones being saved. (Frost's looser version of Mark was that Christ implied one cannot be saved unless one knows how to read poetry.) Each of these positions demands a different kind of reader, a different view of what a reader is supposed to be or do in relation to the poem. These views conflict and, in so doing, represent the conflict in the poet between the need to be entangled with ''other,'' to be engaged with and enriched by the encounter (that is, the poet's social, additive needs), and the need to protect, to keep whole and pure and private the inner core of the self.

Surely this is a conflict every artist experiences: on the one hand, the need to share one's art and thought, one's ''self,'' and with that the need to be recognized; on the other hand, there is the equally strong need to protect that self and that creation. Studying a poet such as Frost, therefore, can help us to understand the complex and ambivalent attitude writers can have toward their readers and the effect such conflicting feelings have on their poetic texts, on what sorts of engagement they will provoke from the reader.

Judith Oster. *Toward Robert Frost: The Reader and the Poet* (Athens: Univ. of Georgia Pr., 1992), pp. 1, 2–4

Regardless of the intellectual, imaginative, or psychological reasons for it, Frost's social vision in the heuristic emblem poems represents in some ways the most remarkable of all his achievements in refusing to accept crucial modern discontinuities. Frost achieves his vision of ''fellowship'' despite being an American, though our culture has historically tended toward acute individualism; despite being an American nature writer, though that tradition has strongly emphasized the need for solitude as a means of apocalyptic preparation; despite being a modern poet, though all of the major poetic traditions since 1798 stress the supremacy of the individual mind; despite, finally, his own ungenerous political theories expressed again and again, not only in conversations and letters but also in many of the ''editorial'' poems of his last thirty years. It is this side of Frost which has driven a number of intelligent critics to attack his social vision as atomistic or worse. Malcolm Cowley, for instance, in a famous attack in 1944, suggests that ''What Frost sets before us is an ideal, not of charity or brotherhood, but of separateness'' or ''self-centeredness.'' Denis Donoghue, more than twenty years later, concludes that Frost is a ''Social Darwinist.'' More recently, even as sympathetic a critic as David Bromwich (like Cowley, basing his conclusions substantially on ''Two Tramps in Mud Time''), sees Frost as a poet of "charity denied." The unsympathetic, ungenerous side of Frost's social vision cannot be wished away—but it is not the only side. At least in "An Unstamped Letter," "The Tuft of Flowers," "Iris by Night," and "Two Look at Two," and in fact in numerous other poems, Frost is capable of celebrating remarkably intense ties between people—though, admittedly, these exist not between groups, or between the individual and a group, but between pairs of human beings. At that level, Frost's social vision is remarkable not just for him but for any twentieth-century American writer.

Thus Frost shows that a poet with a feisty temperament, a genuine relish for imaginative difficulties, and the resources of a centuries-old tradition need not simply or passively accept the great social discontinuity of modern experience any more than the Cartesian or the temporal. Emerson writes that "it is dislocation and detachment from the life of God, that makes things ugly," and that the poet, because he "re-attaches things to nature and the Whole, . . . disposes very easily of the most disagreeable facts." Surely Frost would view the desire to "dispose" of any facts, even the most disagreeable, as a fatal kind of self-deception; he neither does so nor wants to do so. Yet he clearly and consistently is concerned with resisting many of the characteristic modern varieties of "dislocation and detachment," with "re-attaching things to nature and the Whole," and by doing so, fulfilling a major part of the task which Emerson sets for the poet. Using the emblem-reading tradition, modifying it, bending it, playing off it, Frost's nature lyrics move again and again to relocate both the synecdochic emblem and the individual emblem reader in a larger order of being, to show that the emblem—butterfly weed or decaying woodpile or dried-up brook—is never just an isolated thing, and to help the reader "realize," as Thoreau puts it "where we are and the infinite extent of our relations."

George F. Bagby. *Frost and the Book of Nature* (Knoxville: Univ. of Tennessee Pr., 1993), pp. 197–98

[The] halfway place between Earth and Eden is the one Frost characteristically inhabits and the older I get, the more I admire his ability to dwell there resolutely, in a middle state; to stay buoyant, rhythmically and spiritually, while still managing to register the full drag of the gravity of being alive. Hence the continuing appeal of "After Apple Picking" and "Birches." They are not just beguiling evocations of a man on a ladder or a lad in a tree, but poems in which a positive state of mind is matched against an exhausting experience of the world. And the same could be said of the even starker confrontations between consciousness and mystery in "The Most of It" and "An Old Man's Winter Night." . . .

Frost is at his very best when he holds this balance between stark evidences of human aloneness and intimations of human belonging. In the beginning, it was there in "The Tuft of Flowers"; it reappeared constantly, in monologues like "A Servant to Servants" and parables like "Mending Wall" and "For Once Then Something" and "The Most of It," but for me, nowadays, it is embodied most entrancingly in his strangely convincing poem "Two Look at Two." In it, Frost displays an empathy with [D.H.] Lawrence, and a scrupulosity of observation that would have pleased [James] Joyce. But in the way it weaves a colloquial tone and vocabulary into a feat of artful repetition and variation—repetition as the law of increasing returns, as it were—and in the

way it brings sensation to a point where it becomes revelation, the poem is pure Frost.

Seamus Heaney. *Poetry Review.* Winter, 1993–1994 [print version of talk given at ICA, London, November 29, 1993], pp. 31, 32

Frost grounded not only his linguistic practice but his vision in the Emersonian beliefs that every word was once a metaphor and that life itself—our American life—is the source of poetry unmediated by dependence upon the past. We can imagine how wounding to Frost's sense of his own desserts, despite his four Pulitzer Prizes, was the sway of the modernist poets with their practices so implicated in what Eliot had called "the mind of Europe." It was not only his rural subjects that kept Frost's work from winning approbation from academics and reviewers; the very method of his versing, the ways his poems do their work upon the reader, was unrecognized by critics trained only to parse the thickets of allusion offered by the modernist masters. . . .

In . . . Frost's best work, the poetry itself "throws off" its "fixed symbols." The meaning grows out of the language, the syntax, the associations of the words, the rhythms of the speech in which they are spoken. Meaning is dependent upon neither a set of arbitrary, assigned correspondences, nor a specialist's knowledge of arcane sources. In his reliance upon the poem itself as the source of its symbols Frost reflects his debt to Emerson after all. Rejecting the self-centered, spiritualizing aspects of Transcendentalism, Frost nevertheless accepts—and revels in—Emerson's call for personal experience unmediated by the authority of the past. When Frost does invoke the past, drawing on classical legend or Biblical allusion, he undermines the authority of his allusions. His well-gazer's search for Truth rebukes the self-love of Narcissus; his Adamic apple-picker embraces without guilt the sensuous experiences that have fatigued him; his dream-vision holds the possibility of a resurrection without repentance. Frost accepts the world, with which he said he had "a lover's quarrel." Acknowledging that we can grasp no more than half a loaf in our search for absolutes, Frost celebrates our seeking with invented symbols adequate to his skeptical vision. As he said in "The Figure a Poem Makes," his poems do indeed begin in delight and end in wisdom.

Daniel Hoffman. "Robert Frost: The Symbols a Poem Makes." *Gettysburg Review.* Winter, 1994, pp. 104, 111–12

Frost believed that a poem should be written in a single, free-flowing run. He compared composing verse to sliding down a hill on a sled and declared: "I never wrote anything without thinking: 'This is it!'" Like Plato's symbolic horses, whose creative energy had to be harnessed by a charioteer in order to be transformed into art, Frost wrote, in a punning passage, that the first rush of inspiration must be tempered by wordplay in order to avoid the twin dangers of cliché and aestheticism. . . .

A brilliant teacher from youth to old age, Frost had many valuable—and always pragmatic—ideas about the imaginative act, the rush of inspiration, the methods of revision, and the pressures of publication. He was not a tormented, self-destructive poet, but one who loved the play of the imagination, took joy in his creation, and believed that "poetry spoils you for anything else in life." Fond of social life and a great talker, in middle and old age he loved to draw large crowds at lectures around the country. But he also needed and valued solitude and reflection. Reflecting on the apparent laziness of his early years, he declared that loafing had a great deal to do with being creative, and that for proper artistic growth there must be idleness, which had been the making of him.

Jeffrey Meyers. Introduction. In Robert Frost. *Early Frost: The First Three Books* (Hopewell, N.J.: Ecco Pr., 1996), pp. xxxiv–xxxv

BIBLIOGRAPHY

A Boy's Will, 1913 (p); *North of Boston*, 1914 (p); *Mountain Interval*, 1916 (p); *New Hampshire*, 1923 (p); *Selected Poems*, 1923, rev. eds., 1928, 1934; *West-Running Brook*, 1928 (p); *Collected Poems*, 1930; *A Further Range*, 1936 (p); *Selected Poems*, 1936 (English edition); *A Witness Tree*, 1942 (p); *A Masque of Reason*, 1945 (p); *The Poems of Robert Frost*, 1946; *Steeple Bush*, 1947 (p); *A Masque of Mercy*, 1947 (p); *Complete Poems*, 1949; *In the Clearing*, 1962 (p); *The Letters of Robert Frost to Louis Untermeyer*, 1963; *Robert Frost and John Bartlett: The Record of a Friendship*, 1963 (l); *Selected Letters*, 1964; *Robert Frost Speaks*, 1964 (e); *Selected Prose*, 1966 (e); *Interviews with Robert Frost*, 1966; *The Poetry of Robert Frost*, 1969; *A Time to Talk: Conversations and Indiscretions* (recorded by Robert Francis Frost), 1969; *Family Letters of Robert and Elinor Frost*, 1972; *Robert Frost on Writing*, 1973 (e); *Robert Frost: A Living Voice*, ed. Reginald L. Cook, 1974 (contains twelve lectures by Frost in addition to text by Cook); *Collected Poems, Prose, and Plays*, 1995

FUCHS, Daniel (1909–1993)

Though he never quite succeeds, it is impossible to read *Summer in Williamsburg* without being aware of its sincerity, its vitality and—in a way—its importance.... No comment on *Summer in Williamsburg* would be complete without mention of Mr. Fuchs's style, which is extremely competent and incisive.... His talent lies chiefly in the direction of dialogue.... He has captured the very cadence, the accent and inflection, of a local idiom.

Margaret Wallace. *New York Times Book Section*. Nov. 18, 1934. p. 6

With this second novel [*Homage to Blenholt*] Mr. Fuchs performs a rare feat in switching from the naturalistic approach of his first book (*Summer in Williamsburg*) to a racy, caricaturing manner, appealing strongly to the sense of humor. What is still more unusual, he does not direct his satire against Babbitts or intellectuals—the customary targets for satire in America—but sticks to the locale he knows best, that drab Jewish section in Brooklyn known as Williamsburg.... His manner is fundamentally his own. Its main features may be traced to a keen ear for picking up the rich idiomatic language of his characters, an intense dislike (which sometimes gets out of hand) for the social system that smothers them, and an almost morbid sensitiveness to the folly of human beings influenced by a tabloid-movies atmosphere.

Jerre Mangione. *New Republic*. April 1, 1936. pp. 229–30

His novels, of which *Low Company* is the third, are as inclusive as they are terse and clever. Their humor is inimitably Jewish, but few other novelists have conveyed it so unobtrusively, and for the same purpose. It is a humor that consists largely of the homely metaphors that abound in Yiddish, but which sound uproarious only when heard in literal translation. Too many Jewish writers have stopped at that, and as a result their work reads like mimicry. In Mr. Fuchs' hands the humor retains its extravagance and its crude vitality, but it is a humor that is pointed to indicate the desperation that so often lies behind it.

Writing in that spirit, Mr. Fuchs has proved again and again that the ghetto was never destroyed; it was merely moved, piece by piece, from the East Side to Williamsburg and Brownsville and the Bronx.

Alfred Kazin. *New York Herald Tribune Book Section*. Feb. 14, 1937. p. 8

Low Company is the story of petty lives, of petty tragedies. Fuchs hates all his characters. When he writes with pity, it is a merciless, steely, stiletto kind of pity. A few times we are appalled at what happens to the characters and are just about to lavish our sympathy, when the author pours his icy water over every living thing in Neptune Beach. And here we come to the debit side of Fuchs' artistry. Fuchs, at this stage of his writing, has found no place to lay down his burden. His hate is a slow, burning, consuming hate, and he vents it ruthlessly. The superb humor, the comical situations magnificently described in *Low Company*, are actually merciless jabs at his characters. There have been comments that Fuchs, because of his penchant for grotesquerie, stems from Charles Dickens. Nothing, however, could be further from the truth. While Dickens hated many of his characters, he had a great love and compassion for his heroes and heroines. Dickens was a confirmed believer in the happy ending. Fuchs is a child of sorrow.

Albert Halper. *New Republic*. Feb. 24, 1937. p. 90

Sympathy is a dominant note in Fuchs' writing. He has a keen eye, an excellent ear for the speech of his characters, a quick perception of the grotesque, the whimsical, the pathetic, the tragic in crowded urban life. And underlying these capacities is a genuine respect for his characters, for the human animal....

The present novel [*Low Company*], like its predecessors, is constructed almost like a drama. There is considerable dependence on dialogue, there is a fairly strict effort to obtain objectivity, and an ingenious sense of plot and construction is displayed. In fact, the author's gift for construction threatens to become a defect. The concluding pages of *Low Company* unite and complete the novel's many stories in such a fashion that one almost sees the seams and stitchings. Yet I know of few novelists in America today of Fuchs's age who possess his natural talent and energy or his sense of life.

James T. Farrell. *The Nation*. Feb. 27, 1937. p. 244

The first of Daniel Fuchs' novels opens with a "hard mad" summer storm which sends the inhabitants of Williamsburg scurrying for shelter. The last one ends in a steamy heat that promises to bring business at last to the desperate concessionaires of Neptune Beach. In between is a richly knowing account of sudden changes in psychic weather, destructive twisters, brief, illusory periods of sunlight, in the lives of some yearning, trapped, angry, wrong-headed, immensely vocal individuals. They are mostly from Brooklyn, mostly Jews. Mr. Fuchs treats them with satiric relish and yet with a deep sense of identification. . . . Except for the movies and radio programs they name, these novels are not dated in the least. The author deals with the conditions of bad housing, corruption, widespread dishonesty and racketeering that preoccupy New Yorkers today and he deals with them—though his novels are a quarter of a century old—in a way that is fresh and revealing as literature.

Robert Gorham Davis. *New York Times Book Section*. Sept. 10, 1961. p. 5

Very few writers are able to evoke anything out of the environment that depressed them as they grew. Fuchs has been compared to James T. Farrell, but it is clear now that he had greater gifts than Farrell, and did much more than transcribe. His dialogue, from the very beginning, had a flavor of its own; while seemingly realistic it is as artful as Hemingway's or O'Hara's, and read aloud it usually makes one laugh. In this book, as in the others, there are the sensitive and the brutal; they encounter and are astonished by each other, and Fuchs judges not, for they are all human.

Reading the novels again, I was fearful that they might not hold up, but time has neither dimmed nor darkened them, and I suspect they are more readable and compelling today, if only because the problems are different now, and we can meet all of the author's wonderful people simply as people and not as representatives of a condition. They are fixed now, the nice ones, the evil ones, the old, the young, as a wonderful tapestry of "low life" captured with unsentimental warmth.

Hollis Alpert. *Saturday Review*. Sept. 23, 1961. p. 18

If *Summer in Williamsburg* presents a dilemma, and *Homage to Blenholt* is a high-spirited attempt to delay or evade the problem of choice, *Low Company* marks an acceptance of the burdens of commonplace reality. For what constitutes both a major strength in Fuchs' work and a reason, perhaps, for the abrupt termination of his career as a young novelist, is his grim and ironic appreciation of the power of the commonplace, everything in daily existence that erodes ambition and spirit. As Albert Halper, a novelist who is Fuchs' contemporary, remarked of him: "he is a man with a burden. I do not envy him . . . he is a child of sorrow."

Perhaps so. But this child of sorrow, this poet of the Williamsburg streets, wrote some of the most winning fictions we have about American Jewish life. His scope narrow, but his tone pure, Fuchs was that rarity, a "natural" writer with a gift for spontaneous evocation and recall.

Irving Howe in *Proletarian Writers of the Thirties*, edited by David Madden (Southern Illinois). 1968. pp. 104–5

West of the Rockies is a novel about Hollywood, though the people and events it deals with are as far removed from the stardust image as the book itself is from the "blockbuster" treatment accorded to that strange, artificial community by writers less talented if more widely known, than Daniel Fuchs. It is a tightly controlled, perceptive piece of writing which tells of the tenuous, perturbed

relationship between a world-famous Hollywood actress—a star—and a youngish man who works for her agency; and though it is no part of Mr. Fuchs's purpose to reveal sensational examples of tat behind the glamour or vicious backstage wheeling and dealing, we are given, with no sense of strain or contrivance, a sense of the realities of "stardom": of the personal failures which have led to the crisis the characters now face. . . .

Mr. Fuchs develops this notion of dependence and muted anguish with considerable skill, relying not only on what he tells us but on what he deliberately omits in order to convey the pressures and decidedly unglamorous aspects of stardom on Hollywood's terms.

TLS: The Times Literary Supplement. Oct. 15, 1971. p. 1290

How different . . . from any other Jewish fiction of the forties and fifties is a book like Daniel Fuchs's *Summer in Williamsburg*, first published in 1934, ten years before [Bellow's] *Dangling Man*. When Fuchs's novels were reissued in the early sixties much was made of the fabulistic, "poetic" side, as if they could only be appreciated in the wake of a moral allegorist like Malamud. Actually, the great strength of the books is their feeling for the life of the streets, the Runyonesque "low company" of youthful gangs in Williamsburg and Jewish mobsters in the Catskills, a chapter of social history quickly forgotten when the Jews became more respectable and the Jewish novel more morally austere. In Fuchs the moral temperature is low—he is notably ham-handed in portraying the religious life of his Jews, a more inward subject. He is a folklorist, an anthropologist of street life rather than a purveyor of moral parables. For all his freedom from the cant of proletarian writing he remains in essence a 1930s realist; for him life is with the people.

Morris Dickstein. *Partisan Review*. Nov. 1, 1974. p. 42

BIBLIOGRAPHY
Summer in Williamsburg, 1934 (n); *Homage to Blenholt*, 1936 (n); *Low Company*, 1937 (n); *Three Novels*, 1961; *West of the Rockies*, 1971 (n); *The Apathetic Bookie Joint*, 1979 (n)

FULLER, Charles (1939–)

[*The Village: A Party*] leaves you thinking. Mr. Fuller has written a not-too-fanciful fantasy about racial integration that somberly concludes that it will not at present solve anybody's racial problems.

A charismatic black man, married to a white girl, has founded a community for other racially mixed couples. Superficially, the community has been a success, both in terms of the personal happiness of its members and the edification of the world at large; but now its leader has found another woman, and she is black.

Fearing for the community's "image" if their leader is allowed to defect from his dream, the group strikes him down at a birthday party. His widow it is decided, must marry a black man. Utopia has become not just a ghetto but a cell-block.

Mr. Fuller's initial situation is so intellectually provocative that his resolution seems disappointingly melodramatic. Even in a symbolic context, it is as hard to believe that these suburban types would automatically devour their leader as it was to believe a similar situation in Edward Albee's "Everything in the Garden"; in such well-appointed living rooms, discussion always precedes—and generally replaces—action.

However, *The Village* has enough things right with it to make you want to watch Mr. Fuller. His dialogue can crackle—"I knew you before you were black, Nick," the leader's wife tells him bitterly—and he knows how to make a point without words, as when the partygoers are shocked to find themselves pairing off for cards according to race, blacks with blacks, whites with whites.

The argument of Mr. Fuller's play—that integration exacerbates rather than relieves racial tensions—is too important to be treated in the brief fashion allowed here. The play's originality and urgency are unquestionable and so is the talent of the playwright.

> Dan Sullivan. *The New York Times*. November 13, 1968, p. 39.

[*In the Deepest Part of Sleep*] is about the debilitating effect of a mentally disturbed mother on a Philadelphia family in the mid-nineteen-fifties.

As seen through the eyes of a young black adolescent on the brink of manhood, this may be a true experience, at least for the playwright, but it does not hold much interest as theatre.

As was also evident in Mr. Fuller's *Candidate!*, . . . the author has a tendency to overdraw his characters and his situations. . . .

In *In the Deepest Part of Sleep*, the mother, released from the hospital after a breakdown, makes obsessive demands on her son, his step-father and her nurse, who is decidedly provocative to both males in the family.

The situation is an obvious one, but it still might be dramatically viable if it were written with insight or at least if it were played in a natural, straightforward manner.

In the opening minutes the play is stricken by bathos and never fully recovers. . . . [The mother] cries and moans so much that she loses all of our sympathy (and we wonder how the other characters are able to endure her). The play continues, predictably, even, in the end, to a suggestion of an incestuous relationship. . . .

There are several moments in *Deepest Sleep*—just as there were in *Candidate!* (which was about the election of a black mayor in a northern city)—that make it clear that Mr. Fuller is a playwright who should be heard from.

In one touching encounter . . . the mother confesses her sexual craving to her husband, and when rebuffed, switches immediately to verbal attack. In another, the nurse tries to seduce the son, and the playwright is shrewdly observant about the ineptness of adolescence.

Unfortunately these are only flashes of reality in a play that asks for too much indulgence.

> Mel Gussow. *The New York Times*. June 5, 1974, p. 54.

A Soldier's Play is, to put it simply, a major breakthrough for the promising author of *The Brownsville Raid* and last season's *Zooman and the Sign*. This is, in every way, a mature and accomplished work—from its inspired opening up of a conventional theatrical form to its skillful portraiture of a dozen characters to its remarkable breadth of social and historical vision. It's also a play that speaks to both blacks and whites without ever patronizing either

group. Mr. Fuller writes characters of both races well—and he implicates both in the murder of Sergeant Waters. . . .

Waters isn't as simple as he seems in the play's early flashbacks. For all his venom and cruelty, he was also a prideful man who refused to today to whites and who often wanted the best for his fellow blacks. "Who the hell was he?" asks the prosecutor in frustration as the evidence comes in—and it soon becomes apparent that the case can't be solved until that question is resolved.

As the answer comes, Mr. Fuller uses it to illuminate the behavior of every black character in the play, as well as the white society they inhabit. Waters is psychotic, all right, but the basis of his warped, cruel behavior is self-hatred, not hatred—and the cause of that self-hatred is his own recognition of the bankruptcy of his efforts to please whites. Much as he's tried to bury his black roots and as far as he's gone in the Army, Waters just can't escape the demon of racism—that sinking feeling that, for all his achievements, *they still hate you*. And in Water's distorted personality, his men see a magnified, mirror image of what they most fear and hate in themselves—the fear of being destroyed by allowing white racism to define the ambitions of one's life.

While we can see why the men might have been tempted to murder Waters, Mr. Fuller recognizes such an act for what it is—both a symbolic and literal form of self-destruction. The playwright took this same moral position in *Zooman*, which told the story of a contemporary black community that was too cowardly to identify a murderer in its midst. Here, as before, the playwright has compassion for blacks who might be driven to murder their brothers—because he sees them as victims of a world they haven't made. Yet he doesn't let anyone off the hook. Mr. Fuller demands that his black characters find the courage to break out of their suicidal, fratricidal cycle—just as he demands that whites end the injustices that have locked his black characters into the nightmare.

At the same time, Mr. Fuller places his new play in a historical context that gives it a resonance beyond its specific details. As the investigation proceeds, another, larger drama is played out; the soldiers, who have not seen any wartime action, wait in desperate hope that they may get orders for overseas, so that they can prove that "colored boys can fight" Hitler as well as white boys. But in the playwright's view, this aspiration is just another version of Water's misplaced ambition to deny his blackness by emulating whites—and just as likely to end in tragic, self-annihilating doom.

> Frank Rich. *The New York Times*. November 27, 1981, p. 3.

An angry, consuming energy which propels the protagonist towards violence, an irony which humanizes him while depriving the viewer of easy categorizations: these elements characterize Charles Fuller's style. Within an American theatre tradition Fuller's work both acknowledges the seminal position of Amiri Baraka and extends the vision of the tumultuous 1960s beyond a rigid, racial schematization which in conferring upon blacks the status of victims of oppression, seemingly robbed them of any responsibility for or power over the circumstances in which they found themselves.

A former bank loan collector, college counsellor, and city housing inspector, Fuller initially gained a measure of national recognition in 1976 with *The Brownsville Raid*. Though presently out of circulation, the play is of interest because it prefigures the approach adopted in the later *A Soldier's Play. The Brownsville Raid* is a dramatization of the investigation into a 1906 shooting spree which culminated in President Teddy Roosevelt's unwarranted, dishonorable discharge of an entire black infantry brigade. With historical accounts as his starting point, Fuller skilfully interweaves a ''whodunnit'' plot with a compelling portrait of a black corporal who has his faith in the Army shattered when he refuses to comply with his officers' demand for a scapegoat. Both black and white men are presented with strengths and faults; what emerges is a composite picture of men and a society whose vision is distorted by racism.

In both *Zooman and the Sign* and *A Soldier's Play* racism appears not as a specific, external event to which the black protagonists must react; rather, its negative values have been so internalized that, propelled by their own frantic despair, the characters move relentlessly towards self-destruction. In the first play, about a father's search for his daughter's killer, a knife-toting, drug-running, 15-year-old casually admits to the audience at the outset that he is the killer. Although Zooman attempts to mask a mounting sense of entrapment with calculated bravado, his direct conversations with the audience about familial disintegration, unwanted homosexual encounters, and detention for uncommitted crimes characterize him as an alienated youth whose experiences have taught him that ''niggahs can't be heroes,'' that blacks seemingly have no control over the atrophy engulfing their families and communities. These monologues, delivered in a street-wise, frenetic style which is nonetheless reminiscent of black toast traditions and Muhammad Ali's alliterative poetry, have the effect of humanizing Zooman, of placing him in a context where his asocial behavior becomes more understandable, and his affinity to the larger society more apparent.

Just as Zooman believes that blacks are helpless, so too do the neighbors of the slain girl, for no one will come forth as witnesses to the crime. The father's erecting a sign accusing them of moral complicity triggers only hostile recriminations from the neighbors and argument within the family itself. Symbolic of a community's failure to foster a more active, ennobling sense of its own possibilities, the sign occasions the final violence wherein Zooman is accidentally killed in his attempt to tear it down. Another black child lies dead in the street, another family grieves, and another sign goes up as momentary monument to incredible waste.

An ultimately pervasive irony, which empties the landscape of possible victors and reveals instead a society maimed by racism, is equally evident in *A Soldier's Play*. Unlike Zooman, Sergeant Waters espouses the black middle-class values of hard work, education, and racial pride as the means of self-advancement. Like Zooman, Waters, in seeking a sphere in which to exercise a masculine sense of control and dignity, has had only limited success, for he operates within the segregated Army of World War II. The search for his killer triggers a series of flashbacks which reveal him as a vicious, petty tyrant bent upon literally ridding the race of all those blues-singing, hoodoo-oriented men who he says prevent advancement; yet, they also create a measure of sympathy for this ambitious man, consumed by misplaced faith, self-hatred, and guilt.

The eventual identification of two black recruits as Waters's murderers defies the expectation, carefully nurtured by the playwright, that overt white hostility is the motivating factor. Additionally, it raises questions concerning the definition of justice, for the infantrymen have just received their long-awaited orders to ship out, in effect being granted license to kill in Europe a tyranny

similar to what Waters represents at home. Compounding the irony further, Fuller provides a postscript which subverts the dramatic experience: the investigating officer reveals that the entire incident is recorded in military documents as meaningless black-on-black crime; Waters is inadvertently listed as an heroic war casualty; and the entire company is destroyed in combat. Thus, the Army learns nothing from this sorry episode.

To date, Fuller's dramatic world is dominated by driven, destructive men trying to carve out a viable place within a hostile environment. Though his characters inhabit a bleak landscape, his audiences need not: through the dramatic experience they can appreciate how racism distorts an entire society and choose to stop the human destruction.

> Sandra L. Richards. In *Contemporary Dramatists, 5th edition*, ed. K. A. Berney (St. James Press, 1993).

BIBLIOGRAPHY
The Village: A Party, 1968 (d), performed as *The Perfect Party*, 1969; *In My Many Names and Days*, 1972 (d); *Candidate*, 1974 (d); *In the Deepest Part of Sleep*, 1974 (d); *First Love*, 1974 (d); *The Lay Out Letter*, 1975 (d); *The Brownsville Raid*, 1975 (d); *Sparrow in Flight*, 1978 (d); *Zooman and the Sign*, 1980 (d); *A Soldier's Play*, 1981 (d); *We*, 1988 (d); *Jonquil*, 1990 (d)

FULLER, R. Buckminster (1895–1983)

Buckminster Fuller—you are the most sensible man in New York, truly sensitive. Nature gave you antennae, long-range finders you have learned to use. I find almost all your prognosticating nearly right—much of it dead right, and I love you for the way you prognosticate. . . .

To say that you have now a good style of your own in saying very important things is only admitting something unexpected. To say you are the most sensible man in New York is not saying much for you—in that pack of caged fools. And everybody who knows you knows you are extraordinarily sensitive. . . .

Faithfully [I am] your admirer and friend, more power to you— you valuable ''unit.''

> Frank Lloyd Wright. *Saturday Review*. Sept. 17, 1938. p. 14

At a time of crisis in his life Fuller set himself, like Descartes in his Dutch stove-heated compartment, to survey the whole of the human dilemma—all the obstacles that stood in the way of man's survival and in the way of man's potential development. His philosophical starting point was the totality of possible events— ''universe,'' as he called it, defining it in terms of the way it impinges on the human mind. . . .

Fuller's definition of ''universe'' is an attempt to treat *all* experience as finite. . . .

Fuller makes cumulative experience a pivotal factor in change. Experience is finite; it can be stored, studied, directed; it can be turned with conscious effort, to human advantage. . . .

Real wealth to Fuller is thus nothing more than the extent to which man, at a given moment, has harnassed forms of universal energy and, in the process, has developed a re-employable experience.

> Robert W. Marks. *The Dymaxion World of Buckminster Fuller* (Reinhold). 1960. pp. 9–10

Through the more immediate results of Fuller's work, structures of great elegance affording dramatic, functional performance may be viewed around the world. Its greater value, however, may lie in the wide influence of his philosophical approach. His coherent system of thought is a creative synthesis which embraces many significant areas of the social, industrial, scientific, and individual aspects of living. It represents a major attempt to outline a workable and comprehensible cosmology which endeavors to account for all physical and psychophysical phenomena behaviors within a field system of relations encompassing all known scientific laws and hypotheses.

In assuming a finite universe, permeable to human thought (which though not simultaneously "knowable" may yet be comprehended through its rationally co-ordinate patterns), Fuller restores man to a comprehensive position in which he may exercise his full evolutionary initiative toward controlling his destiny. He avoids previous philosophical dilemmas of paired antitheses, like materialism versus idealism, by assuming an integral polarity in phenomena relations, in which apparently exclusive opposites are resolved into places as complementary interactive aspects of a whole process. Within this approach, Value is not ultimately material, but like thought may be externalized in a materially operable principie. Hence ethical assumptions gain new dignity as the embodiment of such Value principles, materially and durably evident in man's universal experience.

> John McHale. *R. Buckminster Fuller* (Braziller). 1962. p. 42

Ideas and Integrities is a difficult book to read from start to finish. It is a much better book to read from finish to start. Each page is, in a sense, a statement of a contemporary problem, followed by a series of incisive, unexpected, wildly imaginative questions. The genius of Richard Buckminster Fuller is that he knows exactly what questions to ask, and in which order. What makes him more than a walking computer is his humanity and his imagination. For whether he likes it or not, Bucky is, above all, an artist and a poet—that rare contemporary poet who does not despair of the human condition.

> Peter Blake. *New York Times Book Section.* July 28, 1963. p. 7

Buckminster Fuller, whose name is high on the campus lists of favored environmental persons, is a comprehensive, all-purpose, long-distance, world-around genius talker who teaches everything to everyone everywhere. Wherever you look, there he is in his blue suit, with wide-open magnified eyes, pouring out his ideas in a flood of words, intoxicated by the universe and fed by an internal stream of energy that re-creates itself as it is used, and that may very well be a conscious effort by the universe to use Fuller to illustrate its own principles. For him, the universe is simply an endless, beginningless, wrap-around environment, "a non-simultaneous complex of unique motions and transformations."

Forty years ago when he first began talking on a broad scale about the universe, what it contained, what to do with it, and how to live in it, he was seldom understood and only rarely appreciated. His thoughts, and the language he used to express them, occasionally reached the outer limits of inscrutability. . . .

Fuller over the years has found his own way to clearer and deeper expression of a philosophy of science, art, and society—an expression that uses the imagery of a fully developed poet, the ideas of a scientist, designer, and practical engineer, and the spiritual energy of an authentic prophet.

> Harold Taylor. *Saturday Review.* May 2, 1970. p. 56

It is impossible to convey the density of illustration or the copiousness of Buckminster Fuller's thought in a brief synopsis. Nor is it possible to draw a hard line between those points in Fuller's thinking where description leaves off and prescription takes over. Science fact and science fiction blur, perhaps by design, in [*Intuition*]. . . . Written partially in English, partially in space-think, the art of saying more with less words, Fuller's non-poems are a sort of physics refresher course cum brainstorm cum moral epistle.

> Victor Howes. *Christian Science Monitor.* May 10, 1972. p. 11

There is an earnestness in Buckminster Fuller's attitude to life that is direct and manly and that inclines a critic to relent from too exclusive a concern with the aims of the poetic craft. . . .

One sees evidence [in *Intuition*] that Buckminster Fuller is indeed exquisitely sensitive to certain forms of beauty. . . . But framing seemly, shapely speech is not among his gifts. That is a misfortune. There is no instrument save language for giving expression to his doctrine, and dressed in the language that he has devised for the purpose that doctrine seems childish and embarrassing. Mr. Fuller is plainly a man who must be judged by his actions, for his intuition fails him when he sets out to speak to his fellow man.

> Emile Capouya. *Saturday Review.* June 24, 1972. p. 67

Bucky had discovered something about the way of his own thought. Though he did not, like Thoreau, polish aphorisms till they resemble souvenirs, yet like the aphorist he thought in discrete energy packets, linear in sequence. The key to clarity was to make these boundaries somehow evident. From this time even the sentences he prints as ordinary prose have a new awareness of internal marking points.

He had discovered, in his own roundabout way, a mode of American poetry, the straightforward sentence collected out of energized units, and analyzed into them again by a visual aid. . . .

Bucky Fuller's satisfactions are conceptual: the domes, a general case, and the worldwide process he has envisaged for so long, a general case as well.

Similarly, the satisfaction he takes from writing (mostly verse now—the published prose comes from lecture transcripts) is that of conveying with clarity the most accurate general statement he can manage. Beauty does not concern him. It is not banished, though, by those enjambed polysyllables. The 1956 poem he dedicated to Dr. Jonas Salk not only resembles Roman and Elizabethan attempts to versify advanced knowledge, it is the nearest thing we have to a Metaphysical poem.

> Hugh Kenner. *Bucky: A Guided Tour of Buckminster Fuller* (Morrow). 1973. pp. 219–20, 222

Whatever Bucky has built or tried has been a demonstration that it is possible, in a practical way, to break out of the limiting conceptions supplied by common knowledge and the standard operating procedures. And . . . in form and structure whatever he has built or tried to build, derives from the views he has developed of the form, structure and play of forces in the universe. Repeatedly he tells his devoted audiences to start with Whole Systems. ''Dig wholes!'' . . .

How far along has Bucky gotten in the fulfillment of these excellent intentions, bringing all the parts of our special knowledge and interests to bear on our well-being? In verbal precision and definition he gets more successful every year. But there are not yet many practical returns. . . .

In a time of specialization, alienation, divisiveness, dissonance, fragmentation of knowledge and all the rest of it, Bucky has come forward with demonstrations, in artifacts and schemes, of healing possibilities. His task, like Thoreau's, has been to work outside the customary practices, as a maker of metaphors and paradigms ''meeting our deepest needs,'' freeing us a little from limiting conceptions, giving us new points of departure.

> Elting E. Morison. *New York Times Book Section.* March 11, 1973. p. 6

In performance what is wrong seems to matter little, because Fuller when performing makes the particular points minor, and the star-spinning from one to the next entrancing.

This may indicate why Fuller is so beloved, and scorned, and even feared. He seems to cast a spell that makes interested listeners into something like followers, and those who seek to dismiss him know that spell-binders have been suspect for a number of centuries. Those who claim to chart the universe are often known for having too easy answers; in response to such people, specialists, who could be trusted, came into being, and they soon demonstrated that the universe could not be charted. They piled up such huge storehouses of specialized knowledge that any one person's knowledge of more than a little bit of it would have to be inaccurate, or superficial, or trivial. So let us accept this. As a knower, as someone speaking about history or chemistry or physics or architecture, Fuller is seldom going to be as accurate, as subtle, as comprehensive as at least some and maybe many specialists in each of these ''subjects'' might be. But is there nothing left? What is left is Fuller's faith. . . .

Sitting on bleachers, watching him at a distance of at least a hundred yards, one could nonetheless feel his presence as something more than charismatic or soothing. He asked and so received and deserved, only for time and patience, not for belief, or if he asked for that, it was only as a way of asking us to believe more in ourselves. That was memorable, and listening to Fuller as he spins his stars is an experience one should have, and probably more than once.

> Roger Sale. *New York Review of Books.* Feb. 7, 1974. pp. 30, 32

BIBLIOGRAPHY

The Time Lock, 1928 (e); *Nine Chains to the Moon*, 1938 (e); *Education Automation*, 1962 (e); *Untitled Epic Poems on the History of Industrialization*, 1962 (p); *Ideas and Integrities*, 1963 (e); *No More Secondhand God, and Other Writings*, 1963 (p); *Operating Manual for Spaceship Earth*, 1969 (e); *Utopia or Oblivion*, 1969 (e); *The Buckminster Fuller Reader*, 1970; *Intuition*, 1972 (p); (with E.J. Applewhite) *Synergetics: Explorations in the Geometry of Thinking*, 2 vols., 1975–79 (e); *And It Came to Pass—Not to Stay*, 1976 (e); *Pound, Synergy, and the Great Design*, 1977 (lectures); *R. Buckminster Fuller on Education*, ed. Peter H. Wagschal and Robert D. Kahn, 1979 (e); *Critical Path*, 1981 (h); *Tetrascroll: Goldilocks and the Three Bears: A Cosmic Fairy Tale*, 1982; *Grunch of Giants*, 1983 (e); (with Anwar Dil) *Humans in Universe*, 1983 (e); *Inventions: The Patented Works of R. Buckminster Fuller*, 1983 (catalog); *The Artifacts of R. Buckminster Fuller: A Comprehensive Collection of His Designs and Drawings*, 4 vols., ed. James Ward, 1984; *Fuller's Earth: A Day with Bucky and the Kids*, ed. Richard J. Brenneman, 1984 (e); *Synergetics Dictionary: The Mind of Buckminster Fuller*, ed. E.J. Applewhite, 1986 (ref); (with Kiyoshi Kuromiya) *Cosmography: A Posthumous Scenario for the Future of Humanity*, 1992 (e)

G

GADDIS, William (1922–)

This 956-page first novel [*The Recognitions*] is easily the most exasperating mélange of genuinely scathing and merely random satire, of shrewd dialogue and chaotic fragments, of apt allusion and pretentious display, of suggestive prose and turgid outpourings that this reader has come upon. With such virtues of good avant-garde writing as audacity, freshness and independence it mixes such faults of the bad as obscurity, formlessness and intellectual arrogance. Inevitably it echoes the devices of *Ulysses* and resembles it in its attitude toward contemporary life, except that Joyce's vision of the decline of man from a godlike Ulysses to a commonplace Dublin Jew seems by contrast wistful and whimsical. For Mr. Gaddis (who, by the way, began this book eight years ago, when he was about twenty-five years old) sees ours as literally a society of forgeries, counterfeits, plagiarisms and fakes. . . .

It would be unjust to treat Mr. Gaddis' book as though it were in any way intended as a conventional novel. Structurally it is a series of symbolic episodes calculated not to tell a story but to suggest the sterility of contemporary life. Like a poem it coheres only in spirit, and this it does by exemplifying throughout half a million words man's degeneration to a point where he can no longer recognize the genuine, no less create it.

Unfortunately *The Recognitions* does not persuade us that it is based on any but a narrow and jaundiced view, a projection in part of private discontent. It is a clinical collection of slides showing organisms of decay magnified grotesquely and stained to an unnatural vividness. Somewhere in this book there is material for a novel and somewhere behind it is a writer with remarkable equipment, but *The Recognitions* itself is a grandiose curiosity.

> Milton Rugoff. *New York Herald Tribune Book Section*. March 13, 1955. p. 6

What [*The Recognitions*] lacks, like all claustrophobic works of art, is imagination. It has plenty of invention and fantasy, but that is something different. Imagination in art is the ability to select significantly: to select in order to communicate a vision.

It is only belated recognition of *The Recognitions* that may now indicate some definite guidelines to the course open to the contemporary novel. And for those who consider the achievements of James Joyce in perfecting many vital aspects of the modern novel—only to bemoan the absence of any major successors to Joyce—a closer examination of Gaddis's first and only novel to date should do much to emphasize the pervasiveness of the Joycean influence and perhaps indicate tendencies of what is to come. . . .

When imitation becomes impossible, it usually follows that a reaction develops instead, but in the case of James Joyce such a reaction could hardly be fruitful: against which Joyce is one to react? the naturalistic Joyce? the symbolistic Joyce? the Joyce of "scrupulous meanness" or the Joyce of "mandarin" involutions? the poet? the storyteller? the chronicler? the moral amoralist or the immoral moralist? With James Joyce, I am suggesting, the twentieth century has produced its most consummate literary artist, and it is to William Gaddis's credit that he has sought and found in Joyce both a direction toward the future and a definite delineation of what has been accomplished, so that *The Recognitions* at once acknowledges its debt and proclaims its individuality. Gaddis is able to do this because the basic element of his work is the delicate balance between originality and imitation, and the book itself as such is able to be a living example of what it *means*.

> Bernard Benstock. *Contemporary Literature*. Summer, 1965. pp. 177–9

Even the most indulgent well-wisher is likely to pick up any novel, especially a first novel, three hundred pages longer than *Ulysses*, with reluctance and read it to the end only with stalwart perseverance, even if stimulated, as in Gaddis's novel, by excellence in conception and execution. Stretches of vexation, frustration, *déjá vu*, and frank boredom make the first reading sluggish; but I read it a second time much more willingly and have perused it again and again eagerly. . . .

Gaddis has published no other novels; but a chapter from a new one appeared in the fall of 1970 in *Dutton Review*, No. 1. At forty-nine, Gaddis is a classic example, apparently, of a young writer of genius shooting the works in his first novel—equal in length, range, and complexity to five novels. Appalled by the disconnectedness of time, Stanley, a character in the book who has devoted his life to finishing a massive composition for the organ, makes a statement that describes *The Recognitions* itself: "It's impossible to accomplish a body of work without a continuous sense of time, so instead you try to get all the parts together into one work that will stand by itself and serve the same thing a lifetime of separate work does, something higher than itself."

> David Madden in *Rediscoveries*, ed. David Madden (Crown). 1971. pp. 292–3

Tony Tanner recently concluded his critical survey of American fiction between 1950 and 1970 [*City of Words*] by claiming that William Gaddis' *The Recognitions* (1955) inaugurated an entire period of American fiction. Tanner's conclusion culminates a long, largely underground history for Gaddis' gigantic novel about forgers and counterfeiters, phony art, onanistic sex, and the false rhetoric of all kinds of religions. Still, few outside of a coterie of devoted followers have read or even heard of *The Recognitions*. Although it surfaced briefly at various times during the last twenty odd years, making its way onto an occasional college reading list, relatively little has been written about the perplexing novel since the initial, antagonistic reviews. A satire so fastidious in its condemnation of the entire modern world—a deliberate counterfeit which itself borrows at random from hundreds of sources and satirizes such living persons as then Senator Richard Nixon—of necessity had to provoke exasperated responses. Because reviewers attacked the novel as being too long, complicated, and nihilistic, the public at large ignored it. We have now had, however, access to some of Gaddis' manuscripts, which may help *The Recognitions* find its rightful aboveground reputation.

The manuscripts reveal Gaddis' intent to satirize the book reviewing world of the 1950s for preferring the kind of work being done by Hemingway and other popular writers of the time. Thus he made no attempt to accommodate reviewers or readers and went so far as to predict they would not read his 956-page long, involuted, fragmented, self-consciously demanding novel. . . .

Peter William Koenig. *Contemporary Literature*. Winter, 1975. pp. 61–2

The most radical feature of *JR* (and the one that may limit its audience to readers possessing powers of super-human endurance) is the form in which it is presented. The book consists of 736 pages of virtually uninterrupted monologue and dialogue, an almost continuous outpouring of language embellished scarcely at all by descriptions of character and setting. People by the dozens move back and forth through thick mists of verbiage, talking to and at and around and behind one another. Yet somehow nobody really listens or quite understands what is being said. This, as it turns out, is entirely appropriate to the subject, which is the debasement of language as both cause and symptom of the corruption of a society which has been abstracted by technology from the concrete realities of feeling and being, and in which the totalitarian obfuscations of bureaucratese, the gibber and jargon of the computer, and the lying Newspeak of Watergate politics, corporate finance, and multimedia education have severed the connection that is supposed to exist between words and the truths they are intended to describe. . . .

Gradually there emerges out of this babble of jargon-demented tongues the perfectly sane, merely obsessive figure of JR, logical end-product of the ongoing situation, supreme example of the utilization potential of a meaningful learning experience. A good old American boy from his perpetually runny nose right down to his torn sneakers with the flapping soles, JR has learned his lessons well and knows by instinct how to apply them manipulatively to achieve, in the classic rags-to-riches tradition, the only goals he has been taught to respect: money, fame, and power. . . .

It is undoubtedly inevitable that the novel promises at almost every point to fall victim to the imitative fallacy, that it is frequently as turgid, monotonous, and confusing as the situation it describes. Yet Gaddis has a strength of mind and talent capable of surmounting this very large difficulty. He has managed to reflect chaos in a fiction that is not itself artistically chaotic because it is imbued with the conserving and correcting power of his imagination. His awareness of what is human and sensible is always present behind his depiction of how far we have fallen from humanity and sense. His vision of what is happening in our world is profound and extremely disturbing. If it should ever cease to disturb, there will be no better proof of its accuracy.

John W. Aldridge. *Saturday Review*. Oct. 4, 1975. pp. 28–30

Like other novels of excess, *JR* is aggressively rhetorical, risking the reader's refusal while offering pointers to its own intentions. In *The Public Burning*, [Robert] Coover uses chapters on *Time* and *The New York Times* to comment on his own novel. The narrator of [Thomas Pynchon's] *Gravity's Rainbow* bobs and weaves among his characters, mixing charitable omniscience with insults to the

reader. There are several episodes in *JR* that reveal the desperation of the communication breakdown that is a central subject of the novel and the methods—what I call recording and redundancy—Gaddis uses to prevent breakdown between his novel and its reader. These methods are risky: although realism and repetition are at first aids to clear communication, in excess they become an assault as Gaddis insistently and thoroughly manifests what a runaway is. Messages among the characters in *JR* fail for many reasons: the sender's intellectual shortcomings or lack of interest, duplicity in language itself, the receiver's distraction or ignorance of the code, interference in or overload of the channels of communication. Throughout the novel sirens, loudspeakers, radios, televisions, and other agents create noise against which communication has to struggle. These problems inspire several experiments by a minor character named Vogel. One of these, teleportation, reflects Gaddis' method in the book, for teleportation attempts to send the messenger rather than just the message. Adopting the roles of recorder, collector, and transmitter rather than narrator, Gaddis "sends the messenger," allows his characters to present themselves as voices. This I call recording because Gaddis does not use certain conventions that would suggest authorial mediation or the transformation of speech into writing. Contexts and speakers are not identified in *JR*. There are no quotation marks in the text; the punctuation within sentences is irregular, usually suggesting the arbitrary pause of a voice rather than the formality of written discourse. The filler, solecisms, false starts, fragments, and repetitions of speech are left in. To further this sense of raw recording, Gaddis includes reproductions of newspaper advertisements, a handwritten school essay, a series of logotypes, and a writer's note cards. Playing back the stupid, pathetic, and ugly noise we hear in our work, media, families, and in our own throats, Gaddis assaults us with an excess of verisimilitude, what is called over and over again in the book "the real." The single most dominant quality of this reality is its instantaneousness. As the clocks splinter into seconds, money-making minutes, the characters are always behind, late, making an abrupt change, rushing, trying to keep up with life that has been pervaded by the quantitative values of the runaway economic system. Fragmentation and trivialization of speech are the minute-to-minute effects of this speeded-up system.

Thomas LeClair. *Modern Fiction Studies*. Winter, 1981–82, pp. 598–99

In recent years we hear William Gaddis spoken of in tones of breathless adoration—the outlaw late modernist, the father-figure to a generation of American novelists, the overcoat from which Pynchon, Gass, and others emerged—or not at all. It is a difficult fate for the working novelist, who has not had the chance to be discussed and evaluated by readers alongside the critics. The reason is simple, and it somewhat indicts us as a culture: Gaddis is very difficult to read. In his second novel *J.R.*, which followed the more traditionally difficult *The Recognitions* (1955) by two decades, he announced a prose style that earned him much esteem and, I suspect, fewer real readers than even the pessimist might suppose. . . .

Readers more familiar with the reputation than the work now have reason to be grateful. For whatever reasons, Gaddis has, in *A Frolic of His Own*, produced his most accessible novel. Less dizzying in its transitions, more topical in presentation, easier on the eye because of its incorporation of diverse texts—legal opinions, long sections of a play—the novel may win Gaddis some of the audience that he deserves. At the same time, it must be said, when placed in the high-altitude ranks of his other work, his new book is not his very best. Top-heavy with legalistic obsession, it skimps on character and thereby undercuts its chances of making a strong moral connection to the material. Even so—and this nicely illustrates Gaddis's anomalous position—it is, in intelligence, wit, and technical follow-through, leagues ahead of most so-called serious novels that are published these days.

Sven Birkerts. *New Republic.* Feb. 7, 1994, pp. 27–28

Is *A Frolic of His Own* that difficult, that exhausting? I devoured it in a weekend in a state of exhilaration and delight. Yes, you do have to keep your wits about when reading Gaddis, but it's a rare privilege these days to be taken this seriously as a reader. Like Henry James, William Gaddis wants the kind of reader on whom nothing is lost. He doesn't talk down or assume you can't make connections. He expects that you've read a few books in your time and read the papers. This is literature, not a TV sitcom.

The point is not whether Gaddis is difficult or not but whether difficulty is such a bad thing in literature. Those who prefer easy listening may want easy reading, but others should find a novel bracing, challenging. In Gaddis's second novel, *J.R.*, Jack Gibbs is asked if his work in progress on technology and the arts is difficult, and he answers, "Difficult as I can make it." The difficulties Gibbs undergoes to get this book written, the breadth of his research and length of time he devotes to the task (after seventeen years he still isn't finished), show what sort of pact should exist between serious writers and serious readers.

Gaddis knows he's difficult (Gibbs is one of his personas in *J.R*)., and consequently lightens the task somewhat by making his books very funny, filling them with all forms of humor, from limericks and low puns to learned wit and Olympian ironies. The absence of a comic element can make some difficult literary works a real grind—Pound's *Cantos*, say, or Broch's *Death of Virgil*—despite their other virtues. On the other hand, the comic element is what makes extremely difficult novels like Joyce's *Finnegans Wake* and Julian Rios's *Larva* such a pleasure to wrestle with. And yet few reviewers convey the idea that Gaddis is essentially a comic novelist and that his books can be great fun—rather than an exercise in masochism—to read.

Steven Moore. *The Nation.* April 25, 1994, p. 505

BIBLIOGRAPHY
The Recognitions, 1955 (n); *JR*, 1975 (n); *Carpenter's Gothic*, 1985 (n); *A Frolic of His Own*, 1994 (n)

GAINES, Ernest J. (1933–)

I can think of no other contemporary American novelist whose work has produced in me anything like the sense of depth, the sense of humanity and compassion, and the sense of honesty that I find in Gaines's fiction. It contains the austere dignity and simplicity of ancient epic, a concern with man's most powerful emotions and the actions that arise from those emotions, and an artistic intuition that carefully keeps such passions and behavior under fictive control. Gaines may be one of our most naturally gifted story-tellers. . . .

From the beginning, Gaines has worked to put into an appropriate form his own sense of history, a sense which has both dictated and arisen from his central subject, the blacks and the whites who live in and around his imaginary town of Bayonne, near Baton Rouge, and who work the land of the plantations that still survive. Gaines has the special feeling for these people and this land that comes from having grown up among them, and having absorbed the quality of their lives without exercising any analytical selectivity as to what he absorbed. Thus, his feelings are strongly attached to the sheer physical texture of this country, and it pervades his fiction: the hot summer sky filled with a hazy sun; the freezing, sleet-ridden days of winter; the monochromatic hues of a brilliantly white sky meeting a brilliantly white earth; the winter darkness in whose heavy overcast the distinction between the earth and the sky are obliterated. Gaines has the intuition of D. H. Lawrence and Thomas Hardy. Like them, he feels a permanent spirit residing in the land, which transcends time and space. His characters are born with the past in their bones, and their lives, whether they stay or leave this place, are dominated by it—this "place" in which the past is embedded. . . .

Whether it is intuitive or learned, Gaines's perception of the world resembles that of a biologist, who sees each living organism passing through time, occupying stages, crossing boundary lines into new and unfamiliar territory. Organic life is postulated on the oscillation between life and death, and these are the realities which Gaines fastens on to.

Jerry H. Bryant. *Iowa Review.* Winter, 1972, pp. 106, 110, 119

While his lands and subjects are consistent, there is an evolution of Ernest Gaines's vision through his four works, as he becomes increasingly concerned with black history and black community. The movement from *Catherine Carmier* to *Miss Jane Pittman* is from personal and racial history rendered as a kind of bondage, a solitary existential nightmare of dead ends and blasted families, toward history sensed as a natural cycle, wheeling slowly through the rebirth of a *people*, toward their inevitable collective liberation. As his vision matures, there is an accompanying shift in Gaines's use of materials and fictional techniques. He moves away from a personal version of the white "existential" novel, later assimilating and adapting folk forms—popular sermons, slave narratives, folk tales, oral histories—re-making the long fictional forms to his own unique ends. . . .

With *Bloodline*, Ernest Gaines sounds a very different emphasis on black history and community. The vision of history as fate, as a cycle from which one cannot escape, is expanded. As the title *Bloodline* suggests, the book is concerned with the living, the organic, and Gaines is writing with a vision of the natural history of a people. The dominant concern through these five stories is with natural patterns of growth and decay, the evolution from childhood to maturity to old age as seen in the lives of people, races, generations, eras. In the shapes of these stories, and in the recurrent images and metaphors, the past, present and future are all of a piece; history is part of a natural process, and humans who live within it find their lives infused with significance.

> Jack Hicks. *Black American Literature Forum.* Spring, 1977, pp. 9, 13

When Ernest Gaines published *The Autobiography of Miss Jane Pittman* in 1971, he secured his footing within the American literary world as an important artist. The critical acclaim was nearly unanimous, and the transformation of the work into a popular television drama embellished that success. But Gaines' quiet vision of endurance was no sudden occurrence. With the patience of a journeyman becoming master of his vision, his view of life had been worked out in three previous books; of these earlier works, *Bloodline*, a cycle of short stories published in 1968, is a minor-keyed masterpiece. This is so, despite an age in which easy praise inflates achievement.

To discuss *Bloodline* properly, one must grant that a writer need not strain with an overreaching ambition to create significance in his fiction; he may instead make his mark by accurately recreating the texture of ordinary life, and leave it to us to discover the subtleties of the specific milieu he knows thoroughly. In this sense, *Bloodline* is a worthy descendant of Turgenev's *Sportsman's Sketches* and Joyce's *Dubliners*. It is equally evocative of ordinary life. Within the specific tradition of Afro-American literature, however, *Bloodline* is of even more pressing importance.

Bloodline has significance because it is in line with, though still different from, past landmarks of Afro-American short fiction. Charles Chesnutt's *Conjure Woman and Other Stories*, Jean Toomer's *Cane*, and Richard Wright's *Uncle Tom's Children*—all, like Gaines' *Bloodline*, concern themselves chiefly with the South, that "old country" of racial memory. In these works, successive generations of particular writers, each with some tie to the South, wrestled to divine the significance of that "old country." The works are important for that reason. Further, with regard to their importance and place in an ethnic short-prose tradition, these works are outstanding precisely because they are very much more than collections of separate pieces. Each writer in his own way—Chesnutt by undermining the Plantation Tradition, Toomer by evoking the mysteries of racial memory, Wright by the programmatic ordering of horror—constructs a whole with far greater significance than that of its separate pieces. In that regard, *Bloodline*, too, urges us beyond the bare sum of its parts, while, even more than its predecessors, accepting the ordinariness of the lives it sketches.

> Todd Duncan. *Callaloo.* May, 1978, pp. 85–86

Ernest Gaines's fiction has been characterized from the first by its quiet force. The characters in his several fine books often raise their voices, but the author declines to raise his. These characters are mainly poor, and mostly black; their lives are seldom far removed from the threat of violence, physical or emotional or both. Sooner or later the violence arrives, and the characters cry out at one another, or to the heavens. Their pain, struggle, bewilderment, joys and agonies are registered with precision and sympathy, but the strong prose that carries their stories is not affected by the fevers or the biases of those it describes.

A swimmer cannot influence the flow of a river, and the characters of Ernest Gaines's fiction—from Catherine Carmier to Miss Jane Pittman, and from Miss Jane to the Rev. Phillip Martin of *In My Father's House*—are propelled by a prose that is serene, considered and unexcited. It is the force of Mr. Gaines's character and intelligence, operating through this deceptively quiet style, that makes his fiction compelling. He is, pre-eminently, a writer who takes his own good time, and in this case [*In My Father's House*] the result of his taking it is a mature and muscular novel. . . .

Not the least of the book's virtues is the variety and richness of its minor characters. Phillip Martin's guilty search into his past takes him, internally, down a long road of memory. Externally it brings him into contact with a number of people—his godmother, an old girlfriend, a former gambling buddy and an embittered young black guerrilla—whose portraits are done with Flaubertian economy but equally Flaubertian vividness. The dialogue is spare, but unerring, and humor will keep slipping in subtly, despite the tragedies behind these lives. The tone of the book is determined by Mr. Gaines's decision—a brilliant one—to set the novel not in the expected context of a sweaty, dripping Louisiana summer, but in the miserable, frigid, sunless Louisiana winter. The sun never shines on this story, and the metaphors that describe the doom of Robert X are, appropriately, metaphors of chill.

There are few blemishes on the book. Now and then a character strays into polemic; once or twice the tone breaks. Perhaps Robert X should not have been allowed to speak at all, for his condemnatory silence is far more eloquent than the little that he eventually says. But these are small blemishes indeed on a book that attempts a large theme, and is fully adequate to it.

> Larry McMurtry. *New York Times Book Section.* June 11, 1978. p. 13

In My Father's House is an important work, showing significant development in Gaines's art and thought, especially in light of his depiction of and reaction to the 1970s. . . .

Gaines's distancing of his readers—and himself—from this novel may not indicate a change in his philosophy, but it does, I think, reflect a change in his attitude toward his characters' potential development. Considered in sequence, Gaines's first three novels show a gradual development in his characters' ability to grow, change, and prevail. All the characters in *Catherine Carmier*, his first novel, are victims of social or environmental forces, while in *Of Love and Dust* Jim Kelly and Marcus Payne achieve growth through fighting the inertia of southern black life and, within limits at least, gain the capacity to shape their lives. Gaines's sense of this power on the part of his characters culminates in the depiction of Jane Pittman, who prevails over seriously adverse circumstances. The *Autobiography* reconciles the dichotomies of the earlier novels: past and present, young and old, man and woman. In *In My Father's House* the reconciliation falls apart. . . .

Gaines's first three novels culminated in Jane Pittman, a character who embodies the positive values in his world. Perhaps he was then faced with the problem of how to create a story which would represent a significant development from such a powerful, heroic figure. In *In My Father's House* Gaines implies that Miss Jane's triumph, both personal and social, may be atypical, that Martin's fall is the more usual human fate. Burdened by a past he cannot escape, by overweening pride and self-esteem, Martin is defeated. Whether he can rise again, as is characteristic of traditional tragic heroes, is problematical. The ending of this novel suggests the ending of his first novel, *Catherine Carmier;* in that the characters are in stasis, immobile, unable to move and break out of the pattern in which they are trapped. The novel ends *we just go'n have to start again.*

Frank W. Shelton. *Southern Review.* Spring, 1981, pp. 340–41, 345

BIBLIOGRAPHY
Catherine Carmier, 1964 (n); *Of Love and Dust,* 1967 (n); *Bloodline,* 1968 (s); *The Autobiography of Miss Jane Pittman,* 1971 (n); *A Long Day in November;* 1971 (juv); *In My Father's House,* 1978 (n); *A Gathering of Old Men,* 1983 (n); *Porch Talk with Ernest Gaines: Conversations on the Writer's Craft,* ed. Marcia Gaudet and Carl Wooton, 1990 (i); *A Lesson before Dying,* 1993 (n); *Conversations with Ernest Gaines,* ed. John Lowe, 1995

GARDNER, Isabella (1915–1981)

Her gravestone reads ISABELLA GARDNER 1915–1981: POET, but when I say that I am writing a biography of Isabella Gardner, I either draw a blank, or am regaled with stories about visits to, and thefts from, that most idiosyncratic Boston museum assembled by Isabella Stewart Gardner, "Mrs. Jack." . . .

It is a biographer's boon if her subject's poems are autobiographical, as Isabella Gardner's so clearly are; for the poetry lover, a poet's life is just one impulse from which good poems may spring. . . .

In the late forties and early fifties Isabella Gardner proved herself to be a consummate craftsman of lyric verse, a magician of sound: quite a number of her poems were set to music. She took all forms, from the obligatory sonnet ("Sonnet for My acquaintances") to the sestina ("The Music Room") to the little known, forbidding "Triolet," Gardner's first published poem. Although she seldom submitted to fixed verse forms, she controlled the chaos of life by end rhyme, alliteration, assonance, and, often, strictly metered iambic lines, as well as the "symbology, inter-relating, universal and associative, of Christianity and myth and magic (and Freud)" (in Gardner letters). . . . In [the] short, incantatory lyric ["Cock-A-Hoop"] above love, death, and war, Isabella Gardner plays witty verbal games—the cocksure soldier is almost a conceit—and alludes to fables and religion, observing with precision and feeling. . . .

Gardner wrote only about a hundred poems all told, thirty of which are now collected for the first time. A number of these "new" works, for instance the earlier mentioned "Triolet" and "Incantate the Cockatrice," are apprentice poems. Gardner's high standards never allowed her to gather such poems in book form; in *Collected Poems* they demonstrate her mastery of technique. They are useful as contrast to Gardner's best poems in which formal devices particularize and therefore emphasize feelings, keeping intense emotions from crossing over to generalized sentimentality.

Other previously uncollected poems, as well as two Villon translations and the late poem written about Allen Tate just after his death ("One Sunday in 1966") show that although Isabella Gardner's output was small and her fame brief, the quality of her work is as monumental as Fenway Court [Isabella Stewart Gardner's grand house, now the Gardner Museum].

Marian Janssen. *Kenyon Review.* Summer, 1991, pp. 152, 157, 160

BIBLIOGRAPHY
Birthdays from the Ocean, 1955 (p); *The Looking Glass,* 1961 (p); *West of Childhood: Poems 1950–1965,* 1965 (p); *Collected Poems,* 1990

GARDNER, John (1933–1982)

Taut, ruminative and in its dignity never solemn, [*The Resurrection*] is an ordeal to read—but a rewarding one. . . . I was reminded here and there of Hermann Broch's *Death of Virgil,* but Mr. Gardner's protagonist is altogether more in this world. The children (to whom he hardly knows how to speak) are deftly drawn in the insouciance of their daily energy; the frozen panic of the wife comes through movingly, and one character—Horne, the mad law-librarian—embodies the notion of malfunctioning demiurge. Mr. Gardner subtly combines them all through devices of hallucination and dream, tense-switching, and italicized thoughts-within-thoughts.

Paul West. *Book Week.* July 17, 1966. p. 12

At times Agathon [in *The Wreckage of Agathon*] whose name in Greek means the Good, stands for the whole Western tradition of humane tolerance, now threatened by the twin fanaticisms of repression and revolution. At others, he is some kind of primordial natural force, a witness to age-long woe and fatality. At still others, when what he calls facticity catches up with him, Agathon is just a slobbish old lecher smelling of onions. In this guise he represents the irreducible, incorrigible lump of humanity that always jams up the bright theoretical machines continually being invented by one Lycurgus or another, and thus saves mankind from betterment.

In this guise, Agathon saves the book too. With his rambling wit, his irrelevancies, rages, blunderings, unfairnesses, with his tender-rough efforts to jerk his friend Peeker to wisdom through the muck of the world, he emerges as one of the scapegrace saints who have adorned literature from Socrates to Gulley Jimson.

Robert Wernick. *Time.* Nov. 9, 1970. p. 86

John Gardner's [*The Wreckage of Agathon*], like [Dan] Jacobson's [*The Rape of Tamar*], is a *tour de force* dealing with ancient historical legend in modern idiom. The resemblance is even closer in that his central figure, a sublimely ridiculous seer named Agathon (a mixture of "Crito" and Joyce Cary's Gulley Jimson, with a touch of Marguerite Yourcenar's Hadrian), believes that, in a world where truth is unknowable and where time's wreckage makes prisoners of us all, vividness of being is the highest wisdom. . . .

The novel is narrated alternately by Agathon and his disciple and mixes the concerns of public and private life. Gardner is ambitious to make his book a statement not merely about justice or about time but also about sex, growing old, and the art of living. His rhetoric and invention maintain considerable energy, but on second reading the liveliness appears more facile than at first. . . .

And the book's numerous aphorisms, though potentially forceful in the proper context, are a good deal less original than the author seems to be claiming, hence a little embarrassing.

David J. Gordon. *The Yale Review*. Spring, 1971. pp. 433–4

Mr. Gardner's *Grendel* is interpretation and elaboration rather than translation—a sophisticated version of what *Beowulf* is ultimately *about* in modern terms. The device that he uses is to present us with a subjective autobiography by an extremely self-conscious Grendel before and immediately after Beowulf's arrival in Denmark. . . .

Mr. Gardner has a disturbing talent. There can be no doubt about that. Grendel, in addition to being the narrator, is much the most sympathetic figure in *Grendel*—in spite of his outrageous behavior and often deplorable opinions. What remains questionable is whether the literary object upon which *Grendel* is parasitic can carry the weight Mr. Gardner imposes on it. *Beowulf*, for all its historic interest, remains obstinately second-rate as a work of literature.

F. W. Bateson. *New York Review of Books*. Dec. 30, 1971. pp. 16–7

One approached Mr. Gardner's new novel [*Grendel*] with caution, suspecting another literary word-game. In the endless search for new objects of compassion, he has taken the monster from *Beowulf* called Grendel, and asks us to examine its predicament: how can Grendel's anti-social tendencies (eating all those brave Scandinavian soldiers) be explained except in terms of childhood deprivation, social rejection on account of physical deformity, horrible smell, etc.?

However, from this whimsical, monumentally silly idea for a novel Mr. Gardner has constructed something of pure delight. Grendel's grudge against humanity may originate in the pique of a rejected suitor when, on his first encounter with men, he is mistaken for a tree fungus, but Mr. Gardner invites us to believe that Grendel had a point. We examine the Beowulf legend for a start, and through it all the legends with which mankind sustains belief in his intrinsic nobility, and see the whole structure as a pack of lies. Squalid, bloodthirsty encounters between frightened men are built into epic battles; ignoble and furtive lusts become by the telling something beautiful and good. Mr. Gardner's book is as funny and as elegantly written as anything I have read for a long time.

Auberon Waugh. *Spectator*. July 1, 1972. p. 14

The Wreckage of Agathon, an inventive if rather baroque meditation on the status of imaginative freedom within an oppressive political order, and *Grendel*, a dazzling revision of the Beowulf story that injects nightmare into the complacencies of our cultural and historical self-imaginings, seemed for all their brilliance more like strokes of theater, bright ideas carried off by extraordinary

powers of execution, than fully explored fictional territories. Both, though thematically "relevant" enough, took place in a remote past, letting us see ourselves in them only around a corner. One wondered if Gardner's art might not require such a corner, if he mightn't be doomed to being a writer who could address us only in asides, winking knowingly from a long way off.

Two readings of [*The Sunlight Dialogues*] now convince me that Gardner is much more than a sleight-of-hand man. Where *Grendel* was, within its limits, virtually perfect, like a masterfully practiced stage-turn, *The Sunlight Dialogues* is ambitious, heroically flawed, contemporary (though with rich mythic resonances), absorbing moment by moment and darkly troubling after it's over.

Gardner is that rare creature, a philosophical novelist.

Thomas R. Edwards. *New York Times Book Section*. Dec. 10, 1972. p. 1

Of course, Gardner's novel [*The Sunlight Dialogues*] can be faulted. Just as he shares with John Updike (and many other American writers) an obsession with entropy, so he reveals something of Updike's straining for self-vaunting but redundant simile. They both should be banned from using the word "like" for a decade. It could also be argued that some of the very long tirades detach themselves from the speakers' characters and swarm around like unattached mists of angry words. But these cavils are minor compared with the high degree of success achieved by this ambitious novel. It is a major fictional exploration into America, no less—the America that is vanishing and the problematical America of today. And without abandoning its fictional premises, it draws us into a sobering meditation on the possible shapes of our immediate future. It tells no lies yet ends with a refusal to accept despair. It does all this at the same time as it involves us in an absorbing and intricately interwoven story. This is a great deal for any one novel to do, and it should be recognized immediately for what it is—a very impressive achievement.

Tony Tanner. *Saturday Review*. Jan., 1973. pp. 79–80

John Gardner's last two novels, *The Wreckage of Agathon* and *Grendel* were short and beautifully compact. They, too, were philosophical novels; that is, they addressed themselves to contradictions and irrational miseries in our society, and they make splendid sense. *The Sunlight Dialogues* is too wordy, too vague of design, to sustain and deliver the same kind of energetic meaning.

Mr. Gardner is a medievalist (he teaches Old and Middle English at Southern Illinois U) and his mind would seem to have been on the sagas of Iceland when he undertook this novel. The sagas wander off in just this way, appending digression to digression, ending up with all the design of a monkey-puzzle tree. And yet John Gardner writes a bold, flexible prose, and his mastery of vernacular is superb. The book is too good to bore; it overwhelms, it hides its climaxes, it strays; it is too damned long.

Guy Davenport. *National Review*. Feb. 2, 1973. p. 159

Like a proper allegory, Gardner's novel operates on two levels. In its frame of realism, *The Sunlight Dialogues* takes place in Batavia, New York, in 1966. The Sunlight Man proves to be a member of a

prominent local family, and in his detailed chronicle of the generations of Hodges, Gardner can perform like a veritable Galsworthy
toward his Forsytes.

But, like a morality play, the novel constantly moves from
specific people and events toward a sort of staged warfare of good
and evil. Clumly is the last tired Apollonian, struggling fecklessly
to enforce the law's jot and tittles as small boys let the air out of his
tires and, in fact, the old American order deflates around him. The
Sunlight Man, a poet, a magician, is in essence a daemonic figure:
the embodiment of all that is newly restless, newly rebellious in the
American spirit.

> Melvin Maddocks. *Atlantic Monthly*. March, 1973. p. 100

Jason and Medeia [is] a tour de force of literary nostalgia and
imitative form.

Jason and Medeia is nothing less than an epic poem in 24 books
(the full Homeric complement) on one of the major cycles of
Greek legend. . . .

Gardner's ambition is evidently to fabricate in English a fourth
"ancient" epic to complement the *Iliad*, the *Odyssey*, and the
Aeneid, as well as a book to stand beside his own novels, which are
very much concerned with myth, wonder and historical fantasy. . . .
Gardner, himself an ingenious translator from the Middle English,
has invented a bizarre variant . . . the open hoax, the instant classic,
a translation without an original. . . .

What remains unclear . . . is why Gardner should have undertaken such a hybrid project. The answer, I'm afraid, lies near at
hand: Gardner is a prolific and learned writer of amazing virtuoso
dexterity, but with little power of judgment or depth of inspiration.
Like another superb technician, Ezra Pound, he needs to hang his
hat on another man's rack, to unravel and reweave someone else's
thread. Always the clever student, full of boyish bravado, he sets
tough tasks for himself—hurdles, challenges—and polishes them
off effortlessly, without really pondering if they were worth doing
at all.

> Morris Dickstein. *New York Times Book Section*, July 1,
> 1973. p. 4

A serious case can be made for how little John Gardner resembles
himself. Now he's an epic poet, now an epic novelist, now a
medieval monster, now a simulated Poe or Melville. He is the latter
two, and more, in this new collection of his short stories [*The
King's Indian*], the title story a remarkable novella, full of marvels.

Gardner is the Lon Chaney of contemporary fiction, a writer
without a personal psychography in his work. He seems sprung not
from life but literature, history and ideas, a man making books with
other books as a starting point, but a writer of enormous range and
inventiveness. His prose is regal.

What he is is a splendid show-off.

> William Kennedy. *New Republic*. Dec. 7, 1974. p. 19

A puzzling absence of criticism attends the works of John Gardner.
He has published five novels since 1966: *The Resurrection* (1966),
The Wreckage of Agathon (1970), *Grendel* (1971), *The Sunlight
Dialogues* (1972), and *Nickel Mountain* (1973); he has also pub-
lished a long poem, *Jason and Medeia* (1973), and a collection of

stories, *The King's Indian* (1974). His works have been praised in
an impressive number of brief reviews; his experiments with
novelistic form have won him recognition as an innovator. But as
prolific, well-received, and innovative as he may be, Gardner has
not yet received the serious critical attention which his works
merit. . . . One can consider the five novels as a group of works
written at the beginning of his career and suppose that they were
written in the following phases: the "very early" phase—*The
Resurrection* and *Nickel Mountain*; the "early" phase—*The Sunlight Dialogues* and *The Wreckage of Agathon*; and the "late"
phase—*Grendel*.

The Resurrection and *Nickel Mountain* share a concern with the
affirmation of life in the face of death. . . . These two novels from
the "very early" phase of Gardner's career resemble each other in
several ways. They share an upstate New York setting, which
Gardner will replace with more fabulous realms in the later novels.
They share an omniscient narrator, presenting plausible characters
who speak convincing dialogue; Gardner will use self-conscious
and unreliable first-person narrators in the later novels. They share
a conventional chronological structure, which will be modified to
more experimental forms in the last three novels. *The Resurrection*
and *Nickel Mountain* share a large, philosophical focus on the
question, posed bluntly and emphatically to James Chandler.
"*What is the meaning of life?*". . . Just as the first two novels share
similar themes and techniques, they also share a similar flaw. At
their worst, they are sentimental; the affirmations made by the
protagonists are not earned nor are they fully credible. . . .

Gardner's last three novels are his best and are distinguished
from the first two by their inclusion of the figure of the alien,
developed to its fullest in *Grendel*. Gardner's three most compelling characters are aliens: the Sunlight Man, Agathon, and Grendel.
Each is an eccentric, estranged from a society he improves through
the biting wit of his alienation; each is pitted against righteousness
and complacency; each is an artist of sorts: the Sunlight Man with
magic, Agathon with fictionalized narrative, and Grendel with
poetic myth. Finally, each is a joker, a sad clown, whose jokes
emerge like black humor from a mood of despair.

The Sunlight Dialogues and *The Wreckage of Agathon* share a
similar theme, in which the metaphysical focus of the earlier novels
is replaced by a social focus. Both novels are about the inadequacy
of law and the need for justice, the narrowness of codified rules and
the need for a broader human understanding.

> Susan Strehle. *Critique*. 18, 2, 1976, pp. 86–88

John Gardner is one of the few American novelists who has
remained fascinated by the man who acts, who wills one thing
intensely enough to get it. A medievalist, Gardner seems to have
kept his faith that "except in the life of a hero, the whole world's
meaningless." *October Light* is a stunningly written tragicomic
novel that searches through the operative myths of national greatness for a surviving American heroism. Sally, an 83-year-old
feminist, and James, her 70-year-old farmer brother, mirror two
heroic strains in the American consciousness, the one intoxicated
by progress; the other devoted to the land and deriving its values from the endless repetitions of nature. Belief in progress
and change and willingness to work the land opened up the
American wilderness. . . .

Missing in his novels is a sense of masculine purpose, of the
hero as the man who can put his power in the service of a

worthwhile cause. Gardner's heroes are willful, self-absorbed narcissists who see determination and merit as the same, and whose heroism involves only the willingness to follow their obsessions wherever they might lead. . . In not making distinctions between the value of one obsession and another, Gardner stalemates his novels.

Gardner's irresolution takes the form of an irony so pervasive it seems to stem from that well of American bitterness that made Herman Melville and Mark Twain, creators of distinctive American heroes, finally black about America's possibilities. Gardner presses his ambivalences into *October Light*, forcing his chauvinism and his nihilism against each other like monuments to two American civilizations. He achieves a disturbing, utterly original novel that gets as close as any book can to that acid cartoon, Grant Wood's "American Gothic."

Josephine Hendin. *New Republic*. Feb. 5, 1977, pp. 31–32

On Moral Fiction . . . will probably be quoted as widely as [William] Gass's *Fiction and the Figures of Life* was a few years ago, not because Gardner's formulations of the new fictional conservatism are particularly brilliant but because he articulates feelings and tastes many disgruntled readers share. Gass's essays had an elegant uselessness; Gardner's appeal is plain talk and righteousness. I have heard "Kill the Aestheticians" murmured in my university library. Gardner responds to this kind of frustration with academic jargon by using words, such as Beauty, Truth, and Goodness, that most critics walked away from years ago. These abstractions come to have a sludge-like quality; Gardner's distinctions often lack precision (a favorite pejorative is "creepy"), and his readings of recent fiction are sometimes militantly unimaginative. But *On Moral Fiction* is still a necessary book because its earnest force requires even the reader who resists it page by page to examine his assumptions about fiction and because no other writer—Tom Wolfe in *The Painted Word* excepted—has reminded us recently that art is by and for human beings.

Gardner finds most contemporary American fiction and its criticism mediocre or worse. Authors lack belief, so they follow the cult of style, fancy surface. If they have values worth communicating, their fiction is too often programmatic and didactic. Criticism accepts this diminished state of fiction while trifling with finer and finer-gauged descriptive categories. What we need, argues Gardner, is a moral fiction, one that improves life through its sane and healthy vision and through its creation of character models for our imitation. The moral artist is the poet-priest who creates by a process of careful imitation, testing his fiction against the larger reality of human experience. A true criticism would judge fiction, at least partially, on moral grounds. This summary does little violence to Gardner's positions. While they are filled out with some explanation of central terms, with references to classic authorities, and with discussions of contemporary writers (John Fowles as hero, William Gass and mostly unnamed nihilists as villains), Gardner's arguments are meant to be fundamental. He insists on a common sense view, an enforced simplicity, and he has the Platonic assurance that we—always it is "we"—know the good but just can't find it.

I think Gardner's assessment of the current literary scene is substantially accurate if our contemporaries are measured against classic or even classic modern writers. His judgments would also be true of the fiction written in the 1870s. Still, we do need to recognize that very few of our writers have the heart or ambition to

be a Melville or a Pynchon. Even Gardner's prescriptions could be persuasive had he not vitiated the basic force of his argument with an inconsistent definition of moral fiction, with narrow assumptions, inflated claims, and limited sympathies. Gardner defines moral fiction both by the exploratory, mimetic process of its composition and by the healthy effects it has without fully considering that a "moral" process can and sometimes does produce a negative, even a nihilistic work. His assumptions—that ordinary language is adequate for interesting fiction, that art communicates very much like other discourses, that the reader should fall into fiction as into a dream—are insistently naive, but even more difficult to accept is Gardner's pride. He proclaims that art and criticism are the only ordering agencies left in our culture, that "true" art—and not just the best art—is necessarily moral, and that the artist is the only true critic. As a reader of his fellow novelists, Gardner is sometimes pettish (his comments on Bellow and Updike), occasionally sloppy, and at least once flatly wrong—when he mistakes what happened in Heller's *Something Happened*. There is little sympathy for satirists, creators of indirect affirmations, and makers of imaginative ornaments. In a world where everything and everyone is used, ordered for a purpose, Gardner would make fiction one more operation, the most efficient persuasion. He forgets fun.

On Moral Fiction does not collapse through its many weaknesses because, ultimately, Gardner sides with great art, an ambitious humane art that displays the writer's love for his craft, his world, and his readers.

Thomas LeClair. *Contemporary Literature*. Autumn, 1979. pp. 509–11

The garden and the machine confront each other anew in Gardner's fiction. The voice of the garden, linked to the pastoral impulse with its love of nature and poetic longings, confronts the voice of the machine, linked to the darker Manichaean belief that the world is mere accident, brute force controls all history, and only outright manipulation will keep things running. The basic pattern of dialogue between the classical/medieval hope for regeneration and redemption, linked to light and often magic, and the modern nihilistic certainty of gloom and despair, linked to darkness and often black magic, informs the basic narrative structure of Gardner's fiction. These voices set off against one another—the human heart in conflict with itself—set up a counterpoint in his fiction, which slowly works itself out in the process of the confrontation itself. Fiction becomes a "dream unfolding in the mind," a spell cast by both opposing camps, defining each other by the pattern of dialogue and conflict between them. . . .

In *The Sunlight Dialogues* Gardner achieves that equilibrium between "radical disunites," that fully wrought balance between the pastoral idyll and Calvinist/Manichaean melodrama, which lies at the heart of the greatest of American literature. Here Clumly, the benevolent watchdog, and Taggert Hodge, the Babylonian anarchist, confront one another in a series of dialogues representing the contradictory impulses of western and, in particular, American culture. The dialogue, in fact, becomes Gardner's basic narrative structure, his basic aesthetic form, in the book. The Babylonian holiness of matter confronts the Judeo-Christian holiness of spirit. The Babylonian love of substance opposes the Judeo-Christian "idle speculation" about abstract relationships between soul and flesh (p. 413). An impersonal universe confronts that "grand American responsibility" for right and wrong (p. 323). Clumly finally realizes that "'we must all be vigilant against growing indifferent to people less fortunate. . . . We have to stay awake, as best we can, and be ready to obey the laws as best as we're able to see them. That's it. That's the whole thing'" (pp. 670, 672). No winners or losers but a constant juggling of contraries, a balance of irreconcilable positions, a continued vigilance in the unrelenting encounter between the "radical disunites" of American culture. The Manichaean interpenetration of each becomes the only certainty, although the pastoral vantage point points the way toward armed reconciliation. . . .

What Henry James referred to as American literature's "rich passion for extremes" can be found in Gardner's fiction. Gardner's hope for human communion and love, however fragmentary and diminished, remains undaunted. He is clearly reworking the American fable for our own troubled contemporary times and not merely delighting in structuralist and "post-modernist" techniques for their own artificer's delight. Like Hawthorne, Melville, and Faulkner before him, he seems intent on dispelling anew the notion of a special American innocence, yet at the same time recognizing the pull and enchantment of the pastoral impulses implicit in that American myth. He's aware of the precariousness in that farther darkness and uses his pastoralism as a vantage point from which to observe and re-create the American heart's unrelenting conflict with itself.

Samuel Coale. In *John Gardner: Critical Perspectives*, ed. Robert A. Morace and Kathryn Van Spanckeren (Southern Illinois Univ. Pr., 1982), pp. 20, 23, 26–27

In recent years, Gardner has been dogged by charges of plagiarism—he was accused of twigging his popularized biographical book *The Life and Times of Chaucer* (1977) with unattributed borrowings from more-serious Chaucerian scholars—and in a foreword to this new book, he conscientiously reels off his sources and influences, perhaps hoping to fend off further charges. He needn't have fussed. The novel *is* patchy and derivative, but that's the least of its worries. . . .

His new novel, I'm afraid, is a whopping piece of academic bull slinging. With *Mickelsson's Ghosts*, John Gardner hasn't so much composed a novel as he has used his mind as a vacuum cleaner to suck up a lot of serious reading and then dump the scruffy contents on the reader's carpet. Gleanings from Nietzsche and Luther and Wittgenstein, ruminations on the significance of Dadaism, trendy little velleities about nuclear strife. . . , deep-think musings on the sovereignty of music, morbid broodings on the lingering shadows of Nazism—time and time again Gardner empties his mind, burying the reader in foothills of lint. . . . What is *Mickelsson's Ghosts* about? Name it: love, guilt, history, family ties, entropy and doom, God's enigmatic silence—the whole shebang. But magisterial themes call for a magisterial style, and the writing in *Mickelsson's Ghosts* is all slap and dribble, a trickling spill of irrelevancies. . . .

Mickelsson's Ghosts . . . is . . . one of those big, noisy books that tries to be about everything and, because of its incoherence, ends up being about nothing. Nabokov describing Pnin's tongue at play among his craggy teeth gives one more to live for than does John Gardner prowling through the mists of history, trying to slip the handcuffs on Heidegger. . . .

Literary critics aren't the only ones thrown from the sled by highbrow slumming; trying to play philosopher in this new novel sends John Gardner for an inglorious spill. As *Grendel* proved, Gardner is at home with myth and legend—he can make you feel the heat of a beastie's breath, the crack of wood on stone. But as a thinker he's hopeless. *Mickelsson's Ghosts* simply won't do.

James Wolcott. *Esquire*. June, 1982, p. 134

BIBLIOGRAPHY
The Resurrection, 1966 (n); *The Wreckage of Agathon*, 1970 (n); *Grendel*, 1971 (n); *The Sunlight Dialogues*, 1972 (n); *Jason and Medeia*, 1973 (p); *Nickel Mountain*, 1973 (n); *The King's Indian: Stories and Tales*, 1974; *The Construction of the Wakefield Cycle*, 1974 (c); *The Construction of Christian Poetry in Old English*, 1975 (c); *Dragon, Dragon*, 1975 (juv); *October Light*, 1976 (n); *A Child's Bestiary*, 1977 (p); *In the Suicide Mountains*, 1977 (fairy tales); *The Life and Times of Chaucer*, 1977 (b); *The Poetry of Chaucer*, 1977 (c); *On Moral Fiction*, 1978 (c); *Freddy's Book*, 1980 (n); *The Art of Living*, 1981 (s); *Mickelsson's Ghosts*, 1982 (n); *On Becoming a Novelist*, 1983 (e); *The Art of Fiction: Notes on Craft for Young Writers*, 1984 (c); (with John R. Maier and Richard A. Henshaw) *Gilgamesh*, 1984 (tr); *Stillness and Shadows*, ed. Nicholas Delbanco, 1986; *On Writers and Writing*, 1994 (c)

GARLAND, Hamlin (1860–1940)

In Hamlin Garland we meet an earnest man—one who believes in his own work so thoroughly that he cannot fail to impress others. His characters are real men and women. He has lived with them, toiled with them, suffered and resented wrong with them. It would be impossible for him to write anything else than those dreary, hopeless stories of life upon Western ranches.

Edwin Markham, 1893 in mss. quoted in *American Literature*. May, 1945. p. 153

Mr. Garland's books seem to me as indigenous in the true sense as any our country has produced. They are western American, it is true, but America is mostly western now. . . . I like being in the company of men who believe so cordially in man's perfectibility; who believe that wrongs can really be righted, and that even in our depraved conditions, which imply selfishness as the greatest personal good, teach that generosity and honesty and duty are wiser and better things. I like stirring adventure without bloodshed, as I find it so often in his pages; I like love which is sweet and pure, chivalry which is in its senses, honor for women which recognizes that while all women ultimately are good and beautiful some women are better and beautifuller than others.

William Dean Howells. *North American Review*. Oct., 1912. p. 526

American criticism, which always mistakes a poignant document for esthetic form and organization, greeted these moral volumes as works of art, and so Garland found himself an accepted artist. No more grotesque miscasting of a diligent and worthy man is recorded in profane history. He had no more feeling for the intrinsic dignity of beauty, no more comprehension of it as a thing in itself, than a policeman. He was a moralist endeavoring ineptly to translate his messianic passion into esthetic terms, and always failing. *A Son of the Middle Border*, undoubtedly the best of all his books, projects his failure brilliantly. It is, in substance, a document of considerable value—a naïve and often illuminating contribution to the history of American peasantry. It is, in form, a thoroughly third-rate piece of writing—amateurish, flat, banal, repellent. Garland got facts into it; he got a sort of evangelical passion. But he couldn't get any charm. He couldn't get any beauty.

H.L. Mencken *Prejudices: First Series* (Knopf). 1919. pp. 134–5

Mr. Garland told his early stories in the strong, level, ominous language of a man who had observed much but chose to write little. Not his words, but the overtones vibrating through them cry out that the earth and the fruits of the earth belong to all men and yet a few of them have turned tiger or dog or jackal and snatched what is precious for themselves while their fellows starve and freeze. Insoluble as are the dilemmas he propounded and tense and unrelieved as his accusations were, he stood in his methods nearer, say, to the humane Millet than to the angry Zola.

Carl Van Doren. *The Nation*. Nov. 23, 1921. p. 596

To us of the Middle Border the Hamlin Garland books are epic. Their unashamed provincialism is their glory. Here is the perfection of the willingly provincial—not on the defensive, not in any challenge, never by a breath apologetic. But completely articulate. . . . Not only to one who knows the land and the people, but to anyone who finds inestimably worth while an honest record of any section of national life—of world life—the Border books are almost intolerably precious. They are the record of that rarest of creatures, the provincial who goes into the world and makes it his own without seeking to "change front"—and then tells the whole progress with power.

Zona Gale. *The Yale Review*. July, 1922. p. 852

Hamlin Garland has been called a realist; he might with better reason be called a romanticist. Like lads romantic, he paused, tired to the bone from plowing, to read of dukes and duchesses and of people with charmed lives. . . .Although he pictures his boyhood as hard, still the book probably considered his masterpiece, *A Son of the Middle Border*, tells of a bright world vanished, a landscape so beautiful that it hurt him to have some parts of it revealed to aliens. At every step, in his description of the terrible toil of his people, the beauty of the natural scene remains.

Ruth M. Raw. *Sewanee Review*. April, 1928. p. 202

What, one wonders, would have happened if he had kept his loyalty to the humble, hapless farmers of (his) early stories? What if he had

extended that loyalty so that it embraced urban as well as rural laborers? He might have avoided the whole period of unhappy experimentation in romanticism, and he might have ended, not as a complacent and garrulous chronicler of past glories, but as the great novelist he once gave promise of becoming.

Granville Hicks. *The Nation*. Oct. 21, 1931. p. 436

Garland's "middle border" had been little treated in literature before, as deliberately chosen subject matter. Here it appeared, simple, humble—oh, so humble!—but with a certain candor, a direct view of life, that was to be its hallmark, and a new note in American culture. The country boy born in Wisconsin, who had declaimed the standard pieces of eloquence in a two-by-four academy in Iowa, who had seen what the pioneer was up against on the burning plains of Dakota, and who in good time had the chance to orient himself amidst the world's store of knowledge in Boston, swore to tell what he knew, without dressing or palliation. Young Garland in the first fresh tide of self-consciousness is almost the very type of intellectual young America, so eager, so serious, so full of his new truth.

Ferner Nuhn. *The Wind Blew from the East* (Harper). 1942. p. 80

The movement, nurtured by Howells, found its major spokesman in Hamlin Garland. . . . When he came to Boston and found the example and personal encouragement of Howells, he wrote his only substantial work of fiction: *Main-Travelled Roads*, the book that almost singlehandedly exploded the myth of the West as the Garden of America, the happy lair of noble primitives surrounded by the soft beneficence of a friendly nature. It was a work, Howells saw immediately, which expressed the sad spirit of the rural Northwest from the experiences of one who had been part of what he saw. Following Howells' precepts, Garland wrote out of his own experience and about the region that he knew best, and for the particular brand of realism which dealt explicitly with the provincial environment out of which an author came, he coined the word "veritism."

Everett Carter. *Howells and the Age of Realism* (Lippincott). 1954. pp. 120–1

BIBLIOGRAPHY

Under the Wheel, 1890 (d); *Main-Travelled Roads*, 1891 (s); *Jason Edwards*, 1892 (n); *A Little Norsk*, 1892 (n); *A Member of the Third House*, 1892 (n); *A Spoil of Office*, 1892 (n); *Prairie Folks*, 1893 (s); *Prairie Songs*, 1893 (p); *Crumbling Idols*, 1894 (e); *Rose of Dutcher's Coolly*, 1895 (n); *Wayside Courtships*, 1897 (s); *The Spirit of Sweet-water*, 1898 (n); (revised edition), *Witch's Gold*, 1906); *Ulysses S. Grant*, 1898 (b); *The Trail of the Goldseekers*, 1899 (t); *Boy Life on the Prairie*, 1899 (n); *The Eagle's Heart*, 1900 (n); *Her Mountain Lover*, 1901 (n); *The Captain of the Gray-Horse Troop*, 1902 (n); *Hesper*, 1903 (n); *The Light of the Star*, 1904 (n); *The Tyranny of the Dark*, 1905 (n); *The Long Trail*, 1907 (n); *Money Magic*, 1907 (n) (published as *Mart Haney's Mate*, 1922); *The Shadow World*, 1908 (e); *The Moccasin Ranch*, 1909 (n); *Cavanagh, Forest Ranger*, 1910 (n); *Other Main-Travelled Roads*,

1910 (s); *Victor Ollnee's Discipline*, 1911 (n); *The Forester's Daughter*, 1914 (n); *They of the High Trails*, 1916 (s); *A Son of the Middle Border*, 1917 (a); *A Daughter of the Middle Border*, 1921 (a); *The Book of the American Indian*, 1923 (s); *Trailmakers of the Middle Border*, 1926 (a); *The Westward March of American Settlement*, 1927 (e); *Back-Trailers from the Middle Border*, 1928 (a); *Prairie Song and Western Story* (selections), 1928; *Roadside Meetings*, 1930 (r); *Companions on the Trail*, 1931 (r); *My Friendly Contemporaries*, 1932 (r); *Afternoon Neighbors*, 1934 (r); *Joys of the Trail*, 1935 (e); *Iowa, O Iowa!* 1935 (p); *Forty years of Psychic Research*, 1936 (m); *The Mystery of the Buried Crosses*, 1939 (e)

GARRIGUE, Jean (1914–1972)

Miss Garrigue's first book of poems is notable for two qualities: an acute introspective sensibility, at its best in such delicate probings of mood and motive as "Letter for Vadya," and an unusual accuracy of physical observation, especially when she is dealing with animals. The verse is relentlessly honest, stripped of tricks—too stripped, perhaps—, alive at every point. . . . Unhappily . . . the greater part of the poems, for all their vitality, are marred by a sloppiness that seems to be the result less of obtuseness than of impatience. There is *brio* enough here, and to spare; but there is a tendency to sag, to go unkempt.

Dudley Fitts. *Saturday Review*. June 19, 1948. p. 26

Her poetry is at once lush and cryptic, extravagant and concise. It is elaborate with color and imagery, rich with alliteration and a frequent Elizabethan elegance. . . . There are occasional overtones of Hopkins and Dylan Thomas in her work, but she is undeniably original and individual as an artist and a craftsman in complete command of her medium. . . . The poetic intensity, the wealth of light and color, and the real distinction of Miss Garrigue's work cannot fail to impress the perceptive and careful reader.

Sara Henderson Hay. *Saturday Review*. Jan. 16, 1954. pp. 19–20

The world of *The Monument Rose* is romantic in its richness and strangeness and curious elaboration of detail. . . . Most of all, though, and for all the elegance in particular words, the character of this poetry is just where it belongs, in the play between rhythms and syntax, the wave-motion so to say, which makes the identity of passage after passage and makes all one and most fine. This thing, the weaving and stitching, is the most neglected part of poetry at present, but attention to it is a mark of mastery, and the gift for it, the melodiousness which is, as Coleridge claimed, the final and distinguishing sign of a poet, is something Miss Garrigue wonderfully has.

Howard Nemerov. *Sewanee Review*. Spring, 1954. p. 317

Leaving aside the poems about Colette, cats, country gardens, etc., her work contains a core of intensely and I should say fully humane poems, which are increasing in proportion to the whole. If they never rise to anything that can be called a pitch, they nevertheless preserve the attractive quietness of steady intellectual warmth. At the same time there can be no doubt that she has a splendid lyrical gift and uses rhyme and meter elegantly. This is a less rare attainment than her others; some of her poems could be transposed to volumes she never wrote and no one would know the difference; but in the best poems her softly modulated rhymes and assonances together with unexpected variations in the length and pace of her lines produce what she (elegantly) calls "a little native elegance": the effect is right and original.

Hayden Carruth. *Hudson Review*. Spring, 1965. p. 134

Miss Garrigue is perhaps more skilled than any other poet writing today with the power to dramatize emotional thresholds between jeopardy and renewal. She has a genius for returning to life's viable starting points following defeats, disappointments, hovering over the twin craters of frustrated love and failed art, owning up to the bleakest shortcomings in the self. In poem after poem, her subject is the failure of events in daily life ever to measure up to her spirit's esthetic craving for perfectability. . . . She relentlessly subjects her keenest life-experiences to the refining "restless eye" of her dream-life. It is because she is able to enjoy all living beauties so much, strictly for themselves, that one is assured of the tragic heroism of her deprivations, of the demands her theology imposes on her responsive being. Her triumph is one of restraint, a succession of inured resistances to all pleasures easy of access, delaying and forestalling her natural gift for spiritual uplift until she has reached the supreme moment in which we are able to "think all things are full of gods." She will settle for nothing short of that arrival, and if she has had to sacrifice the more fashionable virtues of poetry in our time—expressiveness and immediacy—to evolve a middle range, a plateau, of vision (halfway between the language of feelings particularized and the language of elusive dream-states), we can only be as grateful for the qualities her art withholds as for those it affords, for there are rewards to be secured in reading her best poems of a kind that can be found in no other body of work.

Laurence Lieberman. *Poetry*. May, 1968. pp. 121–2

The sumptuary must convince the skeptical reader that so much strenuous emotion is warranted and not just self-indulgence. The overingenious design of Miss Garrigue's poems cannot support so much emotion.

When she restrains her impulse to shock, however, when her self-consciousness is in abeyance, she writes finely and movingly. My favorite poems are "This Swallow's Empire," "A Fable of Berries," most of "Pays Perdu," "Address to the Migrations," with its controlled oratory, "Of a Provincial City," and "Nth Invitation." Miss Garrigue has a gift for song, and many of her best pieces are love ballads which either *Christabel*-like blend romance with black irony, or in the manner of songs in Jacobean plays express a macabre love-wit ("The Strike of the Night" and "Gravepiece"). Beginning with *Country without Maps*, she achieves a comely lyrical calm; the shorter lines provide a welcome enlivening of the rhythm.

Herbert Leibowitz. *Hudson Review*. Autumn, 1968. p. 560

It emerges gradually that Miss Garrigue has taken up her rich, mannered style with her eyes open. There are prose stanzas in this book [*Studies for an Actress*] in which that style is dropped, and they are good. But they do not contain those lines of poetry which appear in her other verse. Her style, then, is the only way in which she can realize her potential for certain thoughts; thoughts which cannot form in the mind unless the emotional conditions are propitious to them and the clock is turned back. They cannot form in this mind and be recognized as poetry unless they resemble what has already been poetry. For she has no vision of a lyric poetry which is new in kind. . . .

In her last book she has made an effort to bring both sensibility and manner up to date; possibly she had at last woken up to the fact that her traditional poetic abilities were strangling her. The mixture is of old and new. But she begins to know herself well enough to hear her own voice.

> Rosemary Tonks. *New York Review of Books*. Oct. 4, 1973. p. 10

Once in a while [in *Studies for an Actress*] there are echoes, strains of the old magic, of the enchantment her poems can convey when she mingles dream and reality, magic and fact. "Pays Perdu" from *Country without Maps* may sum up and distill that essence more perfectly than any other poem of hers. In this volume [*Studies for an Actress*] though I find a diffuseness and uncertainty that may not have been a matter of "failing powers" but rather a function of a new start, an engagement with new material. To our loss Jean Garrigue did not live to finish what she began.

> Louis Coxe. *New Republic*. Oct. 6, 1973. p. 28

BIBLIOGRAPHY
(with others) *Five Young Poets*, 1944; *The Ego and the Centaur*, 1947 (p); *The Monument Rose*, 1953 (p); *A Water Walk by the Villa D'Este*, 1959 (p); *Country without Maps*, 1964 (p); *New and Selected Poems*, 1968; *Chartres and Prose Poems*, 1971 (e, p); *Studies for an Actress, and Other Poems*, 1973; *Selected Poems*, 1992

GASS, William H. (1924–)

The world with which Mr. Gass works [in *Omensetter's Luck*] has long been exhausted, you would think, not only by Sinclair Lewis but by the likes of Sherwood Anderson and Edgar Lee Masters. Certainly all the hip little novelists nowadays have abandoned it for the chic regions of drug addiction and alcohol trauma, jet-set sodomy and the dropout's novel of ideas. Mr. Gass, though he leads us into many a terrifying vision, does not resort to a single routine apocalypse. And yet while the costumes of the book may be historical, its impact is compellingly modern. . . .

Mr. Gass's prose is equal to his design. Among novels I've read in recent years, only Norman Mailer's *An American Dream* has been able to pound such wild music out of pain. Gass, like Mailer, finds the very melody of dread. But whereas Mailer uses the current

counters of urban despair, Gass reaches back to the language of the Bible, of Cotton Mather and the Farmer's Almanac.

> Frederic Morton. *New York Times Book Section*. April 17, 1966. pp. 4, 53

Gass's first novel [*Omensetter's Luck*] . . . received remarkable critical acclaim from all shades of the critical spectrum, and Gass immediately became one of the important writers of his generation. This collection [*In the Heart of the Heart of the Country*]. . .serves to focus the distinctive qualities of his sensibility and style. . . .Gass is "old-fashioned" in his insistence that language is an immediate extension of human feeling and cognition. But what makes him modern is how much he knows—like John Barth, Thomas Pynchon and Walker Percy he is one of the philosopher-novelists who bring a new intellectual power to the basically transcendental American sensibility. It is writing like this that will achieve, if it is at all possible, a saving continuity with tradition as it attempts to save human feeling and individuality for art.

> Jack Kroll. *Newsweek*. April 1, 1968. p. 92B

[Gass] is not much interested in the kind of mirror before which preens that dandy Nabokov whose novels, Gass says, are used "to hold the mirror up to Nabokov." Nor is his interest that blasted cliché which he staunchly rejects, old friend though it may be, of the novel as a mirror to the world. . . .

Gass's own looking glass is like Alice's, not a plane off which images bounce but a medium through which one passes lightly and easily from one realm to another, between the world of God's creation and the world of, say, Henry James's, between philosophy and art, criticism and fiction, phenomena and words. What interests Gass most of all is the relationship between these realms, the boundary (he knows it is there) that one has crossed, and the slightly bumpy sensation one feels at the precise moment of passing through.

> Beverly Gross. *The Nation*. March 22, 1971. p. 376

[In *Fiction and the Figures of Life*] the fictionist, trained as a philosopher, examines the art of fiction, its tools, and its relation to philosophy with thoroughness, speaking always to the point until the consistency of the essays becomes the flaw in the collection.

Though the essays are written with unfailing grace, the reader of Mr. Gass's fiction will find them redundant, for the subject of the fiction is often fiction. In his essay, "The Concept in Fiction," Gass is erudite and analytical about the names of characters. In *Omensetter's Luck* he is convincing. . . .

In the essays he deals brilliantly with a Platonic vision of language and reality, calling for a fiction in which characters, "freed from existence, can shine in essence, and purely Be." But the difference between the stories spilled like all-too-digested dinners from the mouths of old women and the fiction that can "shine in essence, and purely Be" is *demonstrated* in Gass's fiction.

> Earl Shorris. *Harper's Magazine*. May, 1972. pp. 98–9

The Midwest . . . in William H. Gass's story "In the Heart of the Heart of the Country" . . . becomes a metaphor for loneliness, for a sense of the self as stranded in a symbolic geography, almost before the writer has done anything to make this happen. Lives are "vacant and barren and loveless," Gass writes, "here in the heart of the country." "Who cares," he asks later, "to live in any season but his own?"

I suspect that it is because this last question is so central in American writing, and so perfectly rhetorical, not expecting an answer, that the Midwest, with its physical spread and relative emptiness, slips so easily into allegory, has a hard time sustaining itself as a real place in fiction. There is no mention of the Midwest in Gass's *Willie Masters' Lonesome Wife*, but the location is recognizably that of Gass's earlier story: the heart of the heart of the country, the lonely heart of a person looking for love, a lonely mind reaching out for us, then shrinking back, complaining of its isolation even as it wriggles further into solipsism. . . .

Behind the fussiness of much of his book there is a real urgency, a powerful vision of the loneliness inherent in writing (you write because you can't speak, for whatever reason) and of writing as a useful and articulate image for loneliness of other kinds.

> Michael Wood. *New York Review of Books*. Dec. 14, 1972. p. 12

In *The Pleasure of the Text*, Roland Barthes sexualizes the pleasure of reading contemporary fiction and calls for "writing aloud". . . . William Gass' *On Being Blue* is the writer's companion to Barthes' reader's guide, an erotics of writing that defines the productive relation of lay and lie for the novelist. Gass both argues and displays "the use of language, like a lover . . . not the language of love, but the love of language, not matter, but meaning, not what the tongue touches, but what it forms, not lips and nipples, but nouns and verbs." Throughout *On Being Blue* is the kind of "writing aloud" we get from no other American novelist or critic. . . .

At once metaphor and metaphoric, *On Being Blue* is an elegant extension of Gass' plea for the medium of fiction articulated in the essays of *Fiction and the Figures of Life* and in the fictional essay *Willie Masters' Lonesome Wife*. He asks the writer to "give up the blue things of this world in favor of the words which say them" because sex—and most other charged subjects—lacks a sufficient vocabulary, disrupts esthetic form, and turns language into a transparency on a world we only think we know. Blue books come to signify every kind of fiction that makes its reader a voyeur peering through the lens of language, never noting it no matter what its color, to see the supposed subject—politics, city life, the perils of being female, whatever. . . . *On Being Blue* [is] a book no person who loves writing and the sound writing makes should be without.

> Thomas LeClair. *New Republic*. Oct. 9, 1976, p. 38

Mr. Gass is hardly a structuralist philosopher, but he has written works of fiction—*Omensetter's Luck* and *In the Heart of the Heart of the Country* are his best-known works—that give heart to the structuralist enterprise, and his essays may be said to promote the attack on realist aesthetics. . . . [The essays in] *Fiction and the Figures of Life* (1972) . . . constitute the most vigorous anti-realist literary "programme" we have had in our time. His new collection of essays, *The World within the Word*, not as dedicated to system-building as the first, but no less teasing and brilliant, sustains but

does not substantially develop his theory. When the earlier book first appeared, a reviewer for the *New York Times* called it "a defense of 'poesy' in a time of need." The time is always needy, of course, and it is more than "poesy" that Gass defends, but the reviewer was not mistaken to state that Gass "calls our attention to art." To do so, need we say, is to remind us as well of all the things that art is not, and ought never to be asked to be. Gass calls our attention to art not by instructing us in the decipherment of signs or in the chastening of sentiment but by underlining all of the things art will not do, and celebrating the very special things it has to do.

Gass's books are wonderful books because they raise all of the important aesthetic issues in the starkest and most inventive way. The writing is informed by a moral passion and a love of beautiful things that are never compromised by the author's compulsive addiction to aestheticizing formulations. We all know what Gass is writing against, including the tiresome use of novels for purposes of unitary moral uplift and penetrating "word-view." What he detests is the goody sweepstakes, in which works of art are judged not by their formal complexity or nuances of verbal texture but by their ability to satisfy easy moral imperatives. Gass has had some hand in discrediting the kind of righteous moralism that so corrupts ordinary apprehension of the literary arts. That is good. But the essays in his two collections have also served to confuse some readers about the art of reading. In so far as the essays suggest that realism is necessarily a debased aesthetic, they encourage a view of reading as a specialized activity to which we bring special passions—like the passion for form—and from which we rigorously exclude others. That is not, it seems to me, an entirely useful way to record what really goes on when we read a book. Strange to say, I think William Gass knows better than the rest of us what goes on; and one day he may even decide to tell us.

> Robert Boyers. *TLS: The Times Literary Supplement*. Nov. 3, 1978, pp. 1274–75

William Gass is a critic and a professor of philosophy at Washington University in St. Louis and the author of three volumes of fiction, each of which is intelligent and well-crafted but somehow less than memorable. For three decades, he has been laboring over a vast novel about the frustrations of private life in an age of historical enormities. Here is the finished product. Some may seize on it as a postmodern masterpiece, but it is a bloated monster of a book. (At 400,000 words, it is almost one-third longer than Joyce's *Ulysses*.) The bloat is a consequence of sheer adipose verbosity and an unremitting condition of moral and intellectual flatulence. Lest this last description seem gratuitously mean, let me quickly note that Gass's narrator is himself obsessed with farting; history writing, politics, and sex are all repeatedly reduced to a bursting bubble of malodorous gas. At one point Gass's text is actually embellished with a diagram of four farts, labeled *F* to *T*.

Gass's real achievement is to have produced a complete compendium of the vices of postmodern writing. His narrator, William Kohler, is a professor of history at a midwestern university, who records in a secret diary his ruminations about his life, about his colleagues and (very intermittently) about the Nazi genocide, after having completed a major study called *Guilt and Innocence in Hitler's Germany*. The time of writing is the 1960s, when Kohler is in his fifties. . . .

(empty)

From its very beginnings the novel adopts a variety of devices to disrupt the realist tradition. Gass's narrator is an inscriber of what John Barth once designated "the literature of exhaustion." Professorial to the marrow, he inhabits a library, buckles under the weight of the innumerable volumes that he carries in his head. . . . The line between reality and textuality blurs, and everything turns into text. . . .

The Tunnel is equally postmodern in its transgression of the limits of structure. Where modernist novels that break with traditional linear narration . . . replace it with an elaborate structure of recurring motifs and other kinds of formal symmetries and antitheses, the procedure in *The Tunnel* is loose, unimpeded, free-associative flow. The principle of artful selection is renounced. . . .

The mingling of styles, the conjoining of high and low, which critics such as Bakhtin and Auerbach saw as the fulfillment of the modern novel, is pushed here to an extreme and banal limit.

Robert Alter. *New Republic.* March 27, 1995, pp. 29–30

BIBLIOGRAPHY
Omensetter's Luck, 1966 (n); *In the Heart of the Heart of the Country*, 1968 (s); *Fiction and the Figures of Life*, 1971 (c); *Willie Masters' Lonesome Wife*, 1972 (n); *On Being Blue*, 1976 (c); *The World within the Word*, 1978 (c); *Habitations of the Word*, 1985 (e); *The Tunnel*, 1995 (n); *Finding a Form*, 1996 (c); *Cartesian Sonata and Other Novellas*, 1998

GATES, Henry Louis, Jr. (1950–)

Henry Louis Gates, Jr., is a pivotal figure in the generational shift that has been taking place in African American criticism. A former member of the Yale English faculty, currently a distinguished professor at Cornell, and an active member of the MLA [Modern Language Association], Gates has had an enormous influence on literary studies in the United States. Through his scholarship and sponsorship of various conferences and research projects, he is responsible for drawing attention to the richness and diversity of black writing here and abroad and for encouraging critics to draw on recent developments in critical theory as a foundation for examining African American expressive culture. . . .

Like the generation of black artists and critics who preceded him, Gates saw American and European written discourse as historically linked to an oppressive, ethnocentric political order bent on suppressing the cultural heritage of those it subjugates. It was imperative, for this reason, for black critics to derive interpretative practices from the aesthetic principles unique to their own traditions.

The Signifying Monkey is Gates's most important and sustained piece of scholarship to date. Essentially a series of essays linked together through a common theory of the vernacular, it is in effect a major effort at racial retrieval, an attempt to reclaim the Afrocentric roots of African American literature. What makes the work unique is that it does not shy away from establishing a heritage common to black people in the U.S., the Caribbean, South America, and Africa. Moreover, in celebrating the African influence on life in the diaspora, it openly challenges the hegemony of a white Eurocentric

culture that continues to negate, coopt, and absorb black creativity. Gates does not give an historical account of how the West attempts cultural genocide, but he is clear from the outset that he intends to rescue African values from marginalization and degradation and to assert their originality and sovereignty.

In this work, Gates modifies his initial position that there are no determining formal relations between literature and social institutions. Still committed to establishing a theoretical framework for the study of black literature that is text-centered, Gates has been forced to develop a broad cultural approach to accommodate his notion that African American creativity is rooted in the vernacular.

Norman Spencer. *American Book Review.* January-February, 1990, pp. 15, 25

[Kwame Anthony] Appiah's eloquent and extensively researched work [in *In My Father's House: Africa in the Philosophy of Culture*, [1992] makes a formidable statement about the historic inability to frame linguistic resistance to biological racism except in oppositional terms and the consequent reliance on other forms of racial discourse. This discourse of racial solidarity is what limits the positive aspects of Pan-Africanism. But in framing his own argument, Appiah appears to perceive the Afrocentric position (a term he does not use) with a narrow lens. He refers to the rich and varied cultures of precolonial Africa in questioning the existence of a unified African worldview, but it is unclear how this precludes the existence of certain shared values and traditions, especially among coregional cultures. . . . However, in vigorously articulating the complexities and contradictions in the Pan-African movement, Appiah creates a space in which crucial dialogue can continue on "more secure foundations" than that of the reverse discourse of racial essence (176) toward a "reinvigorated Pan-Africanism" based on the continent and the diaspora's "shared contingencies" of histories, geographies, and societies (180).

In his new book, humorously titled *Loose Canons*, well-known African-American literary theorist Henry Louis ("Skip") Gates, Jr., explores the notion and realities of these "shared contingencies," along with the pitfalls of the Pan-African/Afrocentric movement, while responding to the critics of multiculturalism. As the subject moves from the African continent to the diaspora, specifically to the United States, Gates presents a companion text to Appiah's. (Having worked closely together for so long, the two critics have apparently produced a dialogic voice in developing their positions.) Gates directs his analysis to the background of Black Studies, the contentious debate over the literary canon, and finally the relationship of all of these issues to the reality of black people's lives in a postmodern, postslavery society. He writes this book because of his fear that the "mindless celebration of difference for its own sake is no more tenable than the nostalgic return to some monochrome homogeneity." His aim is to "search for a middle way" (xix). . . .

In part 3: "Society" [of his book], Gates returns to an issue underlying the other sections, that "it sometimes seems that blacks are doing better in the college curriculum than they are on the streets" (19). Although he is painfully aware that multicultural studies is not a "panacea" for social problems, Gates also reminds us that tolerance must come with understanding—and of course education. It is in the last essay, "Trading on the Margins," that

Gates unequivocally names his "middle way": he is a cultural pluralist, neither right nor left. Although he is clearly more sympathetic to the cultural left, it is his attack on the left that is most telling. In the binary opposition of literary and cultural center versus margin, the self-appointed "Other" allows the structures to remain intact and those in the margins to remain marginalized— kept in our place. It is, according to Gates, this paradigm—a "colonial" one—that "has started to exhaust its usefulness in describing our own modernity" (189).

Like Appiah, Gates is attempting to set up a new paradigm—in this case, for a multicultural America, no longer based on us–them politics. But, as Gates well knows, the middle ground is not so easy to find.

Gay Wilentz. *College English*. January, 1994, pp. 73–75

The debate about multiculturalism and the literary canon would seem to have been played out by now, rendering old news Henry Louis Gates's collection of essays dating back to 1990 [*Loose Canons*]. But the need for sensible, informed voices like his is increasingly important as we struggle over what we most value in our schools and our national identity. . . .

Gates's most important contribution is to offer a moderate voice that both defends multiculturalism and can think productively about the larger issue of American culture. The key point of debate concerns the American identity. Schlesinger argues passionately for the idea of a unified American culture: "Our task is to combine due appreciation of the splendid diversity of the nation with due emphasis on the great unifying Western ideas of individual freedom, political democracy, and human rights. These are the ideas that define the American nationality—and that today empower people of all continents, races, and creeds." Gates doesn't really disagree but offers a different emphasis. Whereas Schlesinger speaks of needing to appreciate diversity, Gates wishes to highlight it: the only way to transcend divisions "is through education that seeks to comprehend the diversity of human culture. Beyond the hype and the highflown rhetoric is a pretty homely truth: there is no tolerance without respect—and no respect without knowledge."

John Ottenhoff. *Christian Century*. Jan. 19, 1994, p. 53

We read Henry Louis Gates, Jr.'s, memoir because of who he now is: a highly respected scholar and essayist, one of the few preeminent black intellectuals in a culture where, more often than not, the two words together are viewed as a contradiction in terms. But *Colored People* falls short of the criteria for successful memoir. This is both surprising and disappointing, since Gates's achievements over barely four decades as writer, scholar, public intellectual and chairman of Harvard University's Afro-American Studies Program are certainly impressive. I suspect that the story of the forces and influences, adversity, and insight that transformed a poor kid from hardscrabble West Virginia into one of America's leading scholars is inherently fascinating. Unfortunately, that is not the tale we are told in *Colored People*.

Instead, we are given a memoir of Gates's boyhood and early life that seems somehow sanitized. We are left with surface information: that Gates came of age during a period that straddled segregation and desegregation; that he suffered a serious physical disability as an adolescent; that he was an extremely bright and precocious child in a time and place when people didn't know what to do with precocious children, least of all black male precocious children; that for years he competed unsuccessfully with his older brother for his father's affection and attention; that, growing up in a household in which his mother "hated" white folks, many of his early sexual attractions were to white women. . . .

Reading *Colored People*, I sense that Gates has a lot to say but isn't ready to say it, opting instead to charm and amuse. Perhaps memoir is not for him, since it demands a discomfiting degree of personal revelation and introspection. Perhaps the more interesting material can be found in the twenty years since he left West Virginia. The personal, political, and academic journeys, challenges, and machinations that must have attended his near-meteoric rise in the still-segregated academy would make for great reading. I hope that in the future he decides to write that story and tell all. Unfortunately, in *Colored People*, Gates does not tell enough.

Jill Nelson. *The Nation*. June 6, 1994, p. 795

Gates is one of the most gifted and accomplished black academics in American history. He is in many ways an awe-inspiring figure, especially since he has achieved his celebrity by being a literary critic, a somewhat arcane intellectual pursuit. For a man of Gates's stature, then, one must have high standards. And so one is obliged to ask, about *Colored People*, not if it is worth reading (anything that Gates puts on paper is worth reading), but whether it was worth writing. This book makes one worry that Gates's position is foreclosing what he can do as a writer, pressuring him to produce work that seems not as carefully thought-out and crafted as it might be, more preoccupied with the projection of a public image that would please blacks and not alienate whites than with the exploration of the meaning of his consciousness. Gates's talent and intelligence promise a great deal more than this book delivers.

Gerald Early. *New Republic*. July 4, 1994, p. 38

BIBLIOGRAPHY

ed., *Black Literature and Literary Theory*, 1984 (h, c); ed. (with Charles T. Davis), *The Slave's Narrative*, 1985; ed., "*Race*," *Writing, and Difference*, 1986 (e); ed., *The Classic Slave Narratives*, 1987 (anthol); *Figures in Black*, 1987 (h, c); *The Signifying Monkey*, 1988 (c); ed., *Reading Black, Reading Feminist*, 1990 (h, c); ed., *Bearing Witness*, 1991 (b); *The Films of Spike Lee*, 1992 (c); *Loose Canons*, 1992 (c); *The Amistad Chronology of African-American History, 1445–1990*, 1993 (h); ed. (with K.A. Appiah), *Alice Walker: Critical Perspectives*, 1993 (c); ed., *Gloria Naylor: Critical Perspectives*, 1993 (c); ed., *Langston Hughes: Critical Perspectives*, 1993 (c); ed., *Richard Wright: Critical Perspectives*, 1993 (c); ed., *Toni Morrison: Critical Perspectives*, 1993 (c); ed., *Zora Neale Hurston: Critical Perspectives*, 1993 (c); *Colored People*, 1994 (m); *Speaking of Race, Speaking of Sex*, 1994 (e); ed. (with Kwame Anthony Appiah), *Identities*, 1995 (e); (with Cornel West) *The Future of the Race*, 1996 (e); general ed. (with Nellie Y. McKay), *The Norton Anthology of African-American Literature*, 1996; *Thirteen Ways of Looking at a Black Man*, 1997 (e); ed. (with

Kwame Anthony Appiah), *The Dictionary of Global Culture*, 1997 (ref); ed. (with William L. Andrews), *Pioneers of the Black Atlantic: Five Slave Narratives from the Enlightenment, 1772–1815*, 1998; ed. (with Maria Diedrich and Carl Pedersen), *Black Imagination and the Middle Passage*, 1999 (c)

GELBER, Jack (1932–)

For while *The Connection* may not be "art," it is none the less arresting. . . . Though the play's form is unresolved, and some of the writing self-conscious as well as overlong, it is a bit of naturalism not without point and not without talent. . . . *The Connection* creates a distinct sense of authenticity, even in the terrible languor of pace which marks the opening of the proceedings. . . . The result will surely seem unpleasant for spectators eager for either "art" or entertainment, but there is a sort of melancholy in the event, with touches of genuine pathos and even a wretched sort of lyricism. It is as if one had looked for a moment into a corner of our city to breathe the rank air of its unacknowledged dejection. The play reeks of human beings and if we turn completely away from people of any kind we can know little of anything worth knowing.

Harold Clurman. *The Nation*. Aug. 15, 1959. p. 80

. . .Jack Gelber's play, despite obvious literary derivations, soon emerges as highly original and unpredictable. . . . *The Connection* even avoids that over-intellectualization of human behavior which informs the work of Beckett, Ionesco, and Genet. Gelber has managed to assimilate, and sometimes to parody, his borrowed techniques without a trace of literary self-consciousness; and by the use of live jazz . . . as a rhythmic contrast of the dialogue, he has introduced an effective theatrical device all his own. The most striking thing about this work is its Spartan honesty. . . .

Robert Brustein. *New Republic*. Sept. 28, 1959. p. 29

Jack Gelber's *The Connection* . . . skillfully blends jazz with Beckett's theme of waiting. The image of the drug addicts waiting for the arrival of the messenger carrying their drug is a powerful conception. The presence of a jazz quartet improvising onstage lends the play a fascinating element of spontaneity, and the dialogue has a lyricism of pointlessness that equals much of the best writing in the Theatre of the Absurd. But the play is marred by a laborious superstructure of pretense at realism. Author and director appear, and go to great lengths to convince the audience that they are seeing real drug addicts; two film cameramen who are supposed to record the events of the evening are involved in the action, and one is actually seduced into drug-taking. And, finally, the strange, spontaneous, poetic play culminates in a plea for a reform of the drug laws. *The Connection*, brilliant as it is in parts, founders in its uncertainty as to which convention it belongs to— the realist theatre of social reform or the Theatre of the Absurd.

Martin Esslin. *The Theatre of the Absurd* (Doubleday Anchor). 1961. p. 227

It is only when the pose of metaphysician or metaphysical psychologist is assumed, even when the metaphysics are those of nothingness, that the pretense becomes objectionable. The most obvious case of this is Jack Gelber's *The Apple*, played in last season's repertory at the Living Theater.

Gelber had his actors appear to improvise "a life behind the senses," letting them work on the proposition that the spectators— representing people at large—lived mostly on the surface. The actors therefore assailed the spectators (particularly a drunk paranoiac who came up out of the orchestra to assail them) where they were most complacent, and where their complacency most covered up their vileness. A whole bag of tricks was used to show what life was really like. The play succeeded in its task of alienation—but unfortunately to no purpose. For the life behind the senses, at least as Gelber dramatized it, was just as meaningless as it was vile. . . . What was wrong was that he was trying to be political in metaphysical or anti-metaphysical garb.

The Connection wasn't like this. For all its unconventionality it was an honest political drama. It created a mood, a feeling, and despite some sleight-of-hand here and there, as in the excessive use of the jazz, its sincerity was strong enough to make people take it seriously. The irony was that when social protest was really felt and effectively voiced it often transcended itself to become something religious.

L.E. Chabrowe. *Kenyon Review*. Winter, 1963. pp. 146–7

Jack Gelber's rough paean to junkies, *The Connection*, was an early document of hipsterism and it should come as no surprise to find him operating out of the same pad in his first novel, *On Ice*. The title is meant to suggest the cool and precarious existence of Manny Fells, a Village hipster who, on a phony resumé, takes a job as a private eye impersonating a camera salesman in a suburban discount house. As might be expected from this description, Mr. Gelber's theme is "identity" and while his *milieu* is familiar—the post-war world that the Whole Sick Crew of Thomas Pynchon inherited from the whole sick crew of Joseph Heller—he does have some interesting things to say about the difficulty of being your own man these days.

Paul Levine. *Hudson Review*. Autumn, 1964. p. 472

The Connection, in spite of its pretense at documentary technique, makes an almost complete break with the emotional and political objectives of naturalism. In a naturalistic play we accept the illusion created on the stage, and take it for reality: once we assume that the stage is a room with one wall missing, for instance, and that the players do not know they are being watched, we are likely to accept almost anything, as long as it maintains a decent level of verisimilitude. But in *The Connection* we are unsure, since the play won't allow us to make the initial pretense. The person sitting next to a spectator might be an actor—or is he?. . . In *The Connection*, the actors, because they are addicts, cannot maintain the artifice of role-playing; their extra-dramatic needs keep breaking through and, as we have seen, take over the play. Reality keeps rudely displacing the illusionistic performance: it is method-acting with a vengeance.

Louis Kampf. *College English*. Oct., 1966. p. 11

BIBLIOGRAPHY
The Connection, 1959 (d); *The Apple*, 1961 (d); *On Ice*, 1964 (n);
Square in the Eye, 1965 (d) (also titled, *Let's Face It*); *The Cuban
Thing*, 1968 (d); *Sleep*, 1972 (d)

GIBSON, William (1914–)

Gibson's special force is in linking an almost Wordsworthian apprehension of nature to a technique which does combine flow and complexity. He gives an effect of tension rather than of reflectiveness; his sense of a lost paradise is modest. But his feeling for the unity of a natural scene and internal tension seem to come spontaneously in a way that has been rare since the original romantics. . . .

There are defects in the volume, of course—echoes that are occasionally too close, an overenthusiasm now and then for the massing possibilities of the rhythms. But the total effect is of brilliant accomplishment. . . . *Winter Crook* does not establish Gibson for certain as one of the best American poets for the fifties, but it definitely enters him as a possibility.

James Hall. *Poetry*. August, 1948. pp. 278, 281

Mr. Gibson manipulates his complicated story [*The Cobweb*] with admirable skill and a keen, if somewhat hectic, sense of drama. He is a master of dialogue. His characters, remarkably alive, are viewed with clarity and charity; he sees them moving through life with ironical unawareness of the disaffections they often inspire in those nearest them, and at the same time he stirs the reader to pity for them all. . . .

The author's power . . . is such that you will overlook his tendency to go into excessive detail whenever one of his characters enters wardrobe or bathroom. This is the literary paradox in a work that signals the arrival of a brilliant new novelist with the technique and the maturity to command respect at once and anticipation for the future.

Charles Lee. *Saturday Review*. Mar. 13, 1954. p. 19

William Gibson's *Two for the Seesaw* . . . is one of those pleasant plays that obviously belong in the theatre, since they are almost always highly popular. They are the bestsellers of the contemporary stage. No one should cavil at their success. But, I confess with some reluctance, they interest me very little. . . . The play, in short, is a conventional tale without real characters, cemented by jokes and that sense of recognition which is the recognition of clichés and thus supposed by many playgoers to represent a modest realism.

Harold Clurman. *The Nation*. Feb. 1, 1958. p. 107

Although I doubt whether playwright William Gibson would put it so, class distinctions are the hard core of his most adroit and refreshing dramatic duet called *Two for the Seesaw*, a play sustained entirely by the relationship of a Nebraska lawyer called Jerry with a Bronx girl called Gittel. . . . This disparate pair merge their

separate loneliness in an affair, full of tenderness, humor and plain honest earthiness. So fresh and accurate is Mr. Gibson's dialogue, so right his mercurial changes of pace . . . that you almost believe in the affair's reality.

Marya Mannes. *The Reporter*. March 6, 1958. p. 36

Here [in *The Seesaw Log*], at last, a playwright has had the courage and bad manners to chronicle his seventy days of rehearsal and pre-Broadway tryout agony. His log, though necessarily edited, makes no deliberate attempt to be entertaining. It is admirably free of the sort of dramatization one finds in most pre-opening newspaper pieces, or of the color that Lillian Ross put into her brilliant profile of the making of *The Red Badge of Courage*. Not that such articles should avoid being as readable as possible, but to one who has been through such an experience, they never seem to be quite the way it really was.

Lest the reader suspect that *The Seesaw Log* describes a particularly grim case, let it be pointed out immediately that Mr. Gibson had a much happier situation than do most playwrights. . . . Yet despite these unusually favorable circumstances, the playwright found his seventy days as enervating and ungratifying as they are in almost every Broadway show. . . . I don't believe Mr. Gibson *has* complained. He has stated what happened, and what would probably happen if he were to do it all over again. And his statement stands as a penetrating document of our contemporary theatre.

Henry Hewes. *Saturday Review*. March 14, 1959. p. 55

It is something like a stroke of genius then for William Gibson to have thought of prefacing the text of the published play [*Two for the Seesaw*], with a 141-page *Log* describing his experiences in selling, casting, rehearsing and trying it out. For it is one reader's opinion that the *Log* is a more important addition to our theatrical library than the play itself.

Harold Clurman. *New York Times Book Section*. March 15, 1959. p. 5

. . .like the play which preceded it [*Two for the Seesaw*], *The Miracle Worker*—written with the same wit and mounted with equal competence—is essentially a two-character work about the relationship of kindness to love. . . . It is Gibson's penchant for instructing his characters in "mature" behavior which disturbs me most. In common with most playwrights of the modern school, love operates in his plays with all the intensity of an ideology, and the only development his people are permitted is a more accurate apprehension of the proper way to show affection. . . .

I say this with regret because, although his craft is still a little shaky, Gibson possesses substantial literary and dramatic gifts, and an integrity of the highest order. In addition, he brings to his works authentic compassion, wit, bite, and humor, and a lively, literate prose style equalled by few American dramatists. . . .

Robert Brustein. *New Republic*. Nov. 9, 1959. p. 28

Mr. Gibson's book [*The Seesaw Log*] is something more than a book about the theatre. It is also a book about our culture in general.

Mr. Gibson is quite aware of this. In his account of what was entailed in bringing his play *Two for the Seesaw* to the stage, he does not conceive the difficulties he confronted to be merely technical, but also as having to do with the assumptions of the significant part of the population that was to be his audience and with the relation of the writer to these assumptions. For Mr. Gibson the chief cultural interest of his adventure with the theatre presents itself as a personal and moral question. His play, as everyone knows, became a great success and made—is still making—a great deal of money. What Mr. Gibson is concerned to discover is whether in the arduous process of its becoming a success, the play lost some of its truth and the playwright some of his integrity.

Mr. Gibson is an intelligent man and I don't think he misconceives his problem by overrating his play. It is a "little" play, its modesty is one of its virtues. It was written for Broadway and in the hope of its succeeding with Broadway audiences. It challenges none of the vested interests, affronts none of the deep-rooted pieties of this audience. I say this not in order to denigrate the play, which I like, but simply to suggest the level on which Mr. Gibson raises and faces the question of truth and integrity. It is not as if he had written *Ghosts* and had yielded to commercial pressure to change the ending of the play to a happy one. But even a modest comedy about a love affair may be more or less honest, as may any scene in the play, or any speech in a scene.

Lionel Trilling. *Drama Review*. May, 1960. p. 17

BIBLIOGRAPHY

I Lay in Zion, 1947 (d); *Winter Crook*, 1948 (p); *The Cobweb*, 1954 (n); *Two for the Seesaw*, 1958 (d); *The Miracle Worker*, 1959 (d); *The Seesaw Log*, 1959 (m); *Dinny and the Witches*, 1959 (d); *Dinny and the Witches, and The Miracle Worker*, 1960 (d); *A Mass for the Dead*, 1968 (r); *A Cry of Players*, 1968 (d); *American Primitive: The Words of John and Abigail Adams Put into a Sequence for the Theater*, 1972 (d); *The Butterfingers Angel, Mary and Joseph, Herod the Nut and the Slaughter of 12 Hit Carols in a Pear Tree*, 1977 (d); *Golda*, 1978 (d); *Notes on How to Turn a Phoenix into Ashes: The Story of the Stage Production, with the Text, of "Golda,"* 1978 (e, d); *A Season in Heaven; Being the Log of an Expedition after That Legendary Beast, Cosmic Consciousness*, 1978; *Shakespeare's Game*, 1978 (c); *Monday after the Miracle*, 1983 (d); *Goodly Creatures*, 1986 (d); *Handy Dandy: A Comedy But*, 1986 (d)

GINSBERG, Allen (1926–1997)

This poetry is not "rational discourse" such as we find in almost all other American literature of dissidence. Nor is it that flaccid sort of negation, too easy and too glib, that so often reduces the charge in the writing of Patchen and others. . . . It is the fury of the soul-injured lover or child, and its dynamic lies in the way it spews up undigested the elementary need for freedom of sympathy, for generous exploration of thought, for the open response of man to man so long repressed by the smooth machinery of intellectual distortion. . . . Despite his many faults and despite the danger that he will screech himself mute any moment now, is he the real thing?

What we can say, I think, is that he has brought a terrible psychological reality to the surface with enough originality to blast American verse a hair's-breadth forward in the process.

M.L. Rosenthal. *The Nation*. Feb. 23, 1957. p. 162

Among the literary radicals of the West Coast, Allen Ginsberg and his poem "Howl" have acquired a succès d'estime remarkable in both its proportions and its manifestations. The poem so clearly intends to document—and celebrate—several types of modern social and psychological ills that the question of its literary merit seems to me almost irrelevant. . . . Walt Whitman is the poet's chief master. . . . But the virulence of Ginsberg's revolt against modern society comes—if these things really have any literary antecedents—from the verse of the Great Depression: Fearing, Patchen, Richard Wright, et al. . . . It's a very shaggy book, the shaggiest I've ever seen.

Frederick Eckman. *Poetry*. Sept., 1957. pp. 391–3

Ginsberg gets away with it because he is frankly justifying himself (in "Howl"), because his assault on America is a personal cry that rings true, because his hysteria is tempered with humor, and because the dope addicts, perverts, and maniacs he celebrates are not finally glamorized. . . . (But) no new territory is being staked out by these writers—Ginsberg's return to Whitman is a shift in fashion, not the mark of a revolutionary sensibility. . . . The fact is that it takes more than a feeling of "disengagement" from the contemporary world to provide the materials for a genuine avant garde revolt.

Norman Podhoretz. *New Republic*. Sept. 16, 1957. p. 20

In the lines of Ginsberg's *Kaddish* is evoked the passionate and destroyed body of a woman who pursues a world which is not hers and which does not become hers. In the poet's prayer for the dead is the sound of the man wrenched from the past by horror and compassion: in that isolation and clarity is the terror of myth and its sense of the ultimate threats. It is not a poem which could easily be forgotten. Everywhere reflecting Whitman and Lindsay and the width of the American past, the poem moves in its final sections through the heavy bars of the traditional Hebrew prayer. It is a poem of very great power, of very great "mass." It is also a poem of great visual acuity, and often of startling verbal precision, avoiding nothing in its path. It is not, to say again, a poem which could easily be forgotten. . . . But the danger for Ginsberg in the shorter pieces is that there may be nowhere for him to go if he is to rely on declamation, that he might be stuck on too high and too declamatory a note. There need be nothing ephemeral about the lyric poet who responds passionately and in his own way to his own vision, but if the poet begins to ask us to accept a system of opinions and attitudes he must manage the task of rigorous thought.

George Oppen. *Poetry*. Aug., 1962. p. 329

The death of the Jewish mother in Ginsberg's *Kaddish*, and the succession of cultural generations implied in the burden of identity laid by the mother on the son, is unquestionably the most momentous record in English of the problem of the passing of the older sociology and meaning of the Jewish family-centered culture in America. But the mysticism with which Ginsberg faces the problem of the death of Israel is, perhaps, less momentous than the poetry which he makes the vehicle of that problem. . . . We may note that the Jewish symbology becomes available in American poetry just at the point in which the Jewish poet finds it necessary to document the death of the Jewish cultural fact.

The earlier poetry of Ginsberg, that represented primarily by the volume entitled *Howl*, is a great deal more buoyant than the poetry which we are here considering. Between *Howl* and *Kaddish* Ginsberg has lost his humor and gained a kind of horror which even he cannot accommodate to the necessary reticence of the poetic mode. Ginsberg's chief artistic contribution in *Kaddish* is a virtually psychotic candor which effects the mind less like poetry than like some real experience which is so terrible that it cannot be understood. In America, which did not experience the Second World War on its own soil, the Jew may indeed be the proper interpreter of horror.

> Allen Grossman. *Judaism*, Fall, 1962. p. 307

Perhaps the chief accomplishment of his first book, *Howl and Other Poems*, was to give maddened voice to the more depressing statistics of the day—the rise in mental illness, drug addiction, and homosexuality—and to the morally anarchic mood that came in the wake of the war and the cold war, or McCarthyism, and of the Bomb. Now the long poem *Kaddish* lays open the personal experience behind this voice. In accordance with the Hebrew meaning of the title, it is both a hymn of praise to God and an elegiac incantation inspired by the death of the poet's mother. . . . Mr. Ginsberg is merciless in presenting what would normally be the secret wounds of family life.

Still, it is a tender, affectionate poem. The form, even the syntax, is improvisational—piled-up notes on Naomi's habits and sayings and on particular incidents, interwoven with echoes of Hebrew prayer and with the poet's own insights, prophesying, dreaming, and praise of life in the face of the horror.

> M.L. Rosenthal. *The Reporter*. Jan. 3, 1963. pp. 46–7

The lines don't shape, predict, and limit whole-poem forms. Most of the poems might have been shorter or longer. The reason is that external reality (time, place, event) dictates Ginsberg's means, so the means are outside the poem and, though unrecoverable, are more complete there. Certain things happened in a certain city at a certain time: a journal, or cata-travelog of accidentals. Opposite (for clarification) is the internal vision, selecting, transfiguring, making new and whole; the poet servant to the poem that exists apart in terms of its own reality. The unity in Ginsberg's work is Ginsberg in search of unity, so that the poems are fragments of the search. The greater poem is possible when the poem is the sought unity, the poet providing the fragments to the whole from his fragmentary experience.

The poems in this volume [*Reality Sandwiches*] date from 1953 to 1960, poems both before and after *Howl*. They mostly lack the desperately earnest cry for truth and the sung-tension accuracy of Ginsberg at his best.

> A. R. Ammons. *Poetry*. June, 1964. pp. 186–7

Allen Ginsberg is a notoriety, a celebrity; to many readers and nonreaders of poetry he has the capacity for releasing odd energetic responses of hatred and love or amused affection or indignant moralizing. There are even people who are roused to very flat indifference by the friendly near-sighted shambling bearded figure who has some of the qualities of such comic stars as Buster Keaton or Charlie Chaplin. And some of their seriousness.

His latest book *Planet News* grants another revelation of his sensibility. The usual characteristics of his work are there, the rhapsodic lines, the odd collocations of images and thoughts and processes, the occasional rant, the extraordinary tenderness. His poetry resembles the Picasso sculpture melted together of children's toys, or the sculpture of drift-wood and old tires and metal barrels and tin cans shaped by enterprising imaginative young people along the polluted shores of San Francisco Bay. You can make credible Viking warriors from such materials. Ginsberg's poetry works in parallel processes; it is junk poetry, not in the drug sense of junk but in its building blocks. It joins together the waste and loss that have come to characterize the current world, Cuba, Czechoslovakia, the Orient, the United States, Peru. Out of such debris as is offered he makes what poetry he can.

> Thomas Parkinson. *Concerning Poetry*. Spring, 1969. p. 21

What is engaging about *Planet News* is the personality of Allen Ginsberg. This King of May and guru presides over a gentle saturnalia. He is believably "tranquil in his hairy body," his bawdry devotional and his homosexuality as casual and empathic as Whitman's. The poems have a friendly clutter and humor. For those who expect the howls (and howlers) of a Beat publicist for buggery and expanded consciousness, *Planet News* will prove surprising in its chaste and controlled lyricism. Ginsberg is more Ganymede than Jove. From a poet as erotically gregarious and "prophetic" as Ginsberg, one is prepared for a certain amount of the "Gasbag," and his long shaggy prose lines droop at times from all the cosmic weight they must bear. Still, in such poems as "Galilee Shore," "Describe: The Rain on Dasaswamedh," most of "Wichita Vortex Sutra," "City Midnight Junk Strains" (a fine elegy for Frank O'Hara), and in particular, "Wales Visitation," he may not "make Mantra of the American language," but he certainly makes "old human poesy."

> Herbert Leibowitz. *Hudson Review*. Autumn, 1969. p. 501

Allen Ginsberg . . . is the figure who preeminently represents the link between right now and back then; and in a single remarkable poem called, of course, "America," becomes the living memory of our dying memory of the mythological thirties. He included the poem in his first slim collection, *Howl*, a little book which raised a lot of hell, out of which there emerged finally a new life-style and a new metapolitics that has remained at the center of the cultural scene ever since.

> Leslie Fiedler. *The Collected Essays*, vol. 2 (Stein and Day). 1971. p. 253

Ginsberg is one of the most traditionalist poets now living. His work is an almost perfect fulfillment of the long, Whitman,

Populist, social revolutionary tradition in American poetry. In addition he is a latter-day *nabi*, one of those Hebrew prophets who came down out of the hills and cried ''Woe! Woe! to the bloody city of Jerusalem!'' in the streets. *Howl* resembles as much as anything the denunciatory poems of Jeremiah and Hosea. After Ginsberg, the fundamental American tradition, which was also the most international and the least provincial, was no longer on the defensive but moved over to the attack, and soon, as far as youthful audiences were concerned, the literary Establishment simply ceased to exist. It's not that Ginsberg is the greatest poet of the generation of the Fifties, although he is a very good one, it's that he had the most charismatic personality. The only poet in my time to compare with him in effect on audiences was Dylan Thomas, and Dylan Thomas was essentially a performer, whereas Ginsberg meant something of the greatest importance and so his effects have endured and permeated the whole society, and Thomas's have not.

Ginsberg is the only one of his immediate associates who outgrew the nihilistic alienation of the Beat Generation and moved on to the positive counter culture which developed in the Sixties. He was the spokesman of the lost youth of 1955 and he remained a spokesman of the youth who were struggling to found an alternative society in 1970. His influence is enormous, as great in India or Sweden or underground behind the Iron Curtain as it is in America.

> Kenneth Rexroth. *American Poetry in the Twentieth Century* (Herder and Herder). 1971. pp. 170–1

Should it not be declared that with the publication of [Ginsberg's] *Howl* (1956) and [Lowell's] *Life Studies* (1959) our poetry was indubitably changed and indispensably enriched? Before that, it now seems, there were the giants (Eliot, Pound, Williams) struggling with their long poems, and the veteran lyric craftsmen (Frost, Stevens) presenting us with many fine shorter ones. But beyond that—a handful of well-made, intelligent, quite respectable lyrics that, after taking an English course or two, one could produce dutiful analyses of and admire for their wellwrought shapes. Ginsberg and Lowell changed all that, thrusting upon us in their immensely different ways the poem as personal performance. . . .

Often with Ginsberg the solemn and the silly are in too close company for this reader's comfort; it is the lack of complex ideas that for all its incidental virtues finally make his poetry mean less to me than it does to some. But the very idea of reviewing Ginsberg, certainly our most incorrigible poet, has its ludicrous aspect. . . .

> William H. Pritchard. *Hudson Review*. Autumn, 1973. pp. 592–4

Largely because of his deep feeling for [Neal] Cassady, Ginsberg's tender lyrical voice is well-represented in *The Fall of America*. But his ambition in this book to speak, like Whitman, from the self-transcendent perspective of a prophet doesn't come off very well. The data remain data, conceptually unmanaged; the mood of outrage seems childishly insufficient as a mode of emotional mastery over the horrors he describes. As in *The Gates of Wrath*, Ginsberg's strength in this latest book is the strength of his belief in the art of poetry itself. Ginsberg remains an imitator, a disciple whose work is always reminding the reader of the 19th-century Romantic masters. As their disciple, however, Ginsberg has no peer: perhaps it is his own form of maturity as a poet. In any case,

Ginsberg's whole working life has been an illustration of the capacity of that poetry to revitalize itself in the consciousness of people seeking through every mode of communal effort to find grace, a way to survive with others.

> Diane Middlebrook. *Parnassus*. Spring–Summer, 1974. p. 135

Ginsberg insists that the study of consciousness is the primary legitimate tradition in poetry. . . . Ginsberg vowed to dedicate his life and poetics to the realization of Blake's demand that the poet must cleanse the doors of perception. . . .

Robert Lowell and Allen Ginsberg, arguably the best poets of their generation, have perhaps succeeded most notably in surviving their own publicity. They have been able to write good poetry for thirty years in part because the publicity that surrounded them was generated by others who were quick to attend not so much to talent as to popularity. Lowell and Ginsberg became well known in different ways, of course, but both ways grew out of their talents for an endless, often *driven* form of speaking that at one and the same time clarified itself and grew more inclusive of the historical complexity it recorded. This speaking—one often thinks of both poets as ''commentators''—has a confessional cast to it, and both men have made the private order into public occasion more than once. But their fullest voices were achieved through their ability to make the public events they often deplored into something like private musings. The languages they discovered to enable this transformation are sometimes similar; for all the apparent differences in their sensibilities, it might be interesting to see just what lies behind, and inside, their distinctive modes of speech. . . .

The source of Ginsberg's sensibility . . . is the affinity group rather than the nuclear family. In contrast to Lowell's historical burdens, Ginsberg's social and political consciousness, and even his conscience, seems looser and yet more extensive. Lowell's political awareness takes shapes in key epochs, or even key moments, that serve as measures of values, tests of true progress, while at the same time hinting that all is devolutionary. Ginsberg's polis is always a future, utopian one; though he shares Lowell's sense of America's massive failure as a political ''experiment,'' that failure has a different texture, a different moral weight in his poetry than it does in Lowell's.

> Charles Molesworth. *The Fierce Embrace: A Study of Contemporary American Poetry* (Univ. of Missouri Pr., 1979), pp. 37, 39

Allen Ginsberg, in ''Wichita Vortex Sutra,'' seems to have managed both the articulation of particulars and their imaginative transcendence. It appears that Ginsberg's powerful emotional response to the inhumanity that war represents, as it is reflected early in the poem, allows him finally to negate that war, to eliminate it entirely from his system of recognitions. No poem that I have seen dealing with the Vietnam period in American life is so packed with angry details at the beginning—the minutiae of newspapers, radio reports, advertising slogans, all of which tend to falsify reality—and so blithe and ethereal at the end. The personal and poetic transformation Ginsberg works in ''Wichita,'' from almost total submersion in and obsession with political and military detail and dishonesty to final disbelief and liberation from such detail, is most unusual.

Perhaps even more unusual is the fact that this poem was written with the greatest ''projective'' rapidity—actually composed on tape-recorder as the poet traveled southwest through Kansas by car. The transformation occurring at the end—the transcendence of the personal—. . . is effected not through the adoption of *persona*, dramatic projection, or the subordination of present ills by a philosophic consideration of the past, but rather through the ritual act of *mantra*, in which Ginsberg, having described as many civil and military evils as possible, calls upon a rich pantheon of Indian, Christian, and Jewish gods to exorcize those evils and flatly declares the end of war. Surprisingly, the mantra seems to work, not just for Ginsberg, but for the reader as well. . . .

In this work of Ginsberg we have, to my mind, that rare integration of visual and aural, phenomenal and personal attentions which somehow eluded both Denise Levertov and Robert Duncan in their various strivings to personalize and politicize their poetry. We also have a remarkable instance of the success of modern organic/projective poetry from a writer who, for all his uplifted spontaneity, refuses to shut himself off from the validity of the outside world—particularly the natural and human world—and its insistent claim to reality.

> William Aiken. *Modern Poetry Studies*. 10, 2–3, 1981, pp. 232, 240

It seems a strangely sober act to pick up *Collected Poems 1947–1980*, all eight hundred pages of it, and read [Allen] Ginsberg as if he had always, like any poet, asked to be judged by his work. No Jack Kerouac sits beside you beating out the rhythms on coffeehouse tables with the palms of his hands, and assuring you how important Allen's poetry is. This is Ginsberg on his own, sans bells, kids, grandmothers, presenting himself as if he were dead and the twentieth century past and he had fallen into line with the poets of the age to see who will make it into the American literature survey courses of 2001. Yet it does not feel fair to judge him in that company.

If one makes comparisons with Eliot, Pound, Lowell, Stevens, or even with Ransom or Robert Penn Warren, the collected Ginsberg does not stand a chance. What these eight hundred pages prove is that Ginsberg has always been a minor poet; that is, a poet who has produced a few remarkable pieces, but the bulk of whose work shows no philosophical growth (despite its ostentatiously philosophical preoccupations) and rarely any depth. It is no small thing to be a minor poet; few make the list in any century. Ginsberg seems to be aware of his place. In the introduction, he warns that this collection will allow readers to ''observe poetic energy as cyclic, the continuum a panorama of valleys and plateaus with peaks of inspiration every few years.''

So, in fact, we do observe. When one considers that these poems cover thirty-three years of personal and national history, most of them lived feverishly, there is a striking sameness to the body of this work. Only Ginsberg's musical brilliance, his perfect pitch, saves the sameness from monotony. . . .

Does the collected Ginsberg represent the collected us? Certainly not, at least in the sense of reaching the nation's real complications. Still, as a guidebook to the national emotional highlights of the past four decades, the book is indispensable. So, evidently, is Ginsberg. Continually changing shapes and sounds, he has managed to outlast better poets by remaining forever current, urgent, with it, whatever ''it'' happened to be. What a strange national

Moses. But maybe not. The two qualities one takes from this collection are sinful innocence and innocent sin. Allen was always a good boy.

> Roger Rosenblatt. ''A Major Minor Poet.'' [Review of *Collected Poems 1947–1980* by Allen Ginsberg] *New Republic*. 192, March 4, 1985, pp. 33–35

The major thematic pronouncement of [the volume] *Mind Breaths* is one which encourages nourishment of and communion with the inner Self, an inner ''form,'' and which would, as well, suggest that involvement with the tragedies of society is only a hindrance to achieving that inner peace, which is, since all else is ''hopeless,'' the only achievable goal left.

With the thematic suggestions of [the other poems in the volume] as a backdrop, the poem ''Mind Breaths'' stands out as the realization, in poetic form, of an inner peace, an inner calmness, which allows the individual to reflect upon the outer world and to take in the outer world without becoming either actively involved in it or emotionally disturbed by it. ''Mind Breaths'' is the only poem in the volume which shows the poet, as it were, ''acting'' to manage the world around him. Other poems—''Yaweh and Allah Battle,'' ''Yes and It's Hopeless,'' ''What I'd Like to Do,'' ''Hospital Window''—have suggested that one must cultivate the inner Self or achieve an inner peace instead of or before confronting the outer world, but ''Mind Breaths'' is the first and only poem in the volume which depicts the individual actually as having achieved that inner peace and thereby providing an example of, in a sense, the ''solution'' for the individual. . . .

The poem ''Mind Breaths'' thus becomes, in a sense, the centerpiece of the volume, standing as the incarnation—the enactment—of the individual's solution to managing the outer world, a solution which is but longingly hinted at in other poems—or explained, rather than illustrated, in ''Contest of Bards''—and it underscores, finally, the dramatic shift Ginsberg has taken thematically away from earlier volumes.

The point here has not been—as it so often becomes in literary explications—to suggest that the poetry in *Mind Breaths* is ''better'' or ''worse'' than Ginsberg's earlier poetry but to point out that a significant thematic shift is occurring in the poetry which has been hitherto overlooked. Whether this shift is, as [Mark] Shechner and the other critics have suggested it is not, an ''advance in vision'' for Ginsberg is really a moot question. One would, of course, first have to define advance—a word which, when dealing with intangible movements or shifts, is very problematic, and perhaps even more so when talking about poetic ''vision.'' The point is, I believe—and this is what critics have failed to perceive, probably because certain poems in *Mind Breaths* (e.g., the ''songs'') have turned critics away from the entire volume—that the poems of *Mind Breaths* are not rehashing the topics and themes of *Howl* and *Kaddish*. They reveal a changing Ginsberg.

> Jay Dougherty. ''From Society to Self: Ginsberg's Inward Turn in *Mind Breaths*.'' *Sagetrieb*. Spring, 1987, pp. 89–91

The Beats shook up American life in ways other than literature. With their free-and-easy ways, their belief in love and visions and openness, they made the first cracks in the armor and gave America some breathing room after the claustrophobia of the postwar decade. Ginsberg has claimed that the Beat Generation influenced everything from gay liberation, black liberation, and women's liberation to liberation of the word from censorship, the demystification and/or decriminalization of some laws against marijuana and other drugs, and the spread of ecological consciousness.

Some of these claims have been dismissed by critics. The Beats had no obvious connection with the civil rights movement, and most feminist historians are critical of the Beats for their misogyny; it would be ingenious to find the origins of the women's movement among Beat Generation literary activity, except perhaps as a reaction against it.

The gay movement, however, has clear roots in the kind of open-minded comradeship and male bonding found among the early Beats, particularly between Ginsberg and Kerouac, or Kerouac and Cassady. It was a kind of masculine tenderness out of Walt Whitman, virtually unknown in the late forties and early fifties, which later became a prototype in the gay community, what Ginsberg called a "cooperative tender heart."

The bravery of Ginsberg's confessions in *Howl*—"America, I'm putting my queer shoulder to the wheel" or "who let themselves be fucked in the ass by saintly motorcyclists, and screamed with joy"—revelations of homosexuality in the middle of the McCarthy period, made without guilt or shame, was inspirational to homosexuals across the country and heralded the beginnings of the gay liberation movement. Ginsberg held up his gay "marriage" to Peter as exemplary, although he later worried about the harm that may have caused to anyone copying him and was later criticized by sectors of the movement for simply reproducing role stereotypes. He gave dozens of benefit readings for gay causes and championed the cause in interviews and the media. In the history of the struggle to achieve acceptance for homosexuals in American society, Ginsberg was a central figure.

The Beats and their publishers, notably Barney Rosset at Grove Press, played an important role in ending literary censorship, through the trials of *Howl* and *Naked Lunch*. Ginsberg was willing to put himself on the line, whether testifying on behalf of Jack Smith's film *Flaming Creatures*, which had been seized as obscene, or opposing 1988 FCC regulations that prohibited "Howl" from being read aloud on the radio except after midnight. Although Ginsberg often claims the Beat Generation as the genesis of the ideas of sixties youth culture, in most instances, where some lasting influence on society can be shown, it was caused not by the Beat Generation but by Ginsberg himself in his tireless campaigning for what he regards as a better world.

The one continuous thread throughout his life has been to fulfill the vow he made as a teenager, standing on the windswept prow of the Hoboken ferry on his way to take the Columbia University entrance examinations: to devote his life to helping mankind. He became the poet advocate of the underdog, and this has always been his greatest theme. To paraphrase Richard Ellmann on Oscar Wilde, Ginsberg's greatness as a writer is partly the result of the enlargement of sympathy that he demands for society's victims.

It was not an easy ride. Ginsberg's sincerity has been doubted, his methods have often been criticized, his poetry has been ridiculed. Despite that, he has become the most famous living poet on earth, one of America's best known cultural ambassadors, his poetry translated into virtually every language, from Chinese to Serbo-Croatian. He changed the world a little.

Barry Miles. *Ginsberg: A Biography* (New York: Simon & Schuster, 1989), pp. 532–33

It will be forty years in October since Allen Ginsberg gave his historic first reading of "Howl" (in San Francisco), the poem which so spectacularly launched his poetic career and put the Beat Generation on the American literary and cultural map. Looking back at the various outraged responses the poem inspired, the one that now seems strangest is not the (unsuccessful) prosecution for obscenity (some of Ginsberg's poems still can't be broadcast on American radio during the day) but the objection from the literary "establishment" that the poem was wild and wholly lacking in craft. What has become clear over the intervening years is just how systematic and considered Ginsberg's methods are. Indeed, next to this anarchic beatnik, many formalist and traditionalist poets seem like brave improvisers, going it without the kind of aesthetic (and ideological) framework that Ginsberg has always so readily invoked to explain and justify his art. . . .

Now that he's nearly seventy, the record is inevitably dominated by the experience of age and the prospect of death, and it is this subject matter rather than any technical advance that distinguishes *Cosmopolitan Greeting: Poems 1986–1992* from all his earlier volumes.

Nicholas Everett. *TLS: The Times Literary Supplement*. Feb. 10, 1995, p. 7

BIBLIOGRAPHY
Howl, 1956 (p); *Kaddish and Other Poems*, 1961; *Empty Mirror*, 1962 (p); *Reality Sandwiches*, 1963 (p); (with William Burroughs) *The Yage Letters*, 1964 (letters); *Planet News*, 1968 (p); *Airplane Dreams*, 1969 (p); *Indian Journals*, 1970 (p, e); *Kaddish*, 1972 (d); *The Fall of America*, 1973 (p); *Allen Verbatim*, 1974 (e); *The Visions of the Great Rememberer*, 1974; *The Gates of Wrath*, 1973 (p); *Gay Sunshine Interviews*, 1974 (interviews); *The Iron Horse*, 1974 (p); *First Blues*, 1975 (p); *Chicago Trial Testimony*, 1975 (court testimony); *Sad Dust Glories*, 1975 (p); *Madeira and Toasts for Basil Bunting's 75th Birthday*, 1977 (misc); *Mind Breaths*, 1977 (p); *As Ever: The Collected Correspondence of Allen Ginsberg and Neal Cassady*, 1977; *Journals: Early Fifties, Early Sixties*, 1977; *Poems All Over the Place, Mostly 'Seventies*, 1978 (p); *Composed on the Tongue*, 1980 (p); (with Peter Orlovsky) *Straight Hearts' Delight*, 1980 (p, letters); *Plutonian Ode: Poems 1977–1980*, 1981; *Mostly Sitting Haiku*, 1981 (p); *Man Loves*, 1982 (p); *Collected Poems, 1947–1980*, 1984 (r); *White Shroud*, 1986 (p); *Howl: Original Draft Facsimile*, 1986 (p); *Your Reason and Blake's System*, 1988 (lecture); *Cosmopolitan Greetings*, 1994 (p); *Journals Mid-Fifties. 1954–1958*, 1995 (m); *Illuminated Poems*, 1996; *Indian Journals, March 1962–May 1963: Notebooks, Diary, Blank Pages, Writings*, 1996 (misc); *Selected Poems, 1947–1995*, 1996; *Death and Fame: Last Poems, 1993–1997*, 1999

GIOVANNI, Nikki (1943–)

Power and love are what are at issue in Nikki Giovanni's poetry and life. In her earlier poems (1968–1970), these issues are for the most part separate. She writes of personal love in poems of private life; of black power and a public love in political poems. She won her fame with the latter.

In poems such as ["The True Import of the Present Dialogue, Black vs. Negro"], Giovanni speaks for her people in their own language of the social issues that concern them. Her role is that of spokeswoman for others with whom she is kin except for the fact that she possesses the gift of poetry: "i wanted to be / a sweet inspiration in my dreams / of my people. . . ." The quotation is from a later poem in which she is questioning that very role. But as she gains her fame, the concept of poet as "manifesting our collective historical needs" is very much present.

In defining poetry as "the culture of a people," Giovanni, in the statement from *Gemini* quoted earlier, uses "musician" and "preacher" as synonyms for "poet". All speak for the culture; all *speak*, with the emphasis on the sound they make. Making poems from black English is more than using idioms and grammatical idiosyncrasies; the very form of black English, and certainly its power, is derived from its tradition and preeminent usage as an oral language. . . .

The act of naming, of using language creatively, becomes the most powerful action of all—saying, calling fudge love, calling smiling at old men revolution is creative (rather than derivative) action that expresses more than her own powers as woman and poet. In "Seduction" there was a significant gap between language (rhetoric) and action, between male and female. In that fable, men and words were allied and were seen by the woman poet as impotent. The woman was allied with action (love), but she was, in the poem, mute. The man calls her action "counterrevolutionary." Now, in "My House," the woman's action, love (an overt expression of the personal, private sphere), is allied to language. Giovanni brings her power bases together in this poem, her dominion over kitchens, love, and words. No longer passive in any way, she makes the food, the love, the poem, and the revolution. She brings together things and words through her own vision (dream, poem) of them, seeing that language (naming) is action, because it makes things happen. Once fudge has been named love, touching one's lips to it becomes an act of love; smiling at old men becomes revolution "cause what's real / is really real." Real = dream + experience. To make all this happen, most of all there must exist a sense of self on the part of the maker, which is why the overriding tone of the poem is the sense of an "i" who in giving need feel no impotence from the act of taking (both become aspects of the same event). Thus this is *her* house and he makes her happy, thus and only thus—"cause" abounds in this poem, too: this, her poem, can be his poem. Not silly at all.

In bringing together her private and public roles and thereby validating her sense of self as black woman poet, Giovanni is on her way towards achieving in art that for which she was trained: emotionally, to love; intellectually and spiritually, to be in power; "to learn and act upon necessary emotions which will grant me more control over my life," as she writes in *Gemini*. Through interrelating love and power, to achieve a revolution—to be free. She concludes her poem "When I Die" (*My House*) with these lines:

> and if ever touched a life i hope that life knows that i know
> that touching was and still is and will always be the
> true revolution

These words of poetry explain the way to enact a dream, one that is "a real possibility": "that I can be the first person in my family to be free. . .I'm twenty-five years old. A revolutionary poet. I love".

Wherever Nikki Giovanni's life as poet will take her, she will go there in full possession of her self.

Suzanne Juhasz. *Naked and Fiery Forms* (New York: Harper & Row, 1976), pp. 157–58, 173–74

It was the publication of *Black Feeling, Black Talk, Black Judgement* (1968, 1970) that began her rise to national prominence. She captured the fighting spirit of the times with such lines as "Nigger can you kill?" (in "The True Import of Present Dialogue, Black vs. Negro") and "a negro needs to kill / something" ("Records"). These poems were distinguished more by the contrast between the words and the image of their author than by anything else. Also in the volume were a number of personal poems, including gentle satires on sexual politics, and introspective, autobiographical ones, such as "Nikki-Rosa," still one of her best. It talked about growing up, the value of a loving childhood and challenged the stereotype of the angry militant: ". . .they'll/probably talk about my hard childhood/and never understand that/all the while I was quite happy," she wrote.

From the beginning, the personal, feeling poems were juxtaposed against those of violent militancy. But in subsequent books she spurned the latter completely. Her vision in *Black Feeling* which saw "our day of Presence/When Stokely is in/The Black House" ("A Historical Footnote to Consider Only When All Else Fails") narrowed, in her autobiographical essays *Gemini* (1971), to the conclusion that "Black men refuse to do in a concerted way what must be done to control White men." In any case, as she wrote in *My House* (1972), "touching" was the "true revolution" ("When I Die").

But Giovanni's books after *Black Feeling* did more than repudiate violence. As critic Eugene Redmond pointed out, they offered her view from a new perspective: that of the rite of passage toward womanhood. The growing-up motif is a common one in literature, especially among women writers. It has provided some of their most memorable work and, in Giovanni's case, a unifying theme in her work.

Paula Giddings. In Mari Evans, ed. *Black Women Writers (1950–1980)* (New York: Doubleday, 1984), p. 212

Giovanni is a frustrating poet. I can sympathize with her detractors, no matter what the motives for their discontent. She clearly has talent that she refuses to discipline. She just doesn't seem to try hard enough. In "Habits" she coyly declares:

> i sit writing
> a poem
> about my habits
> which while it's not
> a great poem
> is mine

It isn't enough that the poem is hers; personality isn't enough, isn't a substitute for fully realized poems. Even though she has created a compelling persona on the page, she has been too dependent on it. Her ego has backfired. She has written a number of lively, sometimes humorous, sometimes tragic, often perceptive poems about the contemporary world. The best poems in her three strongest books, *Black Feeling, Black Talk, Black Judgement, Re: Creation*, and *Cotton Candy*, demonstrate that she can be a very good poet. However, her work also contains dross: too much unrealized abstraction (flabby abstraction at that!), too much "poetic" fantasy posing as poetry and too many moments verging on sentimentality. In the early 1970s, after severely criticizing Giovanni's shortcomings, Haki Madhubuti said he eagerly awaited the publication of her new book, *Re: Creation*; he hoped that in it she would fulfill the promise of her earlier poetry. Even though it turned out to be one of Giovanni's better books, I find myself in a similar situation to Madhubuti's. I see that not only does Giovanni have promise, she already has written some good poems and continues to write them. Yet I am concerned about her development. I think it is time for her to stand back and take stock of herself, to take for herself the time for reflection, the vacation she says Aretha deserves for work well done. Nikki Giovanni is one of the most talented writers to come out of the Black 1960s, and I don't want to lose her. I want her to write poems which grow out of that charming persona, not poems which are consumed by it. Giovanni must keep her charm and overcome her self-indulgence. She has the talent to create good, perhaps important, poetry if only she has the will to discipline her craft.

> William J. Harris. In Mari Evans, ed. *Black Women Writers (1950–1980)* (New York: Doubleday, 1984), p. 228

Upon reading Nikki Giovanni's early poetry, one immediately notes the ferocity of her verse. Its force, its passion, and its hatred startle, but the 1960s were startling years. Hers is a message of revolution, killing, changing. The cry is for a strong sense of individualism and for an individual who will stand up to effect the changes society demands. The combined volume containing the texts from her two books, *Black Feeling Black Talk/Black Judgement*, illustrates this emphasis. A later volume, *My House*, is much more personal and concentrates on the influences at work on the poet.

The Women and the Men continues that sense of mellowing, of shifting focus and emphasis in the poetry, as the poet stresses personal contacts. It is interesting to note that many of her individual poems are dedicated to specific people, often identified by name or by initials. In the most recent volume, the mellowing is not only evident; it is the thrust of the book.

One critic of contemporary poetry praised Giovanni for her ability to use simple folk and blues rhythms and techniques. That strength is evident in . . . her verses about strong black women she has met.

> Dennis Lloyd. In Ray Willbanks, ed. *Literature of Tennessee* (Macon, Georgia: Mercer University Press, 1984), pp. 197–98

While Giovanni has received more attention first for her militant poems on racial themes and later for her feminist writing, the poems that will finally determine her position in the canon of American poetry are, almost without exception, ones in which place functions not only as a vehicle, but also as a theme. In her most recent work, her themes are becoming increasingly complex, reflecting her maturity as a woman and as a writer. Traditionally in Southern writing, place has been associated with themes of the past and the family; these themes are seen in Giovanni's poems of the late 1960s and the early 1970s, with the added dimension of a desire to understand the faraway places from which black slaves were brought to the American South. Her later poetry reflects a changing consciousness of her role in society as a single woman, the need to adjust her concept of home and family and of the importance of smaller places, such as houses and rooms, to fit her

own life, a life that many American women and men, black and white, can identify with. In her best poems, places grow into themes that convey the universal situation of modern humanity, a sense of placelessness and a need for security. . . .

For her, place is more than an image, more than a surface used to develop a narrative or a theme, just as place functions in the best poetry of the Southern tradition lying behind her work. Further, the changing sense of place in these poems can be seen to reveal Giovanni's developing sense of herself as a woman and as a poet. Suzanne Juhasz, Anna T. Robinson, and Erlene Stetson all emphasize in their recent critical discussions the growing feminist consciousness they find in Giovanni's work. Her use of place is broader than simply a feminist symbol, though, just as her poetry has developed beyond purely racial themes. The relationships of people to places and the ways people have responded to and tried to control places are important themes for Giovanni, as are the ways places sometimes control people. Greatest in thematic significance are the need to belong to a place or in a place and the necessity of moving beyond physical places to spiritual or metaphysical ones.

> Martha Cook. In Tonette Bond Inge, ed. *Southern Women Writers: The New Generation* (Tuscaloosa: University of Alabama Press, 1990), pp. 228, 299

BIBLIOGRAPHY

Black Feeling, Black Talk, 1968 (p); *Black Judgement*, 1968 (p); *Poem of Angela Yvonne Davis*, 1970 (p); *Re:Creation*, 1970 (p); *Gemini: An Extended Autobiographical Statement on My First Twenty-Five Years of Being a Black Poet*, 1971 (a); *Spin a Soft Black Song: Poems for Children*, 1971 (p); *My House*, 1972 (p); *Ego-Tripping and Other Poems for Young People*, 1973 (p); *The Women and the Men*, 1975 (p); *Cotton Candy on a Rainy Day*, 1978 (p); *Vacation Time: Poems for Children*, 1980 (p); *Those Who Ride the Night Winds*, 1983 (p); *Sacred Cows . . . and Other Edibles*, 1988 (p); *Knoxville, Tennessee*, 1994 (p); *Racism 101*, 1994 (nf); *The Genie in the Jar*, 1996 (p); *The Selected Poems of Nikki Giovanni*, 1996 (p); *The Sun is So Quiet*, 1996 (p); *Love Poems*, 1997 (p)

GLASGOW, Ellen (1874–1945)

Miss Glasgow has refused to consider herself less than an artist. She has not written of Virginian life but of human life in Virginia. She has taken two or three years to perfect a book, not because she wanted to be sociologically accurate but because she wanted to be artistically mature, and this sense of pace and dignity, this tacit assumption that the novel is a major work of art—these are the qualities she has brought to her interpretation of immediate environment.

> Howard Mumford Jones. *Saturday Review*. Oct. 16, 1943. p. 20

You have in the work of Ellen Glasgow something very like a complete social chronicle of the Piedmont section of the State of Virginia since the War Between the States, as this chronicle has been put together by a witty and observant woman, a poet in grain, who was not at any moment in her writing quite devoid of malice, nor of an all-understanding lyric tenderness either; and who was not ever, through any tiniest half-moment, deficient in craftsmanship. You have likewise that which, to my first finding, seemed a complete natural history of the Virginian gentlewoman throughout the last half-century, with all the attendant features of her lair and of her general habitat most accurately rendered. But reflection shows the matter to be a great deal more pregnant than I thought at outset; for the main theme of Ellen Glasgow, the theme which in her writing figures always, if not exactly as a Frankenstein's monster, at least as a sort of ideational King Charles's head, I now take to be The Tragedy of Everywoman, As It Was Lately Enacted in the Commonwealth of Virginia.

> James Branch Cabell. *Let Me Lie* (Farrar, Straus). 1947. p. 243

In her comedies as in her serious novels, Ellen Glasgow significantly advances but a single thesis, that man is the enemy of woman. The comedies rout him with ridicule and edged contempt; the serious novels display his dead body as proof of love's futility. . . . In no major work from the publication of *Virginia* which may be reckoned as the author's first demonstration of mature powers, does a man of questing virility appear but to dupe or otherwise humiliate a woman spiritually his superior. . . . Nor is one villainous hero to be confused with the other; such are the author's gifts that each betrayer remains sharply individualized. By multiplying particularized instances, Miss Glasgow seeks to establish the general truth of her proposition, that men, until winnowed by the years, bring only rue in their wake. Rue, that is, to women; for Ellen Glasgow presents masculine character primarily as it subserves feminine.

> Josephine Lurie Jessup. *The Faith of Our Feminists* (H. Smith). 1950. pp. 52–3

Ellen Glasgow was a literary rebel in the first half of her career, a literary ancestor in the second half, but her work has never had the full recognition it deserves. One of our top three women writers, she has been eclipsed by the glow of Willa Cather's lovely fairy tales and by the cool glitter of Edith Wharton's social snobbery. Yet as a literary figure Miss Glasgow was superior to these ladies in many respects, and her best novels are of equal interest and importance with theirs.

> Maxwell Geismar. *The Nation*. Nov. 13, 1954. p. 425

The social historian cannot become personally involved at the expense of his own satirical objectivity, for at that moment true satire becomes impossible. All of which is a way of saying that Miss Glasgow's success at applying blood and irony in pursuit of the social history of Virginia depends upon her own detachment; and too often she is not at all detached, but instead is so intensely engaged and identified with the supposed objects of irony that she can be neither ironic nor realistic. She surrenders her objectivity to the private demands of her characters; instead of creating Dorinda in *Barren Ground*, she becomes Dorinda. Or rather, it is Dorinda who ceases to be a fictional character and becomes an extension of

Miss Glasgow's own life and personality, until it is Miss Glasgow who is undergoing the experience.

It is a good rule of thumb for the Glasgow novels that whenever the author begins identifying a character's plight with her own, begins projecting her personal wishes and needs into the supposedly fictional situation, then to that extent both the character and the novel are weakened. Contrariwise, Miss Glasgow's success as a novelist is in direct proportion to her success in standing away from her characters and letting them find their own fictional level, as created figures in a story.

> Louis D. Rubin. *No Place on Earth* (Texas). 1959. pp. 13–14

In the novels which compose her triptych of manners, Ellen Glasgow explored the meaning for her Virginians of a change in moral attitudes. In these novels she showed plainly that she could neither accept nor wholly reject the code of behavior which had governed polite society or, indeed, all of society in Virginia since colonial times. Earlier she had attacked the features of that code which she found debilitating, or even evil in their effect. Especially had she objected to what she called "evasive idealism." For against all forces in the life of an aristocratic society which prevented men and women from living rich lives, or which protected barbarity, weakness and greed in the name of tradition, Ellen Glasgow sternly waged war. Yet, if she attacked the code as faulty, she could not readily accept what was usually offered as its alternative: the abandonment of all rule in human relationships. . . .

The Sheltered Life (1932) is Ellen Glasgow's finest novel, for in this tragedy of manners she combined most effectively all the elements of her material and art. In it character, action, and atmosphere interact to reveal not only the tragedy in lives shaped by the code of polite behavior and by the pretenses of a cult of Beauty but also the evil lurking in assumptions of innocence. She cast over these people a magic portrayal, a brilliance of life, and a beauty which makes superb the irony in the charm of their outward lives and their darker implications.

> Blair Rouse. *Ellen Glasgow* (Twayne). 1962. pp. 98, 108

It is unfortunate for the artistic stature of her short stories that Miss Glasgow did not continue writing them after 1924. Although she dated *Virginia* (1913) as her first mature work, it is generally agreed that her "major phase" began with *Barren Ground* (1925). This novel, together with *The Sheltered Life* (1932) and *Vein of Iron* (1935), remains unchallenged by anything she wrote in a shorter form. "Jordan's End" gives us a hint of what she might have done if she had taken the short story as seriously as she took the novel, if she had not been so obsessed with her "social history of Virginia."

From our perspective today, we can see that Ellen Glasgow kept maturing stylistically, but that her moral and social concepts solidified in the middle of the 1920's. The rebel of the nineties found herself the conservative of the twenties. Nevertheless, the advice of Walter Hines Page and her own iron vein kept her writing fiction even after she had lost faith in her readers, even when she knew she was celebrating lost values. For this she had earned her status as one of America's leading woman novelists.

> Richard K. Meeker. Introduction to *The Collected Stories of Ellen Glasgow* (Louisiana State). 1963. p. 23

The advantages that she brought to her task and ambition were indeed considerable. Out of her wide reading she selected the mightiest and probably the best models to guide her in her re-creation of the Virginia scene. She used Hardy as her master in rustic atmosphere, George Eliot as her guide in morality, Maupassant for plot, and Tolstoy for everything. She had the richest source material that any author could wish, consisting simply of a whole state and its whole history, a state, too, that occupies the center of our eastern geography and of our history and that not coincidentally has produced more Presidents than any other. And the social range among Miss Glasgow's characters is far greater than that of most twentieth-century novelists, suggesting that of such Victorians as Trollope, Dickens, Elizabeth Gaskell, and, again, George Eliot. . . .

Miss Glasgow had the same range in scenery that she had in human beings, and she could make the transfer without difficulty from the grim mountains and valleys of *Vein of Iron* to the interminable fields of broom-sedge in *Barren Ground* and thence to the comfortable mansions of Richmond and to the smaller gentility of Petersburg and Williamsburg. Highly individual in American letters is her ability to pass with equal authority from country to city, from rusticity to sophistication, from the tobacco field to the drawing room, from irony to tragedy.

Yet for all her gifts and advantages she does not stand in the very first rank of American novelists. She was unable sufficiently to pull the tapestry of fiction over her personal grievances and approbations.

Louis Auchincloss. *Pioneers and Caretakers* (Minnesota). 1965. pp. 86–8

In her novels of manners, Ellen Glasgow repeatedly shows us men and women of wisdom and perception who lack the moral courage to act upon their knowledge and hence are destroyed by societies whose fundamental weakness they recognize but to which they bring not anger or resistance but amusement and retreat. Nowhere is this characteristic more obvious than in her novel *The Sheltered Life* where her protagonist, she claims, is General Archbald. She regards the General as an example of "the civilized mind in a world where even the civilizations we make are uncivilized"; and yet despite that kind of praise, General Archbald is finally a representative figure of his own world, a world that subscribes to a false idealism. At every crucial point he has lacked the quality of character which would have enabled him to make his civilized mind felt as an active force in his decaying civilization.

C. Hugh Holman. *Three Modes of Modern Southern Fiction* (Georgia). 1966. p. 21

In the history of Southern literature Ellen Glasgow's place is assured. She was, simply, the first really modern Southern novelist, the pioneer who opened up for fictional imagination a whole spectrum of her region's experience that hitherto had been considered inappropriate for depiction in polite letters. From the very beginning she meant business, and she had no patience with those who would have literature be anything less or other than an honest portrait of human experience and human meaning. Decades before Faulkner, Wolfe, Warren, Caldwell, Welty, and the others, she did

her best to write about Southern experience as she actually viewed it, not as her neighbors thought she ought to be seeing it. In the words of the historian C. Vann Woodward, "When eventually the bold moderns of the South arrested the reading and theatrical world with the tragic intensity of the inner life and social drama of the South, they could find scarcely a theme that Ellen Glasgow had wholly neglected. She had bridged the gap between the old and the new literary revival, between romanticism and realism."

Louis D. Rubin, Jr. In *Ellen Glasgow: Centennial Essays*, ed. M. Thomas Inge (Univ. Pr. of Virginia, 1976), p. 4

Ellen Glasgow, . . . who died in 1945, is not at all highly regarded at present; yet she was a distinguished American novelist and the first of the Southern women writers . . . to repudiate the "willed heroic vision." Her primary theme, indeed, is the way in which grand ideas and facile goodwill interfere with the capacity to perceive ordinary miserable truths. . . .

What fascinates Ellen Glasgow is the paradox involved in the correlation between integrity and dissembling; in her novels it is always those of the highest moral character who are most reluctant to take account of domestic or social ills. They become adept at pretending. She makes the point over and over: "Her higher nature lent itself to deceit"; ". . . both clung . . . to the belief that a pretty sham has a more intimate relation to morality than has an ugly truth." The characters—most of them at any rate—are not at all critical of society's arrangements, but the author is: she is openly a crusader for social reforms, but she avoids a haranguing note by keeping her tone sardonic rather than impassioned. Benign obtuseness, willed or otherwise, is her target; but she understands how this quality can make life more agreeable for those who possess it. . . .

Ellen Glasgow's objective . . . is to underline the harm occasioned by self-deceits and wilful delusions, and to suggest, as far as possible, a wider social parallel for the personal failures and tragedies her novels depict. At best, her work is authoritative and graceful; and her social observation is always acute.

Patricia Craig. *TLS: The Times Literary Supplement*. Nov. 13, 1981, p. 1319

BIBLIOGRAPHY

The Descendant, 1897 (n); *Phases of an Inferior Planet*, 1898 (n); *The Voice of the People*, 1900 (n); *The Battleground*, 1902 (n); *The Freeman*, 1902 (p); *The Deliverance*, 1904 (n); *The Wheel of Life*, 1906 (n); *The Ancient Law*, 1908 (n); *The Romance of a Plain Man*, 1909 (n); *The Miller of Old Church*, 1911 (n); *Virginia*, 1913 (n); *Life and Gabriella*, 1916 (n); *The Builders*, 1919 (n); *One Man in His Time*, 1922 (n); *The Shadowy Third*, 1923 (s) (English edition, *Dare's Gift*, 1924); *Barren Ground*, 1925 (n); *The Romantic Comedians*, 1926 (n); *They Stooped to Folly*, 1929 (n); *The Old Dominion Edition of the Works*, 1929–1933; *The Sheltered Life*, 1932 (n); *Vein of Iron*, 1935 (n); *The Virginia Edition*, 1938; *In This Our Life*, 1941 (n); *A Certain Measure*, 1943 (c); *The Woman Within*, 1954 (a); *Letters*, 1958; *The Collected Stories*, 1963; *Beyond Defeat: An Epilogue to an Era*, 1966 (n); *Ellen Glasgow's Reasonable Doubts: A Collection of Her Writings*, ed. by Julius Rowan Raper, 1988 (misc)

GLÜCK, Louise (1943–)

Glück's cryptic narratives invite our participation: we must, according to the case, fill out the story, substitute ourselves for the fictive personages, invent a scenario from which the speaker can utter her lines, decode the import, "solve" the allegory. Or such is our first impulse. Later, I think, we no longer care, in "Thanksgiving" for instance, who are the prey and who the predators: we read the poem, instead, as a truth complete within its own terms, reflecting some one of the innumerable configurations into which experience falls. Glück's independent structures, populated by nameless and often ghostly forms engaged in archaic or timeless motions, satisfy without referent. They are far removed from the more circumstantial poetry written by women poets in the last 10 years, but they remain poems chiefly about childhood, family life, love, and motherhood. In their obliquity and reserve, they offer an alternative to first-person "confession," while remaining indisputably personal.

The leap in style from Glück's relatively unformed first book (*Firstborn*, 1968) to *The House on Marshland* suggests that Glück is her own best critic. For myself, I would hope she might follow the advice Keats and Stevens gave themselves, and write a long poem: "All kinds of favors," said Stevens, "drop from it."

Helen Vendler. *The New Republic*. June 17, 1978, pp. 34–37.

Louise Glück is familiar to readers of contemporary American poetry. As early as her debut appearance in Paul Carroll's *Young American Poets* (1968), her work intimated a poet of consequence. There was something about the obvious technical facility and self-lacerating tone that was immediately engaging, not to say arresting. Her first book, *Firstborn* initially published in the United States by the New American Library in 1968, substantiated that impression. In a review of the book, Robert Hass wrote that the poems were "hard, artful, and full of pain," characteristics of the poetic *épistémé* in which they were written.

True to its "confessional" sources, the poetry of *Firstborn* is, as Hass hints, formally strict, musically dense, and thematically elliptical, even obscure. But two poems, "The Egg," and "The Wound," set forth Glück's obsessive subject, abortion, and form a kind of thematic matrix for the book as a whole, focusing its somewhat blurred emphases. And those emphases, the recurring themes of emptiness, sterility and death, are powerfully reinforced by their juxtaposition with the plenitude, fertility, and vitality of the natural world or, one might say, the nature fertility of the physical world. Hence, in the presence of nature ("Ripe things sway in the light / Parts of plants leaf / Fragments"), not the "gored roasts" or "plot / Of embryos," abortion seems unnatural, *contra natura*. Furthermore, what the poems insist in their oblique way is that one can never be done with something like abortion. What is seemingly dead, past, returns—as Freud knew—to haunt the present and future, obsessively alive. Such, at least, is the poetic premise of *Firstborn*. . . .

It is a commonplace that every poet has his or her subject and, as readers, we grant them this. Yet in an art that has been dominated by male obsessions (what Foucault calls the discourse of power), Glück's subject is an uncommonly female one, even as the style and models of *Firstborn* are not. Herein lies the contradictory nature and ambiguous achievement of the book. This is not to say that Glück polemicizes her subject as, I think, Adrienne Rich has recent books. Although "The Egg" and "The Wound" are not wholly successful artistically speaking because of the unresolved disjunction between verse and voice, they are still too rich and complex for the reductionism of "right to-life" or "radical feminist" slogans. Glück is not intent to teach, but to present. And what is presented—sometimes coolly, sometimes fiercely, always forcefully—is not easily dismissed. Which is simply to say that Glück is not a proselytizer but a poet, and an accomplished one at that. . . .

If poems such as "The Racer's Widow," "Cottonmouth Country," and a formal *tour de force*, "Phenomenal Survival of Death in Nantucket," mark a poet of considerable talent at work in *Firstborn*, one not wholly subject to her poetic models, nonetheless the tone that pervades the book is so high-pitched that, finally, there is little of the quiet control that is often a sign of the mature poet. In a review of *The House on Marshland*, Calvin Bedient wrote in the *Sewanee Review* (Spring 1976):

> Her earlier poems are tense performances, the light a little too strong, with Robert Lowell, Sylvia Plath, and Robert Browning [evident in her frequent use of the dramatic monologue] noticeably coaxing from the wings. The poems are brilliant but lack resonance. . . . They suffer from a too-conscious subject and skill.

The House on Marshland however, is a major advance on its predecessor—brilliant and self-conscious as that book was—and evidence of an achieved poetic maturity. In poem after poem the subtle interweaving of myth and music produces an effect that can only be termed spellbinding. On its publication Stanley Kunitz wrote: "Those of us who have waited impatiently for Louise Glück's second book can rejoice that it confirms and augments the impression of a rare and high imagination." Yet that imagination, burdened by a difficult subject which seemed to necessitate a difficult style (or perhaps it was, as a Russian formalist or Glück herself might argue, vice versa), was occulted in *Firstborn*.

Reading *The House on Marshland* though, one senses that Glück could not have written the latter without the poetic travail of the former. The effect, evident from the very first poem of the book, "All Hallows," is a poetry liberated of its creator's designs (and, as Keats knew, of the reader's as well). It also makes possible a situation in which, to paraphrase Heidegger, *poetry speaks us*, author and reader alike. While implicitly criticizing the clipped style of her first book, Glück in a recent, illuminating interview (*Columbia* [Spring/Summer 1981]) credits the transformation to a change in technique.

> *Firstborn* is full of those bullet-like phrases, the nonsentences. When I finished the poems in that book, it was clear to me that the thing I could not continue to do was make sentences like that. The earliest poems in *The House on Marshland* were responses to a dictum I made myself, to write poems that were, whenever possible, single sentences. . . . What it turned out to do was open up all kinds of subject matter that I had not had access to. . . . technical impositions precede change. I had become habituated to a mode of expression that was itself communicative of a certain state of mind and attitude. If you take that. . . . technique away, then by definition you are going to have something else. . . . The atmosphere of spontaneous deadness will go. That was what I thought I was doing from Book 1 to Book 2.

Thus, as Glück notes, the terse voice and clotted verse of *Firstborn* give way to the off-hand tone and matter-of-fact rhythms of, say, "Pomegranate," a representative poem from *The House on Marshland*. . . .

If, as Helen Vendler claims, Glück's poems "are far removed from the circumstantial poetry written by women poets in the last ten years," they also suffer occasionally from a lack of immediacy, a sense of humor or wit (where there is no lessening of intensity, as Eliot defined it) which would leaven her sometimes too deadly serious tone. Certainly Glück's possesses, and is possessed by, a magisterial voice that has made for some astonishing poems. The danger is that it will produce mere magic, rhetoric devoid of the felt experiences of everyday life. This caveat, I suppose, accounts for some of the ambivalence I experienced after reading Glück's third and most recent book of poems, *Descending Figure*. At first glance, it merely seems to repeat the successes of *The House on Marshland*.

However, if Glück's tone and language have not changed appreciably (which readers familiar with her work might find vexing), *Descending Figure* does extend the emotional range of the first two books to accommodate events, one surmises, in the evolution of her personal life. Although still haunted by pain and loss and death, the poems are less obsessed with these topics and so less marked by a rather nostalgic desire for extinct states of being and non-being in general: the world of childhood innocence, the "absolute knowledge" of the womb and tomb. True, there are poems about dead children and deadlier male-female relationships, staples of the first two books, but there are also poems about the poet's husband and son, the domesticities of daily life and its small, though not insignificant, pains and pleasures. . . .

Paradoxically, despite or because of its downward movement toward the things of this world, *Descending Figure* represents a slight upbeat impulse in Glück's poetry, one not perceptible perhaps to the general reader though one, more importantly, which two poets of pain and loss and death, Sylvia Plath and Anne Sexton, never lived to see and write about. "I have survived my life," a speaker in *Firstborn* says. Louise Glück has survived, and *Descending Figure* is a small testament to her canny craft and courage. In the future, no doubt, her poems will not only continue to move and amaze us but reflect more and more those moments when, just as we are waiting on what Rilke calls a "rising happiness" (steigendes *Glück*), "a happy thing *falls*" (*ein Glückliches* fällt). Descending figures such as these are also the stuff of poetry.

Robert Miklitsch. *The Hollins Critic*. October, 1982, pp. 1–13.

[Louise Gluck's *The Wild Iris* is an] innovative, demanding new work by one of our most important poets. *The Wild Iris* returns to the distanced voice of Gluck's early poetry—and to its restrained, meticulous observation of the natural world—but this volume is not recapitulation. It is a foray into new territory, from which emerges a personal mythology giving rise, in turn, to theology.

The Wild Iris weaves three essential voices. The first is the singular, solitary cry of the supplicant. Sometimes devotional, sometimes chaste, sometimes ecstatic, this voice is found in the seven poems entitled "Matins" and the ten called "Vespers"—all of which present the human condition. These poems contain both praise and query, comprising a one-sided debate with the concept of god. The second voice is that of the earthly garden—of flowers

both tended and wild, the anthropomorphized world speaking as from within some innate wisdom. The third voice is a dispassionate divinity as he declares himself, either as a presence in the natural world or as an absence. Together, these fifty-four poems form a single braid; the reader senses both the individual strand and the combined strength.

The poems of *The Wild Iris* are intellectual, wholly realized within the rational mind, and yet they depend not only on an intimate knowledge of nature but also on a respect for (and passionate love of) the natural world. In narrative time, the book's duration is from early spring through early fall—a garden's visible cycle. By giving the garden a voice, Gluck forces us to see ourselves as the plants might see us—silly, foolish creatures obsessed with our mortality. Gluck does not really describe the plants (description alone being of no interest to her); she speaks from *inside* the flowers, giving each a voice and unearthing new knowledge of human behavior by examining the particularities of each variety, whether it is the lamium's predisposition toward shade ("living things don't all require/light in the same degree") or the snowdrop's surprising revival ("I didn't expect/to waken again, to feel/in damp earth my body/able to respond again. . .").

This is a book that should be read at one sitting. The voices combine to create an intense religious experience—even if the god proves to be nonexistent. The effect is one of dazzling austerity. . . .

It is a privilege to watch as a poet breaks new ground. In *The Wild Iris*, Louise Gluck has applied a stringent mind to nature in order to understand not only the self but the definition of faith and/or acceptance. (The acceptance, though, is a dark one: we are given one brief life.) Like [Robert] Frost, Gluck looks for the moment she will see *beyond* and *through*. The poems are simultaneously passionate and remote, as though written with the white heat of a distant star. Their visionary mode may even provide an entry into the snowy fields.

Judith Kitchen. *Georgia Review*. Spring, 1993, pp. 145–59.

Louise Gluck is a poet of strong and haunting presence. Her poems, published in a series of memorable books over the last twenty years, have achieved the unusual distinction of being neither "confessional" nor "intellectual" in the usual senses of those words, which are often thought to represent two camps in the life of poetry. For a long time, Gluck refused both the autobiographical and the discursive, in favor of a presentation that some called mythical, some mystical.

The voice in the poems is entirely self-possessed, but it is not possessed by self in a journalistic way. It told tales, rather, of an archetypal man and woman in a garden, of Daphne and Apollo, of mysteriously significant animal visitations. Yet behind those stories there hovered a psychology of the author that lingered, half-seen, in the poems. Gluck's language revived the possibilities of high assertion, assertion as from the Delphic tripod. The words of the assertions, though, were often humble, plain, usual; it was their hierarchic and unearthly tone that distinguished them. It was not a voice of social prophecy, but of spiritual prophecy—a tone that not many women had the courage to claim.

It was something of a shock, therefore, when Gluck's recent book *Ararat* turned away from symbol to "real life," which was described with a ruthless flatness as though honesty demanded a rock-bottom truth distilled out of years of reflection. In that book Gluck restrained her piercing drama of consciousness, and reined in her gift for poetic elaboration. It was clear that some sort of self-chastisement was underway.

Now, reversing course, she has written a very opulent, symbolic book, full—of all things—of talking flowers. [*The Wild Iris*] is really one long poem, framed as a sequence of liturgical rites: the flowers talk to their gardener-poet; the poet, who is mourning the loss of youth, passion and the erotic life, prays to a nameless god (in Matins and Vespers, many times repeated); and the god, in a very tart voice, addresses the poet. As the flowers are to their gardener-poet, so is she to her gardener-god; the flowers, in their stoic biological collectivity, and their pathos, speak to her, sometimes reproachfully, as she speaks, imploringly, to her god. The god has a viewpoint both lofty and ironic, and repeatedly attacks the self-pity or self-centeredness of the poet. These are dangerous risks for a late twentieth-century poem to take, but Gluck wins the wager of her premises. The human reader, too, is placed in "this isthmus of a middle state" (Pope) between the vegetatively animate world and the severe spiritual world, and shares the poet's predicament. . . .

What a strange book *The Wild Iris* is, appearing in this fin-de-siecle, written in the language of flowers. It is a *lieder* cycle, with all the mournful cadences of that form. It wagers everything on the poetic energy remaining in the old troubadour image of the spring, the Biblical lilies of the field, natural resurrection. It depends, too, on old religious notions of spiritual discipline. It is pre-Raphaelite, theatrical, staged and posed. It is even affected. But then, poetry has a right to these postures. When someone asked Wallace Stevens's wife whether she liked his poems, she answered, "I like Mr. Stevens's poems when they are not affected. But they are so often affected." And so they were. The trouble lay, rather, in Elsie Stevens's mistrust of affectation. It is one of the indispensable gestures in the poet's repertory.

Helen Vendler. *The New Republic.* May 24, 1993, pp. 35–8.

BIBLIOGRAPHY
Firstborn, 1968 (p); *The House on Marshland*, 1975 (p); *The Garden*, 1976 (p); *Descending Figures*, 1980 (p); *The Triumph of Achilles*, 1985 (p); *Ararat*, 1990 (p); *The Wild Iris*, 1992 (p); *Proofs and Theories*, 1994 (e) *Meadowlands*, 1996 (p) *Vita Nova*, 1999 (p)

GODWIN, Gail (1937–)

Back in the days before the Women's Liberation Front changed everything it used to be possible to think of women who wrote novels as a different order of beings from male novelists. Now, we are supposed to think of all women as essentially identical with men, except for some slight variations in plumbing, etc.

Yet the desire to think of women who write as dissimilar in some real and important sense to men who write persists, and Gail Godwin's first novel, it seems to me, has to be thought of in relation to this difference. Her book is very much a woman's novel, and I want to discuss it in those terms. But let me say first that it is an excellent piece of work, shrewdly observed and carefully crafted, deserving of the praise that such established writers as Kurt Vonnegut, John Fowles, and George P. Elliot have already bestowed on it. *The Perfectionists* is, in fact, too good, too clever, and too finished a product to be patronized as a "first novel." It

deserves better; it deserves criticism. And that is what I will try to give it.

The Perfectionists is a novel of domestic life or, more accurately, of sexual partnership. The "perfectionists" of the title are an English psychotherapist, Dr. Empson, and his American wife, Dane, who come to Majorca for something like a belated honeymoon, along with the doctor's three-year-old illegitimate son and one of his female patients. The relationship between husband and wife, as complicated by the strange little boy, is the central concern of the novel, and it is developed with a satiric and symbolic vigor that suggests a combination of Jane Austen and D. H. Lawrence. The eerie tension that marks this complex relationship is the great achievement of the novel. It is an extraordinary accomplishment, which is bound to attract and hold many readers. . . .

My principal criticism of these proceedings has to do with the resolute femininity with which they are presented. By this I mean not that metaphysical womanhood which Dickens perceived behind the pseudonym of "George Eliot" when he reviewed her amazing first novel, *Adam Bede*, but a narrower and pettier kind of thing. The women in this novel are, all of them, more or less interesting, more or less sympathetic. The men, starting with the doctor . . . are all fatuous and self-centered creatures.

This is, then, a woman's novel in a narrow and constricting way. I suspect that Miss Godwin can extend the range of both her sympathy and her satire. I hope that she will want to. From Jane Austen to Iris Murdoch, the great women of our fiction have been metaphysically female and not merely feminine.

Robert Scholes. *Saturday Review.* Aug. 8, 1970, pp. 37–38

Gail Godwin's *The Odd Woman* (1974) does not at first glance seem to be in the currently popular mode of self-conscious fiction—and perhaps for this reason has not attracted the critical attention it deserves. Neither a work as involuted as one by Borges nor a *Kuenstlerroman, The Odd Woman* centers on the relation between literature and life, especially on the effect that literature—and the lies it often tells—has on those who believe it. Of special interest is the novel's focus on fiction's traditional portrayal of women and its effect on women's relations with and reactions to men. . . .

To Jane, a professor of English, literature serves as far more than simply vocation or avocation. It is not just an object of perception but conditions her very mode of seeing. She views her own life through the refracting filter of literature. . . .

The full insight that the literary world has no necessary correlation with the actual world bursts on Jane. Villains in art need not be villains in life. Moreover, her insight confirms the truth of Jane's early wondering whether or not the concept of the self is itself a myth—"Characters were not so wholly good or bad, heroes or villains, anymore," whether or not the very notion of personality—the staple of fiction—is itself false. As the concepts of personality and of heroes and villains die, so does "all the stuff of novels" on which Jane depends to give meaning to her life.

Unfortunately, *The Odd Woman* does not end on an optimistic note of lessons learned. . . . The novel closes with the snow falling, reminding us of Jane's retreat when writing her dissertation, and pointing to another such frozen retreat from the actual world.

Godwin seems to offer a forceful indictment of literature and the harmful effects it can have on its readers. Jane can never be happy except, perhaps, in the safe world of the imagination, the only world which can begin to fulfill the expectations literature has fostered in her. We must go on to ask how Godwin can escape her own indictment of literature, whether her message does not undermine the very novel in which it is embodied. . . .

As Jane notes, Gissing's novel [with the same title] displays his "unrelenting pessimism. It was one of the few nineteenth-century novels she could think of in which every main female character who was allowed to live through the last page had to do so alone. The book's ending depressed her utterly." Godwin might find her defense against the charge she, too, levels against literature in pointing to the pessimistic ending of Jane's story as an example of the truth-telling that we must require from contemporary fiction. Godwin, however, has some of the Jane Clifford in her, and her novel still embodies some of the old attractive lies.

Susan E. Lorsch. *Critique.* 20, 2, 1978, pp. 21, 31

Gail Godwin's newest novel, *Violet Clay,* [is] a terrifying example of sentimentality in the disguise of contemporary sensibility. . . .

None of the novel's characters has been translated by Godwin's imagination into credibility. They speak to each other in prolix and tendentious conversations, so unedited by personality that they are droll. . . .

Well, to be fair, a lot of this is the fault of bad writing, an inability to describe exactly or to transcribe the sound of different voices into anything resembling living language. . . .

But there is worse than this, the basis from which the flabby language, the insubstantial characters, the odd lapses of taste seem to spring; the novel is simply half-baked, half-created, and so far from inevitable that one reads it constantly reminding oneself that it could easily have been avoided. . . .

If the book carries any conviction with it, it is that Violet's esthetic is pretty much molded by her author's, a schoolgirl sensibility in search of vocation. Gail Godwin has been regarded highly as a novelist for some time, certainly since *The Odd Woman* was published in 1974, and I wonder unhappily how much of that regard is due to the fashionable nature of her themes, which can create, without feeling for character, language, ambience, or moral significance, a job lot of current concerns that passes as "Women's Fiction."

Edith Milton. *New Republic.* July 8–15, 1978, pp. 40–41

Gail Godwin, on first reading, seems to stand apart from contemporary women writers. She appears immune to experiments with style and the contemporary raw language of sexuality. Her works are plotted symmetrically in the manner of George Eliot, whom she admires, and at a time when many women writers are primarily concerned with woman's emerging sexuality as well as with her active participation in the outside world, Godwin maintains that the demands of the inner woman are much more complex than this. Inner life, says her heroine, Jane Clifford (*The Odd Woman,* 1974), is as important as outer life. But it is obvious that the author considers the inner life even more important. Her first two novels, *The Perfectionists* (1970) and *Glass People* (1972), are clever, well-executed works about women who attempt to grapple with the domestic life and with sexual partnership. More specifically, the

heroine of *Glass People* is confronted with what she comes to regard as the awful responsibility of freedom.

How to achieve freedom while in union with another person, and impose one's own order on life so as to find self-fulfillment, is the theme which runs through Godwin's works and becomes the major theme of exploration in her third novel, *The Odd Woman.* . . . Where some other women writers maintain a pessimism about the man/woman relationship, Godwin has her heroine doggedly affirm that man and woman can be a unit; man and woman need each other. Yet it is worth noting that the heroine is alone in the end. The open ending, however, indicates that the author is still the writer of freedom, marriage, love, children, and the relationship between generations. Her subsequent work, *Dream Children* (1976), continues these themes with variations.

Anne Z. Mickelson. *Reaching Out: Sensitivity and Order in Recent American Fiction by Women* (Scarecrow, 1979), p. 68

Gail Godwin's heroines have abandoned their soapboxes, and thank goodness for that. Godwin is by now an "established" writer; she has four novels and a collection of short stories to her credit, not to mention a National Book Award nomination. Her complex and fascinating characters, like Jane Clifford in *The Odd Woman* and Violet in *Violet Clay,* have until now suffered from two crippling flaws: they have repeatedly indulged in long, often boring, interior monologues—"meandering and distinctly tedious," huffed novelist Larry McMurtry of an earlier novel—and they have had no sense of humor whatsoever.

However, the news of Godwin's latest novel, *A Mother and Two Daughters,* is good, in fact, very good indeed. Nell, Cate, and Lydia Strickland, the three women who dominate the stage, are—like Violet Clay and Jane Clifford—thoughtful, well-educated, self-analytic people, but Godwin hustles them along at a brisk pace through this long, but definitely never tedious tale. They don't opine about the meaning of love or the perils of George Eliot, but do share with us their attempts to make a good job of an ordinary daily life familiar to us all. . . .

Only a few times in this long novel does Godwin falter. A digression on contemporary fiction seems jarringly self-conscious. The requisite eccentrics are skillfully drawn, but show up right on cue: the overbearing, curious spinster aunt Theodora and the disfigured Uncle Osgood with his heart of gold and his redemptive role for latter-day sinners. The middle-class black couple seem plopped down in order to stir up a few thoughts on prejudice and change. All the characters take themselves very seriously, but it is part of their astonishing strength that they persuade us to do likewise.

Anyone from an average family will find themselves drawing a breath and muttering: "Yes, that's how *I* felt, that's how it always is." Godwin wrote of Jane Clifford in *The Odd Woman*: "Her profession was words and she believed in them deeply. The articulation, interpretation, and preservation of good words." She could have been describing herself. She pilots her cast of characters with infinite care, through turbulence, clouds, and sparkling skies. The smooth landing at the novel's end is deeply satisfying: not a neat tying up of loose ends, but a making sense of the past and a hint of the possibilities of the future. Gail Godwin is not just an established writer, she is a growing writer.

Brigitte Weeks. *Ms.* Jan., 1982, pp. 40–41

In general, Miss Godwin's gifts (like Margaret Drabble's) have been best served by the spacious dimensions of the conventional novel. Her talent lies in creating intelligent woman protagonists—usually middle-class and imaginative, often with artistic aspirations—who struggle to lead examined lives in the face of self-imposed as well as cultural constraints. Blessed with humor as well as perceptiveness, they are nearly always sympathetic, even when they behave badly. (Their amiability can be irritating. I sometimes wish Miss Godwin's characters would behave worse more often; her women often suffer from the excess of politesse common to children of the 1950's.)

In any case, her reflective characters come to life slowly, emerging as much from thought as from action, and Miss Godwin's novels have generally accommodated them. I especially liked the edgy perversity of *The Perfectionists* (1970) and the irony and insight of *The Odd Woman* (1974), as well as the gentler but widening vision of *A Mother and Two Daughters*.

I wish I could be as enthusiastic about *Mr. Bedford and the Muses*, a short novel and five stories. The stories have the more obvious problems, which are at least partly due to brevity and partly to their tucked-in edges. Shapeliness is deadly in short fiction. At best, it creates an excess of charm; at worst, it kills the story on the page. . . .

On its own terms, which are not those of Miss Godwin's larger novels, *Mr. Bedford* is a memorable portrait of the kind of people who might have known Scott Fitzgerald during their "better days." It is wry, haunting and sharp.

> Judith Gies. *New York Times Book Section*. Sept. 18, 1983, pp. 14, 37

BIBLIOGRAPHY
The Perfectionists, 1970 (n); *Glass People*, 1972 (n); *The Odd Woman*, 1974 (n); *Dream Children*, 1976 (s); *Violet Clay*, 1978 (n); *A Mother and Two Daughters*, 1982 (n); *Mr. Bedford and the Muses*, 1983 (n); *A Southern Family*, 1987 (n); *Father Melancholy's Daughter*, 1991 (n); *The Good Husband*, 1994 (n); *Evensong*, 1999 (n)

GOLD, Herbert (1924–)

If it is true that Mr. Gold's novel (*Birth of a Hero*) has a special importance because it represents a turning point in the intellectual's attitude toward the middle class . . . , it must not be overlooked that Mr. Gold writes with charm and talent. He understands the phenomena at which he is smiling, and he communicates adroitly his delighted recognition of the significance of such neglected rituals as the office party and the commuter's daily journey. If we are really at the beginning of a new era of conservatism, we can only hope that the writers who will choose to celebrate the heroic virtues of the middle-aged and the comfortably placed will be able to do so with at least a portion of Mr. Gold's benevolent wit, radical perception, and intellectual vigor.

> Harvey Swados. *The Nation*. Oct. 6, 1951. p. 284

Like Flaubert, Herbert Gold hangs his effects on a faithful reporting of sensations recorded by the five senses. . . . Scenes are strung together necklace-style and motivation is not always clear or credible. Characters have labels and are stuck to them. It's a cerebral performance with a tangle of long, long thoughts, most of them entertainingly presented in colorful, runaway language. A high fidelity ear and eye are at work here.

> James Kelly. *New York Times Book Section*. Feb. 14, 1954. p. 5

The Man Who Was Not With It is itself a carnival, bringing the reader into a strange and fascinating tent. The novel is a spectacular linguistic performance. Herbert Gold's writing is sometimes flashy and full of sideshow guile, but much more often his story is beautifully told, with tough and tender humor. . . . Herbert Gold is no longer a novelist to be watched in the future—his performance is here, and well worth watching right now.

> Alan Harrington. *The Nation*. June 23, 1956. p. 535

Herbert Gold's *The Man Who Was Not With It* belongs to (a) tradition, that of the picaresque, which Mr. Gold has fitted with the existentialist idea of the tragedy of "engagement", in a novel that is exciting both as language and as figuration of destiny. . . . Mr. Gold's story has as its human substance the awful risk inherent in adult faith between men. The picaresque design of the book lies in the adventures of a kid who travels with a carnival. . . . To be "with it and of it" is the carnival lingo for the ultimate loyalty to the strange, spiritually islanded life of the carnival.

> Dorothy Van Ghent. *The Yale Review*. Summer, 1956. p. 632

Gold's intelligence is the brightness of skill, exuberance, and his prized risk-taking. It is the sheer vitality of a talented writer. . . . Herbert Gold . . . seems to have found, evolved, or perhaps been born with, a Baroque style that is exciting and controlled; but he has yet to find a theme thick and heavy enough with significance or rooted deeply enough in the universals of "human nature" . . . to be worthy of this style. . . . The only resonance is that of the word-music; and though rich and various, it sometimes seems like pleasant ornamentation, or fireworks and exhibitionism, and occasionally it reminds me of Parmigianino's mannerist portraits of the long-necked Madonna: exceedingly beautiful, except that a little of such beauty goes a long way.

> Melvin Seiden. *The Nation*. April 25, 1959. pp. 389–90

There are no writers under forty—and there are few of any age—for whom I have more admiration than I have for Herbert Gold. His first novel, *Birth of a Hero*, published while he was still in his twenties, was an extraordinarily perceptive study of love in middle age. He followed it with a dramatic and vivid novel of city life and race conflict, *The Prospect Before Us*, and then came his novel of carnival ways, the drug habit, and young love, rich in carnie talk, *The Man Who Was Not With It*. He has also written several first-rate short stories and some vigorous criticism. In less than ten years he has produced a body of work that establishes him as a central figure in today's literature.

Granville Hicks. *Saturday Review*. April 25, 1959. p. 12

Mr. Gold has an extraordinary talent for style, but also a weakness for it; he is in danger of becoming a *stylist*. As Shakespeare, according to Dr. Johnson, would sometimes trade all sense for the achievement of a pun, Gold will trade it for a frill, or sometimes even a trill. His style is by nature a vehicle of warm and intelligent humor, and when it is properly limited, leashed, and pommeled into obedience, it does its work well and charmingly. Gold can be very, very funny; or expressive; or even brilliant in little perfect flashes of incidental observation or conversation. . . . But often there is a regrettable muddying of perception by style—an overstyling that blinds or distracts or blurs the eye that is supposed to see something more clearly with the style's help.

Richard Foster. *Hudson Review*. Spring, 1961. pp. 146–7

Gold has emerged as a kind of literary hipster, far too cunning to be taken in by any hipster nonsense, but who in his unsentimental coolness, pitiless sense of the contemporary, and inside dopesterism has links with the type.

Even more important, Gold, like very few of our major writers, has tried to stretch language to meet the new requirements of our time. He has used an idiom that is highly permutable, strained perhaps, too shifty; but it reaches out to encompass new states of mind that writers in an easier time did not have to cope with. At its best, it is taut, keyed-up, nervously inventive; at its worst, it is merely artsy-smirky, a pushy, obtrusive prose. And it defines Gold's stance: the novelist as wise guy. . . . Herbert Gold leaves us where we were before. There is a terrible emptiness everywhere. If the older generation of writers dealt with the loss of values, Gold's characters seem never to have had them.

David Boroff. *Saturday Review*. April 20, 1963. pp. 45–6

Mr. Gold is "That most happy fellow" in America, the master of "the going thing." His stories and novels are zeroed in on a new generation who suffer early sorrow, make an early marriage, father children at an early age, and then—surrounded by the symbols of middle-class domesticity—find their hearts festering with unrealized adolescent desires. Divorced in their early thirties, cut adrift in a hustling world that "understands" but never helps, these martyrs to the American fixation on "love" wobble desperately between fantasies of suicide and a second, better union.

The one man who speaks consistently to their condition—who describes it minutely in all its embarrassingly familiar detail and yet never betrays its poignant optimism—is Herbert Gold.

Albert Goldman. *New Republic*. June 8, 1963. p. 23

Herbert Gold's *Salt* is a western of the *Playboy* world. Touching all the conventions of life among the lonely crowd on and off Madison Avenue, Mr. Gold draws a triangle of two old army buddies and the girl whom one of them really loves and the other one merely uses. Pretty Barbara is a small town girl in the big city; poor Dan, a sad sack hero from Cleveland who is trying to forget a divorce; and

suave Peter, a cynical Wall Street junior executive who juggles oranges to keep his balance between love affairs. Around this configuration, Gold paints in the usual local color: Village hipsters, suburban organization men, and, of course, GIRLS, GIRLS, GIRLS.

Gold's ironic sweet-and-sour style is quite good for reproducing the sidewalks of New York—"it's a lovely city at certain intense moments, both hard and cajoling—but what do you do with the rest of the moments?"—but quite inadequate for penetrating beneath the surface. . . . Gold's characters may be looking for love but they will settle for sex; and while there is nothing necessarily wrong with their attitude there is something definitely wrong with the author's. Mr. Gold wants it both ways: to be hip with the hipsters and moral with the moralists; and his final rejection of the New York scene—irritating and unconvincing as it is—is magically consistent with the *Playboy* philosophy of bourgeois bohemianism.

Paul Levine. *Hudson Review*. Autumn, 1963. p. 458

The Man Who Was Not With It—in the few years of its paperback existence rather wildly called *The Wild Life*—is a book to which synopsis can't do justice. It can merely indicate some of the main trends of the story. Herbert Gold has marvelously captured carnival life, with its lures for markers and its fights with rubes, all the excitement and tinsel and struggle. Grack is the most successful of the author's vitalistic characters, and to hear him giving his pitch on the midway, with his "lookee" and his "hee hee hee" and "ho ho ho," is to be in the gusty atmosphere of the fairgrounds. In having Bud tell the story in carnie slang, Gold makes full use of his own ability to handle colorful idiom. It crackles. But the language isn't flashed just for its own sake; it is organic. Through it, the author is able to present nuances of character and investigate the depths of his particular kind of people in a way which would have been less intimate with straight language. Herbert Gold's tendency toward the bizarre in style exactly matches the subject matter in this book.

Harry T. Moore in *Contemporary American Novelists*, ed. Harry T. Moore (Southern Illinois). 1964. pp. 180–1

Gold always seems on the verge of writing the big one. *The Man Who Was Not With It* almost turned a carnival barker's world into a modern myth. *The Age of Happy Problems* was a collection of bright, Gold-plated journalism. His last novel, *Salt*, merely glossed the ways of Madison Avenue. The facile, witty Gold has yet to hit that blend of the comic, realist and moral visions that might make him a first-rank figure. He is currently a *Playboy* intellectual under contract. . . . Coming of age in the Midwest, he never developed that tough-minded desire for battle that is the hallmark of the New York Jewish tradition. Before *Fathers*, in fact, Gold never needed to write a *Jewish* novel. Now that he has, his efforts to establish a family history for himself—to make amends to Sam Gold for having once rejected his gift of life—seem painfully painless, another glittering, but not quite valuable Gold mine of "happy problems."

Howard Junker. *Newsweek*. March 27, 1967. pp. 104A–105

With Mr. Gold's fictional world there can be no finicky discriminations: we go through good times and bad with a brave wonderful family, with a huge supporting cast of uncles, aunts, cousins, school friends, business associates, racketeers. The excitement and the good-heartedness are infectious, without doubt, and there's no denying that Mr. Gold's writing is crisper than it used to be; his book is mercifully free of the gooeyness that characterized his earlier novels.

Still, one has to resist Mr. Gold's eager message that experience, slice it how you like, is just wonderful, though one can see how he came by it. As a novelist he combines the Whitman-style hipster and the Jewish immigrant, as is evident from the opening paragraph of *Fathers*. . . . In his early novel, *The Man Who Was Not With It*, the hipster mode predominated, whereas the new novel is fixed in the denser realities of Jewish family life, and has a correspondingly greater solidity.

Bernard Bergonzi. *New York Review of Books*. June 1, 1967. pp. 30–1

Mr. Gold's novel [*Fathers*] has a curiously seductive quality. I am not usually captivated by this particular form of Jewish excess, which inflates every character into a near-caricature and which drips and runs over with tears-behind-laughter. Mr. Gold can be shockingly corny at times, and his folksiness is always threatening to swamp him. (''Every sky has its own magic if a man knows how to put it there.'') But he can also write with a wonderful and very individual power, canalizing his ferocious energies and creating exactly the effect that he intended. He is funny; he is charming; he is, by the end of the book, irresistible, even if one is left with the uneasy feeling that one should have fought rather harder against him.

Philip Toynbee. *New Republic*. June 17, 1967. p. 21

BIBLIOGRAPHY
Birth of a Hero, 1951 (n); *The Prospect before Us*, 1954 (n); *The Man Who Was Not With It*, 1956 (n); (with R. V. Cassill and James B. Hall) *Fifteen by Three*, 1957 (s); *The Optimist*, 1959 (n); *Love & Like*, 1960 (s); *Therefore Be Bold*, 1960 (n); *The Age of Happy Problems*, 1962 (e); *First Person Singular*, 1963 (e); *Salt*, 1963 (n); *Fathers*, 1967 (n); *The Great American Jackpot*, 1969 (n); *Biafra Goodbye*, 1970 (h); *The Magic Will: Stories and Essays of a Decade*, 1971; *My Last Two Thousand Years*, 1972 (a); *The Young Prince and the Magic Cone*, 1973 (juv); *Swiftie the Magician*, 1974 (n); *Waiting for Cordelia*, 1977 (n); *Slave Trade*, 1979 (n); *He/She*, 1980 (n); *Family: A Novel in the Form of a Memoir*, 1981; *A Walk on the West Side: California on the Brink*, 1981 (e); *True Love*, 1982 (n); *Mister White Eyes*, 1984 (n); *A Girl of Forty*, 1986 (n); *Lovers and Cohorts: Twenty-Seven Stories*, 1986; *Dreaming*, 1988 (n); *Travels in San Francisco*, 1990 (t); *Best Nightmare on Earth: A Life in Haiti*, 1991 (t); *Bohemia: Where Art, Angst, Love, and Strong Coffee Meet*, 1993 (b); *She Took My Arm As If She Loved Me*, 1997 (n)

GOODMAN, Paul (1911–1972)

Paul Goodman's dance poems are based indirectly on the Noh-plays. These are not intended to be dramatic, in the Western sense,

of unfolding an action. Their aim is rather an ''initiation into a true awareness.''. . .

The style—a loose blank-verse interspersed with short lines and with prose—is fluid; the thought is always interesting, and the stylized form allows him to make use of such phrases as ''how curious this is!''—''how strange!''—with full effect. A poet with such a strategic sense as these dance-poems reveal may develop along unexpected lines.

Lloyd Frankenberg. *New Republic*. March 16, 1942. p. 371

Among writers of the non-realistic persuasion, Mr. Goodman is unusually well-educated, imaginative, and witty, and even though, as we follow him from piece to piece, his unremitting literacy and cleverness become a bit wearing, this virtuosity must be to some extent excused as an excess of virtues. [*The Facts of Life*] contains at least one story, the title story, which is entirely delightful, and a play, ''Jonah,'' about the prophet of doom, which is both comic and wise. The fact that the collection as a whole falls short of these two items doesn't of course diminish Mr. Goodman's stature in relation to other writers of his convention. It does, however, tend to confirm an old suspicion that even the method of non-realism cannot forfeit story-telling to disputation and still be sustaining.

Diana Trilling. *The Nation*. July 28, 1945. p. 90

In a sense . . . *The Empire City* is what can always be called ''coterie literature.'' More often than necessary, it is frankly, intimately addressed to the intellectual who has had Utopian dreams, read or written for *Partisan Review*. . . . At the same time, it is a book originating in good will, mature candor, and an urgently fermenting, more than secular morality. . . . The spirit inside, and the text itself, which seems not so much written as whistled, laughed, teased, prayed, come as close to imparting a man's gratuitous love for his own kind as mere language ever can.

Robert Phelps. *New York Herald Tribune Book Section*. June 28, 1959. p. 3

The Empire City unfolds as a series of incidents, antic, lyrical, wry or elegiac, but informed by high spirits that counterbalance a terrifying awareness of degradation. . . . Nothing that we have lived or lived through during the past generation escapes having its absurdities uncovered. . . . It is all funny and sorrowful and not to be denied. . . . Yet Goodman, unlike Kafka, who was content to let the humor, ruefulness and terror speak for themselves, has an irrepressible taste for oratory, a thirties-like itch for declamation that introduces great stretches of tedium into an otherwise fertile landscape.

Richard Gilman. *Commonweal*. July 31, 1959. p. 401

The Community of Scholars beautifully exemplifies Goodman's virtues as a social critic, in a less dramatic way, perhaps, than his classic study of juvenile delinquency, *Growing Up Absurd*, but no less impressively: this is a book that deserves comparison with Newman's *The Idea of a University* or Veblen's *The Higher Learning in America*. The theme here is the disruptive effect of administration and administrative mentality on the proper relation between college students and their teachers in America today, and on the proper relation between the college itself and the surrounding society. As usual with Goodman, the approach is philosophical rather than narrowly political. That is, he does not begin by asking what choices are allowed by the apparently ineluctable forces of the present (in this instance the growth of an administrative apparatus extraneous and even hostile to the process of learning); he begins by asking what are the essential properties and purposes of a college, under what arrangements historically have these properties found their fullest expression, and under what conditions can we plausibly imagine that they might be better realized in the future. [1962]

Norman Podhoretz. *Doings and Undoings* (Farrar). 1964. pp. 99–100

Goodman is by temperament optimistic and busy; one wonders whether he cares very much about seeing his demands realized or whether just making them is sufficient satisfaction. His habit of attributing the evils and neglects of society to mental inadequacy ... is, to my mind, an evasion of the real resistance to change arising from people's historically acquired attachments to property, conventions, superstitions. ... Though, if things were up for a vote, I should oppose most of Goodman's recommendations, I do not doubt that arguing against them would lead me to better opinions than agreeing with almost anyone else. This is another way of saying that Goodman is making an indispensable contribution to democratic thinking.

Harold Rosenberg. *New York Times Book Section.* Jan. 14, 1962. p. 6

Essentially, all of Paul Goodman's poems are about himself, and social and political concepts are present, not programmatically, but because they are interwoven with his private concerns. Thus the erotic is just as likely to be present in a political context as the political in an erotic context, and we gain some beginnings of insight into their still obscure interaction. The relationship between sexual fear and the politics of murder and suicide, and the alternative relationship of an architecture of community and the use of human energy for peace and pleasure: these concepts are as integral to his poetry as Pound's insistence on the reciprocity of monetary reform and just government with precision and vitality of language are to the *Cantos.*

Denise Levertov. *The Nation.* April 13, 1963. p. 310

Intimacy really means everything to [Goodman]. Placing the sharpest value on the spontaneous utterance, the thing to be said, yet schooled, helter-skelter, in the classical tradition, Goodman, predictably, is a glorious mixer. Politically, he blends, I think, Kantian morality with Humean expediency; personally, he "publishes thirty books and rears three children," and indulges his idiosyncrasies. If Hebraic truth is prophetic and for the race, and Christian truth confessional and individual, Goodman irresistibly responds to both. In the novels, whether the naturalism of *Making Do* or the surrealist tinting of *The Empire City,* his heroes, devastatingly impressionable, keep fingering the chinks in the armor, the holes in the fences, wrestling with those parts of the

economy, or the self, unexplored or unwanted. They are, like Goodman, both pariahs and charioteers.

Similarly, the poems. These are rallying songs of innocence and experience—querulous, anecdotal, prayerful, salacious. Often they are hymns to overcoming that which cramps, celebrating that which heightens, or brings together: "Creator Spirit, come." The best, it seems to me, are unpruned or unornamental, zesty and life-giving, if only for the moment. The worst (and, happily, that means the minority) lack everything—fullness of language, flow of images—that poetry must be if it is not to be cactus.

Robert Mazzocco. *New York Review of Books.* May 21, 1970. p. 4

America's inability to accommodate and profit by the whole of Paul Goodman is, for Goodman, properly a sign and symptom of her inability to deal with *any* experience in a spontaneous and inclusive way (though it should be said, in America's defense, that to accommodate the whole of Paul Goodman is a considerable undertaking, one that might make any republic fractious). Goodman's emphasis on a reading of his *Collected Poems* as a whole, as a *Leaves of Grass*-type experience, rather than as a series or even as a scattering of beautiful realizations, lucky hits and near misses, is part of the same impulse towards convergence, unity, completion, connections within the self. ...

Goodman [is], more than any American poet alive, the true heir and disciple of the Good Grey Poet, mining the verge of the inclusive experience; and if he does not have Whitman's genius for suggesting that he is a Cosmos in himself, relying of necessity on the received forms to stiffen his talent, he is apter to catch his own posture, even his own imposture, in a reflexive and restorative irony. The other, public irony is that Paul Goodman's poetry has been obscured—cancelled, as a Sacred Book—by its situation in his canon—if he had written only poems, he would I think have held the place in American poetry today that sexuality, say, has in our assessment of human possibilities—central, flawed, affording occasions for joy and fulfillment.

Richard Howard. *Alone with America* (Atheneum). 1971. pp. 155–6, 162

[Goodman] had been a hero of mine for so long that I was not in the least surprised when he became famous, and always a little surprised that people seemed to take him for granted. The first book of his I ever read—I was sixteen—was a collection of stories called *The Break-up of Our Camp,* published by New Directions. Within a year I had read everything he'd written, and from then on started keeping up. There is no living American writer for whom I have felt the same simple curiosity to read as quickly as possible *anything* he wrote, on any subject. That I mostly agreed with what he thought was not the main reason; there are other writers I agree with to whom I am not so loyal. It was that voice of his that seduced me— that direct, cranky, egotistical, generous American voice. ...

Paul Goodman's voice touched everything he wrote about with intensity, interest, and his own terribly appealing sureness and awkwardness. What he wrote was a nervy mixture of syntactical stiffness and verbal felicity; he was capable of writing sentences of a wonderful purity of style and vivacity of language, and also capable of writing so sloppily and clumsily that one imagined he must be doing it on purpose. But it never mattered. It was his voice, that is to say, his intelligence and the poetry of his intelligence incarnated, which kept me a loyal and passionate addict.

Susan Sontag. *New York Review of Books.* Sept. 21, 1972. p. 10

There was always a coarse-grained Hasidic magic about Goodman's stories, novels and poems. As with Buber, his peak moments were events that happened between people and in community. The Gestalt group work pioneered by Goodman and Perls is really a therapeutically ritualized search for Buber's I-Thou experience—with a heavy admixture of Reichian body mysticism to give it an even greater earthiness and weight. Like Buber, too, (and like the Taoist sages who are so similar to the Hasidic mystics) Goodman had a shrewd eye for how miraculously transfigured the common-place substance of life might be—if only for one zany instant—if only to be followed by the business as usual of benightedness, folly, nastiness and failure. . . .

The patient acceptance of human frailty, the constitutional melancholy and broodiness, both are drawn from the Hasidic masters. . . . The whole nobility of Judaism has always lain in its stubborn trust that the world, such as it is, and people, such as they are, are unique manifestations of the Lord's will and so here is where we must make do.

Theodore Roszak. *Book World.* Oct. 15, 1972. p. 10

Belatedly, in August, I heard of Paul Goodman's death. Shortly before, I'd been reading his last book of poems, *Homespun of Oatmeal Gray*, a book full of frustration and loss. I had thought again, as often in the past ten years, of writing him a letter. His "Drawing the Line" was one of the writings that changed my way of being in the world in the early '60's; that, along with Simone Weil, moved me toward politics. All his work, poetry and prose, was full of vital energy and courage and love for good craft, "healthy speech," the natural world and the human body. Goodman was one of those few contemporary poets for whom there was no apparent split between himself and nature—in his own person he did not seem to suffer from that division, although he certainly suffered from and struggled with its effects on politics and the social order. His sensuality—at least as I read it in his poems—seems all of a piece: grass, water, a Cape Cod beach, city streets, the embrace of another body, the taste of food, are parts of one whole for him, much as they were for Whitman. Like Whitman, he seems to have come by this wholeness through bisexuality (though I think of Whitman as a more truly feminine nature). Whether he was as capable as Whitman of respecting wholeness in others, I do not know.

Adrienne Rich. *American Poetry Review.* Jan.-Feb., 1973. p. 16

[Goodman] belonged among those authors who are remembered less for what they wrote than for who they were. As a teacher he did not bring a new message but evoked the voice that had been slumbering in the imagination of his audience. His thought was neither very original nor in any way systematic. A eulogy that were to try a summary of his ideas could only reveal their contradictions.

I can honor him only by continuing in his own aphoristic, some-what freewheeling style, to free-associate some ideas which might please or displease him.

I believe that Paul was first of all a poet, and the youth of the 1960's listened to him not because he or they were politically radical, but because he opposed Wordsworth to General Motors, free love to the Board of Education, community to big organizations. He was neither a socialist nor an anarchist in the strict sense of those terms, but a rebel who had the courage to say what others dimly guessed or did not admit to themselves: that they did not understand the world into which they were supposed to grow up; that they felt crushed by the demands made on them by their parents, their teachers, their future employers; that all this seemed absurd. Many who, before he said this, had felt stupid, felt free because he had said it.

Henry Pachter. *Salmagundi.* Fall, 1973. p. 54

Many years ago I said in a review that if Paul Goodman had written in French or German he would have been well known all over the world before he was thirty. In a recent book on American poetry I said of him that he taught at Black Mountain a part of the year for many years. The second statement is a mistake. As a matter of fact, the squares on the Black Mountain faculty, particularly the most reactionary (putatively Far Left) German refugees, demanded that he be fired because he was what they considered a "sexual deviant." One thing he certainly was for many years was a leading think tank for the editors of the *Partisan Review*, along with Harold Rosenberg and Lionel Abel. Had Rahv and Phillips not taken exhaustive notes on the conversations of these three mentors, the *Partisan Review* would have had great difficulty ever rising above the intellectual level of the *Reader's Digest*. . . .

All his life he wrote poetry. Did he think of himself as a poet? Was he a poet? . . . One thing he certainly is not is a poet of the international modernist idiom. Twelve dollars and fifty cents worth of poems [*Collected Poems*], four hundred and sixty five pages. There is little evidence that anybody from Baudelaire to many of the youngest poets of the *American Poetry Review* ever existed. The work of a life in poetry—it's the life that matters. This is confessional poetry in a different sense than the use of the term invented by A. Alvarez. He meant the autobiographical case histories of the more or less mad. I think he first applied the term to Sylvia Plath. Paul was far from mad. He was sane and sad. He is one of the very few Americans with a genuine tragic sense of life, that sense that comes from six thousand years of culture, the abiding realization that life is heartbreakingly comic. Never forget, Chekhov called his plays of disorder and early sorrow, suicide and decay "comedies." Paul shared that point of view, a hard thing to do in a country where you are either an optimist or a pessimist or unpublishable.

Kenneth Rexroth. *American Poetry Review.* 3, 3, 1974. p. 48

BIBLIOGRAPHY

The Grand Piano, 1942 (n); *Stop-Light: Noh*, 1945 (pd); *The Facts of Life*, 1945 (s,d); *State of Nature*, 1946 (n); *Kafka's Prayer*, 1947 (c); (with Percival Goodman) *Communitas*, 1947 (e); *The Break-up of Our Camp*, 1949 (s); *The Structure of Literature*, 1954 (e); *The Empire City*, 1959 (n); *Our Visit to Niagara*, 1960 (s); *Growing Up*

Absurd, 1960 (e); *Drawing the Line*, 1962 (e); *Utopian Essays and Practical Proposals*, 1962 (e); *The Community of Scholars*, 1962 (e); *The Lordly Hudson, and Other Poems*, 1962; *Making Do*, 1963 (n); *The Society I Live in Is Mine*, 1963 (e); *Compulsory Mis-Education*, 1964 (e); *People or Personnel*, 1965 (e); *Three Plays*, 1965; *Five Years*, 1966 (m); *Hawkweed*, 1967 (p); *Like a Conquered Province*, 1967 (e); *Adam and His Works*, 1968 (s); *North Percy*, 1970 (p); *New Reformation*, 1970 (e); *Tragedy and Comedy*, 1970 (d); *Homespun of Oatmeal Gray*, 1970 (p); *Speaking and Language*, 1972 (e); *Little Prayers and Finite Experience*, 1972 (misc): *Collected Poems*, 1974

GORDON, Caroline (1895–1981)

Penhally is the triumphant tragedy of a house and the vindication of a mode of life. It is an achievement at once of erudition and of sombre and smouldering passion. It is distinguished by the afterglow of the Greek-Roman-Anglo-Saxon classicism that marked the Old South off from all other lands. . . .

Penhally differs from other historical works which are written from the outside and are at best *tours de force*—more or less reconstitutions. It unites itself to the living school of autobiographic writers in that it is a piece of autobiography. Mrs. Tate [Caroline Gordon] has from her earliest days so lived herself into the past of her race and region that her whole being is compact of the passions, the follies, the exaggerations, the classicisms, the excesses, the gallantries and the leadings of forlorn hopes that brought the Old South to its end. She does not have to document herself in order to evoke Morgan's cavalry raids or conditions of life amongst the slaves in the be-hollyhocked Quarters. She has so lived in the past that it is from her own experience that she distils these things.

So *Penhally* is a chronicle of reality. . . . Her characters have none of the historic over-emphasis that distinguishes the usual romance of escape. Her Southern girls are not over-dimitied, her gallants not over-spurred, her great proprietors not over-lavish. They are in short everyday people—but people of an everyday that is not today. That is a great literary achievement—and a great service to the republic the chief of whose needs is to know how life is constituted.

Ford Madox Ford. *Bookman*. Dec., 1931. pp. 374–6

None Shall Look Back fills out by a . . . discursive method the fortunes of the family in the midst of a war which destroys the social basis of its way of life. *The Garden of Adonis* has for scene the country community about the time of the last depression, when the full effects of defeat have had time to show their marks. *Aleck Maury, Sportsman* is not outside [Caroline Gordon's] subject but treats it in a very special way; and her most recent novel, *The Women on the Porch*, shifts the location to the city, the full-blown symbol of the western progression, or more specifically in American mythology, the end of pioneering. The heroine, the first to marry outside the connection (and this is significant), in her flight from the City with no intention of returning to the family seat instinctively finds her way back, but this time to a place of ghosts and sibyls. But the startling disclosure of the book is the crystallization of what has been gradually emerging, the theme of prevailing

interest. To isolate such a theme . . . is an act of violence and distortion to the work as a whole. Briefly, this theme is what Life, the sly deceiver, does to womankind but particularly to the woman of great passion and sensibility. It is not that men do not come in for their share of sorrows and disappointments; it is, rather, that Life, represented in the only possible hierarchy of institutional and organized society, has a masculine determination. Very subtly the White Goddess reasserts herself as Miss Gordon's Muse. The young girl in ''The Brilliant Leaves,'' the various heroines of *Penhally* (Alice Blair, the dark sister), Lucy of *None Shall Look Back*, and most eloquently the wife of Aleck Maury, are all the same woman. Very few of the male characters—Forrest, Nicholas, Mister Ben the possible exceptions—are able to measure up to the requirements of what the heroine thinks a man should be.

Andrew Lytle. *Sewanee Review*. Autumn, 1949. p. 578

[Caroline Gordon] has not accommodated the austerities of her method to that cultivation of violence and oddity for its own sake, whether in subject-matter or style, which is one of the more distressing infantilisms of an otherwise vital and growing Southern expression in literature. And while there is nostalgia and backward glancing in her early novels of the old South, she sternly reminds herself in the title of one of them that ''None shall look back.'' Thus she loses out, as well, at the popular romancing level of Southern fiction, for she has not gone with the wind.

Caroline Gordon, whose prose is perhaps the most unaffected and uniformly accomplished that is being written by any American woman today, should be seen as the conservator in contemporary Southern fiction of the great classical tradition of the nineteenth century novel as formulated by Stendhal, Flaubert and somewhat later, Henry James. . . .

Miss Gordon's allegiances are clearly formulated [in the preface to the anthology *The House of Fiction*] and in her last novel, *The Strange Children*, her fidelity to the tradition of ''naturalism'' as she has defined it emerges with a mature authority. It is in this finely thoughtful work that her real service to the realm of Southern letters as the conservator of the heritage of ''naturalism'' and thus of the mainstream of the great fiction of the western world is most powerfully demonstrated.

Vivienne Koch in *Southern Renascence: The Literature of the Modern South*, ed. Louis D. Rubin, Jr., and Robert D. Jacobs (Johns Hopkins). 1953. pp. 325–7

The Malefactors marks a new departure in Miss Gordon's fiction. Yet it does have a connection with four novels which precede it. It also illustrates strikingly a change in outlook which these novels represent. *Penhally* and *None Shall Look Back* are full of regret for the vanished order of the Old South where men and women knew their place in the social hierarchy and could depend all their lives on values which their ordered society taught and supported. With *The Garden of Adonis* Miss Gordon moved into the modern Southern world which has lost its connections with the old order. Her men and women must now struggle through the crises of their lives helped only by a sense of decency and the necessity of reconciliation to forestall disaster. There is no way back, not even through nostalgia and grief for a vanished order.

In *The Strange Children* a new note is faintly sounded. . . . This muted emphasis on a religious theme prepares us for its full development in *The Malefactors*. Among the wastrels of talent whom we meet at the fête of the prize bull only Tom and Vera discover the way up and are reborn. Will this, then, be the pattern in Miss Gordon's fiction hereafter? As the South has faded from her novels, religion has taken its place, and the way is up.

Willard Thorp. *Bucknell Review*. Dec., 1956. pp. 14–5

Most of the critics who have written about Miss Gordon have discussed her as a Southern writer—and of course she is. Some of her characters are deracinated Southerners or Middle Westerners, usually intellectuals who have left home. They are invariably unhappy; trouble and disorder trail along their foreign paths and remain with them when they occasionally return home. Miss Gordon has also written many passages, even whole novels, about the land and its healing moral power, which gives one a sense of belonging. She especially likes land that has not given up its fruits and rewards too easily; one appreciates what one has sweated to achieve.

Is Miss Gordon's preoccupation with Art also Southern? Perhaps, but her style is closer to Willa Cather's than it is to Southern rhetoric, even the quiet rhetoric of Katherine Anne Porter. Respect for form is in part Southern—for example, in manners, which cover and control personal likes, dislikes, drives, and ambitions; possibly too in a fairly general disregard for scientific principles and a preference for the arts that bear on personal relationships; and in a more open respect and liking for "elegance." But change comes on apace, and the Southern world of Miss Gordon's youth is no longer what it was. North and South grow more, not less, alike, and at least one or two of her novels seems to acknowledge that this is so.

William Van O'Connor in *South: Modern Southern Literature in Its Cultural Setting*, ed. Louis D. Rubin, Jr., and Robert D. Jacobs (Doubleday). 1961. p. 321

Most of Miss Gordon's fiction belongs close to the heart of the new tradition; in fact, she and her husband [Allen Tate] are responsible for the term, symbolic naturalism, and for its definition. Miss Gordon conspicuously lacks the spontaneity and originality of the more widely read artists in the mode, but she has been one of the most conscientious students of technique and has constantly sought to broaden the range of her subject matter and philosophic understanding. Committed, like her husband, to the conservative agrarian ideal and opposed to modern "progress," she turned immediately to a fictional examination of her heritage, which centers in a rural district on the Kentucky-Tennessee line, adjacent to that of Robert Penn Warren. Only gradually, after an excursion back into Virginia beginnings, did she work her way into the modern era.

Miss Gordon's instinct is for pattern; she works most effectively, therefore, with the historical movement, the family group, the typical, rather than the individual, character. Not until her later novels does she attempt any deep penetration into her protagonists' minds or psychological processes and seldom then does she enter into them with any strongly participative warmth. Her quality as an artist depends upon objective observation and analysis, on a sure control of technique and symbolic extension, rather than upon the arousal of an empathic response to her characters. Perhaps largely for this reason, she has never achieved great popular success, though her work has stood high in critical esteem.

John M. Bradbury. *Renaissance in the South: A Critical History of the Literature, 1920–1960* (North Carolina). 1963. pp. 57–8

In 1953 Caroline Gordon remarked that a trend toward orthodoxy in religion was apparent among fiction writers as it was in the world at large. . . . It is no more surprising that in her quest for the universal myth she should have come to Catholicism than that she should have found, before her conversion, the touchstones of her being in the southern past. She is not, in the forties, a Catholic writer. But the entire, combined force of her need—for order, for tradition, for piety, for absolution and grace, for a shaping world view that would take the place of the shapeless chaos of the world—forced her inevitably and logically toward the Roman Church; and at the end of the decade, in 1951 to be precise, she published her first overtly Catholic novel. She had made the open commitment augured in all her predispositions. The wonder is that writers like Faulkner and Warren, who, for the same reasons, seemed to press toward the same end, had not yet entered the Church a decade later.

Before the Church there were the South and the Past. The elegiac tone Carolina Gordon adopted toward the past derived from her conviction that a total conception of life, life as good, stable, and continuous, had disappeared or been destroyed. A pervasive sense of cultural loss flows through her work. The fragmented lives of her characters are a reflection of this destruction of a whole and coherent cultural pattern that might define life. No force appears in the secular world to act as anchor for man, since neither the cosmopolitanism of urban culture nor the intellectualism that flourishes there provides a satisfactory center for human existence. Nor is the world of nature in itself sufficient. The urgent pessimism of her fiction is the result of her conviction that man's hope and his fate are equally blasted.

Chester E. Eisinger. *Fiction of the Forties* (Chicago). 1963. p. 186

It is the strength of Miss Gordon's work to suggest continually new facets of significance as one lives through the books in his mind. The characters and the incidents form new configurations with the result that the significance of any one of her books enlarges constantly as one reviews it. Her purpose has been from the beginning to suggest that reality is spiritual as well as empiric, immaterial as well as material. Accordingly, she has presented the experience of her characters in time and then again as it reaches beyond time. The ineffable dimensions of her materials she suggests through a discerning use of myth; and in her later books Christianity reinforces their universal implications. . . . As a writer Miss Gordon is the inquiring moralist even before she is the religious writer. Because of her passionate concern with the way life should be, her books are rooted in social realities even as they look toward the visionary. Intelligence, compassion, psychological insight, depth of vision, and stylistic distinction inform a canon of work that impresses always by its comprehensiveness and strength.

> Frederick P. W. McDowell. *Caroline Gordon* (Minnesota). 1966. p. 45

[Caroline Gordon's] fiction dramatizes the myth of the South, as Cooper's does that of the Western migration, James's of Old and New World culture, Proust's of French social change at the end of the nineteenth century. Beginning, in thematic order, with *Green Centuries* and ending with *The Malefactors*, Miss Gordon's fiction shows the movement from loss to acquisition, from rootlessness to stability, from chaos to order, from matter to spirit. In *Green Centuries* the antagonistic natural world drives the exile to certain destruction as he escapes his past (finally, himself) in the pursuit of the unknown. This theme of the natural world as opponent reappears later in *The Garden of Adonis* and particularly in *The Women on the Porch*, as does the central concept of the failure of love between man and woman, in part the result of destroyed cultures or man's warped view of new and different economic systems.

> James E. Rocks. *The Mississippi Quarterly*. Winter, 1967–68. p. 10

Penhally is a completely "rendered" novel, as [Ford Madox] Ford would have said. Its method of presentation—the shifting post of observation in the line of succession among the Llewellyns—allows a remarkable degree of control for such a large subject. Its author has seldom written better. But she was not content with the perfection of a method, and her subsequent books have realized her subject by a variety of means. Her second novel, *Aleck Maury, Sportsman* (1934), for instance, is based on the convention of the old-fashioned memoir. Aleck Maury is the only one of her major characters whom Miss Gordon has granted the privilege of telling his own story, and she thus departs from what with her is a virtual principle. This, the most popular of her novels, can stand by itself, but it gains something from those written after it, as though it were cutting across a territory whose outlines are more fully revealed later on.

> Ashley Brown. *Southern Humanities Review*. Summer, 1968. p. 283

No more than a handful of modern writers have produced short stories which are both technically sound and rich in fictional values.

Such a writer is Caroline Gordon, whose artistic discipline has always been adequate to control the wide range of vision she brings to her fiction. Indeed she tends to crowd into her stories more than their formal limitations would seem to permit: the total experience of a region's history, the hero's archetypal struggle, the complexity of modern aesthetics. In every instance, however, she succeeds in bringing the broad scope of her narrative into focus and in creating the ideal fictional moment, when form and subject are at war and the outcome hangs forever in the balance.

Yet there is a classic simplicity in most of her short stories, an unusual economy of incident and detail which decorously masks their essential thematic complexity. Even the prose is, for the most part, spare in its diction and syntax, particularly in the first-person

narratives, dominated by a tone that is quiet and conversational, the intimate language of the piazza on a warm summer evening.

And it is in this quality that one finds a clue to the origins of Miss Gordon's narrative virtue. For she is still in touch with the oral tradition which in her formative years was a vital element of family life. Like William Faulkner and Katherine Anne Porter, with whom she has much in common, her experience of the nature of being begins in the family, with its concrete relationships, its sense of wholeness, its collective memory.

> Thomas H. Landess. Introduction to *The Short Fiction of Caroline Gordon: A Critical Symposium*, ed. Thomas H. Landess (Dallas). 1972. p. 1

The Glory of Hera is a matchless book—a peak, I think, in the career of a writer devoted to a too familiar, and often belittled, vocation. The uniqueness of the book consists in this: that its author stretches the capacities of the novel so that it can operate authentically in the protean land of ancient Greek myth. It can take on the shapes and assume the colors that make it resemble a luminous mosaic depicting the exploits which were attributed to the god-engendered hero, Heracles. Beginning with Homer's account of the burly bowman, the myth, though revealed piecemeal in many arts, remained the special property of the poets, so astonishing was it, so unbounded, ranging as it did from Heaven to Hell and over all of the perilous borderlands of Earth. The ancients would argue that whatever else might occur, this ineffable stuff could never be captured by a writer of mere prose, by which they would have meant, of course, a chronicler or encyclopedist of some sort. That Caroline Gordon has captured it—indeed she has delivered it quivering and alive from the monstrous darkness of the past—is a triumph for the modern art of prose fiction as well as for the far from modern arts of revivifying immemorial legends.

> Howard Baker. *Southern Review*. Summer, 1973. pp. 523–4

BIBLIOGRAPHY
Penhally, 1931 (n); *Aleck Maury, Sportsman*, 1934 (n); *None Shall Look Back*, 1937 (n); *The Garden of Adonis*, 1937 (n); *Green Centuries*, 1941 (n); *The Women on the Porch*, 1944 (n); *The Forest of the South*, 1945 (s); *The Strange Children*, 1951 (n); *The Malefactors*, 1956 (n); *How to Read a Novel*, 1957 (c); *A Good Soldier: A Key to the Novels of Ford Madox Ford*, 1963 (c); *Old Red, and Other Stories*, 1963; *The Glory of Hera*, 1972 (n); *The Collected Stories of Caroline Gordon*, 1981; *The Southern Mandarins: Letters of Caroline Gordon to Sally Wood, 1924–1937*, 1984

GORDON, Mary (Catherine) (1949–)

The three principal characters in the novel [*Of Men and Angels*] variously mirror and read each other; more exactly, Anne is the central figure "doubled" on two sides by Caroline and Laura. Like Caroline, whose life and work she pores over, Anne is a creative woman and a mother. However, unlike Caroline, Anne has a passionate commitment to motherhood: whereas Caroline was a "bad" mother to her son, "allowing" him to die young (shades of the maternal omnipotence fantasy), Anne is a totally "good" mother to her children and has their safety uppermost in her mind. Caroline, on the other hand, was a good "other" mother to Jane, whose feelings toward her own biological mother were no warmer than (as she puts it) feelings toward "a rather distant cousin" (167). Caroline is therefore split into a murderous and a nurturing mother, depending on whether one looks at Stephen or Jane. But she can also be seen as the "bad" version or double of Anne—a mother who chooses to sacrifice her own child to her work. . . .

The web of connections between the characters in the novel suggests several observations. First, the structural similarity between Caroline and Anne is evident, but so is Anne's greater complexity (and more complicated splitting), which rightly confers on her the title of protagonist, if not necessarily heroine. . . . The second observation my reading suggests is a truism, but significant: in order to survive, a child needs at least one good mother, whether it is the biological mother or an "other" one. Stephen and Laura, who find no nurturing mother, die. Finally, in this novel no child (except perhaps Anne?) has more than one "good" mother. And that raises once again the question of maternal fantasy and its relation to social reality.

Susan Rubin Suleiman. *Signs*. Autumn, 1988, pp. 35–38

[*Temporary*] *Shelter* is an important word in [Mary Catherine] Gordon's work, sought by all of her characters with more or less success. (It is no accident that the title for her collection of short stories [1987] is *Temporary Shelter*.) In the first two novels, love and shelter must be searched for outside the traditional family setting. Both Isabel and Felicitas find themselves members of a family in the extended sense. Struck by Eleanor's jealousy of her friendship with Liz, Isabel realizes, "We are connected. . . . I am not entirely alone" (121). Reflecting on the relationship among her friends, Felicitas's mother Charlotte realizes that "there was something between them, between all of them. They were connected to something, they stood for something. . . . When all of them came together, they were something" (18). It is this "something" that Felicitas rejects, to seek security in the Cavendish menage, "more like a family, and Felicitas needed a lot of support" (156). In *The Company of Woman*, there is only one nuclear family, the one Cyprian leaves behind to enter the priesthood; "I would not be the son of my father, the brother of my brothers, bumbling and heavy and uncouth. I would be part of that glorious company, the line of the apostles. I would not be who I was" (278). the few families in *Final Payments* lack love. Liz and John Ryan find marriage more of a convenience for raising two children than a meaningful relationship. Liz finds fulfillment in a lesbian liaison, while John regularly commits adultery. Cynthia Slade has tricked Hugh into marriage and now taunts him with his infidelities.

John W. Mahon. "Mary Gordon: The Struggle with Love." In Mickey Pearlman. *American Women Writing Fiction: Memory, Identity, Family Space.* (Lexington: Univ. Pr. of Kentucky, 1989), p. 50

The Other Side is a family saga raised several octaves. Here are the failed marriages, the hypocrisy, the old pretense, and the evolving hatred. But Mary Gordon's treatment of these themes is unique.

The story moves in and out of focus on members of the MacNamara family: the parents, gentle, decent Vincent, and high-principled but irascible Ellen, who emigrated from Ireland to America (the "other side") in the early part of the century; their daughters and grandchildren—particularly the cousins Cam and Dan—and their great grandchildren. . . .

Mary Gordon's writing has a gravity which is often mythic in tone. "Her mother is a house she would bring down," thinks the malign Theresa. And indeed there are references throughout to the House of Atreus, as though hinting at a modern Celtic Oresteia. She has a capacity for revealing the tragic in ordinary people, awarding them stature even in their petty vindictiveness. The doom-laden atmosphere, the unity of time and place, the clash of generations, and the unmasking of ancient lies are reminiscent of O'Neill's *Long Day's Journey into Night.*

Mary Flanagan. *New Statesman & Society.* Feb. 2, 1990, p. 34

The bloody wretched Irish, "they could never be happy, any of them . . . unhappiness was bred in the bone, a message in the blood, a code of weakness. The sickle-cell anemia of the Irish: they had to thwart joy in their lives," so carries on, in what seems typical pub-fashion, one of the members of Mary Gordon's big Irish-American family in *The Other Side.* He, Dan, saw it in Ireland, "everywhere he went . . . the doomed service of the ideal, the blatant disregard of present pleasure, . . . in their politics, their architecture . . . their living rooms, their towns, . . . in the jarring printed carpets and the half-glass doors that closed as if they kept out someone dangerous or insane." Well, I'm convinced, but please go on: I like the details, the crazy love/hate thing, the sound of your voice, its rhythms, and the overriding oceanic swell that it all mattered, and does yet. This book is full of marvelous talk, scenes and people: and five generations of a big family, all of whose stories we get to hear. . . . And for each life, a whole America is painted in, beginning with immigrant life in New York, early union organizing, two world wars, the Depression, holding the family together despite all, up to a new slacker America of divorce, scattered households, weaker characters, more money but far less sense, much less beauty. . . . Gordon brings such fresh insight, energy, patience, engagement to each portrait in the gallery that we feel it too, and we read this rambling rich novel with much pleasure, and often surprise.

Alice Bloom. *Hudson Review.* Spring, 1990, p. 163

The novel [*Final Payments*], in fact, implicitly affirms the value of language even in its gloomiest sequences: there are few novelistic characters for whom exactness of word choice and attention to the sheer beauty of language are more important than they are for Isabel Moore. Throughout the book, Isabel has used words like "clarity," "purity," "certainty," and especially "center" with such frequency and care that they begin to seem as solid as the word "bastard" sounded in Archbishop Lefebvre's mouth. Although it is her lover Hugh Slade who, according to Isabel, is able to take words like "devoted" and "duty" and "polish them like stones" (168), it is really Isabel herself who is the novel's primary word polisher. It is through her aesthetic, erotic, humorous care with language that a bridge has been created between the beautiful but rigid (and lost) world of Joseph Moore and the world of temporal humanity: ''That, at least, I owed to my father—making the effort to find the proper words for things'' (152). . . .

And by presenting Isabel's ultimate faith that human beings in the modern world can still articulate a religious vision if they employ a narrative rather than a doctrinal discourse, *Final Payments* seems to be making a larger statement about the efficacy of storytelling for pursuing religious questions; this is a religious novel about the religious value of novels. Gordon demonstrates that narrative can consider religious issues imaginatively, metaphorically, even playfully, without freezing them into dogma. This means that, for Gordon, religious truths cannot be stated definitively; there is no One True (and Literal) Language. But there are plenty of metaphors to weave, tales to spin, jokes to tell. The last words of *Final Payments* are, appropriately, ''There was a great deal I wanted to say.''

John M. Neary. *Essays in Literature.* Spring, 1990, pp. 109–10

BIBLIOGRAPHY
Final Payments, 1978 (n); *The Company of Women*, 1981 (n); *Men and Angels*, 1985 (n); *Temporary Shelter*, 1987 (s); *Spiritual Quests: The Art and Craft of Religious Writing*, 1988 (c, e); *The Other Side*, 1989 (n); *Good Boys and Dead Girls*, 1991 (e); *The Rest of Life*, 1993 (3n); *The Shadow Man*, 1996 (a, b); *Spending: A Utopian Divertimento*, 1998 (n)

GOYEN, William (1918–1983)

Here are the most extravagant feelings, the most absurd recklessness of revealment, at times there is real danger of the fatal drop into over-pathos, over-saying: a boyish tearfulness over some very dubious attachments. . . . To balance this fault, the writing as a whole is disciplined on a high plane, and there are long passages of the best writing, the fullest and richest and most expressive, that I have read in a very long time—complex in form, and beautifully organized, shapely as a good tree, as alive and as substantial.

Katherine Anne Porter. *New York Times Book Section.* Aug. 20, 1950. p. 17

He has the poet's ear for the spoken word and he knows how to use the regionalist's best tools. All of these tales (in *Ghost and Flesh*) but one are set in the dusty county of east Texas, and even in that single exception a young man in a San Francisco hotel room recalls those landscapes, though he has abandoned them. Mr. Goyen knows how these people blending South and West in their inheritance, talk and move and how they dress and what they raise in their gardens and what churches they go to, and his writing takes on strength and richness from that familiarity. He can tell stories in dialect that is fresh and unforced; and he has noted the figures of speech used by country people.

Sylvia Stallings. *New York Herald Tribune Book Section.* Feb. 10, 1952. p. 5

William Goyen's short stories exhibit the same qualities which made his recent literary debut an exciting one: intelligence and sensitivity, an intense and sometimes florid imagination, and an extreme preoccupation with form and language. At their best these stories possess a magical quality rare in contemporary American fiction which marks this Texan as one of the strikingly talented young writers of the last decade. . . . The author examines the problem of the nature of reality in terms of a never-ceasing conflict between the present and the past, between the visible and the invisible.

William Peden. *Saturday Review.* March 22, 1952. p. 17

In a captivating fantasy called *In a Farther Country* William Goyen continues to fabricate the fragile world of super-reality which characterized *The House of Breath*. . . and . . . *Ghost and Flesh*. . . . Events in the story grow not out of rationally plausible circumstance, but occur simply because the author exercising the fiat of a fairy tale, waves his wand and bids them happen. All seem on the verge of vanishing momentarily if removed from the sustaining medium of Mr. Goyen's evocative prose style. That they do not vanish until the end, when the dream is broken, attests to the efficacy of that style and to the talent of a strangely gifted writer.

Jerome Stone. *Saturday Review.* July 23, 1955. p. 27

It is hard to believe that these two books were written by the same man. One, the *Selected Writings*, shows William Goyen to be an extraordinarily rewarding and exciting writer. The other, *Come, the Restorer*, is an embarrassingly bad echo. Of course, Goyen's fiction technique is by its nature a fail-safe gamble. He approaches the problem of fiction in such a way that he can only win or lose— he cannot produce a middling good book.

William Goyen is one of those writers whose reputation has always outrun his sales. When I first read him some 10 years ago, I was told that he was like Malcolm Lowry. Well, I don't see the resemblance—except perhaps in the fervor of his devoted readers. The *Selected Writings* collection brings together some of his out-of-print works, from the years 1950–1963; its intent clearly is to present Goyen as a kind of classic. The book actually includes a short bibliography, articles in three languages to show what a fine and valued writer he is. Now that is a pretentious bit of scholarly trivia—but don't be put off by it. The *Selected Writings* is a book well worth reading. It is not, as the English would say, a ''good read.'' It is dark, mystical, hypnotic, grotesquely powerful. It will probably haunt your dreams. . . .

Goyen is usually classified as a Southern writer, but his regionalism sits lightly on him. He superficially resembles Flannery O'Connor and the early Truman Capote (''Other Voices, Other Rooms''). But the similarities are misleading. Capote and O'Connor were truly regionalists, drawing their support from their background. Goyen is very nearly a completely placeless writer, his landscape the mind's interior.

The *Selected Writings* shows Goyen to be an eccentric, difficult writer. Because of his great concern with his own inner perspective, he is often jumbled in his words and tangled in his wildly grotesque visions. He is primarily a writer of despair, of hopelessness, of pain. There is no relief, no shadow of comfort in his vision, only a kind of frenzied dance of death performed with a curious desperate elegance. A stylish apocalypse, as it were.

Goyen always seems far more interested in expression—the recording of his own visions and thoughts—than in communicating with the reader. And this is basically the reason for the failure of his new novel.

Come, the Restorer is a long private dream of good and evil, of the life and death, of man the angel and man the beast, of creation and destruction. It is like a canvas of Hieronymus Bosch but without Bosch's unifying esthetic tensions. *Come, the Restorer* is a novel without pattern, without plot (except in the crudest sense), without forward motion. Everything is symbolic, and every symbol alters its meaning many times. It is a book in which conventional logic is of no use, no value. This fragmentation is of course quite deliberate. In his freewheeling fashion Goyen pyramids his shifting symbols (a white rattlesnake, a grave in the Garden of Eden, an exploding chemical factory, etc.), relying on their cumulative effect, their overall impression on the reader's emotions rather than his intelligence. Randomness produces unity—at least in theory.

Come, the Restorer is a foolish novel. There is, for example, a long passage in a tropical Garden of Eden (where elemental male and female forces engage in a battle of sexuality) that is embarrassingly silly. It is as if *Green Mansions* were being replayed with Xaviera Hollander in the part of Rima the bird girl.

The novel suffers, moreover, from being too clever. It dies of its own intricacy. Its grotesques are just impossibly exaggerated. . . .

Still, in this day of written-to-order novels, of fiction tailored to meet the expected demands of the market—like a new breakfast cereal or an after-shave lotion—it is encouraging to find a novelist who has enough faith in himself as a writer to be difficult and obscure and inevitably limited in his sales. The serious American novel is still alive!

Shirley Ann Grau. *New York Times Book Section.* Nov. 3, 1974, pp. 73–74

As befits an age of universal solitude, in which art often is *about* art, William Goyen's stories are a testament to the essentiality of telling. He regards such communication as a form of love, a process including seeing and saying: to tell one must know; once one knows he *must* tell. . . .

Goyen's sense of his own work is just as serious: "story telling is a rhythm, a charged movement, a chain of pulses or beats. To write out of life is to catch, in pace, this pulse that beats in the material of life." His affirmations that he wishes "to write out of life" and "record as closely as possible the speech as *heard*" show that he sees himself as a medium of a heritage. Like many of his characters, he passes on an assimilation of actual and imagined material. Though the proportions of the mixture would be impossible to measure, Goyen's concentration on rendering the "true music" in the "marvelous instrument of language . . . *given* to me" is the most distinctive feature of his work.

The willingness to discipline himself in the use of language underlies his entire achievement as a writer. His stories ring with precision because they are language told to someone, not simply private, inchoate voices. . . . *The Collected Stories of William Goyen* (1975) . . . presents his ideas with remarkable continuity and seems to have been his means of experimenting in form and of

finding "a language I thought I could use." Whether he writes of homelessness, fragmentation of individuals, elusiveness of the past, or the miracle of human love, Goyen is playing his main themes—the essentiality of telling—and orchestrating speech to render the "marvelous reciprocity" of a genuine relationship. . . .

Goyen has always written of human relationships—solitary people who fail to connect, solitary people who succeed in loving. The latter have been Goyen's hope: they are alert to surroundings; they have patience and imagination to comprehend others.

Jay S. Paul. *Critique.* 19, 2, 1977, pp. 77–78

The House of Breath is unique in our literature, owing no debts to any literary antecedents. One reason for such uniqueness is that Goyen almost always writes in the first-person singular, and the voice is unquestionably his own—Southwestern, sensitive, searching, deeply rooted in Old Testament locutions. Goyen, exiled in body from the Southwest, can never absent himself from that locale. He has the almost morbid sensibility that comes from the feelings of exile and suppression. . . .

A second reason his work is unique is that his books seem composed through a sort of double process—that of the photograph and that of the poem of the fact and the vision. . . .

Thirdly, Goyen's imagery is often dreamlike, unreal to the point of surrealism, and always intensely personal. He draws upon a personal mythology of rattlesnakes and oil wells, tightrope walkers and flagpole sitters, which is distinctly his own. Goyen is in point a fabulist, making his own myths and creating characters much larger than life. His dreamlike imagery and mythic characters are but two facets of his distinctive style. His stories and novels are all written in prose, but in prose which has many of the characteristics of poetry. It is a style which yokes the exaltations of poetry with the ordinariness of spoken prose. His books are dramatic, but they are not plays. . . .

Like poetry, they give the outlines of life rather than the whole of it (as in many novels). In this respect, Goyen's fiction bears little relationship to the sociological novel, or the novel of environment. . . . Goyen's novels break with the things which are in order to merge with those things which *may be*, including even spirits, which figure prominently in his second book, *Ghost and Flesh.* . . .

From the first—that is, roughly from 1949 onward—his fiction has been of the most intimate kind, surpassing the physical realities in favor of the subjective ones. Events, when they occur in his fiction at all, are related not to character so much as to sensibility. His concern is not for concrete truths, but poetic truths—for the dream, the fantasy, the outrageous. It is this engagement with *all* things, not merely the physical things of this world, which is a part of Goyen's real achievement. . . .

Overall, his work is consistent and at a very high level. And *The House of Breath* is perhaps a masterpiece—still in print twenty-five years after publication.

Nevertheless, it is doubtful that Goyen's fiction has been a creditable influence upon any other writer of note today. His concerns and his style are too highly individual to be of use by others. (Anyone who has attempted to copy his style will find that task near impossible.) Rather than being famous as the founder of a school or a following, Goyen should be noted as a highly individualized voice. He is a fabulous original, like Carson McCullers and

Flannery O'Connor and not many others. In an age of mechanization, he devotes himself to poetry. In an age of plastic, he celebrates
the ghost and the flesh.

> Robert Phillips. *William Goyen* (Twayne, 1979), pp. 33–35,
> 112, 114

William Goyen, who died in August, will be remembered as one of
the great American writers of short fiction. Tapestries of storylike
scenes form his famous first novel, *The House of Breath* (1950),
and the later ones. His special success with the short form grows
essentially from his language, which grips the reader with an
Ancient Mariner's powerful hand while speaking of both the
everyday and the uncanny. Though Goyen was often labeled a
Texas writer, his language was a stylistic accomplishment rather
than a regional or period manner, utterly individual, neither typically Southern nor, as some would have had it more recently, magic-
realist. What may appear at first to be a colloquial narrative often
becomes an intense, songlike prose utterance with verses and
refrains. Goyen himself once remarked that some of his stories
were really anthems.

Arcadio, his only major published work since *Collected Stories*
(1975), is the most intense of these visionary songs of life. Set in his
native Texas, like many of his previous works, it opens with a
typically Goyenesque narrative of a "visitation"—Goyenesque in
that the author characteristically filtered a story through one of its
characters, a witness slightly apart who hears someone else speak
of what happened, and Goyenesque also in that what interested him
most of all was passion and intensity of experience. . . .

The apparition has been evoked by the narrator's memory of his
taciturn uncle, who on another hot night had told him of seeing a
person bathing in secret in the nearby river, someone who seemed
both man and woman. That was Arcadio, a living war and a
reconciliation of opposites, half man and half woman, half "Mescan"
and half Texan, half saintly and half wanton, half truth teller and
half blatant exaggerator.

Framed by the narrator's reminiscence, the novel becomes
Arcadio's account of himself (he seems slightly more male than
female), delivered on a long day to a silent listener—our narrator—
in the shade of an abandoned, vine-tangled railroad trestle over a
dry riverbed. Jesus consorted with publicans and sinners, and
Arcadio recounts a life of spiritual quest in a world of brothels
and jailhouses.

This is a work of profound sympathy for the lost, the displaced,
the crazy, the imprisoned, the homeless, the deformed, the loveless—all the turned-away, whose light we tend to put out by our
fear of them. Amazingly, Arcadio also touches on the reigning
social problems of our day: the environment destroyed, the family
broken and dispersed, loveless sex. He does this in passing,
offering the viewpoint of the outcast, the sinner, whose sense of the
world around him is both true and naïve. Neither Arcadio's
ultimate confrontation with his long-lost family nor the apocalyptic
destruction of cities and people he has witnessed can redeem his
travails or solve the problems around him. Instead, he tells his story
to a silent listener, and his extended aria transforms pitiable sadness
and crazy misdeeds into a reconciliation of violent opposites. His
remembering and singing of others who are gone makes peace with
them and, through his being heard by his listener, makes peace for
them. An early story, "Ghost and Flesh," is perhaps the most
important statement of Goyen's belief that the situation of the

storyteller and the listener is a spiritual one in which guilt, suffering
and sorrow are finally redeemed.

Arcadio's parables and paradoxes restore meaning to the lives
he recounts. His song may be Goyen's finest achievement. The
work of a master fabulist, it was one more courageous foray into
fiction unlike anyone else's, haunting the reader with its tenderness
and ferocity.

> Reginald Gibbons. *New York Times Book Section*. Nov. 6,
> 1983, pp. 14, 36–37

BIBLIOGRAPHY
The House of Breath, 1950 (n); *Ghost and Flesh*, 1952 (s); *In a
Farther Country*, 1955 (n); *The Faces of Blood Kindred*, 1960 (s);
The Fair Sister, 1963 (n); *Arcadio*, 1983 (n); *Had I a Hundred
Mouths: New & Selected Stories, 1947–1983*, 1985 (s); *William
Goyen: Selected Letters from a Writer's Life*, ed. by Robert
Phillips, 1995; *Half a Look of Cain: A Fantastical Narrative*, 1994
(n); *Come, the Restorer*, 1996 (n)

GRAU, Shirley Ann (1929–)

Most of these stories center around Negroes in Louisiana. . . .
These "colored" stories are quite definitely the best of her work.
The reader may be occasionally mildly troubled by Miss Grau's
tendency to blur or confuse her own point of view with that of her
focal characters as she does in the rather unsuccessful story "Miss
Yellow Eyes"; for the most part, though, she writes with considerable control and skill. More important, she sees and hears well;
most important, she understands what she sees and hears. To an
uninitiated ear her dialect is for the most part effective; her people
are almost always convincing. Miss Grau, further, displays considerable variety and flexibility; whether she works in the border-
region of myth and folklore, as she does in the effective title story
of Stanley "the Black Prince" . . .or in the more traditional
medium of the realistic "The Way of a Man," she avoids sensationalism, violence, and whimsy for their own sakes. She writes out
of neither sentimental love not tear-filled despair. Hers is not a
namby-pamby world of dreams, or a darkened alley in which
animals die meaningless deaths. Frustration and violence and death
are present in her world, but so also are serenity and achievement
and life.

> William Peden. *Saturday Review*. Jan. 29, 1955. p. 16

Her basic approach in the stories was one of careful atmospheric
setting. She has used the same technique in the novel [*The Hard
Blue Sky*], painstakingly describing the coast, the islands, the
desolate sweep of marshes, birds, oaks and palms, the packs of wild
dogs that overrun the Isle aux Chiens—her island world, a terrain
outlined minutely and enclosed by water and the hot summer
sky. . . . Miss Grau writes wonderfully well about people—there
isn't character on the island who doesn't come alive, and no two,
even though everyone on the island seems to be more or less
vaguely related, who are alike. Her handling of the relations
between men and women is particularly perceptive, but again it is

her knowledge of and interest in character that reveals so much about these relations. . . . Above all, Miss Grau is a natural story-teller, and her novel has a kind of casual looseness that makes room for many stories, tales which, far from destroying the unity of the book, tighten the fabric of the world she constructs.

    Elizabeth Bartelme. *Commonweal*. July 11, 1958. p. 380

[*The Hard Blue Sky*] belongs in the category of novels which are essentially evocations of a little-known region or place—in this case a small, primitive, storm-swept island off the Louisiana Coast on the edge of a dangerous swamp. The people on the Isle aux Chiens are of mixed French and Spanish descent, and their curious speech is peppered with eroded bits of French. . . . Miss Grau recreates in all its dimensions the singular life of an inbred, almost isolated little world. She is a fine artist, but she has stretched her material too far; it could have been handled more effectively within the compass of a novelette.

    Charles Rolo. *Atlantic Monthly*. Aug., 1958. p. 84

The Hard Blue Sky, to the extent that it needs to be classified, belongs to the old-fashioned school of regionalism. *The House on Coliseum Street* could be Gothic but isn't: . . . it is not even specifically Southern. It is full of the sights and sounds and smells of New Orleans and the surrounding country; that is the kind of writer Miss Grau is. But its essential action could take place anywhere.

    To me *The House on Coliseum Street* is not so exciting as *The Hard Blue Sky*, but it is a good book for Miss Grau to have written at this point in her career. Her control is perfect, and there isn't a scene that doesn't count. Her senses are acute, and, as I have said, they make their contribution to the texture of the novel, but there are no descriptions for the sake of description. The writing, as always, is wonderfully firm. Miss Grau is not exploring new territory, as she was in some of her stories and in *The Hard Blue Sky*, but she has done admirably what she wanted to do, and she has left us with a picture of a young woman that it will be hard to forget.

    Granville Hicks. *Saturday Review*. June 17, 1961. p. 20

The most effective aspect of Miss Grau's work here [*The House on Coliseum Street*], to my reading, is the conveyed awareness of loss and emptiness following the abortion. . . . Joan is haunted by "that first ghost child. Ghost child, lost child" and in her imagination it takes on the aspect of a bit of seaweed, "my seaweed child." This, in what seems to me the novel's furthest imaginative grasp, becomes the ultimate loneliness, the lost "heart ticking away inside. . . . The soft floating seaweed bones."

    But there are only occasional and faint flashes of such imaginative and verbal magic here, magic which lit up page upon page of Miss Grau's memorable first book, *The Black Prince and Other Stories*.

    Coleman Rosenberger. *New York Herald Tribune Book Section*. July 23, 1961. p. 6

Shirley Ann Grau has been demonstrating her gifts as a sensitive observer of human development and growth for some time now. With a few words she can establish a mood, mixing man's emotions with appropriate reflections of them in landscape. . . .

She knows the people, knows the ambiguities of race relations, the devices, pretenses, ironies, absurdities, and incredible frustra-tions. . . . Most significantly, she writes at a time when she can know some answers too. For this is a novel [*The Keepers of the House*] which in its own sudden and firm way has a statement to make. . . . She gathers herself together and ends her story by insisting that deceptions exposed are ultimately if painfully better than compromises and falsehoods endured.

    Robert Coles. *New Republic*. April 18, 1964. pp. 17–19

Shirley Ann Grau is a Southerner who writes about the Deep South with a word choice as fastidious as Willa Cather's and with a passion aroused by the turbulence in her home country. Her new novel, *The Keeper of the House*. . . , a beautifully designed, beauti-fully written book, is a story told in two moods. The first half is the evocation of the William Howland plantation. . . . The tone of the telling changes after [William's grand-daughter] Abigail's mar-riage to handsome John Tolliver. She suspects that he married her for her money, and he did; and she suspects that he is a philanderer, which he is. But she knows that he is a hard worker in his law office, and she loves him; she bears their children and works for his political career, until they are flung apart by the scandal over Old Will's miscegenation. The bitter vengeance that follows is hard to take.

    Edward Weeks. *Atlantic Monthly*. May, 1964. p. 135

BIBLIOGRAPHY

The Black Prince, 1955 (s); *The Hard Blue Sky*, 1958 (n); *The House on Coliseum Street*, 1961 (n); *The Keepers of the House*, 1964 (n); *The Condor Passes*, 1971 (n); *The Wind Shifting West*, 1973 (n); *Evidence of Love*, 1977 (n); *Nine Women*, 1985 (s); *Roadwalkers*, 1994 (n)

GREEN, Paul (1894–1981)

Evidently the numerous short folk-plays which Mr. Green has written have served him well. The image of a primitive society which he projects upon the stage [in *The Field God*] with an apparently effortless ease has an extraordinary depth and solidity, and the minor characters who create it are all conceived with an incisive yet natural humor. But it is not with this that he stops. The wildly passionate story which he tells of a conflict between a primitively powerful love and the religious fanaticism of a remote community is one which is firmly rooted in the manners and traditions of that community. It is no conventional stage plot foisted upon a certain set of characters but something which grows out of the people and their ways—a genuine folk tragedy.

    Joseph Wood Krutch. *The Nation*. May 4, 1927. p. 510

Paul Green's *Wide Fields* . . . is the first venture into a volume of prose by the winner of last year's Pulitzer Prize in drama. It is a collection of pieces about the poor whites of Little Bethel, a North Carolina community. While there is an unevenness in Mr. Green's work on the technical side, every one of his sketches, grave or gay, is informed with fine sincerity, with understanding and a deep sympathy. What is important is his turning to the poor white as literary material, and this sample is proof enough that the neglected field he has begun to work has rich soil. I think this book may be hailed safely enough as the augury of some good novels if Mr. Green decides to take time enough away from his twin loves of the drama and philosophy to turn his hand to fiction.

Herschel Brickell. *Bookman*. June, 1928. pp. 461–2

In Abraham's Bosom is one of the most beautiful and tragic of all modern dramas. The character of Abraham is carried through seven scenes, each showing a crisis in the hero's struggle to broaden his limited mental horizon. But every time he seems on the point of success, he finds himself thwarted. Nor is his tragedy altogether the tragedy of the Negro in a white man's world; his failure lies ultimately within himself. Mr. Green makes no attempt to solve his problem, simply stating it in human terms. . . . He exults in tragedy as the manifestation of man living at his intensest, and the intensity of his thirst for life and ever more life is satisfied with nothing less than life can give him. This is always what we call tragedy, though when it is seen through the eyes of an artist of Mr. Green's stamp, it is a tragedy that burns and purifies like fire.

Barrett H. Clark. *Theatre Arts*. Oct., 1928. pp. 734–5

There are no folk motion pictures, nor "speakies." The pictures are standardized products, turned out wholesale from Hollywood, like a motor car or a breakfast food. But Green's plays could come from no place but the corner of the South where he was born and reared, and their value first is to the cultural life of his own State, and only later to the country at large, exactly as the value of the plays of Yeats, Synge and Lady Gregory was first to Ireland. . . .

He has written with equal understanding about the whites and the blacks in North Carolina, though perhaps as yet his best work is about his black friends, for whom he has intense sympathy without sentimental delusions. Their language and metaphor being more picturesque than that of the whites, he has in writing about them been able more fully and happily, because more naturally, to indulge his poetic flair for rhythmical and heightened speech. In some of his negro plays we can feel something of Synge's power to evoke music and moods from the mere sound of words.

Walter P. Eaton. *The Drama in English* (Scribner). 1930. pp. 328–9

The characters in Mr. Green's play [*The House of Connelly*] are clearly defined; their words—all but the heroine's—are profoundly Southern and have been well heard by the dramatist out of his own Southern life. Sometimes a detail, though tiny, is so startlingly Southern that none but a Southerner could savor its exactness. . . . The uncle's role, rather too long for the sting and pathos intended by it, runs somewhat too far toward the Russian flavor; and his suicide seems to me unconvincing, as well as being both untrue to this Southern type or temperament and harmful to the play's total impression on the memory. *The House of Connelly* remains, notwithstanding, well worth a dozen more facile works. Uncle, girl,

problem or no, it is at its source poetic, by which I mean the richness, quiver and dilation that it often gives to the material presented.

Stark Young. *New Republic*. Oct. 14, 1931. p. 235

I hasten to report, at last, a performance of real importance: Paul Green's *House of Connelly*, as presented by the newly organized Group Theatre. It is important because the author and the assembled actors and directors are trying for something fundamental, something beautiful, careful, conscientious: something worth doing for its own sake. In this they are nearly unique. . . . A pithy description of this play is going the rounds, to the effect that it kills two birds with one stone, *The Seagull* and *The Wild Duck* and it is true that Mr. Green has been influenced by his predecessors, especially Chekhov, more in this play than in any other I know—no doubt because of his theme. . . . Of course when it comes to the form of the play as a whole, there can be no question of comparison with the master. Will Connelly marries Patsy Tate with the approval of their author, and the brash, bright, business-like alliance of these two, with its hopes of profit and rejuvenation, sticks out of the melancholy Russian pattern like a bandaged thumb. Chekhov's vision was comparatively whole as well as essentially tragic; the people he knew, the best he could find, were degenerating. Mr. Green's vision, on the other hand, is partial, tentative, hopeful, and not without its sociological axe to grind.

Francis Fergusson. *Bookman*. Nov., 1931. p. 298

As more short plays began to flow from his pen Green found less need for one-act models. His material found expression in its own language and the simplest narrative form served his dramatic purpose. The society which he pictured in brief snatches of drama was easily drawn, for it had strongly definitive lines. There were plantation owners, poor whites, negroes. The relationships between the three types, and their influence on one another, made drama. Very sensibly Green first recorded this drama in single independent acts as he discovered it. The last few years have shown how he has built upon these early foundations. . . .

In Abraham's Bosom . . . was produced at the end of the year 1926 in the Provincetown Theatre, New York. It was an episodic chronicle in seven scenes that summed up without sentimentality the story of the white man's inconsistency toward the black. In the tortured soul of the play's protagonist, Abraham McCranie—in his failure to establish himself as an educator, in his inability to humiliate his spirit before his weakling white half-brother, in the worthlessness of his son whom he had consecrated to the service of his people—lay the subject for a pure and inevitable tragedy. It gave the playwright full opportunity for the employment of all his gifts—his accuracy of observation, his poetic sensitivity, his philosophic turn of mind. The simplicity of its narrative form was, moreover, wholly fitting to its content.

Carl Carmer. *Theatre Arts*. Dec., 1932. pp. 998–9

Having established himself as one of the more important American playwrights, Paul Green now brings out a long and authentic novel [*This Body the Earth*] about the plight of the white sharecropper in the South. . . . In spite of the structural defects that result from Mr. Green's attempt to impose the technique of the theatre upon the technique of the novel, it is an outstanding addition to the literature of social protest that is being written by Southern writers. . . . [The hero] is defeated, not by himself, but by the agricultural economy of the South. This economy, in Mr. Green's novel, becomes the Nemesis of the old Greek tragedies—merciless, vindictive, hounding a man to death. The implicit moral is that the individual, no matter how rugged, cannot combat a system that makes individuals its prey. . . . Paul Green has written a brave, honest, eloquent book— his most important performance since *In Abraham's Bosom*

      Hamilton Basso. *New Republic*. Nov. 13, 1935. pp. 24–5

Paul Green's play [*Johnny Johnson*] with music by Kurt Weill is a brave and at times successful attempt to project an anti-war play with a sense of humor. Johnny Johnson is a young Middle West American who believes in peace, but takes war propaganda at its face value until he is disillusioned. . . . Had the play itself been less naif, and as good as Mr. Green's lyrics and Mr. Weill's music, it might well have been a landmark in the American theatre.

      Greenville Vernon. *Commonweal*. Dec. 4, 1936. p. 162

Paul Green's plays are a statement of unquestioned fact about the negroes and country whites of the North Carolina lowlands. They are folk plays. With the exception of a few isolated pieces like Roark Bradford's and Marc Connelly's *The Green Pastures* and Dorothy and Dubose Heyward's *Porgy*, Paul Green's work is America's strongest contribution to the perpetuation of the folk-play genre. The type is important in the new American drama. Although it has attracted Broadway, it is not written to satisfy Broadway standards. It is theatre for the people everywhere, and has met encouragement in many scattered centers. So Paul Green writes with a free hand and experiments as much as he likes. . . . The economic problem as Green presents it makes *In Abraham's Bosom* classify as proletarian. This is likewise true of most of the later plays, and especially of the latest, *Johnny Johnson*, produced in New York by the Group Theatre during the season 1936–1937. This play—part fantasy, part musical satire, part symbolic poetry—Green calls " a legend." The hero, " a natural man in a sick world," is white—an idealist like the colored hero of *In Abraham's Bosom*, and as destined to failure. All of Green's plays show that he is a professional philosopher. Every folk idea and custom is a symbol of some significant social truth. But it is the picturing which makes the plays distinguished.

      Vernon Loggins. *I Hear America* (Crowell). 1937. pp. 219–21

Most of his work, perhaps all, springs from a knowledge of the tragic quality of life. He has people singing folksongs in almost every play, but their songs, whether gay or melancholy, have the air of lament and the sob of a people singing to keep up spirit.

    No one writing for the stage has set down more haunting and plaintive lyrics than those given here [*Out of the South*] to the tired mouths of plain people. . . . There is not a play, new or old, in this collection that does not have that high thematic combination of pathos and tenderness and humor running through it.

      Stanley Young. *New York Times Book Section*. June 11, 1939. p. 15

It is not too much to say that Paul Green is the only playwright, with the uncertain exception of Eugene O'Neill, who belongs notably to both the American land and the American theatre. He came to the latter as the natural poet of the Old South. The depth of his commitment to his people, which was from the beginning a commitment to the human race, also made him the laureate of the *New* South aborning not without labor and turbulence. He started in the 1920's as a writer of short plays of local color, moved into a professional Broadway theatre with full-length dramas of the South, and after 1937 started extending his horizons with the writing of epics that encompass historical events for which ordinary playhouses and the resources of realistic plays are patently inadequate. . . .

    In coalescing a number of one-act plays of Negro life into the Pulitzer Prize drama *In Abraham's Bosom*, in 1927, Paul Green enlarged his dramatic scope impressively. . . . *The House of Connelly*, the play with which The Group Theatre opened its momentous career in the 1930's, remains the most poignant drama of the postbellum South, and *Johnny Johnson*, given another Group Theatre production in 1936, is by far the most imaginative and affecting antiwar full-length play in the American theatre.

      John Gassner. Introduction to *Five Plays of the South* by Paul Green (Hill and Wang). 1963. pp. ix, xi

BIBLIOGRAPHY

Day by Day, 1923 (d); *The Scuffletown Outlaws*, 1924 (d); (with Erma Green) *Fixin's*, 1924 (d); *In Aunt Mahaly's Cabin*, 1925 (d); *The Lord's Will and Other Carolina Plays*, (*The Lord's Will, Blackbeard, Old Wash Lucas, The No 'Count Boy, The Old Man of Edenton, The Last of the Loweries*), 1925; *Lonesome Road: Six Plays for the Negro Theatre*, (*In Abraham's Bosom, White Dresses, The Hot Iron, The Prayer-Meeting, The End of the Row, Your Fiery Furnace*), 1926; *The Field God and In Abraham's Bosom*, 1927 (d); *The Man Who Died at Twelve O'Clock*, 1927 (d); *In the Valley and Other Carolina Plays*, (*In the Valley, Quare Medicine, Supper for the Dead, Saturday Night, The Man Who Died at Twelve O'Clock, Unto Such Glory, The No 'Count Boy, The Man on the House, The Picnic, In Aunt Mahaly's Cabin, The Good-Bye*), 1928; *Wide Fields*, 1928 (s); *The House of Connelly*, (with *Potter's Field, Tread the Green Grass*), 1931 (d); *The Laughing Pioneer*, 1932 (n); *Roll Sweet Chariot*, (revision of *Potter's Field*), 1935 (d); *Shroud My Body Down*, 1935 (d); *This Body the Earth*, 1935 (n); *The Enchanted Maze*, 1935 (d); *Hymn to the Rising Sun*, 1936 (d); *Unto Such Glory*, 1936 (d); *Johnny Johnson*, 1937 (d); *The Lost Colony*, 1937 (d); *The Southern Cross*, 1938 (d); *The Enchanted Maze*, 1939 (d); *Out of the South*, 1939 (d coll); *The Field God*, (revised version), 1940; *The Highland Call*, 1941 (d); (with Richard Wright) *Native Son*, 1941 (d); *The Hawthorne Tree*, 1943 (e); *Forever Growing*, 1945 (e); *Salvation on a String*, 1946 (s); *The Common Glory*, 1948 (d); *Dog on the Sun*, 1949 (s); *Dramatic Heritage*, 1953 (e); *Wilderness Road*, 1956 (d); *The Founders*, 1957 (d); *Drama and the Weather*, 1958 (e); *The Confederacy*, 1959 (d); *The Stephen Foster Story*, 1960 (d); *Plough and Furrow*, 1963 (e); *Texas: A Symphonic Outdoor Drama of American Life*, 1967; *Home to My Valley*, 1970 (a); *Trumpet in the Land: A Symphonic Drama of Peace and Brotherhood*, 1972; *The Honeycomb*, 1972 (d); *Land of Nod, and Other Stories*, 1976; *Paul Green's Wordbook: An Alphabet of Reminiscence*, ed. Rhoda H. Wynn, 1990; *Paul Green's War Songs: A Southern Poet's History of the Great War, 1917–1920*, ed. John Herbert Roper, 1993 (p); *A Southern Life: Letters of Paul Green, 1916–1981*, ed. Laurence G. Avery, 1994; *A Paul Green Reader*, ed. Laurence G. Avery, 1998 (misc)

GREGORY, Horace (1898–1982)

Chelsea Rooming House is an extraordinary book; a fresh poetic vision and an individual talent here are loosed to express a great fear and a deep tenderness concerning human life. Mr. Gregory as poet interprets unintellectual humanity hurling itself at doors to which it has no key.... Although Mr. Gregory's poems spring from a strong feeling about social conditions they never become propaganda. The poet is far too intellectual to allow that. Instinctively and rightly he connects the past with the future, throwing a vision of life backwards and forwards along its right plane. The pattern of life is different in each age, but the feeling for life is universal.

Eda Lou Walton. *The Nation*. Dec. 17, 1930. p. 680

Gregory is grouped among writers of social revolution, where he is remarkable for adding the authority of a poet to the authorization, whatever it may be worth, of official orthodoxy. But this destination is incidental to his fundamental qualities. The sincerity and art that have gone into his books should be major assets to any cause, but they are too substantial to need or allow partisan coercion. What is important is that their authority exists before and after the specific issues of subject matter are faced. This is equivalent to saying that Gregory, as a poet, dignifies his beliefs by bringing to them the highest integrity of which the intelligence, socially or practically directed, is capable.

Morton D. Zabel. *New Republic*. June 19, 1935. p. 173

The agrarian pattern is that of the "Eternal Now." It brings the past to us, not as if of antiquarian interest, as a collection of curios in a museum, but as another version of the present. The events of today (and Gregory can note them as concretely as does any barrister's indictment before a Grand Jury) are at the same time fused with a sense of the long perspective, whereby the poet is *close-to* and *remote-from* simultaneously. In his case, a specific intimate event, existing in its particularities but once, is reported with an overtone of migrations and historic sweeps. The poet observes through a screen of myth, so that what he sees bears the markings of this screen upon it.

Kenneth Burke. *Poetry*. July, 1935. pp. 228–9

His technique is particularly interesting. Like Eliot, he is fond of the dissonant chord and unresolved suspense; like Hart Crane, he crowds image upon image to increase sensation and suggest new perspective. But he does not share Eliot's disillusion nor Crane's

disorganization. There is constant control as well as positive belief in Gregory's poetry; his faith is a social faith. His method and manner created a new tone, half-ruminative, half-lyrical, superficially descriptive yet somehow integrated.

Louis Untermeyer. *Saturday Review*. April 12, 1941. p. 15

By temperament Gregory seems happiest as an elegiac poet, celebrating, with his grieving rhetoric, the lost places, the lost persons, the lost world of his inheritance.... Gregory is not and never will be a casual writer. To be sure, he has a strong sense of the contemporary, in both its historic and its idiomatic aspects, but to use the contemporary breezily, *au naturel*, is not his talent: he must work on it imaginatively and break it down into the deep, grave rhythms of his reflective spirit.

Stanley J. Kunitz. *Poetry*. June, 1941. p. 155

Gregory is no less a craftsman than MacNeice. But his material is so much more substantial and it is given such a solid poetic integration that the mechanics of his writing are less assertive than those of MacNeice. Gregory is primarily a dramatic poet with the command of lyric which, in our poetic tradition, has always accompanied true dramatic expression.... Human experience is his material, but he does not patronize or poeticize it. He simply extracts its essence, adding nothing which might artificially dignify it. The inherent dignity of the essential is the beauty of Gregory's poetry.

John L. Sweeney. *The Yale Review*. Summer, 1941. p. 821

It is Mr. Gregory's intention, and high distinction, to be conscientiously contemporary, deriving his imagery from what is most recent in our surroundings.... Yet his effectiveness as a poet of the present depends, paradoxically, on an allegiance felt rather than declared to the past.... Other poets who have shared this doubleness of vision have often yielded to the urge to use it with satiric malice. Mr. Gregory is free of that. One feels behind his sharp awareness of what is about him a depth of terror and a depth of tenderness for the human lot.

George F. Whicher. *New York Herald Tribune Book Section*. May 4, 1941. p. 2

Mr. Gregory is a stubborn formalist. His project is before him and he sticks to it; he foresees and numbers the details that must be attended to in its careful execution, and like a good general he always has a firm thumb on the map. This makes, let us admit it, for a certain rigidity. It is a little as if the resultant poetry were too much done to formula. The right ingredients are there—imagination, tenderness, humor, irony, the pathos of distance, the pathos of the contemporary-ephemeral, the convenient stairway that always leads from the finite to the infinite—but one has the feeling that Mr. Gregory has somehow got them there by a clever and cultivated sort of sleight-of-mind, a trained and studious dexterity.

Conrad Aiken. *New Republic*. Sept. 15, 1941. p. 346

Most of Mr. Gregory's poems do not have regular meters, line lengths, or stanzas; any poet knows how hard it is really to organize a poem without these. But his feeling for speech and tone, his real selectivity, . . . do manage to hold his poems together surprisingly often. . . . He belongs more to the conversational-colloquial half of modern poetry than to the rhetorical-obscure half; his textures often have the particularity and precision and bareness of successful prose. He is an accomplished, sensitive, and complicated poet; honest, too: he never fools his readers without fooling himself.

Randall Jarrell. *The Nation.* Sept. 20, 1941. p. 258

We who have known Gregory's poetry over the last ten years know that a great deal of its force and depth have arisen from an acute perception of the past as being still alive and working in the present day. Gregory is inferior to no poet living; but he has learned to trace out, carefully, just where in the past, both of the strains that made up our present actually got started.

John Gould Fletcher. *New York Times Book Section.* April 16, 1944. p. 3

It may seem a long jump from an early poem called "Salvos for Randolph Bourne" to a late one called "Homage to Circe," but if you examine them side by side you find a similar delicacy of texture, a similar unerringness of choice of detail, and in the later poem a further growth of an ear so intricately modulated it has few rivals this side of Eliot.

Without brains, such facility could be mere dulcet tone. It never is. . . . Horace Gregory has always moved the mind. Now he has ways of twitching at one's nerves also, and latterly, at his best, moving the heart.

Winfield Townley Scott. *New York Herald Tribune Book Section.* Aug. 19, 1951. p. 3

Each of the poems of this collection *Selected Poems* represents a degree of formal attainment, of formal success.

Yet Mr. Gregory is striving for much more. The myths he evokes are in a constant state of flux and as a poet he seeks to integrate himself therein. . . . Each of the poems is some form of question on the essential mystery of man, and some form of lament over the poet's consciousness engaged in a life which limits the consciousness. Mr. Gregory revindicates one of the oldest functions of poetry, envisaged as the reservoir of human unhappiness, and also as the means, the noblest means perhaps, to transcend the unhappiness, to make of it a way of contemplation, a way of understanding.

Wallace Fowlie. *New York Times Book Section.* Aug. 19, 1951. pp. 5, 20

Gregory is, I think, our best chronicler of the universal *devices* of distraction, of the ruses—especially alcohol and opulence—modern man employs against the unthinkable and the inevitable. (If I were ever to meet Gregory, I would expect him to say, before I had

the first one, "Have another drink.") The variations he plays on this nameless hysteria, the settings he gives it, the characters who act it out, are amazing in their aptness. There is a kind of civilized gallows humor in their telling which Gregory uses with what would seem very nearly like sadism if it were not for the underlying pity that one feels also in his rendering of people at bars, official dinners, open-air concerts, or sitting at night in rich apartments in New York with "The city washed away like time beneath us/And nothing there except the perfect view." Yet one wonders, sometimes, if his work doesn't depend a little too much on decor, on descriptions of settings, and such. I won't dwell on this, though, for it really doesn't disturb me more than faintly. I am too much in favor of Gregory's kind of subtlety in depicting the condemned playground that the diseased unconscious makes of our world, the extraordinary ways in which he shows the eruption of the timeless myths into modern life, and the inability of moderns to rise to the myths and their meanings, though they live them, unrecognizing.

James Dickey. *Sewanee Review.* Summer, 1962. p. 494

He belongs to no school or clique. His career both as writer and as teacher has involved a dauntless, even heroic struggle against ill health, and he has had no time, if he were so inclined, for those public readings by which reputations are sometimes enhanced. Amid all the noise of literary politics, he has worked quietly ahead, hardly noticed even when, from time to time, he does receive some award or honor.

His work is not in the least sensational or exhibitionistic. And now that he has brought out his *Collected Poems* at the age of sixty-six, we can see more clearly than before that many of his best poems have been intense, concentrated, and very self-contained; enduring, yet slight and hard to keep in view; quick trout in cold, almost silent streams. Sensuality and violence are often present in these poems, yet are used not as weapons against the reader but as the raw material of the poet's sensibility. After all, "classical restraint" does imply something to be restrained.

M.L. Rosenthal. *The Reporter.* Sept. 10, 1964. p. 50

In an age in which the raw, the raucous, and the personal are increasingly identified with the real, it is natural, even appropriate, that poetry such as Horace Gregory's be given less than its due. This is all the more ironical in that few poets have been as successfully occupied with our day's Medusa-like powers. But now that so much of a lifetime's writing is in, to the discerning, the harvest, as well as the gratitude we should feel for it, must be obvious. . . . From his first poem on he treats the anonymous, buried lives of our world. And he gives them, by discovering their own most private speech, full voice. This voice, awing in its ability to bridge the chasmic distance between dream and reality in these lives, is a constant, growing one in his work.

Theodore Weiss. *Poetry.* Nov., 1964. p. 134

A characteristic feeling of these poems is disquiet. A characteristic form, the monologue or dialogue. A characteristic effect, that of the lucid and haunted. The manner is lucid but it is dealing with shadowy presences or with wind, silence, darkness, or with the forces behind the reality of our times.

This effect of the lucid and haunted is Gregory's particular own. His eye on the world is sharp but his greater concern is to see it in its widest implications—which is, in an essential sense, to mythologize it. His "hellbabies," drunks, salesmen, police sergeants, lonely sensitives, are voices out of the theater of some vaster play—characters, too, of their own void, warped by the pressures of circumstances. . . . Horace Gregory is an old master of the clearcut articulations of the musical line, the incised image, and of the architecture of a poem. His art, subtle like the virtues his poetry lives by, expresses a tragic view in a nervous-veined and noble language.

Jean Garrigue. *New Leader*. Feb. 15, 1965. pp. 23–4

BIBLIOGRAPHY

Chelsea Rooming House, 1930 (p) (English edition, *Rooming House*, 1932); *The Poems of Catullus*, 1931 (tr); *No Retreat*, 1933 (p); *Pilgrim of the Apocalypse*, 1933 (c); *Wreath for Margery*, 1933 (p); *Chorus for Survival*, 1935 (p); *Poems, 1930–1940*, 1941 (p); (with Marya Zaturenska) *A History of American Poetry, 1900–1940*, 1946 (c); ed. *The Portable Sherwood Anderson*, 1949 (coll); (with Jeanette Covert Nolan and James T. Farrell) *Poet of the People: An Evaluation of James Whitcomb Riley*, 1951 (c); *Selected Poems*, 1951; *The Metamorphoses of Ovid*, 1958 (tr); *Amy Lowell*, 1958 (b); *The World of James McNeill Whistler*, 1959 (b); *The Medusa in Gramercy Park*, 1961 (p); *The Dying Gladiators*, 1961 (e); *The Crystal Cabinet*, 1962 (c); *The Love Poems of Ovid*, 1964 (tr); *Collected Poems*, 1964; (with Marya Zaturenska) *The Silver Swan: Poems of Romance and Mystery*, 1966; *Dorothy Richardson*, 1967 (b); *D. H. Lawrence: Pilgrim of the Apocalypse*, 1970 (c); *The House on Jefferson Street: A Cycle of Memories*, 1971 (r); *Spirit of Time and Place*, 1973 (e); *Another Look*, 1976 (p)

GUARE, John (1938–)

Although steeped in Ibsen (frequent references to *A Doll's House*) and Chekhov (one notably funny diatribe against *The Three Sisters*), [*Marco Polo Sings a Solo*] recalls nothing so much as the play Kurt Vonnegut would have written if he could write plays; the same affectionate loathing for humanity, the same manipulation of preposterousness in event and language, the same comic ability to grab a cliché and twist it into life by taking it literally. Above all, the same despair, splashed across an otherwise good-humored farcical entertainment, too thinly to rank as a deep artistic vision but strong enough to put a chill on the jollity, to scatter it across the stage in tiny beads of freeze-dried horror. You feel that, packed into a test tube, Guare's view of life would indeed be powerful enough to freeze the whole world, like Vonnegut's ice-nine. We probably ought to be grateful that he has the kindness to dilute it with sheer playfulness, that his mind cannot resist a purely comic or nonsensical diversion, that he follows so many tracks off in so many directions that returning to the main point becomes a tour de force.

The forces that keep *Marco Polo* from falling apart are the characters' obsessions, carried almost to the degree of Jonsonian

humors: one with heroism and planthood, one with the glow of someone else's family life, one with his stature in the pop-political world of diplomacy. And the glamorous female around whom these three creatures revolve, drained of any feeling at all, sublimates her disgust by going to endless productions of *A Doll's House*. The end is stasis, an emotional icing over that reflects the ice-palace setting. The characters wait, frozen, for the new century, wondering if they have actually lived through any of this one.

Michael Feingold. *The Village Voice*. Feb. 14, 1977, p. 43

The Landscape of the Body is quite simply the best work Guare has ever done. It is the play Guare's supporters have always wanted to see and the one which skeptics, pointing to the brilliant flashes contained within plays that never seemed to find a final structure, doubted Guare could write. With *Landscape* "the world's oldest living promising playwright" (the quote is from Guare's *Rich and Famous*) hands in a masterpiece. . . .

Guare has always defined his plays as being about the conflict between dreams and the world. But it strikes me that Guare at his best is about much more than that. He is a man at once furious at the imperfections of the world—he actually does find it disgusting, as Holahan says in the play, that Joseph Welch made a movie for Otto Preminger—and thoroughly compassionate about what people must do when in battle with this world.

This compassion is not always present in Guare's work, but when it is there, it makes Guare unique among current satirists. Guare is not a social critic standing on the outside and laughing with slight disdain. He is *inside*, and it is from this particularly painful vantage point that the laughter comes. It brings not only criticism but complicity, not righteous anger but a desperate struggle against despair. Guare is an idealist and realist both.

Terry Curtis Fox. *The Village Voice*. Aug. 15, 1977, pp. 34–35

Muzeeka shows Guare's inventiveness and facility. Unrealistic monologues alternate with direct address to the audience as violence erupts out of domesticity. The titular Muzeeka is the canned music of conformism, which overtakes Jack Argue (whose name is an anagram of Guare). Although inspired by the Dionysian dances of the Etruscans, Argue becomes a junior executive for Muzeeka, marries a nice girl, has a suburban house and a baby. On the night his baby is born, he goes to a whore in Greenwich Village for a "Chinese basket job." Glad to be drafted, Argue is soon in Vietnam, where the soldiers fight for television coverage of their skirmishes. When his soldier buddy offers Argue a share in his father's business and marriage to his sister, Argue stabs himself. At home his wife intones patriotic platitudes, the Greenwich Village whore intones hip platitudes, his Vietnam army buddy intones military platitudes, and a stagehand pours the ketchup of Argue's blood. . . .

The House of Blue Leaves . . . [is] a marriage of Feydeau and Strindberg, or a painful domestic situation played as farce. The House of Blue Leaves is an insane asylum, and the inhabitants of a Queens, New York apartment convert it to an insane asylum when they step in and out of three doors and a window. . . .

In marrying Feydeau of the precipitous doors to Strindberg of the restraining straitjacket, Guare complained: "Who says I have to be confined and show a guy slipping on a banana peel? Why can't I take him to the next level and show him howling with pain because he's broken his ass?'' Guare hasn't learned the simple answer: because a broken ass on stage is funny, and the audience will not believe the pain.

By 1972 Guare did not have to think of pain. Not only did *Blue Leaves* win an Obie and the New York Drama Critics Circle award, but also his adaptation of *Two Gentlemen of Verona* (with music by Galt MacDermott) was voted the best musical. Rich and rather famous, Guare wrote *Rich and Famous* about a Broadway playwright with the farcical name of Bing Ringling. One actor plays Bing, and another plays all other male parts, while an actress plays all female parts. . . .

Landscape of the Body (1977) parodies another aspect of New York City, but Guare sees the play as ''people fighting against the death in all our lives.'' Death is grisly soon after the opening scene in which a disguised passenger on the Hyannisport-Nantucket ferry apprehends a woman for beheading her adolescent son. . . .

After these sallies Off-Broadway, Guare returned to Broadway with the small cast, reined fantasy, but unsubdued wit of *Bosoms and Neglect* (1980). His most skilfully constructed plot—a prologue and two acts on three realistic sets—and clearly delineated characters were soon swept off the Great White Way, but they have graced several other theatres in the very year of opening. . . .

Like Neil Simon, John Guare endows his characters with wit at the expense of credibility. Tending to self-indulgence at the expense of drama, Guare seems most recently to be in control of wit and farce. In *The House of Blue Leaves* we were barely introduced to Guare's Strindbergian characters before they were slammed by Feydeauian doors. A decade later farce simmers down to neurosis in *Bosoms and Neglect*, and the Strindbergian note sounds only in a loveless mother-son family, a loveless daughter-father (offstage) family. True to Broadway desire, a new couple finally forms, and yet the coupling bristles with psychological peril. The contemporary avatar of happy endings is person-to-person warmth, however fragile, however improbable. Sentimentality has a new hard edge.

Ruby Cohn. *New American Dramatists: 1960–1980* (Grove, 1982), pp. 36–41

John Guare has just run his second horse in the Lydie Breeze Sweepstakes, while a third is being saddled up for the next race. At this rate, he will soon have the largest stable in the American theater. Let's wish him luck with his final entry. The first two nags haven't shown the stamina to finish the course, and they are being led to the starting post in confusing chronological order.

Gardenia . . . takes place in 1875 and 1884; *Lydie Breeze* . . . is set in 1895. A few of the events remembered in the latter work are dramatized in the former, while some characters only mentioned in *Lydie Breeze* now constitute the central figures of *Gardenia*. That history is happening in *Gardenia*, rather than being recalled, should result in a more active play. It doesn't. Guare is more controlled here, because less distracted by the progress of spirochete bacilli through his characters' veins, but *Gardenia* remains basically undramatized, a disunified sketch in search of another draft. . . .

It is maddening to find this gifted playwright continually betraying his own talents through a failure of craft. Guare usually provides enough material for a dozen plays. I think his dramaturgy

would benefit by his settling on one (how much more powerful *Bosoms and Neglect* would have been had he not diluted a black comedy about death with an irrelevant second act about a cute meet in a psychiatrist's office). We should be grateful that at least one American playwright is willing to create an historical context for his work, but perhaps he should think more about supplementing his readings in revisionist history with some study of Aristotle's *Poetics*. . . .

I await the third play in the trilogy, less out of expectation that it will produce something significant than out of hope that John Guare will finally have gotten this damned Lydie Breeze business out of his system. Perhaps then he can settle down to write a coherent and consistent play—preferably one that observes the unities.

Robert Brustein. *New Republic.* May 19, 1982, pp. 24–25

[John] Guare's early plays—through *Marco Polo*—are whimsical comedies with a dark undercurrent, peopled by unpredictable eccentrics, alternately foolish and violent, for whom everything goes wrong. In *Blue Leaves*, written under the aegis of Strindberg and Feydeau, the director friend of Artie Shaugnessy, the protagonist, flies into New York from Hollywood to mourn his incinerated girlfriend and ends up leaving with Artie's, who's very much alive. *Rich and Famous* takes place on the disastrous opening night of the first produced play (but the eight hundred and forty-third written) by Bing Ringling, the world's oldest living promising young playwright, whose parents end up deserting him for his archrival, the boy next door. *Marco Polo*, set on an island off the coast of Norway in the year 1999, ends just after Tom, whose legs have been eaten by piranhas below the ice floe, makes a remarkable observation: ''I've been reading Chekhov. *Three Sisters.* Those poor girls, all the time trying to get to Moscow. The town they lived in was only forty-eight miles from Moscow. In 1999 that town is probably part of Greater Downtown Moscow. They were in Moscow all the time.''

The evocation of Chekhov is more than coincidental. Guare stands out among his contemporaries for his intricately plot-driven playwriting, filled with both the major reversals and the little ironic surprises—so common in Chekhov—that force characters incessantly to reevaluate their situations. Events never turn out as planned, his characters never get what they want and yet, almost inevitably, they turn their losses into unexpected gain. In a theater dominated by dramas of disillusionment and perdition, Guare has almost single-handedly renovated the classic ironic formula, writing dramas in which recognition issues out of suffering, understanding out of dismay.

David Savran. *In Their Own Words* (New York: Theatre Communications, 1988), pp. 84–85

GUARE: Reality! Everything you do is based on reality. Henry James once said you can soar as high as you can, but you've always got to hang onto a string—the string which holds onto that balloon—and that's a very demanding image. I love to anchor things in reality. My current play, *Six Degrees of Separation*, was inspired in part by an actual event reported in the *Times*. *Bosoms and Neglect* is based on a terribly real event that happened to me. I believe that any reality is there to use and explore. We have nothing else but that.

DIGAETANI: That reminds me of Hwang's *M. Butterfly*, which is also based on a newspaper story. A newspaper story was what gave Leoncavallo the idea for his opera *I Pagliacci*.

GUARE: Most plays are based on a real event.

DIGAETANI: But I think your talent is not historical but comical. What generates the comedy in your writing?

GUARE: I have no idea. I like to make people laugh, I guess. I don't know.

> John L. DiGaetani. *A Search for a Postmodern Theatre: Interviews with Contemporary Playwrights* (Westport, Ct.: Greenwood Pr., 1991), p. 110

BIBLIOGRAPHY

Something I'll Tell You Tuesday, and The Loveliest Afternoon of the Year, 1967 (d); *Cop-Out, Muzeeka, Home Fires: Three Plays*, 1970; *Kissing Sweet, and A Day for Surprises*, 1971 (d); (with Milos Forman) *Taking Off*, 1971 (screenplay); *The House of Blue Leaves*, 1972 (d); *Two Gentlemen of Verona*, 1973 (d, adaptation); *Marco Polo Sings a Solo*, 1977 (d); *Rich and Famous*, 1977 (d); *Landscape of the Body*, 1978 (d); *Bosoms and Neglect*, 1982 (d); *Three Exposures*, 1982 (d); *Gardenia*, 1982 (d); *Lydie Breeze*, 1982 (d); *Six Degrees of Separation*, 1990 (d); *Women and Water*, 1990 (d); *Four Baboons Adoring the Sun*, 1993 (d); *Chuck Close : Life and Work, 1988–1995*, 1995 (b); *The War Against the Kitchen Sink*, 1996 (d)

GUTHRIE, A.B., Jr. (1901–1991)

We shall never know exactly how the mountain men talked; they had no literal reporters. We shall never know as much as we should like about their psychology; they told little of themselves and wrote almost nothing. We do not even know as much as we should just how they dressed, fed. . . . All this has to be patiently reconstructed with historical research, firsthand knowledge of the Western scene, and above all imagination. Mr. Guthrie has not written a great novel (in *The Big Sky*), but he used imagination and study to do an impressive work of reconstruction.

> Allan Nevins. *Saturday Review*. May 3, 1947. p. 10

(On *The Big Sky*) A monument of a book! One of those monuments made out of rough boulders, native to the spot, rolled together to serve as a pedestal for a towering bronze figure of epic size. The first monument raised to the men who in the wild emptiness of those middle plains and beyond, in the mountains which are the spine of our country, preceded the home-making pioneer, a monument to the "mountain man."

> Dorothy Canfield Fisher. *New York Herald Tribune Book Section*. May 4, 1947. p. 1

I can't help feeling that Mr. Guthrie has applied the realistic technique to material of which the reality cannot be captured by the documentary method. This method serves him well in one respect. The brutality and the plain squalor of life in the early West come through. On the other hand, one suspects that its rather solemn and pedestrian compulsions inhibit him in another respect. Though a few tall tales are spun around campfires, he makes very little use of the humorous myth-making which was and still is a constant and indigenous American way of coping with the overwhelming presence. . . . Mr. Guthrie's mountain men would be more believable if they were more legendary—by which I do not mean romantic.

> Margaret Marshall. *The Nation*. May 24, 1947. p. 632

Even more successfully than its predecessor, *The Big Sky*, Mr. Guthrie's second novel (*The Way West*) repossesses the past and gives a sense, not of fiction, but of the Western experience itself as it was totally known a hundred years ago by the men who underwent it, who chose it, and who were re-created by it as Western Americans. Mr. Guthrie writes with modest but sure art, especially in his feeling for the idiom of Western talk and for the narrative style proper to it.

> Robert Gorham Davis. *New York Times Book Section*. Oct. 9, 1949. p. 5

Recollection falters at the attempt to number the troops of fictional tales spawned of Parkman's *Oregon Trail* and the library of overland emigrants' journals. Just as Emerson Hough's *Covered Wagon* was the best of the lot when it appeared, now *The Way West* tops them all; indeed it is another kind of book. They were adventure stories. This is a novel. It is not an action story for action's tumultuous sake, but a story of people.

> Elrick B. Davis. *New York Herald Tribune Book Section*. Oct. 9, 1949. p. 3

What emerges above all from a consideration of *These Thousand Hills*, and a glance back at *The Big Sky* and *The Way West*, is the fact that Mr. Guthrie is moved by a fictional purpose as high and valid as his historical purpose is big, and that the two are soundly related, that he is writing, out of the real events of a real world, something like a spiritual epic of the Northwest.

> Walter Van Tilburg Clark. *New York Times Book Section*. Nov. 18, 1956. p. 54

One of the wonderful things about A. B. Guthrie's novels . . . is that they grow out of a great popular literary tradition—the "Western.". . . We see how a sort of folk literature, become sterile and puerile to the point of absurdity, can be lifted up. And I think its roots have everything to do with its artistry. There's only a slight difference between it and the better tales in the conventional manner. But that slight difference takes this novel out of the rut to a point where it can take its place beside other superior novels growing out of other traditions the world over. It will hold its own.

> Fred T. Marsh. *New York Herald Tribune Book Section*. Nov. 18, 1956. p. 3

BIBLIOGRAPHY
The Big Sky, 1947 (n); *The Way West*, 1950 (n); *These Thousand Hills*, 1956 (n); *The Big It*, 1960 (s); *The Blue Hen's Chick*, 1965 (a); *Arfive*, 1970 (n); *Wild Pitch*, 1973 (n); *Once upon a Pond*, 1973 (juv); *The Last Valley*, 1975 (n); *The Genuine Article*, 1977 (n); *No Second Wind*, 1980 (n); *Fair Land, Fair Land*, 1982 (n); *Playing Catch-Up*, 1985 (n); *Big Sky, Fair Land: The Environmental Essays*, 1988; *Murder in the Cotswolds*, 1989 (n); *A Field Guide to Writing Fiction*, 1991 (e); *Murders at Moon Dance*, 1993 (n)